THE
HISTORY
HIGHWAY

D0024069

REF
e.117
.H55
2006

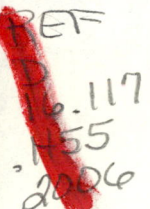

THE
HISTORY
HIGHWAY

A 21st Century Guide to Internet Resources

—— Fourth Edition ——

Edited by

Dennis A. Trinkle and Scott A. Merriman

M.E.Sharpe
Armonk, New York
London, England

DAVID L. RICE LIBRARY
UNIVERSITY OF SOUTHERN INDIANA
EVANSVILLE, IN

#62324884

Copyright © 2006 by M.E. Sharpe, Inc.

All rights reserved. No part of this book may be reproduced in any form
without written permission from the publisher, M.E. Sharpe, Inc.,
80 Business Park Drive, Armonk, New York 10504.

Library of Congress Cataloging-in-Publication Data

The history highway : a 21st-century guide to Internet resources /
[edited by] Dennis A. Trinkle and Scott A. Merriman.— 4th ed.
   p. cm.
  Rev. ed. of: The history highway 3.0. 3rd ed. c2002.
  Includes bibliographical references and index.
  ISBN 0-7656-1630-0 (cloth : alk. paper)—ISBN 0-7656-1631-9 (pbk. : alk. paper)
  1. History—Computer network resources. 2. Internet. 3. History—Research—
Methodology. 4. History—Computer-assisted instruction.
I. Title: The history highway. II. Trinkle, Dennis A., 1968–
III. Merriman, Scott A., 1968– IV. History highway 3.0

D16.117.A14 2006
025.06′90983—dc22   2005033335

Printed in the United States of America

The paper used in this publication meets the minimum requirements of
American National Standard for Information Sciences
Permanence of Paper for Printed Library Materials,
ANSI Z 39.48-1984.

BM (c)	10	9	8	7	6	5	4	3	2	1
BM (p)	10	9	8	7	6	5	4	3	2	1

In honor of the next generation,
Caroline Bradshaw Merriman and John Thomas Trinkle,
and the one before, especially Gayle Trinkle

Contents

Acknowledgments

The idea for *The History Highway* was conceived nearly a decade ago. That the work is now entering its fourth incarnation is a testament to its value to students, instructors, and lovers of history. It is also a tribute to the many individuals who have contributed directly and indirectly to the project over the past ten years. We cannot possibly thank everyone who has played a role in writing, so we hope you know that your efforts and support are recognized and appreciated. We would especially like to thank the contributors to this and past editions of *The History Highway*. We extend our sincere thanks and hearty apologies to Stephen Kneeshaw, whose chapter, "History and Social Studies Organizations," was not correctly attributed to him in the last edition of the work.

Dennis A. Trinkle would like to thank the faculty, staff, and students of DePauw University for their many tangible and intangible contributions to *The History Highway*. DePauw is a lively learning community, and I want to thank President Robert Bottoms and Executive Vice President Neal Abraham for their support and encouragement of my many activities. I also want to especially thank several faculty and staff colleagues who daily make my teaching, research, and work better and more successful: Annette Coon, Aaron Dzuibinsky, Bob Hershberger, Julianne Miranda, Ken Owen, Rick Provine, Nate Romance, and Carol Smith.

I would also like to thank the members of my other professional family—the American Association for History and Computing. In particular, my sincere appreciation is extended to David Staley, Charles Mackay, Jeffrey Barlow,

Kelly Robison, Jessica Lacher-Feldman, Steve Hoffman, and Deborah Anderson. It is a genuine pleasure to work with so many creative and passionate teachers and scholars. Finally, but certainly not least, special thanks to my wife, Kristi, my greatest blessing John Thomas, my brother Keith, my mother Gayle, and all the members of my extended family. Your constant energy and care are a great inspiration.

Scott A. Merriman would like to thank his family, friends, and teachers, both past and present, for their support and guidance. Special thanks to my wife, Jessie, for her assistance, both in this writing effort and in many others, and to my daughter Caroline for all the smiles and ducks that she has brought into my life. I would also like to recognize the History Department of the University of Kentucky, faculty, staff, graduate students, and fellow part- and full-time instructors alike, for their support and encouragement. Especially deserving of gratitude for serving as mentors are, among others, Robert Ireland and Robert Olson. My years at UK have been enriched by my friendships with, among many others, Jessica Flinchum, Amber Fogle, Elizabeth Hill, Stephanie May, Erin Shelor, Jeremiah Taylor, and Jennifer Walton.

In my larger travels, I have been ably assisted by many people, far too many to mention, and I would be remiss if I did not thank at least some of them here. I am truly grateful for my continuing friendships and professional relationships with Jeffrey Barlow, Rowly Brucken, Bud Burkhardt, Randal Horobik, Jen McGee, Kelly Robison, David Staley, and Paul Wexler. I am thankful to my family for their perpetual support. Finally, for all those who have supported me, but who are not specifically mentioned, thanks!

Introduction

More than 60 percent of American households now report that they regularly access the Internet. This figure represents a stunning historical transformation. The number of Web pages is increasing so rapidly that no reliable estimate exists, though best guesses suggest more than 8 billion Web pages. The growth rate and proliferation are staggering and historically unprecedented. Radio, television, and the telephone became part of American daily life at a comparatively glacial pace. Such dizzying expansion and alteration make the Internet a tremendously exciting phenomenon, but also unsettling and unwieldy.

When we wrote the first edition of *The History Highway* in 1996, we lamented that trying to explore and sample the Internet was like trying to sip water from a fire hose. When *The History Highway 2000* appeared, and when *The History Highway 3.0* followed, the metaphor might have been changed to sipping water from a rushing river or Niagara Falls. Today, that first fire hose might be replaced by a roaring ocean. The pace of expansion and change is accelerating.

To novices and even seasoned users, the information superhighway can be information overload at its worst, often more intimidating and frustrating than exciting. For anyone interested in history, however, the Internet simply cannot be ignored. The resources are richer and more valuable than ever. There are hundreds of thousands of sites dedicated to the American Revolution alone. Students can find the complete texts of millions of books, work with previously inaccessible primary documents, and explore thousands of first-rate sites dedicated to historical topics. Publishers can advertise their wares, and professors can find enormous databases devoted to teaching suggestions, online versions of historical journals, and active scholarly discussions on a wide variety of research topics. The Internet is quite simply the most revolutionary storehouse of human knowledge in history.

For most of us, however, whether we are students, professors, librarians, editors, or just lovers of history, there are not enough hours in our already busy days to go chasing information down an infinite number of alleyways, no matter how useful or interesting that information might be. The aim of this book is to offer detailed information about the thousands of quality resources that are out there and how to find them.

Part I is a short primer for those with limited experience using the Internet. It discusses what exists and what you can do with it. It explains how to gain access to the Internet and outlines what types of software are necessary. There is also an important section on the manners and rules that govern the Internet—"netiquette," as seasoned users call it. A valuable new section on evaluating Internet resources has been added to the chapter as well.

Part II is the heart of the book. It lists thousands of sites that will appeal to anyone interested in history and that our specialist section authors have determined to be reliable and useful for the serious study of history. This section will allow you to avoid the helter-skelter databases, such as Yahoo!, Excite, Google, and DogPile, that take you to information regardless of quality and utility. You will not find sites created by first-graders in Indianapolis or by biased, ahistorical groups like the Holocaust Deniers of America. Bon Voyage!

Part I

Getting Started

Chapter 1

The Basics

Dennis A. Trinkle

History of the Internet

Since this book is directed at those interested in history, it seems sensible to begin with a brief history of the Internet itself. The story of the Internet's origins is as varied, complex, and fascinating as the information the Net contains. Ironically, the Net began as the polar opposite of the publicly accessible network it has become. It grew out of the Cold War hysteria surrounding the Soviet launch of Sputnik, the first artificial satellite, in 1957. Amid paranoia that the United States was losing the "science race," President Dwight D. Eisenhower created the Advanced Research Projects Agency (ARPA) within the Department of Defense to establish an American lead in science and technology applicable to the military. After helping the United States develop and launch its own satellite by 1959, the ARPA scientists turned much of their attention to computer networking and communications. Their goal was to find a successful way of linking universities, defense contractors, and military command centers to foster research and interaction, but also to sustain vital communications in case of nuclear attack. The network project was formally launched in 1969 by ARPA under a grant that connected four major computers at universities in the southwestern United States—UCLA, Stanford, the University of California at Santa Barbara, and the University of Utah. The network went online in December 1969. The age of computer networks was born.

In the early 1970s, it became clear to the initial developers of the ARPANET that the system was already stretching past its Cold War origins. Nonmilitary research institutions were developing competing networks of communication, more and more users were going online, and new languages were being introduced that made communication difficult or impossible between networks. To resolve this problem, the Defense Advanced Project Agency (which had replaced ARPA) launched the Internetting Project in 1973. The aim was to create a uniform communications language (a protocol, as the rules governing a computer language are termed) that would allow the hundreds of networks being formed to communicate and function as a single meganetwork. In an amazing display of scientific prowess comparable to the Apollo program, this crucial step in the development of the information superhighway was accomplished in a single year when Robert Kahn and Vinton G. Cerf introduced the Transmission Control Protocol/Internet Protocol (TCP/IP). This protocol made possible the connection of all the various networks and computers then in existence and set the stage for the enormous expansion of the Internet.

Over the next decade, the Department of Defense realized the significance and potential of the Internet, and nonmilitary organizations were gradually allowed to link with the ARPANET. Commercial providers like CompuServe then began making the Internet accessible for those not connected to a university or research institution. The potential for profiting from the Internet fueled dramatic improvements in speed and ease of use.

The most significant step toward simplicity of use came with the introduction of the World Wide Web (Internet), which allows interactive graphics and audio to be accessed. The World Wide Web was the brainchild of Tim Berners-Lee of the European Laboratory for Particle Physics, who created a computer language called hypertext that made possible the interactive exchange of text and graphic images and allowed almost instantaneous connection (linking) to any item on the Internet. Berners-Lee was actually developing this revolutionary language as the Internet was expanding in the 1970s and 1980s, but it was only with the introduction of an easy-to-use Web browser (as the software for interacting with the Web is called) that the Web became widely accessible to the average person. That first browser—Mosaic—was made available to the public by the National Center for Supercomputing Applications at the University of Illinois, Urbana-Champaign, in 1991. Three years later, Mosiac's creator, Marc Andreessen, introduced an even more sophisticated browser that allowed the interaction of sound, text, and images—Netscape Navigator. The next year Microsoft launched a browser of its own—Internet Explorer.

Today, there are many software options for exploring the Internet and access can be purchased through thousands of national and local service providers. A user need no longer be a military researcher or work at a university to "surf the Net." There are now more than 100 million users logging onto the

Internet from the United States alone. Tens of thousands of networks now are connected by TCP/IP, and the Internet forms a vast communication system that can legitimately be called an information superhighway.

Uses of the Internet

This section of Part I will explain the most useful features of the Internet for those interested in history. It will discuss sending and receiving e-mail, reading and posting messages to Usenet newsgroups and discussion lists, logging on to remote computers with telnet, transferring files using the file transfer protocol, and browsing the World Wide Web. The next section will discuss in detail the software packages that perform these tasks and explain exactly how to get online.

Sending and Receiving E-mail

E-mail (electronic mail) is the most popular feature of the Internet. It offers almost instantaneous communication with people all over the world. Rather than taking days or weeks to reach their destination, e-mail messages arrive in minutes or seconds. A professor in Indianapolis, Indiana, can correspond with a student in Delhi, India, in the blink of an eye. A publisher, editor, and author can exchange drafts of a history book they are preparing with no delay. And e-mail does not involve the high costs of international postage, fax charges, or long-distance telephone premiums. E-mail is always part of the basic service arrangement provided with Internet access, and it is quite easy to use with the software packages discussed later.

E-mail Addresses

E-mail addresses are very similar to postal addresses. Like a postal address, an e-mail address provides specific information about where the message is to be sent along the Internet. For example, a friend's address might be something like:

Gkuecker@depauw.edu.

If you look at the end of the address, you will notice the .edu suffix. This means the e-mail message is going to an educational institution. In this case, it is Depauw University, as the second item indicates. Finally, the address reveals that the recipient is your friend Glen Kuecker (Gkuecker). This is just like providing the name, street address, city, state, and zip code on regular mail.

Although the names that individual institutions choose for their Internet addresses vary widely, all addresses in the United States are broken down into the computer equivalent of zip codes. We already noted the .edu in the above message indicates the recipient's account was at an educational institution. There used to be six key three-letter designations (the first six listed below) that provided a clue as to where your e-mail was going or coming from. However, that number has now grown exponentially. The following fourteen categories are just some of the many options available to today's Web surfer:

Category	Meaning
.com	commercial organizations
.edu	educational institutions
.gov	government organizations (nonmilitary)
.mil	military institutions
.net	network service providers
.org	miscellaneous providers
.aero	air-transport industry
.biz	businesses
.coop	cooperatives
.info	unrestricted
.museum	museums
.name	individuals
.pro	accountants, lawyers, and physicians
.country (.xx)	two-letter code designating the Web site's country of origin

A common naming system for American primary and secondary schools has also recently been introduced. This system uses the school name, the k12 designation, and the state where the school is located in the address. A typical address might read:

KeithTrinkle@howe.k12.in.us.

This indicates that a student, teacher, or administrator at Howe High School in Indiana sent the e-mail. The k12.xx.us will always be present in e-mail coming from a primary or secondary school, where the xx will be replaced by the abbreviation for the state.

These designations do not apply to e-mail addresses for accounts located outside the United States, but an equally simple system exists for identifying foreign messages. All mail going to or coming from foreign accounts ends with a two-letter country code. If you have a colleague in France, you might receive an e-mail message ending with .fr. You may receive an e-mail message from an editor in Canada ending in .ca. Or, if you met a historian with similar interests on that last trip through Tanzania, you might soon receive mail ending with .tz. Here is a partial list of these country extensions:

.af	Afghanistan
.al	Albania
.dz	Algeria
.as	American Samoa
.ad	Andorra
.ao	Angola
.ai	Anguilla
.aq	Antarctica
.ag	Antigua and Barbuda
.ar	Argentina
.am	Armenia
.aw	Aruba
.au	Australia
.at	Austria
.az	Azerbaijan
.bs	Bahamas
.bh	Bahrain
.bd	Bangladesh
.bb	Barbados
.by	Belarus
.be	Belgium
.be	Belize
.bj	Benin
.bm	Bermuda
.bj	Bhutan
.bo	Bolivia
.ba	Bosnia-Herzegovina
.bw	Botswana
.bv	Bouvet Island
.br	Brazil
.io	British Indian Ocean Territory
.bn	Brunei Darussalam
.bg	Bulgaria
.bf	Burkina Faso
.bi	Burundi
.kh	Cambodia

.cm	Cameroon
.ca	Canada
.cv	Cape Verde
.ky	Cayman Islands
.cf	Central African Republic
.td	Chad
.cl	Chile
.cn	China
.cx	Christmas Island
.cc	Cocos Islands
.co	Colombia
.km	Comoros
.cg	Congo
.ck	Cook Islands
.cr	Costa Rica
.ci	Côte d'Ivoire
.hr	Croatia
.cu	Cuba
.cy	Cyprus
.cz	Czech Republic
.dk	Denmark
.dj	Djibouti
.dm	Dominica
.do	Dominican Republic
.tp	East Timor
.ec	Ecuador
.eg	Egypt
.sv	El Salvador
.gq	Equatorial Guinea
.er	Eritrea
.ee	Estonia
.et	Ethiopia
.fk	Falkland Islands
.fo	Faroe Islands
.fj	Fiji
.fi	Finland
.fr	France
.gf	French Guiana
.pf	French Polynesia
.tf	French Southern Territories
.ga	Gabon
.gm	Gambia

.ge	Georgia
.de	Germany
.gh	Ghana
.gi	Gibraltar
.gb	Great Britain
.gr	Greece
.gl	Greenland
.gd	Grenada
.gp	Guadeloupe
.gu	Guam
.gt	Guatemala
.gn	Guinea
.gw	Guinea-Bissau
.gy	Guyana
.ht	Haiti
.hm	Heard and McDonald Islands
.hn	Honduras
.hk	Hong Kong
.hu	Hungary
.is	Iceland
.in	India
.id	Indonesia
.ir	Iran
.iq	Iraq
.ie	Ireland
.il	Israel
.it	Italy
.jm	Jamaica
.jp	Japan
.jo	Jordan
.kz	Kazakhstan
.ke	Kenya
.ki	Kiribati
.kp	North Korea
.kr	South Korea
.kw	Kuwait
.kg	Kyrgyzstan Republic
.la	Lao People's Democratic Republic
.lv	Latvia
.lb	Lebanon
.ls	Lesotho
.lr	Liberia

.ly	Libyan Arab Jamahiriya
.li	Liechtenstein
.lt	Lithuania
.lu	Luxembourg
.mo	Macau
.mk	Macedonia
.mg	Madagascar
.mw	Malawi
.my	Malaysia
.mv	Maldives
.ml	Mali
.mt	Malta
.mh	Marshall Islands
.mq	Martinique
.mr	Mauritania
.mu	Mauritius
.yt	Mayotte
.mx	Mexico
.fm	Micronesia
.md	Moldova
.mc	Monaco
.mn	Mongolia
.ms	Montserrat
.ma	Morocco
.mz	Mozambique
.mm	Myanmar
.na	Namibia
.nr	Nauru
.np	Nepal
.nl	Netherlands
.an	Netherlands Antilles
.nt	Neutral Zone
.nc	New Caledonia
.nz	New Zealand
.ni	Nicaragua
.ne	Niger
.ng	Nigeria
.nu	Niue
.nf	Norfolk Island
.mp	Northern Mariana Islands
.no	Norway
.om	Oman

.pk	Pakistan
.pw	Palau
.pa	Panama
.pg	Papua New Guinea
.py	Paraguay
.pe	Peru
.ph	Philippines
.pn	Pitcairn
.pl	Poland
.pt	Portugal
.pr	Puerto Rico
.qa	Qatar
.re	Réunion
.ro	Romania
.ru	Russian Federation
.rw	Rwanda
.sh	Saint Helena
.kn	Saint Kitts and Nevis
.lc	Saint Lucia
.pm	Saint Pierre and Miquelon
.vc	Saint Vincent and the Grenadines
.ws	Samoa
.sm	San Marino
.st	São Tomé and Príncipe
.sa	Saudi Arabia
.sn	Senegal
.sc	Seychelles
.sl	Sierra Leone
.sg	Singapore
.sk	Slovakia
.si	Slovenia
.sb	Solomon Islands
.so	Somalia
.za	South Africa
.es	Spain
.lk	Sri Lanka
.sd	Sudan
.sr	Suriname
.sj	Svalbard and Jan Mayen Islands
.sz	Swaziland
.se	Sweden
.ch	Switzerland

.sy	Syria
.tw	Taiwan
.tj	Tajikistan
.tz	Tanzania
.th	Thailand
.tg	Togo
.tk	Tokelau
.to	Tonga
.tt	Trinidad and Tobago
.tn	Tunisia
.tr	Turkey
.tm	Turkmenistan
.tc	Turks and Caicos Islands
.tv	Tuvalu
.ug	Uganda
.ua	Ukraine
.ae	United Arab Emirates
uk	United Kingdom
.us	United States
.um	United States Minor Outlying Islands
.uy	Uruguay
.uz	Uzbekistan
.vu	Vanuatu
.va	Vatican City State
.ve	Venezuela
.vn	Vietnam
.vg	Virgin Islands (British)
.vi	Virgin Islands (U.S.)
.wf	Wallis and Futuna Islands
.eh	Western Sahara
.ye	Yemen
.yu	Yugoslavia
.zr	Zaire
.zm	Zambia
.zw	Zimbabwe

E-mail Security

Because sending e-mail is so similar to sending a letter by postal service, many people forget that there are two major differences—federal laws discourage anyone from looking at (or intercepting) your mail, and sealed packaging provides a fairly reliable way to detect tampering, but, unfortunately, e-mail is not protected in the same ways. As your electronic message passes through the Internet, it can be read, intercepted, and altered by many individuals.

Some security measures have been developed to protect e-mail just as an envelope secures letters. The latest versions of many programs that process e-mail now include the ability to encrypt messages. Encryption converts your e-mail into a complex code that must be deciphered by an e-mail program or Web browser that is designed to convert the encoded message back into regular text. The latest versions of most e-mail programs include the ability to code and decode encrypted e-mail. If you purchase products and services over the Internet, you will also want to be certain that your account or credit card numbers are insured by some sort of encryption. Nevertheless, it is prudent to keep in mind that no security measure is completely reliable. Remember, too, never to give out your personal information via e-mail or to follow links from e-mails, which could redirect your browser to a false Web site designed to steal your personal information. Cut and paste e-mail addresses to your browser for safety, and only give out personal information using secure encrypted Web sites to sellers or individuals who have your personal trust. Look for the padlock icon at the bottom right-hand corner of some browser windows. If the icon is absent or the padlock open, the site is unencrypted. If the padlock icon is present and closed, the site is encrypted. Other browsers display encryption in different ways. Even on an encrypted site, you should still be sure you are working with a trusted seller before disclosing credit card or other personal data.

Reading and Posting Messages on Newsgroups

For anyone interested in history, newsgroups are another rewarding feature of the Internet. Newsgroups are the electronic equivalent of the old New England town meetings in which anyone could pose a question or make an observation and others could respond to it. Each newsgroup is regulated by a moderator who, like the editor of a newspaper, sets the quality and tone of the posts. There are groups that regularly discuss the Holocaust, the American Revolution, historical publishing, library concerns, and cartography, just to mention a few areas. Though newsgroups are declining somewhat in popularity, in favor of listservs and personal blogs, several remain popular among historians.

Several clues can help you determine the content and nature of groups. Like e-mail addresses, the addresses of newsgroups provide some insight into the nature of the group. Take the newsgroup:

alt.civilwar.

This address indicates that the group discusses the alternative topic—the Civil War. Each newsgroup has a similar address revealing its type and topic. The following categories will aid in determining which of the nearly ten thousand newsgroups are worth investigating:

Category	Meaning
alt.	alternative themes (most groups relating to history carry the alt. designation)
comp.	computer-related topics
misc.	miscellaneous themes
news.	posts about newsgroups
rec.	recreational topics
sci.	scientific discussions
soc.	social concerns
talk.	talk radio–style format

Reading and Posting Messages on Discussion Lists

Discussion lists are a hybrid mixture of e-mail and newsgroups. With discussion lists, the posts and replies that anyone can access in newsgroups are sent by e-mail only to those who have subscribed to the list. As with most newsgroups, there is generally an editor who screens the posts before they are sent to subscribers, maintaining quality and decency. There are discussion lists that target students, professors, editors, publishers, librarians, and general readers. Almost any historical topic imaginable has a list devoted to it. How open the discussion lists are to subscribers is determined by the moderators. Some limit membership to those with special interests, while others permit anyone who wishes to join. Part II discusses the lists focusing on history and explains their qualifications for subscription in more detail.

Part II will also provide more specific instructions on how to subscribe to each group. All discussion lists share a basic subscription format, however. To subscribe (or to unsubscribe), one simply sends an e-mail message to the computer that receives and distributes the messages. This computer is called the listserver (or listserv) because it serves the list. For example, to send a message to a list discussing the history of dogs (H-Dog), you would send the e-mail message:

> Subscribe H-Dog yourfirstname yourlastname

to the e-mail address:

Listserv@ucbeh.san.uc.edu.

The listserv would quickly acknowledge your registration as a member, and e-mail posts from the other list members would begin arriving in your box.

Word of Warning About Discussion Lists

You should be careful to join only subscription lists that are truly of interest and be certain to read your e-mail several times a week. Most discussion lists are very active, sending out fifteen or more messages per day. If you get carried away at first, you may find yourself buried under an avalanche of several hundred e-mail posts awaiting your eager attention. So be careful to subscribe only to those lists that most interest you until you gain a feel for how much mail you are likely to receive.

Blogging

Blogs (Weblogs)—pages in which a single person or group of authors chronicles a particular topic—are of interest to oral historians and others seeking to capture history as it is experienced by the individual. There are two basic types of blogs, individual and interactive. Individual blogs are run by a single person or small group, and all messages posted come from that one person or small community. Interactive blogs allow posts from a much wider group and often spawn their own blogging communities. The environment created by bloggers and their readers is collectively known as the blogsphere.

Like readers of e-mail message chains, blog readers must generally start reading at the end of the blog and work backward, or else read in reverse chronological order, as the newest messages are added to the top of the page. Familiar readers thus will not have to wade through the entire blog to catch up on the most recent information. This convention can be disorienting for those used to standard front-to-back reading, but fans of back-to-front graphic novels can easily adapt to the practice. In interactive blogs, a single topic of great interest can generate a huge volume of posts, called a blog storm or blog swarm.

Blogs usually consist of a list of chronological entries, with the home page either containing all the entries or a hyperlinked entry list to facilitate faster reading. Blogs are equipped with technology that allows the blog owner to moderate conversations in his or her sphere. Bloggers have had an impact on politics already, and those studying their historical impact will doubtless have a challenging task.

Logging Onto a Remote Computer With Telnet

Although more and more libraries are migrating to more user-friendly, icon-based systems, most people who have used an electronic library catalog in the past ten years are familiar with the text-based systems used to search for a book in the library. These machines do not have their own microprocessors, but are linked to a central computer that shares information with all the terminals connected to it. Telnet is a program offered by all Internet service providers that permits your home or office computer to act just like those old terminals at the library. It enables you to temporarily connect to a remote computer and access its information as if it were on your own computer. Telnet has decreased in popularity in recent years as icon-based technology surpassed it in capability and accessibility. Moreover, library databases are now generally available to the public via the Internet without telnet software (though, to be sure, some libraries must still rely on text-based systems.)

Transferring Files With File Transfer Protocol (FTP)

File Transfer Protocol (or FTP) is similar to telnet, but it is still much more widely used. Like telnet, it is a program that connects you to a remote computer. FTP does not allow you to read the material on the remote machine; rather, it allows you to download it to your own computer, or to post your own files to the remote location. You can use FTP to get a copy of the U.S. Constitution or to download a program that teaches you the history of the Vietnam War. Thousands of sites with downloadable files, programs, and historical information are out there waiting to be tapped. Many of the best and most useful FTP sites will be discussed in Part II.

As with telnet, there are many packages that permit FTP access. For now, we will only mention that three main types of FTP access exist: anonymous FTP, identified FTP, and restricted FTP. Anonymous FTP allows anyone to connect to a computer and download information without giving identification. Identified FTP also allows anyone to copy materials, but it requires the provision of e-mail address and name, so the sponsors of the site can maintain statistical information about the use of their site. Restricted FTP is used by some commercial and private institutions that only allow FTP for a fee or for authorized users. Part II specifies which of these categories the sites fall into and explains how to gain access when a fee or password is required.

Browsing the World Wide Web

For most computer users, time on the Internet will mean using a Web browser. The Web is the most popular and fastest growing section of the Internet because it combines text, sound, and graphics to create multimedia sites. History buffs can find everything from an audio track of the "Battle Hymn of the Republic" to short film clips of JFK's assassination to a complete version of the French *Encyclopédie.*

The Web and Web browser packages owe much of their popularity and potential to their multimedia format, but they also profit from their ability to link information. Web page developers can create links to any other page on the Web, so by merely using your mouse to point at a highlighted image or section of text and then clicking the correct mouse button, you can almost instantly bring up that information. Thus, a link on a home page can connect you to any other site, just as a cross-reference in a textbook sends you to other related information. This makes the Internet an amazingly easy-to-use source of information or recreation.

The next section discusses the software that makes connecting to the Web possible, but as with e-mail, you will need to understand Web addresses in order to find information on the Internet. Do not feel intimidated by the techno-talk surrounding the Web. Web addresses, like everything Internet-related, have a technical name, "uniform resource locators," (URL). Every page on the Web has a unique URL. This makes it very easy to go directly to the information you need. They look something like strings of numbers or letters separated by dots (periods) and slashes. For example,

http://mcel.pacificu.edu/JAHC/JAHCiv2/index.html

is simply a link to the *Journal of the Association for History and Computing.* Some addresses are longer than this. Some are shorter. All contain three basic parts. Looking from right to left, the first designation you notice is index.html. This tells you that you are retrieving a file called index in the HTML format. HTML (Hypertext Markup Language) is the standard language of the Web for saving multimedia information. Other possibilities include .gif and .jpeg, which indicate graphic images files, .avi and .wav, which indicate audio files, and .mov, which signals a movie; XML is a markup protocol like HTML, but that also allows metatags, descriptive tags that encode content descriptions. Software can then do more sophisticated searches. Another common protocol is VRML, virtual-reality-modeling language, an Internet standard for rendering three-dimensional graphics.

The middle part of the address—mcel.pacificu.edu/JAHC/JAHCiv2—is just like an e-mail address, specifying what network and computer stores the information so that your software package can find it on the Internet. The .edu extension tells you the information is at an educational institution, and, as with e-mail, there will always be a three-letter code revealing the type of institution that sponsors the site.

The http:// lets you know that the browser is using the Hypertext Transfer Protocol to get the information. This is the standard language that governs the transfer and sharing of information on the Web. If you were using your browser to telnet or FTP, the http:// would be replaced by ftp:// or telnet:// and then the address, showing which function your computer is performing.

Of course, you can use the Internet and profit from the World Wide Web without spending hours studying the technical background, history, and terms. The next chapter tells you how to get on the Internet and what software you need.

Chapter 2

Signing On

Dennis A. Trinkle and Jessica Lacher-Feldman

Getting on the Internet

Dennis A. Trinkle

Once upon a time, getting connected to the Internet was the hardest part of
going online. In the early days, if you did not work for the military or a research institution, you were out of luck. The introduction of commercial providers in the 1980s made access easier to obtain, but it might have cost you as
much as a new car. Today, there are thousands of local and national Internet
service providers, and the competition has made Internet access amazingly
inexpensive. In most markets, you can now get almost unlimited access for
$10 to $25 per month. For those fortunate enough to work for a library, college, university, or publisher, the price is often even better—free. Getting on
the Internet has never been easier or less expensive.

Internet access is offered by three basic categories of service providers—
corporate/institutional, national commercial, and local commercial providers.
For those who do not have access to the Internet at work or school, there are
several factors to consider in choosing a provider. Unless you use a cable modem or DSL, which do not require dial-up access, perhaps most important is
finding a service that offers a local phone number or a toll-free number, so that

you need not pay long-distance charges for your Internet access. The attractiveness of the Internet vanishes quickly in the presence of a $400 phone bill. Fortunately, there are now so many service providers it is usually easy to find a provider that offers a local phone number in your area, even in rural zones. Cable and satellite providers are also scurrying to offer other access options besides telephone connections.

The second consideration is the type of service you desire. Many national and local service providers in your city or state will offer almost unlimited access to the Internet, e-mail, FTP, and other basic services for very affordable rates. (Local service providers can be found by looking in your local phone book under "Internet Service Providers.")

Hardware

Convenient use of the Internet and its many tools is governed by speed. The faster your computer can send and process information, the more pleasurable and productive your time on the Net will be. Thus, there is a simple rule of thumb that guides the purchase of computer equipment for use on the Internet: Buy the best machine you can realistically afford. This does not mean to mortgage your house just to get better equipment. All new computers sold today are more than adequate for exploring the resources described in this book. Even most of those sold within the last four years have enough capacity to handle most Internet functions. More memory (RAM), a faster processor, and a speedier modem will all enable you to interact with the Net more quickly, however.

Software

While many educational institutions and the national service providers such as AOL and CompuServe offer their own software packages with directions and tutorials, those who choose local service providers can select the software they wish to use to access the Internet. Most local service providers will also give new users software needed to access the Internet along with detailed instructions. In principle, however, you can use any package you wish to connect to the Internet through a local provider. This section will present brief descriptions of some of the best packages and explain where to obtain them.

Web Browsers and E-mail Programs

The two powerhouse packages (Web browsers, as they are called) that most Internauts use are Netscape Communicator and Microsoft Internet Explorer. They combine all the tools for accessing the Web and sending e-mail. Both can display the combinations of graphics and text that make the Internet a lively and exciting resource. They are simple to use, come with tutorials and a help feature, and are good choices for all users from novices to experts.

Netscape Communicator and Microsoft Internet Explorer also can both be downloaded on the Internet free of charge. You can download Netscape at the following address (please note, addresses are case sensitive):

http://browser.netscape.com/ns8/.

Microsoft Internet Explorer can be downloaded at:

http://www.microsoft.com/windows/ie/default.mspx.

Netscape and Internet Explorer perform all the functions you need to explore the Internet, including e-mail. However, those who send and receive a lot of electronic correspondence, or who plan to send long files along with their messages, may prefer to use a package designed specifically to handle electronic mail. If you purchased some version of Microsoft Office, you may have received Microsoft Outlook as part of your package (this differs from Microsoft Outlook Express, a scaled-down version of the same program). This is a popular e-mail program that many companies and universities rely upon. Qualcomm's Eudora is also an excellent package for handling e-mail. It is available in free and paid versions, with the paid versions having better features and no ads. It also features an attractive graphic environment and menu, which makes it easy to use.

Eudora is available for download at:

http://www.eudora.com/.

Finally, Pegasus mail is available free from the Mercury Mail Transport system. It is compatible with all operating systems, including Linux. Its author, David Harris, intends to keep the system free to anyone who downloads it, so that information can be exchanged freely. Like Eudora, the system has user-friendly graphics and menus.

Pegasus is available at:

http://www.pmail.com/.

Netiquette and Copyright

There are some basic courtesies that keep the free and open communication of the Internet polite and enjoyable. Here are some netiquette hints that can keep you from accidentally offending someone.

General Netiquette

The most important thing to remember is that Internet communication is just like writing a letter. Electronic messages, however, can be seen by many individuals other than the intended recipient. They can be forwarded to countless people. They can even be printed and posted in public areas. Thus, the golden rule of Internet communication should never be forgotten:

> Never write anything you would not want a stranger to read.

It is also important to remember that e-mail is judged by the same standards as other written communication. Sometimes, the ease and speed of electronic communication lulls users into forgetting to check grammar and spelling. This can lead to your e-mail being forwarded to thousands of individuals, and you do not want people all over the Internet laughing because you innocently asked if it was Vasco de Gama who circumcised the world with a 40-foot clipper.

There are also several special grammatical conventions that govern the Internet. One important rule is not TO WRITE EVERYTHING OUT IN CAPITAL LETTERS or to underline everything, *italicize everything*, or **put everything in bold**. Seasoned e-mail readers consider this the equivalent of shouting at the top of your lungs, and it is considered the mark of a "newbie," or someone who has not yet learned how to behave on the Internet.

Because e-mail lacks a convenient way to convey emotion through text, you will also often encounter special symbols in e-mail correspondence. For example, a :) or :(is often put after a sentence to express happiness or sadness. A 0 may be added to express surprise. A :; may be inserted to indicate confusion, and history buffs who think they are Abe Lincoln may include a =l:-)= somewhere in their messages. Some users may also add full-fledged smiley face icons. These emoticons add a bit of charm to Internet communication, but it is important to remember that they are only appropriate in informal correspondence. They should not be overdone. Too many emotive symbols are considered another mark of a newbie.

Rules for Newsgroups and Discussion Lists and Blog Posts

Besides the netiquette governing general Internet communication, there are also some rules for those who wish to participate in newsgroups, discussion lists, and blogs.

1. Before you make a post to a group or list, it is wise to follow the group's posts for a while. This will help you to know what has already been asked and what type of questions/statements is considered appropriate. Asking repetitive or uninformed questions can get you off to a bad start.
2. Think before you write. Do not send off emotional or ill-considered responses to posts. (This is called "flaming" in Internet parlance.) Take time to consider criticisms, sarcasms, and insults carefully. Remember the Internet is not an anonymous frontier, and online remarks can be just as hurtful as any others. Moreover, it can be more difficult to convey with text an emotion that is easily transmitted by voice. A seemingly innocent remark can come off brash and rude because it was not phrased carefully.
3. Do not send private correspondence to groups or lists. If you just want to thank someone, send the message to the person directly. And be very careful when you reply to a message. The "reply all" feature of your e-mail program is both a boon and a potential bane. You do not want to accidentally tell several thousand readers about your date last night because you replied to the wrong address or to all of the original recipients.
4. Do not post advertisements to groups or lists. This is considered extremely rude and intrusive, and it is the surest way to become the victim of vicious flaming. Internauts are being careful to avoid the spread of junk mail to the Internet. Spam is already prevalent enough without any further contributions.

Copyright

The question of copyright is an important one for students, teachers, librarians, publishers, and all those on the Internet. Everyone wants to know what laws govern copying and sharing information on the Internet, and lawyers and lawmakers are working to develop clear rules that govern electronic mediums. For now, the issues of copyright as they pertain to the Internet are still somewhat hazy, but there are some certainties that can guide your steps.

Most important, all online correspondence, files, and documents are handled like other written documents. They are automatically held to be copyrighted in the individual author's name. When an Internet item is copyrighted by some other party, the copyright holder generally identifies himself or herself at the end of the document.

Students, teachers, and general users will be glad to know that Internet documents can be copied according to the fair use rules that govern printed sources. You can make personal copies of online documents and images, and you can incorporate them in instructional packages (if you are a student, teacher, or librarian) as long as the package is in no way intended to generate a profit, and only a small percentage of the overall work is copied. Other more precise rules governing copyright will undoubtedly be developed in the near future. For now, the safest course seems to be treating Internet sources just like other written documents. Students will be wise to cite their Internet sources *very* carefully and clearly in the texts of their papers or in footnotes. Copying and pasting work directly from the Internet into your term paper, without the use of *both* quotation marks *and* appropriate citation, is a form of plagiarism that is particularly simple to catch.

Evaluating Online Resources
Tools, Tips, and Terms
Jessica Lacher-Feldman

The Web Today

More and more we find ourselves dependent on the World Wide Web as a research tool. The way we seek and find information has changed remarkably: in just the past couple of years, a new term—a verb—has entered into the American linguistic landscape. We find ourselves saying things like "Just Google it. I bet you'll find what you're looking for." The use of Internet search engines as the first and only stop for information has completely changed the way that some students and teachers approach research and information seeking.

The challenge that this notion presents is that many people do not realize that these search engines are not magically verifying the veracity or adequacy of the information that they provide. Spiders and robots crawl the Web and look for terms that appear in the Web sites' content and in metatags. These robots do not discriminate—they grab everything and anything that they are programmed to find and happily give it all back to you in your search results.

As with any research endeavor, it is the responsibility of the end users to verify that the information that they use is good material—that it comes from reliable and unbiased sources and that it was written with no hidden agenda. This section will introduce you to the terms, tips, and tools you need to understand how to evaluate Internet resources, both in their content and their sources.

Information Literacy and Peer Review

As a general rule, much of the content of the World Wide Web has not been written with the same rigorous scholarship that you find in scholarly journals, newspaper articles, and books. The notion of peer review does not necessarily have an impact on the content of the vast majority of the materials on the World Wide Web, though there is certainly an abundance of free and easily accessible materials on the Web that reflects excellent scholarship. For example, numerous free online journals have undergone a rigorous peer review process, such as the *Journal for the Association for History and Computing* (*JAHC*), available online at http://mcel.pacificu.edu/JAHC/JAHCindex.HTM.

Traditionally, academic publishing involved a great deal of editorial control, and the distribution of scholarly work was greatly limited; subscription print journals found their way to libraries and to the offices of professors, and often not much further. Electronic publishing and the Internet have in many ways made it much easier to produce and distribute excellent scholarship to a broader and broader audience. Certainly a wealth of information exists on the Internet, and *The History Highway* helps to demystify much of the historical research information that exists online. The Internet can provide end users of all kinds with the information that they seek.

With all of this at your fingertips, one question needs to remain at the forefront of your mind and should be considered and reconsidered: *Are all Web resources created equal?*

The answer, unfortunately, is no. But that only requires you to be a better information consumer. The Web certainly offers a level of convenience never seen before. The speed with which you can retrieve information on a host of subjects is unprecedented. Students and other information consumers often come to the Internet believing it holds all the information they need for a research paper or other project. This is a dangerous assumption. Researchers and others who use only the Web invariably hinder their scholastic potential and, indeed, their own credibility.

Without question there is a great deal of wonderful, accurate, and valuable information on the Internet. Course syllabi from other colleges and universities shed light on a particular subject and provide still more resources, both print and online. Web sites of archival repositories and other cultural institutions identify and describe their collections online, providing users with authenticated digital surrogates as well as context for some of their holdings. The Internet offers an incredible bounty of information, but as with any type of research, the user must exercise good judgment in evaluating its value, authority, verity, and validity.

There is a term that is used often in describing this ability—information literacy. Information literacy is a skill set that allows individuals to "recognize where information is needed" and "to locate, evaluate, and use effectively the needed information."[1] These skills are critical in the era of the Internet. With the relative ease and access of the Internet, anyone with the ability to use Web development software and access to a bit of Web space can place any material at all online. This accessibility can create numerous challenges for researchers who fail to evaluate the information they retrieve.

The History Highway presents a broad range of history-related Web sites that have been evaluated and recommended by scholars in their respective fields. However, in such a volatile and rapidly evolving and changing environment, a Web site can disappear overnight, leaving frustrated and bewildered researchers behind. There have been efforts to archive the vast amount of information on the Web at given times, taking massive snapshots of the Internet on a regular basis. Sources such as the Internet Archive (http://Internet.archive.org/) are useful tools and excellent resources in researching the evolution of the Internet itself, but the constant shift—loss and gain of the availability of Web sites—remains frustrating for users. Sites are constantly being added and deleted from the Internet. Sites that were once free might begin charging a fee for use, limit access, or change their interface, editorial policy, or even overall mission.

The speed, breadth, and availability of online resources have changed the way that libraries do business, as well as the way a researcher might approach a project. For many researchers, serendipitous browsing of library stacks has been replaced by surfing the Web. There is room in the world for both approaches, and it is certain that one approach is not clearly better than the other.

Over the years, users have developed a degree of trust in regard to print sources. Editors review books and journals, and publishers are committed to printing and distributing these works. The process of publishing an article in an academic journal or a scholarly monograph through a commercial or university press is long and tedious. Copy editors carefully scrutinize these submissions, and a panel or group of peers reviews and edits them long before the material is presented in its final form to the public. Then, these print resources are sometimes reviewed by other journals, adding additional end value to the information they contain. These peer-reviewed sources are traditionally deemed reliable, accurate, and acceptable to use in research.

The Democratization of Information

One of the greatest things about the Web is that anyone with an Internet account, reasonable access to Web development tools, and a little bit of Web space can put something—anything—out there for the world to see. The Internet has democratized the distribution of information by offering this means to self-publish material. Much of the material on the Web has not been scrutinized by anyone. The vast majority of Web sites are not reviewed or refereed, certainly not to the extent that scholarly print materials are reviewed. Independent entities may review and award great Web sites, but they do not necessarily review content; their concern is rather appearance, functionality, and creativity. One such entity is the Webby Awards (http://Internet.webbyawards.com/).While these awards are prestigious, they are not the same as peer review.

The democratization of information—new materials being made available to the public every day—does not make it easier for the end user to do work. In fact, this makes it even more critical for all end users to learn to evaluate the online materials they consider using for research or information. The danger in finding faulty information on the Internet increases exponentially as more and more material is made available. By taking a Web source at face value without first trying to verify the information it contains as well as the source or sources for that information, users run the risk of perpetrating an untruth, not to mention personal and professional embarrassment.

Evaluating Web Sites: What to Look For

Many Web sites indicate on the index or home page that they are endorsed by a particular group or evaluating body. This endorsement does not necessarily hold the same weight as a peer-reviewed journal. However, depending on the endorsing body itself and its agenda, this simple piece of information offers initial evidence of the validity and informational value of the Web site.

With the ability to do research online at any time and from practically any place comes the responsibility to understand and evaluate online materials to make certain that these resources are accurate, unbiased, and of high quality. With practice, common sense, and a few skills, you become a good information consumer. You must develop critical thinking skills and an understanding of how to evaluate online sources—that is, you must gain a degree of information literacy. The ability to evaluate online resources when doing research is an extension of the ability to evaluate print resources and primary source materials. Indeed, developing skills to evaluate online resources has become a critical and absolutely necessary first step in the research process.

The Questions

Content: There are several questions that you need to ask as you view a site for the first time. When you first locate a Web site, take a look at the overall content. Are the title and the author of the site easily identified? Is the author credible? Are the author's credentials clearly listed and verifiable? Does the author document experience and expertise on the subject presented? Does the site represent a specific group or organization? Is this clearly indicated or buried within the site itself?

It is important to identify a corporate entity, political group, or religious body sponsoring the site. These bodies may have hidden agendas, despite the organization's attempt to present clear and unbiased information to its potential end users. Clues to the verity of this kind of site might be present in the URL.

If a Web address ends with .com, then this is corporate or commercial Web site. A site with the .edu suffix is from an educational institution, most likely a college or university. However, it should be noted that individuals affiliated with an institution can often place data on the institution's site. These sites generally display a tilde (~) somewhere in the URL and should be accessed with a bit more caution. The content may or may not be sanctioned by the host institution and may well contain biased or incorrect information. However, the page might just as easily be written by a noted professor in the field. Such a page might look like this:

http://Internet.ua.edu/~jdoe.html.

As a general rule, .gov, .org, and .edu sites contain the most reliable information on the Internet with regard to history and history-related sources.

Purpose: When looking at the content of a particular Web site, you must also seek out the purpose of the material presented. That is to say, does the material appear to be scholarly or popular? Who appears to be the intended audience for this Web site? Is it written for students, scholars, or peers? Does the language talk down to its audience? Does it oversimplify complicated information? Does it use language to complicate a simple or commonly understood topic?

Tone: It is critical to also look at the tone of the material presented. As with print material, the end user must be able to recognize the fundamental differences in language style, as well as the differences between a scholarly and nonscholarly work. A scholarly work is generally intended for a relatively narrow audience and is usually serious in content as well as overall appearance and presentation. (However, good scholars can also use humor in their works to good effect!) Popular works, in direct contrast, are written for a broader audience and therefore have broader appeal. While this may not always be the case, the Web site developed for a popular audience may have more graphics, bolder use of color, and broader, more general topics. For example, compare these two Web sites:

http://Internet.eonline.com/

and

http://mcel.pacificu.edu/JAHC/JAHCindex.HTM.

The first site is divided into numerous components, with several graphics, a scrolling bar of headlines, a slide show of alternating photographs and blinking text, and, most notably, advertising for various products. The second site is a sober white page with a simple graphic and blue and black text, and no advertising. The second site listed here is full of valuable information, but it is evident that neither its strength, nor its focus, is on grabbing the attention of a broad audience. It should be noted, however, that Web design is constantly getting more sophisticated, and even the most scholarly of Web sites now feature Flash, JavaScript, beautiful illustrations, and bold and stylish Web design. As with books, you cannot judge them by their covers—or home pages!

It is also important, as with print sources, to understand that Web sites may contain information that seems appropriate to your work, but does not have the level of scholarly value needed for your research. Some sites, while they do provide valuable information, are not geared toward the scholar or expert in a given field. Another type of site relies upon sensationalism, playing upon the curiosity and gullibility of its readers by using inflammatory language. For example, compare the following two sites:

http://scientificamerican.com

and

http://Internet.weeklyworldnews.com/.

While these two sites are obvious examples of the differences between types of online publications, comparing the style, content, and language serves as a useful exercise in understanding the broad range of online publications available with a simple search. A search for "prehistoric man" will generate results in both of these Web sites. However, the data on the *Scientific American* site is much, much more reliable. (And it does not hurt to note that *Scientific American* is also a peer-reviewed print journal with a Web arm.) While you may never consider using the *Weekly World News* in a research project, information that is just as inflammatory, inaccurate, or fictional exists throughout the Internet in much more subtle guises like the Holocaust Deniers of America.

Scope: You must also consider the scope of the material presented in the site being evaluated. Does the site appear to be narrowly or broadly focused on the subject at hand? How does it compare to other things you have read on this same topic? If the creator appears to have omitted important dates, events, or particular aspects of the issue or topic presented, this should immediately indicate a problem with the site. Has a list of related sources, a bibliography or webliography, been included on the site? If so, does the list appear to be biased in any way? Look at the other URLs listed. How does their inclusion reflect upon the site you are investigating?

Currency: The very basic question of currency is one that must be asked when evaluating a Web site. When was the material last updated? Is there a date for the last update? Does the site include the most recent editions of materials referenced? If the Web site has not been updated for a long time, or if citations refer to outdated editions of other sources, this should be a cause for concern. Though some historical discussions remain valid for years after their sites were last updated, many abandoned sites lack, at best, the most recent findings in a field. Is there more current and accurate information elsewhere? Has an old source been used in order to further an unpopular or outdated opinion? Are these opinions current? Does the language appear old-fashioned? Are the terms used considered politically incorrect or offensive? These biases may be especially evident when researching issues of race, gender, sexuality, or class online. You should consider whether the Internet is the best place to seek out the information you need. While a Web site mounted in 1996 may have the best information available online about a particular event, it is the responsibility of the researcher to verify this information and make certain that the site is the best possible source for the purpose it is being used.

Sources: When researching on the Internet, always seek out the sources used to create a site. All of this information should be clearly stated either on the home or index page or on a bibliography included in the site. Are there accurate and clear citations? Can these citations be readily verified? If the information is not easily accessible or readily available, there may be a problem. Check the links provided on the site. Are the linked sites appropriate, useful, and current?

Style: When it comes to Web sites, style is not just a question of simple aesthetics, but can often indicate if the creator of the site is skilled and serious about the information presented. An attractive Web site suggests to the researcher accuracy and authority, but this is certainly not always the case. In the information age, you must learn to be a good information consumer. This is done not only by reviewing all the components stated above, but also by taking note of things such as navigability, structure, and usability of any given Web site. Is there search capability on the site? If not, how does the lack of a search function interfere with the functionality of the site? How does the writing style correspond to the information in the site and the site's intended audience? All these factors should be noted carefully when considering any Web site for use in research of any kind. All information is not created equal.

Images: The Internet, among its many achievements, has created a venue for sharing information graphically as well as through the written word. Images on the Web can provide excellent historical evidence and are valuable tools for research. Images of handwritten letters, photographs, art, and other materials can be extremely interesting and valuable, enhancing the research experience immensely. But it is necessary to be aware that images can readily be altered in order to provide false evidence to support a controversial belief.

Such alterations of images are especially common in sites created by hate groups, most notably Holocaust deniers, who proliferate on the Internet and actively seek to spread their beliefs to others. Because the Web is accessible to anyone, both end users and creators, it has become an easy, effective way to make available materials that are misleading and perpetrate falsehoods. Some Web sites are blatant in that regard, but others manipulate users into believing that they are looking at vetted, accurate information. You must look for bias by investigating the creator of the site and the creator's agenda. The information may not be readily obvious to the end user. A legitimate nonprofit organization can have an .org Web address, but an .org site does not, by mere definition, house reliable or unbiased information.

When controversial information is presented to an audience in a slick, manipulative fashion, the novice researcher could easily be fooled into taking that information at face value as accurate. It is critical when using digitized surrogates of primary source material, including images of photographs, letters, or other correspondence, to take note of the Web address and trace its origin— verifying the source of that image. Compare these two URLs:

http://rmc.library.cornell.edu/FRENCHREV/Lafayette/exhibit/
ampolimages/iampol_lips.htm

and

http://rmc.library.cornell.edu/FRENCHREV/Lafayette
/images/screen/2_11.jpg

Both URLs are from the same collection but this is not immediately clear. The first offers an image of a handwritten recipe for Martha Washington's famous lip salve; the second is a portion of a letter presented on a page with no support documentation or transcription associated. In this case, the only indication that the material is probably reliable comes from the URL, which shows that the image is based in Cornell's library. While many older online exhibitions or digital collections may serve up images without accompanying information, the information in the URL is often enough to verify the validity and veracity of the image. The second URL here is clearly from a collection of images at Cornell University Library on the French Revolution and on Lafayette. By working from right to left and breaking down the URL, you can readily determine where the image is from and how it is being used, and if, in turn, it is an accurate and valid source.

Without the accompanying URL on the second site, all we have is a digitalized handwritten page with no information about the creator, the context, or anything else. By using a program such as Adobe PhotoShop, an unscrupulous creator of a Web site could alter a document or photograph with relative ease in order to support a personal agenda. While there is no great controversy in lip salve, it is critical to look for possible hidden agendas, as well as physical inconsistencies in the images themselves. Do they look altered? Is there evidence of pixelization or smudging concentrated in one area? Do other photographs on this site have similar problems or issues? Are there higher resolution images available to the end user as well?

Digitized Primary Sources: Digital surrogates, in the form of online exhibitions and collections, have increased dramatically over the past few years. Institutional repositories, digital archives, and virtual collections of all kinds are becoming de rigueur in libraries and archives across the United States and beyond. Theses exhibitions and digital collections provide excellent opportunities to gain access to materials that, without the advent of the Internet and its rich graphics capabilities, would be nearly impossible to see. It is important, however, to keep in mind that materials seen online are surrogates, digital images of an original document. Whether the surrogates are being accessed or made available as preservation copies in the same repository where you are doing your research, or are being accessed from halfway around the world, it is critical to review the URL to determine where these images are from and how they are being used.

Copyright and Fair Use: It is essential to consider issues of copyright and fair use when using any resource, including Web resources. Copyright laws are complicated and confusing to most people, but some general rules must be kept in mind. Even if copyright information is not presented on the Web site or is not made clear or evident, the material most probably still falls under copyright law. While access to the material may be free on the Internet, you must adhere to the same copyright laws as with print material.

Citing Online Resources: The most recent editions of *MLA Handbook for Writers of Research Papers,* the *Chicago Manual of Style,* and the *APA Stylebook* all provide information on citing Internet sources. As in any bibliography, it is important to adhere to a prescribed style. Citation information that might not be readily apparent may be part of a credits or an "about the Web site" page on the site you are referencing. You need to provide the most complete and accurate bibliographical information that you can find.

Bringing It All Together

When doing a search for online sources, it is critical to understand the types of sources you are looking for. A user doing historical research needs to seek out sites that are best suited for the project at hand, such as material presented by experts in the subject matter or cultural agencies that specialize in that particular area. While the Web site for a regional chamber of commerce might offer current demographics information on a given area, that resource will not help you if your research focuses on the same geographic area in the mid-nineteenth century. Before you even begin to search the Web, you should define your research and decide what particular types of Web sites will be most helpful. The sources, whatever they may be, should match your purpose and reflect your goals.

Searching the Web

Using a search engine to seek out information online is a task that many people have grown very comfortable with over the past few years. But there is a question that *must* be considered by anyone doing Web searches: How do you know if you are really doing an effective search? Identify a good search engine by first seeking out the advice of your academic institution's library. As mentioned previously, the ubiquitous google.com has taken over as the number one search engine used not only to search the Internet, but to power specialized searches of institutional sites such as colleges and universities. Google is not the only search engine available, and it is important to try different search engines, using the same search terms, in order to see how your results may vary. Here are some factors to consider:

- The search interface: Is it clear? Easy to use?
- How large is the database?
- Is the material indexed by machine or by people?

- How well do the search capabilities (Boolean searching, advanced searching) work?
- Are the results ranked?
- Is there advertising intermingled with the search results?

When in Doubt. . . . ASK!

Working with online resources can indeed be daunting. While the sites named here are plentiful and excellent, we know that more and more history sites are being added to the Web every day.

Brief courses in online search skills are offered frequently in educational institutions and libraries of all kinds. It is also important to never hesitate to ask a librarian for advice and instruction in online searching. A few minutes of instruction can be extremely valuable and ultimately save time as well. Effective searching is a skill that can be learned. Seek out your local information professionals, those who are trained to pass on their information-seeking skills.

If you have a strong interest in a particular topic, it is a good idea to check the Web frequently for information on that particular subject. Some Web sites offer alerts to new sites and updates to their own that may further your knowledge and interest. Bookmarking sites and printing out key materials for future reference will also save time and effort later on.

By keeping these few principles in mind, developing the skills needed to evaluate online resources is not difficult. *The History Highway* has done some of this work for the searcher by providing online sources that have been scrutinized by scholars in their respective fields. As the Web continues to grow and change, researchers from all levels and disciplines must be prepared to access and to interpret the very best the Web has to offer without risking the use of inaccurate, or inappropriate information. By asking the right questions and approaching online research with a critical eye, an open mind, and an arsenal of evaluative tools, the history researcher can reap the ever-growing bounty of the Internet.

Notes

1. American Library Association (ALA). *A Progress Report on Information Literacy: An Update on the American Library Association Presidential Committee on Information Literacy: Final Report* (Chicago: American Library Association, 1998), available at http://www.ala.org/ala/acrl/acrlpubs/whitepapers/progressreport.htm.

Part II

Internet Sites
for Historians

The history sites on the Internet present an astounding amount of information. No one could ever hope to examine and read everything that is now online. Of course, no one could ever read every book in the Library of Congress, either. This is why the Library of Congress is meticulously organized and cataloged. When you need to find a book or a fact, you can go to an index or turn to a librarian for assistance. There is no single Internet librarian, but the subject-area specialists who have written the following sections offer the same guidance and assistance you would get from a knowledgeable librarian or seasoned teacher. Part II of *The History Highway* is designed to help you find specific information when you are looking for it and guide you to interesting and useful sites that are worth examining for pleasure or serious study.

As you read this guide, you will notice that the historical sites on the Internet have been created by a wide variety of people, ranging from history professors and students to publishers and history buffs. There is also a broad range of content on the Internet. Some sites are scholarly; others are informal. Some are composed entirely of links to other sites. The resources described in *The History Highway* have been screened for quality, utility, and reliability. In an age of information superabundance, however, it is important that everyone become a skilled critic of electronic information. To help you make personal determinations about each site, whenever possible the names and sponsoring institutions or organizations are clearly indicated. Nevertheless, we urge you not to assume that every argument or resource that you encounter on the following pages is credible or valid. Just as many excellent books contain some errors and misinterpretations and every library contains fallacious books, so some of the sites mentioned here contain a mixture.

Chapter 3

Futuring Methods, Practitioners, and Organizations

David J. Staley

In the popular imagination, professionals who think about the future are often confused with science fiction buffs. The relationship between the professional futurist and the science fiction buff is akin to the relationship between the professional historian and the history buff. Professional futurists today use a variety of disciplined techniques and work in very practical settings, such as business, government, think tanks, universities, and nonprofit corporations. Below is a list of several such organizations and futurist practitioners. The goal of this list is to provide a sense of the variety of methods futurists employ, describe their Web sites, and detail the types of problems and situations they seek to address.

Anticipating the Future

http://ag.arizona.edu/futures/

This is the Web site for an online course (but not a formal credit-granting course) at the University of Arizona maintained by Roger L. Caldwell. Links to Tutorials, Tours and Seminars; Paradigms, Driving Forces, and Trends; Scenarios, Foresight and Change; and Futures Related Sites and Resources.

The Arlington Institute

http://www.arlingtoninstitute.org

This is the consulting firm of futurist John Peterson. Click onto the links for scenarios, gaming, group process design, and modeling complex systems, each of which offers an excellent description of these futuring methods. Peterson is especially well known for his examination of "wild cards," which he defines as "low-probability, extremely high-impact events that are social and technological developments or natural phenomena [that are] (a) global in scope and directly affect the human condition; (b) potentially disruptive (negatively and/or positively); (c) intrinsically beyond the control of any single institution, group or individual; and (d) rapidly moving."

Battelle

http://www.battelle.org/forecasts/default.stm

Battelle Memorial Institute is a research and development center that works with both government and business to develop new technologies and products. This site is a link to its "Technology Forecasts" page, which includes the institute's Top 10 list of predictions in areas such as the future of terrorism and security, consumer products, and technology generally. See next entry as well.

Battelle: Dr. Futuring

http://www.battelle.org/dr-futuring/

This is the site of Battelle futurist and thought leader Steven Millett. Includes descriptions of futuring methods such as trend analysis and IFS (Interactive Future Simulations), a tool that uses cross-impact analysis to develop multiple scenarios. Includes a link to the technology forecasts noted above.

Center for International Forestry Research

http://www.cifor.cgiar.org/acm/methods/fs.html

This is a CIFR Web page on "Future Scenarios." Includes a link where you can download a brief guide to the variety of scenario methods and the problems to which they can be applied, especially "adaptive management." The file may take a few minutes to download, but the resource is worth the wait.

The Centre for Future Studies

http://www.futurestudies.co.uk

A UK-based think tank that consults with business and encourages discussion, debate, and creative thinking about the future. Click onto "Recent Publications," which includes topics such as scenarios, nanotechnology, and transport. Site includes access to several PowerPoint presentations as well.

Club of Amsterdam

http://www.clubofamsterdam.com/default.asp

The Club of Amsterdam is "an independent, international think tank that supports thought leaders and knowledge workers to form opinions, visions and agendas about preferred futures." Made up largely of corporate leaders. The site includes a journal and links to articles on a wide array of topics such as nanotechnology, media and entertainment, food and agriculture, and culture and religion. Provides an interesting European perspective on futuring methods and interpretations of the future.

Club of Rome

http://www.clubofrome.org/

The Club of Rome is perhaps best known for its 1972 report *The Limits to Growth,* which predicted dwindling oil supplies by the turn of the (last) century and the resulting effects on economic growth. The Club of Rome is an international think tank that explores "the World Problematique," which it defines as a concept "to describe the set of the crucial problems—political, social, economic, technological, environmental, psychological and cultural —facing humanity." On this site, look especially at the links, the downloadable publications (note that some of these are in languages other than English), and the reports, although these have to be ordered separately. Look carefully for the link "tt30," which is a small think tank for futurists around the age of thirty. Includes a link to its book *Exploring a Worthwhile Future for All.*

Deloitte Touche Tohmatsu

http://www.deloitte.com

A global consulting firm, specializing in thought leadership in technology, media and telecommunications; real estate; manufacturing; life sciences; and other areas. This site has links to Deloitte Research, including downloadable position papers on a variety of trends that affect global business. Click on "Insights and Ideas," then click "Deloitte Research." On this page, click on "Deloitte Research by Category" to find links to research on trends in energy and resources, manufacturing, financial services, and consumer business. A highly recommended site.

DonTapscott.com

http://www.nplc.com/

The Web site of futurist Don Tapscott, who works especially with business strategy. This site contains a few links to his recent publications, which offer a quick view of his thinking.

Foresight International

http://www.foresightinternational.com.au/

According to Richard Slaughter, Foundation Professor of Foresight at Swinburne University of Technology, a director of Foresight International, and one of Australia's leading futurists, a futurist is "someone who has learned how to study the future and how to use this knowledge to enable others to identify options and choices now. By studying the future you can move away from a passive or fatalistic acceptance of what may happen to an active and confident participation in creating the future you want." Includes his essay, "The Making of a Futurist."

Foresight (UK)

http://www.foresight.gov.uk/

Science-based futurist projects sponsored by the British government, such as intelligent infrastructure systems; brain science, addiction and drugs; and cybertrust and crime prevention. The links to each project include project reports, executive summaries, and other reports and publications. The site includes links to other future-related Web sites.

The Foundation on Economic Trends

http://www.foet.org/index.htm

The think tank of noted futurist Jeremy Rifkin, the Foundation on Economic Trends "[examines] emerging trends in science and technology and their likely impacts on the environment, the economy, culture and society." Rifkin is an "activist futurist"; note especially the "Campaigns" link, which include his legal challenges and activist work in the areas of human cloning, the hydrogen economy, civil society, and biotechnology patents. Each link describes the activities of Rifkin and his foundation and links to other useful sites.

Global Business Network

http://gbn.com/

Cofounded by Peter Schwartz and Stewart Brand, the Global Business Network is one of the leading futurist organizations. Schwartz especially has been a pioneer in the application of the scenario method to business strategy. An important site, with access to some articles; look especially at those dealing with scenarios. However, beware: many of the links here require a subscription (which is very expensive).

Institute for the Future

http://www.iftf.org

The site offers no free information, but does provide useful descriptions of the kinds of futuring work the institute performs for business and organizations.

KurzweilAI.net

http://www.kurzweilai.net/index.html?flash=2

This is the site of inventor and forward thinker Ray Kurzweil. The AI in the title refers to "accelerated intelligence," the site informs us. Visitors to the site are guided by Ramona, a photorealistic avatar. Links to articles based around themes such as "How to Build a Brain," "Will Machines Become Conscious?" "Dangerous Futures," "Virtual Realities," "The Singularity" (a reference to the accelerating pace of technological change), and "Living Forever," are of particular interest to Kurzweil. Challenging, outside-the-box thinking, too important to dismiss easily.

The Long Now Foundation

http://www.longnow.org/

The Long Now Foundation "hopes to provide counterpoint to today's 'faster/ cheaper' mind set and promote 'slower/better' thinking" by encouraging a very long-term perspective (the "long now" is defined as 10,000 years). Board members include Brian Eno, Esther Dyson, Peter Schwartz, and Stewart Brand. The foundation has begun a number of "slow" projects, such as the 10,000-Year Clock, the Rosetta Project (an archive of all the world's languages), and the All Species Foundation, which is dedicated to cataloging all of the earth's species.

The Millennium Project: Global Futures Study and Research

http://www.acunu.org/

This is a project sponsored by the American Council for the United Nations University. The project is "a global participatory futures research think tank of futurists, scholars, business planners, and policy makers who work for international organizations, governments, corporations, NGOs, and universities." Includes links to "Future Scenarios for Africa," "Lessons of History," "Environmental Security," and "Applications of Futures Research to Policy." A very useful site, highly recommended.

The Next Twenty Years

http://www.tnty.com/

The Next Twenty Years is a conference series on trends and scenarios in bio-technology, nanotechnology, medicine, and security. The site maintains links to a number of "essays on the future" and both webcasts and transcripts of previous conferences.

On the Horizon

http://horizon.unc.edu

On the Horizon is located at the University of North Carolina-Chapel Hill, whose mission is "to inform educators about the challenges that they will face in a changing world and steps they can take to meet these challenges." This useful site has links to the various projects carried out by the organization, a link to *Innovate: Journal of On-Line Education,* and links to conferences. Look especially at the link for "ON-RAMP," which includes links to a wide array of data and materials.

Plausible Futures Newsletter

http://www.plausiblefutures.com/

Site maintained by the Norwegian futurist Ole Peter Galaasen. In addition to links to news stories on science and technology, includes section on different futuring methods, including scenario planning. The site is filled with data, which makes it both valuable and also a bit user-unfriendly, but worthwhile in any event.

The RAND Corporation

http://www.rand.org

Although not known as a futurist organization per se, the RAND Corporation nevertheless provides useful analysis and environment scanning on a number of important topics that are relevant for futurists. This site is filled with downloadable reports on a wide array of topics, including education, the environment, popula-tion and aging, science and technology, and terrorism and homeland security. Look especially at the "hot topics" link for research on important issues like bioterrorism, Iran, Iraq, surveillance, and social issues in Islamic countries.

Scenario Planning Resources

http://www.well.com/~mb/scenario/

Site maintained by futurist Martin Börjesson. Includes links to articles and reports on scenario methods and their various applications and organizations that employ scenarios. A useful site.

Shaping Tomorrow

http://www.shapingtomorrow.com/

A UK organization that tracks trends in business, government, technology, and society. Many of the features on this site require a subscription, so it may not be useful for schools and teaching purposes; the site is aimed largely at business and government clients (and those who can afford to pay). There is a free e-mail newsletter service that provides summaries of articles. Still, an important site that shows a good range of futuring methods and topics.

Social Technologies

http://www.socialtechnologies.com/

A consulting firm that helps clients look five to ten years forward, then applies those insights to strategic thinking in the present. Much of the site describes the services performed by the firm, but note especially the link to "2025." This provides "immersion in the world of 2025." This link is grouped according to fifteen topics, each providing thoughtful scenarios on topics including the built environment, health, energy, the environment and sustainability, work and leisure, and transportation. Most of the material here requires payment, but there are some free downloads.

Toffler Associates

http://www.toffler.com/default.shtml

An executive advisory firm formed by the noted futurists Alvin and Heidi Toffler. "We help companies and governments create their future in the fast emerging 'Third Wave' economy," they note, referring to their 1991 book on the emergence of the information- and knowledge-based economy. Includes a link to a brief number of publications.

The World Future Society

http://wfs.org

The leading futurist organization in the United States, the World Future Society "strives to serve as a neutral clearinghouse for ideas about the future, [including] forecasts, recommendations, and alternative scenarios." Look especially as the regularly updated "Forecasts" link for predictions in the areas of demographics, government and politics, the economy, technology, and culture and lifestyles. Look also at the "The Future: An Owner's Manual" link, which provides a useful description of different futuring methods and applications.

Chapter 4

Future Issues

David J. Staley

Like historical inquiries, an inquiry about the future requires evidence. Since no "archives of the future" yet exist, the futurist must rely on information and data located in the present, such as statistics, trends, journalistic accounts, and government reports. Futurists call searching for and being receptive to a wide variety of such information "environment scanning." Using the information gathered through environment scanning, the futurist can then infer implications and effects, creating useful representations of the future.

Historians do not examine the whole of the past, but rather tend to light upon certain key issues as historiographically important (varieties of social history and gender history are important to historians right now, for example). Similarly, professional futurists also center upon a few key areas of interest or concern, rather than considering the whole of the future. In addition to serving as excellent ways to scan the environment, the sites listed below are grouped according to those key issues that are currently drawing the attention of futurists:

1. the hydrogen economy and alternative energy
2. the Internet and communications
3. demographic and environmental trends
4. terrorism and security
5. nanotechnology
6. biotechnology
7. intellectual property

The Hydrogen Economy and Alternative Energy

The Alternative Energy Institute

http://www.altenergy.org/

AEI is a nonprofit corporation, and this site provides links to various news reports, syllabi, and case studies from around the world. There is some uncertainty as to the authorship of the site (there is little way to determine who or what interests the AEI represents) but the site does offer a perspective very different from that of official government sites or research labs and universities. Use with caution.

HyWeb—The Hydrogen and Fuel Cell Information System in the Internet

http://www.hyweb.de/

This site is maintained by L-B-Systemtechnik, a German commercial firm that "supports industry, politics and non-governmental organisations in the identification of new products and services, in the development of strategies for the introduction of new products and concepts, with system studies, in finding new partners-networking, in the project management and co-ordination of projects, with strategic consultancy services." Supplies access to articles and other publications that provide a useful European perspective. Quality of the links on the site is uneven, however; therefore use with caution. The site is maintained in both English and German.

IEEE: Investigating the Hydrogen Economy

http://www.ari.vt.edu/hydrogen/

A virtual discussion held by the Institute of Electrical and Electronics Engineers after a conference held in April 2004 titled "The Hydrogen Economy: Its Impact on the Future of Electricity." The site includes links to a discussion (which requires a user login), links to other organizations working with hydrogen, background documents in pdf formats, and abstracts from the presenters at the conference.

U.S. Department of Energy Hydrogen, Fuel Cell and Infrastructure Technologies Program

http://www.eere.energy.gov/hydrogenandfuelcells/

Provides a useful introduction to the main issues concerning the hydrogen economy and the technology of fuel cells. Interesting sections on "The

Hydrogen Future" and teaching materials for elementary, secondary, and university teachers.

The Internet and Communications

Center for the Digital Future

http://www.digitalcenter.org

Supported by the University of Southern California Annenberg Center for the Digital Future, the site includes yearly reports from the project "Surveying the Digital Future: A Longitudinal International Study of the Individual and Social Effects of PC/Internet Technology." This is "a long-term longitudinal study on the impact over time of computers, the Internet and related technologies on families and society." Includes links to the first three annual reports as well as findings from the first World Internet Report and the use of the Internet by Latinos. An important source.

Centre for Quantum Computation

http://www.qubit.org/

Located at Cambridge University, the CQC "conducts theoretical and experimental research into all aspects of quantum information processing, and into the implications of the quantum theory of computation for physics itself." Quantum computing weds aspects of quantum mechanics to information processing. Click on "Research," which links to different working groups, and on "Library" for links to articles, books, and presentations on quantum computing. The "Community" link includes links to researchers (and their home pages). See also "Tutorials." Warning: the information here is quite specialized, but nevertheless provides a useful introduction to the dimensions of the research involved here.

CompSpeak2050: Institute for the Study of Talking Computers and Oral Cultures

http://www.compspeak2050.org

This is the Web site for William Crossman, philosopher and futurist, who maintains that computers and computing will soon evolve into what he calls VIVO (Voice In/Voice Out) "talking computers." One of his more controversial claims is that written language will eventually be phased out and that VIVO will facilitate the creation of a new kind of electronic oral culture by the year 2050.

The site includes links to articles Crossman has published (although note that many of these are published in various European languages) and conferences at which he has presented. Culture Challenging Conceptualization that is important for all futurists to consider.

First Monday

http://www.firstmonday.dk/

An online, peer-reviewed journal dealing with the Internet. Excellent articles on a range of issues, including open source, the politics of information, and the digital divide, especially the Internet in the developing world. Highly recommended.

Future of Computing

http://www.infoweblinks.com/content/futureofcomputing.htm

Sponsored by a textbook publisher, this is a collection of links on issues dealing with quantum, molecular, and DNA computing. Very interesting and useful links for thinking about the future of computing.

The Journal of Digital Information

http://jodi.ecs.soton.ac.uk/

An electronic journal developed by the British Computer Society and Oxford University Press, centering on "the management, presentation and uses of information in digital environments." The journal is organized thematically, although published in traditional "issue" format. These themes are Digital Libraries, Hypermedia Systems, Hypertext Criticism, Information Discovery, Information Management, Social Consequences of Digital Information, and Usability of Digital Information. A useful resource.

Liquid Information

http://www.liquidinformation.org/

Liquid Information is a project developed by Frode Hegland and Doug Engelbart (who developed the mouse). The project aims to "make text more interactive— turning words into hyperwords." In their vision, all the words on a screen would be linked to other forms of information. Click on "Demo" to see, for instance, a live CNN.com page. Click onto any word and a screen pops up, allowing the user to look up the word in a dictionary, to do a Google search, or link to other paragraphs that contain the word. The site is experimental, but suggests a new way of thinking about text on the screen.

Pew Internet and American Life Project:
The Future of the Internet

http://www.pewinternet.org/pdfs/PIP_Future_of_Internet.pdf

A January 2005 report of a survey of technologists, scholars, and members of the public that considers a wide variety of issues, such as the impact of the Internet on news and publishing, security, education, families, and civic engagement. A useful and highly recommended source.

Wired.com

http://wired.com/

The online version of the technology magazine. Not a futurist publication per se, but very good at locating cutting-edge developments and thinking through some of the implications. Covers many types of technologies (including biotechnology and nanotechnology).

Demographic and Environmental Trends

Bureau of Labor Statistics

http://stats.bls.gov/

Includes statistics on employment and unemployment, demographics, occupations, productivity, inflation and consumer spending, business costs, and geography. Includes links to publications and research papers.

Child Trends Databank

http://www.childtrendsdatabank.org/

Reports, tables, and figures on trends in health, social and emotional development, income, education, demographics, and family/community as related to American children. Data are very accessible, as the audience here is journalists, researchers, students, policy makers, and child advocates. Very useful, highly recommended.

A Demographic Perspective on Our Nation's Future

http://www.rand.org/publications/DB/DB320/

A downloadable PDF file of a complete, forty-nine–page book from the RAND Corporation. Considers demographic trends such as declining birthrates, generation gaps, economic disparity, and increasing ethnic diversity. The study then addresses the policy implications of these demographic trends.

Energy Information Administration

http://www.eia.doe.gov/

The Energy Information Administration is a statistical agency of the U.S. Department of Energy. Statistical data on a wide variety of energy sources, including historical data. Look especially at the link to "Projections to 2025," which includes forecasts for such topics as market forces, coal, emissions, and electricity. Site includes links to downloadable publications, press releases, and weekly updates.

Global Trends 2015: A Dialogue About the Future With Nongovernment Experts

http://www.cia.gov/cia/reports/globaltrends2015/#link3

A CIA Web site that is not a traditional intelligence assessment. Considers seven key "drivers" of the future: demographics, natural resources and the environment, science and technology, globalization, national and international governance, future conflicts, and the role of the United States. Site also considers major uncertainties, including asymmetrical warfare, demographic challenges in Europe and Japan, and unpredictable conditions in the Middle East and China. Contains useful charts, graphs, and maps. An excellent resource for thinking about the future.

Google Zeitgeist

http://www.google.com/press/zeitgeist.html

A compilation of trends in Google searches. Interesting way to gauge attitudes in the culture at the moment, although perhaps less useful for spotting longer term trends.

Hispanic Trends

http://www.hispaniconline.com/trends/

Online version of the print magazine *Hispanic Trends*. Online version has compilations of newspaper reports dealing with arts and entertainment, sports, business, politics, and education.

National Statistics, UK

http://www.statistics.gov.uk

British statistics dealing with a range of social trends, from agriculture and commerce to crime, unemployment, and population/migration. Filled with data, although sometimes confusing to navigate. Recommended nevertheless.

Online Trends: A Compendium of Data on Global Change

http://cdiac.esd.ornl.gov/trends/trends.htm

Site maintained by the Carbon Dioxide Information Analysis Center, which is described as "the primary global-change data and information analysis center of the U.S. Department of Energy." Includes trend data on atmospheric trace gas concentrations, greenhouse gas emissions, climate, and ecosystems. This information also includes useful graphics and data sets.

Population Reference Bureau

http://www.prb.org/

The Population Reference Bureau provides "timely and objective information on U.S. and international population trends and their implications." The site incorporates links for educators which include lesson plans. Click onto "Datafinder" for a database of world population and health statistics. "PRB library" links to many useful free publications. The site, which can be searched by topic or by region, includes links to other PRB Web sites, such as the Center for Public Information on Population Research and the Interagency Gender Working Group. Highly recommended.

Trends in Europe and North America

http://www.unece.org/stats/trend/trend_h.htm#ch1

Site maintained by the United Nations Economic Commission for Europe. Note that registration is required to look at the comprehensive data on this site; however, there is a "restricted area" link that provides access, without any registration, to a wealth of useful compilations of statistics covering a wide variety of topics, from energy and environment to families and education. Look especially at the brief but very useful country profiles, which include many tables and charts.

Trends in Japan

http://web-jpn.org/trends/index.html

Very interesting site on trends in Japanese science and education, business and economics, sports, fashion, and popular culture and society. Provides short articles, which are compilations and summaries of Japanese news sources, on each trend.

U.S. Census Bureau

http://www.census.gov/

A necessary resource. Population, economic and business, and geographic data are accessible from this site.

U.S. Department of Justice, Bureau of Justice Statistics

http://www.ojp.usdoj.gov/bjs/welcome.html

Statistics on victims and crimes, prosecution, law enforcement, courts and sentencing, corrections, and drugs. Includes tables and charts.

WHO Statistical Information System (WHOSIS)

http://www3.who.int/whosis/menu.cfm

Site maintained by the World Health Organization. Tabular data on a wide variety of health issues and epidemiological data from countries around the world. Click onto the "Publications" link for several downloadable WHO publications. The "Research tools" link includes geo-referenced databases. Somewhat awkward to navigate, but filled with useful statistical data nevertheless.

Worldwatch Institute

http://www.worldwatch.org/

Worldwatch Institute "offers a unique blend of interdisciplinary research, global focus, and accessible writing that has made it a leading source of information on the interactions among key environmental, social, and economic trends." Main topics include people, nature, economy, and energy. This site includes links to many of the institute's publications (these are not free, although they are moderately priced). Free information is included on the site by following the link under "Research Library." See also the "Press Room" link.

Terrorism and Security

Al Qaeda, Trends in Terrorism and Future Potentialities: An Assessment

http://www.rand.org/publications/P/P8078/

Link to a downloadable PDF document from Bruce Hoffman, of the RAND Corporation. Considers the current and future state of the Al Qaeda network, as well as future trends in terrorism, especially thinking about the forms future terrorist acts might take.

Department of Homeland Security

http://www.dhs.gov/dhspublic/

Includes links to news and press releases. Note especially the links to "Research and Technology."

Facts on International Relations and Security Trends (FIRST)

http://first.sipri.org/

Searchable database on a wide array of trends in international security, such as nuclear weapons, military expenditures, peacekeeping activities, arms production and trade, and conventional weapons holdings. The site is aimed at politicians, journalists, researchers, and the general public.

Future Directions in Terrorism: Implications for Australia

http://www.aspi.org.au/pdf/Terrorism_Creswell_AB.pdf

Not a metasite, but rather a PDF of an address by Aldo Borgu of the Australian Strategic Policy Institute (ASPI), delivered on September 8, 2004, to the Special Operations Command Senior Leadership Group. Lays out what Borgu perceives as "basic facts" about terrorism and its implications for Australia. Asks poignant questions about the future of terrorism. An important perspective from outside the United States.

Homeland Security Institute

http://www.homelandsecurity.org

The Homeland Security Institute's mission is "to assist the Department of Homeland Security (DHS), Science and Technology Directorate and the DHS Operating Elements, in addressing important homeland security issues, particularly those requiring scientific, technical, and analytical expertise." Includes links to the *Journal of Homeland Security,* which has articles, book reviews, interviews, and commentary, and to a newsletter with links to news and press releases.

U.S. State Department: Patterns of Global Terror

http://www.state.gov/s/ct/rls/pgtrpt/

An annual report to Congress from the State Department on the level and scope of terrorist activities across the globe.

Nanotechnology

Foresight Institute

http://www.foresight.org/

According to the site, the Foresight Institute is an "educational organization formed to help prepare society for anticipated advanced technologies," and its advisory board includes notable names from the worlds of business, academics, and medicine. The site includes links to news reports, to a threaded discussion page, and to *Foresight Update*, a publication of the Institute. Very useful site.

The Institute of Nanotechnology

http://www.nano.org.uk

Attached to the University of Stirling Innovation Park (United Kingdom). Site includes links to universities, government research centers, and others engaged in nanotechnological research. Includes links to images, although many of these are PowerPoint quality (they are not very high resolution and just average quality). Users must join in order to view the full Web site, but an associate membership is free. Many parts of the site can be accessed without a login.

Nanotech Now

http://nanotech-now.com/

According to its mission statement, Nanotech Now seeks to "provide a forum and format that helps clarify nanotechnology and nanoscale science, to laymen, general business persons, non-specialists, highly skilled technicians, professionals, and academics. Our most basic intentions are to stimulate public debate, and to provide a single-source information point." Note especially the "Possible Futures" and "Image Gallery" links.

National Nanotechnological Initiative

http://www.nano.gov

The NNI is an association of federal research and development projects. Includes links to media reports on nanotechnology, and an educational resource link for elementary, secondary, and university students and their teachers.

Technology Review.com

http://technologyreview.com/

The online version of the MIT publication. Centers on leading-edge technologies, especially those that are ripe for commercialization. Also useful for keeping up with trends in biotechnology and in computing.

The University of Wisconsin-Madison Materials Research Science and Engineering Center (MRSEC) Interdisciplinary Education Group (IEG)

http://www.mrsec.wisc.edu/edetc/index.html

Site that focuses on nanotechnology as a way to teach science and engineering concepts to college students. Includes links to a wide array of teaching materials, slide libraries, kits, and modules. Intended for science teachers rather than those interested in the future implications of the technology, but accessible nevertheless.

Biotechnology

Bio.com

http://www.bio.com/

This site, which is aimed largely at life scientists and biotech companies, features many industry reports, covering topics such as genomics, proteomics, bioinformatics, and drug discoveries. Bio.com seeks "the exchange of information within the life sciences, biotechnology and pharmaceutical industries." Although these are specialized topics, the articles are written in journalistic fashion and so are accessible.

BioPortal

http://www.bioportal.gc.ca/english/BioPortalHome.asp?x=1

This official site of the Canadian government contains information on "government policy and research activity; business support programs and market intelligence; a virtual library of educational resources; and regulations on biotechnology research and applications."

The Biotechnology and Development Monitor

http://www.biotech-monitor.nl/

An online journal sponsored by the Network University in the Netherlands. The journal presents "critical views on biotech, agriculture, sustainable development and food security issues for developing countries." Most of the articles are written for a broad audience of policy makers, scientists, students, and journalists, and so are user-friendly. Issues are free, but subscriber information is requested. The site also includes an extensive collection of links, grouped by topic, geographic region, and type of organization, and each of these is grouped into subcategories.

Biotechnology Australia

http://www.biotechnology.gov.au/

A Web site sponsored by the Australian government. The "links" link connects to a wide variety of Australian and international Web pages dealing with biotech associations and services and educational institutions.

Biotechnology Industry Organization

http://www.bio.org/

An information, advocacy, and business support group, the Biotechnology Industry Organization provides links to press releases, speeches and publications, government and business reports, and position papers covering topics such as health care, intellectual property, and bioethics. Note especially the link to "Science Updates."

Biotechnology Information Directory Section

http://www.cato.com/biotech/

A metasite sponsored by Cato Research, which is "a full-service contract research and development organization with international resources dedicated to helping pharmaceutical and biotechnology companies efficiently and expeditiously navigate the regulatory approval process in order to bring new drugs, biologics, and medical devices to the people who need them." Does not appear to be related to the Cato Institute. Links to many sites, covering such categories as publications, products, clinical trials, and software.

Biotechnology Law Resources

http://biotech.law.lsu.edu/blaw/

A metasite from Louisiana State University's law school, the site includes links to terrorism and bioterrorism resources, biomedical engineering and the law, and cases and briefs related to biotechnology. Not as extensive as the Working Group on Environmental Justice site listed below, but still useful.

Biozone International

http://www.biozone.co.uk/biolinks/BIOTECHNOLOGY.html

Biozone International is a publishing house in New Zealand that produces educational materials for secondary school students. This site is a metasite with links organized according to topics such as general sites, biotechnology techniques, biotechnology processes, applications in biotechnology, and issues and ethics of biotechnology.

The Center for the Study of Technology and Society

http://www.tecsoc.org/biotech/biotech.htm

This Washington, DC, think tank "examines the interaction of technological change and society. The Center will strive to emphasize and clarify the point that advances in technology are neither inherently good nor inherently evil—but that every new technology has the potential to cause problems, and the capacity to solve problems." This page is its "Biotechnology" page (the Center maintains several other such pages), and it includes useful links to newspaper articles on biotechnology. A very useful site.

Council for Biotechnology Information

http://www.whybiotech.com/

The Council for Biotechnology Information "communicates science-based information about the benefits and safety of agricultural and food biotechnology. Its members are the leading biotechnology companies and trade associations." Site is chiefly composed of articles written by the CBI. Includes sections for consumers, farmers, teachers and students, and journalists.

The Electronic Journal of Biotechnology

http://www.ejbiotechnology.info/

Sponsored by UNESCO, this online journal contains articles dealing with a wide range of biotechnological issues, with particular focus on the impact of biotechnology in the developing world. The site includes links to news, organizations, publications, and other information sources.

European Federation of Biotechnology

http://www.efbweb.org/

The European Federation of Biotechnology is an association "of all national and cross-national Learned Societies, Universities, Institutes, Companies and Individuals interested in the promotion of Biotechnology throughout Europe and beyond." The association is interested in promot[ing] biotechnology in a "socially and ethically acceptable manner" and so is interested in issues of sustainability. The site is a collection of links to Web pages featuring the Federation's sections, working groups, and task groups. These Web pages largely report on the activities of each of these groups and do not contain many reports or publications, but they are useful and inviting nevertheless. Look for "weblinks" to a wide variety of information services, various European associations, and other related sites.

The European Initiative for Biotechnology Education

http://www.eibe.info/

This site features nineteen units dealing with a broad array of topics on biotechnology, such as "Biotechnology and the Environment," "The Human Genome Project," and "Biotechnology: Past and Present." Designed as teaching materials for sixteen to nineteen-year-old (European) students, each unit contains experiments, debate topics, and role-playing activities. Easy-to-access PDF files.

Friends of the Earth Europe

http://www.foeeurope.org/GMOs/Index.htm

A grassroots environmental organization, the site is devoted to issues surrounding biotechnology and genetically modified organisms. Site includes links to a quarterly magazine, *Biotech Mailout*; other FoEE reports and publications; press releases; and European legislation. This antibiotechnology site provides a useful perspective that should be considered.

Union of Concerned Scientists

http://www.ucsusa.org/food_and_environment/biotechnology/page.cfm?pageID=340

The Union of Concerned Scientists aims to "augment rigorous scientific analysis with innovative thinking and committed citizen advocacy to build a cleaner, healthier environment and a safer world." This site is entitled "What Is Biotechnology?" and includes reports and short position papers.

Working Group on Environmental Justice

http://ecojustice.net/biotechnology/

Located at Harvard, this is a metasite that includes links to news reports (and many audio clips) dealing with issues such as biosafety, genetic engineering, intellectual property rights, world trade, and international relations. Extensive list of links.

ZNet: Biotechnology

http://www.zmag.org/biotechwatch.htm

A site maintained by activists against biotechnology. Includes links to organizations as well as to articles—really more like blogs—on biotechnology issues. A challenge especially to global corporations and outside the mainstream, the site offers a useful and provocative perspective nevertheless.

Intellectual Property

The Consumer Project on Technology

http://www.cptech.org/ip/wipo/genevadeclaration.html

The Consumer Project on Technology was started by Ralph Nader. This site includes links to legal documents, government reports, articles, patents, and commentary by CPTech.

Copyfutures: The Future of Copyright

http://lsolum.typepad.com/copyfutures/2004/08/the_future_of_c.html

Copyfutures is the blog for Professor Lawrence Solum's Intellectual Property Seminar at the University of San Diego School of Law. Also includes links to news reports, other blogs, and Web sites of universities and other organizations devoted to copyright issues.

Creative Commons

http://creativecommons.org/

Stanford University law professor Lawrence Lessig's organization, Creative Commons advocates "flexible copyright" for creative works and is one of the driving forces for a relaxation of existing copyright laws. Site includes features on and links to various flexible copyright sites covering music, text, education, images, and audio.

Electronic Frontier Foundation

http://www.eff.org/

Founded by John Perry Barlow (of Grateful Dead fame) and John Gilmore, the Electronic Frontier Foundation is an advocacy group interested in "civil liberties issues related to technology." (Lawrence Lessig belongs to the board.) Site includes links to news reports, legal briefs, and congressional briefings.

IP @ The National Academies

http://search.nap.edu/shelves/ip/

The National Academies are the congressionally chartered National Academy of Sciences, the National Academy of Engineering, the Institute of Medicine, and the National Research Council. Topics here include antitrust, copyright, database protection, international harmonization, technology transfer, and trademarks, among others. Most of the links here are merely order forms for books, but the link to the newsletter is free and useful.

The Motion Picture Association of America

http://www.mpaa.org/home.htm

Links to PDF files stating the movie industry's take on issues of piracy, digital copyright, and creativity. A frequent target of scorn by those advocating for "free culture," but this is a needed site to balance the views of the other advocacy groups listed in this section.

Public Knowledge

http://www.publicknowledge.org/

Public Knowledge defines itself as an "advocacy group working to defend your rights in the emerging digital culture." Lawrence Lessig sits on the board of directors; Siva Vaidhyanathan (author of *Copyrights and Copywrongs: The Rise of Intellectual Property and How It Threatens Creativity*) is on the advisory board. Intended for policy makers, scholars, journalists, and artists, the site is filled with links to data, news reports, analysis of current intellectual property debates, and press releases. The "Issues" link is a good place to start in order to organize all the complex facets of this issue.

Chapter 5

General History

Mary E. Chalmers

Metasites (General and Specific History Categories)

Galaxy

http://www.galaxy.com/cgi-bin/dirlist?node=53033

Galaxy, claiming to be the Internet's first searchable directory, provides links to history sites in thirty-eight categories, including oral and other types of history; treaties, pacts, and agreements; museums; philosophy of history; and this day and week in history.

History of Science, Technology, and Industry

http://echo.gmu.edu/center.php

This Center for History and New Media at George Mason University Web site "catalogues, annotates, and reviews" more than 5,000 sites on the history of science, technology, and industry. Searchable by topic, historical period, and source type, the Web site also provides guidance to find and learn about projects collecting historical materials online.

Tennessee Technological University History Resources

http://www2.tntech.edu/history/

This site is a good starting place for students to find not only historical resources (documents, textbooks, audiovisuals, archives, and so on), but also sources about careers, study, travel, and scholarly groups. Some of the material on the site is directed toward TTU students, but scrolling down reveals resources of broader interest.

Visual Arts Sources and Images

http://library.concordia.ca/research/subjects/arthistory/visualart/
artvisualart.php

This research tool from the library of Montreal-based Concordia University provides access to significant art history guides, museums, and resources for finding visual images of art, architecture, and art history from around the world. Additional sites focus on Canadian resources.

WWW Virtual Library for History

http://vlib.iue.it/history/index.html

http://rmweb.Indiana.edu/history/vl/index.html

The Virtual Library (VL) for History, formerly at the University of Kansas, now has its central catalogue at European University Institute in Italy, with a mirror site at University of Indiana. The VL has grown so much that the catalog is now an "integrated and international network of indexes," accessible by clicking on "WWW VL History." The catalog is searchable through Google and by epoch, country or region, topic, and research methods and materials.

Topic-Specific Sites

Arctic Circle

http://arcticcircle.uconn.edu/index.html

Arctic Circle is an educational site on the peoples, cultures, natural resources, and history of the Arctic region. It explores questions of social equity and environmental justice as connected to the diverse cultures, histories, political economies, and interests of the Arctic Circle. This site also provides extensive links to other Internet materials on culture, science, education, and other related topics. Arctic anthropologist Norman Chance maintains the site.

Collated Web Index of Historians and Philosophers

http://www.scholiast.org/history/histphil.html

This Web site, created by Danish graduate student Peter Ravn Rasmussen, provides available links to ancient, medieval, and modern historians and philosophers. The links, not all of which remain valid, range from online archives to each historian's or philosopher's publications and home page to biographies and notes.

History of Money

http://www.ex.ac.uk/~RDavies/arian/llyfr.html

This site is a good place to start if you want to know about the history of money and related topics. Based on Glyn Davies's *A History of Money from Ancient Times to the Present Day,* the site contains both a chronology of money through time and essays on the Vikings, Celtic coins, third-world debt, the European Union, the U.S. dollar, and more. The site also has Web links to other sites about money, its value, and its history.

Maritime History

http://ils.unc.edu/maritime/home.shtml

This site brings together the vast resources (Web links and library databases) available for researching maritime history. The classification system for the online resources largely follows the fourth edition of R.G. Albion's *Naval & Maritime History: An Annotated Bibliography* and its *Supplement* by B.W. Labaree.

Popular Culture

http://www.uky.edu/Subject/popcul.html

The University of Kentucky Libraries maintains this subject catalog on popular culture. While it has not been updated in a couple of years, most of the URLs are still valid. Find access to top-notch libraries, colleges, and organizations devoted to popular culture as well as a diverse mix of resources on popular culture.

Professional Cartoonists Index

http://cagle.msnbc.com/

Daryl Cagle, the cartoonist for the online magazine *Slate,* maintains this site of newspaper editorial cartoons. The site includes cartoons by cartoonists from around the world, with access to cartoon archives for many of the cartoonists. Currently, the site also has separate sections of cartoons about Iraq and about the War on Terror. In addition, the site provides lesson plans for integrating political cartoons into the classroom.

A Walk Through Time

http://physics.nist.gov/GenInt/Time/time.html

This site, maintained by the National Institute of Standards and Technology, presents a short, illustrated narrative about time through the ages. It begins with a look at ancient calendars and early clocks and continues through mechanization, standardization, and developing technology.

World Rulers

http://rulers.org

A source to find out names of rulers of countries and territories, including subdivisions, often back to 1700. It also has chronological accounts of the changes in status of these entities, including disputed areas. Foreign ministers of the twentieth (and sometimes nineteenth) century are also listed. It also identifies the chronology of leaders of many world religions and international organizations.

Resources for Historians and Students of History

Guide to History Departments Around the World

http://chnm.gmu.edu/resources/departments

The Center for History and New Media at George Mason University manages this searchable database of more than 1,200 history department Web sites.

H-Net Home Page

http://www.h-net.org/

H-Net is an innovative, international organization of scholars and teachers dedicated to developing the potential of the Internet to facilitate "the free exchange of academic ideas and scholarly resources." The site contains links to more than 100 discussion lists, each with its own scholarly or pedagogical focus. Discussions from those lists and peer-reviewed scholarly book reviews are accessible and searchable.

Internet History Sourcebooks

http://www.fordham.edu/halsall

An excellent site for finding primary documents is the Internet Sourcebooks. This site provides copy-permitted primary sources and links to other Web sites of primary sources. Begun as the Medieval History Sourcebook, the site has now expanded to cover ancient, medieval, and modern eras. Additionally, sourcebooks cover a range of regional, topical, and thematic categories.

K–12 Teachers Website for History and Social Studies

http://school.discovery.com/schrockguide/history/histg.html

The administrator for technology for Nauset Public Schools (Cape Cod, Massachusetts) and a former library media specialist, Kathy Schrock has put together a diverse array of links to sites appropriate for K–12 teachers. Besides links to other sites identifying additional resources, she has links to engaging topical sites such as "Wacky Patent of the Month," Nobel winners and related sites, "Evening News Abstracts" since 1968, and newspaper advertisements from 1911 to 1955. She also has guides to U.S. and world and ancient history sites from this URL.

Maps for Historians

http://www.lib.utexas.edu/maps/map_sites/hist_sites.html

This University of Texas Library Web site allows access both to the Perry-Castañeda Library Map Collection (historical maps grouped by geographic region, plus historical astronomical charts) and to historical maps available on the Web.

Chapter 6

Ancient History

TammyJo Eckhart

Any attempt to use one search term to discover all the sources concerning "ancient" cultures will prove to be misleading at worst and unhelpful at best. Terms are inconsistently used, not only on the Internet and the World Wide Web but also between institutions, professionals, and cataloging systems. Instead of just typing in the term "ancient," it may be wisest to try to determine what terms are used most often for the culture and time period you are interested in. If your interest is very new and you are unsure of the correct terminology, try looking for the general regional or cultural term and scan the results for hints as to the time period covered, or find a general site that claims to give an outline of the history of that place and people.

The Web sites included here were tested for ease of access, variety of information, and focus on factual or commercial information. First there are general ancient history sites, which include a variety of geographic and cultural resources. Then Web sites that focus on specific geographic or historic periods are featured. All site links are for English-language versions, though search engines and metalink sites will have links to resources around the world. Knowledge of German, French, Italian, Greek, and Latin is quite useful when researching the ancient world.

General Ancient History Web Sites

Ancient World Mapping Center

http://www.unc.edu/awmc

The Ancient World Mapping Center at the University of North Carolina at Chapel Hill promotes cartography, historical geography, and geographic information science. It has many free maps, as well as information on conferences about studies around the world.

Art History Resources on the Web

http://witcombe.sbc.edu/ARTHLinks.html

In 1995 Chris Witcombe, professor of art history at Sweet Briar College in Virginia, created an extensive metasite of online resources about art history around the world, from the prehistoric to the modern periods. The sections are chronological as well as geographical and include often-overlooked regions such as Oceania and North America. Most of the links have images that are free to educators, but some links require permission before users can download or use them in the classroom.

BUBL LINK

http://bubl.ac.uk/link/a/ancienthistory.htm

This is an index maintained by the Centre for Digital Library Research at the University of Strathclyde, Scotland, with the stated goal of promoting the use of information technology in education. Descriptions and links to a variety of Internet resources are listed by Web site title. The links range from Mesoamerica to Asia and include topics lists, subject bulletin boards, and a Latin dictionary and grammar text, as well as a section for today's news and events relating to any of the cultures covered.

Cindy Renfron: Culinary & Brewing History Links

http://members.aol.com/renfrowcm/links.html

An inclusive site from the well-respected author of books on the history of cooking. Provides links to many sites dealing with different aspects of food and drink in ancient and medieval Europe. Her home page provides a hands-on approach to learning about ancient food.

Encyclopedia Mythica

http://www.pantheon.org/mythica.html

Started in 1995 and still chiefly edited by Micha F. Lindemans, this is a searchable online encyclopedia that boasts over 5,700 entries. The Web site is organized into several areas: mythology, folklore, a bestiary, heroes, an image gallery, and genealogy tables. Several parts of the site are under continuous construction. The site has a staff of specialists from around the world who focus on particular cultures or periods, but it also gathers articles from anyone wishing to submit materials.

The Institute for the Study of Slavery (ISOS)

http://www.nottingham.ac.uk/isos/

Started by Thomas Wiedemann as the International Centre for the History of Slavery in 1998, this organization has expanded beyond the historical study of slavery, but it is still an excellent place to begin research on slavery in any time period. The site and the institute are currently directed by Dick Geary, of the School of History at the University of Nottingham.

International Numismatic Commission

http://www.amnumsoc.org

The home page for the INC provides links to major collections and updates on legal changes relating to numismatics, as well as information about the organization itself. It can be accessed in both English and French.

Modern Western Civilizations

http://www.execulink.com/~bcox/hwm/index.htm

Do not be put off by the site's title; this has excellent links to the subjects of history, art, music, geography, psychology, and sociology for cultures around the world and throughout time. The extensive links are divided into dozens of categories, including organizations, archives, architecture, and even employment resources, which are missing from many other metasites. The sites are not peer-reviewed.

OSSHE Historical & Cultural Atlas Resource

http://www.uoregon.edu/~atlas/

Developed at the University of Oregon in 1996, this site offers a variety of maps from Europe and North America throughout history. It is the continued effort of the Departments of History and Geography along with the New Media Center. Most of the maps require Macromedia Flash to work.

Papyrology Home Page

http://www.users.drew.edu/jmuccigr/papyrology/

Designed and maintained by John D. Muccigrosso, assistant professor at Drew University, this Web site offers links to papyrus collections, images, journals, professional societies, and other papyrology sites. Not regularly updated.

Ancient African History Web Sites

There is a huge gap on the Internet in professional and academically sound sources about ancient Africa. This gap reflects not only a lack of archaeological and written evidence, but also an intense interest in alternative theories that do not meet basic academic standards.

African Timelines

http://www.cocc.edu/cagatucci/classes/hum211/timelines/htimeline.htm

Edited by Cora Agatucci, professor of English at Central Oregon Community College, this site has many links to specific periods and cultures; it also addresses some controversial topics confronting students of ancient history and African history today.

Egyptology.com

http://www.egyptology.com/

Full of links to other online resources about Egypt, the "alternative" sites are set aside from the mainstream and scholarly lists, a large gallery of images, and sections on select individual subjects. There is also a link to the journal *KMT,* where the site's creator, Greg Reeder, is a contributing editor.

Egyptology Resources

http://www.newton.cam.ac.uk/egypt/index.html

Celebrating its tenth year in service with the assistance of the Newton Institute at the University of Cambridge, Egyptology Resources, created and maintained by Nigel Strudwick, tries to find the best resources, research, and organizations focusing on ancient Egypt available on the World Wide Web today. Wide range of materials for professionals, teachers, and students. Updated frequently.

Ancient Asia

Like Africa, the number of countries and the sparse surviving written evidence have left a considerable gap in resources on ancient Asia. It may be best to search for specific countries when looking for information about Asia, then trace the history backward. Some unique sites and metasites are listed below.

Asian Arts

http://www.asianart.com/

Regularly updated and searchable Web site edited by Ian Alsop that provides information about galleries, resources, books, and events related to art throughout Asian history. Also has a forum for questions and discussion.

China WWW Virtual Library

http://sun.sino.uni-heidelberg.de/igcs/

Maintained and regularly updated by the Institute of Chinese Studies, Heidelberg University, this searchable site has links to a wide range of periods and topics and focuses on scholarly resources. It is edited by Hanno E. Lecher with a staff of scholars specializing in Chinese culture and history. Regularly updated.

Harappa: Glimpses of South Asia Before 1947

http://www.harappa.com/

A wonderfully visual site produced by Omar Khan; offers brief information and a multitude of images from the earliest civilizations of the Indus Valley until India's independence from Great Britain in 1947. Includes artistic and scholarly images as well as movies and sound clips.

History of China

http://www.chaos.umd.edu/history/welcome.html

Leon Poon's site is still the best one-stop source for information and links about the earliest civilizations of China. The basic information is legally copied from the *U.S. Army's Area Handbook on China.*

Ancient Europe

This section includes cultures from throughout Europe with the exception of resources focused on Greece or Rome. More detailed information can be found searching by country or culture name.

The Bronze Age in Europe

http://www.geocities.com/Athens/Crete/4162/

Indexed by region along with links to resources on metallurgy, general information, and current exhibits or events related to ancient Europe, this site is regularly updated by B. Sprenzel, a student of European archaeology at the University of Regensburg. It is available in English or German.

The Prehistoric Web Index of Ancient Sites in Europe

http://easyweb.easynet.co.uk/~aburnham/database/

A database of over 2,000 Web resources discussing megalithic sites as well as other archaeological sites in Europe. Indexed by geography and type of structure that survives. Not updated often.

Ancient Greco-Roman World

The greatest number of sites dealing with ancient history is dedicated to Greece and Rome. A few sites focus on other civilizations in the Mediterranean area during the Greco-Roman periods.

Diotima: Women and Gender in the Ancient World

http://www.stoa.org/diotima/

This Web site grew from its beginnings in 1995 under the guidance of Ross Scaife and Suzanne Bonefas to be the best single metasite on gender and women for the ancient Mediterranean world. It includes course syllabi, academic papers, and scholarly articles. It is peer-reviewed by a volunteer editorial board of scholars and updated frequently.

Electronic Resources for Classicists:
The Second Generation

http://www.tlg.uci.edu/~tlg/index/resources.html

This metasite, maintained by Maria C. Pantelia of the University of California at Irvine, offers the most extensive listing of subjects and services available today. It is a must-save site for anyone serious about classics.

Interactive Ancient Mediterranean Project

http://iam.classics.unc.edu/

This provides maps and atlases as well as links to other map sites. It is a cooperative effort of the American Philological Association's Classical Atlas Project, the Departments of Classics and History at the University of North Carolina at Chapel Hill (UNC–CH), and the Classics Department's Apollo Project.

Metis: A QTVR Interface for Ancient Greek
Archeological Sites

http://www.stoa.org/metis/

A Web site created and maintained by Bruce Hartzler, a classics graduate student at the University of Texas, that offers QuickTime "walk-throughs" of more than fifty archaeological sites as well as links to articles about the sites.

The Perseus Digital Library

http://www.perseus.tufts.edu/

One of the standard Web sites for any scholar interested in the ancient Mediterranean. While it offers many links and some translations, it is not a substitute for other sites that have more extensive online e-texts. However, the material here is current and reviewed by the editor, Gregory Crane, frequently. It may take a bit of time to figure out the navigation; advanced knowledge of Greek and Latin will help you find materials.

Ancient Near East

After Greece and Rome, the Near East is the subject of the next largest collection of Internet historical resources found on the Web today. As with Africa, being specific about the culture you are looking for will aid any search.

ABZU

http://www.etana.org/abzu/

This "Guide to Resources for the Study of the Ancient Near East Available on the Internet," maintained by the Oriental Institute at the University of Chicago and funded by Etana, is a clearinghouse for Internet sites, publications, institutions and museums, online discussion groups, and online texts concerning the ancient Near East. It is edited by Charles E. Jones, research archivist—bibliographer.

Ancient Jewish History

http://www.us-israel.org/jsource/Judaism/jewhist.html

Part of the Jewish Virtual Library, an online encyclopedia created by the American-Israeli Cooperative Enterprise, this site has articles, links, images, and even a virtual tour of the lands of Jewish history. The site does have modern political undertones, but the ancient information is still quite valuable.

The Oriental Institute, University of Chicago

http://www.oi.uchicago.edu/OI/default.html

This Web source has evolved from humble beginnings in 1994 to an enormous collection of links to Web sites concerning the ancient Near East, e-texts, catalogs of images, and publication lists, while still focusing on the Oriental Institute, its research, offerings, and running exhibits. The virtual museum shows the layout before 1996, when the facilities were expanded and revised.

Ancient Western Hemisphere

Sources about the ancient peoples of the Western Hemisphere have been traditionally limited to the cultures of Central and South America, and indeed, the majority of Web resources deal only with Mesoamerica. However, this section includes Internet sources dealing with other ancient Western Hemisphere civilizations, as well as the traditional ones, ranging from the North Pole to the tip of Chile and Argentina.

Ancient Mesoamerican Civilizations

http://angelfire.com/ca/humanorigins/index.html

Designed by Kevin L. Callahan of the Department of Anthropology at the University of Minnesota, this site provides links and information about ancient writing, government, religion, and much more for the Maya, Mixtc, Zapotec, and Aztec cultures. The site has an "Automatic Language Translator" for re-searchers whose first language is not English.

Mesoweb

http://www.mesoweb.com/

Directly linked with PARI (Pre-Columbian Art Research Institute), this site offers drawings, rubbings, time lines, maps, site reports, and essays on various topics for the Mesoamerican cultures. Several of the sections are interactive media or animation. There are links to Spanish language Web sites included at the bottom of the page.

Ancient History Web Resources Geared Toward Teaching

All of these recommended sites focus on pedagogical issues. Some offer step-by-step lesson guides and others offer links and images to use in courses, while still others are designed to be a supplement to a class. None of these resources can replace the instructor's own knowledge and skills, though the pages range from elementary to university level. This is the largest section of "Ancient History," since its list includes resources from around the world and targets students, teachers, researchers, and layper-sons alike. Note that some of the civilizations found on these pages are not found elsewhere on the Web at this time and may be the best online source for those cultures.

The Amazing Ancient World of Western Civilization: Act I

http://www.omnibusol.com/ancient.html

The first of a set of online for-credit history courses offered at Foothill College at Los Altos Hills, California, designed and taught by Konnilyn Feig. Professor Feig is a historian whose specialization is not ancient history; thus, the site is geared toward making the past interesting and useful for students and laypeople rather than only experts in antiquity. The course begins with prehistory, looks at non-Western cultures that preceded the better-known Greeks and Romans, spends considerable time on the Greco-Roman world, and finally lists online and offline resources for further exploration. The graphics are kinetic and might be fun for primary and secondary students.

Classical Technology Center

http://ablemedia.com/ctcweb

Part of the AbleOne Education Network, this site provides free Internet and teaching materials created by classics teachers and primarily for classics teachers. The site sponsors, highlights, and recognizes other teaching resources for or approaches to teaching ancient studies by awarding the AbleMedia Bronze Chalice.

Classics Teachers Page

http://www.users.globalnet.co.uk/~loxias/teachers.htm

Andrew Wilson personally checks all of the links listed on this site fairly regularly. Includes information about contests, software, and organizations for classics instructors as well as links to other sites dealing with the ancient Greco-Roman world.

The Detective and the Toga

http://histmyst.org/

Richard M. Heli has compiled an extensive reference on mystery novels and short stories set in the Roman world from its mythic past to the Middle Ages. A good source if you are searching for something to liven up your classes. Arranged multiple ways, including published language of the story, time period, author profiles, and even publishing companies. Updated regularly.

Dr. J's On-Line Survey of Audio-Visual Resources for Classics

http://lilt.ilstu.edu/drjclassics2/Files/greekartandarch.shtm

A unique resource. Janice Siegel reviews three-dimensional online sites that re-create ancient buildings and locations, instructional CD-ROMS, instructional videos, film strips, slide collections, and posters all relating to ancient Greece. Not regularly updated but contains a multitude of materials, most reviewed and containing necessary information about computer or technological requirements for use.

Exploring Ancient World Cultures

http://eawc.evansville.edu/index.htm

Edited by Anthony F. Beavers with the assistance of Patrick Thomas, Alison Griffith, Paul Halsall, Hiten Sonpal, and Bill Hemminger, this is a supplement for courses about the ancient world. Geared toward teachers and students, it provides images, e-texts, basic outlines, and links relating to the early civilizations of China, early Islam, Egypt, Greece, India, medieval Europe, Rome, and the Near East. Started in 1997, the links are regularly updated. The surviving source from the once powerful and important Argos search engine, which is no longer in operation.

Gander Academy: Ancient Peoples/Archeology Theme Page

http://www.stemnet.nf.ca/CITE/peoples.htm

Jim Cornish, fifth-grade teacher at the Gander Academy in Newfoundland, Canada, has collected a unique list of resources exploring the Aztec, Anasazi, Maya, and Inca cultures as well as Chinese dynasties.

History/Social Studies for K–12 Teachers

http://home.comcast.net/~dboals1/boals.html

Maintained by Dennis Boals, this site offers links to a wide variety of WWW resources on ancient civilizations. Links are listed by period, topic, or location and include a guide to critical thinking as well as resources geared toward parents, teachers, students, and even authors. Some updates are made each month, and there is a "special announcements" section that is somewhat political in tone.

Internet Ancient History Sourcebook

http://www.fordham.edu/halsall/ancient/asbook.html

The goal of this Web site, compiled and edited by Paul Halsall, is to provide e-texts for students and instructors to use along with visual and aural materials. Recommended time lines and course outlines for instructors are also included. An acknowledged limit of the site is that many of the translations are well over seventy-five years old. For most secondary and college classes, these will be accurate enough, though certainly not for serious scholarly work. The textual focus is on Greece, Egypt, Mesopotamia, Rome, and the beginnings of Christianity. Persia is also addressed, primarily in secondary and visual form. The links to other Internet history sourcebooks at the top of the page are very useful.

Latinteach

http://www.latinteach.com/

A forum where instructors of Latin meet to share resources, syllabi, and experiences in teaching Latin today; the discussion group is particularly useful. It is a both a list you can subscribe to and a Web site of materials and links.

Mr. Donn's Ancient History

http://members.aol.com/donnandlee/index.html

This site has lesson plans and resources for middle school units ranging from prehistory to the Renaissance and from around the globe. It also has clip art, fonts, games, and other materials to use in your own teaching. The "Daily Life" lessons are particularly interesting for younger students.

Mr. Dowling's Electronic Passport

http://www.mrdowling.com/

Geared toward middle school students, this site offers lessons and links for twenty-two subjects ranging from prehistory to modern issues. Not only are the "facts" given, but basic concepts and methods of history are explained. Mike Dowling is a geography teacher at Roosevelt Middle School in West Palm Beach, Florida.

Online Classics Course Materials

http://www.colleges.org/ctts/courses_frames.html

A searchable database of well over 200 syllabi and related course materials used in classics and other ancient history subjects. Faculty is asked to help the collection grow by submitting their own syllabi and providing links to the course and to their own e-mail so that users can contact them. Created and maintained by the Classics, Teaching and Technology Subcommittee of the American Philological Association. Updated at least twice a year.

The Prehistoric Archeology of the Aegean

http://projectsx.dartmouth.edu/history/bronze_age/

Currently a detailed set of twenty-nine lessons on the history of the prehistoric period, based on the courses of Jeremy B. Rutter, chair of the Classics Department at Dartmouth College. Created in 1996, sadly this promising site has not been updated or expanded since summer 1997, though it has moved to the above new address.

Roman Times

http://darkwing.uoregon.edu/%7Emharrsch/romanwonders.html

Mary Harrosch is not an ancient historian, but this member of the Network and Management Information Systems, College of Education, University of Oregon, loves ancient Rome. Here is a series of links to current research and commercial offerings relating to the Roman world, ranging from popular culture to scholarly articles and studies. An amazing list of what is hot about ancient Rome.

Rome Project

http://www.dalton.org/groups/rome/

Used at the Dalton School, a private elementary school in New York City, this Web site offers a large selection of materials and links designed to aid the study of ancient Rome. However, the information also includes Greek authors and images. The color maps and e-texts that give selections from ancient works are particularly impressive, but they take a long time to download, even on a fast connection.

World Cultures & Geography—Ancient History

http://www.teachersfirst.com/matrix.cfm

Part of the TeachersFirst.com network, this regularly updated site allows primary and secondary teachers to find Internet, mass media, and traditional resources about the ancient world. Sponsored by the Network for Instructional TV, Inc., the site relies on television projects a good deal, but the wide range of materials and the topics and suggestions offered show that the site is truly geared toward making the ancient world come alive to young minds. The "Professional Resources Matrix" addresses concerns about teaching, working with a variety of students, and developing as an instructor.

Chapter 7

Medieval History

Christopher A. Snyder

Because of the prevalence of medieval studies programs, curricula, and scholarship in academe, many of the Internet sites in this category are of an interdisciplinary nature and not solely historical.

The Aberdeen Bestiary Project

http://www.abdn.ac.uk/bestiary/bestiary.hti

The Aberdeen Bestiary, written and illuminated in England around 1200, is considered one of the best examples of its type. The entire manuscript has been digitized and placed online by a team at the Aberdeen University Library. The digitized version, displaying full-page images and detailed views of illustrations and other significant features, is complemented by a series of commentaries and a transcription and translation of the original Latin.

The American Academy of Research Historians of Medieval Spain

http://www.uca.edu/divisions/academic/history/aarhms/

The American Academy of Research Historians of Medieval Spain (AARHMS) is an affiliated society of the American Historian Association and sponsors sessions at both the AHA's annual meeting and at the International Congress of Medieval Studies. Its Web site, maintained by James W. Brodman of the

University of Central Arkansas, offers translations of medieval charters, manuscript images, and book reviews.

Ancient and Medieval Atlas

http://www.roman-emperors.org/Index.htm

This site contains historical maps of Europe for every century from 1 CE to 1500 CE. Maps are in color and clickable. Maintained by Christos Nüssli and affiliated with De Imperatoribus Romanis (see Italian history section) and ORB.

Anglo-Saxon Charters on the World Wide Web

http://www.trin.cam.ac.uk/chartwww/

An online collection of Anglo-Saxon charters, royal diplomas, episcopal confessions, and other early medieval documents. Maintained by Simon Keynes on behalf of the British Academy–Royal Historical Society Joint Committee on Anglo-Saxon Charters on a server at Trinity College, Cambridge.

Anglo-Saxon History: A Select Bibliography

http://www.wmich.edu/medieval/research/rawl/keynesbib/index.html

Despite its name, this is an extensive bibliography of Anglo-Saxon history compiled by Simon Keynes and presented online by the Medieval Institute at Western Michigan University.

Anglo-Saxon Studies: A Select Bibliography

http://bubl.ac.uk/docs/bibliog/biggam/

A good collection of Anglo-Saxon sources in such areas as Old English language and literature, Anglo-Latin and Latin ecclesiastical texts, paleography, history, numismatics, onomastics, and archaeology. Compiled by C.P. Biggam of Strathclyde University Library.

Arthurian Resources

http://www.arthuriana.co.uk/

A good resource for students of Arthuriana, especially those with an interest in the historical and archaeological evidence for King Arthur. Maintained by Thomas Green.

Arthuriana: The Scholarly Journal of Arthurian Studies

http://smu.edu/Arthuriana/

Arthuriana, the quarterly journal of the International Arthurian Society (North American branch), covers many aspects of medieval history and literature. Its Internet site contains article abstracts, bibliographies, a time line and illustrated gazetteer, and Arthurian links.

Arthurnet Links

http://web.clas.ufl.edu/users/jshoaf/Arthurnet.htm

The home page of Arthurnet, an Internet discussion group sponsored by the journal *Arthuriana* and located on the University of Florida server. Mostly a metasite with an excellent collection of links to Arthurian and medieval resources.

The Avalon Project

http://www.yale.edu/lawweb/avalon/medieval/medmenu.htm

A substantial online collection of medieval legal documents at Yale Law School.

Bede's World

http://www.bedesworld.co.uk/

The Museum of Early Medieval Northumbria at Jarrow sponsors a Web page for exploring the world of the Venerable Bede (673–735 CE) through his writings and related archaeological discoveries.

Byzantium: Byzantine Studies on the Internet

http://www.fordham.edu/halsall/byzantium/

One of the most extensive online resources for Byzantine studies. Contains texts, images, syllabi, conference information, essays, and bibliography. Maintained by Paul Halsall at Fordham University.

The Camelot Project

http://www.lib.rochester.edu/camelot/cphome.stm

The Camelot Project is designed to make available in electronic format a database of texts, images, bibliographies, and basic information about King Arthur and the Arthurian legends. The project is sponsored by the University of Rochester and is overseen by Alan Lupack.

CAPITULUM: Research Group for Medieval Church History

http://www.staff.u-szeged.hu/~capitul/capiteng.htm

This Hungarian academic site features some unique links to sites on the crusades, medieval medicine, and more.

Catasto: Census and Property Survey for Florence and Verona in the Fifteenth Century

http://dpls.dacc.wisc.edu/Catasto/

This site provides searchable access to the raw data and documentation files for the "Census and Property Survey for Florentine Domains and the City of Verona in Fifteenth-Century Italy"; David Herlihy and Christiane Klapisch-Zuber are the principal investigators.

Celtic Art & Cultures

http://www.unc.edu/courses/art111/celtic/index.html

This site was developed as part of an art history course at UNC–Chapel Hill. Contains time lines, essays, links, and a remarkable collection of images of Hallstatt, La Tène, and medieval Celtic art.

Celtic Inscribed Stones Project

http://www.ucl.ac.uk/archaeology/cisp/database/

The Celtic Inscribed Stones Project is an online database that includes every nonrunic inscription raised on a stone monument within Celtic-speaking areas (Ireland, Scotland, Wales, Dumnonia, Brittany, and the Isle of Man) in the early Middle Ages (400–1000 CE). The database, maintained by the Department of History and the Institute of Archaeology at University College London, contains over 1,200 inscriptions and is fully searchable.

The Celtic Literature Collective

http://www.ancienttexts.org/library/celtic/ctexts/

An amazing collection of medieval Irish, Welsh, and Arthurian texts (in translation) compiled by Mary Jones. Warning: not all translations are attributed.

Celtic Studies Bibliography

http://www.humnet.ucla.edu/humnet/celtic/csanabib.html

The Celtic Studies Association of North America (CSANA) sponsors this substantial online bibliography, which covers publications in the field up to 2003. Fully searchable. Edited by Karen E. Burgess.

CELT: Corpus of Electronic Texts

http://www.ucc.ie/celt/index.html

The CELT Project at University College Cork is an online resource for contemporary and historical Irish documents in literature, history, and politics.

Centre for Medieval Studies, University of Toronto

http://www.chass.utoronto.ca/medieval/index.shtml

The Web site of one of the most prominent medieval studies centers in the world. In addition to information about the centre's programs and publications, this site has dozens of good links.

Cult of the Saints

http://urban.hunter.cuny.edu/~thead/anthology.htm

This is an anthology of texts illustrative of the medieval cult of the saints. Translations and introductions provided by Thomas Head of the City University of New York.

Deeds of Arms

http://www.nipissingu.ca/department/history/muhlberger/chroniqu/texts/deedsch.htm

Steve Muhlberger of Nipissing University in Canada has collected references to "deeds of arms" or tournaments in dozens of medieval texts (both in the original and in translation).

De Re Militari: The Society for Medieval Military History

http://www.deremilitari.org/

De Re Militari is an international scholarly association established to foster interest in the study of premodern military affairs. It publishes *The Journal of Medieval Military History* and maintains a Web site with a large variety of academic resources.

The Digital Mirror—Treasures

http://www.llgc.org.uk/drych/drych_s004.htm

The National Library of Wales has made accessible online several medieval manuscripts from its collection, including the Black Book of Carmarthen, the Book of Taliesin, the Hengwrt Chaucer, and an eleventh-century astronomy manual.

Digital Scriptorium

http://sunsite.berkeley.edu/Scriptorium/

The Digital Scriptorium at the University of California–Berkeley is an image database of medieval and renaissance manuscripts that unites scattered resources from many institutions into an international tool for teaching and scholarly research.

Diplomatarium Norvegicum

http://www.dokpro.uio.no/engelsk/about_dn.html

A searchable database of transcriptions of some 20,000 diplomas relating to Norway from about 1050 to 1590. Maintained by Bjørn Eithun, University of Oslo.

DScriptorium

http://www.byu.edu/~hurlbut/dscriptorium/

This project, at Brigham Young University, is devoted to collecting, storing, and distributing digital images of medieval manuscripts. Maintained by Jesse Hurlbut.

Dumbarton Oaks Byzantine Studies

http://www.doaks.org/Byzantine.html

The Dumbarton Oaks Research Library and Collection, in Washington, DC, has one of the best collections of Byzantine images, rare books, and research materials in the world. The collection is searchable online.

Early Church Fathers

http://www.tertullian.org/fathers/

This site, edited by Roger Pearse, contains English translations of the works of more than fifty Fathers of the early church.

Early Medieval Forum

http://www.tcnj.edu/~chazelle/emf.html

The Early Medieval Forum, an association of scholars and students in the humanities and social sciences whose work focuses on Europe and the Mediterranean from 500 to 1200, operates a listserv and this directory of Internet resources for the study of the early Middle Ages. Maintained by Celia Chazelle at the College of New Jersey.

Early Medieval Maps

http://gate.henry-davis.com/MAPS/EMwebpages/EM1.html

A good collection of images of medieval maps and cartographic bibliography. Sponsored by Henry Davis Consulting.

Early Medieval Resources for Britain, Ireland and Brittany

http://members.aol.com/michellezi/resources-index.html

This nonacademic site contains good chronologies, bibliographies, links, and translations of early Welsh poetry. Maintained by Michelle Ziegler.

Early Music Institute

http://www.music.indiana.edu/som/emi/

The Web site of the Early Music Institute, at the Indiana University School of Music, offers information about recordings and performances of medieval music and is a gateway to the Thesaurus Musicarum Latinarum, an evolving database of the entire corpus of Latin music theory written during the Middle Ages and the Renaissance.

Epact: Scientific Instruments of Medieval and Renaissance Europe

http://www.mhs.ox.ac.uk/epact/

Epact is an electronic catalog of medieval and Renaissance scientific instruments—astrolabes, armillary spheres, sundials, quadrants, nocturnals, compendia, surveying instruments—from four European museums: the Museum of the History of Science in Oxford, the Istituto e Museo di Storia della Scienza in Florence, the British Museum in London, and the Museum Boerhaave in Leiden.

Essays in Medieval Studies

http://www.luc.edu/publications/medieval/

Essays in Medieval Studies: The Proceedings of the Illinois Medieval Association, published by West Virginia University Press, is available online. The general editor of the online version is Allen J. Frantzen.

Fontes Anglo-Saxonici: A Register of Written Sources Used by Anglo-Saxon Authors

http://fontes.english.ox.ac.uk/

This is a searchable database of all written sources that were incorporated, quoted, translated, or adapted anywhere in English or Latin texts written in Anglo-Saxon England (i.e., England to 1066) or by Anglo-Saxons in other countries. Sponsored by the English faculty of the University of Oxford.

Gregorian Chant Home Page

http://silvertone.princeton.edu/chant_html/

This site is full of links and resources supporting advanced research on Gregorian chant. Maintained at Princeton University by Peter Jeffery.

A Guide to Medieval and Renaissance Instruments

http://www.music.iastate.edu/antiqua/instrumt.html

A unique site featuring replicas of medieval and Renaissance instruments, including images, sound recordings, and bibliographies. Sponsored by the group Musica Antiqua, formed at Iowa State University in 1967.

The Heroic Age

http://members.aol.com/heroicage1/homepage.html

The Heroic Age is a refereed online journal dedicated to the study of northwestern Europe from the late Roman empire to the advent of the Norman empire. Issues include feature articles, essays, book and film reviews, archaeology news, historical biographies, and "Medievalia on the Web."

The Hilandar Research Library

http://cmrs.osu.edu/rcmss/

The Hilandar Research Library at Ohio State University has the largest collection of medieval Slavic manuscripts on microform in the world. Its Web site features an online exhibition and links to medieval Slavic resources.

Hill Monastic Manuscript Library

http://www.hmml.org/

The Hill Monastic Manuscript Library at Saint John's University in Minnesota has several medieval manuscripts in its collection. At its Web site you can view images of these manuscripts, hear audio files of medieval music, and connect to related medieval sites.

The Internet Medieval Sourcebook

http://www.fordham.edu/halsall/sbook.html

One of the first and most extensive online collections of medieval texts, both excerpts and full texts. Though many are older English translations, the site also includes texts in French, Spanish, and Latin, as well as some secondary literature. Searchable, with texts listed under convenient categories as well as by author and title. Maintained at Fordham University by Paul Halsall.

The Labyrinth: Resources for Medieval Studies

http://labyrinth.georgetown.edu/

One of the first and most highly acclaimed medieval Internet sites. In addition to its impressive collection of texts and images, the Labyrinth provides connections to databases, services, texts, and images on other servers around the world. The Labyrinth is sponsored by Georgetown University and is fully searchable.

The Lindisfarne Gospels

http://www.lindisfarnegospels.org/

This site, maintained by the British Library, offers essays, images, bibliography, and links relating to the eighth-century illuminated manuscript.

Maps of Medieval Islam

http://ccat.sas.upenn.edu/~rs143/map.html

An online collection of color maps tracing the development of Islam in the Middle Ages. Part of Barbara R. von Schlegell's course on Islamic religion at the University of Pennsylvania.

Marginality and Community in Medieval Europe

http://www2.kenyon.edu/Projects/Margin/margin.htm

Designed as a class project at Kenyon College, this site has short articles, bibliographies, and links to primary and secondary sources related to heretics, Jews, homosexuals, prostitutes, lepers, and witches in the Middle Ages.

Mediaevum: Medieval Studies on the Internet

http://english.mediaevum.de/

This German metasite has a tremendous variety of links and resources, from addresses of publishers of medieval studies to lists of medieval manuscripts available online. Both English and German language versions (the German is more extensive).

Medica: The Society for the Study of Healing in the Middle Ages

http://www.umm.maine.edu/medica/

The society's Web page offers bibliographies, links, and conference announcements with respect to medieval medicine and healing.

Medieval Academic Discussion Groups

http://www.towson.edu/~duncan/acalists.html

Maintained by Edwin Duncan. Contains descriptions of medieval and related lists and subscription addresses.

Medieval Academy of America

http://www.medievalacademy.org/

The Medieval Academy's Web page has information about publications (including its journal *Speculum*), conferences, awards, and jobs for medievalists.

Medieval & Renaissance Europe— Primary Historical Documents

http://library.byu.edu/~rdh/eurodocs/medren.html

Part of the Primary Historical Documents project at Brigham Young University, this metasite has links to medieval manuscript facsimiles, original language texts, and English translations.

The Medieval and Renaissance Food Homepage

http://www.pbm.com/~lindahl/food.html

This nonacademic site contains a large number of links to medieval texts about food and cooking. Maintained by Greg Lindahl.

The Medieval and Renaissance Internet

http://163.238.8.169/dept/modlang/talarico/medlist.htm

An extensive metasite maintained by Kathryn Talarico of the College of Staten Island.

Medieval Art and Architecture

http://www.pitt.edu/~medart/index.html

Alison Stones of the University of Pittsburgh has a Web site that features images of medieval art and architecture as well as a useful glossary of terms.

Medieval Canon Law

http://faculty.cua.edu/pennington/

The homepage of Ken Pennington (now at Catholic University) includes very useful essays, bibliographies, and texts concerning medieval canon law. Pennington has also made available online his medieval course syllabi.

Medieval English Towns

http://www.the-orb.net/encyclop/culture/towns/towns.html

Stephen Alsford's very useful site provides capsule histories of select English towns, primary sources, and links to other sites on medieval towns. Now part of the ORB project.

Medieval History Lectures

http://www.ku.edu/kansas/medieval/108/lectures/

Lynn Nelson at the University of Kansas has made available online several of her undergraduate medieval history lectures.

The Medieval Institute at Western Michigan University

http://www.wmich.edu/medieval/index.html

The Medieval Institute at Western Michigan University was established in 1961 as a center for teaching and research in the history and culture of the Middle Ages. Its Web site has information about academic programs and its annual conference, the International Medieval Congress, the largest gathering of medievalists in the world.

Medieval Literary Resources

http://andromeda.rutgers.edu/~jlynch/Lit/medieval.html

An excellent metasite with links to primary sources (in several languages), modern criticism, academic sites, journals, and organizations for medievalists. Maintained by Jack Lynch at Rutgers University.

Medieval Narrative Sources: A Chronological Guide

http://www.consulex.hu/ms/centers/biblio/

This extensive, descriptive list of medieval texts is one of many resources made available by the Department of Medieval Studies at Central European University in Budapest.

The Medieval Review

http://www.hti.umich.edu/t/tmr/

This book review journal (formerly the *Bryn Mawr Medieval Review,* now published by Western Michigan University) is searchable and has put all of its reviews since 1993 online.

The Medieval Science Page

http://members.aol.com/McNelis/medsci_index.html

A metasite with links related to all aspects of medieval and Renaissance science. Edited by James McNelis of Wilmington College.

Medieval Studies at UC–Davis

http://medieval.ucdavis.edu/

A good metasite, housed at the University of California at Davis, with lots of links to primary sources.

Medieval Sword Resource Site

http://www.aiusa.com/medsword/

This noncommercial site provides information of interest to students and collectors of medieval European swords and other edged weapons. Good bibliography.

The Medieval Technology Pages

http://scholar.chem.nyu.edu/tekpages/Technology.html

These pages offer scholarly discussion of medieval technological innovations, with time line and bibliography. Maintained by Paul J. Gans at New York University.

Medieval Women: An Interactive Exploration

http://mw.mcmaster.ca/home.html

This is a fun multimedia site, located at McMaster University in Canada, devoted to exploring the lives of medieval women. Good essays, bibliography, and links.

Medioevo Italiano

http://www.medioevoitaliano.org/

This Italian site features a wide array of resources for the study of Italy in the Middle Ages. Published by Angello Gambella and the Medioevo Italiano Project, and available in English, French, German, and Spanish versions.

Ménestral: Un Portail pour les Médiévistes

http://www.ccr.jussieu.fr/urfist/omedirht.htm

This French-language Web site contains links to bibliographies, research centers, archives, and other medieval resources for academic researchers. Sponsored by the University of Paris, Jussieu.

The Middle English Collection

http://etext.virginia.edu/mideng.browse.html

The Middle English Collection at the Electronic Text Center, University of Virginia, includes everything from mystery plays to the works of Chaucer. Fully searchable.

The Mining Co. Guide to Medieval Resources

http://historymedren.miningco.com/

This popular metasite/search engine has devoted a lot of effort to collecting medieval links. The sites represented are a mixed bag, but include online essays, scholarly journals, map collections, and images.

Monastic Matrix

http://monasticmatrix.org/

An ongoing collaborative effort by an international group of scholars of medieval history, religion, history of art, archaeology, and religion as well as librarians and experts in computer technology. Their goal is to collect and make available all existing data about all professional Christian women in Europe between 400 and 1600. The project draws on both textual and material sources, primary and secondary, although its basis is unpublished archival evidence.

NetSERF

http://www.netserf.org/

A metasite with over 1,000 medieval-related links, maintained by Beau Harbin. Also contains medieval-related news items and an excellent glossary of medieval terms.

Old English Pages

http://www.georgetown.edu/cball/oe/old_english.html

The most diverse and useful of the Old English Web sites, maintained by Cathy Ball at Georgetown University. Here are links to dependable history and language sites, plus information about software, courses, manuscript images, and even sound files of spoken Old English poetry.

The Online Medieval and Classical Library

http://sunsite.berkeley.edu/OMACL/

English translations of more than thirty medieval and classical texts (not excerpts). Searchable, with links to other primary source collections. Housed at the University of California–Berkeley and maintained by Douglas B. Killings.

ORB—Online Reference Book for Medieval Studies

http://www.the-orb.net

This is an ambitious project to create an evolving online textbook for medieval studies. Contains links, primary sources and images, instructional materials, bibliographies, and original "encyclopedia" essays on over fifty medieval topics.

Peritia

http://www.ucc.ie/peritia/index.html

Peritia is the journal of the Medieval Academy of Ireland. Its Web site features contents and abstracts from past issues as well as related links. Maintained at University College Cork.

Richard III Society

http://www.richardiii.net/

The Web site of the Richard III Society (London) is dedicated to the study of fifteenth-century England and to the scholarly reassessment of the much-maligned English king. It features essays, links, and information about the society's journal and conference. The North American branch also has an excellent Web site (http://www.r3.org/).

The Robin Hood Project

http://www.lib.rochester.edu/camelot/rh/rhhome.stm

The Robin Hood Project is designed to make available in electronic format a database of texts, images, bibliographies, and basic information about Robin Hood. The project is sponsored by the University of Rochester and is overseen by Alan Lupack.

Rob's Norman Bibliography

http://www.ku.edu/carrie/NormBib/

An extensive online bibliography of primary and secondary sources on the Normans compiled by Robert Helmerichs.

Romiosini: Hellenism in the Middle Ages

http://www.greece.org/Romiosini/

This site, sponsored by the Hellenic Electronic Center, includes essays, maps, genealogies, bibliographies, and photos of Byzantine churches and icons. Maintained by Nikolaos Provatas and Yiannis Papadimas.

Rosala Viking Centre

http://www.rosala-viking-centre.com/

The Web site of this Finnish museum features maps, illustrations, artifact images, and general information about the Vikings.

Russian and East European Studies

http://clover.slavic.pitt.edu/~djb/slavic.html

This metasite contains lots of good links to medieval Slavic resources, including online primary sources. Maintained by David J. Birnbaum at the University of Pittsburgh.

Secrets of the Norman Invasion

http://www.secretsofthenormaninvasion.com/

This unique Web site features essays, primary sources, and aerial photographs relating to the landing of the Normans in England in 1066. Included are photographs of the Bayeux Tapestry. Created by Nick Austin of the Landscape Channel (UK).

SUL Medieval Pages

http://www-sul.stanford.edu/depts/ssrg/medieval/medieval.html

This site at Stanford University Library is a good place for searches for bibliography and e-texts.

The Sutton Hoo Society

http://www.suttonhoo.org/

The Web page of the Sutton Hoo Society contains bibliography, maps, photos, and an interactive tour of the famous Anglo-Saxon royal burial.

The Texas Medieval Association

http://www.towson.edu/~duncan/tmahome.html

The home page of the Texas Medieval Association serves as a good medieval metasite as well as offering information about the organization and its conferences.

The Très Riches Heures du Duc de Berry

http://humanities.uchicago.edu/images/heures/heures.html

Online images of and background text about this early fifteenth-century *book of hours,* considered by many the greatest example of late medieval manuscript illumination.

Viking Heritage

http://viking.hgo.se

A public history initiative launched by a group of Viking researchers, this fully searchable Swedish site offers information about Viking exhibits, images, and bibliography.

Virtuelle Bibliothek—Mittelalterliche Geschichte

http://www.phil.uni-erlangen.de/~p1ges/ma_resso.html

A German-language metasite at the University of Erlangen with extensive links to bibliography, archives, and other electronic resources.

Welsh Castle Index

http://www.castlewales.com/listings.html

This nonacademic site contains an enormous archive of castle photos plus good bibliography and links. Maintained by Jeffrey L. Thomas.

The World of Dante

http://www.iath.virginia.edu/dante/

A hypermedia project for the study of the *Inferno,* using VRML to search and navigate the text. Created by Deborah Parker and the Institute for Advanced Technology in the Humanities at the University of Virginia.

The WWW Virtual Library History Index: Medieval Europe

http://www.msu.edu/~georgem1history/medieval.htm

This extensive metasite is maintained by the Michigan State University Graduate Student Medieval and Renaissance Consortium.

The WSU Anglo-Saxon Homepage

http://www.wmsu.edu/~hanly/oe/503.html

This home page for Michael Hanly's Old English course at Washington State University serves as a good Anglo-Saxon metasite with some images thrown in. Links to other Old English course Web pages.

Chapter 8

Renaissance and Reformation History

Lisa R. Holliday

General Sites

Learner.org

http://www.learner.org/exhibits/renaissance/

Emphasizing historical context, this site discusses the far-reaching impact of the Renaissance on art, music, and literature. It provides numerous links to articles for additional reading.

World Civilizations at Washington State University

http://www.wsu.edu/~dee/REFORM/COUNTER.HTM

This site offers a historical overview of the impact of the Reformation on the Counter-Reformation. In addition, it discusses the aims of the Counter-Reformation and looks at its impact on the later church.

Art and Music

Library of Congress

http://www.loc.gov/exhibits/vatican/music.html

Sponsored by the Library of Congress, this site discusses the character of Renaissance music. It details the works of several Renaissance composers and contains links to images of their writings. This site also contains links to Renaissance displays at the Vatican.

Museum of Science

http://www.mos.org/leonardo/

Sponsored by the Museum of Science, this site provides a broad range of information on Leonardo da Vinci, including a detailed biography and his artistic works as well as his inventions and contributions to science. It offers a detailed bibliography and links to other sites.

Reuteler

http://www.visi.com/~reuteler/leonardo.html

This site is dedicated to Leonardo da Vinci's paintings and sketches. It provides thumbnail images of thirty-nine of da Vinci's works that are available for download. It offers links to biographical accounts of his life as well as commercial sites that sell replicas of da Vinci's works.

Biographical Sites

John Calvin

Christian Classics Ethereal Library

http://www.ccel.org/c/calvin/

This site contains early translations of Calvin's works as well as links to several online articles and encyclopedia entries on Calvin.

New Advent

http://www.newadvent.org/cathen/03195b.htm

A detailed encyclopedia article, this site offers an excellent discussion of Calvin's background, works, and theology. It gives a useful bibliography for further reading.

World Civilizations at Washington State University

http://www.wsu.edu/~dee/REFORM/CALVIN.HTM

This site focuses on Calvin's historical context and contributions to later religious developments. It contains a detailed summary of his thought and works.

Erasmus

Biography.com

http://www.biography.com/search/article.jsp?aid=9288045&search=

This is a brief, but useful biography of Erasmus with links to biographical articles on men who influenced or knew Erasmus.

Erasmus Text Project

http://smith2.sewanee.edu/erasmus/etp.html

Partial collection of Erasmus's works, though the author plans to add more. This site contains links to drawings of Erasmus, biographies, and descriptions of those who knew him well.

Ignatius of Loyola

Christian Classics Ethereal Library

http://www.ccel.org/ccel/ignatius/exercises.html

This site contains translations of Ignatius of Loyola's *Spiritual Exercises*. The files are available for download.

The Life of St. Ignatius Loyola

http://www.luc.edu/jesuit/ignatius.bio.html

Sponsored by Loyola University, this site gives a detailed account of the life of Ignatius of Loyola, including his conversion and the founding of the Society of Jesus.

Martin Luther

ICLnet and Project Wittenberg

http://www.iclnet.org/pub/resources/text/wittenberg/wittenberg-luther.html

This site contains translations of selected works by Martin Luther.

Martin Luther: The Reluctant Revolutionary

http://www.pbs.org/empires/martinluther/

Part of a PBS documentary, this site provides useful information about Luther's life and works, with an emphasis on his religious and historical context.

The Reformation Guide

http://www.educ.msu.edu/homepages/laurence/reformation/Luther/Luther.htm

This is a metasite on Martin Luther. It contains detailed information on Luther's historical context, works, and life as well as outside links and a bibliography.

Reformation.org

http://www.reformation.org/luther.html

This site provides a succinct summary of Luther's works and life. It stresses his historical context and his contribution to later religious developments. In addition, it provides several paintings of Luther, his friends, and his home.

Western Civilization at Western New England College

http://mars.wnec.edu/~grempel/courses/wc2/lectures/luther.html

Part of an online course, this site offers a thorough account of the historical and religious circumstances that precipitated Luther's actions at Wittenberg as well as the development of the Radical Reformers.

Petrarch

Medieval History Sourcebook

http://www.fordham.edu/halsall/source/petrarch1.html

This site provides selections of Petrarch's letters in English translations.

The Petrarchan Grotto

http://petrarch.freeservers.com/

This site offers links to Petrarch's works, in Italian, Latin, and English, as well as information on manuscript traditions. It also provides links to articles on Petrarch and a detailed bibliography.

Petrarch at Peter Sadlon

http://petrarch.petersadlon.com/

This site is dedicated the life and works of Francesco Petrarch and Laura de Noves. It provides detailed information on Petrarch's historical context and his contribution to the humanist movement. In addition, it offers pictures relating to Petrarch's life, translations of his works, links to other sites, and a bibliography.

Literature

Humanism (Rome Reborn: The Vatican Library and Renaissance Culture)

http://www.loc.gov/exhibits/vatican/humanism.html

Sponsored by the Library of Congress, this site details the humanist texts on display at the Vatican Library. It contains detailed summaries of numerous texts and their translators that emphasize historical and literary contexts as well as the conflict that emerged between the Catholic Church and humanist ideals. This site contains links to images of the texts and to other displays at the Vatican.

Notes on Humanism and the Renaissance

http://unr.edu/homepage/nickles/wthonors/humanism-renaissance.htm

A detailed account of the background and trends that defined the humanist movement, emphasizing the distinction between the northern and southern movements. Although this site it does not give links to other sites, it does contain a useful bibliography for further reading.

Medicine

Insecta

http://www.insecta-inspecta.com/fleas/bdeath/

This site provides succinct accounts of the transmission, course, and end of the Black Death. It offers copious pictures and discussion of the impact of the plague on Europe's population, economy, art, and religious life.

Jefferson Village

http://jefferson.village.virginia.edu/osheim/intro.html

This site offers links to firsthand accounts of the plague in English translations.

Military and War

Le Poulet Gauche

http://www.lepg.org/wars.htm

This site gives extensive information on the background, course, and consequences of the Wars of Religion. It provides links for further information on key battles and a detailed bibliography for further reading.

The Thirty Years' War

http://www.pipeline.com/~cwa/TYWHome.htm

This site offers a detailed look at the battles of the Thirty Years' War.

Western Civilization at Western New England College

http://mars.acnet.wnec.edu/~grempel/courses/wc2/lectures/30yearswar.html

In addition to providing accounts of key battles, this site emphasizes the historical context of the Thirty Years' War and the events that precipitated it.

World Civilizations

http://www.wsu.edu/~dee/REFORM/WARS.HTM

This site provides an in-depth look at the historical background and context of the Wars of Religion as well as a thorough look at the impact of the wars on individual European countries.

The Reformation and the Counter-Reformation

Believe

http://mb-soft.com/believe/txc/radrefor.htm

This site offers a succinct but informative look at the various Reformer movements that occurred in Luther's wake. In addition to providing a summary of origins and beliefs, this site also contains a useful bibliography.

The Counter Reformation Guide

http://www.educ.msu.edu/homepages/laurence/reformation/Counter/Counter.htm

This site provides links to primary sources on the Counter-Reformation, including the contributions of Ignatius of Loyola and the Council of Trent.

Eldrbarry

http://www.eldrbarry.net/heidel/anabrsc.htm

This site provides brief accounts of various Radical Reformer groups, including their founders and dates. It contains numerous links to other sites and online articles that are categorized according to group. In addition, it also offers links to detailed bibliographies.

The History Guide

http://www.historyguide.org/earlymod/lecture4c.html

Part of a lecture series on Western Civilization, this article offers an in-depth look at the Reformers, including their relationship to Luther and Calvin and their impact on the Catholic Reformation. It provides links to other sites for additional information on many of the key figures in the Reformation and their beliefs.

Sovereign Grace Community Church

http://www.ritchies.net/p4wk4.htm

Part of a larger church history site sponsored by the Sovereign Grace Community Church, this page gives a detailed account of the formation of the Anabaptists and their beliefs. It considers the relationship between the Anabaptists and other Reformers and explores the impact of the Anabaptists not only in the period following the Reformation, but on the development of later denominations. It provides a few links to early works on Anabaptists and on the Schleitheim Confession.

State-Building and Politics

The Early Modern Period, 1500–1800

http://www.bartleby.com/67/575.html

This site provides a concise look at the development of states in the Early Modern Period and an exploration of the factors that precipitated state development. It gives an individual look at European nations and offers a bibliography for further reading.

Hapsburg

http://www.hapsburg.com/home.htm

This site is dedicated to the history of the Hapsburg dynasty, presented through texts and images. It offers detailed chapters on the Hapsburgs and a thorough bibliography for further reading.

Heraldica

http://www.heraldica.org/topics/national/hre.htm

This very detailed site offers an account of the formation of the Holy Roman Empire, its functions, members, and provinces through the eighteenth century. It summarizes the various offices of the empire, the reigns of the emperors, beginning with Charlemagne, and the territorial possessions of the empire. The site also provides links for further reading.

The Metropolitan Museum of Art: The Holy Roman Empire and the Habsburgs, 1400–1600 A.D.

http://www.metmuseum.org/toah/hd/habs/hd_habs.htm

Sponsored by the Metropolitan Museum of Art, this site offers a brief history of the Holy Roman Empire from its inception in the ninth century to the time of the Hapsburgs and the Reformation. It provides links for additional reading on key figures and to exhibitions at the Met.

Chapter 9

African History

Elisabeth McMahon

Metasites

African Studies Center, University of Pennsylvania

http://www.sas.upenn.edu/African_Studies/

Maintained by Ali Dinar, this site has a number of excellent links to the broader Africana Web community. Of special interest are the materials on the Horn of Africa, including those found under the "Africa Feeds" section. This site also contains a bulletin board with current events, educational information, job and grant opportunities.

African Studies Internet Resources

http://www.columbia.edu/cu/lweb/indiv/africa/cuvl/

The "official" site on African studies for the WWW Virtual Library is maintained by Joseph Caruso, an Africana librarian at Columbia University. The collection on this site is "research oriented" rather than focused on teaching materials.

Africa South of the Sahara

http://www-sul.stanford.edu/depts/ssrg/africa/guide.html

Karen Fung, an Africana librarian at Stanford University, created this site and has actively maintained it for years. It is a searchable site that can also be browsed by country or topic. Fung also includes a section for students on evaluating Africana Web resources.

An A–Z of African Studies on the Internet

http://www.lib.msu.edu/limb/a-z/az.html

This site is run by Peter Limb and Ibra Sene at Michigan State University. The alphabetized organization is good for country-specific information, but less helpful for topics. This site is an invaluable resource for finding listservs focused on Africa. However, there were a number of broken links, and some links led to the African Studies Center, University of Pennsylvania and Africa South of the Sahara sites, Stanford University, California.

Etudes en Sciences Humaines sur l'Afrique Noire

http://www.afriqueindex.com/Categories/sciencesh.htm

A francophone metasite focused on the social sciences and humanities in Africa. The site is indexed by country and topic and contains many Web pages in French that are not found on the anglophone sites.

H-Africa Discussion Network

http://www.h-net.org/~africa/

A gateway site to a variety of listservs that focus on African history and cultures. It includes book reviews of Africana scholarship and a "notable threads" section that covers topics such as "Africa's 100 best books of the twentieth century." Make sure to check the date of the latest post on these lists since some are no longer active.

University of Illinois Center for African Studies

http://www.afrst.uiuc.edu/

This searchable site is one of the best metasites available for researchers because of its sections on libraries, publishing, news sources, research links, and weather information for planning trips. There are good resources on African governments, the U.S. government's role in Africa, and information on human rights in Africa. For teachers, the listing of Africa Outreach centers in the United States is particularly useful.

Specific Sites

Africa

http://www.pbs.org/wnet/africa/

The Public Broadcasting Corporation, *Nature,* and *National Geographic* television co-sponsor this site. It is a great resource for teachers, with many images and information about specific African communities. There are virtual tours of the continent, highlighting the history, music, people, and environments of Africa. Additionally, sections include teaching tools, photo essays, games, and projects for children.

Africa Action

http://www.africaaction.org/index.php

With a motto of "Activism for Africa since 1953," this site offers policy analysis and information, campaign actions, public education, and outreach concerning U.S. policy toward Africa. This site offers a wealth of resources on recent African history through position papers, reports, articles, commentaries, and opinion pieces and an annual policy outlook for the continent. The site is searchable and has several topic bars on most of the most pressing social and economic issues facing Africans.

Africa Confidential

http://www.africa-confidential.com/

This is a subscription news source for the continent that is archived to 1999. The site is useful for finding news as the archive is searchable. A brief overview of each article is available but users are required to pay for full access. Can be useful for finding information about specific topics and dates.

Africa Maps: Perry-Castañeda Library Map Collection

http://www.lib.utexas.edu/maps/africa.html

The Perry-Castañeda collection is an excellent source of maps for the study of the continent. There are maps for individual countries and for Africa as a whole. The maps range in topics, including historical (dating from the early nineteenth century), Islam, political, natural vegetation, and population density.

AfricaNews Online

http://allafrica.com

AllAfrica operates five offices on the continent, gathering articles from news sources across Africa. The site, available in French and English, lists daily

headlines from African media organizations and puts them in a searchable format. No subscription is required for recent information, although it is necessary for archived materials.

Africa Research Central

http://www.africa-research.org/mainframe.html

Billed as a "clearinghouse of African primary sources," this site is maintained
by two well-respected Africana scholars, Kathryn Green and Susan Tschabrun.
This site is searchable by type of repository, country, repository name, and type
of primary sources. The goal of this site is to help researchers outside of Africa
ascertain where sources are located on the continent and to help those in Africa
find the materials that have been removed to other continents (as many materials
have). Recently updated, the site contains information on the needs of African
repositories and grants available from international funding agencies.

African History and Studies

http://www2.tntech.edu/history/african.html

Tennessee Technological University produces this page, which contains a number of links to Africa-related sites. The mixture of site links is interesting but
not entirely related to African history. There were several broken links, although the page is listed as being updated recently.

African History Homepage

http://courses.wcupa.edu/jones/his311.htm#indafrica

Dr. Jim Jones of the history department at West Chester University of Pennsylvania maintains this site for his African history classes. It has a number of
useful time lines, maps (including blank maps of Africa—perfect for quizzes),
some colonial documents, and other useful sources for teaching. Jones also
includes his African history syllabi.

African Internet Resources Relevant to Museums

http://icom.museum/africom/africa1.htm

This page was developed by the International Committee for Documentation of
the International Council of Museums to give information about resources concerning Africa in African and Western museums (in English and French). It is
divided into five sections: African museums, non-African museums, African programs of international organizations, African subject information relevant to museums, and general African Internet resources relevant to museums. While some
links are broken, there is still a wealth of information concerning museums.

African National Congress

· http://www.anc.org.za/

The ANC was a major apartheid-era resistance organization that became the dominant postapartheid political party in South Africa. This site is invaluable to any researcher studying twentieth-century South Africa because of the wealth of government resources, historical documents (ephemera, conference and policy documents, press releases, etc.), and full texts of the Truth and Reconciliation Commission reports. The historical documents section is divided into two parts, the ANC and "World Against Apartheid" documents. It also contains links to numerous related sites, such as the Women's and Youth's Leagues of the ANC.

The African Studies Association (United States)

http://www.africanstudies.org/

This site gives information concerning the history, membership, coordinate organizations, and publications of the African Studies Association of the United States. It is searchable and contains past programs of the yearly conferences.

African Studies at Central Connecticut State University

http://www.ccsu.edu/Afstudy/

The most useful component of this site is the full-text access to *Africa Update*. This online newsletter addresses timely topics in African studies, useful for scholars and teachers. The page also contains links to other Africana sites.

African Timelines: History, Orature, Literature & Film

http://web.cocc.edu/cagatucci/classes/hum211/timelines/htimelinetoc.htm

This site is maintained by Cora Agatucci at Central Oregon Community College. The African time lines she creates are a series of links to historical information and debates concerning African history. This is a deep site of great use to teachers and students. While the formatting of the site is difficult to read at times, it is maintained regularly.

Afrique Francophone

http://www.lehman.cuny.edu/deanhum/langlit/french/afrique.html

This excellent resource for sites on francophone Africa is maintained by Thomas C. Spear, a French professor at Lehman College of the City University of New York. There are a number of categories of links, including sections for all francophone countries in Africa, francophone universities, news media, and cultural, music, and literature sites. There are pages listed here that are not usually included on the main anglophone metasites.

Ancient Egypt: The British Museum

http://www.ancientegypt.co.uk/menu.html

A great teaching tool for K–12 students, this interactive Web site about ancient Egypt was developed by the British Museum. Students can look at images of artifacts and see how they are connected with the story of "ordinary" and "elite" Egyptians. Users can explore an Egyptian temple and pyramid, moving through the rooms into the inner chambers, and learn about the belief system of the Egyptians.

The Atlantic Slave Trade and Slave Life in the Americas: A Visual Record

http://hitchcock.itc.virginia.edu/Slavery/

Funded by the Virginia Foundation for the Humanities, Jerome S. Handler and Michael L. Tuite created this image database concerning the slave trade. Images are classified under the headings Maps: Africa, New World, Slave Trade; Pre-Colonial Africa: Society, Polity, Culture; Capture of Slaves & Coffles in Africa; European Forts & Trading Posts in Africa; Slave Ships & the Atlantic Crossing (Middle Passage); Slave Sales & Auctions: African Coast & the Americas. This valuable collection, searchable by keyword, is a wonderful resource for both researchers and teachers.

BBC World Service Online: Africa

http://news.bbc.co.uk/1/hi/world/africa/default.stm

This site contains news items on all African countries, with an archive going back to November 1997. Audio and video clips are available on the site. It is a useful resource for recent images of Africa, running special exhibits in which Africans give their perspective in pictures and words.

BBC World Service: *The Story of Africa*

http://www.bbc.co.uk/worldservice/africa/features/storyofafrica/index.shtml

The Story of Africa includes the text of twenty-four programs produced by the BBC about African history. It also includes narratives about empires on the continent, with maps and a few images. This site will be useful for educators who need an overview of African history. The audio no longer works for all the programs.

Bulletin d'Anthropologie et d'Histoire Africaines en Langue Française

http://www.up.univ-mrs.fr/%7Ewclio-af/

The *Bulletin of African Anthropology and History* in the French language is housed at the Université de Provence. The site offers the full-text of the bulletin from its beginning in the spring of 1997.

The Congo Cookbook

http://www.congocookbook.com

A fun site geared toward primary and secondary school teachers. The Congo Cookbook lists food projects for the classroom, including various African recipes. Along with the recipes, it gives the cultural and historical contexts for the foods of different regions.

The Core Historical Literature of Agriculture

http://chla.library.cornell.edu/

The Albert R. Mann Library of Cornell University maintains this collection of documents. The site is a searchable, full-text collection of books and journals covering topics such as agricultural economics, crops and their protection, food science, and rural sociology. The materials available cover the early nineteenth to late twentieth centuries and are an excellent resource for Africanists working in the fields of agriculture or environmental history. Keyword searches of the full texts allow researchers to go directly to the pages related to their interests.

Demotic Texts Published on the WWW

http://oi.uchicago.edu/OI/DEPT/RA/ABZU/DEMOTIC_WWW.HTML

While this site has not been updated since 1999, many of the links are still good and a wide variety of images of demotic texts are available. The catalog of papyri from ancient Egypt in the demotic language contains legal, administrative, religious, and literary texts, as well as letters, among other documents. There is also a listing of online collections and archives, bibliographies, directories, and articles concerning demotic texts.

Egypt State Information Service: Nubia

http://www.sis.gov.eg/En/Arts&Culture/Museums/GeneralMuseums/070301000000000009.htm

The history and culture of Nubia are presented here by the State Information Services of the Egyptian government. There is much useful information, including a detailed map, recordings of songs, and images of the region and historical artifacts. However, this is obviously a state-run site.

Exploring Africa

http://exploringafrica.matrix.msu.edu/index.html

This site is maintained by Scott Pennington, the assistant director of MATRIX: The Center for Humane Arts, Letters, and Social Sciences Online. Geared toward K–12 teachers, the site offers curricula, activities, and resources about Africa. A series of teaching modules addresses a variety of topics in African history.

Foreign Policy in Focus

http://www.fpif.org/

This organization describes itself as "a think tank without walls." The Web site has an international focus; however, the section on Africa is easily accessible and contains policy briefs, commentaries, special and policy reports, conflict profiles, and discussion papers on a range of topics as far back as 1997.

The Griffith Institute

http://www.ashmol.ox.ac.uk/Griffith.html

The Griffith Institute of the University of Oxford in England "has the largest specialized Egyptological archive in the world." The Web site is a gateway to these collections, with an index of the archive holdings by author. There are a number of wonderful collections with full-text documents, such as the records of Howard Carter's expeditions in the Valley of Kings. There are some activities for young people as well. This site is useful for both teachers and researchers interested in ancient Egypt.

Historical Graphics: Political Cartoons, Photographs, and Advertising

http://www.boondocksnet.com/gallery/

This Web site, which focuses on American imperialism from the 1890s to 1920s, has interesting graphics related to the Congo Free State and the South African War. It also contains the full text of documents and books related to the Congo Free State, including literary responses by Conrad and Twain. The full text of *The Black Man's Burden: The White Man in Africa from the Fifteenth Century to World War I*, E.D. Morel's 1920 study of the "devastating impact of European interventions and colonialism in Africa," is included. The photographs of the Congo can be found under the sections Stereoscopic Visions of War and Empire and Kodak vs. the King. The South African War is represented by political cartoons, including the famous image of Cecil Rhodes astride Africa.

Human Rights Watch

http://www.hrw.org/

A full-text resource for Human Rights Watch reports on Africa (and the rest of the world). Searchable by country and the themes Arms, Children's Rights, HIV/AIDS and Human Rights, Women's Rights, Prisons, Torture and Abuse, International Justice, LBGT Rights, United Nations, and Refugees. There are also photo essays related to human rights issues in Africa.

INCORE (International Conflict Research)

http://www.incore.ulst.ac.uk/

INCORE is a joint project of the United Nations University and the University of Ulster. Current research projects include Peace Processes, Divided Societies, Management of Diversity, Education & Conflict, Governance & Transition, and the Role of Civil Society. INCORE publications available on the site include occasional papers, research reports, and conference reports. The site is searchable by keyword and has a regional index of country information and reports, although most of these date back to 2001 and earlier.

Internet African History Sourcebook

http://www.fordham.edu/halsall/africa/africasbook.html

Housed at Fordham University, this site was created by Paul Halsall. It contains material extracted from three other Internet History Sourcebooks (Ancient, Medieval, and Modern). The categories listed are African History: General; Africa Origins; Egypt; Other Ancient African Societies; Greek and Roman Africa; Africa and Islam; Ethiopia and Christianity; slavery; European Imperialism; Modern Africa; Gender and Sexuality in Modern Africa; and Further Resources on African History. Although many of the links to other Web sites have been broken, the existing body of documents housed on the site is incredibly useful.

Issues in African History

http://www.uiowa.edu/~africart/toc/history/giblinhistory.html

This essay on African history by James Giblin, a history professor at the University of Iowa, outlines many of the debates in African history. For teachers unfamiliar with the history of Africa, this is an excellent overview.

The Kennedy Center African Odyssey Interactive

http://artsedge.kennedy-center.org/aoi/artsedge.html

This site is divided into two sections. The first section, Visual Arts and Education Resources, contains a group of specially designed exhibits for the African Odyssey project. The second section, Related Links, offers a wealth of resources through links to African art collections across the United States and in Africa as well. For African art, this is one of the best resources on the Web.

Kingdoms of the Medieval Sudan

http://webusers.xula.edu/jrotondo/Kingdoms/welcome.html

Jonathan Rotondo-McCord of Xavier University of Louisiana gives brief overviews of four empires (Mali, Songhay, Hausaland, and Kanem-Bornu) and the themes of trade and Islam in African history. He includes a thoughtful discussion of the region's history, highlighting the differing interpretations of these empires. The site includes a photo gallery and several multiple-choice self-tests. This is a very good site to illustrate the complexities of African history.

The Middle East Network Information Center

http://link.lanic.utexas.edu/menic/

This is a portal site for links on North African countries normally classified under the purview of the Middle East (Algeria, Egypt, Libya, Mauritania, Morocco, Sudan, and Tunisia). Pages are categorized under Arts and Humanities, Business and Economy, Countries and Regions, Education, Government, Health and Science, News and Media, Reference, Social Science, and Society and Culture. The links for K–12 educational resources are especially helpful.

National Records Service, The Gambia: Slave Trade Website

http://www.nrs.gm

Funded by UNESCO and supported by the Gambian government, this site lists information about the precolonial slave trade from The Gambia (made famous in the 1970s by Alex Haley's book *Roots*). The site contains digitized images of documents concerning slavery, maps and a discussion of the ethnic groups living in the region.

Panapress: The Pan African News Agency

http://www.panapress.com

Panapress is a subscription African news site that maintains some free-access stories on a variety of topics. It also has special issues available to all users on topics ranging from the refugee situation across Africa to the African presence at the Olympic Games. It has a number of pictures and is useful for teachers who want to show the array of African news stories. English, French, Portuguese, and Arabic language translation buttons are available for all stories.

Perspectives: The South African War

http://www.pinetreeweb.com/perspectives.htm

A very useful resource for documentary sources on the South African War. The site is maintained by Lewis P. Orans, who has collected a variety of writings from participants in the war, including Arthur Conan Doyle, Robert Baden-Powell, Richard Harding Davis, L.S. Amery, Christian Rudolf de Wet, and C.R.B. Barrett.

Project Gutenberg: Online Book Catalog

http://www.gutenberg.org/catalog/

This site allows free access to a huge collection of full-text books, including works by early explorers in Africa such as David Livingstone, Richard Burton, Henry Stanley, Mungo Park, and Mary Kingsley. Searchable by key word in the title or by author.

PSM Data Bank for the Preparation of History Class

http://www.zum.de/psm/imperialismus/primaer.php3

The PSM Data Bank contains a number of documents on German colonialism in Africa during the late nineteenth and early twentieth centuries. Many of the documents are available in English, though a few are only in German. This is an invaluable site for those studying German colonies in Africa because many of the documents are not otherwise available in the United States.

ReliefWeb

http://new.reliefweb.int/rw/dbc.nsf/doc100?OpenForm

Run by the United Nations Office for the Coordination of Humanitarian Affairs, ReliefWeb was begun in 1996. This remarkable site maintains a searchable listing of current and past (to 1981) emergencies and individual country pages. The country pages give the latest updates on any disasters and categorize them by topic. Each page also includes maps, a country profile, travel information, and key documents concerning humanitarian emergencies. This is a truly wide-ranging site with a wealth of information for historians about humanitarian issues in Africa for the last two and a half decades.

Smithsonian Institution: African History and Culture

http://www.si.edu/history_and_culture/african/

The African section of the Smithsonian Institution Web site contains numerous links to Africa-related Web exhibits built by the staff of the Smithsonian. The exhibits encompass a broad range of African studies, from ancient history to modern studies of dreadlocks, African headgear, and African migration, among others. This is a wonderful portal to show students the vibrancy and richness of Africa.

South African History Online

http://www.sahistory.org.za/pages/mainframes.htm

South African History Online was started in 1999 as a not-for-profit "people's history project." It covers a wide range of materials concerning South African history, especially in the twentieth century. The section titled Egoli, A History of Black Johannesburg, is fascinating in its detail.

United Nations Economic Commission for Africa

http://www.uneca.org/eca_resources/home.htm

This site contains links to ECA documents, conference materials, speeches, policy statements, publications, press releases, meetings, events, and the ECA databases and library. The documents and publications sections go back as far as 1996, including the annual Economic Report on Africa (to 1998).

United Nations High Commissioner for Refugees

http://www.unhcr.ch/cgi-bin/texis/vtx/home

This is a searchable, comprehensive site for information about refugees around the world. It maintains pages for every country, which are divided into the categories of UNHCR news, operations, statistics, background, analysis and policy, and maps. These pages give useful information about conflicts in African countries and up-to-date information as well. The site covers a variety of topics and has quick key links to topical pages. The Teachers Corner includes resources such as books, educational kits, games, pamphlets, brochures, and posters available for use in the classroom.

University of Chicago: Oriental Institute Archaeology Projects

http://oi.uchicago.edu/OI/PROJ/OI_Archaeology.html

This site contains information on a series of ventures in the Near East, including the Nubia Salvage Project and the Giza Mapping Project. The site was originally developed at the University of Chicago by John Sanders, head of the Oriental Institute Computer Laboratory, and Charles Jones, Oriental Institute research archivist. These pages include introductions to the projects, the museum exhibitions, and photos of items in the museum's permanent collections.

WoYaa!

http://www.woyaa.com

Although there are some useful historical Web sites found here, many are of questionable authorship. Ostensibly all of the sites relate to Africa, though some links are actually unconnected to the continent. With the use of good search terms, this site offers some interesting historical information.

Chapter 10

Middle Eastern History

Ranin Kazemi

Metasites

Internet History Sourcebooks Project

http://www.fordham.edu/halsall/

This Web site contains collections of documents and links to texts on various themes, regions, and periods. It is edited by Paul Halsall of Fordham University. See "Internet Islamic History Sourcebook," "Internet Jewish History Sourcebook," "Internet African History Sourcebook," "Internet Indian History Sourcebook," "The Byzantine Studies Page," "Internet Global History Sourcebook," "Internet History of Science Sourcebook," and "Internet Women's History Sourcebook."

Internet Public Library

http://www.ipl.org/

The IPL is housed at the University of Michigan. See the subheadings "Middle East" and "Africa" under "Subject Collections: Regional."

Middle East & Islamic Studies Collection at Cornell University

http://www.library.cornell.edu/colldev/mideast/

Provides numerous links to all aspects of the region, including history and literature.

Middle East in the Google Directory

http://directory.google.com/Top/Society/History/By_Region/Middle_East/

Additional relevant subheadings include "Africa," "Asia," "Europe," "Balkans," "Middle Eastern Studies," and "Islam: History." See Yahoo! entry for similar subheadings.

Middle East in the Yahoo! Directory

http://dir.yahoo.com/arts/humanities/history/by_region/regions/middle_east/ and "Islam" http://dir.yahoo.com/Society_and_Culture/ Religion_and_Spirituality/Faiths_and_Practices/Islam/History/

MidEast, Armenian & Central Asian Studies at UCLA

http://www.library.ucla.edu/libraries/url/colls/mideast/index.html

Selected links to various aspects of the region.

Near Eastern Studies Resources (Princeton University Library)

http://www.princeton.edu/%7Epressman/neareast.htm

Links to libraries, archives, directories, encyclopedias, megasites, databases, and much besides.

Voice of the Shuttle

http://vos.ucsb.edu/browse.asp?id=3918

This is a database that is managed by the University of California, Santa Barbara. This entire section is divided into the following subsections: General Resources, Byzantium, The Crusades, Egypt, Iran (and Persia), Iraq (and Babylon, Mesopotamia), Israel (and Palestine), and Turkey. See also the relevant sites in the following sections: The Middle East under Art History; Archaeology; Middle Eastern & Near Eastern Studies under Area & Regional Studies; Arabic, Persian, and Turkish under Literatures (Other Than English); Arab American under Minority Studies; and Islam and Judaism under Religious Studies.

WWW Virtual Library History Central Catalog

http://vlib.iue.it/history/index.html

This index is maintained by the European University Institute. See the section on Islam under History by Topics; Algeria, Egypt, Morocco, Somalia, Sudan, and Tunisia under History by Countries and Regions: Africa; Armenia, Bahrain, Central Asia, Georgia, Indonesia, India, Iran, Iraq, Israel, Jordan, Kuwait, Lebanon, Oman, Palestine, Qatar, Saudi Arabia, Syria, Turkey, United Arab Emirates, Uzbekistan, and Yemen under Asia; Cyprus and Spain under Europe; and Ancient Near East and Ancient Egypt under History by Eras and Epochs.

Web Sites With Limited Content

Juan R.I. Cole Home Page

http://www-personal.umich.edu/~jrcole/

This Web site is created by Juan Cole of the University of Michigan. It contains syllabi, papers, links, bibliographies, books, translations, documents, and much besides.

The Crusades: Voices and Perspectives

http://www.umich.edu/~iinet/worldreach/assets/docs/crusades/toc.html

This site contains high school materials that can serve as introduction to the history of the Crusades. It is produced by George McDowell. The link "Israeli-Palestinian Conflict" provides related information.

History of Assyrians

http://www.aina.org/aol/peter/brief.htm

A brief account by Peter BetBasoo.

Parthian Empire: History and Coins of Ancient Parthia

http://www.parthia.com/

This Web site, maintained by Chris Hopkins, provides an insightful history of the empire.

Sasankia: The History and Culture of Sasanians

http://sasanika.fullerton.edu/

This Web site aims at presenting the Sasanian Empire on the Internet.

Reference Materials and Primary Sources

Alkhazina

http://www.princeton.edu/~humcomp/alkhaz.html

This Web site provides materials on diverse aspects of early Islamic civilization, including notable sections on Sufism, Islamic scholars, and the arts.

Al-Waraq

http://www.alwaraq.com/

An Arabic digital library, this site contains primary materials by most prominent historians, geographers, philosophers, literati, and religious scholars of the region in the medieval period. Membership is free.

Arab Gateway: Maps of the Arab World

http://www.al-bab.com/arab/maps/maps.htm

Contemporary and historical maps. See also "Middle East Historical Maps."

Avesta: Zoroastrian Archives

http://www.avesta.org/

Archives of materials in Old and Middle Persian. "Most of the texts in these archives are extremely rare."

Bequest Unearthed

http://phoenicia.org/

"The largest web compilation & repository of studies about the origin, history, geography, religion, arts, crafts, trade, industry, mythology, language, literature, music, wars, archaeology, and culture of the Canaanite Phoenicians."

Encyclopedia Iranica

http://www.iranica.com/

This is an important encyclopedia in the field of Middle East history. It covers the greater Iranian cultural world.

Federal Research Division, Library of Congress

http://www.loc.gov/rr/frd/

Through this division, the Library of Congress "provides customized research and analytical services on foreign and domestic topics to the United States Government and District of Columbia agencies." Important research products pertaining to the history of the Middle East include "Country Studies," "Global Gateway," and "Portals to the World." Also, an up-to-date "snapshot of the world [i.e., including the Middle East]" can be readily accessed through CIA—The World Factbook http://www.cia.gov/cia/publications/factbook/index.html.

Islamic Medical Manuscripts Home Page

http://www.nlm.nih.gov/hmd/arabic/arabichome.html

This site discusses "Islamic medicine and science during the Middle Ages and the important role it played in the history of Europe."

Islamic Studies Internet Curriculum Resource

http://www.unc.edu/depts/islamweb/index.html

Links to syllabi, texts, academic organizations, and much besides. Edited by Carl Ernst and Charles Kurzman.

MENALIB: Middle East Virtual Library

http://ssgdoc.bibliothek.uni-halle.de/vlib/html/index.html

This site provides "access to online information and to digital records of printed and other offline media."

Middle East Historical Maps

http://www.lib.utexas.edu/maps/historical/history_middle_east.html

Maintained on the Web site for the University of Texas, Austin.

Middle East Studies Internet Resources

http://www.columbia.edu/cu/lweb/indiv/mideast/cuvlm/index.html

Of particular importance are the sections on bibliographies and Middle East religions, including the Druze faith, Zoroastrianism.

Shi'ite Encyclopedia

http://al-islam1.org/encyclopedia/

This encyclopedia is written from a religious point of view. It could, nonetheless, serve as a starting point for further inquiries about this particular definition of Islam.

Journals and Similar Publications

Annual Egyptological Bibliography

http://www.leidenuniv.nl/nino/aeb.html

Published by the International Associations of Egyptologists in cooperation with the Netherlands Institute for the Near East, Leiden University.

Armenian Forum: A Journal of Contemporary Affairs

http://www.gomidas.org/forum/welcome.htm

Covers a variety of topics, including the recent history of Armenians.

Electronic Journal of Oriental Studies

http://www2.1et.uu.nl/Solis/anpt/ejos/EJOS-VII.0.htm

Published by the Department of Arabic, Persian, and Turkic Languages and Cultures, Utrecht University.

Hugoye: Journal of Syriac Studies

http://syrcom.cua.edu/hugoye/

"Dedicated to the study of the Syriac tradition."

International Journal of Middle East Studies

http://fp.arizona.edu/mesassoc/

Published by the Middle East Studies Associations (MESA) of North America, *IJMES* is one of the most important journals of Middle East studies. The association sponsors a number of other publications and activities.

Iranian Studies

http://www.iranian-studies.com/

The *Journal of the International Society for Iranian Studies* is one of the most prominent periodicals in the field of Iranian studies. The society sponsors a number of activities.

Jerusalem Quarterly File and the Institute for Jerusalem Studies

http://www.jqf-jerusalem.org/inside.html

On the history and contemporary dynamics and trends within the city. The IJS is a branch of the Institute of Palestine Studies.

Journal of American Studies of Turkey

http://www.bilkent.edu.tr/~jast/

American studies sponsored by the American Studies Association of Turkey.

Journal of Maronite Studies

http://www.mari.org/

Sponsored by the Maronite Research Institute.

MIT Electronic Journal of Middle East Studies

http://web.mit.edu/cis/www/mitejmes/intro.htm

"Founded and run primarily by graduate students and young scholars, the journal is committed to publishing scholarly writing on the modern Middle East."

Sudanic Africa: A Journal of Historical Sources

http://www.hf-fak.uib.no/institutter/smi/sa/sahome.html

"Devoted to the presentation and discussion of historical sources on the Sudanic belt."

Listservs and Centers

Adabiyat: Middle Eastern Literary Traditions

http://www.listserv.emory.edu/archives/adabiyat.html

Housed at Emory University and edited by Franklin Lewis, this is perhaps the only listserv in the English-speaking world that is specifically devoted to Middle Eastern literature and literary history.

H-Bahai

http://www.h-net.org/~bahai/

Besides a listserv, this site provides primary texts in Arabic, Persian, and European languages, digitized books, articles, reviews, and other sources about Shaykhism, the Babi and Baha'i faiths, and modern Iran.

H-Mideast-Medieval

http://www.h-net.org/~midmed/

This discussion network is devoted to the study of the Middle East from 500 to 1500 CE. Follow the link "Middle East Medievalists" for further materials concerning this period. See particularly "MEM Resources" links to online manuscripts archives. Other relevant discussion networks on H-Net include H-Gender-MidEast, H-Turk, H-Islamart, and H-Mideast-Politics.

Institute of Ismaili Studies

http://www.iis.ac.uk/home_11.htm

Ismaili communities have long been persecuted in the Middle East. This Web site represents them very well in that scholarly papers as well as texts written by individuals within the community have been published here. See particularly the "Research" link.

Institute of Turkish Studies

http://www.turkishstudies.org/

The Institute of Turkish Studies is the "only non-profit, private educational foundation in the United States devoted solely to supporting and encouraging development of Turkish Studies in American higher education." See also "Ottoman and Turkish Studies at Harvard" http://www.fas.harvard.edu/~turkish/turk_stud_Harvard.html.

Jewish Studies Network

http://www.h-net.org/~judaic/

Discussion network, book reviews, newsletters, preprint articles, syllabi, and much more.

University of Michigan Center for Middle Eastern and North African Studies

http://www.umich.edu/%7Eiinet/cmenas/

There are a number of similar centers at other important universities. They typically have a section on their Web sites in which they provide online resources and outreach materials, including links, sometimes annotated, on the history and the other aspects of the Middle East. They include The Middle East Institute, Columbia University http://www.sipa.columbia.edu/REGIONAL/MEI/index.shtml, Center for Middle Eastern Studies at the University of Chicago http://www.cmes.uchicago.edu/, and Harvard University Center for Middle Eastern Studies http://www.fas.harvard.edu/~mideast/.

Chapter 11

Asian History

Jeffrey G. Barlow

The last few years have been stable ones for Asian studies on the Web. While some older sites have disappeared, in general the excellent sites endure. Many of these sites have been continuously upgraded to enhance their authority and usability. An important change is the increasing number of sites now available in local languages; these may be more useful to specialists in some cases.

The WWW Virtual Library (WWWVL) remains the place to begin for almost any search in Asian studies.

Please note that a Web page with live links to all the sites mentioned here can be found at http://mcel.pacificu.edu/MCEL/Barlow/research.html.

Metasites

The Asian Studies WWW Monitor

http://coombs.anu.edu.au/asia-www-monitor.html

This site contains frequent updates on issues affecting the WWW in East Asia. It is updated at frequent intervals and could serve as a useful site for studying the WWW in Asia, as well as a point to begin many searches dealing with contemporary issues.

Asian Studies WWW Virtual Library

http://vlib.org/AsianStudies.html

This is another important metasite, the Asian Studies WWW Virtual Library formerly at the Universita de Venenzia, relocated to Harvard, then moved to the VLIB.org servers. Fortunately, this site has been broadened to further enhance its authority.

Guide to Online Bookstores in Asian Studies

http://www.ciolek.com/WWWVLPages/AsiaPages/VLBookshops.html

These shops have a strong Internet presence, including online ordering procedures in most cases.

World Area Studies Resources

http://www.wcsu.ctstateu.edu/socialsci/area.html

This metasite, sponsored by Western Connecticut State University, is one of those surprising sites which appear to be largely the work of a single zealous individual, in this case, J. Bannister. It covers not only Asian studies but many other areas as well and has won a number of awards.

WWW Virtual Library—Alphabetic Catalog

http://vlib.org/Home.html

The topical catalog for the WWWVL is found at this site.

WWW Virtual Library—Asian Studies

http://coombs.anu.edu.au/WWWVL-AsianStudies.html

In Asian studies the grandest of the sites is this metasite at the Australian National University (Coombs), maintained by T. Matthew Ciolek. The Coombs site is staggering in its extent and will lead the visitor to literally thousands of additional sites in every conceivable field of Asian studies. An index of its importance is that every scholar I queried mentioned Coombs as an important site.

WWW Virtual Library—Regional Studies

http://vlib.org/Regional.html

This is the Virtual Library Regional Studies page of the WWW Virtual Library (WWWVL), a massive cataloging project where experts in that field maintain each topic or division. Almost any search in any field should begin here, but particularly one in Asian history.

Area or Country Studies Sites

East Asia

Asian-Pacific Economic Cooperation

http://www.apecsec.org.sg/

This is an area-wide site maintained by the organization for Asian-Pacific Economic Cooperation. It is a gigantic site with many free downloads of publications. This would be particularly useful for those working in recent history, and in economic issues, of course.

Search Engines: Asia Databases

http://www.ciolek.com/SearchEngines.html#asia

The metasites listed above are a useful gateway into Asia on the Web, but subject area sites devoted to geographic areas or to individual countries are also very important. A good place to begin for country-specific search engines is here. For unknown reasons the site now opens with a listing of search engines, likely to be very familiar to anyone desiring specific searches in the Asian studies area. But scrolling down to "Simple Search Engines, Asia Databases" will reveal a wide variety of search engines in individual countries of Asia. Most are commercial sites, but as they contain search engines for sites specific to that country or culture, each is an important resource for that country and will presumably uncover materials not found in larger sites or search engines. The "Annotated Guide to WWW Search Engines," now in three parts, edited by T. Matthew Ciolek, is very useful.

China

European Association of Sinological Librarians

http://www.uni-kiel.de/easl/easl.html.

This very useful site is maintained by the European Association of Sinological Librarians. This site provides entry into a wide variety of collections and resources in Chinese studies.

Mao Zedong Internet Library

http://www.marxists.org/reference/archive/mao/

This site is an example of the high degree of politicization of the Chinese studies field, as well as an example of how scholars may benefit from it. This is an extensive online archive of the works of Mao Zedong. This very useful site seems to relocate frequently. You may have to search "Mao Zedong, works of" to turn it up in the future.

U.S. Embassy—China

http://www.usembassy-china.org.cn/

The Web site of the U.S. embassy in Beijing has many useful resources for study of or travel to the Peoples Republic of China.

WWW Virtual Library Internet Guide to Chinese Studies

http://sun.sino.uni-heidelberg.de/igcs/

This site is maintained by Hanno Lecher at Leiden University and is also part of the China WWW Virtual Library.

Taiwan

Academia Sinica

http://www.sinica.edu.tw/ (Chinese Language)

http://www.sinica.edu.tw/main_e.shtml (English Language)

This is the Web site of the central scholarly institution in Taiwan, the Academia Sinica. The site is a true treasure for Asian historians as it permits full-text retrieval of 92 million characters of ancient Chinese texts.

The China Post

http://www.chinapost.com.tw/

This is Taiwan's premier English-language newspaper and should probably be the first stop for those interested in current events in Taiwan.

Index of Taiwanese Organizations

http://www.taiwandc.org/index.html

This site now provides not only recent political news regarding Taiwan, but also important international articles. It seems to represent the Greens much more than the KMT.

Taiwan-Government (Information Office)

http://www.gio.gov.tw

This site contains a broader treatment of the government and politics of Taiwan than the one directly above. While its purposes are primarily commercial, it provides good information and is frequently updated.

Japan

Japan Policy Research Institute

http://www.jpri.org/

The Japan Policy Research Institute, begun by Chalmers Johnson, is a very active, rapidly growing site with a great deal of information relating to historical and contemporary issues affecting Japan and U.S.-Japanese relations. Many of its resources are now available only via passwords and membership.

U.S.-Japan Technology Management Center

http://asia.stanford.edu/

The U.S.-Asia Technology Management Center at Stanford University (formerly the U.S.-Japan Technology Management Center) has long been one of the important centers for contemporary economic issues in Japanese studies. It also hosts many important sites such as that of the Japanese Diet. The "J-Guide" accessible from this site is also the WWW Virtual Library for Japanese Studies.

Korea

WWW Virtual Library for Korean Studies

http://www.skas.org/

This site, once at Duke University, is now maintained by the Society of Korean-American Scholars. It seems to serve organizational purposes as well as research ones. Its links to Korean-American centers are particularly useful here.

South Asia

WWW Virtual Library—South Asia

http://www.columbia.edu/cu/libraries/indiv/area/sarai/

This is the South Asian metasite for the WWW Virtual Library, found at the South Asia Resource Access on the Internet site (SARAI) at Columbia University and maintained by David Magier. Of all the Virtual Library sites, this has one of the cleanest and most useful opening pages, from which users can move quickly to a wide range of specific materials.

Southeast Asia

Southeast Asia Guide

http://www.library.wisc.edu/guides/SEAsia/

The Southeast Asian site at the University of Wisconsin, Madison, is impressive. It is very easy to use in that the opening or splash page loads quickly and the site quickly opens to a wide variety of well-considered and deeply arrayed resources. It needs updating, but is still extremely useful.

WWW Virtual Library—Southeast Asia

http://iias.leidenuniv.nl/wwwvl/southeast.html

This is the WWW Virtual Library for Southeast Asian studies, hosted at the International Institute for Asian Studies at the University of Leiden. The site contains good portals for eleven different countries of this region.

Vietnam

The History of the ARVN

http://mcel.pacificu.edu/mcel/barlow/TR2/tianrong2/arvnhist.htm

This site, which I maintain, is one of the few with a statement by ARVN (Army of the Republic of Vietnam, Saigon) veterans.

Edwin E. Moïse's Vietnam War Bibliography

http://www.clemson.edu/caah/history/facultypages/edmoise/
bibliography.html

A wonderful bibliography is maintained at this site by the scholar Edwin Moïse of Clemson. This site is an example of what one scholar can do to assist others less knowledgeable in teaching a particular area.

Pacific University Asian Studies Resource Page

http://mcel.pacificu.edu/as/home/resources.html

This site has some original materials in it: these pages contain many interviews with American veterans and have received considerable attention.

Saigon Times

http://www.saigontimesweekly.saigonnet.vn/

This is the site of the *Saigon Times,* a weekly newsmagazine from Saigon. It has many useful resources.

Vietnam Online

http://www.vietnamonline.net/

This is a useful commercial site in Hanoi. It is a compilation of diverse databases, primarily commercial ones.

The Wars for Vietnam: 1945–1975

http://vietnam.vassar.edu

An excellent university site is this Vietnam War site at Vassar. It is not, however, apparent when this site was last updated, nor who maintains it.

Asian Art

Beijing Palace Museum

http://www.dpm.org.cn/english/default.asp

This is the site of the Beijing Palace Museum. As an Internet site, it rivals the National Palace Museum in Taipei, discussed below.

Jacques-Edouard Berger Foundation

http://www.bergerfoundation.ch

This site includes a wonderful trove of professionally produced photographs of Asian sites and Asian art.

National Palace Museum

http://www.npm.gov.tw/index.htm

This is the site of the National Palace Museum, Taiwan, which is among the great Chinese art collections of the world.

The Shanghai Museum

http://www.shanghaimuseum.net/en/index.asp

The Shanghai Museum, now arguably the world's most modern museum of Chinese artifacts, at last has a Web site that is well worth visiting.

WWW Virtual Library—Asian Art

http://www.nyu.edu/gsas/dept/fineart/html/chinese/index.html

This is the WWW Virtual Library for Asian art, hosted by the indefatigable Nixa Cura, who updates it regularly.

WWW Virtual Library—Museums and Exhibitions

http://vlmp.museophile.com

This site provides a list of world museums on the Internet, indexed by country and region. It is regularly updated and contains many recent additions.

Philosophy and Religion

Buddhism in Europe

http://www.sunderland.ac.uk/~os0dwe/bs10.html

One site worth mentioning, although it has not been updated for several years, is that hosted by Martin Baumann in the United Kingdom. It contains a wonderful series of links to English-language bibliography on Buddhism in Europe.

Buddhist Palace

http://mcel.pacificu.edu/mcel/omm/

This site, maintained at Pacific University, is a very complex and interactive guide to Buddhism with an emphasis upon the Lotus Sutra. Fair disclosure requires that I mention that I had a hand in its creation.

Chinese Philosophical e-Text Archive

http://www.wesleyan.edu/~sangle/etext/index.html

This site is the wonderful Chinese Philosophical e-Text project, which provides originals and translations of classical texts. It is based at Wesleyan University. It has not been updated in several years, but most of the content consists of classical Chinese texts in any event.

Resources for the Study of East Asian Language and Thought

http://www.human.toyogakuen-u.ac.jp/~acmuller/index.html

This site, maintained by an individual enthusiast, Charles Muller, professor of East Asian Philosophy and Religion at Toyo Gakuen University, Chiba, opens into a number of Buddhist and Japanese resources. Muller also shows a degree of thoughtfulness too often lacking in Asian-related sites in that he provides links necessary to download useful software for viewing his site and other encoded ones. This site also contains the Electronic Buddhist Texts Initiative, a promising resource for scholars and students in this field.

WWW Virtual Library—Religions

http://www.vlib.org/Religion.html

This site is the index for the WWW Virtual Library in Religions. However, this site is not highly developed for religions outside East Asia, though it improves steadily.

WWW Virtual Library—Taoism

http://www.religiousworlds.com/taosim/index.html

This is the WWW Virtual Library site for Taoism, the best entry point for this religion/philosophy. This Web site has not been revised since spring 2004.

Organizations

Asia Society

http://www.asiasociety.org/

This site is maintained by the Asia Society, a nonprofit, nonpartisan, educational institution. The Asia Society presents a wide range of programs, including major art exhibitions, performances, international corporate conferences, and contemporary affairs programs. It has many useful materials for K–12 teachers, a rarity in this field.

Association for Asian Studies

http://www.aasianst.org/

The Association for Asian Studies, with its many regional associations, is the leading professional organization for Asianists.

Miscellaneous and Much to Be Discouraged

Asian Studies Papers

http://www.asianstudiespapers.com/

This is the site of a web-based term paper factory specializing in Asian studies. This site now includes Papers-On-Japan.com, China-Research-Papers.com, and Essaysite.com. Anyone teaching in this area who uses the WWW as a teaching tool should become familiar with the papers sold here. Explain to your students that the penalty for ordering from this site is a sanction known to the Chinese in earlier eras as "extinction through five generations." In checking student papers for plagiarism, a simple Google search on a unique string of text will probably turn up the original. If not, this site will provide a free one-page sample of each of the papers listed, which might well prove definitive evidence.

Chapter 12

Australian and New Zealand History

Christine de Matos

Australia

General History and Metasites

Australian Council of Professional Historians Associations, Inc. (ACPHA)

http://www.historians.org.au/

The ACPHA is a national body representing professional historians in Australia. The site hosts links to professional historians' bodies in each state and territory, as well as an extensive list of links to other Australian history-related Web sites.

Australian Federation Full Text Database

http://setis.library.usyd.edu.au/oztexts/fed.html

Funded by the New South Wales Centenary of Federation, this Scholarly Electronic Text and Image Service (SETIS) database provides digital access to texts of the debates surrounding Federation in Australia (1901).

Australian Heritage Bibliography

http://www.heritage.gov.au/heraindex.html

Formerly known as HERA, this site contains a searchable bibliographic database on significant places in Australia's natural and cultural environment, produced by the Australian Heritage Commission.

Australian History Resources

http://www.austudies.org/info/docs.html

This is a vast collection of links to various Internet sites focusing on Australian history, with an emphasis on primary sources. These links include major Australian archives, documents, e-journals, historical societies, and resources on Australia held in the United States.

Australian Jewish Genealogical Society, Inc.

http://www.ajgs.org.au/

Australian Jewish Historical Society, Inc.

http://www.ajhs.info/

These two sites provide access to information on Australian Jewish history, including Jewish archives, publications, historical sites, and genealogical resources.

Australian Literary and Historical Texts

http://setis.library.usyd.edu.au/oztexts/ozlit.html

This Web project provides free online and fully text-searchable access to over a hundred Australian literary texts from the seventeenth to the early twentieth century. The site was developed and is maintained by the Scholarly Electronic Text and Image Service (SETIS) at the University of Sydney library.

Bright Sparcs

http://www.asap.unimelb.edu.au/bsparcs/bsparcshome.htm

Bright Sparcs is a register of archival material and resources on the heritage of Australia's developments in science, technology, engineering, and medicine. The site also includes information and classroom ideas for teachers.

Chinese Heritage of Australian Federation

http://www.chaf.lib.latrobe.edu.au/

An online research portal into the contributions of the Chinese community to the development of the Australian nation, this site has been developed jointly by La Trobe University (Australia), the Chinese Museum (Australia), and

Shanghai's East China Normal University. The site has many resources, including access to more than a dozen databases, Chinese stories of Federation (1901), and teaching resources.

City of Sydney History

http://www.cityofsydney.nsw.gov.au/AboutSydney/HistoryAndArchives/

As the home page describes, this site aims to allow the user to explore "Sydney's history through images, text, memories and voices." Users have access to online exhibitions, notices of events, archival records (via Archives Investigator or Archive Pix), and general historical information. One excellent resource is *Barani,* a separate Web page and an interactive resource for research on the indigenous history of Sydney.

Documenting Democracy

http://www.foundingdocs.gov.au/

Developed as a cooperative project between eight Australian archives, with the support of the National Council for the Centenary of Federation, this site aims to tell the story of the development of democracy in Australia through key documents.

Endeavour Project: Journals of James Cook's First Pacific Voyage

http://coombs.anu.edu.au/~cookproj/home.html

A hypermedia project exploring the use of digital technology in advancing the intellectual skills of the cross-cultural historian, this site allows users and students to explore the journals of James Cook, Joseph Banks, and John Hawkesworth. Maps and other historical documents are also available on the site. Together these resources provide an online historical exploration of the encounters between the European voyagers and the peoples of the Pacific.

First Fleet Online

http://cedir.uow.edu.au/programs/FirstFleet/

An online resource for teaching and learning about the First Fleet (1787–1788), this site has been provided by the University of Wollongong. It contains a database on the convicts of the First Fleet, plus letters, diary entries, and stories.

Gold 150

http://www.anmm.gov.au/gold150/gold150.htm

Gold 150 is a Web project sponsored by Sovereign Hill, the National Maritime Museum, the University of Ballarat, and the Australia Foundation to mark 150 years of Australian gold rush history. The site includes images, documents, essays, and guides to further resources on the gold rushes.

Matthew Flinders Collection

http://www.sl.nsw.gov.au/flinders/

To commemorate the bicentenary of Matthew Flinders's circumnavigation of the Australian continent, the State Library of New South Wales has developed this site in order to place its collection of materials online. Included in the electronic archive are manuscripts, maps and charts, biographies, time lines, and realia.

New South Wales Heritage Office

http://www.heritage.nsw.gov.au

A resource for research on heritage in Australia, this site includes the Online Heritage Databases. One fine resource is the New South Wales Heritage Office project, Maritime Heritage Online, and under the "For Students" link, a connection to the excellent New South Wales education site, Teaching Heritage.

Oral History Association of Australia

http://www.ohaa.net.au

Membership details, conferences, publications, and links to other oral history Web sites can be found on this site.

Papers of Sir Joseph Banks

http://www.sl.nsw.gov.au/banks/

The State Library of New South Wales holds approximately 10,000 manuscript pages of Sir Joseph Banks (1743–1820), a naturalist who sailed with Captain James Cook on the *Endeavour,* including correspondence, reports, invoices and accounts, journals, and a small quantity of maps, charts, and watercolors.

PictureAustralia

http://www.pictureaustralia.org/

The PictureAustralia database provides a central Web-based search point to locate images of Australian history and heritage held in a number of participating Australian cultural institutions.

Royal Australian Historical Society

http://www.rahs.org.au/

The aim of the RAHS is to encourage Australians to learn more about their history. The Web site contains information about the society and its affiliates, notice of events, and some resources, including *Images of Federation,* a collection of digitized photographs, and *An Historical Guide to Sydney's Green Plaques,* a list of places, people, or events commemorated in Sydney's history.

Society of Australian Genealogists

http://www.sag.org.au/

An important point of call for the serious genealogist, the SAG site hosts information about the society; notification of seminars, conferences, and workshops; an online catalog to references and resources; and a number of databases, which include a Ticket of Leave index, a Ships Muster index, a Soldiers and Marines index, and a Sydney Streets index.

Women in Politics in South Australia

http://www.parliament.sa.gov.au/history/html/women.shtm

South Australia was the first state in Australia (indeed, one of the first places in the world) to grant women's suffrage in 1894. This site, hosted by the State Library of South Australia and sponsored by the Women's Suffrage Centenary Steering Committee, examines the role of women in politics in South Australia and the wider historical context.

Aboriginal and Torres Strait Islander History

Aboriginal Studies WWW Virtual Library

http://www.ciolek.com/WWWVL-Aboriginal.html

Part of the general WWW Virtual Library, this site boasts a wide collection of links to Aboriginal studies Internet sites.

Australian Institute of Aboriginal and Torres Strait Islander Studies

http://www.aiatsis.gov.au

The institute's Web site provides information on indigenous research, seminars, and family history.

The Hidden Histories

http://www.museum.vic.gov.au/Hidden_Histories/

The Hidden Histories Project, sponsored by the Museum of Victoria and the Department of Education, Employment and Training (Victoria), aims to document the oral histories of Koori (indigenous) communities and to increase the wider community's understanding of Koori culture.

The Koori History Website

http://www.kooriweb.org/foley/indexb.html

A comprehensive place to research indigenous history, this site includes everything from political cartoons and newspaper articles to essays and photographs. Links to other indigenous-related sites, as well as more general Australian studies sites, are provided.

Mabo—The Native Title Revolution

http://www.mabonativetitle.com/

This site is a multimedia resource for teachers, students, and researchers on the landmark 1992 High Court ruling on indigenous land rights and native title, named after its principle plaintiff, Edward Koiki Mabo. The ever-expanding online database contains text, and audio and visual material related to native title and land rights issues, and teacher study notes are also available.

Mura Gadi

http://www.nla.gov.au/muragadi/

Mura Gadi, meaning "pathways for searching," is an online database at the National Library of Australia. It enables users to search the library's collections for resources on Aboriginal and Torres Strait Islander peoples. The collection includes oral histories, manuscripts, and images.

Archives, Libraries, Museums, and Journals

Archives of Australia

http://www.archivenet.gov.au/archives.html

This site links researchers to the various state and territory government archives in Australia.

Australia Museums and Galleries Online

http://amol.org.au

Developed by the Heritage Collections Council, this site provides guides to the collections, and other useful information, of over 1,000 Australian museums and galleries. There are also resources for museum workers, including the *Open Museum Journal.* Note that this site is about to undergo major changes; thus the URL may also change. The new name for the body and site will become the Collections Australia Network (CAN).

Australian Trade Union Archives

http://www.atua.org.au/atua.htm

The ATUA is an online gateway for researchers of labor or employer history to search or browse archival and published material held in Australian repositories. A time line of Australian labor history and links to similar sites are also provided.

Australian War Memorial

http://www.awm.gov.au/

Research on Australia's involvement in overseas conflicts necessitates a visit to the Australian War Memorial's Web site. It includes searchable databases on the memorial's vast collection (art, books, film, official and private records, photographs, roll of honor, sound recordings), the Australia-Japan Research Project, current events, and an online journal, *Journal of the Australian War Memorial.*

Directory of Archives in Australia

http://www.archivists.org.au/directory/asa_dir.htm

The Directory of Archives is a comprehensive database of information about archives in Australia, developed by the Australian Society of Archivists, and the Australian Science Archives Project.

The Electronic Journal of Australian and New Zealand History

http://www.jcu.edu.au/aff/history/

The School of Humanities at James Cook University supports this peer-reviewed forum.

Jessie Street National Women's Library

http://www.jessiestreetwomenslibrary.com/

With the aim of promoting "awareness of the cultural and literary heritage of Australian women," this site includes information about the collection, links to search the collection, and short biographies of "Fabulous Women."

National Archives of Australia

http://www.naa.gov.au/

This is an essential starting point for historical research pertaining to the Australian Commonwealth government. The site has general information about the archives, an online database to search the collection, links to other archives, and notices of events and exhibits.

The National Archives of Ireland Transportation Records

http://www.nationalarchives.ie/topics/transportation/search01.html

The National Archives of Ireland has developed this site to provide an online facility to search for the records of convicts sent from Ireland to Australia from 1788 to 1868.

National Library of Australia

http://www.nla.gov.au

The National Library of Australia provides an exhaustive entry point for information on Australian history, both within its own collections and on the Internet. The site also houses a number of databases and guides useful for research on Australian history. These include the Register of Australian Archives and Manuscripts (RAAM), Australian Journals OnLine (AJOL), Australian History on the Internet, Australian Periodical Publications 1840–1845, Federation Gateway, Rare Maps Digitisation Project, South Seas: Voyaging and Cross-cultural Encounters in the Pacific (1760–1800), and the Australian Libraries Gateway.

New Zealand

General History and Metasites

GenEoNZ: New Zealand and Maori Genealogy

http://www.geocities.com/Heartland/Park/7572/nz.htm

Listed on this site is a huge range of sources and services for genealogy in New Zealand.

Heritage Images Online

http://www.aucklandcity.govt.nz/dbtw-wpd/heritageimages/apphoto.htm

This site allows the photographic collection at the Auckland City Libraries to be viewed and searched by keyword.

New Zealand: Ancient and Modern History

http://www.enzed.com/hist.html

This site is part of the larger eNZed Web site, which provided links to information on New Zealand. It is a very comprehensive index, including everything from the arrival of the Maori to recent economic reforms.

New Zealand Electronic Text Centre

http://www.nzetc.org/

This site is an electronic archive, founded in 2001, to provide ever-expanding free and open access to texts and images that focus on New Zealand and the Pacific Islands. Currently included are texts on sport, World War II, and modern New Zealand.

New Zealand Historic Places Trust

http://www.historic.org.nz/

Information concerning historic and culturally significant places in New Zealand can be found on this site.

New Zealand Society of Genealogists, Inc.

http://homepages.ihug.co.nz/~nzsg/

Genealogy news, school project resources, research collection services, and membership information can all be found on this Web site. Forms and charts for genealogists can be downloaded as PDF files.

NZHistory.net.nz

http://www.nzhistory.net.nz/index.html

The NZHistory site aims to be the "first port of call" for research on New Zealand's history. As well as links to Internet sites, it has a discussion forum and online quizzes to test your knowledge of New Zealand's history.

Professional Historians Association of New Zealand/Aotearoa

http://www.phanza.org.nz/

The PHANZA provides information for members, prospective members, and clients, access to PHANZA e-journal, and access to their newsletter *Phanzine*.

The Treaty of Waitangi

http://www.treatyofwaitangi.govt.nz/

This is the official government Web site designed to increase public awareness and knowledge of the Treaty of Waitangi. Included are copies of the treaty in English and Maori, the historical background to the treaty, a time line, a treaty awareness research study, and list of online resources.

WWW Virtual Library History: New Zealand

http://www.vlib.iue.it/history/oceania/NewZealand/index.html

This virtual history site provides a very comprehensive index to Web sites dealing with many aspects of New Zealand's history.

Archives, Libraries, and Museums

National Archives of New Zealand

http://www.archives.govt.nz/index.html

The National Archives Web site contains information about its holdings, government discussion papers, and links to other sites.

National Library of New Zealand

http://www.natlib.govt.nz/

As well as information about the collections, catalogs, and digital resources of the National Library, links are provided to digital collections, including the online image database, Timeframe and Papers Past, the library's newspaper digitization project.

National Register of Archives and Manuscripts (NRAM)

http://www.nram.org.nz

The NRAM site is a database that helps archivists and researchers locate archival collections held in museums, local government bodies, libraries, historical societies, community repositories, and in-house business, religious, and sporting archives throughout New Zealand.

New Zealand Museums Online

http://www.nzmuseums.co.nz/

This site provides access to a database of information on museums in New Zealand, searchable by collection, region, or name.

Chapter 13

Canadian History

David Calverley

Metasites

Canada's Digital Collections

http://collections.ic.gc.ca/

Billed as the largest Canadian history resource on the Internet, this site has over 600 digital resources available to researchers and students. The majority of the sites, however, are more suited for secondary and first and second year undergraduate students than academic scholars. The sites maintained vary in range from national historical events to local and regional resources and stories.

Canadian Archival Resources on the Internet

http://www.usask.ca/archives/menu.html

This site provides links to numerous Canadian archives and archival resources on the Internet organized by province, region, academic institution, and theme. There are also links to colleges and universities that offer archivist training programs. Not all the links are useful as each archive maintains its own Web site. Some of the archives provide searchable databases of their holdings that are useful for historians considering an extensive research trip.

Canadian Museum of Civilization Corporation

http://www.civilisations.ca/

A stepping-stone into Canada's numerous federal museums, this is a crucial site for those interested in these institutions and the history that each is
dedicated to. This site links into numerous elements of Canadian history,
covering social, military, political, archaeological, and Aboriginal histories that are too numerous to provide a complete listing. Some outstanding
specific links are offered later in this chapter.

Libraries and Archives Canada

http://www.collectionscanada.ca/

The National Library of Canada and the National Archives of Canada can
be accessed through this site. By clicking on "Search Archival Materials,"
the user accesses a number of primary documents and resources, as well as
search tools to locate call and reference numbers for the archives' extensive holdings. This is particularly useful for those resources on microfilm
that can be lent to the researcher's local or university library. By clicking
on "Browse by selected topics," users can access a number of online resources. The "Amicus" link allows users to search the National Library of
Canada's holdings. Included with the National Library is a new feature: the
Canadian Thesis Portal. Users can download theses written since 1998 as
PDF files. Both the National Library and the National Archives sites maintain numerous links to educational resources pertaining to various aspects
of Canadian history.

General Sites

The Applied History Research Group

http://www.ucalgary.ca/applied_history/tutor/

Based at the history department at the University of Calgary, the AHRG is
composed of senior undergraduate and graduate students who research various topics in Canadian history and then produce fairly comprehensive Web
sites highlighting their findings. This is primarily a secondary resource as
few primary documents are made available on the site. Canadian subjects
include The Peopling of Canada, Calgary and Southern Alberta, Canada's
First Nations, Colonial North America, and Peopling North America.

Archives of Ontario

http://www.archives.gov.on.ca/

Users can search the AO's collection on this Web site. The databases available are very useful and fully searchable, covering a range of materials from general resource searches to more theme-specific databases. In addition, the site offers very thorough histories of various events and themes in Ontario history with links for unfamiliar terms, and primary documents, photographs, and maps. These histories are changed periodically.

Canadian Constitutional Documents

http://www.solon.org/Constitutions/Canada/English/index.html

The Solon Law Archives contains important Canadian political and constitutional documents. The earliest is Charles II's charter to the Hudson's Bay Company in 1670 and the most recent is the 2001 constitutional amendment that renamed Newfoundland the "Province of Newfoundland and Labrador." This is an excellent primary resource site for anyone interested in the main events of Canada's political and constitutional development.

Canadian Department of National Defence— History Directorate

http://www.forces.gc.ca/hr/dhh/engraph/home_e.asp

This is a very well developed and useful Web site. It contains numerous downloadable books and pamphlets written by departmental historians. An important primary document resource, which can also be downloaded, is the Canadian Military Headquarters Reports about Canada's various roles in World War II. Also provided on this site is a list of the department's library holdings. This is an excellent research site for those interested in Canada's military history.

The Canadian Encyclopedia

http://www.thecanadianencyclopedia.com/
index.cfm?PgNm=Homepage&Params=A1

Academics and leading researchers and writers in various fields of Canadian history write entries for the encyclopedia. A search engine makes it very accessible. The entries are suitable for beginning research into almost any topic in Canadian history, although the information here should be supplemented with more detailed sources.

Department of Indian Affairs and Northern Development—Historical Treaty Information Site

http://www.ainc-inac.gc.ca/pr/trts/hti/site/maindex_e.html

This site provides downloadable research reports on Canada's Indian treaties, written by leading scholars in the field. The site also provides numerous links to a large variety of other sites about First Nations' history in Canada. Included on this site is an excellent bibliography of further print resources. This is a useful site to access treaty documents and other primary sources concerned with Canada's First Nations.

Dictionary of Canadian Biography

http://www.biographi.ca/EN/

The DCB is one of the most important research sources on the Internet for Canadian history. Started in the 1970s, the DCB began as a print resource written by specialists. A fully searchable database of this twelve-volume work makes this an indispensable research tool. Volume twelve takes Canadian history into the 1920s. A useful bibliography of both primary and secondary resources is provided at the end of each entry. It is a resource to use after gaining some background knowledge on the event or person one is studying.

Early Canadiana On-Line

http://www.canadiana.org/eco/index.html

This site contains 1.6 million scanned pages of early Canadian primary documents and a fully searchable database. These generally are previously published, but out-of-print documents. There are resource links with short essays, biographies, and documents suitable for senior high school and first- and second-year undergraduate students. There are also a number of links to lesson plans and educational resources for teachers. The free version gives users substantial access to documents, but there is also a subscription service for full access to this resource. The site is maintained by the Canadian Institute for Historical Microreproductions.

European Exploration From Earliest Times to 1497

http://www.heritage.nf.ca/exploration/early_ex.html

Maintained by the Newfoundland provincial government, this site contains general information about the early exploration and settlement of northeastern North America from the Vikings to John Cabot, as well as descriptions of early nautical techniques. There are few primary documents on this site, but a number of useful maps clearly outline the explorers' routes. Bibliographies and links to important archival sites and maritime history sites round out this Web page nicely.

A History of the Native People of Canada

http://www.civilisations.ca/archeo/hnpc/npint00e.html

This site is maintained by the Canadian Museum of Civilisation. It offers a précis summary of all the chapters in J.V. Wright's two-volume work, *A History of the Native People of Canada*. It is concerned mainly with precontact First Nations. Although a very useful source, it was written for those with substantial previous knowledge in this field.

The *Jesuit Relations* and the History of New France

http://www.collectionscanada.ca/jesuit-relations/index-e.html

This site contains links to Reuben Gold Thwaites's translation of the *Relations* on the Early Canadiana Web site. Maintained by the National Library and National Archives of Canada, it contains an excellent essay on the historical context of the *Jesuit Relations*. A similar site is offered at *The Jesuit Relations and Allied Documents, 1610–1671* (http://puffin.creighton.edu/jesuit/relations/). This is a more useful Web page since the *Relations* can be downloaded. There is also a search engine to find specific information in the *Relations*.

The Prime Ministers of Canada

http://www.primeministers.ca/

This site contains useful biographies of all of Canada's prime ministers. Of particular interest are the short interview snippets with leading historians and commentators. One weakness, however, is the lack of primary source material. The site is therefore cursory in its treatment of Canada's leaders and should be supplemented with appropriate entries from the *Dictionary of Canadian Biography*.

The War of 1812 Website

http://www.militaryheritage.com/1812.htm

Although a commercial Web site, this site provides excellent articles and primary documents pertaining to the War of 1812. A number of primary documents are also provided. Links on this page lead to a similar site about the Seven Years' War/French and Indian War (1756–1763). There is one glaring weakness on this site: there is no information about the importance of First Nations allies to the British in Upper Canada.

Chapter 14

Latin and South American History

Kathleen A. Tobin

Metasites

H-LatAm

http://www.h-net.org/~latam/

A discussion network created by Humanities Net (H-Net) at Michigan State University. It puts scholars in contact with other Latin American history scholars around the world and provides access to reviews, papers, archives, etc.

Integration in the Americas

http://www.unites.uqam.ca/gric/integration.htm

Maintained by the University of Quebec at Montreal, this site contains a vast number of links related primarily to commerce and trade in the Americas. A valuable resource for scholars of international economic relations.

Internet Resources for Latin America

http://lib.nmsu.edu/subject/bord/laguia/

This site, compiled and maintained by Milly E. Malloy at New Mexico State University, is an excellent collection of links to databases, library sources, Web directories, and online books. Very valuable in all areas of research on Latin America.

Latin America Data Base

http://www.ladb.unm.edu

A news and educational service on Latin America and an online publisher and information center. Access to articles in its online publications (*Sourcemex, NotiCen,* and *NotiSur*) requires a subscription, but the site also includes a wealth of information through links.

Latin America Home Page

http://www.casahistoria.net/latam.html

Created by a former instructor in Argentina to provide history students with guidance and access to valuable Web sites, this site is a good place to start when doing any kind of research in Latin American history.

Latin American Network Information Center

http://www.lanic.utexas.edu

This is the best place to start in conducting research on Latin America. Categorized by country, by topic, and by source of information, the collection of sites is comprehensive.

Latin American Studies Links

http://www.unl.edu/LatAmHis/LatAmLinks.html

Categorized by topics and sources, this site is a collection of links addressing a variety of subjects. Contains teaching resources, government sites, university sites, and sources for topics such as economics, labor, and human rights. Maintained by DeeAnna Manning in the Department of History at the University of Nebraska, Lincoln.

Political Database of the Americas

http://www.georgetown.edu/pdba/

Provides access to a substantial number of government documents and reference materials important to all Latin American countries. Reference materials include extensive bibliographies and links to organizations. Available in English, Spanish, French, and Portuguese.

Zona Latina: Latin American Media & Marketing

http://www.zonalatina.com/

An excellent source of news information. Through this site, researchers have access to newspapers and articles from across the political spectrum.

General History

The Conference on Latin American History

http://www.h-net.org/~clah/index.php

Home page of the Conference on Latin American Studies (CLAH), an organization that promotes the study and improved teaching of Latin American history. The site provides information about the organization and includes links useful to students and professionals in the field. It is affiliated with the American Historical Association (AHA).

The Council on Hemispheric Affairs

http://www.coha.org/

This is the home page of the Council on Hemispheric Affairs, an independent organization that monitors U.S.-Latin American relations. It offers information on politics, economics, and diplomatic issues, plus thorough investigative reports.

Historical Text Archive

http://historicaltextarchive.com

Compiled and edited by Donald J. Mabry, a retired professor and now independent scholar, this site contains articles, e-books, essays, documents, and photos on all aspects of history, many of them dealing with Latin America.

Library of Congress/*Handbook of Latin American Studies* Online

http://lcweb2.loc.gov/hlas/

An online version of the *Handbook,* with an extensive bibliography on Latin America. This format allows scholars to search thousands of works selected by humanities and social science scholars. It also offers abstracts and complete bibliographic information.

Oxford Latin American Economic History Database

http://oxlad.qeh.ox.ac.uk/

Hosted by the Latin American Centre at Oxford University, this site is aimed at social and economic historians of Latin America. It allows scholars to research a wealth of statistical data from Latin American regions (population, government expenditures, etc.) for the period from 1900 to 2000.

RetaNet, Resources for Teaching About the Americas

http://retanet.unm.edu/

This Web site, designed for secondary educators, acts as an interactive learning community of teacher peers. It offers lesson plans, curriculum materials, and news sources.

Society for Latin American Studies

http://www.slas.org.uk/

Home page of the Society for Latin American Studies, the principal association of Latin American studies scholars in the United Kingdom. It holds links to other associations in the UK and elsewhere, as well as information links. Maintained by Katie Willis of the Department of Geography at the University of London.

Sources and General Resources on Latin America

http://www.oberlin.edu/faculty/svolk/latinam.htm

Compiled by Steven Volk of the Department of History at Oberlin College, this site contains a wide variety of Web sources including bibliographies, databases, maps, and primary source documents, organized by topic and by country.

USAID: Latin America and the Caribbean

http://www.usaid.gov/locations/latin_america_caribbean/

This official Web site of the U.S. Agency for International Development provides current projects and links to country and region profiles created by USAID.

Pre-Columbian Latin America

Anthro.Net: The Andes

http://home1.gte.net/ericjw1/andes.html

Contains bibliographic references and links to Internet sources for Andean archaeology and ethnography.

Foundation for the Advancement of Mesoamerican Studies

http://www.famsi.org/

This Web site for the Foundation for the Advancement of Mesoamerican Studies contains maps, information on Maya writing, and links to many pre-Columbian Web sites.

Indigenous Peoples

http://lanic.utexas.edu/la/region/indigenous/

From the Latin American Network and Information Center, this page provides links to information on indigenous groups in Latin America and their histories. Categorized by region and by ethnic group.

MEXonline: Mexico Pre-Columbian History

http://www.mexonline.com/precolum.htm

Links to general sites promoting pre-Columbian history and archaeology. Some sites are devoted specifically to the Maya, the Aztecs, or other indigenous groups.

Colonial Latin America

Bibliography on History of Ideas in Colonial Latin America

http://www.h-net.org/~latam/bibs/bibideas.html

This is simply a bibliography, but it is a solid one offering an extensive list of sources. Housed on the H-LatAm section of Humanities Net.

Colonial Latin America

http://www.college.emory.edu/culpeper/BAKEWELL/

This site contains an extensive chronology of colonial Latin American history and links to interactive "ThinkSheets" exploring numerous topics. Also a good source for early maps and primary source documents. Excellent source for students.

Internet Modern History Sourcebook: Colonial Latin America

http://www.fordham.edu/halsall/mod/modsbook08.html

Part of the Internet History Sourcebooks Project, an independent project given Web space and support by Fordham University. It offers links to articles and documents relevant to colonial Latin American history.

Resources in Colonial Latin American History

http://lib.ollusa.edu/netguides/newspain.htm

Compiled by Steven Wise, reference/instruction librarian at Our Lady of the Lake University in San Antonio, Texas. Provides links to reference materials, primary sources, secondary sources, and Internet sources.

Central America and the Caribbean

AfroCuban History: A Time Line, 1492–1900

http://www.afrocubaweb.com/history.htm

This site contains a thorough time line, plus links to some related sites. It also contains very valuable sources examining race and identity in the history of Cuba.

Association of Caribbean States

http://www.acs-aec.org

This Web site of the Association of Caribbean States, established in 1994 to promote cooperation among its members, has links to news, trade information, and various projects. In English, French, and Spanish.

Caribbean Community and Common Market

http://www.caricom.org/

The Web site of CARICOM is a good source of information on its member countries.

Central America Panorama

http://www.elpanorama.net/

Source of news and information on various countries in Central America categorized by country. Available in English, Spanish, and German.

History of Cuba

http://www.historyofcuba.com/cuba.htm

This site is compiled by J.A. Sierra, an independent scholar. It is one of the few such sites that remains politically neutral. It contains brief synopses of historical episodes, a valuable timetable and bibliography, and links to primary source documents.

Latin American Network Information Center: Caribbean Nations

http://lanic.utexas.edu/region/caribbean.html

LANIC source, offering links and information on Caribbean countries. Categorized by country.

Latin American Network Information Center: Caribbean Regional Resources

http://lanic.utexas.edu/la/region/caribe/

LANIC source, offering links and information on the Caribbean region. Categorized by topic.

United Nations Economic Commission for Latin America and the Caribbean

http://www.eclac.cl/

This Web site of CEPAL, one of five regional commissions of the United Nations. This site provides links to publications, press releases, analysis and research reports, and statistical information. Available in English and Spanish.

Argentina

Argentine History: General

http://www.historiadelpais.com.ar/

Thorough history of Argentina, including military, political, and social history perspectives. Available only in Spanish.

Latin American Network Information Center: Argentina

http://www.lanic.utexas.edu/la/argentina/

LANIC source on Argentina. Provides links to organizations, newspapers, and educational institutions in Argentina or containing information about Argentina.

Bolivia

Boliviaweb

http://www.boliviaweb.com

Aimed toward a general audience, but contains some good links to information about Bolivian history and culture.

Brazil

The Brazilian Institute of Geography and Statistics

http://www.ibge.gov.br/

Provides statistical information and analysis of Brazilian development. Indicators include population, agriculture, industry, trade, and natural resources. Available in Portuguese and English.

Brazilian National Government

http://www.brasil.gov.br/

Official Web site of the Brazilian government. Information on policies, projects, socioeconomic indicators, public utilities, and social services. Only in Portuguese.

Chile

Chilean National Library of Congress

http://www.bcn.cl/

Electronic access to the Chilean National Library of Congress. This site is very valuable to scholars researching Chilean law. Provides links to historic legislative documents. Only in Spanish.

Latin American Network Information Center: Chile

http://www.lanic.utexas.edu/la/chile/

Valuable source of links on Chile. Information on business, economy, education, the environment, history, human rights, etc.

National Institute of Statistics

http://www.ine.cl/

Offers statistical information and analysis on development and related indicators of population, agriculture, mining, energy, labor, etc. Only in Spanish.

Colombia

Gobierno En Linea

http://www.gobiernoenlinea.gov.co/

Official Web site of the Republic of Colombia. Contains links to government documents and history. Provides numerous links to government departments and organizations related to education, social welfare, energy, agriculture, etc. Only in Spanish.

Republic of Colombia

http://www.colostate.edu/Orgs/LASO/Colombia/colombia.html#History

This Web site, created and maintained by the Latin-American Student Organization, contains general information about history and geography and links to organizations, universities, newspapers, and municipal resources.

Ecuador

Ecuador

http://newbabe.pobox.com/~leer/ecuador

Very good information source on Ecuador, with links to newspapers, educational institutions, government, and economic organizations.

Indigenous Peoples in Ecuador

http://abyayala.nativeweb.org/ecuador/

Good source of links to information about the indigenous people and to indigenous organizations. Some information is in Spanish, some in English.

Mexico

Latin American Network Information Center: Mexico

http://www.lanic.utexas.edu/la/mexico/

Valuable list of links from and about Mexico. Provides access to organizations, educational institutions, newspapers, and academic research resources.

Mexican Archives Project

http://www.lib.utexas.edu/benson/Mex_Archives/Collection_list.html

List of rare books and manuscripts held in the Benson Latin American collection at the University of Texas library. The collection also contains many works in Latin American studies and Mexican American and Latino studies. This site describes the holdings of rare books and manuscripts.

Mexico Online: History

http://www.mexonline.com/history.htm

History page of Mexico Online. Provides general information on Mexican history, plus links to primary source documents, constitutions, and biographies.

Peru

Parliamentary Portal of Peru and the World

http://www.congreso.gob.pe/

Official Web site of Congress. Contains general information about the country and a wealth of information about Peru's government. Links to organizations, legislation, and documents. Only in Spanish.

Venezuela

Embassy of the Bolivarian Republic of Venezuela in the United States of America

http://www.embavenez-us.org

Web site of the Venezuelan embassy in the United States, providing information on government, economy, business, culture, and tourism. Has numerous links to government organizations, documents, and services available to Venezuelan citizens.

Republica Bolivariana de Venezuela

http://www.venezuela.gov.ve/

Official Web site of the Republic of Venezuela. Much of the site is devoted to the powers and policy of the president, but a deeper look into the site finds significant information on history, culture, the economy, the indigenous people, etc. Only in Spanish.

Selected Library Catalogs With Major Latin American Holdings

Biblioteca Nacional: Argentina

http://www.bibnal.edu.ar/

Biblioteca Nacional: Brazil

http://www.bn.br/

Biblioteca Nacional: Chile

http://www.bibliotecanacional.cl/

Biblioteca Nacional: Panama

http://www.binal.ac.pa/

Biblioteca Nacional: Peru

http://www.binape.gob.pe/

Biblioteca Nacional: Portugal

http://www.biblioteca-nacional.pt/

Biblioteca Nacional: Spain

http://www.bne.es/

Duke University Libraries

http://www.lib.duke.edu/

Stanford University Libraries: Latin American and Iberian Collections

http://www-sul.stanford.edu/depts/hasrg/latinam/index.html

Tulane University Latin American Library

http://lal.tulane.edu

University of California at Berkeley Library

http://www.lib.berkeley.edu/

University of Florida Library

http://www.uflib.ufl.edu/

University of Illinois Latin American and Caribbean Library

http://www.library.uiuc.edu/lat/

University of Miami Library

http://www.library.miami.edu/

University of North Carolina at Chapel Hill Libraries

http://www.lib.unc.edu/

University of Texas Library Online

http://www.lib.utexas.edu/

Vanderbilt University Library

http://www.library.vanderbilt.edu/

Chapter 15

European History

General European History

Patrick Callan

BBC Renaissance Secrets

http://www.open2.net/renaissance2/index.html

This interactive BBC Web site explores four main topics: Venice as a "second-hand" city, Renaissance hospitals, an assassination attempt on Elizabeth I, and Gutenberg's movable type printing. The concept of "Doing History" encourages visitors to examine essays about historical evidence and knowledge and learn more about the historian's craft.

Discovery and Reformation

http://www.wsu.edu/~dee/REFORM/REFORM.HTM

Thomas Hooker of Washington State University offers an introduction to European history from the period of exploration through the Reformation, the Counter-Reformation, and the wars of religion. The site has a comprehensive list of Internet resources to strengthen the quality of the introduction.

Encyclopedia of the 1848 Revolutions

http://www.cats.ohiou.edu/~Chastain/

This is an exemplary site, showing how the international community of historians can collaborate in producing an innovative and challenging site, expanding historical awareness and understanding in a manner rarely encountered on the Internet. Hosted by James G. Chastain, at Ohio University, it calls on over 170 extensive articles on the experience of the revolutions throughout Europe, from Ireland in the west to Russia in the east. The authors are specialists in their fields, and the net result is a top quality resource.

Enduring Popularity of Courtly Love

http://members.aol.com/KLStoner/essays/courtly_love.html

Kay Stoner's essay "The Enduring Popularity of Courtly Love" examines a driving force of the high period of medieval love literature, prevailing from 1100 to 1300. Well annotated, the site combines judicious use of narrative and quotation.

Essays in History

http://etext.lib.virginia.edu/journals/EH/

An exceptional site containing a treasure trove of serious articles on European history from the journal *Essays in History*.

Eurodocs

http://library.byu.edu/~rdh/eurodocs/

This exceptional site, dealing with countries of western and central Europe, hosts primary documents dealing with political, economic, social, and cultural topics.

European Integration History Index

http://vlib.iue.it/hist-eur-integration/Index.html

This European Union site provides Internet resources on the history of Europe after World War II. It describes the process of political, economic, and cultural integration and cooperation between various European countries, mainly for the period after 1945.

Lectures on Modern European Intellectual History

http://www.historyguide.org/intellect/intellect.html

Steven Kreis presents a lecture series ranging from ancient Sumer to the fall of Soviet-style communism in 1989. In summary, it is an online textbook in Western Civilization.

Le Poulet Gauche

http://www.lepg.org/index.html

Authored by three talented enthusiasts who started the site to illuminate aspects of "re-living history." A fictional tavern called Le Poulet Gauche, in Calais, France, is the starting point for a consideration of France in the 1500s.

ORB

http://the-orb.net

ORB is an academic site, written and maintained by medieval scholars for the benefit of their fellow instructors and serious students. All articles have been judged by at least two peer reviewers. Authors are held to high standards of accuracy, currency, and relevance to the field of medieval studies. It also contains many original essays by historians.

Turning the Pages

http://www.bl.uk/collections/treasures/digitisation1.html

This British Library site brings the most advanced technology to exploring treasures of literature, such as Leonardo da Vinci's notebooks, the Lindisfarne Gospels, and the Sforza Hours. As reader, you literally turn the pages.

Twenty-Five Lectures on Modern Balkan History

http://www.lib.msu.edu/sowards/balkan/

A series of twenty-five lectures prepared by Stephen Sowards looks briefly at early Ottoman rule in the Balkans and then moves on to consider the principal events and controversies down to 1996. Worth noting are the legacy of nationalism from the 1948 revolution in Hungary and Romania, the Balkan Causes of World War I, and modern topics such as the Yugoslav Civil War (to 1995).

WESSWeb

http://www.dartmouth.edu/~wessweb/index.html

This site aims to provide specialists in Western European studies with professional information and data concerning ongoing and recent Western research efforts.

British History

Ian Morley

Metasites

Anglo-Saxon Charters

http://www.trin.cam.ac.uk/chartwww/

Maintained by Trinity College, Cambridge University, this site is concerned with different documents about British life from about 675 to 1066 CE. Supported by the British Academy and the Royal Historical Society, this wide-ranging site provides a plethora of information on Saxon history and incorporates, for instance, a searchable edition of the entire body of Anglo-Saxon royal charters and digital images of charters held by the British Library.

Early-Modern and Modern Periods

http://www.fordham.edu/halsall/mod/modsbook.html

Focusing on post–sixteenth-century affairs, this site includes both broad subjects and more specialized themes, such as philosophies and aspects of industrialization. With literally thousands of sources, this site incorporates subjects often excluded from other general history-centered Web sites, like "studying history," i.e., historiography and the use of sources materials in the research process.

History of Britain: Hamden Public Library

http://www.hamdenlibrary.org/Links/history.html#British%20History

All-embracing historical Web site that links to history Web sites about, for instance, the Victorian period and World War I. Relating not only to British history sites, this comprehensive Web site by Hamden Public Library covers wider cultural and historical fields, such as European history, ancient history, and Renaissance and Reformation history—subjects that have at one time or another influenced the evolution of British society.

History of Britain: Marquette University

http://www.marquette.edu/library/sites/history.html#britain

Marquette University's site hyperlinks to, for example, the British Library and British Official Publication Collaborative Publications Reader Service as well as sites detailing British history since 1800. The site also links to the popular H-Albion Web site, a discussion network for British and Irish history that is part of the larger H-Net Web system (hosted by Michigan State University).

History of Britain: Primary Documents

http://library.byu.edu:80/~rdh/eurodocs/uk.html

Developed by Brigham Young University, this site is composed of important documents relating to Britain from ancient times to the twentieth century. Furthermore, the Regional, Local and Family History section provides access to a range of sites focusing on parts of Irish, Scottish, and Welsh history, as well as details of London's past like the Crystal Palace of 1851.

History of Britain: Reference and Archives

http://vlib.iue.it/history/europe/uk/uk.html

This virtual library site, with its slight political history stress, provides numerous maps, bibliographies, and biographies as well as links to respected organizations, associations, and libraries. Links can be also found for subjects such as prime ministers, members of Parliament, and writers as well as biographies of noted persons from various past ages. Additionally, the site has military history links and provides access to a number of valuable source materials.

Medieval Britain

http://www.geocities.com/profviano/medieval/2general.html

This site has extensive resources connected to medieval culture, people, literature, and military conflicts as well as links to sites about more generalized history. Links are given to subjects such as medieval English literature and medieval linguistics and word meaning, as well as metasites specializing in medieval history.

Nineteenth-Century Britain

http://www.britainexpress.com/History/Victorian_index.htm

This site provides information about life, people, law, art, and many of the most significant cultural events during the Victorian era. By way of example, this site takes account of the significance of people such as Gothic architect and designer A.W.N. Pugin; celebrated craftsman, designer, and writer William Morris; and the premier architect of Regency England, John Nash. Furthermore, brief details are provided of British life and prominent events at the beginning and end of Queen Victoria's reign.

Philosophies, Politics and Nationhood

http://www.multcolib.org/homework/eurohist.html

Web guide from Multnomah County Library (Oregon) emphasizing topics such as political, military, and royal matters in Britain and also the wider European context. Links as well to a small number of metasites focusing on limited aspects of European history, parts of which are of relevance to British events and developments.

General Sites

BBC Online History

http://www.bbc.co.uk/history/

With an abundant number of sections, this site makes it possible to delve into the many eras and prominent cultural fields in British history. In addition the site contains pieces of writing by noted academics and also a "Multimedia Zone" with animations, galleries, games, and virtual tours. Special links are provided to the wide variety of themes included in many of the BBC's world-renowned historical documentary series.

British History: Britannia

http://britannia.com/history/

A comprehensive Web site about the evolution of Britain that consists of data about monarchs, distinguished individuals, the church, the British Empire, historical periods, historical places (regions), and architecture, for example. Also includes a British Life section about the arts, government, and sports in the contemporary context.

British History: Wars and Conflict

http://www.british-history.com/

Essentially focusing on military history, this site chronicles countless battles and wars in Britain and the British Empire from the Roman era through World War II, providing concise details of conflicts such as the Battle of Rorke's Drift (1879) during the Anglo-Zulu War in South Africa, as popularized by the film *Zulu*.

The British Isles

http://www.great-britain.co.uk/history/history.htm

Acknowledging the richness of the history of Britain, this site provides access to subdivisions and eras of British life dating from about 4000 BCE to the twentieth century, with individual sections about the history of Ireland, Scotland, and Wales. By covering topics like ancient archaeology, the Romans, the Normans, the Tudors, Oliver Cromwell, the growth and fall of the British Empire, and King George I, II, and III, the site thus provides a thorough outline of significant British people and events.

British Monarchy: Official Web Site

http://www.royal.gov.uk/output/Page1.asp

Provided by the British government, this site chronicles the history of the monarchy in Britain and provides a wealth of information about the present queen, the royal family, her art collection, and her places of residence. With a vast number of pages, this site more than adequately explains both the role of the queen in modern British society and the evolution of the royal line up to the twenty-first century through the unfolding of numerous past royal dynasties.

Channel 4 History

http://www.channel4.com/history/

The content of this site (often updated) is closely associated with television documentaries and programs made by Channel 4. Nonetheless, supplementary information is also given about some social matters in Britain, such as battles or the monarchy. The "Search History" facility provides access to information regarding historical periods from 1000 BCE to the year 2000.

Encyclopedia of British History, 1500–1980

http://www.spartacus.schoolnet.co.uk/Britain.html

Instructive Web site with a search engine facility. Information can be found on a vast number of subjects, such as the monarchs and royal families, politicians, political groups, parliamentary developments, ethnic minorities, towns and cities, trade unions, the Industrial Revolution, railways, World War I, and the histories of Scotland and Wales. With its inclination toward political and cultural matters, this site is particularly useful for anyone interested in the social history of Britain.

Historic Britain: Places to Visit

http://www.nationaltrust.org.uk/main/w-index.htm

This site belongs to the National Trust, one of the foremost organizations for preserving British cultural heritage. The site provides useful introductory information for both visitors and researchers with links to over 300 celebrated places of historical or cultural importance. A search engine is provided and a clickable regional map gives instantaneous access to buildings or gardens owned by the National Trust within a specified part of the British mainland. A small number of virtual tours are also presented within the site.

History of the British Isles: Timeline

http://www.historique.net/history.html

Provides a time line of prominent events in British history from the prehistoric period to the twentieth century. Clicking on the time line opens up more detailed overviews of each historical age. Although many past events are just briefly described, the site nonetheless introduces the cultural expansion of Britain through time. Also somewhat briefly details historical matters such as feudalism and noted persons such as Geoffrey Chaucer.

Roman and Prehistoric Britain

Pre-Historic Archaeology

http://www.stonepages.com/

Detailed site providing a catalog and description of numerous ancient historical archaeological sites in England, Ireland, Scotland, and Wales, such as Stonehenge, Skara Brae, and Bry Celli Ddu. Contains a major glossary of terms associated with archaeology and links to literally hundreds of well-known and less familiar archaeological sites scattered across Britain.

Roman Archaeology

http://www.hadrians-wall.org/

Thorough investigation of arguably one of Britain's most famous historic constructions and a present UNESCO World Heritage Site, Hadrian's Wall—an evocative reminder of Britain's Roman legacy. Provides details of the Hadrian's Wall Tourism Partnership, the organization formed to develop tourism in the West Cumbrian region of northern England where the ancient wall is located.

Roman Britain: Britannia

http://www.romanbritain.freeserve.co.uk/

Highlights Britannia, the province of the Roman Empire that is today known as Britain. With a somewhat military perspective, the site nevertheless concurrently expresses the cultural nature of Roman life in Britain. Contains chapters on the Roman army in Britain; the Roman-British background, including information about Boudica, the leader of the British rebellion against the Romans; books and source materials; and coins. Auxiliary information is also given on ancient Egypt due to the author's interest in this field.

Roman Britain: Roman-Britain.org

http://www.roman-britain.org/main.htm

Clickable maps, references, and details about ancient Britain, the native British tribes and their major sites of habitation, the Romans, the Romano-British peoples, the geography of Britain, and the architecture and constructions of Roman Britain, such as Hadrian's Wall and the Antonine Wall. With clickable computerized maps, the site shows the location of not only military forts but important sites of habitation and settlement, for example.

Roman Britain: Timeline

http://www.britannia.com/history/romantime.html

Extensive time line following major events in the history of Roman Britain, beginning with the invasion in 55 BCE and ending with Britain's independence from Rome in 410 CE. With a built-in clickable facility, information and pictures or maps concerning significant places and people can be immediately accessed within the large Britannia.com Web site. Consequently, an ample amount of data is provided about Roman life in Britain.

Viking and Saxon Britain

Anglo-Saxon England

http://www.mnsu.edu/emuseum/prehistory/vikings/angsaxe.html

Site emphasizes Saxon society, particularly the reign of King Cnut and the role of the church, while also offering links to documents about the Saxon invasion of England. An extensive bibliography and an exhaustive appendix of material relating to Cnut's reign are also provided. Furthermore, the site links to the Anglo-Saxon Web ring, which is a catalog of sites related to the history and archaeology of Anglo-Saxon England and the Old English language and its literature.

Saxon History: Village Net Local History

http://www.villagenet.co.uk/history/0200-anglosaxons.html

Uncomplicated site that explains key groups of Saxon people, Saxon places, and basic urban settlement expressions from the Saxon language. Contains a list of villages with histories stretching to the Saxon era, providing basic details of the settlements' past as well as present-day amenities.

Medieval Britain

Early-Medieval Britain and Ireland

http://www.postroman.info/

This site highlights Britain's development from 350 to 850 CE, a period often referred to as the Dark Ages or sub-Roman period when Roman rule declined and the Saxons invaded. Materials within this site are referenced to well-known books, and many key points are directly quoted from source materials, providing a highly factual content. The site is simply laid out so it is easy to follow the authors' points of discussion.

Medieval: Internet Medieval Sourcebook

http://www.fordham.edu/halsall/sbook.html

This is an online version of the Internet History Sourcebooks Project at Fordham University's History Department. It contains an array of resources on the medieval era. Affiliated as well with the Online Reference Book for Medieval Studies, the site has many links to sites on not only British but also European medieval history and moreover has a massive variety of materials, maps, and texts about historic British law (Saxon law, Norman law, common law, etc.), for example.

Medieval: Time Reference

http://www.timeref.org/

Follows Britain's progress from Alfred the Great to the late 1400s, incorporating the social and cultural changes introduced by the Normans following their invasion in 1066. Contains key dates, key places, time lines, and clickable maps. Each part of this large site contains a wide variety of relevant materials. For example, the architecture section, with its colorful photographs and three-dimensional reconstructions, has information about a range of building types: castles, abbeys, monasteries, and cathedrals. A massive A to Z people index includes the rulers of Scotland and France, earls, and barons.

Early Modern History

The Stuarts (1603–1714) and House of Orange

http://www.great-britain.co.uk/history/restore.htm

Short introduction to the royal monarchs who preceded and followed the British Civil Wars and Interregnum during the mid-1600s. Links are given within the site to the other British royal dynasties, highlighting the main social and cultural issues within each age of history but providing little more than an overview of each epoch.

The Tudors (1485–1603)

http://www.englishhistory.net/tudor.html

Information centers on the Tudor kings and queens, their relatives, and noted persons in Tudor society. Access is also given to numerous primary and secondary documents. Site contains a search engine. Countless portraits of the Tudors and their contemporaries may also be found on this in-depth Web site.

Tudors, Stuarts and Other Monarchs

http://www.britannia.com/history/h6f.html

Consists of a detailed (clickable) list of all British monarchs from about 800 CE to the present day, including Saxon, Danish, and Norman kings and all succeeding royal houses. Biographies, some short in length and some with links to contextual matters, of each monarch are given. Information chronologically begins with the House of Wessex in the ninth century and ends with the House of Windsor, the present-day royal family.

The Georgians

Georgian England: The Georgian Period

http://www.britainexpress.com/History/Georgian_index.htm

Short articles on "The Three Georges," i.e., King George I, II, and III, in addition to details about daily life in the Georgian period (primarily the 1700s). Notice is also given to architectural developments and the most noted designer of the time, John Nash, who is still considered one of the greatest architects in British history. Landscaped gardens, country houses, canals and waterways, plus the Baroque form of architecture all receive due consideration.

Victorian History

The British Empire

http://www.britishempire.co.uk/

Evocative site dedicated to both the good and not so good aspects of British colonial expansion. Discussing all aspects of the British Empire, the site contains a number of detailed academic papers, time lines, a discussion board, a map room, and a section on the British armed forces, among other parts. The input of eminent academic writers to this site ensures that the standard of material is of a high level. A search engine is provided.

Victorian Britain

http://www.learningcurve.gov.uk/victorianbritain/

Site focusing on both the social developments and the troubles of Victorian life in order to stimulate debate as to whether Britain in the 1800s was a great nation or not. With sections titled, for instance, "A Healthy Nation?," "A Divided Nation?" and "A Lawless Nation?," the site provides source materials and a list of questions so as to provoke both understanding and debate from the reader. With its support for historical discourse, the site forms a notable resource for teachers who want to introduce significant social issues (such as public health, social welfare, social class, crime and disorder, etc.) of Victorian history to their students.

Victorian Life: The Victorian Web

http://www.victorianweb.org/

Funded by the University Scholars Program at the National University of Singapore, this comprehensive site uses both primary and secondary sources to give abundant information relating to life in Victorian Britain. With a massive amount of material embedded within this site, the principal social, economic, artistic, and cultural issues in Victorian society are noted and provided for. A lengthy list of periodicals, books, and Web sites easily allows for further research of any matter discussed within the site.

The Twentieth Century

The Garden City

http://www.letchworthgardencity.net/

Overview of the Garden City, an idea that came to influence not only housing but emergent statutory British town planning—the first modern town planning system in the world—and the design of living environments for working people in Britain from the Edwardian period up to 1939 and the onset of World War II. With its broad nature, this site highlights both the historical conception of the Garden City and its manifestation, Letchworth Garden City, but also the settlement's modern-day character and community spirit.

National Health Service

http://www.nhs.uk/england/aboutTheNHS/history/default.cmsx

History of the National Health Service (NHS), a major component of the social welfare reform introduced after the end of World War II in 1945. Split into a number of sections, each covering about a ten-year period, this site briefly highlights the major issues of the NHS, such as administration, management, and financial cost, as well as the changing political times that have influenced the form and development of a major British social welfare institution that is respected worldwide.

Political Evolution

http://www.britannia.com/history/nar20hist.html

A long narrative outline of the domestic and overseas political policy changes in Britain throughout the twentieth century, including policies concerning the British Empire. The site notes matters of significance such as the development of trade unions and working-class solidarity, changes in British trade strategy and foreign trade rules, the emergence of the wider social welfare system, the impact of World War I on British society, the Irish situation and ultimately Ireland's independence from British rule, the Great Depression, World War II, post-1945 reform, the decline of the British Empire, the rise of British technological innovations, the problems of Northern Ireland, and the philosophies championed by prime ministers Margaret Thatcher, John Major, and Tony Blair.

World War One

http://www.bbc.co.uk/history/war/wwone/index.shtml

BBC site covering World War I—the Great War, as it is also known—in vast detail. Attention, for instance, is given to the war in context, social debates, the campaigns and battles, and how to search archives for family and military records. Biographies and a thorough time line provide for easy comprehension of the main persons and events during the Great War, while the "Multimedia Zone," with movies, photographs, soldier's letters, three-dimensional models, battlefield tours, animations, and audio files of war poetry, bring the true nature of the war to life.

World War Two

http://www.bbc.co.uk/history/war/wwtwo/

A large-scale BBC-maintained site with time lines, details of battles and influential persons during the war, galleries, and multimedia files. Like the BBC World War I site, this World War II site contains an array of source materials, some written by specialists in this particular field of British military history.

Eastern European and Russian History

Alexander Zukas

Metasites

Armenian Embassy Web Site

http://www.armeniaemb.org/DiscoverArmenia/Index.htm

This site has a large collection of Armenian links on the Internet arranged alphabetically, without annotations. There are several history-related sites linked here, dealing mainly with the Armenian genocide of 1915–1916. Maintained by the Embassy of the Republic of Armenia in Washington, DC.

A Belarus Miscellany

http://misc.home.by/

A collection of links to resources from and about Belarus. Organized by subject and features a separate history links page, which in turn contains annotated links to onsite and external resources. Maintained by Peter Kasaty and hosted by the University of Tennessee in Knoxville. Mirror site in Belarus.

CeltoSlavica

http://www.celtoslavica.de/links/links_slavica.html

A part of the larger CeltoSlavica New Age–style Web site, which publishes legends, myths, poems, and songs of Celtic and Slavic peoples, this metasite deals with the spiritual and religious aspects of Slavic life. History links are scattered throughout the site, within areas dedicated to various countries and themes like "sacred images." Maintained by Markus Osterrieder of CeltoSlavica and hosted in Germany.

Central Eurasia Project Resource Page

http://www.eurasianet.org/

This site focuses on Georgia, Armenia, Azerbaijan, Turkey, Tajikistan, Uzbekistan, Kyrgyzstan, Kazakhstan, Turkmenistan, Afghanistan, and

Mongolia. Each of those Central Eurasian countries has a separate resource page, with links grouped according to subjects, with some history links, although the amount and quality of the material varies from country to country. Maintained by the Soros Foundation.

Cilicia.com

http://www.cilicia.com/

A large Armenian information site with extensive resources and outside links. Many of the history-related links are located on the Armenian Genocide page. External links are grouped together following the internal resources, and it is easy to distinguish one from another. Maintained by Raffi Kojian and hosted by Cilicia.com. Part of the Armenian Web Ring.

Friends and Partners History

http://www.friends-partners.org/friends/history/index.html

This metasite provides links to resources in Russian, Soviet, and American history, as well as to historical documents, such as the constitutions of the Russian Federation and the United States and the 1867 Alaska treaty. Many of the links lead to Russian language resources. Hosted and maintained by Friends and Partners, a Russo-American citizens' organization.

Funet Russian Archive

http://www.funet.fi/pub/culture/russian/index.html

A links and resources site on Russia and the former Soviet Union. History-related links are located at Funet Russian Archive Index and Links, which is arranged alphabetically. The whole site itself is at its best in providing onsite historical resources. Maintained by and hosted by Finnish University and Research Network, Espoo, Finland.

History/Social Studies Web Site for K–12 Teachers

http://home.comcast.net/~dboals1/boals.html

An important metasite in that it is virtually the only site to provide links to history resources specifically chosen for K–12 teachers. The Russian area is large (over one hundred links) with links to general resources and resources of specific interest to schoolteachers. Maintained by Dennis Boals and hosted by Xplore Company.

H-RUSSIA WWW Links

http://www.h-net.org/~russia/links/

A selection of links to Russian resources from H-Net. History materials are available on the chronology of Russian history and primary sources from the Kievan period onward. A wealth of teaching resources covers medieval, early modern, and modern Russian history, the history of the Soviet Union, political theory, arts and literature, and interdisciplinary topics. The site, hosted by Michigan State University, also provides extensive bibliographic links.

Illustrated History of Russia and the Former USSR

http://www.friends-partners.org/oldfriends/mes/russia/history.html

This is a collection of links to sites dealing with artifacts, photographs, and other graphic material from the various periods in Russian history, from the era of Genghis Khan to the July 1996 presidential elections in Russia.

Index of Resources for History

http://vlib.iue.it/hist-russia/Index.html

This site hosts extensive links to resources in Russian history organized chronologically (from pre-Kievan Russia to the Russian Federation) and topically (women, military, science and technology, etc.) with links to a wonderful series of maps. There are also links to reference sites, Web publications, and Russian search engines. The site is maintained by Serge Noiret and Inaki Lopez Martin at the European University Institute in Florence, Italy.

Institute of Baltic Studies

http://www.ibs.ee/

An Estonian site with links to resources on Estonia and other Baltic states. Organized by subject. History subject area is small, with both internal and external links listed together. Highlight: Department of History, University of Tartu site, with its Electronic Library of Estonian History page. Maintained and hosted by the Institute of Baltic Studies in Estonia.

Internet Resources for Russian Studies

http://src-h.slav.hokudai.ac.jp/link/index-e.html

This is probably the best metasite for materials on Russia, including Siberia and Asian Russia, central Eurasia, the Commonwealth of Independent States, and Eastern Europe. The materials are very well organized geographically (by region and country) and by subject (journals, institutions for research and exchange, culture, politics and economics, ethnicity and history, and society and life). Many of the links on this metasite lead to resources compiled within the former Soviet Union that cannot be found on other metasites. Most of the links are reliable in their connection. The site is maintained by the Slavic Research Center at Hokkaido University in Japan.

Medieval Russia—Medieval History Net Links

http://historymedren.about.com/od/russia/

A small but well-organized metasite on medieval Russian history. There are links to chronologies of Russian history, overviews of Russian ruling houses and medieval Russian cities, compilations of medieval Russian law, maps of medieval Russia, and articles on the Mongols, the Oprichnina of Ivan IV, the Novgorod Chronicle, and Russian medieval arms and armor. The site is maintained by About.com.

Orthodox Christian Resources on the Internet

http://www.iconwall.org/links/

This well-designed metasite is unique in bringing together the links related to the Russian and other Slavic Orthodox churches. Arranged by subject. History page is small but very useful. Highlights: Ecumenical Orthodox Church History, a comprehensive history of the Orthodox Church, including the Russian church. The site is maintained by Catherine Hampton and is hosted by Icon Wall in conjunction with Human Rights Web. Not all links are functional and the site has not been updated recently.

Russia—The Armed Forces

http://www.russiansabroad.com/russian_history_320.html

This site provides a survey of imperial Russian military history since Peter the Great, Russian and Soviet military doctrine and principles, geopolitical views, Russia's military and security relations with former members of the Soviet Union, China, and NATO, nuclear armaments, force and command structure, and the defense industry. The site is maintained by RussiansAbroad.

Russia on the Web

http://www.valley.net:80/~transnat/index.html#Russia

A well-designed metasite with links to Russian sources. Organized by subject with a small history page. Many of the sites on this page can, however, be found on other, larger metasites. Hosted by the Transnational Institute.

Russian and East European Network Information Center

http://reenic.utexas.edu/reenic/index.html

A large metasite with links to resources on Russia, the countries of the former Soviet Union, and Eastern Europe. Most country pages have a history subject listing, but these are not abundant in resources. The site is at its best as a starting point to other relevant metasites on the World Wide Web. Maintained by the Center for Russian, East European and Eurasian Studies at the University of Texas in Austin.

Russian and East European Studies Web (REESWeb)

http://www.ucis.pitt.edu/reesweb/

A deceptively extensive metasite that has a searchable database of useful links for Russian and Eastern European history. Users can find material on REESWeb by using the "browse subject" or "search keyword" functions. The "browse subject" function is the most useful as it narrows searches to items held on REESWeb and the item list is wide-ranging and covers various subjects, geographic regions, cultures, and time periods. Given the sparse nature of the initial REESWeb splash page, users can find help formulating their queries by checking out the REESBrowse Hints and Tips page. One highlight of the site is an abbreviated version of the ArcheoBiblioBase directory and bibliographic database for Russian archives, covering the fourteen federal archives in Russia, as well as larger regional and local archives. It includes a number of significant finding aids to many of the archives as well as other information on their holdings, location, and access. Gives links to comparable sites in Belarus, Ukraine, and other areas. ArcheoBiblioBase is in English or Russian. REESWeb is maintained by the Center for Russian and East European Studies at the University of Pittsburgh.

Russian History

http://www.departments.bucknell.edu/russian/history.html

A well-organized and well-maintained Russian metasite. The links are generally arranged in chronological order, although there are large thematic sections. A number of links lead to photographic and genealogical material, as well as Russian and Soviet historical documents. Maintained by Bucknell University in Lewisburg, Pennsylvania.

Russian History on the Internet

http://www.bol.ucla.edu/~jseaman/

This metasite contains links on Russian history and culture in the period from 1801 to 1991. The site needs updating but the links are useful. The main strengths of the site are links to the Alexander Palace Russian History Web sites, Chronology of Russian History, and archival resources and a (slightly dated) bibliography of materials related to Russian history. The site is maintained by James Seaman at UCLA and focuses on his areas of interest.

Russian Military History: Sword of the Motherland

http://www.russianwarrior.com/

Sword of the Motherland is devoted to the study of the Russian military from the 1830s to the modern era. The site highlights military life during the peasant rebellions in the 1850s, the Crimean War, the conquest of Central Asia, wars with the Ottoman and Japanese Empires, the period of World War I and the Bolshevik Revolution, the consolidation of Stalin's power, the era of the Spanish Civil War and World War II, the Cold War, and the post-Soviet era. The link to each era contains a brief synopsis of the times and detailed information about the weapons, uniforms, and field gear. The background of various weapons designers as well as what could be found in the civilian world of the era is presented as well. The site is extensively cross-linked so that discovering information about related topics is easy. It is maintained by the Sword of the Motherland Foundation.

The Russian Revolution

http://www.barnsdle.demon.co.uk/russ/rusrev.html

A fairly small but very useful metasite with particular emphasis on the February and October Revolutions of 1917 and the Russian Civil War. It also contains links to political parties, figures, and movements; images and maps; and critiques of the events in the years after the Russian Revolutions of 1917. Privately maintained by David Barnsdale.

Russian Studies

http://www.departments.bucknell.edu/russian/

A well-organized and well-maintained Russian studies metasite, it covers not only Russian history but also history-related topics like Russian culture, media, politics, economics, and geography. The history links are chronological as well as thematically organized. Under "culture" users will find literature, art, feminism, folklore, and holidays, among other topics of interest to students and scholars. There are also links to Russian and Soviet historical documents. The site is maintained by the Russian Studies Program at Bucknell University in Lewisburg, Pennsylvania.

The Society for Romanian Studies

http://www.huntington.edu/srs/

This site contains a large Romanian Studies Internet Gateway, with links to outside sites on Romania, organized by subject. Although history is not one of those subjects, a significant number of history-related links can be found in the Scholarly Publications and Cities areas. Maintained by Paul E. Michelson and hosted by Huntington College in Huntington, Indiana.

UNCG's Slavic Studies Trails

http://www.uncg.edu/~lixlpurc/russian.html

A collection of links to resources on and from Poland, Russia, and Ukraine. The Russian links are the most numerous and reliable, and some of them lead to history sites. This site is best used as a starting point to other larger and more history-oriented metasites. Maintained by the Department of German and Russian at the University of North Carolina at Greensboro.

World History Compass

http://www.worldhistorycompass.com/whlindex.htm#Europe Index

A large and important metasite with links to history materials throughout the world. Russian, former Soviet Union, and East European links are indexed under Europe where in turn they are indexed under separate countries. No annotations for sites are provided. Maintained by Schiller Computing, in Stratford, Connecticut, and hosted by LexiConn Internet Services of the same city.

WWW Virtual Library—History Central Catalogue

http://vlib.iue.it/history/index.html

A part of the WWW Virtual Library, this site is an important starting point for research in history. Russian and Eastern European resources are located in the Europe section by individual country. The links are not annotated. The site is maintained by Serge Noiret and Inaki Lopez Martin at the European University Institute in Florence, Italy.

Reference Sites

ArcheoBiblioBase

http://www.iisg.nl/~abb/

An important information source on federal and regional archives of the Russian Federation. The information for each archive includes name, address, phone number and e-mail, hours, outline of holdings, library facilities, and finding aids. Maintained by Patricia Kennedy Grimsted in collaboration with Rosarkhiv, the Federal Archival Service of Russia, and hosted by the International Institute of Social History in Amsterdam, the Netherlands.

Armenian Research Center

http://www.umd.umich.edu/dept/armenian/

A U.S.-based resource site that deals with various aspects of Armenian history and culture. The most useful part of the site is a collection of bibliographies on Nagorno-Karabakh conflict and Armenian genocide, which constitutes an important starting point in a study of these two topics. Maintained by the Center for Armenian Research and Publication and hosted by the University of Michigan-Dearborn.

Brokgaus Online

http://www.agama.com/bol/

The core material presently at this site is the *Brokgaus-Efron Encyclopedia* and the pre-Revolutionary dictionaries by Pavlenkov, Mikhelson, and Starchevskii. The encyclopedia is a very important source of information on pre-Revolutionary Russia, a source that may not be readily available elsewhere. The site is in Russian, and knowledge of the language, as well as a Russian-English keyboard, is needed to access the site. Compiled and maintained by Sergei Moskalev and jointly hosted by Agama WWW Server and Cityline Internet Service Providers (Moscow).

A Chronology of Russian History

http://www.departments.bucknell.edu/russian/chrono.html

A chronology of Russian history, the site is "divided into four arbitrary periods": Kievan-Appanage (860–1689), Imperial (1689–1916), Soviet (1917–1991), and post-Soviet (1991 to the present). "A fifth page displays related chronologies on specialized subjects."

The House of Romanov

http://www.departments.bucknell.edu/russian/facts/romanov.html

The detailed family tree of the Romanov tsars and emperors who ruled Russia between 1613 and 1917. The site appears to be under construction, and key figures in the dynasty will have links to more detailed information about themselves and their contribution. Maintained by Robert Beard and hosted by the Russian Studies Department of Bucknell University in Lewisburg, Pennsylvania.

The House of Rurik

http://www.departments.bucknell.edu/russian/facts/rurik.html

The detailed family tree of the Rurik Dynasty, Russia's first ruling dynasty, descended from Viking princes. The site appears to be under construction, and key figures in the dynasty will have links to more detailed information about themselves and their contribution. Maintained by Robert Beard and hosted by the Russian Studies Department of Bucknell University in Lewisburg, Pennsylvania.

H-RUSSIA WWW Site

http://www.h-net.msu.edu/~russia/

H-RUSSIA, a member of H-NET, encourages scholarly discussion of Russian and Soviet history. Makes available diverse bibliographical, research, and teaching aids, and features a review project. Maintained by H-NET Humanities & Social Sciences Online and hosted by Michigan State University.

Lomonosov Moscow State University Faculty of History Electronic Resources Library

http://www.hist.msu.ru/ER/English/index.htm

This site contains very useful links to materials not available from other metasites. Materials available include electronic historical texts like the Legal Code of 1649, databases in Russian, digital sources, links for historical sources in Russian, a short list of links for historical sources in English, and links for reference books in Russian. The site is hosted and maintained by the Faculty of History at Lomonosov Moscow State University.

The Lost Churches of Kyiv

http://www.iprinet.kiev.ua/oldkiev/

This site is an important reference source on the churches in the Ukrainian capital destroyed during the Stalinist era. Each link leads to a separate page with a photograph of the church in question, and a description of its history and the circumstances of its destruction. Maintained and hosted by the Global Ukraine ISP under the auspices of the Ukraine Online project.

Moldova History Index

http://www.workmall.com/wfb2001/moldova/moldova_history_index.html

This site focuses on Moldovan history since the start of the Soviet period with some links to pre-Soviet history. The source for the historical information is the Library of Congress Country Studies. Helen Fedor maintains the site.

Moldova: Important Events

http://www.timisoara.com/msoccer/eventsMOLDOVA.htm

A chronology of the history of Moldova, from Roman times (105 CE) to the present. Maintained and hosted by the Embassy of Moldova in Washington, DC.

Political Leaders, 1945–2001

http://www.terra.es/personal2/monolith/00index.htm

A continually updated index of leaders of the countries in the world, from 1945 to the present day. Heads of states, prime ministers, and the leaders of ruling parties are featured. Some countries also have picture links.

Reference Sources: Russian History and Literature

http://www.lib.berkeley.edu/Collections/Slavic/russref.html

This online bibliography of reference material is extremely useful as a starting point in research on Russian and Soviet history and literary heritage. Sources listed include general guides, encyclopedias, serial reference publications, and guides to archival materials and émigré sources. Library of Congress classification numbers are provided. Maintained by Allan Urbanic and hosted by the Library of the University of California at Berkeley.

Russian Encyclopedias

http://www.encyclopedia.ru/

This is the main page for a number of Russian encyclopedias, general and subject-specific, all of which are searchable for free. Along with a link to the Brokgaus and Kirill and Mefodius encyclopedias, there are also links to a legal encyclopedia and a great biographical encyclopedia. The *Brokgaus-Efron Encyclopedia* is a very important source of information on pre-Revolutionary Russia, a source that may not be available elsewhere. The site is in Russian and knowledge of the language, as well as a Russia-English keyboard, is needed to access the site.

Russian History

http://hulmer.allegheny.edu/history.html

A short chronology of Russian history, from early Russia to the Bolshevik Revolution of 1917. Concentrates on the rulers of Russia during this period. Hyperlinks to a glossary of related terms. Maintained by Kristen Magee and hosted by Allegheny College in Pennsylvania.

Russian Revolution in Dates

http://www.barnsdle.demon.co.uk/russ/datesr.html

A detailed chronology of the Russian Revolution, from Bloody Sunday in January 1905 to the death of Lenin in 1924. Privately maintained by David Barnsdale as a part of his Russian Revolution site.

Sources on Russia & the FSU (Former Soviet Union)

http://www.vwc.edu/wwwpages/dgraf/places.htm

A general metasite, organized by region, with links to Russia and the former Soviet Union, Central Europe, and the Balkans, among other regions. Related metasites with Russian links: Exhibits and Museums, Military History. Maintained by Professor Dan Graf and hosted by Virginia Wesleyan College.

Soviet Leaders

http://en.wikipedia.org/wiki/List_of_leaders_of_the_Soviet_Union

This site features extensive biographies of all major Soviet leaders from Lenin to Gorbachev as well as minor leaders who held high posts in the Communist Party or Soviet state (e.g., secretary-general of the Communist Party, chairman of the Presidium of the Supreme Soviet, president of the Soviet Union, etc.). A great number of internal links in the biographies connect them to major themes in Soviet history. The site is hosted by Wikipedia.

Ukraine—History

http://www.infoukes.com/history/

Ukrainian history is covered in this site from prehistory to the present with a focus on key events. The site is openly nationalistic and anti-Soviet. Much of the material provides a nationalistic Ukrainian view on Ukrainian activities in World War II (i.e., the integration of the 1st Division of the Ukrainian National Army into the German Wehrmacht) as resistance to Soviet occupation. The site is managed and hosted by InfoUkes, an Internet-based Canadian information resource about Ukraine and Ukrainians.

WWW Virtual Library History: Lithuania

http://vlib.iue.it/history/europe/lithuania.html

A part of the WWW Virtual Library, this site is an important starting point for research in Lithuanian history. The site is replete with links to maps, reference materials, bibliographies, libraries, research centers, universities, historical articles dealing with topics from ancient to modern Lithuanian history, Jews of Lithuania, and Vilnius in old photographs. The site is maintained by Lynn H. Nelson in conjunction with Serge Noiret and Inaki Lopez Martin at the European University Institute in Florence, Italy.

Online Exhibitions and Virtual Tours

The Abel-Powers Connection

http://www.wfu.edu/users/kotwbj2/

This site contains a detailed biography of Rudolf Abel (alias William Fischer) and his activities as a legendary Soviet spy in Britain and the United States. The site features an online exhibit of photographs and documents associated with Abel, who was arrested in 1957 and freed in 1962 in exchange for U-2 pilot Francis Gary Powers, whose life is also included on the site. The site is maintained by Bryan Kotwicki and Alex Gelb, who maintain that Powers might have been a Soviet double agent who staged the U-2 crash, and hosted at Wake Forest University.

The Alexander Palace Web Sites

http://www.alexanderpalace.org/

The palaces showcased include the Alexander Palace, the Great Catherine Palace of Tsarskoe Selo, and the Yelagin Palace of St. Petersburg. Each of the sites includes a virtual tour of the palace in question, its history, and its connection with the various members of the Romanov dynasty. Other exhibits showcased include the Romanov Jewels. Maintained by Alexander Palace Association and hosted by PalasArt Web Design and Hosting of Austin, Texas.

Aleksandr Rodchenko

http://www.moma.org/exhibitions/1998/rodchenko/index.html

This site is a retrospective. Aleksandr Rodchenko (1891–1956) was a consummate artist in all media; his painting, design work, and photography were fundamental to the founding of abstract art in Revolutionary Russia. Rodchenko was deeply committed to the ideals of the Revolution, and his work cannot be understood apart from the turbulent and world-historical changes in Russia in the 1920s and 1930s. His work included portraits of famous Soviet artists, actors, and intellectuals in that period.

Beyond the Pale: The History of Jews in Russia

http://www.friends-partners.org/partners/beyond-the-pale/

This site explores the history of Jews in Russia and the Soviet Union. The exhibition explores Jewish life from the Middle Ages to the resurgence of anti-Semitism in the post-Soviet period. Each section outlines the events, policies, and ideas of the time and is accompanied by images of artifacts, paintings, and photographs. English and Russian versions available. Maintained by M.F. Miller and Matvey B. Palchuk. Hosted by Friends and Partners.

The Chairman Smiles

http://www.iisg.nl/exhibitions/chairman/

An online exhibition of posters from the former Soviet Union, Cuba, and China. The Soviet section features thirty-three posters dating between 1919 and 1938. A brief introduction is followed by images of the posters. Each image contains an explanatory note, giving the author, translation of the slogan, and a brief historical background. Maintained and hosted by the International Institute of Social History in Amsterdam, the Netherlands.

Estonia: Land, People, Culture

http://www.erm.ee/vanast/pysi/engpages/

An online version of the permanent exhibition at the Estonian National Museum in Tallinn. The site covers all historical facets of Estonian life, including peasant life, holidays and festivities, and regional peculiarities, through tsarist, interwar, Soviet, and post-Soviet eras. Maintained and hosted by the Estonian National Museum in Tallinn, Estonia.

The Face of Russia

http://www.pbs.org/weta/faceofrussia/

An online companion to the acclaimed PBS series of the same name. This well-developed site includes an interactive time line of Russian history and culture, description of the series, and reference material. Maintained and hosted by the Public Broadcasting Service in Alexandria, Virginia.

The Jewels of the Romanovs

http://www.alexanderpalace.org/jewels/welcome.html

This Web site was designed as an introduction to the exhibition that traveled across the United States in 1996 and 1997. The Web site contains about forty objects that are part of the total exhibit. There are ecclesiastical objects, jewelry, paintings, and costumes from the 300 years of the Romanov Dynasty, which ruled Russia from 1613 until 1917. The site is hosted and maintained by the Alexander Palace Web site and designed by Bob Atchison.

The Kremlin in Moscow

http://www.moscow-taxi.com/sightseeing/kremlin/

This site offers a brief but solid history of the Kremlin. It also contains links to numerous Web pages with photos and descriptions of the Kremlin's most famous features: its walls and towers, State Armory, the Cathedrals of the Assumption, of St. Michael the Archangel, and of the Annunciation, Ivan the Great Bell Tower, Church of the Deposition of the Robe, Great Kremlin Palace, State Kremlin Palace, Patriarch's Palace, Faceted Palace, Terem Palace, the Arsenal, Presidium, Senate Building, Tsar Bell, and Tsar Cannon. The site, which is easy to navigate, is hosted by Moscow Hotels and Optima Worldwide Corporation.

Medieval and Early Modern Russia and Ukraine

http://faculty.washington.edu/dwaugh/rus/ruspg1.html

This Web page provides links to resources for the teaching and learning of the early history of the areas encompassed primarily by today's Ukraine and the European parts of Russia and some adjoining regions of Eastern Europe. The particular focus is on the culture of the Orthodox East Slavs; the period covered extends to approximately 1700. The emphasis is on material available in English.

Nicholas and Alexandra

http://www.nicholasandalexandra.com/

This online exhibition proceeds chronologically, from the youth and courtship of Nicholas II and Alexandra to their exile and execution in Yekaterinburg in 1918. The site also contains Russian maps of the period, a Nicholas and Alexandra time line, list of the Romanov rulers, and related links. Maintained and hosted by Broughton International, an organizer and promoter of exhibitions based in St. Petersburg, Florida.

Pictures of Russian History

http://metalab.unc.edu/sergei/Exs/His/His.html

A selection of illustrations completed by S. Ivanov from 1908 to 1913 for *Pictures of Russian History,* published in Moscow. The original work was in a series of albums, and it gives an important insight into how the history of Russia was perceived in the Russian Empire at the beginning of the twentieth century.

Revelations From the Russian Archives

http://lcweb.loc.gov/exhibits/archives/

The documents presented in this exhibition come from the archives of the Communist Party of the Soviet Union and cover a wide range of chronological periods and themes, such as Lenin's attitudes, Stalin's purges, Chernobyl, and the changes in relations between the Soviet Union and the United States. Each page describes the historical background of a given theme, then presents scanned images of illustrative documents relating to that theme and period, together with translations. Maintained and hosted by the Library of Congress.

The Romanovs: Their Empire, Their Books

http://www.nypl.org/research/chss/slv/exhibit/roman.html

This exhibit presents a selection of items from a collection of over 3,000 Romanov volumes acquired by the New York Public Library during the 1920s and 1930s, organized thematically according to six broad areas: Empire, War, Exploration, Work and Leisure, Culture, and Faith. Each area contains a short summary and one or two sample illustrations. Maintained by R. Davis and hosted by the New York Public Library.

Russian Art From the Hulmer Collection

http://hulmer.allegheny.edu/

An online exhibition of Russian religious art bequeathed to Allegheny College by Eric C. Hulmer. Maintained by Amelia Carr and hosted by Allegheny College in Pennsylvania.

The Russian Church and Native Alaskan Cultures

http://lcweb.loc.gov/exhibits/russian/s1a.html

This online exhibit deals with the relationship between the Russian Orthodox Church and the native peoples and cultures of Alaska and the Aleutian Islands between 1741 and 1915. It includes scanned images of the lithographs, documents, and photographs that illustrate the various facets of the relationship between the Russian Orthodox missionaries and the native Alaskans and Aleutians. Maintained and hosted by the Library of Congress.

Russian Empire, 1895–1910

http://cmp1.ucr.edu/exhibitions/russia/russia.html

A selection of photographs from Moscow, St. Petersburg, and Kiev dating from 1895 to 1910, part of the Keystone-Mast collection of some 900 stereoscopic images of Russia, housed at the California Museum of Photography. Maintained and hosted by the California Museum of Photography at the University of California at Riverside.

Russian Icons

http://www.auburn.edu/academic/liberal_arts/foreign/russian/icons/

A large collection of digitized images of Russian icons dating from the twelfth to the late seventeenth century. Maintained by George Mitrevski as part of his resources page and hosted by Auburn University in Alabama.

Soviet War Photography

http://www.schicklerart.com/exh/sovietwar/

A collection of thirty-three Soviet World War II photographs by the country's most noted master photographers of the time. Covers a wide range of topics, from the partisans gathering to thwart the Nazi advance into Belorussia to the subsequent war crimes trials at Nuremberg in 1946. Maintained and hosted by Howard Schlicker Fine Arts of New York.

Treasures of the Czars

http://www2.sptimes.com/Treasures/

An exhibition of the tsars' treasures that was mounted in 1995 at the Florida International Museum in St. Petersburg, Florida. The site contains the exhibits as well as historical information about the Ruriks and the Romanovs, including an interactive time line of the tsars, and a detailed tour of the exhibition itself. Maintained and hosted by *St. Petersburg Times* of St. Petersburg, Florida, as a part of its Web site.

Virtual Tour of Budapest

http://www.fsz.bme.hu/hungary/budapest/bptour/bptour.htm

Part of a larger Web site on the history of Budapest, this virtual tour leads the viewer through the Castle District, the Royal Palace, the inner city, the Parliament building, Gellert Hill, Margaret Island, along the banks of the Danube, and down famous avenues and boulevards. Created by Marót Miklós, Rohonyi Katalin, and György Pataki and hosted by the Department of Control Engineering and Information Technology at the Technical University of Budapest.

Virtual Tour of Prague

http://www.virtourist.com/europe/prague/

This tour is part history and part modern-day exploration of the beautiful Central/Eastern European city of Prague. The photographs are stunning and the brief texts that accompany them highlight important historic features of the city and key events in Prague's history. Enric Corberó maintains the site, which is hosted by Virtourist.

Virtual Tour of St. Petersburg

http://saint-petersburg.com/virtual-tour/index.asp

This site offers a wonderful virtual tour of St. Petersburg. Links are provided to Web pages on the Peter and Paul Fortress, the Cabin of Peter the Great, the Summer Palace of Peter the Great, Peterhof, St. Petersburg State University, Menshikov Palace, the Hermitage, St. Isaacs Cathedral, Nevsky Prospect, Mikahilovsky Castle, and the cruiser *Aurora,* among other sights. The site is easy to navigate and is hosted by Moscow Hotels and Optima Worldwide Corporation.

Yevgeni Khaldei

http://www.schicklerart.com/exhibitions/khaldei/exhibit/exhibit.html

A selection of the photographs by Yevgeni Khaldei, one of the most preeminent Soviet news photographers of the World War II era. The photographs include such famous images as the raising of the Soviet flag over the Reichstag, the seated portrait of Churchill, Truman, and Stalin at the Potsdam Conference, and the images of the Nuremberg Trials. Maintained and hosted by Howard Schlicker Fine Arts of New York.

Online Archives

The Armenian Genocide

http://www.armeniapedia.org/index.php?title=Armenian_Genocide

This site aims to provide documentary material concerning the massacres of Armenians in the Ottoman Empire in 1915–1916. Section I provides a summary of Armenian history prior to the genocide, section II is a summary of events leading up to the genocide, section III briefly describes the genocide, and section IV discusses life after the genocide. The site also contains the map of Armenia's border with Turkey as drawn by President Woodrow Wilson.

Armenian National Institute

http://www.armenian-genocide.org/

The Armenian National Institute is an organization based in Washington, DC. Its Web site has an extensive research area, which contains photographs, a selection of documents from American and British archives, statements from various official sources on the Armenian genocide, and reprints of press coverage of the massacres in the United States between 1915 and 1920.

Cold War Document Library

http://wwics.si.edu/index.cfm?topic_id=1409&fuseaction=library.Collection

An online collection of documents connected with the Cold War and the participation of various powers (e.g., Soviet Union, United States, and China) in it. Maintained and hosted by the Woodrow Wilson International Center for Scholars as part of its Cold War International Project site.

The Development of the R.S.F.S.R.

http://www.marxists.org/history/ussr/index.htm

A significant repository of the material relating to the establishment and the early days of the Soviet Union, in the form of the RSFSR (Russian Soviet Federative Socialist Republic). Contains Soviet documents on foreign policy and American-Soviet relations, the constitution of the RSFSR, and photographs of leading Bolsheviks and leaders of the White movement. Maintained by Brian Basgen and hosted by the Marxists Internet Archive.

From Marx to Mao

http://www.marx2mao.com/

An online archive of English translations of works by leading socialist thinkers, from Marx and Engels to Mao Zedong. The material related to Russian history is featured in the online collection of works, arranged chronologically, by Lenin and Stalin. The works are mostly sources from the English editions published by the Foreign Languages Publishing House in Moscow in 1950s and 1960s. The site is maintained by David J. Romagnolo.

Marxist Writers

http://www.marxists.org/archive/

This site provides English translations of selected works of important Marxist theorists and activists, both Russian and non-Russian. The Russian Marxists include Lenin, Stalin, Nikolai Bukharin, Leon Trotsky, Anatoly Lunacharsky,

Maxim Gorky, David Riazanov, and Alexandra Kollentai, among others. The archives of Lenin and Stalin also contain digitized photographs. The site is maintained by the Marxists Internet Archive and hosted at Marxists.org.

Modern Customs and Ancient Laws in Russia

http://www.yale.edu/lawweb/avalon/econ/kovalm.htm

A series of six lectures on the ancient laws of Russian society and their influence on nineteenth-century Russian customs, delivered in 1891 by Maxime Kovalevsky, a prominent Russian thinker in the field. Maintained and hosted by the Avalon Project at Yale Law School.

Modern History Sourcebook: Catherine the Great

http://www.fordham.edu/halsall/mod/18catherine.html

A selection of materials in English translation related to Catherine the Great. Includes the characterization of Catherine by Baron de Breteuil, the French diplomat in Moscow; Catherine's proposals for the Russian law code; and an excerpt of her decree on the serfs. Maintained by Paul Halsall and hosted by Fordham University of New York.

Moscow Trials 1936, Court Proceedings

http://art-bin.com/art/omoscowtoc.html

An online version of the official transcript of the 1936 trial of Zinoviev and others accused of belonging to the so-called Trotskyite-Zinovievite United Terrorist Center. This was one of the first large show trials in the Stalinist Soviet Union and it led to the execution of Zinoviev, Kamenev, and other members of the Left Opposition. Maintained and hosted by the *Art Bin* online magazine in Sweden.

Patriotic History

http://www.lants.tellur.ru/history/index.htm

This Russian-language site has a wealth of information on Russian history. The highlights of the archive, however, are the online versions of the classic works of Russian history, including *Lectures* by V.O. Kliuchevskii and *The History of Russia from the Earliest Times* by S.M. Soloviev. Maintained by Oleg Lantsov and hosted by Tellur Network Technologies of Moscow.

The Peace Treaty of Brest-Litovsk

http://www.lib.byu.edu/~rdh/wwi/1918/brestlitovsk.html

A complete text of the peace treaty of Brest-Litovsk, which took Russia out of World War I, set the stage for invasion by various powers, and was a starting point for the Russian Civil War. Maintained by Jane Plotke as part of the World War I Document Archive and hosted by the Brigham Young University Library.

Russian History Home Page

http://www.dur.ac.uk/~dm10www/Russhist.html

An important and useful online archive providing Russian historical texts in English. A wide chronological and thematic range of documents is provided, from the medieval Russian chronicles describing the founding of the city of Kiev to documents on the trial of Soviet dissidents in the 1960s. Maintained by John Slatter and hosted by the University of Durham in the United Kingdom.

Russian History on the Internet

http://www.bol.ucla.edu/~jseaman/

This metasite contains links on Russian history and culture in the period from 1801 to 1991. The site needs updating but the links are useful. The main strengths of the site are links to the Alexander Palace Russian History Web sites, Chronology of Russian History, and archival resources and a (slightly dated) bibliography of materials related to Russian history. The site is maintained by James Seaman at UCLA and focuses on his areas of interest.

Russian Philosophy on the Intelnet

http://www.emory.edu/INTELNET/rus_philosophy_home.html

An archive of material connected with Russian philosophers and the history of Russian philosophy of the nineteenth and twentieth centuries. Features an overview of the history of Russian philosophy, the major ideas of four Russian thinkers (Vladimir Solovyov, Nikolai Fedorov, Vasily Rozanov, and Nikolai Berdyaev), a portrait gallery, related links, and a number of other works. Maintained by Mikhail N. Epstein, associate professor in the Department of Russian, Eurasian, and East Asian Languages and Cultures at Emory University.

The Song of Igor's Campaign

http://lib.ru/NABOKOW/slovo.txt

A translation of the *Song of Igor's Campaign (Slovo o polku Igoreve)*. This Russian epic poem is an important primary source of early medieval Russian history. The poem is translated by Vladimir Nabakov, and the site contains a link to the original text.

VENONA Home Page

http://www.nsa.gov/venona/index.cfm

VENONA was the code name used for the U.S. Signals Intelligence effort to collect and decrypt the text of Soviet KGB and GRU messages from the 1940s. These messages provided extraordinary insight into Soviet attempts to infiltrate the highest levels of the U.S. government. The site features the images of the VENONA documents, the chronology of the project, and the document release monographs. Maintained and hosted by the National Security Agency at Fort Meade, Maryland.

Accounts and Opinions

Armenia-Azerbaijan Conflict

http://www.geocities.com/fanthom_2000/mfa-bulletin.html

The Information Bulletin of the Ministry of Foreign Affairs of the Azerbaijan Republic from 1996 presents an Azeri perspective, "Concise Historical Information on Azerbaijan and the Roots of the Armenian-Azeri Conflict." The first section presents a brief history of Azerbaijan and its claims to Karabakh, and the second section discusses the background, causes, and essential elements of the conflict with Armenia from the official Azeri perspective. The site is maintained by Tabib Huseynov, an Azeri student in the United States, and hosted on the GeoCities Web site.

Armenian History

http://www.armenianhistory.info/index.htm

This site provides an extensive history of Armenia and Artsakh-Karabakh province, covering forty centuries of history with a glossary of famous Armenians, historical terms, and historical sites by Yuri Babayan. The site is a good place to encounter a detailed Armenian narrative on the history of Armenia, as well as its neighbors and conquerors, that validates Armenian culture, myths, and history as well as claims to Nagorno-Karabakh.

Azerbaijan's History

http://www.azeris.com/history/index.htm

An easily navigated Web site, it contains links to ancient Azerbaijan, medieval Azerbaijan, Azerbaijan with the Russian Empire, Azerbaijan Democratic Republic (1918–1920), Azerbaijan with the Soviet Union (1921–1991), and the

Republic of Azerbaijan to the present. There are hyperlinks to modern and historical maps of Azerbaijan as well as historical books about Azerbaijan and links to Web sites with further information on Azeri history. The site is maintained by the Global Azerbaijani Network.

The Cossack Page

http://en.wikipedia.org/wiki/Cossack#History_of_Cossacks

Containing a brief history of the Cossack movement in Russia and Ukraine from its medieval beginnings to its post-Soviet revival, this site also explains Cossack organization, image, and terms, and it includes links to other sites concerned with Cossack history. The site is hosted by Wikipedia.

Did Lenin Lead to Stalin?

http://www.geocities.com/CapitolHill/2419/lensta.html

An analysis of Lenin and his connection to Stalin from an anarchist perspective. Argues that Lenin actively pursued policies that eventually became the hallmarks of Stalinism, namely socialism in one country, one-party rule, and totalitarianism. Maintained by Andrew Flood and hosted by the Capitol Hill server of the GeoCities.

"The Establishment of the Kiev Rus'"

http://xyz.org.ua/russian/win/discussion/hold_rus.rus.html

An online article in Russian (a Ukrainian version is available as well) by Sergei Datsyuk tracing the establishment, the rise, and the eventual demise of the Kievan Rus' and the lessons that can be learned from this medieval state by the modern Ukrainian state in its economic, social, and cultural policies. Maintained and hosted by the *XYZ Online Magazine* of the Ukraine.

Estonian Cultural History: A Short Overview

http://www.einst.ee/publications/cult_history/

Providing a concise historical overview of the history of Estonia from prehistoric times to the present, this Web site portrays the country's history from a distinctly nationalist point of view. The period after 1980 and the drive for independence is represented in the greatest detail and as leading to the country's best period, after the breakup of the Soviet Union in 1991. World War II Estonia is presented as the victim of double aggression from the Soviet Union and Nazi Germany. There are hyperlinks to other material in the Estonia County Guide site. The site is maintained and hosted by the Estonian Institute, a foundation associated with the Estonian Ministry of Culture.

Estonian History

http://www.estonica.org/eng/teema.html?kateg=43

Estonian history is presented in a series of hyperlinks in this Web site hosted by *Estonica,* an encyclopedia about Estonia, compiled by the Estonian Institute. The site, which is easy to navigate, begins with the Estonian Middle Ages and continues through Swedish rule, the Baltic Landestaat period, a period of "national awakening" under Russian rule (which is not mentioned in the title), the period of independence from 1918 to 1940, and the "Soviet era and the restoration of independence." The period of independence gets another treatment in a Supplementary Texts section of links. In general, the tone of the article is balanced and evenhanded.

Factory Committees in the Russian Revolution

http://flag.blackened.net/revolt/talks/russia_fac.html

A discussion by Ray Cunningham of the factory committee's role in establishing the eight-hour day and other improvements to workers' conditions following the February Revolution of 1917. Maintained by Workers Solidarity Movement, an Irish anarchist group, and hosted by Flag.Blackened.Net server.

Funet Russian Archive Directory

http://www.funet.fi/pub/culture/russian/history/

This site contains an online version of *A Brief History of Russia and the Soviet Union* (1971) which was used to train American military personnel. It also contains a detailed chronology of Russia with relevant links, and numerous miscellaneous accounts on different periods in Russian history. Maintained and hosted by Timo Hamalainen.

History & Culture of Russia

http://www.interknowledge.com/russia/rushis01.htm

An overview of the history of Russia, in which the authors aim to go beyond the usual "compendium of hazy legends and sensationalist rumors." Throughout the text there are hyperlinks to other Russian material. Maintained by the Russian National Tourist Office and hosted by InterKnowledge Corporation.

History of Belarus (Great Litva)

http://www.belarusguide.com/as/history/history.html

A history of Belarus from the sixth century CE to the present, this site includes a chronology of Belarus, followed by sections dealing with the Grand

Duchy of Litva (a medieval Belarusian state and the Belarusian Renaissance); "Rzecz Pospolita Polsko-Litewska" (Commonwealth of the Kingdom of Poland and the Grand Duchy of Lithuania); the Napoleonic war, Belarusian revival, and Belarusian uprising of 1863–1864; World War I, the end of the Russian Empire, and the founding of the Belarusian Democratic Republic; World War II; the postwar Byelorussian Soviet Socialist Republic (BSSR); and the Republic of Belarus, the independent state proclaimed in 1992. The sections provide excerpts from recent works in Belarusian history, dealing with such sensitive areas as the nature of the Grand Duchy of Lithuania, Cossack wars, Stalinist repression and executions of Belarusians in the 1930s, and Belarusian collaboration with, and resistance to, the Nazis in World War II. This commercial Web site is maintained by Ryhor Hajduk, Kirill Yurchenko, and Alies' Arciukhovich.

History of Kazakstan

http://members.tripod.com/~kz2000/history/

This page, part of a more general Kazakstan Online site, deals with the history of Kazakhstan and especially the origins of the various ethnic groups that have populated the country throughout the ages. More modern historical events connected with Kazakhstan are dealt with in the chronology of Kazakhstan. Maintained by Yerzhan Yerkin-uly and hosted by Tripod Inc.

History of Modern Russia

http://mars.acnet.wnec.edu/~grempel/courses/russia/

This site features, among other things, a complete set of forty-eight course lectures by Gerhard Rempel, professor emeritus at Western New England College. These lectures deal with a wide variety of topics in Russian history, from the democratic tradition in medieval Russia to the 1989 revolutions in Eastern Europe. Maintained by Rempel and hosted by Western New England College in Springfield, Massachusetts.

A History of Russia

http://palimpsest.lss.wisc.edu/~creeca/

Online versions of lectures on the history of Russia from 800 to 1917, delivered in 1987 by Michael Petrovich, professor of Balkan and Russian History at the University of Wisconsin-Madison. The lectures are in RealAudio format, with maps and images displayed. Maintained and hosted by the Center for Russia, East Europe and Central Asia, University of Wisconsin-Madison.

The History of Russian Navy

http://www.neva.ru/EXP096/book/book-cont.html

An online version of the book by the same name, which gives a detailed overview of the history of the Russian navy from the times of Kievan Rus´ to the Bolshevik Revolution. Illustrated, but no references are provided. Maintained and hosted by RUSNet of St. Petersburg, as part of the Russian Pavilion in the 1996 Internet World Exhibition.

"An Inquiry into a Scandinavian Homeland for the Rus´"

http://www.geocities.com/Athens/9529/scanrus.htm

Online version of "An Inquiry into a Scandinavian Homeland for the Rus´," a paper by Hugh R. Winfrey, in which the author examines the Scandinavian origins of the founders of Russia. Well written and extensively footnoted, with a large bibliography. Maintained by Hugh R. Winfrey and hosted by GeoCities.

Kievan Rus´ and Mongol Periods

http://unx1.shsu.edu/~his_ncp/Kievan.html

The information on this Web site is excerpted from *Russia: A Country Study,* ed. Glenn E. Curtis (Washington, DC: Federal Research Division of the Library of Congress, 1996). The study investigates the origins of the Russian state, starting with Kievan Rus´ as the first East Slavic state, and examines the dizzying ethnic diversity of the region of present-day Ukraine. The article ends with the Mongol invasion and the fall of Kievan Rus´, which left a powerful legacy for later Russian states like Muscovy. The site is hosted by Sam Houston State University in Huntsville, Texas.

The Kronstadt Uprising, 1921

http://www.islandnet.com/~citizenx/kronstadt.html

An online account and analysis of the Kronstadt uprising in Soviet Russia's Baltic fleet in 1921, written by Brian R. Train. Examines the events that led to the uprising, its causes and effects, and the connection between the uprising and other events in Soviet history at the time. Bibliography included.

Moldova

http://www.moldova.org

An informational site on all aspects of Moldova. The history section provides brief accounts of Moldova's early and recent history, with a chronology of important events connected with Moldova and its predecessors. The site is sponsored by the Moldova Foundation, a nonprofit organization that operates a nonpolitical, nongovernmental, and noncommercial country portal.

Republic of Azerbaijan

http://www.azembassy.com/azerbaijan/browse.htm

This official Web site of the Azerbaijani embassy to the United States offers a brief, informative outline of Azeri history since prehistory. In keeping with the official viewpoint of the site, the responsibility for the conflict over Nagorno-Karabakh is placed squarely on Armenian aggression.

The Russian Post-Emancipation Household

http://www.ub.uib.no/elpub/1995/h/506006/Hovedoppgave.pdf

This master's thesis in history by Herdis Kolle of the University of Bergen in Norway examines Russian peasant households in two villages in the Moscow area following the emancipation of the serfs in 1861. Covers demography, family life, and the occupations pursued by the freed peasants. Maintained by the Department of History at the University of Bergen.

Eastern Europe

Reference Sites

APAP Recommendations

http://www.informatics.sunysb.edu/apap/recomm/index.html

Bibliographies on all aspects of Polish history and society. History-related topics include general Polish history, Polish military history, and the Holocaust and Polish-Jewish relations. Maintained by John Radzilowski on behalf of the Association of Polish-American Professionals and hosted by the Department of Informatics at the State University of New York at Stony Brook.

Historical Text Archive—Europe

http://historicaltextarchive.com/sections.php?op=listarticles&secid=12

This section contains extensive links to Web sites about European history. While not exclusively focused on Eastern Europe, there are links to information about Russia, Yugoslavia, Hungary, and other countries. Each link notes the number of visitors.

Hungarian History Page

http://www2.4dcomm.com/millenia/dates.htm

A collection of materials, in English and Hungarian, relating to the history of Hungary and Hungarian people from 5000 BCE to modern days. Text, digitized maps, and links to other Hungarian history sites are included. The site is still under construction. Maintained as part of the Hungarian Heritage Homepage site and hosted by Global Internet Services, 4D Communications Inc.

Hungary: Battles for Freedom 1848–49

http://hungary.ciw.edu/1848–49/index.html

This reference source provides a day-by-day account of the Revolution of 1848 in Hungary and the role of various figures in it, including military and political leader Louis Kossuth. Materials include text, illustrations, and an 1890 recording of Louis Kossuth. Includes a photo gallery of Kossuth and the memorials in the United States and Hungary connected with him.

Hungary in 1848–1849

http://h-net2.msu.edu/~habsweb/sourcetexts/hungsources.html

This strong selection of documents, from 1848 to 1852, focuses on the impact of the revolutions on Hungary, including communications between King Ferdinand and the Hungarian Diet, and the Hungarian Declaration of Independence, April 14, 1849.

The Imperial House of Hapsburg

http://www.hapsburg.com/

This site on the Hapsburg monarchy is hosted by Juraj Liöiak, of McGill University, Montreal, Canada. While difficult to navigate, it contains worthwhile information on the origins of the dynasty, its symbols, the Holy Roman Empire, and the achievements of the Hapsburgs. However, it does not develop the history of the dynasty as comprehensively as it might.

New Sources on the 1968 Soviet Invasion of Czechoslovakia

http://www.gwu.edu/~nsarchiv/CWIHP/BULLETINS/b2a4.htm

http://www.gwu.edu/~nsarchiv/CWIHP/BULLETINS/b3a3.htm

A historiographical essay by Mark Kramer on the new sources of information about the 1968 Soviet invasion of Czechoslovakia that became available since the late 1980s and the collapse of the Eastern bloc and the Soviet Union.

Maintained by the Cold War International History Project and hosted by the School of Engineering and Applied Science at George Washington University.

Polish Kings

http://projects.edte.utwente.nl/masters/spizewsk/pl_kings/pl_kings.htm

A well-designed reference site dealing with the Polish monarchy from 960 CE to 1795 and the partition of Poland between Russia and Prussia. Features sections on Polish royal dynasties, a time line of Polish monarchy, and an alphabetical listing of all Polish kings, among other things. The site is intended as a teaching resource for setting up lessons about rulers in Poland. Maintained by Justyna Lanzing-Spizewska and hosted by the University of Twente in Enschede, the Netherlands.

Romania

http://risc.ici.ro/docs/romania.html

A comprehensive reference site dealing with various periods of Romanian history, from the late Middle Ages to modern days. One of the aims of this site is to debunk the commonly held myths about Romanian history. Much of the site is divided into geographical areas roughly corresponding to what the compilers of the site see as traditional Romanian regions, most of which have historical material. The site is still under construction. Maintained and hosted by the Research Institute for Informatics in Bucharest.

Online Archives

Hungarian Electronic Library (MEK)

http://www.mek.iif.hu/

The Hungarian Electronic Library (MEK), established in 1993, currently consists of some 2,500 documents. The History collection is a significant one, with areas covered including the general history of Hungary, local and regional history, history of neighboring countries, and related subjects. Texts are mainly in Hungarian, but a significant number of English texts are available as well. Maintained by Moldován István and Drótos László and hosted by the National Information Infrastructure Development Program of the government of Hungary. Best viewed with a Central European character set.

Hungarian History

http://www.net.hu/corvinus/

A collection of digitized texts on Hungarian history from Corvinus Library in Hungary. American and Hungarian (translated) historical texts are presented, as are important memoirs of the witnesses to various periods in Hungarian history. The texts can be read online or be downloaded as Microsoft Word files. Links to other Hungarian sites. Maintained and hosted by Hungary.Network.

The Wolf Lewkowicz Collection

http://web.mit.edu/maz/wolf/

Between 1922 and 1939, Wolf Lewkowicz of Poland engaged in a lengthy, intimate correspondence in Yiddish with his nephew Sol J. Zissman. This correspondence consists of 179 letters, which document various aspects of life in the Jewish community in Poland, culminating with the Holocaust, which took the lives of Wolf Lewkowicz and most of his family. Translated from Yiddish. Family photographs and recordings of excerpts of some of the letters are included here. Maintained by Marc Zissman and hosted by WWW Server, Massachusetts Institute of Technology.

Accounts and Opinions

A.I.P.C.—Polish History

http://www.ampolinstitute.org

Currently under reconstruction, this Polish history site features a brief history of Poland, including portraits of all Polish kings, and the chronology of Polish history from 966 CE to the present. Maintained and hosted by the American Institute of Polish Culture in Miami, Florida.

Backward Through the Looking Glass:
The Yugoslav Labyrinth in Perspective

http://www.demog.berkeley.edu/~gene/looking.glass.html

This is an extensive, detailed academic essay by E.A. Hammell (University of California, Berkeley) about the deep-seated roots of the ethnic conflicts in the Yugoslav area, from the Roman Empire to the modern conflict.

Brief History of Hungary

http://www.users.zetnet.co.uk/spalffy/h_hist.htm

By the author's own admission, this is a "broad outline" of the history of Hungary. Arranged in reverse chronological order, going back to the tenth century, it includes links to downloadable texts and books and to online archives on Hungarian history. Maintained by Stephen Pálffy and hosted by Zetnet Internet Service in the United Kingdom.

Bulgaria.com—History of Bulgaria

http://www.bulgaria.com/history/index.html

This section of the Bulgaria.com site is divided into two parts. The first provides a chronological account of the country's history, from prehistoric antiquity to 1944, and the second provides biographies of Bulgarian rulers, from pre-Christian khan Kubrat to post-Communist president Zhelyu Zhelev. Both sections are well translated and illustrated. Maintained and hosted by Bulgaria.com in Santa Clara, California.

Bulgarian History and Politics

http://www.b-info.com/places/Bulgaria/ref/05HIST.shtml

The Bulgarian History and Politics site contains a bibliography for Bulgarian history from medieval times to the present. Each source listed in the bibliography is described fully, and there are accompanying pictures.

The Czech Republic—History

http://www.travel.cz/travel/history.asp

A detailed chronology of Czechoslovakia, its predecessor and successor states, as well as the peoples living in the territory of the country, from prehistory to current days. Well written and illustrated. Maintained by Gabriela Beranova and hosted by Tom's Travel in Prague.

Documents on Bosnia

http://www.mtholyoke.edu/acad/intrel/bosnia.htm

A substantive list of documents, texts, and contemporary material on Bosnia, hosted by Vincent Ferraro, professor of International Politics at Mount Holyoke University.

The Hungarian Revolution of 1956 & How It Affected the World

http://www.cserkeszek.org/scouts/webpages/zoltan/1956.html

Zoltán Csipke examines the causes of the Hungarian Revolution of 1956 in relation to the independence struggle of the Hungarian people, the events of the revolution, and its effects throughout Hungarian society and the world in general. Privately maintained by Csipke and hosted by Cserkeszek Online, the official site of the Hungarian scout troops 8 and 49 in the Los Angeles area.

Hungary: Essential Facts, Figures & Pictures

http://www.mti.hu/hungary/default.htm

An online version of the book by the same name published by the Hungarian News Agency. A historical overview, from the Magyar settlement to the present day, is featured, with some of the sections still under construction.

Intermarium

http://www.columbia.edu/cu/sipa/REGIONAL/ECE/intermar.html

This online journal provides an electronic medium for noteworthy scholarship and provocative thinking about the history and politics of Central and Eastern Europe following World War II. Jointly maintained by Andrzej Paczkowski, Institute for Political Studies, Polish Academy of Sciences, and John S. Micgiel, Institute on East Central Europe, Columbia University. Hosted by School of International and Public Affairs at Columbia University.

Jews in Poland

http://www.cyberroad.com/poland/jews.html

This site outlines the history of Poland's Jewish community from 965 to the outbreak of World War II in 1939 and discusses the condition of Jews in Poland during the war and today. Maintained by LNT Poland and hosted by Cyberville Webworks.

"The Magyars of Conquest-Period Hungary"

http://www.net.hu/Magyar/hungq/n0141/p3.html

In this article for the *Hungarian Quarterly,* Gyula László, a retired professor of Eötvös University, examines Byzantine and Arabic sources on the arrival of Magyars to present-day Hungary, in support for his argument that the Magyars arrived in two separate waves, centuries apart. Maintained and hosted by Hungary.Network Ltd.

Romania—History

http://home.sol.no/~romemb/history.htm

A detailed outline of Romanian history, from Roman times to modern days. Illustrated with images of historical landmarks, artifacts, portraits, and photographs of Romanian rulers and statesmen. Maintained by the Romanian Embassy in Oslo, Norway, and hosted by Scandinavia Online.

Twenty-Five Lectures on Modern Balkan History

http://www.lib.msu.edu/sowards/balkan/

This series of online lectures deals with the turbulent history of the modern Balkans from 1500 to current days. While most of the lectures deal with the Balkans proper, a number examine the Eastern European states of Hungary and Romania. Compiled and maintained by Steven W. Sowards and hosted by Michigan State University Libraries.

The Warsaw Uprising

http://www.princeton.edu/~poland/uprising/

An account of the Warsaw Uprising of 1944 by the Polish Resistance. An overview of the situation before the uprising, followed by accounts of the events of August and September 1944 and the aftermath. Maps and photographs of the uprising and the key people involved are also provided. The page is still under construction. Maintained by Marcin Porwit and hosted by the Department of Computer Science at Princeton University.

French History

Mary E. Chalmers

Metasites

French History Web Links

http://www.georgetown.edu/faculty/schneidz/web.html

Professor Zoë Schneider at Georgetown University links French historians to what they would find valuable: bookstores; museums, images, and multimedia; maps; professional resources; e-texts; archives and libraries; an e-mail directory of French historians; and gateways to sites for French medieval and modern history.

La France à travers les ages: Links

http://www.as.wvu.edu/mlastinger/

West Virginia University French professor Michael Lastinger's home page links to France Through the Ages cover an eclectic range of topics (and often multiple links within each topic) from Caesar and Asterix to Jean Jaurès and surrealism. This site also has links on the nineteenth century, Émile Zola, French literature, and French cinema.

WESS French Studies Web: History

http://www.library.yale.edu/wess/frenhist.htm

WESS French Studies Web (http://www.library.uiuc.edu/ala/alawess/index.html), a site useful to French historians in its own right, has a site specifically devoted to the history of France, Belgium, Switzerland, Luxembourg, and Monaco. It provides links to primary, secondary, and tertiary sources, libraries, archives, and collections.

Libraries, Archives, Primary Sources

Bibliothèque nationale de France (BNF)

http://www.bnf.fr/

The home page for France's national library, this site includes general information about the library and current events, virtual exhibitions, and online catalogs. It is now possible to reserve documents and a seat in the library and to request photocopies online.

Gallica—BNF Online Texts

http://Gallica.bnf.fr/

The BNF has undertaken to create free online access to important works in its collections. The selection of 70,000 texts and 80,000 images focuses on francophone culture. It samples images and dictionaries, encyclopedias, periodicals, and other texts from the Middle Ages to the nineteenth century. It also includes thematic dossiers on texts by Zola and Proust, travels in France, Italy, and Africa, great French writers, and savant societies, among others.

History of France: Primary Documents

http://library.byu.edu/~rdh/eurodocs/france.html

Part of Eurodocs, this subset on France provides transcriptions, facsimiles, and translations of primary sources, both textual and image, from antiquity to the present. It also has legal and government documents, including all French constitutions since 1789 and the Napoleonic Code; regional, local, and family history; and historical collections.

Internet History Sourcebooks

http://www.fordham.edu/halsall/

This expansive collection of primary sources from ancient to modern history is classroom usable (often excerpts of long texts) and copyright free or copy-permitted. French sources are findable through scanning the chronological, thematic categories and reviewing the information and links within.

The National Archives

http://www.archivesnationales.culture.gouv.fr/

This site has the online catalogs for the National Archives, which consists of five centers: the Centre Historique of National Archives and the Centre for Contemporary Archives for pre- and post-1958 sources respectively, the Centre for Archives of Overseas Territories, the Centre for Archives of the Workplace, and the National Centre for Microfilms.

The Project for American and French Research on the Treasury of the French Language (ARTFL)

http://humanities.uchicago.edu/orgs/ARTFL/

ARTFL has created multiple searchable databases of French texts, many of which are only accessible from subscribing institutions. FRANTEXT, the main database, has nearly 2,000 French texts (Renaissance to twentieth century) copied mostly from scholarly print editions (novels, correspondence, verse, journalism, drama, treatises, theater) in literary criticism, history, biology, economics, and philosophy. Other databases include French Women Writers (more than 100 texts), Diderot's *Encyclopédie,* and various dictionaries (seventeenth century to the present).

Repositories of Primary Sources

http://www.uidaho.edu/special-collections/eur01.html

The Special Collections and Archives of the University of Idaho Library maintains this site of primary sources for European countries (A-M, Andorra-Malta, is the range of countries the site covers). The French section contains links to national, institutional, departmental, municipal, and diocesan archives.

General Historical and Cultural Sources

Bibliography for French History: 1500–Present

http://www.library.yale.edu/rsc/history/frenhist.htm

Susanne Roberts, librarian for European history at Yale University, maintains this extensive bibliography of French history sources of all types (bibliographies, dissertations, library catalogs, periodicals, government publications, and statistical and book review sources) and primary sources sorted by format (print, microformat, e-text, manuscript, and archival).

Le Ministère de la culture et de la communication

http://www.culture.gouv.fr/

The French Ministry of Culture and Communication, which oversees the National Archives, maintains this vast resource of cultural events, virtual exhibits, and searchable databases for images and documents in many cultural fields.

The Louvre

http://www.louvre.fr/

The official Web page of the Louvre museum provides a visual and textual history of the palace and the museum and access with descriptions to selected works from its collection. The site also has information on visiting the museum, on past (since June 1998), present, and upcoming exhibits at the museum, and on its educational efforts.

The Musée d'Orsay

http://www.musee-orsay.fr/

The official Web page for the Musée d'Orsay gives a history of the building and the museum, describes the history of the collection and of the various media techniques, identifies new acquisitions and pieces in the collection on loan, and provides a small sampling of art from the collection. It has visitor information and an extensive listing of upcoming events.

Paris Maps

http://www.columbia.edu/cu/arthistory/courses/parismaps/

This collection of one hundred slides by Columbia University art history professor Barry Bergdoll shows sectional maps of Paris from 1716 to 1887.

Old Regime History and Before

The Age of Charles V (1338–1380)

http://www.bnf.fr/enluminures/aaccueil.htm

This site contains 1,000 illuminations presented in a French National Library exhibit titled The Age of Charles V (1338–1380). The illuminated texts are taken from seven manuscripts (fourteenth and fifteenth centuries), including Froissart's *Chronicles*. The illuminations are organized by manuscript, by historical subject, and by theme (history, religion, science and technology, sports and entertainment, and miscellaneous).

Château de Versailles

http://www.chateauversailles.fr/

This official site of the Château de Versailles, available in several languages, provides practical information about visiting the château as well as historical information. The French-language site also includes educational materials and additional links to exhibits, related sites, and research information. High-quality snapshots (both visual and textual) provide a beautiful, informative window into the château and its history, the gardens, and some of its masterpieces. Through other snapshots, viewers learn about the Sun King's daily routine, the life of a courtier, entertainment, seats of power, and meals.

Great Archeological Sites

http://www.culture.gouv.fr/culture/arcnat/en/

This Web site provides access to sites exploring the Tautavel Man (450,000 years ago), the Lascaux (30,000 years) and Chauvet (15,000 years) caves and their prehistoric paintings, a fortress and a capital city from Gaul (2,000+ years), a medieval church and a town of peasant knights (1,000+ years), and underwater and aerial archaeology.

Images of Medieval Art and Architecture

http://www.pitt.edu/~medart/index.html

This site concentrates on images of medieval churches throughout France and England by University of Pittsburgh art professor Allison Stones. It also has a glossary of medieval art and architecture. In collaboration with the University of Pittsburgh's Digital Research Library, Stones is creating a searchable image database of medieval monuments. The first church completed for this database, Vézelay in Burgundy (ninety-one images), is linked to this site.

International Society for Eighteenth-Century Studies

http://www.c18.org/

This site is a collaborative effort by libraries, specialists, learned societies, and others to create virtual access to library catalogs, bibliographies, e-texts, research tools, and scholarly Internet sites. Currently the site has information about conferences and exhibits, annotated bibliographies of significant figures from the long eighteenth century, several e-text projects (such as the Linnaean Correspondence and Rousseau's *Julie*), professional resources and journals, calls for papers, and the home pages of people working on the eighteenth century. The site also includes Rutgers University professor Jack Lynch's links to scholarly electronic sources for the eighteenth century.

Labyrinth: Old French

http://labyrinth.georgetown.edu/display.cfm?Action=
View&Category=French,%20Old

Labyrinth, an important electronic resource for medieval studies, is sponsored by Georgetown University. The "French, Old" subcategory provides access to multiple manuscript resources on Chrétien de Troyes, Marie de France, twelfth- to thirteenth-century Provençal poetry (from ARTFL), medieval drama, and other e-texts.

La Nouvelle France Resources

http://www.culture.gouv.fr/culture/nllefce/fr/

This site provides access to information about la Nouvelle France, including a brief illustrated history and a Jesuit missionary's annual account of the Sault Mission (1667–1685). For research purposes, it includes useful listings of regions, cities, and organizations (libraries, archives, chambers of commerce, and museums), with contact information and summaries of their relevant holdings.

French Revolution to the Present

Encyclopedia of 1848 Revolutions

http://cscwww.cats.ohiou.edu/~chastain/index.htm

Begun in 1986, this encyclopedia, with contributors worldwide, continues to be updated. Its articles cover the Revolutions and responses to them in Western and Eastern Europe and in the larger world, including West Africa and Australia.

Foundation Napoléon

http://www.napoleon.org

http://www.napoleonica.org

The Foundation Napoléon, founded in 1987, encourages the telling of Napoleonic history (both first and second empire) by operating a library and two Web sites (above), publishing Napoleonic studies, offering research grants and prizes, and supporting other Napoleonic organizations. The first Web site, for general use, includes explanatory information and appropriate visuals for the imperial family, places, books, paintings, symbols and key dates (politics, battles, economy and society, and arts and science), and the Republican calendar. It also has e-texts, bibliographies, a directory of Napoleonic films, and a searchable database of images. The second site provides online access to Napoleonic documents, mostly from the Library of the Conseil d'Etat.

Liberty, Equality, Fraternity: Exploring the French Revolution

http://chnm.gmu.edu/revolution/index.html

Sponsored by the American Social History Project (City University of New York) and the Center for History and New Media (George Mason University), this site is a model for interactive, scholarly sites exploring historical topics. French Revolution historians Lynn Hunt and Jack Censor were principal authors of this Web site and the corresponding book and CD-ROM (Penn State University Press). The site combines twelve topical essays, thirteen maps, a time line, and a glossary with over 600 source documents (250 images, 350 texts, and 13 songs).

Napoleonic Literature

http://www.napoleonic-literature.com/

This site is dedicated to reproducing out-of-copyright material related to the Napoleonic era. It includes histories and memoirs, fiction and drama, poetry, and bibliographies. It also provides a historical and literary chronology with links to literary works if available.

The Siege and Commune of Paris, 1870–1871

http://www.library.northwestern.edu/spec/siege/index.html

The Special Collections Library at Northwestern University has digitized over 1,200 photographs and images, including several dozen caricatures, from its Siege and Commune collection. The collection also includes (not online) 1,500 caricatures, 68 newspapers, 1,000 posters, and lots of books and pamphlets.

Vichy Web Page

http://artsweb.bham.ac.uk/vichy/govts.htm

This page from University of Birmingham (UK) professor Simon Kitson provides access to some primary documents from Vichy and extensive links on Vichy and the Resistance, as well as on general and thematic information about France in World War II.

German History

Alexander Zukas

Metasites

DINO—Wissenschaft—Geschichte

http://webkatalog.dino-online.de/?path=100-539-2481-3610-2506

Of the various German-language search engines, DINO (Deutsches InterNet-Organisationssystem) offers the most convenient and extensive listing of history-oriented sites. The DINO history section is divided into subcategories by time period and special interest.

German History

http://www.phil.uni-erlangen.de/~p1ges/heidelberg/gh/gh.html

This section of the WWW Virtual Library is a directory of resources arranged by epoch and historical subfield. Although the sections are uneven, it is a useful starting point for exploration.

Habsburg Home Page

http://www2.h-net.msu.edu/~habsweb/

H-German Home Page

http://www2.h-net.msu.edu/~german/

Both of these sites, which are sponsored by the H-Net group of electronic discussion lists, provide a variety of resources, including archives of discussion threads, book reviews, news about professional conferences and meetings, teaching materials, and selected links to other sites of historical interest. H-German focuses on the scholarly study of German history of all time periods. Habsburg is devoted to "the community within H-Net dealing with the culture and history of the Habsburg Monarchy and its successor states in central Europe from 1500 to the present" (Habsburg welcome). Material provided by these sites may be in English or German.

Virtual Library Germany

http://www.phil.uni-erlangen.de/~p1ges/vl-dtld-e.html

The Virtual Library Geschichte is the historical section of the Virtual Library Deutschland hosted at the University of Erlangen in Germany and constitutes a branch of the Virtual Library History hosted at the European University Institute in Florence, Italy. The Virtual Library Geschichte presents academically valuable German-language Web sites on historical topics in a systematic fashion, summarizes their contents, and assesses their quality. Each of the referees is an expert in his or her field. The hyperlinked material is grouped by epoch (prehistory, ancient, medieval, early modern, nineteenth century, and twentieth century) and by region, theme, and area of interest. This site houses a collection of historical metaindexes at German universities, with a link to resources on German history. The site is available in both English and German. (The German version is at http://www.phil.uni-erlangen.de/~p1ges/vl-dtld.html.)

WWW Virtual Library–Germany

http://www.neha.nl/w3vl/countries.html

This metasite provides an alphabetical and geographical (by continent and country) breakdown of the Economic and Business links within the WWW Virtual Library. The Germany entry provides links to scholarly conferences, associations and societies, research institutions, archives and libraries, museums, Internet metasites, data archives, and individual Web sites on economic, business, and labor history. The Economic and Business History section of the WWW Virtual Library is maintained and hosted in Amsterdam by the Netherlands Economic History Archive.

General History Sites

Archives in Austria/Archive in Österreich

http://my.bawue.de/~hanacek/info/aarchive.htm

Andreas Hanacek compiled this directory of the street addresses, phone numbers, e-mail addresses, and Web sites of Austrian state and provincial archives.

They are arranged by region (Land) with the national archives and the Vienna archives listed separately. The main pages are in German. Most of the text is addresses and literature citations. Key German terms are listed and translated on an English-language Web page. All cited locations, administration districts, and countries are given in German spelling. The list is hosted by Baden-Württemberg E-Net.

Archives in the Federal Republic of Germany/ Archive in der Bundesrepublik Deutschland

http://my.bawue.de/~hanacek/info/darchive.htm

Andreas Hanacek maintains this Web site with a list of the street addresses, phone numbers, and Web sites (where available) of archives in the Federal Republic of Germany. The links are grouped by archive area: governmental (domestic), religious, business, military, and special. Within each area is a further breakdown by region or province (North Rhine-Westphalia, Bavaria, etc.) or church type (Catholic, Protestant, etc.). The main pages are in German. Most of the text is addresses and literature citations. Key German terms are listed and translated on an English-language Web page. All cited phone numbers are given in the "within Germany" form. Dialing from abroad requires the caller to add the national area code for Germany. All cited locations, administration districts, and countries are given in German spelling. The list is hosted by Baden-Württemberg E-Net.

Austrian Historical Bibliography/ Österreichische Historische Bibliographie

http://www.uni-klu.ac.at/groups/his/OHB-Datenbank/ohb-datenbank.htm

This searchable database corresponds to annual printed volumes, beginning in 1945, that report professional publications in Austrian history. Books, periodical articles, conference proceedings, dissertations, and essay collections are included. Produced at the Institut für Geschichte an der Universität Klagenfurt. For scholars only.

Dachau Concentration Camp Memorial Site/ KZ-Gedenkstaette Dachau

http://www.kz-gedenkstaette-dachau.de/ (German version)

http://www.kz-gedenkstaette-dachau.de/englisch/content/index.htm (English version)

This site, run by the Dachau Concentration Camp Memorial Museum, is in German and English. It contains short, vivid articles on the history of the concentration camp, maps, prisoners, slave labor, suffering and death in the camp, the last months of the camp, and liberation. The site contains a virtual tour of Dachau as well as links to other concentration camp memorial sites (e.g., Buchenwald, Auschwitz, Mauthausen). The site's home page features a quote from Eugen Kogon, a former inmate at Buchenwald and author, "Dachau—the significance of this name will never be erased from German history. It stands for all concentration camps which the Nazis established in their territory."

Data Bank on the Revolution in Baden 1848/49/ Das Informationssystem zur Revolution von 1848/49

http://www.ruf.uni-freiburg.de/histsem/badrev/

This site contains a wealth of primary information on the Revolution of 1848 to 1849, especially in Baden. Collective biographies and documents draw on the resources of the "Erinnerungsstätte für die Freiheitsbewegungen in der deutschen Geschichte" (Memorial Foundation for Movements of Liberty in German History) at the Rastatt division of the Federal German Archives. Users can search for information by communities and towns, individuals, and themes. There is also a lexicon of terms. The site is in German and maintained by a project team at the University of Freiburg.

Deutschland: Könige, Kaiser, Staatschefs

http://userpage.chemie.fu-berlin.de/diverse/bib/de-kks.html

This reference site provides birth and death dates and periods of rule for German leaders from Charlemagne to Gerhard Schroeder. Compiled by Burkhard Kirste of the Freie Universitat, Berlin.

Die Körpermassaker im deutschen Bauernkrieg von 1525

http://www.sfn.uni-muenchen.de/forschung/koerper/fwarb_de.html

Florian Welle writes an interesting history of the Peasant War by focusing on the body, the bodies of peasants and the bodies of the nobility and knights, and how these distinct bodies made a difference to the outcome of the struggle. She treats psychological issues as well as issues of bodily nutrition, training, and protection. The topic of the body is a new and growing research area in history and this Web site makes a valuable contribution to that discourse.

Encyclopedia of 1848 Revolutions

http://www.cats.ohiou.edu/~Chastain/index.htm

This comprehensive Web site includes the works of authors from around the world who have contributed articles to the only complete history of all the

1848 revolutions. Organized by James Chastain of Ohio University, this encyclopedia covers every aspect, personality, and region of the world in which a popular revolt occurred in 1848. Germany and France are particularly well represented. The authors of the articles are well-known historians of the era.

The Example of Dachau/Zum Beispiel Dachau

http://members.aol.com/zbdachau/index.htm (German version)

http://members.aol.com/zbdachau/indexe.htm (English version)

The infamous concentration camp at Dachau, outside Munich, is represented by the official memorial site listed above and by this one created by the Study Group for the Investigation of the Contemporary History of Dachau. It is in German and English. Some citizens of Dachau (former camp inmates) founded the group, and later the Web site, to protest the selective memory of their fellow citizens of Dachau and demonstrate that the past was neither forgotten nor dead in Dachau. They researched the history of the city to uncover the cause and the structures that once made possible a totalitarian regime in Germany. They seek insight into the daily life of the citizens of Dachau in those times and the suffering of the inmates of the concentration camp under the SS. This is a valuable site for lessons in civic-inspired history.

The First World War

http://www.dhm.de/lemo/html/wk1/index.html

This is another outstanding German Historical Museum site. Like the site on the Second Empire, this site contains a wealth of information on Germany, this time during World War I. It investigates the conduct of the war, internal politics, industrial output and control, economic life, research, war propaganda, art, and daily life. It also hosts recordings of speeches by Kaiser Wilhelm II. The site is in German.

Fredericus Rex: Prussia's King Frederick the Great

http://members.tripod.com/~Nevermore/king.html

Ursula Grosser Dixon, a novice historian, has compiled a wonderful and very readable site on Frederick the Great and his contribution to German history. She discusses his military campaigns, his daily life, his social and political reforms, his "enlightened despotism," and his relations with Voltaire. This site is a good place to start understanding the life and times of this important Hohenzollern monarch.

Friedrich der Grosse

http://www.bieli.de/fried_1.htm

This is an extensive article in German about the military campaigns fought by Frederick the Great in the eighteenth century. The author, Stefan Bielenberg, maintains the Web site and presents pictures, battle reports, troops dispositions, and tactics of Frederick's great battles that helped forge Prussia into the leading state in Germany in the early modern period. The site is in German.

German Archives on the Internet/Deutsche Archive in Internet

http://www.uni-marburg.de/archivschule/deuarch.html

This German-language site is a directory of links to individual archival repositories on the Web arranged by archival category: governmental, municipal, church, literary, economic, parliamentary, political parties and organizations, university, institutional, and media archives. There are also links to European and overseas archives as well as business and labor association archives. The site is maintained by Karsten Uhde and sponsored by the Institut für Archivwissenschaft, Archivschule Marburg (the Institute for Archival Science at the Archive School of the University of Marburg).

German, Austrian, Swiss Cultural History

http://courseweb.stthomas.edu/paschons/culthist.html

This site has several useful components: a bibliographical dictionary of several hundred prominent persons from German-speaking Europe (in German); a chronology of important events in German and world history; and a calendar of significant events in the German-speaking countries, arranged by month and date (in English). Created by Paul A. Schons of the University of St. Thomas.

German Historical Museum, Berlin/Deutsches Historisches Museum, Berlin

http://www.dhm.de/

An overview of the museum founded amid some controversy in 1987 and devoted to the history of the German nation. The site provides general information about the aims and organization of the museum as well as its collections and exhibitions. In addition, descriptions and images of selected items from the permanent collections and selections from previous exhibitions are available. In German and English.

The German Peasants' Revolt: Der Bauernkrieg von 1525

http://www.geocities.com/Vienna/Strasse/9298/zuefallig/bauernkrieg.htm

The Peasant War was a major event in sixteenth-century Germany. This Web site provides a general overview of the conflict, its origins, place in the agrarian crisis of the age, conduct, revolutionary nature, dispersion across southern Germany, and outcome.

Haus der Geschichte der Bundesrepublik Deutschlands

http://www.hdg.de/

The Haus der Geschichte der BRD presents the history of the two postwar German states—the Federal Republic of Germany and the German Democratic Republic—with particular emphasis on the development of political institutions. In German and English.

History of Austria, Austro-Hungarian Empire: Primary Documents

http://library.byu.edu/~rdh/eurodocs/austria.html

History of Germany: Primary Documents

http://library.byu.edu/~rdh/eurodocs/germany.html

The EuroDocs site at Brigham Young University is the most comprehensive resource for primary documents in German and Austrian history. Documents may be in a variety of formats and in German or English. The time period covered spans from the end of the classical period to the present. Highlights include the works of Marx and Engels and the World War I Document Archive. Compiled by Richard Hacken.

Living Virtual Museum Online, German Historical Museum, Berlin/Ledendiges virtuelles Museum Online (LeMO), Deutsches Historisches Museum, Berlin

http://www.dhm.de/lemo/home.html

LeMO is a Web-based tour through German history in the twentieth century sponsored by the German Historical Museum and the Historical House of the Federal Republic of Germany. The Historical Museum prepared the first half of the online exhibit (up to 1945) while the Historical House prepared the material for the post-1945 era. Fraunhofer-Institut für Software- und Systemtechnik created all three-dimensional virtual reality "experiential worlds" by means of VRML. These three-dimensional worlds allow easy navigation through the site chronologically and are tied to the visual, textual, and film and sound media. The main divisions of the HTML-based part of the Web site are Imperial Germany, the First World War Weimar Germany, the Third Reich, the Second World War, Postwar Germany, Divided Germany, Germany United, and Germany Today. The site, in German, is packed with visual and textual material that will reward students of twentieth-century German history.

Martin Luther Historical Site

http://www.luther.de/

This site is a good source of information about the life and times of Germany's most famous religious reformer. It includes a detailed biography, discussion of the historical background, and legends associated with Martin Luther's life. In German and English.

The Marx/Engels Archive

http://www.marxists.org/archive/marx/

This is an extraordinary collection of the major works, as well as lesser-known publications, of two famous Germans, Karl Marx and Friedrich Engels, hosted at the University of Colorado. Of particular interest to historians of Germany beyond the well-known classics of Marxist literature also hosted at this site are *The German Ideology,* articles by Marx in *Rheinische Zeitung, Critique of Hegel's Philosophy of Right, Deutsche-Französische Jahrbücher, The Peasants' War in Germany, Revolution and Counter-Revolution in Germany, The Prussian Military Question and the German Workers's Party, Critique of the Gotha Program, Reformists in Germany's Social-Democratic Party,* and *The Peasant Question in France and Germany.*

The National Socialist Regime/Das NS-Regime

http://www.dhm.de/lemo/html/nazi/

The German Historical Museum has created an immense academic site where students of German Nazism can explore in detail issues raised by the Hitler regime. The site explores the establishment of the Nazi regime, its domestic and foreign policies, and its economy, as well as art and daily life under the Nazis. It also discusses the Olympic Games in Berlin in 1936, anti-Semitism, and German resistance to Hitler. The number of links and informative sites is astonishing. There is a chronology of events for each year from 1933 to 1939. This richly illustrated, German-language site contains some video clips and a "collective memory" section of memoirs and interviews with people who lived through the Nazi experience.

Philipp Melanchthon

http://www.melanchthon.de/

An online exhibition commemorating the 500th anniversary of the birth of the reformer and humanist. The site details Melanchthon's life and involvement in the Protestant Reformation. In German and English. The Kommunale Datenverarbeitungsgesellschaft Wittenberg created this site and the site on Martin Luther.

The Protestant Reformation

http://history.hanover.edu/early/prot.html

The Internet Archive of Texts and Documents, which organized this site on the Reformation, is a creation of faculty and students in the History Department of Hanover College. The principal goal of the archive is to make primary texts and secondary sources on the Internet available to students and faculty for use in history and humanities classes. This site hosts primary texts from the Lutheran Reformations, Reformed Reformations, Radical Reformations, the English Reformation, and the Scottish Reformation. Secondary sources and links to scholarly sites on the Reformation are included on the site.

Prussia/Preussen

http://www.preussenweb.de/preussstart.htm

Developed by Reinhard Nelke, Prussian Web houses a wealth of information on the state of Prussia, which existed as a kingdom from 1701 to 1918 and as a state within Germany from 1918 to 1947, when it was abolished by the Allies after World War II. The historical overview describes the growth of Prussia after 1701 to become the most powerful state in northern Germany and the one that unified a "small" Germany, which excluded Austria, in 1871. Besides the extensive historical overview, the site contains maps of Prussia's growth, a list of its provinces and rulers since 1134, an extensive treatment of its army's history, links to biographies of important Prussians, links to other sites on Prussian history, and a bibliography. This German-language site is a strategic place to start the study of Prussian history on the Web.

The Radical Reformation, Thomas Münzer

http://www.bopsecrets.org/rexroth/communalism3.htm

Thomas Münzer has been closely associated with the 1525 Peasant Revolt in Germany. A Protestant dissenter, he broke with Martin Luther and became an important religious radical of the Reformation. This site, hosted by the Bureau of Public Secrets in Berkeley, California, places Münzer's thoughts and actions within the context of sixteenth-century German society and the Reformation itself. The site, featuring material by Kenneth Rexroth, a famous poet and social critic, explores the turbulent ideologies and politics of the period, the Peasant Revolt, and its aftermath.

Reformation

http://www.mun.ca/rels/reform/index.html

This site, maintained by Hans Rollmann of the Memorial University of Newfoundland, provides links to texts, translations, and images of major Reformation figures—Martin Luther, Philipp Melanchthon, John Calvin, Ulrich Zwingli, and Heinrich Bullinger—as well as links to Anabaptist, Mennonite, and Counter-Reformation sites. The site is hosted by the Department of Religious Studies at the Memorial University of Newfoundland (Canada).

Second German Empire (Das Kaiserreich)

http://www.dhm.de/lemo/html/kaiserreich/index.html

The German Historical Museum has created a monumental and scholarly site where students of the German Empire from 1871 to 1918 can explore issues surrounding foreign policy, domestic policy, industry economics, science, education, art, culture, daily life, and anti-Semitism. The site has a chronology of events for each year from 1900 to 1914. The site is richly illustrated, has some videos, and is in German.

The Thirty-Years War

http://mars.acnet.wnec.edu/~grempel/courses/wc2/lectures/30yearswar.html

The Thirty Years' War (1618–1648) was a general European war fought mainly in Germany. The war devastated Germany: it took almost 200 years for the German territories to recover from its effects. Gerhard Rempel of Western New England College maintains this Web page on the Thirty Years' War. He provides an excellent overview of the war, its causes, its course, and its impact on Europe and Germany in particular.

The Thirty Years War, 1618–1648

http://www-geschichte.fb15.uni-dortmund.de/fnz/thirty.html

Stephanie Marra of the University of Dortmund maintains this Virtual Library page on the Thirty Years' War. The links to primary and secondary resources and essays are extensive. The page provides links to a museum presentation of the war, biographies, chronologies, the Peace of Westphalia, and a well-developed presentation of the history of the war by Christopher Atkinson.

Virtual Library Geschichte "Drittes Reich"

http://www.geschichte.fb15.uni-dortmund.de/links/NS_-
_Zeit_und_Zweiter_Weltkrieg/

This page devoted to the Third Reich, compiled by Ralf Blank of the Ruhr-Universität, Bochum, is one of the standouts of the German History section of the WWW Virtual Library (above). It offers information about various aspects of the Nazi regime, including "Politik," "Wirtschaft," and "Widerstand."

Virtual Library: History: German History, 19th Century

http://www.phil.uni-erlangen.de/~p1ges/heidelberg/gh/e6.html

The Virtual Library carries dozens of links to important Web sites on nineteenth-century German history, including the Napoleonic Wars, the Congress of Vienna, "Vormärz," the Revolutions of 1848–1849, the Wars of Unification and the Second Reich, and Bismarck. This is the place to start investigating nineteenth-century Germany on the Web.

WebMuseen: Museen und Ausstellungen im deutschsprachigen Raum

http://webmuseen.de/

This site provides information and links for museums of all types in Germany, Austria, and Switzerland. The "Themen" option allows a search for historical museums.

The Weimar Republic/Virtual Library Geschichte: Die Weimarer Republik

http://www.dhm.de/lemo/html/weimar/index.html

This German Historical Museum site maintains the high scholarly standards and accessibility of the other German Historical Museum sites discussed previously. It begins with an explanation of the Revolution of 1918 and continues to investigate the formation of the Weimar Republic, domestic policy, foreign policy, industrial developments and economic troubles, intellectual life, art and culture, daily life, anti-Semitism, and the forerunners of Nazism. The site has a chronology of events for each year of the republic, from 1918 to 1933, and is in German.

Willkommen bei der Bundesregierung Deutschlands

http://www.bundesregierung.de/

Auswäertiges Amt

http://www.auswaertiges-amt.de/

Der Bundespraesident

http://www.bundespraesident.de/

Deutscher Bundestag

http://www.bundestag.de/index.htm

These official sites of the German federal government are good starting points for recent history and political events. Of particular historical interest is the site of the Auswäertiges Amt (Foreign Ministry), with information about its organization, history, and publications.

The Witch Hunts

http://www.kings.edu/womens_history/witch/index.html

This is an interactive Web site developed by Brian Pavlac that is housed at King's College in Wilkes-Barre, Pennsylvania. It includes a simulation of a witch hunt in Germany in 1628. Germany was the center of witch hunts in the early modern period and this site tries to dispel myths about who were accused of witchcraft and why. The material is organized into the following areas: Ten Theories about the Causes of the Witch Hunts, Ten Common Errors and Myths about the Witch Hunts, a time line, an annotated bibliography on witch hunts, and the witch hunt simulation. The site makes a valuable teaching aid but its set of academic resources makes it useful to scholars as well.

World War II/Der Zweite Weltkrieg

http://www.dhm.de/lemo/html/wk2/index.html

This German Historical Museum site provides comprehensive treatment of German involvement in World War II. The site covers the following areas in great detail: the course of the war, domestic and foreign policy, industry and economy, daily life, the Holocaust, resistance, and art and culture. The quality of the material and information provided is impressive. There is a chronology of events for each year from 1939 to 1945. This German-language site is richly illustrated, with video clips and a "collective memory" section of memoirs and interviews with people who lived through the war. The site is highly recommended for anyone seeking to understand German involvement in World War II and how academics and other Germans see the war today.

Irish History

Patrick Callan

The 1798 Rebellion

http://www.bbc.co.uk/history/state/nations/irish_reb_01.shtml

Professor Thomas Bartlett presents a valuable overview of the 1798 rebellion, including its origins and its legacy.

The 1916 Rising

http://www.bbc.co.uk/history/war/easterrising/

This site is a tremendous introduction to the influential 1916 rising. The site indicates the events leading up to 1916, the insurrection itself, and its aftermath, through essays, profiles, photographs, an extensive sound archive, music, images, and newspapers from the period.

The Act of Union

http://www.actofunion.ac.uk/

The Act of Union Virtual Library brings together pamphlets, newspapers, parliamentary papers, and contemporary manuscript material relating to the 1800 Act of Union between Ireland and Britain.

A to Z of Ancient Ireland

http://home.iprimus.com.au/selliot/ireland/a_to_z_of_ancient_ireland.htm

This extensive glossary of terms associated with Celtic Ireland runs the gamut from *airbre druad* (or "druid's hedge") to "yew sticks" used by magicians. It is based on a text, *Ancient Ireland: The User's Guide,* by Conan Kennedy.

Battle of the Boyne, William of Orange

http://www.bbc.co.uk/northernireland/learning/william/

This BBC site is very diverse, touching on a wide range of topics—the childhood of William of Orange, his marriage, his wars, his reign, and his special relationship with Ireland.

Bawnboy Workhouse

http://users.ox.ac.uk/~peter/workhouse/Bawnboy/Bawnboy.shtml

Photographs of the remains of a typical workhouse give a flavor of the scale of these publicly funded buildings that gained so much notoriety during the famine period.

George Berkeley, Philosopher

http://www.maths.tcd.ie/pub/HistMath/People/Berkeley/

Biographical guide to Ireland's most eminent philosopher, lectures and essays on his philosophy, and selections from his works.

CAIN Web Service

http://cain.ulst.ac.uk/

CAIN (Conflict Archive on the Internet) is the most comprehensive and scholarly site dealing with the modern conflict in Northern Ireland. It covers themes such as education, employment, discrimination, housing, law and order, and women and the conflict.

CELT: Corpus of Electronic Texts

http://www.ucc.ie/celt/

This site (Corpus of Electronic Texts) contains a wide range of primary material, including material on Irish language texts. The site contains primary materials on the history of the early twentieth century, including six books by James Connolly, founder of the Irish Socialist Republican Party and *The Path to Freedom* by Michael Collins.

Celtic Ireland

http://www.unc.edu/courses/art111/celtic/

A collection of pictures, maps, time lines, a glossary, and quizzes. The site includes links to high Crosses, the Gallarus Oratory on the Dingle Peninsula, St. Kevin's Kitchen, and the grounds of Glendalough.

Chronicon: An Electronic Journal

http://www.ucc.ie/chronicon/

This electronic journal provides scholarly articles on Irish history, high-quality postgraduate reports, and a historians' forum.

Michael Collins

http://www2.cruzio.com/~sbarrett/mcollins.htm

Suzanne Barrett's brief, well-written biography includes a bibliography relating to Collins.

The "Confessio" of Saint Patrick

http://www.robotwisdom.com/jaj/patrick.html

Kidnapped at sixteen years of age and sold into slavery in Ireland, St. Patrick went on to convert the Irish to Christianity. His "Confessio," originally written in Latin, offers a clear and enthralling view of life in the British Isles.

Michael Davitt: Mayo's Most Famous Son

http://www.mayo-Ireland.ie/Mayo/News/ConnTel/CTHistry/MlDavitt.htm

Davitt, founder of the National Land League, died in Dublin in 1906 at the age of sixty. By the time of his death, "land for the people" had largely become a reality, prison reform had begun, and he himself had become an international champion of liberty.

Famine Records

http://www.nationalarchives.ie/topics/famine/famine.html

This article is an attempt to bring to the attention of those interested in famine research—whether at the local or national level—collections in the National Archives that span the famine period. There is a searchable index of the relief commission papers from 1845 to 1847.

The Famine: *The Times* and Donegal

http://www.vindicator.ca/history/famine/timesDonegal.asp

Thomas Campbell Foster's very detailed reports from County Donegal, published originally in *The Times* (London), in 1845, provide excellent material on the local famine. This site also includes materials on the Ballyshannon workhouse.

The Fenians in the USA

http://www.aladin.wrlc.org/gsdl/collect/fenian/fenian.shtml

Click in search box for titles, subjects, and people to gain access to a rich and varied set of documents relating to the history of the Fenian Movement in the United States and the 1798 Rebellion. Superb material on John O'Mahony,

James Stephens, John Mitchel, O'Donovan Rossa, and other Fenian leaders. The quality of reproduction is exceptionally high.

The Great Irish Famine Curriculum

http://www.nde.state.ne.us/SS/irish_famine.html

Developed in New York, this curriculum places the events of the famine in the context of human rights education. It contains a detailed account of the famine, with teacher notes and many ancillary activities to boost understanding of the famine.

The Great War, 1914 to 1918: 16th (Irish) Division

http://freespace.virgin.net/sh.k/xvidiv.html

This site on the 16th (Irish) Division, seen as the nationalist counterpart to the 36th (Ulster) Division in the Great War, features a history, material about its famous chaplain, Father William Doyle, reproductions of photographs, illustrations, and other information from the division's scrapbook.

The Great War, 1914 to 1918: 36th (Ulster) Division

http://www.irishsoldier.org/ulster_division.html

This site offers a brief outline of the military experiences of the 36th (Ulster) Division, which become an important symbolic element of Ulster unionism after the war.

The Great War, 1914 to 1918: General Context

http://www.tcd.ie/General/Fusiliers/

Dealing with Ireland's history during the Great War, this site covers the home rule bill, the National Volunteers, living conditions in Dublin, the history of the Dublin Fusiliers regiment, its main battles, and some of its soldiers (such as poet Francis Ledwidge).

The Great War, 1914 to 1918: Kildare Region

http://kildare.ie/hospitality/historyandheritage/athyheritage/ww1.htm

Showing the Great War's impact on Ireland, this site provides extensive text of articles from the *Kildare Observer* for 1914 and 1915, with a comprehensive list of casualties from the Kildare area. This innovative site shows the importance of the Internet for bringing primary material to public attention.

The Great War, 1914 to 1918: Memories

http://www.irishsoldier.org/

The site of the Somme Heritage Center commemorates the involvement of the 36th (Ulster) and 16th (Irish) Divisions in the Battle of the Somme and the 10th in Gallipoli, Salonika, and Palestine. Included is a brief history of the 36th Division, as well as featured interviews with veterans of World War I.

The Great War, 1914 to 1918: Royal Dublin Fusiliers

http://www.greatwar.ie/

This very comprehensive site, hosted by the Royal Dublin Fusilier Association, includes information on Irish battalions in the British army, as well as Ireland's experience in World War I.

Ireland: History in Maps

http://www.rootsweb.com/~irlkik/ihm

A series of twenty-four maps of Ireland, ranging from the earliest habitation through the Celts, the Normans, and the Plantations, up to the 1840s. Each map is complemented by an explanatory text and links.

Ireland in the 1950s

http://migration.ucc.ie/oralarchive/testing/breaking/index.html

This magnificent site presents extensive information about individuals living in or leaving Ireland during the harsh days of the 1950s. Fifty profiles of individuals are presented in a summary interview, a broadcast of each interview, and facsimiles of family documents and photographs. This is primary source history at its most vibrant.

Ireland's Ancient Stone Monuments

http://www.stonepages.com/

This multinational site has a magnificent section on Ireland's court and passage tombs, stone circles, dolmens, standing stones, cairns, and hill forts. Navigation is very easy. The site includes a helpful glossary and an active map that locates monuments and brings the user to the individual pages.

Ireland's National Police Force

http://www.esatclear.ie/~garda/

The Garda Síochána Historical Society has excellent material on the history of Irish policing from 1770 to 1922 and many modern controversies.

The Irish Constitution

http://www.maths.tcd.ie/pub/Constitution/index.html

A copy of the 1937 constitution, which provides the touchstone for many contemporary debates in Ireland today.

The Irish Diaspora

http://memory.loc.gov/learn/educators/workshop/european/
wimmlink.html#ellis

The American Library of Congress has gathered together fifteen sites on the Irish famine and Irish emigration, providing a comprehensive list of the available materials in this complex and important area.

Irish Diaspora Studies

http://www.brad.ac.uk/acad/diaspora/

Irish diaspora studies is the name given to the worldwide, scholarly, interdisciplinary study of Irish emigration and its social, linguistic, economic, cultural, and political causes and consequences. The site is modest in content, but very valuable in terms of insight and scholarship, focusing on reviews, discussion papers, and notes and queries.

Irish Famine, 1845–50

http://vassun.vassar.edu/~sttaylor/FAMINE/

This site features superb graphic material showing scenes from the famine, mainly drawn from the *Illustrated London News,* the *Cork Examiner,* and the English magazine *Punch.* The site also hosts over a hundred illustrations relating to the famine experience. The graphics show laborers, their cabins, beggars, landlords, evictions, funerals, and emigration to America.

Irish Famine, 1845–50

http://www.bbc.co.uk/history/state/nations/famine_01.shtml

This excellent BBC site is an excellent synopsis of the famine, with some modern perspectives considered, such as "An Artificial Famine?"

Irish History: Curriculum History

http://www.scoilnet.ie

This site is targeted at second level schools in Ireland; the "resource finder" search feature yields much curriculum material, suitable for use in schools, on a multitude of historical topics.

Irish History: Discussion Site

http://www2.h-net.msu.edu/~albion/

H-Albion is a discussion network for British and Irish history. Entering "Ireland" into the search box produces a superb range of opinions and articles. The range of topics and the expertise of the list contributors make this an essential site for those interested in researching Irish history.

Irish History: General Sites

http://bubl.ac.uk/link/i/irishhistory.htm

This is a quality site, recommending sound links with plenty of history content and variety. Interestingly, sites are cataloged by subject, as well as by Dewey classification. An exceptional introductory site.

Irish History Magazine

http://www.historyireland.com/

This magazine, covering all aspects of Irish history, is not totally online, but there are many examples of interviews with historians and many extraordinary articles, including "The Age of Ulysses" and "Father Flanagan's Visit to Ireland 1946."

Irish Parliamentary Statutes, 1922 to 2004

http://www.bailii.org/ie/legis/num_act/

This is a comprehensive list of the legislation passed by the Irish Dáil.

The Irish Times

http://www.ireland.com

The Irish Times hosts this site, which frequently features special supplements on items of historical interest, with items relevant to Northern Ireland's recent history under the heading "Path to Peace."

Labor History

http://flag.blackened.net/revolt/ireland_history.html

This index of articles from the alternative perspective of labor history covers topics from the 1798 rebellion and the Irish famine to the Catholic Church, the 1916 rising, and the history of the Irish Republican Army.

National Archives of Ireland

http://www.nationalarchives.ie/

This Web site provides general information about the National Archives. The potential of the site has been limited by the very small scale of documentation available online. The site includes seventeen facsimiles related to the 1798 rebellion, with introductory and explanatory information. It briefly covers topics such as foreign affairs, agriculture, and law, with a selection of research guides on subjects including the Irish famine, and information about the transportation of Irish emigrants to Australia between 1791 and 1868.

National Library of Ireland, Case Studies

http://www.scoilnet.ie/hist/article_topic.aspx?id=801&nav=false

This site, hosted by Scoilnet, the Irish educational portal, features six detailed case studies, including the Lordship of Tír Eoghain, Elizabethan Dublin, and Meiler Magrath's Clerical Career. Three others relate to more modern history, including the Elections of 1885 and 1886, the Gaelic Athletic Association from 1884 to 1891, and the 1919 Dublin strike and lockout.

Newgrange Monuments

http://www.knowth.com

This site features excellent images and descriptions of the tombs in the Newgrange area.

Nineteenth-Century Ireland

http://www.qub.ac.uk/english/socs/ssnci.html

This site by the Society for the Study of Nineteenth-Century Ireland lists information about its activities and members, but also hosts a links segment on nineteenth-century history that is very rewarding.

Northern Ireland, 1885 to 2004

http://www.ark.ac.uk/

A joint resource between the two Northern Ireland universities, the Northern Ireland Social and Political Archive sets out to make social science and political information on Northern Ireland available. The specialist section and the publication areas have many valuable resources.

Northern Ireland, 1970–2000

http://www.bbc.co.uk/northernireland/learning/history/stateapart/

A State Apart is an interactive chronicle covering the thirty years of conflict in Northern Ireland, prepared by BBC Northern Ireland.

Northern Ireland, 1990s

http://www.rascal.ac.uk/

RASCAL is a new electronic gateway to research resources in Northern Ireland. It makes social and political information on Northern Ireland available to the widest possible audience.

Northern Ireland Election Results

http://www.ark.ac.uk/elections/

Nicholas Whyte, a PhD from Queen's University of Belfast, posted this well-moderated text on the history of Westminster parliamentary elections and constituencies, providing links to local political parties.

Northern Ireland, Twentieth-Century Voices

http://www.bbc.co.uk/northernireland/history/taleofthecentury/index.shtml

BBC Northern Ireland presents a series of radio broadcasts on Northern Ireland's history from 1900 to 1999.

Nuzhound News Archive

http://www.nuzhound.com

This site allows surfers to access a special index of Irish history articles published in Irish newspapers during the previous few years, giving an indication of many controversies and anniversaries in Irish historiography.

The Orange Order

http://www.grandorange.org.uk/

Hosted by the Orange Order, the site contains a series of historical articles on subjects as diverse as the Glorious Revolution of 1688 and 1689, the Battle of the Boyne, and the opposition to home rule from 1886 to 1921.

Parliamentary Papers Relating to Ireland, 1801 to 1922

http://www.eppi.ac.uk/

The Enhanced British Parliamentary Papers on Ireland, 1801–1922 Project digitizes British Parliamentary Papers relating to Ireland, from 1801 to 1922, one of the principal resources for the study of modern Irish history. This searchable database has major social inquiries and census information, reports on economic, educational, and scientific subjects, cultural and linguistic institutions, and political and military developments.

Primary Sources

http://library.byu.edu/~rdh/eurodocs/ireland.html

Part of the Eurodocs site, this site contains Irish documents ranging from the Bull of Pope Adrian IV in 1155 to the 1999 report of the Independent Commission on Policing for Northern Ireland (the Patten Report), as well as extensive links to other sites.

Princess Grace Irish Library, Monaco

http://www.pgil-eirdata.org/

This continues to be the most comprehensive and accessible site on Irish studies. Intended as a "scholars' notebook," it has the capacity to become a site of first resort for people looking for meaningful information on Irish history, although the ambit of the site is much wider. The PGIL Author Dataset contains comprehensive biographical and bibliographical information on 4,500 Irish writers, with extracts from their works and commentaries upon them. A first-class site.

Ulster Covenant, 1912

http://www.proni.gov.uk/ulstercovenant/index.html

The Public Record Office of Northern Ireland has compiled a superb introduction to this famous demonstration of unionist solidarity, when unionists signed a pledge to oppose home rule.

Ulster Plantation

http://www.bbc.co.uk/history/war/plantation/

The Plantation of Ulster began in the seventeenth century when English and Scottish Protestants settled on land confiscated from the Gaelic Irish. Through essays, audio, photographs, and interactive maps, users can discover how the plantation transformed Gaelic Ulster.

Unionist View of Northern Ireland

http://www.cruithni.org.uk/index.html#overview

This brief overview of Ulster history reflects a unionist perspective and is a useful reciprocal to the many sites reflecting nationalist or republican sentiment on the Internet.

A View of the Present State of Ireland

http://darkwing.uoregon.edu/~rbear/veue1.html

Author of the well-known poetry classic *The Faerie Queen,* Edmund Spenser penned an acerbic memoir, *A View of the Present State of Ireland,* in 1596, reflecting the gulf between the English overlords and the native Irish.

The Wild Geese Today: Erin's Far Flung Exiles

http://www.thewildgeese.com

This comprehensive guide to over 450 Irish Web sites has a general bibliography. The eclecticism of its authors makes it a curio with many nuggets, including substantial information on the role of the Irish in the American Civil War.

Workhouse Living Conditions

http://www.iol.ie/~gartlan/fampt1.htm

This Web site features the conditions in the Carrick-on-Shannon workhouse.

Italian History

Richard Wojtowicz

Metasites

Art History

http://witcombe.sbc.edu/ARTHLinks.html

Maintained by Christopher L.C.E. Witcombe of Sweet Briar College. Italian art history sources appear in the sections Prehistoric Art, Ancient Greece & Rome, Art of the Middle Ages, 15th-Century Renaissance Art, 16th-Century Renaissance Art, 17th-Century Baroque Art, 18th-Century Art, 19th-Century Art, 20th-Century Art, 21st-Century Art, and Museums & Galleries.

Brigham Young University Italian Index

http://frenital.byu.edu/classes/ita1420/

Index of links to all areas of Italian history including Paleolithic, Etruscans, Ancient Rome, Middle Ages, Humanism, Renaissance, Late Renaissance, Baroque, 1700s, Romanticism, Risorgimento, and Contemporary Themes.

Subcategories include Art, Literature, and Music; Biographies; Countries and Economy; Cultural Anthropology; History and Philosophy; Indexes and Bibliographies; Science and Techniques; and Urbanism.

BUBL LINK Catalogue of Internet Resources: Italian History

http://bubl.ac.uk/link/I/italianhistory.htm

List of resources including Archaeological Resource Guide for Europe Geographical Index, Fondazione Gramsci (research and documentation center), Futurism, Italian Life Under Facism, Leaning Tower of Pisa, Medici Archive, Renaissance and Baroque Architecture, and Sistine Chapel in Rome.

DMOZ Open Directory Project: Italy History

http://dmoz.org/Regional/Europe/Italy/Society_and_Culture/History/

Sites on ancient Rome, Etruscans, archaeology, architecture, Catholicism, wars, Amadeo Bordiga, Giuseppe Garibaldi, Nicolo Machiavelli, Giuseppe Mazzini, and Benito Mussolini. Under the "see also" section on this page, for those who read Italian, take a look at the World: Italiano: Società: Storia.

History of Italy—Primary Documents

http://www.lib.byu.edu/~rdh/eurodocs/italy.html

Offers links to selected sites and documents encompassing the formation of Latin Christendom through the Medici period to World Wars I and II and the present.

H-Italy Italian History

http://www2.h-net.msu.edu/~italy/

A member of H-Net Humanities and Social Sciences OnLine. H-Italy offers scholars information on Italian history. The site provides links to announcements for conferences and seminars, calls for papers and grant opportunities, jobs, discussion, literature reviews, resources, arts and architecture, Italian literature, museums and exhibitions, and other assorted links at H-Italy Links. A search facility allows the user to search H-Italy for keywords or all H-Net logs.

Hyperwar European Theater of Operations: The Mediterranean

http://www.ibiblio.org/hyperwar/ETO/Med/index.html

Materials on World War II operations in Italy and the Mediterranean, mostly from U.S. Army sites. Operations include Sicily and the Allied campaigns on the mainland.

Internet Ancient History Sourcebook: Rome

http://www.fordham.edu/halsall/ancient/asbook09.html

This site covers Roman historians, Etruscans, Roman foundations, republican institutions, Carthaginian war, imperial expansion, civil wars and revolution, the Principate, law, military, empire and provinces, literature, art and architecture, education, economics, slavery, daily life, religion, gender and sexuality, and modern perspectives. Each subdivision covers numerous additional sites.

Italian History—University of Colorado, Colorado Springs

http://web.uccs.edu/history/globalhistory/italy.html

Provides links for general sources, ancient Rome, and the Roman Empire.

Italian Renaissance Persona

http://www.georgetown.edu/labyrinth/subjects/italy/italy.html

Provides connections to Web resources on Italian culture, Italy, and Italian language. This page is no longer maintained, but still has some valuable links. The Labyrinth Library Italian Bookcase accesses some sites for Boccacio's *Decameron,* but suffers some dead links for Dante. The suggested link to *The Labyrinth* provides links to Italian and other medieval studies materials.

Medieval Italy

http://www2.kumc.edu/itc/staff/rknight/Italian.htm

Offers a list of outside sites for Italian texts, an online encyclopedia, warfare, manuscript illumination, clothing of the period, and maps. This site is sponsored by a local branch of the Society for Creative Anachronism.

Society for Italian Historical Studies

http://faculty.valenciacc.edu/ckillinger/sihs/

Links to Italian history sites and historical documents.

Western European Studies Section: Italian Studies Web

http://www.library.yale.edu/wess/italian.html

The Italian Studies Web of this section contains contributions from Italian studies bibliographers nationwide. The Web is a joint effort of Yale University Libraries, Brigham Young University Libraries, and the University of Illinois at Urbana-Champaign. It gives links to WWW Gateways for and to Italy, Libraries and Book Trade, a Reference Shelf, Newspapers and Periodicals, Associations, and Subject Resources. This site strives for quality.

The WWW Virtual Library—Italian History Index

http://vlib.iue.it/hist-italy/Index.html

The index has an editorial board to select the "Best of the Italian History Index" and specific page maintainers. Introduces links under the categories Reference, Geographical, Chronological, Topical, and Other subdivisions. The Other subdivision leads to Italian search engines, libraries and publishers, Italian institutions and universities, maps, and historical maps.

Content Sites

Timeline of Italian History

http://pirate.shu.edu/~connelwi/Timeline.htm

Seton Hall students and interested visitors have compiled a detailed time line here. The site also provides a link to an Italian-American History Timeline.

Timeline of the Italic Peninsula

http://www.fiu.edu/~honors/italy/time line.htm

This time line covers 3,000 years of Italian history from pre-Etruscan Italic tribes to the Italian Republic.

Ancient Italy Through the Goths

The Decline and Fall of the Roman Empire by Edward Gibbon

http://www.ccel.org/g/gibbon/decline/home.html

Gives the complete text of this classic.

De Imperatoribus Romanis

http://www.roman-emperors.org/indexx.htm

This "Online Encyclopedia of Roman Emperors" provides extensive information on the emperors and empresses of Rome with hyperlinks to other related names, bibliographies, and maps. Works in Internet Explorer.

The Etruscan World

http://www.museum.upenn.edu/new/worlds_intertwined/etruscan/main.shtml

From the University of Pennsylvania Museum, this site outlines topics from the earliest Etruscans, the orientalizing period, and daily life in Etruria through the Etruscan language, Etruscans and religion, and the final days of the Etruscans.

Lombards

http://www.bartleby.com/65/lo/Lombards.html

Columbia Encyclopaedia article discusses these Germanic people in Italy.

The Origin and Deeds of the Goths by Jordanes

http://www.ucalgary.ca/~vandersp/Courses/texts/jordgeti.html

Translated by Charles C. Mierow for students of ancient history at the University of Calgary. Jordanes was of Gothic Ancestry and wrote in the sixth century CE.

The Ostrogoths

http://www.fordham.edu/halsall/source/theodoric1.html

These letters were written for Theodoric, the most Romanized of Germanic kings, by his secretary Cassiodorus.

Charlemagne

Charlemagne

http://www.newadvent.org/cathen/03610c.htm

Catholic Encyclopaedia entry includes Charlemagne's involvement with Italy.

Charlemagne's Biography

http://www.chronique.com/Library/MedHistory/charlemagne.htm

Charlemagne the King from Will Durant's *Story of Civilization,* 1950.

Otto I and Otto II

Otto I

http://www.newadvent.org/cathen/11354a+.htm

Otto I, the Great, of Germany, from the *Catholic Encyclopedia.*

Otto II

http://www.newadvent.org/cathen/11355a.htm

"Catholic Encyclopaedia entry on Otto II."

The Medieval Period

Bellarmine's Biography

http://es.rice.edu:80/ES/humsoc/Galileo//People/bellarmine.html

Biography of Robert Cardinal Bellarmine (1542–1621), admonisher of Galileo.

Bellarmine's Letter on Galileo's Theories

http://www.fordham.edu/halsall/mod/1615bellarmine-letter.html

Full text of Bellarmine's letter on Galileo's theories, 1615.

Galileo Galilei

http://www.fordham.edu/halsall/mod/galileo-tuscany.html

Letter to the Grand Duchess Christina of Tuscany, 1615.

History of Florence and of the Affairs of Italy by Niccolo Machiavelli

http://www.worldwideschool.org/library/books/hst/european/
HistoryofFlorenceandoftheAffairsofItaly/chap0.html

Includes Books I to VIII.

Medieval Sourcebook: Giorgio Vasari

http://www.fordham.edu/halsall/source/vasari1.html

"Life of Leonardo da Vinci," in Vasari's *Lives of the Most Eminent Italian Architects, Painters, and Sculptors,* 1550.

Southern Italy in the Early Middle Ages

http://faculty.cua.edu/pennington/Naples/LectureTwo/EarlyMiddleAges.htm

Provides a time line and maps for Moslems, Normans, and Byzantines in southern Italy.

Renaissance Italy

Byzantines in Renaissance Italy

http://www.the-orb.net/encyclop/late/laterbyz/harris-ren.html

Jonathan Harris's *Byzantines in Renaissance Italy* with bibliography.

The Civilization of the Renaissance in Italy

http://www.idbsu.edu/courses/hy309/docs/burckhardt/burckhardt.html

Online version of the 1878 translation of Jacob Burkhardt's six-part book, *The Civilization of the Renaissance in Italy*. Information on despots, dynasties, republics, the papacy, individualism, antiquity, humanism, universities, literature, science, aesthetics, society, morality, and religion.

The Italian Renaissance

http://www.ibiblio.org/wm/paint/glo/renaissance/it.html

Essay on the Italian Renaissance provides further links to specific artists and their works such as Giotto de Bondone, Sandro Botticelli, Andrea Mantegna, Giovanni Bellini, Leonardo da Vinci, Michelangelo, Raphael, and Titian.

Papal States

Maps of the Papal States

http://www.duesicilie.org/mappe.html

Includes maps showing the extent of the Papal States during different periods.

"Papal States: Exiles and Political Prisoners"

http://www.cats.ohiou.edu/~Chastain/ip/papstaex.htm

"Papal States: Exiles and Political Prisoners," from *The Encyclopedia of Revolutions of 1848*.

Papal States Pre-1849

http://www.cats.ohiou.edu/~Chastain/ip/papalsta.htm

Pre-1849 overview of the Papal States.

The Unification Period

Garibaldi

http://www.fordham.edu/halsall/mod/1860garibaldi.html

Report on the Conquest of Naples, 1860.

Italian Unification

http://www.fordham.edu/halsall/mod/1861italianunif.html

Documents of Italian unification, 1846–1861.

King Victor Emmanuel

http://www.fordham.edu/halsall/mod/1871victoremm.html

Emmanuel's address to Parliament, Rome, 1871.

Twentieth-Century Italy

World War I

"The Italian Front, 1915–1918"

http://www.worldwar1.com/itafront/

La Grande Guerra's "The Italian Front, 1915–1918," gives information on weapons and equipment, battles, casualties, geography, diplomacy and operations, and who's who on the front.

Italy's Declaration of War

http://www.lib.byu.edu/~rdh/wwi/1915/italydec.html

Italian premier Antonio Salandra's Declaration for the Allies, May 23, 1915.

Fascism

Benito Mussolini

http://www.fordham.edu/halsall/mod/mussolini-fascism.html

"What Is Fascism?," 1932.

Fascism in Italy

http://www.library.wisc.edu/libraries/dpf/Fascism/Home.html

Selections from the Fry Collection at the University of Wisconsin on everyday life under fascism.

Maps

Italy, northern part—Kingdom

http://www.hicleones.com/callmap-e.php?tekst=10081&map=Italy%2C
%20northern%20part%20-%20Kingdom

Italy, southern part—Kingdom

http://www.hicleones.com/callmap-e.php?tekst=10082&map=Italy%2C%
20southern%20part%20-%20Kingdom

Map of the Italian Kingdom

http://www.hicleones.com/callmap-e.php?tekst=10080&map=Italy
%20-%20Kingdom

The three maps above come from the site Historical-Geographical Encyclopedia of the World (1880–1898)—Maps.

Italy Maps

http://www.lib.utexas.edu/maps/italy.html

Historical maps for Italy from the Perry-Castañeda Library Map Collection.

More Maps of the world

http://oddens.geog.uu.nl/index.php

See "Odden's Bookmarks" at the above URL for more maps.

MultiMap.com

http://www.multimap.com/

See maps of Italy by clicking on the chosen area of the map of Europe. This is handy if you do not have a print atlas on hand.

Mediterranean History

James P. Cousins

General Sites

Babelmed

http://www.babelmed.net/index.php?lingua=en

Babelmed is a site that offers historical data from the Mediterranean as it relates to contemporary social and cultural issues. In addition to news from the Mediterranean, the site offers its readers the opportunity to review books, explore Mediterranean art galleries, and discuss topics related to Mediterranean history.

H-Mediterranean

http://www.h-net.org/~mediter

H-Mediterranean is a part of the H-Net project based out of Michigan State University. The H-Mediterranean site provides the user with information about publications, future conferences, and job opportunities in Mediterranean studies. The site also contains a cross-disciplinary discussion board.

The Mediterranean World in Late Antiquity

http://ccat.sas.upenn.edu/jod/wola.html

A site containing materials related to a variety of subjects and persons associated with the Mediterranean world in late antiquity (200–700 CE). It is both a source of, and a gateway to, primary materials, bibliographies, and sites of general interest.

Medlib

http://www.unesco.org/webworld/build_info/medlib.html

Medlib is a project that seeks to create a virtual library for materials related to Mediterranean history. In addition to information on the project, the site contains links to online archives and library collections in the Mediterranean.

Perseus Digital Library

http://www.perseus.tufts.edu

Sponsored by a number of public and private organizations, the Perseus Project is a Tufts University–based collection of primary source documents. A range of documents from the ancient Mediterranean world is included, both the original language and an English translation.

Archaeology

The Archaeology of the Ancient Mediterranean Sea

http://archaeology.about.com/od/mediterraneansea

This site provides links to pages containing information on the study of archaeology in and around the Mediterranean Sea.

Archaeology Resources

http://www.geocities.com/i_georganas/main.html

This site features a linked listing of related academic journals, bibliographies, online resources, and search engines. This site also includes a directory of universities and colleges that offer programs in Mediterranean archaeology.

Mediterranean-archaeology.net

http://www.mediterranean-archaeology.net

A site containing general information, bibliographies, and links to pages devoted to the study of archaeology in Spain, Italy, Sardinia, and the eastern Mediterranean.

Maps and Cartography

Ancient Routes

http://www.ancientroute.com

A site that examines and charts ancient Mediterranean trade routes. Each route under consideration is accompanied by extensive background information, pictures, maps, and links to related Internet sources.

Interactive Ancient Mediterranean

http://iam.classics.unc.edu

This is an online atlas that provides users access to modern maps of the ancient, premodern, and modern Mediterranean world. Maps are arranged by country or region and are offered in a number of formats for purposes of instruction.

Yale University's Mediterranean Map Collection

http://www.library.yale.edu/MapColl/med.htm

This is an online collection of medieval Mediterranean maps. These maps are a part of the Yale University collection, which consists of over 215,000 maps available for download.

Organizations and Journals

The Canadian Institute for Mediterranean Studies

http://www.utoronto.ca/cims/files/abouteng.htm

The Canadian Institute for Mediterranean Studies supports a variety of projects related to the study of the Mediterranean. Membership information, including subscriptions to the institute's bulletin, is included.

Dikemes: International Center for Hellenic and Mediterranean Studies

http://www.dikemes.gr

Home page of Dikemes, an Athens-based nonprofit institution that offers intensive summer programs in subjects related to Mediterranean studies. Descriptions of programs and application materials are available for download.

Fares Center for Eastern Mediterranean Studies

http://farescenter.tufts.edu

This is a Tufts University Web site that provides information on upcoming conferences and lectures. The site also provides a directory of Mediterranean studies programs from other North American universities.

Institute for Mediterranean Studies

http://www.studies.org

Home page of the Institute for Mediterranean Studies, a nonprofit foundation that supports archaeological excavations and publications and offers a number of educational videos related to the Mediterranean.

Mediterranean Studies Association

http://www.mediterraneanstudies.org

This is the home page of the Mediterranean Studies Association. The site contains information related to the association's annual journal and conference schedule.

Society for the Medieval Mediterranean

http://www.leeds.ac.uk/smm/Main.html

A site devoted to the interdisciplinary study of the Mediterranean from the eighth to sixteenth centuries of the Common Era. The society supports a journal, and submission criteria are provided.

History of Art and Culture

Bibliography on Music in the Mediterranean World

http://faculty.washington.edu/snoegel/music.html

This page offers citations of over 500 works related to the history of Mediterranean music.

Detroit Institute of Arts: Permanent Collection— Ancient Art

http://www.dia.org/collections/ancient/greece/greece.html

A site that offers pictures of ancient Mediterranean sculptures and pottery. Pictures are hyperlinked to pages that provide detailed discussions of the work.

Diotima: Women & Gender in the Ancient Mediterranean World

http://www.stoa.org/diotima

A Web site that contains interdisciplinary resources for anyone interested in the study of gender in the ancient Mediterranean. The site includes bibliographic data, essays, links to similar pages, and access to specialized search engines.

Musicians of the Mediterranean

http://research.umbc.edu/eol/3/index.html

This is an online journal that contains articles and book reviews related to the history of Mediterranean music. The site also contains links to audio files of relevant pieces.

Perseus Art & Archaeology

http://www.perseus.tufts.edu/art&arch.html

This site, an extension of the Perseus Project, provides information and pictures of architecture, sculpture, coins, and pottery of the ancient to medieval Mediterranean. Over 33,000 pictures are available for viewing and download.

Nordic (Scandinavian) History

Mary Anne Hansen

Metasites

CultureNet Sweden

http://www.kultur.nu/

CultureNet Sweden provides links to hundreds of Web sites containing and presenting Swedish culture. Note the "in English" link option in the lower right-hand corner. This site links to archives, libraries, museums, and other cultural institutions.

European History: Scandinavia

http://www.library.cmu.edu/Research/Humanities/History/scandinavia.html

This site from Carnegie Mellon University Libraries provides links to diverse areas of Scandinavian studies.

Legends: The Viking World

http://www.legends.dm.net/sagas/viking.html

Created by Paula Kate Marmor, this site provides links to a variety of Viking-related Web sites.

Medieval Studies

http://www.uib.no/cms/links/links.htm

Compiled by the University of Bergen Centre for Medieval Studies, the vision of this site is to enhance understanding of Europe as a whole, from the Middle Ages to today.

Scandinavian Studies Research Guide

http://www.lib.byu.edu/estu/euro/scand.html

Maintained by the Harold B. Lee Library at Brigham Young University, this site is a comprehensive resource for Scandinavian research on the Web.

General History Sites

Antique Maps of Iceland

http://kort.bok.hi.is/

The National and University Library of Iceland has digitized every antique map in its collection older than 1900 and made them freely available on the Internet.

Bombs and Babies

http://www.hist.uib.no/bomb/

The project Bombs and Babies—Oral History on the Web was launched in August 1997 as a pilot collaboration project between the departments of history at the University of Bergen and University College London. The site presents students' work on oral history dealing with childhood memories from World War II. Includes audio clips of interviews.

A Brief History of Iceland

http://www.iceland.is/history-and-culture/

Created by the Icelandic Ministry for Foreign Affairs, this site provides an overview of Icelandic history and culture.

Country Studies: Finland

http://countrystudies.us/finland/

This Web site contains the online versions of books previously published in hard copy by the Federal Research Division of the Library of Congress as part of the Country Studies/Area Handbook Series sponsored by the U.S. Department of the Army between 1986 and 1998. Each study offers a comprehensive description and analysis of the country or region's historical setting, geography, society, economy, political system, and foreign policy.

Danish Data Archives

http://www.dda.dk/

The Danish Data Archives (DDA) is a national data bank for researchers and students in Denmark and abroad. The DDA, an independent unit within the Danish State Archives, provides demographic and social data.

Database of Wall Paintings in Danish Churches

http://www.panoramas.dk/kalkmalerier/

The Department of History at the University of Copenhagen has created Danske Kalkmalarier, an online database containing 5,320 images of wall paintings from Danish churches. The site also provides statistical data, articles, and literature on art and related topics.

The Demographic Data Base

http://www.ddb.umu.se/index_eng.html

Hosted by the University of Umeå, the Demographic Data Base makes available historical data from parish registers and parish statistics for researchers from both Sweden and abroad.

The Digital Archive of Norway

http://digitalarkivet.uib.no/

The Digital Archive of Norway is a cooperative effort between the Department of History at the University of Bergen and the Regional State Archives of Bergen, part of the National State Archives. The archive contains searchable nominative records from censuses, parish registers, emigration lists, and military records of Norway.

The Documentation Project

http://www.dokpro.uio.no/engelsk/index.html

Hosted by the University of Oslo, this site contains information on diverse aspects of Norwegian language, history, and culture. It has searchable databases on a number of historical sources, including the Diplomatarium Norvegicum, a large collection of Norwegian official documents prior to 1570. The collection contains 90,000 documents today in a searchable full-text database in the original language (Norse or Latin), with a Norwegian abstract.

Facts About Genealogy in Denmark

http://www.genealogi.dk/factwors.htm

First published in 1970, and still useful today, this article provides basic information for anyone who wishes to do genealogical research in Denmark. The article is also updated with links to a number of sites useful for genealogical research in Denmark.

Foreningen Forn Sed

http://www.forn-sed.no/main/english/english.htm

Foreningen Forn Sed is a religious society for those who believe in Norwegian folklore, the spirits and entities the folklore represents, and the gods and other beings from the Norse pantheon. The purpose of the society is to keep alive the old traditions, beliefs, and ways and to foster interest in the popular faith and the Norse cultural heritage.

Greenland Guide Index

http://www.greenland-guide.dk/default.htm

Greenland Guide is a comprehensive resource for virtual exploration of Greenland's culture, history, and travel.

History of Finland: A Selection of Events and Documents

http://www.histdoc.net/history/history.html

Maintained by Pauli Kruhse, this site contains a large number of primary sources on Finnish history, spanning from 1249 to 1944.

How to Trace Your Ancestors in Norway

http://digitalarkivet.uib.no/sab/howto.html

The Royal Norwegian Ministry of Foreign Affairs has published *How to Trace Your Ancestors in Norway* in nine editions from 1958 to 1996. This edition, written by the head of the State Archive of Bergen, has an extensive introduction explaining how to trace ancestors in Norway and giving a good overview of Norwegian nominative source material.

H-Skand

http://www.h-net.org/~skand/

H-Skand is a Web site for the H-Net discussion list of the same name. H-Skand focuses particularly on research and teaching interests, new scholarship in the field, discussions of Scandinavian historiography, and the sharing of knowledge and experience about the teaching of Scandinavian history, including posting and discussion of course syllabi and reading lists.

Info About Denmark

http://www.ambmoskva.um.dk/en/menu/InfoDenmark/

The Royal Danish Ministry of Foreign Affairs, in cooperation with the editors of the *Danish National Encyclopedia*, provides an in-depth description and general history of Denmark on this site. The chapters are written by leading Danish experts.

The Ninety-Two Medieval Churches of Gotland

http://www.algonet.se/~sorengra/churches/mapindexeng.html

This site describes ninety-two medieval churches in Gotland, Sweden, with texts and images. Users can click on maps to locate a church or search through an index.

Norway Heritage Project

http://www.norwayheritage.com/ships/

The information on this site is for research and educational purposes. The site contains the names of ships known to have left Norway for America between 1825 and 1925, including passenger lists.

The Norwegian Historical Data Centre

http://www.rhd.uit.no/indexeng.html

The Norwegian Historical Data Centre is a national institution under the Faculty of Social Science at the University of Tromsø. The Web site contains searchable online census material from 1865.

Norwegian Historical Statistics—1994

http://www.ssb.no/english/subjects/00/histstat/

Historical Statistics—1994 is a useful reference for anyone seeking knowledge about the development of Norwegian society from the nineteenth century onward. There is a summary for every item and English text in figures and tables. The statistics are produced and published by the governmental bureau of statistics.

Norwegian Social Science Data Services

http://www.nsd.uib.no/english/

"The Norwegian Social Science Data Services is a national center servicing the research community. Its main objective is to secure access for the Norwegian research community to data and to provide various services." The center's material is arranged into three groups: "Regional Data, Individual Data, and Data on the Political System."

The Online Medieval and Classical Library

http://sunsite.berkeley.edu/OMACL/

This collection of electronic texts includes Scandinavian texts in English translation, such as the Old Norse *Heimskringla,* by Snorri Sturluson, and the Danish *Gesta Danorum* by Saxo Grammaticus.

Project Runeberg

http://www.lysator.liu.se/runeberg/

Coordinated by Linköping University, Sweden, Project Runeberg is an initiative to publish free electronic editions of Nordic literature. It contains over 200 texts, ranging from old Norse sagas to novels of Strindberg.

Swedish Institute

http://www.si.se/

The official Swedish site containing information about Sweden in general and an overview of both Swedish history and the Sami people of Sweden.

The Viking Answer Lady

http://www.vikinganswerlady.com/index.html

Created by Christie L. Ward as a result of her passion for researching Viking lore, the Viking Answer Lady is a comprehensive Web site for research into a variety of topics concerning the Viking Age.

Virtual Finland

http://virtual.finland.fi/

An official Finnish Web site produced by the Ministry for Foreign Affairs of Finland, containing information on a wide range of topics, including history.

The World of the Vikings

http://www.worldofthevikings.com/

A guide to Viking resources on the Internet, this site is a gateway to topics such as mead, ships, sagas, and runes. This site offers a World of the Vikings CD-ROM for purchase, but also provides access to numerous freely available resources.

Chapter 16

United States History

General United States History

John A. King

General Sites

AcademicInfo: US History Gateway

http://www.academicinfo.net/histus.html

Although this site is a bit cumbersome to navigate and is plagued by advertising, it is vast in its annotated listing of Web sites related to American history—there are thousands of links! Its list of digital collections, for example, contains links to many primary source collections on the Web, while its Teaching US History section has links to sites specifically designed with classroom applications in mind. Sites are organized here both thematically and chronologically.

The Adoption History Project

http://www.uoregon.edu/~adoption/

This Web site provides a very complete treatment of the history of adoption in the United States, primarily in the twentieth century. This site is easy to use, and it has a nice repository of primary sources on the topic.

AMDOCS: Documents for the Study of American History

http://www.ku.edu/carrie/docs/amdocs_index.html

Part of the Digital Collection at the University of Kansas, AMDOCS provides a vast collection of primary sources in American history. The chronological organization makes it easy to locate both specific documents and documents representative a particular time period. Documents are mostly political in nature (presidential documents, Supreme Court decisions, treaties, political tracts, etc.), but some literary pieces and song lyrics are included as well.

The Authentic History Center

http://www.authentichistory.com/

The Authentic History Center presents artifacts from American popular culture, dating back to the antebellum period. Organized chronologically, the site includes audio files (songs, speeches, and radio broadcasts of major events, among other items), documents (a small collection of letters and diaries), and a substantial number of images of various types (posters, photographs, cartoons, and even some comic books!).

The Avalon Project

http://www.yale.edu/lawweb/avalon/avalon.htm

The Avalon Project, housed at Yale University, is a collection of legal, political, and diplomatic documents from the earliest years of the United States to the present. The collection includes not only official documents such as treaties and addresses, but also some private correspondence, presidential papers, and other materials. This is one of the best places to find the full text of a treaty or act.

Biography of America

http://www.learner.org/biographyofamerica/

From the Annenberg/CPB project, the Biography of America is a series of twenty-six lectures in video format, embedded with music and images, given by prominent historians. Each video episode is viewable online, and the Web site contains supplemental time lines, maps, Webographies, and interactive activities for each episode.

Digital History

http://www.digitalhistory.uh.edu/

Like the Gilder Lehrman site (below), Digital History provides a vast array of narratives of the major periods of U.S. history (see the "Guides" portion of the Web site), as well as features on special topics in American history, such as "science and technology" and "ethnic America." A wide variety of primary sources complements the descriptive sections of the Web site. Digital History also includes a separate section for teachers, with excellent handouts and fact sheets, lesson plans, background information, and other teaching aids.

Diving America: Religion and the National Culture

http://www.nhc.rtp.nc.us:8080/tserve/divam.htm

The National Humanities Center presents in this Web site a broad collection of articles, all richly illustrated, on the significance of religion in America from the seventeenth to the twentieth century. In addition, the site provides an extremely thoughtful teacher's guide for teaching each of the twenty-five articles in the collection. This is an excellent place to learn about any topic in American religious history, from religious pluralism to African-American religion to Islam in America.

Documenting the American South

http://docsouth.unc.edu/

Documenting the American South is an effort of the University of North Carolina to provide online access to the Southern perspective in American history by publishing online documents from its special collections. Documents include government documents, diaries, slave narratives songs, and many other texts on topics as wide-ranging as Carolina history to religion to World War I. The texts are diverse in their representation of race, gender, economic status, occupation, age, and other demographic criteria.

Eyewitness to History

http://www.eyewitnesstohistory.com/index.html

Although this site does not limit itself to U.S. history, much on the site is relevant. The site provides eyewitness accounts of historical events, "history through the eyes of those who lived it," as the Web site proclaims. It does contain some very interesting documents, which could be useful complements to textbook reading in a survey course. For example, students might enjoy reading William Bradford's description of his time on the *Mayflower,* the testimonies of those surrounding President James Garfield after he had been shot, Sheriff Pat Garrett's account of his shooting of Billy the Kid, or Branch Rickey's account of his meeting with Jackie Robinson in 1945, resulting in Robinson's signing with the Los Angles Dodgers, breaking the color barrier in major league baseball.

From Revolution to Reconstruction . . . and what happened afterwards

http://odur.let.rug.nl/~usa/

This is probably the best place on the Web to find a narrative of American history from pre-Columbian to present times. The narrative on this site is

essentially a compilation of several publications of the United States Information Agency. In a limited number of hyperlinks in the texts, the site enhances
the USIA accounts with a nice collection of biographies and bibliographies.

The Gilder Lehrman Institute of American History

http://www.gilderlehrman.org/

The Gilder Lehrman Institute presents online twenty "modules" covering the
major periods in American history, from the colonial period to 9/11. Each
module includes a narrative overview of the period; a unique selection of ten
or so primary sources; visual aids, including maps, graphs, and images; lesson
plans; guided readings of primary sources; and recommended Web sites, books,
films, and other resources.

History Matters

http://historymatters.gmu.edu/

From George Mason University, the History Matters Web site is designed especially for teachers of American history, but contains resources that should be
helpful to any student of American history as well. The site contains a rich
collection of primary sources along with instructive guides for interpreting
them. In addition, the site includes articles on various topics in the teaching of
American history; a very impressive annotated list of Web sites in American
history, organized chronologically and topically; sample syllabi; lesson plans
incorporating the use of the World Wide Web; and samples of students' work.

Jensen's Web Guides

http://tigger.uic.edu/~rjensen/0.htm

Professor Richard Jensen of the University of Illinois has prepared guides to
historical research on the Web in the following fields: American political history, politics research (general), military history, the Civil War and Reconstruction, Thomas Jefferson, railroad history, the Vietnam War, and world
populations. The guides on political and military history are especially useful.
The guides are quite comprehensive, including both electronic and print resources. Jensen updates his guides regularly, indicating sites that he especially
recommends, and he is usually accurate.

Kingwood College Library

http://kclibrary.nhmccd.edu/research.htm

Designed specifically for researchers, the Kingwood College Library (in
Kingwood, Texas) research page has a splendid collection of links to pages

and Web sites on American history, highlighted by decade-by-decade discussions of American cultural history. These pages are detailed expositions of American cultural history, with illustrations and a plethora of hyperlinks embedded in the text to related Web sites. A similar set of pages exists for American popular music.

Library of Congress Web Sites

http://www.loc.gov/

The Library of Congress has much to offer students of American history, both at the Library itself and online. The home page of the Library of Congress provides links to the subsites below, as well as a catalog search, "ask a librarian," a link to the "global gateway" for doing research on world affairs, and general information and news about the library.

Library of Congress: American Memory

http://memory.loc.gov/ammem/index.html

The result of a fifteen-year project of the Library of Congress and other libraries and archives to digitize the "American experience," the American Memory site presents over 9 million documents, including maps, still and moving images, and recorded sound. The materials are organized into a hundred collections, but the archive is easily searchable by term, category, time period, and document type. This is easily the richest collection of American history primary sources to be found online.

Library of Congress: Especially for Researchers

http://www.loc.gov/rr/

The Especially for Researchers page provides all the instruction necessary for doing research effectively in the collections of the Library of Congress, either in person or online. Links to digital collections, databases, interlibrary loan, and finding aids are all located here.

Library of Congress Exhibitions Gallery

http://www.loc.gov/exhibits

This is a collection of online exhibitions from the Library of Congress. Much of the material here can also be accessed via the American Memory Web site. Those included in this collection are excellent and wide-ranging, including an outstanding one on the role of religion in American life to the mid-nineteenth century, another on the contributions of Bob Hope, and many other topics.

Library of Congress: The Learning Page

http://memory.loc.gov/learn/

The Learning Page is specifically dedicated to teachers. In addition to information on professional issues, the page contains many lesson plans, activities, and instructions and recommendations on using the digital collections of the Library of Congress in the classroom.

Library of Congress: Thomas

http://thomas.loc.gov/

Another site sponsored by the Library of Congress, Thomas is the primary site for "legislative information on the Web." The site contains the full text of the *Congressional Record* from the 101st Congress (1989–1990) to the present, and many materials from Congresses as far back as the 93rd (1973–1974). Additionally, Thomas includes information on the workings of the legislative branch of government and various historical collections, including several primary source collections and congressional biographies and bibliographies dating back to the First Continental Congress (1774).

National Archives and Records Administration

http://www.archives.gov/

The NARA site contains a plethora of documents, as well as an electronic "Exhibit Hall" containing more than thirty online exhibits on important themes in American history, including "100 milestone documents in American history." The site is especially useful for teachers, as its "Digital Classroom" contains not only a great many lesson plans, but also a variety of teaching aids (including very effective document analysis worksheets) for using primary sources in the classroom.

National Park Service: Links to the Past

http://www.cr.nps.gov/

Links to the Past is the home page for the National Park Service's excellent collection of historical information. Ranging from special features to the Web sites for individual parks and Web courses on history, archaeology, and preservation, the site offers a wealth of information useful to history students, teachers, and scholars. Especially good for teachers are the lesson plans prepared by the Park Service, under the title "Teaching with Historic Places" (http://www.cr.nps.gov/nr/twhp/). These are some of the most well-prepared and interesting lesson plans for American history on the Web, incorporating primary texts, secondary readings, images, maps, background information, and a variety of study questions and activities for students.

Nature Transformed: The Environment in American History

http://www.nhc.rtp.nc.us:8080/tserve/nattrans/nattrans.htm

Similar to the Diving America Web site Nature Transformed is a National Humanities Center project. A very thorough and richly illustrated survey of American environmental history, the site provides an excellent overview of the topic. Articles, such as "The Columbian Exchange," "The Puritan Origins of the American Wilderness Movement," and "Roads, Highways, and Ecosystems," are all complemented by detailed and original teachers' guides for using the resources of the Web site in the classroom.

Oyez: U.S. Supreme Court Multimedia

http://www.oyez.org/oyez/frontpage

The Oyez site provides concise summaries of all major cases heard by the Supreme Court and, for many recent cases, provides audio excerpts of the reading of the Court's decisions. The Oyez site also provides biographies of all the justices who have served on the Supreme Court. The Oyez content can be easily searched or browsed. Oyez also provides a link to FindLaw, the Web site where the full text of court decisions can be located, along with other information of interest to legal scholars.

PBS: *American Experience*

http://www.pbs.org/wgbh/amex/

One of the best television series on the history of America, PBS's *American Experience* has covered political, economic, cultural, and technological topics in American history. Many of the episodes have companion Web sites, found here, with special features, biographies, time lines, bibliographies, teachers' guides, and transcripts of the programs.

Professor Donna M. Campbell's "American Literature" Site

http://www.wsu.edu/~campbelld/index/html

Although Professor Donna Campbell's Web site is focused primarily on topics in American literature, there is much here useful to students of history. Naturally, history and literature are interrelated, and everything on the Web site, such as the section on American authors, is discussed in its proper historical context. The time line is actually two time lines, one of developments in literature and a corresponding time line of developments in social history, and topics in "Literary Movements" include not only the movements one would expect, but jeremiads, slave narratives, travel narratives, and other genres that should appeal to the historian.

The Smithsonian

http://www.si.edu/

The national museum of the United States, the Smithsonian Institution has published online an extensive and wide-ranging array of materials and exhibits based on its vast collections. While the history and culture exhibits are the most relevant to historians, exhibits in other collections also may be useful. In addition to exhibit-specific lesson plans, the Smithsonian site also has a special section for teachers, including lesson plans.

Tax History Project

http://www.taxhistory.org/

The Tax History Project Web site is an excellent one for anyone wishing to learn more about tax history in the United States and, even more broadly, about American economic history. Rich in images and audio files, the site includes the "Tax History Museum," which chronicles the history of taxation in the United States (though it is weak on the later part of the twentieth century), as well as information on presidential tax returns; discussions of special topics, such as the debate over taxation in the *Federalist Papers;* a collection of images; and an extensive collection of articles on specific topics in tax history.

U.S. Census Bureau

http://www.census.gov/population/www/index.html

The U.S. Census Bureau Web site contains the most recent census data, as well as historical census data dating back to the first official census in 1790. Users should also consult the Historical Census Data Browser (http://fisher.lib.virginia.edu/collections/stats/histcensus/), which allows users to sort, manipulate, and map census data, to the county level, from 1790 to 1960. The data includes both demographic and economic statistics.

WWW Virtual Library—History: United States

http://vlib.iue.it/history/USA/

This site is a vast resource for researchers of American history. Its links are organized both chronologically and thematically. This would be an excellent starting place for a research project, as there seems to be nary a topic that is not represented by the links on this site.

State Histories

State governments, state archives, state museums, state historical preservations societies, and universities are responsible for many good Web sites and resources online for state, regional, and local history. Many provide excellent case studies and/or examples of state history with the broader context of general American history. These Web sites showcase both interactive historical presentations and some very rich resources from the collections of state archives that could be windfalls for researchers. Users should also examine Chapter 30, "State and Provincial Historical Societies," later in this volume. Here are some of the best examples of this kind of Web site:

Adirondack History Network

http://www.adirondackhistory.org/

Although its featured topics are somewhat limited in number, the exhibits on this Web site are original and informative, and they also encourage users to consult the online digital archives of the Adirondack Museum for further research. Mostly centered in the Gilded Age and Progressive Era, some topics included are "Women's Work" and "Mose Ginsberg: From Immigrant Peddler to Honored Citizen."

Exploring Florida

http://fcit.usf.edu/florida/

This site contains over 4,500 images and 3,000 maps, in addition to movies, audio files, documents, and other sources, documenting the history of Florida. The site offers an impressive collection of historical texts that could be integrated into a U.S. history course, including topics ranging from colonial life to railroad building, urbanization, and ethnicity and diversity.

Kansas History On-line

http://www.kansashistoryonline.org/ksh/Index.asp

Some portions of this site are still under construction, but the site provides a very detailed outline of Kansas history, highlighting many major themes and developments in American history (e.g., sectionalism, the frontier, reform movements). There are also several featured topics, such as buffalo and Bloody Kansas, which are treated in great detail.

The Library of Virginia

http://www.lva.lib.va.us/whoweare/exhibits/index.htm

The state Library of Virginia maintains a number of online exhibits on topics ranging from slave revolts to roots music and from women's history to art history. The exhibits are narratives that are richly illustrated and are complemented by extensive selections of digitized documents from the state archives.

Maryland State Archives Museum On-line

http://www.mdarchives.state.md.us/msa/educ/exhibits/html/exhibit.html

One of the state archives with the best presence online, the Maryland State Archives Museum On-line offers several excellent exhibits, such as Maryland in Focus, a robust collection of images documenting Maryland's history, as well as an extensive presentation of primary sources from the state's history, covering all periods from the colonial to the recent.

Washington State History Museum

http://www.wshs.org/

In its virtual "Great Hall of Washington History," the Washington State History Museum provides the experience of its brick-and-mortar Great Hall online. Visitors can explore a variety of themes in American history, such as early encounters, pioneer life, and art history, through this virtual tour. In addition, like many state and local museums, the Washington State History museum has published the full text of many articles in its journal, *COLUMBIA,* online. Readers can find articles here on such diverse topics as environmental history, labor history, and sport history.

The Way We Lived in North Carolina

http://cepa.newschool.edu/het/

Based on the publication of a book by the same name, this Web site details the social history of North Carolina through narrative text and the generous use of images and maps.

Publishing Companies' Web Sites

Bedford/St. Martins's History Resource Center

http://www.bedfordstmartins.com/history/

Students and teachers should be fond of this Web site. The site contains documents, images, maps, and a nice complement of secondary sources on a variety of topics. In addition, short "critical thinking" modules focus on particular issues in U.S. history. Instructors will find the maps archive useful, with over 600 maps, including printable blank maps. Students will find the student study guides that accompany the Bedford texts invaluable, as they include chapter summaries, terms lists, multiple choice quizzes, some very fine map exercises, and many other activities. Registration is required for students and instructors, but is free and does not require the use of a Bedford/ St. Martin's textbook.

Wadsworth's American History Resource Center

http://www.wadsworth.com/history_d/special_features/ext/ am_hist/AmerHis-ch01.html

Teachers and students alike will find the American History Center an extremely useful resource. The site is easy to use and highly interactive. Some of the features are intertwined with Wadsworth's *American Journey* textbook. The site contains documents, images, maps, animated features on immigration and demographics, and an interactive time line with links to further information about the people and events on the time line.

African-American History

Mary Anne Hansen

Metasites

Academic Info: African-American History: An Annotated Resource of Internet Resources on Black History

http://academicinfo.net/africanam.html

This extensive listing provides quality sites on African-American history for researchers, university students, and teachers. The site lists and briefly describes metaindexes, digital libraries and archives, online publications, museum presentations, library and archival catalogs, resources for teaching, and some topics such as Martin Luther King, jazz, and slavery. It is a useful source for locating primary materials. The directory is created and kept updated by Academic Info, a private organization compiling subject indexes for respected Web sites on a wide range of topics.

African American History and Culture

http://www.si.edu/resource/faq/nmah/afroam.htm

This is a list of the Smithsonian's resources on African-American history and culture.

African-American West

http://www.wsu.edu:8080/~amerstu/mw/af_ap.html#afam

This multicultural American West metasite links to numerous Web resources about blacks in the history of the American West. Local sites included.

American Identities: African-American

http://xroads.virginia.edu/~YP/african.html

Produced by the University of Virginia American Studies Program, this site links to a wide range of sites, some of them historical. Although these and other related sites are hosted at the University of Virginia, they are not directly connected.

A–Z of African Studies on the Internet

http://www.lib.msu.edu/limb/a-z/az.html

A–Z of African Studies on the Internet is another general clearinghouse of links to African and African-American sites. Two Michigan State University librarians, Peter Limb and Ibra Sene, maintain the site.

Black History Pages

http://blackhistorypages.com/

This directory site provides links to a wide variety of Web sites having to do with black history.

Black Soldiers in the Civil War

http://www.academicinfo.net/africanamcw.html

This site links to several other sites about African-American history during the Civil War, including Buffalo Soldiers.

Christine's Genealogy Web Site

http://ccharity.com/

Important for black history as well as genealogy, this privately maintained site contains a variety of governmental documents and lists. Although the contents are scattered and searching is somewhat difficult, materials include immigration records to Liberia, a Freedmen's Bureau list of "outrages," lists of lynchings, census records, and similar records useful in both research and teaching. Also links to black history by members of local communities.

Classic African-American Literature

http://curry.edschool.virginia.edu/go/multicultural/sites/aframdocs.html

Links to online sites of classic African-American documents, some more historical than literary. This site also contains a wide range of documents, familiar and unknown, many of them useful in teaching history. Part of the Multicultural Paths Project at the University of Virginia.

Historical Text Archive: African-American History

http://historicaltextarchive.com/

A metasite created by a professor at Mississippi State University who publishes high-quality articles, books, essays, documents, historical photos, and links, screened for content, for a broad range of historical subjects. It includes a wide variety of links, including some to black history in particular states and regions, exhibits about blacks, primary sources, genealogy sites, and teaching materials. Although Mississippi State University hosts the site, the university takes no responsibility for it.

Social Studies School Services: Black History

http://www.socialstudies.com

This commercial organization offers lesson plans, student exercises, RealVideo clips of materials it sells, catalogs of its other materials, reviews of other sites, and links. Extensive, but materials are not guaranteed for accuracy.

General Sites

Aboard the Underground Railroad

http://www.cr.nps.gov/nr/travel/underground/

Aboard the Underground Railroad: A National Register of Historic Places Travel Itinerary introduces travelers, researchers, historians, preservationists, and anyone interested in African-American history to the fascinating people and places associated with the Underground Railroad. The itinerary currently provides descriptions and photographs of sixty historic places that are listed in the National

Park Service's National Register of Historic Places, America's official list of places important in our history and worthy of preservation. It also includes a map of the most common directions of escape taken on the Underground Railroad and maps of individual states that mark the location of the historic properties.

African-American Community

http://www.cmstory.org/african/default.htm

A large collection of online photographs and other information about African-Americans for Charlotte and Mecklenberg County, North Carolina, sponsored by the local public library.

African-American Heritage

http://www.cr.nps.gov/aahistory/

Provides an extensive listing of resources on the subject, including a list of physical locations, along with relevant Web sites that are important in African-American history.

African American Labor History Links

http://www.afscme.org/about/aframlink.htm

Created by the American Federation of State, County and Municipal Employees, the nation's largest and fastest-growing public service employees union.

African-American Mosaic: A Library of Congress Resource Guide for the Study of Black History and Culture

http://lcweb.loc.gov/exhibits/african/intro.html

The major site and starting place for African-American materials online from the Library of Congress and a rich sampling of its larger collections. Included are a comprehensive text and images from the nearly 500 years of the black experience in the Western Hemisphere. Lesser-known topics include Liberia, abolitionists, western migration, and documents from the Works Progress Administration, the Federal Writers Program, and the Daniel Murray Pamphlet collection. Items within the African-American Mosaic can be searched online. The American Odyssey is separate from the American Mosaic.

African-American Resources at the University of Virginia

http://etext.lib.virginia.edu/subjects/African-American-html

This site contains an initial online group of texts of documents and images relating to slavery assembled by a special seminar of the Rare Books Division of the Library of the University of Virginia.

African-American Resources: Electronic Text Center

http://etext.lib.virginia.edu/speccol.html

An extensive collection of original documents ranging from nineteenth-century African-American issues to dozens of letters from notable individuals, including Mildred Carr and Thomas Jefferson.

African Americans in the West

http://www.library.csi.cuny.edu/westweb/pages/black.html

This section of WestWeb provides information about African-Americans in the West. Like much of the rest of WestWeb, it is constantly changing and developing. Under "Texts" users will find examples of primary texts, such as the letters of African-American GIs in World War II and secondary texts, such as critical essays and historical studies (coming soon). Under "Resources" are biographies of Western African-Americans, bibliographies, and teaching materials. Under "Links to Other Sites," users will find a collection of links to sites dealing with various issues in African-American history, such as overland migration, the Black Panthers, and cowboy history. Finally, under "Images," users will find both general collections that include some images of Western African-American history and direct links to pictures available online.

African Genesis: Black History

http://afgen.com/history.html

This site offers contemporary and historic information concerning black America and the African diaspora. The music section is concentrated on jazz, gospel, blues, and a little bit of soul. In the history section are articles on abolitionists and African-American pioneers. The religion section is currently restricted to African traditional religions. In the African American Griot News section there are news articles and reports of interest to black America and the Diaspora.

AfriGeneas

http://www.afrigeneas.com/

AfriGeneas is a site devoted to African-American genealogy, to researching African ancestry in the Americas in particular and to genealogical research and resources in general. It is also an African ancestry research community featuring the AfriGeneas mail list, the AfriGeneas message boards, and daily and weekly genealogy chats.

Africans in America

http://www.pbs.org/wgbh/aia/home.html

An ambitious site with many of the strengths and weaknesses of original public television production. Extensive documents, text, maps, and images are included along with careful lesson plans for teachers. Although the impressive panel of scholars who assisted with the project is listed, little attention is given throughout to the identity and qualifications of writers and speakers, creating problems for students trying to put materials in historical context.

Afro-American Sources in Virginia: A Guide to Manuscripts

http://www.upress.virginia.edu/plunkett/mfp.html

This is an electronic edition of a print guide jointly produced by Michael Plunkett of the University Press of Virginia and the University of Virginia's Electronic Text Center.

American Slave Narratives: An Online Anthology

http://xroads.virginia.edu/~hyper/wpa/wpahome.html

Texts, photos, and recordings of some selected Works Progress Administration interviews are presented online. Developed for classroom use at the University of Virginia.

Archives of African-American Music and Culture

http://www.indiana.edu/~aaamc/index.html

This is a large database dedicated to all aspects of African-American music and culture, including many links to related sites. The site is a project of the Department of Afro-American Studies at Indiana University.

Behind the Veil: Documenting African-American Life in the Jim Crow South

http://cds.aas.duke.edu/btv/

This is a major project to collect and make accessible oral histories and photographs recording the experiences of African-Americans in the Jim Crow South.

The Center for Documentary Studies at Duke University is responsible for the project, with involvement from other universities and communities.

Black History and Classical Music

http://chevalierdesaintgeorges.homestead.com/History.html

This Web site provides an introduction to black history and classical music. It includes a black history quiz and previews to companion pages.

Black Pioneers and Settlers of the Pacific Northwest

http://www.endoftheoregontrail.org/blakbios.html

Produced by the End of the Oregon Trail Interpretive Center, this site provides a time line of blacks in the state, biographies and photographs of early African-Americans there, discussion of the state's exclusion legislation and slavery, and a bibliography of sources.

Charlotte Hawkins Brown Memorial, North Carolina Historic Sites

http://www.ah.dcr.state.nc.us/sections/hs/chb/chb.htm

This excellent site, created by the North Carolina Division of Archives and History, gives information about Charlotte Hawkins Brown, a leading black educator, and the school that she founded. Online texts of documents by and about her give insight into her own thought. Very extensive bibliographies give references to manuscript collections, theses, and primary material. Articles and reports, books, and pamphlets are listed for those doing additional research.

Civil Rights in Mississippi Digital Archive

http://www.lib.usm.edu/~spcol/crda/

This important site makes available to a wider audience the oral histories collected in the fall of 1997 by the staff members at the University of Southern Mississippi's Center for Oral History and Cultural Heritage and at the Tougaloo College Archives. It contains online texts of interviews, searchable in various ways, and a bibliography. The Mississippi State Legislature, Mississippi Department of Archives and History, and the Mississippi Humanities Council funded the project.

Database of United States Colored Troops in the Civil War

http://www.itd.nps.gov/cwss/

The United States National Park Service and the Civil War Soldiers and Sailors created this database and made it available online. In addition to 235,000 names, information is presented in about 180 histories of USCT units and regiments and links to sites about the most significant Civil War battles in which African-Americans fought. Click on US Colored Troops under Origin in the database to limit your search to African-Americans.

A Deeper Shade of History

http://www.seditionists.org/black/bhist.html

A Deeper Shade of History is one of the premier resources on African-American history, film, and literature. Created and maintained by Charles Isbell of MIT, it is an excellent resource for biographies, with well-developed accounts of figures such as Thurgood Marshall and Paul Robeson.

Desegregation of the Armed Forces: Project Whistlestop Harry S. Truman Digital Archives

http://www.trumanlibrary.org/whistlestop/study_collections/ desegregation/large/

The Truman Presidential Library has digitized Truman's Executive Order 9981, calling for desegregation of the armed forces, and other documents from the study leading up to that decision.

Duke University Library and John Hope Franklin Research Center for African and African-American Documentation

http://scriptorium.lib.duke.edu/franklin/collections.html

In association with Duke Library's Digital Scriptorium, the Franklin Center publishes digitized versions of finding aids, subject guides, and materials from selected collections. Exhibits include African-American Women; Retrieving African-American Women's History; and Third Person, First Person: Slave Voices from the Special Collections Library, Duke University.

Exploring *Amistad* at Mystic Seaport: Race and the Boundaries of Freedom in Antebellum Maritime America

http://amistad.mysticseaport.org/main/welcome.html

This site, produced by the Mystic Seaport Museum, is one of the best teaching sites focusing on a particular event and its participants. Included are a brief narrative, a time line, and links to other sites. The online historical documents related to the capture of the ship and its occupants provide little-known information, and the teacher's guide presents a variety of activities, including a reenactment of the capture.

Faces of Science: African-Americans in the Sciences

http://webfiles.uci.edu/mcbrown/display/faces.html

Faces of Science looks at the past, present, and future of African-Americans in the sciences. It presents biographies of famous African-Americans grouped by scientific discipline, examines the percentages of doctorates granted to African-Americans in each area of the sciences, offers a wealth of statistical and demographic data, and contains links to other related sites.

The Frederick Douglass Papers Project

http://www.iupui.edu/~douglass/

Information about the project at Indiana University—Purdue University at Indianapolis to edit and publish Douglass's papers not included in the Yale edition of Douglass's works. The site includes links to other sites and a bibliography of recommended sources.

Freedmen and Southern Society Project

http://www.history.umd.edu/Freedmen/

Scholars at the University of Maryland are in the process of editing a multivolume collection of papers from the National Archives by and about men and women who became free from slavery during and after the Civil War. The project is funded by the National Endowment for the Humanities.

Harlem 1900–1940: An African-American Community

http://www.si.umich.edu/CHICO/Harlem

This impressive site was created at the School of Information at the University of Michigan as part of its Cultural Heritage Initiatives for Community Outreach. Items came from the Schomberg Center and include digitized texts and photographs. Suggestions for teachers using the materials and links to other related sites are also presented.

History Makers

http://thehistorymakers.com/

The initial goal of the History Makers site is to complete 5,000 interviews of both well-known and unsung African-Americans within the next five years, creating an archive of unparalleled importance and exposing the archival collection to the widest audience possible. Not since the WPA project of the 1930s, when teams of writers and researchers were sent throughout the South to conduct 2,300 mostly hand-recorded interviews with former slaves, has there been such a methodic and wide-scale attempt to capture the testimonies of African Americans.

Inventory of African-American Historical and Cultural Resources in Maryland

http://www.sailor.lib.md.us/MD_topics/his/af_am.html

A very extensive listing by county of structures, historical sites, and collections materials in Maryland relating to African-American history. The Maryland Commission on African-American History and Culture supports the project.

Martin Luther King Jr.

http://www.seattletimes.com/mlk/index.html

One of the best sites about King for classroom teachers and students. Produced by the *Seattle Times,* it includes editorials, interviews, news columns, and photographs from the newspaper. King is presented in historical context, with a series of classic pictures from the civil rights movement. The study guide provides probing questions relating to King's holiday and larger questions of racial equality.

Martin Luther King Jr. Papers Project of Stanford University

http://www.stanford.edu/group/King/

The scholars at Stanford University who are editing and publishing King's writings have begun to make a sampling of his papers available online, including some of his most well-known documents. In addition, the site contains a bibliography file containing about 2,700 references to published works dealing with King and the civil rights movement.

Museum of African Slavery

http://jhunix.hcf.jhu.edu/~plarson/smuseum/welcome.htm

The Museum of African Slavery in the Atlantic is designed to provide accurate, engaging, and provocative information to the public about the history of slavery. The site is aimed at primary and secondary students and their teachers. The primary author is Pier M. Larson, a professor of African history at Johns Hopkins University.

National Archives and Records Administration

http://www.archives.gov/

Primary documents about African-Americans from the National Archives and teaching activities for using them in the classroom. Topics include the *Amistad* case, black soldiers in the Civil War, and Jackie Robinson. Other African-American materials can be found by searching the National Archives Digital Library. See also John H. White: Portrait of Black Chicago content at this site.

National Civil Rights Museum

http://www.civilrightsmuseum.org/

This site discusses the National Civil Rights Museum in Memphis, Tennessee. It contains a virtual tour of the museum's exhibits and their aims. Color and black-and-white photos are included. In addition to the tour, there are links to related sites, membership information, and admission.

Negro League Baseball

http://www.negroleaguebaseball.com/

This site provides information on Negro League baseball, including team histories and player profiles.

North American Slave Narratives, Beginnings to 1920

http://metalab.unc.edu/docsouth/neh/neh.html

Books, pamphlets, and broadsides written by fugitive and former slaves before 1920 are being collected and put online by scholars at the University of North Carolina. This National Endowment for the Humanities project, when complete, will include all such works.

Prairie Bluff

http://www.prairiebluff.com/

B.J. Smothers's private Web genealogy project, this site provides links to cemetery records and other documents and resources, especially in the South.

Schomburg Center for Research in Black Culture

http://www.nypl.org/research/sc/sc.html

The Schomburg Center for Research in Black Culture at the New York Public Library is a national research library devoted to collecting, preserving, and providing access to resources documenting the experiences of peoples of African descent throughout the world.

Selected Library African-American Online Catalogs

http://www.library.ucla.edu/libraries/url/colls/africanamer/cats.htm

A listing of some online catalogs of African-American materials created and maintained by the UCLA Libraries. A good source for locating materials, even though not all such collections are included.

This Is Our War

http://www.afro.com/history/OurWar/intro.html

A series of articles written by black war correspondents during World War II for the *Baltimore Afro-American*. This is part of a larger site on black history produced by the newspaper.

Voices of the Civil Rights Era

http://www.voicesofcivilrights.org/

Voices of the Civil Rights Era is an audio archive, sponsored by Webcorp, containing different views of the future from Malcolm X, Martin Luther King Jr., John F. Kennedy, and others.

W.E.B. DuBois Virtual University

http://members.tripod.com/~DuBois/

This private site is a clearinghouse for information on DuBois. It offers links to online texts by and about DuBois, a bibliography of articles and dissertations in print about him, and a list of DuBois scholars.

Women and Social Movements in the United States, 1600–2000

http://womhist.binghamton.edu/projectmap.htm

This site from the University of New York-Binghamton contains about twenty document sets, dealing with African-American women's history. Compiled for college and high school classrooms, this site contains materials by and about black women seldom found elsewhere. The project is funded by the National Endowment for the Humanities.

Writing Black USA

http://www.learnnc.org/bestweb/writeblack

Writing Black USA contains full-text essays, books, and poems documenting the African-American experience in the United States from colonial times to the present.

Native American History
J. Kelly Robison

Native American History—General Links

American Indian Studies

http://www.csulb.edu/projects/ais/

This site, created by Troy Johnson at California State University, Long Beach, contains a useful list of links to Native American sites, including recognized and nonrecognized tribal sites, history sites, and activist sites. Also includes a large number of images of Native Americans from the precontact period to the present.

Bureau of Indian Affairs, U.S. Department of the Interior

http://www.doi.gov/bureau-indian-affairs.html

The Bureau of Indian Affairs has information on the tribes, tribal governments, some history, the treaties, and documents on current affairs in Native America. The documents make this site important for researchers and teachers delving into the current situation among Native Americans. The index page is a clearinghouse of Web sites and other governmental sites dealing in some way with Native peoples.

First Nations Site

http://www.dickshovel.com

This very political site, maintained by Jordan S. Dill, contains many internal pages that are generally diatribes against the system rather than anything of real value to the historian. However, the list of offsite links makes this site a good resource.

Images of Native America: From Columbus to Carlisle

http://www.lehigh.edu/~ejg1/natmain.html

Professor Edward J. Gallagher's students at Lehigh University created a series of online essays on how Europeans and Euro-Americans imagined Native peoples. The essays are nicely written and contain links to related sites.

Native American Documents Project

http://www.csusm.edu/projects/nadp/nadp.htm

Located at California State University at San Marcos, this site contains primary material related to allotment and the Rogue River War, Indian Commissioner reports of the 1870s, and some digitized versions of legislation such as the Dawes Act.

Native American History and Culture

http://www.si.edu/resource/faq/nmai/start.htm

An excellent starting place for information on Native American history and culture. Includes online Smithsonian exhibits; resources for teachers, parents, and students; and a quite extensive list of readings for various topics. No links, but this site in itself is worth looking into.

NativeWeb

http://www.nativeweb.org/

An extensive collection of links and articles both for and about indigenous peoples in the Americas. These links and articles are not just of a historical nature, but also contain political, legal, and social materials. Includes search engines, message boards, lists of Native events, and articles about what is currently happening in Native America. An excellent site from which to begin research.

Recommended American Indian Web Sites

http://www.public.iastate.edu/~savega/amer_ind.htm

The list of links in this site by Susan A. Vega García can be found in many other locations, but the list of links to e-journals pertaining to Native issues is impressive.

This Day in North American Indian History

http://americanindian.net/

Phil Konstantine's Native American history and culture Web site seems, at first glance, an amateurish attempt by a history buff to have something on the Web. However, despite the somewhat cheesy "Moons" and other such things,

Konstantine's links page includes an incredible 8,000 links. "Dates" is well worth clicking on.

Native American History—Topical

1492: An Ongoing Voyage

http://www.ibiblio.org/expo/1492.exhibit/Intro.html

This digital exhibit from the Library of Congress contains numerous short essays on life in the Americas and in Europe prior to the European voyages. The "voyage" then continues through a brief view of European conquest of the Americas from the Caribbean to the shores of North America. The thumbnail images within the essays are wonderful visual descriptors of the topics and can be viewed in larger format.

The Avalon Project: Relations Between the United States and Native Americans

http://www.yale.edu/lawweb/avalon/natamer.htm

A superb collection of primary documents relating to Native peoples compiled and digitized by the Yale Law School Avalon Project. The main focus of this site is treaties between the U.S. government and tribes. The site also includes statutes, presidential addresses, and a few court cases involving Native Americans. Although the list of documents on the main Native American page is relatively small, a search of the site will produce many other statutes in HTML format.

The Aztec Calendar

http://www.azteccalendar.com

Created by Rene Voorburg, this nicely done site examines the Aztec calendar. The opening screen depicts the current date in Aztec glyphs. Also contains a calculator that converts any date to its Aztec equivalent. The introduction is a brief, but thorough, essay on the calendar and its meaning.

Cahokia Mounds State Historic Site

http://www.cahokiamounds.com/cahokia.html

Run by the Illinois Historic Preservation Agency, Cahokia is the site of a pre-European city across the river from St. Louis, Missouri. The site lists upcoming events at the park and some information on the archaeology and history of Cahokia. This site seems to be a continual work in progress since it has very few new items posted within the past two years.

National Indian Law Library

http://www.narf.org/nill/Nillindex.html

This site, maintained by the Native American Rights Fund, contains an extensive list of tribal documents, including constitutions and codes. Of equal interest are the links to Supreme Court cases concerning Native issues and extensive links on Native law issues, including primary documents and secondary resources.

Native American Authors

http://www.ipl.org/div/natam/

Part of the Internet Public Library, this section of the larger site can be browsed by author, title, or tribal affiliation. There is no search engine or subject browsing, however. Individual title "cards" contain basic bibliographic information plus some works by the authors.

Native American Nations

http://www.nativeculturelinks.com/nations.html

An alphabetical listing of Web sites either maintained by Native nations themselves or dedicated to a particular nation.

Sipapu: The Anasazi Emergence into the Cyber World

http://sipapu.ucsb.edu/

The site not only begs the reader to explore Anasazi architecture and archaeology, but also asks for contributions. The research section contains a database of Chaco outliers (great house communities) and a bibliography of related print works. It also links to several scholarly papers on the Anasazi. One interesting item is a wonderful little toy that allows 360-degree viewing of the Great Kiva of Chetro Ketl at Chaco Canyon National Monument. Created by John Kanter at the University of California at Santa Barbara.

American West

J. Kelly Robison

The American West is generally thought of as the region of the United States west of the Mississippi River, though sometimes as the area west of the ninety-eighth line of meridian. Yet Western historians also study westward expansion, which brings in that area between the Appalachian Mountains and the Mississippi River. For many years, the "frontier" and the West have been synonymous, harking back to the debate over Frederick Jackson Turner's frontier thesis. In practice, thus, Western American history encompasses a wide scope of place and time. Chronologically, Western History embraces the entirety of human history of the West; from the beginnings to the present day. The study of the American West is a diverse field and the following World Wide Web sites reflect that diversity.

General Resources

America's West—Development and History

http://www.americanwest.com/

Though, at first glance, this site seems hokey and interested solely in the much-mythologized "Old West," it does contain a nicely organized series of pages of useful links to other sites.

New Perspectives on *The West*

http://www.pbs.org/weta/thewest/

The Web site for the PBS special on the American West produced by Ken Burns. An extensive site with links to a wide range of primary documents, articles on various Western topics, and biographies of Western figures.

WestWeb: Western History Resources

http://www.library.csi.cuny.edu/westweb/

A growing collection of topically organized links to Western history resources created and maintained by Catherine Lavender of the City University of New York. The site is broken down into thirty-one different chapters, each of which contains numerous links to sites that specialize in that topic. Some of the topic chapters also contain image thumbnails linked to National Archives photographs. The site is indexed. This site should be the first place anyone interested in Western history sites on the Web should go.

The American West—Topical

Buffalo Soldiers and Indian Wars

http://www.buffalosoldier.net

Although this site concentrates almost exclusively on the role of African-American soldiers in the campaigns against Native peoples, it provides a nice synopsis of that topic. Links embedded within the text (there are photographs as well) go to shorter essays on particular individuals or events or offsite to other pages that cover a topic in more detail.

California Heritage Collection

http://sunsite.Berkeley.EDU/calheritage/

From the Bancroft Library, this site is a collection of over 30,000 images of California's history and culture. The site, part of the Online Archive of California, also includes resources for K–12 instructors. Because of the sheer volume of images, some pages take a long time to load.

California Mission Studies Association

http://www.ca-missions.org/

Dedicated to the study and preservation of California's missions, this organization's Web site contains articles on the missions, a nice glossary of mission-related terms, and some wonderful photographs. The site also maintains both annotated and nonannotated links pages.

Frederick Jackson Turner, "The Significance of the Frontier in American History" (1893)

http://www.library.csi.cuny.edu/dept/history/lavender/frontier.html

Although brief, this page by Catherine Lavender contains not only a link to the hypertext of Turner's "Frontier Thesis," but also links to other sites on Turner and a short, but excellent, bibliography. For the teacher of Western history, Lavender has included a number of questions about the thesis that students could, and perhaps should, use in their examination of Turner.

Ghost Town Gallery

http://www.ghosttowngallery.com

This site is fun rather than of deep interest to the serious research historian. The reader can access photographs of the various ghost towns through either a listing by state or through a clickable map. Some information about the towns, such as dates of founding and significance, are given, though the reader could wish for more.

The Interactive Santa Fe Trail Homepage

http://www.kansasheritage.org/research/sft/

Created for Kansas Heritage, this site's most interesting feature is its extensive list of other sites related to the Santa Fe Trail. The sizable bibliography of

Santa Fe Trail books and articles, print and online, primary and secondary, is also worth looking into. This site is a great starting point from which K–12 students can explore the history of the trail and the people who used it.

The Japanese-American Internment

http://www.geocities.com/Athens/8420/main.html

Contains a time line of the Japanese-American internment, basic information on the camps, and remembrances of internees. Numerous links to other Web sites and to primary documents are also available on this site by John Yu.

The Lewis and Clark Expedition

http://www.pbs.org/lewisandclark/

The Ken Burns PBS production companion site. Contains excerpts from the Corps of Discovery journals, a time line of the journey, maps of the expedition, and numerous other related materials. Also contains interviews with authorities on the expedition and classroom resources for teachers.

Mountain Men and the Fur Trade: Sources of the History of the Fur Trade in the Rocky Mountain West

http://www.xmission.com/%7Edrudy/amm.html

A resource for the study of the fur trade era. This site contains transcribed primary documents from the fur trade era, digitized business records, and a nice collection of digitized images of artifacts and art from the period. A nicely done site.

Multicultural American West

http://www.wsu.edu:8080/~amerstu/mw/

Essentially an online, annotated bibliography of sites relevant to the study of the American West. As the site's name implies, most of the resources and links are related to ethnicity in the West. The number of links and resources, including documents and first-person accounts, is impressive. Designed by Washington State University's American Studies program.

The Overland Trail

http://www.over-land.com/

A site dedicated to Ben Holladay's Overland Trail, created by Elizabeth Larson. Contains a large amount of information, including a clickable map to articles. The articles range from those strictly about the route and stopovers to Indian problems along the route. Links to other sites are categorized by topic and include brief descriptions.

The Silent Westerns: Early Movie Myths of the American West

http://xroads.virginia.edu/~HYPER/HNS/Westfilm/west.html

Mary Halnon's site devoted to the portrayal of the West in silent film. The brief, but excellent essays on the early film industry and mythologized elements in the Western movies are supplemented by footnotes and images of early films and silent movie stars.

Utah History Encyclopedia

http://www.media.utah.edu/UHE/

Just as the name implies, the UHE is encyclopedic in style and scope. Over 200 contributors wrote close to 600 articles, containing more than 200 photographs, on topics in Utah history. The site does not contain a search engine, though this hardly matters since the frames version of the site lists topics alphabetically and navigation is easy as long as readers know what they are looking for.

The Vigilantes of Montana: Secret Trials and Midnight Hangings

http://montana-vigilantes.org/

This site, maintained by Louis Schmittroth, contains a wealth of information on the Montana vigilantes. The site contains online books and articles by well-known Montana historians. The politics of the site are apparent, but the information contained within is well worth perusing.

Who Killed William Robinson?

http://web.uvic.ca/history-robinson/

A wonderful resource for teachers, this site by Ruth Sandwell and John Lutz takes the reader through a historical mystery to determine the identity of a murderer. Contains primary documents and asks pertinent questions dealing with race, politics, and settlement.

Women Artists of the American West, Past & Present

http://www.sla.purdue.edu/waaw/

Created by Susan Ressler of Purdue University and Jerrold Maddox of Penn State, this online exhibit of female artists provides essays on those artists or particular groups of artists. The Web site is originally from a distance-learning course, as the syllabus makes abundantly clear. But the syllabus also ties together the various elements of the site into a coherent framework.

Colonial American History (1492–1763)

Edward Ragan, Scott A. Merriman, and Dennis A. Trinkle

Metasites

From Revolution to Reconstruction

http://odur.let.rug.nl/~usa/usa.htm

This metasite, maintained by the Arts Faculty of the University of Groningen, Netherlands, is a massive resource for all aspects of American history. The site is divided into five general sections: Outlines, Essays, Documents, Biographies, and Presidents. This site is organized around several U.S. Information Agency publications: *An Outline of American History, An Outline of the American Economy, An Outline of American Government,* and *An Outline of American Literature.* While the text of these outlines has not been changed, they have been enriched with hypertext links to relevant documents, original essays, and other Internet sites. Currently this site contains over 3,000 relevant HTML documents.

Institutions (Museums, Libraries, Historical Societies, and Online Organizations)

Archives of Maryland Online

http://aomol.net/html/index.html

The site is sponsored by the Maryland State Archives. At present, it "provides access to over 471,000 historical documents that form the constitutional, legal, legislative, judicial, and administrative basis of Maryland's government." Researchers can gain access to full-text documents from Maryland's entire executive, legislative, and judicial history. This is a bold initiative to provide access to "records that are scattered among a number of repositories and that often exist only on rapidly disintegrating paper."

Colonial Williamsburg

http://www.history.org/

The official Web site for Colonial Williamsburg, one of the most extensive historical reconstructions in the United States. The well-illustrated site offers tourist information, educational resources, a colonial dateline, a historical glossary of names, places, and events in Colonial Williamsburg, photos of buildings and people, articles from *Colonial Williamsburg: The Journal of the Colonial Williamsburg Foundation,* and an extensive section on colonial lifestyles.

Common-place

http://www.common-place.org/

Common-place is sponsored by the American Antiquarian Society and the Gilder Lehrman Institute of American History in association with the Florida State University Department of History. It bills itself as a "common place for exploring and exchanging ideas about early American history and culture" in a way that is "a bit friendlier than a scholarly journal, [and] a bit more scholarly than a popular magazine." Published quarterly, this online journal includes essays, books reviews, roundtable discussions, and an open forum for commenting on articles that appear in *Common-place.*

H-OIEAHC Discussion Network

http://www.h-net.msu.edu/~ieahcweb/

This is the Web site of the H-OIEAHC discussion list, which is sponsored by the Omohundro Institute of Early American History and Culture (OIEAHC). Affiliated with H-Net, this group focuses on colonial and early American history. Its Web pages contain information about the discussion list and allow users to subscribe. They also include calls for papers, conference announcements, bibliographies, book reviews, articles, and links to related sites, including the Omohundro Institute.

Jamestown Rediscovery Project

http://www.apva.org/jr.html

The Jamestown Rediscovery Project, sponsored by the Association for the Preservation of Virginia Antiquities, is a ten-year comprehensive excavation of Jamestown that began in 1994. This site offers photographs and progress reports on the project to date, two online exhibits, and plans for the future.

The Library of Virginia Digital Library Program

http://www.lva.lib.va.us/dlp/index.htm

The Library of Virginia's Digital Library Program is an internationally recognized effort to preserve, digitize, and provide access to significant archival and library collections. Users can search births, deaths, marriages, wills, and Bible records, genealogy and biography databases, photograph collections, and maps, gazetteers, and geographical resources, among other things. Perhaps the most stunning accomplishment is the Land Office Patents and Grants Database, which is searchable by keyword and provides links to scanned copies of the original Virginia land patents. All in all, this is a remarkable tool for Virginia historians and genealogists.

Plimoth-on-Web: Plimoth Plantation's Web Site

http://www.plimoth.org

The official Web site for the living history museum of seventeenth-century Plymouth. Like the living history museum, the Web site brings 1627 Plimoth back to life.

Religion and the Founding of the American Republic

http://www.loc.gov/exhibits/religion/religion.html

This online exhibit, sponsored by the Library of Congress, is a nuanced presentation of America's rich religious traditions. Divided into sections that include downloadable JPEG images and scanned texts, the exhibit explores America's history as a seventeenth-century religious refuge. It also examines the Great Awakening of the eighteenth century and its influence on the religious attitudes of the American Revolution. Additional sections discuss the separation of church and state as well as the religious diversity of the early republic.

Society of Early Americanists Home Page

http://www.hnet.uci.edu/mclark/seapage.htm

The SEA aims to further the exchange of ideas and information among scholars of various disciplines who study the literature and culture of America up to approximately 1800. The society publishes a newsletter, operates an electronic bulletin board, and maintains the Web site. The site contains an excellent list of links on colonial and early American history.

Topical Histories

1492: An Ongoing Voyage

http://www.ibiblio.org/expo/1492.exhibit/Intro.html

1492: An Ongoing Voyage is an electronic exhibit of the Library of Congress. The site weaves images and text to explore what life was like in pre- and post-Columbian Europe, Africa, and the Americas. The site examines the effect that the discovery of America had on each continent, stressing the dark elements of colonization. There are excellent maps, documents, artwork, and supporting text.

1755: The French and Indian War Home Page

http://web.syr.edu/~laroux/

Created by Larry Laroux, a professional writer, this site serves as a prologue to Laroux's forthcoming book *White Coats,* which will examine the soldiers who fought in the French and Indian War of 1755. The site is presently under construction, but Laroux eventually aims to include histories of important battles, a list of French soldiers who fought in the war, and other statistical records. The site already contains a brief narrative account of the war, along with some interesting information and trivia.

Iroquois Oral Traditions

http://www.indians.org/welker/iroqoral.htm

This Web site is part of the American Indian Heritage Foundation's Indigenous Peoples' Literature page. The tradition of De-Ka-Nah-Wi-Da (the chief who brought peace and power in the traditional stories) and Hiawatha, who between them, were traditionally credited with creating the Iroquois Confederation, is recounted here along with over twenty other Iroquoian stories about the people of the longhouse and their place in the world. Many of these stories were translated into English and recorded in the late nineteenth and early twentieth centuries.

Jonathan Edwards

http://www.jonathanedwards.com/

Mark Trigsted of Flower Mound, Texas, has created what he describes as the "World's Largest Edwards Web Site." And he may be right. Trigsted has transcribed nearly a hundred of Edwards's sermons on topics such as judgment, doctrine, shepherding, and charity. In addition to sermons, Trigsted has included extensive excerpts from Edwards's writings on theology, science, and religious revival in the eighteenth century.

Salem Witchcraft Trials: 1692 (Famous Trials in American History)

http://www.law.umkc.edu/faculty/projects/ftrials/salem/salem.htm

Doug Linder, a professor of law at the University of Missouri-Kansas City Law School, has compiled many of the relevant Salem witchcraft documents as part of his Famous Trials Web site. Linder has included a detailed chronology, several maps, selected images, information on the legal procedure in witch-craft cases, and brief biographies of all major participants in the trials. Also included is a wealth of relevant transcribed documents, such as Cotton Mather's *Memorable Providences,* the arrest warrants, examinations and evidence, various petitions, and several letters from New England governor William Phips. The evidence is presented objectively without the myriad of odd historical explanations.

Salem Witch Museum

http://www.salemwitchmuseum.com/

This site primarily presents travel information, including a map of witch trial sites with links to photographs. Also offered is an interactive FAQ section on witch trials and local history. Other resources are being added rapidly.

The Thanksgiving Tradition

http://www.plimoth.org/Library/Thanksgiving/thanksgi.htm

The research, education, and public relations departments at Plimoth Plantation: The Living History Museum of 17th-Century Plymouth present a cornu-copia of information on the American Thanksgiving tradition. Included at this site are relevant primary documents, essays, a sample menu, and a list of alternate claimants for the "first Thanksgiving."

Virtual Jamestown: Jamestown and the Virginia Experiment

http://www.virtualjamestown.org/

Created by Crandal Shifflett, professor of history at Virginia Tech, the "Virtual Jamestown Archive is a digital research, teaching, and learning project that explores the legacies of the Jamestown settlement." Included are links to primary documents and images; digitized, 360-degree reconstructions of the fort; discussion of Indian, African, and English life around Jamestown; and time lines. This site has been included in the NEH EDSITEment Project. If you cannot go to Jamestown in person, this is the next best thing.

Wampum—Treaties, Sacred Records

http://www.kstrom.net/isk/art/beads/wampum.html

This site offers information on the construction and meaning of wampum to Native America. Included are images and descriptions along with links that provide more detail.

Documents and Images

18th Century Documents

http://www.yale.edu/lawweb/avalon/18th.htm

This first-rate collection of documents is part of the Avalon Project at Yale Law School. Included here are many of the significant American colonial legal documents of the eighteenth century. These documents detail the Anglo-American imperial relationship and the major political conflicts of the era of the American Revolution, as well as those of the early American national period. There are links to document sets such as *The Federalist Papers,* the state and federal constitutions, and early presidential papers.

American Colonist's Library: A Treasury of Primary Documents

http://www.edline.net/pages/Catholic_Central_High_School/Classes/03842501/library

Compiled by Richard Gardiner, a history instructor at University Lake School (Hartland, Wisconsin), the American Colonist's Library is a comprehensive gateway to the early American primary source documents that are currently available online. Included in the list are links to historical sources that influenced American colonists, online collections of the work of major early American political leaders, the text of the Acts of Parliament concerning the American colonies, numerous American Revolution military documents, and much more. The hundreds of documents are grouped chronologically from 500 BCE to 1800 CE. As the site boasts, "if it isn't here, it probably is not available online anywhere."

American Historical Images on File: The Native American Experience

http://www.csulb.edu/projects/ais/nae/

This collection of historical images of Native American peoples was developed by Professor Troy Johnson of California State University, Long Beach. The images span the chronological range of Native America, from Paleo-Indians to the present. They are presented here with full permission of Facts On File, Inc., but take note of the copyright details before you use them for your own purposes.

A Briefe and True Report of the New Found Land of Virginia

http://docsouth.unc.edu/nc/hariot/hariot.html

This Web site includes the transcription of the 1590 folio edition of Thomas Hariot's *A Briefe and True Report of the New Found Land of Virginia,* which is "the first original book in English relating to what is now America, written by one of the first Englishmen to attempt new world colonization." The images from Hariot's volume, which were based on John White's watercolors and engraved by Theodore de Bry, are reproduced here in facsimile.

Colonial Charters, Grants and Related Documents

http://www.yale.edu/lawweb/avalon/states/statech.htm

The Avalon Project at Yale Law School has compiled a wide range of colonial-era charters. Many of the documents are general charters granted to individuals, such as *Priviledges and Prerogatives Granted by Their Catholic Majesties to Christopher Columbus* (1492) and Queen Elizabeth's 1584 charter to Sir Walter Raleigh. Organized by colony, the site includes founding documents as well as updated charters and related material.

Columbus and the Age of Discovery

http://muweb.millersville.edu/~columbus/

A searchable database of over 1,100 text articles pertaining to Columbus and themes of discovery and encounter. The site, which allows unrestricted access, was built by the History Department of Millersville University of Pennsylvania in conjunction with the U.S. Christopher Columbus Quincentenary Jubilee Commission of 1992.

Early America

http://earlyamerica.com/earlyamerica/index.html

The main focus of Early America is primary source material from eighteenth-century America. The site is the public access branch of the commercial American Digital Library, which sells reproductions of hundreds of early American documents from the Keigwin and Mathews Collection of eighteenth- and nineteenth-century historical documents, as well as images, maps, and other items.

Gottlieb Mittelberger, *On the Misfortune of Indentured Servants* (1754)

http://odur.let.rug.nl/~usa/D/1601–1650/mittelberger/servan.htm

In 1750 the German immigrant Gottlieb Mittelberger arrived in Philadelphia, where he taught school. When he returned to Germany in 1754, he wrote this account describing the miserable life that servants endured in the colonies.

The Jesuit Relations and Allied Documents: 1610 to 1791

http://puffin.creighton.edu/jesuit/relations/

This impressive undertaking is the work of Rev. Raymond A. Bucko, a Jesuit priest and professor of anthropology at Creighton University in Omaha, and Thom Mentrak, a historical interpreter at the Ste. Marie Among the Iroquois Museum in Syracuse, New York. This site contains the scanned and transcribed version of the seventy-one-volume edition edited by Reuben Gold Thwaites in the late nineteenth century. *The Jesuit Relations* began as private reports between the Jesuit missionaries in New France and their superiors in Paris. The Jesuits made extensive reports on the native peoples they encountered, making this source a must for serious research into Huron and Haudenosaunee (Five Nations) culture in the seventeenth century.

John White Drawings/Theodore de Bry Engravings

http://www.virtualjamestown.org/images/white_debry_html/introduction.html

By a special licensing agreement with the British Museum, Virtual Jamestown (see above) has digitized a collection of John White's fabulous watercolors that depict coastal Algonquian life around the Roanoke colony in 1585. These watercolors were the basis of Theodore de Bry's engravings.

The Leslie Brock Center for the Study of Colonial Currency

http://etext.lib.virginia.edu/users/brock

This Web site seeks to take some of the confusion out of understanding and working with colonial currencies. Included here are eighteenth-century pamphlets and other contemporary writings that relate to currency, as well as more recent articles on the various colonies and currencies and links to additional resources covering currency rates and monetary history.

Mayflower History

http://www.mayflowerhistory.com/

Caleb Johnson, a *Mayflower* descendant, has authored this detailed site about the people who settled at Plymouth colony. Includes a *Mayflower* passenger list with biographies for each passenger and a history of the voyage and early settlement. There is also a genealogy of the early Plymouth settlers along with passenger lists from other voyages to Plymouth colony. The site also contains full-text primary sources from the first three decades of Plymouth settlement as well as links to *Mayflower* societies, museums, and other resources.

Notes on the State of Virginia

http://etext.lib.virginia.edu/toc/modeng/public/JefVirg.html

Constructed as a series of answers to questions posed by foreign observers, Thomas Jefferson's *Notes,* first published in 1787, provides a unique description of the natural and human landscapes of Virginia in the late eighteenth century. This e-text version is sponsored by the University of Virginia Library Electronic Text Center.

Perry-Castañeda Library Map Collection (University of Texas)

http://www.lib.utexas.edu/maps/histus.html

The University of Texas Library presents its impressive collection of historical maps in JPEG format for convenient downloads. These historical maps of the United States are categorized under the following headings: Early Inhabitants, Exploration and Settlement, Territorial Growth, Military History, and Later Historical Maps. Also included are links to additional historical map resources.

The Plymouth Colony Archive Project at the University of Virginia

http://www.people.virginia.edu/~jfd3a/

The Plymouth Colony Archive presents a collection of searchable texts, including seminar analysis of various topics, biographical profiles of selected colonists, probate inventories, wills, "Glossary and Notes on Plymouth Colony," and "Vernacular House Forms in Seventeenth-Century Plymouth Colony: An Analysis of Evidence from the Plymouth Colony Room-by-Room Probate Inventories 1633–1685," by Patricia E. Scott Deetz and James Deetz. The site itself is maintained by the Deetzs, pioneers in material culture studies.

Rare Map Collection—Colonial America

http://www.libs.uga.edu/darchive/hargrett/maps/colamer.html

The Hargrett Rare Book and Manuscript Library at the University of Georgia has digitized an impressive collection of rare maps. The Colonial America section includes maps that date from 1625 through 1774. In addition, there are links to maps from earlier and later periods.

Theodore de Bry Copper Plate Engravings

http://www.csulb.edu/projects/ais/woodcuts/

This collection of historical images of Native peoples is the digitized versions of copperplate engravings made by the Flemish engraver and publisher Theodore de Bry. The engravings are based on the watercolor paintings of the sixteenth-century English explorer John White. The site was developed by Professor Troy Johnson of California State University, Long Beach.

Revolutionary America
Robert Lee

Metasites

American Revolution

http://www.americanrevolution.org/

This comprehensive metasite contains over 1,900 links to nearly every topic on the American Revolution available through the Internet. The links are broken down into three sections—for historians, genealogists, and reenactors—and spread out over 300 pages. Visitors may also peruse a vast and growing library of exclusive content. The Scholar's Showcase, featuring historical essays and e-books, especially warrants a visit.

Eighteenth-Century Resources

http://www.andromeda.rutgers.edu/~jlynch/18th/

A self-described "labor of love" by Jack Lynch, an English professor at Rutgers University, this metasite houses an expansive collection of links covering the "very long" eighteenth century. Topics run the gamut of arts and sciences, with an emphasis on British history and literature. In assembling the site, Lynch targeted the needs of students and researchers, providing links to e-texts, professional resources, and Web pages of other eighteenth-century scholars.

WWW Virtual Library: Revolutionary Era, 1765–1783

http://vlib.iue.it/history/USA/ERAS/revolutionary.html

Dr. Lynn H. Nelson launched the Virtual Library at the University of Kansas in 1993 and the site has since been transferred to the domain of the European University Institute in Florence, Italy. It has a voluminous, bulleted index with a spartan design that allows visitors to follow chronological, geographical, or topical orientations across a bevy of sites. Relevant content also appears in a separate index covering the constitutional era, 1786–1800.

General Sites

The Adams Family Papers: An Electronic Archive

http://www.masshist.org/digitaladams/aea/index.html

The Massachusetts Historical Society's collection of John Adams's papers cuts across the revolutionary era and offers valuable insight into Massachusetts politics, the fledgling American government, international affairs, and the personal lives of the Adams family. The archive is divided into three sections: John Adams's diary, his autobiography, and his correspondence with his wife, Abigail Adams. In addition to illuminating eighteenth-century courtship and married life, John and Abigail's letters provide a female perspective on the events of the period.

The American Revolution and Its Era: Maps and Charts of North America and the West Indies, 1750–1789

http://memory.loc.gov/ammem/gmdhtml/armhtml/armhome.html

This large and growing Web site will eventually display digital images of over 2,000 period maps and charts held by the Library of Congress. Simply put, there is no better online resource on the geography of North America as it was visualized during the revolutionary era.

The American Revolution Educational New Media Project

http://independence.nyhistory.org/

Funded by the U.S. Department of Education, this Web site initiates the New-York Historical Society's plan to bring its vast revolutionary era records to the

Internet. The project's first installment, an online exhibition titled Independence and Its Enemies in New York, showcases dozens of digital documents, games for students, and lesson plans for educators.

The American Revolution: Lighting Freedom's Flame

http://www.nps.gov/revwar/

The National Park Service created Lighting Freedom's Flame to promote awareness of federally owned revolutionary parks. The invitingly designed site integrates links to relevant national parks with stories from the period, biographies of major figures, and various educational resources for students and teachers. It also offers virtual tours of these parks, announces upcoming public history events, and features a section on the "unfinished Revolution." The emphasis falls as much on the Revolution's legacy as the war itself, providing an interesting introduction to the subject of public memory.

American Revolution

http://www.americanrevolution.com/

This site features a wealth of material on the Revolution, organized in over fifty topical links. All the information is put forth in a straightforward, encyclopedic style, interlaced with hyperlinks to simplify navigation. Topics range widely, including traditional discussions of military and political issues, social histories of the roles played by women, African-Americans, and immigrants, and even some quirky accounts like the "History of Yankee Doodle Dandy."

The American Revolution

http://theamericanrevolution.org

Along with two time lines and short biographies of political figures, this site contains solid accounts of key battles in the American Revolution. Each brief description includes a battle synopsis and an analysis of the event's place in the scope of the war, as well as humanizing details like the temperature, weather, and casualty statistics. In an attempt to build the relationship between online and traditional secondary sources, most pages direct readers to recent monographs pertinent to the topic at hand.

Archiving Early America

http://earlyamerica.com

Web surfers undeterred by a few flashy ads will be rewarded with this site's archive of eighteenth-century primary sources, including images of period maps, newspapers, and pamphlets, all displayed in their original format. The content varies from the well-known Articles of Confederation to a rare issue of *The Maryland Gazette* recounting George Washington's trip to the Ohio Valley in 1754. There are also sections on notable women, famous obituaries and portraits, and an online journal, *The Early American Review.*

Avalon Project at the Yale Law School: 18th Century Documents

http://www.yale.edu/lawweb/avalon/18th.htm

This frequently updated site should be one of the first stops for students and researchers looking for primary sources on revolutionary America. It archives full-text transcriptions of state constitutions, colonial acts and edicts, government treaties, political pamphlets, and various other records of eighteenth-century history, law, and diplomacy. The documents appear in alphabetical order, but the site's user-friendly format also permits navigation by subject or time frame. A search function on a full copy of *The Federalist Papers* is one of the project's many useful features designed to expedite research.

Bibliographies of the War of American Independence

http://www.army.mil/cmh-pg/reference/revbib/revwar.htm

These extensive bibliographies, amassed by the U.S. Army Center of Military History, are a helpful source to consult before venturing out to the library. However, the bibliographies were originally compiled for the 1983 publication *The Continental Army* and the site was last updated in 2000, so be sure to heed the introduction's advice to cross-reference.

The Black Patriots Foundation

http://www.blackpatriots.org/

Over 5,000 blacks fought in the American Revolution. An initiative to restore the memory of their contributions led to the founding of the Black Patriots Foundation in 1985. Its Web site, part of that effort, includes an e-book copy of the classic work *The Colored Patriots of the American Revolution,* links on the American Revolution and black history, and information on the memorial to the black patriots being built on the National Mall.

Documents From the Continental Congress and Constitutional Convention, 1774–1789

http://memory.loc.gov/ammem/collections/continental

One of American Memory's many revolutionary era collections, this site features hundreds of keyword-searchable broadsides and other records on the

Continental Congress and Constitutional Convention. The broadsides cover the well-known drafting and ratification of the Constitution, but also pertain to Congress's more workaday tasks of holding committee meetings and issuing resolutions. The additional documents include petitions, political pamphlets, diplomatic and financial reports, and papers from state and local governments. To see how some of these documents have been interpreted, check out the online exhibits, Declaring Independence: Drafting the Documents and Religion and the Founding of the American Republic, available through the site's related resources page.

The History Place: American Revolution

http://www.historyplace.com/unitedstates/revolution/index.html

The History Place's six-part time line spans from early colonial history up to 1790 and is especially detailed during the war years from 1775 to 1783. Its simple format makes it easy to get a general sense of the chronology of the Revolution or quickly find specific dates. For anyone taking a course or writing a paper on this era, this site merits a bookmark.

The Thomas Jefferson Papers

http://memory.loc.gov/ammem/collections/jefferson_papers/index.html

As a slave owner whose articulation of natural rights in the Declaration of Independence framed the Revolution, Jefferson is a case study in the complexities of early American life. The Library of Congress holds 27,000 Jefferson documents and has greatly simplified serious research by posting digital images of many of them on its American Memory page. The papers come in a variety of forms, including correspondence, addresses, legal documents, and scientific writings. Students and teachers looking for a more public history-oriented introduction to Jefferson will find one at the media-rich Monticello home page at http://www.monticello.org/.

Journals of the Continental Congress

http://lcweb2.loc.gov/ammem/amlaw/lwjc.html

Between 1904 and 1937, the Library of Congress published the thirty-four-volume *Journals of the Continental Congress, 1774–1789,* based on the original journals kept by Secretary Charles Thompson and on other congressional records. The American Memory project has digitized the work and equipped it with a search function, bringing easy access to this immense chronicle of the legislative process that transformed America from a confederation of rebellious colonies into a unified nation under the current Constitution.

Loyalist, British Songs & Poetry of the American Revolution

http://users.erols.com/candidus/music.htm

This small site displays the lyrics to ten British songs and the names of their tunes. Humorous ditties like "The Congress" offer a novel way to access the Loyalist perspective. Just as valuable as the page itself are its links to other Loyalist resources, including a link to *Plain Truth,* James Chalmers's rejoinder to Thomas Paine's *Common Sense.*

Omohundro Institute of Early American History & Culture

http://www.wm.edu/oieahc/

This Web page is an online hub for scholars studying early America. Visitors will find recent tables of contents for *The William & Mary Quarterly,* conference and colloquia announcements, the institute's newsletter, and a variety of links. The page also provides access to the institute's H-Net discussion forum, an excellent resource designed for (but not limited to) academics.

The Online Institute for Advanced Loyalist Studies

http://www.royalprovincial.com/

This Web page provides an interesting introduction to the Tory worldview during the American Revolution. A good—albeit far from comprehensive—sampling of documents related to the Loyalist experience appears in the sections titled History and Military. The site is aimed chiefly at those interested in military research, genealogy, and living history, but could also be used effectively for class discussions on point of view in historical narratives.

Thomas Paine National Historical Association Web Archive

http://www.thomaspaine.org/newarch.html

Thomas Paine did as much as anyone to foment the Revolution when he published *Common Sense* in 1776. Along with biographies of Paine and a chronology of his writings, this site hosts a full-text archive of Paine's corpus—essential reading for anyone interested in the ideology of the Revolution.

RevWar75

http://www.revwar75.com/

Primarily for researchers interested in the microhistory of the Continental Army and, to a lesser extent, the British Crown Forces, this site dons an impressive index of surviving orderly books. Since its inception, the site has grown to include a library with scholarly articles and primary sources pertaining to the life of the common soldier, as well as indexes of land and sea battles and Revolutionary War articles from the journal *Military Collector & Historian.* Those studying specific military units or campaigns will find this page particularly helpful.

Spy Letters of the American Revolution

http://www.si.umich.edu/spies/

Covert intelligence on enemy location, troop strength, and strategy gathered by spies and traitors was an integral component of the execution of the Revolutionary War. This online exhibit, assembled from the Sir Henry Clinton Collection at the University of Michigan, offers a rare window into the intelligence operations of the American and British armies. The site provides multifaceted access to primary sources on subjects ranging from the infamous Benedict Arnold to lesser-known female spies.

The Sullivan-Clinton Campaign: History, The Iroquois & George Washington

http://sullivanclinton.com/

This multimedia site focuses on the Sullivan-Clinton Campaign against the Iroquois in 1779, with a particular emphasis on Indian dispossession in New York. Along with contemporary texts and brief articles, the site features photo galleries, original animation, and interactive maps that together provide an excellent overview of the Six Nations role in the Revolution.

USHistory

http://www.ushistory.org/

The Independence Hall Association in Philadelphia developed this "Congress of Web sites" focused on Pennsylvania in the revolutionary era. On these colorful and informative pages, Web surfers can take a virtual tour of Philadelphia's Historic Mile, delve into the myth and history of the American flag at Betsy Ross's house, be introduced to the life of Benjamin Franklin, and learn the history of the Liberty Bell. Additional sections on Valley Forge, Brandywine Battlefield, and the Philadelphia Campaign of 1777 analyze Pennsylvania as a military front.

George Washington: A National Treasure

http://www.georgewashington.si.edu/index.html

This online companion to the National Portrait Gallery's touring exhibition of Gilbert Stuart's George Washington portraiture is a study in national memory.

The centerpiece is an interactive version of the iconic Landsdowne portrait that highlights the painting's symbolism. The site's "Patriot Papers," which follow the exhibition across the country, tell Washington-inspired stories and the "Town Hall" hosts discussion forums. Along with puzzles for kids, there are educational aids for teachers and families. The links page functions as an authoritative metasite on Washington. From here, the general public can visit the virtual Mount Vernon and researchers can access extraordinary digital archives at the Library of Congress and the University of Virginia.

Early United States History (1783–1860)

Edward Ragan

Metasites

From Revolution to Reconstruction

http://odur.let.rug.nl/~usa/usa.htm

This metasite, maintained by the Arts Faculty of the University of Groningen, Netherlands, is a massive resource for all aspects of American history. The site is divided into five general sections: Outlines, Essays, Documents, Biographies, and Presidents. This site is organized around several U.S. Information Agency publications: *An Outline of American History, An Outline of the American Economy, An Outline of American Government,* and *An Outline of American Literature.* While the text of these outlines has not been changed, they have been enriched with hypertext links to relevant documents, original essays, and other Internet sites. Currently this site contains over 3,000 relevant HTML documents.

The Making of America

http://www.umdl.umich.edu/moa/

The Making of America is a digital library of primary sources in American social history from the antebellum period through Reconstruction. Contained in this collection are approximately 8,500 books and 50,000 journal articles on subjects as far ranging as education, psychology, American history, sociology, religion, and science and technology. The project, sponsored by the University of Michigan and Cornell University, "represents a major collaborative endeavor in preservation and electronic access to historical texts." These texts are searchable by keyword with links to digitized copies of the nineteenth-century imprints. This is an outstanding site for those who need access to nineteenth-century documents.

Nineteenth-Century Documents Project

http://www.furman.edu/~benson/docs/

Lloyd Benson has prepared an extensive collection of primary documents. The period is categorized topically, and all topics seem to emphasize increased sectional differences and the coming of the Civil War. The documents are grouped under the following headings: Early National Politics, Slavery and Sectionalism, the Nebraska Bill, the Sumner Caning, the Dred Scott Decision, John Brown's Raid on Harpers Ferry, an 1850s Statistical Almanac, the 1860 Election, Secession and War, and the Post–Civil War Era.

Institutions (Museums, Libraries, Historical Societies, and Online Organizations)

American Treasures of the Library of Congress

http://lcweb.loc.gov/exhibits/treasures/

This is a substantial virtual exhibit from the Library of Congress collections that contains a variety of items, including letters by Thomas Jefferson and John Quincy Adams's notes from the *Amistad* case. Substantial detail and historical context are provided for each component of the collection. Jefferson, whose personal library became the core of the Library of Congress, arranged his books into three types of knowledge, corresponding to three faculties of the mind: memory (history), reason (philosophy), and imagination (fine arts).

Amistad: Race and the Boundaries of Freedom in Antebellum Maritime America

http://amistad.mysticseaport.org/main/welcome.html

This site is part of the Mystic Seaport Museum. It contains information on the *Amistad* slave ship, the revolt of its cargo, and the Supreme Court trial of its slave mutineers. The focus of this site is living history. A time line of events is provided as are classroom lessons for teachers.

The Early America Review

http://www.earlyamerica.com/review/

This electronic "Journal of Fact and Opinion on the People, Issues and Events of 18th-Century America" is edited by Don Vitale. The journal contains wide-ranging articles about the social, political, and military developments of this period. An excellent example of the ways in which modern scholarship seeks to combine traditional formats with technology.

Historic Mount Vernon—The Home of Our First President, George Washington

http://www.mountvernon.org

Visitors to the official Mount Vernon Web site will find information designed to meet a variety of needs. In addition to a virtual tour of the house and grounds, this site contains a biography of Washington written at the fifth-grade level, teaching aids such as quizzes, and an electronic image collection.

The Gerrit Smith Virtual Museum

http://www.NYHistory.com/gerritsmith/index.htm

The New York History Net has detailed information about the abolitionist leader Gerrit Smith. Includes a biographical essay, bibliography, and portrait gallery of Smith and his family. This site was developed in cooperation with the Syracuse University Library Department of Special Collections and Hamilton College (Clinton, New York), both of which hold substantial portions of the Gerrit Smith's papers.

Topical Histories

African Canadian Heritage Tour

http://www.ciaccess.com/~jdnewby/heritage/african.htm

The African Canadian Heritage Tour celebrates the history of those who made the arduous journey to freedom in Canada via the Underground Railroad. This site is the central Internet presence for a collection of five historical sites that provide information about the Underground Railroad and the African-Canadian settlement of southwestern Ontario: the Buxton Historical Site and Museum, the North American Black Historical Museum, the Sandwich Baptist Church, the Uncle Tom's Cabin–Josiah Henson Interpretive Site, and the Woodstock Institute Sertoma Help Centre.

Abolition: The African-American Mosaic

http://www.loc.gov/exhibits/african/afam005.html

The Library of Congress provides information on the history of the antislavery movement in America that led to the formation, in 1833, of the American

Anti-Slavery Society. Includes references to Library of Congress holdings such as abolitionist publications, minutes of antislavery meetings, handbills, advertisements, songs, and appeals to women. Demonstrates the tradition of the abolition movement in America before 1833.

The American Whig Party (1834–1856)

http://odur.let.rug.nl/~usa/E/uswhig/whigsxx.htm

Essay by Hal Morris that describes the rise of the American Whig Party as an opposition to President Andrew Jackson's kinglike tendencies. Included is a history of the Whig Party and links to biographies of Whig presidents and political leaders in America.

John Brown

http://www.pbs.org/weta/thewest/people/a_c/brown.htm

This PBS-sponsored site contains a biography of the radical abolitionist John Brown.

James Fenimore Cooper (1789–1851)

http://odur.let.rug.nl/~usa/LIT/cooper.htm

Kathryn VanSpanckeren's literary biography evaluates James Fenimore Cooper's role in the development of the American novel. Traces the familial and cultural influences that led Cooper to create Natty Bumppo, his chief protagonist.

Chronology of the Secession Crisis

http://members.aol.com/jfepperson/secesh.html

James F. Epperson charts the chronology of events that culminated with the firing upon Fort Sumter, South Carolina. The site includes links to relevant documents.

Democracy in America: De Tocqueville

http://xroads.virginia.edu/~HYPER/DETOC/home.html

The American studies program at the University of Virginia maintains this site, which explores American democracy in the 1830s. De Tocqueville traveled across the United States in the 1830s, and his itinerary, letters, and journal entries are here combined with cultural artifacts from the period to provide a glimpse of American democracy and culture in the early nineteenth century. Among other topics, this site examines issues of gender, race, and religion for the period.

The Founding Fathers

http://www.archives.gov/national-archives-experience/charters/
constitution_founding_fathers.html

The National Archives and Records Administration has compiled biographies of the delegates to the Constitutional Convention of 1787. This is an excellent place to start when studying the U.S. Constitution and the Founding Fathers.

Benjamin Franklin: A Documentary History

http://www.english.udel.edu/lemay/franklin/

J.A. Leo Lemay, the Henry Francis du Pont Winterthur Professor of Colonial American Literature at the University of Delaware, gives visitors a peek into the research that he is doing for a Franklin biography. He offers a detailed chronology of Franklin's life that is divided into three stages: early life, professional interests, and political career. Each event in Franklin's life is verified with citations that are connected to a bibliography of primary documents.

Benjamin Franklin: Glimpses of the Man

http://www.fi.edu/franklin/rotten.html

The Franklin Institute maintains this site, which celebrates the life and work of Benjamin Franklin. It emphasizes his work as statesman, printer, scientist, philosopher, musician, economist, and inventor.

Horace Greeley (1811–1872)

http://equinox.unr.edu/homepage/fenimore/greeley.html

David H. Fenimore of the University of Nevada, Reno, offers a detailed biography of Greeley complete with photographs, quotations, a Greeley bibliography, and links to related information.

Sarah Grimké, Angelina Grimké (Biographies)

http://www.gale.com/free_resources/whm/bio/grimk_sisters.htm

Gale Publishing has created these biographies of Sarah Grimké and Angelina Grimké that focus on their work for abolition and women's suffrage.

Thomas Jefferson: A Film by Ken Burns

http://www.pbs.org/jefferson/

This PBS-sponsored site is the online version of Ken Burns's documentary about Thomas Jefferson. It features selections of Jefferson's writings used in the film, the transcripts of interviews conducted for the film, tips for educators on teaching about Jefferson, and classroom activities for students.

The Thomas Jefferson Memorial Foundation

http://www.monticello.org

The Thomas Jefferson Memorial Foundation has prepared a virtual tour of life at Monticello to demonstrate how Jefferson spent an average day. Included here is a discussion about Jefferson's interests, inventions, family, slaves, and grounds. Lengthy essays seek to explain Jefferson's world to the twentieth-century student. Links connect the reader to additional information about Monticello, its owner, inhabitants, and visitors. "The Jefferson-Hemings DNA Testing: An On-Line Resource" is a valuable link for understanding the current controversy about Jefferson's legacy.

Lewis & Clark

http://www.pbs.org/lewisandclark/

This is the PBS-sponsored online companion to Ken Burns's documentary series on the Lewis and Clark expedition. The site includes biographies for all members of the Corps of Discovery along with equipment lists, time lines, maps, and excerpts from the journals kept. Also included are short histories of the Native American tribes that were encountered on the journey. Burns discusses the making of the series, and PBS provides teaching resources. Overall, this is an excellent site.

Manifest Destiny

http://odur.let.rug.nl/~usa/E/manifest/manifxx.htm

This essay by Michael Lubragge traces the history of this concept in America.

The Mexican-American War (1846–1848)

http://www.pbs.org/kera/usmexicanwar/

This PBS-sponsored site is the online companion to the television documentary. The site provides a detailed analysis of the war from both sides with the perspective that "there are many valid points of view about a historical event." The war is placed in its larger context as a war for North America. Also included here are a bibliography, a teacher's guide, a time line of events, historical analysis by experts, and information on the making of the documentary. This site is available in Spanish and English.

The Mexican-American War, 1846–1848

http://www.dmwv.org/mexwar/mexwar.htm

Sponsored by the Descendants of Mexican War Veterans, this site offers a history of the war with sections on the countdown to war, the various conflicts fought across Mexico and California, and the peace that followed. Also provided are maps, documents, images, and links to related resources.

Mountain Men and the Fur Trade: Sources of the History of the Fur Trade in the Rocky Mountain West

http://www.xmission.com/~drudy/amm.html

This site is devoted to the mountain men of the Rocky Mountains through 1850. It includes digitized personal and public records and a bibliography for further reading.

New Perspectives on *The West*

http://www.pbs.org/weta/thewest/

This is the PBS-sponsored online companion to the eight-episode documentary on the American West produced by Ken Burns and Stephen Ives. Burns and Ives introduce the production and provide a time line with relevant biographies of key figures. Also included are sample primary source documents that were used to create the series and links to related sites.

Orphan Trains of Kansas

http://www.kancoll.org/articles/orphans/

Connie Dipasquale and Susan Stafford present their research about children brought to Kansas from New York on Orphan Trains. This site includes firsthand accounts, a time line, newspaper descriptions, and partial name lists of children on the Orphan Train.

Peabody Museum: The Ethnography of Lewis and Clark

http://www.peabody.harvard.edu/Lewis_and_Clark/

The Peabody Museum of Archaeology and Ethnology at Harvard University has developed this site to examine the cultural implications of the Lewis and Clark expedition. Included here are artifacts (with detailed descriptions) from Native Americans, route maps, and a resources page with links.

Politics and Sectionalism in the 1850s

http://odur.let.rug.nl/~usa/E/1850s/polixx.htm

Stephen Demkin has written this essay that examines the major political issues of the 1850s, such as the Compromise of 1850, the Kansas-Nebraska Act, and the Dred Scott decision. Also included are links to related sites.

Presidents of the United States

http://www.whitehouse.gov/history/presidents/index.html

The official White House Web site provides excellent biographies of the presidents along with links to relevant documents and biographies of the first ladies.

Presidents of the United States

http://www.ipl.org/div/potus/

The Internet Public Library has produced a useful collection of presidential Web sites. Sections contain presidential election results, cabinet members, notable events, and links to Internet biographies. The information here is laid out in a very accessible format.

A Roadmap to the U.S. Constitution

http://library.thinkquest.org/11572/?tqskip=1

Jonathan Chin and Alan Stern of ThinkQuest have developed this site on the U.S. Constitution. The authors have tried to re-create the milieu out of which the Constitution emerged. In addition to providing an annotated copy of the Constitution, essays explore the origins of this document. The authors also examine constitutional crises and the relevant Supreme Court decisions. This site provides a discussion board for those with specific questions.

Secession Era Editorials Project

http://history.furman.edu/~benson/docs/index.htm

Lloyd Benson of the Furman University Department of History has reproduced newspaper editorials from four critical events that highlighted America's growing sectional divide. Included are the Kansas-Nebraska Bill (1854), the caning of Massachusetts senator Charles Sumner by South Carolina representative Preston Brooks (1856), the *Dred Scott* decision (1857), and the raid on Harpers Ferry by radical abolitionist John Brown (1859). The project includes "at least one complete run of editorials from each major political party in each state of the Union." Users can search the editorials by text. Benson has also developed "mapping and statistical tools for placing the editorials into their analytical context."

"The Star Spangled Banner"

http://odur.let.rug.nl/~usa/E/banner/bannerxx.htm

Amato F. Mongelluzzo offers an essay that relates the events and dispels several myths surrounding the creation of this poem that became the national anthem.

Henry David Thoreau Home Page

http://www.walden.org/Institute/index.htm

This site, sponsored by the Walden Woods Project, the Thoreau Society, and the Thoreau Institute, is the essential Thoreau site. Emphasized here are Thoreau's biography, images, electronic texts, and scholarly analysis of Thoreau's work.

To the Western Ocean: Planning the Lewis and Clark Expedition

http://www.lib.virginia.edu/exhibits/lewis_clark/ch4.html

The site is part of a map exhibition at the Tracy W. McGregor Room, Alderman Library, University of Virginia. To the Western Ocean is the fourth chapter of a larger exploration of nation building and mapmaking. This site is valuable because it places the Lewis and Clark expedition into a larger historical context.

Uncle Sam: An American Autobiography

http://xroads.virginia.edu/~CAP/SAM/home.htm

The American studies program at the University of Virginia has created this site to discuss the origin of this American icon. The forgotten origin of Uncle Sam during the War of 1812 is placed alongside his evolution as a symbol and national icon, including his official adoption and standardization by the U.S. State Department in the 1950s.

The Valley of the Shadow

http://valley.vcdh.virginia.edu/

Edward L. Ayers, the Hugh P. Kelley Professor of History at the University of Virginia, has developed this massive archive of primary sources that concern the experiences of Franklin County, Pennsylvania, and Augusta County, Virginia, in the years just preceding the Civil War. These two counties were "separated by several hundred miles and the Mason-Dixon line." The document archive includes newspapers, letters, diaries, photographs, maps, church records, population census, agricultural census, and military records. Students can research and write their own histories from the documents provided. The project is primarily intended for secondary schools, community colleges, libraries, and universities. This research is available in CD-ROM form from W.W. Norton Publishers (http://www.wwnorton.com).

War of 1812

http://www.army.mil/cmh-pg/books/amh/amh-06.htm

This is a discussion of the War of 1812, from *American Military History* (chapter 6). This e-text is sponsored by the Army Historical Series, Office of the Chief of Military History, U.S. Army. The war is presented as an outgrowth of the Napoleonic Wars. The major battles are narrated in detail as are comparisons of American and British military capabilities and strategies.

"Woman of Iron"

http://womenshistory.about.com/library/prm/blwomanofiron1.htm

"In 1825 Rebecca Lukens took over her late husband's iron mill. The company still thrives—a testament to the management abilities of this pioneering woman CEO." This article by Joseph Gustaitis is sponsored by *American History* magazine.

Documents and Images

"Across the Plains in 1844"

http://www.pbs.org/weta/thewest/resources/archives/two/sager1.htm

This account was written by Catherine Sager Pringle circa 1860. It is reprinted here from S.A. Clarke's *Pioneer Days in Oregon History,* vol. 2 (1905).

The *Amistad* Case

http://www.archives.gov/digital_classroom/lessons/amistad_case/
amistad_case.html

The National Archives and Records Administration provides all relevant documents related to the *Amistad* slave mutiny. This site also includes teaching ideas that are based on the National Standards for History and the National Standards for Civics and Government.

The Annapolis Convention

http://www.yale.edu/lawweb/avalon/annapoli.htm

The Annapolis Convention assembled to discuss economic issues faced by the states under the Articles of Confederation. It resolved to explore alternatives to the Articles. This site contains the report of the commissioners from the states on September 14, 1786, and links to the Articles of Confederation, the Madison debates, the *Federalist Papers,* and the U.S. Constitution.

The Articles of Confederation

http://www.yale.edu/lawweb/avalon/artconf.htm

The Articles of Confederation established a central government for the thirteen colonies after the American Revolution. It was a weak system in which the separate states held the balance of power. This site contains a full-text copy of the Articles and links to the Annapolis Convention, the Madison debates, the *Federalist Papers,* and the U.S. Constitution.

The Bill of Rights

http://www.archives.gov/national_archives_experience/charters/
bill_of_rights.html

The National Archives and Records Administration provides coverage of the Bill of Rights. Included here is a high-resolution image of the document.

Boundaries of the United States and the Several States

http://www.ac.wwu.edu/~stephan/48states.html

Ed Stephan of Western Washington University has created a charming animated map that depicts the territorial growth of the United States. This site allows students to visualize how national, territorial, and state boundaries changed over time.

Cherokee Nation v. Georgia

http://www.pbs.org/weta/thewest/resources/archives/two/cherokee.htm

This is a full-text copy of the decision handed down by Supreme Court chief justice John Marshall in 1831, which dealt with the forced removal of Native Americans from Georgia and other Southern states. The decision held that the Native Americans had rights and were "domestic dependent nations," a status between independent countries and tribes without rights.

The Confessions of Nat Turner

http://docsouth.unc.edu/turner/turner.html

This is the complete text of *The Confessions of Nat Turner* (1831). Nat Turner led a large slave revolt in 1831, and after his capture he allegedly made these confessions.

The Constitution of the United States

http://www.archives.gov/national-archives-experience/charters/
constitution.html

This site is maintained by the National Archives and Records Administration. The Founding Fathers page features the biographies of the fifty-five delegates to the Constitutional Convention. Users can read a transcription of the complete text of the Constitution. This page also provides links to biographies of each of the thirty-nine delegates who signed the Constitution. The article "A More Perfect Union" is an in-depth look at the Constitutional Convention and the ratification process. A quiz section gives visitors the chance to test their knowledge.

The Federalist Papers

http://www.yale.edu/lawweb/avalon/federal/fed.htm

These essays were authored by John Jay, Alexander Hamilton, and James Madison, and argue in favor of constitutional ratification. The collection is searchable by keyword and linked to relevant documents such as the Articles of Confederation, the Annapolis Convention, the Madison debates, and the U.S. Constitution.

The Federalist Papers

http://www.law.emory.edu/FEDERAL/federalist/

These essays were authored by John Jay, Alexander Hamilton, and James Madison. First published in 1787–1788, they supported the Constitution. They serve as bold statements of American political theory, and this online version makes them more accessible than ever before, as it is keyword searchable and each essay is also individually available.

FindLaw: U.S. Constitution

http://www.findlaw.com/casecode/constitution/

This site contains all the articles and amendments to the U.S. Constitution. Each item is completely annotated with explanations and references. Through hyperlinks, users can access the full-text version of relevant Supreme Court decisions. Each decision is placed in its historical context along with pertinent theories of law and government. This is an invaluable resource for legal professionals.

First-Person Narratives of the American South

http://docsouth.unc.edu/fpn/index.html

This site contains an outstanding collection of electronic texts that document the American South. It includes diaries, autobiographies, memoirs, travel accounts, and ex-slave narratives. The focus is on first-person narratives of marginalized populations: women, African-Americans, enlisted men, laborers, and Native Americans.

"A Girl's Life in Virginia Before the War"

http://docsouth.unc.edu/burwell/menu.html

This memoir by Letitia M. Burwell describes Southern plantation life before the Civil War. It was originally published in 1895.

Godey's Lady's Book

http://www.history.rochester.edu/godeys/

Selections from the popular nineteenth-century women's magazine, *Godey's Lady's Book*. Issues from the 1850s include "For the Home," "Nor Just for Ladies," and "Fashion Corner" sections. Visitors to this site will find an informative glimpse into the daily life of the mid-nineteenth-century middle class.

"A Grandmother's Recollections of Dixie"

http://docsouth.unc.edu/bryan/menu.html

This is a collection of letters from Mary Norcott Bryan to her grandchildren. It was published in 1912. Her letters shed light on Southern plantations before the Civil War.

Historical Maps of the United States

http://www.lib.utexas.edu/maps/map_sites/hist_sites.html#US

The University of Texas at Austin has digitized the Perry-Castañeda Library Map Collection. This is an excellent source for digitized copies of rare maps.

"The Hypocrisy of American Slavery"

http://www.historyplace.com/speeches/douglass.htm

This speech was given by Frederick Douglass on July 4, 1852, in Rochester, New York. See elsewhere in this section Douglass's speech given the following day titled, "What to the Slave Is the Fourth of July?"

The Jay Treaty

http://odur.let.rug.nl/~usa/D/1776–1800/foreignpolicy/jay.htm

The Jay Treaty between Great Britain and the United States was the most controversial issue of George Washington's presidency. It was proclaimed in February 1796. Its real significance was that it represented Britain's recognition of American nationality.

Thomas Jefferson on Politics and Government: Quotations From the Writings of Thomas Jefferson

http://etext.virginia.edu/jefferson/quotations/

This site, sponsored by the University of Virginia, contains an extensive collection of Jefferson quotations. The stated goal of this site is to constitute a "fair statement of the complete political philosophy of Thomas Jefferson." Also included are a brief biography of Jefferson and links to related sites.

John Brown: An Address by Frederick Douglass

http://www.mdcbowen.org/p5/jb/douglass.htm

This speech by Frederick Douglass can be found at the Library of Congress Web site. It is a tribute to John Brown, a radical abolitionist who, in 1859, raided the federal arsenal at Harpers Ferry, Virginia, in a mad attempt to foment a slave revolt. Brown was hanged by the Virginia authorities. His last words were: "I, John Brown, am now quite certain that the crimes of this guilty land will never be purged away but with blood." Douglass memorialized Brown as a true hero of the abolitionist cause.

"A Journey to the Seaboard States" (1856)

http://odur.let.rug.nl/~usa/D/1851–1875/olmsted/jourxx.htm

This essay by Frederick Law Olmsted focuses on slavery and the plantation system. It was written in 1856 while Olmsted was on a journalistic assignment for the *New York Daily Times*. Olmsted was critical of slavery as both cruel and inefficient.

Kentucky Resolution (1799)

http://odur.let.rug.nl/~usa/D/1776–1800/constitution/kent1799.htm

This was Thomas Jefferson's republican response to the Federalists' Alien and Sedition Acts. The resolution advanced the state compact theory and argued that states retained the right to notify Congress when it had exceeded its authority.

The Louisiana Purchase Treaty

http://www.archives.gov/exhibits/american_originals_iv/sections/louisiana_purchase_treaty.html

This online exhibit by the National Archives presents images of the document that was signed in Paris in 1803, along with a transcription of the text.

The Madison Debates

http://www.yale.edu/lawweb/avalon/debates/debcont.htm

The Debates in the Federal Convention of 1787 was created from notes taken by James Madison during the Constitutional Convention held in Philadelphia between May 14 and September 17, 1787. The debates are searchable by keyword or can be accessed according to specific dates. Also contained here are links to the Articles of Confederation, the Annapolis Convention, the *Federalist Papers,* and the U.S. Constitution.

John Marshall

http://odur.let.rug.nl/~usa/D/1801–1825/marshallcases/marxx.htm

Here are the major decisions written by Chief Justice John Marshall, including *Marbury v. Madison* and *Cherokee Nation v. Georgia.* Also included is a biography of Marshall.

The Monroe Doctrine

http://odur.let.rug.nl/~usa/D/1801–1825/jmdoc.htm

The Monroe Doctrine was an early statement on American foreign policy. It was taken from President James Monroe's annual message to Congress on December 2, 1823.

North American Slave Narratives

http://docsouth.unc.edu/neh/index.html

This large collection of American slave narratives is part of the Documenting the American South project sponsored by the University of North Carolina at Chapel Hill. This is an excellent resource for better understanding the slaves' world in the antebellum South.

The Prairie Traveler: A Hand-book for Overland Expeditions

http://www.kancoll.org/books/marcy/

This survival guide and handbook, written by Captain Randolph B. Marcy, U.S. Army, was published in 1859.

The Proclamation of Neutrality (1793)

http://odur.let.rug.nl/~usa/D/1776–1800/foreignpolicy/neutr.htm

President George Washington proclaimed American neutrality during the wars of the French Revolution.

Scanned Originals of Early American Documents

http://www.law.emory.edu/FEDERAL/conpict.html

Scanned originals of the Constitution, the Bill of Rights, and the Declaration of Independence.

The Sedition Act of July 14, 1798

http://www.yale.edu/lawweb/avalon/statutes/sedact.htm

This act, passed by Congress on July 14, 1798, made it a federal crime to speak against the U.S. government. It is perhaps the most repressive law in American history.

"Slavery a Positive Good"

http://douglassarchives.org/calh_a59.htm

This speech was given on the floor of the U.S. Senate by John C. Calhoun in 1837.

Treaty of Greenville (1795)

http://odur.let.rug.nl/~usa/D/1776–1800/indians/green.htm

This is the complete text of the American Indian treaty that formally opened the Northwest Territory for settlement.

Uncle Tom's Cabin

http://xroads.virginia.edu/~HYPER/STOWE/stowe.html

The American Studies program at the University of Virginia provides an e-text of Harriet Beecher Stowe's 1852 novel.

Virginia Resolution (1798)

http://www.yale.edu/lawweb/avalon/virres.htm

This was James Madison's republican response to the Federalist's Alien and Sedition Acts. It advanced the state compact theory, which argued that the federal government could operate only within its constitutionally defined limits.

Virginia Statute for Religious Freedom (1786)

http://religiousfreedom.lib.virginia.edu/sacred/vaact.html

This act was drafted by Thomas Jefferson in 1777. An amended version passed the Virginia legislature in 1786. It served as the precedent for the religious freedom article in the Bill of Rights.

"What to the Slave Is the Fourth of July?"

http://douglassarchives.org/doug_a10.htm

This speech was delivered by Frederick Douglass on July 5, 1852. See elsewhere in this section, Douglass's speech given the day before in Rochester, New York, titled "The Hypocrisy of American Slavery."

American Civil War History

Jeffrey W. McClurken

Metasites

The American Civil War Home Page

http://sunsite.utk.edu/civil-war/

Started in 1994, this is one of the oldest Civil War link sites, yet it remains useful because of its helpful categories and the sheer number of links.

Civil War and Reconstruction: Jensen's Guide to WWW Resources

http://tigger.uic.edu/~rjensen/civwar.htm

Built by an academic historian, this guide is a good place to start, given its topical and chronological categories of links to scholarly sites and primary source documents.

The Civil War Index Page

http://www.homepages.dsu.edu/jankej/civilwar/civilwar.htm

This site contains more specific subcategories, and more commercial links, than other metasites.

United States Civil War Center

http://www.cwc.lsu.edu/

Based at LSU, the Civil War Center has indexed over 9,000 Civil War Web sites, from scholarly sites to popular sites covering movies, quotes, reenactors, and vendors.

Library of Congress

This institution has worked to make accessible online numerous primary documents from its extensive collections, many of which relate to the Civil War.

Library of Congress: African American Odyssey

http://lcweb2.loc.gov/ammem/aaohtml/exhibit/aointro.html

The Web companion to an exhibit of materials from the Library of Congress. The sections on slavery, abolition, the Civil War, and Reconstruction are particularly useful.

Library of Congress: Civil War Maps

http://lcweb2.loc.gov/ammem/collections/civil_war_maps/

This impressive site includes an essay on the history of Civil War mapping and over 2,000 images of Civil War–era maps, atlases, and charts.

Library of Congress: Civil War Treasures From the New York Historical Society

http://memory.loc.gov/ammem/ndlpcoop/nhihtml/cwnyhshome.html

This site houses a broad selection of manuscripts, sketches, posters, and photographs that includes, but goes beyond, the New York area in its focus.

Library of Congress: Abraham Lincoln Papers

http://memory.loc.gov/ammem/alhtml/malhome.html

Heavy on research and light on context, this site contains over 20,000 documents, including letters, speeches, and notes from Lincoln.

Library of Congress: Selected Civil War Photographs

http://memory.loc.gov/ammem/cwphtml/cwphome.html

This collection includes over a thousand original pictures from the Civil War, many of them linked to a war chronology, and some historical context on photography.

National Park Service (NPS)

As part of its educational mission, the NPS and its many parks and historic places have made many primary documents and scholarly articles available to Web researchers.

Camp Life: Civil War Collections

http://www.cr.nps.gov/museum/exhibits/gettex/index.htm

Based on an exhibit at the Gettysburg Park, the site is an interesting virtual tour of the material culture of Civil War soldiers' daily life.

Civil War Archaeology

http://www.cr.nps.gov/seac/civilwar/index.htm

This site details NPS efforts at excavations at Fort Pulaski, Shiloh, and Andersonville, the notorious Confederate prison, giving a brief history of each location.

Civil War Soldiers and Sailors System (CWSS)

http://www.itd.nps.gov/cwss/

The CWSS is one of the most important research sites for the Civil War. It contains the names and basic information for over 6 million soldiers and sailors from both sides. The site also has many regimental histories, summaries of 364 battles, listings of Medal of Honor winners and prisoners of war, and a section on the key roles played by black soldiers.

NPS Battlefields and Historic Sites

Each NPS park or historic location has its own Web site, many of which are useful for Civil War researchers. Many of these Web sites include maps, battle summaries, scholarly articles, educational opportunities, and excerpts from letters, diaries, and memoirs. The following are some of the best.

> Antietam National Park–http://www.nps.gov/anti/home.htm
> Appomattox Courthouse National Historic Park—http://www.nps.gov/apco/index1.htm
> Clara Barton National Historic Site—http://www.nps.gov/clba/

Fredericksburg and Spotsylvania National Military Park—http://www.nps.gov/frsp/vc.htm

Gettysburg National Military Park—http://www.nps.gov/gett/home.htm

Lincoln Home National Historic Site—http://www.nps.gov/liho/index.htm

Petersburg National Battlefield Park—http://www.nps.gov/pete/mahan/PNBhome.html

Vicksburg National Military Park—http://www.nps.gov/vick/home.htm

General Sites

American Civil War

http://spec.lib.vt.edu/civwar/

Virginia Tech's Special Collections has transcribed small collections of letters from several Union and Confederate soldiers.

American Civil War Collection

http://etext.virginia.edu/civilwar/

Constituting one segment of the University of Virginia's Electronic Text Center, this site includes several large diaries and hundreds of letters from and to ordinary soldiers, as well as Civil War–related fiction and poetry.

Battlefield Medicine in the American Civil War

http://www.civilwarmedicine.aphillcsa.com/index.html

This site, although not scholarly in presentation, conveys the dark side of Civil War medicine with graphic pictures and excerpts from primary documents.

Captain Richard W. Burt: Civil War Letters From the 76th Ohio Volunteer Infantry

http://my.ohio.voyager.net/~lstevens/burt/

This bare-bones site offers transcriptions of letters, poems, and materials related to this Ohio soldier's wartime experience.

Civil War Diaries at Augustana College Library

http://www.augustana.edu/library/SpecialCollections/civi11.html

Two diaries of Illinois soldiers were scanned and transcribed for this site.

Civil War Diary of Bingham Findley Junkin

http://www.iwaynet.net/~lsci/junkin/

This site is a transcription of a brief diary from a Pennsylvania enlisted soldier.

Civil War Letters of Samuel S. Dunton

http://home.pacbell.net/dunton/SSDletters.html

Plainly presented, these transcriptions of a New York soldier's letters home discuss his time in Baltimore, Washington, and Louisiana.

Civil War Resources From the Virginia Military Institute Archives

http://www.vmi.edu/archives/cwsource.html

The staff of VMI's archives has produced an excellent site combining various primary documents from more than sixty of their collections with secondary narratives on a variety of topics, including Stonewall Jackson, the Battle of New Market, and life in the Shenandoah Valley.

Civil War Women

http://scriptorium.lib.duke.edu/collections/civil-war-women.html

http://scriptorium.lib.duke.edu/collections/african-american-women.html

These Web sites present Duke University's three transcribed collections about women during the war, featuring the papers of Rose Greenhow, the Confederate spy and propagandist (first site), and three collections of Duke's material on African-American women from the Civil War era, including letters from slave women to their slaveholders and family members (second site).

Dwight Henry Cory Letters

http://homepages.rootsweb.com/~lovelace/cory.htm

Posted by a descendant of Cory, the site includes transcriptions of letters between the Ohio cavalry officer and his future wife.

Documenting the American South

http://docsouth.unc.edu/

This site showcases the impressive records of the University of North Carolina's Southern Historical Collection. Click on "Collections" to see digitized primary sources including autobiographies, slave narratives, and material on the Southern home front during the Civil War. (See also a collection of soldiers' letters at http://www.lib.unc.edu/mss/exhibits/civilwar/.)

Freedmen and Southern Society Project

http://www.history.umd.edu/Freedmen/

This site, part of a multivolume series publishing records in the National Archives relating to African-Americans during the war, contains examples of dozens of transcribed documents.

Ulysses S. Grant Association

http://www.lib.siu.edu/projects/usgrant/

The association has published twenty-six volumes of Union general Ulysses S. Grant's papers. The site includes a very useful chronology, linked to excerpts from his memoirs and other primary documents.

H-CivWar

http://www.h-net.org/~civwar/

This site is the Web presence for the H-CivWar discussion list. The site includes archived posts, subscription information, and related book reviews by scholars.

HarpWeek

http://www.harpweek.com/

This subscription site presenting *Harper's Weekly* (1857–1912) has an extensive free section on nineteenth-century topics, including articles on political cartoons, literature, race relations, and Constitutional amendments.

Robert E. Lee Papers

http://miley.wlu.edu/LeePapers/

Washington and Lee University makes available images of nearly fifty letters written by the school's most famous president and Confederate general. The site also includes a link to hundreds more transcribed letters from Lee.

Letters From an Iowa Soldier in the Civil War

http://www.civilwarletters.com/home.html

This attractively presented site contains fifteen letters from Private Newton Scott to his future wife, Hannah Cone.

Overall Family Civil War Letters

http://www.geocities.com/Heartland/Acres/1574/

This site presents transcribed and scanned letters from an Ohio family whose husband and father served and died of disease. Unlike many other online collections of letters, the site includes lots of context, including short biographies for nearly all of the people mentioned in the letters.

The Papers of Jefferson Davis

http://jeffersondavis.rice.edu/

The fifty documents selected from the fifteen-volume publication of the works of the Confederacy's president include his letters and speeches, as well as pictures and scholarly information on Davis and his family.

Pearce Civil War Documents Collection

http://www.nav.cc.tx.us/library/civilwar/full_text.htm

This small, well-organized, online collection is a sample of documents available at Navarro College in Texas. The site is very usable; however, other than letters from Captain L.D. Bradley of Texas, there is only one letter each from various other soldiers.

Secession Era Editorials Project

http://history.furman.edu/~benson/docs/

Sponsored by Furman University, this site includes transcriptions of newspaper editorials from all over the nation, representing all political parties, on four topics key to the coming of the Civil War: the Kansas-Nebraska Act, the caning of Charles Sumner, the Dred Scott case, and John Brown's raid.

Shotgun's Home of the American Civil War

http://www.civilwarhome.com/

This large, sweeping site, created by a passionate amateur, includes extensive secondary material from various articles, as well as extensive primary source records, including large excerpts from the Official Records of the War of the Rebellion.

Valley of the Shadow Project

http://jefferson.village.virginia.edu/vshadow2/

Based at the University of Virginia's Center for Digital History and started by historian Edward Ayers in 1993, the Valley Project brings together all available information on one Northern county (Franklin County, Pennsylvania) and one Southern county (Augusta County, Virginia) up to and during the Civil War years. The documents assembled by a team of scholars include searchable transcriptions of diaries, letters, newspapers, images, military records, and maps.

Women Soldiers of the Civil War

http://www.archives.gov/publications/prologue/1993/spring/women-in-the-civil-war-1.html

This is an online version of an article by scholar DeAnne Blanton that explores the role of women who fought as men in the two armies. The site also contains photographs and records from the National Archives.

Gilded Age and Progressive Era History

Jeremy Boggs

Metasites and Directories

American Memory

http://memory.loc.gov/ammem/

One of the preeminent history sites available, American Memory provides access to a plethora of materials held by the Library of Congress. Users can browse the content by topic or collection, or search all collections by keyword. The site also provides guides to help teachers incorporate the American Memory project into classroom learning. The site is currently undergoing an extensive but elegant redesign.

Gilded Age and Progressive Era Resources

http://www2.tntech.edu/history/gilprog.html

Maintained by the Department of History at Tennessee Tech, this site contains a growing list of sites useful to those interested in the history of the Gilded Age and Progressive Era.

History Matters

http://historymatters.gmu.edu/

This site is a joint project of the Center for History and New Media at George Mason University and the American Social History Project and Center for Media and Learning at the City University of New York. It contains invaluable resources for history teachers at the secondary and collegiate levels. Visitors can learn how to interpret documents, search various primary sources available on the site, and search reviews of other history-related sites.

Presidents

Ulysses S. Grant, 1869–1877

http://www.mscomm.com/~ulysses/

Webmaster Candace Scott has collected and made available numerous documents written by Ulysses S. Grant and his family and friends. Photos, letters, and interviews with various members of Grant's family are available.

Rutherford B. Hayes, 1877–1881

http://www.americanpresident.org/history/rutherfordbhayes/

This site contains a brief biography of Hayes's life, as well as links to images and other Web resources.

James A. Garfield, 1881

http://www.americanpresident.org/history/jamesgarfield/

A detailed biography of Garfield, who served only one hundred days as president before being assassinated.

Chester A. Arthur, 1881–1885

http://www.americanpresident.org/history/chesterccrthur/

A solid biography that details Arthur's life and links to his papers, images of him, and articles about him.

Grover Cleveland, 1885–1889 and 1893–1897

http://www.americanpresident.org/history/grovercleveland2/

Cleveland was deemed the "Guardian President" for his then record use of the veto power. This site provides a thorough overview of his life before and during his presidency.

Benjamin Harrison, 1889–1893

http://www.americanpresident.org/history/benjaminharrison/

Harrison's legacy continues to be debated, and the reasons for this are detailed in this short biography. The site also links to images of him, including a cartoon, and related articles.

William McKinley, 1897–1901

http://www.americanpresident.org/history/williammckinley/

McKinley served as president during the Spanish-American War. During his presidency he also sent over 2,000 soldiers to China to help suppress the Boxer Rebellion. McKinley won a second term in 1900, but he was assassinated a year later. This biography details his time in office and the historical contexts in which he served as president.

Theodore Roosevelt, 1901–1909

http://www.americanpresident.org/history/theodoreroosevelt/

Author, politician, and "Rough Rider," Roosevelt became William McKinley's vice president in 1901 and later took office after McKinley's assassination. This site provides an interesting discussion of the life of Roosevelt.

William Howard Taft, 1909–1913

http://www.americanpresident.org/history/williamhowardtaft/

This site provides a detailed biography of the twenty-seventh president, covering his life before and after his term in office.

Activists, Authors, Businessmen, and Inventors

Alexander Graham Bell Family Papers

http://memory.loc.gov/ammem/bellhtml/bellhome.html

Another splendid project in the American Memory collection, this site provides visitors access to the papers of Alexander Graham Bell and his family. Among the materials presented are family papers, written correspondence, laboratory notebooks, and various articles written by Bell. This is a rich resource for anyone interested in learning more about this influential inventor.

Andrew Carnegie

http://www.pbs.org/wgbh/amex/carnegie/

A companion to PBS's documentary titled *The Richest Man in the World,* this site contains insightful material related to Andrew Carnegie. A time line traces events during Carnegie's life. The gallery provides images and commentary, and the People and Events section gives detailed biographical information on Carnegie as well as a discussion of the Homestead Strike in 1892.

Eugene V. Debs

http://www.eugenevdebs.com

This site, created by the Eugene V. Debs Foundation, details the life and work of Debs, an ardent Socialist and supporter of labor rights, who was arrested for his involvement in organizing the 1893 strike against the Pullman Company.

Thomas A. Edison Papers

http://edison.rutgers.edu

A joint project of Rutgers University, the National Park Service, the New Jersey Historical Society, and the Smithsonian Institution, this site contains an impressive searchable database of Edison's papers and drawings. Access to newspapers and patents is also available, as well as biographic information on Edison.

Emma Goldman Papers

http://sunsite.berkeley.edu/Goldman/

This site provides access to a number of primary sources related to this political and social activist.

The Jack London Collection

http://sunsite.berkeley.edu/London/

This site, a project of the library at the University of California, Berkeley, gives visitors access to a variety of materials related to Jack London. Materials include audio clips, letters and postcards, and pictures. A brief biography of London, written by Dr. Clarice Stasz, is also available.

Poet at Work: Recovered Notebooks From the Thomas Biggs Harned Walt Whitman Collection

http://memory.loc.gov/ammem/wwhtml/wwhome.html

Visitors to this site can access four notebooks and a cardboard butterfly kept by Walt Whitman. These materials disappeared from the Library of Congress in 1942, but were recovered in 1995.

John D. Rockefeller Biographical Sketch

http://archive.rockerfeller.edu/bio/jdrsr.php

Maintained by the Rockefeller Archive Center, this site provides a brief biography of Rockefeller. Other links on the site take users to a detailed bibliography of published material on Rockefeller as well as a section titled In Their Own Words, where visitors can read materials published by Rockefeller at the turn of the century. An interactive family tree traces the Rockefeller family from 1897 to the present.

Mark Twain in His Times

http://etext.lib.virginia.edu/railton/

Using resources available in the Barrett Collection of American Literature at the University of Virginia Library, Steven Railton has created an engaging site that explores the life and writing of Mark Twain. Railton has gathered a number of manuscripts, contemporary reviews, images, and exhibits related to Mark Twain. The site is maintained by the Electronic Text Center at the University of Virginia.

Booker T. Washington Papers

http://www.historycooperative.org/btw/

Created by History Cooperative and the University of Illinois Press, this site contains images as well as access to the published version of the *Booker T. Washington Papers*, published by the University of Illinois Press. The papers are searchable and can be printed.

Consumerism and Popular Culture

America at Work, America at Leisure: Motion Pictures from 1894–1915

http://memory.loc.gov/ammem/awlhtml/

This American Memory site contains 150 motion pictures that show various leisurely and sporting activities, including calisthenics, boxing, football games, and parades.

American Variety Stage: Vaudeville and Popular Entertainment, 1870–1920

http://memory.loc.gov/ammem/vshtml/vshome.html

Over 600 scripts, programs, and photos make up this American Memory collection on the early history of vaudeville.

Baseball Cards, 1887–1914

http://memory.loc.gov/ammem/bbhtml/bbhome.html

Part of the American Memory collection, this site contains over 2,100 baseball cards from 1887 to 1914.

Cartoons of the Gilded Age and Progressive Era

http://history.osu.edu/Projects/USCartoons/GAPECartoons.htm

This site, which is part of The Ohio State University Department of History's Cartoon Collections, features a number of cartoons about such topics as the antitrust movement, imperialism and its opponents, and the 1900 presidential campaign.

Emergence of Advertising in America, 1850–1920

http://scriptorium.lib.duke.edu/eaa

This is a rich resource of nearly 9,000 advertisements from the 1850s to the 1920s. Created and maintained by the John W. Hartman Center and Digital Scriptorium at Duke University. Users can search or browse the advertisements by topic or keyword.

Red Hot Jazz Archive: A History of Jazz Before 1930

http://www.redhotjazz.com

Webmaster Scott Alexander has gathered a number of documents that detail the development of jazz music. Several films of musical performances are available, as well as a number of essays on the historical development of jazz and biographical sketches of influential musicians of the time.

Industrialization and Urbanization

Child Labor in America, 1908–1912: Photographs of Lewis W. Hine

http://www.historyplace.com/unitedstates/childlabor/

Lewis W. Hine became an investigative photographer for the National Child Labor Committee in 1908, after a career as a teacher. The more than sixty photographs contained in this site are part of his work documenting working conditions of children across the United States.

City Sites: Multimedia Essays on New York and Chicago, 1870s–1930s

http://www.artsweb.bham.ac.uk/citysites/

A project by the University of Birmingham and the University of Nottingham in the United Kingdom, this site contains interactive essays on the history of New York and Chicago. The site is an interesting use of the Web for publication, offering readers a refreshing view of the urban histories of these two cities.

Panoramic Maps, 1847–1929

http://memory.loc.gov/ammem/pmhtml/panhome.html

This American Memory project provides access to a variety of panoramic maps of U.S. cities. Visitors can access the maps by subject, keyword, or geographic location. The maps offer an interesting view of how Americans perceived their urban landscapes.

San Francisco Historical Photograph Collection

http://sfpl.lib.ca.us/librarylocations/sfhistory/sfphoto.htm

The San Francisco Public Library has made available photographs and printed material related to San Francisco from 1850 to the present. Users can search for photographs, browse by subject, or locate images using an interactive map of the city.

Urban Experience in Chicago: Hull-House and Its Neighbors, 1889–1963

http://www.uic.edu/jaddams/hull/urbanexp/index.htm

This site by the University of Illinois at Chicago and the Jane Addams Hull-House Museum gives visitors access to valuable primary source documents, photographs, and essays pertaining to the history of Hull-House. Elegantly designed, this site includes a historical narrative, a time line, maps of the neighborhood, and resources for teachers.

Politics and Government

Finding Precedent: *Hayes v. Tilden,* the Electoral College Controversy of 1876–1877

http://elections.harpweek.com/controversy.htm

HarpWeek created this site to inform students and the public about the controversy surrounding the election in 1876–1877. The site contains images and cartoons from *Harper's Weekly* as well as an overview of the controversy, biographies on important figures, and a discussion of its resolution.

Foreign Relations of the United States

http://libtext.library.wisc.edu/FRUS/

A project of the University of Wisconsin Libraries, this site gives readers access to digital copies of *Foreign Relations of the United States,* a publication by the State Department's Office of the Historian. The collection can be searched or browsed, and an index is available for volumes covering the years 1861 to 1899 and 1900 to 1918.

The Presidential Election, 1860–1912

http://elections.harpweek.com/

This site, also created by HarpWeek, provides a concise overview of each presidential election between 1860 and 1912. Along with the overview, the site contains political cartoons from each election with explanations of the cartoons.

Uniting Mugwumps and the Masses: *Puck's* Role in Gilded Age Politics

http://xroads.virginia.edu/~MA96/PUCK/home.html

An online master's thesis by Daniel Henry Backer, this site explores the history of the mugwumps. The mugwumps were Republicans who, in the 1884 presidential election, supported Democrat Grover Cleveland instead of the Republican candidate, James Gillespie Blaine. Backer's site provides analysis of the magazine *Puck* and the political cartoons it contained. A cartoon archive provides access to twenty images that are used throughout the site.

Race, Class, and Gender Issues

African American Perspectives: Pamphlets From the Daniel A.P. Murray Collection, 1818–1907

http://memory.loc.gov/ammem/aap/aaphome.html

This American Memory collection provides access to published material written in the nineteenth century. Most of the publications were printed between 1875 and 1900. Authors of the materials include, among others, Booker T. Washington and Frederick Douglass.

By Popular Demand: "Votes for Women" Suffrage Pictures, 1850–1920

http://memory.loc.gov/ammem/vfwhtml/vfwhome.html

Thirty-eight pictures, including photographs of picketers and protesters, are available in this American Memory collection. Also included in the collection are cartoons commenting on the suffrage movement, antisuffrage demonstrations, and portraits of influential people during the movement.

A Coal Miner's Work

http://people.cohums.ohio-state.edu/kerr6/courses/History563/
A%20Coal%20Miner's%20Work.htm

Written by K. Austin Kerr and sponsored by The Ohio State University, this site explores the life and times of late nineteenth-century coal miners.

The Dramas of Haymarket

http://www.chicagohistory.org/dramas/index.htm

A project by the Chicago Historical Society and Northwestern University, this site explores the Chicago Historical Society's Haymarket Affair Digital Collection. Organized like a drama—with a prologue, five acts, and an epilogue—the Dramas of Haymarket interprets documents available on the Haymarket affair in engaging fashion. The site is rich in multimedia, and hyperlinks to other relevant resources allow visitors to engage the material from different perspectives.

Images of African Americans From the Nineteenth Century

http://digital.nypl.org/shomburg/images_aa19/

Sponsored by the Schomburg Center for Research in Black Culture at the New York Public Library, this site contains hundreds of images that reveal the lives of African-Americans in the nineteenth century.

Votes for Women: Selections From the National American Woman Suffrage Association, 1848–1921

http://memory.loc.gov/ammem/naw/nawshome.html

This American Memory collection contains 167 pamphlets, books, and other resources that contribute to the history of the suffrage movement. Papers of prominent suffragists, including Susan B. Anthony, Elizabeth Cady Stanton, and Alice Stone Blackwell, are available.

Women Working, 1870–1930

http://ocp.hul.harvard.edu/ww/

A project by Harvard University Libraries, this site provides a detailed account of the lives of women workers. Pamphlets, diaries, letters, and images are available so users can explore the lives of working women, including teachers, actresses, secretaries, farm laborers, and factory workers.

War and Imperialism

Anti-Imperialism in the United States, 1895–1935

http://www.boondocksnet.com/ai/index.html

If readers can ignore the moving advertisements on this site, they can take advantage of the hundreds of documents available on the anti-imperialism movement. The site contains speeches, essays, and cartoons from the era, as well as current discussion of the materials.

The Crucible of Empire: The Spanish-American War

http://www.pbs.org/crucible/

Created by the Public Broadcasting Company, this site provides related resources for a film produced by PBS also called *The Crucible of Empire*. The site includes a time line as well as discussion of various aspects of the Spanish-American War, including yellow journalism and music of the 1890s.

Events—Spanish-American War

http://www.history.navy.mil/photos/events/spanam/eve-pge.htm

This site, created by the Navy Historical Center, contains a number of images from the Spanish-American War.

The Spanish-American War in Motion Pictures

http://memory.loc.gov/ammem/sawhtml/sawhome.html

This American Memory site contains a searchable and browsable index of various films that depict the Spanish-American War. The films were produced by the Edison Manufacturing Company and the American Mutoscope and Biography Company.

A War in Perspective, 1898–1998

http://www.nypl.org/research/chss/epo/spanexhib/index.html

Created and maintained by the New York Public Library, this site contains a brief but thorough summary of various aspects of the Spanish-American War.

The World of 1898: The Spanish-American War

http://www.loc.gov/rr/hispanic/1898/

Part of the American Memory collection, this site houses various documents and resources pertaining to the Spanish-American War and the people involved. Users can browse the material through the subject index or look at specific resources, such as maps, literary commentary, and personal narratives.

The Age of Franklin D. Roosevelt

Anne Rothfeld

Metasites

American Memory

http://lcweb2.loc.gov/ammem

American Memory, maintained by the Library of Congress, is ideal for anyone interested in American history, and researchers may want to visit this Web page first. The Web site contains Age of Roosevelt topics including New Deal programs, election and inauguration, and correspondence and ephemera. Researchers can browse by collection names and search by all collections.

New Deal Network

http://newdeal.feri.org

The Franklin and Eleanor Roosevelt Institute sponsors this Web site, which is the starting point for historical figures and events of the Age of Roosevelt. New Deal Network offers primary source materials and photographs, both of which are searchable by topics and dates. This site hosts the H-US 1918–45, a moderated H-Net discussion list for teachers and historians.

Historical Figures

Herbert C. Hoover

Herbert C. Hoover Presidential Library and Museum

http://www.hoover.nara.gov

The Hoover Presidential Library and Museum constructed this Web site, which contains information on his presidency, education modules, and research guides to both the Hoover presidential papers and the papers of Rose Wilder Land and her mother, children's author Laura Ingalls Wilder. Rose Wilder wrote one of the first biographies of Hoover, published in 1919. This Web site, which is the best place to start for topics on Hoover, is updated weekly and has links to related sites.

White House—Herbert Hoover

http://www.whitehouse.gov/history/presidents/hh31.html

Maintained by the White House staff, this page has biographies of President Hoover and the first lady, Lou Henry Hoover, with links to the text of the president's inaugural address and to the Hoover Presidential Library.

Huey P. Long

Every Man a King: Excerpts From Huey Long's Autobiography

http://www.ssa.gov./history/huey.html

Constructed by the Social Security Administration, this Web site contains excerpts from Huey Long's autobiography, *Every Man a King*, published in 1933.

Long was a showy politician, popular in the early 1930s, who advocated reallocation of wealth.

My First Days in the White House: Excerpts From Huey Long's "Second Autobiography"

http://www.ssa.gov./history/hueywhouse.html

The Social Security Administration also maintains this page, which includes excerpts from all eight chapters of Long's 1935 book, *My First Days in the White House*.

Anna Eleanor Roosevelt

Eleanor Roosevelt Center at Val-Kill

http://www.ervk.org

Val-Kill was Eleanor Roosevelt's cottage along the Hudson River. The Val-Kill Center's purpose is "to preserve Eleanor Roosevelt's home as a vibrant living memorial, a center for the exchange of significant ideas and a catalyst for change and for the betterment of the human condition." The Center maintains this page to provide information on Roosevelt and some photographs of her. There is an extensive list of useful links to topics and issues concerning her.

Eleanor Roosevelt Resource Page

http://personalweb.smcvt.edu/smahady/ercover.htm

This is a wonderful place to start any Internet search relating to Eleanor Roosevelt. The site, authored by Sherry S. Mahady, contains biographical and bibliographical information, quotes from scholars and peers, documents from Roosevelt's column, newspaper articles, letters from her papers and the National Archives, video clips, and links to other sites with information, pictures, and documents pertaining to the first lady.

Franklin D. Roosevelt

FDR Cartoon Collection database

http://www.nisk.k12.ny.us/fdr

This award-winning site, constructed by Paul Bachorz of Niskayuna High School in Niskayuna, New York, contains an extensive collection of over 30,000 FDR cartoons taken from newspapers and magazines during the 1930s and 1940s. There are also links to other Web sites, suggestions for school teachers, and Roosevelt's inaugural addresses.

Franklin D. Roosevelt Library and Museum

http://www.fdrlibrary.marist.edu

Created by the staff of the Roosevelt Presidential Library, this site provides short biographies of the president and the first lady. Additionally, the site contains several guides to the collections at the Roosevelt Presidential Library. Increasingly, the library is putting documents online. Now accessible is a collection of several thousand documents from the White House safe files during the Roosevelt years. Finally, there is an exceptional, copyright-free, online photograph database.

White House—Franklin D. Roosevelt

http://www.whitehouse.gov/history/presidents/fr32.html

The White House staff maintains this site, which contains short biographies of Franklin and Eleanor Roosevelt. There are links to the texts of FDR's inaugural addresses.

The Great Depression

African Americans and the New Deal

http://newdeal.feri.org/texts/subject.htm

This location, part of the New Deal Network, contains dozens of documents relating to blacks and the New Deal.

American Memory: FSA-OWI Photographs

http://lcweb2.loc.gov/ammem/fsowhome.html

American Memory, maintained by the Library of Congress, is a wonderful Web site for all topics in American history. It has thousands of primary sources that relate to the Age of Roosevelt. This particular location contains over 160,000 (including 1,600 in color) Farm Security Administration and Office of War Information photographs covering the years 1935 to 1945.

Dust Bowl Refugees in California

http://www.sfmuseum.org/hist8/ok.html

The Museum of the City of San Francisco maintains a Web site on California history, which has this section on dust bowl refugees. It contains primary sources and photographs.

A New Deal for the Arts

http://www.archives.gov/exhibits/new_deal_for_the_arts/index.html

The National Archives and Records Administration maintains an online version of this exhibit. The page has several good examples of New Deal art in various forms, including paintings, photographs, and posters.

The Trials of the Scottsboro Boys

http://www.law.umkc.edu/faculty/projects/FTrials/scottsboro/scottsb.htm

This location is part of the larger Famous American Trials Web site created by Doug Linder. The page on the Scottsboro boys contains a short history, biographical and bibliographical information, photographs, and trial documents.

Social Security Administration Online History

http://www.ssa.gov/history

The U.S. Social Security Administration built this page, which contains oral histories, video and audio clips, documents, photographs, brief biographies, and guides to the Social Security Administration archives.

Supreme Court Decisions (Legal Information Institute)

http://www.law.cornell.edu/supct/index.html

The Legal Information Institute and Cornell University sponsor this U.S. Supreme Court decisions Web site, which is an excellent place to gain quick access to decisions from the Wagner Act to Japanese relocation. This Web site contains an "Archives of Decisions" searchable by topic, author, or party. The site also contains general information on the U.S. Supreme Court.

The Voices From the Dust Bowl: The Charles L. Todd and Robert Sonkin Migrant Worker Collection, 1940–1941

http://memory.loc.gov/ammem/afctshtml/tshome.html

This page, part of American Memory, contains oral histories, photographs, and dozens of other primary documents relating to the dust bowl.

Works Progress (later Projects) Administration (WPA) Folklore Project and Federal Writers' Project

http://lcweb.loc.gov/ammem/wpaintro/

This American Memory site has several thousand WPA Folklore Project and Federal Writers' Project documents representing over 300 authors from twenty-four states from 1936 to 1940. The Library of Congress collection includes 2,900 documents. Searchable by keywords or by state.

WPA Murals and Artwork From Lane Technical High School Collection

http://www.lanetech.org

Maintained by Flora Doody, the director of Lane Technical High School's Artwork Restoration Project, this site has lots of WPA artwork, including eleven frescoes, two oil on canvas murals, an oil on steel fire curtain, two mahogany carved murals, and two concrete cast fountain statues. The site also contains artwork created for the General Motors Exhibition at the Century of Progress, Chicago's World Fair (1933–1934). Click on "Murals" at the above site to find the murals and artwork.

WPA's California Gold Northern California Folk Music From the Thirties

http://memory.loc.gov/ammem/afcchtml/cowhome.html

This American Memory Web site "includes sound recordings, still photographs, drawings, and written documents from a variety of European ethnic and English- and Spanish-speaking communities in Northern California. The collection comprises thirty-five hours of folk music recorded in twelve languages representing numerous ethnic groups and 185 musicians." This collection is well documented and easy to use. Search by musical instruments, ethnic groups, or performers.

World War II—Home Front

Alexander Zukas

German Prisoners of War in Clinton, Mississippi

http://www2.netdoor.com/~allardma/powcamp2.html

Mike Allard's site has minimal text but some interesting pictures of German prisoners at the POW camp in Clinton, Mississippi.

The Homefront During World War II

http://www.gettysburg.edu/~mbirkner/fys120/homefront.html

Professor Michael Birkner of Gettysburg College created this Web site for his first-year seminar class. The site hosts oral histories of the residents of Adams

County, Pennsylvania, a photo gallery of Gettysburg College during the war, advertising from the war years, and excerpts from the *Gettysburg Times* concerning everyday life on the home front. The site clarifies how the war affected small-town America.

The Japanese American Internment

http://www.geocities.com/Athens/8420/main.html

This is a rich and very developed site concerning the internment of Japanese-Americans during World War II. Included are sections on prewar intelligence reports on the loyalty of Japanese-Americans, the politics of internment, the state of mind and intentions of policy makers, life in the camps, the impact of the camps on those detained, and firsthand accounts by survivors. The site, maintained and regularly updated by C. John Yu, contains a large number of links to other Web sites exploring issues surrounding the internment of Japanese-Americans.

Japanese-American Internment and San Francisco

http://www.sfmuseum.org/war/evactxt.html

This site, maintained by the Museum of the City of San Francisco, contains dozens of newspaper articles about Japanese-American removal, photographs (including those by Dorothea Lange), contemporary accounts, and related information about internment.

Japanese American Internment at Harmony

http://www.lib.washington.edu/exhibits/harmony/

The University of Washington Libraries created this Web page about the internment camp in Puyallup, Washington, which contains primary source material including letters, the camp newspaper, drawings, pictures, and other documents. It is a useful place to begin an Internet search about internment.

Japanese American Internment in Arizona

http://jeff.scott.tripod.com/japanese.html

Jeffrey Scott, a specialist in Arizona history, maintains this page on the Gila River and Poston internment camps in Arizona. The site briefly describes the circumstances of Japanese internment and provides links to sites dedicated to the pictorial representation of these two camps, to books dealing with the camps, and to sites of photographic collections. The site also provides a list of manuscript sources and ephemera relating to the Arizona internment camps. The site is hosted on the Tripod.com domain.

Japanese American Internment (Resource Page for Teachers)

http://www.umass.edu/history/institute_dir/internment.html

The History Institute at the University of Massachusetts at Amherst sponsors this site, which is perhaps the best place to start searching for material on the internment of Japanese-Americans. Well organized and with dozens of Web links to documents, pictures, and related camp information, this site, designed for K–12 teachers, provides rich primary sources for classroom curricula.

Japanese Internment Camps During the Second World War

http://www.lib.utah.edu/spc/photo/9066/9066.htm

This online photograph exhibit, sponsored by the University of Utah Special Collections Department, displays a sampling of the library's collections concerning the internment of Japanese-Americans, particularly at the Topaz and Tule Lake camps.

The Lions' History: Researching World War II Images of African Americans

http://www.archives.gov/research/african-americans/ww2-pictures/index.html

Barbara Lewis Burger of the National Archives gathered this remarkable series of photos after immersing herself in African-American military history and researching life on the home front in the 1940s. Her intent was to produce a publication that fills a visual documentation void while at the same time stimulates interest in both black history and the holdings of the National Archives. This Web site does achieve both goals.

OWI Photographs

http://lcweb2.loc.gov/ammem/fsowhome.html

This site contains thousands of photographs of the home front taken for the Office of War Information during the war years. It is part of the American Memory project maintained by the Library of Congress.

Pictures of World War II

http://www.archives.gov/research/ww2/photos/images/thumbnails/index.html

The National Archives has a treasure trove of images from World War II. The war was documented on a huge scale by thousands of photographers and artists who created millions of pictures. American military photographers representing all the armed services covered the battlefronts around the world. Every activity of the war was photographed. On the home front, the many federal war agencies produced and collected pictures, posters, and cartoons on such subjects as war production, rationing, and civilian relocation. Among the areas covered in this photo ensemble are leaders, the home front, supply and support, rest and relaxation, aid and comfort, and victory and peace. If a picture is worth a thousand words, then little more needs to be said.

Rosie the Riveter and Other Women World War II Heroes

http://www.u.arizona.edu/~kari/rosie.htm

This site contains short vignettes about women's roles in World War II. Women worked as factory laborers, nurses and doctors, soldiers, journalists, prostitutes, and subjects of propaganda art. The site provides a different perspective on the war and some little-known information. A number of World War II propaganda posters illustrate the points in the texts.

Rutgers Oral History Archives of World War II

http://fas-history.rutgers.edu/oralhistory/orlhom.htm

The Rutgers World War II oral history project was funded by the Rutgers class of 1942 and directed by G. Kurt Piehler. The Web site has several dozen oral histories from veterans and civilians available for download (in Adobe Acrobat format).

San Francisco During World War II

http://www.sfmuseum.org/1906/ww2.html

This site maintained by the Museum of the City of San Francisco has information about San Francisco during the war years. Most of the primary sources on this site come from the *San Francisco News*.

Topaz Camp

http://www.millardcounty.com/topazcamp.html

Millard County, Utah, hosts this site, which provides a brief overview of Topaz, a Japanese-American relocation camp located in Millard County during World War II. The site explains the background to the relocation of Japanese-Americans, life in the camp, and conditions in the desert. The site also boasts picture postcards of the camp.

What Did You Do in the War, Grandma? Rhode Island Women During World War II

http://www.stg.brown.edu/projects/WWII_Women/tocCS.html

An oral history of Rhode Island women during World War II, written by students in the Honors English Program at South Kingstown High School, this site provides not only information about lesser-known aspects of the war, but also a good model of action for teachers interested in using the Internet for class projects.

World War II Posters: Powers of Persuasion

http://www.archives.gov/education/lessons/wwii-posters

The National Archives and Records Administration maintains this page, which has thirty-three war posters and one sound file. The page is divided into two categories representing the two psychological approaches used in rallying public support for the war.

WWII Propaganda Poster Collection From Northwestern University Library

http://www.library.northwestern.edu/govpub/collections/wwii-posters/

The Northwestern University Library's Government Publications division maintains this site, which has a searchable database of 300 wartime posters.

World War II—Military History

Alexander Zukas

504th World War II HomePage

http://www.ww2-airborne.us/units/504/504.html

An example of the many sites dedicated to military units, this one chronicles the experiences of the 504th Parachute Infantry Regiment during World War II.

Achtung Panzer

http://www.achtungpanzer.com/panzer.htm

One of the many enthusiast sites dedicated to German armor. This one features many illustrations, tables of technical data, and a large number of links to other World War II sites.

A-Bomb WWW Museum

http://www.csi.ad.jp/ABOMB/

This online project is a Japanese-hosted Web site designed to inform visitors about the effects of atomic weapons on Hiroshima and Nagasaki and to encourage discussions about world peace. The Hiroshima City University Department of Computer Science produced the site that gives a different perspective on the dropping of atomic weapons on Japan from that usually found in the United States. The creators of the Web site state that "The Web site is neither meant to condemn nor condone the bombing, but is meant as a way for people to express their views on how to achieve peace, on what peace is, and other thoughts about peace." Although the site is a somewhat random collection of material, it provides a useful entry for teachers to present the issues surrounding the use of atomic weapons at the end of World War II for student discussion and to discuss the cultural legacy of the bomb.

Armies of the Second World War

http://books.stonebooks.com/armies/

A rich online database of day-by-day orders of battle and information about hundreds of division-, brigade-, and regiment-sized units in World War II, this database covers Commonwealth, Dominion, Colonial, and Exile armies, as well as minor Allied armies in Europe, Africa, and western Asia from September 1, 1939, through May 7, 1945. The site will be expanded to include further theaters of the war.

Atomic Bomb Decision

http://www.dannen.com/decision/index.html

This site contains full-text documents on the decision to use the atomic bomb. Most of the originals are in the U.S. National Archives. The documents contain the positions of those who argued for and against the use of atomic weapons on human targets in the months leading up to the dropping of the atomic bomb on Hiroshima.

The Battle of Britain

http://www.raf.mod.uk/bob1940/bobhome.html

This is a detailed, extensive Web site devoted to the aerial battle over Great Britain in 1940. It is hosted by the Royal Air Force and contains the official reports of the battle and a day-by-day account of the four-month battle.

BBC Online: World War Two

http://www.bbc.co.uk/history/war/wwtwo/index.shtml

This British Broadcasting Corporation Web site covers numerous topics on the war such as campaigns and battles, politics, the British home front, and the Holocaust. A multimedia zone offers interactive maps, photographs, and audio and video clips. WW2 People's War, linked to this site, is a new Web site from BBCi (BBC Interactive) History, aspiring to create a new national archive of personal and family stories from World War II.

China Defensive, 1942–1945: The China Theater of Operations

http://www.army.mil/cmh-pg/brochures/72–38/72–38.htm

This account of World War II in China was prepared in the U.S. Army Center of Military History by Mark D. Sherry. In it he explains the differences between the Chinese, European, and Pacific war fronts, what the United States hoped to achieve in China, and the ultimate result of U.S. interventions, supplies, and strategic intentions. The site helps fill out the picture of World War II in this major theatre of the war.

Codebreaking and Secret Weapons in World War II

http://home.earthlink.net/~nbrass1/enigma.htm

This site deals with some of the secret weapons developed by the combatants in World War II and how the Allies found out about the ones the Axis had developed. The site provides a window on the clandestine but militarily significant aspects of the war.

Dad's War: Finding and Telling Your Father's World War II Story

http://members.aol.com/dadswar/index.htm

If you can tolerate the small promotional effort for his works on writing personal history, Wes Johnson has done a service with this index of personal histories and initial instructions for writing the history of a family member who served in World War II (and, by extension, any war).

East Anglia: The Air War

http://www.stable.demon.co.uk/

Contains a series of informative essays with illustrations concerning various air forces and the aircraft flown during World War II. The site also provides an excellent index of links to related Web pages and a bibliography of print reference works.

Feldgrau.com: A German Military History Research Site, 1919–1945

http://www.feldgrau.com/

A detailed Web site developed by an independent scholar working on a number of projects related to German World War II military history. It covers "the history of the units and formations of the various military, paramilitary, and auxiliary forces from 1933–45." Includes discussions of various battles and a bibliography of nearly 500 titles.

Guadalcanal Campaign

http://www.history.navy.mil/photos/events/wwii-pac/guadlcnl/guad-1.htm.

This site is hosted by the Naval Historical Center of the U.S. Department of the Navy. It is the official U.S. Navy interpretation of the battle of Guadalcanal, with a large number of combat photographs and a brief narrative of the battle. This site is part of an extensive Web site commemorating the battle with links to other pages dealing with different aspects of the fighting.

Hyperwar: A Hypertext History of the Second World War

http://www.ibiblio.org/hyperwar/

A linked anthology of articles related to World War II, many of them discussing specific battles in detail, along with links to other sources.

Imperial Japanese Navy Page

http://www.combinedfleet.com/

Enthusiast Jon Parshall has created a detailed index to links about the Japanese navy during World War II, including detailed histories of individual vessels.

The Luftwaffe Home Page

http://www.ww2.dk/

This site provides data on the Luftwaffe and an index of links to Luftwaffe-related Web pages.

A Marine Diary: My Experiences on Guadalcanal

http://www.gnt.net/~jrube/index2.html

Entries from the diary of a Marine who served at Guadalcanal, with a large set of links to related World War II resources on the Internet.

Midway

http://www.history.navy.mil/photos/events/wwii-pac/midway/midway.htm

This is a Department of the Navy Naval Historical Center site. It contains a detailed narrative and excellent photographs of the battle. This is a good place to start gathering information about this important battle, often considered the turning point of the war in the Pacific. The site contains an FAQ section and a list of related resources.

Nanjing Massacre Archive

http://www.cnd.org/njmassacre/index.html

The *China News Digest* hosts this extensive site on the famous Nanjing Massacre in 1937–1938 in China, including the war crimes testimony and trial after the war.

Naval Air War in the Pacific

http://www.daveswarbirds.com/navalwar/

Photos and paintings of American air combat during World War II.

Normandy: 1944

http://normandy.eb.com/

Encyclopedia Britannica's multimedia examination of the Normandy invasion.

Open Directory Project: World War II

http://dmoz.org/Society/History/By_Time_Period/Twentieth_Century/Wars_and_Conflicts/World_War_II/

This comprehensive directory contains over 800 Web sites on World War II including Air Forces (96), Arts and Literature (14), Atomic (55), Primary Sources (6), Education and Academic (4), Holocaust (285), Land Forces (37), Naval Forces (79), People (191), Regional (123), Theaters of Operations (175), War Crimes (4) and Weapons and Equipment (54).

The Pacific War: The U.S. Navy

http://www.microworks.net/pacific/

This page, which forms a conscious complement and counterpoint to the Imperial Japanese Navy page above, wants to inform visitors of the U.S. Navy's contribution to the overall victory that ended World War II with as much awesome detail as can be mustered. Comparing the information on both Web sites will give the student of World War II naval warfare an excellent overview of the military strength and tactics of these two major Pacific powers. The sites also contain short profiles of naval leaders and personal histories of veterans.

A People at War

http://www.archives.gov/exhibits/a_people_at_war/a_people_at_war.html

This site presents an online exhibition by the National Archives. It includes a brief discussion of events leading up to the war and links to related sites. Focuses on the people who served rather than providing a traditional history of the war.

Propaganda Leaflets of the Second World War

http://www.geocities.com/CapeCanaveral/4503

Most of the propaganda leaflets shown in these pages are anti-Nazi (airdropped by the UK/U.S. Allied Air Forces), although some Nazi leaflets are shown here also. The Web site author warns that some images and texts in the Nazi propaganda leaflets may be disturbing or offensive on religious, racial, or ethnic grounds. The material, which is produced exactly from the originals, provides visitors with good comparisons on the use of symbols and propaganda during the war.

Red Steel

http://www.algonet.se/~toriert/

Enthusiast Thorleif Olsson's extensive Web site on Russian tanks and armored vehicles.

Return to Midway

http://www.nationalgeographic.com/features/98/midway/

National Geographic has created this multimedia site featuring images and streaming video of the wrecks of the carriers sunk at the Battle of Midway.

The Russian Campaign, 1941–1945: A Photo Diary

http://www.geipelnet.com/war_albums/otto/ow_011.html

This site is a diary of a German soldier along with pictures he took of his experiences with an antitank battalion on the Russian front. It covers the whole span of the Russian campaign and provides an on-the-ground look at the fortunes of German troops and rare scenes of the fighting between German and Russian forces.

Second World War Encyclopedia

http://www.spartacus.schoolnet.co.uk/2WW.htm

This online encyclopedia is a Spartacus Educational Web site that enables research on individual people and events of the war in detail. The individual
sections include Background to the War, Nazi Germany, Chronology of the
War, Political Leaders, European Diplomacy, Major Offensives, the Home Front,
British Military Leaders, U.S. Military Leaders, German Military Leaders, Japanese Military Leaders, Russian Military Leaders, French Military Leaders, the
Armed Forces, the Air War, the Sea War, the Resistance, Scientists and Inventors, Resistance in Nazi Germany, French Resistance, the Holocaust, War Artists, Weapons and Tactics, Women in the War, Secret Agents, and Soldiers,
Sailors and Pilots.

U-Boat Net

http://uboat.net/

A comprehensive study of the German U-boat, including maps, technology,
and profiles of more than 1,100 German submarines employed during World
War II.

What Did You Do in the War, Grandma?: Rhode Island
Women During World War II

http://www.stg.brown.edu/projects/WWII_Women/tocCS.html

An oral history of Rhode Island women during World War II, written by students in the Honors English Program at South Kingstown High School, this
site provides not only information about lesser-known aspects of the war, but
also a good model of action for teachers interested in using the Internet for
class projects.

Women Come to the Front: Journalists, Photographers,
and Broadcasters During World War II

http://lcweb.loc.gov/exhibits/wcf/wcf0001.html

This Library of Congress site documents the work of eight female war correspondents, most of whom worked overseas while a few covered the home front.
The site provides some corrective to the male-dominated discussions of World
War II life at the front while documenting continued male prerogative in the
periodical business.

The Women's Army Corps

http://www.army.mil/cmh-pg/brochures/wac/wac.htm

The U.S. Army has developed this online article about the Women's Army Corps during World War II.

The World at War

http://www.euronet.nl/users/wilfried/ww2/ww2.htm

Wilfried Braakhuis has created an extremely detailed time line of the war, with illustrations, statistics, and a very large number of links, organized by relevant dates. This graphic-intensive site takes a while to load, but is worth looking at.

World War Two in Europe

http://www.historyplace.com/worldwar2/time line/ww2time.htm

Part of the History Place, a large Web site dedicated to assisting students and educators, this is a World War II time line with links to illustrations and short articles on specific events.

World War II on the Web

http://www.geocities.com/Athens/Oracle/2691/welcome.htm

An index to more than 400 Web sites concerned with World War II, many of them highly specialized.

World War II Poster Collection

http://www.library.northwestern.edu/govpub/collections/wwii-posters/

This collection of hundreds of World War II posters from the U.S. government is hosted by Northwestern University. The posters range from the mundane to the shocking, from recruiting posters to those exhorting greater patriotism and sacrifice as well as secrecy. Taken together, the posters provide an excellent window on wartime culture, at least as officially propagated by the U.S. government.

World War II Resources

http://metalab.unc.edu/pha/index.html

An extensive collection of historical documents from World War II based at the University of North Carolina-Chapel Hill.

World War II Seminar

http://history.sandiego.edu/gen/classes/ww2/175.html

Class materials for a World War II history course from the University of San Diego, including an extended bibliography and several time lines created by students.

World War II Sites

http://home.comcast.net/~dboals1/a-part1a.html#WORLD%20WAR%20II

This is an excellent directory to over 200 Web sites on all aspects of World War II. The major purpose of this directory is to encourage the use of the World Wide Web as a tool for learning and teaching and to provide some help for teachers in locating and using the resources of the Internet in the classroom. This directory is a superb place to start searching for Web sites on World War II.

The World War II Sounds and Pictures Page

http://www.earthstation1.com/wwii.html

Sounds, video, and images of many items related to World War II. The site includes aircraft, warships, propaganda posters, and other assorted images.

The World War II Study: North Africa

http://www.topedge.com/panels/ww2/na/index.html

In this site, many issues regarding the North Africa campaign of the Allies from 1940 to 1943 receive a fresh look. The author examines the importance of North Africa to the Allies and Axis and dispels myths about the campaigns and personalities of the North African theater. He provides a time line of the conflict and considers supply issues, troop levels, weaponry, commanders, tactics, and high-command disputes.

World War II Timeline

http://history.acusd.edu/gen/WW2Timeline/start.html

A fairly good and general time line for World War II. Includes a very valuable list of additional links. Also has a number of interesting pictures, maps, documents, and a good bibliography. Includes some student pages. A first-rate site by Steve Schoenherr of the University of San Diego's History Department.

World War II Web Sites

http://connections.smsd.org/veterans/wwii_sites.htm

This site serves as a gateway to World War II sites appropriate for students and teachers. Links revolve around the following topics: The Rise of Fascism—Germany, Italy and Japan, Holocaust, Pearl Harbor and America's Response, D-Day and the War in the Pacific, The Home Front, Plans for Peace and the Atomic Bomb, Personalities, Literature, Propaganda, Women in the War, and Miscellaneous. Updated regularly, the site leads users to movie clips, virtual tours, stories of the war, biographies, films, and photographs.

The Cold War

Alexander Zukas

1948: The Alger Hiss Spy Case

http://www.thehistorynet.com/ah/blalgerhiss/index2.html

This links to a June 1998 *American History* article by James Thomas Grey that examines the Alger Hiss case and the issues that still remain unresolved fifty years later.

The 1956 Hungarian Revolution: A History in Documents

http://www2.gwu.edu/~nsarchiv/NSAEBB/NSAEBB76/

Hosted by the National Security Archive at The George Washington University, this site contains parts of this National Security Archive Electronic Briefing Book edited by Malcolm Byrne. The book is a compilation of new government documents from Hungarian, Russian, and U.S. archives, which shed light on the Soviet decision to invade Hungary in 1956 and the U.S. responses to that invasion. Twelve of the 120 documents in the book are reproduced on this Web site.

The Alger Hiss Story

http://homepages.nyu.edu/~th15/

Hosted at New York University and dedicated to students, scholars, archivists, teachers, and a general audience, this is an engaging, comprehensive site that re-creates one of the most important legal cases in U.S. history during the Cold War—a case that helped launch McCarthyism. The site strives to be an authoritative portal to primary information about Alger Hiss, the Hiss case, and the early Cold War years, including new scholarship, newly released official documents from various governments and government agencies, and archival material, such as trial testimony, court and government records, and commentary, collected in many libraries and online repositories. It also functions as the digitized and online counterpart to the Alger Hiss Papers at the Harvard Law School Library. Acting in tandem with the Harvard collection, this Web site posts a complete summary of the charges against Hiss and takes a comprehensive look at the case for the defense. Among the many interesting leads to explore through the site are exclusive new interviews with eyewitnesses and others, Freedom of Information Act releases of government documents, grand jury secret testimony, and House Un-American Activities Committee files released in 2001.

American Experience: Race for the Superbomb

http://www.pbs.org/wgbh/pages/amex/bomb

This PBS companion site explores a top secret U.S. Cold War program to build a weapon more powerful than the atomic bomb dropped on Japan. The site includes audio clips, a time line, primary documents, and other educational materials.

The Avalon Project: Documents in Law, History, and Diplomacy

http://www.yale.edu/lawweb/avalon/coldwar.htm

Maintained by the Yale University Law School, this site contains basic documents under the following headings: American Foreign Policy 1941–49; the United States Atomic Energy Commission proceedings in the Matter of J. Robert Oppenheimer; The Warsaw Security Pact: May 14, 1955; State Department Papers Relating to the Foreign Relations of the United States, Vol. X, Part 1, 1958–60; the U-2 Incident: 1960; the RB-47 Airplane Incident: July–September 1960; and the Cuban Missile Crisis.

The Berlin Airlift

http://www.wpafb.af.mil/museum/history/postwwii/ba.htm

This Web site is part of the larger online exhibit titled "U.S. Air Force Museum, Post–World War II History Gallery 1946–50s." The focus is primarily military. The site is a good source of information and images of the aircraft used to airlift provisions to the inhabitants of Berlin.

Berlin Wall Online

http://www.dailysoft.com/berlinwall/

Heiko Burkhardt developed this site chronicling the history of the Berlin Wall from a (West) German point of view. Replete with interesting facts, maps, photographs, stories of escape attempts, and an archive of related documents and material, the site places the Berlin Wall into the context of Cold War politics and German history. Some East German documents and resources are available on the site as are links to the British National Archives and the German Propaganda Archive (which highlights only Nazi and East German propaganda).

Chronology of Russian History: The Soviet Period

http://www.pbs.org/weta/faceofrussia/timeline-index.html

Part of a PBS Web site on the history of the Russian people called the *Face of Russia*, this interactive time line details major cultural, political, military, and social events of twentieth-century Russia and the Soviet Union. Clicking on the highlighted images and text brings up expanded content and images. Users can scroll through the time line chronologically or jump to a specific period using the key at the top of the page. The complete time line chronicles Russian culture since about 850 CE and includes streaming audio and video clips, still images, and text.

CIA and Assassinations: The Guatemala 1954 Documents

http://www.gwu.edu/~nsarchiv/NSAEBB/NSAEBB4/index.html

The National Security Archive is an independent, nongovernmental research institute and library located at The George Washington University in Washington, DC. The archive collects and publishes declassified documents acquired through the Freedom of Information Act. On May 23, 1997, the CIA released several hundred records that verified the CIA's involvement in the infamous 1954 coup in Guatemala at the height of the Cold War politics of "brinkmanship." Some of these documents, including an instructional guide on assassination found among the training files of the CIA's covert Operation PBSUCCESS, are stored on this site.

CNN—*Cold War*

http://cnn.com/SPECIALS/cold.war/

This Web site was created to accompany the twelve-part series on the Cold War airing on CNN in the winter and spring of 1998–1999. The Web site is a valuable resource because it provides an extraordinary diversity of materials, including multimedia and audio clips, interactive maps, primary documents, newspaper and journal coverage of the events, and transcripts of interviews that formed the basis for the series.

Cold War Guide

http://www.cold-war.info/

The Cold War Guide is a project of Roman Studenic of Bratislava, Slovakia, which provides a centralized database about the events of the Cold War and about the roles people, states, and government agencies played in it. It is a metasite that provides basic information and links to other sources that provide more detail. The Cold War Guide offers an index of all entries in an encyclopedia format, a time line of events, and an archive of texts, essays, and various data that includes more encyclopedia entries.

Cold War Hot Links: Web Resources Relating to the Cold War

http://www.stmartin.edu/~dprice/cold.war.html

David Price, an anthropologist at St. Martin's College in Lacey, Washington, has compiled an impressive list of links to Web sites that contain primary sources, essays, and analyses examining the impact of the Cold War on American culture.

Cold War International History Project

http://wwics.si.edu/index.cfm?topic_id=1409&fuseaction=topics.home

The Cold War International History Project (CWIHP) Web site was established at the Woodrow Wilson International Center for Scholars in Washington, DC, in 1991. The project supports the full and prompt release of historical materials by governments on all sides of the Cold War. In addition to Western sources, the project has provided translations of documents from Eastern European archives that have been released since the collapse of communism in the late 1980s. Users may join discussion groups and download issues of the *Bulletin* issued by CWIHP.

The Cold War Museum

http://www.coldwar.org/

In 1996, Francis Gary Powers Jr. and John C. Welch founded the Cold War Museum to preserve Cold War history and honor Cold War veterans. The Cold War Museum, a Smithsonian Affiliate Museum, endeavors to maintain a historically accurate record of the people, places, and events of the Cold War that will enable visitors to reflect upon the global geopolitical climate of that period (1940s to 1990s). On its Web site, the museum displays artifacts and memorabilia associated with various Cold War–related events such as the Marshall Plan, the Berlin Air Lift, the Korean War, the building of the Berlin Wall, the U-2 Incident, the Cuban Missile Crisis, the Vietnam War, President Mikhail Gorbachev's glasnost, the fall of the Berlin Wall, and the collapse of the Soviet Union.

A Concrete Curtain: The Life and Death of the Berlin Wall

http://www.wall-berlin.org/gb/berlin.htm

This site contains a detailed history of the Berlin Wall from its creation to its destruction. Part of an exhibition comprising around a hundred photographs for the Deutsches Historisches Museum in Berlin, the site is a good place to start examining the historical and cultural significance of "The Wall."

The Costs of the Manhattan Project

http://www.brook.edu/FP/PROJECTS/NUCWCOST/MANHATTN.HTM

These estimates were prepared by the Brookings Institute and are part of the larger U.S. Nuclear Weapons Cost Study Project.

Cuba

http://bubl.ac.uk/link/c/cuba.htm

This metasite on Cuba is hosted and maintained by the Centre for Digital Library Research at Strathclyde University in Scotland under the acronym BUBL. The site has links to a Castro speech database, maps, political resources, and material on tourism and the economic impact of U.S. sanctions on Cuba.

The Cuban Missile Crisis

http://www.personal.psu.edu/staff/r/x/rxb297/CUBA/MAIN.HTML

This site is a wonderful place to start researching the Cuban Missile Crisis. It contains excellent links to primary and secondary source materials at the Library of Congress, the Federation of American Scientists, the State Department, the National Security Archive, and in Premier Nikita Khrushchev's memoirs, among other sources. The site provides an overview of the crisis and discusses its causes, UN and Turkish involvement, and the outcome of the crisis.

The Cuban Missile Crisis, 1962

http://www.state.gov/www/about_state/history/frusXI/index.html

This is the site for volume 11 of *Foreign Relations of the United States,* which is the official U.S. Department of State volume of documents dealing with the

Cuban Missile Crisis. The entire volume or excerpts can be read online. A very important source for the official documents dealing with this crisis.

The Cuban Missile Crisis, 1962

http://www.fas.org/irp/imint/cuba.htm

The Federation of American Scientists maintains this metasite. It contains links to online State Department documentation, analysis of President John Kennedy's advisers, transcripts of ExComm (Executive Committee) deliberations, and photographic evidence of the Soviet presence in Cuba until the 1980s.

The Cuban Missile Crisis, October 18–29, 1962

http://www.hpol.org/jfk/cuban/

This Web site contains audio files of a set of tape recordings released by the John F. Kennedy Library in October 1996. These recordings were made in the Oval Office. They include President Kennedy's personal recollections of discussions, conversations with his advisers, and meetings with the Joint Chiefs of Staff and members of the president's executive committee. Transcripts of the audio files are included. A rich source of information on the American perspective of the crisis.

Documents Relating to American Foreign Policy: The Cold War

http://www.mtholyoke.edu/acad/intrel/coldwar.htm

The International Relations Program at Mount Holyoke College maintains this Web site. Organized by years from pre-1945 to recent retrospectives on the meaning and significance of the Cold War, this site contains hundreds of links to both primary and secondary source material—especially useful to students and researchers because of the variety of sources available.

Documents Relating to American Foreign Policy: Cuban Missile Crisis

http://www.mtholyoke.edu/acad/intrel/cuba.htm

This collection of links allows researchers and students access to newspaper coverage of the crisis. The Web site contains important links to information relating to Soviet and Cuban perspectives on the crisis. Links to essays and books by the most influential historians of this crisis are also provided.

Famous American Trials: Rosenbergs Trial, 1951

http://www.law.umkc.edu/faculty/projects/ftrials/rosenb/ROSENB.HTM

Professor Douglas Linder of the University of Missouri-Kansas City School of Law created this site. The Web site contains links to a wealth of firsthand materials, including excerpts from the trial transcript, the judge's sentencing statement, excerpts from appellate court decisions, images, the Rosenbergs' final letter to their sons, and a link to the Perlin Papers, a collection of about 250,000 pages that relates to the investigation, trial, and execution of Julius and Ethel Rosenberg. The papers were declassified in the 1970s.

Fifty Years From Trinity

http://www.seattletimes.com/trinity/supplement/internet.html

The *Seattle Times* compiled this list of Internet resources relating to the development of the atomic bomb and nuclear energy.

For European Recovery: The Fiftieth Anniversary of the Marshall Plan

http://www.loc.gov/exhibits/marshall/marsintr.html

This Library of Congress Web page accompanied an exhibit on the fiftieth anniversary of the Marshall Plan in 1997. Besides an overview of the plan and a time line, the site has links developed by the National Library of the Netherlands and other European libraries: the rationale for the Marshall Plan, communist critiques of the plan, Soviet opposition, a negative view of aid to Europe, a Dutch view, benefits for the U.S. economy, among others. There are also the complete texts of books on the Marshall Plan: *The Marshall Plan and the Future of U.S. European Relations, The Marshall Plan and You* (a Dutch book from 1949), *Kiplinger's Magazine's How to Do Business Under the Marshall Plan,* and W. Averill Harriman's album, *The Marshall Plan at the Mid-Mark.*

Harvard Project on Cold War Studies

http://www.fas.harvard.edu/~hpcws/

This annotated set of links relating to the study of the Cold War is prepared and maintained by the Davis Center for Russian Studies at Harvard University. The project intends to build on the achievements of the Cold War International History Project and the National Security Archive. The site also contains links to Harvard University's new *Journal of Cold War Studies.*

Institute for the History of the 1956 Hungarian Revolution

http://www.rev.hu/index_en.html

Dedicated to the study of the 1956 uprising in Hungary, the institute's Web site contains links to numerous aspects of the uprising. The institute, located in Budapest, has produced a multimedia CD-ROM on the history of the 1956 revolt and the site contains links to studies on Hungarian history since World War II, an oral history archive, a photo-documentary archive, and a database (in Hungarian) of biographies, oral history interviews and extracts from trial records, bibliographical data (books, articles, and audiovisual documents), and accounts of events and institutions. The institute considers itself the successor of the Imre Nagy Institute of Sociology and Politics, which operated in Brussels between 1959 and 1963, and other Western émigré organizations, and its purpose is to establish a genuine account of the events in Hungary from the point of view of those who participated in the revolt.

An Introduction to National Archives Records Relating to the Cold War

http://www.archives.gov/research/cold-war/

Hosted by the National Archives, this metasite was compiled primarily by Tim Wehrkamp. It "identifies several representative series and data sets of textual, electronic, still picture, and motion picture records that document U.S. government policies, programs, and actions during the Cold War. The compilers have chosen a selection of records that illustrate the range and content of National Archives and Records Administration (NARA) holdings relating to this period. These records by no means represent all NARA-held documentation concerning the topic. The intended audience for this publication is graduate students and other researchers new to the field of Cold War history who may be unfamiliar with NARA records relating to the era." It would be a good place for them to begin their research.

The National Security Archive Homepage

http://www.gwu.edu/~nsarchiv/

The National Security Archive is an independent, nongovernmental research institute and library located at The George Washington University in Washington, DC. The archive collects and publishes declassified documents gathered through the Freedom of Information Act (FOIA). The archive boasts the world's largest nongovernmental library of declassified documents, including thousands of documents relating to nuclear history, U.S.-Japanese relations, the Cuban Missile Crisis, and other crises of the 1960s and 1970s.

The Real Thirteen Days: The Hidden History of the Cuban Missile Crisis

http://www.gwu.edu/~nsarchiv/nsa/cuba_mis_cri/

The National Security Archive has created an extensive Web site on the Cuban Missile Crisis. It includes essays titled "Turning History on Its Head" by Philip Brenner, "The Declassified Documents" by Peter Kornbluh and Laurence Chang, "The Most Dangerous Moment in the Crisis" by Jim Hershberg, and "Annals of Blinksmanship" by Thomas Blanton. Visitors can hear audio clips of White House meetings, read the documents exchanged between the White House and the Kremlin, see the U-2 surveillance photos of the Russian missile installations, and read a detailed chronology of events relating to the Cuban Missile Crisis from 1959 to 1992. This revisionist site is dedicated to dispelling myths about the crisis, especially the myth of calibrated brinkmanship—the belief that if you stand tough you win and that nuclear superiority made the difference in moments of crisis.

Secrets of War

http://www.secretsofwar.com/

This is the companion site to the History Channel's twenty-six-part documentary series titled *Sworn to Secrecy: Secrets of War,* which was aired in 1998. The site contains transcripts and links to maps, images, and other information relating to the history of espionage.

A Select Bibliography of the U-2 Incident

http://www.eisenhower.utexas.edu/u2.htm

This brief bibliography is located at the Dwight D. Eisenhower Presidential Library.

Senator Joseph McCarthy: A Modern Tragedy

http://www.foxvalleyhistory.org/mccarthy/

This archive contains film and audio clips from Senator Joseph McCarthy's speeches and appearances on television.

Soviet Archives Exhibit

http://metalab.unc.edu/expo/soviet.exhibit/entrance.html#tour

The Library of Congress developed this online exhibit where visitors can browse images of documents from the Soviet archives. The two main sections of this exhibit are the Internal Workings of the Soviet System and The Soviet Union and the United States. The section on postwar estrangement includes commentary on Soviet perspectives on the Cold War and the Cuban Missile Crisis.

Space Race

http://www.nasm.si.edu/galleries/gal1114/

The space race was a high-profile area of the Cold War competition between the United States and the Soviet Union, the most powerful nations in the world after World War II. For a half-century, the two superpowers competed for supremacy in a global struggle on the earth, in air, at sea, and in space that was tied to an arms race and a drive for military primacy. This U.S. National Air and Space Museum site contains links to the military origins of the space race, the Soviet challenge in space, the race to the moon, espionage from space, and building a permanent U.S. presence in space.

The U-2 Incident 1960

http://www.yale.edu/lawweb/avalon/u2.htm

The Avalon Project at Yale University developed this Web site on the U-2 incident in 1960. It is a useful starting place to find the basic diplomatic documents, including the exchange of notes between the United States and Soviet governments, public statements by State Department officials, and the documentation maintained by the State Department in the *Foreign Relations of the United States* series.

The Venona Project

http://www.nsa.gov/venona/index.cfm

VENONA was the code name used for the U.S. Signals Intelligence effort to collect and decrypt the text of Soviet KGB and GRU messages from the 1940s. These messages provided extraordinary insight into Soviet attempts to infiltrate the highest levels of the U.S. government. The National Security Agency has declassified over 3,000 messages related to VENONA and made them available at its home page.

The Wars for Vietnam

http://vietnam.vassar.edu/

This site, produced by students at Vassar College, provides an overview of the Vietnam War, primary documents and photos from the American and Vietnamese sides, detailed accounts of the battles of Ia Drang Valley, and links to other related sites. Many of the documents are from Vietnamese archives in Hanoi.

General Twentieth-Century United States History

John Barnhill

Metasites

Digital History/Could You Have Passed the 8th Grade in 1895?

http://www.digitalhistory.uh.edu/

This American history site has time lines, videos, interactive time lines, graphics, standard bibliographies, links, and written content. The test from 1895 is in the multimedia section. It even has an "ask a historian" section—one of the best new sites.

Economic History

http://www.tntech.edu/history/economic.html

This site combines associations, archives, journals, and specialized sites in business and economic history and contemporary issues. Plus, it has historical price calculators. This page is part of the broader Tennessee Tech site that is old but still solid.

History Matters: The U.S. History Survey on the Web

http://historymatters.gmu.edu/

Everything anyone could ever need to teach the American History survey—making history relevant to current events, using primary documents, secrets of teachers, using the Web, and the reference desk.

Librarians Index to the Internet

http://lii.org/search?query="United+States+History"
+"20th+century";searchtype=subject

Nothing fancy, just good solid search capability for just about any topic—and it stays current—good starting point.

U.S. Diplomatic History Resources Index

http://faculty.tamu-commerce.edu/sarantakes/stuff.html

This site ties to associations, archives, bibliographies, book reviews, journals, funding—a great starting point for the vast topic of American diplomatic history. It also has an index from "archive" to "White House."

WWW Virtual Library—History: Internet & W3 (World Wide Web)

http://vlib.iue.it/history/internet/index.html

This site includes an atlas, biographies, and bibliographies and is organized topically and chronologically by decade (including the eighteenth century). It is current as of 2004 and the starting point for history of the Net. It is, after all, a subset of the WWW Virtual Library, which has been growing and improving for more than a decade, a millennium by Net standards.

Google: U.S. History 20th Century

http://directory.google.com/Top/Society/History/By_Time_Period/
Twentieth_Century/

Nothing fancy—just many links by decade and by topic.

General Sites

America 1900

http://www.pbs.org/wgbh/pages/amex/1900/index.html

PBS sites based on the *American Experience* programs are generally well put together. This program features life in 1900, and the site describes the film and includes a searchable database.

The American Experience

http://www.pbs.org/wgbh/amex/index.html.

The PBS program *American Experience* deals with arts, politics, technology, and culture through use of time lines, maps, and illustrations. Chronological, alphabetical, and thematic indexes allow easy access to materials supporting the films. Topics cover a range from the racehorse Seabiscuit through the Golden Gate Bridge to aviator Charles Lindbergh. Teacher's guides and bibliographies are also included.

American Memory Collection

http://memory.loc.gov/ammem/ammemhome.html

Collections range from photographer Ansel Adams to the Wright Brothers, with over a million documents, photos, and recordings. "Ask a librarian" has links to other Library of Congress sources as well as the National Archives, Virtual Reference, and much more. Inquiries get a reply in five days the site promises.

American Temperance and Prohibition

http://prohibition.osu.edu/default.htm

Nice variety of materials on the rise of the American prohibition movement. Material includes cartoons and photos and lots of text on events and major figures. The Ohio State University also has sites pertaining to immigration, lynching, and Ohio-specific topics, mostly dating to 1997 but still with live links.

Anti-Imperialism in the United States, 1898–1935

http://www.boondocksnet.com/ai/index.html

For teachers and interested persons alike this is the best anti-imperialism site, with cartoons and an extensive array of documents, including full-length works. It presents one side of the issue, and not even the side that won out—it needs to be used in conjunction with a good site on imperialism, such as the Age of Imperialism (http://www.smplanet.com/imperialism/toc.html).

Apollo Lunar Surface Journal

http://www.hq.nasa.gov/office/pao/History/alsj/frame.html

Although this site on the Apollo missions dates from 1995, updates continue, and it works well. No bad links, and as the site has grown it remains a good source for mission summaries, crew information, and photos.

CIA and Assassinations: The Guatemala 1954 documents

http://www.gwu.edu/~nsarchiv/NSAEBB/NSAEBB4/index.html

Because this is a representative sample of the National Security Archive, it deserves examination. The NSA digs the documents out and puts them online in a straightforward array. Mostly, as in the case of the CIA and the 1954 coup, the material addresses matters unflattering to America's self-image.

Civil Rights Coalition for the 21st Century

http://www.civilrights.org/index.html

This site has a solid history of civil rights with links to many legal cases, a comprehensive set of links to civil rights organizations' sites, and an extensive issues section. It is a bit untidy, but that seems to be where civil rights is today. See especially the "Research Center."

Detroit Photos Home Page From the Library of Congress

http://memory.loc.gov/ammem/detroit/

With a bit more text, the 25,000 transparencies and glass negatives on this Library of Congress American Memory site could be invaluable. As it is, the Detroit Photographic Company photos give a good impression of turn-of-the-century life.

Digger Archives

http://www.diggers.org/

The diggers were a short-lived San Francisco commune that tried to provide street theater and free stores in the late 1960s. The site tries to preserve that history while linking to current groups clinging to those days and those values. Interesting.

The Digital Classroom

http://www.archives.gov/digital_classroom/index.html

The National Archives helps educators to teach using primary documents. This site includes a set of ten units on the twentieth century. The site also provides lesson plans, links to additional sources, a documentary analysis worksheet, and information about summer workshops for educators and electronics workshops for their classes.

The *Enola Gay* Controversy

http://www.lehigh.edu/~ineng/enola/

Originally designed for a university course at Lehigh University, Pennsylvania, the site remains valuable for its thorough treatment of the controversy over the Smithsonian's *Enola Gay* display, now removed. It shows clearly what can go wrong when historians and the public disagree on the meaning of an event. Extensive bibliography and links to other sites.

Famous Trials of the Twentieth Century

http://www.umkc.edu/famoustrials

This site looks at many famous trials from Socrates to O.J. Simpson, and its twentieth-century trials range from Bill Haywood to the Scopes "monkey" trial and from Charles Manson to President William Jefferson Clinton. Included are crime scene maps, evidence, transcripts, and verdicts. The site contains links to Linder's Constitutional Law pages, which are also well done—even a page of Supreme Court humor and a provocative section on evil—and to other famous trials such as those of Fatty Arbuckle and Patty Hearst.

The Forest History Society

http://www.lib.duke.edu/forest/index.html

Niche history taken seriously becomes an organization such as this, with an oral history program, publications, a searchable photograph database, a bibliography with 33,000 citations, and even a suggested middle school curriculum. The Forest History Society library and archives are at Duke University.

For European Recovery: The Fiftieth Anniversary of the Marshall Plan

http://lcweb.loc.gov/exhibits/marshall/

This site shows how the Library of Congress uses its resources to present a historical event, in this case the anniversary of the Marshall Plan. The site contains extracts from *The Marshall Plan and the Future of U.S.-European Relations,* the twenty-fifth anniversary document. The site also provides a fairly extensive explanation of the plan's rationale and chronology. It lacks audio and video, but it is a good representative exhibit of the Library of Congress and the plan, and it links to the Marshall Foundation (http://www.marshallfoundation .org/), which includes a filmography, annotated bibliography, and more.

The Emma Goldman Papers

http://sunsite.Berkeley.EDU/Goldman/

An online exhibit based on the 20,000 documents, images, and moving pictures in the Emma Goldman Papers Project housed at the University of California-Berkeley, is the entry point to a site that also includes a recommended curriculum for teaching the life of the radical Goldman as well as the issues that formed her times—women's rights, immigration, and other issues still unresolved. The site exemplifies what is best in archive sites—eye appeal and good content. Of course, it also has a page of "Emmarabilia" for sale, as well as a solicitation for money to fund the continuation of the site.

Kennedy Assassination Home Page

http://mcadams.posc.mu.edu/home.htm

This page remains the best balanced of the online sources on the Kennedy assassination, and its links are to the best materials. The owner does note that most of the assassination links are to conspiracy sites and that the books he recommends are not necessarily the best, just those necessary for a balanced understanding before digging further.

Kingwood College Library American Cultural History: The Twentieth Century

http://kclibrary.nhmccd.edu/decades.html

A component of a site designed for easy access by students to research a broad range of topics, the cultural history section is arranged by decade, with a historical overview and essays on fads and fashions, technology, the arts, and literature and music. The overall page at http://kclibrary.nhmccd.edu/research.htm has music site links, including the Rock and Roll Hall of Fame and lots of rock 'n' roll sites.

Mining History, Museums and Disasters

http://www.msha.gov/history.htm

The material is mostly text and photos on mining history. Tidily arranged discussions deal with canaries, emergency vehicles, African-Americans, Asian and children workers, and more. Links to state museums and memorials are extensive, but some links are bad. Take a minute to read "'Oh God, For One More Breath': Early 20th Century Tennessee Coal Miners' Last Words" at http://historymatters.gmu.edu/d/62/.

National Archives

http://www.nara.gov/

The National Archives and Records Administration has a good search capability, an online exhibit with samples of its records, and information on its services—records management, archives, and training at locations throughout the United States. The Web site barely scratches the surface of the 4 billion records NARA has in its custody, but it is the starting point for finding material and finding out how to find more.

National Civil Rights Museum

http://www.civilrightsmuseum.org/about/about.asp

The Lorraine Motel in Memphis, Tennessee, where Martin Luther King was assassinated, is now part of the National Civil Rights Museum. When the motel property experienced a succession of failures, the Martin Luther King, Jr. Memorial Foundation saved it. The museum includes archives and exhibits on the broad history of civil rights, not just King and his assassination. It is a good example of how sometimes it is necessary to change in order to preserve.

New Deal Network

http://newdeal.feri.org/index.htm

Coverage of the 1930s on this site includes documents, photos, good links, and, of course, lesson plans and such. It includes the H-Net discussion list, H-US 1918–45, which includes current news, teaching resources, and opportunities for teachers and historians to talk about the period.

Oyez: U.S. Supreme Court Multimedia

http://www.oyez.org/oyez/frontpage

The audiophile will really enjoy the hours of arguments before the Supreme Court of the United States. Others might find more of interest in the photos and biographies of current and former justices. Further information for some, but not all, justices is in the links to transcripts, lists of cases, and other material. The virtual tour of the court is interesting as well.

Presidential Elections, 1860–1996

http://fisher.lib.virginia.edu/elections/maps/

This site maps popular vote totals for every presidential election between 1860 and 1996 and electoral results from 1900 through 1996. It also includes a detailed look at the 2000 election and links to related sites. Hopefully, 2004 will get that treatment too. Includes links to related sites.

Presidential Libraries

http://www.archives.gov/presidential_libraries/presidential_records/
presidential_records.html

This site lists presidential libraries from Hoover to Clinton, with an overview of the libraries and links to the library sites. Address, fax, and e-mail information helps too.

Presidential Speeches

http://odur.let.rug.nl/~usa/P/

This Groningen, Netherlands, project is a good example of a European American studies site, and it even includes an extended discussion of the genesis and methodology of the project. It includes mostly State of the Union and inaugural addresses, presidential biographies, and links to other sources.

Redstone Arsenal Historical Information

http://www.redstone.army.mil/history/welcome.html

This is an exceptionally good government military history (as in done by historians hired by the military) site using photos and videos and a range of textual materials to cover the U.S. Army's aviation and missile command. Contents include oral histories, chronologies, and information about specific types of weapons. Pluses include the links and the lightly humorous touch within the text.

Jonas Salk, Biography

http://www.achievement.org/autodoc/page/sa10bio-1

Salk developed the polio vaccine. This site is more than strictly a biography though. It is part of the Academy of Achievement site, which seeks to use historical figures as role models. Another use for history: "Achievement TV is an electronic forum that allows students to learn from outstanding individuals of our time while, at the same time, satisfying core curriculum requirements."

Skylighters

http://www.skylighters.org/

This site is the official home of the 225th AAA Searchlight Battalion Veterans. As well as being a good place to learn about World War II, it is a good example of the military reunion genre. It has a chronology, links, and oral histories. And, if you do not like this one, go to the World War II Web ring linked at the bottom of the page.

United States Entry into World War I: A Documentary Chronology

http://edsitement.neh.gov/view_lesson_plan.asp?id=471

EDSITEment provides a lesson plan for teaching high school students the topic while giving them practice in using Web resources to make historical judgments. This site includes course objectives, complementary lessons, and more.

Veterans History Project

http://www.loc.gov/folklife/vets/vets-home.html

This project is attempting to capture the stories of America's 25 million living veterans, or a fair sample thereof. The site includes audio, visual, and text material, a searchable database, a short course, student guide, and links to other oral history projects.

Watergate

http://www.washingtonpost.com/wp-srv/national/longterm/watergate/splash1a.htm

Where else but at the *Washington Post* would a user look for the Watergate scandal? Bob Woodward and Carl Bernstein, who broke the case and brought down President Richard Nixon, were *Post* reporters. The site has a time line, a Where Are They Now? section, and a May 2005 article on the disclosure of the identity of "Deep Throat" that ended a two-decades-long mystery.

White House Historical Association

http://www.whitehousehistory.org/

This site is a good example of the charitable nonprofit approach to history. The WHHA site mixes education and entertainment and a bit of fund-raising. It includes recommended lessons as well as a tour. There is also music and animation—and the obligatory gift shop. But the content is quite extensive too—with multipage time lines of topics ranging from African-Americans to *The West Wing,* to music.

Chapter 17

Women's History

Melissa Ooten

African-American Women: Online Archival Collections at Duke

http://scriptorium.lib.duke.edu/collections/african-american-women.html

The Digital Scriptorium from the Special Collections Library of Duke University offers the rare opportunity for users to access and read letters written by slave women online. It also offers links to other materials on African-American women's history.

Agents of Social Change

http://www.smith.edu/libraries/libs/ssc/curriculum/index.html

This document collection from the Sophia Smith Collection at Smith College seeks to reach middle and high school students. It contains some information online and offers a guide to the collections housed at Smith. These collections include the papers of attorney Constance Baker Motley, attorney Mary Kaufman, pacifist Jessie Lloyd O'Connor, and feminist Gloria Steinem as well as the records of the Women's Action Alliance and the National Congress of Neighborhood Women.

American Women's History: A Resource Guide

http://www.mtsu.edu/~kmiddlet/history/women.html

This site, from Middle Tennessee State University, offers a variety of indexed and linked material. It includes both a subject index and a state index of sources on topics ranging from advice literature and public speaking to material culture and quilts. The site also offers advice on how to find both primary and secondary sources, available both on- and offline.

Elizabeth Blackwell: "That Girl There Is a Doctor in Medicine"

http://www.nlm.nih.gov/hmd/blackwell/index.html

This site chronicles the life of Elizabeth Blackwell, the first American woman to receive the MD degree. It is the online version of a 1999 exhibit held at the National Library of Medicine in Bethesda, Maryland. The Web site is divided into four different periods of Blackwell's life: admission into medical school, college life, graduation, and career.

The Chinese in California, 1850–1925

http://lcweb2.loc.gov/ammem/award99/cubhtml/cichome.html

While this Library of Congress American Memory site is not devoted specifically to women, it does contain significant amounts of material on women. A subject search of "women" calls up a variety of source material, in particular images of both white women and Chinese women in various settings, most notably San Francisco's Chinatown.

Civil Rights in Mississippi Digital Archive

http://avatar.lib.usm.edu/%7Espcol/crda/index.html

This archive from the McCain Library and Archives at the University of Southern Mississippi contains several oral interviews of women who worked in the civil rights movement. Selected manuscripts and photographs can also be found through the site, along with a history of the civil rights movement in Hattiesburg and a civil rights time line. At present, the site is best used for listening to the oral histories of women activists and in finding useful links to other civil rights Web sites.

Civil War Women: Primary Sources on the Internet

http://scriptorium.lib.duke.edu/women/cwdocs.html

This bibliography from Duke University provides a starting point for researching women during the Civil War era. Users can find links to scanned letters, diaries, and documents, and a list of photographs that include women in the Library of Congress and National Archives.

Documenting the American South

http://docsouth.unc.edu/

Documenting the American South, from the University of North Carolina, houses an extensive collection of primary resources for the study of Southern history and Southern women. Searchable by collection, title, author, or subject, this database contains a number of works by women.

Documents From the Women's Liberation Movement— Duke Special Collections

http://scriptorium.lib.duke.edu/wlm/

This online archival collection from Duke University's Special Collections can be searched by keyword or by subject. A diverse set of documents include "Women Rap About Sex," the Radicalesbians' "The Woman-Identified Women," a photo essay on "What Sort of Man Reads Playboy," and Anne Koedt's "The Myth of the Vaginal Orgasm." Unlike other sites, Duke includes a significant number of documents that address women's sexualities.

Feeding America: The Historic American Cookbook Project

http://digital.lib.msu.edu/projects/cookbooks/

Michigan State University Libraries and the Institute of Museum and Library Services present the Feeding America project. This project provides an online collection of some of the most important American cookbooks from the late 1700s to the early 1900s. Full text exists for dozens of the cookbooks, and they are fully searchable.

The Emma Goldman Papers

http://sunsite.berkeley.edu/Goldman/

This site contains anarchist Emma Goldman's papers. Goldman was deported from the United States following imprisonment for protesting the draft during World War I. It includes links to two exhibitions introducing Goldman, including one at the Jewish Women's Archive, another important site for women's history (http://www.jwa.org/index.html). Accessible online primary sources include selections from her several books, her published essays and speeches, and third-person accounts of Goldman's life and work.

A Historical Investigation into the Past: Lizzie Borden/Fall River Project

http://ccbit.cs.umass.edu/lizzie/

This project, developed by the History Department and the Center for Computer-Based Instructional Technology at the University of Massachusetts-Amherst, encourages users to examine the evidence of the Lizzie Borden axe murder trial and to draw their own conclusions about Borden's life. The digital archive contains documents and illustrations from Borden's trial, material on the surrounding community of Fall River (including the 1880 census, a visitor's guide, poll tax payment, and a city directory), and late nineteenth-century newspaper articles and literature to give students a broad context in which to interpret the components of class, gender, race, and region that may have affected Borden's trial.

Internet Women's History Sourcebook

http://www.fordham.edu/halsall/women/womensbook.html

Derived from three major online sourcebooks, this site, from Paul Halsall of Fordham University, offers information specific to women's history in ancient, medieval, and modern times. Included regions range from ancient Egypt to North America, Latin America, and southeast Asia, just to name a few. Links are also provided to articles and materials that provide a context for the historical study of women.

Japanese American Relocation Digital Archives

http://jarda.cdlib.org/

This site, from the Online Archive of California, provides a historical overview of the World War II relocation of Japanese-Americans in the United States. Materials relevant to women constitute a large part of the database, including hundreds of photographs and artistic works. In all, the archive contains over 10,000 images and over 20,000 pages of electronic transcripts, all searchable.

Jewish Women's Archive

http://www.jwa.org/index.html

The Jewish Women's Archive divides its information into "discover," "teach," and "research." The teaching section of the site offers suggestions on integrating Jewish women's histories into the curriculum and the research area contains a virtual archive, searchable by a person's name, subject, occupation, or location.

The Lesbian History Project

http://www-lib.usc.edu/~retter/main.html

The Lesbian History Project is most useful for the large number of links it provides, including links to current and archived journals, dissertations and theses, course syllabi, images, and one to a history of Southern Californian lesbians, including a chronology.

Making It Their Own: Women in the West

http://scholar.library.csi.cuny.edu/westweb/pages/women.html

This section of Catherine Lavender's WestWeb focuses exclusively on Western women. It contains several primary sources, including journals, diaries, letters, and autobiographies from individuals such as Willa Cather and Leslie Marmon Silko. The primary texts are evenly divided between Native American and white women. Life history manuscripts from the Folklore Project of the WPA Federal Writers' project are also included.

Mother Jones Collection

http://libraries.cua.edu/MotherJones/

This site contains information on the life and work of labor activist and union organizer Mary Harris Jones, known popularly as Mother Jones, from the Terence Powderly and John Mitchell collections at Catholic University. Separate letter, picture, and subject indexes guide users through the available sources.

National Women's History Project

http://www.nwhp.org/

This Web site, from the nonprofit educational corporation the National Women's History Project, seeks to both celebrate and educate about women's historical accomplishments. The site's Biography Center lists dozens of women whose accomplishments the project believes deserve recognition. For each woman, the site lists an outline of her life as well as further resources on her both in print and online. The site is also dedicated to promoting Women's History Month each March.

New York Triangle Shirtwaist Fire

http://www.ilr.cornell.edu/trianglefire/

This site is devoted to the Triangle Shirtwaist fire of New York City, which took the lives of 146 immigrant workers in 1911. The user-friendly site contains the story and its aftermath, including links that introduce the topic, discuss sweatshop and strike conditions in garment factories before the 1911 fire, and detail funerals, protests, investigations, and reform attempts. Primary sources available through the site include testimonials from factory workers, letters written to factory owners and managers, songs of labor activists, and numerous newspaper and magazine accounts. The site also includes excerpts from the Factory Investigating Commission of New York State in 1912 that was established as a result of the fire to investigate factory conditions throughout the state.

The Pill: American Experience

http://www.pbs.org/wgbh/amex/pill

The Pill, the PBS Web site accompanying the film of the same name, contains a synopsis and transcript of the film, along with primary sources, especially concerning the 1960 approval of the birth control pill. Further Reading provides contemporary books and Web sites. Website Features allows users to vote on issues concerning medical insurance and the pill and to submit their own personal comments and questions about the pill and birth control in general. Questions about the pill will be answered by Harvard Medical School professor Dr. Daniela Carusi.

The Eleanor Roosevelt Papers, The Human Rights Years, 1945–1962

http://www.gwu.edu/~erpapers/index.html

The Eleanor Roosevelt Papers, a research center associated with George Washington University, presents this project focusing on Roosevelt's human rights advocacy spanning the years after she left the White House. Users can access information on her life and works written both by and about her. Sources include letters, speeches, newspaper columns, book excerpts, and articles. Separate sections are devoted to information on how to teach Eleanor Roosevelt and on human rights advocacy.

Salem Witch Trials: Documentary Archive and Transcription Project

http://etext.virginia.edu/salem/witchcraft/home.html

This documentary archive, from the University of Virginia and the Danvers Archival Center, is one of the most sophisticated on the subject. Available documents include three volumes of transcribed court records. Interactive maps of the village allow users to track the locale of both the accused and their accusers across the spring of 1692. Holdings from several archives including the Boston Public Library, the Massachusetts Historical Society, and the Peabody Essex Museum have also been scanned and are available in their original form for users' perusal. Contemporary books supplement the documents to set the documents in their historical context.

Tejano Voices

http://libraries.uta.edu/tejanovoices/

The Center for Mexican American Studies Oral History Project at the University of Texas at Arlington presents seventy-seven Tejano and Tejana voices speaking about racial discrimination in Texas during the post–World War II era. The site offers brief biographies, interview summaries and transcripts, photographs of the interviewees, and the opportunity to listen to the recorded interviews. About two dozen of the interviews were conducted with women.

The Ten O'Clock News

http://main.wgbh.org/ton/

This Web site houses 532 tapes from the WGBH-Boston Media Archives and Preservation Center. This collection focuses on stories related to African-Americans aired on the news from 1974 to 1991. The site can be searched by keyword and browsed by category, and video clips are available for many of the featured stories. While not devoted specifically to women, the site does include several stories about women and gender in Boston's African-American communities.

Urban Experience in Chicago: Hull House and Its Neighborhoods

http://www.uic.edu/jaddams/hull/urbanexp/contents.htm

This interpretive site from the University of Illinois at Chicago seeks to situate the history of Hull House into the broader context of its surrounding urban environs. Six major sections constitute the site: Historical Narrative, Timeline, Images, Geography, Teacher's Resources, and Search. In the historical narrative, each chapter has its own subsections including relevant newspaper articles, letters, memoirs, images, and unpublished manuscripts. Users can search for specific material either by author, title, or word or phrase, or they can browse document keywords.

Votes for Women: Selections From the National American Woman Suffrage Association Collection, 1848–1921

http://memory.loc.gov/ammem/naw/nawshome.html

http://memory.loc.gov/ammem/vfwhtml/vfwhome.html

The first site's collection consists of over 160 items from NAWSA. It includes a variety of materials including diaries and book-length studies of suffrage movements and postcards. The second site includes thirty-eight photographs, including portraits, some parades, and pictures of women voting.

WASP (Women Airforce Service Pilots)

http://www.twu.edu/wasp/

This site, maintained by Texas Woman's University, offers information on Women Airforce Service Pilots (WASPs) from the World War II era. It includes information on related archival collections, photographs, and news updates. Of particular interest is the online Oral History Project containing WASPs' oral history transcripts and an "Ask an Archivist" option for asking a question via e-mail.

Who Was Martha Ballard?

http://www.dohistory.org/martha/

This site, from DoHistory, centers on the invaluable eighteenth-century diary of midwife Martha Ballard, who resided in Maine. The time line keeps track of notable events in Ballard's life and her community, along with notable events in the fields of science and medicine and in the history of Maine and the United States.

Women Come to the Front: Journalists, Photographers, and Broadcasters in WW II

http://www.loc.gov/exhibits/wcf/wcf0001.html

This Library of Congress site highlights the careers of eight women during World War II. The site features the work of photographer Therese Bonney, photographer Toni Frissell, photojournalist Marvin Breckinridge Patterson, journalist Clare Boothe Luce, columnist and radio broadcaster Janet Flanner, photographer Esther Bubley, photographer Dorothea Lange, and correspondent May Craig. Extensive displays of the work of each individual are accessible.

Women and Social Movements in the United States, 1600–2000

http://womhist.binghamton.edu

This site contains over four dozen document projects revolving around more than a thousand primary source documents. About half of the projects are available for free; the other half are only accessible through subscription. Available for free, projects range in time from the American Revolution to the present and include a wide range of women. The expanded subscription version of the Web site, jointly published by the Center for the Historical Study of Women and Gender at the State University of New York at Binghamton and Alexander Street Press (both of these also collaborate on the site as a whole), contains an invaluable database of books, pamphlets, and additional primary source projects, although access to the database requires subscription.

Women in World History

http://www.womeninworldhistory.com

This site provides resources for learning about women globally. "Lessons" offer thirteen curriculum initiatives for exploring women's history in the classroom, and "essays" contextualize the histories of women from different historical time periods and areas of the world.

Women's Diaries

http://oldsite.library.upenn.edu/etext/collections/diaries/?

From the Schoenberg Center for Electronic Text and Image at the University of Pennsylvania Library, this site offers online access to the manuscripts of six women's diaries dating from the mid-nineteenth to the mid-twentieth century.

Women Working: 1870–1930

http://ocp.hul.harvard.edu/ww/

This site from Harvard University provides online access to manuscripts and images related to working women's histories. The collection contains over 2,000 books and pamphlets, 1,000 images, and 5,000 scanned pages. Users can both browse and search the collections.

WWW Virtual Library Women's History

http://www.iisg.nl/w3vlwomenshistory/

Maintained by the International Institute of Social History, this site lists institutions, organizations, archives, library collections, and online resources related to women's history. Conference announcements related to women's history themes are also included.

Chapter 18

World History

David Koeller

The academic study of world history focuses on the interactions and connections among the people, civilizations, and regions of the world. In choosing Web sites for inclusion in this list, therefore, I have focused on sites that are global or interregional in scope and, with a few exceptions, have excluded those that, while global in scope, treated each region or people in isolation.

Metasites

Academic Info: World History Gateway

http://www.academicinfo.net/hist.html

While this site has a large collection of links to a variety of history resources, including some world history resources, it is often difficult to distinguish the resource links from the many advertisements. The site is operated by Academic Info and maintained by Mike Madin.

History Link 101

http://historylink101.com/

An extensive list of links maintained by Eric Rymer, a public school teacher in Ohio, and designed for school teachers. Pages are listed by subject and culture and in a picture gallery. There are extensive navigation aids with provisions to easily use the site to present a lesson plan. To also simplify things for the busy teacher, each of the sites is rated on its content and its visual appeal. This site is still expanding and will be a very impressive tool when finished.

The World History Compass

http://www.worldhistorycompass.com/index.htm

This metasite has such an extensive collection of links on such a wide range of subjects that anyone teaching or studying world history will find it useful. However, the site has not been updated so many of the links are dead. The site is provided by Schiller Computing and serves as a way to draw customers to its online bookstore.

WWW Virtual Library History Central Catalogue

http://vlib.iue.it/history/index.html

This is an excellent collection of links to hundreds of articles on most aspects of history. There are, however, few references that are specifically world history. This would be a good place for a comparative history project, however. This site was originally developed by Lynn H. Nelson at the University of Kansas. It is now being maintained by Serge Noiret and Inaki Lopez Martin at the European University Institute, Florence, Italy.

World History Sites

The Encyclopedia of World History

http://www.bartleby.com/67/

This is the online version of the famous *World History Encyclopedia,* first developed by William Langer several decades ago and now edited by Peter Stearns, both major figures in the field of world history. The print version is a marvelous resource. Unfortunately, the Web version is little more than the print version with a search function. With the right use of hyperlinks, this could be a tremendous resource.

Fleet Gazelle

http://www.cultures.com/

http://www.mesoweb.com/

http://www.mythweb.com/

Fleet Gazelle publishes a number of educational CD-ROMs and has three Web sites to advertise them. The first and most relevant for the study of world history features several short multimedia pieces mostly on preurban societies. The second, MesoWeb, is dedicated to the study of MesoAmerican cultures. Finally, MythWeb is devoted to Greek mythology, with some resources for teaching mythology. All three sites feature impressive graphics, animations, and extensive teacher guides.

Frank Smitha's World History

http://www.fsmitha.com/index.html

Frank Smitha is an amateur historian who has developed a set of very impressive online world history interpretive essays that could be profitably used as a world history textbook. They cover world history from antiquity to the present. The essays are impressive not only for their scope, but also for their balance and emphasis on the interconnectedness of history. Also included at the site are excellent map and image collections, and a detailed time line.

History of the World

http://www.camelotintl.com/world/index.html

Camelot International is a British apartment locator company that maintains this Web site as a service to its customers. In addition to a series of articles linked to chronologies, there are also some interesting film clips. The articles are unsigned but appear to be of good quality.

History World

http://www.historyworld.net/

There are a number of ways to access the information at this site. The unique "WhoWhatWhere" feature allows users to find out what was happening at a particular place at a particular time. There are also time lines and a "tours" feature. It is not a scholarly site, although there are a few longer articles.

H-World Homepage

http://www2.h-net.msu.edu/~world/

This is the Web site for the H-World online discussion group. This discussion group, sponsored by the National Endowment for the Humanities and Michigan State University, composed of those who have a teaching or research interest in world history, has among its members leaders in the field of world history. This site is both an archive of the group's discussions and a resource for world historians. The list's postings are arranged both chronologically and by thread. A search engine is also available. Besides the discussion archives, the site includes course syllabi for teaching world history at the secondary, college, and graduate levels, bibliographies on many world history topics, reviews of recent scholarship, and teaching aids, most drawn from the list's discussions.

Hyper History

http://hyperhistory.com/online_n2/History_n2/a.html

This site shows the real potential of the Internet for teaching and studying history. The site consists of an image-mapped chronology of world history from prehistory to the present. The events listed on the chronology are then hyperlinked to a very brief description of the event. The site is global in scope and offers a fine set of maps comparing events in different parts of the world at a particular moment in time.

The Internet Global History Sourcebook

http://www.fordham.edu/halsall/global/globalsbook.html

One of the series of sourcebooks developed by Paul Halsall. This site focuses on the interaction among cultures. While there have been no additions to the site since 2000, the primary sources found here are still an important resource.

The Journal of World-Systems Research

http://jwsr.ucr.edu/index.php

The *Journal of World-Systems Research* is an electronic journal, distributed free over the Internet. As the name suggests, it is "dedicated to scholarly research on the modern world-system and earlier, smaller intersocietal networks." World-system theory is one of the important approaches to the study of world history, and this Web site and journal are an important resource for learning of the latest scholarship in this field.

National Center for History in the Schools

http://www.sscnet.ucla.edu/nchs/

The National Center for History in the Schools has developed standards for world history in grades five through twelve. This site provides an online version of those standards. In addition, the Center also has samples from its sourcebook *Bring History Alive!* to help teachers meet these standards.

United Nations Organization: Cyber School Bus

http://www.un.org/Pubs/CyberSchoolBus/index.html

Student and teacher resources for ages ten to eighteen. Includes information on the UN member states, quizzes, and curriculum modules on global poverty, human rights, and other issues. While focused on contemporary events, there is some material for those interested in comparative world cultures.

WebChron: The Web Chronology Project

http://www.thenagain.info/WebChron/index.html

While there are many Web sites of chronologies, WebChron is unique in that it attempts to present a global chronology, it uses hyperlinks to "nest" detailed chronologies "inside" more general chronologies, and it describes many of the events using student-written articles. This nesting allows users to get a sense of how one period relates to another and how events in one region of the world correspond to events in other regions. Because the articles are student projects, their quality is uneven, but many are excellent.

World Civilizations: An Internet Classroom and Anthology

http://www.wsu.edu:8080/%7Edee/WORLD.HTM

Developed by Richard Hooker of Washington State University for a course for first-year college students, this site integrates a world cultures text, written principally by Hooker, with primary source readings and links to other Web resources. While very impressive in its graphic presentation and its treatment of the cultures represented, the focus of the course and of the site is the development of the cultures and not on their interaction.

World History Archives

http://www.hartford-hwp.com/archives/index.html

"A collection of documents for teaching and learning about world history from a working class perspective." The site contains more 11,000 primary and secondary sources arranged by region and theme. The site is administered by Haines Brown and reflects his interests, but is a very useful resource for studying contemporary world history.

The World History Association

http://www.thewha.org/

The official Web site of the World History Association, the leading organization for world historians. It contains a series of links to many of the resources listed here as well as a series of links to teaching resources, including course syllabi.

The World History Reader

http://www.wsu.edu:8080/~wldciv/world_civ_reader/

An advertisement for a now out-of-print world history reader, this site nevertheless has some useful excerpts from primary sources. The editor of the anthology is Paul Brians of Washington State University. While many of the translators are mentioned by name, the site gives little other information about the source of the translation. Many of the sources are taken from old translations, but some appear to have been done specifically for this anthology.

World History Sources

http://chnm.gmu.edu/worldhistorysources/

Maintained by the Center for History and New Media and developed through a grant by the National Endowment for the Humanities, this site is designed to help teachers of Advanced Placement world history courses.

World History: Specific Aspects

Exploring Ancient World Cultures

http://eawc.evansville.edu/

This site provides links to essays, texts, and images of the ancient world. This is not a true world history site since there is little on the comparison or interaction of these societies, but there is good information for study and the foundation for comparison. This site is under the general editorship of Anthony F. Beavers and is housed at the University of Evansville.

Women in World History Curriculum

http://www.womeninworldhistory.com/

Developed by Lynn Reese to promote her Women in World History Curriculum, for which this site is an advertisement, it provides some very useful resources for teaching about women in world history. Especially impressive is a page devoted to the role of women in the Industrial Revolution that shows through the use of primary source material the differences and inequities in the roles of men and women.

Chapter 19

History of Computers

Hugh Randall

Apple-history.com

http://www.apple-history.com/frames/?

Traces the history of the Apple personal computer, offering images and information for every model.

Charles Babbage Institute

http://www.cbi.umn.edu/

Maintains a searchable image database, as well as a database of over 300 oral histories relating to the history of computers and technology.

Babbage

http://www-history.mcs.st-andrews.ac.uk/history/Mathematicians/Babbage.html

A comprehensive biography of Charles Babbage (1791–1871), the first man to envision a programmable computer and developer of the steam-powered, punch card–fed analytical engine.

The Computer Comes Home: A History of the Personal Computer

http://www.computer-museum.org/exhibits/pccomeshome/index.html

An online exhibit tracing the history of the personal computer.

Computer History Museum

http://www.computerhistory.org/

Home page of the Computer History Museum, located in Mountain View, California.

Computer Languages History

http://www.levenez.com/lang/

Provides links to the histories of over fifty programming languages, as well as a detailed flowchart tracing the development and genealogy of these languages.

The ENIAC Story

http://ftp.arl.army.mil/~mike/comphist/eniac-story.html

A history of the first electronic digital computer, developed by the Ordnance Department of the U.S. Army.

Bill Gates: Before Microsoft

http://ei.cs.vt.edu/~history/Gates.Mirick.html

Biography of Microsoft founder Bill Gates.

Graphical User Interface Gallery

http://toastytech.com/guis/

Provides background information and images of various graphical user interfaces (GUIs). This site also traces the development of the GUI through a graphical time line.

History of Computing Hardware

http://en.wikipedia.org/wiki/History_of_computing_hardware

A comprehensive overview of the history of computing hardware, replete with numerous links to related topics. Wikipedia, the provider of this free, online encyclopedia, offers a number of excellent entries on computer-related topics.

Hobbes' Internet Time Line

http://www.zakon.org/robert/internet/time line/

A time line of the most significant events in the early development of the Internet.

IBM Archives

http://www-03.ibm.com/ibm/history/

Contains online exhibits, documents, and multimedia related to the history of IBM.

Steve Jobs

http://ei.cs.vt.edu/~history/Jobs.html

Biography of Steve Jobs, cofounder of Apple Computer.

Douglas W. Jones's Punched Card Index

http://www.cs.uiowa.edu/~jones/cards/index.html

Material relating to the history of punch cards.

Making the Macintosh Home Page

http://library.stanford.edu/mac/

This site includes a number of primary sources, images, and interviews documenting the development and history of the Apple Macintosh computer.

The Museum of HP Calculators

http://www.hpmuseum.org/

Maintains information on Hewlett-Packard calculators manufactured between 1968 and 1986, as well as a collection of HP advertisements.

Old-Computers.com: The Museum

http://www.old-computers.com/museum/default.asp

Traces the genealogy of computers, offering a wealth of technical information relating to individual makes and models, as well as an extensive collection of images.

A Short History of the Internet by Bruce Sterling

http://www.library.yale.edu/div/instruct/internet/history.htm

This site provides a useful introduction to the early years of the Internet, more specifically ARPANET, the first decentralized computer network in the United States.

TLC: A Brief History of Hacking

http://tlc.discovery.com/convergence/hackers/articles/history.html

A Web site to accompany The Learning Channel program *Hackers: Outlaws and Angels*. Offers a brief overview of the history of computer hacking.

Triumph of the Nerds

http://www.pbs.org/nerds/

Companion site to the PBS program *Triumph of the Nerds: The Rise of Accidental Empires*. Includes a time line, biographical information on individuals featured on the program, and the full transcript of the show.

University of Virginia Computer Science: Computer Museum

http://www.cs.virginia.edu/brochure/museum.html

Site includes images of the many artifacts located in the University of Virginia's computer museum.

Chapter 20

History of Science

Scott A. Merriman

General Directories and Indexes

ECHO Virtual Center: Science, Technology and Industry

http://echo.gmu.edu/index.php

The Center for History and New Media maintains this site focusing on science, technology, and industry. Users can survey sites in a number of areas or perform a keyword search. The site also links to sites that give users the opportunity to record their recollections of scientific events, such as the New York City blackout or electric vehicles. This is a good place to begin research.

History of Science on the World Wide Web

http://www.ou.edu/cas/hsci/rel-site.htm

This Web site is the work of the History of Science Department at the University of Oklahoma. It contains links to many of the other resources listed here, as well as more libraries, archives, and research centers of note. There is no annotation or order to the list, apart from some very general top-level categories, but the list is small enough to scroll through. This site is useful for the number of links to subject indexes on the history of various scientific disciplines.

H-Med-Sci-Tech

http://www.h-net.msu.edu/~smt/

H-Med-Sci-Tech is a moderated and active listserv on all aspects of history of science, medicine, and technology. To subscribe to the History of Medicine, Science, and Technology listserv, follow the directions at the site.

Internet History of Science Sourcebook

http://www.fordham.edu/halsall/science/sciencesbook.html

This page and other Internet history sourcebooks have been created and are maintained by Paul Halsall. Halsall provides teachers with chronologically organized links to public domain texts, commentaries, and other Web sites. His sections on Greco-Roman scientific philosophy and culture, science in Latin Christendom, and Islamic science are particularly strong; non-Western scientific topics are not as well represented, and there is minimal annotation. This is a useful resource for undergraduate educators.

History of Astronomy

The Galileo Project

http://galileo.rice.edu/

The Galileo Project is a hypertext source of information on the life and work of Galileo Galilei (1564–1642) and the science of his time. The Office of the Vice President of Computing of Rice University supports the project, and it represents the collective efforts of Drs. Albert Van Helden and Elizabeth Burr and their students.

The History of Astronomy Home Page

http://www.astro.uni-bonn.de/%7Epbrosche/astoria.html

This is the most extensive metasite for the history of astronomy. It is maintained on behalf of Commission 41 (History of Astronomy) of the International Astronomical Union and the Working Group for the History of Astronomy in the Astronomische Gesellschaft.

History of Biology

Caduceus-L

http://www.hshsl.umaryland.edu/caduceus/

Caduceus-L is a moderated electronic discussion list that provides a forum for exchanging information on any aspect of the history of the health sciences. To subscribe: Send the command sub caduceus-l [your name] to listproc@list.ab.umd.edu, or visit the Web page.

History of Biomedicine

http://www.mic.ki.se/History.html

This site, maintained at the Karolinska Institute in Sweden, is extremely thorough. Links are divided by categories, including extensive sections on traditional Indian, Chinese, and Islamic biomedicine. There are also links to resources on the history of diseases and indigenous cultures. Many of the links are extremely general. The site does not have a search feature.

History of Medicine

http://www.nlm.nih.gov/hmd/index.html

The National Library of Medicine, a division of the National Institutes of Health, maintains this Web site. The most important resource is Medline, NLM's bibliographic index to literature published since 1965 in the history of medicine and related topics. It currently contains about 13 million citations and is updated weekly. Another major resource is the searchable database of nearly 100,000 images from the NLM's print and photo collection. These images are digitized, but one can order high-resolution prints from the library.

Natural History Caucus, Special Libraries Association

http://www.lib.washington.edu/sla/

The home page of the SLA Natural History Caucus is aimed at special librarians working in natural history museums and repositories, but contains useful resources for the historian as well. There is a hyperlinked, alphabetical list of natural history libraries around the world. However, these are not annotated. There is a similar list of natural history museums around the world, organized by geographical region. There are also hyperlinked lists of bibliographies, some of which are annotated, and other resources that are oriented to scientists.

History of Chemistry

Chem-Hist

Chem-Hist seeks to promote information and communication among historians of chemistry and of the chemical industry. To join, send mail to MAISER@LISTSERV.NGATE.UNI-REGENSBURG.DE with the following command in the body of your message: subscribe CHEM-HIST.

Classic Papers in Chemistry

http://dbhs.wvusd.k12.ca.us/webdocs/Chem-History/Classic-Papers-Menu.html

This Web site is maintained by ChemTeam and John L. Park, a high school chemistry teacher. Although many of the chemistry resources are aimed at educators and students, the Classic Papers section contains a growing list of historical works in chemistry (mostly excerpted). Unfortunately, it is not clear which papers have been excerpted and which sections have been removed.

Selected Classic Papers From the History of Chemistry

http://web.lemoyne.edu/~giunta/papers.html

This page, maintained by Carmen Giunta at Le Moyne College, is a companion Web page to John Park's Classic Papers in Chemistry page listed above. There are more papers (although some links point to the ChemTeam site) and more annotations. The papers are divided by subject category, but there is no searchable index. Giunta notes when papers are excerpted. This Web site contains an extensive collection of papers, but some links are unique to the ChemTeam Web site and are not cross-linked here.

History of Mathematics

The MacTutor History of Mathematics Archive

http://www-history.mcs.st-and.ac.uk/~history/index.html

This searchable Web site, maintained at the University of St. Andrews in Scotland, contains biographies of mathematicians of note (accessible chronologically or alphabetically), images, references, information on famous curves, bibliographies, and links to other resources. The generally informal tone and the lack of primary references make this site more suitable for teaching purposes than for research.

Women in Mathematics

http://www.scottlan.edu/lriddle/women/women.htm

This Web site is part of an ongoing project of mathematics students at Agnes Scott College in Atlanta, Georgia. This resource is best for K–12 teachers and students. The biographical essays are fairly brief and contain some references and photographs.

History of the Physical Sciences

American Institute of Physics: Center for History of Physics

http://www.aip.org/history/

The AIP has a long history of promoting study of the history of physics. Its semiannual newsletter since 1994 is online, is updated regularly, and contains articles, announcements, reports on archival materials, bibliographies, and funding and conference opportunities. The Niels Bohr Library catalog, finding aids to various archival collections, the Emilio Segrè Visual Archives photo collection catalog, online exhibits, and an extensive list of related links make this collection useful to scholars and teachers.

Contributions of Twentieth-Century Women to Physics

http://cwp.library.ucla.edu/

Sponsored by the American Physical Society, this Web site is maintained by physicist Nina Byers at the University of California, Los Angeles. The site contains a searchable archive of biographies, indexed by subfield of physics. The research for the biographies was verified by working physicists around the world. The information may be more useful as an educational tool than as a research tool, since there are relatively few links to primary resources or mentions of archival collections related to each scientist.

History of Oceanic and Atmospheric Science Locator

http://www.lib.noaa.gov/docs/windandsea4.html#HistoryOceanic

Although this site is only part of a much larger Web page, there are no other metasites that deal with this subject. The page points to biographical information and other National Oceanic and Atmospheric Administration resources.

Map History/History of Cartography

http://www.maphistory.info/

Tony Campbell, the map librarian at the British Museum in London, maintains this exceptional Web site. It is an extensive and extremely well-organized collection of resources for both the scholar and the amateur. It contains links to both paper and electronic resources, including reference books, map listservs, grants, societies, and commercial venues.

NOAA History

http://www.history.noaa.gov/

This site makes available many of the historical resources of the National Oceanic and Atmospheric Administration. The site contains a catalog of the entire map and chart collection of the Office of Coast Survey, as well as biographical sketches of important people (these were drawn from official newsletters), an extensive photo library, and stories, songs, and poems.

History of Psychology

History and Philosophy of Psychology Web Resources

http://www.psych.yorku.ca/orgs/resource.htm

This site is maintained by Christopher D. Green at York University in Canada and is shared by several divisions of the American Psychological Association, the Canadian Psychological Association, and other international professional organizations. It contains links to relevant professional organizations, archives and manuscript collections, full-text documents, and other related sites.

Resource Guide: History of Psychology

http://pages.slu.edu/faculty/josephme/resguides/psyhist.html

Miriam E. Joseph of the University of St. Louis compiled this library guide. It is a good resource for students and teachers interested in the history of psychology. It contains annotations to relevant and useful books, reference works, overviews, journals, citation indexes, manuscript collections, and Web sites.

Miscellaneous Science Resources

Catalog of the Scientific Community in the Sixteenth and Seventeenth Centuries

http://galileo.rice.edu/lib/catalog.html

This catalog, originally compiled by the late Dr. Richard S. Westfall of the Department of History and Philosophy of Science at Indiana University and now part of the Galileo project at Rice University, contains extensive biographical profiles of sixteenth- and seventeenth-century scientific personalities. The database can be searched by any of twenty fields, including means of support, religion, and nationality. In addition to biographical information, Westfall included known references to the scientist. One shortcoming is that there is no way to browse the list of scientists.

The Faces of Science: African Americans in the Sciences

http://webfiles.uci.edu/mcbrown/display/faces.html

This Web site is maintained by Princeton University. In addition to biographical profiles of numerous African-American scientists, inventors, and doctors, the Web site also contains links to electronic conferences on this topic, historical data on doctoral degrees awarded to African-Americans, and bibliographies. This site is probably best suited to teachers, both university and K–12, who are interested in the historical role of African-Americans in science, and those who are interested in increasing the numbers of African-Americans in the sciences.

The Medieval Science Page

http://members.aol.com/mcnelis/medsci_index.html

The Web site is maintained by James McNelis, the editor in chief of *Envoi: A Review Journal of Medieval Literature*. The site contains a large amount of information, even if it is not frequently updated. Annotated links are organized by topic and include links to scholarly listservs, full-text documents, classic texts, and other materials. The list is not searchable, but instead is organized in linear fashion.

WISE: Archives of Women in Science and Engineering

http://www.lib.iastate.edu/spcl/wise/miss.html

This Web site is the informational page of Iowa State's collection of records and papers of women in science, one of the largest in the United States. There are some K–12 resources, virtual exhibits, and bibliographies, and this Web site is very useful for its collection list.

International History of Science and Medicine

ASAPWeb: Australian Science Archives Project

http://www.asap.unimelb.edu.au/

ASAP is an organization that is working to identify and preserve scientific records of enduring value, both those from the past and those that are being created today. One feature on the Web site is Bright Sparcs, a searchable database of biographical information on Australian scientists in history. Where appropriate, there are links to information on archival repositories and online sources that house information on the scientist. Other important resources include a biographical and bibliographic database of Australian physicists to 1945 and information on Australian archival repositories.

Chi Med: The History of Chinese Medicine Webpage

http://www.albion.edu/history/chimed/

This Web site is maintained at Albion College in Michigan. In addition to an international list of scholars working in the field, this Web site has (somewhat dated) links to numerous online resources, bibliographies, syllabi, conference and grant listings, and research institutions. There is also subscription information for a listserv devoted to junior faculty and graduate students doing research in this area.

Historical Health Information Locator Service (Canada)

http://www.fis.utoronto.ca/research/ams/hilscan/

This service is, according to the Web site, "a national research service based at the University of Toronto's Centre for Research in Information Studies dedicated to expanding awareness of and access to historical resources relating to Canadian healthcare and medicine." This site serves researchers, archivists, and custodians of Canadian health care collections. The site contains a list of Internet and print resources and contact information. The site may be removed in the future, but is a good resource for as long as it is available.

WWW Virtual Guide to the History of Russian and Soviet Science and Technology

http://web.mit.edu/slava/guide

This guide was established and is maintained by Dr. Slava Gerovitch, a lecturer in the science, technology, and society program at MIT. There is an extensive list of archival collections, journals, scholars, relevant Russian institutions, and course syllabi. The site is fairly easy to navigate, but does not have search capability. This unique site is useful for both research and teaching.

Chapter 21

History of Technology

Mark McCallon

Metasites

ECHO—Exploring and Collecting History Online

http://echo.gmu.edu/

Centralized guide to Web sites that chronicle the history of technology. Sponsored by George Mason University's Center for History and New Media.

H-Sci-Med-Tech Links Page

http://www.h-net.org/~smt/

Web site and discussion list for scholars studying the history of technology, medicine, and science. A link to other Web sites and bibliographies complements the online content.

Internet Public Library—History of Science & Technology

http://www.ipl.org/div/subject/browse/hum30.03.30/

The Internet Public Library is a growing archive of Web sites created by the University of Michigan School of Information Science. The section devoted to science and technology has links to Web sites for specialists and general historians.

University of Delaware Library—Internet Resources for History of Science and Technology

http://www2.1ib.udel.edu/subj/hsci/internet.htm

Created by David L. Langenberg, this excellent, up-to-date Web site provides a thorough list of links to resources in many subject areas. Especially helpful are the links to online exhibits and databases honoring inventors and scientists.

World History Compass: History of Technology

http://www.worldhistorycompass.com/tech.htm

Although the site has not been updated recently, there are some excellent links to museums and universities in the United States and Europe.

Yahoo—History—Science and Technology

http://dir.yahoo.com/Arts/Humanities/History/By_Subject/
Science_and_Technology/

The editors of the Yahoo search engine maintain this directory of Web sites that includes both general technology history and subject-specific resources for medicine, television, automobiles, and the Internet.

General Sites

Charles Babbage Institute Center for the History of Information Technology

http://www.cbi.umn.edu/index.html

The Charles Babbage Institute is a historical archives and research center at the University of Minnesota created to promote the study of the history of computing, information processing, and software design. Included on the Web site are transcripts from more than 300 interviews with influential scientists and photographs from the historical archives of the Burroughs Corporation.

Computer History Museum

http://www.computerhistory.org/

The Computer History Museum is the largest history museum for preserving the history of the computing revolution from 1945 to 1990. The Web site for the museum presents a detailed time line of computing history with biographical sketches and photographs. Also included are online exhibits on microprocessors, visible storage, and the Internet.

Devices of Wonder

http://www.getty.edu/art/exhibitions/devices/html/

An online exhibit at the Getty Museum, Devices of Wonder explores the history of unusual scientific instruments and optical devices that educate and entertain. Videos and animation enhance the site.

DSpace at Massachusetts Institute of Technology

http://dspace.mit.edu/

DSpace is an ambitious project to house the digital projects of MIT faculty and researchers. Included in the site are technical reports, working papers, conference proceedings, and images that chronicle the history of technology. The site is still new so many items are not available yet.

EarlyCinema.com

http://www.earlycinema.com

This Web site chronicles the early technological developments in motion pictures. A detailed time line introduces the researcher to various devices and techniques used in early filmmaking. A film section is to be added shortly.

Thomas A. Edison Papers

http://edison.rutgers.edu/

Over 180,000 document images from the Edison National Historical Site and Archives are available on this site. Patents, newspaper clippings, and sketches by and about Edison can be found on this outstanding site.

The Engines of Our Ingenuity

http://www.uh.edu/engines/

Written and hosted by John Lienhard, this weekly radio program about technological innovations is heard nationally on NPR. The Web site contains the transcript for each show with additional graphics and classroom materials.

Epact—Scientific Instruments of Medieval and Renaissance Europe

http://www.mhs.ox.ac.uk/epact/

Epact is an electronic catalog of over 500 scientific instruments from four European museums, including several quadrants and sundials. Included on the Web site are descriptions and photographs of each image. Thematic articles and essays supplement the instruments to give details on how the main types of instruments operated.

Greatest Engineering Achievements of the 20th Century

http://www.greatachievements.org/

Maintained by the National Academy of Engineering, this Web site examines the top twenty inventions and innovations of the twentieth century, including the automobile and the Internet. For each achievement, a detailed history with a time line is presented.

Historic American Buildings Survey/Historic American Engineering Record

http://memory.loc.gov/ammem/collections/habs_haer/

Part of the Library of Congress's American Memory Project, this important online archive traces the history of buildings and engineering technologies in America. The archive includes extensive collections of photographs, drawings, and written histories for more than 35,000 historic structures and places from pre-Columbian times to the twentieth century.

ICOTEC—International Committee for the History of Technology

http://www.icohtec.org/

ICOTEC was established to foster international cooperation for the study and development of the history of technology. Included on the Web site are the table of contents to *ICON* (the organizational journal) and the online newsletter.

IEEE History Center (Institute of Electrical and Electronics Engineers)

http://www.ieee.org/organizations/history_center/

The IEEE History Center is an electronic clearinghouse of information on the history of computing and engineering technologies. Available online are books, biographies and oral histories of electrical engineers, and a comprehensive bibliography of sources on the history of computing.

IEEE Virtual Museum

http://www.ieee-virtual-museum.org/

This online museum contains award-winning exhibits that explore the history of electricity and electronics. Biographies and links to related Web sites demonstrate the relevance of engineers and engineering to society.

Institute and Museum of the History of Science— Exhibits and Learning

http://www.imss.fi.it/espo/

The Web site for this museum located in Florence, Italy, includes an online catalog of photographs and descriptions on display at the museum and many online exhibits. Also includes extensive digital libraries devoted to the works of Galileo and a selected group of works on the history of glass.

Imperial War Museum's Collections Online

http://www.iwmcollections.org.uk/

The Imperial War Museum chronicles the history of warfare in the twentieth century. Included in the online archives are photographs, documents, films, and art. Highlights of the Web site include information on war machines, media technologies, and aircraft used by the British.

Lawrence Livermore National Laboratory—Timeline of Laboratory History

http://www.llnl.gov/time line/

This time line chronicles the accomplishments of the Livermore National Laboratory, one of the premier scientific centers in the world, over the past fifty years. Detailed stories enhance the multitude of graphics and videos available. Also includes links to laboratory reports and related Web sites.

Lemelson Center for the Study of Invention & Innovation

http://invention.smithsonian.org/

The Lemelson Center has played a key role in providing resources to foster an appreciation for inventors and their inventions. The Web site contains many virtual exhibits and video clips spanning all time periods. Also included is the invention archive at the American History Archives Center.

Linda Hall Library of Science, Engineering, and Technology

http://www.lindahall.org/

The Linda Hall Library contains one of the most extensive collections of materials related to science, technology, and engineering in the world. Several outstanding online exhibits can be viewed through the Web site. Also, a significant digital library of star atlases and historical indexes is available.

Making the Modern World

http://www.makingthemodernworld.org.uk/

An excellent example of an educational site, this highly graphical tour provides stories about science and invention from the eighteenth century until today. Sponsored by the Science Museum, its multimedia exhibits include learning modules, guided tours, time lines, and images.

Newton Project

http://www.newtonproject.ic.ac.uk/intro.html

Hosted by the Imperial College in London, the aim of this project is to produce a complete online edition of Isaac Newton's scientific and nonscientific works. A comprehensive catalog of his works and online editions of many of his personal and scientific papers are available on the Web site.

Smithsonian Institution Libraries Galaxy of Knowledge— Industry & Technology

http://www.sil.si.edu/galaxy/industry.cfm

The Imaging Center at the Smithsonian has created this interesting collection of materials gathered from the libraries at the Smithsonian Institution. Included are interesting collections on the Panama Canal, the Wright Brothers, and early astronomical instruments.

Society for the History of Technology (SHOT)

http://www.shot.jhu.edu/index.html

Formed in 1958, the society encourages the study of the history of technology and its impact on society and culture. The Web site includes links to the table of contents for the society's journal and announcements of awards and conferences. There are also links to other credible Web resources.

Time-Warp Project

http://www.time-warp.org/

This entertaining site is an attempt to archive the development of technologies from 1900 to the present. For each decade, descriptions of different devices used in the homes of that time period are presented with description and photographs.

"To Fly Is Everything . . ."

http://invention.psychology.msstate.edu/

The detailed account of the invention of the airplane is presented in this comprehensive digital library of documents and images from the nineteenth and early twentieth centuries. Especially interesting is the correspondence between Wilbur Wright and Octave Chanute, the engineer of the Herring/Chanute glider that formed the basis for the Wright Brothers' design.

Transistor Legacy: Then and Now

http://www.lucent.com/minds/transistor/

Made available through Bell Labs, this Web site provides an overview of the transistor, including its history and its uses.

Vintage Calculators Web Museum

http://www.vintagecalculators.com/

Produced by Nigel Tout, photographs and descriptions of over 100 handheld, desktop, and mechanical calculators are available. Also, books and manuals pertaining to the history of the calculator have been added to the site.

Walk Through Time

http://physics.nist.gov/GenInt/Time/time.html

Created by the National Institute of Standards and Technology, this online exhibit presents the evolution of time measurement from ancient times to the atomic clocks of today. A helpful bibliography provides additional resources on time measurement.

Chapter 22

Holocaust Studies

Anne Rothfeld

Amcha

http://www.amcha.org/

Amcha is the support organization of Israeli centers for Holocaust survivors and the children of survivors.

Anne Frank Center USA

http://www.annefrank.com/

The site for the Anne Frank Center USA, with educational information for teachers and students, information on the center's traveling exhibit, and activities at the center.

Anne Frank House

http://www.annefrank.nl/

The official Web site for the Anne Frank House, this site gives viewing information, exhibition information, a keyword and book list, and information about and photos of her famous diary.

Bulgarian Jews During World War II

http://www.b-info.com/places/Bulgaria/Jewish/

An archive of articles, letters, and other documents that attempts to explain the experience of Jews in Bulgaria and why not a single Bulgarian Jew was deported to the Nazi death camps during World War II. Also includes a bibliography and link section.

Cybrary of the Holocaust

http://remember.org

An impressive resource for both teachers and students of the Jewish Holocaust. This Web site includes a wide variety of texts, artwork, discussion forums, eyewitness accounts, poetry, photographs, and bibliographies. All content is donated by users and participants.

The Desert Holocaust Memorial

http://www.palmsprings.com/points/holocaust/

A photo and information page for a memorial site in Rancho Mirage, California. This Web site has an impressive number of Holocaust-related links.

The Forgotten Camps

http://www.jewishgen.org/ForgottenCamps/

An extensive site devoted to several of the lesser known concentration camps, work camps, police camps, transit camps, and similar facilities. This page was created by Vincent Chatel, son of a survivor, and Chuck Ferree, a witness and camp liberator. It is also accessible in a French version.

H-Holocaust

http://www.h-net.msu.edu/~holoweb/

The Web location for the Humanities and Social Science Online initiative's Holocaust discussion list. Includes an opportunity to join the list, as well as scholarly reviews, academic announcements, course syllabi, and an entire log of H-Holocaust messages. Other related H-Net listservs include H-German, H-Judaic, and H-Antisemitism.

Holocaust Education Resources for Teachers

http://www.Holocaust-trc.org/

Sponsored by the Holocaust Education Foundation, this site offers lesson plans, curricula, essays and publications, bibliographies, and a vast array of information and links for those intending to teach about the Holocaust.

The Holocaust History Project

http://www.holocaust-history.org/

An archive of documents, photographs, recordings, book reproductions, and essays regarding the Holocaust, with a focus on direct refutation of Holocaust denial.

The Holocaust Memorial Center: Illuminating the Past, Enlightening the Future

http://www.holocaustcenter.com/

The first American Holocaust memorial, the Web site for this museum and archive in Farmington Hills, Michigan, contains exhibits, an archive of documents and artifacts, and an oral history archive. An interesting addition is the Life Chance exhibit, an interactive role-playing scenario wherein you make choices which determine if you would have lived or died during the Holocaust.

Holocaust: Non-Jewish Victims

http://www.holocaustforgotten.com/

A site dedicated and devoted to the more than 5 million people, other than Jews, who were slaughtered during the Holocaust.

Holocaust Pictures Exhibition

http://www.phdn.org/histgen/schmitz/indexeng.html

A collection of thirty-seven photos with documentation and commentary, which is also available in French.

The Holocaust Ring

http://www.einsatzgruppenarchives.com/holoring.html

A list of Web pages that all contribute to Holocaust understanding, study, research, or dynamics. Membership is required.

Holocaust Understanding and Prevention by Alexander Kimel

http://www.kimel.net/

Informative site, recommended by the History Channel, created by Holocaust survivor Alexander Kimel. Contains a wide variety of documents, memoirs, and poetry by Holocaust survivors, an online magazine on Holocaust issues, and an excellent collection of links to other sites.

KZ Mauthausen-GUSEN Info-Pages

http://www.gusen.org/

An archive of documentation and information about the Mauthausen-GUSEN death camps, considered the worst of all the Nazi camps.

Louisiana Holocaust Survivors

http://www.southerninstitute.info/holocaust_education/
holocaust_education.html

With space contributed by the Southern Institute for Education and Research, this is a Web site–based archive of the stories of Louisiana residents who survived the Holocaust.

Mauthausen Concentration Camp Memorial

http://www.mauthausen-memorial.at/

Web site for the Mauthausen concentration camp memorial. Contains documentation and information about the camp, available in numerous languages.

The Nizkor Holocaust Educational Resource

http://www2.ca.nizkor.org/index.html

The Nizkor Project Web site is the home page of an international multimedia project, spearheaded by Canada-based archivist Ken McVay (http://veritas.nizkor.org/~kmcvay/), which aims to counter those who deny the Holocaust. It is an extremely well-documented and rich resource, containing over 4,000 documents, and is one of the world's largest online collections of Holocaust-related materials.

To Save a Life: Stories of Jewish Rescue

http://www.humboldt.edu/~rescuers/index.html

The text from a previously unpublished work by Ellen Land-Weber that tells the stories of nine Jews who were rescued from the Holocaust and the six people who saved them.

The Simon Wiesenthal Center

http://www.wiesenthal.com/

The Simon Wiesenthal Center in Los Angeles is dedicated to chronicling the history of human rights and the Holocaust. The center's online site contains exhibits, glossaries, articles, and information on the center's activities.

Survivors of the Shoah Visual History Foundation

http://www.vhf.org/

Founded by film director Steven Spielberg in 1994, this nonprofit foundation is dedicated to videotaping and archiving interviews of Holocaust survivors all over the world, using the latest technology. The site offers information on the project, repositories, production status, and access to over 45,000 testimonies.

Teaching the Holocaust

http://www.socialstudies.com/c/@c0kc44xusXy6Y/Pages/holo.html

A collection of links to resources and materials for teaching about the Holocaust.

Teaching the Holocaust Through the Use of Stamps, Pictures, Texts, and Paintings by Children in the Holocaust

http://mofetsrv.mofet.macam98.ac.il/~ochayo/einvert.htm

An interdisciplinary computer-based resource for teaching about the Holocaust through stamps, pictures, texts, and paintings by children who were in the Holocaust. Offers a complete teacher's guide, dictionary, and teaching unit. Also available in a Hebrew version.

The United States Holocaust Memorial Museum

http://www.ushmm.org/

The official site of the U.S. Holocaust Memorial Museum. Offers information on exhibits and activities of the museum, as well as an array of documents and contact information. The museum, a memorial to everyone who perished in the Holocaust, focuses on photographic and cinematic exhibits.

The Wolf Lewkowicz Collection

http://web.mit.edu/maz/wolf/

The Wolf Lewkowicz Collection is made up of 178 letters translated into English (the original Yiddish is also available) from a man in Poland to his nephew in the United States, written between 1922 and 1939. Lewkowicz was later sent to Treblinka, where he died. Photos and sound recordings are also available. A list of names and a chronology of the letters is included to help researchers.

Women and the Holocaust: A Cyberspace of Their Own

http://www3.sympatico.ca/mighty1/

A collection of essays, tributes, bibliographies, poetry, and personal reflections that focus on women's experiences during the Holocaust,

Yad Vashem: The Holocaust Martyrs and Heroes Remembrance Authority

http://www.yadvashem.org/

Yad Vashem is the Jerusalem-based Holocaust memorial established in 1953. The Web site consists of online exhibits, information about the memorial center and its research, calls for papers, and a vast collection of publications. The Central Database of Shoah Victims' Names, which contains over 3 million individual records, is now available.

Chapter 23

Law, Civil Liberties, and Civil Rights History

Richard P. Mulcahy

Law

Avalon Project

http://www.Yale.edu/lawweb/avalon/avalon.htm

The Avalon Project at Yale University Law School offers access to a wide variety of documents relating to American legal history. The documents are arranged according to period and are cross-referenced. Selections range from the Mayflower Compact (complete with the names of its signatories) and Thomas Paine's *American Crisis,* to Lincoln's two inaugural addresses, the Gettysburg Address, the Yalta Accords, and twenty-first century documents. The site is also linked to Project DIANA, which is listed as "An Online Human Rights Archive." This site is a very thorough, valuable resource for both advanced scholars and students alike.

Charters of Freedom

http://www.archives.gov/national_archives_experience/charters/charters.html

This site's purpose is to make important documents in America's history, including the Bill of Rights, the Declaration of Independence, and the Constitution, available to both students and educators. The site also features informational items, such as an overview of the Constitutional Convention and additional information on the Articles of Confederation, the forerunner to the Constitution.

Digital Classroom

http://www.archives.gov/education/index.html

This site offers a wonderful resource for serious students and educators. Its main sections include Teaching with Documents, Conducting Research, Locating Publications, and Growing Professionally. Under Teaching with Documents, users can access topics ranging from the Lewis and Clark Expedition to the Great Depression and World War II. An essential resource for any instructor interested in exposing students to primary documentary materials and how they are used in historical research.

Famous Trials

http://www.law.umkc.edu/faculty/projects/ftrials/ftrials.htm

This site is maintained by Douglas Linder at the University of Missouri-Kansas City School of Law. It features a total of forty trials. Newly added to the site are the Hiss-Chambers spy case, the McMartin preschool case, and the trial of John Hinckley Jr. Each of these sections features full narratives and original documents such as briefs and trial transcripts, as well as graphics of the people and evidence involved. In addition, the site's presentations reflect the findings of mainstream scholarship relative to the cases it covers. It is the very best site of its kind on the World Wide Web.

Federalist Papers

http://www.law.ou.edu/hist/federalist

This site offers access to the complete collection of the *Federalist Papers,* a series of short articles written by Alexander Hamilton, James Madison, and John Jay in support of the ratification of the Constitution of the United States. The papers provide great insight into the constitution relative to the framers' original intent and have been so used in various Supreme Court decisions. This site is well designed, provides access to each of the papers in a readily accessible plain-text format, and is highly recommended.

Tarlton Law Library Virtual Library

http://tarlton.law.utexas.edu/vlibrary/

This site's resources are divided into two broad categories: guides to traditional manuscript sources and guides to electronic and online resources. Online resources include research databases, legal research on the Web, electronic resource tutorials, general reference resources, and online search strategies. The site also features a special section dealing with Aztec and Mayan law, law in popular culture, and U.S. Supreme Court decisions. Highly recommended.

Civil Liberties

The Alger Hiss Story

http://Homepages.nyu.edu/~th15/

This site deals specifically with the Hiss-Chambers spy case. It is one of the most extensive sites on a single topic currently available on the World Wide Web, although it also raises the question of civil liberities in general. Written from the point of view that Hiss was innocent, the site features a chronology, video clips, articles, and an extensive critique of the VENONA traffic, which allegedly confirmed Hiss's guilt. Well researched and effectively argued, this site provides an excellent counterpoint to other resources, such as the Famous Trials Web site, reviewed above, that argue that Hiss was guilty. Highly recommended.

The American 1950s

http://www.writing.upenn.edu/~afilreis/50s/home.html

This site, maintained through the University of Pennsylvania's Department of English, is a substantial clearinghouse for information on the 1950s, with special reference to McCarthyism and the Cold War. Among new items on the site are a video file featuring a thirty-second commercial for Dwight Eisenhower from the 1952 presidential election, a short biography of Zero Mostel, an actor who had been blacklisted, a summary of author Lillian Hellman's FBI file, and an article comparing America's anxieties about nuclear war in the 1950s to current fears about terrorist attacks. This site is highly recommended for all users.

American Radicalism Collection

http://www.lib.msu.edu/coll/main/spec_col/radicalism/index.htm

This site provides a guide to Michigan State University's radicalism collection, including access to online versions of Industrial Workers of the World pamphlets, appeals for the Rosenbergs, the Sacco and Vanzetti case, and writings by Margaret Sanger on birth control. These documents provide excellent insight relative to the era's mainstream and oppositional cultures.

Banned Books Online

http://Onlinebooks.library.upenn.edu/banned-books.html

This page offers information on past and recent efforts to ban various works, including *Ulysses, The Origin of Species,* and *Tom Sawyer.* For example, the site reports on a 1996 effort by a New Hampshire school board to remove Shakespeare's *Twelfth Night* from the curriculum, as the school board claimed the play promoted "alternative lifestyles." Even more important, the site offers not only a list of banned works, but complete texts as well. The information it presents makes it a useful resource for anyone interested in freedom of thought.

The File Room

http://www.theFileroom.org

Similar to the previous site, this site offers access to information about censorship efforts worldwide, including the United States. Of particular interest are the case studies it provides on recent censorship efforts in the United States, especially those involving institutions such as schools. With these, the site lists its sources of information. This very informative site is well worth visiting.

McCarthyism

http://www.spartacus.schoolnet.co.uk/USAred.htm

This site is part of Britain's Spartacus Online Encyclopedia. This is a beginner's site for anyone interested in McCarthyism, civil liberties, or the Cold War. It offers basic information on a number of interrelated topics, including the WPA Federal Art Project, the Hollywood Ten, Elizabeth Bentley, a woman who accused, generally falsely, many people of spying in 1945, and Alger Hiss, whom the United States officially accused of being a Soviet spy. This site is recommended for the novice or anyone needing quick information.

Civil Rights

Anti-Defamation League: The Holocaust and Related Issues

http://www.adl.org/holocaust

This site deals with the Holocaust and related issues, such as Holocaust deniers and the Lipstadt case (in which historian Debra Lipstadt won a libel case filed against her by Holocaust denier David Irving). The site offers a great deal of information, especially personal narratives, about the "hidden children" and the controversy involving Pope Pius XII's decision that Jewish children hidden by Catholics should not be returned to their own families after the war. The site also presents an excellent review of Roberto Benigni's movie *Life Is Beautiful.* It is highly recommended for anyone interested in the Holocaust and the toll it continues to take.

The Civil Rights Documentation Project

http://www.usm.edu/crdp/index.html

This site, maintained by the University of Southern Mississippi, provides access to oral history interviews on the civil rights movement in Mississippi from the early 1960s through the 1970s. The site lists those interviewed, provides transcripts and outlines of the subject matters discussed, and includes a biographical sketch of the interviewee. Persons interviewed include civil rights activists who went to Mississippi to take part in the Freedom Rides and Freedom Schools, as well as those who were born and raised in Mississippi. The site is an important and invaluable tool for the serious educator and researcher.

Civnet

http://www.civnet.org

Civnet is maintained by Civitas International, which describes itself as "a worldwide, non-governmental organization for civic education." The site offers links to articles and speeches on civic matters, as well as myriad links to news organizations, journals, and museums. It also provides information to educators on how to teach concepts of citizenship and the rights and responsibilities that go with it. A very useful and informative site.

Greensboro Sit-Ins: Launch of a Civil Rights Movement

http://www.sitins.com

On February 1, 1960, the so-called Greensboro Four sat at a "white only" lunch counter at a Woolworth's in Greensboro, North Carolina, and demanded to be served. This tactic became a staple in the arsenal of nonviolent protest.The site includes a bibliography on the civil rights movement, biographical sketches of the four original protestors, and an extensive civil rights time line dating from 1865. It features an extensive collection of photographs relating to the Greensboro Four, as well as video and audio selections. The site links to the National Civil Rights Museum, the NAACP, and a site created to mark the anniversary of the integration of Little Rock Central High School.

National Civil Rights Museum

http://www.civilrightsmuseum.org

The site features a virtual tour of the National Civil Rights Museum, which presents a useful narrative about the civil rights struggle. Students can get basic information on such figures as Frederick Douglass, Harriet Tubman, and William Lloyd Garrison. The site also contains still pictures of several of the museum's exhibits, including a city bus from the Montgomery, Alabama, bus boycott. This site offers a good basic introduction to the history of the civil rights movement.

Chapter 24

Modern Military History

S. Mike Pavelec

Here are a few modern military history (defined as from 1898 to 2005) Web sites for initial research into the field of academic military history. These Web sites are slanted toward the technology side of military history. There are many more; these are some of the most reliable and helpful sites for beginning (and continuing) researchers.

The Best of the List

Air and Space Power Chronicles

http://www.airpower.maxwell.af.mil/

The U.S. Air Force's journal site. A good place for information on the scholarly pursuits at the Air University at Maxwell Air Force Base, Alabama.

BUBL LINK: A Catalogue of Internet Resources

http://www.bubl.ac.uk/link/m/militaryhistory.htm

A British site of compiled military history Web sites by one of Britain's best search networks.

eHistory.com

http://www.ehistory.com

A Web site dedicated to electronic history (history on the Web). Formerly independent, it is now being run through The Ohio State University's Department of History. Look for vast improvements in the content of this great site for research and images.

Eye Witness to History

http://www.eyewitnesstohistory.com/

A collection of firsthand accounts of historical events. The Web site covers a variety of topics; see specifically the valuable military history entries and information.

Federation of American Scientists

http://www.fas.org/main/home.jsp

A collection of the latest analyses on current U.S. military capabilities. Further information is provided on world military systems and capabilities.

Globalsecurity.org

http://www.globalsecurity.org

An informative Web site dedicated to historical and current military operations and analysis. Includes interesting and informative military history documents and articles.

The Historical Text Archive

http://www.historicaltextarchive.com/

An independent Web site dedicated to articles, texts, and books on history and historical research. Good content on military history.

The History Guy

http://www.historyguy.com/

A history Web site with good information and resources. See especially the military history section.

The History Net

http://www.historynet.com

A clearinghouse for history on the Web; especially rich in resources and articles on military history.

Military History

http://www.militaryhistory.about.com/

An informative Web site dedicated to all aspects of military history. Site contains good articles and information from a number of sources.

Military History Online

http://www.militaryhistoryonline.com/

Another well-built Web site dedicated to all aspects of military history. Of particular interest are well-written articles with references on a number of military history topics.

OnWar.com

http://www.onwar.com/

A starting place for research on individual wars, rebellions, and uprisings across time. Especially helpful time lines and chronologies of human conflict.

The Society for Military History

http://www.smh-hq.org/

The main Web site for the academic organization dedicated to the scholarly pursuit of military history. Also a useful place to start when looking for academic historians, their conferences, and academic military history articles and research.

University of North Texas Department of History, Center for the Study of Military History

http://www.hist.unt.edu/military.htm

An excellent academic-sponsored Web site with multiple links for military history research and documentation.

The War Times Journal

http://wtj.com/

An online journal full of information and resources on military history.

The West Point Atlas Home Page

http://www.dean.usma.edu/history/web03/atlases/atlas%20home.htm

This Web site of the U.S. Army school at West Point provides atlases for all American wars; see especially the extensive coverage of World War II and Vietnam.

The Women's Army Corps Veterans Association

http://www.armywomen.org/

This WAC Web site, dedicated to women in uniform, is a valuable historical research tool with images and links.

Archives, Documents, and Primary Research

The Avalon Project at Yale Law School

http://www.yale.edu/lawweb/avalon/20th.htm

A great place for online documents, specifically twentieth-century documents. The Yale Law School has dedicated extensive time and effort to making primary documents available online.

EuroDocs: Primary Historical Documents From Western Europe

http://www.lib.byu.edu/~rdh/eurodocs/index.html

A Brigham Young University library project presenting primary historical documents from Europe, including a great wealth of treaties in translation for English research.

The National Archives (formerly the Public Record Office), England

http://www.nationalarchives.gov.uk/default.htm

The Web site dedicated to the British counterpart of the American National Archives and Records Administration. This site is the gateway for research in Britain.

National Archives and Records Administration (NARA)

http://www.archives.gov/index.html

The Web site dedicated to the National Archives of the United States. A starting place for online research and contact information for the holdings and archivists at the National Archives in Washington, DC.

National Museum of the U.S. Air Force

http://www.wpafb.af.mil/museum/

The best site for the beginner and advanced researcher on American airpower.

Smithsonian National Air and Space Museum

http://www.nasm.si.edu/

The main Web site for the Smithsonian's excellent collection of archives and artifacts.

The World War I Document Archive

http://www.gwpda.org/

An excellent research guide and Web site dedicated to World War I documents and archives. See especially the Maritime War subsection.

Spanish American War (1898–1902)

The Spanish American War Centennial Web Site

http://www.spanamwar.com/

A Spanish American War Web site with extensive information and images. The best Web site for information devoted to this war.

The World of 1898: The Spanish-American War

http://www.loc.gov/rr/hispanic/1898/

The Library of Congress Hispanic Division's Web site on Hispanic perceptions of the Spanish-American War. Good time lines, images, articles, and references.

Boer War (1899–1902)

Anglo Boer War Museum

http://www.anglo-boer.co.za/

A Web site dedicated to the Boer War from the South African (white) perspective. The Anglo Boer War Museum sponsors the Web site.

The Boer War: South Africa (1899–1902)

http://www.geocities.com/Athens/Acropolis/8141/boerwar.html

A personal Web site with valuable information and research on the Boer War.

Russo-Japanese War (1904–1905)

The Russo-Japanese War Research Society

http://www.russojapanesewar.com/

A Web site dedicated to the Russo-Japanese War of 1904–1905. A very interesting and informative site for important information on an underinvestigated war.

World War I (1914–1918)

The Aerodrome

http://www.theaerodrome.com/

An excellent starter site for World War I aviation research.

The Great War and the Shaping of the Twentieth Century

http://www.pbs.org/greatwar/

The PBS site dedicated to World War I and its aftermath.

Over the Front: The League of WWI Aviation Historians

http://overthefront.com/main/index.html

A group dedicated to World War I Aviation scholarship and research. The league publishes the journal *Over the Front* and is the sister organization of *Cross and Cockade* in England.

The War at Sea (WWI)

http://www.gwpda.org/naval/n0000000.htm

World War I naval warfare Web site with wonderful research and information. There are extensive bibliographies on World War I naval history. Part of the excellent World War I Document Archive.

World War One: Trenches on the Web

http://www.worldwar1.com/

One of the best sites for research and finding aids on World War One. See especially The Great War Society Within Trenches on the Web.

Russian Civil War (1917–1922)

Allied Intervention in the Russian Civil War

http://www.regiments.org/wars/ww1/russia.htm

An English site dedicated to lists and bibliography of Allied intervention in the Russian Civil War. Also presents time lines and biographies.

Russian Civil War

http://www.spartacus.schoolnet.co.uk/RUScivilwar.htm

An encyclopedic reference tool on the Russian Civil War.

Chaco Wars (1927–1929, 1932–1935)

The Chaco War

http://www.american.edu/TED/ice/chaco.htm

The American University's case study on the Chaco war and its relevance in history.

The Gran Chaco War

http://worldatwar.net/chandelle/v1/v1n3/chaco.html

A useful Web site—with images and maps—on the Gran Chaco War between Bolivia and Paraguay. Useful information on this overlooked conflict.

Spanish Civil War (1936–1939)

History of the Spanish Civil War

http://dwardmac.pitzer.edu/Anarchist_Archives/spancivwar/
spancivwarhis.html

A Pitzer College (Claremont, California) Web site dedicated to the history of the Spanish Civil War. See especially the information on the American volunteers in the war, the Abraham Lincoln Brigade.

Spanish Civil War

http://www.spartacus.schoolnet.co.uk/Spanish-Civil-War.htm

A student-sponsored Web site full of encyclopedic resources and information.

The Spanish Revolution and Civil War, 1936–1939

http://www.geocities.com/capitolhill/9820/

A Spanish Civil War site from the leftist perspective. Within the site there are numerous links to other Spanish Civil War sites and resources. Of particular interest is a digital reproduction of the music for "L'Internationale" available to play on the Web site.

World War II in Europe (1939–1945)

Achtung Panzer

http://www.achtungpanzer.com/panzer.htm

Extensive resources and links on World War II German tank and armored warfare.

The Air War

http://www.stable.demon.co.uk/

Extensive resources and information on the air war over Western Europe, specifically information on the British, Americans, and Germans.

Axis History Factbook

http://www.axishistory.com/

An amateur Web site dedicated to Germany and the Axis in World War II. Useful information and images presented by a dedicated amateur historian and academic political scientist.

The Battle of Britain Historical Society

http://www.battleofbritain.net/

The introductory Web site for both the Royal Air Force Fighter Command Battle of Britain and the Battle of Britain Historical Society. Both have excellent resource material on the famous aerial struggle over England in World War II.

Feldgrau.com—The German Armed Forces, 1919–1945

http://www.feldgrau.com/

An informative site on research materials and topics on the German armed forces leading up to and during World War II.

Hyperwar: A Hypertext History of the Second World War

http://www.ibiblio.org/hyperwar/

An individual attempt to link multiple resources on World War II. There is a good bibliography as well as valuable information and resources on the war.

The Luftwaffe, 1933–1945

http://www.ww2.dk/

This Luftwaffe site has good information and useful links for Luftwaffe research and discussion groups.

Sword of the Motherland

http://www.russianwarrior.com/

An excellent Web site dedicated to Russian and Soviet military history. See especially the World War II pages, resources, and links under the "Great Patriotic War."

UBoat.net

http://uboat.net/

Extensive resources and links on German World War II submarines and their operations.

The Warbirds Resource Group

http://www.warbirdsresourcegroup.org/

A resource site for all manner of World War II aircraft and aviation research.

World War II in the Pacific (1939–1945)

The Hiroshima Archive

http://www.lclark.edu/~history/HIROSHIMA/

Lewis and Clark College's (Portland, Oregon) site dedicated to the documents and controversy surrounding the atomic bomb dropped on Hiroshima in August 1945.

Imperial Japanese Navy

http://homepage2.nifty.com/nishidah/e/index.htm

A Web site dedicated to the Imperial Japanese Navy (IJN). It is maintained by an individual whose credentials cannot be verified, but the site has very interesting and authentic nuts-and-bolts data on the IJN.

Imperial Japanese Navy Page

http://www.combinedfleet.com/

A Web site dedicated to the Imperial Japanese Navy of World War II.

A Marine Diary: My Experiences on Guadalcanal

http://www.gnt.net/~jrube/indx2.html

An American marine's recollection of his ordeal at Guadalcanal complete with images and information on this important Pacific battlefield.

National Atomic Museum—The Manhattan Project Display

http://www.atomicmuseum.com/tour/manhattanproject.cfm

The National Atomic Museum in Albuquerque, New Mexico, and the Web site dedicated to the history of the American Manhattan Project and the development of the atomic bomb during World War II.

The Pacific War: The U.S. Navy

http://www.microworks.net/pacific/

A helpful resource guide to World War II U.S. Navy Pacific theater campaigns and information.

Chinese Civil War (1945–1949)

The Chinese Civil War at Eduseek.com

http://www.eduseek.com/navigate.php?ID=497

An encyclopedic reference to the Chinese Civil War with good links, including an animated map of the war.

Handbook for the Chinese Civil War

http://www.nwc.navy.mil/chinesecs/

Professor Andrew Wilson of the Naval War College's Strategy and Policy Department presents a basic reader and good source of information on the Chinese Civil War.

Cold War—U.S. Versus USSR

Cold War Bibliography

http://www.cmu.edu/coldwar/bibl.html

Carnegie Mellon University's Web site (somewhat dated—from 2000—but watch for updates) on the Cold War. A lot of good information directly garnered from the Cold War Science and Technology Colloquium.

Cold War Hot Links

http://www.stmartin.edu/~dprice/cold.war.html

A Web site dedicated to links on Cold War information by Professor David Price of St. Martin's College in Lacey, Washington.

The Cold War Museum

http://www.coldwar.org/

The Web site of the museum dedicated to the Cold War. Informative time lines, documents, and images.

Documents Relating to American Foreign Policy: The Cold War

http://www.mtholyoke.edu/acad/intrel/coldwar.htm

Within Professor Vincent Ferraro's personal Web site, he has posted this Cold War documents page. See his other documents pages for even more important information.

Journal of Cold War Studies

http://www.fas.harvard.edu/~hpcws/journal.htm

Harvard's academic journal dedicated to Cold War studies helps researchers stay updated on the latest research on the Cold War.

The Korean War (1950–1953)

The Korean War

http://www.korean-war.com/

A Web site with excellent resources and links on Korean War history. See especially the extensive bibliography.

The Korean War Project

http://koreanwar.org/

The starting place for Korean War research and information.

The Korean War Veterans Association

http://www.kwva.org/

A valuable resource for locating and contacting veterans of the Korean War.

French Indochina (1945–1954)

Air War Over French Indochina

http://hedgehoghollow.com/awoic/

A good Web site devoted to the French phase of the Indochinese War (to 1954) and all the air forces involved. Good images, links, and source references.

Dien Bien Phu

http://www.dienbienphu.org/english/

A Web site dedicated to the preservation of the French perspective of the battle of Dien Bien Phu.

Cuban Missile Crisis (1962)

The Cuban Missile Crisis, 1962

http://www2.gwu.edu/~nsarchiv/nsa/cuba_mis_cri/

George Washington University's Cuban Missile Crisis Web site. Complete with documents, photos, and analysis of the crisis.

The United States in Vietnam (1954–1975)

The Lyndon Baines Johnson Library and Museum— University of Texas

http://www.lbjlib.utexas.edu/

The Gerald R. Ford Library and Museum— University of Texas

http://www.ford.utexas.edu/

These two excellent Web sites focus on the American presidencies during and immediately after the American involvement in the Vietnam War. The University of Texas is also sponsoring its Vietnam War Declassification Project at http://www.ford.utexas.edu/library/exhibits/vietnam/vietnam.htm, which will offer more documents, resources, and images in the near future.

The Vietnam Project

http://www.vietnam.ttu.edu/

Texas Tech University's Vietnam Project, complete with resources, document archives, and extensive oral interviews.

Vietnam War Bibliography

http://www.clemson.edu/caah/history/FacultyPages/EdMoise/bibliography.html

Dr. Edwin Moise of Clemson University in South Carolina provides a bibliography and detailed links relating to his Vietnam Wars classes and a history of the Vietnam Wars in general. An excellent research tool on the conflicts in Southeast Asia.

The VietnamWar.net

http://www.vietnamwar.net/

A nonacademic site dedicated to the Vietnam War, with documents and resources.

Vietnam: Yesterday and Today

http://servercc.oakton.edu/~wittman/

Professor Sandra Wittman of Oakton Community College in Skokie, Illinois, presents this Web site dedicated to online Vietnam resources.

The Wars for Vietnam, 1945–1975

http://vietnam.vassar.edu/

Vassar College's Vietnam Wars Web site, complete with documents and images.

The Arab-Israeli Wars (1948–1981)

The Arab-Israeli Conflicts in Maps

http://www.jafi.org.il/education/100/maps/

Well-illustrated maps pertaining to the history of Israel and Palestine.

The Arab-Israeli Wars

http://english.aljazeera.net/NR/exeres/A5179275–0F1D-40A2-A3AB-3745424C6EFC.htm

Content and links on the Arab-Israeli Wars from the Arab perspective.

Army Area Handbook

http://lcweb.loc.gov/frd/cs/iltoc.html

The U.S. Army Area Handbook on Palestine and the conflict in the Middle East, published by the Library of Congress, Federal Research Division.

The Israeli Defense Force Homepage

http://www1.idf.il/DOVER/site/homepage.asp?clr=1&sl=EN&id=-8888&force=1

The IDF Homepage with detailed information on the history of the IDF and conflicts in the area since 1948.

The Jewish Virtual Library

http://www.jewishvirtuallibrary.org/

An informative Web site with a number of documents and articles relating to the Arab-Israeli Wars from the Israeli perspective.

The Falklands War (1982)

The Falkland Islands Conflict, 1982

http://www.falklandswar.org.uk/

An excellent site for initial research on the British Falklands campaigns of 1982.

Grenada (Operation Urgent Fury) (1983)

Special Operations: Grenada, 1983

http://www.specialoperations.com/Operations/grenada.html

An interesting Web site dedicated to Operation Urgent Fury in Grenada as well as additional information on Operation Just Cause in Panama in 1989. Good bibliographical references.

The Persian Gulf War I (1990–1991)

Desert Storm.com

http://www.desert-storm.com/

A Web site dedicated to the history and documentation of the Desert Storm campaign.

Fog of War—The 1991 Air Battle for Baghdad

http://www.washingtonpost.com/wp-srv/inatl/longterm/fogofwar/fogofwar.htm

An in-depth analysis of the air war during Desert Storm.

Operation Desert Storm: 10 Years After

http://www2.gwu.edu/~nsarchiv/NSAEBB/NSAEBB39/

The George Washington University's National Security Archive collection on the documents relating to the postwar analyses of the 1991 Persian Gulf War.

Operation Desert Storm/Desert Shield

http://www.gulflink.osd.mil/timeline/

Good information on the dual campaigns in the Persian Gulf War of 1991.

Gulf War II—Operation Iraqi Freedom (2003–present)

Defend America

http://www.defendamerica.mil/

The U.S. Department of Defense Web site with ongoing coverage of the Iraq War.

Iraq War Information

http://www.iraqwar.info/

A Web site dedicated to current information on the Iraq War.

Operation Iraqi Freedom

http://www.centcom.mil/Operations/Iraqi_Freedom/iraqifreedom.asp

Central Command's Web site devoted to current information on the war in Iraq.

Operation Iraqi Freedom

http://www.jfsc.ndu.edu/library/publications/bibliography/
operation_iraqi_freedom.asp

The National Defense University's first look at the publications, articles, and resources on the Iraq War.

Overviews: Air Power

The Aerial Reconnaissance Archives

http://www.evidenceincamera.co.uk/index.htm

A useful place to start for aerial reconnaissance information, history, and images.

Redstone Arsenal Historical Information

http://www.redstone.army.mil/history/

A Web site dedicated to the history of the U.S. missile program. Interesting documents, images, articles, and monographs on missile history.

U.S. Air Force Historical Research Agency

http://www.au.af.mil/au/afhra/

The U.S. Air Force's office for historical research. A wonderful and reliable site to start researching U.S. airpower history.

U.S. Air Force Historical Studies

http://www.airforcehistory.hq.af.mil/

A starting place for U.S. Air Force historical research.

Overviews: Army

U.S. Army Center of Military History

http://www.army.mil/cmh-pg/

A starting place for U.S. Army historical research.

Overviews: Defense

The U.S. Department of Defense

http://www.defenselink.mil/

The U.S. Department of Defense Web site, dedicated to information and news.

Overviews: Navy

American Merchant Marine at War

http://www.usmm.org/

A starting place for U.S. Merchant Marine historical research.

The Battleship Page

http://www.battleship.org/

A site dedicated to extensive information on U.S. Naval battleship history and information.

Haze and Gray and Underway—Naval History and Photography

http://www.hazegray.org/

A Web site dedicated to world naval history. It covers most of the world's navies and is particularly interesting to researchers on American naval history. This Web site has *The Dictionary of American Fighting Ships* online as well as a list of all U.S. warships of all time.

The Naval Institute

http://www.usni.org/

A self-titled Independent Forum on National Defense that provides information and images on naval technology and capabilities as well as naval history. The Naval Institute maintains the Web site and publishes through the Naval Institute Press and the journals *Proceedings* and *Naval History*.

The Naval Vessel Register

http://www.nvr.navy.mil/

The U.S. Department of Defense register of U.S. Navy warships provides information on all the current U.S. Navy ships.

Naval Weapons of the World

http://www.navweaps.com/

A Web site on historical as well as modern naval weapons from around the world. Loaded with helpful information on naval (shipboard) weapons with good images.

U.S. Marine Corps History and Museum Division

http://hqinet001.hqmc.usmc.mil/HD/

A starting place for U.S. Marine Corps historical research.

U.S. Naval Historical Center

http://www.history.navy.mil/

A starting place for U.S. Navy historical research. See especially (and for starters) the navy's excellent resources and images on the Battle of Midway at the "Midway Night" link.

Warships1

http://www.warships1.com/

A Web site dedicated to the historic documentation of naval ships and weapons.

Museum Locators

There are far too many museums to list separately—this Web site is a great museum locator:

Yahoo Index of Military History Museums and Memorials

http://dir.yahoo.com/Arts/Humanities/History/By_Subject/Military_History/Museums_and_Memorials/

A comprehensive guide to museum and memorial listings and Web sites. Hosted by Yahoo.com.

Chapter 25

Historiography

Ranin Kazemi

Metasites

Bibliographies in the Google Directory

http://directory.google.com/Top/Reference/Bibliography/History/

Bibliographies on specific themes, regions, and periods. It may also prove useful to check "Bibliographies in the Yahoo! Directory" (http://dir.yahoo.com/Arts/Humanities/History/Bibliographies/) .

Historians in the Google Directory

http://directory.google.com/Top/Society/History/Historians/

This is certainly not an exhaustive list of important historians, but it provides a good starting point. Parallel and additional categories may also be found in the Yahoo! Directory (http://dir.yahoo.com/Arts/Humanities/History/Historiology/Historians/).

Internet History Sourcebooks Project

http://www.fordham.edu/halsall/

Collections of documents and links to texts on various themes, regions, and periods. This Web site is edited by Paul Halsall of Fordham University. For materials on historiography see Studying Ancient History, (http://www.fordham.edu/halsall/ancient/asbook01.html), Studying [Medieval] History, (http://www.fordham.edu/halsall/sbook1a.html), and Studying [Modern] History. Some of the materials might in fact be identical.

Internet Public Library

http://www.ipl.org/

The Internet Public Library is maintained by the School of Information at the University of Michigan. It provides links to digital libraries and important resources and institutions in various fields, including history. See entries under History, Philosophy, History of Arts and Humanities, History of Social Sciences, and Books.

Philosophy of History in the Google Directory

http://directory.google.com/Top/Society/Philosophy/Philosophy_of_History/

Of the two categories listed on the Web site, "Philosophers" is the more important since it gives links to a number of philosophers whose works are extremely important in historical studies. There are also specific Web pages on aspects of the philosophy of history. The parallel category in the Yahoo! Directory is "Historiology" (http://dir.yahoo.com/Arts/Humanities/History/Historiology/). See particularly "Historiography in the Yahoo! Directory" (http://dir.yahoo.com/Arts/Humanities/History/Historiology/Historiography/).

Voice of the Shuttle

http://vos.ucsb.edu/index.asp

This database, managed by the University of California, Santa Barbara, has a section on history. The materials under the subsection Historiography are organized under three main rubrics: General History Resources (by far the most important of the three), Paradigm-Setting Works of History Writing, and Theoretical or Methodological Works. The materials under General History Resources will also prove beneficial for the links to databases that provide annotated links, archives, electronic documents, maps, and other historical resources.

WWW Virtual Library History—Central Catalogue

http://vlib.iue.it/history/index.html

This index, maintained by the European University Institute, provides links on various aspects of historical studies. Pertinent materials to historiography may be found under the category titled Research: Methods and Materials.

General Web Sites

EServer.org: History and Historiography

http://eserver.org/history/

This site includes original works published online by the EServer and links to historical and historiographical materials. The EServer is based at Iowa State University.

Historians and Philosophers: A Collated Web Index

http://www.scholiast.org/history/histphil.html

This Web site, created and maintained by a history student at the University of Copenhagen, has a list of historians and philosophers whose works have been consequential to historical inquiries. The materials are organized under four periods: Classical Period, Medieval and Renaissance Period, Early Modern Period, and Modern Period. The Modern Period is broken up into three different subperiods. Some of the links might not work, and the entries are of uneven value.

Labyrinth

http://labyrinth.georgetown.edu/

This Web site provides links to numerous electronic resources in medieval studies. Users need to know what types of historiographical questions and texts or else what intellectuals they seek information on in order to utilize this index effectively.

Philosophy of History Archive

http://www.nsu.ru/filf/pha/

This Web site is maintained by Professor Nikolai Rozov of Novosibirsk State University. Contrary to its claim, it is not a comprehensive archive of materials on the philosophy of history and theoretical history. Nonetheless, it provides some additional points of departure for the student of historical method.

Digital Libraries

Archive for the History of the Economic Thought

http://socserv.socsci.mcmaster.ca/~econ/ugcm/3ll3/

Presented here are the full texts of works by important historians and intellectuals whose output is important to history writing, including Emile

Durkheim, G.W.F. Hegel, David Hume, Karl Marx, Charles de Secondat Montesquieu, Thomas Paine, Jean-Jacques Rousseau, Arnold Toynbee, Max Weber, and Xenophon.

Electronic Texts for the Study of American Culture

http://xroads.virginia.edu/~HYPER/hypertex.html

Classical studies of American history and works of historiographical importance, for instance, by Francis Parkman, Alexis de Tocqueville, and Frederick Jackson Turner.

Eliohs: Electronic Library of Historiography

http://www.eliohs.unifi.it/

A virtual collection of texts that have particular historiographical value. Some of the authors represented here are Sir Thomas More, Sir Francis Bacon, Michel-Guillaume-Saint-Jean de Crèvecoeur, Edward Gibbon, David Hume, Jean-Jacques Rousseau, Adam Smith, Voltaire, Jacob Burckhardt, Charles Darwin, Alexis de Tocqueville, Lord Acton, Herbert Butterfield, and Frederick Jackson Turner.

Gallica: bibliothèque numérique de la Bibliothèque nationale de France

http://gallica.bnf.fr/

This digital library provides electronic texts of many important French works, including those of French historians.

Internet Classics Archive

http://classics.mit.edu/index.html

The English translations of the works of some Greco-Roman writers and six classical Iranian and Chinese authors. The Web site also gives links to the Perseus Digital Library.

Perseus Digital Library

http://www.perseus.tufts.edu/

An "evolving digital library" funded by a number of institutions including the Digital Libraries Initiative Phase 2 and Tufts University. Of particular historiographical importance are the texts under Classics, including works by Herodotus, Strabo, Thucydides, and Tacitus.

Major Figures

Fernand Braudel Center

http://fbc.binghamton.edu/

This is the Web site for the Fernand Braudel Center at Binghamton University, State University of New York. The Braudel Center was founded in 1976 "to engage in the analysis of large-scale social change over long periods of historical time." Because of their particular methodological approach, the scholarly activities sponsored by the center might be of interest to those who inquire about historical methodology in general.

Collingwood and British Idealism Centre

http://www.cf.ac.uk/euros/collingwood/

A starting point to inquire about R.G. Collingwood, a central figure in any inquiry about historical methodology. The center is housed at Cardiff University.

The Foucault Pages at CSUN

http://www.csun.edu/~hfspc002/foucault.home.html

Materials and links on this contemporary French thinker.

Institute for Vico Studies

http://www.vicoinstitute.org/

The only Giambattista Vico center in the English-speaking world, the institute was founded in 1974 at Emory University, and its Web site provides a starting point for studies of this Italian historian.

Marxists Internet Archives

http://www.marx.org/

A wealth of materials by and on Karl Marx and those who were influenced by his thought.

Voltaire Society of America

http://humanities.uchicago.edu/homes/VSA/

A good starting point for inquiries about this eighteenth-century French intellectual.

Aspects of Historiography

Aragonese Historiography

http://eserver.org/history/aragonese-historiography.txt

This essay, published by the EServer, pertains to the essentials of Aragonese historiography.

Classical Historiography for Chinese History

http://www.sscnet.ucla.edu/history/elman/ClassBib/

Bibliographies for classical Chinese historiography.

Iranian Historiography

http://www.iranica.com/articles/v12f3/v12f3036.html

A collection of articles in *Encyclopedia Iranica* on Iranian historiography before and after the advent of Islam.

National Center for History in the Schools

http://nchs.ucla.edu/

The NCHS has published over sixty teaching units on aspects of U.S. and world history. It promotes a standards-based approach to teaching history in schools, emphasizing the National Standards for History.

World History Archives

http://www.hartford-hwp.com/archives/index.html

A Web site that contains numerous documents to "support the study of world history from a working-class and non-Eurocentric perspective." Under World Historiography, users find a number of texts of uneven quality.

Writing Tips and Standards

http://personal.stthomas.edu/gwschlabach/courses/writing.htm

These practical tips and suggestions for undergraduates are edited by Gerald Schlabach of the University of St. Thomas, St. Paul, Minnesota. See particularly A Sense of History: Some Components and Ten Commandments of Good Historical Writing.

Journals

Cromohs: Cyber Review of Modern Historiography

http://www.cromohs.unifi.it/

There are many articles and full-text materials in this electronic journal. See particularly Useful Resources to find indexed links to relevant Web sites.

History and Theory

http://www.historyandtheory.org/

This is the Web site of the international journal *History and Theory*, "devoted to the theory and philosophy of history." It provides a link to H-History and Theory, an academic discussion network on the subject (http://www.h-net.org/~hist-thr/), which is also managed by this journal.

Histos: The Electronic Journal of Ancient Historiography

http://www.dur.ac.uk/Classics/histos/

This journal is administered at the University of Durham. It publishes all its materials both online and in "fully-edited and hard-copy format."

Storia della Storiografia: History of Historiography

http://www.cisi.unito.it/stor/home.htm

The Web site of the international journal *Storia della Storiografia*. The journal was founded in 1982 and is presently located at the University of Turin.

Teaching History: A Journal of Methods

http://www.emporia.edu/socsci/journal/

The Web site of the journal *Teaching History*, which was founded in 1976 and whose goal is to provide "history teachers at all levels with the best and newest teaching ideas for their classrooms." The journal is housed at Emporia State University.

Chapter 26

Historic Preservation and Conservation

Anne Rothfeld

Advisory Council on Historic Preservation

http://www.achp.gov

Created by the independent federal agency that advises the president and Congress on historic preservation issues, this Web site offers links to historic preservation officers throughout the United States and information about the National Historic Preservation Act of 1966.

American Institute for Conservation of Historic and Artistic Works

http://aic.stanford.edu/

This organization of professional conservators shares its expertise on how to care for prized possessions, from paintings and photographs to home videotape. AIC's Web site also offers literature discussing the care of materials, including paper and photographs, and advice on how to locate and select a professional conservator.

Built in America: Historic American Buildings Survey and Historic American Engineering Record, 1933–Present

http://memory.loc.gov/ammem/awhhtml/awpnp6/nabshaer.html

As part of its American Memory project, the Library of Congress has begun digitizing the vast documentation of American architecture, engineering, and design collected by the Historic American Buildings Survey and the Historic American Engineering Record. As the materials are made available online, they can be searched by keyword, subject, and geographic area.

CoOL: Conservation OnLine

http://palimpsest.stanford.edu

From Stanford University Libraries, information on a wide range of conservation topics of interest to libraries, archives, museums, and their user community, including digital imaging and the conservation and use of electronic records.

Council on Library and Information Resources

http://www.clir.org/

Offers online publications related to current issues in the preservation of library materials. Many full-text articles and reports are available.

Heritage Conservation and Historic Preservation

http://www.slv.vic.gov.au/services/conservation/guides/

The State Library of Victoria in Australia has assembled this online library about conservation issues. International in scope, the many topics addressed by articles and accompanying Web links include information about caring for cultural objects such as books and paper, film and photographs, and sound and magnetic materials.

Keeping Our Word: Preserving Information Across the Ages

http://www.lib.uiowa.edu/ref/exhibit

This virtual version of an exhibit by the University of Iowa Libraries addresses the issues of preserving materials from cave paintings and clay tablets to electronic media. The exhibit includes links for doing further research on preservation issues.

Links to the Past: National Park Service Cultural Resources

http://www.cr.nps.gov

A site of great scope and depth, this project of the National Park Service is the place to start for information about visiting historic places throughout the national parks system, teaching with historic places, and working at historic locations as a national parks volunteer. Online exhibits cover topics such as the life of Frederick Douglass and camp life at Gettysburg, and virtual tours take Web visitors to historic places in Detroit, Seattle, and other regions of the country. The site also serves as the gateway to programs such as Tools for Teaching, the Historic American Buildings Survey and Historic American Engineering Record, and the National Register of Historic Places.

National Archives and Records Administration—Archives and Preservation Resources

http://www.archives.gov/preservation/index.html

From the experts at the National Archives, information about preserving documents and photographs. NARA's Web page includes guidance on general preservation, preparations for emergencies, and specifications for proper storage.

National Center for Preservation Technology and Training

http://www.ncptt.nps.gov

This project within the National Park Service includes an extensive, annotated database of online resources in archaeology, history, historic architecture and landscapes, and conservation of materials and objects. The database includes links for subscribing to listservs related to preservation and conservation.

National Preservation Institute

http://www.npi.org

This organization offers online registration for its numerous training seminars in historic preservation and cultural resources management.

National Trust for Historic Preservation

http://www.nthp.org

This private, nonprofit organization dedicated to saving historic buildings, neighborhoods, and landscapes offers a site with information about the group's mission and many projects, including its annual list of the nation's most endangered places. A link to its *Preservation* magazine offers tables of contents, book reviews, and excerpts from some other features of the magazine. This site links to the National Trust's Main Street Center, which works to revitalize historic and traditional commercial areas and provides information about the history and preservation of Main Street communities and advice for organizing a Main Street revitalization project.

Northern States Conservation Center

http://www.collectioncare.org

Northern States Conservation Center of Saint Paul, Minnesota, here offers numerous articles about the management and preservation of museum collections, including advice about museums' use of the World Wide Web.

PreserveNet

http://www.preservenet.cornell.edu

Incorporating the PreserveNet Information Service and the PreserveNet Law Service, this Web site at Cornell University includes extensive links to preservation organizations, education programs, conferences and events, and job and internship opportunities. The Law Service offers texts of major state and federal preservation legislation and models for preservation ordinances. This is also the host site for the Guide to the African-American Heritage Preservation Foundation Inc.

RLG DigiNews

http://www.rlg.org/preserv/diginews

RLG DigiNews, a bimonthly electronic newsletter by the Research Libraries Group in cooperation with the Cornell University Library Department of Preservation and Conservation, focuses on preservation through digital imaging. Back issues to 1997 are available and searchable.

The Society of Architectural Historians

http://www.sah.org

International in scope, this organization's collection of Internet resources promotes the study of historical architecture and includes links to collections of images of historic buildings. A searchable guide to master's programs and degrees in architecture history is available.

State Historic Preservation Legislation Database

http://www.ncsl.org/programs/arts/statehist_intro.htm

The National Conference of State Legislatures offers this database of state legislation and constitution articles governing historic places, archaeological locales and materials, and significant unmarked burial areas. The database is searchable through state name and topic area.

World Heritage

http://whc.unesco.org/pg.cfm

Home page for the UNESCO project that encourages the preservation of cultural and natural heritage locations around the world. This Web site includes information about more than 500 World Heritage places, including those considered endangered. The Web site, which appears in both English and French, comprises searchable links including news, reports, and events.

World Monuments Fund

http://www.wmf.org/

The Web site of this private, nonprofit organization working to safeguard works of art and architecture includes information about the fund's international list of the hundred most endangered monuments.

Chapter 27

Urban History

Martin V. Minner

Metasites

H-Urban Web Links

http://www2.h-net.msu.edu/~urban/weblinks/index.htm

H-Urban's links page, an exhaustive collection of Web sites, is the indispensable place to start when looking for online urban history resources.

Perry-Castañeda Map Collection: U.S. Historical City Maps

http://www.lib.utexas.edu/maps/historic_us_cities.html

Provides links to hundreds of historical city maps listed alphabetically by city name. Includes links to useful map sites and collections.

Bibliographies

Serial Bibliography Project: Urban and Planning History

http://www.amst.umd.edu/Research/serial/histurb.html

An annotated bibliography of journals covering urban and planning history. Part of a larger American studies bibliographic project at the University of Maryland.

The Urban Past: An International Urban History Bibliography

http://www.uoguelph.ca/history/urban/citybib.html

A thorough bibliography compiled by Gilbert Stelter, professor emeritus at the University of Guelph. Offers a broad chronological scope and global perspective.

Urban Planning, 1794–1918: An International Anthology of Articles, Conference Papers, and Reports

http://www.library.cornell.edu/Reps/DOCS/homepage.htm

An online anthology of planning history documents compiled and annotated by historian John W. Reps. Also provides a lengthy bibliography of sources not included in the anthology.

Journals and Organizations

H-Urban

http://www2.h-net.msu.edu/~urban/

The H-Urban discussion network is an electronic forum for scholars, professionals, and graduate students interested in urban history and urban studies. Its site provides announcements, reviews, a job guide, teaching resources, and Web links.

Journal of Urban History

http://www.sagepub.com/

Provides subscription information, submission guidelines, and a list of editorial board members.

Perspectivas Urbanas/Urban Perspectives

http://www.etsav.upc.es/urbpersp/

An online journal in Spanish and English on planning theory and history.

Planning Perspectives

http://www.tandf.co.uk/journals/titles/02665433.asp

A journal on history, planning, and the environment. Provides a sample copy and table of contents.

Planum

http://www.planum.net/

An online European journal on planning.

Société Française d'Histoire Urbaine

http://www.sfhu.msh-paris.fr/home.htm

The site for the French Society of Urban History provides information about the organization and includes a list of recent French works in the field.

Society for American City and Regional Planning History

http://www.urban.uiuc.edu/sacrph/index.html

Provides membership information, a newsletter, and announcements of conferences and publications.

Urban Affairs Association

http://www.udel.edu/uaa/

Membership information, meeting announcements, job listings, and information on the *Journal of Urban Affairs*.

Urban History

http://www.journals.cup.org/owa_dba/owa/
ISSUES_IN_JOURNAL?JID=UHY

Provides abstracts of the contents of recent issues of the British journal *Urban History*.

Urban History Association

http://www.unl.edu/uha/UHA.html

A newsletter, membership information, conference and award announcements, and a page of urban history links.

Urban History Review/Revue d'histoire urbaine

http://www.hist.umontreal.ca/u/urbanhistory/home.html

Offers abstracts in English and French for recent issues of this journal of Canadian urban history.

Selected Urban History Sites

The Ancient City of Athens

http://www.stoa.org/athens/

A photographic archive on ancient Athens for students and teachers.

Aquae Urbis Romae: The Waters of the City of Rome

http://www.iath.virginia.edu/waters/

An interactive cartographic project dealing with the impact of water systems on the development of Rome since 753 BCE. Visitors can build their own maps and examine the city's topography in three dimensions.

The Black Renaissance in Washington, DC

http://www.dclibrary.org/blkren/index.html

Provides biographies, a bibliography, links, and a time line.

Brooklyn Daily Eagle Online

http://www.brooklynpubliclibrary.org/eagle/

This useful project provides online access to the *Brooklyn Daily Eagle* from 1841 to 1902. Searching is by date or keyword.

The Buffalo History Works

http://www.buffalohistoryworks.com/

A variety of exhibits and archives compiled by the Buffalo and Erie County Historical Society.

Building the Washington Metro

http://chnm.gmu.edu/metro/

A history of the Washington, DC, subway in text and images, with sections on planning, engineering, architecture, construction, and operation.

Centennial Exhibition Digital Collection: Philadelphia, 1876

http://libwww.library.phila.gov/CenCol/index.htm

A history of the Centennial Exhibition of 1876 with an interactive map and teaching resources.

Centre for Metropolitan History

http://www.history.ac.uk/cmh/cmh.main.html

A useful site on London history, including links to research projects, publications, and archives.

Chicago Historical Society

http://www.chicagohs.org/

An important urban history site providing access to the Chicago Historical Society's exhibits, research collections, and online projects. Two of the site's many noteworthy projects deal with the Great Chicago Fire and the Haymarket bombing.

Chicago Imagebase

http://tigger.uic.edu/depts/ahaa/imagebase/

Based at the University of Illinois at Chicago, the Imagebase provides an impressive collection of digitized images pertaining to Chicago's built environment.

City Sites: Multimedia Essays on New York and Chicago, 1870s–1930s

http://artsweb.bham.ac.uk/citysites/

An electronic book examining the visual and literary cultures of New York and Chicago from a multidisciplinary perspective. This site is part of the 3 Cities project at the Universities of Birmingham and Nottingham.

The Encyclopedia of Cleveland History

http://ech.cwru.edu/

Contains all the articles from *The Encyclopedia of Cleveland History* and *The Dictionary of Cleveland Biography,* additional articles, and high-resolution photographs.

The Five Points Site

http://r2.gsa.gov/fivept/fphome.htm

An archaeological exploration of New York City's Five Points section.

Greenwood's Map of London 1827

http://users.bathspa.ac.uk/greenwood/

Based on a detailed 1827 map of the city of London, this site enables visitors to zoom in on a selected portion of the city. Provides links to present-day maps and aerial photographs to permit comparison with the city of 1827.

Harlem, 1900–1940: An African-American Community

http://www.si.umich.edu/CHICO/Harlem/index.html

An exhibition based on material from the Schomburg Center for Research in Black Culture at the New York Public Library. Includes text, photographs, and teaching resources.

Harlem: Mecca of the New Negro

http://etext.lib.virginia.edu/harlem/

A digital version of *Survey Graphic* magazine's special issue in March 1925 devoted to the Harlem Renaissance. Provides the issue's entire contents in text and JPEG formats.

Historic Pittsburgh

http://digital.library.pitt.edu/pittsburgh/index.html

A broad-based site providing access to digitized books, maps, image collections, finding aids, and census records.

History of Mumbai

http://theory.tifr.res.in/bombay/history/

An introduction to the history of Mumbai (Bombay).

LaGuardia and Wagner Archives

http://www.laguardiawagnerarchive.lagcc.cuny.edu/defaulta.htm

Provides finding aids and a searchable database for the collected papers of New York mayors Fiorello LaGuardia, Robert Wagner, Abraham Beame, and Edward Koch.

Levittown: Documents of an Ideal American Suburb

http://tigger.uic.edu/~pbhales/Levittown.html

Offers family and commercial photographs of Levittown along with a primer on Levittown, Long Island, history.

Lewis Mumford Center for Comparative Urban and Regional Research

http://www.albany.edu/mumford/

Among the center's online projects are *Children in Newcomer and Native Families* and *Census 2000,* an analysis of changes in metropolitan areas' racial and ethnic composition.

The Living City

http://www.livingcityarchive.org/htm/home.htm

A digital library project dealing with public health in New York from the 1860s to the 1920s. Includes a searchable database of documents in PDF format, an annotated time line, and exhibits.

Los Angeles and the Problem of Urban Historical Knowledge

http://cwis.usc.edu/dept/LAS/history/historylab/LAPUHK/index.html

A pioneering multimedia essay published by the History Cooperative in conjunction with the December 2000 issue of the *American Historical Review.* Explores historical study of the metropolis through the theme of "mapping."

Los Angeles: Past, Present & Future

http://www.usc.edu/isd/archives/la/

Based in large part on archival resources at the University of Southern California, this site provides links to many sites on Los Angeles across time.

Milwaukee Urban Archives

http://www.uwm.edu/Library/arch/

Online exhibits include photographs, postcards, documents, and video clips.

Monuments and Dust: The Culture of Victorian London

http://www.iath.virginia.edu/mhc/

A collaborative effort by scholars in England and the United States, this site seeks to bring together visual, statistical, and textual sources on Victorian London. Includes a three-dimensional model of the Crystal Palace, site of the Great Exhibition of 1851.

Museum of the City of New York

http://www.mcny.org

Many online-only exhibits complement the museum's on-site offerings. Some of the recent exhibitions deal with the World Trade Center, and aviation.

Museum of the City of San Francisco

http://www.sfmuseum.org/

Offers online exhibitions ranging from the 1849 Gold Rush to 1960s rock music.

New York Public Library

http://www.nypl.org/research/chss/spe/art/photo/photo.html#online

Provides online access to the exhibition Berenice Abbott: Changing New York, 1935–1938, and to two projects on Lewis Hine: Work Portraits, 1920–1939, and Construction of the Empire State Building, 1930–1931.

Places in Time: Historical Documentation of Place in Greater Philadelphia

http://www.brynmawr.edu/iconog/frdr.html

The collaborative effort of several organizations, this site brings together a broad collection of images, documents, and links.

San Diego History

http://www.sandiegohistory.org/index.html

Includes a photo gallery, online exhibitions, and articles from the *Journal of San Diego History*. Tours of San Diego's 1915 and 1935–1936 expositions feature maps, stereographic views, and postcards.

The Siege and Commune of Paris, 1870–1871

http://www.library.northwestern.edu/spec/siege/

Provides more than 1,200 digitized, searchable photographs and images from the Siege and Commune of Paris.

Skyscraper Museum

http://www.skyscraper.org

An impressive collection of online projects including a three-dimensional model of Manhattan, virtual walking tours, and an interactive animation depicting the forces shaping Manhattan's skyscrapers.

Social Life of Cities

http://www.wfu.edu/academics/sociology/sociallifeofcities/

A collection of photographs dealing with public space, collective memory, urban design, and architecture.

The Triangle Factory Fire

http://www.ilr.cornell.edu/trianglefire/

A compilation of primary and secondary material from the Cornell University Library on the Triangle factory fire of 1911. Useful for student papers.

Urban Experience in Chicago: Hull-House and Its Neighborhoods, 1889–1963

http://www.uic.edu/jaddams/hull/urbanexp/contents.htm

Provides documents, images, and interpretive narratives on Jane Addams, Hull-House, and Chicago's Near West Side neighborhood.

The Urban Landscape

http://scriptorium.lib.duke.edu/diap/

A searchable database of 1,000 images from the Rare Book, Manuscript, and Special Collections Library at Duke University on the urban landscape.

USC Digital Archive

http://digarc.usc.edu:8089/cispubsearch/

The University of Southern California's Digital Archive provides access to a number of collections dealing with the Southern California metropolitan area.

U.S. Steel Gary Works Photography Collection

http://www.dlib.indiana.edu/collections/steel/

A selection of photographs from Indiana University Northwest's Calumet Regional Archives dealing with the Gary steel works and life in the city of Gary.

Virtual Greenbelt

http://www.otal.umd.edu/~vg/

Provides images, oral history interviews, and other sources on the New Deal–era planned community of Greenbelt, Maryland.

Chapter 28

Living History and Historic Reenactment

Bambi L. Dingman and
Jessie Bishop Powell, Merriman

Metasites

The Costume Page

http://www.costumepage.org/tcpsupp.html

This is the definitive source for costuming information on the Web, conveniently sorted by period of interest. Links to costume suppliers, accessories, and patterns for every time period.

Histrenact: The Historical Reenactment Web Site

http://www.montacute.net/histrenact/welcome.htm

Links to general suppliers and craftsmen, historical information, online reenactment information, and societies that re-create different time periods.

Reconstructing History Patterns

http://www.reconstructinghistory.com/patterns/partners.html

Links to general suppliers for Celtic, medieval, and Victorian costuming.

General Sites

ALHFAM

http://www.alhfam.org/

Home of the Association for Living History, Farm and Agricultural Museums. The association's Web page has conference information, employment classifieds for living history specialists, planning tips for living history locations, and extensive links to living history organizations throughout the world.

American Longrifle Association

http://www.liming.org/alra/

A period trekking group and umbrella organization spanning the years 1750 to 1850. A calendar of events can be found online, as well as photographs and a bibliography.

Angelcynn

http://www.ancientworlds.net/aw/Group/32408

All content is related to Anglo-Saxon living history representing the period 400 to 900 CE: clothing and appearance of the early Christian Anglo-Saxons, weapons and armor, history, and related links.

Buckskins and Black Powder

http://www.hogheavenmuzzleloaders.com/index02.htm

This excellent site has links to a variety of black powder and buckskinning sites on the Web. Also includes information about black powder clubs, the fur trade era, and re-creating history.

Butler's Rangers

http://iaw.on.ca/~awoolley/brang/brang.html

This corps of rangers served in the American Revolution and is re-created at living history events today. Information about the rangers, both past and present, can be found on this site, as well as historical source material and other information.

C & D Jarnagin Company

http://www.jarnaginco.com/

A provider of fine wares for the period 1750 through 1865, with a full complement of uniforms and equipment for American troops.

Camp Chase Gazette

http://www.campchase.com/

A well-known publication devoted to American Civil War re-creation. The online edition contains informative articles, a virtual roster of Civil War reenactors, upcoming events, and other relevant information.

Camp Life

http://www.cr.nps.gov/museum/exhibits/gettex/index.htm

Gettysburg National Park holds the largest Civil War collection in the National Park System, with more than 40,000 cataloged items. A unique aspect of the collection is that many of the pieces are common, everyday items that allow visitors a glimpse into the lives of the soldiers who owned them. Now a portion of the collection can be viewed online in this virtual museum of photographs and artifacts devoted to everyday camp life.

Castle Keep Ltd.

http://www.reenact.com/

Living history information and supplies for reenactors, categorized by period of interest, from medieval times to the twentieth century.

The Civil War Artillery Page

http://www.cwartillery.org/artillery.html

Information about organization and drill, weapons, ammunition, equipment, history, and reenactment of field and foot artillery units of the American Civil War.

Civil War Reenactors Home Page

http://www.cwreenactors.com/

This Web site offers photos, history, trivia, event reviews, and related links for reenactors and Civil War enthusiasts.

Clothing of the Ancient Celts

http://www.reconstructinghistory.com/celtic/

The primary focus of this Web page is on prehistoric and classical Celtic culture and costuming, with a wealth of information about hair, jewelry, dyes, textiles, and links to other Celtic sites.

Company of Saint George

http://www.chronique.com/george.htm

Fostering the spirit of chivalry by portraying a tournament company of the fourteenth and fifteenth century. Ceremony information, upcoming events, and a discussion about the role of historic interpreters can be found at this site. The site was last updated in 1997, but it remains accurate in its depictions.

Coon 'n Crockett Muzzleloaders

http://www.coon-n-crockett.org/cnc~home.htm

This page is loaded with information about the club, the muzzleloading hobby, photos, and upcoming events.

Elizabethan Fencing and the Art of Defence

http://jan.ucc.nau.edu/~wew/fencing.html

An interesting page related to the art of fencing and swordplay. Topics include period masters, terminology, types of blades, and links to other fencing sites on the Web.

Elizabethan Period Costumes

http://www.renfaire.com/Costume/index.html

A source of information on Elizabethan clothing, patterns, and footwear.

Fall Creek Sutlery

http://fcsutler.com/

Supplies for Civil War reenactors and Victorian era enthusiasts.

Flintlock FAQ

http://members.aye.net/~bspen/flintlockfaq.html

A beginner's guide to flintlock shooting with a concise history of flintlock weapons and answers to questions about flintlock performance.

French and Indian War—Mohican History Links

http://www.mohicanpress.com/m008021.html

The information provided here will be of interest to French and Indian War reenactors. Links to both Mohican and colonial history.

French and Indian War Webpage

http://web.syr.edu/~laroux/lists/alpha.html

Though the site itself appears not to have been updated since 2000, its lists of soldiers, companies, and battles will prove useful to the French and Indian War reenactor.

GI Journal

http://www.militaria.com

Articles of interest to World War I and World War II reenactors and links to division Web pages, reproduction uniforms, and military history magazines.

The Gunfighter Zone

http://www.gunfighter.com

A Web site for reenactors of the Old West and members of Cowboy Action Shooting groups, with links to discussion boards, suppliers, books, magazines, and informative articles.

Historic Enterprises

http://www.historicenterprises.com/

Specializes in highly accurate handmade replicas of museum examples. Although it is a commercial site, it includes a great deal of historical information and interesting photos of the company's work.

The Historical Maritime Society

http://www.hms.org.uk/

Re-creates British Navy life from 1793 to 1815 (Napoleonic War period).

Historical Reenactors

http://novaroma.org/via_romana/reenactments/index.html

Costuming information, reenactment guidelines, and a listing of reenactment groups portraying military and civilian life during the Roman era, compiled and presented by Nova Roma, an organization dedicated to the study and restoration of ancient Roman culture.

19th Indiana Volunteer Infantry, Co. A

http://www.19thindiana.com/

Civil War reenactors and nineteenth-century civilian impressionists. This Web page has an event schedule, company newsletter and historical information.

Japanese Internment Camps

http://www.teacheroz.com/Japanese_Internment.htm

Links to various pieces of information regarding life in America's Japanese internment camps during World War II.

Jas. Townsend & Son

http://jas-townsend.com/

A mail-order company specializing in historic clothing, camp gear, tents, books, music, knives, tomahawks, oak kegs, and other assorted items for the period 1750 to 1840.

1st Kansas Volunteer Infantry and Kansas Women's Relief Corps

http://www.firstkansas.org/

Maintained by Jeremy Birket, this site was last updated in July 2004. It contains information about the company's participation in the Civil War.

King's Arms Press and Bindery

http://www.kingspress.com/

Specialized reprints of eighteenth-century books and pamphlets, including drill books and regulations, as well as military treatises.

Knighthood, Chivalry and Tournaments Resource Library

http://www.chronique.com/

Information on books, battle accounts, codes of conduct, armoring techniques, and more. Also includes a lengthy index of sites related to chivalry, armor, and reenactment groups.

Le Poulet Gauche

http://www.lepg.org/

A compendium of information on the history, daily life, and culture of six-teenth-century France. Le Poulet Gauche was formed by a group of Bostonians who re-created a sixteenth-century alehouse. Their Web site, last updated in January 2004, offers information on food, drink, gaming, clothing, fencing, tradesmen, and suppliers.

Links to the Past

http://www.cr.nps.gov/colherit.htm

An extensive Web page from the National Park Service with online archives for many historic locations, as well as battle summaries, battlefield information, national landmarks, and online exhibits.

Longshot's Rendezvous

http://www.wizzywigweb.com/longshot/

A source of rendezvous information for mountain men, buckskinners, and muzzleloaders of Missouri and Illinois. Also includes a guide to getting started in rendezvous and links to other sources.

28th Massachusetts Volunteer Infantry, Co. A, C, & H

http://www.28thmass.org/

A well-designed Web page with information for historical research and reenacting.

Medieval/Renaissance Food Homepage

http://www.pbm.com/~lindahl/food.html

A comprehensive site containing recipes, primary sources, clip art, medieval cooking articles, and food publications. Users may join the mailing list by sending the message to "subscribe sca-cooks" majordomo@ansteorra.org.

Milieux: The Costume Site

http://www.milieux.com/costume/

A comprehensive list of links to costuming sites with diversified themes, such as medieval costuming, armor, Civil War uniforms, colonial garb, and modern accessories.

Morningside Books

http://www.morningsidebooks.com

Noted for its Civil War collection and as a recognized dealer of Don Troiani artwork.

Mountain Men and the Fur Trade

http://www.xmission.com/~drudy/amm.html

An online research center devoted to the history and traditions of trappers, explorers, and traders, with a digital collection, bibliography, an archive of trade records, and links to Web sites related to the fur trade era.

National Renaissance Faire Directory

http://Renaissance-Faire.com/Locations.htm

A listing of Renaissance Faires around the country with links to Web pages and event information. Users of a dial-up server must be patient: the page takes a little while to load.

NetSerf

http://www.netserf.org/

A huge index arranged by subject matter and with links to all things medieval—including religion, culture, art, and literature.

47th New York State Volunteers, "Washington Grays"

http://www.awod.com/gallery/probono/cwchas/47ny.html

A federal reenacting unit. The Web page has an extensive unit history and Civil War reenactment information.

5th New York Volunteer Infantry, Co. A, Duryée's Zouaves

http://www.zouave.org/

An excellent Civil War company Web page with a detailed history, roster, and extensive photo gallery.

Northeastern Primitive Rendezvous

http://www.frontiernet.net/~oakhill/

Guns, clothing, and accessories for the period 1640 to 1840.

North/South Alliance

http://www.nsalliance.org/

Information on the First Confederate and First Federal Divisions in the American Civil War and an event listing. Most documents are PDF.

The Northwest Territory Alliance

http://www.nwta.com/main.html

This group strives to re-create the lifestyle, culture, and arts of the Revolutionary War era with an accurate representation of uniforms, weaponry, and battlefield tactics. This Web site offers forms and documents useful to reenactors, an event schedule, chronology of events in the War for Independence, pattern lists, and publications.

The Patriots of Fort McHenry

http://www.bcpl.net/~etowner/patriots.html

This organization hopes to preserve the historical legacy of the patriots who defended Baltimore in 1814. Fort McHenry is best known as the scene of the battle that Francis Scott Key witnessed and wrote about in the "Star Spangled Banner."

Plimoth Plantation

http://www.plimoth.org/

Plimoth Plantation's Pilgrim Village brings to life the Plymouth of 1627. This Web site has plenty of information about the village and also includes educational information for reenactors. This is a wonderful source of information for anyone who wishes to interpret in the first person.

Pre-1840's Buckskinning

http://www.living-history.net

Contains a lengthy list of rendezvous groups around the United States, publications, trader events, and buckskinning classifieds. Last updated in 2003.

Proper Elizabethan Accents

http://www.renfaire.com/Language/index.html

Pronunciation guide, drills, and vocabulary to perfect your accent for the Faire.

Reenactor Net

http://www.reenactor.net/

A list of links to reenactor Web sites, categorized by time period. Regularly updated.

Regia Anglorum

http://www.regia.org/

A society with a vast number of resources available for portraying the British people as they were a hundred years before the Norman Conquest. The Web site has membership and contact information.

64th Regiment of Foot

http://freenet.vcu.edu/sigs/reg64/

Members of the 64th Regiment portray British infantry soldiers from the time of the Revolutionary War. Their Web page has information on the British army, regimental colors, the Brown Bess, women and the army, and plenty of primary reference material.

Renaissance Faire Overview

http://www.renfaire.com/General/faire.html

An introduction to attending Renaissance Faires and a description of what to expect.

Renaissance Magazine

http://www.renaissancemagazine.com

Well-known to reenactors as an informative print magazine, the online version is packed with useful information as well, including past features on books, music, movies, and products and links to related Web sites.

The Rolls Ethereal

http://jducoeur.org/rolls/

This is an online directory for members of the Society for Creative Anachronism, with hundreds of searchable listings.

Roman Life

http://www.dl.ket.org/latin1/things/romanlife/

This site contains historical information on Roman life and directions for making Roman-style costumes.

Roman Orgy

http://homepage.sunrise.ch/mysunrise/julien.courtois/orgy/

An excellent site with information about the art of Roman cooking, recipes, historical documents, and links to related sites.

The 42nd Royal Highland Regiment, "The Black Watch"

http://www.42ndrhr.org/index.php

This well-designed site is a terrific source of information on period music, dancing, uniforms, and everything related to the "Black Watch" of the late 1700s in North America.

SCA Dance, Music, and Minstrel Homepages

http://www.pbm.com/~lindahl/dance.html

http://www.pbm.com/~lindahl/music.html

http://www.pbm.com/~lindahl/minstrel.html

Links to the SCA's dance, music, and minstrel pages respectively. These pages offer primary sources, articles, and sound files related to Renaissance music and dance.

SCRIBE's History Archives

http://www.faire.net/SCRIBE/archives/History.Htm

These pages contain hundreds of text files related to the history of the Renaissance and the Middle Ages, including listings of Renaissance Faire participants, guilds, groups, song lyrics, and events around the country. Images and articles related to period crafts such as Celtic knot work, heraldic crests, brewing, cooking, blacksmithing, and textiles can also be found at this site.

Second Panzer Division

http://www.panzerdivision.org/

The largest and best-equipped German reenacting unit in North America. Its Web site has information about equipment and tactics, a bibliography, and links to other World War II reenactors. It contains a disclaimer to the effect that the group exists for educational purposes and its reenactors are prohibited from anti-Semitic activities.

Shadows of the Past

http://www.sptddog.com/sotp/

This organization's guide to reenacting the Old West, with articles, historical resources, photographs, literature, and links to related sites.

Society for Creative Anachronism (SCA)

http://www.sca.org/

The SCA is dedicated to researching and re-creating pre–seventeenth-century European history. This site has a huge amount of information on topics related to medieval history, including official documents, events, the art of combat, and more.

1st South Carolina Artillery, C.S.A.

http://www.awod.com/gallery/probono/cwchas/1scart.html

Reenacts the history of the men who manned the artillery of the Confederate defenses of the South Carolina coast during the American Civil War. The Web site has history, photos, and a bibliography.

A Stitch Out of Time

http://home.earthlink.net/~wymarc/

Medieval embroidery techniques for the ninth through sixteenth centuries.

Trev's Rendezvous Down Under

http://www.geocities.com/Yosemite/Trails/1878/

This site has contact information for many groups that are accessible only through e-mail, as well as for organizations that are already on the Internet.

20th Century Fashion: Women's Fashion: 1940s

http://www.costumegallery.com/1940.htm

Fabric rationing in the 1940s affected the way people dressed. This Web site gives information about American women's fashion in this period.

U.S. Civil War Center

http://www.cwc.lsu.edu

The Civil War Center is an attempt to index all the Civil War sites on the Web. There are links to national parks, battlefields, roundtables, reenacting groups, events, and events. This should be one of the first stops for people interested in re-creating the American Civil War.

U.S. Regulars Civil War Archive

http://www.usregulars.com/

Library of key works on Civil War strategy, tactics, and drill used by the regular army and volunteers and at the U.S. Military Academy at West Point.

Welcome to Fort Erie and the War of 1812

http://www.iaw.on.ca/~jsek/

Helpful information about the Fort Erie siege and the War of 1812 reenactment units.

White Oak Society, Inc.

http://www.whiteoak.org/

This Web site has a wealth of information about rendezvous and the fur trade era, from interpreters who portray authentic characters of the eighteenth century.

World War I Trenches on the Web

http://www.worldwar1.com/

A compendium of information for the World War I reenactor. This history of the Great War has a reference library, war poster reproductions, interesting articles, and reenactor photographs. Last updated in 2004.

World War II Women and the Homefront

http://www.teacheroz.com/WWIIHomefront.htm

Site contains a multitude of links to help reenactors authentically create American women's experience of World War II.

Chapter 29

Genealogy

Samuel Dicks

Genealogists have created many Internet sites and other research tools that are also of use to biographers, social and military historians, and other scholars. Probate, military, census, immigration, naturalization, marriage, and land records are among the many kinds of materials genealogists have accumulated on the Internet. The Internet makes it easy to identify the kinds of materials available before a trip is planned, make contact with others working on the same family lines, and find other ways to obtain detailed information. Cyndi's List and RootsWeb (see below), as well as search engines and published reference works, provide additional research tools. The single most useful reference work is *The Source: A Guidebook of American Genealogy,* published by Ancestry.com (see below) and available at most public libraries.

Most Useful Sites

American Family Immigration History Center (Ellis Island Records)

http://www.ellisislandrecords.org

From 1892 to 1924 over 22 million people entered the United States through Ellis Island. The ships' manifest records ordinarily include the immigrant's given name and surname, ethnicity, last place of residence, name of ship and departure port, arrival date, age, gender, and marital status, along with the location of their name on the manifest. Numerous other Web sites, including Ancestry.com and RootsWeb.com, provide background on the Ellis Island experience. If you are searching for passenger records before 1892, the Immigrant Ships Transcribers Guild (http://www.immigrantships.net/) is compiling a list of earlier ship passengers.

Ancestry.com

http://ancestry.com

This is the best-known and most useful subscription Internet site for genealogists. On-screen indexed copies of federal censuses, military indexes, vital records, British records, a genealogy periodical index of the Allen County Public Library in Fort Wayne, Indiana, with over a million articles, and many other sources for people not easily found elsewhere are here. Some materials are also available without membership or with free trial memberships. Some libraries also subscribe to this site and make it free to their patrons. There is an interesting free daily Internet genealogy newsletter.

Cyndi's List of Genealogy Sites on the Internet

http://cyndislist.com/

Cyndi Howell's Web site is the best-known and most comprehensive genealogy site, with over 200,000 links to states, counties, provinces, nations, military records, ethnic, religious, and other sites too numerous to note. Users who browse through Cyndi's List slowly over several days will discover many other helpful sites that are little known.

Family History Library (LDS Church, Salt Lake City)

http://www.familysearch.org/

The Church of Jesus Christ of Latter-day Saints maintains the world's largest family history library, and a large amount of information from the library continues to be added to this Web site. Local Family History Centers, commonly operated by volunteers in Mormon churches in many cities, can provide additional information and arrange for the borrowing of microfilm. Church records from overseas and local government records are among the many holdings that may be accessed online or, in some cases, by visiting a local center. Holdings available for low cost on CD-ROM include the Freedmen's Bank Records (a major African-American database), the 1880 U.S. Federal Census, the 1881 Censuses for the British Isles and Canada, and Vital Records (Birth, Marriage, Death) for Mexico and the Scandinavian countries. There are forms, teaching aids, and a great deal more at this Web site. Check the various site subheadings, such as Research Guidance, Web Sites, and Family History Library Catalog.

Heritage Quest

http://heritagequest.com/

This is a commercial Web site that has items you may wish to purchase or consult, but more important, many state, local, and university libraries include this extensive collection among the Internet databases available free to their patrons. The Heritage Quest database includes the U.S. censuses, Revolutionary War pension files, early local histories and family genealogies, and many other materials, all of which can be accessed through a place or name word search. This site is often overlooked by novices, but is much too important to ignore, especially if you can gain free access with a library password. Check with your local library or genealogical society to see if it is available in your area.

The National Archives and Records Administration

http://www.archives.gov/research_room/genealogy/

The National Archives has one of the most useful sites provided by the federal government. Census schedules (1790–1930); alien, immigration, and naturalization records; ship passenger records; military and military pension records; and Native American records are among the sources most commonly used by genealogists. (Most naturalization records before November 27, 1906, are in county courthouse or state records. The "naturalization" section on this site explains how citizenship of wives, children, and veterans was handled differently in earlier periods.) Many of the microfilmed materials, including census schedules and military pension indexes, are also in the thirteen regional branches of NARA, which can be accessed from this site. Useful articles from the NARA journal, *Prologue,* may be found at "Genealogy Notes." The sites relating to the census schedules provide an explanation of the Soundex system, an index made in the 1930s for Social Security applicants who were born before birth certificates were common. Soundex takes into account different spellings and acts as an index for most censuses since 1880. A Soundex converter that allows users to list several surnames at once is http://www.bradandkathy.com/genealogy/yasc.html.

For casualty or other military records, see http://www.archives.gov/research_room/arc/topics/highlights.html.

RootsWeb

http://rootsweb.com/

Rootsweb is the oldest and largest free genealogy site. Its home page lists large numbers of other useful sites including the Social Security Death Index (SSDI), which provides information on individuals with death claims since the early 1950s. One of its best-known features is the Rootsweb Surname List (RSL), a sort of international bulletin board where users can connect with others pursuing the same surnames. There are connections to many other state and local sites and other resources, plus a free, informative weekly Internet newsletter.

State Historical Societies and Archives

http://www.ohiohistory.org/links/arch_hs.html

Most states have a state historical society and a state archives. The historical society will probably include microfilm copies of newspapers and census records, private papers donated to the society, early state and local histories, and other publications relating to the region. A state archive is ordinarily the custodian of official state papers, such as those of the governor or adjutant general (some states had censuses for years ending in 5, such as 1895, and adjutant general records are useful for military records for state militias in war time). Newspapers and other materials may also be in a state library or a state historical library. The Ohio Historical Society provides links to most state historical societies and archives; other state societies, archives, and libraries can be located at the Cyndi's List or RootsWeb sites (see above).

U.S. Bureau of Land Management: General Land Office Records

http://www.glorecords.blm.gov/

This is one of the most useful federal sites for genealogists and historians. The transfer of land titles from the federal government to individuals and much more can be found here. Surname searches may also bring forth maps and copies of the original documents.

USGenWeb

http://usgenweb.org./

The USGenWeb Project, manned by volunteers, is one of the most useful sites for quickly accessing states and counties. Users can click an individual state in the left margin to go to state and county sites for all fifty states, and many other links. Additional local sites, sometimes by private parties, may also be obtained by using a search engine and the name of the county and state or by searching for local historical or genealogical societies or public libraries.

U.S. Immigration and Naturalization Service

http://uscis.gov/graphics/aboutus/history/

Now part of the Department of Homeland Security and recently renamed U.S. Citizenship and Immigration Services, this site provides much detail on immigration and naturalization records, Chinese immigrant files, and other topics, as well as useful teaching aids.

U.S. Vital Records Information

http://vitalrec.com/index.html

Modern state and territory sites for finding birth, marriage, divorce, and death records are available here. Some records are available online and may be accessed at county or state links.

Additional Sites

The 10,000 Year Calendar

http://calendarhome.com/tyc/

Genealogists and historians are often stuck with incomplete dates expressed as "the Sunday after Christmas" or "Friday, November 23." This is the most elaborate of various sites that provide a calendar for any month of any year desired. There is also information on calendar changes, Mayan and Chinese calendars, and other related topics. For a simpler perpetual calendar, go to http://www.timeanddate.com/calendar/.

African-American Genealogy: Christine's Genealogy Website

http://ccharity.com/

This provides information and links to most other sites that deal with African-American genealogy. Also see the African-American page on Cyndi's List.

African-Native American Genealogy

http://www.african-nativeamerican.com/

Black Indian Slaves, Indian Territory Freedmen, and Frontier Slave Narratives are among the many resources included on this site.

AfriGeneas: African Genealogy in the Americas

http://www.afrigeneas.com/

AfriGeneas includes a guide for beginners, research sites, articles, message boards, and much more of interest to genealogists and historians. Many state and local historical societies also have extensive materials on African-American history, including early newspapers and manuscripts.

Amistad Research Center (Tulane University)

http://www.amistadresearchcenter.org/

This major research center includes extensive manuscripts, oral histories, photographs, and other materials from the Abolitionist era and the American Missionary Society to the Harlem Renaissance and beyond. It also includes material on Native Americans, Puerto Ricans, Appalachian whites, Asian-Americans, and Mexican-Americans, among others. Included in its collection are correspondence and other materials of many people involved in antislavery and civil rights movements.

Civil War Soldiers and Sailors

http://www.itd.nps.gov/cwss/

The National Park Service, in conjunction with the National Archives and Records Administration and various military and genealogy organizations, has developed this computerized database of Civil War soldiers and sailors, both Union and Confederate. Individuals not listed here may be located at various state or local Web sites, including state archives and historical societies. Union pension file indexes are also available at NARA branches and other locations with the use of Soundex, or at Ancestry.com (fee-based). Confederate records are in various state archives. Also see 1883 and 1890 U.S. veterans' censuses for Union veterans or dependents (only available for some states)—some of them are on the Internet at http://www.arealdomain.com/pensioners1883.html.

The Commonwealth War Graves Commission

http://www.cwgc.org/cwgcinternet/search.aspx

This commemorative site provides personal and service details for the 1.7 million soldiers from throughout the British Commonwealth who died in World War I or World War II. Also includes civilian casualties and other information.

Family Tree Maker Online

http://familytreemaker.genealogy.com/

Family Tree Maker has one of the largest software programs for genealogists. It also provides much free information on its Web site.

The Federation of East European Family History Societies (FEEFHS)

http://feefhs.org/

This is a major Web site for Central and Eastern European countries, from Switzerland and Germany to eastern Russia, whose emigrants have ethnic links with those peoples currently in the United States and throughout the world.

Helm's Genealogy Toolbox

http://www.genealogytoolbox.com/

Matthew L. Helm's site is one of the oldest and best-known sites for a wide variety of information and links.

International Black Sheep Society of Genealogists

http://blacksheep.rootsweb.com/

An organization for those with horse thieves or other scoundrels among their ancestors; the site has many interesting stories and useful links.

JewishGen

http://www.jewishgen.org/

JewishGen is the primary Internet source for those engaged in Jewish genealogy. It connects with numerous databases, including JewishGen Family Finder, which connects people searching the same ancestral towns and surnames. For locating Holocaust survivors, see the Holocaust Global Registry at this site.

Native American Enumerations

http://www.us-census.org/native/

Because Indians on reservations were not considered citizens and therefore not counted in determining congressional districts until 1924, they were not included in the ten-year federal censuses, but were counted at various times in special enumerations. This site provides a detailed explanation and connections to the available sources. Also see http://www.accessgenealogy.com/native/.

For Native American mailing lists, see http://lists.rootsweb.com/index/other/ Ethnic-Native/.

The Online Genealogical Database

http://gentree.com/gentree.html

This site contains links to all known databases on the Web. Family sites are included only if a database is available for searching.

Tracing Your Native American Genealogy (Carolyne's Genealogy Helper)

http://www.angelfire.com/tx/carolynegenealogy/

Tracing Native American family history presents unusual difficulties. Carolyne Gould provides help through the maze of confusing resources.

USGS National Mapping Information Query Form

http://geonames.usgs.gov/pls/gnis/web_query.gnis_web_query_form

For those doing genealogical research, this Geological Survey Query Form is useful for locating obscure population centers, cemeteries, and other sites in the United States. In most cases, users can obtain the coordinates and also maps indicating the locations. Many Canadian sites may be seen at http://atlas.gc.ca/site/english/sitemap/index.html. Maps for other places in the world are at http://uk2.multimap.com.

Chapter 30

State and Provincial Historical Societies (Canada and United States)

Thomas Saylor

Metasite

National Council on Public History
http://www.ncph.org/
Listing of publications, resources, activities, and useful links.

Canada

Canada's National History Society
http://www.historysociety.ca/
Extensive listing of archives, government departments, libraries, museums, organizations, and publications.

Historical Society of Alberta

http://www.albertahistory.org/

British Columbia Historical Federation

http://www.bchistory.ca/

Fédération des Sociétés d'histoire du Quebec

http://www.histoirequebec.qc.ca/

Manitoba Historical Society

http://www.mhs.mb.ca/

Newfoundland Historical Society

http://www.infonet.st-johns.nf.ca/providers/nfldhist/

The Ontario Historical Society

http://www.ontariohistoricalsociety.ca/

Prince Edward Island Museum and Heritage Foundation

http://www.gov.pe.ca/peimhf/

Royal Nova Scotia Historical Society

http://nsgna.ednet.ns.ca/rnshs/

Saskatchewan History and Folklore Society

http://www.shfs.ca/

Yukon Historical and Museums Association

http://www.yukonalaska.com/yhma/

United States

Alabama Department of Archives and History

http://www.archives.state.al.us/

Alaska Historical Society

http://www.alaskahistoricalsociety.org/

Arizona Historical Society

http://www.ahs.state.az.us/

http://www.arizonahistoricalsociety.org/

Arkansas Historical Association

http://www.uark.edu/depts/arkhist/home

California Historical Society

http://www.californiahistoricalsociety.org/

Colorado Historical Society

http://www.coloradohistory.org/

Connecticut Historical Society

http://www.chs.org/

The Historical Society of Delaware

http://www.hsd.org/

Florida Historical Society

http://www.florida-historical-soc.org/

Georgia Historical Society

http://www.georgiahistory.com/

The Hawaiian Historical Society

http://www.hawaiianhistory.org/

Idaho State Historical Society

http://www.idahohistory.net/

Illinois State Historical Society

http://www.historyillinois.org/

Indiana Historical Society

http://www.indianahistory.org/

State Historical Society of Iowa

http://www.iowahistory.org/

The Kansas State Historical Society

http://www.kshs.org/

Kentucky Historical Society

http://history.ky.gov/

Louisiana Historical Society

http://www.louisianahistoricalsociety.org/

Maine Historical Society

http://www.mainehistory.org/

Maryland Historical Society

http://www.mdhs.org/

Massachusetts Historical Society

http://www.masshist.org/

Michigan Historical Center

http://www.michigan.gov/hal/0,1607,7-160-17445_19273—,00.html

Minnesota Historical Society

http://www.mnhs.org/

Mississippi Department of Archives and History

http://www.mdah.state.ms.us/

Missouri Historical Society

http://www.mohistory.org/

Montana Historical Society

http://www.his.state.mt.us/

Nebraska State Historical Society

http://www.nebraskahistory.org/

Nevada Historical Society

http://dmla.clan.lib.nv.us/docs/museums/reno/his-soc.htm

New Hampshire Historical Society

http://www.nhhistory.org/

New Jersey Historical Society

http://www.jerseyhistory.org/

Historical Society of New Mexico

http://www.hsnm.org/

New York Historical Society

http://www.nyhistory.org/

North Carolina Office of Archives and History

http://www.ah.dcr.state.nc.us/

State Historical Society of North Dakota

http://www.state.nd.us/hist/

Ohio Historical Society

http://www.ohiohistory.org/

Oklahoma Historical Society

http://www.ok-history.mus.ok.us/

Oregon Historical Society

http://www.ohs.org/

The Historical Society of Pennsylvania

http://www.hsp.org/

Rhode Island Historical Society

http://www.rihs.org/

South Carolina Historical Society

http://www.schistory.org/

South Dakota State Historical Association

http://www.sdhistory.org/

Tennessee Historical Society

http://www.tennesseehistory.org/

Texas Historical Commission

http://www.thc.state.tx.us/

Texas State Historical Association

http://www.tsha.utexas.edu/

Utah State Historical Society/Division of State History

http://history.utah.gov/

Vermont Historical Society

http://www.vermonthistory.org/

Virginia Historical Society

http://www.vahistorical.org/

Washington State Historical Society

http://www.washingtonhistory.org/wshs/

West Virginia Division of Culture and History

http://www.wvculture.org/

Wisconsin Historical Society

http://www.wisconsinhistory.org/

Wyoming State Historical Society

http://wyshs.org/

Chapter 31

History Book Sources
on the Internet

Mariah Hudson

Book Search Networks

In the past few years the trend in bookselling on the Internet has been the consolidation of independent sellers' book holdings onto large book search network sites. These search networks have greatly contributed to the ease of locating academic and popular books by minimizing search efforts. Another advantage of search networks is that many compare prices and offer multiple copies of the same title, allowing users to select the book condition. Many search sites also offer a quality guarantee and have standardized no-hassle return policies. Almost all Web sites now take credit cards or Paypal. When available, the listing will indicate the number of categories for browsing and the approximate number of titles currently available.

Advanced Book Exchange

http://www.abebooks.com

ABE claims to be the world's largest online bookseller, and the selection of history titles is truly impressive. ABE offers used and new, rare and out-of-print books and is one of the best sites for locating books published before

1900. It offers more than 365,000 titles on general history, 380,000 titles on military history, and 47,000 titles on medieval and Renaissance history. Unfortunately, ABE does not have subcategories by time period, which would make browsing easier.

Alibris

http://www.alibris.com

Alibris offers new and used books, only a small proportion of which are rare books. Alibris is well indexed with fifty-five geographic and topical search categories. Browsing is made easy by clearly indexed subtopics; there are fifteen topics under U.S. history and twenty under military history. A separate textbook search is available.

Amazon.com

http://www.amazon.com

Amazon is teamed up with Borders and offers mostly new books, though some used books are available through independent sellers who list books on the site. History books are organized by thirteen geographic and topical categories. There are eight searchable subcategories for U.S. history and sixteen for military history. One noteworthy feature is Amazon's searchable selection of historical journals, documentaries, software, and DVDs.

Antiqbook

http://www.antiqbook.com/

Antiqbook sells primarily used books and specializes in antiquarian works, making this a first stop for rare or out-of-print European works and a highly recommended site for antiquarian and rare book searches in general. This site includes selections from hundreds of individual sellers. Many of the sellers are in Europe; however, there are over a hundred history booksellers in the United States. The Antiqbook site is well organized and cross-indexed by geographic region, time period, and subspecialty.

Barnes and Noble

http://www.bn.com

Barnes and Noble features popular new works and a limited selection of used books provided by independent dealers. While its prices are not significantly lower than the cover price, fast shipping and local in-store searches are two features that make this site worthwhile if you need a book in a hurry. Two unique features are searches by Nobel Prize or National Book Award winners and finalists, and searches by price. The prereserve feature gives the option of preordering soon-to-be-released books.

Best Book Buys

http://www.bestwebbuys.com/books

Currently listing 195,584 history books on eighty-five topics, this well-categorized site has one of the largest selections of new books online. Best Book Buys searches and compares prices at several of the major book dealers on the Internet, including Alibris, Amazon, and Barnes and Noble. BBB is a recommended site for in-print books searches and price comparisons.

Biblio

http://www.biblio.com

Biblio sells from the inventories of hundreds of independent booksellers. It claims to have 14 million new and used books, of which 10 percent are history titles. Biblio has an extensive collection of African-American, military, regional and women's histories. A community bulletin board offers a forum to exchange ideas with other collectors.

Bibliology

http://www.bibliology.com

Though Bibliology has a poor interface for general searches, making browsing nearly impossible, it has a large selection of rare books from sellers around the globe and coordinates the sale of primary documents and manuscripts from private dealers. A recommended primary document source.

Bookfinder

http://www.bookfinder.com

Bookfinder searches all the major book networks, including Amazon, Powell's, and Alibris. Bookfinder is best for specific book searches. While the specificity of the search function makes browsing tedious, one useful feature is a search for books in different languages (mainly French, German, and Spanish).

Books and Book Collecting at Trussel

http://www.trussel.com/f_books.htm

Trussel does not sell books, but provides a wealth of information on local resources and dozens of independent dealers.

Half.com

http://half.ebay.com

Half offers new and used books at half off the cover price or less. Half, a subsidiary of eBay, displays books for sale through eBay on the bottom of the screen with price information, which is helpful for comparing prices and makes searching eBay unnecessary. This site allows individuals to list books and has an extensive selection of academic and popular books. History titles are listed with nonfiction works.

International League of Antiquarian Booksellers

http://www.ilab-lila.com

ILAB coordinates the sale of books and documents through its member sites, of which there are hundreds. ILAB has some of the most specific search features available and offers access to the inventories of small booksellers across the globe, making it one of the best book search networks for rare and antiquarian books.

Massachusetts and Rhode Island Antiquarian Booksellers

http://www.mariab.org

MARIAB, an organization for sellers of rare books in New England, has been in business for twenty-nine years. Though MARIAB does not sell books, it has detailed information on the holdings of over 150 booksellers, as well as dozens of online catalogs and search services. This site is a must stop for locating rare early American books and primary sources.

Tom Folio

http://www.tomfolio.com

Tom Folio is an extensive search network site, hosting more than a hundred American bookstores listed by region as well as many more international sellers. There are ten geographic search categories with tens of thousands of new and used titles available.

Independent Book Sellers

Although books search networks have improved the ease of finding fairly common books, individual booksellers are by no means an obsolete search source. Independent booksellers may provide a better selection of scholarly, rare, and antiquarian books, because networks often offer only a fraction of a seller's inventory and may exclude less common works. The list below represents a few of the many independent sellers that do not list inventory on search networks or those whose collections are not fully listed elsewhere. The location is listed for booksellers who have bookshops; the rest are online only. Specialized bookstores frequently offer a phone search for titles and documents that are not online. Many also offer book location services.

2ndHandBooks.com

http://www.2ndHandBooks.com
E-mail: books@2ndHandBooks.com

Used rare and out-of-print books. Specialties: U.S., Africa, Renaissance, medieval, European, natural history. Number of history titles: thousands. Location: Metairie, Louisiana.

Alden Books

http://www.aldenbooks.com/
E-mail: info@aldenbooks.com

New and used scholarly works. Specialties: North America, Asia. Number of history titles: 2,500+.

Asia Book Room

http://www.OldBookroom.com
E-mail: books@AsiaBookroom.com

Specialty: Asia, Middle East, Pacific, Africa. Number of history titles: 15,000+. Location: Australia.

Book Close Outs

http://www.bookcloseouts.com
E-mail: service@bookcloseouts.com

Popular new and used bargain books. Specialty: ancient, Asian, biography, world. Number of history titles: 10,300. Location: New York City; Ontario, Canada.

Books Unlimited

http://www.booksunlimited.com
E-mail: otierney@booksunlimited.com

New and used popular books, some scholarly works. Specialty: general, U.S. history. Number of history titles: 10,000+. Location: Denver.

Comenius-Antiquariat

http://www.comenius-antiquariat.com/english
E-mail: 2005@comenius-antiquariat.ch

Used and rare books, many of which are in German. Specialty: Swiss history. Number of history titles: 6,500+. Location: Switzerland.

Ed Conroy Bookseller

http://www.edconroybooks.com
E-mail: info@edconroybooks.com

Primarily used books. Specialties: military, modern European. Number of history titles: 35,000+.

D.K. Publishers Distributors Ltd.

http://www.dkpdindia.com
E-mail: order@dkpd.com

New books. Specialty: India, Asia. Number of titles: 75,000, more than 10 percent in history. Location: India.

E-books

http://www.ebooks.com/

E-books offers recent academic and popular history books as digital selections on forty-four topics and regions. Selection is limited, but downloading makes purchasing convenient. Specialties: U.S., European, ancient history. Number of history titles: 1,000+.

Editions

http://www.nleditions.com
E-mail: info@nleditions.com

Primarily new or gently used; all hardback. Selections are updated weekly. Specialties: none, but 2,000 U.S. titles. Number of history titles: 20,000+ online, 70,000 not listed online, but accessible by phone. Location: Boiceville, New York.

Ground Zero Books Ltd.

http://www.groundzerobooksltd.com
E-mail: info@groundzerobooksltd.com

New, used, scholarly, rare, and out-of-print military history books. Specialties: military, the history of war. Number of history titles: 53,000+.

Great Northwest Bookstore

http://www.greatnorthwestbooks.com
E-mail: gnworders@greatnorthwestbooks.com

Primarily used books; much of the extensive stock is not yet online. GNB offers phone searches for unusual or rare titles. Specialty: American, Western. Number of history titles: 40,000+. Location: Portland, Oregon.

History Wiz books

http://books.historywiz.org
E-mail: eeyore@books.historywiz.org

New and used books. The collections of eighteenth-century, African-American, and American Revolution titles make this a worthwhile site for Americanists. Specialties: European, U.S., world. Number of history titles: 1,000+.

Labyrinth Books

http://www.labyrinthbooks.com
E-mail: books@labyrinthbooks.com

New and used book selection dedicated to scholarly and university press works. Specialties: European, world, women's, U.S., New York City. Number of titles: 155,000, of which more than 25 percent are history. Location: New York City.

David M. Lesser, Fine Antiquarian Books LLC

http://www.lesserbooks.com
E-mail: dmlesser@lesserbooks.com

Dedicated to American history, David M. Lesser offers used and rare American books and documents. Specialties: American colonial and Revolution. Number of history titles: 10,000+. Location: online site also offers print catalogs.

Parmer Books

http://www.stairway.org/parmer/index.html
E-mail: ParmerBook@aol.com

Primarily used and academic; most of Parmer's stock is historical. Specialties: Western, Pacific, exploration. Number of history titles: 4,000. Location: San Diego.

The Personal Navigator

http://www1.shore.net/~persnav/
E-mail: persnav@shore.net

Used rare and antiquarian books and documents. Specialties: military, American, nineteenth-century. Number of history titles: 1,000+.

Mark Post, Bookseller

http://www.markpostbooks.com
E-mail: markpost1@earthlink.net

Primarily used antiquarian and rare books. Specialties: America, Europe, colonial Africa. Number of history titles: 3,300+. Location: San Francisco.

Powell's

http://www.powells.com/
E-mail: help@powells.com

Highly recommended site for new, used, rare, and out-of-print works with a large proportion of academic books. Specialties: U.S., European, military. Number of history titles: over 100,000. Location: Portland, Oregon.

Prairie Reader Bookstore

http://www.prairie-reader.com
E-mail: info@prairie-reader.com

New, used, and rare books and documents. Specialties: Western, U.S., Colorado. Number of history books: 20,000.

Primary Source On-Line History Bookstore

http://www.historesearch.com/bookstore.html
E-mail: jmike@snowcrest.net

New and used scholarly monographs and textbooks. Specialties: ancient, Western. Number of history titles: 1,000+.

Serendipity Books

http://members.iinet.net.au/~serendip/
E-mail: books@serendipitybooks.com.au

New and used academic titles. Specialties: Australia, Southeast Asia. Number of history books: 11,000+. Location: Perth, Western Australia.

Xerxes Books

http://www.xerxesbooks.com
E-mail: catra@xerxesbooks.com

Offers used and out-of-print books. Highly recommended site for works published before 1900. Specialties: scholarly, general history. Number of history titles: 27,000. Location: Glen Head, New York.

Chapter 32

History and Social Studies Organizations

Stephen Kneeshaw

American Historical Association

http://www.historians.org/

The American Historical Association traditionally has served historians in all disciplines through a variety of member services. In recent years the AHA has given more time and attention to the needs of precollegiate teachers. The home page for the AHA provides information on the association and on more than a hundred affiliated societies, selected articles from the newsletter *Perspectives,* a calendar of historical events, and a "primer" on how the AHA serves K–12 teachers in history. Some sections of the Web site are available only to members.

The Historical Society

http://www.bu.edu/historic/index.html

By its self-description, the Historical Society wishes "to revitalize the study and teaching of history by reorienting the historical profession toward an accessible, integrated history free from fragmentation and over-specialization." The society offers historians an open forum for "frank debate" on issues critical to the historical profession. The Web site includes a table of contents for *The Journal of the Historical Society* and *Historically Speaking* (newsletter) and snippets of the published materials, but full access requires membership in the society.

The History Cooperative

http://www.historycooperative.org

Although technically not an "organization," the History Cooperative provides online connection to the journals of several professional associations, including the *American Historical Review* and the *Journal of American History*. This service began in 2000 as a cooperative venture of the American Historical Association, the Organization of American Historians, the University of Illinois Press, and the National Academy Press. Users can access electronic versions of articles in current issues and some past issues. Many of the journals are "ungated," but some, such as the *AHR* and *JAH,* require membership for full access.

History News Network

http://hnn.us/

Developed and run through the Center for History at George Mason University, the History News Network offers a daily listing of materials that should interest historians who teach and those who prefer research. In sections such as Hot Topics, Breaking News, and Culture Watch, readers can follow developing stories, read the thoughts of historians from a wide range of print and online sources, and get daily thoughts from historians-as-bloggers who respond to the contemporary events. The Teacher's Lounge provides a useful section on Memories and teaching suggestions for 9/11 and also discusses other notable events.

H-NCH—National Coalition for History

http://www.h-net.org/~nch/

H-NCH is "the official electronic voice" of the National Coalition for History (formerly the National Coordinating Committee for the Promotion of History), which supports history and historians in the political circles of Washington, DC, and the American states. The Web site provides a connection to past issues of *Washington Updates* (1997–present), describing the work of NCH and its lobbying successes.

National Council for History Education

http://www.history.org/nche

The NCHE Web site is more useful than many organizational sites because it goes well beyond descriptions of NCHE and its programs. For example, History Links sends a user to a diverse mix of sites: Web sites for historical organizations; history education sites; links of interest to social studies educators;

and repositories of primary sources, promoted as "a listing of over 3000 websites
. . . for the research scholar."

NCSS Online—National Council for the Social Studies

http://www.ncss.org

NCSS Online offers Web-based information services for the National Council
for the Social Studies, the largest umbrella organization for social studies educators. This site promotes NCSS, which is to be expected, but it also provides
links for professional development, standards and curriculum, and teaching
resources.

Organization of American Historians

http://www.oah.org/

The Organization of American Historians is the premier professional association for United States history. But beyond its service to college and university
teachers and researchers, OAH serves precollegiate history teachers through
such means as the *OAH Magazine of History* and outreach programs described
on this Web site. A link to History Teaching Units introduces lesson plans for
grades 6–12 based on primary documents developed by the OAH in concert
with the National Center for History in the Schools at the University of California at Los Angeles.

Society for History Education—*The History Teacher*

http://www.csulb.edu/~histeach/

This Web site for the Society for History Education, which publishes *The History Teacher,* links the organization and the journal together through the Web
server at California State University at Long Beach, where the journal is housed.
The Web site provides a current table of contents for current and past issues of
The History Teacher, links to related organizations, and contact information
for the society and the journal.

Chapter 33

Maps and Images

Martin V. Minner

Maps—Metasites

Cartographic and Spatial Data on the Internet

http://www.lib.uchicago.edu/e/su/maps/mapweb.html

A collection of map links compiled at the University of Chicago. Emphasizes Chicago and Illinois.

Map History/History of Cartography

http://www.maphistory.info/index.html

A gateway site with thousands of map history links for professional historians and amateur researchers. A companion site provides links to many map images.

Odden's Bookmarks

http://oddens.geog.uu.nl/index.php

An extensive site at Utrecht University providing a searchable list of more than 22,000 links to cartographic sites, map collections, and other map resources.

Perry-Castañeda Map Collection— Historical Map Web Sites

http://www.lib.utexas.edu/maps/map_sites/hist_sites.html

Compiled by the Perry-Castañeda Library at the University of Texas, this site offers a wide-ranging list of links to historical map Web sites. The scope is global.

Selected Map Sites

Alabama Maps

http://alabamamaps.ua.edu/

More than 6,000 digitized maps from the University of Alabama Map Library.

Cartographic Modeling Lab

http://cml.upenn.edu/

The University of Pennsylvania's Cartographic Modeling Lab provides resources for Geographic Information Systems (GIS) research and offers online versions of the lab's projects.

Civil War Maps

http://lcweb2.loc.gov/ammem/collections/civil_war_maps/

Offers digitized Civil War maps from the Library of Congress, the Virginia Historical Society, and the Library of Virginia.

Color Landform Atlas of the United States

http://fermi.jhuapl.edu/states/

Provides a variety of maps for each of the fifty states, including topographical maps, satellite images, county maps, and scans from an 1895 atlas.

Cultural Maps

http://xroads.virginia.edu/~MAP/map_hp.html

An American studies project at the University of Virginia, this site seeks to create an American historical atlas examining the physical landscape as well as mapmakers' mental and cultural terrain.

Early Washington Maps: A Digital Collection

http://www.wsulibs.wsu.edu/holland/masc/xmaps.html

A searchable collection of maps and bird's-eye views from Washington State University.

Earth Sciences and Map Library, University of California-Berkeley

http://library.berkeley.edu/EART/MapCollections.html

Several thousand digitized maps, including a strong California collection.

Harvard Map Collection

http://hcl.harvard.edu/maps/

Provides detailed online viewing of two sixteenth-century Mercator globes.

Historical City Maps

http://www.library.yale.edu/MapColl/cities.html

Yale University Library's online collection of American and European city maps.

Historic Cities

http://historic-cities.huji.ac.il/historic_cities.html

A project at the Hebrew University of Jerusalem featuring a worldwide collection of historical city maps.

IEG-Maps

http://www.ieg-maps.uni-mainz.de/

A collection of Central European maps since 1812 at the Institute for European History in Mainz.

John R. Borchert Map Library, University of Minnesota

http://www-map.lib.umn.edu/map_libraries.phtml

Provides research tools and a substantial list of map library links.

Lewis & Clark: The Maps of Exploration 1507–1814

http://www.lib.virginia.edu/small/exhibits/lewis_clark/home.html

Based on an exhibit at the University of Virginia's Alderman Library, this site examines the Lewis and Clark expedition and the history of North American cartography from Columbus to Jefferson.

Library of Congress Geography and Maps: An Illustrated Guide

http://www.loc.gov/rr/geogmap/guide/

This site, an introduction to the Library of Congress's cartographic collections, features selected images in a variety of subject areas.

Making Sense of Maps

http://historymatters.gmu.edu/mse/maps/

An introduction to the use of maps as historical evidence. Includes interactive exercises and a bibliography.

Map Collections: 1500–2004

http://lcweb2.loc.gov/ammem/gmdhtml/gmdhome.html

Part of the Library of Congress's American Memory project, this site provides online images in the following subject areas: cities and towns, conservation and the environment, discovery and exploration, cultural landscapes, military battles and campaigns, transportation, and general maps.

Map Division, New York Public Library

http://www.nypl.org/research/chss/map/map.html

Provides sample images from the library's map collections.

MapHist

http://www.maphist.nl/

The MapHist e-mail discussion group for map historians maintains an online archive of maps that have been discussed on the list.

Maps of the Pimería: Early Cartography of the Southwest

http://dizzy.library.arizona.edu/branches/spc/set/pimeria/welcome.html

Based on maps from the University of Arizona Library Map Collection, this exhibit examines the cartographic history of the region of New Spain encompassing what is now southern Arizona and northern Sonora.

National Geographic: Maps and Geography

http://www.nationalgeographic.com/maps/

The online version of *National Geographic* provides a variety of map resources.

The Newberry Library

http://www.newberry.org/

The Newberry Library's site includes bibliographic material on the library's maps and history of cartography collections and sample images.

New York State Historical Maps

http://www.sunysb.edu/libmap/nymaps.htm

Offers annotated online maps of New York State from 1556 to 1895.

Osher Map Library

http://www.usm.maine.edu/~maps/

This site provides online versions of exhibits that have appeared at the Osher Map Library and Smith Center for Cartographic Education at the University of Southern Maine.

Philadelphia—Maps and Geographic Information

http://www.library.upenn.edu/datasets/philamaps.html

Provides a variety of historical and contemporary maps of Philadelphia.

The Ryhiner Map Collection

http://biblio.unibe.ch/stub/ryhiner/

Thousands of digitized maps, with an emphasis on Switzerland.

University of Georgia Rare Map Collection

http://scarlett.libs.uga.edu/darchive/hargrett/maps/maps.html

The University of Georgia's Hargrett Rare Book and Manuscript Library provides online images of many historical maps from its collection, with an emphasis on maps of Georgia.

University of Michigan Map Library

http://www.lib.umich.edu/maplib/

Online maps of Michigan and a collection of Web links.

The U.S. Civil War Center

http://www.cwc.lsu.edu/links/links3.htm#Maps

The U.S. Civil War Center, a division of Louisiana State University Libraries Special Collections, has compiled a list of links to Civil War maps. Other portions of the site provide links to images and multimedia.

The Walker Collection: Maps of Asia Minor and the Middle East, 1511–1774

http://www.lib.unimelb.edu.au/collections/maps/digital/walker.html

A completely digitized collection of 135 maps at the University of Melbourne.

Images—Metasites

ArtServe

http://rubens.anu.edu.au/

The Australian National University's ArtServe site provides links to worldwide art and architecture sites, primarily emphasizing the Mediterranean region, Japan, and India.

Images Canada: Picturing Canadian Culture

http://www.imagescanada.ca/index-e.html

A gateway site offering search capabilities in numerous Canadian image collections.

Mother of All Art and Art History Links Page

http://www.art-design.umich.edu/mother/

An annotated collection of links to visual resources, image collections, online exhibitions, and museums. Sections on Africa, Asia, and the Middle East, as well as on Europe and the Americas, make this metasite a valuable resource for world history.

Rotch Visual Collections

http://libraries.mit.edu/rvc/index.html

The Rotch Visual Collections at the Massachusetts Institute of Technology offer a useful page of links to image collections on the Web, organized by subject area.

Selected Image Sites

American Memory

http://memory.loc.gov/ammem/amtitle.html

The American Memory site, produced by the National Digital Library Project of the Library of Congress, provides access to more than 9 million digitized primary source items on U.S. history and culture. Some of the best image collections are "Suffering Under a Great Injustice": Ansel Adams's Photographs of Japanese-American Internment at Manzanar; Edward S. Curtis's The North American Indian; Daguerreotype Portraits and Views, 1839–1864; America from the Great Depression to World War II: Photographs from the FSA-OWI, 1935–1945; Panoramic Photographs: Taking the Long View, 1851–1991; Small-Town America: Stereoscopic Views from the Robert Dennis Collection, 1850–1920; and Touring Turn-of-the-Century America: Photographs from the Detroit Publishing Company, 1880–1920.

American Museum of Photography

http://www.photography-museum.com/

Galleries of historical interest deal with slavery, spirit photography, and Commodore Matthew Perry's expedition to Japan.

Center for Creative Photography

http://www.library.arizona.edu/branches/ccp/ccphome.html

Offers an index of the center's collection of more than 60,000 photographs as well as selected online images. The center maintains more than one hundred collections of papers, manuscripts, and artifacts pertaining to photographers and photographic organizations.

Center for Documentary Studies

http://cds.aas.duke.edu/index.html

The Center for Documentary Studies promotes documentary work encompassing photography, filmmaking, oral history, folklore, and writing.

Charles Cushman Collection

http://www.dlib.indiana.edu/collections/cushman/

A searchable archive of more than 14,000 Kodachrome slides taken by the amateur photographer Charles Cushman from 1938 to 1969.

Chicago Imagebase

http://tigger.uic.edu/depts/ahaa/imagebase/

A project at the University of Illinois at Chicago providing a broad selection of digitized images pertaining to Chicago's built environment.

Collected Visions

http://cvisions.cat.nyu.edu/mantle/

The Collected Visions project offers a provocative perspective on how photographic images shape personal memory. The site invites visitors to submit photographs and to create photo essays from their own photographs or from other visitors' submissions.

The Daguerreian Society

http://www.daguerre.org

The Daguerreian Society's site features a selection of digitized daguerreotype images and informative explanatory text. The site's resource page offers a history of the daguerreotype, nineteenth- and twentieth-century published sources, a bibliography, and information on the daguerreotype process.

Denver Public Library Photography Collection

http://photoswest.org/

This site features exhibits based on the photography collection in the Denver Public Library's Western History/Genealogy Department.

Digital Media Lab, University of Virginia

http://www.lib.virginia.edu/clemons/RMC/DML/index.html

Offers thousands of digitized images. Recent projects include The Atlantic Slave Trade, Viewing Pompeii, and the Tibet and Himalayan Digital Library.

Frank Lloyd Wright: Designs for an American Landscape, 1922–1932

http://www.loc.gov/exhibits/flw/flw.html

The online version of an exhibit at the Library of Congress, this site integrates many of Wright's drawings into an essay on his work. The project includes images of hypothetical study models based on Wright's drawings.

George Eastman House International Museum of Photography and Film

http://www.eastmanhouse.org/

The George Eastman House, an important resource for research in the history of photography, offers many digitized photographs, stereo views, and lantern slides.

Images From the History of Medicine

http://www.ihm.nlm.nih.gov/

Provides online access to almost 60,000 images in the prints and photographs collection of the U.S. National Library of Medicine's History of Medicine Division. Includes portraits, caricatures, and graphic art.

Images of African Americans From the 19th Century

http://digital.nypl.org/schomburg/images_aa19/

A selection of images from the New York Public Library's Schomburg Center for Research in Black Culture. The archive can be searched by keyword or subject area.

Japanese Old Photographs in Bakumatsu-Meiji Period

http://oldphoto.lb.nagasaki-u.ac.jp/unive/

More than 5,000 digitized photographs of Japan from 1860 to 1899, made available by Nagasaki University Library.

LIFE

http://www.life.com/Life/lifeclassic.html

Front covers from 1936 to 1972, the period when *LIFE* was published weekly, can be searched by keyword or date. The site also offers a selection of photographs.

Motion Picture & Television Reading Room

http://lcweb.loc.gov/rr/mopic/

The Library of Congress offers many early motion pictures online in QuickTime, MPG, and Real Media formats. Subject areas and periods range from popular entertainment in the 1870s to the consumer economy of the 1920s.

Museum of the City of New York

http://www.mcny.org

Many of the museum's online exhibitions on New York history make use of images. Among the site's photographic projects is New York During the War:

Photographs from the Office of War Information. Other exhibitions of historical interest are Looking North: Upper Manhattan in Photographs, 1896–1939; Gotham Comes of Age: New York Through the Lens of the Byron Company, 1892–1942; and Berenice Abbott: Changing New York.

National Aeronautics and Space Administration

http://www.nasa.gov/multimedia/highlights/index.html

NASA's multimedia gallery features a searchable archive of hundreds of thousands of still images. The gallery also provides access to NASA-related audio, video, and works of art.

National Archives and Records Administration: Exhibit Hall

http://www.archives.gov/exhibit_hall/index.html

Features numerous exhibitions of historical images including Picturing the Century, a photographic retrospective of the twentieth century; Powers of Persuasion, a collection of World War II propaganda posters; Panoramic Photography, a sampling of panoramic images; and Portrait of Black Chicago, an exhibition of photographs of 1970s Chicago.

National Museum of Photography, Film & Television

http://www.nmpft.org.uk/home.asp

Provides an introduction to the museum's collections and online images.

New York Public Library

http://www.nypl.org/research/chss/spe/art/photo/photo.html#online

Provides online access to the exhibition Berenice Abbott: Changing New York, 1935–1938 and to two projects on Lewis Hine: Work Portraits, 1920–1939 and Construction of the Empire State Building, 1930–1931.

Online Archive of California

http://www.oac.cdlib.org/

Provides image searching in many collections throughout California.

Photographs From the *Chicago Daily News:* 1902–1933

http://memory.loc.gov/ammem/ndlpcoop/ichihtml/

A major collection of more than 55,000 images by *Chicago Daily News* photographers. The photographs are from the Chicago Historical Society and have been made available through the American Memory site at the Library of Congress.

Princeton University: Seeley G. Mudd Manuscript Library

http://www.princeton.edu/~mudd/

Features recent exhibits from the library including photographs and audiovisual items. Among recent exhibits is Testing Boundaries: Cartoon Visions of Roosevelt's Third Term.

Royal Photographic Society

http://www.rps.org/index.html

Offers an archive of recent exhibitions held at the society's Octagon Galleries in Bath.

The Siege and Commune of Paris, 1870–1871

http://www.library.northwestern.edu/spec/siege/

Provides more than 1,200 digitized, searchable photographs and images from the Siege and Commune of Paris.

Small Towns, Black Lives

http://www.blacktowns.org

Created by Wendel White, professor of art at Richard Stockton State College of New Jersey, this project presents documentary images of historically African-American communities in southern New Jersey. The project includes photographs, documents, video clips, and panoramic images.

Smithsonian Institution

http://photo2.si.edu/

Offers numerous online exhibitions and a searchable database of images. A few of the projects of historical interest are Magic Lanterns, Magic Mirrors: A Centennial Salute to Cinema, Recent Presidential Inaugurals, and Reflections on the Wall: The Vietnam Veterans Memorial.

Temple of Liberty: Building the Capitol for a New Nation

http://www.loc.gov/exhibits/us.capitol/s0.html

A Library of Congress exhibit on the history and meaning of the U.S. Capitol, including many maps, prints, architectural drawings, and photographs from the eighteenth to the twentieth centuries.

They Still Draw Pictures

http://orpheus-1.ucsd.edu/speccoll/tsdp/

A collection of more than 600 drawings made during the Spanish Civil War by schoolchildren in Spain and in French refugee centers. The images are from the Southworth Spanish Civil War Collection at the University of California–San Diego.

UCR/California Museum of Photography

http://www.cmp.ucr.edu/

An outstanding site based on the museum's collection of historical and contemporary images. More than 33,000 stereographic images from the museum's Keystone Mast Collection are available online. Visitors to the site can use 3-D red/blue glasses to simulate the effect of a stereoscopic viewer. The site features numerous exhibits and searchable image collections.

United Nations Photo

http://www.un.org/av/photo/

Provides a selection of images from the United Nations Photo Library. The site's history section includes a time line of images from the League of Nations to the present.

Chapter 34

Resources for Teachers of History
K–12 and College

Stephen Kneeshaw

Metasites

Academic Info

http://www.academicinfo.net/table.html

Academic Info is a subject directory designed for college-level use that provides both annotated listings of Internet sites and gateways to specialized materials. The site offers metaindexes, general directories, and teaching materials to serve needs at many academic levels. Especially useful is the section on U.S. history—Academic Info U.S. History, with a fully annotated directory of Internet resources divided into sections such as period gateways, diversity gateways, and topical resources.

Digital Librarian: A Librarian's Choice of the Best of the Web—History

http://www.digital-librarian.com/history.html

Self-described as "a librarian's choice of the best of the Web" (and run by Margaret Vail Anderson of Cortland, New York), the Digital Librarian covers virtually every academic discipline, many of which are linked to the history page. This site provides an entry point for such diverse topics as the ancient world, genealogy, Judaica, Latin America, the Middle East, and women's resources. For elementary teachers, there are useful connections to children's literature and resources. Lists are alphabetized and annotated briefly, but there is no internal search mechanism.

Index of Resources for Historians

http://vlib.iue.it/history/index.html

http://rmweb.indiana.edu/History/VL/index.html.

The oversight of this valuable Web site has switched from the University of Kansas to the European University Institute in Florence, Italy, but this remains an exceptional metasite with more than 3,000 connections arranged alphabetically by subject and name. There are no annotations, but subject breakdowns make this an easily usable Web site. The list emphasizes college and university-level history, but some sites are geared specifically to K–12 audiences. Some sections are foreign-language–based rather than English (e.g., Brazil in Portuguese and Holocaust in German), making them difficult for many American users to access. Users also can access the full index via a mirror site at Indiana University (the second URL above).

Internet Public Library

http://www.ipl.org

The Internet Public Library is an easy-to-use metasite organized by "subject collections" and "ready references." History Web sites (available through arts and humanities or social sciences) have been organized by documents and sources, eras, regions, and topics, with subheadings in each area allowing users to break down their searches in close detail. Short but descriptive annotations for each Web site make the IPL easy to manage for students as well as teachers.

Lesson Plans and Resources for Social Studies Teachers

http://www.csun.edu/~hcedu013/index.html

This site, maintained by Marty Levine at California State University, Northridge, should be the first gateway accessed by elementary and secondary history teachers who want to sample the wealth of the World Wide Web. A clickable table of contents on the opening page leads to nine areas such as Lesson Plans and Teaching Strategies, Other Social Studies Resources (including government and museum sites), Teaching Current Events, and Newsgroups and Mailing Lists. The lengthy lists of links are alphabetized and annotated for a quick reading of contents.

The Ten Best Sites

AMDOCS: Documents for the Study of American History

http://www.ku.edu/carrie/docs/amdocs_index.html

This Web site, managed at the University of Kansas, provides users with one of the broadest Web-based lists of documents for American history available on the WWW. Documents range from the fifteenth century into the twenty-first century, from Columbus's letter to Ferdinand and Isabella in 1494 to the presidential debates of 2004. The list is set to both chronological eras (e.g., Age of Exploration, the Civil War) and presidential administrations, making it easy to locate documents for any given time in American history.

American Memory

http://rs6.loc.gov

The rich collections of the Library of Congress come to life in words and pictures in American Memory. This rapidly growing site, now with more than 125 collections online (up from forty-two three years ago), includes documents, maps, photographs and prints, motion pictures, and sound recordings. An easy-to-use search engine and a list of entries alphabetized by subjects and titles provides entry to topics ranging from baseball cards, Civil War images, and the conservation movement (one of my favorites) to Ansel Adams (photographs from the internment camp at Manzanar), posters from the WPA, and the dust bowl.

The Digital Classroom

http://archives.gov/digital_classroom/index.html

The Digital Classroom, from the National Archives and Records Administration (NARA), encourages teachers at all levels to use documents in their classrooms. This is NARA's complement to American Memory from the Library of Congress. The Web site delivers documentary materials from the National

Archives, lesson plans, and suggested methods for teaching with primary documents. The topics available online span a wide range—literally A to Z—from the *Amistad* case to the Zimmerman telegram. NARA also provides a reproducible set of document analysis worksheets for written documents, photographs, cartoons, posters, maps, artifacts, sound recordings, and motion pictures that history teachers will find easy to use and attractive for their students.

ERIC—Educational Resources Information Center

http://www.eric.ed.gov/

Reorganized under the auspices of the Department of Education in 2004, ERIC (formerly AskERIC) provides a centralized database to search the ERIC online systems that contain more than 1.1 million entries dating back to 1966. Users also can access more than 100,000 full-text documents. The search engine offers several options: keywords, title, author, or ERIC number. For students and teachers, ERIC will be a valuable source to track down information on every conceivable topic, pointing to resources for teaching, research, and writing.

History Matters

http://historymatters.gmu.edu

Designed for secondary and college teachers in American history, History Matters combines the efforts of the American Social History Project at the City University of New York and the Center for History and New Media at George Mason University. With an express purpose to "focus on the lives of ordinary Americans," History Matters delivers teaching materials, first-person documents, interactive exercises, "syllabus central," and threaded discussions on teaching history. A keyword search option allows users easy access to materials in the site.

History/Social Studies Web Site for K–12 Teachers

http://my.execpc.com/~dboals/boals.html

As the name suggests, this site focuses on the needs of K–12 classroom teachers in locating and using the resources of the Internet. A clickable table opens a wide range of topics, including K–12 resources, archaeology, genealogy, geography, American history, and non-Western history. This site provides a gateway to some 600 locations, including lesson, commercial, project, and general sites. The one downside is that the lists are not alphabetized, although they do provide brief but useful annotations.

Kathy Schrock's Guide for Educators

http://school.discovery.com/schrockguide

Kathy Schrock created and maintains one of the best-known Web sites for educators. This "categorized list of sites" on the Internet, which Schrock updates often "to include the best sites for teaching and learning," covers the whole span of academic subjects. Clicking the link for history and social studies opens connections to American and world history as well as general history and social studies sites. Schrock's annotations give brief but useful signposts to the various links.

SCORE History–Social Science

http://score.rims.k12.ca.us

Schools of California Online Resources for Education (SCORE) designed this Web site primarily for K–12 teachers in California, but the site will be useful to teachers in all states. SCORE links users to resources and lessons by grade level, resources by theme and topic, virtual projects and field trips, and more. All the materials have been evaluated and rated on a 1 to 5 scale by a team of educators, assuring quality control in such areas as accuracy, grade appropriateness, depth, and variety.

Studying and Teaching History

http://www.tntech.edu/history/study.html

This fine Web site from Tennessee Technological University offers a database of valuable materials for history teachers and students on a wide range of topics. Currently available are study guides for history classes from several universities, reference works, guides for research and writing, links for oral history, maps and audio-visual materials, portfolios, living history and reenactments, studying and teaching history at K–12 levels, and graduate schools.

Teaching History: A Journal of Methods

http://www.emporia.edu/socsci/journal/main.htm

Designed and maintained at Emporia State University, Kansas, by the publication team for the journal *Teaching History,* this site reflects the main objective of the journal, to provide teachers at all academic levels "with the best and newest teaching ideas for their classrooms." Besides information on the journal, this site provides links to a rich list of resources in nine history-related categories, from American and world history to genealogy, writing aids, and teaching resources.

WWW Resources for History Teachers

Agents of Social Change

http://www.smith.edu/libraries/ssc/curriculum/index.html

Working with a grant from NEH, Smith College, Massachusetts, processed eight manuscript collections addressing issues centered on the major theme of "agents for social change." Smith took as its mission "to reach beyond the traditional community of archival users—beyond senior scholars, graduate students and undergraduates" and to design lesson plans directed toward middle and high school students. Through this Web site students can get better acquainted with such diverse topics as the fight for civil rights, for urban reform, and for women's rights from the 1930s into the 1980s.

The Avalon Project: Documents in Law, History, and Diplomacy

http://www.yale.edu/lawweb/avalon/avalon.htm

History teachers frequently use documents to enrich lesson plans and illustrate key ideas. The Avalon Project from the Yale Law School provides connections to a wealth of documents from pre-eighteenth century into the twenty-first century. The one downside is the listing of documents (within a century-based format) in alphabetical rather than chronological order. But a list of major collections and a search engine within the project make this a user-friendly Web site that is accessible for all grade levels.

Awesome Library

http://www.awesomelibrary.org/

Awesome Library for teachers, librarians, students, and parents gives users links to all teaching fields and to more than 26,000 reviewed resources. Under the social studies link, users can click into history and lesson plans or make connections to specialized history-related fields such as conservation, current events (including hunger and civil liberties), holidays, multicultural resources, and terrorism.

Biographical Dictionary

http://www.s9.com/biography

Biographical Dictionary offers biographies of more than 28,000 men and women "who have shaped our world from ancient times to the present day." Users can search the list by names, birth or death years, professions, literary and artistic works, and other keywords, making these men and women easily accessible for students and teachers.

Center for Teaching History With Technology

http://thwt.org/

As the name suggests, the Center for Teaching History with Technology provides a variety of materials to aid teachers at K–12 levels (with carryover value for college-level teaching) who wish to incorporate technology into their classrooms. The Web site is easy to navigate, using links brought together under "resources." Teachers will find activities, games, quizzes, and e-texts, as well as lesson plans, PowerPoint tips, and Advanced Placement resources.

Center for the Liberal Arts at the University of Virginia

http://www.virginia.edu/cla/

This Web site is dedicated to "opportunities for continuing content education for K–12 teachers," although many of the materials are appropriate for college and university levels as well. Clicking on "History" takes the user to a wonderful collection of Web sites on American history, geography, government, world history, and Virginia state history, which, of course, is rich in early American and Civil War–related topics.

Core Documents of U.S. Democracy

http://www.gpoaccess.gov/coredocs.html

This Web site from the Government Printing Office delivers more than the title suggests. Beyond such cornerstone documents as the Declaration of Independence, Constitution, and Bill of Rights, and Supreme Court decisions, users get a statistical abstract of the United States, a weekly compilation of presidential documents, and more. This Web site will be useful for history teachers who bring current events into their classrooms.

Ditto.com

http://www.ditto.com

For teachers wanting to liven up PowerPoint and lecture presentations and bring more visuals into their classrooms, Ditto.com provides "visual search of the web using pictures." The search engine is fast and user-friendly, but teachers might feel overwhelmed with the number of choices. For example, searches on topics such as Vietnam, Yellowstone, and Civil War provide thousands of images. For each visual, source information is available to ensure proper citations.

EDSITEment

http://edsitement.neh.gov/

EDSITEment provides subject-based connections to top humanities sites in four fields: art and culture, literature and language arts, foreign languages, and history and social studies. EDSITEment draws from collections "from some of the world's great museums, libraries, cultural institutions, and universities." All the sites have been "reviewed for content, design, and educational impact in the classroom." The materials are set into grade-specific categories from K–2 through 9–12, with many of the 9–12 materials suitable for college and university classrooms.

FREE: Federal Resources for Educational Excellence

http://www.ed.gov/free/index.html

FREE is the result of a "partnership" of teachers and more than fifty federal agencies to develop Internet-based learning modules and learning communities. The agencies include the CIA, FBI, National Park Service, Library of Congress, National Archives and Records Administration and White House. A site map provides connections to various topic areas, including the social studies. Topics are arranged alphabetically with the sponsoring agency identified. Brief annotations give good direction for users.

From Revolution to Reconstruction . . . and What Happened Afterwards

http://odur.let.rug.nl/~usa/

This hypertext Web site comes largely from materials prepared by the United States Information Agency, starting with "an outline of American history." This Netherlands-based site delivers one of the best collections of materials on American presidents, including full texts of inaugural addresses and State of the Union speeches.

Helping Your Child Learn History

http://www.ed.gov/pubs/parents/History/

This Web site, aimed primarily at parents, brings history to life for children, especially ages four through eleven. The suggestions, of course, are equally pertinent for lower-grade teachers. Topics include History Education Begins at Home (e.g., "history is a habit"), History as Story (e.g., "cooking up history"), and History as Time (e.g., "put time in a bottle").

The Heritage Education Network (THEN)

http://histpres.mtsu.edu/then/

Many indifferent students turn on to history when teachers introduce them to family and local history. THEN—The Heritage Education Network—provides a nice mix of resources for teachers who want to make "nearby history" part of their curriculum. As the Web site notes, "Heritage Education is the use of local cultural and historic resources for teaching the required curricula of grades K–12." In fact, it can work at the college level too. Run through Middle Tennessee State University, THEN spotlights such diverse resources as family history, historic buildings and structures, cemeteries, farms, and photographs. THEN also provides a list of contacts in each of the fifty states, including local historical societies and state agencies, who can assist in program development.

The History Channel

http://www.historychannel.com

This Web site provides an easy gateway into video materials from the History Channel. The History Store is the place to order videos, but this is more than just a commercial site. The speeches and video section lets students "watch, listen, [and] explore" such diverse characters as Franklin D. Roosevelt, Neil Armstrong, Martin Luther King Jr., Babe Ruth, and Yasir Arafat. Classroom materials, including vocabulary terms, discussion questions, and extended activities, are available online to accompany videos.

The History Net: Where History Lives on the Web

http://www.thehistorynet.com

The History Net, with its clickable list of historical times and topics along the edge, might seem to be just another history Web site. In fact, its major role is to provide links to published articles on times and topics, using journals such as *Civil War Times, Military History, Vietnam, British Heritage, Wild West,* and *American History.* The Web site also provides discussion forums related to topics addressed by the journals.

History Now: American History On-Line

http://www.historynow.org

This new Web site started in late 2004 is from the Gilder Lehrman Institute of American History (a sure sign of quality) and appears in journal form. History Now will offer four "issues" per year, with each separate issue focusing, through documents, on a topic with significance in American history, such as American elections and slavery. From the Teacher's Desk offers lesson plans for different grade levels, and Interactive History delivers interactive time lines, maps, and more. Topic specialists offer their thoughts in short but pointed essays in The

Historian's Perspective. This Web site operates much in the manner of the *Magazine of History* from the OAH, focusing on one topic per "issue," providing teachers with a variety of ideas to bring into their classrooms.

The History Place

http://www.historyplace.com/index.html

The History Place provides a variety of links that will be useful to history teachers, especially at the secondary level. At this point, the site emphasizes American history, but there are strong sections on Hitler and the Holocaust, the Irish potato famine, and genocide in the twentieth century. Other European topics are "in development." Users will find time lines (e.g., the Civil War "with quotes and photos"), photographs, and "points of view," which are reviews and reflections from established writers and historians. The site also offers "movie reviews" for films with historical themes.

History Timelines on the Web

http://history.searchbeat.com/

The title promises time lines, but this Web site delivers much more that will be useful to history teachers and students at all levels. For example, the section on the Depression and New Deal includes a short history of the era, an annotated list of online resources, a section on people, places, and events, and links to collections of photographs, as well as time lines.

H-Net Teaching

http://www.h-net.msu.edu/teaching

H-Net Teaching provides a gateway to several Web sites on teaching maintained by H-Net (Humanities and Social Science Online) at Michigan State University. Each of these Web sites includes edited, threaded discussions on topics of interest to list subscribers and archives, complete with search mechanisms, on previous discussions. H-Net Teaching includes the following:

EDTECH—on educational technology

H-AfrTeach—teaching African history and studies

H-High-School—teaching high school history and social studies (an indispensable site for secondary history teachers)

H-Mmedia—high-tech teaching, multimedia, CD-ROM

H-Survey—teaching United States history survey courses (a must-see site for college American survey teachers)

H-Teach—teaching history at all levels (my personal favorite of the H-Net sites with enlightening discussions on a wide range of important topics for history teachers)

H-W-Civ—teaching Western Civilization courses (a companion to H-Survey).

Internet History Sourcebook Project

http://www.fordham.edu/halsall/

This Web site provides a gateway to a collection of public-domain and copy-permitted historical texts developed and maintained by Paul Halsall of Fordham University. The three key "sourcebooks" cover ancient history, medieval history, and modern history. In addition, Halsall has developed several subsidiary sourcebooks that draw from the three key sourcebooks. The subsection on multimedia and history in the modern history sourcebook is rich in audio and visual materials that will enliven teaching and learning.

Learning Space—Social Studies for Washington Students and Teachers

http://www.wscss.org/

The Learning Space provides many links specific to a single state, here Washington State, but the site has great value for all history teachers. Using general indicators such as social studies subjects, frameworks, and teacher resources, the Learning Space links users to broad topics (American and world history) as well as specialized topics such as flags, Lewis and Clark, and Native Americans.

The Library in the Sky

http://www.nwrel.org/sky/index.asp

Run by the Northwest Regional Educational Laboratory in Portland, Oregon, the Library in the Sky offers more than 1,200 links to educational resources for teachers, librarians, students, and parents, in every field of study. History and the social studies get enough attention to make this a useful site for the K–12 community.

Marco Polo: Internet Content for the Classroom

http://www.marcopolo-education.org/index.aspx

Started in 1997 as a nonprofit consortium of educational organizations, Marco Polo provides K–12 teachers access to seven content-based Web sites tied to national standards plus professional development resources. Teachers will find lesson plans keyed to specific grade levels, downloadable worksheets, links to other Web sites, and more. Content partners include EDSITEment (for the humanities—from NEH) and Xpedition (for geography—from *National Geographic*).

National Center for History in the Schools

http://www.sscnet.ucla.edu/nchs

The National Center for History in the Schools, located at the University of California, Los Angeles, publishes online the National Standards for United States History, K–4 and 5–12, the National Standards for World History, and the Revised Standards for History. In addition, Bring History Alive introduces sourcebooks for U.S. and world history, grades 5–12, with more than 1,200 activities arranged by grade level and keyed to the revised standards (available for purchase rather than free use by teachers).

National Portrait Gallery

http://www.npg.si.edu

The National Portrait Gallery, a branch of the Smithsonian Institution, provides online access to many of its collections that teachers and students can tap for PowerPoint and lecture presentations. This will be the only way to access National Portrait Gallery collections during a multiyear renovation (from January 2000 to July 2006). The Web site includes several virtual past exhibitions and the permanent collection of the NPG, including the Hall of Presidents. For some of the special exhibitions, teacher resources packets are available.

Our Documents—100 Milestone Documents

http://www.ourdocuments.gov

Promising "to help us think, talk, and teach about the rights and responsibilities of citizens in our democracy," this Web site introduces "100 milestone documents" that shaped the American experience. A teacher sourcebook delivers an annotated time line, key themes, and lesson plans. The Web site also provides quick links to curriculum standards and ideas for librarians, making this useful across many grade levels.

ParkNet—National Park Service

http://www.nps.gov

The National Park Service, through ParkNet, delivers one of the best Web sites run and maintained by a U.S. government agency. "History and Culture" and "Interpretation and Education" (link to "Learn NPS") provide entry points to a variety of teaching resources, including lesson plans, Parks in Your Curriculum, and Teaching with Historic Places (which gets a full description below). The Parks and Recreation heading opens links for all NPS properties. Some of these—Olympic National Park in Washington State, for example—have expanded Web sites that provide attractive resources for teachers such as lesson plans that they can pick up and use with ease.

Popular Songs in American History

http://www.contemplator.com/america/index.html

This innovative Web site provides "tunes, lyrics, information, historical background and tune related links" for a wide range of songs from the seventeenth century into the early twentieth century. The songs are arranged by time frame and topic (e.g., gold rush, Civil War, and cowboys). For each song, users get a brief introduction, lyrics, and music. One notable section, developed "in response to requests," spotlights sea shanties and songs of the sea.

Project Gutenberg

http://www.promo.net/pg

One of the best-known early WWW sites, Project Gutenberg, started in 1971, provides digital versions of classic works in world history and literature for the classroom. The collection now numbers more than 13,000 electronic books (e-Books) in more than thirty languages. An in-site search engine—called an online book catalog—allows users to find e-texts by checking alphabetical lists of authors and titles, which can be downloaded via FTP or the Web. Two lists—on the top hundred books and authors of the week—make interesting browsing.

Smithsonian Institution Social Studies Lesson Plans

http://smithsonianeducation.org/educators/indexhtml

Under the heading Field Trips, the Smithsonian Center for Education and Museum Studies provides detailed information that will aid teachers preparing students for visits to the Smithsonian Institution or to other museums (see Teaching Strategies and Preparation Materials). Teachers can jump quickly to lesson plans and easily identify useful resources with a search engine keyed to subject, grade level, and keyword. The section on Heritage Teaching Resources will prove useful to teachers looking for materials to celebrate "heritage months" in their classrooms.

Teachers Helping Teachers

http://www.pacificnet.net/~mandel/

Teachers Helping Teachers opened in 1995 under the direction of Scott Mandel, a classroom teacher in California, who updates the site each week during the school year. Now with more than 4 million hits—testimony to its value for teachers—the site provides lesson plans (all submitted by teachers) for K–12 grade levels. Many of these plans are easily adaptable to a variety of teaching situations. Another useful section is links to educational resources on the Web that have been alphabetized by subject.

Teaching With Historic Places

http://www.cr.nps.gov/nr/twhp/index.htm

This site, run through the National Park Service, focuses on the teaching opportunities presented by properties on the National Register of Historic Places. The purpose is to "turn students into historians as they study primary sources, historical and contemporary photographs and maps, and other documents, and then search for the history around them in their own communities." The NPS provides lesson plans (categorized according to the National Standards for United States History for Grades 5–12), education kits, and workshops to facilitate the integration of historic places into the curriculum. In a nice invitation to get teachers to add new materials, the NPS also provides an online author's packet to "help [teachers] create materials to convey the meaning and importance of these places to students from upper elementary to high school."

THOMAS: Legislative Information on the Internet

http://thomas.loc.gov/#thomas

THOMAS bills itself as "legislative information on the Internet." It is certainly that and much more. Run through the Library of Congress, THOMAS follows the work of the U.S. Senate and House of Representatives, providing summaries, status reports, and full texts of legislation in Congress. The site also provides directories for members of Congress, making it a critical tool for teachers who use current events in their classrooms.

Timelines of History

http://timelines.ws

Timelines of History operates with a simple format: Click on dates (centuries, decades, years, even months for the most recent dates) and follow time. The time lines include American and world history. Other sections allow users to search time by countries, American states, cities (notably New York City and San Francisco plus others off site), and subjects of various sorts, such as disasters, environment, pop and rock music, technology, women, and writers. Regular updates keep this Web site current (literally up to date), making it a useful resource for teachers and students.

United States Department of Education

http://www.ed.gov

The official home page of the U.S. Department of Education is a good place to learn about federal educational initiatives. The "teachers" link opens some useful sites such as FREE (described above) and GEM (Gateway to Educational Materials). Those who are interested also can find a variety of policy documents online at this site.

Virtual Field Trips Site

http://www.field-guides.com/

This Web site provides a way for teachers to take their students around the world without leaving their classrooms. They can "travel" to Antarctica; visit deserts, oceans, salt marshes, and volcanoes; encounter dinosaurs, fierce creatures, and insects ("a creepy crawly experience"); and then live through hurricanes and tornadoes. At the individual field trip sites, users will find terms to learn, concepts, and teachers' resources.

Words and Deeds in American History

http://lcweb2.loc.gov/ammem/mcchtml/corhome.html

Here is one more site from the Library of Congress (LOC). Actually an off-shoot of American Memory (described above), Words and Deeds gives a condensed collection of manuscript materials (with some ninety "representative documents") that can enrich the teaching and study of history. The LOC has provided a detailed description to accompany each document and links to other resources in the library's collection that connect to the documents.

Chapter 35

Electronic Journals

Jeremy Boggs

Metasites

Directory of Open Access Journals

http://www.doaj.org

DOAJ is a directory dedicated to increasing the use of open-access journals in all fields. The site currently lists thirty-eight history journals. Readers can browse the journal listings and search articles. DOAJ is a project of Lund University Libraries, Sweden.

History Cooperative

http://www.historycooperative.org

A joint project by the American Historical Association, the Organization of American Historians, the University of Illinois Press, and the National Academy Press, this site provides access to eighteen journals. Four of the journals— *American Historical Review, Journal of American History, Western Historical Quarterly,* and *William and Mary Quarterly*—are only accessible through a subscription, but the rest of the journals are free to read. Conference notes and links to other resources are also available on the site.

JSTOR

http://www.jstor.org

JSTOR is a comprehensive archive of past articles in major journals in the discipline of history. Visitors can search for articles in a variety of ways or browse past volumes of journals. JSTOR holds over sixty journals in history, eleven journals in the history of science and technology, and numerous journals in other fields. Subscription required.

Oxford Journals Online

http://www.oxfordjournals.org/

Oxford University Press provides electronic versions of a number of history and history-related journals. The journals are available by subscription, and readers can search and browse issues. Many journals in OJO also have RSS (Really Simple Syndication) feeds.

Individual Journals

49th Parallel

http://www.49thparallel.bham.ac.uk/about.htm

49th Parallel covers interdisciplinary approaches to the study of American and Canadian history and culture. Disciplines covered in the journal include history, literature, and cultural studies.

African Studies Quarterly

http://www.africa.ufl.edu/asq/

Published by the Center for African Studies at the University of Florida, this journal contains refereed articles on a variety of topics related to African studies and the history of Africa. The journal, which has been published since 1997, includes articles and book reviews in HTML and PDF formats.

B.C. Asian Review

http://www2.arts.ubc.ca/bcar/

B.C. Asian Review is a refereed journal maintained by the Department of Asian Studies at the University of British Columbia, in Vancouver, Canada. The journal started in 1991, but has been available online since 1997. Focusing on a wide range of topics related to Asian history and culture, *B.C. Asian Review* contains articles and book reviews. The archive section is browsable both by issue and by geographic area.

Bryn Mawr Classical Review

http://ccat.sas.upenn.edu/bmcr/

Published since 1990, *Bryn Mawr Classical Review* contains refereed articles on all topics and fields related to classical studies. The archives of the journal are searchable by keyword, but readers can also browse past articles by year. Articles are published individually, and an index lists article authors and review authors. The journal also contains the archives of the *Bryn Mawr Electronic Resources Review* (http://ccat.sas.upenn.edu/bmcr/bmerr/), an online journal dedicated to reviewing Web sites, CD-ROMs, and other media related to classical studies. Readers can subscribe to the journal by sending an e-mail to the editors.

Common-Place

http://www.commonplace.org

http://www.historycooperative.org/cpindex.html

This journal publishes articles, reviews, and discussion on early American history and culture. The site is elegantly designed and provides resources to a variety of readers. *Common-Place* is a project of the American Antiquarian Society and the Department of History at Florida State University.

Cromohs

http://www.cromohs.unifi.it

Cromohs (*Cyber Review of Modern Historiography*) is an academic, peer-reviewed journal on modern historiography. Articles are written in Italian and English, and the journal has been online since 1996.

Delaware Review of Latin-American Studies

http://www.udel.edu/LASP/DeRLAS.html

Maintained by the Department of Latin-American Studies at the University of Delaware, this journal has published issues biannually since 1999. Besides publishing articles and book reviews on all topics related to the history and culture of Latin America, the journal contains links to conference notes, recent scholarship in Latin-American studies, and a profiles section that contains interviews with Latin-American studies scholars about their research and teaching.

E-Journal of Portuguese History

http://www.brown.edu/Departments/Portuguese_Brazilian_Studies/ejph/

This journal is relatively new, having published three issues since 2003. The journal is a joint project of Brown University and the University of Porto in Portugal.

The Electronic Journal of Australian and New Zealand History

http://www.jcu.edu.au/aff/history/

Hosted by James Cook University in Australia and an extension of the H-Net listserv H-ANZAU (History of Aotearoa New Zealand and Australia), this journal publishes research articles, information related to the history of Australia and New Zealand, and other resources relevant to the journal's focus. The journal is searchable by keyword, and readers can browse the contents of current and past issues. Articles are published in HTML format, and book reviews published since 2002 are available through H-Reviews.

Electronic Journal of Contemporary Japanese Studies

http://www.japanesestudies.org.uk/index.html

EJCJS publishes articles, reviews, and information related to the history, politics, and society of contemporary Japan. While most of the articles focus on recent developments in Japan, a number of articles discuss historical topics and developments. Besides peer-reviewed articles the journal also contains a section entitled Discussion Papers, in which scholars can share their research with the public in an effort to improve the arguments of the papers. A Bulletin section features calls for papers, research funding, and various lectures, exhibitions, and workshops related to contemporary Japanese studies.

Electronic Journal of Oriental Studies

http://www2.1et.uu.nl/Solis/anpt/ejos/EJOS-1.html

Online since 1998, the *EJOS* publishes academic work on a variety of topics related to Oriental studies. The journal is published by the Department of Arabic, Persian and Turkic Languages and Cultures at Utrecht University, Netherlands.

Eras

http://www.arts.monash.edu.au/eras/

Eras is a peer-reviewed journal created by postgraduate students at Monash University, Australia. The journal contains academic work in a variety of disciplines, including history, religion, and archaeology.

Essays in History

http://etext.lib.virginia.edu/journals/EH/

Essays in History, published online from 1990 to 2000, was sponsored by the Corcoran Department of History and the Electronic Text Center at the University of Virginia. The journal, published and peer-reviewed by graduate students, published scholarship on a variety of topics and fields in history.

Heroic Age

http://members.aol.com/heroicage1/homepage.html

Heroic Age publishes research on the medieval history of northwestern Europe (Britain, Ireland, and surrounding areas). The journal publishes academic articles, reviews, news, and editorials.

History of Intellectual Culture

http://www.ucalgary.ca/hic/

A peer-reviewed academic journal with contributors across the globe, *History of Intellectual Culture* provides a venue for studying the historical developments of ideas and ideology. Published annually since 2001, the journal contains articles in both HTML and PDF formats as well as links relevant to the journal's subject matter.

Intersections

http://wwwsshe.murdoch.edu.au/intersections/issue10_contents.html

Intersections, which has published ten issues since 1998, focuses on historical and theoretical considerations of gender in Asian contexts. Sponsored by the School of Asian Studies at Murdoch University in Australia, the journal not only strives to present innovative interpretations in gender history, it also "explores new ways of 'doing' history" through digital media.

Journal for Millennial Studies

http://www.mille.org/publications/journal.html

Created by the Center for Millennial Studies, *Journal for Millennial Studies* published five issues from 1998 to 2001. Articles and book reviews in this journal focused on the history and culture of millennia, apocalypse, and utopia.

Journal for Multimedia History

http://www.albany.edu/jmmh/

Sponsored by the History Department at the University of Albany, State University of New York. Although the journal has not published a new issue since

2000, past issues contain interesting articles that succeed at combining various media in their analyses.

Journal of Arabic and Islamic Studies

http://www.uib.no/jais/jais.htm

This journal publishes articles and reviews on all topics related to the history and culture of Arabic and Islamic civilization. The online version of the journal is supported by the Section of Middle Eastern Languages and Cultures at the University of Bergen, the Institute of Ancient Near Eastern Studies at Charles University, Prague, and the Department of Islamic and Middle Eastern Studies at the University of Edinburgh.

Journal of Southern Religion

http://jsr.fsu.edu

Journal of Southern Religion is a peer-reviewed academic journal on all topics related to the history of religion in the American South. The journal is sponsored by the Association for the Study of Southern Religion, with assistance from Florida State University and Louisiana State University.

Journal of the Association for History and Computing

http://mcel.pacificu.edu/JAHC/JAHCindex.htm

JAHC advances interest in the innovative use of computers and new media in the teaching, researching, and publishing of history. The primary journal of the American Association for History and Computing, it has been published three times a year since 1998 and caters to an audience of scholars, teachers, and history enthusiasts.

Limina

http://www.arts.uwa.edu.au/limina/index.html

Limina is published by faculty and postgraduate students in the Discipline of History at the University of Western Australia. Published annually since 1995, articles are available online in PDF format.

Media History Monographs

http://www.elon.edu/dcopeland/mhm/mhm.htm

MHM, which publishes scholarship on the history of journalism and media, is sponsored by Ohio University School of Journalism and the School of Communications, Elon University, North Carolina. The site has published issues biannually from 1998 to 2001 and annually from 2001 to 2005. *MHM* devotes itself to publishing works of scholarship that are too lengthy for journal articles, but not large enough to be considered books.

Michigan Journal of History

http://www.umich.edu/~historyj/index.html

Michigan Journal of History is a student-run journal that publishes research by undergraduate students. Published annually since 2001, the journal is sponsored by the Department of History at the University of Michigan.

Mirator

http://www.cc.jyu.fi/mirator/

Mirator is an academic, peer-reviewed journal on medieval studies. The journal is sponsored by the Department of History and Ethnology, University of Jyväskylä, Finland.

Nordic Notes

http://www.ssn.flinders.edu.au/scanlink/nornotes/index.php

Published annually since 1997, *Nordic Notes* contains peer-reviewed articles, reviews, and editorials on all aspects of Scandinavian studies.

The North American Journal of Welsh Studies

http://spruce.flint.umich.edu/~ellisjs/journal.html

This journal contains work presented originally at conferences sponsored by the North American Association for the Study of Welsh Culture and History. The journal has published four issues since 2001.

The North Star: A Journal of African American Religious History

http://northstar.as.uky.edu

Sponsored by the University of Kentucky and the American Academy of Religion, *North Star* publishes work by senior and junior scholars on all aspects of the history of African-American religion. The journal also highlights new publications, research, and resources related to African-American religion.

Ohio History

http://publications.ohiohistory.org/ohstemplate.cfm?action=intro

Ohio History is the journal of the Ohio Historical Society. All volumes of *Ohio History* since 1887 are available.

Screening the Past

http://www.latrobe.edu.au/screeningthepast/

Screening the Past publishes academic work on visual media and history. The journal was created in December 2004 and features an international "cast" of editors and contributors.

Signs: Electronic Edition

http://www.journals.uchicago.edu/Signs/journal/home.html

Published by the University of Chicago Press, *Signs* is a peer-reviewed journal focusing on women's studies.

Studies on Asia

http://www.isp.msu.edu/studiesonasia/

Studies on Asia is published by the Asian Studies Center at Michigan State University and sponsored by the Midwest Conference on Asian Affairs. The journal features academic work on Asian history and culture, translations, poetry and prose, and pedagogical commentary.

Chapter 36

Libraries

Jessie Bishop Powell, Merriman

Library of Congress

Library of Congress

Library of Congress http://www.loc.gov

Library of Congress catalog http://catalog.loc.gov/

Library of Congress authorities http://authorities.loc.gov/

The Library of Congress's Web page provides a digital gateway to a variety of online collections and government sites, including the U.S. Copyright Office. The Library of Congress collects in all areas *except* medicine and technical agriculture. Most items are available through interlibrary loan.

On the Web site, researchers can search the library's holdings, including some links to digitized materials. Basic searching allows standard library searches, including title, author, and International Standard Book Numbering (ISBN). A more specific guided search allows for Boolean and index limits. Searchers, particularly historians, should be aware that many materials cataloged before 1980, while available to the public, are not represented in the digital catalog. Some collections are represented with collection level catalog records only, meaning that individual items within the collections are not shown in the online catalog.

Metasites (American and Worldwide)

East Asian Libraries Cooperative

http://pears.lib.ohio-state.edu/

A project of Ohio State University, this catalog aims to support researchers interested in East Asia.

ETANA: Electronic Tools and Ancient Near Eastern Archives

http://www.etana.org/

ETANA is the project of several American Oriental studies programs, funded by the Andrew W. Mellon Foundation and a National Science Foundation grant. In addition to housing the Abzu database for studies of the Near East, ETANA also contains digitized versions of some of the core texts for ancient Near East studies and a digital library with archaeological data.

National Libraries of the World

http://www.publiclibraries.com/world.htm

Contains links to many nations' public libraries.

Public Libraries.com

http://www.publiclibraries.com/

Lists contact information, including Web sites, for many U.S. public libraries. The section is organized by state and includes links to metasites for state and presidential libraries (below).

Presidential Libraries

http://www.publiclibraries.com/presidential_library.htm

Lists contact information, including Web sites, for all eleven presidential libraries.

RLG

http://www.rlg.org/

Research libraries belonging to RLG (RedLightGreen) offer digital and print access to a variety of collections. The RLIN (Research Libraries Information Network) database has been frozen and replaced by RLIN21, and these catalogs are both accessible only to members. However, the Web site also offers links to a variety of research-oriented articles and the RedLightGreen research database, which is available to the general public.

State Libraries

http://www.publiclibraries.com/state_library.htm

Lists contact information for most official state libraries.

Yale's Other Libraries Page

http://www.library.yale.edu/orbis/othercats.html

Though designed for Yale students, this page represents an excellent collection of library and research links, including information about Yale's Special Catalogs and a link to the Center for Research Libraries (CRL).

American Libraries and Collections

American Memory: Historical Collections of the National Digital Library

http://memory.loc.gov/ammem/index.html

American Memory contains items that the Library of Congress considers important to U.S. cultural history. The most recently cataloged records have the highest-level information, while older collections may have less detailed information online. Most collections are searchable and many have finding aids such as subject and author lists.

The Beinecke Library

Beinecke library home page: http://www.library.yale.edu/beinecke/

ORBIS: http://orbis.library.yale.edu/

Searchable through ORBIS, Yale's online catalog, the Beinecke Library, Yale's rare books and manuscripts library, also offers access to its events and educational programs, as well as searcher tips on its own home page.

CRL: The Center for Research Libraries

http://www.crl.edu/catalog/index.htm

A consortium of college and university libraries from all over the United States, CRL holds materials important to researchers that librarians could no longer keep on their own institutions' shelves. Member libraries and their patrons may access these materials. Currently, 98 percent of the nearly 5 million entries in the CRL's catalog are available online, including books, newspapers, serials, microforms, archival collections, and other research materials.

The Getty Research Institute for the History of Art and the Humanities

http://opac.pub.getty.edu

Collections available in the Getty include Western art, archaeology, and architecture from the Bronze Age to the present. There are also extensive collections on the conservation of cultural heritage and historic preservation and an unparalleled auction catalog collection with more than 110,000 volumes of materials from the late seventeenth century to the present. Included in the Special Collections are artists' journals and sketchbooks, albums, architectural drawings, early guidebooks, emblem books, prints, and drawings. The Getty Collection's strengths are French, German, Russian, Italian, and American avant-garde materials, futurism, Dada, surrealism, the Bauhaus, Russian constructivism, and Fluxus. Many items from the research library are available for interlibrary loan.

The Hagley Library

http://www.hagley.lib.de.us/

Located in Deleware, the Hagley Museum and Library's focus is American business and technological history.

The Kinsey Institute for Research in Sex, Gender and Reproduction

http://www.indiana.edu/~kinsey/

Collections searchable via KICAT at Indiana University catalog (IUCat): http://www.iucat.iu.edu/

KICAT does not contain records for all items in the Kinsey library, nor does it contain records for the institute's art and archival collections. Records are continually being added to the online catalog as part of the library's retrospective conversion project. For help in using the library's holdings of sex-related magazines, films and videos, newspapers and tabloids, pulp fiction, and books still cataloged according to Dr. Kinsey's system of categories, users must consult with library staff.

Labriola National American Indian Data Center at Arizona State University

Labriola: http://www.asu.edu/lib/archives/labriola.htm

ASU's online catalog: http://catalog.lib.asu.edu/

The Labriola National American Indian Data Center, part of the ASU Libraries, brings together current and historic government, culture, religion and worldview, social life and customs, tribal history, and information on individuals from the United States, Canada, Sonora, and Chihuahua, Mexico. All materials held by the center are searchable via ASU's online catalog.

The Library Company of Philadelphia

http://www.librarycompany.org/

Founded in 1731 by Benjamin Franklin, the Library Company of Philadelphia has over half a million items covering American history and culture from the seventeenth to the nineteenth century. The online catalog, WolfPAC, currently has nearly 100 percent of the library's rare book collection and roughly 10,000 graphic materials. It also includes records from the union catalog of the Philadelphia Area Consortium of Special Collections Libraries (PACSCL): the Academy of Natural Sciences, the Balch Institute for Ethnic Studies, Saint Charles Borromeo Seminary, the Philadelphia Museum of Art, the Rosenbach Museum and Library, the Presbyterian Historical Society, the Athenaeum, and the Historical Society of Pennsylvania. Several other PACSCL member libraries have, or will soon have, catalogs available through the PACSCL Web site or through their individual institution's Web site. These include the American Philosophical Society, the Free Library of Philadelphia, the University of Pennsylvania, Winterthur, the Hagley Museum and Library, Temple University, the College of Physicians of Philadelphia, the Wagner Free Institute of Science, Bryn Mawr, Haverford, and Swarthmore.

The Lilly Library

http://www.indiana.edu/~liblilly/

Searchable at the Indiana University Catalog (IUCat): http://www.iucat.iu.edu

The Lilly Library's online resources include searchable indexes of the manuscript collections, chapbook collection, and French Revolution documents.

National Center for Education Statistics

http://nces.ed.gov/

The National Center for Education Statistics offers digital access to many of its reports and selected publications at this address.

The Newberry Library

http://www.newberry.org/nl/collections/virtua.html

Currently, about 20 percent of the Newberry Library's collection is searchable. Online records exist for materials cataloged by the library since 1978. (This includes some materials published before 1978, but cataloged later by the library.) Starting in 2004, the library began a retrospective conversion from catalog cards to online MARC records for approximately 725,000 items.

The New York Public Library

http://catnyp.nypl.org/

CATNYP is the online catalog of the Research Libraries of The New York Public Library. This catalog includes nearly 2 million records for materials added to the collections before 1972 and nearly 2 million records for materials added to the collection after that time. A very few items are still only to be located in catalog cards or retrospective collections. Publisher G.K. Hall's 800-volume *Dictionary Catalog of The Research Libraries* is one such retrospective catalog.

OhioLink

http://www.ohiolink.edu

This is the communal catalog for all libraries (public, private, college, and university) in Ohio.

Online Archive of California

http://www.oac.cdlib.org/

This site is a compilation of items contributed to the California Archives, including the Bancroft Library, and the California Heritage Digital Image Access Database.

RedLightGreen

http://www.redlightgreen.com

A project of the RLG corporation, and a massive searchable database, RedLightGreen is currently available to the general public (unlike RLIN and RLIN21) and offers a search of over 120 million books, and tells whether they are at your local library.

The Schlesinger Library, Radcliffe College

http://www.radcliffe.edu/schles/

http://holliscatalog.harvard.edu/

The Schlesinger Library is the foremost library on the history of women in America. Its holdings of audiovisual materials, books, ephemera, manuscripts, oral histories, periodicals, and photographs document the social history of women in the United States, primarily during the nineteenth and twentieth centuries—including the recently acquired papers of the late chef Julia Child. It is searchable via Harvard's online catalog, HOLLIS. To search for manuscript and archival collections, users should choose the Expanded Search option in HOLLIS.

Schomburg Center for Research in Black Culture

http://www.nypl.org/research/sc/sc.html

(Holdings searchable via CATNYP, the New York Public Library catalog, http://catnyp.nypl.org)

The Schomburg Center for Research in Black Culture is a national research library devoted to collecting, preserving, and providing access to resources documenting the experiences of peoples of African descent throughout the world. The center provides access to, and professional reference assistance in, the use of its collections to the scholarly community and the general public through five research divisions. The center's collections include art objects, audio and videotapes, books, manuscripts, motion picture films, newspapers, periodicals, photographs, prints, recorded music discs, and sheet music.

University of Oklahoma Western History Collections

Library catalog: http://libraries.ou.edu/eresources/catalog/

Western History Collection: http://libraries.ou.edu/info/info.asp?id=22

This collection aims to provide research opportunities into the development of the Trans-Mississippi West and Native American cultures. Catalog information for many of the materials within the Western History Collections may be accessed through the University of Oklahoma Libraries online catalog. Inventories of several individual collections can be found at the library's Western History Collections page.

Ten Largest Research Libraries in the United States*

1. Harvard University
http://hollisweb.harvard.edu/

2. Yale University
http://orbis.library.yale.edu/

3. University of Illinois at Urbana-Champaign
http://www.library.uiuc.edu/

4. University of Texas at Austin
http://utdirect.utexas.edu/lib/utnetcat/

5. University of California at Berkeley
Bancroft Library (GLADIS): http://sunsite5.berkeley.edu:8000/

UC Berkeley Library Guide: http://www.lib.berkeley.edu/Catalogs/guide.html

6. University of California at Los Angeles
http://www2.1ibrary.ucla.edu/

7. University of Michigan, Ann Arbor
http://www.lib.umich.edu

8. Stanford University
http://jenson.stanford.edu

9. Columbia University
CLIO: http://www.columbia.edu/cu/lweb/

Pegasus: http://pegasus.law.columbia.edu/

EduCat: http://educat.tc.columbia.edu/

Library of the Jewish Theological Seminary: http://alpha3.jtsa.edu:4525/F

*Digest of Education Statistics, U.S. Department of Education. National Center for Education Statistics, 2002, 492, table 420.

10. The University of Chicago

http://www.uic.edu/depts/lib/

Selected Worldwide Libraries
and Collections

ABZU: Oriental Institute Research Archives

http://www.etana.org/abzu/

Rebuilt in partnership with ETANA (Electronic Tools and Ancient Near Eastern Archives), ABZU is a guide to resources for the study of the ancient Near East. Created, compiled, and updated by Charles E. Jones, research archivist at the Oriental Institute's Research Archives at the University of Chicago, the catalog consists of primary and secondary indexes of information.

Bibliothèque Nationale de France

http://www.bnf.fr/

Home page of the French National Library, in French, with an English gateway under construction. The above link is to the summary page for all four catalogs, including GALLICA—an effort to chronicle nineteenth-century France through digitized images and sound.

British Library Integrated Catalogue

http://catalogue.bl.uk/

Manuscript catalog: http://www.bl.uk/catalogues/manuscripts.html

British Library Integrated Catalogue provides access to the major catalogs of the British Library in London and Boston Spa. The collections include humanities, social science, hard science, and technology. There are also business collections cataloged from 1975 to the present, as well as all music cataloged from 1980 to the present and all humanities reference materials cataloged before 1975 (including the archives and materials of the former India Office and colonial Africa). In the older reference materials, the appearance of "D-" before items means the original was destroyed during World War II and has since been replaced. Finally, all serials from 1700 to the present are included in the catalog.

EuroDocs: Primary Historical Documents From Western Europe

http://www.lib.byu.edu/~rdh/eurodocs/

Compiled by Richard Hacken, a librarian at Brigham Young University, this list of links connects to Western European (mainly primary) historical documents that are transcribed, reproduced and, in some cases, translated.

Japan's National Diet Library

http://www.ndl.go.jp/en/index.html

This site offers English-language access to Japan's National Diet Library Web page. It contains links to both Japanese-only and English-language searches of its catalog.

The National Archives—UK

http://www.nationalarchives.gov.uk

Britain's national archives Web site is searchable online. Some documents have been scanned into the site and are viewable via the DocumentsOnline link. There is also a catalog of immigration into Britain in the last 200 years at the MovingHere link, as well as access to documents from the Macmillan government of 1957–1963, digital datasets collections, and collections related to medieval and early modern taxation.

The National Library of China

http://www.nlc.gov.cn/english.htm

Non–Chinese-speaking visitors to this site submit questions to librarians who then search for the information. The site, which is fully searchable in English, explains the collections of China's National Library. Regrettably, English-speaking visitors cannot search the library's actual collections.

OLIS—Oxford's Bodleian Library

http://www.bodley.ox.ac.uk/

OLIS, Oxford University Library's online catalog:
http://www.lib.ox.ac.uk/olis/

The library is searchable through OLIS, Oxford University Library's online catalog. Most materials found in the Bodleian Library are available for inter-library loan.

Chapter 37

Archives and Manuscript Collections

Donnelly Lancaster

Information for Researchers

Introduction to Archives

http://www.umich.edu/~bhl/bhl/refhome/refintro.htm

This Web page is a brief, general introduction to archives and manuscript materials. It clearly states in the text that it provides helpful, basic information for those researchers unfamiliar with special collections. Hyperlinks provide examples of materials and additional information on researching at the library.

Library Research Using Primary Sources

http://www.lib.berkeley.edu/TeachingLib/Guides/PrimarySources.html

This site is a comprehensive, detailed introduction to archives and manuscript use. Not only does it answer the question "What Are Primary Sources?" but it also provides step-by-step strategies and instructions that patrons can use to find the information they seek.

Primary Sources at Yale

http://www.library.yale.edu/instruction/primsource.html

This site contains a detailed introduction to finding primary sources along with instructions. Tailored to the Yale University library resources, it includes finding aids to collections. It also contains information on how to use bibliographic tools and gives links to comprehensive lists of such tools available at Yale's Sterling Library.

Using Archives: A Practical Guide for Researchers

http://www.collectionscanada.ca/04/0416_e.html

This is found on the National Archives of Canada or Library and Archives Canada Web site. It is listed as an online publication. Unlike some of the other sources listed in this chapter, this resource contains more narrative description and instruction than lists, tables, and bibliographies.

Information for Archivists

Archives of the Archivist Listserv

http://listserv.muohio.edu/archives/archives.html

This site contains the archives of the Archives Listserv, maintained by the Society of American Archivists. The listserv is an open forum for discussion about archival issues. The archives Web site contains postings dating back to 1993. A search option allows users to search by date, subject, or author.

Archives Resource Center

http://www.coshrc.org/arc/index.htm

Sponsored by the Council of State Historical Records Coordinators, the Web site contains information and links to educational programs, state archives, and other facilities, training available on the Web, and programs that educate on the use of primary sources. In addition, it contains lists, with Web sites when available, of a variety of information useful to archivists and those interested in the profession, including lists of archival associations, state agencies, forms used by institutions, and fees charged by institutions for services.

CoOL Conservation OnLine

http://palimpsest.stanford.edu/

The result of a project of the Preservation Department of Stanford University Libraries, this Web site contains vast resources on conservation and related issues. Resources may be searched by author name or by subject. Users are invited to submit additional resources.

Introduction to Archival Organization and Description: Access to Cultural Heritage

http://www.getty.edu/research/conducting_research/standards/introarchives/

An excellent resource for students or those new to the archival profession, this site provides a concise, step-by-step introduction to archival theory and work. An excellent section on processing provides the reader with an over-the-shoulder view of this often mentioned and rarely disseminated piece of the archival workflow. Maintained on the Getty Institute Web site and funded by the J. Paul Getty Trust, the Web site was created by prominent members of the American archival community.

Society of American Archivists

http://www.archivists.org/

The Society of American Archivists is the preeminent organization for archivists in the United States. Its Web site contains information about the organization itself and its activities, as well as online resources for education, employment, and publications.

Archives, Manuscripts, and
Special Collections

Metasites

ArchiveNet

http://www.archiefnet.nl/index.asp?taal=en

Maintained by the Historical Centre Overijssel, this site focuses on the Netherlands and Flanders, providing links to repositories in provinces and towns there.

In addition, the site provides links to repositories around the world. The site is primarily in Dutch with sections in English.

Gabriel: The Gateway to Europe's National Libraries

http://www.kb.nl/gabriel/index.html

Launched as a pilot project in 1995, this metasite for forty-three libraries from forty-one member nations in the Conference of European National Librarians allows users to search the collections of all libraries. There are links to each of the forty-three libraries' Web sites along with the language option for each site. In addition, the site contains additional information about the national libraries of Europe, including online exhibits and a news bulletin board dating to 1995.

Guide to the Archives of Intergovernmental Organizations

http://www.unesco.org/archives/guide/uk/index.html

A joint project of the United Nations Educational, Scientific and Cultural Organization (UNESCO) and the International Council on Archives, Section of Archivists of International Organizations, this Web site contains a list of the archives of about eighty intergovernmental organizations. A history of the organization, description of materials held, and rules and guidelines for archival use and access are among the information provided about each archive.

Ready, 'Net, Go! Archival Internet Resources

http://www.tulane.edu/~lmiller/ArchivesResources.html

Created and maintained by Tulane University's Howard-Tilton Library's Special Collections Division, this metasite is clear, concise, and easy to use. Its introductory language is geared to a general audience, and the site contains links to archival resources on the Net, organized by category.

Repositories of Primary Resources

http://www.uidaho.edu/special-collections/Other.Repositories.html

Maintained by Terry Abraham, head of Special Collections and Archives at the University of Idaho, this site contains lists of links to other repositories around the world. The sites are arranged by geographic region. In addition, there are lists of Web sites for organizations, other metasites, and other useful sites for archivists and researchers. Updated monthly, this is an excellent starting point for any researcher seeking primary sources.

Area Specific Sites

Africa

Africa Research Central: A Clearinghouse of African Primary Sources

http://www.africa-research.org/

Sponsored by California State University, Fullerton, this Web site includes a searchable database of libraries, museums, and archives in Africa. Users may search by country, type of repository, repository name, material sought, or keyword within the holdings description. Users may also browse through repository links and descriptions alphabetically by country. In addition, the institutions have a searchable database of their preservation wish lists.

Africa South of the Sahara: Libraries/Archives

http://www-sul.stanford.edu/depts/ssrg/africa/libs.html

Sponsored by the Stanford University Library, this metasite contains links to Internet resources related to Africa and is organized by both country and topic. Within the topical index, the links are annotated and contain valuable information for researchers. In addition, the site is searchable. Researchers interested in Africa should consult this site before venturing further.

Schomburg Center for Research in Black Culture

http://www.nypl.org/research/sc/sc.html

Located at the New York Public Library, the Schomburg Center contains vast holdings related to African-Americans. Its excellent Web site offers online exhibits, a large number of finding aids to its manuscript collections, searchable access to digital images of its visual holdings, and an online catalog for its books.

Asia and the Pacific

Directory of Archives in Australia

http://www.archivists.org.au/directory/asa_dir.htm

Maintained by the Australian Society of Archivists, this is a directory of archival repositories in Australia.

National Archives of Japan

http://www.archives.go.jp/index_e.html

An excellent Web site for those researching Japanese history and interested in the archives' holdings, this site offers an introduction for first-time users to the site and to archives in general. Finding aids to collections are available and easy to use, as are digital images.

National Archives of Singapore

http://www.museum.org.sg/NAS/nas.shtml

This user-friendly Web site should be the first stop for those interested in Singapore's history. The site's features make it easy to search different collections and types of materials, including online exhibits. The site provides easy access to Web sites of the other members of the National Heritage Board, including the Singapore History Museum, Singapore Art Museum, Heritage Conservation Centre, and Asian Civilizations Museum.

Canada

Canada Archival Resources on the Internet

http://www.archivescanada.ca/english/index.html

Developed and maintained by the Canadian Council of Archives, this Web site is geared toward a wide audience, from a school-age child doing a report for class to a scholar doing research. A search engine allows the user to search for material across Canada. Search results include information about collections along with physical location of material and any digital material available. Users may also view online exhibits and search for digitized material. Available in French and English.

Europe—Eastern

PIASA Archival Information Center

http://www.piasa.org/archives.html

This Web site is part of the Polish Institute of Arts and Sciences of America, Inc. (PIASA) Web site. PIASA does not hold archives collections itself, but the Archival Information Center provides links to archival collections around the world relating to Polish history.

Slavic and Eastern European Library, University of Illinois Urbana-Champaign

http://www.library.uiuc.edu/spx/

Although the library holds more than 670,000 volumes related to Slavic and Eastern European countries, the archives and manuscripts held by the library are hard to find on the main library's Web site. A link to the Russian and Eastern European Library (http://web.library.uiuc.edu/ahx/russia/russia.htm) identifies archives and manuscripts related to Russia and other former Soviet Union countries. Links to Internet resources by country contain links to Web sites administered by repositories and agencies in those countries rather than holdings at the Slavic and Eastern European Library. This is an excellent gateway to Eastern European archives and manuscripts.

Slovene Archives

http://www.pokarh-mb.si/index.php?is=2&L=1&L=2

The introductory page is in English and provides only a small amount of information about the archive and its holdings. The introduction page also links to a database searchable in Slovenian only.

Europe—Western

Archives Hub

http://www.archiveshub.ac.uk/

An excellent source for finding archival materials from colleges and universities throughout the United Kingdom, the Hub provides helpful information about everything from the site itself to a glossary of archival terms. The Hub, developed and maintained by representatives from different archives in the United Kingdom, allows users to search the almost 190,000 descriptions of holdings in ninety colleges and repositories in the United Kingdom.

Archives in Germany

http://home.bawue.de/~hanacek/info/earchive.htm

This helpful site about archival resources in Germany provides users with a glossary of terms they might encounter while doing online research, as well as links to different Web sites for repositories in Germany.

ARCHON Archives Online

http://www.archon.nationalarchives.gov.uk/archon/

This is the Web site of the National Archives of the United Kingdom. The Web site includes numerous search mechanisms that allow the user to search for a variety of records, including census records, wills, tax records, and cabinet records. Searching the records is free, but there is a small fee to see some records.

Bundesarchiv Online

http://www.bundesarchiv.de/

This site is in the German language only; the English version is under construction.

Latin America

Benson Latin American Collection, University of Texas at Austin

http://www.lib.utexas.edu/benson/

The Benson Latin American Collection holds materials about Latin America and Latinos in the United States. The Web site contains online exhibits of digital materials. Users may browse through finding aids for manuscript collections and search the online catalog for other materials in the Benson Collection's holdings.

H-LatAm Archives

http://www.h-net.org/~latam/archives/

Displayed partially in Spanish and English, this site contains information about holdings and access to more than twenty repositories.

Latin American Library Tulane University

http://lal.tulane.edu/

The Web site contains a list of manuscript collections, along with finding aids for a portion of the collections.

Military History and Peace Collections

Hoover Institution on War, Revolution, and Peace Library and Archives

http://www-hoover.stanford.edu/hila/

This Web site provides users with access to complete finding aids to a wide variety of manuscript collections dealing with the military, politics, war, and peace around the world.

National Archives and Records Administration (NARA)

http://www.archives.gov/

The National Archives holds vast resources documenting the activities of all branches of the U.S. armed forces.

Swarthmore College Peace Collection

http://www.swarthmore.edu/Library/peace/

This Web site contains access to lists of manuscript collections, photographic collections, artifacts, and other collections. Some of these lists include links to complete finding aids. In addition, the site includes links to repositories with similar collections.

U.S. Army Military History Institute

http://carlisle-www.army.mil/usamhi/

This institute holds unofficial historical records relating to the U.S. Army. The Web site contains descriptions of its archival holdings. In addition, the site contains links to similar repositories for other branches of the armed forces.

Virginia Military Institute Archives

http://www.vmi.edu/archives/

The VMI Archives Web site provides researchers with access to some of their 450 manuscript collections. These collections include personal papers of military personnel who served in the nineteenth and twentieth centuries. The lists of manuscript collections include descriptions, and many have online finding aids and/or digital images of the collections themselves.

Russia and the Former Soviet Union

Estonian Historical Archives

http://www.eha.ee/

Users may choose to read the English version of the Web site, which provides a catalog and other databases for searching the archives' holdings. Some of the databases, however, are offered only in Estonian.

National Library of Russia

http://www.nlr.ru:8101/eng/

Most of the materials that users may access on this site are current published materials rather than manuscripts and archives. There is a database, however, for eighteenth- and nineteenth-century books. In addition, the site contains a link to the Virtual Reference Library, which has links to repositories in other former Soviet states.

State Archives of Latvia

http://www.arhivi.lv/engl/en-lvas-frame.htm

This Web site is in English with searchable databases of its holdings in a mixture of Latvian and English.

United States

Congressional Collections at Archival Repositories

http://www.archives.gov/records_of_congress/repository_collections/

Provides users with links to archival repositories that hold congressional collections. These links are arranged by repository, state, and congressional member's name.

The Library of Congress

http://www.loc.gov/

The largest library in the world, the Library of Congress holds over 128 million items. Funded by the United States Congress, the library is the oldest federal cultural institution in the country. The American Memory collection, which makes available to users over 5 million items online, is an excellent resource for those interested in research using primary sources.

National Archives and Records Administration

http://www.archives.gov/

The National Archives, which holds the nation's official records and those of its federal officials, has a Web site offering excellent resources for researchers of all ages. In addition, the National Archives directs the presidential library program. Its Web site includes searchable catalogs providing access to vast sources documenting American history.

Presidential Libraries

http://www.archives.gov/presidential_libraries/

Contains information about the presidential libraries and links to the individual libraries' Web sites.

State Archives and Historical Societies

http://www.ohiohistory.org/textonly/links/arch_hs.html

A list of state archives and historical societies' Web pages.

Topic Specific Sites

African-Americans

African American Archives, Manuscripts, and Special Collections

http://www2.1ib.udel.edu/subj/blks/internet/afamarc.htm

This University of Delaware Library Web site includes an excellent list of links to repositories holding African-American collections.

Amistad Research Center

http://www.amistadresearchcenter.org/

Located at Tulane University in New Orleans, the Amistad Research Center holds materials related primarily to African-Americans, as well as other minority groups in the United States. Its holdings are significant, but only a few finding aids to these holdings are available on the Web site at present. There is a list of manuscript collections.

Moorland Spingarn Research Center, Howard University

http://www.founders.howard.edu/moorland-spingarn/

Located at Howard University, Washington, DC, this center's holdings include 175,000 volumes, thousands of journals, 17,000 feet of manuscript and archival materials, and about 100,000 prints, photographs, and maps relating to African-American history. The site, however, does not provide information about any of these holdings.

Sexuality

Human Sexuality Collection, Cornell University

http://rmc.library.cornell.edu/HSC/

The Web site contains descriptions and links to finding aids for numerous manuscript collections. Users may search for published material through the online catalog. In addition, there are lists of available periodicals and helpful annotated bibliographies that describe and highlight some of their books.

Kinsey Institute for Research, Indiana University

http://www.indiana.edu/~kinsey/

The Web site contains information about some of the Kinsey Institute's manuscript, archive, art, photography, film, and video collections. The Web site also has a searchable catalog, but this does not contain records for all of their holdings.

United States Immigration History

California Ethnic and Multicultural Archives (CEMA), University of California Santa Barbara

http://cemaweb.library.ucsb.edu/cema_index.html

This Web site includes information about manuscript collections, arranged by ethnicity, including African-American, Asian/Pacific American, Chicano/Latino, and Native American. Some collections have brief descriptions of a few words, while others contain links to complete finding aids along with digital images. Users can also follow links to the Online Archive of California for additional finding aids. In addition, the Web site includes excellent links to other related collections in the United States.

Chicano Research Collection, Arizona State University

http://www.asu.edu/lib/archives/chicano.htm

The collection focuses on Mexican-Americans in Arizona and the Southwest, and the Web site contains descriptions of some manuscript collections. Online exhibits featuring digital images illuminate the Mexican-American experience. Links to other web resources for Mexican-American history make this Web site a must for users researching Mexican-Americans.

Immigration History Research Center, University of Minnesota

http://www.ihrc.umn.edu/

This Web site features a user-friendly search engine for searching descriptions of the collections, or the user can browse through an alphabetical list of collections. Users may also search a separate database of images. The Web site includes a helpful list of links to other Web sites for similar collections.

Women

Archives for Research on Women and Gender, University of Texas, San Antonio

http://www.lib.utsa.edu/Archives/WomenGender/

The collections housed here focus on women and gender issues in south Texas. An annotated guide to resources around the United States and the world makes this site stand out.

The Arthur and Elizabeth Schlesinger Library on the History of Women in America, Harvard University

http://www.radcliffe.edu/schles/index.php

The library holds over 2,500 manuscript collections in women's history. Although users cannot browse through lists of collections, the online catalog on the Web site provides access to finding aids for some of the collections.

Sallie Bingham Center for Women's History and Culture, Duke University

http://scriptorium.lib.duke.edu/women/

This Web site contains helpful information about the Bingham Center's holdings, including annotated subject guides to resources.

Sophia Smith Collection, Smith College

http://www.smith.edu/libraries/libs/ssc/home.html

The Web site gives access to finding aids not only from the Sophia Smith Collection, but also links to the Five College Finding Aid Database, which holds over 900 finding aids from Smith College, Mt. Holyoke College, Amherst College, Hampshire College, and the University of Massachusetts Amherst. The Smith Collection Web site also provides subject lists of manuscript collections in its holdings. Links to other women's history resources on the Web make this a valuable site for researchers.

Chapter 38

Special Collections

Anne Rothfeld

Metasites

ARCHON: Archives On-Line

http://www.archon.nationalarchives.gov.uk/archon/

The main gateway to repositories with manuscript material for British history, ARCHON is a key British resource for both archivists and researchers. The Royal Commission on Historical Manuscripts maintains the site. Researchers will be most interested in the British National Register of Archives (NRA). The NRA leads researchers to a wide variety of manuscript collections, including papers of individuals of note, estates, local authorities, and societies, located both inside and outside the United Kingdom. Users may search the indexes by name of individual or corporate body, type of corporate body, and place name.

Gateway to Library Catalogs

http://lcweb.loc.gov/z3950/

This important search gateway will lead the researcher to descriptions of holdings for a large number of manuscript and archival repositories, predominantly, but not exclusively, in the United States. Select from one of three straightforward, fill-in-the-blank search forms. This electronic catalog derives from the print source, the *National Union Catalog of Manuscript Collections*, a project of the Library of Congress. Check the List of RLIN Library Identifiers on the search forms to see a list of the participating institutions.

Repositories of Primary Sources

http://www.uidaho.edu/special-collections/Other.Repositories.html

With over 5,000 links, this Web site is by far the most complete listing of Web sites for actual (not virtual) archives and special collections departments. Updated frequently by Terry Abraham of the University of Idaho, the site arranges its links by geographical region (continent, country, state, and province). Additional Lists is a good jumping-off point for other archive and special collections metasites.

UK Archival Repositories on the Internet

http://www.archivesinfo.net/uksites.html

Originating out of a University of London master's project by Simon Wilson, this site—mainly targeted at archivists—provides two important listings of archival links useful to researchers: UK Archival Repositories on the Internet and Overseas Archival Repositories on the Internet. One of the best features of these lists is the annotations prepared by the site's author, briefly indicating each site's contents.

UNESCO Archives Portal

http://portal.unesco.org/ci/en/ev.php-URL_ID=5761&URL _DO=DO_TOPIC&URL_SECTION=201.html

Not nearly as complete as Terry Abraham's Repositories of Primary Sources, this UNESCO site is worth knowing about for the important role UNESCO plays in helping archives around the world. This listing of over 4,000 links covers archives in Europe, North America, Latin America, Asia, and the Pacific as well as international archival organizations, professional associations, archival training, international cooperation, and Internet resources.

General Sites

Africa Research Central: A Clearinghouse of African Primary Sources

http://www.africa-research.org

A collaboration between a history professor and an academic librarian at California State University, San Bernardino, this site assists researchers to locate often scarce information about archives, libraries, and museums with primary source collections related to Africa. The site focuses on repositories in Africa, but also provides information for those in Europe and North America. An important mission of the site is to alert researchers to the preservation crisis under way in many countries in Africa and indicate ways to help. The Web site is available in French.

American Memory: Historical Collections for the National Digital Library

http://lcweb2.loc.gov/ammem/

Over one hundred multimedia collections containing over 9 million digitized documents, photographs, recorded sound, moving pictures, and text selected from the Library of Congress's vast Americana holdings cover topics as diverse as twentieth-century architectural design and ballroom dancing. The collections may be searched by keyword or browsed by titles, topics, or collection type. A fun spin-off is Today in History, which presents people, facts, and events associated with the current day's date. Finally, educators are particularly targeted in the Learning Page with activities, lesson ideas, and other information to help teachers use the primary source material at American Memory in their classrooms.

Annuaire des archives et des bibliothèque nationales, des bibliothèque parlementaires et des centres nationaux d'information scientifique et technique de la Francophonie

http://www.bief.org

This directory, originally published in print form in 1996, has been converted into a searchable Web database by the publishers, Canadian-based BIEF (Banque internationale d'information sur les États francophones). The directory includes basic contact information for the national archives and libraries of forty-seven francophone countries. Further descriptive information about many of the listed institutions can be found in a BIEF companion Web site, titled Profis géo-documentaires des états et gouvernements membres des sommets francophones. Together, these databases are an important source of scarce information about archives for many small, non-Western countries. The Web site is available in French and English.

Archives and Knowledge Management: Scholarly Online Resource Evidence and Records

http://www.dcn.davis.ca.us/~vctinney/archives.htm

Created and maintained by V. Chris and Thomas M. Tinney Sr., retired genealogical specialists, this Web site includes links to resources of particular interest to genealogists, such as Genealogy on the Web and the Salt Lake City LDS Family History Center. The Tinney Family organizes links to archives, libraries, and many other types of resources in a variety of categories, from Business and Community and Geography to Religion and Surnames.

Archives in Deutschland

http://www.uni-marburg.de/archivschule/deuarch.html

This list of archival resources, maintained by Dr. Karsten Uhde of the Archivschule Marburg in Germany, brings together links of interest to both archivists and researchers. Historians and genealogists will find the following pages particularly useful: Archives in Germany, listing German archives by type (state, city, church, etc.); Archives in Europe; Non-European Archives; and Genealogy.

Archives of American Art

http://americanart.si.edu/museum_info/index.cfm

The Smithsonian maintains the Archives of American Art (AAA) and its Web site to provide researchers with access to "the largest collection of documents on the history of the visual arts in the United States." With 13 million items, including the papers of artists, dealers, critics, art historians, museums, and art-related organizations of all kinds, the Smithsonian's claim can easily be believed. The letters, sketchbooks, diaries, and other paper archives are supplemented with a large oral history interview collection and a sizable photograph collection. General collection descriptions of AAA treasures can be found in the Smithsonian online catalog (SIRIS) as well as RLIN, and the Smithsonian is beginning to make more detailed finding aids available as well.

Archives of Traditional Music at Indiana University

http://www.indiana.edu/~libarchm/

A Web site that provides information about an important and unusual archive of ethnographic sound materials housed at Indiana University. The largest such university-based archive in the United States, the Archives of Traditional Music preserves commercial and field recordings of vocal and instrumental music, folktales, interviews, and oral history from the state of Indiana, the United States, and the diverse cultures of the world. Holdings can be searched using Indiana University's online catalog, IUCAT.

ArchivesUSA

http://archives.chadwyck.com/

Chadwyck-Healey Inc. has developed a product that is an important tool for researchers interested in locating archival material in the United States. Although ArchivesUSA is a subscription service and therefore not available for free over the Web, it is an important resource that some libraries and archives make available to the public. ArchivesUSA integrates the entire print edition of the National Union Catalog of Manuscript Collections with other sources of information to create a more complete record for a greater number of repositories than is available through RLIN AMC.

The Avalon Project at Yale Law School: Documents in Law, History and Diplomacy

http://www.yale.edu/lawweb/avalon/avalon.htm

Directed by William C. Fray and Lisa A. Spar, the Avalon Project is a major source of digital primary source documents in the fields of law, history, economics, politics, diplomacy, and government. Access to the documents is by time period (mainly century), author/title, and subject. Major collections include the Nuremberg Trials Collection and the Native American Treaty Collection. A recent addition to the digital repository is the Cuban Missile Crisis and Aftermath section, with over 250 documents (including editorial notes), prefatory essay, and lists of persons and abbreviations—a good example of the Avalon Project's aim to not simply mount static text, but to add value.

Black Film Center/Archive

http://www.indiana.edu/~bfca/

By and about African-Americans, the historic 700 films housed at the Black Film Center/Archive at Indiana University consist of both Hollywood and independent efforts. Supplementing the films and videotapes are interviews, photographs, and other archival material. The Web site gives access to descriptions of the repository's holdings, the Frame by Frame database, and related Internet sites.

Canadian Archival Resources on the Internet

http://www.archivescanada.ca/car/menu.html

A comprehensive list of links to Canadian archives and associated resources on the Internet, this guide is the work of two Canadian archivists: Cheryl Avery of the University of Saskatchewan Archives and Steve Billinton of the Archives of Ontario. Researchers can locate archives by name, type (provincial, university, municipal, religious, and medical), and Canadian region or find links to archival educational resources, associations, listservs, and multirepository databases.

Directory of Archives in Australia

http://www.asap.unimelb.edu.au/asa/directory/asa_dir.htm

The updated Web version of a directory originally printed in 1992, this directory of Australian archives allows researchers to browse archives alphabetically and by Australian states and to search them by keyword. There are also handy lists of links to Australian archives and finding aids on the Web.

Directory of Corporate Archives in the United States and Canada

http://www.hunterinformation.com/corporat.htm

The fifth edition of this important print directory, put out by the Society of American Archivists, Business Archives Section, has recently moved to the Web. From Amgen to Walt Disney Corporation, each corporate archive entry supplies contact information, type of business, hours of service, conditions of access, and holding information. "Corporate" is interpreted broadly and includes "professional associations" ranging from the American Psychiatric Association to the International Longshoreman's Union. The directory may be searched by name of corporation, name of archivist, or geographical location.

DPLS Online Data Archive

http://dpls.dacc.wisc.edu/archive.html

The Data and Program Library Service at the University of Wisconsin is creating access to a large selection of archival machine-readable datasets (raw data and documentation files) that can be downloaded for use by social science researchers. The datasets, listed in reverse chronological order or alphabetically by title, cover raw data from an extremely diverse range of historical and current topics, such as French Old Regime bureaucrats (1661–1790), vegetation change in the Bahamas (1972), and the effects of the Learnfare Program (1993–1996).

EuroDocs: Primary Historical Documents From Western Europe: Selected Transcriptions, Facsimiles and Translations

http://library.byu.edu/~rdh/eurodocs/

Aiming to provide digitized documents that shed light on "key historical happenings" in political, economic, social, and cultural history, EuroDocs links to a wealth of digitized resources organized under twenty-three Western European countries from Andorra to Vatican City. Documents are also accessible from pages devoted to medieval and Renaissance Europe and to Europe as a supernational region. EuroDocs is a project of Richard Hacken, European studies bibliographer, at the Harold B. Lee Library, Brigham Young University in Provo, Utah.

Guía preliminar de fuentes documentales etnográficas para el estudio de los pueblos indígenas de Iberoamérica

http://www.lanic.utexas.edu/project/tavera/

An important guide in the Spanish language, made available on the Web, the Guía describes the holdings related to indigenous peoples at hundreds of libraries and archives throughout Latin America, the United States, and Europe. A project of La Fundación Histérica Tavera in Spain, the Guía is organized by country and type of archive (civil or ecclesiastical) and provides contact information and holdings descriptions for all of the institutions listed.

Historical Maps: The Perry-Castañeda Library Map Collection

http://www.lib.utexas.edu/maps

A wonderful collection of digitized historical maps from all regions of the world offered by the Libraries at the University of Texas at Austin. Maps are organized by continent (including the polar regions and oceans) and each map listing gives both publication information and file size. Although most maps are in JPEG format in the 200 to 300K range, some map files are much larger, so users should expect some slow load times. The site also includes Historical Maps at Other Web Sites with links to other historical map collections.

History of Medicine—National Library of Medicine

http://www.nlm.nih.gov/hmd/

The History of Medicine Division at the National Library of Medicine houses one of the world's largest history of medicine collections. The collection consists of print and nonprint materials including archival resources, photographs, and historical audiovisuals that document the history of medicine, health, and disease in all time periods and cultures. Arabic and Persian manuscripts dating back to the eleventh century are available.

International Institute of Social History

http://www.iisg.nl

Founded in 1935 in the Netherlands, IISH is one of the world's largest archival and research institutions in the field of social history, particularly labor history. Its 2,700 archival collections cover a range of topics not always well represented in traditional archives, like anarchism, revolutionary populism in nineteenth-century Eastern Europe, the French Revolution and Utopian socialism, and World War II resistance movements. Collections may be identified using an online catalog, a list of archival collections, or other finding aids. Other IISH resources include the William Morris Archive on the Web, Occasio (a collection of digital social history documents), and numerous electronic publications. The institute's image collections are highlighted by a number of virtual exhibitions with titles like The Chairman Smiles and Art to the People.

National Archives and Records Administration

http://www.archives.gov

NARA's Web site is a rich source of information for historians, genealogists, teachers, and students. For historians, the Research Room organizes information about historical archival records by branch of government and type of material. For genealogists, the Genealogy Page publishes not only practical information about using NARA's facilities nationwide, but also a growing list of "quick guides" on census, military, immigration, and other types of records. Teachers and students will appreciate the Digital Classroom: Primary Sources, Activities, and Training for Educators and Students, with reproducible documents and teaching activities. The Online Exhibit Hall is a showcase for NARA treasures. Finally, NARA's Archival Research Catalog (ARC) is a searchable database that contains and describes more than 1,235,359 cubic feet of selected NARA holdings in Washington, DC, and Maryland (Archives II), the regional archives, and presidential libraries, including 106,215 digital copies of selected textual documents, photographs, maps, and sound recordings.

New York Public Library for the Performing Arts

http://www.nypl.org/research/lpa/lpa.html

"The world's most extensive combination of circulating, reference and rare archival collections" in the performing arts, this Web site describes the library's important collections of recordings, videotapes, autograph manuscripts, correspondence, sheet music, stage designs, press clippings, programs, posters, and photographs in the areas of dance, music, and theater.

Online Archive of California

http://www.oac.cdlib.org/

The Online Archive of California is an umbrella site bringing together information on a steadily increasing number of archival institutions in California. Its most important resource is a centralized database of over 8,000 searchable electronic finding aids, which allows a level of precision searching for archival materials not available in more traditional online library catalogs, like RLIN AMC. Digital images of photographs and correspondence are also available.

Social Science Data Archives–Europe

http://www.nsd.uib.no/cessda/europe.html

A map of Europe organizes links to fourteen important European social science data archives, with separate links to similar non-European institutions. Maintained by the Council of European Social Science Data Archives (CESSDA), this Web site also allows researchers to search the holdings of eleven electronic data repositories through its Integrated Data Catalogue.

Television News Archive

http://tvnews.vanderbilt.edu/

Vanderbilt University holds "the world's most extensive and complete archive of television news," including 30,000 evening news broadcasts and 9,000 hours of special news-related programming. These news broadcasts have been consistently recorded and preserved by the archive since 1968. The Web site makes several searchable indexes available, including Network Television Evening News Abstracts, Special Reports and Periodic News Broadcasts, and Specialized News Collections (containing descriptive summaries of news material for major events like the Persian Gulf War of 1991). The archive is willing to loan videotapes to researchers worldwide.

United States Holocaust Memorial Museum

http://www.ushmm.org/research/collections

The Archive of the Holocaust Memorial Museum in Washington, DC, has gathered together 13 million pages of microfilmed documents, 50,000 photo images, 200 hours of historical motion picture footage, 250 documentary or feature films, and 2,900 oral interviews—all related to the Holocaust, its origins, and aftermath. The document and photographic archives may be searched individually or together using the USHMM Information Access query form available at the Web site.

USIA Declassified Historical Information

http://dosfan.lib.uic.edu/usia/

Pursuant to Executive Order 12958, the United States Information Agency Declassification Unit prepares a listing of declassified documents in order to alert the general public, especially academic researchers, to information no longer classified. Researchers may do keyword searching of this listing or browse by broad topic, from Africa to Youth, to find the titles of more than 5,300 classified and unclassified one-cubic-foot boxes of records coming from the National Archives and many other document-holding federal agencies.

Women and Gender Project, UTSA Archives

http://www.lib.utsa.edu/Archives/WomenGender/

This guide to the archives, libraries, and other repositories on the Web with archival materials by or about women is maintained by the Archives for Research on Women and Gender Project at the University of Texas at San Antonio. Arranged by states in the United States (plus a link devoted to institutions outside of the United States), each listing includes annotations indicating which materials in a given collection may be of interest to researchers in the field of women's history.

Chapter 39

Digital Collections

Sarah Ferentinos,
Jessie Bishop Powell, Merriman

A wide variety of digitized selections from primary documents is available through the Internet. The following list comprises selected examples of the Internet's potential to render archives accessible to researchers. Except where noted, these sites are in English and contain large and/or well-maintained digital collections

Metasites

Berkeley Digital Library SunSITE Digital Collections

http://sunsite.berkeley.edu/Collections/

The links available from this Web site cover a variety of digital text and image collections. The subjects range from literature to gay, lesbian, bisexual, and transgender history to collections of maps, sheet music, manuscripts, and individuals' papers.

Library Exhibits on the Web

http://www.sil.si.edu/SILPublications/Online-Exhibitions/

Maintained by the Smithsonian Institution Libraries, this list contains links to digital exhibits curated by libraries and manuscript repositories. Most exhibits have a historical focus. The list can now be searched by subject terms.

Individual Digital Collections

American Memory From the Library of Congress

http://memory.loc.gov/ammem/index.html

The American Memory Web site contains digitized copies of photographs, documents, sound recordings, and motion pictures from the Library of Congress Americana collections. The site currently houses 127 collections, with new ones added monthly.

Berkeley Digital Library SunSITE

http://sunsite.berkeley.edu/

This site offers both digital collections of archival material and resources for the development of such collections. The Catalogs & Indexes page lists databases for finding historical documents, while the Collections section links to primary documents available for perusal on the Web.

The Digital Past

http://www.digitalpast.org/

Twenty Illinois libraries, all part of the North Suburban Library System, contributed historic collections to this digital archive. Holdings include cemetery lists, medical ledgers, newspaper clippings, photographs, and a collection of documents pertaining to the Nazi Party's attempt to stage a demonstration in Skokie, Illinois, in 1978.

Digital Sources Center, Michigan State University

http://digital.lib.msu.edu/

The special collections division of the Michigan State University Library has undertaken an ambitious digitization project of its holdings on selected topics. These collections include American radicalism, cookbooks, early French writings, comics, temperance, and botany, among others. Many collections are only available to users logging in from the MSU campus.

Early Canadiana Online

http://www.canadiana.org/eco/index.html

Maintained by the Canadian Institute for Historical Microreproductions (CIHM), this digital collection of primary sources contains thousands of books and pamphlets documenting Canadian history from European contact to the early twentieth century. The full text of each of these documents is searchable and is available in PDF format.

Gallica-France

http://gallica.bnf.fr/

Not surprisingly, the Web site of Gallica, la bibliothèque numérique de la Bibliothèque nationale de France, is entirely in French. This endeavor of the French National Library aims to digitize major contributions to French history and culture. The offerings cover the period from the Middle Ages to the nineteenth century and pertain to philosophy, literature, and the sciences as well as history. To date, over 80,000 documents have been added, including text, prints, audio, and video. Images appear in TIFF and PDF formats.

The Library of Virginia Digital Collections

http://www.lva.lib.va.us/whatwehave/index.htm

A gold mine for genealogists, the Library of Virginia Digital Collections site contains over eighty databases, including many digitized versions of old card catalogs. Not all collections are digitized, so it may be worthwhile to contact the library with questions. Digitized catalogs include indices of Virginia marital records, birth and death certificates, wills, land deeds, war pensions, and court proceedings, as well as numerous manuscript collections. Most of the online documents are maps and photographs, although some family Bible records are also included.

Making of America

http://www.hti.umich.edu/m/moagrp/

The Making of America project provides the text of 8,500 books and 50,000 journal articles published in the United States, primarily between 1850 and 1877. The collection includes scientific writings, religious tracts, and publications in the then-emerging fields of education and psychology. Users can access the material through specific searches or by browsing lists of holdings.

National Archives and Records Administration (NARA) Online Exhibit Hall

http://www.archives.gov/exhibit_hall/index.html

NARA Archival Research Catalog: http://www.archives.gov/research_room/arc/index.html

The Online Exhibit Hall of NARA offers numerous exhibits on United States history, as well as showcasing individual documents of great import. Two exhibits deal with different aspects of World War II, and When Nixon Met Elvis contains documents and photos surrounding this odd event of 1970. The American Originals exhibit provides access to documents of the nation's most moving events, such as the Louisiana Purchase Treaty and John F. Kennedy's Inaugural Address. Additional digital documents can be accessed from the NARA Archival Research Catalog.

Prints and Photographs: An Illustrated Guide

http://www.loc.gov/coll/print/guide/

The Library of Congress maintains this rich resource of prints and photographs in its collections. The guide is divided into six thematic portfolios: An American Gallery; Pictorial Journalism; Politics and Propaganda; Architecture, Design, and Engineering; American Landscape and Cityscape; and The World at Large (featuring depictions of other countries). Each section offers an introduction to the theme and images that illustrate the topic. Each image is accompanied by an annotation describing its significance. The site includes a chronology of the library's acquisition of substantial print and photograph collections.

Rare Book, Manuscript, and Special Collection Library at Duke University

http://scriptorium.lib.duke.edu/

This site showcases Duke's award-winning Digital Scriptorium, an online collection of historical items from the library's holdings. The documents are accompanied by informational essays providing historical context, transcriptions (where applicable), and links to related information. The scriptorium's selections reflect the strengths of the library: African-Americans, women, advertising, and music. Much of Duke's impressive papyrus collection is also represented. From this site, users can also access an impressive array of subject guides to Duke's collections.

San Diego Historical Society

http://www.sandiegohistory.org

Oral history: http://www.sandiegohistory.org/audio/audiofile.htm

The San Diego Historical Society provides an extensive array of historical information on its Web site. The society has digitized many historical postcards and compiled numerous photographs and informational articles, particularly on the Panama-California Exposition (1915–1916) and the California Pacific Exposition (1935–1936). In addition, visitors can access biographical sketches of dozens of past residents of San Diego and peruse an online photo gallery that includes early motorcycles, diners, and amusement parks. Finally, visitors can listen to excerpts from oral history interviews in the society's collections or read accounts of colorful moments in San Diego history from Rick Crawford's *Stranger than Fiction*. With an eye toward the quirky, this site is a delightful introduction to the history of San Diego.

Special Collections Digital Center, University of Virginia

http://www.lib.virginia.edu/small/services/digitalservices.html

The Special Collections Digital Center of the University of Virginia serves both as a gateway to the unique library holdings of the university and a clearinghouse of information on digitization. The Collections section of the site provides access to such treasures as Thomas Jefferson's handwritten letters, Sanborn fire maps of the Charlottesville, Virginia, area, Walt Whitman's personal notebooks, and photographs of early twentieth-century African-American life. The Exhibitions section leads to nearly two dozen online exhibits. For those seeking further guidance on the process of digitization, the Information section offers links to a variety of educational sites on the topic.

Treasures From Europe's National Libraries

http://www.theeuropeanlibrary.org/portal/index.htm

Part of the Gabriel site described in the Archives chapter, this site brings together the "treasures" of forty libraries throughout Eastern and Western Europe. Visitors can browse the digital collection by document type, subject, country of origin, or time period, and each item is accompanied by a brief description of its significance. The presentation more resembles a museum exhibit than a research database, however, as complete multipage documents are not included.

Chapter 40

Archival Exhibitions Online

Jessica Lacher-Feldman

For the historian or student of history, what better way is there to gain an understanding of the "stuff of history" than by looking at the real *stuff* of history—archival materials. These items give users insight into the past in ways that the creators of those original documents never could have anticipated.

Archives and special collections repositories of all kinds in both the United States and around the world are the keepers of these touchstones of the past. Rare documents, one-of-a-kind materials, and collections of every conceivable format and size fill these archives, and it is the archivist's responsibility to preserve and provide access to their contents. Because of their often remote physical locations and their overall missions, most archives have traditionally offered limited access to relatively few initiated individuals, mainly scholars doing academic research.

Some repositories have a physical exhibition space that allows them to highlight these rare materials in a selective and contextual way, much as museums traditionally display their holdings. But again, access is limited, and the nature of the exhibitions themselves limits use.

The continuing use of the Internet has changed this notion completely. The missions and goals of most archival repositories have changed significantly in order to reflect this new tool to promote and disseminate their holdings to a broader and broader audience. This chapter focuses solely on online archival exhibitions, which are entirely different from archival exhibitions in the physical realm. (See the chapters on special collections and on archives and manuscript collections.) There are two distinct types of online archival exhibitions. One is an exhibition that is created solely for online presentation. The other is an online presentation in conjunction with a physical exhibition of the same name and title. These online exhibitions highlight collections, provide context, foster collaboration between institutions and between institutions and scholars, and present these unique materials to a worldwide audience.

Repositories present these materials online for a host of reasons—to publicize the collections or a specific item, to draw attention to a particular event or milestone in the repository or host institution, or to complement a physical exhibition being held simultaneously in the repository. An online archival exhibition differs from an online collection of materials in that the exhibition is contextualized and curated. That is, the materials have been brought together from disparate collections within the same repository or from multiple repositories and presented in a narrative, linear, or educational fashion for viewers to explore. The images of the physical items, the additional information about those items, and the way that the information is presented are beneficial for students, teachers, and lifelong learners.

The following are some outstanding online archival exhibitions that take advantage of the dynamic opportunities afforded by the Internet. These exhibitions reflect several different areas of interest. Users interested in exploring new and exciting online exhibitions should bookmark and revisit these Web sites often, as the exhibits and materials are updated frequently. The primary metasite, listed below and hosted at the Smithsonian Institution, is an excellent starting point to explore the bounty of archival exhibitions online.

Metasites

The Smithsonian Institution

http://www.sil.si.edu/SILPublications/Online-Exhibitions/

The Smithsonian Institution maintains a searchable database with links to library and archival institutions on the Web. It has grown to include over 3,000 links to online exhibitions from libraries, archives, and museums around the world.

American Memory: The Library of Congress

http://memory.loc.gov/ammem/index.html

Categorized by subject, American Memory provides users access to vast amounts of materials of all types. It serves as a "digital record of American history and creativity," chronicling historical events, people, places, and ideas. The materials are from the Library of Congress and repositories all over the United States.

Selected Online Archival Exhibitions

Across the Generations: Exploring U.S. History Through Family Papers

http://www.smith.edu/libraries/libs/ssc/atg/

This exhibition features examples of materials from family collections in the Sophia Smith Collection at Smith College, offering viewers an understanding of how to use these very personal materials in interpreting American history.

A. Einstein: Image and Impact

http://www.aip.org/history/einstein/

A historical investigation of the work and impact of one of the greatest minds of the twentieth century. This exhibition from the American Institute of Physics features photographs, compelling narrative, and accompanying historical essays.

Anne Frank, The Writer: The Unfinished Story

http://www.ushmm.org/museum/exhibit/online/af/htmlsite/

This exhibition from the United States Holocaust Memorial Museum features oral histories, interviews, photographs, and other materials on Anne Frank, including her writings beyond the internationally known diary.

Book of the Month: The University of Glasgow

http://special.lib.gla.ac.uk/exhibns/index.html

This online exhibition continues to build every month with a new featured item from the University of Glasgow's special collections. Since August 1999, the special collections staff has addressed the lack of physical exhibition space by presenting new items from the university's holdings—both images and insightful texts—to the rest of the world.

Downtown New York Web Walk

http://www.skyscraper.org/WEB_PROJECTS/WEB_WALK/
webwalk_intro.htm

This innovative and beautifully designed online exhibition from the Skyscraper Museum provides virtual walking tours of lower Manhattan.

From Domesticity to Modernity: What Was Home Economics?

http://rmc.library.cornell.edu/homeEc/default.html

This brilliantly executed exhibition from Cornell University's Kroch Library on the evolution of the field and study of home economics features oral histories, photographs, biographies, and many other resources.

The Great Baltimore Fire of 1904

http://www.mdch.org/fire/

This online exhibition features an interactive historical map, satellite imaging, historic photographs, and film footage of the Baltimore fire. It contains materials from several repositories, including the Enoch Pratt Free Library in Baltimore and the Library of Congress.

In Motion: The African-American Migration Experience

http://www.inmotionaame.org/

This exhibition from the Schomburg Center for Research in Black Culture at the New York Public Library uses Flash and other tools to provide insight into the African-American migration experience and the African diaspora in America.

Wet With Blood: The Investigation of Mary Todd Lincoln's Cloak

http://www.chicagohistory.org/wetwithblood/index.htm

This informative and innovative exhibition from the Chicago Historical Society combines historical narrative with conservation and science to present the evidence surrounding the assassination of President Abraham Lincoln.

Chapter 41

Environmental History

David Calverley

Metasites

American Society for Environmental History

http://www.h-net.org/~environ/ASEH/welcome_IE4.html

ASEH is one of the most important environmental history organizations in North America. This site provides information about available academic positions in environmental history and upcoming conferences such as the annual conference sponsored by ASEH. The Resources link provides connections not only to additional Web sites, but also to online essays concerned with various historiographical themes in environmental history. Through the Publications link users can access a number of online versions of the society's quarterly journal *Environmental History*. The journal (available on the History Cooperative Web site) is useful not only for its articles, but for the extensive annotated bibliography in each issue of books, articles, and academic theses in environmental history.

Environmental History on the Internet

http://www.cnr.berkeley.edu/departments/espm/env-hist/eh-internet.html

Although this site provides a large collection of links, it is not well developed as the links are simply listed with the appropriate title and affiliation but no annotation. Furthermore, some of the links are no longer active. Researchers can use the broken links and Web site titles to search the Internet; patience and typing will lead to the updated Web sites and URLs. Despite these shortcomings, the variety of links provided (ranging from local to national to international environmental history) makes this a useful site for researchers and students.

H-Environment

http://www.h-net.org/~environ/

H-Environment is part of the larger H-Net (History Network) system, which is maintained to develop various Internet-based historical resources. This particular discussion chain on environmental history contains links to bibliographies, scholarly reviews of recent monographs, syllabi in environmental history universities from around the world, and various Web pages. It also provides a very useful discussion list to join for users interested in environmental history. List members can post requests for information and aid from other members, often receiving detailed responses in return. Online debates and discussions are also lively and at times entertaining. This is a scholarly site, but useful for students seeking bibliographic help from other listserv members.

General Sites

American Museum of Natural History

http://www.amnh.org/

This site offers links pertaining to various environmental historical issues. Of particular interest is the Resources to Learning link that highlights a number of the Web pages and resources maintained by the museum.

Association for Environmental Archaeology

http://www.envarch.net/

Very academic in its structure and content, this association's Web site contains links to archaeological and related sites that are concerned with the environment. The association lists upcoming conferences and provides its newsletter to download (as PDF files) and a listing of articles in its journal, *Environmental Archaeology: The Journal of Human Palaeoecology.*

Cultural Environmental Studies

http://www.wsu.edu/~amerstu/ce/ce.html

Maintained by Wisconsin State University, this site attempts to meld environmental history with other subfields of history: women's history, ethnic studies, regional studies, etc. It provides useful resources, including links to "learning modules" dealing with various elements of environmental history. There are also links to a variety of sites ranging from pop culture depictions of the environment to indigenous peoples, environmental art, justice, and writings. In addition, the site offers an excellent annotated bibliography of print resources.

Environmental History of Latin America: On-Line Bibliography

http://www.stanford.edu/group/LAEH/index.html

This site is useful for its extensive bibliography (over 600 references). The bibliography is divided by region (Amazon, Andes, Brazil, etc.). Regional bibliographies contain books (with some links to reviews) and articles. There are also several bibliographies providing information about video documentaries and Internet links pertaining to Latin America.

Environmental History Timeline

http://www.radford.edu/~wkovarik/envhist/

Bill Kovarik of Radford University, Virginia, maintains this site. The time line portion of the site is very detailed, providing a good overview of world environmental history. The site includes a useful bibliography of print resources and an interesting history of events in American environmental history, such as the addition of lead to gasoline and the resulting environmental and health problems that occurred.

The Evolution of the Conservation Movement, 1850–1920

http://lcweb2.loc.gov/ammem/amrvhtml/conshome.html

Maintained by the Library of Congress, this site offers an excellent overview of U.S. environmental history through its detailed chronology. The chronology has embedded links to various primary and secondary documents on the Web page. Of particular interest to senior researchers is the access provided to the Library of Congress's digitized environmental collection, complete with call numbers and links for each item to other archival materials. There are also streaming videos of the collection's films, such as the building of the Theodore Roosevelt Dam. This site should be supplemented with the library's Conservation and Environment map link (http://memory.loc.gov/ammem/gmdhtml/cnsvhome.html).

Nature Transformed: The Environment in American History

http://www.nhc.rtp.nc.us/tserve/nattrans/nattrans.htm

Operated by the National Humanities Center, this site offers useful short essays for teachers who want to incorporate environmental history into their classrooms. Leading U.S. historians and high school teachers worked to create the site, and senior U.S. scholars such as Shepard Krech III and Alfred Crosby wrote the essays. Each essay offers a strong general overview of key issues in American environmental history in addition to a number of useful links to various Web sites concerned with the same topic.

The Time Line of Waste

http://www.st-andrews.ac.uk/%7Ewaste/timeline/index.htm

Maintained by the Arts and Humanities Research Board Research Center for Environmental History at the University of Stirling in Scotland, this site is part of the center's research projects into waste management and wastelands. The site offers a basic chronological breakdown, starting in the year 500 CE and divided into sections continuing to the late twentieth century, of perceptions and policy treatment of wastewater and wastelands in Europe. The clear, straightforward writing provides a useful overview of this particular facet of environmental history. This Web site is very useful for senior high school and junior undergraduate students and for teachers who want to integrate environmental history into their classrooms.

U.S. Environmental History

http://www.mtsu.edu/~lnelson/Environmental-History.html

Dr. Lynn Nelson of Middle Tennessee State University maintains this site as part of his environmental history course. It is useful for its astounding number of links to various government, nongovernmental, academic, and professional organizations concerned with environmental history and environmental themes—links that some of the other Web sites listed in this chapter overlook. There are also links to biographies of important individuals in environmental history. While the site is designed simply, the first section provides page links to various sections on the Web page. These links are well maintained and direct the researcher to other online resources.

Chapter 42

Immigration History

Pamela Grey

Ancestors in the Americas

http://www.cetel.org/

http://www.pbs.org/kbyu/ancestors/resourceguide/

This Public Broadcasting Service video series, at the first site, focuses on the immigration of Asians to the Americas from the 1700s through the 1900s. The series uses a "documemoir" approach involving personal narrative. Narrated QuickTime video clips can be played without additional software. Primary documents, a time line, and viewer guides provide materials and questions that are appropriate for secondary or college-level courses. The site also has an extensive listing of snail mail addresses and links. The second site is a more extensive related research site, Ancestors: Resource Guide.

The Cabildo Online Project

http://lsm.crt.state.la.us/cabildo/cab8.htm

This site gives a brief overview of both forced immigration to New Orleans and the arrival of those who came as a less expensive alternative to entry at New York Harbor: New Orleans was the second leading port of entry between 1820 and 1860.

Center for Immigration Studies

http://www.cis.org/

This conservative think tank is devoted "exclusively to research and policy analysis of the economic, social, demographic, fiscal, and other impacts of immigration on the United States." The site is organized around topical themes and features timely immigration news and an interactive question and answer book. It is an excellent resource for the conservative protectionist viewpoint.

The Data and Program Library Service

http://dpls.dacc.wisc.edu/slavedata/index.html

The University of Wisconsin-Madison, through this site, offers an online data archive of the movement of forced labor during the eighteenth and nineteenth centuries. The site lists slave ship movements, raw data, and documentation of the slave ships and trade between England, Cuba, France, Brazil, and Virginia during the two centuries.

Digital History: Using New Technology to Enhance Teaching and Research

http://www.digitalhistory.uh.edu/historyonline/ethnic_am.cfm

Jointly sponsored by the History Department and the School of Education at the University of Houston, this site includes a searchable index of 1,500 links and more than 400 annotated documents, maps, speeches, and films. Linked primary print sources include African-American, Mexican-American, Native American, and Asian-American voices; a chronology of immigration history; and a featured online exhibit on Chinese immigrants and the Transcontinental Railroad. Separate links include stereopticon slides of Irish-American immigrants and readings on Italian-Americans. The Huddled Masses is a guided reading giving definitions, suggested study questions, and movies appropriate for secondary and college students.

The History Channel's Ellis Island Scrapbook

http://www.historychannel.com/ellisisland/index2.html

This interactive Ellis Island scrapbook provides photographs and narratives of immigrants' experiences on Ellis Island.

The Immigration History Research Center

http://www.ihrc.umn.edu/

This center, founded in 1965 at the University of Minnesota, aims to provide information about immigration. The goal of Collections Online: A Digital

Library of American Immigration and Ethnic History (COLLAGE) is to provide "public access to primary documents for K–12 education." Users can search with an online tool for photographs, documents, and text passages from sites including the International Institute of San Francisco, the National Park Service, and the National Trust for Historic Preservation. Over thirty ethnic groups are represented in the collections.

Immigration: Library of Congress

http://memory.loc.gov/learn/features/immig/alt/introduction.html

This project of the American Memory Collection of the Library of Congress links to a wide variety of immigrant experiences. Among those featured are Native American, African, German, Irish, Scandinavian, Italian, Japanese, Mexican, Chinese, Cuban, Puerto Rican, Polish, and Russian. Images can be used at any grade level. Text is appropriate for advanced upper elementary classes through college level. Each immigrant group is examined in detail through text, artifacts, and images. Topical lesson plans, resources, and bibliographies are linked from the site.

The Lower East Side Tenement Museum

http://www.tenement.org/

This virtual museum experience provides teaching materials, artifacts, and the tenement. The virtual tour takes visitors through the lives of the 10,000 residents who lived at 97 Orchard Street between 1870 and 1915 in an effort to promote understanding, historical perspective, and tolerance of the immigrant experience on Manhattan's Lower East Side. The site uses QuickTime panorama and RealPlayer applications in a video and audio tour illustrating the lives of the immigrants who called the rooms home. Excavation details and examination of individual artifacts are a highlight of the site. The museum is a founder of the International Coalition of Historic Site Museums of Conscience.

The Making of America (MoA)

http://moa.cit.cornell.edu/moa/ (Cornell)

http://www.hti.umich.edu/m/moagrp/ (Michigan)

This joint project of Cornell University and the University of Michigan was funded by the Andrew W. Mellon Foundation. MoA includes more than 70,000 digital images and 3.5 million pages covering the history of the United States from the antebellum period through Reconstruction. Cornell adds over 910,000 pages to this joint project. Images are appropriate for classes from middle school through college. Selected images can be used at the elementary levels.

The Migration Policy Institute

http://www.migrationpolicy.org/research/usimmigration.php

This is an independent think tank dedicated to the study of the worldwide movement of people. The page referenced above provides background papers for journalists and policy makers, links to statistics and analysis on refugee protection, immigration policy, and bibliographic materials.

Jacob Riis' *How the Other Half Lives*

http://www.cis.yale.edu/amstud/inforev/riis/title.html

Jacob Riis documented the immigrant experience in an early forerunner of the field of photojournalism. This site presents a hypertext edition of *How the Other Half Lives: Studies Among the Tenements of New York,* which was originally published in 1890.

Statue of Liberty—Ellis Island Foundation, Inc.

http://www.ellisisland.org/

This site provides a search of passenger arrival records. Users enter the name, gender, and approximate date of birth of an immigrant to call up records. The database includes over 25 million names. Links include secondary and college-level material about starting genealogical research. Free registration is necessary to view immigration records.

Statue of Liberty National Monument and Ellis Island

http://www.americanparknetwork.com/parkinfo/sl/index.html

This Web site provides facts about the Statue of Liberty and the Ellis Island immigrant station. It features a time line, statistics on immigration, and the newcomer photographs of Augustus Sherman. The site is an excellent introduction to basic photography that uses the Statue of Liberty as a focal point in asking students to tell their own family stories through photography.

The Story of Africa: Slavery

http://www.bbc.co.uk/worldservice/africa/features/storyofafrica/index_section9.shtml

In this radio series the BBC World Service gives a detailed history of peoples of the African continent, resistance movements, the Atlantic slave trade, the journey, and resettlement efforts.

Talking Walls: The Barracks on Angel Island

http://www.riverdeep.net/talkingwalls/angelisland/

Angel Island Immigration Station Foundation http://www.aiisf.org/

Angel Island Immigration Station http://people.lib.ucdavis.edu/tss/punjab/angelisland.html

Angel Island was the Pacific gateway for West Coast immigration from 1910 until 1940.

The first site introduces Angel Island to elementary age visitors. The second provides background material on the island and the immigrant experience. The third site provides current photos of the island and an interactive link to island arrival records. It is geared for high school or college readers.

UNESCO: Virtual Visit of Goree Island

http://webworld.unesco.org/goree/

This interactive video tour, with text, details the experiences of forced African laborers who were taken from the prison called "The House of Slaves," constructed in 1776, in the present-day Republic of Senegal.

The University of California, Riverside, Keystone-Mast Collection, California Museum of Photography

http://photo.ucr.edu/projects/immigration

Stereoscopic photographic slides produced by the Keystone View Company, Underwood and Underwood, and the H.C. White Company illustrate immigration from 1900 to 1920. The slides show Ellis Island and the immigrant experience in New York City.

U.S. Citizenship and Immigration Services

http://uscis.gov/graphics/index.htm

This site offers a comprehensive overview of the government agency, required forms, laws and regulations, and a glossary of terms. The site is presented at a high school reading level. The Web page also offers links to immigration statistics, U.S. Customs and Border Protection, and the Student Exchange and Visitor information.

U.S. Citizenship and Immigration Services: History, Genealogy, and Education

http://uscis.gov/graphics/aboutus/history/

This site has specific links to the National Archives and catalogs immigration points of entry by state and territory and includes Chinese Immigrant files.

U.S. Immigration on the Internet Modern History Sourcebook Project

http://www.fordham.edu/halsall/mod/modsbook28.html

This metasite includes arguments for and against immigration, links to sites arranged by ethnicity and race, and primary documents related to immigration.

Chapter 43

Oral History

Thomas Saylor

Organizations

American Association for State and Local History

http://www.aaslh.org/

Oral history is just one of the subjects given coverage at this extensive and well-developed site. More than a dozen historical programs (each with a separate link) and professional development pages are two of its strengths.

American Folklife Center

http://www.loc.gov/folklife/

Extensive information available at this Library of Congress site includes the September 11, 2001 Documentary Project and the substantial Veterans History Project (World War II oral histories, documents, etc.). The Archive of Folk Culture holdings can be researched here, too, and the Collections and Special Presentations Online page showcases diverse projects across the United States. Also, the Resources in Ethnographic Studies page is a treasure trove of hundreds of organizations, scholarly societies, and educators' resources.

Canadian Oral History Association/Société canadienne d'histoire orale

http://oral-history.ncf.ca/

Skeletal site provides contact information for the association and a helpful reference site. Their other pages are waiting for development.

H-Oralhist

http://www.h-net.org/~oralhist/

H-Oralhist, a member of the H-Net Humanities and Social Sciences On-Line initiative, is a network for scholars and professionals active in studies related to oral history. It is affiliated with the Oral History Association. Users can subscribe to the listserv and check these pages: Discussion Networks, Reviews, and Job Guide. There are also several Resources links.

International Oral History Association

http://www.ioha.fgv.br/

Central site for the primary international oral history organization. Information on IOHA conferences, a newsletter archive, and a resources page are the strengths of this site.

National Council on Public History

http://ncph.org/index.html

The official site of the NCPH, this site's best feature is its excellent collection of links to history organizations and societies, museums, and Web sites. In addition, there is information on the NCPH and several of its publications.

Oral History Association

http://omega.dickinson.edu/organizations/oha/

The primary oral history organization in the United States maintains this site, based at Dickinson College in Carlisle, Pennsylvania. It includes information on the OHA, regional oral history organizations, and some resources.

Oral History Society

http://www.oralhistory.org.uk/

This is the central site for this British organization and thus a guide to membership and regional organizations. All visitors will find especially useful information on these pages: Copyright and Ethics, and Resources (print and online).

Institutes and Projects

Alexander Street Press

http://www.alexanderstreetpress.com/

Founded in 2000, this company in Alexandria, Virginia, develops and markets electronic collections of historical sources. Its extensive product line of more than twenty databases includes a variety of different historical subject areas. The oral history area gives access to hundreds of collections in various locations.

American Century Project

http://www.americancenturyproject.org/

This twentieth-century U.S. history project, crafted by Glenn Whitman of Saint Andrew's Episcopal School in Maryland, with a dozen themes ranging from World War II to civil rights to the Gulf War. There is an archive of interviews and an extensive listing of print and online resources for designing and doing oral history projects, classroom assessment tools, and links to other projects. This is an excellent resource for secondary teachers seeking to integrate oral history into their classrooms.

American Memory

http://memory.loc.gov/ammem/

This Library of Congress Web site contains primary source collections on themes in American history, including some oral histories, with searchable databases. The Using Oral History page has teacher material (including downloadable lesson plans) and student lessons.

Baylor University Institute for Oral History

http://www3.baylor.edu/Oral_History/

Helpful is the Oral History Workshop on the Web, with these well-written pages: Introduction to Oral History (planning a project, ethical and legal considerations, equipment, interviewing tips, transcribing); Tips for Family Oral History; and Transcribing Style Guide. The site also includes a searchable database of the institute's more than 700 interviews, conducted since 1970.

Center for the Study of History and Memory

http://www.indiana.edu/~cshm/

This Indiana University Web site includes resources, interviewing techniques, and a guide to the center's archive holdings (unfortunately, no posted transcripts). The Oral History and Memory in the Classroom page contains a helpful annotated list of projects useful for K–12 educators.

Centre for Popular Memory

http://www.popularmemory.org/about1.htm

A relatively new project, this site from the University of Cape Town in South Africa documents South Africa's apartheid past and recent developments.

Foxfire Project

http://www.foxfire.org/

Founded in 1966, this project is aimed at educators, especially K–12. Students make connections with their community, incorporating oral history as part of the learning process. Site includes pages for the Foxfire Approach to Teaching and Learning, Materials for Teachers, and the *Foxfire Newsletter.*

Michigan Oral History Association

http://www.h-net.org/~oralhist/moha/

Most helpful is the Oral History Centers and Collections page, with descriptions of numerous oral history projects and links.

Oral History Project of the World War Two Years and Prisoner of War Oral History Project

http://people.csp.edu/saylor/OHP/OHPhomepage.htm

http://people.csp.edu/saylor/POWproject/POWhome.htm

These projects contain an archive of more than forty complete interviews with Minnesota women and men, civilians and service veterans, speaking on their experiences from 1941 to 1946. Also some visual images and links to oral history resources.

Presidential Oral History

http://www.millercenter.virginia.edu

This easy-to-navigate site from the Miller Center of Public Affairs at the University of Virginia has an emphasis on the American presidency. Separate pages include Presidential Recordings (some audio clips), "Presidential Oral History," and American Political Development.

Regional Oral History Office

http://bancroft.berkeley.edu/ROHO/

This well-organized site created by the Bancroft Library at the University of California–Berkeley features projects developed by the ROHO, and resources, collections, and education pages. Easy to navigate.

Rutgers Oral History Archives: World War II, Korea, Vietnam, Cold War

http://fas-history.rutgers.edu/oralhistory/home.html

An affiliated center of the Department of History at Rutgers, this quality site contains more than 340 interview transcripts (browsable by theme), as well as assorted photos, letters, diaries, and other documents.

United States Holocaust Memorial Museum

http://www.ushmm.org

The Web site of the Holocaust Memorial Museum in Washington, DC, contains a Personal Histories page with interview transcriptions and video clips from dozens of Holocaust survivors, thematically organized (e.g., children, ghettos, liberation). Site also contains a wealth of other Holocaust-related information.

University of Hawai'i Center for Oral History

http://www2.soc.hawaii.edu/css/oral_hist/index.htm

The focus of this site is on the peoples of Hawai'i during the twentieth century. Projects developed by the center, each with a separate page, include Communities; Ethnic Groups; Government; Historical Events; Individual Lives; and Occupations. Resources page includes links to various sources.

Utah Oral History Consortium

http://utahoralhistory.org/

The Utah Oral History Consortium describes itself as "an informal group of individuals with an interest in operating oral history programs, conducting and transcribing interviews, and preserving transcripts and audio and video recordings of oral histories and making them available for research." The Web site includes a number of Utah oral history projects and provides contact information for organizations in the state.

Veterans History Project

www.loc.gov/folklife/vets

A project of the American Folklife Center of the Library of Congress, this is the largest and most complete collection of World War II oral histories in the United States. Information on how to participate, an archive of audio and text interviews with veterans from all service branches and theaters, photographs, and a searchable database help to make this an excellent source.

What Did You Do in the War, Grandma?

http://www.stg.brown.edu/projects/WWII_Women/tocCS.html

This site contains oral histories of Rhode Island women during the World War II years. A project of South Kingstown High School (Rhode Island), the site contains twenty-five complete interview transcripts. There are possible classroom applications, as the site also contains information for teachers.

The Whole World Was Watching: An Oral History of 1968

http://www.stg.brown.edu/projects/1968

This Web site is a joint project between South Kingstown High School (Rhode Island) and Brown University's Scholarly Technology Group. It contains transcripts, audio recordings, and edited stories of a series of interviews conducted in 1998. This project has possible classroom applications, as the site also contains pages on Issues from the Interviews, Reference Material, and Classroom Oral History.

Chapter 44

Business and Economic History

Mark McCallon

Metasites

Leiden University's Business History and Economic History Sites

http://www.geschiedenis.leidenuniv.nl/index.php3?m=&c=376

http://www.geschiedenis.leidenuniv.nl/index.php3?m=&c=642

These sites provide many links to Web sites pertaining to the history of business and economics around the world. The sites are divided geographically and chronologically with links to corporate histories, trade and economic associations (such as NAFTA and the EU), and Web sites for specific industries' history.

Librarians' Index to the Internet—Business

http://lii.org/

A highly selective directory of authoritative Web links, the Librarians' Index includes a list of Web sites pertaining to business resources, labor history, and economics.

Social Science Information Gateway—
Business and Economics

http://www.esrc.bris.ac.uk/

This service provides links to scholarly resources in business and economics. Types of resources include museums, archives, organizations, and mailing lists. A unique feature of the Web site is the ability to find information about other scholars who are interested in similar research.

WebEC—World Wide Web Resources in Economics

http://www.helsinki.fi/WebEc/

Created by the University of Helsinki, WebEC is an excellent resource for locating scholarly information on the history of economics. The site is divided into subject categories and contains a wealth of Web links to sources on economic theory and systems. Over 1,400 links are available on the site.

WWW Virtual Library—Economic and Business History

http://www.neha.nl./w3vl/

The Netherlands Economic History Archive maintains this Web site of outstanding Web sites to assist business and economic historians. The Web site is well organized by subject with new sites added often.

Yahoo!—History—Business and Economics

http://dir.yahoo.com/Arts/Humanities/History/By_Subject/Business/

http://dir.yahoo.com/Social_Science/Economics/History/

The editors of the Yahoo search engine maintain this directory of Web sites for general history and subject-specific resources.

General Sites

Business and Economic History Online

http://www.thebhc.org/publications/BEHonline/beh.html

Business and Economic History Online publishes a large selection of papers from the Business History Conference annual meeting. Also included on the site is the entire run of the journal *Business and Economic History* from 1975 to 1999.

Economic and Business Historical Society

http://www.ebhsoc.org/

The society supports economic and business history research through annual conferences and refereed publications. Included on the Web site are links to publications and other sites.

EH.Net—Economic History Services

http://eh.net/

EH.Net provides a wide range of services to historians and social scientists interested in the field of economics. The Web site includes numerous links to Web sites, mailing lists, and course syllabi. The "How Much Is That?" service allows users to compare exchange rates, interest rates, wages, inflation, and other variables between the past and today. The *EH.Net Encyclopedia of Economic and Business History* is available free on the Web site.

HBS *Working Knowledge*—Business History

http://hbswk.hbs.edu/topic.jhtml?t=bizhistory

Published by the Harvard Business School, the *Working Knowledge* newsletter provides up-to-date information on books and Web sites pertaining to the history of business and management. The Web site contains links to online exhibits and organizations that are deemed outstanding by the staff of the Baker Library at the Harvard Business School.

Library of Economics and Liberty

http://www.econlib.org/

The Library of Economics and Liberty explores the study of economics and markets. Available on the Web site are editions of classic texts in economics and related disciplines, reading lists, and annotated bibliographies.

McMaster University Archive for the History of Economic Thought

http://socserv.mcmaster.ca/econ/ugcm/3113/

This large archive attempts to collect in a single place the primary texts of many of the major economists and schools of thought. Over one hundred authors are represented on the site.

Accounting and Finance Sites

Association of Chartered Accountants in the United States—History of Accounting

http://www.acaus.org/acc_his.html

John R. Alexander has written a detailed overview of the history of accounting from ancient times to the present. Also includes a bibliography of additional readings.

Beyond Face Value: Depictions of Slavery in Confederate Currency

http://www.cwc.lsu.edu/BeyondFaceValue/beyondfacevalue.htm

Created by the United States Civil War Center, this online exhibit displays hundreds of images of Confederate currency and notes. A scholarly article discussing the economic climate of the Confederacy and an extensive bibliography are also available on the Web site.

Museum of American Financial History

http://www.financialhistory.org/

The museum commemorates the spirit and wonders of capitalism and entrepreneurship in America. Online exhibits include the history of the Dow Jones and a history of bank note engraving. A list of links to other Web sites is also available.

Tax History Project

http://www.taxhistory.org/

A public service initiative from the publication *Tax Analysts,* this outstanding Web site provides a wealth of information about the history of U.S. public finances. A virtual museum of American tax history provides a chronological overview of the history of American taxation with images and text. The Web site also contains entertaining material such as cartoons and posters, as well as copies of tax returns filed by the American presidents.

Virtual Museum & Archive of the SEC and Securities History

http://www.sechistorical.org/

Created by the Securities and Exchange Commission Historical Society, this virtual museum makes available primary source materials on the growth of U.S. and international capital markets since the beginning of the SEC in 1934. Papers, photos, oral histories, and a time line are all available on the Web site.

Advertising and Public Relations Sites

Campaigns That Have Made a Difference—The Ad Council

http://www.adcouncil.org/campaigns/historic_campaigns/

Memorable public service campaigns from 1942 to 2001 are available on this Web site. A detailed description is given for each campaign, along with video clips and photographs.

Emergence of Advertising in America, 1850–1920

http://scriptorium.lib.duke.edu/eaa/

This collection contains over 9,000 images related to the early history of advertising in America. The collection is divided into various categories representing hundreds of consumer products and services.

Marketing in the Modern Era—Trade Catalogs and the Rise of Nineteenth-Century Advertising

http://www.library.hbs.edu/hc/exhibits/trade/

The Baker Library at the Harvard Business School's Web site contains images representing the value of trade catalogs as a tool for historical research. Cover art and images of consumer products and machines are available on the Web site with a brief description of each artifact.

Museum of Public Relations

http://www.prmuseum.com/

This PR museum was established in 1997 as an archive for the history of public relations programs in America. The Web site contains online exhibits honoring pioneers in the field including Edward Bernays, often called the father of public relations, Moss Kendrix, one of the first major African-American public relations executives, and others.

Prosperity and Thrift: The Coolidge Era and the Consumer Economy, 1921–1929

http://memory.loc.gov/ammem/coolhtml/coolhome.html

The Prosperity and Thrift online exhibit pulls together a variety of source materials on the origins of the mass consumer economy in the United States during the 1920s. The collection of materials strongly emphasizes advertising and marketing and the government's role in the economy during President Calvin Coolidge's administration.

Sears Archives

http://www.searsarchives.com/

The Sears Archives is an extensive collection of stories, photographs, and brand histories that chronicle the history of the company and its famous catalog from 1886 to the present. Interesting photographs of the earliest stores and model homes are depicted on the site.

Labor and Industry Web Sites

Airline History

http://airlines.afriqonline.com/

Maintained by Sarah Ward, this Web site contains detailed histories for more than 650 airlines around the world, along with updated information on the current status of various airlines. The site also gives histories of commercial aircraft that were used throughout the twentieth century. For many of the aircraft, photos are available.

Directory of Corporate Archives in the United States and Canada

http://www.hunterinformation.com/corporat.htm

Maintained by the Society of American Archivists, Business Archives Section, this Web site provides an extensive list with Web links to companies that maintain historical records or contract with consulting firms to maintain the records for them. For each entry, the contact person, holdings information, and a description are given. The site is organized alphabetically by company name and geographically by state.

Early Office Museum

http://www.officemuseum.com/

The Early Office Museum collects antique office equipment and business technology made before 1920. Many images from the museum are found on this Web site with detailed descriptions of the items. Online exhibits including antique communications devices and equipment used at the 1876 Centennial Exposition make this a great educational site.

From Carbons to Computers: The Changing American Office

http://www.smithsonianeducation.org/educators/lesson_plans/carbons/start.html

This online exhibit sponsored by the Smithsonian Institution explores the changes in the American workplace from the 1830s to the present. A detailed historical time line and an extensive list of Web links highlight the innovations and ideas that have shaped workplace environments and changed the way people do business.

Inside an American Factory: Films of the Westinghouse Works, 1904

http://memory.loc.gov/ammem/papr/west/

Part of the Library of Congress American Memory project, this online exhibit contains twenty-one films depicting the operations of the Westinghouse factories in 1904. Exterior and interior scenes depict male and female workers performing their duties. A textual history of the Westinghouse companies and the working conditions of the time enhances the rich multimedia content available on the site.

Women Working, 1870–1930

http://ocp.hul.harvard.edu/ww/

The first resource set published by the Harvard Open Collections project, this large compilation of books, pamphlets, photographs, and manuscripts explores the role of women in the U.S. economy from the end of the Civil War to the Great Depression. Topics covered include working conditions, educational opportunities, and legislation.

Chapter 45

Natural History

Lakita Edwards

Encyclopedia Smithsonian: Natural History

http://www.si.edu/resource/faq/nmnh/start.htm

A compendium of Smithsonian natural history programs organized by subject area. This site also includes selected links, reading lists, and online exhibits.

The Exploratorium's Ten Cool Sites: Natural History

http://www.exploratorium.edu/learning_studio/cool/natural_history.html

The Exploratorium is a unique museum focused on making science come alive for students through engaging, hands-on activities. Since 1995, Ten Cool Sites has been a staple on the Exploratorium's Web site, providing links to educational sites on various topics. The listing for natural history includes active links from 1995 to the present, including Web sites from PBS and *National Geographic*.

The Field Museum

http://www.fieldmuseum.org/

Founded to house the anthropological and biological collections from the World's Columbian Exposition of 1893, the Field Museum is a cultural institution dedicated to disseminating research, enhancing education, and engaging the public in the areas of science and history.

National Conservation Training Center: Conservation Library

http://training.fws.gov/library/

Part of the U.S. Fish and Wildlife's National Conservation Training Center, this library database offers search options for publications from the Fish and Wildlife Service as well as a digital archive of the service's public domain still photos.

National Park Service: Nature & Science

http://www.nature.nps.gov/

Created by the National Park Service, this site provides students and educators, researchers, and the general public with key information on conservation and critical issues affecting the over 380 National Park System units.

Naturalist Center

http://www.mnh.si.edu/museum/VirtualTour/Tour/Ground/NatCenter/

Part of the Smithsonian Museum of Natural History, the Naturalist Center is a study center dedicated to providing artists, students and teachers, collectors, and the general public with hands-on learning experiences. This site features a virtual tour of the Naturalist Center as well as links to the main page of the Museum of Natural History.

NatureServe

http://www.natureserve.org/

NatureServe is a nonprofit conservation organization, representing an international network of nature heritage programs. This Web site features natural history conferences and workshops, environmental data for download, and descriptions of NatureServe projects throughout the United States and Canada.

National History Book Service Environment Bookstore

http://www.nhbs.com/

British-based bookseller dedicated to providing all in-print publications spanning the natural history disciplines.

Ology: The Museum's Science Website for Kids

http://www.ology.amnh.org/

From the American Museum of Natural History, a site dedicated to reaching young audiences. This site is supported by an interactive interface for young students to explore the museum's collection and learn about natural history. Also includes a link to guides for educators to incorporate into after-school programs.

University of California Museum of Paleontology: UCMP Express

http://www.ucmp.berkeley.edu/subway/subway.html

From the University of California Museum of Paleontology, a comprehensive resource center on natural history, including links to other organizations, museums, journals, and major publishers of natural history.

Chapter 46

Popular Culture

Aaron Marcavitch

Metasites

Eserver

http://eserver.org

Eserver, formerly the English Server, is a massive collection of links to a wide range of topics, most of which focus on popular culture. Art, architecture, feminism, music, and poetry are examples of the highlighted sites.

Google Directory of Social History and Popular Culture

http://directory.google.com/Top/Society/History/By_Topic/Social_History/ Pop_Culture/

This site provides a quick link to many sites dedicated to popular culture. While some are less informative than others, this is a useful first stop before delving deeper into the subject.

History of American Pop Culture

http://web.uccs.edu/history/ushistory/popcult.html

This Web site from the University of Colorado at Colorado Springs Web site is good for links to various popular culture Web sites. The list is selective, providing a good starting point for researchers.

Journals and Organizations

Americana: The Institute for the Study of American Popular Culture

http://www.americanpopularculture.com/

This site provides access to *Americana,* a scholarly, refereed journal. The rest of the site includes sections with articles on various aspects of popular culture.

H-Net: Popular Culture Association and American Culture Association

http://www.h-net.org/~pcaaca/

This Web site provides sign-up for the listserv discussion group, access to the discussion logs, and information on the organization itself. Conference and prize announcements are made on the site.

Journal of Popular Culture

http://www.msu.edu/~tjpc/

This journal, the official publication of the Popular Culture Association, is a "peer-reviewed journal founded in 1967 by Ray and Pat Browne." The site provides submission requirements and a table of contents for recent issues.

Selected Sites

Many sites are not academically focused, but are personal in nature. This list provides sites covering a breadth of topics.

The 1920s Experience

http://www.angelfire.com/co/pscst/

This site, true to its name, explores the art, literature, music, entertainment, and fads and fashions from the second decade of the twentieth century. Each section provides links to a few informative paragraphs about each topic.

American Diner Museum

http://www.americandinermuseum.org

This new museum, based in Providence, Rhode Island, is dedicated to preserving and interpreting the diner in American life. Currently it is developing a new museum Web site.

American Highway Project

http://www.highwayproject.org/

This well-designed site provides documentation of the roadside and transportation. Focused on clean black-and-white photography of roadside architecture, it provides a comprehensive link section for roadside Web sites.

The Atlas of Popular Culture in the Northeastern United States

http://www.geography.ccsu.edu/harmonj/atlas/atlasf.html

This collection of articles on local foods (burgers, wings, etc.), sports, and regions is still under development. John Harman of the Department of Geography at Central Connecticut State University has produced articles providing extensive information on the history and development of the various subjects that he discusses.

BGSU's Popular Culture Program

http://www.bgsu.edu/departments/popc/

Bowling Green State University has the only such degree program in America. Within the site, there are links to the Browne Popular Culture Library, events listings, and the Center for Popular Culture.

Crazy Fads

http://www.crazyfads.com/

Crazy Fads provides interesting information about popular culture items like pet rocks, goldfish swallowing, flagpole sitting, and three-dimensional movies. Although the articles are short, the site does provide a research starting point for the various decades of the twentieth century.

The Crossroads Project

http://xroads.virginia.edu/

American Studies at the University of Virginia, also known as the Crossroads project, provides a wealth of knowledge about American topics. Hypertexts, cultural maps, information on the 1930s, teaching resources, and a wide range of PDF versions of journal articles are all part of this site.

Emergence of Advertising in America

http://scriptorium.lib.duke.edu/eaa/index.html

This Web site details the advertising in America from 1850 to 1920. Drawn from the Rare Book, Manuscript, and Special Collections Library at Duke University, the site allows searching of a wide range of topics. The site provides quality photographs, scans of broadsheets, and much more. This is an excellent resource for the researcher of early popular culture.

History of American Popular Culture

http://www.ithaca.edu/faculty/mtrotti/popculture.html

Michael Trotti at Ithaca College in New York posted his syllabus, which provides external links and readings for students. The site creates a basic primer where users can learn about popular culture as part of the American experience.

Kinsey Institute for Research in Sex, Gender, and Reproduction

http://www.indiana.edu/~kinsey/

This site provides information on the Kinsey Institute, jobs, grants, education opportunities, and human sexuality links. While it does not provide a great deal of information on popular culture, Kinsey's work has revolutionized modern popular sexual culture.

Levittown: Documents of an Ideal American Suburb

http://tigger.uic.edu/~pbhales/Levittown.html

This Web site provides insight into the development of one of modern pop cultures biggest influences—the suburb. The site provides in-depth articles about Levittown and provides wonderful images of the place. Of particular interest is the section on Building Levittown. The site provides a link to another Levittown site at http://www.newsday.com/community/guide/lihistory/.

National Historic Route 66 Federation

http://www.nationa166.com/

The National Historic Route 66 Federation is an organization dedicated to public education and rallying support for the preservation of the historic road and the communities it passes through. The site provides links to various other sites, many of which are more focused on the popular culture of the "Mother Road."

Nuke Pop

http://www.wsu.edu/~brians/nukepop/

Nuke Pop looks at nuclear imagery in popular culture. Paul Brian's overview of the magazines and comics throughout the nuclear age provides interesting insight into the culture of that era.

PopMatters

http://popmatters.com/

PopMatters, an online magazine about modern popular culture, includes reviews and articles highlighting music, film, television, books, the Internet, and computers.

PopPolitics

http://www.poppolitics.com/

This site discusses the connection between popular culture and politics. The site provides forums, articles and web logs about politics and its interaction of modern popular culture.

Popular Culture and Historical Analysis

http://www.wsu.edu/~amerstu/pop/hist.html

The Web site Popular Culture: Resources for Critical Analysis provides in-depth study of popular culture. This subsection includes a bibliography and several good links to other sites.

Popular Culture: From Baseball to Rock and Roll

http://www.loc.gov/exhibits/british/brit-7.html

The Library of Congress provides this interesting look at the intersection of American popular culture and British popular culture. This exhibit is filled with images and links to the original collection.

Roadside America

http://www.roadsideamerica.com/

This site offers links, directions, and details on a variety of roadside places around America. It focuses on several different specific types of roadside artifacts, including Muffler Men, large fiberglass structures that are erected by the side of the road. Links to various lesser-known museums across America, including the American Dime Museum, which shows off all sorts of oddities that existed in dime carnivals, and Alienville U.S.A., a Web site on Rosewell, New Mexico. Of particular interest to those seeking information on popular culture is the Electronic Map, which provides a quick, easy way to search for popular sites.

Space Age City

http://www.spaceagecity.com/

This collection focuses on "googie" and "tiki" architecture. Popular culture's influence on architecture is evident on this site where a section on the writings of Ray Bradbury contrasts with the information on architecture. Googie architecture included huge domes and starbursts in its designs and tiki architecture used many island themes, including palm trees and buildings shaped like island huts.

Victorian Web

http://www.victorianweb.org/

This site, while providing a wealth of information on the Victorian period in general, has several areas that are central to early popular culture. Of particular interest are the areas labeled "Visual Arts" and "Theater and Popular Entertainment," which provide a great deal of knowledge about Victorian popular culture, including bibliographies, articles, and other research material.

Chapter 47

Online Reference Desk

Anne Rothfeld

Metasites

Avalon Project at Yale Law School

http://www.yale.edu/lawweb/avalon/avalon.htm

Documents in law, history, and diplomacy from the pre-eighteenth, eighteenth, nineteenth, and twentieth centuries. "The Avalon Project will mount digital documents relevant to the fields of Law, History, Economics, Politics, Diplomacy and Government. We do not intend to mount only static text but rather to add value to the text by linking to supporting documents expressly referred to in the body of the text."

Center for History and New Media

http://chnm.gmu.edu

The center shows historical works in new media and offers a forum to discuss the usage of archival sources in historical research and presentation. In addition, the center's Web pages provide electronic access to extensive directories, journals, sources, and professional discussions related to historical issues. The center's resources are designed to benefit professional historians, high school teachers, and students of history.

Google

http://www.google.com

The world's largest search engine—for free!

History Cooperative

http://www.historycooperative.org

A collaboration between the American Historical Association, the Organization of American Historians (OAH), the University of Illinois Press, and the National Academy Press, this Web site is a gateway to full-text articles in recent journals including *American Historical Review* and *Journal of American History.* Access to some portions of the Web site is restricted.

History Departments Around the World

http://chnm.gmu.edu

Sponsored by the Center for History and New Media at George Mason University, a search engine of university history departments.

H-Net Humanities and Social Sciences Online

http://www.h-net.org/

H-Net is an international organization of historians, teachers, and students of history contributing to discussion of numerous historical subjects thematically, geographically, and chronologically. H-Net offers discussion listservs, job announcements, book reviews, and calls for papers. Each list is monitored by a committee of scholars.

InfoMine

http://infomine.ucr.edu/

Created by librarians, InfoMine is a gateway of resources for faculty, students, and research staff at the university level. Organized by topics and material medium, this reference tool contains databases, electronic journals, electronic books, bulletin boards, listservs, online library card catalogs, articles, and directories of researchers.

Internet Public Library (IPL), Reference Center

http://www.ipl.org/ref

Provides all the basic reference information and specific subject areas of a regular brick-and-mortar library. When users click on a topic, IPL takes them to additional subject-related sites. Links are subdivided and annotated.

Research-It! Your One-stop Reference Desk

http://www.iTools.com

A metasearch site for information. Each area has its own search screen. Hosted by iTools!, the site is broken into sections or "tools" including language, research, financial, maps, people search, and a link to other links.

Scout Report for Social Sciences and Humanities

http://scout.wisc.edu/

Since 1994, the Internet Scout Project of the Computer Sciences Department at the University of Wisconsin-Madison has been offering a selective collection of Internet resources, covering a myriad of topics. The Scout Report staff consists of content specialists aiming at an audience of faculty, students, staff, and librarians in the social sciences and humanities. Subscription is free with no solicitations and pop-up ads, and the report conveniently arrives in your e-mail inbox.

Archives

ArchivesUSA: Integrated Collection and Repository Information

http://archives.chadwyck.com

Fee-based service providing information and access to primary source holdings of over 5,500 repositories, indexes to over 149,000 special collections, and links to over 5,000 online finding aids. ArchivesUSA includes three major references: Directory of Archives and Manuscript Repositories in the United States (DAMRUS); National Union Catalogue of Manuscript Collections (NUCMC); and National Inventory of Documentary Sources in the United States (NIDS). ArchivesUSA is updated quarterly.

Historical Text Archive

http://www.historicaltextarchive.com

Now with its own domain name, the site is divided into three sections: articles, e-books, and Web links. Organized by geographical and topical subject headings, this site provides links to other sites. Sites focus on the studying and teaching of history.

Manuscripts Catalogue

http://molcat.bl.uk/

The British Library's Department of Manuscripts catalog covers accessions from 1753 to the present day in all types of handwritten materials, with the focus on Western languages. Users can search the multiple catalogs by name, language, year, and other modifiers.

Repositories of Primary Sources

http://www.uidaho.edu/special-collections/Other.Repositories.html

With over 5,000 links, this Web site is by far the most complete listing of Web sites for actual (not virtual) archives and special collections departments. Updated frequently by Terry Abraham of the University of Idaho, the site arranges its links by geographical region (continent, country, state, and province). Additional Lists is a good jumping-off point for other archive and special collections metasites.

Acronyms

Acronym Finder

http://www.acronymfinder.com

Searches over 398,000 common acronyms with definitions, including technology, telecommunications, computer science, and military acronyms. Contains search hints and links to other acronym sites.

Almanacs

CIA World Factbook 2000

http://www.cia.gov/cia/publications/factbook

Complete resource of statistics, maps, and facts for over 250 countries and other entities. The *Factbook* is in the public domain. The site has links to other excellent resources, including Chiefs of State and Cabinet Members of Foreign Governments and selected task force reports. Prepared by the CIA with information provided by numerous federal agencies, including Bureau of the Census, Bureau of Labor Statistics, Department of State, Defense Intelligence Agency, and U.S. Board on Geographic Names.

Biographies

Biographical Dictionary

http://www.s9.com/biography

Includes over 28,000 notable men and women from ancient times to the present day. Users can search the database by name, birth year, death year, and other keywords. Links to biography-related sites, arranged by subject, and has tips for students and teachers on how to use this resource in the classroom.

Biography.com

http://www.biography.com

Searchable database with over 25,000 biographical entries and over 2,500 video clips. Features discussions and materials for the classroom.

Copyright

Intellectual Property Law

http://www.cs.utexas.edu/users/ethics/prop_rights/IP.html

Connects visitors to Web site links including patents, trademarks, intellectual property law, and copyright.

U.S. Copyright Office

http://www.loc.gov/copyright

Housed in the Library of Congress in Washington, DC, this is the main office for copyright information on usage and copyright registration. The site describes how to file for a copyright, what can be copyrighted, and the terms of a copyright. Includes copyright information regarding digitization, the Digital Millennium Copyright Act, legislation, and publications.

Corporations

Directory of Corporate Archives in the United States and Canada

http://www.hunterinformation.com/corporat.htm

The fifth edition of this important print directory, put out by the Society of American Archivists, Business Archives Section, has recently moved to the

Web. From Amgen to Walt Disney Corporation, each corporate archive entry supplies contact information, type of business, hours of service, conditions of access, and holding information. "Corporate" is interpreted broadly and includes professional associations ranging from the American Psychiatric Association to the International Longshoreman's Union. The directory may be searched by name of corporation, name of archivist, or geographical location.

Dictionaries and Thesauri

The Alternative Dictionaries

http://www.notam.uio.no/~hcholm/altlang

Contains foreign words and expressions that would not be found in a standard dictionary. Over 3,100 words and phrases in 120 different languages. Readers and users can add words to the site.

Merriam-Webster Dictionary

http://www.m-w.com/dictionary.htm

Sponsored by Merriam-Webster Inc. Full definitions with an online thesaurus available. Features words recently added, word of the day, and word games.

Oxford English Dictionary On-line

http://www.oed.com/

Fee-based service. Second edition is now available.

Roget's Thesaurus

http://www.thesaurus.com

Like Merriam-Webster, this is the print version now searchable with links to other words and phrases, word of the day, and word games.

Wordsmyth English Dictionary-Thesaurus

http://www.wordsmyth.net

Through this Web site, researchers can search words exactly or as a phrase, find definition and pronunciation guides, and access additional dictionaries with words of the week.

YourDictionary.com

http://www.yourdictionary.com

A portal linking over 2,500 multilingual dictionaries, thesauri, and other sites relating to words and phrases in over 300 languages. Grammar guides in selected languages are also available.

Dissertations and Theses

UMI's On-Line Dissertation Services

http://www.umi.com/umi/dissertations/

This site links to published and archived dissertations and theses, including those available for purchase. Maintains a comprehensive bibliography of over 2 million doctoral dissertations and master's theses. A listing of best-selling dissertations is also available.

Encyclopedias

Encyclopedia Britannica Online

http://www.eb.com

This is a fee-based resource. Content is taken from the print edition and also includes information from *Britannica Books of the Year, Nations of the World, Merriam-Webster's Collegiate Dictionary,* 13,000 graphics and illustrations, and links to related Web sites.

Encyclopedia.com

http://www.encyclopedia.com

Because knowledge is cool, this user-friendly Web site offers a free encyclopedia featuring more than 57,000 articles from the *Columbia Electronic Encyclopedia,* sixth edition. Users can search over 32 million full-text documents, photographs, and maps provided by HighBeam Research.

Symbols.com—Encyclopedia of Western Signs and Ideograms

http://www.symbols.com

Site contains over 2,500 Western signs with discussions of histories, uses, and meanings. Search using the graphic index or the word index.

FAQs (Frequently Asked Questions)

Encyclopedia Smithsonian

http://www.si.edu/resource/faq

Encyclopedia Smithsonian features answers to Smithsonian's frequently asked questions with links to available Smithsonian resources. Topics are filed alphabetically.

Flags

Flags of the World (FOTW)

http://www.fotw.ca/flags

Users can view more than 9,800 pages about flags and over 18,000 images. Site contains news and reports posted to the site's mailing list, and flags can be searched by country, title, maps, and keywords. There is also a glossary and bibliography.

General

Find-A-Grave

http://www.findagrave.com/index.html

This site locates the graves of famous people. Database is organized by last name and geographic location and some photos of graves are included. Users can search by name, location, claim to fame, and date. Database currently contains over 7.2 million names.

The HistoryNet: Where History Lives on the Web

http://www.thehistorynet.com

Contains an archive of different topical areas including eyewitness accounts, historic travel, and people profiles. The site has links to history magazines and newspaper articles and sponsors daily quizzes and factoids.

HyperHistory Online

http://www.hyperhistory.com/online_n2/History_n2/a.html

A 3,000-year time line is available to access over 2,000 files with relevant maps, biographies, and brief histories of people, places, and events. The People section reaches from 1000 BCE to the present for over 800 individuals in science, culture, religion, and politics. The History section displays time lines for major civilizations. The Events section continually grows on the site, ranging from 1790 to the present.

Internet Scout Project

http://scout.wisc.edu/

Published every Friday on the Web and by e-mail, this site provides valuable information about new electronic and online resources, free of charge. Subject report areas include social sciences, science and engineering, business and economics, and the site's general weekly report. Librarians and educators contribute to the site offering reviews of useful and not so useful pages. Searchable archives.

Geographic Names and Maps

Getty Vocabulary Names

http://www.getty.edu/research/conducting_research/vocabularies/

Sponsored by the Getty Research Institute, this site currently has information for the Art and Architecture Thesaurus (AAT), the Union List of Artist Names (ULAN), and the Getty Thesaurus of Geographic Names (TGN). AAT contains over 133,000 terms and notes for describing fine art, archival materials, and material culture. ULAN contains over 225,000 names and biographical information about artist and architects. The TGN currently has over a million geographic names and places. Users can search displays by using geographic hierarchy displays, definition or description of term, other known names, and sources.

Perry-Castañeda Library Map Collection

http://www.lib.utexas.edu/maps/

Links to historical maps at other Web sites. Scope of site includes historical maps from Africa, Asia, the Pacific, North America, South America, Europe, and the Middle East. Also includes astronomical maps.

USGS Mapping Information—Geographic Names Information System (GNIS)

http://geonames.usgs.gov/

This Web site contains over 2 million physical and cultural geographic features in the United States supplied by the Geographic Names Information System and U.S. Board on Geographic Names (BGN). Includes a search engine and links to online geographic resources.

Government and State Resources

FedStats

http://www.fedstats.gov

Statistical information gateway for over a hundred federal government agencies and departments. Users can search FedStats by topic for information on demographics, education, and labor. Each site provides annotated links. Includes the Statistical Abstract of the United States.

Social Statistics Briefing Room

http://www.whitehouse.gov/fsbr/ssbr.html

Access to current federal social statistics on crime, demographics, education, and health. Links are produced and provided by numerous federal agencies.

THOMAS: U.S. Congress on the Internet

http://thomas.loc.gov/

Users can search for congressional bills, the *Congressional Record,* committee bills, and historical documents. FAQs regarding THOMAS Are available.

Grants

FinAid! The Smart Student Guide to Financial Aid

http://www.finaid.org/

"One of the most comprehensive annotated collections of information about student financial aid on the web." Includes links to loans, scholarships, and military aid; information on other types of aid; and tips for applying for aid.

The Foundation Center: Your Gateway to Philanthropy on the World Wide Web

http://fdncenter.org

A subscription-based Web site, the Foundation Center provides grant information, funding trends and analysis, libraries and locations, and Foundation Center publications. Searchable links to over 80,000 private, commercial, and corporate funding sources.

Indices

Librarians' Index to the Internet

http://lii.org

Annotated subject-directory to over 7,900 Web resources arranged by subject. The index is linked to over 200 history-related sites. Using the available search engine can focus a search.

Internet Tutorials

Evaluating Internet Resources

http://library.albany.edu/internet/evaluate.html

Discusses what elements should be included in a reliable Web site and why, including the intended audience, the source of the content, the accuracy and comprehensiveness of the content, and the style and functionality of the page.

Searching the Internet: Recommended Sites and Search Techniques

http://library.albany.edu/internet/search.html

Discusses and describes searching tips for successful usage of subject directories and search engines within Web pages.

Libraries

The Library of Congress

http://www.loc.gov/

America's oldest federal cultural institution and the world's largest library. The library's collection contains over 128 million items and includes the largest map, film, and television collections in the world. Its primary mission is to serve the research needs of the U.S. Congress, but the Library assists all Americans through its popular Web site American Memory, which currently contains over 5 million images.

The National Agricultural Library

http://www.nal.usda.gov/

NAL is the primary source of agricultural information for researchers, educators, policy makers, consumers of agricultural products, and the public. The library is one of the world's largest and most accessible agricultural research libraries. Users can search for books and journal articles in NAL's online catalog, AGRICOLA.

National Library of Education

http://www.ed.gov/NLE/

NLE is the federal government's main resource for education information.

National Library of Medicine

http://www.nlm.nih.gov/

The National Library of Medicine is the world's largest biomedical library. Users can search for books and journal articles on NLM's online catalog, LocatorPlus.

Listservs

H-Net

http://www.h-net.org

For historians, librarians, and archivists, H-Net hosts over a hundred different topical listservs and includes a call for papers page, conference announcements, and employment.

Tile.Net: The Comprehensive Internet Reference

http://tile.net

Users can search for discussion lists, newsgroups (usenet), and FTP sites by entering a subject search. All the results are linked to a page describing the listing and how to subscribe.

Quotations

John Barlett's Familiar Quotations (1901)

http://www.bartleby.com/bartlett

Sponsored by Columbia University's Bartleby Library Archive. Includes English and French writers and wisdom from the ancients. Users can browse by author or search by keyword. Indices are available to browse by author, both alphabetically and chronologically.

The Quotations Page

http://www.quotationpage.com

Read motivational quotes of the day on numerous topics including successes, families, authors, and sports.

Statistics

Historical U.S. Census Data Browser

http://fisher.lib.virginia.edu/collections/stats/histcensus/

Descriptions of people and economy of the United States for each state and county from 1790 to 1960. Information on individuals is not available.

Statistical Abstract of the United States

http://www.census.gov/statab/www

Excellent resource for statistical information: demographics, employment, industrial production, and government financial information. Online information covers data from 1995 to 2005.

U.S. Census Bureau: U.S. Gazetteer

http://tiger.census.gov/cgi-bin/gazetteer

Census data from 1990 on all incorporated municipalities in the United States. Maps provided.

Student and School Information

American Universities

http://www.clas.ufl.edu/CLAS/american-universities.html

An alphabetical listing of universities and colleges in the United States offering undergraduate and advanced degrees.

CollegeNet

http://www.collegenet.com

Search engine helps students find the ideal college by using such categories as region, sports, major, and tuition. Users can also find scholarships and financial aid, college Web applications, and information on college recruiting. Virtual tours allow users to see campuses from the desktop with links to the schools' Web sites.

Peterson's College Search and Guide: Colleges, Career Information, Test Prep, and More

http://www.petersons.com

Prospective students can find their ideal college by major, region, and size of student population. This education resource has links to colleges and universities, graduate programs, and international programs. Users can search the database by keywords and subject specialty.

U.S. News and World Report Online: Graduate School Rankings

http://www.usnews.com/usnews/edu/grad/rankings/rankindex_brief.php

This site helps prospective students find graduate programs meeting their requirements. Includes methodology of rankings.

U.S. News and World Report Online: Undergraduate School Rankings

http://www.usnews.com/usnews/edu/college/rankings/rankindex_brief.php

Users can locate a school by using categories from the most expensive school to one with the best marching band! Includes an explanation of the magazine's methodology of rankings.

Style Manuals and Usage

MLA Online

http://www.mla.org/style

This official site for the Modern Language Association (MLA) provides explanations of the *MLA Handbook for Writers of Research Papers* and *MLA Style*

Manual and Guide to Scholarly Publications, especially on citing electronic resources. Official site for Modern Languages Association (MLA).

Strunk's Elements of Style

http://www.columbia.edu/acis/bartleby/strunk

The print edition online.

Glossary

ActiveX: Downloadable Microsoft technology used on the Internet. These controls are activated by the Web browser and perform a variety of different functions, such as allowing users to view Microsoft Word documents via the Web browser, play animated graphical effects, and display interactive maps. As the name suggests, they make the Web page active, and they provide the same functions as Java Applets.

animated GIF File: A special type of GIF file. A collection of GIFs, presented one after the other with each picture slightly different from the previous one, gives the impression of a video.

applet: A brief program written in the Java programming language that can only be used as part of a Web page.

ASCII (American Standard Code for Information Interchange): A way of formatting data so that it can be read by any program, whether DOS, Windows, or Mac.

av (audiovisual): The file extension assigned to the final draft of an AV document.

BBS (bulletin board system): This term usually refers to small, dial-up systems, which local users can call directly. BBS users generally work asynchronously, meaning that they do not have to be connected to the Web the entire time they are uploading, downloading, and posting messages.

bit: The smallest unit of information understood by a computer. A bit can take a value of 0 or 1. A byte is made up of eight bits, which is large enough to contain a single character. A kilobyte is equivalent to 1024 bytes. A megabyte is equivalent to 1024 kilobytes. A gigabyte is equivalent to 1024 megabytes. A terabyte is equivalent to 1024 gigabytes. A petabyte is equivalent to 1024 terabytes and 9,007,199,254,740,992 bits.

blog: A Web log, which is a log on the Web of a person's (or group's) ideas normally on a certain subject, such as American history or current events, and contain the log and posts about the ideas.

broadband: This refers to a variety of ways to access the Internet, all of them faster than dial-up. Included in this category are cable modems, wireless connections, and DSL lines. Availability greatly varies, and people in urban areas generally have more access than those in rural areas.

browser: A program used to access the World Wide Web. The most popular browsers—Netscape, Linux, AOL, and Internet Explorer—allow users to interact audiovisually with the World Wide Web. AOL provides its own browser solely for its subscribers to use.

burn: To record music or data from a computer onto a storage device (usually a CD or DVD).

cable modem: A modem that works through a cable TV network to send and receive information.

client: A synonym for Web browser or browser.

desktop: The screen that appears once a computer has started up and launched its operating system, but before any programs are launched. This is the background that appears on the base screen of the computer.

dial-up: A type of modem that works through telephone lines to send and receive information. Also, the act of using such a modem.

discussion list: A program that allows an asynchronous discussion between various members of the list by sending a message from one member to all the rest and then allowing the rest to respond. Most discussion lists also have archives of past messages.

DNS (domain name system): DNS is the system that locates addresses on the World Wide Web. When a DNS error message is given by a browser, it means the address it is looking for cannot be found.

document: On the World Wide Web, documents are files or a set of files that can be accessed with a Web browser. Also, most people use the term to refer to any word-processing file.

download: The process of getting a file or files from a remote computer, which is a computer other than the one on a user's desk or local area network.

DSL (digital subscriber line): A faster way to access the Internet than the standard dial-up process, often available through the phone company but generally more expensive.

e-mail: Sending typed messages and attachments through an electronic mail network.

encryption: A method of converting data into unreadable code so that prying eyes cannot understand the content.

FAQ (frequently asked questions): A document that contains answers to the most frequently asked questions about a given topic.

file: A collection of data stored on a disk or other storage device under a certain name.

flame: The practice of sending extremely negative or insulting e-mail.

Flash: A program developed by Macromedia Corporation used by many Web sites to present graphics quickly on Web pages.

FTP (file transfer protocol): A tool for moving files from a computer site to a user's local service provider's computer, from which they can be downloaded.

GIF (graphic interchange format): A set of standards for compressing graphic files so that they occupy less space in a computer's memory or on a storage device. CompuServe and Unisys developed GIF.

hits: Internet slang for both the number of times a site is accessed and for the number of sites found when using any Web search engine.

H-Net (Humanities and Social Studies Online): An organization dedicated to exploiting the potential of electronic media for history. H-Net was originally supported by the National Endowment for the Humanities, the University of Illinois–Chicago, and Michigan State University. Now, H-Net is supported by grants, donations, and job ads paid for by the universities advertising. H-Net sponsors discussion lists, Web sites, book reviews, conferences, and other activities.

home page: The designated beginning point for accessing a World Wide Web site.

HTML (Hypertext Markup Language): One computer language used to construct documents on the World Wide Web. Most home pages are written in HTML.

HTTP (Hypertext Transfer Protocol): A method of coding information that enables different computers running different software to communicate information. It permits the transfer of text, sounds, images, and other data.

hypertext: Data that provides links to other data, allowing users to move from one resource to another.

icon: A graphic image that is used to represent (and usually activate) a file or program.

Internet: The worldwide network of computers that are linked together using the Internet protocol TCP/IP.

ISP (Internet service provider): Any organization that provides connections to the Internet.

Java: A programming language developed by Sun Microsystems that allows programmers to create interactive applications that can be run within Web browsers on any type of computer. Java programs are referred to as applets.

JavaScript: A programming language for developing Internet applications. A Web browser interprets JavaScript statements embedded in an HTML page to create interactivity.

JPEG (Joint Photographic Experts Group): This is now the standard format for compressing graphic files so they occupy less space in a computer's memory or on a storage device.

kbps (kilobits per second): A unit frequently used to measure how fast data is transferred between devices on a network. One KBPS is 1,000 bits per second.

LAN (local area network): A group of computers connected together by cable or some other means so they can share common resources.

link: A connection point that takes the user from one document to another or from one information provider to another.

Listserv: A computer that serves a discussion group by processing, distributing, and storing messages and files for all members of the list.

log in: To gain access to a remote computer system or network by typing a login name and password.

login name (user-ID): The name used for security purposes to gain access to and identify oneself on a network or computer system.

modem: A way to connect to the Internet. A modem can operate through a phone line (dial-up or DSL) or through a TV (cable modem). Generally a user must both buy a modem (although a modem may come with the computer) and pay for service from an Internet service provider (ISP) in order to gain access to the Web.

MPEG (Moving Pictures Expert Group): This is the standard for compressing video images so they occupy less space in a computer's memory or on a storage device.

netiquette: Etiquette for the Internet.

network: A group of interconnected computers.

nickname: A name used in place of a real name. Aliases are often shorter or cleverer than a person's real name, and they offer a measure of privacy in the online community.

page: Either a single screen of information on a Web site or all of the information on a particular site.

PDF (portable document format): A file type developed by Adobe Systems to allow the preservation of complex formatting and symbols.

POP (post office protocol): A standard for exchanging e-mail between a user's computer and an Internet service provider.

RAM (random access memory): The memory that a computer uses to temporarily store and manipulate information. RAM does not hold information after a computer is turned off.

RealAudio: Software that allows sound files to be transmitted from the Internet back to the user's computer in streams, allowing the experience of immediate and simultaneous playing.

rip: To copy music or data from a CD or DVD onto a computer. The first user burns the information from a computer onto a CD or DVD and then a second user rips the information from the storage device onto another computer.

SMTP (simple mail transfer protocol): An accepted standard used extensively on the Internet to allow the transfer of e-mail messages between computers.

snail mail: A term that e-mail users employ to describe the traditional mail or post office service.

spam: To send e-mails to people who in no way asked for that information. Spamming is usually done as bulk e-mailing in order to hassle people, to promote a product, or to send a virus. Named for the Monty Python sketch in which a restaurant served almost nothing but Spam.

TCP/IP (transfer control protocol/Internet protocol): Essentially this is the most basic language on the Internet. The rules of TCP/IP govern the sending of packets of data between computers on the Internet, and they allow for the transmission of other protocols on the Internet, such as HTTP and FTP.

telnet: An Internet protocol enabling users to log on to a remote computer.

T-1 line: A leased Internet line connection. The maximum speed at which data can be transmitted is 1.45 megabits per second on a T-1 line.

UNIX: Like DOS or Windows, UNIX is an operating system run by most of the computers that provide access to the Internet.

URL (Uniform Resource Locator): The address for an Internet site.

USENET: A network of newsgroups dedicated to thousands of different topics.

User-ID (Login name): The name used for security purposes to gain access to and identify oneself on a network or computer system.

Web browser: A program used to access the World Wide Web. The most popular browsers—Netscape and Internet Explorer—allow users to interact audiovisually with the World Wide Web.

Webmail: An e-mail program, based at a Web site, that allows users to pick up their e-mail wherever they are in the world, as long as they have access to the Web. Users log onto a Web site to pick up their e-mail rather than having to access the server at their own institution. Useful and becoming a more universal way to administer and access e-mail.

WiFi (wireless access): A pun on "HiFi"(high fidelity), WiFi is the term used to describe any computer or location capable of making a wireless Internet connection.

Windows Media Player: A program, available for computers using Windows, that allows users to play audio and video files.

.wma: Windows Media Audio. This extension refers to an audio file that is playable by the Windows Media Player on a Windows-based machine.

.wmv: Windows Media Video. This extension refers to a video file that is playable by the Windows Media Player on a Windows-based machine.

WWW (World Wide Web): An Internet service that enables users to connect to all the hypermedia documents on the Internet. The Web is like a network within the Internet.

Zip: Zip files (or Zipped files) are files that have been compressed by a software package to reduce the amount of space that the data take up. The file type is popular on the Internet because smaller files can be sent faster. To create or open a Zip file, a user needs a special software package such as WinZip or PKUNZIP. The .zip extension indicates a Zip file.

About the Editors and Contributors

Jeffrey G. Barlow holds the Matsushita Chair of East Asian Studies and is a professor of history, Pacific University, Forest Grove, Oregon. He is also faculty coordinator for the Berglund Center for Internet Studies and edits its journal, *The Journal of Education, Community, and Values: Interface on the Internet*. His interests are East Asian history, the ethnohistory of the Sino-Vietnamese frontier, and history and computing.

John Barnhill is an independent scholar in Oklahoma (PhD, Oklahoma State University) whose publications deal with immigration, civil rights, energy, and other aspects of the twentieth-century United States. He is author of *From Surplus to Substitution: Energy in Texas* and numerous articles and reviews.

Jeremy Boggs is a PhD student in the Department of History and Art History, George Mason University, and a graduate assistant at the Center for History and New Media. His research interests include nineteenth-century U.S. cultural history, race and racism in U.S. history, and history and new media. Jeremy is currently working on a project that assesses the current state of historical scholarship on the Web and an annotated index of online history journals. Jeremy maintains a blog, ClioWeb, at http://www.clioweb.org.

Patrick Callan is a deputy principal and lecturer at Maynooth-National University of Ireland. He received his BA, MA, and PhD from University College, Dublin, and he is a frequent speaker, writer, and lecturer in Ireland on the future of education and technology.

David Calverley has a PhD in history from the University of Ottawa (1999). His particular specialty is Canadian history (with a focus on First Nations history). He has taught postsecondary students and currently is teaching secondary-level history at the Crescent School in Toronto. His book, *Who Controls the Hunt? Ontario's Game Act, the Canadian Government and the Ojibwa, 1800–1940,* is under consideration for publication by McGill-Queen's University Press.

Mary E. Chalmers teaches European history at Butler University, Indianapolis, Indiana, and is currently president of the American Association for History and Computing. She has taught European and world history for almost a decade at a variety of institutions.

James P. Cousins is a doctoral student at the University of Kentucky, having received his MA from University of Kentucky in 2004 and his BA from Ohio State University in 1999. He was a contributing translator of the *Suda On Line Project of Byzantine Lexicography,* among other publications and research efforts.

Christine de Matos has taught history and computing over the past nine years at the University of Sydney; the University of Technology, Sydney; and the University of Western Sydney. She is currently a doctoral candidate at the University of Western Sydney. Her dissertation explores Australians and the Left in Japan during the Allied Occupation from 1945 to 1949. Recent publications include a paper on the use of computing technology in bachelor of arts degrees and another on the Australian Labor government's policy toward the democratization of Japan from 1945 to 1949. She is currently the manager of the Web site for the Professional Historians Association (NSW, http://www.phansw.org.au).

Samuel Dicks holds a doctorate from the University of Oklahoma and has been a member of the history faculty at Emporia State University since 1965. He is the publication director of *Teaching History: A Journal of Methods* and edits its Internet Web site. In addition to courses in ancient and medieval history, he also teaches historiography and an introductory class in genealogy.

Bambi L. Dingman is a freelance writer from New Jersey. She has been the French and Indian War editor for *Smoke and Fire News,* an internationally recognized living history newspaper, and has also written for *Recreating History Magazine.*

She currently serves as the regimental adjutant for the Seventh Vermont Infantry Regiment as part of the Web-based project Vermont in the Civil War.

TammyJo Eckhart is a PhD candidate in ancient history at Indiana University in Bloomington. She focuses on issues of gender and sexuality, mythology, and slavery. Her minor fields are folklore and comparative women's history. Her research has been published in *Aeon: A Journal of Myth and Science,* her book reviews appear regularly in *The Women's Classical Caucus Newsletter,* and she is a contributor to Salem Press's *Encyclopedia of the Ancient World.*

Lakita Edwards currently serves as the education specialist at Harpers Ferry Center, the media design center for the National Park Service. She received her her EdM in arts in education from Harvard University and her BA from Simon's Rock College, Great Barrington, Massachusetts, in art history and psychology. As a Student Conservation Association alumna, Lakita participated in the pilot of the North American Community Service Project (NACS) in 2002, where she worked with three distinct communities across North America. Her interdisciplinary academic interests include enhancing the impact of the arts in experiential learning and exploring ways to effectively engage diverse audiences through educational media.

Sarah Ferentinos is associate editor of the *OAH Magazine of History,* published by the Organization of American Historians, and a PhD candidate in U.S. history at Indiana University. She holds an MA in history and an MLS, with a concentration in special collections.

Pamela Grey holds a PhD in American history from the University of Southern California. Her emphasis is western history (multicultural–Native Americans), and her dissertation is a biography of Y.B. Burke, the first African-American congresswoman from California. Her personal area of research is architecture and the American West. She currently focuses on teaching history through historical images and photography. She also is a photographer and has worked as an architectural historian.

Mary Anne Hansen is an assistant professor at Montana State University Libraries. She has authored numerous articles and presented papers at several scholarly conferences, including the Association of College and Research Libraries Biennial Conference.

Lisa R. Holliday is a graduate student at the University of Kentucky, where she is completing her dissertation. Her research interests include early Christian history, Roman culture, and intellectual history.

Mariah Hudson is a PhD student in early American history at The Ohio State University in Columbus, Ohio, where she teaches early American history. Her research interests are in urban development and gender, ethnicity, and race in the nineteenth century trans-Mississippi West. For her dissertation, she is writing a comparative study of public health systems and their relationship to mortality in Cleveland, Savannah, Denver, and Atlanta. Mariah holds an MA in American studies from the University of Dallas (2001), where she studied American economic history, and a BA in English from the University of Oregon (1999).

Ranin Kazemi is a second-year MA student in the Department of History at The Ohio State University. Islamic history is his primary academic focus. He acquired his BA degree in English and history from Middle Tennessee State University in May 2002. His interests within his primary field include Iranian history, cultural and intellectual exchange between Iran and its neighbors, and social and intellectual movements on the greater Iranian plateau.

John A. King holds degrees in history and political science from Emory University, Atlanta, Georgia, and Vanderbilt University in Nashville, Tennessee, including a PhD in history, with an emphasis on Chilean history and U.S.-Latin American relations. He taught at Vanderbilt University as a teaching fellow and instructor and served as a history professor at Belmont University in Nashville, Tennessee, before coming to Ransom Everglades Schools in Florida in 1999. He is currently also a member of the adjunct faculty at Barry University, Florida, teaching courses on modern America, the history of Florida, and the contemporary world.

Stephen Kneeshaw is professor of history at College of the Ozarks in southwest Missouri. He is also involved with the teacher education program, specifically history and social studies education. He completed his BA in history and English at the University of Puget Sound and his MA and PhD in American history at the University of Colorado, Boulder. Since 1972 he has been on the history faculty at College of the Ozarks, where he was named the first recipient of the college's Distinguished Faculty Award for excellence in teaching, scholarship, and service. He has held fellowships for study and research at the Newberry Library, Chicago, Illionois, Harvard, MIT, and the U.S. Military Academy at West Point. Steve is the founder and editor of *Teaching History: A Journal of Methods* and for several years has presented workshops on "Active Teaching and Learning" at high schools and colleges. His publications cover a wide range of topics from diplomatic history-to-history education, active learning, and writing to learn.

David Koeller received his MA and PhD from the University of California, Berkeley, and is a specialist in the German Enlightenment. He is an associate professor of history at North Park University, Chicago, Illionis, and has taught world history for many years. He also serves as a member of the World History Association and recently won a grant from the Ameritech Corporation to help develop the WebChron Web Chronology Project.

Jessica Lacher-Feldman serves as the public and outreach services coordinator at the W.S. Hoole Special Collections Library at the University of Alabama. As part of the libraries faculty, she coordinates reference services and instruction, curates archival exhibitions, arranges public events, and manages the Hoole Web site. A native of New York state, Jessica holds a BA in French studies and master's degrees in history and library science (archives concentration) from the State University of New York at Albany. She is active in the American Association for History and Computing, the Society of American Archivists, and the Society of Alabama Archivists.

Donnelly Lancaster is a faculty member of the University of Alabama Libraries, where she is archival access coordinator for the W.S. Hoole Special Collections Library and manages the manuscript department. She holds a master's degree in history with an emphasis in archival studies from Auburn University. A former junior fellow of the Library of Congress Manuscript Division, she is an active member of the Society of American Archivists and the Society of Alabama Archivists and serves on the editorial board of *Provenance,* the journal of the Society of Georgia Archivists.

Robert Lee is a manuscript cataloger for the Gilder Lehrman Collection, on deposit at the New York Historical Society. He works with archival holdings concerning the political and social history of the United States, focusing on the periods of the American Revolution and the early republic.

Aaron Marcavitch is currently finishing his thesis (on standardized roadside architecture) for an MA in public history from Middle Tennessee State University. He already holds a BS in historic preservation from Roger Williams University in Rhode Island. Aaron lives on Nantucket with his wife, Andrea, working at the Nantucket Historic District Commission as assistant administrator. He is a member of the board for the Recent Past Preservation Network and is the webmaster for the Vernacular Architecture Forum. He maintains a personal Web site at http://www.marcavitch.com.

Mark McCallon is business reference librarian and assistant director for the Margaret and Herman Brown Library at Abilene Christian University (ACU) in Abilene, Texas. He has contributed articles to several business and general history encyclopedias, including *Encyclopedia of African American Business* and *African American National Biography.* He has also served as electronic resources and technology librarian at ACU.

Jeffrey W. McClurken worked on the *Valley of the Shadow* online project at the University of Virginia for fifteen months. He graduated from Johns Hopkins University, Baltimore, Maryland, in 2002 with a PhD in American history. He is currently completing a manuscript titled, "After the Battle: Reconstructing the Confederate Veteran Family in Pittsylvania County and Danville, Virginia, 1860–1900." He is an assistant professor of history at the University of Mary Washington, in Fredericksburg, Virginia.

Elisabeth McMahon is currently completing her PhD in East African history at Indiana University. She is also currently teaching a course on African civilizations. She previously served as the managing editor of the journal *Africa Today.*

Scott A. Merriman teaches at the University of Kentucky and the University of Maryland University College. He received his PhD in modern American history from the University of Kentucky in 2003. He has previously taught history at the University of Cincinnati, Northern Kentucky University, Midway College in Kentucky, and Thomas More College in Kentucky. His books include *The History Highway: A Guide to Internet Resources, The History Highway 2000: A Guide to Internet Resources, The History Highway 3.0: A Guide to Internet Resources,* and *History.edu: Essays on Teaching with Technology.* He currently is an associate editor for *Journal of the Association for History and Computing.* He has contributed to the *Register of the Kentucky Historical Society, Historical Encyclopedia of World Slavery, American National Biography, American Decades Primary Sources,* and *Buckeye Hill Country,* among other publications.

Martin V. Minner is a PhD candidate at Indiana University who specializes in urban history and photographic history. His current research is on civic politics and cultural memory in Newark, New Jersey. He is also a technical communication consultant and has worked in software development and computer publishing.

Ian Morley is a former student at the Universities of Humberside, Leicester, and Sheffield in England. With a PhD in British urban history, he has researched the development of the Victorian urban model, civic design, and urban futures. He has numerous publications and has presented at international conferences in many countries, including Malaysia, Singapore, Taiwan, New Zealand, Russia, the United States, England, Spain, and Italy. He also acts as teaching editor to the H-Urban Web site (part of the H-Net online forum) and is curriculum issues editor for the *Academic Exchange Quarterly.*

Richard P. Mulcahy is currently an associate professor of history and director of the Division of Social Sciences with the University of Pittsburgh, Titusville. The author of a number of refereed articles and book chapters, he currently has a book dealing with social policy in Appalachia.

Melissa Ooten received her MA in history from the College of William and Mary, Virginia, in 2001. She currently teaches history and women's studies there, and she defended her dissertation, "Screen Strife: Movie Censorship in Virginia, 1922–1965," in the fall of 2005.

S. Mike Pavelec received his PhD in history from The Ohio State University in 2004. He is an assistant professor of history at Hawaii Pacific University and teaches classes within the Master's in Diplomacy and Military Studies program. He is an active contributor to the historical field with recent book reviews, presentations, and upcoming publications. His first book, *The Development of Turbojet Aircraft in Germany, Britain, and the United States: A Multi-national Comparison of Aeronautical Engineering 1935–1946*, is undergoing revisions for publication with Texas A&M University Press. He focuses on military history, aviation history, science and technology studies, and the interaction between technology and society.

Jessie Bishop Powell, Merriman received a master's degree in English from the University of Kentucky in 2000 and a master's degree in library and information science from the same institution in 2001.

Edward Ragan received his PhD in early American and Native American history from Syracuse University. Currently, he is a visiting assistant professor at the State University of New York, College of Environmental Science and Forestry. His dissertation explores seventeenth-century Anglo-Indian relations in Virginia. Through his research, he has become involved with Virginia Indians in their efforts to gain federal acknowledgment. He has worked most closely with the Rappahannock Tribe. In 2002, he drafted the recognition petition that the Rappahannocks submitted to the United States Congress and the Bureau of Indian Affairs. In addition, he works with the Rappahannock's community education and cultural recovery programs.

Hugh Randall received his BS and MA in history from Central Michigan University and is currently working on his PhD at The Ohio State University. He has recently contributed to *France and the Americas: Culture, Politics, History* (2005) and *Encyclopedia of the New American Nation* (2005).

J. Kelly Robison teaches at San Juan College in New Mexico. He holds a PhD in American history from Oklahoma State University and an MA in American history from the University of Montana. His research and teaching focus is the history of the American West and Native America, with a special emphasis on the Spanish borderlands and cross-cultural acculturation. He is also interested in the use of computer technology in teaching and researching history. He is a consulting editor for the *Journal of the Association for History and Computing*.

Anne Rothfeld is an information specialist at the University of Maryland, Baltimore. She earned her MA in library science from the Catholic University of America, Washington, DC, concentrating in special collections and archives. Previously she was the archivist technician at the U.S. Holocaust Memorial Museum in Washington, DC.

Thomas Saylor is associate professor of history and director of the Faculty Scholarship Center at Concordia University, St. Paul, Minnesota. He studied at the University of Akron, Ohio, and the University of Rochester, New York, where he received his doctorate in 1993. Professionally active in the field of oral history, since 2001 he has founded and directed two oral history projects dealing with World War II. He is the author of *Remembering the Good War* (2005), on the varied experiences of women and men in the Upper Midwest between 1941 and 1945. He is currently working on a book on Minnesotans held as POWs during World War II, having completed more than seventy-five interviews across the nation.

Christopher A. Snyder is acting chair of the department of history and politics at Marymount University in Arlington, Virginia. He taught at Emory University, Atlanta, Georgia, and the College of William and Mary in Virginia before coming to Marymount, and he is a fellow of the Society of Antiquaries of Scotland. His books include *Sub-Roman Britain (AD 400–800): A Gazetteer of Sites* (1996) and *An Age of Tyrants: Britain and the Britons, AD 400–800* (1998).

David J. Staley is director of the Harvey Goldberg Program for Excellence in Teaching at The Ohio State University. He is executive director of the American Association for History and Computing. His areas of interest include visual thinking, historical methodology, the history of science and technology, and the philosophy of history. His publications include *Computers, Visualization and History: How New Technology Will Transform Our Understanding of the Past* (M.E. Sharpe, 2003).

Kathleen A. Tobin received her PhD in history from the University of Chicago. She currently works as assistant professor of Latin American studies at Purdue University Calumet in Hammond, Indiana. Her interests are U.S.-Latin American relations and population policy.

Dennis A. Trinkle is the chief information officer for Valparaiso University. He previously served as Tenzer University Professor in Instructional Technology and chief information officer at DePauw University. He received his BA from DePauw University and his MA and PhD from the University of Cincinnati. He also served for nearly a decade as the executive director of the American Association for History and Computing (http://www.theaahc.org). He has published broadly on technology, teaching, and history. His books include *The History Highway: A Guide to Internet Resources; Writing, Teaching, and Researching History in the Electronic Age; History.edu: Essays on Teaching with Technology; The History Highway 2000: A Guide to Internet Resources;* and *The History Highway 3.0: A Guide to Internet Resources.*

Richard Wojtowicz is a reference librarian and assistant professor at Montana State University, Bozeman. He received his MS in library and information science from the University of Illinois, Urbana-Champaign (2000), his MA in the history of science and technology from Montana State University (1989), and his BA in geography from State University of New York at Buffalo (1973). In 1989, he compiled *Blacks Who Stole Themselves: Advertisements for Runaways in the Pennsylvania Gazette, 1728–1790* with Billy G. Smith. He is presently working on an environmental history of the Yellowstone River basin.

Alexander Zukas is an associate professor of history at National University in San Diego. He received his PhD in history from the University of California, Irvine, in 1991. He has written on the European working class and gender history, innovative approaches to the teaching of world history, and using music and theater to teach historical subject matter. His publications include the articles "Lazy, Apathetic, and Dangerous: The Social Construction of Unemployed Workers in the Late Weimar Republic," *Contemporary European History* (forthcoming); "Cyberworld: Teaching World History on the World Wide Web," *The History Teacher* (August 1999); "Age of Empire," *Radical History Review* (Winter 1997); and "Different Drummers: Using Music to Teach History," *Perspectives* (October 1996). He is currently working on articles about teaching world history courses on the Internet, the phenomenology of teaching online, Karl Korsch's Marxism, unemployed workers in the Ruhr region of Germany during the Weimar Republic, and the ecology of the Ruhr from 1850 to 1930. He serves as director of the Institute for Community and Oral History of the Center for Cultural and Ethnic Studies at National University.

Index

CD INSTRUCTIONS

The PDF file, The History Highway.pdf, can be read by opening it in Acrobat Reader 7. Acrobat Reader 7 is provided on the disc for PCs that do not have Acrobat Reader. Click on it to install it. If you experience problems with this reader, or require a Mac version, go to http://www.adobe.com/products/acrobat/ for a free download of the appropriate reader for your system.

LICENSE AGREEMENT

This is a legal agreement between you (the "end user") and M.E.Sharpe, Inc. By breaking the seal on this package, you have agreed to be bound by the terms of this agreement. If you do not agree to the terms of this agreement, return the CD-ROM in its original packaging to M.E.Sharpe, Inc. This copy is licensed to you for use under the following conditions:

Permitted Uses/You May:
• Use the software on any compatible computer, provided the software is used on only one computer and by one user at a time.
• Use the software on a network, file service, or virtual disk, provided that you have a copy of the print edition of The History Highway and the program disk.

Prohibited Uses/You May Not:
• Make copies of the program disk.
• Distribute, rent, sublicense, or lease the software.
• Alter, modify, or adapt the software, including but not limited to, translating, decompiling, disassembling, or creating derivative works.

This license and your right to use the software automatically terminate if you fail to comply with any provision of this License Agreement.

M.E.Sharpe, Inc., 80 Business Park Drive, Armonk, New York 10504

Collins
COBUILD
English
Usage

DISCARD
DISCARD

THE UNIVERSITY
OF BIRMINGHAM

second edition 2004

© HarperCollins Publishers 1992, 2004

latest reprint 2004

HarperCollins Publishers
Westerhill Road, Bishopbriggs, Glasgow G64 2QT
Great Britain

www.collins.co.uk

Collins®, COBUILD® and Bank of English® are registered
trademarks of HarperCollins Publishers Limited

ISBN 0-00-716346-0

Corpus Acknowledgements

We would like to acknowledge the assistance of the many hundreds of individuals
and companies who have kindly given permission for copyright material to be
used in the Bank of English. The written sources include many national and
regional newspapers in Britain and overseas; magazine and periodical publishers;
and book publishers in Britain, the United States and Australia. Extensive spoken
data has been provided by radio and television broadcasting companies; research
workers at many universities and other institutions; and numerous individual
contributors. We are grateful to them all.

Note

Entered words that we have reason to believe constitute trademarks have been
designated as such. However, neither the presence nor the absence of such
designation should be regarded as affecting the legal status of any trademark.

All rights reserved. No part of this book may be reproduced, stored
in a retrieval system, or transmitted in any form or by any means,
electronic, mechanical, photocopying, recording or otherwise,
without the prior permission in writing of the Publisher.

A catalogue record for this book is available from the British Library

Typeset by Wordcraft, Glasgow

Printed and bound in Great Britain by William Clowes Ltd, Beccles and London

Second edition

Founding Editor-in-Chief
John Sinclair

Publishing Director
Lorna Knight

Editorial Director
Michela Clari

Managing Editor
Maree Airlie

Project Manager
Alison Macaulay

Editor
Maggie Seaton

Lexicographers
Bob Grossmith, Gill Francis, Liz Potter

US Consultant
Orin Hargraves

Editorial Assistance
Sue Ogden

First edition

Editor-in-Chief
John Sinclair

Editorial Director
Gwyneth Fox

Senior Editors
Elizabeth Manning
John Todd

Assistant Editor
Ann Hewings

Editorial Assistance
Ramesh Krishnamurthy
Alyson McGee
Christina Rammell
Keith Stuart

Computer Officer
Zoe James

Secretary
Sue Crawley

HarperCollins Publishers
Annette Capel, Lorna Heaslip, Douglas Williamson

We would like to thank Mona Baker for her useful comments on the text, Louise Ravelli
for assistance on the grammar entries, and Paul Laurent for checking American Usage.
We would also like to thank the people who suggested points to include in the book,
in particular Maksymilian Baranowski, Abkarovits Endre, Francisco Gomes de Matos,
Yuan Kele, Wolf Paprotté, and Martin Warren.

Contents

Introduction

I am very pleased to introduce the new second edition of the Collins COBUILD English Usage. With the help of the Bank of English®, now totalling 524 million words, our compilers have been able to study how people actually use language, and to use their studies to update and revise this book

Usage is the vital detail of language, involving aspects of grammar, meaning, idiom, variety and purpose. It concentrates on the individuality of expression, and most of its statements concern the way words are arranged to express a particular meaning or to do a particular job. There is no generality in most of the statements in this book, because usage deals with all the things that are not covered by the generalities.

Grammar properly deals with broad general statements, like the distinction between count and uncount nouns, or transitive and intransitive verbs. Each of these divides into sub-classes and sub-sub-classes and so on until eventually we get down to the unusual behaviour of just one or two words. The point of grammar is now lost, and the detailed patterns of usage can be set out individually.

There is no strict dividing line, and many grammars for teaching are heavily biased towards usage. It is, after all, the usage end of grammar that most learners need. However powerful the generalities, learners are eventually measured by the actual words and phrases they use, and so they are probably more concerned about the precise points of usage than the abstract notions of countability or transitivity.

A traditional dictionary does not give much usage information, though some modern dictionaries, like the COBUILD range, show a lot through the choice of typical real examples. Dictionaries of idioms come close to usage, but the special meaning that we associate with an idiom is not usually a feature of a usage statement.

More and more nowadays, reference books are trying to help a user produce competent language. Previously they were mainly useful for understanding language. The pressure is on to provide guidance about every detail of usage. Native speakers of English have had usage books for many years, and language professionals like journalists have long had style books and compendiums of usage. Everyone needs a reference book of this kind, and the non-native user of English is no exception. This Usage book is suitable for students from intermediate to advanced level, and for teachers of English.

In order to make this edition even easier for students and teachers to use, we have divided the book into three separate sections: Grammar, Usage and Topics. Each section is clearly marked in the shaded area at the side of each page. All the entries in each section are in strict alphabetical order, with cross references. One feature of COBUILD is that we try to list all the words or phrases that are used in the same way, rather than just giving one or two examples. The lists are very helpful for language production, for example those in the Grammar entry on Complements give information on what verbs take what sort of complements.

The Usage Section

A large number of the entries in the Usage section of the book are short notes on individual words and phrases. Two words may be easily confused, like 'comprehensive' and 'comprehensible'. One word may require another, for example 'afford' requires 'can', 'could', or 'be able to'. Using the evidence from our vast American corpora, we have increased the coverage of American English for this new edition. Where American and British English are different, this is clearly pointed out, so that you do not eat chips when you want crisps, or buy pants when you want trousers. A careful distinction is made between 'disabled', 'handicapped' and 'crippled' and other words which to some people are very sensitive.

The Grammar Section

In this book, we provide a number of entries on grammatical categories in order to link the facts of usage with the broader issues of grammar. Beyond this level the reader must turn to the Collins COBUILD English Grammar for fuller treatment.

The Topic Section

There are also a number of long entries on important usage topics such as Invitations and Punctuation. In these entries a large number of points are gathered together and presented so that the whole entry can be consulted, or just one or two of the points. There are frequent sub-headings to help users find a particular point, so that the entry can be used for quick reference.

The examples

Above all, COBUILD rests its authority on actual examples. Thousands of real extracts from the growing Bank of English® are used to demonstrate the usage points, and each of them is chosen as an appropriate model, so that it can be confidently followed. The English that people invent to illustrate a point is not part of the real communication and may be quite misleading.

If you are fluent in a language you cannot always bring to mind all the details of your actual usage, because it is below your conscious awareness. Hence you may not be able to produce an example that is really reliable.

At COBUILD there is no problem, except to select the very best from a huge range of real examples. These examples are not just 'based on' a corpus, but are actual citations from a corpus, and we hope to convince users that real examples are the only reliable evidence of usage.

The Bank of English

Since 1980 COBUILD has been gathering real language for its files. Each document or transcript is carefully indexed and put into a form suitable for the COBUILD computers to handle. At present, the total number of words in our corpus stands at some 524 million words.

The corpus is called the Bank of English®, and it is a unique resource that powers all the COBUILD publications. The texts are carefully selected; although 524,000,000 words sounds a lot, there is so much now available from computer typesetting that a lot of skill is needed to make the corpus a faithful record of current English. Hundreds of tape recordings are made and carefully transcribed so that the spoken language is well represented, and all sorts of small-scale documents, local publications, letters etc. are gathered to balance the big output of the newspaper presses.

We are most grateful to the large number of contributors who have generously allowed their language to be used as a source of our knowledge, understanding and exemplification.

Cobuild is always keen to know how the reference books and dictionaries are appreciated, and we have set up an e-mail address (**cobuild@ref.collins.co.uk**) for your comments and criticisms, so that future editions can continue to meet your needs.

John Sinclair

Founding Editor-in-Chief

Emeritus Professor of Modern English Language, University of Birmingham

President, The Tuscan Word Centre

Guide to the Usage

The aim of this book is to help learners of English to use individual words correctly and to choose the right words and structures for the meaning they want to convey. Each entry is based on the latest evidence from the *Bank of English* ® corpus, which now totals over 524 million words, so that both learners and teachers will find the book useful as an authoritative reference on how English is actually used today. For this edition, hundreds of new examples have been added to keep the information given up-to-date and relevant.

To help you find what you want more easily, this new second edition of the Collins COBUILD English Usage has been divided into three sections: Usage, Grammar and Topics. The following pages look at each of these in turn. You will also find an index at the back of the book to show you where to find specific items. The Contents Page on page v lists the entries in the Grammar and Topics sections.

THE USAGE SECTION

There are several types of **Usage** entries, and these are explained below.

Entries for individual words

The entries for individual words explain how to use the word, for example by saying which preposition should be used after the word, or whether you should use a 'to-' infinitive or an '-ing' form after it:

> 1 **used as a noun**
> A **desire** is a feeling that you want something or want to do something. You usually talk about a **desire for** something or a **desire to do** something.

This book deals with words which are known to cause problems for learners. For extra clarity, we often explicitly mention what learners should not say, as well as what they should say. These comments should be useful for learners who are drawing false parallels between their own language and English, or between different words in English. Common errors are clearly marked like this:

> ⚠ **WARNING: Homework** is an uncount noun. You do not talk about 'homeworks' or 'a homework'. Note that you do not say 'I have made my homework', you say 'I have **done** my homework'.

When drawing the learner's attention to a way in which a word or expression cannot be used, we give the word or expression that should be used instead, if there is one:

> However, you do not say that you 'accept to do' what someone suggests. You say that you **agree to do** it.
> *The princess agreed to go on television.*
> *She agreed to let us use her flat while she was away.*

Entries for easily confused words

If two or more words are sometimes confused with each other, all the words are given in the entry heading. For example, the entry headed **accept – except** explains the differences between 'accept' and 'except':

---

accept - except

Do not confuse **accept** /əks<u>e</u>pt/ with **except** /ɪks<u>e</u>pt/.

1 **'accept'**

Accept is a verb. If you **accept** something you have been offered, you agree to take it.

I protested that I couldn't <u>accept</u> as a present something she so clearly adored.

2 **'except'**

Except is a preposition or conjunction, used to introduce the only thing or person that a statement does not apply to.

All the boys <u>except</u> Piggy started to giggle.

⇨ See **Usage** entries at **accept** and **except**.

Other entries distinguish between words which have similar basic meaning, but are used in slightly different ways:

---

called - named

You use **called** or **named** when you are giving the name of someone or something. **Named** is less common than **called**, and is not usually used in conversation.

Did you know a boy <u>called</u> Desmond?
We pass through a town <u>called</u> Monmouth.
Anna had a boyfriend <u>named</u> Shorty.

You can use **called** either after a noun or after **be**.

Komis asked me to appear in a play <u>called</u> Katerina.
The book was <u>called</u> The Goalkeeper's Revenge.

You only use **named** immediately after a noun.

The victim was an 18-year-old girl <u>named</u> Marinetta Jirkowski.

There are also entries which point out differences between British and American English usage, where these might be confusing:

---

1 **'post' and 'mail'**

The public service by which letters and parcels are collected and delivered is usually called the **post** in British English and the **mail** in American English. **Mail** is also sometimes used in British English, for example in the name **Royal Mail**.

There is a cheque for you in the <u>post</u>.
Winners will be notified by <u>post</u>.
Your reply must have been lost in the <u>mail.</u>

Entries dealing with groups of words

In some entries, larger groups of words which have a similar basic meaning but different shades of meaning are explained. For example, in the entry at **beauty**, there is an explanation of the differences between the following words: attractive, beautiful, good-looking, gorgeous, handsome, pretty, stunning. Each of these words is illustrated by an example to show the differences in usage and meaning. These entries have a vocabulary-building function, and could be exploited especially with more advanced students. The following entries deal with larger groups of words:

beauty	dignity	newness	strangeness
cook	fatness	obedience	stubbornness
crippled	forcefulness	old	thinness
curiosity	madness	pride	tools
damage	meanness	retarded	work

Some entries contain graded lists of words – that is, lists of words which indicate different degrees of something. For example, the entry at **happy – sad** shows a range of adjectives that are used to indicate how happy or sad someone is. Words indicating roughly the same degree are on the same line, preceded by a grey dot. The words on each line are then arranged in order of frequency. So, in the the entry at **happy – sad**, 'ecstatic' is more common than 'elated', and 'elated' is more common than 'euphoric'. Each word is illustrated by an example from the corpus.

The following Usage entries contain graded lists:

> happy – sad
> like – dislike
> pleased – disappointed
> small – large

There are also the following graded lists of adjuncts in the **Grammar** entry at **Adjuncts**: adjuncts of:

> frequency (never – always)
> duration (briefly – always)
> degree (little – enormously)
> extent (partly – completely)
> probability (conceivably – definitely)

There is a graded list of adverbs of degree used in front of adjectives in the **Grammar** entry at **Adverbs.**

THE GRAMMAR SECTION

The **Grammar** entries in this book contain basic grammatical information, together with information on particularly difficult grammatical points.

The longer entries in this section have a 'menu' at the start of the entry to help you find what you need easily:

Questions

1 'yes/no'-questions	6 'wh'-questions
2 'be'	7 'wh'-word as subject
3 'have'	8 'wh'-word as object or adverb
4 negative 'yes/no'-questions	9 questions in reply
5 answers to 'yes/no'-questions	10 indirect ways of asking questions

---

There is a Glossary of grammatical terms on pp 804–810, which acts as an index to the grammar entries.

THE TOPICS SECTION

The **Topic** entries in this book deal with topics of various kinds. They tell you about the words, structures and expressions that you use when you are talking about a particular situation, such as age or money, or when you are in a particular situation, for example when you are saying goodbye or thank you. Some of the Topic entries tell you about particular groups of words that have a common characteristic or use, for example abbreviations or words that are used to refer to groups. There are also entries on punctuation and spelling. The longer Topic entries have a 'menu' at the beginning to help you to find what you need easily:

Addressing someone

1	position of vocatives	5	addressing relatives
2	writing vocatives	6	addressing a group of people
3	addressing someone you do not know	7	vocatives showing dislike
4	addressing someone you know	8	vocatives showing affection
		9	other vocatives

In Topic entries, we sometimes make a distinction between formal and informal ways of saying something. People use informal expressions when speaking to friends and relatives. They use formal expressions when speaking to people they do not know well or when they are in a formal situation such as a meeting. Formal expressions tend to be used especially by older people.

GENERAL POINTS

Register information

We have tried to make it clear which words and expressions are used in conversation and which are mainly used in writing:

---

2 **'pick' and 'select'**
Pick and **select** have very similar meanings to **choose**. **Select** is more formal than **choose** or **pick**, and is not usually used in conversation.

Words and expressions used in conversation are often also used in pieces written in an informal, conversational style, such as letters to friends and non-serious articles in magazines. Similarly, words and expressions used in writing are also often used in formal speech, for example in news broadcasts and lectures.

When a word, expression, or structure occurs only in novels and written descriptions of events, we say that it occurs only 'in stories'. For example 'dress' is used to mean 'put on your clothes' in stories, but in conversation you would say 'get dressed'. Words described as 'literary', such as the verb 'desire' and the adjective 'infamous', are used in poetical writing and passionate speeches.

If we say that a word or expression is not used 'in modern English', we mean that you may come across it in a book written some time ago, but it would not sound natural in writing today, and should definitely not be used in conversation. For example, in modern English, 'have' is used with words referring to meals, not 'take'. If a word is described as 'old-fashioned', it occurs in old books and may still be used by older people today, but is becoming uncommon.

If we say that a word or expression is not used 'in standard English', we mean that speakers of some varieties of English use it, but it would be regarded as incorrect by most people. A word that is described as 'neutral' is used simply to show that someone or something has a particular quality. A word that is 'complimentary' or 'shows approval' indicates that you admire the person you are describing. A word that is 'uncomplimentary' or 'shows disapproval' indicates that you disapprove of the person or do not find them attractive.

American English

The use of American English is increasingly important in the modern world, and to reflect this, coverage of American English has been extended for this edition, with more examples from our American corpora, and more points covered. Differences between British and

American English usage are also clearly indicated, using a flag symbol:

 There is often a difference between British and American usage. For example, British speakers usually say 'He **had** a bath', while American speakers say 'He **took** a bath'.

Examples

The Collins COBUILD English Usage gives thousands of examples of Usage, all of which are taken from the Bank of English corpus, and show English as it is really used. For this edition, many examples have been replaced to ensure that coverage is up-to-date and relevant, and new examples have been added, for example in the graded lists (see above), to show you how the words are used in context.

Cross references

When information about the use of a word, or additional relevant information, is to be found in another entry, a cross-reference is given, using an arrow symbol, and explaining which section of the book to look in:

> ⬛1 **'previously' and 'before'**
> If you are talking about a period measured back from some earlier time, you use **before** or **previously**.
> *He had died a month <u>before</u>.*
> *She had rented the flat some fourteen months <u>previously</u>.*
> ⇨ See **Usage** entry at **before**.

Warning boxes and information points

When a word or structure causes particular problems for learners, information about the problem can be found in a Warning box within the entry:

> ⚠ **WARNING:** To **pass** an exam always means to succeed in it. It does not mean to take part in it.

Other points which learners should be careful to note are preceded by an 'information' symbol:

> ⓘ You do not say that someone is 'engaged with' the person they are going to marry.

Numbered headings

Many entries have numbered headings which draw attention to the particular use or structure that is being dealt with, or to a word that is being contrasted with another word.

Pronunciation Guide

Vowel sounds

ɑː	heart, start, calm
æ	act, mass, lap
aɪ	dive, cry, mind
aɪə	fire, tyre, buyer
aʊ	out, down, loud
aʊə	flour, tower, sour
e	met, lend, pen
eɪ	say, main, weight
eə	fair, care, wear
ɪ	fit, win, list
iː	feed, me, beat
ɪə	near, beard, clear
ɒ	lot, lost, spot
oʊ	note, phone, coat
ɔː	more, cord, claw
ɔɪ	boy, coin, joint
ʊ	could, stood, hood
uː	you, use, choose
ʊə	lure, pure, cure
ɜː	turn, third, word
ʌ	but, fund, must
ə	the weak vowel in butter, about, forgotten
i	the weak vowel in very
u	the first weak vowel in tuition

Consonant sounds

b	bed, rub
d	done, red
f	fit, if
g	good, dog
h	hat
j	yellow
k	king, pick
l	lip, bill
m	mat, ram
n	not, tin
p	pay, lip
r	run
s	soon, bus
t	talk, bet
v	van, love
w	win
x	loch
z	zoo, buzz
ʃ	ship, wish
ʒ	measure
ŋ	sing
tʃ	cheap, witch
θ	thin, myth
ð	then, loathe
dʒ	joy, bridge

Stress is shown by underlining the vowel in the stressed syllable, as in 'accept /əksept/'

Letters

These are vowel letters:

a e i o u

These are consonant letters:

b c d f g h j k l m n p q r s t v w x y z

The letter y is sometimes used as a vowel, for example in 'shy' and 'myth'

Pronunciation Guide

Vowel sounds

a	heart, start, calm
a	max, fat
ave	cave, try, mine
are	fire, trial, buy, or
ow	out, down, loud
ou	four, lower, sour
e	me, lene, her
er	ray, man, weight
ea	far, care, wear
e	bell, win, lip
u	bread, the bear
ea	near, rand, clear
n	for, corpus
oo	note, phone, coat
oi	more, for, claw
oi	boy, oil, join
u	could, stood, food
ue	you, use, choose
u	fine, pure, cure
u	fur, bird, word
A	bug, paint, most
e	the weak vowel in butter, about, character
i	the weak vowel in very
o	the first weak vowel in tuition

Consonant sounds

b	bed, rub
d	done, red
f	fit
g	good, go
h	hot
l	alley
k	king, rick
l	lip, bill
m	mat, ram
n	not, fin
p	pay, lip
r	run
s	soon, bus
t	talk, set
v	van, love
w	win
z	fizz, fox, buzz
zh	ship, wish
zh	measure
ng	sing
ch	cap, witch
th	thin, myth
th	then, lost, e
j	joy, bridge

Stress is shown by underlining the vowel in the stressed syllable, as in accept (akscpt).

Letters

These are vowel letters:

a e i o u

These are consonant letters:

b c d f g h j k l m n p q r s t v w x y z

The letter y is sometimes used as a vowel, for example in shy and myth.

Usage Section

Usage Section

A a

a - an

1 'a' and 'an'

You use **a** and **an** when you are talking about a person or thing for the first time. **A** and **an** are called the **indefinite article**. You only use **a** and **an** with singular count nouns. The second time you refer to the same person or thing, you use **the**.

She picked up a book.
The book was lying on the table.
After weeks of looking we eventually bought a house.
The house was in a small village.

You can describe someone or something using **a** or **an** with an adjective and a noun, or with a noun and a qualifier.

His brother was a sensitive child.
The information was contained in an article on biology.
I chose a picture that reminded me of my own country.

(i) Note that you do not omit **a** or **an** in front of a noun when the noun refers to someone's profession or job. For example, you say 'He is **an** architect'. You do not say 'He is architect'.

She became a lawyer.
'I'm a writer and an artist, not a scientist,' he says.

2 'a' or 'an'?

You use **a** in front of words beginning with consonant sounds and **an** in front of words beginning with vowel sounds.

Then I saw a big car parked nearby.
… an empty house.

You use **an** in front of words beginning with 'h' when the 'h' is not pronounced. For example, you say 'an honest man'. You do not say 'a honest man'.

…in less than an hour.
… an honest answer.

An is used in front of the following words beginning with 'h':

heir	heirloom	honorary	honourable	hourly
heiress	honest	honour	hour	

You use **a** in front of words beginning with 'u' when the 'u' is pronounced /juː/ (like 'you'). For example, you say 'a unique occasion'. You do not say 'an unique occasion'.

He was a University of London law student.
They could elect a union member.

A is used in front of the following words beginning with 'u':

ubiquitous	unilateral	universe	use	utensil
unanimous	unilateralist	university	used	uterus
unicorn	union	uranium	useful	utilitarian
unification	unique	urinal	useless	utility
uniform	unisex	urinary	user	utopian
uniformed	unit	urine	usual	
uniformity	united	usable	usually	
unifying	universal	usage	usurper	

USAGE

You use **an** in front of an abbreviation when the letters are pronounced separately and the first letter begins with a vowel sound.

Before she became <u>an MP</u>, she was a psychiatric social worker.
He has <u>an</u> FA Cup winner's medal with Tottenham.

3 'a' meaning 'one'

A and **an** are used to mean 'one' in front of some numbers and units of measurement.

⇨ See **Topic** entries at **Numbers and fractions** and **Measurements**.

ability - capability - capacity

Do not confuse **ability** with **capability** and **capacity**.

1 'ability'

You often use **ability** to say that someone can do something well.

He had remarkable <u>ability</u> as a musician.
…the <u>ability</u> to bear hardship.

2 'capability'

A person's **capability** is the amount of work they can do and how well they can do it.

…a job that was beyond the <u>capability</u> of one man.
…the director's ideas of the <u>capability</u> of the actor.

3 'capacity'

If someone has a particular **capacity**, a **capacity** for something, or a **capacity** to do something, they have the qualities required to do it. **Capacity** is a more formal word than **ability**.

…their <u>capacity</u> for hard work.
…his <u>capacity</u> to see the other person's point of view.

a bit

⇨ See **Usage** entry at **bit**.

able - capable

Able and **capable** are both used to say that someone can do something.

1 'able'

When you say that someone is **able** to do something, you mean that they can do it either because of their knowledge or skill, or because it is possible.

He wondered if he would be <u>able</u> to climb over the rail.
They were <u>able</u> to use their profits for new investments.

If you use a past tense, you are saying that someone has actually done something.

We were <u>were able</u> to reduce costs.

⇨ See **Usage** entry at **can - could - be able to.**

2 'capable'

When you say that someone is **capable of** doing something, you mean either that they have the knowledge and skill to do it, or that they are likely to do it.

The workers are perfectly <u>capable</u> of running the organization themselves.
She was quite <u>capable</u> of falling asleep.

You can say that someone is **capable of** a particular feeling or action.

He's <u>capable</u> of loyalty.
Bowman could not believe him <u>capable</u> of murder.

You can also use **capable of** when talking about what something such as a car or machine can do.

The car was <u>capable of</u> 110 miles per hour.

3 **'able' or 'capable'**

If you describe someone as **able** or **capable,** you mean that they do things well.
One of the brightest and <u>ablest</u> members of the government.
He's certainly a <u>capable</u> gardener.

about

1 **'about'**

You use **about** when you mention what someone is saying, writing, or thinking.
It was wonderful to hear Brian talking <u>about</u> John.
I'll have to think <u>about</u> that.

You can say that a book is **about** a particular subject or that it is **on** that subject.
The author is writing a book <u>about</u> the Outer Hebrides.
…Anthony Daniels' book <u>on</u> Guatemala.

You can also use **about** to say what a novel or play deals with. You do not use 'on'.
Ultimately, this is a novel <u>about</u> ethics.
…a story <u>about</u> growing up.

2 **'about to'**

If you are **about to** do something, you are going to do it soon.
You are <u>about to cross</u> the River Jordan.
I was <u>about to go</u> home.

⚠ **WARNING:** You do not use an '-ing' form in sentences like these. You do not say, for example, 'You are about crossing the River Jordan'.

⇨ For more information on **about** , see **Usage** entry at **around - round - about.**

above - over

Above and **over** are both used to talk about position and height. If something is higher than something else and the two things are imagined as being positioned along a vertical line, you can use either **above** or **over.**
He opened a cupboard <u>above</u> the sink.
She leaned forward until her face was <u>over</u> the basin.

However, if something is higher than something else but the two things are regarded as being wide or horizontal rather than tall or vertical, you have to use **above.**
The trees rose <u>above</u> the row of houses.

Above and **over** are both used to talk about measurements, for example, when you are talking about a point that is higher than another point on a scale.
Any money earned <u>over</u> that level is taxed.
…everybody <u>above</u> five feet eight inches in height.

⚠ **WARNING:** You do not use **above** in front of a number when you are talking about a quantity or number of things or people. For example, you do not say 'She had above thirty pairs of shoes'. You say 'She had **over** thirty pairs of shoes' or 'She had **more than** thirty pairs of shoes'.
They paid out <u>over</u> 3 million pounds.
He saw <u>more than</u> 800 children, dying of starvation.

⇨ For more information about approximate numbers, see **Topic** entry at **Measurements.**

You use **over** to say that a distance or period of time is longer than the one mentioned.
…a height of <u>over</u> twelve thousand feet.
Our relationship lasted for <u>over</u> a year.

USAGE

Above and over are also both used to talk about people's rank or importance. You use **above** to talk about people who are more important and in a higher position than other people.

…behaving as if she was in a position _above_ the other staff.

If someone is **over** you, they give orders or instructions to you.

…an officer in authority _over_ him.

absent

If someone is **absent from** a meeting, ceremony, or place, they are not there.

Gary O'Neil has been _absent from_ training because of a stomach virus.
…children who are frequently _absent from_ school.

(i) Note that you use **from** after 'absent' in sentences like these. You do not use 'at'.

If it is clear what meeting, ceremony, or place you are talking about, you can simply say that someone is **absent.**

The Mongolian delegate to the assembly was _absent._

Absent is a fairly formal word. In conversation, you say that someone is **not at** a meeting, ceremony, or place, or that they are **not there.**

She _wasn't at_ Molly's wedding.
The boy _wasn't at_ home at the time of the tragedy.
At the time when she most needed me I _wasn't there._

accept

If you **accept** something that you have been offered, you agree to take it.

Müller _accepted_ a glass of port.

1 advice and suggestions

If you accept someone's advice or suggestion, you decide to do what they advise or suggest.

If she _accepts_ the advice, she feels happier.
I knew that they would _accept_ my proposal.

However, you do not say that you 'accept to do' what someone suggests. You say that you **agree to do** it.

The princess _agreed to go_ on television.
She _agreed to let_ us use her flat while she was away.

2 situations and people

If you **accept** a difficult or unpleasant situation, you recognize that it cannot be changed.

…unwillingness to _accept_ bad working conditions.
The astronaut _accepts_ danger as being part of the job.

However, you do not say that you 'cannot accept' a person you strongly dislike. You say that you **cannot stand** them or **cannot bear** them.

She said she _couldn't stand_ him.
I _can't bear_ the sight of him.

accept - except

Do not confuse **accept** /əksept/ with **except** /ɪksept/.

1 'accept'

Accept is a verb. If you **accept** something you have been offered, you agree to take it.

I protested that I couldn't _accept_ as a present something she so clearly adored.

2 'except'

Except is a preposition or conjunction, used to introduce the only thing or person that a statement does not apply to.

All the boys except Piggy started to giggle.

⇨ See **Usage** entries at **accept** and **except**.

acceptable

You say that something is **acceptable** when it is satisfactory, or when people do not object to it.

To my relief he found the article acceptable.
Are we saying that violence is acceptable?

You do not say that someone is 'acceptable' to do something. You say that they are **willing** to do it.

Ed was quite willing to let us help him.
Would you be willing to go to Berkhamsted?

accommodation

Accommodation is a room or rooms to stay, work, or live in. In British English, **accommodation** is an uncount noun. You do not talk about 'accommodations' or 'an accommodation'.

There is a shortage of accommodation.
…student accommodation.
The centre provides accommodation for 5,360 civil servants.

Speakers of American English sometimes talk about **accommodations**.

All in all, these accommodations are superb, unique and a great place to spend the night!

accompany

If you **accompany** someone somewhere, you go there with them.

She asked me to accompany her to the church.

Accompany is a fairly formal word. In conversation, you say **go with** or **come with**.

I went with my friends to see what it looked like.
He wished Ellen had come with him.

However, there is no passive form of **go with** or **come with**. If you want to use a passive form, you must use **accompany**.

He was accompanied by Clare Boothe Luce, his second wife.
She came out of the house accompanied by Mrs Jones.

accord

If you do something **of** your **own accord,** you do it freely and because you want to do it.

She knew they would leave of their own accord.

⚠ **WARNING:** You must use 'own' in sentences like these. You do not say, for example, 'She had gone of her accord'.
You also do not say that someone does something 'on' their own accord.

according to

1 **'according to'**

If you say that something is the case **according to** a particular person, book, or document, you mean that you got the information from that person, book, or document.

According to Dr Santos, the cause of death was drowning.
The road was forty miles long according to my map.

ⓘ Note that in coversation, instead of saying 'According to George, the roads are very slippery this morning', you often say 'George **says** the roads are very slippery this morning'.

USAGE

Arnold says they do this in Essex as well.
The announcement says a general election might be possible before the end of next year.

2 'in my opinion'

If you want to emphasize that what you are saying is your own opinion, you say '**In my opinion…**' or '**In our opinion…**'.

In my opinion we face a national emergency.
The temple gets crowded, and in our opinion it's best to visit it in the evening.

> ⚠ **WARNING:** You never say 'according to me' or 'according to us'. You also do not use **according to** and **opinion** together. You do not say, for example, 'According to the bishop's opinion, the public has a right to know'. You say '**The bishop's opinion is that** the public has a right to know'.
> *The psychiatrist's opinion was that this is a case of depression.*
> *The general opinion is that French wines are the best.*

⇨ For more information on expressing opinions, see **Topic** entry at **Opinions**.

account

⇨ See **Usage** entry at **bill - check - account**

accuse - charge

1 'accuse'

If you **accuse** someone **of** doing something wrong, you say that they did it.

He accused them of drinking beer while driving.
He is accused of killing ten young women.

ⓘ Note that you do not say that you accuse someone 'for' doing something wrong.

2 'charge'

When the police **charge** someone **with** committing a crime, they formally accuse them of it.

He was arrested and charged with committing a variety of offences.

accustomed to

1 'accustomed to'

If you are **accustomed to** something, you have become familiar with it and you no longer find it strange. **Accustomed to** usually comes after verbs such as **be**, **become**, **get**, or **grow**.

It did not get lighter but I became accustomed to the dark.
I am not accustomed to being interrupted.

ⓘ Note that you do not say that someone is 'accustomed with' something.

2 'used to'

In conversation, you do not usually say that someone is 'accustomed to' something. You say that they are **used to** it. **Used to** usually comes after **be** or **get**.

The company is used to much stronger growth.
I was beginning to get used to the old iron bed.

You can say that someone is **accustomed to doing** something or **used to doing** something.

The bank president is accustomed to working in the Elysée Palace.
We are used to queueing.

> ⚠ **WARNING:** You do not say that someone is 'accustomed to do' something or is 'used to do' something.

If you **accustom yourself to** something, you accept it and become familiar with it.
He sat very still, trying to accustom himself to the darkness.

actual

1 **'actual'**
You use **actual** to emphasize that the place, object, or person you are talking about is the real or genuine one.
The predicted results and the actual results are very different.
The interpretation bore no relation to the actual words spoken.

> ⚠ **WARNING:** You only use **actual** in front of a noun. You do not say that something 'is actual'.

2 **'current' and 'present'**
You do not use 'actual' to describe something which is happening, being done, or being used at the present time. Instead you use **current** or **present**.
The store needs more than $100,000 to survive the current crisis.
Is the present situation really any different from many others in the past?

actually - really

Actually and **really** are both used to emphasize statements.

1 **'actually'**
You use **actually** when you are saying what the truth is about something, often in contrast to other things that might have been said or thought.
All the characters in the novel actually existed.
This load had actually been dispatched three months previously.

You also use **actually** when you are mentioning something that is very surprising. You put **actually** in front of the surprising part of what you are saying.
I was actually cruel sometimes.
He actually began to cry.

It can also be used to be precise or to correct someone.
'Mr Hooper is a schoolteacher.'–'A university lecturer, actually.'
We couldn't actually see the garden.

> ⚠ **WARNING:** You do not use **actually** to emphasize that something is happening now, rather than in the past or future. Instead you use **presently, at present,** or **right now.**
> ⇨ See **Usage** entries at **presently** and **now.**

2 **'really'**
You use **really** in conversation to emphasize something that you are saying.
I really think he's sick.

When you use **really** in front of an adjective or adverb, it has a similar meaning to 'very'.
This is really serious.
⇨ See **Usage** entry at **really.**

advice - advise

1 **'advice'**
Advice /ədvaɪs/ is a noun. If you give someone **advice**, you tell them what you think they should do.

USAGE

One woman went to a psychiatrist for <u>advice.</u>
She promised to follow his <u>advice.</u>

Advice is an uncount noun. You do not talk about 'advices' or 'an advice'. However, you can talk about **a piece of advice.**

What's the best <u>piece of advice</u> you've ever been given?
Could I give you one last <u>piece of advice?</u>

2 **'advise'**

Advise /ədvaɪz/ is a verb. If you 'advise' someone to do something, you say that you think they should do it.

He <u>advised</u> her to see her own doctor.
He <u>advised</u> me not to buy it.

⚠ **WARNING:** You do not use 'advise' without an object. You do not say, for example, 'He advised to leave as quickly as possible'. If you do not want to say who is receiving the advice, you say '**His advice was** to leave as quickly as possible'.

John's <u>advice was</u> to wait until the date of the hearing.

advocate

⇨ See **Usage** entry at **lawyer.**

affect - effect

1 **'affect'**

Affect /əfɛkt/ is a verb. To **affect** someone or something means to change or influence them in some way.

…the ways in which computers can <u>affect</u> our lives.
The disease <u>affected</u> Jane's lungs.

2 **'effect'**

Effect /ɪfekt/ is usually a noun. An **effect** is a change or event which occurs because something else has happened.

…the <u>effect</u> of noise on people in the factories.
This has the <u>effect</u> of separating students from teachers.

You can say that something **has a** particular **effect on** something else.

Improvement in water supply can <u>have a dramatic effect on</u> health.
Clearly the lottery has had a <u>significant effect</u> on our business.

Effect is sometimes a verb. If you **effect** something that you are trying to achieve, you succeed in achieving it. This is a formal use.

Production was halted until repairs <u>could be effected.</u>

afford

If you **can afford** something, you have enough money to buy it.

…those who <u>can afford</u> private education.
Do you think one day we'll <u>be able to afford</u> a new sofa?

Afford is almost always used with **can, could,** or **be able.** You do not say that someone 'affords' something.
The amount of money that someone **can afford** is the amount they are able to spend on something.

It's more than I <u>can afford.</u>
They paid a thousand usually, sometimes more if they <u>could afford</u> it.

You say that someone **can afford to have** something or **can afford to do** something.

…a situation where everybody <u>can afford to have</u> a car.
I <u>can't afford to rent</u> this flat.

You do not say that someone 'can afford having' something or 'can afford doing' something.

⚠ **WARNING:** You do not use a passive form of **afford.** You do not say that something 'can be afforded'. Instead you say that people **can afford** it.
Nobody buys second-hand binoculars any more. People can afford new ones now.

afloat

If someone or something is 'afloat', they are floating on water rather than sinking.
By kicking constantly he could stay afloat.
Her hooped skirt kept her afloat and saved her.

⚠ **WARNING:** You do not use 'afloat' in front of a noun. You do not talk, for example, about an 'afloat boat'.

afraid - frightened

1 **'afraid' and 'frightened'**

If you are **afraid** of someone or something, you feel fear because you think they may harm you.
They were afraid of you.
The guards were so afraid that they trembled.

You can also say that you are **frightened** of someone or something. **Frightened** has the same meaning as 'afraid'.
You're frightened of Alice.
Everyone here is frightened of the volcano.

If you are unwilling to do something because you think it might be harmful or dangerous, you can say that you are **afraid to do** it or **frightened to do** it.
Many assaults go unrecorded because victims are afraid to come forward.
What is the use of freedom if people are frightened to go out?

⚠ **WARNING:** **Afraid** is only used after verbs such as **be** and **feel.** You do not use it in front of a noun. You do not talk, for example, about 'an afraid child'. However, you can talk about 'a **frightened** child'.
He was not going to act like a frightened kid.

2 **another meaning of 'afraid'**

Afraid has another meaning. You use it to say that you are worried that something unpleasant might happen and you want to avoid it. When you use **afraid** like this, it is usually followed by a report clause.
She was afraid that I might be embarrassed.

You can also say that you are **afraid of doing** something. For example, instead of saying 'I was afraid that I might get lost', you can say 'I was **afraid of getting** lost'.
She was afraid of being late for school.
He was terribly afraid of offending anyone.

3 **'I'm afraid...'**

You use **'I'm afraid...'**, **'I'm afraid so'**, and **'I'm afraid not'** to express regret in a polite way. **'I'm afraid so'** means 'yes'. **'I'm afraid not'** means 'no', and both of these expressions are used as responses to questions.
I'm afraid I can't agree.
'I hear she's leaving. Is that right?'– 'I'm afraid so.'
'Can you come round this evening?'– 'I'm afraid not.'

USAGE

after - afterwards - later

1 **'after' used as a preposition**

If something happens **after** a particular time or event, it happens during the period that follows that time or event.

Dan came in just <u>after</u> midnight.
We'll hear about everything <u>after</u> dinner.

You can say that someone does something **after doing** something else.

<u>After leaving</u> school he worked as an accountant.
Frank Brown was released from prison <u>after serving</u> three years.

⚠ **WARNING:** You do not say that someone is 'after' a particular age. You say that they are **over** that age.

She was well <u>over</u> fifty.

You do not use 'after' to say that something is at the back of something else. The word you use is **behind.**

2 **'after' used as an adverb**

You can also use 'after' as an adverb, but only in expressions like **soon after**, **shortly after**, and **not long after**.

Douglas came round to see me, and <u>soon after</u> I met him again at a friend's.
<u>Shortly after</u>, Fania called me.
<u>Not long after</u> she started dragging the go-cart down the narrow streets.

⚠ **WARNING:** You do not use **after** as an adverb on its own. You do not say, for example, '~~I met him after~~'. You say 'I met him **afterwards**' or 'I met him **later**'.

Somebody will hear you and may repeat it <u>afterwards</u>.
I'll join you <u>later</u>.

3 **'afterwards'**

Instead of 'after', you can use another adverb, **afterwards**. There is no difference in meaning.

She died <u>soon afterwards</u>.
<u>Shortly afterwards</u> her marriage broke up.
Her husband lost his fortune in the Wall Street crash and died <u>not long afterwards</u>.

4 **'afterward'**

 Afterward is also sometimes used, especially in American English.

I left <u>soon afterward</u>.
<u>Shortly afterward</u>, he made a trip from L.A. to San Jose.

5 **'later'**

You can use **later** to refer to a time or situation that follows the time when you are speaking.

I'll go and see her <u>later</u>.

A little, **much**, and **not much** can also be used with **later**.

<u>A little later</u>, the lights went out.
I learned all this <u>much later</u>.

You can use **after, afterwards,** or **later** following a phrase that mentions a period of time, in order to say when something happens.

… <u>five years after</u> his death.
She wrote about it <u>six years afterwards</u>.
<u>Ten minutes later</u> he left the house.

⚠ **WARNING:** In standard English, you do not use 'after' as an adverb when mentioning a specific period of time. You do not say, for example, 'I met him a month after'. You say 'I met him a month **afterwards** or 'I met him a month **later**'.
That was actually done about eight months underlineunderlineafterwards.
I returned some three or four weeks later.

after all

You use **after all** when you are mentioning an additional point which confirms or supports what you have just said.
After all, we don't intend to put him on trial.
It had to be recognized, after all, that I was still a schoolboy.

You also use **after all** to say that something is the case or may be the case in spite of what had previously been thought.
Perhaps it isn't such a bad village after all.
Can it be that these people are actually sincere after all?

⚠ **WARNING:** You do not use 'after all' when you want to introduce a final point, question, or topic. Instead you use **finally** or **lastly**.
Finally I want to say something about the heat pump.
And finally, a word about the winner and runner-up.
Lastly I would like to ask about your future plans.

afternoon

The **afternoon** is the part of each day which begins at noon or lunchtime and ends at about six o'clock, or after it is dark in winter.

1. **the present day**
You refer to the afternoon of the present day as **this afternoon.**
I rang Pat this afternoon.
Can I take it with me this afternoon?

You refer to the afternoon of the previous day as **yesterday afternoon.**
Doctors operated on the injury yesterday afternoon.

You refer to the afternoon of the next day as **tomorrow afternoon.**
I'll be home tomorrow afternoon.

2. **single events in the past**
If you want to say that something happened during a particular afternoon in the past, you use **on.**
Olivia Davenport was due on Friday afternoon.
The box was delivered on the afternoon before my departure.

If you have been describing what happened during a particular day, you can then say that something happened **that afternoon** or **in the afternoon.**
That afternoon I walked into Ironstone.
I left Walsall in the afternoon and went by bus and train to Nottingham.

If you are talking about a day in the past and you want to mention that something had happened during the afternoon of the day before, you say that it had happened **the previous afternoon.**
He had spoken to me the previous afternoon.

If you want to say that something happened during the afternoon of the next day, you say that it happened **the following afternoon.**
I arrived at the village the following afternoon.

In stories, if you want to say that something happened during an afternoon in the past, without saying which afternoon, you say that it happened **one afternoon.**

One afternoon as I sat working in my office I heard a knock at the door.

You can also say, for example, that something happened **one November afternoon** or **on a November afternoon.**

He told me his story one cold March afternoon.
I visited it on a warm May afternoon.

3 talking about the future

If you want to say that something will happen during a particular afternoon in the future, you use **on.**

The semi-finals will be on Wednesday afternoon.

If you are already talking about a day in the future, you can say that something will happen **in the afternoon.**

We will arrive at Pisa early in the morning, then in the afternoon we will go on to Florence.

If you are talking about a day in the future and you want to say that something will happen during the afternoon of the next day, you say that it will happen **the following afternoon.**

I leave on Thursday, arriving in Cairo at 9.45pm, then fly to Luxor the following afternoon.

4 regular events

If something happens or happened regularly every afternoon, you say that it happens or happened **in the afternoon** or **in the afternoons.**

In the afternoon we go for a drive.
He is usually busy in the afternoons.
In the afternoon he would take a nap.
I went to the bookstore in the afternoons.

If you want to say that something happens regularly once a week during a particular afternoon, you use **on** followed by the name of a day of the week and **afternoons.**

The estate is going to be opened to the public on Sunday afternoons.
On Saturday afternoons she used to serve behind the counter.

American English uses **afternoons** as an adverb and doesn't require phrases with 'on' or 'in'.

She worked afternoons and nights at her parents' shop.

5 exact times

If you have mentioned an exact time and you want to make it clear that you are talking about the afternoon rather than the early morning, you add **in the afternoon.**

We arrived at three in the afternoon.

afterward

⇨ See **Usage** entry at **after - afterwards - later.**

afterwards

⇨ See **Usage** entry at **after - afterwards - later.**

aged

This word is pronounced in two different ways.

⇨ For information on **aged** /eɪdʒd/, see **Topic** entry at **Age.**
⇨ For information on **aged** /eɪdʒɪd/, see **Usage** entry at **old.**

aggressive

⇨ See **Usage** entry at **forceful.**

USAGE

ago

You usually use **ago** to say how long it is since something happened. For example, if something happened five years **ago**, it is now five years since it happened.

We met two years ago.
We got married about a year ago.

When you are talking about an event in the past, you use the simple past tense with **ago**. For example, you say 'He **died** four years ago'. You do not say 'He has died four years ago'.

Seven years ago, she gave birth to their daughter, Nelly.
I did it just a moment ago.

You only use **ago** when you are talking about a period of time measured back from the present. If you are talking about a period measured back from some earlier time, you use **before** or **previously**.

The centre had been opened some years before.
The sinking had taken place nearly two years previously.

⚠ **WARNING:** You do not use **ago** and **since** together. You do not say, for example, 'It is three years ago since it happened'. You say 'It happened **three years ago**' or '**It is three years since** it happened'.

He died two years ago.
It is two weeks now since I wrote to you.

You also do not say, for example, 'It has been happening since three years ago'. You say that it has been happening **for three years.**

I have lived here for nearly twenty years.
I have known you for a long time.

agree

1 **'agree with'**

If you **agree with** someone about something, you both have the same opinion about it.

My friend agreed with me that it was ridiculous.

If you **agree with** an action or suggestion, you approve of it.

I agree with what they are doing.

Note that you do not say that you 'agree' an action or suggestion or 'are agreed with' it.

2 **'agree to'**

If you **agree to** something that is suggested or proposed, you say that you will allow it to happen or be done.

He had agreed to the use of force.

However, you do not say that someone 'agrees to' an invitation. You say that they **accept** it.

He readily accepted our invitation to speak about his case.

If you **agree to do** something that you have been asked to do, you say that you will do it.

She agreed to let us use her flat.
She finally agreed to come to the club on Wednesday.

Note that you do not say that you 'agree doing' something.

3 **'agree on'**

If people reach a decision together about something, you can say that they **agree on** it.

The warring sides have agreed on an unconditional ceasefire.

4 **'agree that'**

You can say what their decision is using **agree** and a 'that'-clause.

They agreed that all existing sanctions should be maintained.

The passive form **'It was agreed that…'** is often used.

It was agreed that something had to be done.

5 **'be agreed'**

When a decision is made, you can say that the people making it **are agreed.** This is a formal use. In conversation you can say **'Do we all agree?'**

Are we agreed, gentlemen?

So, do we agree that we change that paragraph?

---

aim

Someone's **aim** is what they intend to achieve.

My aim is to play for England.

It is our aim to have this matter sorted quickly.

You can say that someone does something **with the aim of** achieving a particular result. You do not say that someone does something 'with the aim to achieve' a result.

They had left before dawn with the aim of getting a grandstand seat.

The purpose of the meeting was to share information with the common aim of finding Louise safe and well.

---

alight

If something is **alight,** it is burning.

The fire was safely alight.

A candle was alight on the chest of drawers.

To **set** something **alight** means to cause it to start burning.

…paraffin that had been poured on the ground and set alight.

⚠ **WARNING:** You do not use **alight** in front of a noun. You do not say, for example, ~~'People rushed out of the alight building'.~~ You say 'People rushed out of the **burning** building'.

---

alike

If two or more things or people look **alike,** there seems to be no difference between them.

They all looked alike to me.

If two or more things or people are **very alike** or **very much alike,** they are very similar.

We are a close family and very alike.

Monty and Jeremy were very much alike.

If two or more things are **exactly alike,** there is no difference between them.

No two proteins are exactly alike.

⚠ **WARNING:** You do not use 'alike' in front of a noun. You do not say, for example, ~~'They wore alike hats'~~ or ~~'They wore exactly alike hats'.~~ You say 'They wore **similar** hats' or 'They wore **identical** hats'.

The twins insist on wearing similar clothes.

…three little girls in identical dressing gowns.

---

alive

If you say that a person or animal is **alive,** you mean they are not dead.

I think his father is still alive.

She knew the seal was alive.

> ⚠ **WARNING:** You never use 'alive' in front of a noun. You do not say, for example, 'I have no alive relatives' or 'There are many problems transporting alive animals'. Instead you use **living** to talk about people, or **live** /laɪv/ to talk about animals.
> *I have no living relatives.*
> *There are many problems in transporting live animals.*

Alive can also be used after words like **very** and **so** to say that someone enjoys life and is full of energy.
Young people are so alive and exciting.
Floyd felt more alive than he had for years.

---

all

1 used as a determiner

You use **all** immediately in front of the plural form of a noun to talk about every thing or person of a particular kind.
There is built-in storage space in all bedrooms.
All pupils will be expected to learn how to use information technology.

You can use **all** immediately in front of an uncount noun when you are making a general statement about something.
All crime is some kind of revolutionary activity.

When you use **all** in front of the plural form of a noun, you use a plural form of a verb after it.
All boys like to eat.

When you use **all** in front of an uncount noun, you use a singular form of a verb after it.
All pollution is simply an unused resource.

2 used with other determiners

If you want to say something about every thing or person in a group, you use **all**, followed by **the**, **these**, **those**, or a possessive determiner, followed by the plural form of a noun.
Staff are checking all the books to make sure they are suitable.
He has done all these things.
She likes all those children so much.
All my friends must have known.

If you want to say something about the whole of a particular thing, you use **all**, followed by **the**, **this**, **that**, or a possessive determiner, followed by an uncount noun or the singular form of a count noun.
I've read all the stuff that's been written about them.
All this time, Atara and I had been keeping watch.
I want to thank the people of New York for all their help.

🏴 You can put **of** between **all** and a determiner. This use is more common in American English than in British English.
All of the defendants were proved guilty.
All of these religions are closely bound to particular cultures.
I would rather burn all of my money than give it to her.
It will probably never be possible to establish the exact truth about all of their activities.

3 used in front of pronouns

You can use **all** or **all of** in front of the pronouns **this**, **that**, **these**, and **those**.
Oh dear, what are we going to do about all this?
…the agony all of this must have caused.
Were you really interested in all that?

USAGE

Maybe <u>all of that</u> is true, but that's not what the narrative is about.
I got <u>all these</u> for two quid.
<u>*All of these*</u> *are reasons to be cheerful.*

However, in front of personal pronouns you must use **all of**. You do not use 'all'.

Drink it, <u>all of you.</u>
It would be impossible to list <u>all of it</u> in one programme.

You do not use 'we' or 'they' after **all of**. Instead you use **us** or **them**.

He discussed it with <u>all of us.</u>
<u>*All of them*</u> *were taken on a guided tour of the State Bedrooms.*

4 used after the subject

All can also be used after the subject of a clause. For example, instead of saying 'All our friends came', you can say 'Our friends **all** came'.

● When there is no auxiliary, **all** goes in front of the verb, unless the verb is **be**.

Their names <u>all began</u> with S.
We <u>all felt</u> a bit guilty.

● If the verb is **be**, **all** goes after **be**.

They <u>were all</u> asleep.
This <u>is all</u> new to me.

● If there is an auxiliary, you put **all** after it.

It <u>will all be</u> over soon.
We <u>don't all have</u> your advantages.

● If there is more than one auxiliary, you put **all** after the first one.

The bedroom dresser drawers <u>had all been pulled</u> open.

● **All** can also come after the direct or indirect object of a verb when this object is a personal pronoun.

We treat them <u>all</u> as if they were china.
I really do hate you <u>all.</u>

5 used as a pronoun

All can itself be a pronoun with the meaning 'everything' or 'the only thing'. It is often used like this in front of a relative clause.

It was the result of <u>all</u> that had happened previously.
<u>*All*</u> *I did was wash the little girl's ears.*
<u>*All*</u> *I've got is a number.*

All is sometimes used as the subject of a sentence to refer to every person in a group. This is a rather formal use. In more informal English, **everyone** is often used instead.

<u>*All*</u> *were sitting as before.*
<u>*All*</u> *were agreed that the consensus had broken down.*
<u>*Everyone*</u> *in the street was shocked when they heard the news.*

⚠ **WARNING:** You do not use a noun group beginning with **all** as the subject of a negative sentence. You do not say, for example, 'All the children are not noisy'. Instead you use **none** or **not all**. However, there is a difference in meaning. '**None** of the children are noisy' means 'Not one of the children is noisy'. '**Not all** of the children are noisy' means 'Some of the children are not noisy'.

After **none** you can use either a singular or plural form of a verb.

<u>*None*</u> *of these suggestions <u>is</u> very helpful.*
<u>*None*</u> *of us <u>were</u> allowed to go.*

When you use **not all** with the plural form of a noun, you use a plural form of a verb after it.

allow - permit - let - enable

Not all footballers <u>complain</u> that they play too often.
Not all the houses we get offered <u>have</u> central heating.

When you use **not all** with an uncount noun or the singular form of a count noun, you use a singular form of a verb after it.

Not all British industry <u>is</u> delighted.

6 'both'

Do not confuse **all** with **both**. You use **all** when you are talking about three or more things. You use **both** when you are talking about just two things.

There is built-in storage space in <u>all</u> bedrooms.
She cried out in fear and flung <u>both</u> arms up to protect her face.

⇨ See **Usage** entry at **both**.

7 'every'

Every has a similar meaning to **all**. 'Every teacher was consulted' means the same as 'All the teachers were consulted'.
However, there is a difference between **all** and **every** when you use them with expressions of time. For example, if you spend **all day** doing something, you spend the whole of one day doing it. If you do something **every day,** you keep doing it each day.

We can stay here and drink wine <u>all night.</u>
The airport was closed <u>all day</u> after its first serious accident.
She told me that she came that way <u>every day.</u>
…a dozen places like it were advertised <u>every evening</u> in the local paper.

8 'whole'

Whole and **the whole of** also have a similar meaning to **all** and **all of.** For example, 'the **whole** building' and '**the whole of** the building' both mean the same as 'all the building' and '**all of** the building'. However, **all** and **whole** have different meanings in front of the plural form of a noun. If you say 'All the buildings have been destroyed', you mean that every building has been destroyed. If you say '**Whole** buildings have been destroyed', you mean that some buildings have been destroyed completely.

I've taken <u>all</u> my sulphur pills.
… <u>all</u> the cooking utensils.
<u>Whole</u> sections of the suburb have been leveled.
There were <u>whole</u> speeches I did not understand.

allow - permit - let - enable

Allow, permit, and **let** are all used to say that someone is given permission to do something, or is not prevented from doing something. **Permit** is a formal word.

1 'allow' and 'permit'

Allow and **permit** are followed by an object and a 'to'-infinitive clause.

He agreed to <u>allow me to take</u> the course.
Her father would not <u>permit her to eat</u> sweets.

You can say that people **are not allowed to** do something or **are not permitted to** do something.

Visitors <u>were not allowed to</u> walk about unescorted.
Customers <u>are not permitted to</u> converse with the artistes.

You can also say that something **is not allowed** or that it **is not permitted.**

Running <u>was not allowed</u> in the school.
Picnics <u>are not permitted</u> within the Festival Enclosure.

2 'let'

Let is followed by an object and an infinitive without 'to'.

<u>Let me go</u> to the party on Saturday. I won't be late.

You do not use **let** in any passive constructions.

USAGE

3 'enable'

Do not confuse any of these words with **enable**. To **enable** someone to do something means to give them the opportunity to do it. It does not mean to give them permission to do it.

Contraception enables women to plan their families.
The new test should enable doctors to detect the disease early.

all right

If you say that something is **all right,** you mean that it is satisfactory or acceptable.

Is everything all right, sir?

All right is the usual spelling. **Alright** is sometimes used, but many people think this spelling is incorrect.

almost - nearly

1 used to modify adjectives and noun groups

Almost and **nearly** both mean 'not completely' or 'not quite'. They are usually used in front of adjectives or noun groups.

The hay was almost ready for cutting.
We're nearly ready now.
I spent almost a month in China.
He spent nearly five years in the Leningrad special hospital.
It was made of wood like almost all the houses.
She liked doing nearly all the things we liked doing.

2 used to modify verbs

Almost and **nearly** can also be used with verbs. If there is no auxiliary, you put **almost** or **nearly** in front of the verb.

Fanny almost fainted.
Then she nearly died from a drug overdose.

If there is an auxiliary, you put **almost** or **nearly** after the auxiliary.

Some have almost reached International Master level.
Dougal had nearly run out of food.

If there is more than one auxiliary, you put **almost** or **nearly** after the first one.

I 've nearly been drowned in it three times.

⇨ For a graded list of words which are used with verbs to indicate extent, see section on **extent** in **Grammar** entry at **Adjuncts**.

3 used to modify adjuncts

Almost and **nearly** can also be used in front of some time adjuncts such as **every morning** and **every day**, and in front of some place adjuncts such as **there** and **home**.

We took to going out almost every evening.
I used to ride nearly every day.
We are almost there.
I think we are nearly there.

However, **nearly** is hardly ever used in front of adverbs ending in '-ly'. You should use **almost** in front of these adverbs.

She said it almost crossly.
Your boss is almost certainly there.

4 used with 'like'

You can say that one thing is **almost like** another.

It made me feel almost like a hostess.

You do not usually say that one thing is 'nearly like' another.

5 used with time expressions

You can use **almost** or **nearly** in front of time expressions. If it is **almost** or **nearly** a particular time, it will be that time soon.

It was <u>almost</u> 10 p.m.
It's <u>almost</u> supper-time.
By now it was <u>nearly</u> five past ten.

⚠ **WARNING:** Note that you only use **almost** or **nearly** like this after **be**. You do not say, for example, ~~'They arrived at almost five o'clock'~~. Instead you say '**It was almost** five o'clock **when** they arrived'.
It was <u>nearly</u> nine o'clock <u>when</u> Simon made his appearance.
It was <u>almost</u> dark <u>when</u> we got back.

6 used with negatives

You can use **almost** in front of negative words such as **never**, **no**, **none**, **no-one**, **nothing**, and **nowhere**.

A handbag was considered personal and <u>almost never</u> looked into.
There is <u>almost no</u> leadership at all.
I sold a picture by reducing the price to <u>almost nothing</u>.
She had <u>almost nowhere</u> to go.

You cannot use 'nearly' in front of negative words like these.
However, you can use **nearly** after **not** to emphasize a negative statement. For example, instead of saying 'The room is not big enough', you can say 'The room is **not nearly** big enough'.
It's <u>not nearly</u> so nice.
We <u>don't</u> do <u>nearly</u> enough to help.
I <u>haven't</u> done <u>nearly</u> as much as I would like.

You cannot use **almost** after 'not' like this.

7 adding modifiers

You can use **very** or **so** in front of **nearly**.

We were <u>very nearly</u> at the end of our journey.
Now they were <u>very nearly</u> men.
…the American who <u>so nearly</u> won the Open Championship in 1970.
…the family that had challenged the Corleone power, and had <u>so nearly</u> succeeded.

In conversation, you can also use **pretty** in front of **nearly**.

I came across a paragraph about a girl I'd <u>pretty nearly</u> forgotten.
'Do you know that thirty miles is eight hours solid marching?'–'Is it?'– '<u>Pretty nearly</u>.'

You cannot use 'very', 'so', or 'pretty' in front of **almost**.

alone - lonely

1 'alone'

If you are **alone**, you are not with any other people.

I wanted to be <u>alone</u>.
Barbara spent most of her time <u>alone</u> in the flat.

⚠ **WARNING:** You do not use 'alone' in front of a noun. For example, you do not talk about ~~'an alone woman'~~. Instead, you say 'a woman **on her own** '.
Some health farms attract couples; others are popular with people <u>on their own</u>.

2 'lonely'

Do not confuse **alone** with **lonely**. If you are **lonely**, you are unhappy because you do not

USAGE

have any friends or anyone to talk to. **Lonely** is used either in front of a noun or after a verb like **be** or **feel**.

He had befriended a lonely little boy.
She must be very lonely here.

along

You use **along** to indicate that someone or something moves or occurs in or next to something long and narrow such as a road or a river.

Tim walked along Ebury Street.
…the trees all along Bear Creek.
The current passes along this wire here.

⚠ **WARNING:** You do not use 'along' to describe movement from one side of an area to another. For example, you do not talk about going 'along' a desert. Instead you use **through** or **across**.

…hitch-hiking through Arizona.
He wandered across Hyde Park.

When someone or something goes into a hole and comes out the other side, you do not say that they go 'along' the hole. You say that they go **through** it.

I managed to crawl through the hole and when I came out there were flames everywhere.

a lot

⇨ See **Usage** entry at **lot**.

aloud - loudly

1 **'aloud'**

If you say something **aloud,** you say it so that other people can hear you.

In no previous war could men say aloud what was on their minds.

If you read **aloud** a piece of writing, you say the words so that people can hear what has been written.

She read aloud to us from the newspaper.

2 **'loudly'**

If you do something **loudly,** you make a lot of noise when you do it.

The audience laughed loudly.

already

1 **referring to an action**

You use **already** to say that something has happened before now, or that it has happened sooner than expected. When referring to an action, speakers of British English use a perfect tense with **already.** They put **already** after **have**, **has**, or **had**, or at the end of a clause.

We've already agreed to wait.
He had already invited Dougal Haston.
I've had tea already, thank you.
I can't stop him working – he's cleared half the site already.

Some speakers of American English use the simple past tense instead of the present perfect tense. For example, instead of saying 'I have already met him', they say 'I **already** met him' or 'I met him **already** '.

You already woke up the kids.
I told you already – he's the professor.

2 **referring to a situation**

Already is also used to say that a situation exists at an earlier time than expected.

● If there is no auxiliary, you put **already** in front of the verb, unless the verb is **be**.

They already exercise considerable influence in all western countries.
By the middle of June the Campaign already had more than 1000 members.

● If the verb is **be**, you put **already** after it.

It was already dark.
Satellites are already beyond absolute human control.
By the time he got home, Julie was already in bed.

● If there is an auxiliary, you put **already** after the auxiliary.

…animal species which are already considered endangered.

● If there is more than one auxiliary, you put **already** after the first one.

Portable computers can already be plugged into TV sets.

● If you want to emphasize that a situation exists at an earlier time than expected, you can put **already** at the beginning of a sentence.

Already the company is three quarters of the way to the target.
Already a bud on one of the roses was on the point of blooming.

alright

⇨ See **Usage** entry at **all right**.

also - too - as well

You use **also**, **too**, or **as well** when you are giving more information about something.

1 **'also'**

● **Also** is usually used in front of a verb. If there is no auxiliary, you put **also** immediately in front of the verb, unless the verb is **be**.

I also began to be interested in cricket.
They also helped out.

● If the verb is **be**, you put **also** after it.

I was also an American.
Knowledge, which is in many ways our blessing, is also our curse.

● If there is an auxiliary, you put **also** after the auxiliary.

From April you will also have to pay national insurance on the cost of the policy.
The basic symptoms of the illness were also described on the card.

● If there is more than one auxiliary, you put **also** after the first one.

We'll also be hearing about the work of Una Woodruff.
If that light blows, then every other light on the circuit will also have gone.

● **Also** is sometimes put at the beginning of a clause.

She has a reputation for brilliance. Also, she is gorgeous.

ⓘ Note that you never put **also** at the end of a clause.

2 **'too'**

You usually put **too** at the end of a clause.

Now the problem affects middle-class children, too.
It was a pretty play, and very sad too.

In conversation, **too** is used after a word or phrase when you are making a brief comment on something that has just been said.

'His father kicked him out of the house.'–'Quite right, too.'
'They've finished mending the road.'–'About time, too!'

Too is sometimes put after the first word group in a clause.

I wondered whether I <u>too</u> would become one of its victims.
Physically, <u>too,</u> the peoples of the world are incredibly mixed.

However, the position of **too** can make a difference to the meaning of a sentence. 'I am an American **too** ' can mean either 'Like the person just mentioned, I am an American' or 'Besides having the other qualities just mentioned, I am an American'. However, 'I **too** am an American' can only mean 'Like the person just mentioned, I am an American'.

He was playing well, <u>too.</u>
Now we have the financial backing <u>too.</u>
Nerissa, <u>too,</u> felt miserable.
Macdonald, <u>too,</u> was alarmed by the violence.

In British English, you do not put **too** immediately after a link verb or an auxiliary. You do not say, for example, 'I am too an American'. In American English **too** can be used in this way to contradict a negative statement.

'Oh, you aren't fat,' the stylish lady said. 'Ooooo <u>I am too,</u>' Mrs. Turpin said.

You also do not put **too** at the beginning of a sentence.

⇨ For information on other uses of this word, see **Usage** entry at **too**.

3 'as well'

As well always goes at the end of a clause.

Filter coffee is definitely better for your health than boiled coffee. And it tastes nicer <u>as well.</u>
They will have a rough year next year <u>as well.</u>

4 negatives

You do not usually use 'also', 'too', or 'as well' in negative clauses. You do not say, for example, '~~I'm not hungry and she's not hungry too~~'. You say 'I'm not hungry and she's not hungry **either** '. You can also say 'I'm not hungry and **neither is she** ' or 'I'm not hungry and **nor is she** '.

Teddy Boylan wasn't at the ceremony, <u>either.</u>
'I don't normally drink at lunch.'– <u>'Neither do I.'</u>
'No thank you, I don't smoke.'– <u>'Nor do I.'</u>

alternate - alternative

1 'alternate'

Alternate actions, events, or processes keep happening regularly after each other.

…the <u>alternate</u> contraction and relaxation of muscles.

If something happens on **alternate** days, it happens on one day, then does not happen on the next day, then happens again on the day after it, and so on. Things can also happen in **alternate** weeks, months, or years.

We saw each other on <u>alternate</u> Sunday nights.
The two courses are available in <u>alternate</u> years.

2 'alternative'

You use **alternative** to describe something that can be used, had, or done instead of something else.

But still people try to find <u>alternative</u> explanations.
There is, however, an <u>alternative</u> approach.

Note that in American English, **alternate** is sometimes used with this meaning.

How would a clever researcher rule out this <u>alternate</u> explanation?

Alternative can also be a noun. An **alternative** to something is something else that you can have or do instead.

Food suppliers are working hard to provide organic <u>alternatives</u> to everyday foodstuffs.
A magistrate offered them a Domestic Education course as an <u>alternative</u> to prison.
There is no <u>alternative</u> to permanent storage.

You can also say that someone has two or more **alternatives,** meaning that they have two or more courses of action to choose from.

If a man is threatened with attack, he has five <u>alternatives:</u> he can fight, flee, hide, summon help, or try to appease his attacker.

alternately - alternatively

1 **'alternately'**

You use **alternately** to say that two actions or processes keep happening regularly after each other.

Each piece of material is washed <u>alternately</u> in soft water and coconut oil.
She became <u>alternately</u> angry and calm.

2 **'alternatively'**

You use **alternatively** to give a different explanation from one that has just been mentioned, or to suggest a different course of action.

It is on sale there now for just £9.97. <u>Alternatively</u>, you can buy the album by mail order for just £10.
<u>Alternatively</u>, you can use household bleach.

although - though

1 **used as conjunctions**

You use **although** or **though** to introduce a subordinate clause in which you mention something which contrasts with what you are saying in the main clause. **Though** is not used in very formal English.

It was not for myself that I wanted the old piano, <u>although</u> I could play a little.
It wasn't entirely my decision, <u>though</u> I think that generally I agree with it.

You can put 'even' in front of **though** for emphasis.

She wore a fur coat, <u>even though</u> it was a very hot day.

Note that you do not put 'even' in front of **although.**

⚠ **WARNING:** When a sentence begins with **although** or **though,** you do not use 'but' or 'yet' to introduce the main clause. You do not say, for example, 'Although he was late, but he stopped to buy a sandwich'. You say 'Although he was late, **he stopped** to buy a sandwich'.

Although he was English, <u>he spoke</u> fluent and rapid French.
Though he hadn't stopped working all day, <u>he wasn't</u> tired.

You also do not use **although** or **though** in front of a noun group. You do not say, for example, 'Although his hard work, he failed his exam'. You say '**In spite of** his hard work, he failed his exam' or '**Despite** his hard work, he failed his exam'.

<u>In spite of</u> poor health, my father was always cheerful.
<u>Despite</u> her forcefulness, Cindy was uncertain what to do next.

2 **'though' used with clauses ending in a complement or adverb**

When a clause beginning with **though** ends with a complement, you can bring the complement forward to the beginning of the clause. For example, instead of saying 'Though he was tired, he insisted on coming to the meeting', you can say '**Tired though he was,** he insisted on coming to the meeting'. This is a formal use.

<u>Tempting though it may be to follow this point through</u>, it is not really relevant and we had better move on.
I had to accept the fact, <u>improbable though it was.</u>
<u>Astute business man though he was,</u> Philip was capable at times of extreme recklessness.

USAGE

When a clause beginning with **though** ends with an adverb, you can often put the adverb at the beginning of a clause.

Some members of the staff couldn't handle Murray's condition, hard though they tried.

However, when a clause beginning with **although** ends with a complement or adverb, you cannot move the complement or adverb to the beginning of the clause.

3 'though' used as an adverb

Though is sometimes an adverb. You use it when you are making a statement which contrasts with what you have just said. You usually put **though** after the first word group in the sentence. In conversation, you can also put **though** at the end of a sentence.

It might be worth your while to go to court. This is tricky, though, and you'll need expert advice.
Fortunately though, this is a tale with a happy ending.
For Newcastle, though, it was the climax of a hectic year.
I can't stay. I'll have a coffee though.

(i) Note that **although** is never an adverb.

altogether

1 'altogether'

Altogether means 'completely'.

The noise had stopped altogether.
…an altogether different kind of support.

⇨ For a graded list of words used to indicate extent, see section on **extent** in **Grammar** entry at **Adjuncts**.

You also use **altogether** to show that an amount is a total.

You will get £340 a week altogether.

2 'all together'

Do not confuse **altogether** with **all together**. You use **all together** to say that a group of people or things are together or do something together, and that none of them is missing.

It had been so long since we were all together – at home, secure, sheltered.

always

If something **always** happens in particular circumstances, it is certain to happen in those circumstances. If something has **always** been the case, there has never been a time when it was not the case.

When **always** has one of these meanings, it is used with a verb in a non-continuous tense.

● If there is no auxiliary, **always** goes in front of the verb, unless the verb is **be**.
Talking to Harold always cheered her up.
A man always remembers his first love.

● If the verb is **be**, you usually put **always** after it.
She was always in a hurry.
There is always someone to lift the baby up.

● If there is an auxiliary, you usually put **always** after it.
I 've always been very careful.
He 's always been so kind to us all.

● If there is more than one auxiliary, you usually put **always** after the first one.
She had always been allowed to read whatever she wanted.

If you say that something is **always** happening, you mean that it happens often and repeatedly and that this is annoying or surprising. When you use **always** like this, you use it with a verb in a continuous tense.

Uncle Harold was <u>always</u> fussing and worrying.
The bed was <u>always</u> collapsing.

⚠ **WARNING:** You do not use 'always' in comparisons, negative sentences, or questions to mean 'at any time in the past' or 'at any time in the future'. Instead you use **ever**. For example, you do not say ~~'They got on better than always before'~~. You say 'They got on better than **ever** before'.

…the biggest shooting star they had <u>ever</u> seen.
Neither of us would <u>ever</u> again get a job in films.
How will I <u>ever</u> manage to survive alone?

⇨ For a graded list of words used to indicate frequency, see section on **frequency** in **Grammar** entry at **Adjuncts**.

a.m.
⇨ See **Topic** entry at **Time**.

among

1 **'among' and 'between'**

If you are **among** a group of people or things, you are surrounded by them.

James wandered <u>among</u> his guests.
<u>Among</u> his baggage was a medicine chest.

You do not say that you are 'among' two people or things. You say that you are **between** them.

Myra and Barbara sat in the back, the baby <u>between</u> them.
She put the cigarette <u>between</u> her lips.
The island is midway <u>between</u> São Paulo and Porto Alegre.

Note that the form **amongst** is sometimes used, but is more formal than **among**.

The old farmhouse, hidden <u>amongst</u> orchards and fields of maize.

2 **dividing**

You can say that something is divided **among** or **between** a group of people. There is no difference in meaning.

…his estate, which he divided <u>among</u> his brothers and sisters.
Different scenes from the play are divided <u>between</u> five couples.

Note that the form **amongst** is sometimes used, but is more formal than **among**.

I heard that flour was being distributed <u>amongst</u> the citizens.

3 **differences**

You do not use **among** when you are talking about differences. You do not say, for example, ~~'I couldn't see any difference among the three chairs'~~. You say 'I couldn't see any difference **between** the three chairs'.

There was an important difference <u>between</u> the political analysts and the military ones.
For the 1997 election, while experts could tell the difference <u>between</u> the three main parties, the computer did not.

⇨ See **Usage** entry at **between**.

amount

An **amount** of something is how much of it you have, need, or get.

…the <u>amount</u> of salt lost in sweat.
I was horrified by the <u>amount</u> of work I had to do.

You can talk about a **large amount** or a **small amount**. You do not talk about a 'big amount' or a 'little amount'.

Use only a <u>small amount</u> of water at first.
The army gave out only <u>small amounts</u> of food.
There is no proof that <u>larger amounts</u> will prevent more colds.

When you use **amount** in the plural, you use a plural verb with it. For example, you say 'Large amounts of money **were** wasted'. You do not say 'Large amounts of money was wasted'.
Increasing amounts of force <u>are</u> necessary.
Very large amounts of money <u>are</u> required.

⚠ **WARNING:** You do not talk about an 'amount' of things or people. For example, you do not say ~~There was an amount of chairs in the room~~'. You say 'There **were a number** of chairs in the room'. When you use **number** like this, you use a plural verb with it.
A <u>number</u> of provisional bids were received.
A small <u>number</u> of law firms <u>have</u> picked up some major deals.

an
⇨ See **Usage** entry at **a - an**.

and
And can be used to link noun groups, adjectives, adverbs, verbs, or clauses.

1 linking noun groups
When you are talking about two things or people, you put **and** between two noun groups.
I'll give you a nice cup of tea <u>and</u> a ginger biscuit.
…a friendship between a boy <u>and</u> a girl.

When you are linking more than two noun groups, you usually only put **and** in front of the last one.
It's not just dogs, cats <u>and</u> other pets that are being mistreated.
We need volunteers, cars, trucks <u>and</u> drivers to check designated areas.

2 linking adjectives
● You put **and** between two adjectives when they come after verbs such as **be**, **seem**, and **feel**.
The room was large <u>and</u> square.
The bed felt cold <u>and</u> hard.

● When there are more than two adjectives after one of these verbs, you usually only put **and** in front of the last one.
We felt hot, tired, <u>and</u> thirsty.
The child is generally outgoing, happy <u>and</u> busy.

● When you use two or more adjectives in front of a noun, you do not usually put **and** between them.
…a <u>beautiful pink</u> suit.
… <u>rapid technological</u> advance.

● However, if the adjectives are colour adjectives, you must use **and**.
…a <u>black and white</u> swimming suit.

● Similarly, if you are using adjectives which classify a noun in a similar way, you use **and**.
…a social <u>and</u> educational dilemma.

You also use **and** when you put adjectives in front of a plural noun in order to talk about groups of things which have different or opposite qualities.
Both <u>large and small</u> firms deal with each other regularly.
… <u>European and American</u> traditions.

> ⚠ **WARNING:** You do not use 'and' to link adjectives when you want them to contrast with each other. For example, you do not say ~~'He was fat and agile'~~. You say 'He was fat **but** agile'.
> *We are poor but happy.*
> *…a small but comfortable hotel.*

3 **linking adverbs**
You can use **and** to link adverbs.
Mary was breathing quietly and evenly.
They walk up and down, smiling.

4 **linking verbs**
You use **and** to link verbs when you are talking about actions performed by the same person, thing, or group.

I was shouting and swearing.
They just sat and chatted.

If you want to say that someone does something repeatedly or for a long time, you can use **and** after a verb, and then repeat the verb.
They laughed and laughed.
Isaacs didn't give up. He tried and tried.

In conversation, you can sometimes use **and** after **try** or **wait** instead of using a 'to'-infinitive clause. For example, instead of saying 'I'll try to get a newspaper', you say 'I'll try **and** get a newspaper'. Note that in sentences like these you are describing one action, not two.
I'll try and answer the question.
I prefer to wait and see how things go.

> ⚠ **WARNING:** You only use **and** like this when you are using the future tense of **try** or 'wait', or when you are using the infinitive or imperative form.

If you **go and** do something or **come and** do something, you move from one place to another in order to do it.
I'll go and see him in the morning.
She would come and hold his hand.

In conversation, if you say that someone **has gone and** done something, you are expressing annoyance at something foolish that they have done.
He plastered it six months ago and that was bad enough but now he has gone and painted it peach.

5 **linking clauses**
And is often used to link clauses.

I came here in 1972 and I have lived here ever since.

When you are giving advice or a warning, you can use **and** to say what will happen if something is done. For example, instead of saying 'If you go by train, you'll get there quicker', you can say 'Go by train **and** you'll get there quicker'.
Do as you're told and you'll be all right.
Do that again and I'll break your legs.

You do not normally put **and** at the beginning of a sentence, but you can sometimes do so when you are writing down what someone said, or writing in a conversational style.
Send him ahead to warn Eric. And close that door.
I didn't mean to scare you. And I'm sorry I'm late.

USAGE

6 omitting repeated words

When you are linking verb groups which would contain the same auxiliary, you do not need to repeat the auxiliary.

John had already showered and changed.

Similarly, when you are linking nouns which would have the same adjective, preposition, or determiner in front of them, you do not need to repeat the adjective, preposition, or determiner.

… the young men and women of England.
My mother and father worked hard.

7 'both' for emphasis

When you link two word groups using **and,** you can emphasize that what you are saying applies to both word groups by putting **both** in front of the first word group.

They feel both anxiety and joy.

⇨ See **Usage** entry at **both**.

8 negative sentences

You do not normally use 'and' to link groups of words in negative sentences. For example, you do not say 'She never reads and listens to stories'. You say 'She never reads **or** listens to stories'.

He was not exciting or good looking.

⇨ See **Usage** entry at **or**.

However, you use **and** when you are talking about the possibility of two actions occurring at the same time. For example, you say 'I can't think **and** talk at the same time'. You also use **and** if two noun groups occur so frequently together that they are regarded as a single item. For example, **knife** and **fork** are always joined by **and** even in negative sentences such as 'I haven't got my knife **and** fork'.

Unions haven't taken health and safety as seriously as they might have done.

When two noun groups are regarded as a single item like this, they almost always occur in a fixed order. For example, you talk about your **knife and fork,** not your 'fork and knife'.

⇨ For a list of pairs of words of this kind, see **Topic** entry at **Fixed pairs.**

anger

Angry is normally used to talk about someone's mood or feelings on a particular occasion. If someone is often angry, you can describe them as **bad-tempered.**

Are you angry with me for some reason?
She's a bad-tempered young lady.

If someone is very angry, you can describe them as **furious.**

Senior police officers are furious at the blunder.

If they are less angry, you can describe them as **annoyed** or **irritated.**

The Premier looked annoyed but calm.
…a man irritated by the barking of his neighbour's dog.

Typically, someone is **irritated** by something because it happens constantly or continually. If someone is often irritated, you can describe them as **irritable.**

anniversary - birthday

1 'anniversary'

An **anniversary** is a date which is remembered or celebrated because a special event happened on that date in a previous year.

…the anniversary of the first moonwalk.
It's the 100th anniversary of Hitchcock's birth.

2 **'birthday'**

Note that you do not refer to the anniversary of the date when you were born as your 'anniversary'. You call it your **birthday.**

On my twelfth birthday *I received a letter from my father.*
It was 10 December, my daughter's birthday.

announcement - advertisement

1 **'announcement'**

An **announcement** is a public statement giving information about something.

The government made a public announcement *about the progress of the talks.*
The announcement *gave details of small increases in taxes.*

2 **'advertisement'**

An **advertisement** is an item in a newspaper or on television which tries to persuade you to buy something, or which gives you information about an event or job vacancy.

…an advertisement *for Black and White whisky.*
…an advertisement *for an assistant cashier.*

Note that the abbreviated forms **advert** (in British English) and **ad** are also commonly used.

The advert *is displayed at more than 4000 sites.*
…a 60-second TV ad.

another

1 **used to mean 'one more'**

Another thing or person of a particular kind means one more thing or person of that kind. **Another** is usually followed by a singular count noun.

Could I have another *cup of coffee?*
He opened another *shop last month.*

You can use **another** with 'few' or a number in front of a plural count noun.

Within another few *minutes reports of attacks began to come in.*
The woman lived for another ten *days.*

⚠ **WARNING:** You do not use 'another' immediately in front of a plural count noun or an uncount noun. You do not say, for example, 'Another men came into the room'. You say '**More** men came into the room'.

We ought to have more *police officers, and more of them on the streets.*
We need more *information.*

2 **used to mean 'different'**

Another thing or person also means a different thing or person from the one you have been talking about.

It all happened in another *country.*
He mentioned the work of another *colleague, John Lyons.*

Some other is sometimes used with a similar meaning.

I will have to think of some other *way of getting across to Europe.*
They talked about some other *guy they knew.*

⚠ **WARNING:** As with the previous meaning, you do not use 'another' in front of a plural count noun or an uncount noun. You do not say, for example, 'They arrange things better in another countries'. You say 'They arrange things better in **other** countries'.

Other people must have thought like this.
…toys, paints, books and other *equipment.*

3 used as a pronoun

Another is sometimes a pronoun.

I saw one girl whispering to <u>another.</u>

answer

1 used as a verb

When you **answer** someone who has asked you a question, you say something back to them. You can either say that someone **answers** a person or that they **answer** a question.

I didn't know how to <u>answer</u> her.
I tried my best to <u>answer</u> her questions.

(*i*) Note that you do not 'answer to' someone who has asked you a question, or 'answer to' their question.

2 used as a noun

An **answer** is something that you say to someone when they have asked you a question.

'Is there anyone here?' I asked. There was no <u>answer.</u>

An **answer to** a problem is a possible solution to it.

At first is seemed like the <u>answer to</u> all my problems.

(*i*) Note that you do not talk about an 'answer for' a problem.

anti-social - unsociable

1 'anti-social'

Anti-social behaviour is harmful or annoying to other people.

…the growing use of the computer by <u>anti-social</u> elements as a weapon of crime.
Don't let your children develop an <u>anti-social</u> habit such as bullying.

 Note that the American spelling of this word is **antisocial**.

2 'unsociable'

People who do not like the company of other people are sometimes described as **anti-social,** but another word used to describe such people is **unsociable.**

She was an awkward and <u>unsociable</u> girl.

anxious

1 'anxious about'

If you are **anxious about** someone or something, you are worried about them.

I was quite <u>anxious about</u> about George.

2 'anxious to'

If you are **anxious to do** something, you want very much to do it.

We are most <u>anxious to find out</u> what really happened.
He seemed <u>anxious to go.</u>

(*i*) Note that you do not say that someone is 'anxious for doing' something.

3 'anxious for'

If you are **anxious for** something, you want to have it, or you want it to happen.

…civil servants <u>anxious for</u> promotion.
He was <u>anxious for</u> a deal, and we gave him the best we could.

4 'anxious that'

If you are **anxious that** something should happen, you want it to happen very much.

Lyons was most <u>anxious that</u> this should happen.
My parents were <u>anxious that</u> I go to college.

(*i*) Note that when you use a 'that'-clause after **anxious,** you usually use **should** in it.

5 **'anxious' and 'nervous'**

Do not confuse **anxious** with **nervous**. If you are **nervous**, you are rather frightened about something that you are going to do or experience.

I began to get <u>nervous</u> about crossing roads.
Both actors were exceedingly <u>nervous</u> on the day of the performance.

any

1 **'any'**

You use **any** to say that something is true about each thing or person of a particular type, about each member of a group, or about each part of something.

You use **any** in front of a singular count noun to talk about each thing or person of a particular type.

Consult <u>any large dictionary</u> for proof.
…things that <u>any man</u> might do under pressure.

You use **any** in front of a plural count noun to talk about all things or people of a particular type.

One must beware of <u>any forecasts about fuel supplies.</u>
The patients know their rights like <u>any other consumers.</u>

You use **any** in front of an uncount noun to talk about an amount of something.

Throw <u>any vegetable matter</u> to the pig.

When you use **any** in front of a singular count noun or an uncount noun, you use a singular form of a verb with it.

Any book that attracts children as much as this <u>has</u> to be taken seriously.
While any poverty <u>remains,</u> it must have the first priority.

When you use **any** in front of a plural count noun, you use a plural form of a verb with it.

Before any decisions <u>are</u> made, ministers are carrying out a full enquiry.

2 **'any of'**

You use **any of** in front of a plural noun group beginning with **the**, **these**, **those**, or a possessive to talk about each thing or person belonging to a particular group.

It was more expensive than <u>any of the other magazines.</u>
<u>Any of the local boatmen</u> will take you to the caves.
Milk in <u>any of these forms</u> is just as nutritious as when it comes straight from the cow.
Current rates can be obtained on request at <u>any of our branches.</u>

You can use either a plural or singular form of a verb with **any of** and a plural noun group. The singular form is more formal.

Find out if any of his colleagues <u>were</u> at the party.
There is no sign that any of these limits <u>has</u> yet been reached.

You use **any of** in front of a singular noun group beginning with **the**, **this**, **that**, or a possessive to talk about each part of something.

Im not going to give you <u>any of the land.</u>
I feel horribly guilty taking up <u>any of your precious time.</u>

You can also use **any of** in front of the pronouns **this**, **that**, **these**, **those**, **it**, **us**, **you**, or **them**.

Has <u>any of this</u> been helpful?
I don't believe <u>any of it.</u>
'We had numerous chances and didn't take advantage of <u>any of them</u> ,' Pardew said.

Note that you do not use **any** without **of** in front of these pronouns.

You can use either a plural or singular form of a verb with **any of** and the pronouns **these**, **those**, **us**, **you**, and **them**.

We would hotly contest the idea that any of us <u>were</u> middle class.
I don't think any of us <u>wants</u> that.

3 used in questions and negatives

Any is used, especially after **have**, in questions and negative sentences.

Do you have any facts to back up all this?

He said he hadn't any feelings about his own childhood.

⇨ For more information about this use, see **Usage** entry at **some**.

4 used as a pronoun

Any can also be a pronoun.

Discuss it with your female colleagues, if you have any.

The meeting was different from any that had gone before.

anybody

⇨ See **Usage** entry at **anyone - anybody**.

any more

1 'any more'

If you want to say that something that happened in the past does not happen now, you say that it does not happen **any more**. You can also say that something is not the case **any more**. **Any more** usually comes at the end of a clause.

There was no noise any more.

He can't hurt us any more.

People just do not care any more.

Note that you do not say that something does not happen 'no more'.

 Any more is sometimes spelled **anymore** in American English.

The land isn't valuable anymore.

2 'no longer'

Instead of saying that something 'does not happen any more', you can say that it **no longer happens**. This is a fairly formal use.

● You put **no longer** in front of the verb, unless the verb is **be**.

We no longer feed infants in this way.

Their clothing no longer gave effective protection against the heat.

● If the verb is **be**, you put **no longer** after it.

That is no longer the case.

● If you use a modal, you put **no longer** between the modal and the main verb.

They can no longer gather food for themselves.

Ralph could no longer make himself heard.

● In writing, **no longer** is sometimes put at the beginning of a clause, followed by an auxiliary or modal or **be**, and then the subject.

No longer were they isolated from each other.

No longer can boys and girls pick up their skills from their mothers and fathers.

You do not use **no longer** like this in conversation.

3 'any longer'

Instead of saying that something 'does not happen any more' or 'no longer happens', you can say that it **does not happen any longer**. This use is less common. **Any longer** goes at the end of a clause.

She could not doubt it any longer.

anyone - anybody

1 'anyone' and 'anybody'

You use **anyone** or **anybody** to talk about people in general, or about each person of a particular kind. There is no difference in meaning between **anyone** and **anybody**.

Anyone can miss a plane.
Anybody can go there.
If anyone asks where you are, I'll say you've just gone out.
If anybody wants me for anything, tell them I'll be back soon.

☐2 **used in questions and negatives**

Anyone and **anybody** are very commonly used in questions and negative sentences.

Was there anyone behind you?
There wasn't anyone in the room with her.

⇨ For more information about this use, see **Usage** entry at **someone - somebody**.

☐3 **'any one'**

Do not confuse **anyone** with **any one**. You use **any one** to emphasize that you are referring to only one of something.

There are about 350,000 properties for sale at any one time in Britain.

anyplace

⇨ See **Usage** entry at **anywhere**.

anything

☐1 **'anything'**

You use **anything** to talk about a thing or event which might exist or happen, or about each thing or event of a particular kind.

The situation is very tense; anything might happen.
'Do you like beer?'–'I like anything alcoholic.'

☐2 **used in questions and negatives**

Anything is very commonly used in questions and negative sentences.

Why do we have to show him anything?
I did not say anything.

⇨ For more information about this use, see **Usage** entry at **something**.

any time

If you can do something **any time** or **at any time,** you can do it whenever you want to.

If you'd like to give it a try, just come any time.
They can leave at any time.

When you use **any time** without 'at', you can spell it **anytime.**

I could have left anytime.
We'll be hearing from him anytime now.

If you want to say that something can be done whenever a particular thing is needed, you can use **any time** with a 'that'-clause, usually without 'that'.

Any time you need him, let me know.
Any time the banks need to increase rates on loans they are passed on very quickly.

Any time is also used in negative sentences to mean 'some time'.

We mustn't waste any time in Athens.
I haven't had any time to learn how to use it properly.

When you use **any time** to mean 'some time', you do not spell it 'anytime'.

anyway

☐1 **'anyway'**

You use **anyway** when you are adding a remark to something you have just said. Usually the remark is something you have just thought of, and makes your previous statement seem less important or relevant.

If this doesn't work, I'll find a gun and shoot myself. I'm serious. That's what I feel like doing, anyway.

I decided to postpone the idea of doing a course, and anyway I got accepted by the Council.

2 **'any way'**

Do not confuse **anyway** with **any way**. **Any way** usually occurs in the phrase **in any way**, which means 'in any respect' or 'by any means'.

He never threatened her in any way.

I am not connected in any way with the medical profession.

If I can help her in any way, you have only to speak to me.

anywhere

1 **'anywhere' and 'anyplace'**

Anywhere means in any place, or in any part of a particular place.

It is better to have it in the kitchen than anywhere else.

They are the oldest rock paintings anywhere in North America.

 Some speakers of American English say **anyplace** instead of 'anywhere'.

The fact is we're afraid to go anyplace alone.

Airports were more closely watched than anyplace else.

2 **used in questions and negatives**

Anywhere is very commonly used in questions and negative statements.

Is there an ashtray anywhere?

I decided not to go anywhere.

⇨ For more information about this use, see **Usage** entry at **somewhere**.

apart

1 **'apart'**

If two people are **apart**, they are not in each other's company.

They could not bear to be apart.

ⓘ Note that you do not use 'apart' in front of a noun.

2 **'apart from'**

You use **apart from** when you mention an exception to a statement that you are making.

Apart from Ann, the car was empty.

She had no money, apart from the five pounds that Christopher had given her.

When **apart** is used in sentences like these, it must be followed by **from** and not by any other preposition.

 Note that in American English **aside from** is often used instead of **apart from**.

Aside from the location, we knew little about this park.

apartment

⇨ See **Usage** entry at **flat - apartment**.

apologize

If you **apologize to** someone, you say you are sorry.

Afterwards George apologized to him personally.

ⓘ Note that **apologize** must be followed by **to** in sentences like these. You do not say that you 'apologize' someone.

If you **apologize for** something you have done, or **apologize for** something someone else has done, you say you are sorry about it.

Later, Bred apologized to Savchenko for the conduct of a few members of the company.

I apologize for being late.

appeal

In British English, if someone **appeals against** a legal decision or sentence, they formally ask a court to change the decision or reduce the sentence.

He appealed against the five year sentence he had been given.

 Speakers of American English do not use 'against' after **appeal.** They say that someone **appeals** a decision.

Casey's lawyer said he was appealing the interim decision.

appear

1 'appear'

When something **appears,** it moves into a position where you can see it.

A glow of light appeared over the sea.

You also use **appear** to say that something becomes available for people to read or buy.

His second novel appeared under the title 'Getting By'.
It was about the time that video recorders first appeared in the shops.

When you are mentioning the date or period when something became available, you often use **there.** For example, instead of saying 'In the 1960s a new type of car appeared', you can say 'In the 1960s **there appeared** a new type of car'.

In 1992 there appeared The Private Years, the first volume of The Selected Letters of Bertrand Russell.
As early as the mid-twenties there appeared on the market chairs, tables and stools designed by Wijdveldt.

(*i*) Note that in sentences like these you must use **there.** You do not say, for example, 'In the 1960s appeared a new type of car'.

2 'appear to'

If something **appears to** be the case, it seems to be the case. Similarly, if something **appears to** be a particular thing, it seems to be that thing. **Appear to** is more formal than 'seem to'.

I don't appear to have written down his name.
Their offer appears to be the most attractive.

apply

1 request formally

If you **apply** to have something or to do something, you write asking formally to be allowed to have it or do it.

I've applied for another job.
Sally and Jack applied to adopt another child.

2 another meaning of 'apply'

Apply has another meaning. If you **apply** something to a surface, you put it onto the surface or rub it into it. This is a formal use of **apply,** which usually occurs only in written instructions.

Apply a little liquid wax polish.

(*i*) In conversation and in most kinds of writing, you do not say that you 'apply' something. You say that you **put** it **on, rub** it **on, rub** it **in,** or **spread** it **on.**

...the cream that she put on to soothe her sunburn.
Try a little methylated spirit rubbed on with a soft cloth.
Rub in linseed oil to darken it.

USAGE

appreciate

If you **appreciate** something that someone has done for you, you are grateful to them because of it.

Thanks. I really appreciate your help.

We would much appreciate guidance from an expert.

You can use **appreciate** with **it** and an 'if'-clause to say politely that you would like someone to do something. For example, you can say 'I would **appreciate it if** you would deal with this matter urgently'.

We would really appreciate it if you could come.

(i) Note that you must use **it** in sentences like these. You do not say, for example, 'I would appreciate if you would deal with this matter urgently'.

approach

If you **approach** something, you get nearer to it.

He approached the front door.

…Nancy heard footsteps approaching the galley.

(i) Note that **approach** is not followed by 'to'. You do not say, for example, 'He approached to the front door'.

approve

If you **approve of** someone or something, you have a good opinion of them.

His mother had not approved of Julie.

Steve approved of the whole affair.

Note that you do not say that you 'approve to' someone or something.

If someone in authority **approves** a plan or idea, they formally agree to it and say that it can happen.

The White House approved the exercise.

The directors quickly approved the new deal.

(i) Note that for this meaning of **approve** you do not use 'of'.

arise - rise

Both **arise** and **rise** are irregular verbs. The other forms of **arise** are **arises, arising, arose, arisen.** The other forms of **rise** are **rises, rising, rose, risen.**

When an opportunity, problem, or new state of affairs **arises,** it begins to exist. This is the most common meaning of **arise.**

He promised to help Rufus if the occasion arose.

A serious problem has arisen.

When something **rises,** it moves upwards.

Clouds of birds rose from the tree-tops.

When someone who is sitting **rises,** they stand up. This is a formal use. In conversation, it is more usual to say **stand up.** You can also use **rise** to say that someone gets out of bed in the morning. This is also a formal use. In conversation, it is more usual to say **get up.**

⇨ See **Usage** entry at **rise - raise.**

armchair

⇨ See **Usage** entry at **chair - armchair.**

army

An **army** is a large organized group of people who are armed and trained to fight. In British English, after **army** you can use either a singular or plural form of a verb.

The army is in a high state of readiness.

The army are clearing up quite a bit of the land.

USAGE

 In American English, the singular form of the verb is preferred.

The U.S. army is involved in small construction projects.

around - round - about

1 **talking about movement**

When you are talking about movement in no particular direction, you can use **around** and **round** as well as **about**.

It's so romantic up there, flying around in a small plane.
I spent a couple of hours driving round Richmond.
Police constables walk about with guns on their hips.

2 **being present or available**

When you are talking about something being generally present or available, you can use **around** or **about,** but not **round,** as adverbs.

There is a lot of talent around at the moment.
There are not that many jobs about.

⚠ **WARNING: Round** has a lot of other meanings, as a noun, verb, and adjective. You cannot use **about** in these cases.

3 **used as a preposition or adverb**

Around has the same meaning as **round**, when **round** is a preposition or an adverb.

She was wearing a scarf round her head.
He had a towel wrapped around his head.
The earth moves round the sun.
The satellite has passed once more around the earth.
Think of what's happening politically round the world.
…the growth of vigilante societies around the country.
He swung round and faced the window.
The large lady turned around in a huff.

 Around is more common in American English than in British English.

4 **used in phrasal verbs**

You can also use **around** instead of 'round' as the second part of some phrasal verbs.

Don't wait for April to come round before planning your vegetable garden.
When interview time came around, Purcell was nervous.
Irving got round the problem in a novel way.
An impasse has developed and I don't know how to get around it.

 Around Note that American English uses only **around** in these cases.

5 **meaning 'approximately'**

In conversation, **around** and **round about** are sometimes used to mean 'approximately'.

He owns around 200 acres.
I've been here for round about ten years.

ⓘ Note that you do not use 'round' like this.

arrival

When someone arrives at a place, you can talk about their **arrival** there. This is a rather formal use.

His arrival was hardly noticed.
A week after her arrival, we had a General School Meeting.

If you want to say that something happens immediately after someone arrives at a place, you can use a phrase beginning with **on**. Note that you must use **on**, not 'at', in sentences like these. You do not say, for example, 'At his arrival in London, he went straight to

Oxford Street'. You can say 'On his arrival in London, he went straight to Oxford Street'.

On his arrival in Singapore he hired a secretary and rented his first office.
The British Council will book temporary hotel accommodation on your arrival in London.

The possessive determiner is often omitted. For example, instead of saying 'on their arrival', you can just say **on arrival.**

The principal guests were greeted on arrival by the Lord Mayor of London.
On arrival at the Station hotel in Dumfries he acknowledges a few familiar faces.

arrive - reach

1 'arrive'

You use **arrive** or **reach** to say that someone comes to a place at the end of a journey.
I'll tell Professor Hogan you 've arrived.
He reached Bath in the late afternoon.
You usually say that someone **arrives at** a place.
…by the time we arrived at Victoria Station.
…from the moment he had arrived at the Harlowes' bungalow.

However, you say that someone **arrives in** a country or city.
He had arrived in France slightly ahead of schedule.
The American Ambassador to Mexico arrived in Quito today.

⚠ **WARNING:** You never say that someone 'arrives to' a place.
You also do not say that someone 'arrives at home' or 'arrives in home'. You say that they **arrive home.**
We arrived home and I carried my suitcases up the stairs behind her.

You do not use a preposition after **arrive** in front of **here, there, somewhere,** or **anywhere.**
I arrived here yesterday.
When we arrived there, we went to the garage.
Beautiful women, after all, rarely arrive anywhere on time.

2 'reach'

Reach always takes a direct object. You do not say that someone 'reaches at' a place or that they 'have just reached'.
It was dark by the time I reached their house.

3 another meaning

Arrive at and **reach** can both be used to say that someone eventually makes a decision or finds the answer to something.
It took us several hours to arrive at a decision.
They were unable to reach a decision.
I had arrived at a conclusion on the basis of the only facts then available to me.
The commission could not reach a conclusion because of inadequate data.

Come to can be used in a similar way.
Kwezi thought for a while, then seemed to come to a decision.
I came to the conclusion that I could not afford to move.

arrogant

⇨ See **Usage** entry at **proud.**

as

1 used in time clauses

If something happens **as** something else happens, it happens while the other thing is happening.

She wept bitterly <u>as</u> she told her story.
The play started <u>as</u> I got there.

You also use **as** to say that something is done whenever something happens.
Parts are replaced <u>as</u> they grow old.

ⓘ Note that you do not use 'as' simply to mean 'at the time that'. For example, you do not say '~~As I started work here, the pay was £2 an hour~~'. You say '**When** I started work here, the pay was £2 an hour'.

⇨ See **Usage** entry at **when**.

2 | **used to mean 'because'**

As is often used to mean 'because' or 'since'.
She bought herself an iron <u>as</u> she felt she couldn't keep borrowing Anne's.
<u>As</u> he had been up since 4 a.m. he was no doubt now very tired.

⇨ See **Usage** entry at **because**.

3 | **used with adjectives**

You can use **as** in front of an adjective to say how someone or something is regarded or described.
He regarded them <u>as snobbish.</u>
They regarded manual work <u>as degrading.</u>
Officials described him <u>as brilliant.</u>

⚠ **WARNING:** You do not use 'as' after comparative adjectives. You do not say, for example, '~~The trees are taller as the church~~'. You say 'The trees are taller **than** the church'.
She was much older <u>than</u> me.

4 | **used in prepositional phrases**

You can also use **as** in prepositional phrases to say how someone or something is regarded, described, treated, or used.
He was regarded <u>as something of a troublemaker.</u>
If Pluto had been discovered today, it would never be classified <u>as a planet.</u>
I treated business <u>as a game.</u>
I wanted to use him <u>as an agent.</u>

You can also use **as** in prepositional phrases to say what role or function someone or something has.
He worked <u>as a clerk.</u>
He served <u>as Kennedy's ambassador to India.</u>
Bleach removes colour and acts <u>as an antiseptic and deodoriser.</u>

5 | **used in comparisons**

In writing, **as** is sometimes used to compare one action to another.
He looked over his shoulder <u>as</u> Jack had done.
She pushed him, <u>as</u> she had pushed her son.

Like and **the way** are used in a similar way.

⇨ See **Usage** entry at **like - as - the way**.

You can also use **as** in front of some prepositional phrases, especially at the beginning of a sentence. For example, instead of saying 'She took a holiday in April, as she had done in previous years', you can say '**As in previous years,** she took a holiday in April'.
<u>As in previous attacks</u> there was no warning of the bomb.

When you have just made a statement, you can use **as** as a conjunction to indicate that the statement also applies to another person, thing, or group. After **as** you use **be**, **have**, an auxiliary, or a modal, then the subject.
Our daughter feels that way, <u>as do our sons.</u>

USAGE

⚠ **WARNING:** You do not usually use 'as' in front of a noun group when you are comparing one thing or person to another. You do not say, for example, 'She sang ~~as a bird~~'. You say 'She sang **like** a bird'.

He swam <u>like</u> a fish.
I am a worker <u>like</u> him.
Children, <u>like</u> animals, are noisy at meal times.

However, you can make a comparison using **as,** an adjective or adverb, and another **as.** For example, you can say 'You're just **as bad as** your sister'.
⇨ For more information about this use, see **Usage** entry at **as ... as.**

as ... as

1 in comparisons

When you are comparing one person or thing to another, you can use **as** followed by an adjective or adverb followed by another **as.**

You're just <u>as bad as</u> your sister.
...huge ponds <u>as big as</u> tennis courts.
The meal was <u>as awful as</u> the conversation.
She wanted to talk to someone <u>as badly as</u> I did.

After these expressions, you can use either a noun group and a verb, or a noun group on its own.

You're as old as <u>I am.</u>
...some man as old as <u>Father.</u>
François understood the difficulties as well as <u>he did.</u>
I can't remember it as well as <u>you.</u>

If you use a personal pronoun on its own, it must be an object pronoun such as **me** or **him.** It used to be considered correct to use a subject pronoun such as 'I' or 'he', but this now sounds very old-fashioned.

He looked about as old as <u>me.</u>

If you use a personal pronoun and a verb, you must use a subject pronoun.

The teacher is just as sensitive as <u>they are.</u>
...somebody who's as bad at it as <u>I am.</u>

2 using modifiers

You can put words and expressions such as **almost, just,** and **at least** in front of **as ... as** structures.

I could see <u>almost as well</u> at night <u>as</u> I could in sunlight.
It is <u>just as bad</u> to overfeed pets <u>as</u> it is to underfeed them.
He may be <u>at least as unpopular as</u> the President.

3 used with negatives

You can also use **as ... as** structures in various kinds of negative sentence.

They <u>aren't as clever as</u> they appear to be.
I <u>don't</u> notice things <u>as well as</u> I used to.
You've <u>never</u> been <u>as late as</u> this without telephoning.
There is <u>no one as dangerous as</u> an idealist with a machine gun.

So is sometimes used instead of the first 'as', but this use is not common.

Strikers are <u>not so important as</u> a good defence.
I had seldom seen him looking <u>so pleased with himself as</u> he was now.

4 used to describe size or extent

You can use expressions such as **twice, three times,** or **one fifth** in front of **as ... as** structures. You do this when you are indicating the size or extent of something by comparing it to something else.

…volcanoes <u>twice as high as</u> Everest.
This animal is <u>three times as popular</u> with girls <u>as</u> with boys.
Water is <u>eight hundred times as dense as</u> air.

5 **using just one 'as'**

If it is very clear what you are comparing someone or something to, you can omit the second **as** and the following noun group or clause.

A megaphone would be <u>as good</u>.
This fish is <u>twice as big</u>.

ashamed - embarrassed

1 **'ashamed'**

If you are **ashamed**, you feel guilty because you believe you have done something other people will judge to be wrong or unacceptable.

She had behaved badly and was <u>ashamed</u>.
They were <u>ashamed</u> to tell their people how they had been cheated.

You say that someone is **ashamed of** something or someone.

He felt <u>ashamed of</u> his selfishness.
It's nothing to be <u>ashamed of</u>.
I'm <u>ashamed of</u> his firm, and I'm <u>ashamed of</u> you.

2 **'embarrassed'**

If you are **embarrassed**, you are upset because you think something makes you seem foolish.

The Belgian looked <u>embarrassed</u>.
She had been too <u>embarrassed</u> to ask her friends.

You say that someone is **embarrassed by** something or **embarrassed about** it.

He seemed <u>embarrassed by</u> his brother's outburst.
I felt really <u>embarrassed about</u> it.

(*i*) Note that you do not say that someone is 'embarrassed of' something.

as if

1 **'as if' and 'as through'**

You can use **as if** or **as though** at the beginning of a clause when you are describing how someone or something looks, or how someone behaves.

It's a wonderful item and in such good condition that it looks <u>as though</u> it was bought yesterday.
He lunged towards me <u>as if</u> he expected me to aim a gun at him.

Many people think it is incorrect to use 'was' in clauses of this type. They say you should use **were** instead.

He looked at me as if I <u>were</u> mad.
She remembered it all as if it <u>were</u> yesterday.

However, in conversation people usually use **was**.

The secretary spoke as though it <u>was</u> some kind of password.
He gave his orders as if this <u>was</u> only another training exercise.

You can use **was** or **were** in conversation, but in formal writing you should use **were**.

2 **'like'**

Some people say **like** instead of 'as if' or 'as though'.

He looked <u>like</u> he felt sorry for me.
Shaerl put up balloons all over the house <u>like</u> it was a six-year-old's party.

This use is generally regarded as incorrect.

USAGE

ask

You say that someone **asks** a question.

He started <u>asking</u> Diana a lot of questions.

(*i*) Note that you do not say that someone 'says' a question.

1 reporting questions

You also use **ask** when you are reporting questions. After **ask** you usually use a noun group and an 'if'-clause or 'wh'-clause.

When you report a question to which the answer is 'yes' or 'no', you usually use **ask** with an 'if'-clause.

She <u>asked</u> him <u>if his parents spoke French.</u>
Someone <u>asked</u> me <u>if the work was going well.</u>

You can also use a clause beginning with 'whether'.

I <u>asked</u> Professor Bailey <u>whether he agreed.</u>

When you report a question to which the answer is not 'yes' or 'no', you usually use **ask** with a 'wh'-clause.

I <u>asked</u> him <u>what he wanted.</u>
He <u>asked</u> me <u>where I was going.</u>

⚠ **WARNING:** In the 'wh'-clause, the subject and the verb do not change places. You do not say, for example, '~~He asked me when was the train leaving~~'. You say 'He asked me when **the train was** leaving'.

You can say that someone **asks** someone else their name or their age.

He <u>asked</u> me my name.

You can say that someone **asks** someone else the time.

Whenever the butler came by, she <u>asked</u> him the time.

You can also say that someone **asks** someone else's opinion about something.

I <u>was asked</u> my opinion about the new car.

You do not need to say who a question is addressed to if this is already clear from the context.

A young man <u>asked if we were students.</u>
She <u>asked why he was so silent.</u>
I <u>asked how they liked the film.</u>

⚠ **WARNING:** You never use 'to' when mentioning who a question is addressed to. You do not say, for example, '~~He asked to me my name~~'.

2 direct reporting

You can use **ask** when reporting directly what someone says.

'How many languages can you speak?' he <u>asked.</u>
'Have you met him?' I <u>asked.</u>

3 reporting requests

You also use **ask** when you are reporting requests. When someone says that they want to be given something, you report this using **ask** and **for**. For example, if a man says 'Can I have a bunch of roses?', you report this as 'He **asked for** a bunch of roses'.

We <u>asked for</u> the bill.
An Italian came in and <u>asked for</u> a loaf of white bread.

When someone says that they want to speak to another person, for example on the telephone, you say that they **ask for** that person.

He rang the office and <u>asked for</u> Cynthia.
He lifted the telephone and <u>asked for</u> the Prime Minister's private office.

When someone tells another person that they want them to do something, you report this using **ask** and either a 'to'-infinitive clause or an 'if'-clause.

He asked her to marry him.
He was asked to leave.
Two teenage girls ask me if I will take a photograph of them together.
I asked him if he would mind not smoking.

asleep
⇨ See **Usage** entry at **sleep - asleep**.

as long as

1 used in conditionals
You can use **as long as** or **so long as** to say that one thing is true only if another thing is true. For example, if you say 'As long as you are under 16, you can take part in activities' you mean 'If you are under 16, you can take part in activities'.

(*i*) Note that you use a simple tense after **as long as** and **so long as**.

You can look as long as you don't touch.
We were all right as long as we kept our heads down.
The president need not step down so long as the elections are held under international supervision.

2 duration
You also use **as long as** to say that something lasts for a long period of time, or for as much time as possible.

Any stomach-ache that persists for as long as one hour should be seen by a doctor.
But I love football and I want to keep playing as long as I can.
She hesitated as long as she dared.

(*i*) Note that you do not use 'so long as' in this way.

⚠ **WARNING:** You do not use 'as long as' when you are talking about distances. You do not say, for example, 'I followed him as long as the bridge'. You say 'I followed him **as far as** the bridge'.

assertive
⇨ See **Usage** entry at **forceful**.

assignment - homework

1 'assignment'
An **assignment** is a task that someone is given to do, usually as part of their job.

My first major assignment as a reporter was to cover a large-scale riot.

An **assignment** is also a piece of academic work given to students.

The course has heavy reading assignments.
When class begins, he gives us an assignment and we have seven minutes to work at it.

🇺🇸 In American English, an **assignment** is also a piece of work given to schoolchildren to do at home.

2 'homework'
Work given to schoolchildren to do at home is also called **homework**.

He never did any homework.

⚠ **WARNING:** Homework is an uncount noun. You do not talk about 'homeworks' or 'a homework'. Note that you do not say 'I have made my homework', you say 'I have **done** my homework'.

USAGE

assist - be present

1 'assist'

If you **assist** someone, you help them. **Assist** is a fairly formal word.

We may be able to <u>assist</u> with the tuition fees.
He was asked to <u>assist</u> in keeping the hotel under surveillance.

2 'be present'

If you want to say that someone is there when an event or occasion happens, you say that someone **is present** at an event or occasion.

He <u>had been present</u> at the dance.
Howard insisted on <u>being present.</u>

as soon as

As soon as is a conjunction. You use **as soon as** to say that something will happen immediately after something else has happened.

<u>As soon as</u> we get the tickets we'll send them to you.

(*i*) Note that you usually use the simple present tense after **as soon as.** You do not use a future tense. You do not say, for example, 'I will call you as soon as I will get back to my room'. You say 'I will call you as soon as I **get** back to my room'.

Ask him to come in, will you, as soon as he <u>arrives.</u>
I promised the girls I'd call as soon as Daniel <u>comes</u> out of surgery.

When you are talking about the past, you use the simple past tense after **as soon as.**

As soon as she <u>got</u> out of bed the telephone stopped ringing.

assume

⇨ See **Usage** entry at **suppose - assume.**

assure - ensure - insure

1 'assure'

If you **assure** someone that something is true or will happen, you tell them that it is definitely true or will definitely happen, often in order to make them less worried.

'I can <u>assure</u> you that neither of our two goalkeepers will be leaving,' O'Leary said.

2 'ensure' and 'insure'

To **ensure** that something happens means to make certain that it happens.

His reputation was enough to <u>ensure</u> that he was always welcome.

 In American English, this word is usually spelled **insure.**

I shall try to <u>insure</u> that your stay is a pleasant one.

3 'insure'

Insure has another meaning. In both British and American English, if you **insure** your property, you pay money to a company so that if the property is lost, stolen, or damaged, the company will pay you a sum of money.

<u>Insure</u> your baggage before you leave home.

as though

⇨ See **Usage** entry at **as if.**

as usual

⇨ See **Usage** entry at **usual - usually.**

as well

⇨ See **Usage** entry at **also - too - as well.**

as well as

1 linking noun groups

If you say that something is true of one person or thing **as well as** another, you are emphasizing that it is true not only of the second person or thing but also of the first one.

Women, <u>as well as</u> men, have a fundamental right to work.

2 linking adjectives

You can also use **as well as** to link adjectives. When you do this, you are emphasizing that something has not only the second quality you mention but also the first one.

It has symbolic <u>as well as</u> economic significance.

3 linking clauses

You can use **as well as** in a similar way to link clauses. However, the second clause must be a non-finite clause beginning with an '-ing' form.

She was an individual <u>as well as being</u> the airport manager's wife.
She negotiates the licences <u>as well as ordering</u> the equipment.

⚠ **WARNING:** You do not use a finite clause after **as well as.** You do not say, for example, ~~'She negotiates the licences as well as she orders the equipment'.~~

---

at

1 place or position

At is used to talk about the position of something, or about the place where something happens.

There was a staircase <u>at</u> the end of the hallway.
He said I was to be <u>at</u> a certain place in the Kaiserstrasse at 3 p.m.

You often use **at** to mean 'next to' or 'beside'.

The boat was anchored <u>at</u> Westminster Bridge.
Captain Imrie stopped me <u>at</u> the door.

You say that someone sits **at** a table or desk, for example when they are eating or writing.

She was sitting <u>at</u> the dressing table.
I was sitting <u>at</u> my desk reading.

If you want to mention the building where something exists or where something happens, you usually use **at.**

…the exhibition of David Jones' work <u>at</u> the Tate Gallery.
Dr Campbell told of his examination of Meehan <u>at</u> Ayr Police Station on July 15th.
We had dinner <u>at</u> a restaurant in Attleborough.
He lived <u>at</u> 14 Burnbank Gardens, Glasgow.

In British English, you say that someone is **at** school or **at** university.

He had done some acting <u>at</u> school.
After a year <u>at</u> university, Benn joined the RAF.
He was just starting his final year <u>at</u> University College, London.

🇺🇸 Speakers of American English usually say that someone is **in** school.

They had met <u>in</u> high school.

⇨ See **Usage** entry at **school - university.**

You say that someone stops **at** a particular place during a journey.

We pulled in for lunch <u>at</u> a roadhouse.
We docked <u>at</u> Panama.

You say that something happens **at** a meeting, ceremony, or party.

He made his remarks <u>at</u> a press conference.
The whole village were out <u>at</u> a funeral.

USAGE

Teenagers often drink socially <u>at</u> parties, clubs and discos.
He had a fight <u>at</u> a high school dance.

2 time

At is also used to say when something happens.
You use **at** when you are mentioning a precise time.

<u>At</u> 2.30 a.m. he returned.
It is scheduled to be shown <u>at</u> 9pm on Easter Sunday.

If you want to know the precise time when something happened or will happen, you can say **'At what time…?'** but people usually say **'What time…?'** or **'When…?'**

<u>What time</u> does the boat leave?
'We are having a party on the beach.'– '<u>What time?</u>' –'At nine.'
<u>When</u> is the press conference?
'I'll be there this afternoon.'– '<u>When</u>?'

You can say that something happened or will happen **'at** dawn,**'' at** dusk', or **'at** night'.

She had come in <u>at</u> dawn.
It was ten o'clock <u>at</u> night.

However, you say that something happened or will happen **'in the** morning,'**'in the** afternoon', or **'in the** evening'.

If something happens **at** a meal time, it happens while the meal is being eaten.

<u>At</u> dinner we had another in our series of conversations.
He told her <u>at</u> lunch that he couldn't take her to the game tomorrow.

You say that something happens **at Christmas** or **at Easter**.

She sends a card <u>at</u> Christmas.
What will happen to me <u>at</u> Easter?

However, you say that something happens **on** a particular day during Christmas or Easter.

I expect they even play cricket <u>on</u> Christmas Day.
<u>On</u> Easter Monday I headed for a hotel called the Europejski.

In British English, **at** is used with **weekend**.

Relatives are relied on to provide food <u>at</u> the weekend and during holidays.

 American speakers usually use **on** or **over** with **weekend**.

I had a class <u>on</u> the weekend.
The Museum threw a party <u>over</u> the weekend.

at first

⇨ See **Usage** entry at **first - firstly**.

athletics - athletic

1 'athletics'

Athletics consists of sports such as running, the high jump, and the javelin.

He has retired from active <u>athletics.</u>

Athletics is an uncount noun. You use a singular form of a verb with it.

Athletics <u>was</u> developing rapidly.

 Note that the American term for this is **track and field**.

She never competed in <u>track and field.</u>

2 'athletic'

Athletic is an adjective. It can mean 'relating to athletics'.

… <u>athletic</u> trophies.

However, when you use **athletic** to describe a person, you mean that they are fit, healthy, and active. You do not mean that they take part in athletics.

… <u>athletic</u> young men.

at last
⇨ See **Usage** entry at **last - lastly**.

at present
⇨ See **Usage** entry at **presently**.

attempt
⇨ See **Usage** entry at **try - attempt**.

attendant
An **attendant** is someone whose job is to help people in a place such as a filling station or museum.
She stopped the car and told the attendant to fill it up.

You do not refer to someone who works in a shop selling goods to customers as an 'attendant'. A person like this is called a **shop assistant**.
I tell the male shop assistant what I am looking for and why.

 In American Engish, this person is called a **sales clerk**.
…a sales clerk at the Soul Shack record store.

attention
If you give something your **attention,** you look at it, listen to it, or think about it carefully.
When he felt he had their attention, he began.
He switched his attention back to his magazine.

You can also say that someone **pays attention to** something.
Look, pay attention to what I'm saying.
There's far too much attention being paid to these hooligans.

(*i*) Note that you do not say that someone 'pays attention at' something.

attorney
⇨ See **Usage** entry at **lawyer**.

attractive
⇨ See **Usage** entry at **beautiful**.

audience
You refer to all the people who are watching or listening to a play, concert, film, or television play as the **audience**. You can use either a singular or plural form of a verb with **audience**.
Yesterday the audience was rather larger.
The television audience were able to hear some of the comments.

You can also use **audience** to refer to the people who read a particular writer's books or hear about someone's ideas.
…the need for intellectuals to communicate their ideas to a wider audience.

aural - oral

1 **'aural'**
Aural means 'relating to your ears and your sense of hearing'. **Aural** is pronounced /ɔːrəl/ or /aʊrəl/.
I have used written and aural material.

2 **'oral'**
Oral means 'relating to your mouth'. It also describes things that involve speaking rather than writing. **Oral** is pronounced /ɔːrəl/.
…an oral test in German.

USAGE

Both **aural** and **oral** are fairly formal words. They are used mainly to talk about teaching methods and examinations.

autumn

In British English, **autumn** or **the autumn** is the season between summer and winter.
Saturday was the first day of <u>autumn.</u>
She had waited throughout <u>the autumn.</u>

If you want to say that something happens every year during this season, you say that it happens **in autumn** or **in the autumn**.
<u>In autumn</u> the hard berries turn a delicate orange.
Most births occur in spring, while birth rates are lowest <u>in the autumn.</u>

(*i*) Note that you do not say that something happens 'in the autumns'.

 In American English, autumn is referred to as **the fall.**
In <u>the fall</u> we are going to England.

avoid

If you **avoid** something, you take action to prevent it from happening to you.
…a book on how to <u>avoid</u> a heart attack.
The pilots had to take emergency action to <u>avoid</u> a disaster.

If you **avoid doing** something, you make sure that you do not do it.
Thomas turned his head, trying to <u>avoid breathing in</u> the smoke.
You must <u>avoid giving</u> any unnecessary information.

Note that you do not say that you 'avoid to do' something.

⚠ **WARNING:** If you cannot control or change the way you behave, you do not say that you 'can't avoid' it. You say that you **can't help** it or that you **can't help yourself.**
It was so crowded, I <u>couldn't help</u> leaning on him a little.
You know what his temper's like, he just <u>can't help himself.</u>

If someone does not allow you to do what you want to do, you do not say that they 'avoid' you doing it. You say that they **prevent** you **from** doing it.
My only idea was to <u>prevent</u> him <u>from</u> speaking.

await

If you **await** something, you expect it to come or happen, and you are often not intending to take any action until it comes or happens.
Daisy had remained behind to <u>await</u> her return.
We will <u>await</u> developments before deciding whether he should be allowed to continue.
We must <u>await</u> the results of field studies yet to come.

Await is a fairly common word in formal writing, but you do not usually use it in conversation. Instead you use **wait for,** often followed by an object and a 'to'-infinitive. For example, instead of saying 'I awaited her reply', you say 'I **waited for her to reply** '.
I <u>waited for Kate to return.</u>
They just <u>waited for me to die.</u>

awake

Awake, wake, awaken, waken, and **wake up** can all be intransitive verbs to say that someone becomes conscious again after being asleep. They can also be transitive verbs to say that someone makes you conscious when you have been asleep.
Awake and **wake** are irregular verbs. Their past tenses are **awoke** and **woke,** and their past participles are **awoken** and **woken.**

1 **'awake' and 'wake'**

Awake and **wake** are fairly common in writing, especially as intransitive verbs.

I awoke from a deep sleep.

I sometimes wake at four in the morning.

2 **'awaken' and 'waken'**

Awaken and **waken** are old-fashioned or literary words. They are usually transitive verbs.

She was awakened by a loud bang.

When she was asleep nothing wakened her.

3 **'wake up'**

In ordinary conversation, you use **wake up**.

…young babies waking up at night and crying.

Ralph, wake up!

They went back to sleep but I woke them up again.

4 **other meanings**

You can say that something **awakens** your interest or feelings.

My first visit to a theatre awakened an interest which never left me.

The experience awakened my enthusiasm for science afresh.

If you **wake up to** a problem or a dangerous situation, you become aware of it.

The Church must wake up to the financial problems of the clergy.

The West began to wake up to the danger it faced.

5 **'awake' used as an adjective**

Awake can also be an adjective. If someone is **awake**, they are not asleep.

An hour later he was still awake.

Lynn stayed awake for a long time.

Awake is usually used after verbs like **be**, **stay**, **keep**, and **lie**, but it can also be used with verbs like **shake** and **prod** to say that someone wakes someone else up.

You would have to shake her awake.

Wendy would nudge me awake.

Awake is sometimes used after a noun.

She was the last person awake.

He was walking more like a somnambulist than a person fully awake.

⚠ **WARNING:** You never use **awake** in front of a noun. You do not say that someone is 'very awake'. You say that they are **wide awake** or **fully awake**.

He was wide awake by the time we reached my flat.

She rose, still not quite fully awake.

---

award

⇨ See **Usage** entry at **reward - award**.

aware - familiar

1 **'aware of'**

If you are **aware of** something, you are conscious of it, or you know that it exists.

Ralph was aware of the heat for the first time that day.

People became aware of American jazz.

2 **'familiar with'**

If you know or understand something well, you do not say you are 'aware of' it. You say you are **familiar with** it.

I am of course familiar with your work.

You will probably already be familiar with some of this story.

USAGE

away - far

1 'away'

If you want to state the distance of a particular place from where you are, you can say that it is that distance **away.**

…Durban, which is over 300 kilometres <u>away.</u>
It is <u>a long way from</u> London.
Anna was still <u>a long way away.</u>

2 'far'

Far is used in negative sentences and questions about distance, but not usually in affirmative sentences.

⇨ See **Usage** entry at **far.**

awful - awfully

1 'awful'

The adjective **awful** is used in two ways:

In conversation, you use it to say that something is very unpleasant or of very poor quality.

Isn't the weather <u>awful?</u>
Gas smells <u>awful.</u>
The road is <u>awful;</u> narrow and bumpy.

In writing or conversation, you also use **awful** to say that something is very shocking or distressing.

…an account of that <u>awful</u> war.
My husband had an <u>awful</u> death.

2 'awfully'

The adverb **awfully** is used in a completely different way. It is used in front of an adjective to emphasize that someone or something has a quality to a great extent.

You're an <u>awfully</u> kind person, Dr Marlowe.
I'm <u>awfully</u> sorry.
It's getting <u>awfully</u> dark.

ⓘ Note that **awfully** is only used in conversation, and is a rather old-fashioned word. It is more usual to use **very, really,** or **extremely.**

awhile - a while

1 'awhile'

Awhile is an adverb used after a verb. It means 'for a short period of time'.

I may have to stay there <u>awhile.</u>
Can't you just wait <u>awhile?</u>

ⓘ Note that it is more common to use **for a while**, especially in British English.

2 'a while'

A while is an indefinite period of time. You can say that someone does something **for a while** or **after a while.**

<u>For a while</u> it looked as if it might work.
They walked on in silence <u>for a while.</u>
<u>After a while,</u> we drove off.

You can use adjectives such as **short, little,** or **long** in front of **while.**

I'm going to have to leave you on your own for <u>a short while.</u>
…a book that I read <u>a little while</u> ago.

B b

back

1 **used with an intransitive verb**

You use **back** with an intransitive verb to say that someone returns to a place where they were before.

In six weeks we've got to go back to West Africa.
I went back to the kitchen.
I'll come back after dinner.

2 **'be back'**

In conversation, instead of saying that someone will 'come back', you often say that they will **be back**.

I imagine he'll be back for lunch.
Pete will be back from holiday next week.

⚠ **WARNING:** You never use 'back' with the verb **return**. You do not say, for example, 'He returned back to his office'. You say 'He **returned** to his office'.

I returned from the Middle East in 1956.

3 **used with a transitive verb**

You use **back** with a transitive verb to say that someone or something is taken or sent to a place where they were before. **Back** usually goes after the direct object.

We brought Dolly back.
He took the tray back.

When the direct object is a pronoun, **back** always goes after it.

I brought him back to my room.
She put it back on the shelf.

However, when the direct object is a long noun group, or a noun group followed by a relative clause, you put **back** in front of the noun group.

He recently sent back his rented television set.
He put back the silk sock which had fallen out of the drawer.
He went to the market and brought back fresh food which he cooked at home.

4 **returning to a former state**

Back can also be used to say that someone or something returns to a state they were in before.

He went back to sleep.
...a £30 million plant which will turn all the waste back into sulphuric acid.

5 **used as a noun**

Back is also a noun. Your **back** is the part of your body from your neck to your waist that is on the opposite side to your chest and stomach.

We lay on our backs under the ash tree.
She tapped him on the back.

The **back** of an object is the side or part that is towards the rear or farthest from the front.

Many relatives sat at the back of the room, some visibly upset.
Keep some long-life milk at the back of your refrigerator.

The **back** of a door is the side which faces into a room or cupboard.

Pin your food list on the back of the larder door.

The **back** of a piece of paper is the side which has no writing on, or the side which you look at second.

Sign on the <u>back</u> of the prescription form.

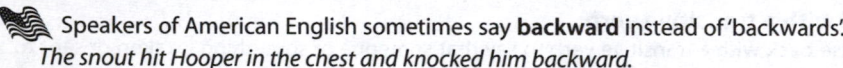 Note that in British English you do not talk about the 'back side' of a door or piece of paper. However, in American English, this construction is common.

Be sure to read the <u>back side</u> of this sheet.

backward

⇨ See **Usage** entry at **backwards**.

backwards

1 'backwards'

If you move or look **backwards,** you move or look in the direction your back is facing.

The hummingbird can fly <u>backwards.</u>
He overbalanced and stepped <u>backwards</u> onto a coffee cup.
Lucille looked <u>backwards</u> at the once-lovely site where her great-great-grandparents' graves had lain.

If you do something **backwards,** you do it the opposite way to the usual way.

Listen to the tape <u>backwards.</u>

ⓘ Note that **backwards** is only an adverb.

2 'backward'

Speakers of American English sometimes say **backward** instead of 'backwards'.

The snout hit Hooper in the chest and knocked him <u>backward.</u>

In both British and American English, **backward** is an adjective. A **backward** movement or look is one in which someone or something moves or looks backwards.

She took a <u>backward</u> step.
Without a <u>backward</u> glance, he walked away.

When **backward** is an adjective, it can only be used in front of a noun.

⇨ For another meaning of **backward,** see **Usage** entry at **retarded.**

back yard

⇨ See **Usage** entry at **yard.**

bad - badly

1 'bad'

Something that is **bad** is unpleasant, harmful, or undesirable.

I have some very <u>bad</u> news.
Candy is <u>bad</u> for your teeth.
The weather was <u>bad.</u>

The comparative and superlative forms of 'bad' are **worse** and **worst.**

Her marks are getting <u>worse</u> and <u>worse.</u>
…the <u>worst</u> thing which ever happened to me.

2 'badly'

You do not use 'bad' as an adverb. You do not say, for example, ~~The Conservatives did bad in the elections~~. You say 'The Conservatives did **badly** in the elections'.

I cut myself <u>badly.</u>
The room was so <u>badly</u> lit I couldn't see what I was doing.

When **badly** is used like this, its comparative and superlative forms are **worse** and **worst.**

We played <u>worse</u> than in our previous two matches.
…the <u>worst</u> affected areas.

Badly has another meaning which is quite different. If you need or want something **badly,** you need or want it very much.

We need the money badly.
I want you so badly.
I am badly in need of advice.

For this meaning of **badly,** you do not use the comparative and superlative forms 'worse' and 'worst'. Instead you use the forms **more badly** and **most badly.**

She wanted him more badly than ever.
Of the three sports, the one that most badly needs to build up new stars is basketball.

⇨ Many other words and expressions can be used in a similar way to this meaning of **badly.** For a graded list, see section on **degree** in **Grammar** entry at **Adjuncts.**

bag

A **bag** is a container made of paper or plastic which is used to carry things.

…a bag of sugar.
…a plastic bag full of sticky labels.

ⓘ Note that a **bag of** something can refer either to a bag and its contents, or just to the contents.

When he went to bed he put a bag of salt beside his head.
He ate a whole bag of sweets.

A **bag** is also a container with handles or a strap, which you use to carry things such as shopping.

He was carrying a red shopping bag.

You can refer to a woman's handbag as her **bag.**

She opened her bag and took out a handkerchief.

 In American English, pieces of luggage are usually referred to as **bags.** Some British speakers also use **bags** with this meaning.

The porter took her bags.

Most British speakers refer to a large piece of luggage as a **case** or **suitcase.**

They left their cases piled beside the car.
She arrived dragging and bumping her heavy suitcase.

baggage
⇨ See **Usage** entry at **luggage - baggage.**

bake
⇨ See **Usage** entry at **cook.**

band - tape

1 **'band'**

A **band** is a narrow strip of material such as cloth or metal which is joined at the ends so that it can be fitted tightly round something.

…a panama hat with a red band.
A man with a black band around his arm stood alone.
Her hair was in a pony tail secured with a rubber band.

2 **'tape'**

You do not refer to the magnetic strips on which sounds are recorded as 'bands'. You call them **tapes.**

Do you want to put on a tape?
His manager persuaded him to make a tape of the song.

USAGE

bank - bench - seat

1 'bank'

The **bank** of a river or lake is the ground at its edge.

…30 miles of new developments along both <u>banks</u> of the Thames.
Leaving her mask and flippers on the <u>bank,</u> she plunged straight into the pool.

A **bank** is also a place where you can keep your money in an account.

You should ask your <u>bank</u> for a loan.

2 'bench' and 'seat'

You do not refer to a long, narrow seat in a park or garden as a 'bank'. You call it a **bench** or a **seat.**

Rudolf sat on the <u>bench</u> and waited.
She sat on a <u>seat</u> on the promenade.

---

banknote

1 'banknote'

A **banknote** is a piece of paper money.

Some of the <u>banknotes</u> were unbelievably dirty.

2 'note'

In British English, a banknote is usually referred to as a **note.**

He handed me a ten pound <u>note.</u>

3 'bill'

 A piece of American paper money is called a **bill,** not a banknote.

He took out a five dollar <u>bill.</u>

⇨ For another meaning of **bill,** see **Usage** entry at **bill - check.**

---

bar

 In American English, a place where you can buy and drink alcoholic drinks is called a **bar.**

Leaving Rita in a <u>bar,</u> I made for the town library.

In British English, a place like this is called a **pub.**

We used to go drinking in a <u>pub</u> called the Soldier's Arms.

⇨ See **Usage** entry at **pub.**

In British English, the rooms in a pub where people drink are called the **bars.** In a hotel, club, or theatre, the place where you can buy and drink alcoholic drinks is also called a **bar.**

…the terrace <u>bar</u> of the Continental Hotel.

---

bare - barely

1 'bare'

Bare is an adjective. If something is **bare,** it has no covering.

The doctor stood uneasily on the <u>bare</u> floor.
He put his hand on my <u>bare</u> leg.

2 'barely'

Barely is an adverb. It has a totally different meaning from **bare.** You use **barely** to say that something is only just true or possible.

He was so drunk he could <u>barely</u> stand.
His voice was <u>barely</u> audible.

> ⚠ **WARNING:** You do not use 'not' with **barely**. You do not say, for example, 'The temperature was not barely above freezing'. You say 'The temperature was **barely** above freezing'.
> If you use an auxiliary or modal with **barely**, you put the auxiliary or modal first. You say, for example, 'He **can barely** read'. You do not say 'He barely can read'.
> *His career at Internazionale <u>had barely</u> begun when he was told he should never play football again.*
> *He <u>could barely</u> get his words out.*

Barely is sometimes used in longer structures to say that one thing happened immediately after another. For example, you can say 'We had **barely** started the meal when Jane arrived'.

ⓘ Note that you use **when** or **before** after **barely**. You do not use 'than'. You do not say, for example, 'We had barely started the meal than Jane arrived'.
The ship had <u>barely</u> cleared the harbour <u>when</u> an Italian customs cutter raced after her.
I had <u>barely</u> said my name <u>before</u> he had led me to the interview room.

barrister

⇨ See **Usage** entry at **lawyer**.

bass - base

These words are both usually pronounced /beɪs/.

1 **'bass'**

A **bass** is a male singer who can sing very low notes.
…the great Russian <u>bass</u> Chaliapin.

A **bass** saxophone, guitar, or other musical instrument is one that has a lower range of notes than other instruments of its kind.
The girl vocalist had been joined by the lead and <u>bass</u> guitars.

A **bass** is also an edible fish that is found in rivers and the sea. There are several types of **bass**.
They unloaded their catch of cod and <u>bass</u>.

> ⚠ **WARNING:** Note that this sense of the word **bass** is pronounced /bæs/.

2 **'base'**

The **base** of something is its lowest edge or part.
…the switch on the lamp <u>base</u>.
I had back pain starting at the <u>base</u> of my spine and shooting up it.

bath - bathe

1 **'bath'**

In British English, a **bath** /bɑːθ/ is a long rectangular container which you fill with water and sit in while you wash your body.
In those days, only quite wealthy families had <u>baths</u> of their own.

🇺🇸 In American English, a container like this is called a **bathtub** or a **tub**.
I spent hours in the warmth of the <u>bathtub</u>.
I lowered myself deeper into the <u>tub</u>.

If you **bath** someone, you wash them in a bath.
She will show you how to <u>bath</u> the baby.
We <u>bathed</u> and dried Sandy together.

USAGE

You do not say that people **bath** themselves. British speakers say that someone **has a bath.**

I'm going to <u>have a bath.</u>

2 'bathe'

 American speakers say that someone **takes a bath** or, more formally, that they **bathe** /beɪð/.

I <u>took a bath,</u> my second that day.
After golf I would return to my apartment to <u>bathe</u> and change.

Bathe is not used with this meaning in British English. In British English, when someone **bathes,** they swim or play in a lake or river or in the sea.

It is dangerous to <u>bathe</u> in the sea here.

This use of **bathe** is now rather old-fashioned. In modern English, you usually say that someone **goes swimming** or **goes for a swim.** American speakers sometimes say that someone **takes a swim.**

She's <u>going for a swim.</u>
I went down to the ocean and <u>took a swim.</u>

 In both British and American English, if you **bathe** a cut or wound, you wash it.

He <u>bathed</u> the cuts on her feet.
She had watched her mother <u>bathe</u> his face and bandage his hands.

ⓘ Note that **bath** and **bathe** both have the present participle **bathing** and the past tense and past participle **bathed.** However, **bathing** and **bathed** are pronounced /bɑːθɪŋ/ and /bɑːθt/ when they relate to 'bath', and /beɪðɪŋ/ and /beɪðd/ when they relate to 'bathe'.

---

be

1 forms

Be is the most common verb in English. It is used in many different ways.
The present tense forms of **be** are **am, are,** and **is,** and the past tense forms are **was** and **were. Be** is both an auxiliary and a main verb.

…a problem which <u>is getting</u> worse.
It <u>was</u> about four o'clock.

⇨ See **Grammar** entry at **Auxiliaries.**

Am, is, and **are** are not usually pronounced in full. When you write down what someone says, you usually represent 'am' and 'is' using **'m** and **'s.**

<u>I'm</u> sorry,' I said.
'But <u>it's</u> not possible,' Lili said.
'Okay,' he said. 'Your <u>brother's</u> going to take you to Grafton.'

You can also represent 'are' using **'re,** but only after a pronoun.

<u>We're</u> winning,' he said.

You can also use the forms **'m, 's** and **'re** when you are writing in a conversational style.

⇨ See **Grammar** entry at **Contractions.**

2 used as an auxiliary

Be is an auxiliary when forming continuous tenses and passives.

She <u>was</u> watching us.
Several apartment buildings <u>were</u> destroyed.

⇨ See **Grammar** entry at **Tenses.**

In conversation, **get** is often used to form passives.

⇨ See **Usage** entry at **get.**

3 used as a main verb

You use **be** as a main verb when you are describing things or people or giving information about them. After **be,** you use a **complement.** A complement is either an adjective or a noun group.

We were <u>very happy.</u>
He is now <u>a teenager.</u>

⇨ See **Grammar** entry at **Complements.**

4 | **indicating someone's job**

When **be** is followed by a noun group indicating a unique job or position within an organization, you do not have to put 'the' in front of the noun.

At one time you wanted to <u>be President.</u>

ⓘ Note that **make** is sometimes used instead of 'be' to say how successful someone is in a particular job or role. For example, instead of saying 'He will be a good president', you can say 'He will **make** a good president'.

5 | **indicating age and cost**

You can talk about a person's age by using **be** followed by a number.

Rose Gibson <u>is twenty-seven.</u>

You can also use **be** to say how much something costs.

How much <u>is</u> it?
It <u>'s</u> five pounds.

⇨ For further information, see **Topic** entries at **Age** and **Money.**

6 | **with prepositional phrases**

You can use many kinds of prepositional phrase after **be.**

He was still <u>in a state of shock.</u>
I'm <u>from Dortmund</u> originally.
…people who are <u>under pressure.</u>

7 | **with 'to'-infinitives**

You sometimes use 'to'-infinitive clauses after **be.**

The talks <u>are to begin</u> tomorrow.
What <u>is to be done</u> ?

⇨ For further information, see **Grammar** entry at **'To'-infinitive clauses.**

8 | **in questions and negative clauses**

When you use **be** as a main verb in questions and negative clauses, you do not use the auxiliary 'do'.

<u>Are</u> you O.K?
<u>Is</u> she Rick's sister?
I <u>was</u> not surprised.
It <u>was</u> not an easy task.

9 | **in continuous tenses**

Be is not usually a main verb in continuous tenses. However, you can use it in continuous tenses to describe someone's behaviour at a particular time.

You'<u>re being</u> very silly.

10 | **'be' and 'become'**

Do not confuse **be** with **become. Be** is used to indicate that someone or something has a particular quality or nature, or is in a particular situation. **Become** is used to indicate that someone or something changes in some way.

Before he <u>became</u> Mayor he had been a tram driver.
It was not until 1845 that Texas <u>became</u> part of the U.S.A.

⇨ See **Usage** entry at **become.**

11 | **after 'there'**

Be is often used after **there** to indicate the existence or occurrence of something.

USAGE

Clearly <u>there is</u> a problem here.
<u>There are</u> very few cars on this street.
<u>There was</u> nothing new in the letter.

> ⚠ **WARNING:** You cannot use **be** without **there** to indicate that something exists or happens. You cannot say, for example, '~~Another explanation is~~' or '~~Another explanation must be~~'. You must say '**There is** another explanation' or '**There must be** another explanation'.
> ⇨ See **Usage** entry at **there**.

12 **after 'it'**

Be is often used after **it** to describe something such as an experience, or to comment on a situation.

<u>It was</u> very quiet in the hut.
<u>It was</u> awkward keeping my news from Ted.
<u>It's</u> strange you should come today.

⇨ See **Usage** entry at **it**.

13 **'have been'**

If you have visited a place and have now come back from it, British speakers say that you **have been** there.

I <u>have been</u> to Santander many times.
I've <u>been</u> there before.

⇨ See **Usage** entry at **go**.

be able to

⇨ See **Usage** entry at **can - could - be able to**.

beach - shore - coast

1 **'beach'**

A **beach** is an area of sand or pebbles next to the sea or a lake. You can relax or play on a beach, or use it as a place to swim from.

He wandered off along the <u>beach.</u>

2 **'shore'**

The **shore** of a sea, lake, or wide river is the land along its edge. The **shore** can be smooth and sandy or very rocky.

…the waves breaking against the <u>shore.</u>

3 **'coast'**

The **coast** is the border between the land and the sea, or the part of a country that is next to the sea.

He landed on the <u>coast</u> of South Carolina.
…the industrial cities of the <u>coast.</u>

bear

1 **'bear'**

Bear is one of several verbs which can be used to talk about people experiencing unpleasant situations. The other forms of 'bear' are **bears, bore, borne**.

You use **bear** in positive sentences when you are talking about a very unpleasant situation. Typically, you talk about someone **bearing** pain or hardship, meaning that they accept it in a brave way.

It was painful, of course, but he <u>bore</u> it.
He <u>bore</u> his sufferings manfully.

2 'endure'
Endure is used in a similar way.
Many have to endure pain without specialist help.

3 'can't bear'
Bear is often used in negative sentences. If you say that you cannot **bear** something or someone, you mean that they are so annoying or irritating that you do not want to be involved with them in any way.
I couldn't bear staying in the same town as that man.
I can't bear him!

4 'can't stand'
Stand is used in a similar way.
He kept on nagging and I couldn't stand it any longer.
She said she couldn't stand him.

5 'tolerate' and 'put up with'
If you **tolerate** or **put up with** something, you accept it, although you do not like it or approve of it.
…the tendency to tolerate extremes of human behaviour.
The local people have to put up with gaping tourists.

bear - bare

These words are both pronounced /beə/.

1 'bear'
Bear can be a noun or a verb.
A **bear** is a large, strong wild animal with thick fur and sharp claws.
The bear reared on its hind legs.
If you **bear** a difficult situation, you accept it and are able to deal with it.
This disaster was more than some of them could bear.

⇨ See **Usage** entry at **bear**.

To **bear** something also means to carry or support it. This is a fairly formal use.
His ankle now felt strong enough to bear his weight.

2 'bare'
Bare is usually an adjective. Something that is **bare** has no covering.
…her bare feet.
The walls were bare.

⇨ See **Usage** entry at **bare - barely**.

beat

If you **beat** someone or something, you hit them several times very hard.
His stepfather used to beat him.

The past tense of 'beat' is **beat,** not 'beated'. The past participle is **beaten.**
The rain beat against the window.
Helmuth had been beaten severely by the gamekeeper.

If you **beat** someone in a game, you defeat them.
Arsenal beat Oxford United 5–1.

beauty

The following words can all be used to describe someone who is nice to look at:

attractive	good-looking	handsome	stunning
beautiful	gorgeous	pretty	

USAGE

1 'attractive', 'gorgeous' and 'good-looking'

Attractive and **gorgeous** are also used to describe young children, but **good-looking** is not.

She had grown into a chubby <u>attractive</u> child, with a mop of auburn curls like her mother's.

2 'handsome'

Handsome is used more often to describe men than women. It is used to describe any man who has regular, pleasant features. However, it is only used to describe women when their features are large and regular rather than small and delicate.

He was a tall, dark, and undeniably <u>handsome</u> man.
In the 1930's the ideal woman was classically <u>handsome</u> rather than childishly pretty.

3 'beautiful' and 'pretty'

Beautiful and **pretty** are generally used to describe women and children rather than men. Only very young boys are described as **pretty,** not older boys, because this word implies a delicate, feminine appearance.

…a <u>beautiful</u> young girl with long hair.
Our mother was laughing and looking <u>pretty</u> and happy.
'Such a <u>pretty</u> baby,' clucked Mrs Morrison.

4 'stunning'

You can also describe a woman as **stunning,** especially when she has made herself look particularly attractive or is wearing very attractive clothes.

An onlooker said the bride looked <u>stunning</u> in a full-length ivory dress.

5 degree of beauty

If you say that someone is **beautiful,** you are implying that they are nicer to look at than if you said they were **attractive, good-looking, handsome,** or **pretty.** If you say that someone is **gorgeous** or **stunning,** you mean that they are extremely nice to look at.

⚠ **WARNING:** You can describe someone's appearance by saying that they **look nice** or **look wonderful,** but if you call someone **a nice man** or **a wonderful woman,** or say that they **are nice** or **are wonderful,** you are describing their character, not their appearance. Similarly, **lovely** is more often used to describe someone's character than their appearance.

---

because

1 'because'

You use **because** when you are giving the reason for something.
If someone asks a question beginning with 'Why?', you can reply using **because.**
'Why shouldn't I come?'–'<u>Because</u> you're too busy.'

If you have said that something is the case and you want to say why it is the case, you usually add a reason clause beginning with **because.**

I couldn't see Helen's expression, <u>because</u> her head was turned.
Rudolph's father did the shopping, <u>because,</u> he said, his wife was extravagant.

2 'as' and 'since'

In writing, the reason clause is sometimes put first, and **as** or **since** is used instead of 'because'.

<u>As</u> the gorilla is so big and powerful, it has no real enemies.
<u>Since</u> she did not make enough money to live in her own house, she went back to live with her mother.

⚠ **WARNING:** When you use **as** or **since** at the beginning of a sentence, you do not put an expression such as 'that is why' at the beginning of the second clause. You do not say, for example, ~~'As you have been very ill yourself, that is why you will understand how I feel'~~. You simply say 'As you have been very ill yourself, **you will understand** how I feel'.

If you want to say that there is a special reason for something, you can use words like **especially** or **particularly** in front of **as** or **since.** When you do this, you put the reason clause after the main clause.

I was frightened when I went to bed, <u>especially as</u> my room was so far up.
It was nice to have someone to talk to, <u>particularly as</u> it looked as if I was going to be there all night.

③ **'for'**
In stories, **for** is sometimes used instead of 'because'. This is an old-fashioned use.
This was where he spent a great deal of his free time <u>for</u> he had nowhere else to go.
His two older sisters slept downstairs, <u>for</u> they had to be up first.

④ **'because of'**
Sometimes you use a noun group instead of a clause when you are mentioning the reason for something. When you do this, you put **because of** in front of the noun group.
Many families break up <u>because of</u> a lack of money.
<u>Because of</u> the heat, the front door was open.

become

① **'become'**
When something or someone **becomes** a particular thing, they start being that thing.
When you feed a current through the coil, it <u>becomes</u> a magnet.
Anybody can <u>become</u> a qualified teacher.

The past tense of 'become' is **became,** not 'becomed'.
We <u>became</u> good friends at once.
The smell <u>became</u> stronger and stronger.

The past participle is **become.**
Would you say that life <u>has become</u> a lot easier for you?
The notion <u>had become</u> very popular in the United States.

When **become** is followed by a singular noun group, the noun group usually begins with a determiner.
Portugal became <u>a colonial power.</u>
I became <u>a construction engineer.</u>
…the aristocratic young man who becomes <u>his friend.</u>

However, when the noun group refers to a unique job or position within an organization, the determiner can be omitted.
In 1960 he became <u>Ambassador to Hungary.</u>
He went on to become <u>head of one of the company's largest divisions.</u>

The following words can be used to mean 'become'. Note that these words can only be followed by an adjective. You do not use a noun group after them.

② **'get'**
Get is very often used to mean 'become'. In conversation, you usually say **get** rather than 'become'.
It <u>was getting</u> dark.
She began to <u>get</u> suspicious.
If things <u>get</u> any worse, you'll have to come home.

3 'grow'

In written English, **grow** is sometimes used to mean 'become'. You use **grow** to say that someone or something gradually changes to a particular state or condition.

Some of her ministers are growing impatient.
The sun grew so hot that they were forced to stop working.

4 'come'

Come can be used with **loose** or **unstuck** to say that something gradually becomes loose or unstuck.

A buckle had come loose, the pin digging into his skin.
Some of the posters came unstuck.

If a dream, wish, or prediction **comes true**, it actually happens.

My wish had come true.

5 'go'

If you want to say that someone feels a sudden change in their body, you use **go**.

I went numb.
He went cold all over.
Their mouths went dry.

You use **go** to say that something suddenly becomes slack or limp.

The rope went slack.
He went as limp as an armful of wet laundry.

If you want to say that someone becomes blind or deaf, you usually use **go**.

She was bedridden and going blind.

If you want to say that someone becomes mad, or starts behaving as if they are mad, you use **go**.

His sister went insane.
I'd go crazy if I wasn't involved in my work.
Uncle Nick went wild with excitement.

There are also several expressions in which **go** is used to mean 'become'. For example, you say that a plan or scheme **goes wrong** or **goes awry**, that a telephone **goes dead**, or that someone's mind **goes blank**.

Something must have gone wrong with the satellite link.
I answered the phone and the line went dead.

In some expressions, **go** is used to say that a person or organization changes their legal status. For example, you say that someone **goes bankrupt**, that a company **goes public**, or that a school **goes comprehensive**.

If the firm cannot sell its products, it will go bankrupt.

6 'go' and 'turn'

In British English, you sometimes use **go** or **turn** to mean 'become'. If you want to say that something becomes a different colour, you use **go** or **turn**.

Her hair was going grey.
The grass had turned brown.

 Note that in American English, **go** is rarely used like this.

If you want to say that a person's face suddenly changes colour, you use **go** or **turn**. For example, you say that someone **goes** or **turns** pale.

Ralph went crimson.
He turned bright red.
I went white. I just felt numb. I just couldn't believe it.

(i) Note that you do not say that someone 'gets pale' or 'becomes pale'.

before

1 indicating time

If something happens **before** a time or event, it happens earlier than that time or event.

We arrived just <u>before</u> two o'clock.
It was just <u>before</u> Christmas.
<u>Before</u> the First World War, farmers used to use horses instead of tractors.

You also use **before** when you are talking about the past and you want to refer to an earlier period of time. For example, if you are describing events that took place in 1986, you refer to 1985 as 'the year **before**'.

The two had met in Bonn <u>the weekend before.</u>
The quarrel of <u>the night before</u> seemed forgotten.

You use **before last** to refer to a period of time that came before the last one of its kind. For example, if today is Wednesday 18th September, you refer to Friday 13th September as **last** Friday and Friday 6th September as 'the Friday **before last**'.

We met them on a camping holiday <u>the year before last.</u>
I have not slept since <u>the night before last.</u>

2 indicating position

Before is sometimes used to mean 'in front of'. This is a formal or old-fashioned use. It is more common to use **in front of** with the same meaning.

He stood <u>before</u> the panelled door leading to the cellar.
The tea had been set <u>before</u> them.
The German model stood <u>in front of</u> a mirror adjusting her hair.

When someone has to appear in a court of law, you can say that they are brought **before** the judge or magistrate.

All three had been taken <u>before</u> a magistrate.

When a proposal is being considered by a parliament, you can say that it is **before** the parliament.

…the Legal Services Bill now <u>before</u> Parliament.

You also use **before** or **in front of** when you are talking about the order in which things appear in speech or writing. For example, if you are describing the spelling of the word 'friend', you can say that the letter 'i' comes **before** or **in front of** the letter 'e'.

If the verb is 'be', 'certainly' can come either <u>before</u> or after the verb.
You can put 'both' immediately <u>in front of</u> a single noun group when it refers to two people or things.

begin

⇨ See **Usage** entry at **start - begin - commence**.

behaviour

Someone's **behaviour** is the way they behave.

I had been puzzled by his <u>behaviour.</u>
…the obstinate <u>behaviour</u> of a small child.

 Note that the American spelling of this word is **behavior**.

behind

1 used as a preposition

If you are **behind** something, you are near the part of it that is considered to be its back.

They parked the motorcycle <u>behind</u> some bushes.
Just <u>behind</u> the cottage was a sort of shed.

USAGE

⚠ **WARNING:** You do not use 'of' after **behind**. You do not say, for example, ~~They parked the motorcycle behind of some bushes~~'.

2 used as an adverb
Behind can also be an adverb.

The sun was almost directly <u>behind.</u>
I walked on <u>behind,</u> kicking up the dead leaves.

---

believe

1 'believe'
If you **believe** a person or **believe** what they say, you accept that what they say is true.

He knew I didn't <u>believe him.</u>
It all sounded so straightforward that I <u>believed it</u> myself.
Don't <u>believe a thing you read</u> in that paper.

If you **believe** that something is the case, you think that it is the case.

I <u>believe</u> some of those lakes are over a hundred feet deep.
China makes you <u>believe</u> that everything is possible.

⚠ **WARNING: Believe** is not used in continuous tenses, even when you are talking about something which is happening now. You do not say, for example, '~~I am believing you~~'. You say 'I **believe** you'.

I <u>believe</u> you have to look at the positive side of things.
I <u>believe</u> that these findings should be fairly presented to your readers.

2 'don't believe'
Instead of saying that you 'believe that something is not' the case, you usually say that you **don't believe that it is** the case.

I just <u>don't believe that Allen or you had anything to do with Stryker's death.</u>

3 'believe' before an object and a 'to'- infinitive
Believe can be followed by an object and a 'to'-infinitive. For example, instead of saying 'I believed that she was clever', you can say 'I **believed her to be** clever'. This is a rather formal use.

I <u>believed him to be</u> right.
He still <u>believed himself to be</u> a failure.

4 passive forms
Similarly, you can say either that **it is believed that** something is the case, or that something **is believed to** be the case. For example, you can say 'It **is believed that** the building is 700 years old' or 'The building **is believed to** be 700 years old'.

It <u>is believed that</u> two prisoners have escaped.
She <u>is widely believed</u> to have presidential aspirations of her own.
The kidnappers <u>are believed to</u> be seeking a ransom.

5 'believe so'
If someone asks you if something is the case, you can say 'I **believe so**'.

'Can he be trusted?' – '<u>I believe so.</u>'

ⓘ Note that when you are asked if something is the case, you do not say '~~I believe it~~'.

5 'believe in'
If you **believe in** God or in such things as ghosts or Father Christmas, you think that they exist. If you **believe in** such things as miracles, you think that they happen.

I don't <u>believe in</u> ghosts.
Only 29 per cent of the population <u>believe in</u> a personal God.

If you **believe in** an idea or policy, you are in favour of it because you think it is good or right, or will have the desired result.

Socialists <u>believe in</u> liberty.
You don't really <u>believe in</u> freedom.

belong

1 indicating possession

If something **belongs to** you, you own it or it is yours.

Everything you see here <u>belongs to</u> me.
You can't take the cart home because it <u>belongs to</u> Harry.

When **belong** is used with this meaning, it must be followed by **to**. You do not say, for example, 'This bag belongs me'. You say 'This bag **belongs to** me'.

⚠ **WARNING: Belong** is not used in continuous tenses. You do not say, for example, 'This money is belonging to my sister'. You say 'This money **belongs to** my sister'.

The flat <u>belongs to</u> a man called Jimmy Roland.
One of the rooms <u>belongs to</u> my niece, Judy.

2 another meaning of 'belong'

You can also use **belong** to say where someone or something ought to be. **Belong** is used on its own, or is followed by an adjunct such as **here**, **over there**, or **in the next room**.

I don't <u>belong here</u>, mother. I'm not like you.
The plates don't <u>belong in that cupboard.</u>
They need to feel they <u>belong.</u>

below

⇨ See **Usage** entry at **under - below - beneath**.

beneath

⇨ See **Usage** entry at **under - below - beneath**.

beside - besides

1 'beside'

If one thing is **beside** another, it is next to it or at the side of it.

<u>Beside</u> the shed was a huge wire birdcage.
I sat down <u>beside</u> my wife.

2 'besides' used as a preposition

Besides means 'in addition to' or 'as well as'.

What languages do you know <u>besides</u> Arabic and English?
The farm possessed three horses <u>besides</u> Clover.
Then you can make something else <u>besides</u> bombs?

3 'besides' used to link clauses

You can use **besides** to introduce a non-finite clause beginning with an '-ing' form. For example, you can say 'He writes novels and poems, **besides working** for the BBC'.

ⓘ Note that you do not say 'He writes novels and poems besides he works for the BBC'.

Education must sow the seeds of wisdom, <u>besides implanting</u> knowledge and skills.
<u>Besides being</u> good company, he was always ready to have a go at anything.

4 'besides' used as an adverb

Besides can also mean 'in addition to the thing just mentioned'.

He needed so much else <u>besides.</u>

You can also use **besides** when you are making an additional point or giving an additional reason which you think is important.

I'll only be gone for five days, and <u>besides</u> , you're going to be doing some fun things while I'm gone.

best

Best is the superlative form of both 'good' and 'well'.

⇨ See **Usage** entry at **good - well**.

If you **do your best,** you try as hard as you can to achieve something.

⇨ See **Usage** entry at **do**.

better

1 **used as a comparative**

Better is the comparative form of both 'good' and 'well'. You do not say that something is 'more good' or is done 'more well'. You say that it is **better** or is done **better.**

The results were <u>better</u> than expected.
Milk is much <u>better</u> for you than lemonade.
Some people can ski <u>better</u> than others.
We are <u>better</u> housed than ever before.

You can use words such as **even**, **far**, **a lot**, and **much** in front of **better.**

This wise old gentleman knew him <u>even better</u> than Annette did.
I decided that it would be <u>far better</u> just to wait.
I like it <u>a lot better</u> than asparagus.
I always feel <u>much better</u> after it.

2 **another meaning of 'better'**

Better is also used to say that someone has recovered from an illness or injury.

Her cold was <u>better.</u>
I hope you'll be <u>better</u> soon.

3 **'had better'**

If you say that someone **had better** do something, you mean that they ought to do it. **Had better** is always followed by an infinitive without 'to'.

I <u>had better</u> introduce myself.
I <u>'d better go</u>.

⚠ **WARNING:** In standard English, you must use **had** in sentences like these. You do not say ~~'I better introduce myself'~~ or ~~'I better go'~~.

In negative sentences, **not** goes after **had better.**

I <u>'d better not</u> let her go.

⚠ **WARNING:** In standard English, you do not say that someone 'hadn't better' do something.

4 **'better still'**

You use **better still** when you are mentioning something you have just thought of which is an improvement on something else that has been mentioned.

How about some Bach to begin with? Or, <u>better still,</u> Vivaldi?
Serve with a good dollop of the rhubarb compote on the side, and some new potatoes (<u>better still</u> , roast the potatoes in the oven).

5 **'rather'**

You do not use 'better' on its own when you are correcting a mistake you have made, or when you think of a more appropriate word than one you have just used. You do not say, for example, '~~Suddenly there stood before him, or better above him, a gigantic woman~~'.

You say 'Suddenly there stood before him, or **rather** above him, a gigantic woman'.
He explained what the Crux is, or <u>rather</u> , what it was.

between

1 describing position

If something is **between** two things, it has one of the things on one side of it and the
other thing on the other side of it.
The revolver lay <u>between</u> the two bodies.
The island of Santa Catarina is roughly midway <u>between</u> São Paulo and Porto Alegre.

You can also say that someone puts something **between** two things.
She put the cigarette <u>between</u> her lips and lit it.

⚠ **WARNING:** You do not usually say that something is **between** several things. You say
that it is **among** them.
⇨ See **Usage** entry at **among.**

2 differences

You talk about a difference **between** two things or people.
I asked him whether there was much difference <u>between</u> British and European law.

3 choosing

When someone makes a choice, you say that they choose **between** two things or people.
It was difficult to choose <u>between</u> Hobson and the other British finalist, Peter Donohoe.

You say that someone chooses between one thing or person **and** another.
They must choose between home-ownership <u>and</u> furnished renting.

beware

If you tell someone to **beware of** a person or thing, you are warning them that the
person or thing may harm them.
<u>Beware of</u> the dog.
I would <u>beware of</u> companies which depend on one product only.

Beware is only an imperative or infinitive. It does not have any other forms such as
'bewares', 'bewaring', or 'bewared'.

bid

1 'bid' in offers of payment

If you **bid** for something that is being sold, you offer to pay a particular amount of
money for it. When **bid** has this meaning, its past tense and past participle is **bid.**
He <u>bid</u> a quarter of a million pounds for the portrait.

2 'bid' in greetings and farewells

People used to use **bid** with expressions like **good day** and **farewell**. This use still occurs
sometimes in stories. When **bid** has this meaning, its past tense is either **bid** or **bade** and
its past participle is either **bid** or **bidden.**
The old woman brought him his coffee and shyly <u>bid</u> him a goodbye.
We <u>bade</u> Nandron a goodbye which was not returned.
Tom <u>had bid</u> her a good evening.
We <u>had bidden</u> them good night.

ⓘ Note that in modern English, you use **say** instead of 'bid' in sentences like these.
I <u>said</u> good evening to them.
Gertrude had already had her supper and had <u>said</u> good night to Guy.

However, when you use **say,** the indirect object goes after the direct object. You do not
say 'I said them good evening'.

USAGE

big - large - great

Big, large, and great are used to talk about size. They can all be used in front of count nouns, but only **great** can be used in front of uncount nouns.

1 describing objects

Big, large, and great can all be used to describe objects. **Big** is the word you usually use in conversation. **Large** is more formal. **Great** is used in stories to indicate that something is very impressive because of its size.

'Where?'–'Over there, by that big tree.'
A leopard frequently retreats to a large tree when it has made a kill.
A great tree had fallen across one corner.

2 describing amounts

You use **large** or **great** to describe amounts.

She made a very large amount of money.
…drugs taken in large quantities.
Young people consume great quantities of chips.

You do not use 'big' to describe amounts.

3 describing feelings

When you are describing feelings or reactions, you usually use **great**.

He has great hopes for the future.
To my great astonishment she started to tell me about how she had first seen him.

When 'surprise' is a count noun, you can use either **big** or **great** in front of it.

The fact that the Government's policy does not make sense should not come as a big surprise.
It will be no great surprise if Zimbabwe beat England.

You do not use 'large' to describe feelings or reactions.

4 talking about qualities

When you are talking about qualities, you use **great**.

…little girls who may or may not turn into adults of great beauty.
The book brought back those early days of the war with great clarity.

You do not use 'big' or 'large' to talk about qualities.

5 describing problems

When you are describing a problem or danger, you use **big** or **great**.

The biggest problem at the moment is unemployment.
The greater the threat, the less tolerance there can be.

You do not usually use 'large' to describe a problem or danger.

6 indicating importance

Great is also used to say that a person or place is important or famous.

…one of the greatest engineers of this century.
…the great cities of the Rhineland.

7 used with other adjectives

In conversation, you can use **great** and **big** together, or you can use either **great** or **big** with another adjective of size. You do this to emphasize the size of something. When you use **great** and **big** together, you always put **great** first.

…a great big gaping hole.
…somewhere out there in the big wide world.
…an enormous great grin.

You do not use adjectives of size together like this in formal writing.

⇨ For a list of adjectives which are used to describe how large or small something is, see Usage entry at **small - large**.

> ⚠ **WARNING:** You can say that someone is in **great** pain, but you do not usually use 'big', 'large', or 'great' to describe an illness. Instead you use adjectives such as **bad, terrible,** or **severe.**
>
> *The child has a bad cold with fever.*
> *I started getting terrible headaches.*
> *The child is then likely to develop a severe anaemia.*

bill - check - account

1 'bill' and 'check'

In British English, a **bill** is a piece of paper showing how much money you owe for a meal in a restaurant.

Two women at the next table paid their bill and walked out.

 In American English, a piece of paper like this is called a **check.**

He waved to a waiter and got the check.

⇨ For another meaning of **check,** see **Usage** entry at **cheque - check.**

When you have to pay for things such as electricity or gas, you get a **bill.**

If you are finding it difficult to pay your gas bill, please let us know quickly.

 In American English, a **bill** is also a piece of paper money.

⇨ See **Usage** entry at **banknote.**

2 'account'

When you have an **account** with a bank, you leave your money in the bank and take it out when you need it.

billfold

⇨ See **Usage** entry at **wallet.**

billion

A **billion** is a thousand million, or 1,000,000,000.

In January 1977, there were 4 billion people in the world.

In Britain, some people use **billion** to refer to a million million, or 1,000,000,000,000.

bit

1 'a bit'

A bit means 'to a small extent or degree'.

She looks a bit like his cousin Maureen.
He was a bit deaf.
The bunch of poppies was getting a bit droopy.
You're doing it a bit better now.
Tonight he has been a bit naughty.

ⓘ Note that you cannot use 'a bit' with an adjective when the adjective is in front of a noun. You do not say, for example, 'He was a bit deaf man'.

⇨ Many other words and expressions can be used in a similar way to **a bit.** For graded lists, see section on **degree** in **Grammar** entry at **Adjuncts** and section on **grading adverbs** in **Grammar** entry at **Adverbs.**

2 'a bit of'

In conversation, you can use **a bit of** in front of **a** and a noun. You do this to make a statement seem less extreme.

Our room was a bit of a mess too.
This question comes as a bit of a shock at first.

USAGE

3 'a bit' with negatives

You can add **a bit** at the end of a negative statement to make it more strongly negative.

I don't like this a bit.
She hadn't changed a bit.

4 'not a bit'

You can use **not a bit** in front of an adjective to emphasize that someone or something does not have a particular quality. For example, if you say you are **not a bit** hungry, you mean you are not hungry at all.

They're not a bit interested.
I've found everyone so friendly, but not a bit inquisitive.

5 'for a bit'

For a bit means 'for a short period of time'.

She was silent for a bit.
Why can't we stay here for a bit?

6 used as the past tense of 'bite'

Bit is also the past tense of **bite**.

⇨ See **Usage** entry at **bite**.

bite

When a person or animal **bites** something, they use their teeth to cut into it or through it. The past tense of **bite** is **bit**, not 'bited'. The past participle is **bitten**.

My dog bit me.
You are quite liable to get bitten by an eel.

blame - fault

1 'blame' used as a verb

If you **blame** someone **for** something bad that has happened, you say or think that they are responsible for it.

The rest of the family blamed her for indirectly causing Sonny's death.
I was blamed for the theft.

2 'to blame'

If someone is **to blame** for something bad that has happened, they are responsible for it.

It was a terrible failure for which I knew I was partly to blame.
The study found schools are not to blame for the laziness of their pupils.
Huge budget deficits were partly to blame for the high levels of interest rates.

3 'fault'

You do not say that something is someone's 'blame'. You say that it is their **fault**.

It's not my fault.
This was all Jack's fault.
It's all the fault of a girl called Sarah.

4 'at fault'

If someone is **at fault**, they have made a mistake which has undesirable consequences.

We failed to explain that to the public and we are at fault in that.

ⓘ Note that you do not say that someone is 'in fault'.

blind

Blind can be an adjective, a verb, or a noun.

1 used as an adjective

If someone is **blind**, they cannot see, because there is something wrong with their eyes.

He is ninety-four years of age and he is <u>blind,</u> deaf, and bad-tempered.

(i) Note that you do not say that 'someone's eyes are blind'.

2 used as a verb

If something **blinds** you, it makes you blind.
The acid went on her face and <u>blinded</u> her.

If something **blinds** you to a situation, it prevents you from being aware of it. This is the most common use of the verb **blind**.
He never let his love of his country <u>blind</u> him to his countrymen's faults.

3 used as a noun

You can refer to all the blind people in a country as **the blind**.
What do you think of the help that's given to <u>the blind?</u>

A **blind** is a wide roll of cloth or paper which you can pull down over a window in order to keep the light out, or to prevent people from looking in.
She slammed the window shut and pulled the <u>blind.</u>

 In American English, a device like this is sometimes called a **shade** or **window shade**.

blow up
⇨ See **Usage** entries at **explode** and **inflate**.

board

1 'board'

If you **board** a bus, train, plane, or ship, you get on it or into it.
Griffiths took a taxi to the Town station and <u>boarded</u> a train there.
Decker <u>boarded</u> another ship, the Panama.

2 'on board'

When you are **on board** a bus, train, plane, or ship, you are on it or in it.
He ran out of the bar, not stopping until he was <u>on board</u> a city bus.
There were 13 Britons <u>on board</u> the Swiss-owned plane.

> ⚠ **WARNING:** You do not use 'of' after **on board**. You do not say, for example, ~~'There were 13 Britons on board of the Swiss-owned plane'.~~

boat - ship

1 'boat'

A **boat** is a small vessel for travelling on water, especially one that carries only a few people.
John took me down the river in the old <u>boat.</u>
…a fishing <u>boat.</u>

2 'ship'

A larger vessel is usually referred to as a **ship**.
The <u>ship</u> was due to sail the following morning.

However, in conversation large passenger ships which travel short distances are sometimes called **boats**.
She was getting off at Hamburg to take the <u>boat</u> to Stockholm.

> ⚠ **WARNING:** When you are describing the way in which someone travels, you do not say that they travel 'by the boat' or 'by the ship'. You say that they travel **by boat** or **by ship**.
> *We are going <u>by boat.</u>*
> *They were sent home <u>by ship.</u>*

bonnet - hood

1 'bonnet' and 'hood'

In British English, the metal cover over the engine of a car is called the **bonnet**.

 In American English, it is called the **hood**.

I unlocked the boot and laid the tools on the <u>bonnet.</u>

…the raised <u>hood,</u> under which I had bent to watch the mechanic at work.

2 other meanings

Both **bonnet** and **hood** have other meanings:

A baby's **bonnet** is a hat which ties under the baby's chin.

A **hood** is part of a coat, jacket, or cloak which you can pull up over your head to protect you from bad weather.

boot - trunk

1 'boot' and 'trunk'

In British English, the **boot** of a car is the space at the back or front where you put luggage or other things.

 In American English, this part of a car is called the **trunk**.

Is the <u>boot</u> open?

Each car had been carrying a large supply of gasoline in the <u>trunk.</u>

2 other meanings

Both **boot** and **trunk** have other meanings:

A **boot** is a kind of heavy shoe.

He sat on a kitchen chair, reached down and pulled off his <u>boots</u>.

A **trunk** is a large case or box with strong, rigid sides.

He gave me a tin <u>trunk</u> filled with my grandfather's sketchbooks.

The **trunk** of a tree is the large main stem from which the branches grow.

… the gnarled <u>trunk</u> of a birch tree.

border - frontier - boundary

1 'border'

The **border** between two countries is the dividing line between them.

They crossed the <u>border</u> into Mexico.

…the German-Polish <u>border.</u>

2 'frontier'

You refer to a border as a **frontier** when it is guarded and separates countries which have different political systems or are in dispute about something.

This decision left only three thousand soldiers to guard the entire <u>frontier.</u>

…the abolition of <u>frontier</u> controls.

You talk about one country's border or frontier **with** another.

…a small Dutch town a mile from the <u>border with</u> with Germany.

Spain reopened its <u>frontier with</u> Gibraltar.

3 'boundary'

The **boundary** of an area of land is its outer edge. You can talk about the **boundary** of a region or local administrative area.

You have to stay within your county <u>boundary</u>.

…the <u>boundary</u> of the Snowdonia National Park.

> ⚠ **WARNING**: You do not talk about the 'boundary' of a country. Instead you talk about
> its **borders**.
> …the <u>borders</u> of Turkey.
> *Meanwhile, along Afghanistan's <u>borders,</u> matters are no less confused.*

bore

1 **'bore'**
Bore is a verb, and it is also the past tense of the verb 'bear'.
⇨ See **Usage** entry at **bear**.

If something or someone **bores** you, you do not find them interesting, and you do not
want to concern yourself with them any longer.
His brand of conservatism <u>bores</u> many of his countrymen.
There had been a time when they enjoyed his company, but now he <u>bored</u> them.

2 **'bored'**
You can say that you are **bored with** something or someone.
Tom was <u>bored with</u> the film.
They never seem to get <u>bored with</u> each other.

3 **'boring'**
Do not confuse **bored** with **boring**. If you say that something is **boring,** you mean that it
bores you.
Was it a <u>boring</u> journey?
…all those <u>boring</u> evenings with people I never wanted to see.

born - borne

Both these words are pronounced /bɔːn/.

1 **'born'**
When a baby **is born,** it comes out of its mother's body at the beginning of its life.
My mother was forty when I <u>was born.</u>

You often say that a person **was born** at a particular time or in a particular place.
Caro <u>was born</u> on April 10th.
Mary <u>was born</u> in Glasgow in 1899.

> ⚠ **WARNING**: You do not say that someone 'has been born' at a particular time or in a
> particular place.

2 **'borne'**
If something **is borne** somewhere, it is carried there. **Borne** is the past participle of the
verb 'bear'. This is a formal use. It is more common to say that something **is carried**
somewhere.
The coffin <u>was borne</u> down the aisle.
The torch <u>was carried</u> into the stadium by Ken Read and Cathy Priestner.

borrow - lend

If you **borrow** something that belongs to someone else, you take it, with or without their
permission, intending to return it.
Could I <u>borrow</u> your car?
I <u>have borrowed</u> my father's wire-cutters from the tool shed.

If you **lend** something you own to someone else, you allow them to have it or use it for a
period of time.
I often <u>lend</u> her money.
One of the grandest paintings in England <u>has been lent</u> to the National Gallery.

USAGE

(i) Note that you do not normally talk about borrowing or lending things that cannot move. You do not say, for example, 'Can I borrow your garage next week?' You say 'Can I **use** your garage next week?'

He wants to <u>use</u> the phone.

Similarly, you do not usually say 'He lent me his office'. You say 'He **let me use** his office'.

She brought them thermoses of coffee and <u>let them use</u> her bath.

bosom

⇨ See **Usage** entry at **breast**.

both

1 used for emphasis

When you link two word groups using **and**, you can put **both** in front of the first word group for emphasis. For example, if you want to emphasize that what you are saying applies to each of two things or people, you put **both** in front of the first of two noun groups.

By that time <u>both Robin and Drew</u> were overseas.
<u>Both she and Dixon</u> were completely safe.
<u>Both Islam and Hinduism</u> are world religions.
They feel <u>both anxiety and joy.</u>

Similarly you can put **both** in front of the first of two adjectives, verb groups, or adjuncts.

Herbs are <u>both beautiful and useful.</u>
These headlines <u>both mystified and infuriated</u> him.
Young artists are winning prestigious prizes <u>both here and abroad.</u>

The word group after **both** should be of the same type as the word group after **and**. For example, you say 'I told **both** Richard **and** George'. You do not say 'I both told Richard and George'.

2 used with one noun group

You can put **both** immediately in front of a single noun group when it refers to two people or things. For example, you can say '**Both boys** were Hungarian'. You can also say '**Both the boys** were Hungarian' or '**Both of the boys** were Hungarian'. There is no difference in meaning.

<u>Both sons</u> later became involved in drugs.
<u>Both the kings</u> under whom he served had financial difficulties.
<u>Both of the diplomats</u> blushed when the company thanked them.

⚠ **WARNING:** Note that you do not say 'Both of boys were Hungarian' or 'The both boys were Hungarian'. You also do not use 'two' after **both**. You do not say 'Both the two boys were Hungarian'.

You can use either **both** or **both of** in front of noun groups beginning with **these**, **those**, or a possessive determiner.

The answer to <u>both these questions</u> is 'yes'.
<u>Both of these houses</u> were described by Aubrey.
I've got <u>both their addresses.</u>
<u>Both of their homes</u> are built near the sea.

3 used in front of pronouns

You can also use **both** or **both of** in front of the pronouns **these** and **those**.

The other two key councils, Wandsworth and Westminster, are in London. And in <u>both these</u>, the Conservatives increased their vote.
It's especially important for children to get into the habit of eating properly and exercising so that they can accept <u>both of these</u> as the normal way of life.

However, in front of personal pronouns you must use **both of.**

This plan of yours is certain to lead to unhappiness for both of you.
Luca was too strong for both of them.

You do not use 'we' or 'they' after **both of.** Instead you use **us** or **them.**

Both of us went to Balliol College, Oxford.
Both of them were admitted to Michael's house by one of the bodyguards.

4 used after the subject

Both can also be used after the subject of a sentence. For example, instead of saying 'Both my sisters came', you can say 'My sisters **both** came'.

● When there is no auxiliary, **both** goes in front of the verb, unless the verb is **be.**

They both got into the boat.
We both love dancing.
Tony and Nigel both laughed noisily.

● If the verb is **be, both** goes after **be.**

They were both schoolteachers.
We were both there.

● If there is an auxiliary, you put **both** after it.

Shearson Lehman and James Capel have both expressed an interest.
They have both had a good sleep.
Mark, we 're both talking rubbish.

● If there is more than one auxiliary, you put **both** after the first one.

They shall both be put to death.

● **Both** can also come after a personal pronoun when the pronoun is the direct or indirect object of the verb.

The commissioners looked curiously at them both.
Mrs Bond is coming over to see us both next week.

5 negative sentences

You do not usually use 'both' in negative sentences. For example, you do not say 'Both his students were not there'. You say '**Neither of** his students was there'.

⇨ See **Usage** entry at **neither.**

Similarly, you do not say 'I didn't see both of them'. You say 'I didn't see **either of** them'.

⇨ See **Usage** entry at **either.**

6 used as a pronoun

Both can also be a pronoun.

A child should be receiving either meat or eggs daily, preferably both.
Both were desperately in love with Violet.

⚠ **WARNING:** You do not use 'both' to talk about more than two things or people. Instead you use **all.**

⇨ See **Usage** entry at **all.**

---

bottom

1 'bottom' and 'behind'

Your **bottom** is the part of your body that you sit on. You can use **bottom** in conversation and in most kinds of writing.

Her bottom was pressed firmly against the wall.

USAGE

 Speakers of American English usually say **behind** rather than 'bottom'.

I've never had my <u>behind</u> on a bicycle.

2 'buttocks'

In formal writing, you refer to this part of your body as your **buttocks**.

…the muscles on his shoulders and <u>buttocks.</u>

3 'bum' and 'butt'

In conversation, some British speakers say **bum** instead of 'bottom', and some American speakers say **butt**. It is best to avoid both these words as many people think they are impolite.

boundary

⇨ See **Usage** entry at **border**.

box-car

⇨ See **Usage** entry at **carriage**.

brackets

⇨ See **Topic** entry at **Punctuation**.

brake

⇨ See **Usage** entry at **break - brake**.

brand

A **brand** of a product is the version made by one particular manufacturer. You usually use **brand** to talk about foods, or about other products which do not last for a long time.

There used to be so many different <u>brands</u> of tea.
It also sells other <u>brands</u> including Mulberry.

ⓘ Do not confuse **brand** with **make**. You use **make** to talk about products such as machines or cars, which last for a long time.

⇨ See **Usage** entry at **make**.

break - brake

These words are both pronounced /breɪk/.

1 'break'

If you **break** something, you damage it badly, usually by hitting it or dropping it so that it divides into two or more pieces.

I tried to <u>break</u> the porthole, but with no success.
The next morning she had another mishap, <u>breaking</u> the mirror on her dressing table.

The past tense of **break** is **broke,** not 'breaked'. The past participle is **broken.**

She stepped backwards onto a cup, which <u>broke</u> into several pieces.
He <u>has broken</u> a window with a ball.

⇨ See **Usage** entry at **broken**.

⇨ Note that several other words can be used with a similar meaning to **break**. See **Usage** entry at **damage**.

2 'brake'

A **brake** is a device on a vehicle which makes it slow down or stop.

He took his foot off the <u>brake.</u>

Brake is also a verb. When a vehicle or its driver **brakes,** the driver makes the vehicle slow down or stop by using the brake or brakes.

The taxi <u>braked</u> to a halt.

breakfast

Your **breakfast** is your first meal of the day. You eat it in the morning, just after you get up.

They had hard-boiled eggs for breakfast.
I open the mail immediately after breakfast.

⇨ See **Topic** entry at **Meals**.

breast - bust - bosom

1 'breast'

A woman's **breasts** are the two soft, round pieces of flesh on her chest that can produce milk to feed a baby.

…a beggar girl with a baby at her breast.
…women with small breasts.

2 'bust'

A woman's breasts can be referred to as her **bust,** especially when you are talking about their size. Note that **bust** refers to both breasts together. You do not talk about a woman's 'busts'.

She has a very large bust.

Bust is also used to talk about the measurement around the top part of a woman's body at the level of her breasts.

'Bust 34' means that the garment is a size 12.

3 'bosom'

A woman's breasts can also be referred to as her **bosom** /bʊzəm/. This is an old-fashioned or literary word.

…hugging the cat to her bosom.

breathe - breath

1 'breathe'

Breathe /briːð/ is a verb. When people or animals **breathe,** they take air into their lungs and let it out again.

It was difficult for him to breathe.
Always breathe through your nose.

2 'breath'

Breath /breθ/ is a noun. Your **breath** is the air which you take into your lungs and let out again when you breathe.

Piggy let out his breath with a gasp.
I could smell the whisky on his breath.

briefly

⇨ See section on **duration** in **Grammar** entry at **Adjuncts**.

bring - take - fetch

1 'bring'

If you **bring** someone or something with you when you come to a place, you have them with you.

He would have to bring Judy with him.
Please bring your calculator to every lesson.

The past tense and past participle of 'bring' is **brought**.

My secretary brought my mail to the house.
I 've brought you a present.

If you ask someone to **bring** you something, you are asking them to carry or move it to the place where you are.
Bring me a glass of Dubonnet.

⚠ **WARNING:** You do not say that you 'bring' a small child to bed. You say that you **put** the child to bed.
A baby may learn to resist being put to bed by furious crying.
Most parents change the nappies before they put the child back to bed.

2 'take'
If you **take** someone or something to a place, you carry or drive them there.
It's his turn to take the children to school.

If you **take** someone or something with you when you go to a place, you have them with you.
She gave me some books to take home.
Don't forget to take your umbrella.

3 'fetch'
If you **fetch** something, you go to the place where it is and return with it to the place where you were before.
I don't want you to fetch anything for me.
I went and fetched another glass.

bring up - raise - educate
1 'bring up'
When you **bring up** a child, you look after it until it is grown up, and you try to give it particular beliefs and attitudes.
Tony was brought up strictly.
The great majority of them have been brought up in working-class homes.

You can use adverbs such as **well** or **badly** in front of **brought up.** If you say that a young person is **well brought up,** you mean that their behaviour shows that they were taught how to behave properly when they were a child.
She's a nicely brought up girl, anyone can see that.
She was a good, properly brought up young woman.

⇨ See **Usage** entry at **grow.**

2 'raise'
 In American English, **raise** can be used to mean 'bring up'.
Henry and his wife May have raised ten children.
I was raised as a Catholic.

Note that Americans do not say that someone is 'well raised'.

3 'educate'
Do not confuse **bring up** or **raise** with **educate.** To **educate** a child means to teach it various subjects, usually at school.
Many more schools are needed to educate the young.
He was educated at Haslingden Grammar School.

Britain - British - Briton
1 'Britain'
Britain or **Great Britain** consists of England, Scotland, and Wales. The **United Kingdom** consists of England, Scotland, Wales, and Northern Ireland. The **British Isles** refers to Britain, Ireland, and all the smaller islands around the coast.

2 **'British'**

The nationality of someone from the United Kingdom is **British,** although some people prefer to call themselves **English, Scottish, Welsh,** or **Northern Irish.** It is incorrect and may cause offence to call all British people 'English'.

You can refer to all the people who come from Britain as **the British.**

I don't think the British are good at hospitality.
The British have always displayed a healthy scepticism towards ideas.

The British can also be used to refer to a group of British people, for example the British representatives at an international conference.

The British have made these negotiations more complicated.
The British had come up with a bold and dangerous solution.

3 **'Briton'**

In writing, an individual British person can be referred to as a **Briton.**

The youth, a 17-year-old Briton, was searched and arrested.

⇨ For more information on talking about nationality, see **Topic** entry at **Nationality words.**

broad

⇨ See **Usage** entry at **wide - broad.**

broken

Broken is the past participle of the verb **break.**

He has broken a window with a ball.

Broken is also an adjective. A **broken** object has split into pieces or has cracked, for example because it has been hit or dropped.

He sweeps away the broken glass under the window.
…a long table covered in broken crockery.
He glanced at the broken lock he was still holding in his free hand.

If a machine or device is not functioning because there is something wrong with it, you do not usually say that it 'is broken'. You say that it **does not work** or **is not working.**

One of the lamps didn't work.
Chris sits beside him with sweaters on because the heater doesn't work.
The traffic lights weren't working properly.

bruise

⇨ See **Usage** entry at **damage.**

bum

⇨ See **Usage** entry at **bottom.**

burglar

⇨ See **Usage** entry at **thief - robber - burglar.**

burgle - burglarize

In British English, if you **are burgled** or if your house **is burgled,** someone breaks into your house and steals things.

Gesher had recently been burgled.

 American speakers usually say that a house **is burglarized.**

Her home had been burglarized.

burst

When something **bursts** or when you **burst** it, it suddenly splits open, and air or some other substance comes out. The past tense and past participle of 'burst' is **burst,** not 'bursted'.

USAGE

As he braked, a tyre <u>burst.</u>

If you **burst** into tears, you suddenly begin to cry.
When the news was broken to Meehan he <u>burst into tears.</u>

ⓘ Note that you do not say that someone 'bursts in tears'.

⚠ **WARNING:** Do not confuse **burst** with **bust.** If you **bust** something, you break or damage it so badly that it cannot be used.

⇨ See **Usage** entry at **bust.**

bus - coach

A **bus** is a large motor vehicle which carries passengers by road from one place to another. In Britain, a comfortable bus that carries passengers on long journeys is called a **coach.**

I'm waiting for the <u>bus</u> back to town.
The <u>coach</u> leaves Cardiff at twenty to eight.

 In America, vehicles for long journeys are usually called **buses.**
In the far horizon a silvery Greyhound <u>bus</u> appears.

If you are on a bus or coach journey, you say that you are travelling or going **by bus** or **by coach.**

I don't often travel <u>by bus.</u>
It is cheaper to travel to London <u>by coach</u> than by train.

ⓘ Note that you do not say that you are travelling 'by a bus' or 'by the coach'.

When someone enters a bus or coach at the beginning of their journey, you usually say that they **get on** it.
When I <u>get on</u> a bus and I see an advert, I read it.

When someone leaves a bus or coach at the end of their journey, you usually say that they **get off** it.
A man of his description was seen <u>getting off</u> a bus near the scene of the murder.

ⓘ Note that you do not say that someone 'goes into' a bus or coach, or 'goes out of' it.

business

1 **used as an uncount noun**

Business is work relating to the production, buying, and selling of goods or services.
There are good profits to be made in the hotel <u>business.</u>
Are you in San Francisco for <u>business</u> or pleasure?

⇨ There are a number of other nouns which refer to activities which people are paid to do. For more information on these words, see **Usage** entry at **work.**

⚠ **WARNING:** You do not refer to a discussion connected with business as 'a business'. You do not say, for example, 'We've got a business to see to'. You say 'We've got **some business** to see to'.
There is a possibility we may do <u>some business</u> with one of the major software companies in the United States.
We've still got <u>some business</u> to do. Do you mind just sitting?

2 **used as a count noun**

A **business** is a company, shop, or organization which produces and sells goods or provides a service.
He set up a small travel <u>business.</u>

bust

Bust can be a verb, an adjective, or a noun. The past tense and past participle of the verb is either **bust** or **busted**.

1 used as a verb

If you **bust** something, you break or damage it so badly that it cannot be used. Note that you only use **bust** with this meaning in conversation. You do not use it in formal writing.

She found out about Jack <u>busting</u> the double-bass.

In informal English, if someone **is busted,** the police arrest them.

They <u>were busted</u> for possession of cannabis.

2 used as an adjective

In conversation, if you say that something is **bust,** you mean that it is broken or very badly damaged.

That clock's been <u>bust</u> for weeks.

 Note that in American English, the adjective is **busted** not 'bust'.

There he found a small writing table with a <u>busted</u> leg.

If a company **goes bust,** it loses so much money that it is forced to close down. You do not use this expression in formal English.

The company almost <u>went bust</u> in February.

3 used as a noun

A woman's **bust** is her breasts.
⇨ See **Usage** entry at **breast.**

but

You use **but** to introduce something which contrasts with what you have just said.

1 used to link clauses

But is usually used to link clauses.

It was a long walk <u>but</u> it was worth it.
I try and see it their way, <u>but</u> I can't.

You do not normally put **but** at the beginning of a sentence, but you can do so when you are replying to someone, or writing in a conversational style.

'Somebody wants you on the telephone.'–'<u>But</u> nobody knows I'm here.'
I always thought that. <u>But</u> then I'm probably wrong.

2 used to link adjectives or adverbs

You can also use **but** to link adjectives or adverbs which contrast with each other.

…a small <u>but</u> comfortable hotel.
We are poor <u>but</u> happy.
Quickly <u>but</u> silently she darted out of the cell.

3 used with negative words to mean 'only'

But is sometimes used after negative words such as **nothing, no-one, nowhere,** or **none.** A negative word followed by **but** means 'only'. For example, 'We have **nothing but** carrots' means 'We only have carrots'.

The crew of the ship gave them <u>nothing but</u> bread to eat.
John had lived <u>nowhere but</u> the farm.
It's better to trust <u>no one but</u> yourself.

4 used to mean 'except'

But is also used after **all** and after words beginning with **'every-'** or **'any-'.** When **but** is used after one of these words, it means 'except'. For example, 'He enjoyed everything **but** maths' means 'He enjoyed everything **except** maths'.

Thomas Hardy spent all <u>but</u> a few years in his native Dorset.

USAGE

He ate everything <u>but</u> the beetroot.
There would be no time for anything <u>but</u> work.
Could anyone <u>but</u> Balmain have done it?

5 **'but for'**

But for is sometimes used to introduce the only factor that prevents something from happening. This use only occurs in writing.

The figure would have been higher <u>but for</u> delays in the delivery of the planes.

6 **'but one'**

In British English, **but** is also used in the phrases **last but one** and **next but one**. If you say that something is the **last but one** in a series, you mean that it is the one before the final one.

It'd be the <u>last</u> job <u>but one.</u>
This is what you were asked to do in the <u>last but one</u> quiz.

In American English, the expression that is used is **the second to the last**.

It's <u>the second to the last</u> paragraph in the section.

If you say that something is the **next but one** in a series, you mean that it is the one after the next one.

She has bought a property <u>next</u> door <u>but one</u> to mine.

butt

⇨ See **Usage** entry at **bottom**.

buttocks

⇨ See **Usage** entry at **bottom**.

buy

When you **buy** something, you obtain it by paying money for it. The past tense and past participle of **buy** is **bought**, not 'buyed'.

I'm going to <u>buy</u> everything that I need in good time.
Never <u>buy</u> anything white that must be dry-cleaned.
Many people have their cars <u>bought</u> for them by the firm they work for.

If you pay for a drink that is drunk by someone else, you say that you **buy** them the drink.

Let me <u>buy</u> you a drink.

(i) Note that you do not say that you 'pay' someone a drink.

by

1 **used in passives**

By is most often used in passive sentences. If something is done or caused **by** a person or thing, that person or thing does it or causes it.

He was brought up <u>by</u> an aunt.
The defending champion, John Pritchard, was beaten <u>by</u> Chris Boardman.
This view has been challenged <u>by</u> a number of workers.
I was startled <u>by</u> his anger.
His best friend was killed <u>by</u> a grenade.

When an '-ed' word is used like an adjective to describe a state rather than an action, it is not always followed by **by**. Some '-ed' words are followed by **with** or **in**.

The room was <u>filled with</u> pleasant furniture.
The railings were <u>decorated with</u> thousands of bouquets.
The walls of her flat are <u>covered in</u> dirt.

2 **used with time expressions**

If something happens **by** a particular time, it happens at or before that time.

He can cook the tea and be out <u>by</u> seven o'clock.
<u>By</u> 1940 the number had grown to 185 million.
I arrived a mile outside the town <u>by</u> mid-afternoon.

(*i*) Note that **by** can only be used with this meaning as a preposition. You do not use it as a conjunction. You do not say, for example, 'By I had finished my lunch, we had to start off again'. You say '**By the time** I had finished my lunch, we had to start off again'.

<u>By the time</u> I went to bed, I was absolutely exhausted.

3   **used to describe position**

You can use **by** to say that someone or something is at the side of a person or object.

I sat <u>by</u> her bed.
There were lines of parked cars <u>by</u> each kerb.

Next to is used in a similar way.

She sat down <u>next to</u> him on the sofa.
…a dark alley <u>next to</u> the house.

⚠ **WARNING:** You do not use 'by' with the names of towns or cities. You do not say, for example, 'I was by Coventry when I ran out of petrol'. You say 'I was **near** Coventry when I ran out of petrol'.

…on a country road <u>near</u> Belfast.
Mandela was born <u>near</u> Elliotdale.

4   **saying how something is done**

By can be used with various nouns to say how something is done. You do not usually put a determiner in front of the noun.

The money will be paid <u>by cheque</u>.
We heard from them <u>by phone</u>.
I always go <u>by bus</u>.

However, if you want to say that something is done using a particular object or tool, you often use **with**, rather than 'by'. **With** is followed by a determiner.

Clean mirrors <u>with a mop</u>.
He brushed back his hair <u>with his hand</u>.

After **watch**, **look**, or **see** you usually use **through** followed by a determiner.

Mrs Mellor could be seen <u>through</u> the window, motionless in a chair.

You can use **by** with an '-ing' form to say how something is achieved.

Make the sauce <u>by boiling</u> the cream and stock together in a pan.
He then tries to solve his problems <u>by accusing</u> me of being corrupt.

by far
⇨ See **Usage** entry at **very**.

C c

café - coffee

1 'café'

A **café** /kæfeɪ/ is a place where you can buy drinks and light meals or snacks. In Britain, **cafés** do not sell alcoholic drinks. **Café** is often spelled **cafe.**

…a waiter from a nearby <u>café</u>.
Inside the <u>cafe</u> it was dark and cool.

2 'coffee'

Coffee /kɒfi/ is a hot drink.

…a cup of <u>coffee</u>.

call

1 attracting attention

If you **call** something, you say it in a loud voice, usually because you are trying to attract someone's attention.

'Edward!' she <u>called</u>. 'Edward! Lunch is ready!'
I could hear a voice <u>calling</u> my name.
'Here's your drink,' Boylan <u>called</u> to him.

2 telephoning

If you **call** a person or place, you telephone them.

<u>Call</u> me when you get home.
Grechko <u>called</u> the office and complained.

When you use **call** like this, it is not followed by 'to'. You do not say, for example, 'I called to him at his London flat'. You say 'I **called** him at his London flat'.

3 visiting

If someone **calls on** you, or if they **call,** they make a short visit in order to see you or deliver something.

He <u>had called on</u> Seery at his London home.
Goodnight. Do <u>call</u> again.
The postman <u>calls</u> about 7 o'clock every morning.

 Call is not used like this in American English.

You can also say that someone **pays a call on** you or **pays** you **a call.** These expressions are used in both British and American English.

Last month, Ayling <u>paid a call on</u> the Deputy Prime Minister.
A few weeks after we moved in, old Pee Wee Stevenson <u>paid</u> us <u>a call.</u>

called - named

You use **called** or **named** when you are giving the name of someone or something. **Named** is less common than **called,** and is not usually used in conversation.

Did you know a boy <u>called</u> Desmond?
We pass through a town <u>called</u> Monmouth.
Anna had a boyfriend <u>named</u> Shorty.

You can use **called** either after a noun or after **be.**

Komis asked me to appear in a play <u>called</u> Katerina.
The book was <u>called</u> The Goalkeeper's Revenge.

can - could - be able to

You only use **named** immediately after a noun.

The victim was an 18-year-old girl <u>named</u> Marinetta Jirkowski.

---

camp bed

⇨ See **Usage** entry at **cot - crib - camp bed**.

---

can - could - be able to

These words are used to talk about ability, awareness, and the possibility of something being the case. They are also used to say that someone has permission to do something. These uses are dealt with separately in this entry. **Can** and **could** are called **modals**.

⇨ See **Grammar** entry at **Modals**.

Both **can** and **could** are followed by an infinitive without 'to'.

I envy people who can <u>sing</u>.
I could <u>work</u> for twelve hours a day.

1 negative forms

The negative form of **can** is **cannot** or **can't**. **Cannot** is never written 'can not'. The negative form of **could** is **could not** or **couldn't**. To form the negative of **be able to**, you either put **not** or another negative word in front of **able**, or you use the expression **be unable to**.

Many elderly people <u>cannot</u> afford telephones.
My wife <u>can't</u> sew.
It was so black you <u>could not</u> see a hand in front of your face.
They <u>couldn't</u> sleep.
We <u>were not able to</u> give any answers.
We <u>were unable to</u> afford the entrance fee.

2 ability: the present

Can, could, and **be able to** are all used to talk about a person's ability to do something. You use **can** or **be able to** to talk about ability in the present. **Be able to** is more formal than **can**.

You <u>can</u> all read and write.
The sheep <u>are able to</u> move around and they <u>can</u> all lie down.
…people who <u>are unable to</u> appreciate new ideas.

Could is also used to talk about ability in the present, but it has a special meaning. If you say that someone **could** do something, you mean that they have the ability to do it, but they do not in fact do it.

We <u>could</u> do a great deal more in this country to educate people.

3 ability: the past

You use **could** or a past form of **be able to** to talk about ability in the past.

He <u>could</u> run faster than anyone else.
A lot of them <u>couldn't</u> read or write.
I <u>wasn't able to</u> do these quizzes.

If you say that someone **was able to** do something, you usually mean that they had the ability to do it and they did it. **Could** does not have this meaning.

After treatment he <u>was able to</u> return to work.
The farmers <u>were able to</u> pay the new wages.

If you want to say that someone had the ability to do something but did not in fact do it, you say that they **could have done** it.

You <u>could have given</u> it all to me.
You <u>could have been</u> a little bit tidier.

If you want to say that someone did not do something because they did not have the ability to do it, you say that they **could not have done** it.

I <u>couldn't have gone</u> with you, because I was in London at the time.

USAGE

If you want to say that someone had the ability to do something in the past, although they do not now have this ability, you say that they **used to be able to** do it.

I used to be able to make it happen.
You used to be able to see the house from here.

4 ability: the future

You use a future form of **be able to** to talk about ability in the future.

I shall be able to answer that question tomorrow.

5 ability: report structures

Could is often used in report structures. For example, if a man says 'I can speak Arabic', you usually report this as 'He said he **could** speak Arabic'.

Ferguson said I could ask for a transfer if after six months I still don't like it.

6 ability: 'be able to' after other verbs

Be able to is sometimes used after modals such as **might** or **should**, and after verbs such as **want, hope,** or **expect.**

I might be able to help you.
You may be able to get extra money.
You should be able to feel this.
She would not be able to drive to inland cities alone here.
You're foolish to expect to be able to do that.

You do not use **can** or **could** after any other verbs.

7 'being able to'

You can use an '-ing' form of **be able to.**

…the satisfaction of being able to do the job.

There is no '-ing' form of **can** or **could.**

8 awareness

Can and **could** are used with verbs such as **see, hear,** and **smell** to say that someone is or was aware of something through one of their senses.

I can smell gas.
I can't see her.
I could see a few stars in the sky.

(i) Note that this is the most common way of expressing awareness through one of your senses. For example, if you become aware of a phone ringing, you say 'I **can hear** a phone ringing'. You do not say 'I hear a phone ringing'.

9 possibility: the present and the future

Could and **can** are used to talk about possibility in the present or future.

You use **could** to say that there is a possibility that something is or will be the case.

Don't eat it. It could be a toadstool.
There could be something in the blood.
He was jailed in February 1992 and could be released next year.

Might and **may** can be used in a similar way.

It might be a trap.
Kathy's career may be ruined.

⇨ See **Usage** entry at **might - may.**

⚠ **WARNING:** You do not use 'could not' to say that there is a possibility that something is not the case. Instead you use **might not** or **may not.**

It might not be possible.
It may not be easy.

If you want to say that it is impossible that something is the case, you use **cannot** or **could not.**

You <u>cannot</u> possibly know what other damage your action may have caused.
You <u>can't</u> talk to the dead.
It <u>couldn't</u> possibly be poison.

You use **can** to say that something is sometimes possible.
Such shifts in opinion <u>can</u> sometimes have a snowball effect.

10 possibility: the past

You use **could have** to say that there is a possibility that something was the case in the past.

He <u>could have</u> been doing research on his own.

Might have and **may have** can be used in a similar way.
The teacher <u>might have</u> known the local policeman.
It <u>may have</u> been a dead bird.

You also use **could have** to say that there was a possibility of something being the case in the past, although it was not in fact the case.
It <u>could have</u> been worse.
He <u>could have</u> made a fortune as a lawyer.

⚠ **WARNING:** You do not use 'could not have' to say that there is a possibility that something was not the case. Instead you use **might not have** or **may not have.**
She <u>mightn't have</u> known what the bottle contained.

If you want to say that it is impossible that something was the case, you use **could not have.**
She <u>couldn't have</u> been drunk because she had had hardly anything to drink.
The man <u>couldn't have</u> thought at all.

11 permission

Can and **could** are used to say that someone is allowed to do something.
You <u>can</u> take out money at any branch of your own bank.
He <u>could</u> come and build in my wood.

Cannot and **could not** are used to say that someone is or was forbidden to do something.
You <u>can't</u> bring outsiders into a place like this.
'May I speak to Mr Jordache, please?' – 'No, you <u>can't</u>.'
Samantha Stone felt that if she <u>couldn't</u> have dinner then no one should.

⇨ See also **Topic** entry at **Permission.**

cancel
⇨ See **Usage** entry at **delay - cancel - postpone.**

candy
⇨ See **Usage** entry at **sweets - candy.**

cannot
⇨ See **Usage** entry at **can - could - be able to.**

capability
⇨ See **Usage** entry at **ability - capability - capacity.**

capacity
⇨ See **Usage** entry at **ability - capability - capacity.**

car

⇨ See **Usage** entry at **carriage**.

care

1 'care'

If you **care** about something, you feel that it is very important or interesting and you are concerned about it.

…people who care about the environment.
We teased him because all he cared about was birds.
I'm too old to care what I look like.

If you do not **care** about something, it does not matter to you.

She couldn't care less what they thought.
Who cares where she is?

2 'care for'

If you **care for** people or animals, you look after them.

You must learn how to care for children.
With so many new animals to care for, larger premises were needed.

If you **do not care for** something, you do not like it. This is a rather old-fashioned use.

I didn't much care for the way he looked at me.

If you ask someone if they **would care for** something, you are asking them if they would like to have it or do it. This is also a rather old-fashioned use.

Would you care for a cup of tea?

3 'take care'

To **take care of** someone or something or **take good care of** them means to look after them.

It is certainly normal for a mother to want to take care of her own baby.
He takes good care of my goats.

ⓘ Note that you do not say that someone 'takes care about' someone else or 'takes a good care of' them.

If you **take care of** a task or situation, you deal with it.

There was business to be taken care of.
If you'd prefer, they can take care of their own breakfast.

You also use **take care** when you are telling someone to be careful about something.

Take care what you tell him.
Take great care not to spill the mixture.

Take care and **take care of yourself** are also ways of saying goodbye.

'Night, night, Mr Beamish,' called Chloe. 'Take care.'

careful - careless - carefree

1 'careful'

If you are **careful**, you do something with a lot of attention.

She told me to be careful with the lawnmower.
He had to be careful about what he said.
This law will encourage more careful driving.

2 'careless'

If you are **careless**, you do things badly because you are not giving them enough attention. **Careless** is the opposite of **careful**.

I had been careless and let him wander off on his own.
Some parents are accused of being careless with their children's health.

3 **'carefree'**
Someone who is **carefree** has no worries and can therefore enjoy life.
When he was younger, he was <u>carefree</u>.
…his normally <u>carefree</u> attitude.

carnival
⇨ See **Usage** entry at **fair - carnival**.

carousel
⇨ See **Usage** entry at **roundabout**.

carriage - car - truck - wagon

1 **'carriage'**
Carriage is one of several nouns which are used to refer to vehicles pulled by railway engines.
In British English, a **carriage** is one of the separate sections of a train that carries passengers.
The man left his seat by the window and crossed the <u>carriage</u> to where I was sitting.

2 **'car'**
 In American English, these sections are called **cars**.
He arrived in town in a private railroad <u>car</u>.

In British English, **car** used to be part of the name of some special kinds of railway carriage. For example, a carriage might be called a **dining car**, a **restaurant car**, or a **sleeping car**. These terms are no longer used officially, but people still use them in conversation.

He made his way into the <u>dining car</u> for breakfast.

3 **'truck' and 'wagon'**
In British English, a **truck** is an open vehicle used for carrying goods on a railway.
…a long <u>truck</u> loaded with bricks.

 In American English, this vehicle is called a **freight car** or a **flatcar**.
The train, carrying loaded containers on <u>flatcars</u>, was 1.2 miles long.
… the nation's third-largest railroad <u>freight car</u> maker.

In British English, a **wagon** is a vehicle with a top, sides and a sliding door, used for carrying goods on a railway.
The pesticides ended up at several sites, almost half of them in railway <u>wagons</u> at Bajza station.

 In American English, vehicles like these are usually called **boxcars**.
A long train of <u>boxcars</u>, its whistle hooting mournfully, rolled into town from the west.

ⓘ Note that a **truck** is also a large motor vehicle used for transporting goods by road.
⇨ See **Usage** entry at **lorry - truck**.

carry - take

1 **'carry' and 'take'**
Carry and **take** are usually used to say that someone moves a person or thing from one place to another.
He picked up his suitcase and <u>carried</u> it into the bedroom.
My father <u>carried</u> us on his shoulders.
She gave me some books to <u>take</u> home.
It's his turn to <u>take</u> the children to school.

> ⚠ **WARNING:** Do not confuse **carry** and **lift**. When you **carry** something, you move it from one place to another without letting it touch the ground. When you **lift** something, you move it upwards using your hands or a machine. After you have lifted it, you may **carry** it to a different place.

2 transport

You can also say that a ship, train, or lorry **is carrying** goods of a particular kind. Similarly you can say that a plane, ship, train, or bus **is carrying** passengers.

…tankers _carrying_ Iranian crude oil.
…the Pakistani airliner _carrying_ 145 passengers and crew.
…dozens of trains _carrying_ commuters to work.

Take can be used in a similar way, but only if you say where someone or something is being taken to. You can say, for example, 'The ship **was taking** crude oil **to Rotterdam**', but you cannot just say 'The ship was taking crude oil'.

…the first of several aircraft planned to _take_ British aid _to the area._

You can say that a small vehicle such as a car **takes** you somewhere.

The taxi _took_ him back to Victoria.

ⓘ Note that you do not say that a small vehicle 'carries' you somewhere.

---

case

1 'in case'

You use **in case** or **just in case** to say that someone has something or does something because a particular thing might happen.

I've got the key _in case_ we want to go inside.
We tend not to go too far from the office, _just in case_ there should be a bomb scare that would prevent us getting back.

> ⚠ **WARNING:** After **in case** or **just in case**, you use a simple tense or **should**. You do not use 'will' or 'shall'.
> You do not use 'in case' or 'just in case' to say that something will happen as a result of something else happening. You do not say, for example, 'I will go in case he asks me'. You say 'I will go **if** he asks me'.
> He qualifies this year _if_ he gets through his exams.

2 'in that case'

You say 'in that case' or 'in which case' to refer to a situation which has just been mentioned and to introduce a statement or suggestion that is a consequence of it.

'The bar is closed,' the waiter said. '_In that case,_' McFee said, 'allow me to invite you back to my flat for a drink.'
I greatly enjoy these meetings unless I have to make a speech, _in which case_ I'm in a state of dreadful anxiety.

3 'in this respect'

You do not use 'in this case' to refer to a particular aspect of something. For example, you do not say 'Most of my friends lost their jobs, but I was very lucky in this case'. You say 'Most of my friends lost their jobs, but I was very lucky **in this respect**'.

The children are not unintelligent - in fact, they seem quite normal _in this respect._
But most of all, there is that intangible thing, the value of the brand. _In this respect,_ Manchester United, the most famous football club in the world, is unique.

---

cast

If you **cast** a glance in a particular direction, you glance in that direction.

Carmody <u>casts</u> an uneasy glance at Howard.
Out came Napoleon, <u>casting</u> haughty glances from side to side.

(i) The verb **cast** has several other meanings. Note that for all its meanings its past tense and past participle is **cast**, not 'casted'.

He <u>cast</u> a quick glance at his friend.
He <u>cast</u> his mind back over the day.
He <u>had cast</u> doubt on our traditional beliefs.
Will <u>had cast</u> his vote for the President.

casualty
⇨ See **Usage** entry at **victim**.

cause

1 used as a noun
The **cause of** an event is the thing that makes it happen.
Nobody knew the <u>cause of</u> the explosion.
Disease or illness is not a <u>cause of</u> this type of mental slowness.

(i) Note that you use **of**, not 'for', after **cause**.

You do not use 'because of' or 'due to' with **cause**. You do not say, for example, ~~The cause of the fire was probably due to a dropped cigarette~~. You say 'The cause of the fire **was** probably a dropped cigarette'.
The report said the main cause of the disaster <u>was</u> the failure to secure hatches and watertight doors.
The cause of the symptoms <u>appears to be</u> inability to digest gluten.

2 used as a verb
To **cause** something means to make it happen.
We have a good idea what <u>causes</u> an earthquake.
Any acute infection can <u>cause</u> headaches.

You can say that something **causes someone to do** something.
…a blow to the head which <u>had caused him to lose</u> consciousness.
It <u>had caused her to be</u> distrustful of people.

You do not say that something 'causes that someone does' something.

certain - sure

1 having no doubts
If you are **certain** or **sure** about something, you have no doubts about it.
He felt <u>certain</u> that she would disapprove.
I'm <u>sure</u> she's right.

2 definite truths
If it is **certain** that something is true, it is definitely true. If it is **certain** that something will happen, it will definitely happen.
It is <u>certain</u> that he did not ask for the original of the portrait.
It seemed <u>certain</u> that the satellite had burned up completely on re-entering the earth's atmosphere.
It is <u>certain</u> that they will have some spectacular successes.
It seems <u>certain</u> that they will both have to stay in prison for the rest of their lives.

(i) Note that you do not say that it is 'sure' that something is true or will happen.

3 'be certain to' and 'be sure to'
Instead of saying that it is certain that someone or something will do something, you can say that they **are certain to do** it or **are sure to do** it.

I'm waiting for Cynthia. She 's certain to be late.
The growth in demand is certain to drive up the price.
These fears are sure to go away as the baby gets older.
The telephone stopped ringing. 'It 's sure to ring again,' Sarah said.

Instead of saying that it is certain that someone will be able to do something, you often say that they **can be certain of** doing it or **can be sure of** doing it.

I chose to go private so I could be certain of having the best care possible.
It was the only way he could be sure of catching Rodenko by surprise.
You can always be sure of controlling one thing – the strength with which you hit the ball.

4 emphasis

You do not use words such as 'very' or 'extremely' in front of **certain** or **sure**. If you want to emphasize that someone has no doubts or that something is true, you use words such as **absolutely** and **completely**.

We are not yet absolutely certain that this report is true.
Whether it was directed at Eddie or me, I couldn't be completely certain.
Can you be absolutely sure that a murder has been committed?
She felt completely sure that she was pregnant.

---

certainly

1 emphasizing and agreeing

Certainly is used to emphasize statements. You often use **certainly** when you are agreeing with something that has been said or confirming that something is true.

It certainly looks wonderful, doesn't it?
Ellie was certainly a student at the university but I'm not sure about her brother.

⚠ **WARNING:** Do not confuse **certainly** and **surely**. You use **surely** to express disagreement or surprise.

Surely you care about what happens to her.

Both British and American speakers use **certainly** to agree with requests and statements.

'It is still a difficult world for women.' – 'Oh, certainly. '

Note that American speakers also use **surely** in this way.

'Can I have a drink?' – 'Why, surely. '

2 position in sentence

Certainly is usually used to modify verbs.

● If there is no auxiliary, you put **certainly** in front of the verb, unless the verb is **be**.

The letters certainly added fuel to the flames of her love for Tom.
It certainly gave some of her visitors a fright.

● If the verb is **be**, **certainly** can go either in front of it or after it. It usually goes after it.

It was certainly acceptable to Bach and Mozart.
The so-called electronic brains are certainly the most spectacular.
That certainly isn't true.

● If there is an auxiliary, you usually put **certainly** after the auxiliary.

...a large building that would certainly be empty and available.
They can certainly be quite big enough for a diver to put his foot into.
He decided he 'd certainly proved his point.

● If there is more than one auxiliary, you usually put **certainly** after the first one. **Certainly** can also go in front of the first auxiliary.

He will certainly be able to offer you advice.

They <u>would certainly have been accused</u> of cowardice.
The roadway <u>certainly could be widened.</u>

● If you use an auxiliary without a main verb, you put **certainly** in front of the auxiliary.

'I don't know whether I've succeeded or not.'–'Oh, you <u>certainly have</u> .'
'Do you think this was a film that needed making?'–'Yes, I <u>certainly do.</u>'

● You can also put **certainly** at the beginning of a sentence.

The stock markets fear a further rise in interest rates. <u>Certainly</u>, the City thinks the
government acted too late.
For many years union representatives have found themselves battling with employers.
<u>Certainly,</u> there will be many such struggles in the future.
<u>Certainly</u> it was not the act of a sane man.

3 'almost certainly'

If you think that something is the case, but you are not quite sure about it, you can say
that it is **almost certainly** the case.

She will <u>almost certainly</u> be left with some brain damage.
I am <u>almost certainly</u> being watched.

(*i*) Note that you never put 'nearly' in front of **certainly**.

⇒ Many other words can be used to say how certain you are about something. For a graded
list, see section on **probability** in **Grammar** entry at **Adjuncts**.

4 'certainly not'

You say **certainly not** when you want to say 'no' in a strong way, usually in answer to a
question.

'Had you forgotten?'– '<u>Certainly not.</u>'
'Leave me alone, please.'– '<u>Certainly not.</u> You agreed to finish it and we are relying on you.'

chair - armchair

1 'chair'

A **chair** is a piece of furniture for one person to sit on, with a support for the person's
back. When a chair is a very simple one, you say that someone sits **on** it.

Anne was sitting <u>on an upright chair.</u>
Sit <u>on this chair,</u> please.

When a chair is a comfortable one, you usually say that someone sits **in** it.

He leaned back <u>in his chair</u> and looked out of the window.

2 'armchair'

An **armchair** is a comfortable chair with a support on each side for your arms. You always
say that someone sits **in** an armchair.

He was sitting quietly <u>in</u> his <u>armchair,</u> smoking a pipe and reading the paper.

chairman - chairwoman - chairperson

1 'chairman'

The **chairman** is the person who is in charge of a meeting or debate.

The vicar, full of apologies, took his seat as <u>chairman.</u>

The head of an organization is often referred to as its **chairman**.

…Sir John Hill, <u>chairman</u> of the Atomic Energy Authority.

2 'chairwoman'

In the past, **chairman** was used to refer to both men and women, but it is now not often
used to refer to a woman. The woman in charge of a meeting or organization is
sometimes referred to as the **chairwoman**.

Margaret Downes is this year's <u>chairwoman</u> of the Irish Institute.

USAGE

3 'chairperson' and 'chair'

The person in charge of a meeting or organization is also sometimes referred to as the **chairperson** or **chair**. These words can be used to refer to either a man or a woman.

...*Ruth Michaels, chairperson of the Women Returners' Network.*
You should address your remarks to the chair.

chance

1 'chance'

If it is possible that something will happen, you can say that there is **a chance that it will happen** or **a chance of it happening.**

There is a chance that Labour could actually increase its majority.
If we play well there is a chance of winning 5-0.

If something is fairly likely to happen, you can say that there is **a good chance** that it will happen.

There was a good chance that I would be killed.
We've got a good chance of winning.

If something is unlikely to happen, you can say that there is **little chance** that it will happen. If you are sure that it will not happen, you can say that there is **no chance** that it will happen.

There's little chance that the situation will improve.
There's no chance of going home.

If someone is able to do something on a particular occasion, you can say that they have **the chance to do** it.

You will be given the chance to ask questions.
Visitors have the chance to win a digital camera.

2 'chances'

You can talk about someone's **chances of doing** something. For example, if someone will probably achieve something, you can say that their **chances of achieving** it are good.

What are your chances of becoming a director?
Single women have relatively equal chances of achieving white-collar work.

(i) Note that you do not talk about someone's 'chances to achieve' something.

3 'by chance'

If something happens **by chance,** it was not planned.

Many years later he met her by chance at a dinner party.

4 'luck'

Note that if you say that something happens **by chance,** you are not saying whether it is a good thing or a bad thing. If something good happens without being planned, you refer to it as **luck,** not 'chance'.

I couldn't believe my luck.
How can we ever be rescued except by luck?

charge

⇨ See **Usage** entry at **accuse - charge.**

cheap - cheaply

1 'cheap' as an adjective

Cheap goods or services cost less than other goods or services of the same type.

... *cheap red wine.*
... *cheap plastic buckets.*
A solid fuel cooker is cheap to run.

2 **'cheap' as an adverb**

In conversation, **cheap** can also be an adverb, but only with verbs which refer to the buying, selling, or hiring of things.

I thought you got it very <u>cheap</u>.
You can hire boots pretty <u>cheap</u>.

3 **'cheaply'**

With other verbs, the adverb you use is **cheaply**.

You can play golf comparatively <u>cheaply</u>.
In fact you can travel just as <u>cheaply</u> by British Airways.

4 **'low'**

You do not say that things such as wages, costs, or payments are 'cheap'. You say that they are **low**.

If your family has a <u>low</u> income, you can apply for a student grant.
…tasty meals at a fairly <u>low</u> cost.

check

⇨ See **Usage** entries at **cheque - check** and **bill - check - account**.

checkroom

⇨ See **Usage** entry at **cloakroom - checkroom**.

cheerful

⇨ See **Usage** entry at **glad**.

cheers - cheerio

1 **'cheers'**

People often say **cheers** to each other just before drinking an alcoholic drink.

I took Captain Imrie's chair, poured myself a small drink and said <u>'Cheers!'</u>
<u>Cheers,</u> Helen. Drink up.

Some British people also say **cheers** instead of 'thank you' or 'goodbye'.

'Here you are.' – 'Oh, <u>cheers.</u> Thanks.'
'Thanks for ringing.' – 'OK, <u>cheers.</u>' – 'Bye bye.' – <u>'Cheers.'</u>

2 **'cheerio'**

Cheerio is a more common way of saying goodbye. It is used mainly in British English.

I'll give Brigadier Sutherland your regards. <u>Cheerio</u>.

chef - chief

1 **'chef'**

A **chef** /ʃef/ is a cook in a hotel or restaurant.

Her recipe was passed on to the <u>chef</u>.
…a <u>chef</u> trained at Maxim's to produce rich and imaginative menus.

2 **'chief'**

The **chief** /tʃiːf/ of a group or organization is its leader.

…the police <u>chief</u>.
…Jim Stretton, <u>chief</u> of UK operations.

chemist - pharmacist

1 **'chemist'**

In British English, a **chemist** is a person who is qualified to prepare and sell drugs and medicines.

…the pills the <u>chemist</u> had given him.

USAGE

2 'pharmacist'

 In American English, someone like this is usually called a **pharmacist**.

The boy was eighteen, the son of the <u>pharmacist</u> at the Amity Pharmacy.

3 another meaning of 'chemist'

In both British and American English, a **chemist** is also a person who studies chemistry or who does work connected with chemical research.

…a research <u>chemist.</u>

chemist's - drugstore - pharmacy

1 'chemist's'

In Britain, a **chemist's** or **chemist** is a shop where you can buy medicine, cosmetics, and some household items.

I found her buying bottles of vitamin tablets at the <u>chemist's.</u>
He bought the perfume at the <u>chemist</u> in St James's Arcade.

2 'drugstore'

 In the United States, a shop where you can buy medicine and cosmetics is called a **drugstore**. In some drugstores, you can also buy simple meals and snacks.

…eating strawberry ice-cream sodas at Nagle's <u>drugstore</u>.

3 'pharmacy'

A **pharmacy** is the place within a chemist's or drugstore, or within a supermarket or other business where you can get prescription drugs.

…the <u>pharmacy</u> section of the drugstore.

In Britain, a chemist's can also be referred to formally as a **pharmacy**.

cheque - check

1 'cheque'

In British English, a **cheque** is a printed form on which you write an amount of money and say who it is to be paid to. Your bank then pays the money to that person from your account.

Ellen gave the landlady a <u>cheque</u> for £80.
I'd like to pay by <u>cheque</u>.

2 'check'

 In American English, this word is spelled **check**.

They sent me a <u>check</u> for $520.

In American English, a **check** is also a piece of paper showing how much money you owe for a meal in a restaurant.

He waved to a waiter and got the <u>check.</u>

In British English, a piece of paper like this is called a **bill**.

chief

⇨ See **Usage** entry at **chef - chief**.

childish - childlike

1 'childish'

You say that someone is **childish** if you think they are behaving in a silly or immature way.

…Penny's selfish and <u>childish</u> behaviour.
Don't be so <u>childish.</u>

2 'childlike'

You describe someone's voice or appearance as **childlike** when it seems like that of a child.

Her voice was fresh and <u>childlike</u>.

She looked at me with her big, <u>childlike</u> eyes.

chips

 In British English, **chips** are long, thin pieces of potato fried in oil. Pieces of potato like these are called **fries** or **french fries** in American English.

…fish and <u>chips</u>.

They go out to a place near the Capitol for a steak and <u>fries</u>.

 In American English, **chips** or **potato chips** are very thin slices of potato that have been fried until they are hard and crunchy. Pieces of potato like these are called **crisps** in British English.

…a bag of <u>potato chips</u>.

…a packet of <u>crisps</u>.

choose

1 'choose'

When you **choose** someone or something from a group of people or things, you decide which one you want.

Why did he <u>choose</u> these particular places?

The past tense of 'choose' is **chose**, not 'choosed'. The past participle is **chosen**.

I <u>chose</u> a yellow dress.

Miles Davis <u>was chosen</u> as the principal soloist on both works.

2 'pick' and 'select'

Pick and **select** have very similar meanings to **choose**. **Select** is more formal than **choose** or **pick**, and is not usually used in conversation.

Next time let's <u>pick</u> somebody who can fight.

They <u>select</u> books that seem to them important.

3 'appoint'

If you **appoint** someone to a job or official position, you formally choose them for it.

It made sense to <u>appoint</u> a banker to this job.

The Prime Minister <u>has appointed</u> a civilian as defence minister.

4 'choose to'

If someone **chooses to do** something, they do it because they want to or because they feel it is right.

Some women <u>choose to manage</u> on their own.

The majority of people do not <u>choose to be</u> a single parent.

The way we <u>choose to bring up</u> children is vitally important.

You do not say that someone 'picks to do' something or 'selects to do' something.

chord - cord

These words are both pronounced /kɔːd/.

1 'chord'

A **chord** is a number of musical notes played or sung together to produce a pleasant sound.

He played some random <u>chords</u>.

USAGE

2 **'cord'**

Cord is strong, thick string. A **cord** is a piece of this string.

She tied a cord around her box.

A **cord** is also a length of wire covered with plastic which connects a piece of electrical equipment to an electricity supply.

Christian name - first name - forename - given name

1 **'Christian name'**

In British English, a person's **Christian name** is the name given to them when they were born or when they were christened. Many people have two or more Christian names. Christian names come in front of a person's surname.

Do all your students call you by your Christian name?

'You remember their mother's Christian name?' – 'Margaret, I think.'

2 **'first name'**

 In American English, **Christian name** is not used. American speakers talk about a person's **first name**. British people who are not Christians also use **first name**.

At some point in the conversation Boon had begun calling Philip by his first name.

3 **'forename'**

On official forms, you are usually asked to write your surname and your **first name** or **forename**. **Forename** is only ever used in writing.

4 **'given name'**

 In American English, **given name** is sometimes used instead of 'first name' or 'forename'.

⇨ For more information about names, see **Topic** entry at **Names and titles**.

church

A **church** is a building in which Christians hold religious services.

The church has two entrances.

…St Clement's Church, Sandwich.

You use **church** immediately after a preposition when you are talking about a religious service held in a church. For example, if someone goes to a service in a church, you say that they go **to church.**

None of the children goes to church regularly.

People had heard what had happened at church.

Will we see you in church tomorrow?

I saw him after church one morning.

A **Church** is one of the groups of people within the Christian religion, for example Catholics or Methodists. You can refer to all the people and officials who belong to one of these groups as **the Church.**

The Church should indeed speak on the matter.

Surely the Church ought always to support peaceful change and reconciliation.

cinema

⇨ See **Usage** entry at **film**.

class - form - grade

1 **'class'**

A **class** is a group of pupils or students who are taught together.

If classes were smaller, children would learn more.

I had forty students in my class.

2 **'form'**

In many British schools and in some American private schools, **form** is used instead of 'class'. **Form** is used especially with a number to refer to a particular class or age group.

…the fifth _form._

She's in _Form_ 5.

3 **'grade'**

 A **grade** in an American school is similar to a **form** in a British school.

…a boy in the second _grade._

classic - classical

1 **'classic' used as an adjective**

A **classic** example of something has all the features or characteristics which you expect something of its kind to have.

This statement was a classic illustration of British politeness.

It is a classic example of the principle of 'less is more'.

Classic is also used to describe films or books which are judged to be of outstanding quality.

…one of the _classic_ works of the Hollywood cinema.

…Brenan's _classic_ analysis of Spanish history.

2 **'classic' used as a noun**

A **classic** is a book which is well-known and thought to be of a high literary standard.

We had all the standard classics at home.

Classics is the study of the ancient Greek and Roman civilizations, especially their languages, literature, and philosophy.

She obtained a first class degree in Classics.

3 **'classical'**

Classical music is music written by composers such as Mozart and Beethoven. Music of this kind is often complex in form, and is considered by many people to have lasting value.

I spend a lot of time reading and listening to classical music.

… _classical_ pianists.

Classical is also used to refer to things connected with ancient Greek or Roman civilization.

… _classical_ mythology.

Truffles have been savoured as a delicacy since classical times.

client

⇨ See **Usage** entry at **customer - client.**

cloakroom - checkroom

A **cloakroom** is a room where you leave your hat and coat, especially in a place of entertainment.

…a _cloakroom_ attendant.

 In American English, a room like this is sometimes called a **checkroom.**

In British English, **cloakroom** is also a polite word for a toilet.

⇨ See **Usage** entry at **toilet.**

 In American English, a **checkroom** is also a place where luggage can be left for a short time, especially at a railway station.

USAGE

close - closed - shut

If you **close** /kləʊz/ something such as a door, you move it so that it covers or fills a hole or gap.

He opened the door and <u>closed</u> it behind him.

You can also say that you **shut** something such as a door. There is no difference in meaning. The past tense and past participle of 'shut' is **shut,** not 'shutted'.

I <u>shut</u> the door quietly.

Both **closed** and **shut** can be adjectives.

All the other downstairs rooms are dark and the shutters are <u>closed</u>.
The windows were all <u>shut.</u>

However, only **closed** can be used in front of a noun. You can talk about a **closed** window, but not a 'shut' window.

He listened to her voice coming faintly through the <u>closed</u> door.

You can use either **close** or **shut** to say that work or business stops for a short time in a shop or public building.

Many libraries <u>close</u> on Saturdays at 1 p.m.
What time do the shops <u>shut?</u>

You can say that a road, border, or airport **is closed.**

Police said the border <u>was closed</u> without notice around midnight local time.

You do not say that a road, border, or airport 'is shut'.

Close is sometimes used to say that something is brought to an end.

He needs another $30,000 to <u>close</u> the deal.
The case is <u>closed.</u>

You do not use **shut** with this meaning.

⚠ **WARNING:** Do not confuse the verb **close** with the adjective **close** /kləʊs/. If something is **close** to something else, it is near to it.

⇨ See **Usage** entry at **near - close.**

closet

⇨ See **Usage** entry at **cupboard.**

clothes - clothing - cloth

1 **'clothes'**

Clothes /kləʊðz/ are things you wear, such as shirts, trousers, dresses, and coats.

I took off all my <u>clothes.</u>

⚠ **WARNING:** There is no singular form of **clothes.** You cannot, for example, talk about 'a clothe'. In formal English, you can talk about a **garment,** a **piece of clothing,** or an **article of clothing,** but in ordinary conversation, you usually name the piece of clothing you are talking about.

2 **'clothing'**

Clothing /kləʊðɪŋ/ is the clothes people wear. **Clothing** is an uncount noun. You do not talk about 'clothings' or 'a clothing'.

Wear protective <u>clothing</u>.
Some locals offered food and <u>clothing</u> to the refugees.

3 **'cloth'**

Cloth /klɒθ/ is fabric such as wool or cotton which is used for making such things as clothes.

…*strips of cotton <u>cloth.</u>*
The women were weavers of <u>cloth.</u>

(*i*) Note that when **cloth** is used like this, it is an uncount noun.

A **cloth** is a piece of fabric used for cleaning or dusting. Note that the plural form of 'cloth' is **cloths,** not 'clothes'.
Clean with a soft <u>cloth</u> dipped in warm soapy water.
Don't leave damp <u>cloths</u> in a cupboard.

coach
⇨ See **Usage** entry at **bus - coach.**

coast
⇨ See **Usage** entry at **beach - shore - coast.**

coat
A **coat** is a piece of clothing with long sleeves which you wear over your other clothes, especially in order to keep warm.
She was wearing a heavy tweed <u>coat.</u>
Get your <u>coats</u> on.

You only use **coat** to refer to a piece of clothing which is worn outdoors. Knitted clothes which cover the upper part of your body and which you can wear indoors are called **cardigans, jumpers,** or **sweaters.**

coffee
⇨ See **Usage** entry at **café - coffee.**

cold
If you want to emphasize how cold the weather is, you can say that it is **freezing,** especially in winter when there is ice or frost.
…a <u>freezing</u> January afternoon.

In summer, if the temperature is below average, you can say that it is **cool.** In general, **cold** suggests a lower temperature than **cool,** and **cool** things may be pleasant or refreshing.
This is the <u>coldest</u> winter I can remember.
A <u>cool</u> breeze swept off the sea; it was pleasant out there.

If it is very **cool** or too **cool,** you can also say that it is **chilly.**
It was decidedly pleasant out here, even on a <u>chilly</u> winter's day.

collaborate - co-operate

1 **'collaborate'**
When people **collaborate** on a project, they work together in order to produce something. For example, two writers can **collaborate** to produce a single piece of writing.
Anthony and I <u>are collaborating</u> on a paper for the conference.
The film was directed by Carl Jones, who <u>collaborated</u> with Rudy de Luca in writing it.

2 **'co-operate'**
When people **co-operate,** they help each other.
…an example of the way in which human beings can <u>co-operate</u> for the common good.

If you **co-operate** with someone who asks for your help, you help them.
The editors agreed to <u>co-operate.</u>
I couldn't get the RAF to <u>co-operate.</u>

 The spelling **cooperate** is sometimes used, and is preferred in American English.
They are willing to <u>cooperate</u> in the training of medical personnel.

USAGE

college

A **college** is an institution where students study after they have left school.

Computer Studies is one of the many courses at the local technical college.
…the Royal College of Music.

You use **college** immediately after a preposition when you are talking about someone's attendance at a college. For example, you say that someone is **at college**.

He hardly knew Andrew at college.
He says you need the money for college.
What do you plan to do after college?

 In American English, you usually say that someone is **in college**, not **at college**.

⇨ See **Usage** entry at **school - university**.

colour

When you are describing the colour of something, you do not normally use the word **colour**. You do not say, for example, 'He wore a green colour tie'. You say 'He wore a **green** tie'.

She had blonde hair and green eyes.
…a bright yellow hat.

However, you sometimes use the word **colour** when you are asking about the colour of something, or when you are describing a colour in an indirect way.

What colour was the bird?
The paint was the colour of grass.

ⓘ Note that in sentences like these you use **be**, not 'have'. You do not say 'What colour has the bird?' or 'The paint has the colour of grass'.

You also use the word **colour** when you are using more unusual colour words. For example, you can say that something is **a bluish-green colour**.

The plastic is treated with heat until it turns a milky white colour.
There was the sea, a glittering cream colour.

You can also say, for example, that something is **bluish-green in colour**.

The leaves are rough and grey-green in colour.

You can also add the suffix **-coloured** to the name of a colour.

…a cheap gold-coloured bracelet.
He selected one of his most expensive cream-coloured suits.

 Note that the American spellings of 'colour' and '-coloured' are **color** and **-colored.**

come

1 **'come'**

You use **come** to talk about movement towards the place where you are, or towards a place where you have been or will be.

Come and look.
Eleanor had come to visit her.
You must come and see me about it.

The past tense of 'come' is **came**. The past participle is **come**.

The children came along the beach towards me.
A ship had just come in from Turkey.

2 **'come' or 'go'?**

When you are talking about movement away from the place where you are, you use **go**, not 'come'. You also use **go** when you are describing movement which is neither towards you nor away from you.

⇨ For more information on talking about movement, see **Usage** entry at **go**.

ⓘ Note that you use **here** with **come** and **there** with **go**.

> *Elizabeth, <u>come</u> over <u>here</u>.*
> *I still <u>go there</u> all the time.*

If you invite someone to accompany you somewhere, you usually use **come**, not 'go'.

> *Will you <u>come</u> with me to the hospital?*
> *<u>Come</u> and meet Roger.*

In some situations, you can use **come** or **go** to show indirectly whether you will be in a place that you are referring to. For example, if you say 'Are you **going** to John's party?', you are not indicating whether you yourself are going to the party. However, if you say 'Are you **coming** to John's party?', you are showing that you will definitely be there.

3 **'come' in stories**

When you are saying what happened to someone else, for example in a story, you use **come** to talk about movement towards that person.

> *She looked up when they <u>came</u> into the room.*
> *He thought he'd have another drink before the train <u>came</u>.*

In stories, if someone **comes to** a place, they arrive there.

> *She eventually <u>came to</u> the town of Peconic.*

4 **'come and'**

You use **come and** with another verb to say that someone visits you or moves towards you in order to do something.

> *<u>Come and see</u> me whenever you feel depressed.*
> *She would <u>come and hold</u> his hand.*

5 **used to mean 'become'**

Come is sometimes used to mean 'become'.

> *One of my plaits <u>came</u> undone and I burst into tears.*
> *Remember that some dreams <u>come</u> true.*

⇨ See **Usage** entry at **become**.

come from

If you **come from** a particular place, you were born there, or it is your home.

> *'Where do you <u>come from</u>?' –'India.'*
> *I <u>come from</u> Zambia.*

ⓘ Note that you do not use a continuous tense in sentences like these. You do not say, for example, '~~Where are you coming from?~~' or '~~I am coming from Zambia~~'.

come to

⇨ See **Usage** entry at **arrive - reach**.

come with

⇨ See **Usage** entry at **accompany**.

comic - comical

When people or things seem amusing or absurd, you can describe them as **comic** or **comical**.

> *Everything began to appear strange and <u>comic</u>.*
> *There is something slightly <u>comical</u> about him.*

Comic is also used to describe things which are intended to be funny. When **comic** has this meaning, you only use it in front of a noun.

…her talent for grotesquely <u>comic</u> voices.
He first appeared on stage with his father, performing <u>comic</u> songs at the age of seven.

Comic appears with this meaning in several compounds, such as **comic opera**, **comic strip**, and **comic relief**.

Comical is not usually used to describe things which are intended to be funny.

commence

⇨ See **Usage** entry at **start - begin - commence**.

comment - commentary

1 'comment'

A **comment** is something you say which expresses your opinion of something.

People in the town started making rude <u>comments.</u>
It is unnecessary for me to add any <u>comment.</u>

2 'commentary'

A **commentary** is a description of an event that is broadcast on radio or television while the event is taking place.

We gathered round the radio to hear the <u>commentary.</u>
…a <u>commentary</u> on the Cheltenham Gold Cup.

comment - mention - remark

1 'comment'

If you **comment on** a situation, or make a **comment** about it, you give your opinion on it.

Mr Cook has not <u>commented</u> on these reports.
I was wondering whether you had any <u>comments.</u>

2 'mention'

If you **mention** something, you say it, but only briefly, especially when you have not talked about it before.

He <u>mentioned</u> that he might go to New York.

3 'remark'

If you **remark on** something, or make a **remark** about it, you say what you think or what you have noticed, often in a casual way.

Visitors <u>remark</u> on how well the children look.
General Sutton's <u>remarks</u> about the conflict.

committee

A **committee** is a group of people who represent a larger group or organization and who make decisions or plans on behalf of that group or organization.

A special <u>committee</u> has been set up.

In British English, you can use either a singular or plural form of a verb after **committee**.

Since 1963 the Committee <u>has</u> struggled, unable to shake off its weaknesses.
The National Executive Committee <u>have</u> their travelling expenses paid.

 Note that American speakers usually use only a singular verb form with **committee**.
The North American planning committee <u>has</u> recommended 28 possible topics.

common

If something is **common**, it is found in large numbers or it happens often.

The rhesus is one of the <u>commonest</u> monkeys in India.
Today, it is <u>common</u> to see adults returning to study.

You do not use a 'that'-clause after **common**. You do not say, for example, 'It is quite

~~common that motorists fall asleep while driving~~. You say 'It is quite common **for motorists to fall asleep** while driving'.

It is common <u>for a child to become</u> deaf after even a moderate ear infection.
It is quite common <u>for dogs to be poisoned</u> in this way.

company

A **company** is a business organization that makes money by selling goods or services.
He is a geologist employed by an oil <u>company</u>.

In British English, you can use either a singular or plural form of a verb after **company**.
The company <u>has</u> taken on 1600 more highly-paid staff.
The company <u>have</u> quickly established an enviable reputation since their foundation in 1984.

 Note that American speakers usually use only a singular verb form with **company**.
Another major American company <u>has</u> announced massive layoffs and other cost-cutting measures.

compare

☐1 **'compare'**
When you **compare** things, you consider them and discover their differences or similarities.
It's interesting to <u>compare</u> the two prospectuses.

When **compare** has this meaning, you can use either **with** or **to** after it. For example, you can say 'It's interesting to compare the new prospectus **with** the old one' or 'It's interesting to compare the new prospectus **to** the old one'.
…studies <u>comparing</u> Russian children <u>with</u> those in Britain.
I haven't got anything to <u>compare</u> it <u>to</u>.

☐2 **'be compared to'**
Compare has another meaning. You use it to say that one person or thing is said to be like another one.
As an essayist he <u>is compared</u> frequently <u>to</u> Paine and Hazlitt.
…a computer virus can <u>be compared to</u> a biological virus.

When you use **compare** like this, you must use **to** after it. You do not use 'with'.

complain

☐1 **'complain about'**
If you **complain about** something, you say that it is wrong or unsatisfactory.
Mothers <u>complained about</u> the lack of play space.
She never <u>complained about</u> the weather.

(*i*) Note that you do not use 'over' or 'on' after **complain**. You do not say, for example, '~~Mothers complained over the lack of play space~~' or '~~She never complained on the weather~~'.

☐2 **'complain of'**
You can also say that someone **complains of** something. However, if you **complain of** something, you are usually drawing someone's attention to it, as well as saying that it is wrong or unsatisfactory.
Women <u>complain of</u> pressure on them to get jobs.
Rioters in both countries <u>complained of</u> police brutality.

If you **complain of** a pain, you say that you have it.
He <u>complained of</u> a headache.

complement - compliment

These words can both be verbs or nouns. When they are verbs, they are pronounced /ˈkɒmplɪment/. When they are nouns, they are pronounced /ˈkɒmplɪmənt/.

1 **'complement'**

If one thing **complements** another, they increase each other's good qualities when they are brought together.

Nutmeg, parsley and cider all complement the flavour of these beans well.
Current advances in hardware development nicely complement British software skills.

A **complement** is an adjective or noun group which comes after a link verb such as **be**.

⇨ See **Grammar** entry at **Complements**.

2 **'compliment'**

If you **compliment** someone, you tell them that you admire something that they have or something that they have done.

They complimented me on the way I looked each time they saw me.
She is to be complimented for handling the situation so well.

A **compliment** is something that you do or say to someone to show your admiration for them.

She took his acceptance as a great compliment.

You say that you **pay** someone a compliment.

He knew that he had just been paid a great compliment.

complete

Complete is usually an adjective. For some of its meanings, you can use words like **more** and **very** in front of it.

1 **used to mean 'as great as possible'**

You usually use **complete** to say that something is as great in degree, extent, or amount as possible.

You need a complete change of diet.
They were in complete agreement.

When **complete** has this meaning, you do not use words like 'more' or 'very' in front of it.

2 **used to talk about contents**

Complete is also used to say that something contains all the parts that it should contain.

I have a complete medical kit.
…a complete set of all her novels.

When two things do not contain all the parts that they should contain but one thing has more parts than the other, you can say that the first thing is **more complete** than the second one.

For a more complete picture of David's progress we must depend on his own assessment.

Similarly, if something does not contain all the parts that it should contain but contains more parts than anything else of its kind, you can say that it is the **most complete** thing of its kind.

…the most complete skeleton so far unearthed from that period.

3 **used to mean 'thorough'**

Complete is sometimes used to mean 'thorough'. When **complete** has this meaning, you can use words like **very** and **more** in front of it.

She followed her mother's very complete instructions on how to organize a funeral.
You ought to have a more complete check-up if you are really thinking of going abroad.

4 **used to mean 'finished'**

Complete is also used to say that something such as a task or new building has been finished.

USAGE

It'll be two years before the process is <u>complete</u>.
…blocks of luxury flats, <u>complete</u> but half-empty.

When **complete** has this meaning, you do not use words like **more** or **very** in front of it.

completely

⇨ See section on **extent** in **Grammar** entry at **Adjuncts**.

compliment

⇨ See **Usage** entry at **complement - compliment**.

composed

⇨ See **Usage** entry at **comprise**.

comprehensible - comprehensive

1 **'comprehensible'**

If something is **comprehensible**, you can understand it.

The object is to make our research readable and <u>comprehensible</u>.
…language <u>comprehensible</u> only to the legal mind.

2 **'comprehensive'**

If something is **comprehensive**, it is complete and includes everything that is important.

…a <u>comprehensive</u> list of all the items in stock.
Linda received <u>comprehensive</u> training after joining the firm.

comprehension - understanding

1 **'comprehension'**

Both **comprehension** and **understanding** can be used to talk about someone's ability to understand something.

He noted Bond's apparent lack of <u>comprehension</u>.
The problems of solar navigation seem beyond <u>comprehension</u>.
A very narrow subject would have become too highly technical for general <u>understanding</u>.

2 **'understanding'**

If you have an **understanding** of something, you have some knowledge of it, or you know how it works or what it means.

The past decade has seen huge advances in our general <u>understanding</u> of how the ear works.
The job requires an <u>understanding</u> of Spanish.

(i) Note that you cannot use 'comprehension' with this meaning.

Understanding has another meaning. If there is **understanding** between people, they are friendly towards each other and trust each other.

What we need is greater <u>understanding</u> between management and workers.

comprehensive

⇨ See **Usage** entry at **comprehensible - comprehensive**.

comprise

1 **'comprise'**

You say that something **comprises** particular things when you are mentioning all its parts.

The village's social facilities <u>comprised</u> one public toilet and two telephones.

2 **'be composed of' and 'consist of'**

You can also say that something **is composed of** or **consists of** particular things. There is no difference in meaning.

The body is composed of many kinds of cells, such as muscle, bone, nerve, and fat.
The committee consists of scientists and engineers.

Some people say that something 'is comprised of' particular things, but this is generally thought to be incorrect.

⚠ **WARNING:** You do not use a passive form of **consist of**. You do not say, for example, 'The committee is consisted of scientists and engineers'.

3 **'constitute'**

Constitute works in the opposite way to the verbs just mentioned. You say that the parts of something **constitute** the whole.

Shop assistants now constitute the largest single occupation group.

You can also say that a number of things **constitute** a fraction of a whole.

Volunteers constitute more than 95% of The Center's work force.

4 **'make up'**

Make up can be used in either an active or passive form. In its active form, it has the same meaning as **constitute**.

Women now make up two-fifths of the British labour force.

In its passive form, it is followed by **of** and has the same meaning as **be composed of**.

All substances are made up of molecules.
Nearly half the Congress is made up of lawyers.

⚠ **WARNING:** You do not use a continuous form of any of these verbs. You do not say, for example, 'The committee is consisting of scientists and engineers'.

conceited

⇨ See **Usage** entry at **proud**.

concentrate

If you **concentrate on** something, you give special attention to it, rather than to other things.

Concentrate on your driving.
He believed governments should concentrate more on education.

You can say that someone **is concentrating on** something.

They are concentrating on saving life.
One area Dr Blanch will be concentrating on is tourism.

ⓘ Note that you do not say that someone 'is concentrated' on something.

When something **is concentrated in** a place, it is all in that place, rather than being spread around in several places.

Modern industry has been concentrated in a few large urban centres.

concerned

1 **used after a link verb**

The adjective **concerned** is usually used after a link verb such as **be**.

If you **are concerned about** something, you are worried about it.

He was concerned about the level of unemployment.
I've been concerned about you lately.

If a book, speech, or piece of information **is concerned with** a subject, it deals with it.

This chapter is concerned with changes that are likely to take place.

ⓘ Note that you do not say that a book, speech, or piece of information 'is concerned about' a subject.

2 **used after a noun**

Concerned can also be used immediately after a noun. You use it to refer to people or things involved in a situation that you have just mentioned.

We've spoken to the lecturers concerned.
Some of the chemicals concerned can cause cancer.

Concerned is often used with this meaning after the pronouns **all**, **everyone**, and **everybody**.

It was a perfect arrangement for all concerned.
This was something of a relief to everyone concerned.

concerto - concert

1 **'concerto'**

A **concerto** /kənˈtʃeətoʊ/ is a piece of classical music written for one or more solo instruments and an orchestra.

…Beethoven's Violin Concerto.

1 **'concert'**

Note that you do not call a performance of music given by musicians a 'concerto'. You call it a **concert** /ˈkɒnsət/.

She had gone to the concert that evening.

condominium

⇨ See **Usage** entry at **flat - apartment**.

confidant - confident

1 **'confidant'**

Confidant /ˈkɒnfɪdænt/ is a noun. A **confidant** is a person who you discuss your private problems and worries with. You use the spelling **confidante** when the person is a woman.

…Colonel House, a friend and confidant of President Woodrow Wilson.
She became her father's only confidante.

2 **'confident'**

Confident /ˈkɒnfɪdənt/ is an adjective. If you are **confident** about something, you are certain that it will happen in the way you want.

He was confident that the problem with the guidance mechanism could be fixed.
I feel confident about the future of British music.

People who are **confident** are sure of their own abilities.

… a witty, young and confident lawyer.
His manner is more confident these days.

conform

If you **conform**, you behave in the way that you are expected to behave.

You must be prepared to conform.

You also use **conform** to say that something is what is wanted or required. When you use **conform** like this, you use either **to** or **with** after it.

Such a change would not conform to the present wishes of the great majority of people.
Every home should have a fire extinguisher which conforms with British Standards.

conscious - consciousness - conscience - conscientious

1 **'conscious'**

Conscious is an adjective. If you are **conscious** of something, you are aware of it.

USAGE

She became <u>conscious</u> of Rudolph looking at her.
I was <u>conscious</u> that he had changed his tactics.

If you are **conscious,** you are awake, rather than asleep or unconscious.

The patient was fully <u>conscious</u> during the operation.

2 **'consciousness'**

Consciousness is a noun. You can refer to your mind and thoughts as your
consciousness.

We assume that the brain is the seat of <u>consciousness</u> and intelligence.
Doubts were starting to enter into my <u>consciousness.</u>

If you **lose consciousness,** you become unconscious. If you **regain consciousness** or
recover consciousness, you become conscious again after being unconscious. These are
fairly formal expressions.

He fell down and <u>lost consciousness.</u>
He began to <u>regain consciousness</u> just as Koch was leaving.
She died in hospital without <u>recovering consciousness.</u>

In more informal English you can say that you **pass out** or **come round**.

He felt sick and dizzy, then <u>passed out.</u>
When I <u>came round,</u> I was on the kitchen floor.

3 **'conscience'**

Conscience is a noun. Your **conscience** is the part of your mind which tells you whether
what you are doing is right or wrong.

My <u>conscience</u> told me to vote against the others.
Their <u>consciences</u> were troubled by stories of famine and war.

4 **'conscientious'**

Conscientious is an adjective. Someone who is **conscientious** is very careful to do their
work properly.

We are generally very <u>conscientious</u> about our work.
She seemed a <u>conscientious,</u> rather earnest young woman.

consider

If you **consider** something, you think about it carefully.

He had no time to <u>consider</u> the matter.
The government is being asked to <u>consider</u> a plan to fix the date of the Easter break.

You can say that someone **is considering doing** something in the future.

They <u>were considering opening</u> an office on the West Side of the city.
He <u>was considering taking</u> the bedside table downstairs.

(i) Note that you do not say that someone 'is considering to do' something.

considerably

⇨ See section on **degree** in **Grammar** entry at **Adjuncts**.

consist of

⇨ See **Usage** entry at **comprise**.

constant - continual - continuous

You can use **constant, continual,** and **continuous** to describe things that happen or exist
without stopping.

1 **'constant'**

You describe something as **constant** when it happens all the time or never goes away.

He was in <u>constant</u> pain.
Eva's <u>constant</u> criticism.

2 **'continual'**

Continual is usually used to describe something that happens often over a period of time.

…his continual drinking.
… continual demands to cut costs.

Continual can only be used in front of a noun. You do not use it after a verb.

3 **'continuous'**

If something is **continuous**, it happens all the time without stopping, or seems to do so.

…days of continuous rain.
…a continuous background noise.

Continuous can be used either in front of a noun or after a verb.

The exercise should be one continuous movement.
The change was gradual and by no means steady and continuous.

4 **'continual' or 'continuous'**

If you are describing something undesirable which continues to happen or exist without stopping, it is better to use **continual** rather than **continuous**.

Life is a continual struggle.
It was sad to see her the victim of continual pain.

Continual can also be used to describe things which happen repeatedly.

He still smoked despite the continual warnings of his nurse.
Valenti's face was handsome though bloated by continual drinking.

It is usually regarded as incorrect to use **continuous** to describe things which happen repeatedly.

constantly

⇨ See section on **frequency** in **Grammar** entry at **Adjuncts**.

constitute

⇨ See **Usage** entry at **comprise**.

consult

If you **consult** someone, you ask them for their opinion or advice.

If your baby is losing weight, you should consult your doctor promptly.
She wished to consult him about her future.
If you are renting from a private landlord, you should consult a solicitor to find out your exact position.

 Some speakers of American English say **consult with** instead of 'consult'.

The Americans would have to consult with their allies about any military action in Europe.
They consult with companies to improve worker satisfaction and productivity.

contemporary

⇨ See **Usage** entry at **new**.

content

Content can be a noun, an adjective, or a verb. When it is a noun, it is pronounced /kɒntent/. When it is an adjective or verb, it is pronounced /kəntent/.

1 **used as a plural noun**

The **contents** of something such as a box or room are the things inside it.

…pouring out the contents of the bag.

(i) Note that **contents** is a plural noun. You cannot talk about 'a content'.

The **contents** of something such as a document or tape are the things written in it or recorded on it.

He knew by heart the <u>contents</u> of the note.

2 used as an uncount noun

The **content** of something such as a speech, piece of writing, website, or television programme is the information it gives, or the ideas or opinions expressed in it.

I was disturbed by the <u>content</u> of some of the speeches.

BBC radio and television both now carry more current affairs <u>content</u> than does the popular press.

The website <u>content</u> includes issues of the newsletter.

3 used as an adjective

If you are **content to do** something or are **content with** something, you are willing to do it, have it, or accept it.

A few teachers were <u>content to pay</u> the fines.

Children are not <u>content with</u> glib explanations.

If you are **content,** you are happy and satisfied. **Content** is not used with this meaning in front of a noun.

He says his daughter is quite <u>content.</u>

I probably feel more <u>content</u> singing than at any other time.

4 'contented'

You can also use **contented** to say that someone is happy and satisfied. **Contented** can be used in front of a noun or after a verb.

…firms with a loyal and <u>contented</u> labour force.

For ten years they lived like this and were perfectly <u>contented.</u>

⇨ Several other words can be used with a similar meaning to **content** or **contented.** For a list of these, see **Usage** entry at **happy - sad.**

5 'content' used as a verb

If you **content yourself with** doing something, you are satisfied with it and do not try to do other things.

Most manufacturers <u>content themselves with</u> updating existing models.

continent

1 'continent'

A **continent** is a very large area of land surrounded or almost surrounded by sea. A continent usually consists of several countries. Africa and Asia are continents.

…the South American <u>continent.</u>

2 'the Continent'

When people talk about **the Continent,** they mean the mainland of Europe, especially central and southern Europe.

On <u>the Continent,</u> the tradition has been quite different.

Sea traffic between the United Kingdom and <u>the Continent</u> was halted.

continual

⇨ See **Usage** entry at **constant - continual - continuous.**

continually

⇨ See section on **frequency** in **Grammar** entry at **Adjuncts.**

continuous

⇨ See **Usage** entry at **constant - continual - continuous.**

contrary

1. **'on the contrary'**

You say **on the contrary** when you are contradicting a statement that has just been made.

'You'll get tired of it.'–'On the contrary. I shall enjoy it.'

You also use **on the contrary** to introduce a positive statement which confirms a negative statement that you have just made.

There was nothing ugly about her dress: on the contrary, it had a certain elegance.

2. **'on the other hand'**

You do not say 'on the contrary' when you are going to mention a situation that contrasts with one you have just described. You do not say, for example, 'I don't like living in the centre of the town. On the contrary, it's useful when you want to buy something'. You say 'I don't like living in the centre of the town. **On the other hand,** it's useful when you want to buy something'.

It's certainly hard work. But, on the other hand, a man who wishes to have a career has to make a great many sacrifices.

control

Control can be a verb or a noun.

1. **used as a verb**

If someone **controls** something such as a country or an organization, they have the power to take all the important decisions about the way it is run.

The Australian administration at that time controlled the island.
His family had controlled the Times for more than a century.

(i) Note that when **control** is a verb, it is not followed by a preposition.

2. **used as a noun**

Control is also used as a noun to refer to the power that someone has in a country or organization. You say that someone has control **of** a country or organization, or control **over** it.

The restructuring involves Mr Ronson giving up control of the company.
The first aim of his government would be to establish control over the republic's territory.

3. **another meaning**

Control is used in the names of the parts of an airport, sea terminal, or border crossing where your documents and luggage are officially checked to make sure that they are in order.

…passport and customs controls.

However, you do not use **control** as a verb to mean 'check' or 'inspect'. You do not say, for example, 'My luggage was controlled'. You say 'My luggage **was checked**' or 'My luggage **was inspected**'.

He offered me a cigar while the baggage was being checked.
The guard took his ID card and inspected it.

convince - persuade

1. **'convince'**

If you **convince** someone of something, you make them believe it is true.

These experiences convinced me of the drug's harmful effects.
It took them a few days to convince me that it was possible.

Some speakers use **convince** with a 'to'-infinitive to say that one person makes another person decide to do something, by giving them a good reason for doing it.

USAGE

Lyon did his best to <u>convince</u> me to settle in Tennessee.
I hope you will help me <u>convince</u> my father to leave.

2 'persuade'

Using 'convince' in this way is generally regarded as incorrect. Instead you should use **persuade**.

Marsha was trying to <u>persuade</u> Posy to change her mind.
They had no difficulty in <u>persuading</u> him to launch a new paper.

convinced

If you are **convinced** of something, you are sure that it is true or genuine.

I am <u>convinced</u> of your loyalty.
He was <u>convinced</u> that her mother was innocent.

You do not use words such as 'very' or 'extremely' in front of **convinced.** If you want to emphasize that someone has no doubts about something, you use words such as **fully** or **totally** in front of **convinced.**

To be <u>fully convinced</u> that reading is important, they have to find books they like.
I am <u>totally convinced</u> it was an accident.
We are <u>absolutely convinced</u> that this is the right thing to do.
Some people were <u>firmly convinced</u> that a non-human intelligence was attempting to make contact.

⚠ **WARNING:** You do not use a 'to'-infinitive after **convinced.** You do not say, for example, 'He is convinced to have failed'. You say 'He is **convinced that he has** failed'.

cook

1 'cook' used as a noun

A **cook** is someone who cooks meals as their job.

Each house had a <u>cook</u> and an assistant <u>cook.</u>

You can also describe anyone's ability to cook by using **cook** with an adjective. For example, you can say that someone is **a good cook** or **a bad cook.**

Are you <u>a good cook</u>?
Appuhamy was <u>an excellent cook.</u>

2 'cook' used as a verb

If you **cook** a meal or a particular type of food, you prepare it for eating and then heat it, for example in an oven or saucepan.

As dawn broke we began to <u>cook</u> our breakfast.
We <u>cooked</u> the pie in the oven.

ⓘ Note that **cook** is only used to talk about food, not drinks.

Several other verbs can be used to talk about the preparation of food and drinks:

3 'make'

If you **make** a meal or a drink, you combine foods or drinks together to produce something different. Note that someone can **make** a meal without heating anything.

I <u>made</u> his breakfast.
I <u>have made</u> you a drink.

4 'prepare'

Prepare is used in two ways. If you **prepare** food, you clean or cut it so that it is ready to be used.

<u>Prepare</u> the vegetables, cut into small chunks and add to the chicken.

To **prepare** a meal or drink means the same as to **make** it (see above). This is a fairly formal use.

USAGE

5 'get'

If you **get** a meal, you prepare it or cook it. You can also say that someone **gets** a meal **ready**. If you **get** a drink, you either mix drinks together or pour a drink.

Then I'd <u>get</u> the tea <u>ready</u>.
I was downstairs <u>getting</u> the drinks.

6 'fix'

 In American English, if you **fix** a meal or drink, you **make** it (see above).

Sarah <u>fixed</u> some food for us.
Morris <u>fixed</u> himself a stiff drink.

There are many verbs which refer to different ways of cooking things:

7 'bake', 'roast'

When you **bake** or **roast** something, you cook it in an oven without liquid. You **bake** bread and cakes, but you **roast** meat. When you **roast** potatoes, you cook them in an oven in some fat. You can also **roast** a large piece of meat or a bird over a fire.

How did you learn to <u>bake</u> cakes?
I personally would rather <u>roast</u> a chicken whole.

(i) Note that you use **roast**, not 'roasted', to describe meat and potatoes that have been roasted.

…a traditional <u>roast</u> beef dinner.

8 'grill', 'toast', 'broil'

When you **grill** or **toast** something, you cook it under or over strong heat. You **grill** meat and vegetables, but you **toast** slices of bread.

 Speakers of American English usually use **broil** rather than 'grill'.

<u>Grill</u> the meat for 20 minutes each side.
<u>Toast</u> the bread lightly on both sides.
I'll <u>broil</u> the lobster.

9 'boil', 'poach', 'steam'

When you **boil** something, you cook it in boiling water. When you **poach** something, you cook it gently in shallow hot water. You can also **steam** something; that is, cook it in the steam rising from a pan of hot water.

I'd peel potatoes and put them on to <u>boil</u>.
<u>Poach</u> the eggs for 4 minutes.
Leave the vegetables to <u>steam</u> over the rice for the 20 minutes cooking time.

10 'fry'

When you **fry** something, you cook it in hot fat or oil.

<u>Fry</u> the breadcrumbs until golden brown.

11 'casserole', 'stew', 'braise'

When you **casserole, stew,** or **braise** something, you cook it fairly slowly in a liquid or sauce.

If you <u>casserole</u> chicken pieces, take the skin off first.
<u>Stew</u> the apple and blackberries to make a thick pulp.
… <u>braised</u> cabbage.

cooker

A **cooker** is a metal oven and hot plate that you use for boiling, grilling, or roasting food.
The food was warming in a saucepan on the <u>cooker</u>.

USAGE

 In American English, this machine is called a **range.**

Baking soda will put out most electrical fires, so keep a box of it near your <u>range.</u>

ⓘ Note that you do not refer to a person who cooks meals as a 'cooker'. You call them a **cook.**

⇨ See **Usage** entry at **cook.**

co-operate

⇨ See **Usage** entry at **collaborate - co-operate.**

cord

⇨ See **Usage** entry at **chord - cord.**

corn

 In American English, **corn** is usually used to refer to the kernels of a particular type of maize, served as a vegetable. In British English, this vegetable is called **sweetcorn.**
In British English, **corn** is used to refer to any type of cereal plant growing in a particular area, for example wheat, barley, or maize.

corner

A **corner** is a place where two sides or edges of something meet.
…a television set in the <u>corner</u> of the room.

When two streets meet, you refer to each of the places where their edges meet as a **corner.**
There is a telephone box on the <u>corner.</u>

You usually say that something is **in** a corner. However, you use **on** when you are talking about the corner of a street.
Peel was working <u>in the corner</u> of a room.
… <u>in one corner</u> of the small, square playground.
…the garage <u>on the corner</u> of the street.
The drugstore was <u>on the corner</u> of the block.

cost

⇨ See **Usage** entry at **price - cost.**

cot - crib - camp bed

1 'cot' and 'crib'

 In British English, a **cot** is a bed for a baby. A cot has high sides to prevent the baby from falling out. In American English, a bed like this is called a **crib.**
Have your baby's Moses basket or <u>cot</u> beside your bed.
I asked for a <u>crib</u> to put the baby in.

2 'cot' and 'camp bed'

 In American English, a **cot** is a narrow bed for an adult. It is made of canvas fitted over a frame, and you can fold it up. You take it with you when you go camping, or you use it as a spare bed at home. In British English, a bed like this is called a **camp bed.**
His bodyguards slept on the <u>cots.</u>
I ended up on a <u>camp bed</u> in the lounge.

could

⇨ See **Usage** entry at **can - could - be able to.**

council - counsel

1 **'council'**

Council /kaʊnsəl/ is a noun. A **council** is a group of people who run a local area such as a town, city, or county.

…*Wiltshire County Council.*

Some other groups of people who run organizations are also called **Councils.**

…*the Arts Council.*

…*the British Council of Churches.*

2 **'counsel'**

Counsel /kaʊnsəl/ is usually a verb. If you **counsel** someone, you give them advice about their problems.

Part of her work is to counsel families when problems arise.

Someone's **counsel** is the lawyer who gives them advice on a legal case and speaks on their behalf in court.

Singleton's counsel said after the trial that he would appeal.

country

1 **'country'**

A **country** is one of the political areas which the world is divided into.

Indonesia is the fifth most populous country in the world.

Does this system apply in other European countries?

2 **'the country'**

You refer to land which is away from towns and cities as **the country.**

We live in the country.

There was a big move of people away from the country to the towns.

⚠ **WARNING:** When you use **country** like this, the only determiner you can use with it is **the.** You do not say, for example, 'I like living in Paris, but my parents prefer to live in a country'.

couple

⇨ See **Usage** entry at **pair - couple.**

course

A **course** is a series of lessons or lectures on a particular subject. It usually includes reading and written work that a student has to do. You say that someone takes a course **in** a subject.

The department also offers a course in Opera Studies.

…*the Special Honours course in Latin.*

ⓘ Note that you do not say that someone takes a course 'of' a subject.

In British English, the people who are taking a course are referred to as the people **on** the course.

There were about 200 people on the course.

🇺🇸 In American English, they are referred to as the people **in** the course.

How many are there in the course as a whole?

craft

A **craft** is an activity such as weaving, carving, or pottery that involves making things skilfully by hand, often in a traditional way. When **craft** has this meaning, its plural form is **crafts.**

It's a pity to see the old crafts dying out.

A **craft** is also a vehicle such as a boat, hovercraft, or submarine that carries people or things on or under water. When **craft** has this meaning, its plural form is **craft.**

There were eight destroyers and fifty smaller <u>craft.</u>

crazy
⇨ See **Usage** entry at **madness.**

credible - credulous - creditable

1 'credible'
If something is **credible,** it can be believed.

His latest statements are hardly <u>credible.</u>
This is not <u>credible</u> to anyone who has studied the facts.

ⓘ Note that **credible** is most commonly used in negative sentences.

2 'credulous'
People who are **credulous** are always ready to believe what other people tell them, and are easily deceived.

<u>Credulous</u> women bought the mandrake root to promote conception.

3 'creditable'
A performance, achievement, or action that is **creditable** is of a reasonably high standard.

He polled a <u>creditable</u> 44.8 percent.
Their performance was even less <u>creditable.</u>

crib
⇨ See **Usage** entry at **cot - crib - camp bed.**

crime
A **crime** is an illegal action for which a person can be punished by law. You usually say that someone **commits** a crime.

A <u>crime has been committed.</u>
The police had no evidence of him <u>having committed</u> any actual <u>crime.</u>

ⓘ Note that you do not say that someone 'does' a crime or 'makes' a crime.

crippled
In the past, when someone had a physical condition that severely affected their life, people used to say that they were **crippled** or refer to them as **a cripple.** Nowadays, these words are avoided because they are thought to be offensive.

The adjectives **disabled, handicapped,** and **physically handicapped** are often used to describe people who have a condition of this kind. **Handicapped** and **physically handicapped** are used especially to describe someone who is born with the condition. You can also say that someone is **in a wheelchair,** if they are unable to walk.

The most sensitive ways of referring to people with a restricting physical condition are to call them **people with disabilities** or **people with special needs.**

Those who will gain the most are <u>people with disabilities</u> and their carers.
Employers are not prepared to pay for the training of <u>young people with special needs.</u>

crisps
⇨ See **Usage** entry at **chips.**

criterion
A **criterion** is a standard by which you judge or evaluate something.

The most important <u>criterion</u> for entry is that applicants must design and make their own work.

The plural of 'criterion' is **criteria,** not 'criterions'.
The Commission did not apply the same criteria to advertising.

⚠ **WARNING: Criteria** is only used in its plural form. You do not talk about 'a criteria' or 'this criteria'.

critic - critical - critique

1 **'critic'**
Critic /krɪtɪk/ is a noun. A **critic** is a person who writes reviews and expresses opinions in newspapers or on television about books, films, music, or art.
What did the New York critics have to say about the production?
…comments by a couple of television critics.

2 **'critical'**
You do not use **critic** as an adjective. The adjective which means 'relating to the work of a critic' is **critical.** When **critical** has this meaning, you only use it in front of a noun.
I was planning a serious critical study of Shakespeare.

3 **'critique'**
Critique /krɪtiːk/ is a noun. A **critique** is a written analysis and judgement of a situation or of a person's work. **Critique** is a formal word.
…an intelligent and incisive critique of our society.
In 1954, Golub published 'A Critique of Abstract Expressionism'.

4 **'review'**
You do not refer to an item written in a newspaper by a critic as a 'critique'. You call it a **review.**
…a book review.
He hadn't even given the play a bad review.

critique
⇨ See **Usage** entry at **critic - critical - critique.**

cry - weep

1 **'cry'**
Cry can be a verb or a noun. The other forms of the verb are **cries, crying, cried.** The plural of the noun is **cries.**
If you **cry,** tears come out of your eyes because you are unhappy, afraid, or in pain.
Helen began to cry.
Feed the baby as often as it cries.
If the baby cried at night, Nick would comfort him.
We heard what sounded like a little girl crying.

In conversation, you can say that someone has a **cry.**
She felt a lot better after a good cry.

2 **'weep'**
Weep means the same as **cry. Weep** is an old-fashioned word which is now used only in stories. The past tense and past participle of 'weep' is **wept,** not 'weeped'.
The girl was weeping as she kissed him goodbye.
James wept when he heard the news.

3 **another meaning of 'cry'**
In a story, if someone **cries** something, they shout it.
'Come on!' he cried.
He cried out angrily, 'Get out of my house!'

USAGE

A **cry** is something that someone shouts.

When she saw him she uttered a <u>cry</u> of surprise.

We heard <u>cries</u> of 'Help! Please help me!' coming from the river.

cup - glass - mug

1 'cup'

A **cup** is a small, round container, usually with a handle, from which you drink hot drinks such as tea and coffee. When you are not holding a cup, you usually rest it on a **saucer.**

…a china <u>cup</u>.

John put his <u>cup</u> and saucer on the coffee table.

 In American English, a **cup** is also standard unit of measurement used in cooking.

Sprinkle 2 <u>cups</u> coconut heavily over the top and sides of the cake.

2 'glass'

You do not refer to a container made out of glass and used for cold drinks as a 'cup'. You call it a **glass.**

I put down my <u>glass</u> and stood up.

He poured Ellen a <u>glass</u> of wine.

3 'mug'

A **mug** is a large deep cup with straight sides and a handle, used for hot drinks. You do not rest a **mug** on a saucer.

He spooned instant coffee into two of the <u>mugs</u>.

cupboard - wardrobe - closet

1 'cupboard'

A **cupboard** is a piece of furniture with doors at the front and usually shelves inside.

The kitchen <u>cupboard</u> is stocked with tins of soup and food.

2 'wardrobe'

A **wardrobe** is a tall cupboard, usually in a bedroom, which has space for hanging clothes.

The master bedroom has an en suite bathroom and a walk-in <u>wardrobe</u>.

3 'closet'

 A cupboard or wardrobe is sometimes built into the wall of a room, rather than being a separate piece of furniture. In American English, a built-in cupboard or wardrobe is called a **closet.**

Clothes hang limp in the <u>closet</u>.

curb - kerb

1 'curb'

Curb can be a noun or a verb.

If you **curb** something, you control it and keep it within definite limits.

…proposals to <u>curb</u> the powers of the Home Secretary.

You must <u>curb</u> your extravagant tastes.

You can say that someone imposes a **curb** on something.

This requires a <u>curb</u> on public spending.

Another year of wage <u>curbs</u> is inevitable.

2 'kerb'

 Curb is also the American spelling of the noun **kerb.** There is no difference in

pronunciation. The **kerb** is the raised edge between a pavement and a road.
The taxi pulled into the kerb.
I pulled up at the curb.

curiosity

The following words can all be used to describe a person who is eager to find out about someone's life, or about an event or situation:

curious	inquisitive	interested	nosy	prying

1 **'curious'**
Curious is a neutral word, which does not show approval or disapproval.
Steve was intensely curious about the world I came from.

2 **'interested'**
Interested is usually complimentary when it is used to talk about someone's interest in a person's life.
She put on a good show of looking interested.

3 **'nosy' and 'prying'**
Nosy and **prying** are used to show disapproval.
'Who is the girl you came in with?'–'Don't be so nosy.'
Computer-based records can easily be protected from prying eyes by simple systems of codes.

(i) Note that **prying** is usually used with **eyes**.

4 **'inquisitive'**
Inquisitive is sometimes used to show disapproval, but it can also be neutral or even complimentary.
Mr Courtney was surprised. 'A ring, you say?' He tried not to sound inquisitive.
Up close, he was a man with inquisitive sparkling eyes and a fresh, very down-to-earth smile.

currant - current

These words are both pronounced /kʌrənt/.

1 **'currant'**
Currant is a noun. A **currant** is a small dried grape.
…dried fruits such as currants, raisins and dried apricots.

2 **'current' used as a noun**
Current can be a noun or an adjective.
A **current** is a steady and continuous flowing movement of some of the water in a river or lake, or in the sea.
The child had been swept out to sea by the current.

A **current** is also a steady flowing movement of air, or a flow of electricity through a wire or circuit.
I felt a current of cool air blowing in my face.
There was a powerful electric current running through the wires.

3 **'current' used as an adjective**
Current is used to describe things which are happening or being used now, rather than at some time in the past or future.
Our current methods of production are far too expensive.

⇨ Several other words can be used with a similar meaning to **current**. For more information on these, see **Usage** entry at **new**.

USAGE

custom

⇨ See **Usage** entry at **habit - custom.**

customer - client

1 **'customer'**

A **customer** is someone who buys something, especially from a shop.

She's one of our regular <u>customers.</u>

2 **'client'**

A **client** is a person or company that receives a service from a professional person or organization in return for payment.

…a solicitor and his <u>client.</u>

cut

If you **cut** something, you use something such as a knife or pair of scissors in order to remove a piece of it or damage it. The past tense and past participle of 'cut' is **cut,** not 'cutted'.

She <u>cut</u> the cake and gave me a piece.

…the shiny crumpled pictures which she'd carefully <u>cut</u> out of the Sears catalogue.

⇨ For information on words with a similar meaning, see **Usage** entry at **damage.**

D d

damage

1 'damage' and 'harm'

Damage is one of several verbs which refer to ways of causing injury or harm. **Damage** and **harm** are the most general verbs.

It is important for a child to learn that one should not damage someone else's property.
Too much detergent cannot harm a fabric, so long as it has been properly dissolved.

2 severe damage

The following verbs refer to severe damage or harm:

defile	destroy	mangle	pull apart	ruin	wreck
desecrate	devastate	mutilate	ravage	vandalize	

The statue was destroyed.
Shops, cars and houses were ruined in the blasts.

Defile and **desecrate** are used to refer to damage done to something precious, pure, or sacred.

They began to find their places of worship desecrated with blood and mud.

3 damage to someone's body

The following verbs refer to damage done to a person's body:

bruise	injure	stab	wound

Every year thousands of people are injured in accidents at work.
During the war he had been wounded in Africa.

Injure and **wound** are the most general terms, although **wound** is used mainly to refer to injuries caused in fighting. If someone **is bruised**, their skin is not broken but a purple mark appears. People **are stabbed** with something pointed, such as a knife.

⇨ See also **Usage** entries at **injure** and **wound.**

4 spoiling

The following verbs refer to acts which spoil the appearance or surface of something:

deface	disfigure	scar	smudge	stain
discolour	mark	smear	spoil	

He was strongly cautioned against defacing the walls with obscenities.
When he untied the bundle in his kitchen, there were five oily guns staining the white cloth.

Deface, disfigure, mark, and **spoil** are the most general terms.

5 cutting

The following verbs are used to refer to damage done with a knife, axe, or other sharp instrument:

cut	hack	nick	scratch	slice
chop	lacerate	pierce	sever	slit
gash	lop off	score	slash	

Their clothes were slashed to ribbons.
The wire had been neatly severed.

USAGE

If you **cut, chop, hack, lop, slash,** or **slice** part of something **off,** you remove it.

Most of my hair had to be <u>cut off.</u>

Only **lop** has to be used with **off**; you can use the other five verbs without 'off' to refer to damage that does not remove part of the object.

You can also **sever** part of something. **Sever** is a formal word.
One constable's hand <u>was severed</u> by a sword blow.

If you **score** or **scratch** something, you make a thin line in its surface. If you **nick** something, you make a small cut in it. The other verbs refer to bigger or deeper cuts.

6 **dividing into pieces**

The following verbs refer to dividing something hard by force into two or more pieces, or dividing one part of it from another:

break	crack	shatter	snap	split
chip	fracture	smash	splinter	

A crowd of youths started <u>smashing</u> windows.
<u>Crack</u> the eggs into a bowl.

If you **chip** or **splinter** something, you break a small piece of it off. If you **crack** something, a line appears where two parts of it are no longer joined. The other verbs refer to more serious damage.

You **tear, rip,** or **shred** cloth or paper.
She took the cheque and <u>tore</u> it into pieces.
A twig <u>ripped</u> a hole in my sleeve.

You **burst** something that is completely full of air or liquid, such as a balloon.

If you **crumble, crush,** or **pulverize** something, you press it so that it becomes a mass of small pieces.
I <u>crumbled</u> bread in my hands.
Peel and <u>crush</u> the garlic.

7 **changing the shape**

The following verbs refer to acts which damage something by changing its shape:

bend	dent	squash
crumple	flatten	twist

He <u>crumpled</u> each picture and threw it on the floor.
The large bronze urns <u>were dented</u> beyond restoring.

Crush can also be used with this meaning when you are talking about cloth or paper.
Her dress had got <u>crushed.</u>

dare

The verb **dare** has two meanings.

1 **main meaning**

In its main meaning, it is normally used only in negative sentences and questions.
If you say that someone **daren't** do something, you mean that they do not have enough courage to do it.
I <u>daren't</u> ring Jeremy again.

 Note that in American English, the contraction 'daren't' is not used. American English uses the full form **dare not** instead.
I <u>dare not</u> leave you here without protection.

If you are talking about the past, you say that someone **did not dare** do something or **didn't dare** do something. In formal writing, you can say that someone **dared not** do something.

She <u>did not dare</u> leave the path.
I <u>didn't dare</u> speak or move.
He <u>dared not</u> show that he was pleased.

A 'to'-infinitive is sometimes used after **did not dare.**

She <u>did not dare to</u> look at him.
He <u>did not dare to</u> walk to the village.

In other kinds of negative sentence, you can use an infinitive with or without 'to' after **dare.**

No one <u>dares</u> disturb him.
No other manager <u>dared to</u> compete.

In 'yes/no'-questions, you put the base form **dare** in front of the subject without using an auxiliary or modal. After the subject, you use an infinitive without 'to'.

Should she write to the girl? <u>Dare</u> she write?
<u>Dare</u> she go in?

(i) Note that you use the base form whether you are talking about the present or the past. In 'wh'-questions, you use a modal such as **would** in front of **dare.** After **dare,** you can use either a 'to'-infinitive or an infinitive without 'to'.

Who <u>would dare to</u> tell him?
What bank <u>would dare</u> offer such terms?

2 **'I dare say'**

You say **I dare say** or **I daresay** to indicate that you think that something is probably true.

It's worth a few pounds, <u>I dare say,</u> but no more.
Well, <u>I daresay</u> you've spent all your money by now.

(i) Note that **I dare say** is a fixed phrase which cannot be varied. You do not say, for example, 'You dare say' or 'I dare to say'.

3 **used as a transitive verb**

In its other meaning, **dare** is a transitive verb. If you **dare** someone to do something dangerous, you challenge them to do it.

I <u>dare</u> you to spend the night in the graveyard.

data

Data is information, usually in the form of facts or statistics that can be analysed or used in further calculations.

Such tasks require the worker to process a large amount of <u>data.</u>
This will make the <u>data</u> easier to collect.

Data is usually regarded as an uncount noun and is used with a singular form of a verb.

…the latest year for which data <u>is</u> available.
…whenever the data <u>involves</u> confrontation between nuclear powers.

People usually say **this data,** rather than 'these data'.

Processing <u>this data</u> only takes a moment.
He may be incapable of transferring <u>this data</u> correctly to a patient's records.

However, some people think these uses are incorrect. They say that **data** is the plural form of the noun 'datum', and should therefore be used with a plural form of a verb. They also say that you should talk about **these data,** not 'this data'.

The economic data <u>are</u> inconclusive.
To cope with <u>these data,</u> hospitals bought large mainframe computers.

It is probably best in any kind of formal or scientific writing to use a plural form of a verb with **data** and to talk about **these data** rather than 'this data'. In other situations, you can use either form.

USAGE

day

1 **'day'**

A **day** is one of the seven twenty-four hour periods in a week.

The attack occurred six days ago.
Can you go any day of the week? What about Monday?

You also use **day** to refer to the time when it is light and when people are awake and doing things. When **day** has this meaning, you can use it either as a count noun or an uncount noun.

The days were dry and the nights were cold.
…a typical working day.
They had waited three days and three nights for this opportunity.
The festivities would go on all day.

2 **'today'**

You refer to the actual day when you are speaking or writing as **today.**

I hope you're feeling better today.
I want to get to New York today.

Today is also used to refer to the present period in history.

Today we are threatened on all sides by financial and political crises.

3 **'the other day'**

You use **the other day** to indicate that something happened fairly recently.

We had lunch the other day at our favourite restaurant.
The other day, I met one of the world's finest violinists.

4 **referring to a particular day**

If you want to refer to a particular day when an event happened or will happen, you usually use a prepositional phrase beginning with **on.**

We didn't catch any fish on the first day.
On May Day we sat as honoured foreign guests in T'ien-an Men Square.
On the day after the race try to jog.

If you have already been talking about events that happened during a particular day, you can say that something else happened **that day.**

Then I took a bath, my second that day.
Later that day Mason was taken by police car from Barlinnie back to the High Court.

You can also say that something had happened **the day before** or **the previous day.**

The day before Kate had worn scarlet shorts for tennis.
My belongings had been taken from me the previous day.

You can also say that something happened **the next day** or **the following day.**

The next day the revolution broke out.
We were due to meet Hamish the following day.

When you have been talking about a particular day in the future, you can say that something will happen **the following day** or **the day after.**

The selectors will meet tomorrow evening and their team will be named the following day.
I could come the day after.

5 **'every day'**

If something happens regularly on each day, you say that it happens **every day.**

You would see her there every day in the summer.
Third, eat at least five portions of fruit and vegetables every day.

⚠ **WARNING:** Do not confuse **every day** with the adjective **everyday.**
⇨ For an explanation of the differences, see **Usage** entry at **everyday - every day.**

6 | **'these days' and 'nowadays'**
You use **these days** when you are talking about things that are happening now, in contrast to things that happened in the past.

If you need medical help abroad these days, it can run into a small fortune.
Bob was drunk, as usual these days.

Nowadays is used in a similar way.

Kids nowadays are lazy.
Why don't we ever see Jim nowadays?

7 | **'in those days'**
You say **in those days** when you are describing a situation in the past which no longer exists.

In those days there were only a handful of professional cricketers in Australia.
Life was so much simpler in those days.

8 | **'one day'**
You use **one day** to say that something will happen at some indefinite time in the future.

Maybe he'll be Prime Minister one day.
Don't cry, Julie, I'll come back one day, I promise.

In stories, **one day** is used when a writer has just described a situation and is mentioning the first of a series of events.

One day a man called Cayley came in to pay his electricity bill.

9 | **other uses**
There are several ways in which **day** or **days** can be used to refer to a particular period in history.

In Shakespeare's day, women's parts were played by male actors.
She wrote in the early days of the republic.
In these days of vaccination measles and mumps are not so common as they used to be in my young days.

ⓘ Note that when you use **day** or **days** like this in an adjunct, the preposition you use in the adjunct is always **in**.

dead

1 | **used as an adjective**
Dead is usually an adjective. Someone who is **dead** is no longer living. You can use **dead** to talk about someone who has just died, or about someone who died a long time ago.

The body of the dead woman lay covered by the steps of the farmhouse.
He was shot dead in a gunfight.

You can also say that animals or plants are **dead**.

The disease was caused by using protein from dead sheep in cattle feed.
Mary threw away the dead flowers.

⚠ **WARNING:** Do not confuse **dead** with **died**. **Died** is the past tense and past participle of the verb 'die'. You do not use **died** as an adjective.

2 | **used as a noun**
You can refer to a group of people who have died as **the dead**.

Among the dead was a five-year-old girl.

deaf

If someone is **deaf**, they are unable to hear anything, or unable to hear very well.

She was deaf as well as short-sighted.

ⓘ Note that you do not say that someone's 'ears are deaf'.

USAGE

deal

1 **'a great deal' and 'a good deal'**

A **great deal** or a **good deal** of something is a lot of it. **A great deal** is more common than **a good deal**.

There was a great deal of concern about energy shortages.
She drank a good deal of coffee with him in his office.

(*i*) Note that these expressions can only be used with uncount nouns. You can talk, for example, about **a great deal of money**, but not about 'a great deal of apples'.

A great deal and **a good deal** can also be adjuncts. If you do something **a great deal** or **a good deal**, you spend a lot of time doing it.

They talked a great deal.

⇨ For a graded list of similar adjuncts, see section on **degree** in **Grammar** entry at **Adjuncts**.

2 **'deal with'**

When you **deal with** a situation or problem, you do what is necessary to achieve the result you want.

They learned to deal with any sort of emergency.

The past tense and past participle of 'deal' is **dealt** /dɛlt/, not 'dealed'.

When they had dealt with the fire, another crisis arose.

If a book, speech, or film **deals with** a particular subject, it is concerned with it.

The book deals with the pursuit of Rommel's army after El Alamein.
The film deals with a strange encounter between two soldiers.

3 **'deal in'**

If someone **deals in** a particular type of goods, they sell them.

They deal in antiques.
...the New Power Group, which deals in heavy machinery.

definitely

⇨ See **Usage** entry at **surely**.

delay - cancel - postpone - put off

1 **'delay'**

If you **delay** doing something, you do it at a later time.

The government delayed granting passports to them until a week before their departure.
Try and persuade them to delay some of the changes.

If a plane, train, ship, or bus **is delayed**, it is prevented from leaving or arriving on time.

The coach was delayed for about five hours.
The flight has been delayed one hour, due to weather conditions.

2 **'cancel', 'postpone' and 'put off'**

Cancel and **postpone** are used to talk about events that have been arranged in advance. To **cancel** an event means to decide officially that it will not take place.

The performances were cancelled because the leading man was ill.
The powerboat championships at Poole were cancelled yesterday because of poor weather.

To **postpone** or **put off** an event means to arrange for it to take place at a later time than was originally planned.

The crew did not know that the invasion had been postponed.
This is not a decision that can be put off much longer.
The Association has put the event off until October.

delighted - delightful

[1] **'delighted'**

If you are **delighted,** you are very pleased and excited about something.

He was <u>delighted</u> with his achievement.
He was <u>delighted</u> to meet them again.

You do not use words such as 'very' or 'extremely' in front of **delighted.** If you want to say that someone is extremely pleased and excited, you can say that they are **absolutely delighted.**

They were <u>absolutely delighted</u> with François from the start.

You do not use words such as 'fairly', 'quite', or 'almost' in front of **delighted.**

⇨ For a graded list of words that indicate how pleased someone is, see **Usage** entry at **pleased - disappointed.**

[2] **'delightful'**

Do not confuse **delighted** with **delightful.** If you say that someone or something is **delightful,** you mean that they are very pleasant and attractive.

Her children really are <u>delightful</u>.
…a <u>delightful</u> room.

delusion

⇨ See **Usage** entry at **illusion - delusion.**

demand

Demand can be a noun or a verb.

[1] **used as a noun**

A **demand** for something is a firm request for it.

…his <u>demands</u> for stronger armed forces.
There have been <u>demands</u> for services from tenants up there.

[2] **used as a verb**

If you **demand** something, you ask for it very forcefully.

They <u>are demanding</u> higher wages.
I <u>demand</u> to see a doctor.
She <u>had been demanding</u> that he visit her.

(*i*) Note that when **demand** is a verb, you do not use 'for' after it.

demonstration

A **demonstration** is a public meeting or march in which people show their opposition to something or their support for something. You usually say that people **hold** or **stage** a demonstration.

French students <u>held</u> violent <u>demonstrations</u> against plans to lower the legal minimum wage for first-jobbers.
Hundreds of people <u>staged a demonstration</u> outside the UN.

(*i*) Note that you do not say that people 'make' a demonstration.

deny

[1] **'deny'**

If you **deny** an accusation or a claim, you say that it is not true.

The accused women <u>denied</u> all the charges brought against them.
He <u>denied</u> that he was involved.
Green <u>denied</u> doing anything illegal.

(*i*) Note that **deny** must be followed by an object, a 'that'-clause, or an '-ing' form. You say, for example, 'He accused her of stealing, but she **denied it** '. You do not say 'He accused her of stealing but she denied'.

2 'say no'

If someone answers 'no' to an ordinary question in which they are not accused of anything, you do not say that they 'deny' what they are asked. You do not say, for example, 'I asked him if the train had left, and he denied it'. You say 'I asked him if the train had left, and he **said no**'.

She asked if you'd been in and I <u>said no.</u>
I asked her whether we could have a party and she <u>said no.</u>

3 'refuse'

If someone says that they will not do something, you do not say that they 'deny' it. You say that they **refuse to do** it or **refuse**.

Three employees were dismissed for <u>refusing to join</u> a union.
We asked them to play a game with us, but they <u>refused.</u>

depart

⇨ See **Usage** entry at **leave**.

depend

1 'depend on'

If you **depend on** someone or something or **depend upon** them, you need them in order to survive.

At college Julie had seemed to <u>depend on</u> Simon more and more.
Uruguay's economy <u>has depended</u> heavily <u>on</u> its banking sector.
The factories <u>depend upon</u> natural resources.

You also use **depend on** to say that something will only happen if something else is the case.

The success of the meeting <u>depends</u> largely <u>on</u> whether the chairman is efficient.

⚠ **WARNING: Depend** is never an adjective. You do not say, for example, that someone or something 'is depend' on another person or thing. You say that they are **dependent** on that person or thing.

2 'depending on'

You use **depending on** to say that something varies according to particular circumstances.

This training takes a variable time, <u>depending on</u> the chosen speciality.
There are, <u>depending on</u> the individual, a lot of different approaches.

3 'it depends'

Sometimes people answer a question by saying '**It depends**', rather than 'yes' or 'no'. They usually then explain under what circumstances something might happen or be the case.

Hansen: How are you on puzzles, Mr. Hill? Hill: <u>It depends.</u> Sometimes I do well, and other times I don't.

dependent - dependant

1 used as an adjective

If you are **dependent on** someone or something, you need them in order to survive.

At first, a patient may feel very <u>dependent on</u> the nurses.
...those who are entirely <u>dependent</u> for their welfare <u>on</u> the public services.
All competitively priced newspapers became <u>dependent on</u> advertising.

ⓘ Note that you do not use any preposition except **on** after **dependent**.

2 **used as a noun**

In British English, your **dependants** are the people who you support financially, such as your children.

…shorter or more flexible working hours for people with <u>dependants</u>.

 In American English, this noun is usually spelled **dependent**.

Employees and their <u>dependents</u> are seeking help in greater numbers.

descend

To **descend** means to move downwards to a lower level.

The valley becomes more exquisite as we <u>descend</u>.
The lift <u>descended</u> one floor.

Descend is a formal or literary word. When someone or something moves downwards to a lower level, you normally say that they **go down** or **come down**.

When the last customers left, he <u>went down</u> to the basement.
He stood at the foot of the stairs calling for her to <u>come down</u>.

describe

The verb **describe** can be used either with a direct object or with a 'wh'-clause.

1 **used with a direct object**

When you **describe** someone or something, you say what they are like.

Can you <u>describe your son</u>?
Next he <u>described a drive</u> on a Saturday afternoon.

You can use **describe** with a direct object and an indirect object. The direct object goes first.

He <u>described the murderer</u> in detail <u>to Detective Lieutenant Lipes</u>.
She <u>described the feeling to me</u>.

2 **used with a 'wh'-clause**

Describe can be used in front of various kinds of 'wh'-clause.

The man <u>described what he had seen</u>.
He <u>described how he escaped</u> from prison.

You can use **describe** with an indirect object and a 'wh'-clause. The indirect object goes first.

I can't <u>describe to you what it was like</u>.
I found it difficult to <u>describe to him what had happened</u> in Patricia's house.

⚠ **WARNING:** When you use **describe** with an indirect object, you must put **to** in front of the indirect object. You do not say, for example, '~~I can't describe you what it was like~~'.

description

A **description of** someone or something is an account of what they are like.

They now had a <u>description of</u> Calthrop and a photograph of his head and shoulders.
…his <u>description of</u> army life in Northern Ireland.
…a detailed <u>description of</u> the house.

ⓘ Note that you do not use any preposition except **of** after **description**.

desert - dessert

1 **'desert'**

Desert can be a noun or a verb. The noun and the verb are pronounced differently. A **desert** /dezət/ is a large area of land where there is very little water or rain, no trees, and very few plants.

…the Sahara <u>Desert</u>.

When people or animals **desert** /dɪzɜːrt/ a place, they leave it, with the result that it becomes empty.

Poor farmers <u>are deserting</u> their parched farm fields and coming here looking for jobs.

If one person **deserts** another, they leave them and no longer help or support them.

Mrs Roding's husband <u>deserted</u> her years ago.

If a member of the armed forces **deserts,** he or she leaves without permission and without intending to return.

I knew something was wrong when he <u>deserted</u> from the army a couple of years ago.

2 'dessert'

Dessert /dɪzɜːrt/ is sweet food served at the end of a meal.

For <u>dessert</u> there was ice cream.

desire

Desire can be a noun or a verb.

1 used as a noun

A **desire** is a feeling that you want something or want to do something. You usually talk about a **desire for** something or a **desire to do** something.

…a tremendous <u>desire for</u> liberty.
Stephanie felt a strong <u>desire for</u> coffee.
He had not the slightest <u>desire to go</u> on holiday.

(*i*) Note that you never talk about a 'desire for doing' something.

2 used as a verb

If you **desire** something, you want it. This is a formal or literary use.

She had remarried and <u>desired</u> a child with her new husband.
Everything you <u>desire</u> can be found in India.

(*i*) Note that when **desire** is a verb, you do not use 'for' after it.

despite

⇨ See **Usage** entry at **in spite of - despite.**

dessert

⇨ See **Usage** entry at **desert - dessert.**

destroy - spoil - ruin

1 'destroy'

If you **destroy** something, you damage it so completely that it can no longer be used.

Several apartment buildings <u>were destroyed</u> by the bomb.
I <u>destroyed</u> the letter as soon as I had read it.

⇨ For information about other words that can be used to describe severe damage, see **Usage** entry at **damage.**

2 'spoil' and 'ruin'

If someone or something prevents an experience from being enjoyable, you do not say that they 'destroy' the experience. You say that they **spoil** it or **ruin** it.

Go and welcome your guests. I hope I've not <u>spoiled</u> things.
The evening had been <u>spoiled</u> by Charles Boon and Mrs Zapp.
Back injury is an unpleasant complaint to suffer from. It's <u>ruined</u> many people's holidays.
The weather had completely <u>ruined</u> their day.

detail - details

1 'detail'

A **detail** is an individual feature or element of something.

I can still remember every single <u>detail</u> of that night.
He described it down to the smallest <u>detail.</u>

2 **'details'**

If you obtain **details** of something, you obtain information about it.

You can get <u>details</u> of nursery schools from the local authority.
A pamphlet with further <u>details,</u> describing the course, is available from the Arts Registry.

ⓘ Note that you do not say that you obtain 'detail' of something.

deter

To **deter** someone **from doing** something means to prevent them from doing it or to persuade them not to do it.

During the war, a flood would not <u>have deterred</u> me <u>from going</u> there on foot.
This did not <u>deter</u> Ealing council <u>from passing</u> a motion commending the police for their 'courage and patience'.

ⓘ Note that you do not say that something deters someone 'to do' something.

device - devise

1 **'device'**

Device /dɪvaɪs/ is a noun. A **device** is an object that has been made or built for a particular purpose, such as recording or measuring something.

...a <u>device</u> that could measure minute quantities of matter.
...an electronic <u>device.</u>

⇨ For information on other words used to refer to useful objects, see **Usage** entry at **tools.**

2 **'devise'**

Devise /dɪvaɪz/ is a verb. If you **devise** a plan, system, or machine, you have the idea for it and you work it out or design it.

The challenge was to <u>devise</u> a proposal that kept costs to a minimum.
Year by year we <u>devise</u> more precise instruments with which to observe the planets.

die

When a person, animal, or plant **dies,** they stop living. The other forms of **die** are **dies, dying, died.**

We thought we were going to <u>die.</u>
Every day people <u>were dying</u> there.
Blake <u>died</u> in January, aged 76.

When someone dies as a result of a disease or injury, you can say that they **die of** the disease or injury or **die from** it.

An old woman <u>dying of</u> cancer was taken into hospital.
His first wife <u>died from</u> cancer in 1971.
Many of the injured sailors <u>died of</u> their wounds.
Simon Martin <u>died from</u> brain injuries caused by blows to the head.

ⓘ Note that you do not use any preposition except **of** or **from** after **die** in sentences like these.

⇨ See also **Usage** entry at **dead.**

die - dye

These words are both pronounced /daɪ/.

1 **'die'**

Die is a verb. When a person, animal, or plant **dies,** they stop living. The other forms of 'die' are **dies, dying, died.**

USAGE

⇨ See **Usage** entries at **die** and **dead**.

2 'dye'

Dye is both a noun and a verb. If you **dye** something such as hair or cloth, you change its colour by soaking it in a coloured liquid. This liquid is called a **dye**. The other forms of the verb 'dye' are **dyes, dyeing, dyed**.

She mixed finely pounded indigo leaves to <u>dye</u> her cloth deep blue.
Dip them in a yellow <u>dye</u>.

---

differ

If two things are different from each other in some way, you can say that one thing **differs from** the other. **Differ** is a fairly formal word.

Schoolchildren's needs <u>differ from</u> those of adults.
How does it <u>differ from</u> what's happening in Poland?
The problems the Chinese face <u>differ</u> importantly <u>from</u> those facing Africa.

(*i*) Note that you do not use any preposition except **from** after **differ**.

difference - distinction

1 'difference'

The **difference** between things is the way or ways in which they are not the same.

Is there much <u>difference</u> between British and European law?
There is an essential <u>difference</u> between computers and humans.
Look at their <u>difference</u> in size.

If something **makes a difference** to a situation, it changes it.

This insight into the causes of truancy certainly <u>makes a difference</u> to staff attitudes.
The fact that she considered herself engaged to Ashton <u>made no difference</u> to his feelings for her.

2 'distinction'

If someone points out that two things are different, you do not say that they 'make a difference' between the things. You say that they **make a distinction** or **draw a distinction** between them.

It is important to <u>make a distinction</u> between claimants who are over retirement age and those who are not.
I don't like <u>making a distinction</u> between male writers and female writers.
He <u>draws a distinction</u> between art and culture.

---

different

1 'different'

If one thing is **different from** another, it is unlike the other thing in some way.

The meeting was <u>different from</u> any that had gone before.
Health is <u>different from</u> physical fitness.

Many British people say that one thing is **different to** another. **Different to** means the same as **different from**.

Work can be said to be <u>different to</u> a career.
Morgan's law books were <u>different to</u> theirs.

(*i*) Note that some people object to this use. In conversation, you can use either **different from** or **different to**, but in writing it is better to use **different from**.

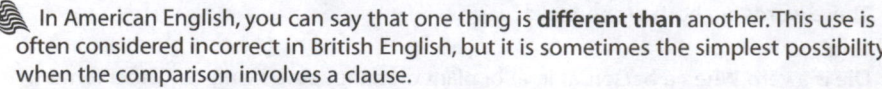 In American English, you can say that one thing is **different than** another. This use is often considered incorrect in British English, but it is sometimes the simplest possibility when the comparison involves a clause.

I am no <u>different than</u> I was 50 years ago.

2 **'very different'**

If there is a great difference between two things, you can say that one thing is **very different from** the other.

The firm is now <u>very different from</u> the firm of the 1980's.

ⓘ Note that you do not say that one thing is 'much different' from another.

If two things are quite similar, you can say that one thing is **not very different from** the other or **not much different from** the other.

I discovered that things were <u>not very different from</u> what I had seen in New York.
Hedda's story is <u>not much different from</u> that of many battered women.

3 **'no different'**

If two things are alike, you can say that one thing is **no different from** the other.

The fields seemed <u>no different from</u> equivalent fields in Iowa.

ⓘ Note that you do not say that one thing is 'not different' from another.

difficulty

1 **'difficulty'**

A **difficulty** is something that prevents you from doing something easily.

There are a lot of <u>difficulties</u> that have to be overcome.
The main <u>difficulty</u> is a shortage of time.

2 **'have difficulty'**

If you **have difficulty doing** something or **have difficulty in doing** something, you are unable to do it easily.

More and more couples seem to <u>be having difficulty starting</u> a family.
She was a girl who <u>had</u> great <u>difficulty in learning</u> to read and write.

ⓘ Note that you do not say that someone 'has difficulty to do' something.

dignity

The following words can all be used to describe someone who behaves in a calm, serious way:

dignified	grave	pompous	solemn	stuffy
formal	po-faced	self-important	staid	

1 **'dignified'**

Dignified is a complimentary word.

Doctors were respected everywhere. They always looked clean and <u>dignified</u>.

2 **'formal', 'grave' and 'solemn'**

Formal, grave, and **solemn** are neutral words, which do not show approval or disapproval.

'How is your mother?' Daintry asked with <u>formal</u> politeness.
…as she explains the concept of gross national product to her <u>solemn</u> students.

3 **'staid'**

Staid is fairly uncomplimentary.

The others are a pretty <u>staid</u> lot.

4 **'po-faced' 'pompous', 'self-important' and 'stuffy'**

Po-faced, pompous, self-important, and **stuffy** are used to show disapproval. **Po-faced** and **stuffy** are not used in formal writing.

He was somewhat <u>pompous</u> and had a high opinion of his own capabilities.
His irrepressible irreverence has frequently landed him in trouble with the <u>stuffy</u> and <u>self-important</u>.

USAGE

dinner - lunch - luncheon

1 'dinner'

People usually call their main meal of the day **dinner.** Some people have this meal in the middle of the day, and others have it in the evening.

Tell him his <u>dinner</u>'s in the oven.

I haven't had <u>dinner</u> yet.

2 'lunch'

People who call their evening meal 'dinner' usually refer to a meal eaten in the middle of the day as **lunch.**

What did you have for <u>lunch</u>?

I'm going out to <u>lunch</u>.

3 'luncheon'

Luncheon is a formal word for 'lunch'.

…a private <u>luncheon</u> at the Aldwych club.

⇨ See **Topic** entry at **Meals.**

directly - direct

1 'directly' and 'direct'

Directly is most commonly used to say that something does not involve an intermediate stage or action, or another person.

They denied having negotiated <u>directly</u> or indirectly with the terrorists.

Plants get their energy <u>directly</u> from the sun.

I shall be writing to you <u>directly</u> in the next few days.

Instead of saying that you receive something 'directly' from someone, you can say that you receive it **direct** from them.

Other money comes <u>direct</u> from industry.

If it does emerge that you are out of pocket, you will be reimbursed <u>direct</u>.

Similarly, instead of saying that one person writes 'directly' to another, you can say that they write **direct** to them.

I should have written <u>direct</u> to the manager.

2 movement

Directly is also used to talk about movement. If you go **directly** to a place, you go there by the shortest possible route, without calling anywhere else.

I had expected to spend a few days in New York, then go <u>directly</u> to my place in Cardiff-by-the-Sea.

You can also say that someone goes **direct** to a place.

Why hadn't he gone <u>direct</u> to the lounge?

⚠ **WARNING:** If you can travel to a place by one plane, train, or bus, without changing to another plane, train, or bus, you do not say that you can go there 'directly'. You say that you can go there **direct.**

You can't go to Manchester <u>direct</u>. You have to change trains at Birmingham.

3 looking at something

If you look straight at a person or thing, you can say that you are looking **directly** at them.

She turned her head and looked <u>directly</u> at them.

4 position

If something is **directly** above, below, opposite, or in front of something else, it is exactly in that position.

USAGE

The sun was almost directly overhead.
I take a seat almost directly opposite the governor.

5 **saying when something happens**

You can also use **directly** to say that something will happen very soon. This is a rather old-fashioned use. In more modern English, **very soon** or **in a moment** are used instead.

She's in a meeting at the moment but she will be here directly.
We'll be up directly. Just take your own things with you.

If you say that you will do something **directly,** you mean that you will do it immediately. This is also a rather old-fashioned use.

I'll move back into my old room directly.
Harrowby asked me to show you to his room directly.

If something happens **directly after** something else, it happens immediately after it.

Directly after the meeting, a senior cabinet minister spoke to the BBC.
Honeysuckle should be pruned directly after flowering.

In British English (but not American English), **directly** is also used as a conjunction to say that one thing happens immediately after another.

Directly he heard the door close, he picked up the telephone.
Directly I saw the word Pankot it occurred to me that you must have known Colonel Layton and his family.

dirty

Something that is **dirty** has dust, mud, or stains on it and needs to be cleaned.

… dirty marks on the walls.

You can also say that a person is **dirty.**

The children were hot, dirty, and exhausted.

You do not use words such as 'completely' or 'absolutely' with **dirty.** If you want to emphasize that someone or something is covered in a lot of dirt, you say that they are **very dirty** or **really dirty.**

'I'm very dirty because of the gas crisis down here and I can't face a cold shower,' she said.
Before washing soak really dirty blankets in the bath.

disabled

⇨ See **Usage** entry at **crippled.**

disagree - refuse

1 **'disagree'**

If you **disagree with** a person, statement, or idea, you have a different opinion of what is true or correct.

I disagree completely with John Taylor.
I disagree with much of what he says.

ⓘ Note that you do not use any preposition except **with** when you are mentioning the person, statement, or idea that you disagree with.

You can say that you **disagree with** someone **about** something.

I disagree with them about cycle maintenance.

You can also say that two or more people **disagree about** something.

He and I disagree about it.
Historians disagree about the date at which these features ceased to exist.

2 **'refuse'**

If someone indicates that they will not do something, you do not say that they 'disagree' to do it. You say that they **refuse** to do it.

USAGE

Don't let a sleepy baby <u>refuse</u> to be put to bed.
The pupils <u>had refused</u> to go home for their lunch.

⇨ See **Usage** entry at **refuse**.

disappear

If someone or something **disappears,** they go or are taken to a place where they cannot be seen or cannot be found.

I saw him <u>disappear</u> round the corner.
She <u>disappeared</u> down the corridor.
Tools <u>disappeared</u> and were never found.
…a certain tin of fruit that <u>disappeared</u> from the school larder.

ⓘ Note that you do not use **disappeared** as an adjective. If you cannot find something because it is not in its usual place, you do not say that it 'is disappeared'. You say that it **has disappeared.**

He discovered that a pint of milk <u>had disappeared</u> from the pantry.
By the time the examiners got to work, most of the records <u>had disappeared.</u>

disappointed

⇨ See **Usage** entry at **pleased - disappointed**.

disc - disk

In British English, a **disc** is a flat circular object.

A traffic warden pointed out that I had no car tax <u>disc</u> on the windscreen.
…an identity <u>disc.</u>

 In American English, this word is spelled **disk**.

…the <u>disk</u> identity in Johnson's lower back.

In both British and American English, a **disk** is also a flat circular plate which is used to store large amounts of information for use by a computer.

The <u>disk</u> is then slotted into a desktop PC.
The image data may be stored on <u>disk.</u>

discourage

To **discourage** someone **from doing** something means to make them less willing to do it.

She wants to <u>discourage</u> him <u>from marrying</u> the girl.
The rain <u>discouraged</u> us <u>from going</u> out.

ⓘ Note that you do not say that you discourage someone 'to do' something.

discover

⇨ See **Usage** entry at **find**.

discuss

If you **discuss** something with someone, you talk to them seriously about it.

She could not <u>discuss</u> his school work with him.
We need to <u>discuss</u> where we go from here.
We <u>discussed</u> whether to approach officials Thurgood knew in the police department.

ⓘ Note that **discuss** is always followed by a direct object, a 'wh'-clause, or a 'whether'-clause. You cannot say, for example, 'I discussed with him' or 'They discussed'.

discussion - argument

1 'discussion'

If you have a **discussion** with someone, you have a serious conversation with them.

My next discussion with him took place a year later.
After the lecture there was a discussion.

You say that you have a discussion **about** something or a discussion **on** something.
I had been involved in discussions about this with Ted and Frank.
We're having a discussion on leisure activities.

2 **'argument'**

You do not use **discussion** to refer to a disagreement between people, especially one that results in them shouting angrily at each other. This kind of disagreement is usually called an **argument**.
He and David had been drawn into a ferocious argument.
I said no, and we got into a big argument over it.

disease

⇨ See **Usage** entry at **illness - disease**.

disinterested - uninterested

1 **'disinterested'**

You use **disinterested** to describe someone who is not involved in a situation and can therefore make fair decisions or judgements about it.
I'm a disinterested observer.

Some people also use **disinterested** to say that someone is not interested in something or someone.
Her mother had always been disinterested in her.

2 **'uninterested'**

However, this use is often regarded as incorrect. Instead of 'disinterested', it is better to say **uninterested**.
Lionel was uninterested in the house.
Etta appeared totally uninterested.

disk

⇨ See **Usage** entry at **disc - disk**.

dislike

If you **dislike** someone or something, you find them unpleasant.
From what I know of him I dislike him intensely.
She disliked the theatre.

You can say that someone **dislikes doing** something.
I dislike falling below the standard I have set for myself.
I grew to dislike working for the cinema.

ⓘ Note that you do not say that someone 'dislikes to do' something.

⇨ For a graded list of words and expressions used to indicate how much someone likes or dislikes something, see **Usage** entry at **like - dislike**.

dismount - get off

1 **'dismount'**

If you **dismount** from a bicycle or horse, you get down from it so that you are standing next to it.
The police officer dismounted from his bicycle.
It is sometimes necessary to dismount and lead the horse for a while.

2 **'get off'**

Dismount is a formal word. You normally say that someone **gets off** a bicycle or horse.

The wind got so strong that I could no longer bicycle against it; I <u>got off</u> and walked.
He had <u>got off</u> his horse and come into the woods.

---

dispose - get rid of

1 **'dispose'**

If you **dispose of** something that you no longer want or need, you throw it away or give it to someone.

Miles of telex tape had to be <u>disposed of</u>.
…the safest means of <u>disposing of</u> nuclear waste.

ⓘ Note that you must use **of** after **dispose**. You do not say that someone 'disposes' something.

2 **'get rid of'**

Dispose is a fairly formal word. In conversation, you usually say that someone **gets rid of** something.

Now let's <u>get rid of</u> all this stuff.
There was a lot of rubbish to <u>be got rid of</u>.

---

disqualified

⇨ See **Usage** entry at **unqualified - disqualified**.

---

dissatisfied

⇨ See **Usage** entry at **unsatisfied - dissatisfied**.

---

distance

⇨ For information on ways of expressing distance, see **Topic** entry at **Measurements**.

---

distasteful

⇨ See **Usage** entry at **tasteless - distasteful**.

---

distinct - distinctive - distinguished

1 **'distinct'**

If one thing is **distinct** from another, there is an important difference between them.

Our interests were quite <u>distinct</u> from those of the workers.
…a tree related to but quite <u>distinct</u> from the European beech.

You describe something as **distinct** when it is clear and definite.

I have the <u>distinct</u> feeling that my friend did not realize what was happening.
A <u>distinct</u> improvement had come about in their social outlook.

2 **'distinctive'**

You use **distinctive** to describe things which have a special quality that makes them easy to recognize.

Irene had a very <u>distinctive</u> voice.

3 **'distinguished'**

A **distinguished** person is very successful, famous, or important.

His grandfather had been a <u>distinguished</u> professor at the University.
Limousines dropped off <u>distinguished</u> visitors.

---

distinction

⇨ See **Usage** entry at **difference**.

---

distinguished

⇨ See **Usage** entry at **distinct - distinctive - distinguished**.

disturb - disturbed

1 **'disturb'**

If you **disturb** someone, you interrupt what they are doing and cause them inconvenience.

If she's asleep, don't <u>disturb</u> her.

Sorry to <u>disturb</u> you, but can I use your telephone?

2 **'disturbed'**

The adjective **disturbed** usually has a different meaning. If someone is **disturbed**, they are very upset emotionally and need special care or treatment.

…emotionally <u>disturbed</u> youngsters.

disused - unused - misused

1 **'disused'**

A **disused** place or building is no longer used for its original purpose and is now empty.

The sculpture was stored in a <u>disused</u> lorry factory.

2 **'unused'**

Something that is **unused** has never been used.

A pile of <u>unused</u> fuel lay nearby.

3 **'misused'**

When something **is misused**, it is used in a wrong or careless way.

He wanted to prevent science from <u>being misused.</u>

In some cases pesticides <u>are</u> deliberately <u>misused.</u>

dive

If you **dive**, you jump head-first into water with your arms straight above your head.

He taught me to swim and <u>dive</u> and water-ski.

You also use **dive** to say that someone jumps or rushes in a particular direction.

You can <u>dive</u> off left into St James's Place.

In British English, the past tense for both senses of 'dive' is **dived**. In American English, it is usually **dove** /<u>douv</u>/.

She <u>dived</u> into the water and swam away.

I <u>dove</u> right in after her.

The cashier <u>dived</u> for cover when a gunman opened fire.

Many survivors, though dazed, immediately <u>dove</u> into the debris to free the injured.

do

Do is one of the most common verbs in English. Its other forms are **does, doing, did, done.** It can be an auxiliary or a main verb.

1 **used as an auxiliary**

⇒ For general information on the use of **do** as an auxiliary, see **Grammar** entry at **Auxiliaries.**

⇒ For information on **do** as an auxiliary in questions, see **Grammar** entries at **Questions** and **Question tags.**

⇒ For information on **do** as an auxiliary in negative clauses, see **Usage** entry at **not** and **Grammar** entry at **Imperatives.**

Do has two other special uses as an auxiliary:

2 **used for emphasis**

You can use it to emphasize a statement. The forms **do, does,** and **did** can all be used in this way.

I <u>do feel</u> sorry for Roger.

It <u>does seem</u> strange, his disappearing at the moment.

USAGE

I wanted to go over to the Ramsey's. Later that day, I did drive by.

You can use **do** in front of an imperative when you are urging someone to do something or accept something.

Do help yourself.
Do have a chocolate biscuit.

3 used to focus on an action

You can also use **do** as an auxiliary to focus on an action performed by someone or something.

When you use **do** like this, you put **what** at the beginning of the sentence, followed by a noun or noun group and the auxiliary **do**. After **do**, you put **is** or **was** and an infinitive with or without 'to'.

For example, instead of saying 'Carolyn opened a bookshop', you can say '**What Carolyn did was to open** a bookshop' or '**What Carolyn did was open** a bookshop'.

What Stephen did was to interview a lot of old people.
What it does is draw out all the vitamins from the body.

You can use **all** instead of 'what' if you want to emphasize that just one thing is done and nothing else.

All he did was shake hands and wish me luck.
All she ever does is make jam.

4 used as a main verb

Do is used as a main verb to say that someone performs an action, activity, or task.

We did quite a lot of work yesterday.
I did all the usual things to raise money.
Every decade there is a census which is done in detail.

Do is often used with '-ing' nouns referring to jobs connected with the home, and with nouns referring generally to work.

He does all the shopping and I do the washing.
Have you done your homework yet?
The man who did the job had ten years' training.
He has to get up early and do a hard day's work.

In conversation, **do** is often used instead of more specific verbs. For example, if you **do your teeth,** you brush your teeth. If you **do the flowers,** you arrange some flowers.

Do I need to do my hair?
She had done her breakfast dishes.

⚠ **WARNING:** You do not normally use **do** when you are talking about creating or constructing something. Instead you use **make.**

I like making cakes.
Sheila makes all her own clothes.
An electric blender makes soups, purees and puddings in a few seconds.
Chimpanzees not only use tools but make them.

⇨ See **Usage** entry at **make.**

5 'do your best'

If you **do your best,** you try as hard as you can to achieve something.

I'm sorry. I did my best.

After **do your best** you can use a 'to'-infinitive.

We do our best to make sure it's up-to-date information.
Certainly OPEC countries did their best to obstruct negotiations.

ⓘ Note that you do not say that someone 'makes their best'.

6 **repeating 'do'**

In questions and negative clauses, you often use **do** twice. You use it first as an auxiliary to form the question or negative verb group, and then repeat it as the main verb. The main verb is always in the infinitive form without 'to'.

What <u>did</u> she <u>do</u> all day when she wasn't working?
If this exercise hurts your back <u>do not do</u> it.

7 **'do about'**

You use **about** after **do** in questions and negative clauses when you are talking about ways of dealing with a problem.

What do you <u>do about</u> children's education?
Really there is nothing we can <u>do about</u> it.

(i) Note that you do not use any preposition except **about** in clauses like these.

doubt

Doubt can be a noun or a verb.

1 **used as a noun**

A **doubt** is a feeling of uncertainty about something.

Frank had no <u>doubts</u> about the outcome of the trial.
I had moments of <u>doubt</u>.

2 **'no doubt'**

You add **no doubt** to a statement to say that you are assuming that something is true, although you cannot really be certain about it.

As Jennifer has <u>no doubt</u> told you, we are leaving tomorrow.
The contract for this will <u>no doubt</u> be widely advertised.

If you say **there is no doubt that** something is true, you mean that it is certainly true.

<u>There's no doubt that</u> it's going to be difficult.
<u>There was no doubt that</u> he was in a highly excitable condition.

(i) Note that you must use a 'that'-clause after **there is no doubt.** You cannot use an 'if'-clause or a 'whether'-clause.

⇒ Many other words and expressions can be used to say how certain you are about something. For a graded list, see section on **probability** in **Grammar** entry at **Adjuncts.**

3 **'without doubt'**

Another way of emphasizing that something is true is to add **without doubt** to a statement. This is a rather formal use.

Hugh Scanlon became <u>without doubt</u> one of the most powerful men in Britain.

Note that speakers of American English usually say **without a doubt** rather than **without doubt** , and this expression is not regarded as formal.

It is the best-tasting tomato, <u>without a doubt</u>.

4 **used as a verb**

If you **doubt** whether something is true or possible, you think it is probably not true or possible.

I <u>doubt</u> whether it would have more than a limited appeal.
I <u>doubt</u> if Alan will meet her.

If someone says that something is the case, or asks you if something is the case, you can indicate that you think it is unlikely by saying **'I doubt it'.**

'I believe I know you.'–'<u>I doubt it.</u> I'm Frederica Potter.'
'Do your family know you're here?'– '<u>I doubt it.</u>'

(i) Note that you do not say 'I doubt so'.

USAGE

doubtful - dubious - suspicious

1 'doubtful'

If you feel **doubtful** about something, you are unsure about it or about whether it will happen or be successful.

Do you feel insecure and <u>doubtful</u> about your ability?
It was <u>doubtful</u> he would ever see her again.

2 'dubious'

If you are **dubious** about something, you are not sure whether it is the right thing to do.

Alison sounded very <u>dubious.</u>
The men in charge were a bit <u>dubious</u> about taking women on.

If you describe something as **dubious,** you think it is not completely honest, safe, or reliable.

...his <u>dubious</u> abilities as a teacher.

3 'suspicious'

If you are **suspicious** of a person, you do not trust them and think they might be involved in something dishonest or illegal.

I am <u>suspicious</u> of his intentions.
Miss Lenaut had grown <u>suspicious.</u>

If you describe something as **suspicious,** it suggests behaviour that is dishonest, illegal, or dangerous.

He listened for any <u>suspicious</u> sounds.
...in <u>suspicious</u> circumstances.

downstairs

If you go **downstairs** in a building, you go down a staircase towards the ground floor.

He went <u>downstairs</u> and into the kitchen.
His two older sisters slept <u>downstairs,</u> for they had to be up first.

(*i*) Note that you do not use 'to', 'at', or 'in' in front of **downstairs.**

downward

⇨ See **Usage** entry at **downwards**.

downwards

1 'downwards'

In British English, if you move or look **downwards,** you move or look towards the ground or the floor.

...a lift that is plummeting <u>downwards</u> at speed.
She gazed <u>downwards.</u>

Downwards is only used as an adverb.

2 'downward'

Speakers of American English usually say **downward** instead of 'downwards'.

The blood from the wound spread <u>downward.</u>
He kept his head on one side as he spoke, looking <u>downward.</u>

In both British and American English, **downward** is an adjective. A **downward** movement or look is one in which someone or something moves or looks downwards.

She made a bold <u>downward</u> stroke with the paintbrush.
...a <u>downward</u> glance.

When **downward** is an adjective, you can only use it in front of a noun.

dozen

1 'dozen'

You can refer to twelve things as **a dozen** things.

… *a dozen eggs.*

When he got there he found more than a dozen men having dinner.

(i) Note that you use **a** in front of **dozen**. You do not talk about 'dozen' things.

You can talk about larger numbers of things by putting a number in front of **dozen**. For example, you can refer to 48 things as **four dozen** things.

On the trolley were two dozen cups and saucers.

They had come in demanding three dozen chocolate chip cookies for a party.

(i) Note that you use the singular form **dozen** after a number. You do not talk about ~~'two dozens cups and saucers'~~. You also do not use 'of' after **dozen**. You do not say ~~'two dozen of cups and saucers'~~.

2 'dozens'

In conversation, you can use **dozens** to talk vaguely about a very large number of things. **Dozens** is followed by **of** when it is used in front of a noun.

She's borrowed dozens of books.

There had been dozens of attempts at reform.

---

draught - draft

Draught and **draft** are both pronounced /drɑːft/.

1 used as nouns

In British English, a **draught** is a current of air coming into a room or vehicle.

The draught from the window stirred the papers on her desk.

They used to open the windows and doors to create a draught.

 In American English, this is spelled **draft**.

A draft of steamy air blew out at them and Meers said, 'Jesus, we left the heat on'.

In British English, **draughts** is a game played by two people with round pieces on a board like a chessboard. This game is called **checkers** in American English.

In both British and American English, a **draft** of a letter, book, or speech is an early version of it.

…the change from the first draft to the final printed version.

He showed me the draft of an article he was writing.

2 'draft' used as a verb

Draft can also be a verb. In both British and American English, when people **are drafted** somewhere, they are moved there to do a particular job.

Extra staff were drafted from Paris to Rome.

 In American English, if you **are drafted,** you are ordered to serve in one of the armed forces.

I was drafted into the navy.

He took a temporary job while he was waiting to be drafted.

In British English, you usually say that someone **is called up**.

He was was called up for National Service in 1950 and served as a driver with the Royal Signals.

---

dream

Dream can be a noun or a verb. The past tense and past participle of the verb is either **dreamed** /driːmd, dremt/ or **dreamt** /dremt/.

USAGE

 Dreamt is not usually used in American English.

1 used as a noun

A **dream** is an imaginary series of events that you experience in your mind while you are asleep.

In his <u>dream</u> he was sitting in a theatre watching a play.

You say that someone **has** a dream.

The other night I <u>had</u> a strange <u>dream.</u>
Sam <u>has bad dreams</u> because soon he will be going to prep school.

(i) Note that you do not usually say that someone 'dreams' a dream.

A **dream** is also an unlikely situation or event that you often think about because you would like it to happen.

My <u>dream</u> is to have a house in the country.
His <u>dream</u> of becoming President had come true.

2 used as a verb

When someone experiences imaginary events while they are asleep, you can say that they **dream** something happens or **dream that** something happens.

I <u>dreamed</u> Marnie was in trouble.
Daniel <u>dreamed that</u> he was back in Minneapolis.

You can also say that someone **dreams about** someone or something or **dreams of** them.

Last night I <u>dreamed about</u> you.
I <u>dreamed of</u> ants converging on us from the whole estate.

When someone thinks about a situation that they would like to happen, you can say that they **dream of having** something or **dream of doing** something.

He <u>dreamed of having</u> a car.
For over a century every small boy <u>dreamed of becoming</u> an engine driver.

You do not say that someone 'dreams to have' something or 'dreams to do' something.

---

dress

1 'dress' and 'get dressed'

When someone **dresses,** they put on their clothes. This use of **dress** occurs mainly in stories.

When he had shaved and <u>dressed,</u> he went down to the kitchen.
Finally he <u>dressed,</u> choosing a thin silk polo-necked sweater.

In conversation, you do not usually say that someone 'dresses'. You say that they **get dressed.**

Please hurry up and <u>get dressed</u>, Morris.
I <u>got dressed</u> and went downstairs.

If you say that someone **dresses** in a particular way, you mean that they usually wear clothes of a particular type.

Over 40? No problem, just <u>dress</u> like a teenager.
I really must try to make him change the way he <u>dresses.</u>

2 'dressed in'

If you want to describe someone's clothes on a particular occasion, you can say that they are **dressed in** something.

He was <u>dressed in</u> a black suit.
He saw people coming towards him dancing, <u>dressed in</u> colourful clothes and feathers.

When a person's clothes are all the same colour, you can say that they are **dressed in** that colour.

All the girls were <u>dressed in</u> white.

3 **'dress up'**

If you **dress up,** you put on different clothes so that you look smarter than usual. People **dress up** in order to go, for example, to a wedding or to an interview for a new job.

I can't be bothered to dress up this evening.

You can say that someone is **dressed up.**

You're all dressed up. Are you going somewhere?

If someone **dresses up as** someone else, they wear the kind of clothes that person usually wears.

He used to dress up as a clown.

⚠ **WARNING:** You only use **dress up** to say that someone puts on clothes which are not their usual clothes. If someone normally wears smart or attractive clothes, you do not say that they 'dress up well'. You say that they **dress well.**

They all had enough money to dress well and buy each other drinks.
We are told by advertisers and fashion experts that we must dress well and use cosmetics.

drink

Drink can be a verb or a noun.

1 **used as a transitive verb**

When you **drink** a liquid, you take it into your mouth and swallow it. The past tense of 'drink' is **drank,** not 'drinked' or 'drunk'.

I drank some of my ginger beer.
We drank a bottle of whisky together.

The past participle is **drunk.**

He was aware that he had drunk too much whisky.

Drunk is also an adjective.

⇨ See **Usage** entry at **drunk - drunken.**

2 **used as an intransitive verb**

If you use **drink** without an object, you are usually referring to the drinking of alcohol.

I never drink alone.
You shouldn't drink and drive.

If you say that someone **drinks,** you mean that they regularly drink too much alcohol.

Her mother drank, you know.
He paid someone to investigate Mr Williams and found he drank and brawled.

If you say that someone **does not drink,** you mean that they do not drink alcohol at all.

She said she didn't smoke or drink.

3 **used as a count noun**

A **drink** is an amount of liquid that you drink.

I asked her for a drink of water.
Lynne brought me a hot drink.

To **have a drink** means to spend some time, usually with other people, drinking alcoholic drinks.

I'm going to have a drink with some friends this evening.

Drinks usually refers to alcoholic drinks.

The drinks were served in the sitting room.
After a few drinks he would get his clarinet out.

4 **used as an uncount noun**

Drink is alcohol.

There was plenty of food and drink at the party.
We are trying to keep him away from drink.

drown

When someone **drowns,** they die because their head is under water and they cannot breathe. You can either say that someone **drowns** or that they **are drowned.** There is no difference in meaning.

She had fallen into the sea and <u>drowned.</u>
They jumped in the river and <u>were drowned.</u>

drugstore

⇨ See **Usage** entry at **chemist's - drugstore - pharmacy.**

drunk - drunken

Drunk is the past participle of the verb 'drink'.

⇨ See **Usage** entry at **drink.**

1 'drunk' used as an adjective

Drunk is also an adjective. If someone is **drunk,** they have drunk too much alcohol and are not in complete control of their behaviour.

The colonel was so <u>drunk</u> that he could barely get his words out.
She was being driven home by an extremely <u>drunk</u> young man.

When someone drinks too much alcohol and loses control of their behaviour, you say that they **get drunk.**

He had decided that he was never going to <u>get drunk</u> again.
We all <u>got</u> happily <u>drunk.</u>

2 'drunken'

Drunken has the same meaning as 'drunk' but it is only used in front of a noun. You do not say that someone 'is drunken'.

…stiffer penalties for <u>drunken</u> drivers.
Groups of <u>drunken</u> hooligans smashed windows and threw stones.

You use **drunken** rather than 'drunk' to describe the behaviour of people who are drunk.

…a long <u>drunken</u> party.
I descended into a deep <u>drunken</u> sleep.

You also use **drunken** rather than 'drunk' to describe people who are often drunk.

Where will she go? Back to her <u>drunken</u> husband in Canada?

dubious

⇨ See **Usage** entry at **doubtful - dubious - suspicious.**

due to

If an event **is due to** something, it happens or exists as a direct result of it.

His death <u>was due to</u> natural causes.
My desire to act <u>was due to</u> Laurence Olivier's performance in 'Hamlet'.

Due to is sometimes used to introduce the reason for an undesirable situation.

<u>Due to</u> repairs, the garage will be closed next Saturday.
The flight has been delayed one hour, <u>due to</u> weather conditions.

This use is fairly common, but some people object to it. Instead of saying 'due to', you can say **owing to** or **because of.**

<u>Owing to</u> the heavy rainfall many of the roads were impassable.
I missed my flight <u>owing to</u> a traffic hold-up.
<u>Because of</u> the law in Ireland, we had to work out a way of getting her over to Britain.
Police closed the Strand <u>because of</u> smoke billowing over the road.

dull - blunt

1 'dull'

If you say that something is **dull,** you mean that it is not interesting.

I thought the book <u>dull</u> and unoriginal.
It will be so <u>dull</u> here without you.

2 'blunt'

In modern English, if a knife is no longer sharp, you do not say that it is 'dull'. You say that it is **blunt.**

Scrape off as much as possible with a <u>blunt</u> knife.

during

1 'during' and 'in'

You usually use **during** to say that something happens continuously or often from the beginning to the end of a period of time.

She heated the place <u>during</u> the winter with a huge wood furnace.
This was evident in the weekly column he wrote for the Guardian <u>during</u> 1963-1964.

In sentences like these, you can almost always use **in** instead of **during.** There is very little difference in meaning. When you use **during,** you are usually stressing the fact that something is continuous or repeated.

⇨ See **Usage** entry at **in.**

You can also use **during** to say that something happens while an activity takes place.

<u>During</u> my years as a pediatrician I learned that child abuse was quite common.
<u>During</u> his visit, the Pope will also bless the new hospital.

You can sometimes use **in** in sentences like these, but the meaning is not always the same. For example, 'What did you do **during** the war?' means 'What did you do while the war was taking place?', but 'What did you do **in** the war?' means 'What part did you play in the war?'

2 single events

Both **during** and **in** can be used to say that a single event happened at some point in the course of a period of time.

He had died <u>during</u> the night.
His father had died <u>in</u> the night.
She left Bengal <u>during</u> the late Spring of 1740.
Mr Tyrie left Hong Kong <u>in</u> June.

It is more common to use **in** in sentences like these. If you use **during,** you are usually emphasizing that you are not sure of the exact time when something happened.

⚠ **WARNING:** You do not use 'during' to say how long something lasts. You do not say, for example, 'I went to Wales during two weeks'. You say 'I went to Wales **for** two weeks'.

duty

⇨ See **Usage** entry at **obligation - duty.**

dye

⇨ See **Usage** entry at **die - dye.**

E e

each

1 | used as a determiner

You use **each** in front of the singular form of a count noun to talk about every person or thing in a group. You use **each** rather than 'every' when you are thinking about the members of a group as individuals.

Each applicant has five choices.
They would rush out to meet each visitor.
Each country is subdivided into several districts.

2 | 'each of'

Instead of using 'each', you can sometimes use **each of**. For example, instead of saying 'Each soldier was given a new uniform', you can say '**Each of** the soldiers was given a new uniform'. **Each of** is followed by a determiner and the plural form of a count noun.

Each of the books has little bits of paper protruding from its pages.
Each of these phrases has a different meaning.
They inspected each of her appliances with care.

You also use **each of** in front of plural pronouns.

He stood smoking his pipe for a good three minutes, making eye contact with each of us.
They were all just sitting there, each of them thinking private thoughts.
Each of these would be a big advance in its own right.

When you use **each of** in front of a plural noun or pronoun, you use a singular form of a verb after the noun or pronoun.

Each of these cases was carefully locked.
Each of us looks over the passenger lists.

⚠ **WARNING:** You never use **each** without **of** in front of a plural noun or pronoun.

If you want to emphasize that something is true about every member of a group, you can say **each one of** instead of 'each of'.

This view of poverty influences each one of us.
An expert lecturer can make each one of his listeners feel that they are the object of his attention.

⚠ **WARNING:** You do not use words such as **almost**, **nearly**, or **not** in front of 'each'. You do not say, for example, 'Almost each house in the street is for sale'. You say 'Almost **every** house in the street is for sale'.

They show great skills in almost every aspect of school life.
Nearly every town has its own opera house.
Not every secretary wants to move up in the world.

You also do not use 'each' or 'each of' in a negative clause. You do not say, for example, 'Each boy did not enjoy football' or 'Each of the boys did not enjoy football'. You say '**None of** the boys enjoyed football'.

None of them are actually African.
None of these suggestions is very helpful.

⇨ See **Usage** entry at **none**.

3 | used after the subject

Each is sometimes used after the subject of a clause. For example, instead of saying 'Each of them received a new pair of boots', you can say '**They each** received a new pair of boots'. In constructions like these, the subject and the verb are always plural.

They each chose a word from the list.
We each have our private views about it.

This type of construction is often used to indicate that an amount relates to each member of a group separately and not to the whole group. For example, if you say 'Arsenal and Everton **each** scored two goals', you are indicating that four goals were scored altogether, not two.

Italy, the UK and Germany each have 2 Commissioners and the other states have 1 each.

When you are talking about an amount like this, you often put **each** at the end of the clause.

They cost eight pounds each.
All three groupings polled 32 per cent each.
…large aluminium cylinders, weighing several tons each.

4 **used as a pronoun**

Each can be used as a pronoun to mean 'each person' or 'each thing'.

Cournoyer, Lemaire, Savard, Lapointe, each is now past thirty.
None of the earlier stages are self-sufficient. Each is a preparation for the next.
If there is more than one convenient hostel, you could spend a few nights at each.

Each one is sometimes used instead of 'each'.

The canoes went skimming down the river with five or six women in each one.
Babies are individuals. This means each one needs to be closely watched.

5 **referring back to 'each'**

You usually use a singular pronoun such as **he**, **she**, **him**, or **her** to refer back to an expression containing **each**.

Each boy said what he thought had happened.

However, when you are referring back to an expression such as **each person** or **each student** which does not indicate a specific sex, you usually use **they** or **them**.

There was to be a flat rate charge for each individual, irrespective of where they lived.

⇨ For a fuller discussion of these uses, see **Usage** entry at **he - she - they**.

each other - one another

1 **uses**

You use **each other** or **one another** when you are talking about actions or feelings that involve two or more people together in an identical way. For example, if Simon likes Louise and Louise likes Simon, you say that Simon and Louise like **each other** or like **one another**. **Each other** and **one another** are sometimes called **reciprocal pronouns**. **Each other** and **one another** are usually the direct or indirect object of a verb.

We help each other a lot.
They sent each other gifts from time to time.
The birds greet one another or change places on the nest.

You can also use them as the object of a preposition.

Terry and Mark were jealous of each other.
They didn't dare to look at one another.

2 **possessives**

You can form possessives by adding **'s** to **each other** and **one another**.

I hope that you all enjoy each other's company.
Apes spend a great deal of time grooming one another's fur.

3 **differences**

There is very little difference in meaning between **each other** and **one another**. **One another** is fairly formal, and many people do not use it at all. Some people prefer to use

USAGE

each other when they are talking about two people or things, and **one another** when they are talking about more than two. However, it is not usual to make this distinction.

easily

⇨ See **Usage** entry at **easy - easily**.

east

1 'east'

The **east** is the direction which you look towards in order to see the sun rise.

Ben noticed the first faint streaks of dawn in the east.
A stiff wind blows up-river from the east.

An **east** wind blows from the east.

It has turned bitterly cold, with a cruel east wind.

The **east** of a place is the part that is towards the east.

…old people in the east of Glasgow.
…a plane which travelled on to the east of the continent.

East occurs in the names of some countries and regions.

…the former Portuguese colony of East Timor.
This beautiful flower grows in grassy places, mainly in East Anglia.
…tribes such as the Masai in East Africa.

⇨ See **Topic** entry at **Capital letters**.

2 'eastern'

However, you do not usually talk about the 'east' part of a country. You talk about the **eastern** part.

…the eastern part of Germany.

Similarly, you do not talk about 'east Europe' or 'east England'. You say **eastern** Europe or **eastern** England.

…the economies of Central and Eastern Europe.
…a scheduled early morning flight from Nancy in eastern France.
…the Eastern Mediterranean.

easterly

If something moves in an **easterly** direction, it moves towards the east.

The yacht was continuing in an easterly direction.

However, an **easterly** wind blows **from** the east.

There was an icy easterly wind blowing off the sea.

The **most easterly** of a group of things is the one that is furthest to the east. The form **easternmost** is also used with the same meaning.

…Indonesia's most most easterly province.
This is the easternmost point in North America.

eastward

⇨ See **Usage** entry at **eastwards**.

eastwards

1 'eastwards'

If you move or look **eastwards**, you move or look towards the east.

They were pressing on eastwards towards the city's small airfield.
I looked out through the window and could see eastwards as far as the distant horizon.

Eastwards is only used as an adverb.

2 'eastward'

 In American English and old-fashioned British English, **eastward** is often used instead of 'eastwards'.

The two cousins hurried <u>eastward</u> against the sharp wind.
He walked back into the field, scanning <u>eastward</u> for dark figures.

In both British and American English, **eastward** is sometimes used as an adjective in front of a noun.

…the <u>eastward</u> expansion of the City of London.

easy - easily

1 'easy'

Something that is **easy** can be done or achieved without effort or difficulty.

Both sides had secured <u>easy</u> victories earlier in the day.
Competitions in the Spectator are never <u>easy</u>.

The comparative and superlative forms of **easy** are **easier** and **easiest**.

This is much <u>easier</u> than it sounds.
This was in many ways the <u>easiest</u> stage.

You can say that **it is easy to do** something. For example, instead of saying 'Riding a camel is easy', you can say '**It is easy to ride** a camel'. You can also say 'A camel **is easy to ride**'.

It is always very <u>easy to be</u> cynical about politics.
The house <u>is easy to keep</u> clean.

2 'easily'

Easy is not an adverb, except in the expressions **go easy**, **take it easy**, and **easier said than done**. If you want to say that something is done without difficulty, you say that it is done **easily**.

Put things in a place where you can find them quickly and <u>easily</u>.
Belgium <u>easily</u> beat Mexico 3-0.

The comparative and superlative forms of **easily** are **more easily** and **most easily**.

Milk is digested <u>more easily</u> when it is skimmed.
These are the foods that are <u>most easily</u> contaminated with poisonous bacteria.

economic

⇨ See **Usage** entry at **economics**.

economical

⇨ See **Usage** entry at **economics**.

economics

1 'economics'

Economics is a noun. It usually refers to the study of the way in which money, industry, and trade are organized.

…the science of <u>economics</u>.
…a degree in <u>economics</u>.

When **economics** has this meaning, it is an uncount noun. You use a singular form of a verb with it.

<u>Economics</u> <u>deals</u> with man in his environment.

If you want to say that something relates to the subject of economics, you use **economics** in front of another noun.

…an <u>economics</u> degree.
…Hull University's <u>economics</u> department.

(i) Note that you do not talk about an 'economic' degree or an 'economic' department.

The **economics** of an industry are the aspects of it which are concerned with making a profit.

…the economics of the timber trade.

When **economics** is used with this meaning, it is a plural noun. You use a plural form of a verb with it.

When this happens, the economics of the industry are dramatically affected.

2 **'economy'**

Economy is a noun. The **economy** of a country or region is the system by which money, industry, and trade are organized there.

New England's economy is still largely based on manufacturing.
Unofficial strikes were damaging the British economy.

Economy is also careful spending or the careful use of things in order to save money.

His seaside home was small for reasons of economy.

3 **'economies'**

If you make **economies,** you try to save money by not spending it on unnecessary things.

It might be necessary to make a few economies.
They will make economies by hiring fewer part-time workers.

4 **'savings'**

However, you do not refer to the money that someone has saved as their 'economies'. You refer to this money as their **savings.**

She drew out all her savings.
Her savings were in the Post Office Savings Bank.

5 **'economic'**

Economic is an adjective. You use it to describe things connected with the organization of money and trade in a country or region. When **economic** has this meaning, you only use it in front of a noun. You do not use it after a verb.

…radical economic reforms.
What has gone wrong with the economic system during the last ten years?

If you say that something is **economic,** you mean that it makes a profit, or does not result in money being lost. When **economic** has this meaning, it can go either in front of a noun or after a verb.

It is difficult to provide an economic public transport service.
We have to keep fares high enough to make it economic for the service to continue.

6 **'economical'**

Economical is also an adjective. It can be used to say that something is cheap to operate or use.

…small, economical cars.
This system was extremely economical because it ran on half-price electricity.

You can also say that a person is **economical** when they do not spend much money.

⇨ Several other words can be used with a similar meaning. For more information, see **Usage** entry at **mean.**

---

economies

⇨ See **Usage** entry at **economics.**

---

economy

⇨ See **Usage** entry at **economics.**

edit - publish

[1] **'edit'**

If you **edit** a text, you examine it and make corrections to it so that it is suitable for publication.

I am indebted most particularly to Mrs Maria Jepps, who checked and edited the entire work.

[2] **'publish'**

Do not confuse **edit** with **publish**. When a company **publishes** a book or magazine, it prints copies of it, which are then sent to shops to be sold.

His latest book of poetry will be published by Faber in May.

educate

⇒ See **Usage** entry at **bring up - raise - educate**.

effect

⇒ See **Usage** entry at **affect - effect**.

effective - efficient

[1] **'effective'**

Something that is **effective** produces the results that it is intended to produce.

… effective street lighting.

Such conditions would make an effective public transport system possible.

[2] **'efficient'**

A person, machine, or organization that is **efficient** does a job well and successfully, without wasting time or energy.

You need a very efficient production manager.

Engines and cars can be made more efficient.

effeminate

⇒ See **Usage** entry at **female - feminine - effeminate**.

efficient

⇒ See **Usage** entry at **effective - efficient**.

effort

If you **make an effort** to do something, you try hard to do it.

Daintry made one more effort to escape.

Little effort has been made to investigate this claim.

(*i*) Note that you do not say that someone 'does an effort'.

either

[1] **used as a determiner**

You use **either** in front of the singular form of a count noun to say that something is true about each of two people or things.

Many children don't resemble either parent.

In either case, Robert would never succeed.

[2] **'either of'**

Instead of using **either**, you can use **either of**. For example, instead of saying 'Either answer is correct', you can say '**Either of** the answers is correct'.

You could hear everything that was said in either of the rooms.

They didn't want either of their children to know about this.

You use **either of** in front of plural pronouns.

I don't know <u>either of them</u> very well.
He was better dressed than <u>either of us</u>.

⚠ **WARNING:** You do not use **either** without **of** in front of a plural noun or pronoun.

Some people use a plural form of a verb after **either of** and a noun group. For example, instead of saying 'I don't think either of you is wrong', they say 'I don't think either of you **are** wrong'.

It's a wonder either of you <u>are</u> here to tell the tale.

This use is acceptable in conversation, but in formal writing you should always use a singular form of a verb after **either of**.

3 **used as a pronoun**

Either can be used on its own as a pronoun. This is a fairly formal use.

<u>Either</u> is acceptable.
I was given two computer print-outs; my name was not on <u>either</u>.

4 **used in negative statements**

You can use **either** or **either of** in a negative statement to emphasize that the statement applies to both of two things or people. For example, instead of saying about two people 'I don't like them', you can say 'I don't like **either of** them'.

She could not see <u>either</u> man.
There was no sound from <u>either of</u> the flats.
'Which one do you want?'–'I don't want <u>either</u>.'

5 **used to mean 'each'**

When you use **either** in front of **side** or **end**, it can have the same meaning as 'each'. For example, 'There were trees on **either side** of the road' means 'There were trees on each side of the road'.

…a narrow road which had small houses built on <u>either side</u> of it.

If you say that two things are on **either side** of something, you mean that one thing is on one side of it and the other thing is on the other side.

The two ladies sat in large armchairs on <u>either side</u> of the stage.
Trenches were dug at <u>either end</u> of the street, closing it to all vehicles.

6 **used as an adverb**

When one negative statement follows another, you can put **either** at the end of the second one.

I can't play tennis and I can't play golf <u>either</u>.
'I haven't got that address.'–'No, I haven't got it <u>either</u>.'

⇒ For other ways of linking two negative statements, see **Usage** entries at **neither** and **nor**.

either ... or

1 **used in affirmative statements**

You use **either** and **or** when you are mentioning two alternatives and you want to indicate that no other alternatives are possible. You put **either** in front of the first alternative and **or** in front of the second one.

Recruits are interviewed by <u>either</u> Mrs Darby <u>or</u> Mr Bootle.
He must have concluded that I was <u>either</u> naive <u>or</u> impudent.
I was expecting you <u>either</u> today <u>or</u> tomorrow.
People <u>either</u> leave <u>or</u> are promoted.
<u>Either</u> she goes <u>or</u> I go.

In conversation, **either** is not always used immediately in front of the first alternative; it is sometimes used in front of a verb earlier in the sentence. For example, instead of saying 'I will ring you either today or tomorrow', people sometimes say 'I will **either** ring you today or tomorrow'.

I suppose you <u>either</u> find it funny or boring.
'How much money do you normally have in your wallet?' – 'I <u>either</u> have £50 <u>or</u> nothing.'

This use is acceptable in conversation, but you should avoid it in formal writing.

2 **used in negative statements**

You use **either** and **or** in negative statements when you are emphasizing that a statement refers to both of two things or qualities. For example, instead of saying 'I haven't been to Paris or Rome', you can say 'I haven't been to **either** Paris **or** Rome'.

He was not the choice of <u>either</u> Dexter <u>or</u> the team manager.
Dr Kirk, you're not being <u>either</u> frank <u>or</u> fair.
This should not be disastrous <u>either</u> morally <u>or</u> politically.

⇨ See also **Usage** entry at **neither … nor.**

elder - eldest - older - oldest

1 **'elder'**

The **elder** of two people is the one who was born first.

Posy was the <u>elder</u> of the two.

If you have a sister or brother who was born before you, you can refer to them as your **elder** sister or brother.

He had none of his <u>elder</u> brother's charm.

2 **'eldest'**

The **eldest** of a group of people, especially the brothers and sisters in a family, is the one who was born first.

Gladys was the <u>eldest</u> of four children.
Her <u>eldest</u> son was killed in the First War.

3 **'older' and 'oldest'**

Elder and **eldest** are slightly formal, and many people do not use them at all. Instead of 'elder' and 'eldest' you can use **older** and **oldest.**

He's my <u>older</u> brother.
Six of their children were there, including the <u>oldest</u>, Luke.

You can use **older** and **oldest** in some ways in which you cannot use 'elder'. For example, you can use **older** after **be**, **get**, or **grow**, and in front of **than**.

Try it when you <u>are</u> a little <u>older</u>.
We're all <u>getting older</u>.
As he <u>grew older</u>, his fascination with bees developed into an obsession.
Harriet was ten years <u>older than</u> I was.

You cannot use 'elder' in any of these ways.

You can also use **older** and **oldest** to talk about things.

On <u>older</u> houses there may be guarantees for treatment against woodworm.
It claims to be the <u>oldest</u> insurance company in the world.

You cannot use 'elder' or 'eldest' to talk about things.

elderly

⇨ See **Usage** entry at **old.**

elect

1 **used as a verb**

Elect is usually a verb. When people **elect** someone, they choose that person to represent them, by voting for them.

They met to <u>elect</u> a president.
Why should we <u>elect</u> him Mayor?
You could <u>be elected</u> as an MP.

⚠ **WARNING:** You only say that someone **is elected** when they are chosen by voting. If they are chosen in some other way, you use another word such as **appoint**, **choose**, **select**, or **pick**.
⇨ See **Usage** entry at **choose**.

2 used as an adjective
Elect is sometimes added after words such as **president** or **governor** to indicate that someone has been appointed to a post but has not officially started to carry out their duties. When **elect** has this meaning, it is only used immediately after a noun.
…*the President elect.*

⚠ **WARNING:** You do not use 'elect' as an adjective simply to say that someone has been elected by voting. Instead you use **elected** in front of a noun.
…*a democratically elected government.*
…*the newly elected president.*

electric - electrical - electronic

1 'electric'
You use **electric** in front of nouns to talk about machines or devices that use electricity.
…*an electric motor.*
I switched on the electric fire.

2 'electrical'
You use **electrical** when you are talking in a more general way about machines, devices, or systems which use or produce electricity. **Electrical** is typically used in front of nouns such as **equipment**, **appliance**, and **component**.
… *electrical appliances such as dishwashers and washing machines.*
…*shipments of electrical equipment.*

You also use **electrical** to talk about people or organizations connected with the production of electricity or electrical goods.
… *electrical engineers.*
…*the electrical and mechanical engineering industries.*

3 'electronic'
You use **electronic** to talk about a device which has transistors or silicon chips which control and change the electric current running through the device, or to describe a process or activity using electronic devices.
…*expensive electronic equipment.*
… *electronic surveillance systems.*

elevator
⇨ See **Usage** entry at **lift**.

else

1 used with 'someone', 'somewhere' and 'anything'
You use **else** after words such as **someone**, **somewhere**, or **anything** to refer to another person, place, or thing, without saying which one.
… *someone else's house.*
Let's go somewhere else.
I had nothing else to do.

2 used with 'wh'-words
You can use **else** after most 'wh'-words. For example, if you ask 'What else did they do?', you are asking what other things were done besides the things that have already been mentioned.

What else do I need to do?
Who else was there?
Why else would he be so willing to plead guilty?
Where else could they live in such comfort?
How else was I to explain what had happened?

(*i*) Note that you do not use 'else' after 'which'.

3 **'little else' and 'much else'**
Else is often used after **little** and **much**. If you say, for example, 'There was **little else** I could do', you mean that there were not many additional things that you could do.
There was little else he could say.
The firm had grown big by bothering about profits and very little else.
My excuse was that I had so much else to do.

4 **'or else'**
Or else is a conjunction with a similar meaning to 'or'. You use it to introduce the second of two possibilities.
You are either a total genius or else you must be absolutely raving mad.
It's likely that someone gave her a lift, or else that she took a taxi.

You also use **or else** when you are mentioning the undesirable results that will occur if someone does not do a particular thing.
You've got to be very careful or else you'll miss the turn-off into our drive.

embark
⇨ See **Usage** entry at **go into**.

embarrassed
⇨ See **Usage** entry at **ashamed - embarrassed**.

emigration - immigration - migration

1 **'emigrate', 'emigration', 'emigrant'**
If you **emigrate**, you leave your own country and go to live permanently in another country.
He received permission to emigrate to Canada.
He had emigrated from Germany in the early 1920's.

You refer to the process by which people leave their own country in order to live somewhere else as **emigration**.
Famine and emigration made it the most depopulated region on the island.

People who emigrate are called **emigrants**.
Thousands of emigrants boarded Cunard ships for the New World.

2 **'immigrant', 'immigration'**
When emigrants arrive in the country where they intend to live, they are referred to as **immigrants**.
…a Russian immigrant.
A ship carrying 54 illegal immigrants sailed into the harbour yesterday.

You refer to the process by which people come to live in a country as **immigration**.
She asked for his views on immigration.
… immigration procedures.

3 **'migrate', 'migration', 'migrant'**
When people **migrate**, they temporarily move to another place, usually a city or another country, in order to find work.
The only solution people can see is to migrate.
Millions have migrated to the cities.

USAGE

This process is called **migration.**
Housebuilding in the south-east has accelerated, encouraging migration from the north.
Migration for work is accelerating in the Third World.

People who migrate are called **migrants** or **migrant workers.**
… migrants looking for a place to live.
In South America alone there are three million migrant workers.

4 **another meaning of 'migrate'**
When birds or animals **migrate,** they move from one place to another at the same time each year.
Texas is the first landfall of most birds migrating north.
Every spring they migrate towards the coast.

employ - use

1 **'employ'**
If you **employ** someone, you pay them to work for you.
The companies employ 7.5 million people between them.
He was employed as a research assistant.

If something **is employed** for a particular purpose, it is used for that purpose. You can say, for example, that a particular method or technique **is employed.**
A number of ingenious techniques are employed.
The methods employed are varied, depending on the material in question.

You can also say that a machine, tool, or weapon **is employed.**
Similar technology could be employed in the major cities.
What matters most is how the tools are employed.

2 **'use'**
However, **employ** is a formal word when it is used to talk about such things as methods or tools. You usually say that a method or tool **is used.**
This method has been extensively used in the United States.
These weapons are used against human targets.

employment
⇨ See **Usage** entry at **work.**

enable
⇨ See **Usage** entry at **allow - permit - let - enable.**

end

1 **'end'**
When something **ends** or when you **end** it, it stops.
The current agreement ends on November 24.
He refused to end his nine-week-old hunger strike.

2 **'end with'**
If you **end with** something, it is the last of a series of things that you say, do, or perform.
He ended with the question: 'When will we learn?'
Whatever the concert was, we always ended with 'Spread a Little Happiness'.

3 **'end by'**
If you **end by doing** something, it is the last of a series of things that you do.
I ended by saying that further instructions would be given to him later.
We talked of various things and he ended by playing me some Bach on the piano.

4 **'end up'**
End up is used in conversation to say what happens to someone at the end of a series of

events. You can say that someone **ends up** in a particular place, that they **end up with** something, or that they **end up** doing something. You do not use 'end up' in formal writing.

I had to change to another train and I ended up at Banbury, which is 20 miles away.
She was afraid to close the window and ended up with a cold.
We ended up taking a taxi there.

endure
⇨ See **Usage** entry at **bear**.

engaged
When two people have agreed to marry each other, or have announced formally that they are going to be married, you can say that they are **engaged**.

They were not officially engaged.
…an engaged couple.

You can also say that each person is **engaged**.

He's just got engaged.
As an engaged girl, she would be unable to accept invitations from other men.

You say that someone is **engaged to** the person they are going to marry.

Sonny was formally engaged to Sandra.

ⓘ You do not say that someone is 'engaged with' the person they are going to marry.

engine
⇨ See **Usage** entry at **machine - motor - engine**.

engineer - engine driver

1 **'engineer'**

An **engineer** is a skilled person who uses scientific knowledge to design and construct machinery, electrical devices, or roads and bridges.

He trained as a civil engineer and worked on the M4 motorway.
…a brilliant young mining engineer.

An **engineer** is also a person who repairs mechanical or electrical devices.

The telephone engineer can't come until Wednesday.

In American English, a person who drives a train is also called an **engineer**.

An engineer pulled his freight train into a siding.

2 **'engine driver'**

In British English, a person who drives a train is called an **engine driver**.

Every little boy has an ambition to be an engine driver.

English
English can be an adjective or a noun.

1 **used as an adjective**

English means 'belonging or relating to England, its people, or its language'.

My wife's English.
…an English pub.
…the English language.

English is sometimes used to mean 'belonging or relating to Great Britain'. However, it is better to avoid this use, as it may cause offence to people who come from Scotland, Wales, or Northern Ireland.

2 **used as a noun**

English is the language spoken in Britain, the United States, and many other countries.

Do you speak English?

Half the letter was in Swedish and half in English.

English is also the study of the English language or English literature.

Karen obtained A levels in English, French, and Geography.

…an English lesson.

People who come from England are sometimes referred to as **the English.**

The English love privacy.

You can sometimes refer to a group of English people, for example supporters of the England football team, as **the English.**

Why do so many of us love to see the English being beaten in sport?

3 **'Englishman' and 'Englishwoman'**

You do not refer to a single English person as an 'English'. You refer to them as an **Englishman** or an **Englishwoman.**

Not a single Englishman was arrested.

…a beautiful Englishwoman.

⇨ See also **Usage** entry at **Britain - British - Briton.**

enjoy

1 **'enjoy'**

If you **enjoy** something, you get pleasure and satisfaction from it.

I enjoyed the holiday enormously.

Enjoy is normally only a transitive or reflexive verb. You do not say 'I enjoyed'. However, some American speakers say '**Enjoy!**', meaning 'Enjoy yourself'.

2 **used with a reflexive pronoun**

If you experience pleasure and satisfaction on a particular occasion, you can say that you **enjoyed yourself.**

I've enjoyed myself very much.

People often say '**Enjoy yourself**' to someone who is going to a social occasion such as a party or a dance.

Enjoy yourself on Wednesday.

3 **used with an '-ing' form**

You can say that someone **enjoys doing** something or **enjoys being** something.

I used to enjoy going for long walks.

They enjoyed being in a large group.

ⓘ Note that you do not say that someone 'enjoys to do' or 'enjoys to be' something.

enough

1 **after adjectives and adverbs**

You use **enough** after an adjective or adverb to say that someone or something has as much of a quality as is needed.

We have a long enough list.

It seemed that Henry had not been careful enough.

The student isn't trying hard enough.

If you want to say who the person or thing is acceptable to, you add a prepositional phrase beginning with **for.**

That's good enough for me.

If you find that the white wine is not cold enough for you, ask for some ice to be put in it.

If you want to say that someone has as much of a quality as they need in order to do something, you add a 'to'-infinitive after **enough.**
The children are <u>old enough to travel to school on their own.</u>

You can also use a 'to'-infinitive after **enough** to say that something has as much of a quality as is needed for someone to be aware of it or to do something with it. Between **enough** and the 'to'-infinitive you put a prepositional phrase beginning with **for.**
It's not even <u>big enough for him to have a kitchen.</u>

Another way of saying that something has as much of a quality as is needed for something to be done with it is simply to add a 'to'-infinitive after **enough.** For example, instead of saying 'The boat was close enough for me to touch it', you can say 'The boat was **close enough to touch** '.
None of the crops was <u>ripe enough to eat.</u>
Some employers claim that women don't stay <u>long enough to train.</u>

⚠ **WARNING:** You do not use a 'that'-clause after **enough** when you are saying what is needed for something to be possible.

Enough is sometimes used after an adjective to confirm or emphasize that something or someone has a particular quality.
It's a <u>common enough</u> dilemma.

When you make a statement of this kind, you often add a second statement that contrasts with it.
She's <u>likeable enough,</u> but very ordinary.

2   used as a determiner
Enough is used in front of the plural form of a count noun to say that there are as many things or people as are needed.
They need to make sure there are <u>enough bedrooms</u> for the family.
I asked Professor Bailey whether there were <u>enough women</u> going into engineering.

You can also use **enough** in front of an uncount noun to say that there is as much of something as is needed.
We had <u>enough room</u> to store all the information.
He hasn't had <u>enough exercise.</u>

3   'enough of'
You do not use **enough** immediately in front of a noun group beginning with a determiner, or in front of a pronoun. Instead you use **enough of.**
All parents worry about whether their child is getting <u>enough of the right foods.</u>
There was <u>enough of an economic surplus</u> to support a church-building program.
They haven't had <u>enough of it.</u>

When you use **enough of** in front of a plural noun or pronoun, you use a plural form of a verb with it.
Eventually enough of these shapes <u>were</u> collected.
There <u>were</u> enough of them to form an identifiable group.

When you use **enough of** in front of a singular or uncount noun or a singular pronoun, you use a singular form of a verb with it.
There <u>has</u> always been enough of the colonial tradition to make it easy to evoke these responses.
There <u>is</u> enough of it for everybody.

4   used as a pronoun
Enough can be used on its own as a pronoun.
I've got <u>enough</u> to worry about.
<u>Enough</u> has been said about this already.

5 **'not enough'**

You do not use **enough,** or **enough** and a noun, as the subject of a negative sentence. You do not say, for example, 'Enough people didn't come'. You say '**Not enough** people came'.

Not enough has been done to help them.
Not enough attention is paid at the design stage of the machinery.

6 **modifying adverbs**

You can use adverbs such as **nearly, almost, just, hardly,** and **quite** in front of **enough.**

This was nearly enough to lose them their chance of winning.
At present there is just enough to feed them.
There was hardly enough time to get the by-pass completed.

You can also use these adverbs in front of an expression consisting of an adjective and **enough.**

We are all nearly young enough to be mistaken for students.
Some of these creatures are just large enough to see with the naked eye.
…children who are hardly old enough to be out on their own.

7 **used with sentence adverbs**

You can use **enough** after sentence adverbs like **interestingly** or **strangely** to draw attention to a surprising quality in what you are saying.

Interestingly enough, there were some questions that Brian couldn't answer.
I find myself strangely enough in agreement with John for a change.
Funnily enough, old people seem to love bingo.

enquire

⇨ See **Usage** entry at **inquire - enquire.**

ensure

⇨ See **Usage** entry at **assure - ensure - insure.**

enter - go into - come into

1 **'enter'**

If you **enter** a room or building, you go into it.

Colonel Rolland entered a small cafe.

Enter can be used without an object.

They stopped talking as soon as they saw Brody enter.

2 **'go into' and 'come into'**

Enter is a rather formal word, and you do not usually use it in conversation. Instead you say that someone **goes into** or **comes into** a room or building.

He shut the street door behind me as I went in.
Boylan came silently into the room.

(*i*) Note that you never say that someone 'enters' a car, train, ship, or plane.

⇨ For more information, see **Usage** entry at **go into.**

entirely

⇨ See section on **extent** in **Grammar** entry at **Adjuncts.**

envious - enviable

1 **'envious'**

If you are **envious,** you wish you had something such as a possession, quality, or ability that someone else has.

We see them doing things we are not allowed to do, and are envious.

You say that you are **envious of** a person or **envious of** something that they have.

…a girl who is deeply envious of her brother.
They may be envious of your success.

2 **'enviable'**

You use **enviable** to describe a possession, quality, or ability that someone has, and that you wish you had yourself.

They have enviable reputations as athletes.
She learned to speak foreign languages with enviable fluency.

equally

You use **equally** in front of an adjective to say that a person or thing has as much of a quality as someone or something else that has been mentioned.

He was a superb pianist. Irene was equally brilliant.

ⓘ You do not use 'equally' in front of **as** when making a comparison. You do not say, for example, 'He is equally as tall as his brother'. You say 'He is **just as tall as** his brother'.

Severe sunburn is just as dangerous as a heat burn.
He was just as shocked as I was.

⇨ See **Usage** entry at **as … as.**

equipment

Equipment consists of the things you need for a particular activity.

…kitchen equipment.
…fire-fighting equipment.

Equipment is an uncount noun. You do not talk about 'equipments' or 'an equipment'. You can refer to a single item as a **piece of equipment**.

He knows how vitally important a piece of equipment your radio is.
The leader carried a number of pieces of equipment with him.

error

An **error** is a mistake.

The doctor committed an appalling error of judgement.
… errors in grammar.

You can say that something is done **in error**. This is a fairly formal use.

They had arrested him in error.
Another village had been wiped out in error.

In conversation, you usually say that something is done **by mistake**.

I opened the door into the library by mistake.

ⓘ Note that you do not say that something is done 'by error'.

escape

The verb **escape** has several meanings. For some of these meanings, it is a transitive verb. For others, it is an intransitive verb.

1 **used as a transitive verb**

If you **escape** a situation that is dangerous, unpleasant, or difficult, you succeed in avoiding it.

They are also emigrating to escape mounting economic problems there.
He seemed to escape the loneliness of extreme old age.
They want to escape responsibility for what they have done.

If you cannot **escape** a feeling or belief, you cannot help having it.

One cannot escape the feeling that there is something missing.
It is difficult to escape the conclusion that they are actually intended for the black market.

USAGE

2 **used as an intransitive verb**

If you **escape from** a place where you are in danger, you succeed in leaving it.

Last year thousands escaped from the country in small boats.

If you **escape from** a place such as a prison, you get out of it and are free.

In 1966 the spy George Blake escaped from prison.
Even if he managed to escape, where would he run?

ⓘ Note that you do not say that someone 'escapes' a prison or any other place.

If you **escape** when someone is trying to catch you, you avoid being caught.

The two other burglars were tipped off by a lookout and escaped.

3 **'get away'**

Get away can be used with the same meaning.

George Watin got away and is presumed to be living in Spain.

---

especially - specially

1 **used in front of adjectives**

These adverbs have a similar meaning when they are used in front of adjectives. For example, you can emphasize that something is very useful by saying that it is **especially** useful or **specially** useful.

He found his host especially irritating.
…a pub where the beer was specially good.

 Note that speakers of American English would only use **especially** in this structure.

2 **used in other positions**

When **especially** and **specially** are not used in front of adjectives, their meanings are different.

You use **especially** to indicate that what you are saying applies more to one thing or situation than to others.

He was kind to his staff, especially those who were sick or in trouble.
Double ovens are a good idea, especially if you are cooking several meals at once.

When **especially** relates to the subject of a sentence, you put it immediately after the subject.

Children's bones, especially, are very sensitive to radiation.

You use **specially** to say that something is done or made for a particular purpose.

They'd come down specially.
…a specially designed costume.
The school is specially for children whose schooling has been disrupted by illness.

---

ethic - ethics - ethical

1 **'ethic'**

A particular **ethic** is an idea or moral belief that influences the behaviour and attitudes of a group of people.

…the ethic of public service.
…the Protestant work ethic.

2 **'ethics'**

Ethics are moral beliefs and rules about right and wrong. When you use **ethics** with this meaning, it is a plural noun. You use a plural form of a verb with it.

Such action was a violation of medical ethics.

Ethics is also the study of questions about what is morally right or wrong. When **ethics** has this meaning, it is an uncount noun. You use a singular form of a verb with it.

We are only too ready to believe that ethics is a field where thinking does no good.

3 **'ethical'**

Ethic is never an adjective. The adjective that means 'relating to ethics' is **ethical**.

…an <u>ethical</u> problem.

He had no real <u>ethical</u> objection to drinking.

---

even

1 **position**

You use **even** to indicate that what you are saying is surprising. You put **even** in front of the surprising part of your statement.

<u>Even</u> Anthony enjoyed it.

She liked him <u>even when she was quarrelling with him.</u>

I shall give the details to no one, not <u>even to you.</u>

However, **even** usually goes after an auxiliary or modal, not in front of it.

You <u>didn't even enjoy</u> it very much.

They <u>may even give</u> you a lift in their van.

They <u>wouldn't even talk</u> to me.

2 **used with comparatives**

You use **even** in front of a comparative to emphasize that someone or something has more of a quality than they had before. For example, you say 'The weather was bad yesterday, but it is **even worse** today'.

He became <u>even more suspicious</u> of me.

They were <u>even more drunk</u> than they had been when we hired them.

You also use **even** in front of a comparative to emphasize that someone or something has more of a quality than someone or something else. For example, you say 'The train is slow, but the bus is **even slower**'.

Barber had something <u>even worse</u> to tell me.

The identification of Tutankhamun's mother is <u>even more difficult.</u>

3 **'even if' and 'even though'**

Even if and **even though** are used to introduce subordinate clauses. You use **even if** to say that a possible situation would not prevent something from being true.

<u>Even if</u> you disagree with her, she's worth listening to.

I hope I can come back, <u>even if</u> it's only for a few weeks.

Even though has a similar meaning to 'although', but is more emphatic.

Gregory, Platt, and Lydon will play <u>even though</u> they are not fully fit.

I was always afraid of men, <u>even though</u> I had lots of boyfriends.

⚠ **WARNING:** If you begin a sentence with **even if** or **even though,** you do not put 'yet' or 'but' at the beginning of the main clause. You do not say, for example, ~~'Even if you disagree with her, yet she's worth listening to'~~.
However, you can use **still** in the main clause. This is a very common use.

<u>Even though</u> the news is six months old, BBC staff are <u>still</u> in shock.

But <u>even if</u> they do change the system, they've <u>still</u> got an economic crisis on their hands.

4 **'even so'**

You use **even so** to emphasize that something is true in spite of what you have just said.

Their feathers are constantly shed and renewed. <u>Even so</u> they need constant care.

The bus was only half full. <u>Even so,</u> a young man asked Nina if the seat next to her was taken.

---

evening

The **evening** is the part of each day between the end of the afternoon and the time when you go to bed.

USAGE

1 the present day

You refer to the evening of the present day as **this evening.**

Come and have a drink with me this evening.
I came here this evening because I particularly wanted to be on my own.

You can refer to the evening of the previous day as **yesterday evening,** but it is more common to say **last night.**

'So you saw me in King Street yesterday evening?' –'Yes.'
I met your husband last night.
I've been thinking about what we said last night.

You refer to the evening of the next day as **tomorrow evening** or **tomorrow night.**

Gerald's giving a little party tomorrow evening.
Will you be home in time for dinner tomorrow night?

2 single events in the past

If you want to say that something happened during a particular evening in the past, you use **on.**

She telephoned Ida on Tuesday evening.
On the evening after the party, Dick went to see Roy.

If you have been describing what happened during a particular day, you can say that something happened **that evening** or **in the evening.**

That evening the children asked me to watch television with them.
He came back in the evening.

If you are talking about a day in the past and you want to mention that something had happened during the evening of the day before, you say that it had happened **the previous evening** or **the evening before.**

Duggan had registered the previous evening at a hotel.
Fanny picked up the grey shawl Bet had given her the evening before.

If you want to say that something happened during the evening of the next day, you say that it happened **the following evening.**

Mopani arrived at Hunter's Drift the following evening.
I told Patricia that I would take her to Cranthorpe the following evening.

In stories, if you want to say that something happened during an evening in the past, without saying which evening, you say that it happened **one evening.**

One evening I drove out to Winndom.
We had him to supper one evening when Paul was here.

You can also say, for example, that something happened **one April evening** or **on a Saturday evening.**

One mild May evening he asked me over to inspect it.
Mac picked me up on a Friday evening.

3 talking about the future

If you want to say that something will happen during a particular evening in the future, you use **on.**

The winning project will be announced on Monday evening.
I will write to her on Sunday evening.

If you are already talking about a day in the future, you can say that something will happen **in the evening.**

The school sports day will be on June 22 with prizegiving in the evening.

4 regular events

If something happens regularly every evening, you say that it happens **in the evening** or **in the evenings.**

A 2-year-old may keep climbing out of bed in the evening to rejoin the family.

In the evening I like to lay breakfast as this is one less job for the morning.
And what do you do in the evenings?

Note that in American English, **evenings** can be an adverb, and does not require phrases with 'in' or 'on'.

Canadian teenage girls insist on going out evenings with friends.

However, if you want to say that something happens regularly once a week during a particular evening, you use **on** followed by the name of the day and **evenings.**

Am I no longer allowed to play chess on Monday evenings?
We would all gather there on Friday evenings.

Here again, American English does not require 'on'.

Friday evenings he packed up to go and stay in his father's new apartment in the suburbs.

5 **exact times**

If you have mentioned an exact time and you want to make it clear that you are talking about the evening rather than the morning, you add **in the evening.**

He arrived about six in the evening.

eventually - finally

Do not confuse **eventually** and **finally.**

1 **'eventually'**

When something happens after a lot of delays or complications, you can say that it **eventually** happens.

Eventually they got to the hospital.
I found Victoria Avenue eventually.

You can also use **eventually** to talk about what happens at the end of a series of events, often as a result of them.

Eventually, they were forced to return to England.

2 **'finally'**

You say that something **finally** happens after you have been waiting for it or expecting it for a long time. When you use **finally** like this, you put it in front of the verb, if there is no auxiliary.

When John finally arrived, he said he'd lost his way.
The heat of the sun finally became too much for me.

If there is an auxiliary, you put **finally** after it.

Parliament had finally legalized trade unions.

You can also use **finally** to show that something happens last in a series of events.

The sky turned red, then purple, and finally black.

You can also use **finally** to introduce a final point, ask a final question, or mention a final item.

Finally, Carol, are you encouraged by the direction education is taking?

ever

1 **'ever'**

Ever is used in negative sentences, questions, and comparisons to mean 'at any time in the past' or 'at any time in the future'.

Neither of us had ever skied.
I don't think I'll ever be homesick here.
Did he ever play football?
I'm happier than I've ever been.

2 **'yet'**

You do not use 'ever' in questions or negative sentences to ask whether an expected

USAGE

event has happened, or to say that it has not happened so far. You do not say, for example, 'Has the taxi arrived ever?' or 'The taxi has not arrived ever'. The word you use is **yet.**

Have you had your lunch yet?
It isn't dark yet.

⇨ See **Usage** entry at **yet.**

3 **'always'**

You do not use 'ever' in positive sentences to say that there was never a time when something was not the case. You do not say, for example, 'I've ever been happy here'. The word you use is **always.**

She was always in a hurry.
Talking to Harold always cheered her up.

⇨ See **Usage** entry at **always.**

4 **'still'**

You do not use 'ever' to say that something is continuing to happen. You do not say, for example, 'When we left Lowestoft, it was ever raining'. The word you use is **still.**

Unemployment is still falling.
She was still beautiful.
I was still a schoolboy.

⇨ See **Usage** entry at **still.**

5 **'ever since'**

If something has been the case **ever since** a particular time, it has been the case all the time from then until now.

'How long have you lived here?'–'Ever since I was married.'
We have been devoted friends ever since.

6 **'ever so' and 'ever such'**

In conversation, you can use **ever so** in front of an adjective to emphasize the degree of something.

They are ever so kind.

If the adjective is part of a noun group, you use **ever such** instead of 'ever so'. **Ever such** always goes in front of **a** or **an.**

I had ever such a nice letter from her.

 You do not use 'ever so' or 'ever such' in formal writing, and neither of these constructions is common in American English.

7 **'ever' with 'wh'-words**

Sometimes people use **ever** after a 'wh'-word at the beginning of a sentence. They do this to express surprise. For example, instead of saying 'Who told you that?', they say '**Who ever** told you that?'

Who ever would have thought that?
'I'm sorry. I'd rather not say.'–'Why ever not?'
How ever did you find me?

When these questions appear in writing, **what ever, where ever,** and **who ever** are sometimes written as single words: **whatever, wherever,** and **whoever.**

Whatever is the matter?
Wherever did you get this?
Whoever heard of a bishop resigning?

However, many people consider these forms to be incorrect, and it is better to write **what ever, where ever,** and **who ever** as two separate words. **How ever** and **why ever** are always written as two separate words.

every

1 **'every'**

You use **every** in front of the singular form of a count noun to indicate that you are referring to all the members of a group and not just some of them.

She spoke to every person at the party.
I agree with every word Peter says.
This new wealth can be seen in every village.

2 **'every' and 'all'**

You can often use **every** or **all** with the same meaning. For example, 'Every dog should be registered' means the same as 'All dogs should be registered'.
However, **every** is followed by the singular form of a noun, whereas **all** is followed by the plural form.

Every child is entitled to be educated at the state's expense.
All children love to build and explore.

⇨ See **Usage** entry at **all**.

3 **'each'**

Instead of 'every' or 'all', you sometimes use **each**. You use **each** when you are thinking about the members of a group as individuals.

Each customer has the choice of thirty colours.
Each meal will be served in a different room.

⇨ See **Usage** entry at **each**.

4 **referring back to 'every'**

You usually use a singular pronoun such as **he**, **she**, **him**, or **her** to refer back to an expression beginning with **every**.

Every businessman would do without advertising if he could.

However, when you are referring back to an expression such as **every student** or **every inhabitant** which does not indicate a specific sex, you usually use **they** or **them**.

Every passenger and crew member is the doctor's patient, and there's no escape from them.

⇨ For a fuller discussion of these uses, see **Usage** entry at **he - she - they**.

5 **used with expressions of time**

You use **every** to indicate that something happens at regular intervals.

They met every day.
Every Monday Mr Whymper visited the farm.

(*i*) **Every** and **all** do not have the same meaning when they are used with expressions of time. For example, if you do something **every morning**, you do it regularly each morning. If you do something **all morning**, you spend the whole of one morning doing it.

He used to walk into his club every afternoon at three o'clock.
Her voice was hoarse. 'You have a cold?'–'No. It's just from talking all afternoon.'
He had been running three miles every day.
That person has been following us all day.

6 **'every other'**

If something happens, for example, **every other** year or **every second** year, it happens one year, then does not happen the next year, then happens the year after that, and so on.

We only save enough money to take a real vacation every other year.
It seemed easier to shave every second day.

everybody

⇨ See **Usage** entry at **everyone - everybody**.

USAGE

everyday - every day

1 **'everyday'**

Everyday is an adjective. You use it to describe something which is normal and not exciting or unusual in any way.

…the everyday problems of living in the city.
A paint finish can transform something everyday and mundane into something more elaborate.

2 **'every day'**

Every day is an adjunct. If something happens **every day,** it happens regularly each day.

Shanti asked the same question every day.

---

everyone - everybody

1 **'everyone' and 'everybody'**

You usually use **everyone** or **everybody** to refer to all the people in a particular group. There is no difference in meaning between **everyone** and **everybody.**

The police had ordered everyone out of the office.
There wasn't enough room for everybody.

You can also use **everyone** and **everybody** to talk about people in general.

Everyone has the right to freedom of expression.
Everybody has to die some day.

In conversation, **everyone** and **everybody** are sometimes used to mean 'a lot of people'.

…the war that everyone had said could never happen.
'Do you know him at all?'–'Everybody knows Lonnie.'

After **everyone** or **everybody** you use a singular form of a verb.

Everyone wants to find out what is going on.
Everybody is selling the same product.

2 **referring back**

When you are referring back to **everyone** or **everybody,** you usually use **they, them,** or **their.**

Will everyone please carry on as best they can.
Everybody had to empty their purses.

⇨ For a discussion of these uses, see **Usage** entry at **he - she - they.**

3 **'every one'**

Do not confuse **everyone** with **every one.** You use **every one** to emphasize that something is true about each one of the things or people you are mentioning.

He read every one of my scripts.
She turned her attention to her friends. Every one had had a good education.

---

everything

You use **everything** to refer to all the objects, actions, activities, or facts in a particular situation.

I don't agree with everything he says.
I will arrange everything.

After **everything** you use a singular form of a verb.

Usually everything is very informal.
Everything happens much more quickly.

ⓘ Note that **everything** is always written as one word. You do not write 'every thing'.

everywhere

Everywhere is an adverb. If you say that something happens or exists **everywhere,** you mean that it happens or exists in all parts of a place or area.

Tap water is drinkable everywhere in the Algarve.
People everywhere are becoming aware of the problem.

You do not usually use a preposition in front of **everywhere.** You do not say, for example, 'He has been to everywhere'. You say 'He has been **everywhere**'. However, you can use **from** with **everywhere.**

They heard from everywhere the lovely clear voices of women singing.
…a strange light that seemed to come from everywhere at once.

 In informal American English, **everyplace** and **every place** are often used instead of 'everywhere'.

He seems to be everyplace and have an opinion about everything.
Almost every place we go we find some type of weapons.

evidence

Evidence is anything that you see, hear, or read which causes you to believe that something is true or has really happened.

We saw evidence everywhere that a real effort was being made to promote tourism.
There was no evidence of quarrels between them.

Evidence is an uncount noun. You do not talk about 'evidences' or 'an evidence'. However, you can talk about a **piece of evidence.**

The finding is the latest piece of evidence that vaccines will in future play an important part in the fight against cancer.
It was one of the strongest pieces of evidence in the Crown's case.

exam - examination

An **exam** or **examination** is an official test that you take part in to show your knowledge or ability in a particular subject. **Exam** is the word most commonly used. **Examination** is more formal and is used mainly in written English.

I was told the exam was difficult.
…a three-hour written examination.

When someone takes part in an exam, you say that they **take** it or **sit** it.

Many children want to take these exams.
After the third term we'll be sitting the exam.

 Note that speakers of American English generally use **take** instead of 'sit'.

In conversation, you can also say that someone **does** an exam.

There is no set time to do this exam.

If someone is successful in an exam, you say that they **pass** it.

Larry passed university exams at sixteen.
They cannot hope to get the kind of job they want even if they pass all their exams.

> ⚠ **WARNING:** To **pass** an exam always means to succeed in it. It does not mean to take part in it.

If someone is unsuccessful in an exam, you say that they **fail** it.

He failed the written paper.
I passed the written part but then failed the oral section hopelessly.

You also say that someone **passes in** or **fails in** a particular subject.

I've been told that I'll probably pass in English and French.
I took it in case I should fail in one of the other subjects.

example 176

USAGE

example

1 'example'

If something has the typical features of a particular kind of thing, you can say that it is an **example** of that kind of thing.

It's a very fine example of traditional architecture.
This is yet another example of British consumers being exploited and asked to pay more.

When someone mentions an example of a particular kind of thing, you say that they are **giving** an example of that kind of thing.

Could you give me an example?
Let me give you an example of the sort of thing that happens.

(*i*) Note that you do not say that someone 'says' an example.

2 'for example'

When you mention an example of something, you often say **for example**.

Japan, for example, has two languages.
There must be some discipline in the home. For example, I do not allow my daughter Zoe to play with my typewriter.

(*i*) Note that you do not say 'by example'.

except

You use **except** to introduce the only thing, person, or group that your main statement does not apply to.

1 used with a noun group

You usually use **except** in front of a noun group.

Anything, except water, is likely to block a sink.
All the boys except Peter started to giggle.

You can use **except** in front of object pronouns such as **me**, **him**, or **her**, or in front of reflexive pronouns such as **himself** or **herself**.

There's nobody that I really trust, except him.
Audrey had allowed no one inside the room except himself.

However, you do not use 'except' in front of subject pronouns. You do not say, for example, 'There's no one here except I'.

⚠ **WARNING:** Do not confuse **except** with **besides** or **unless**. You use **except** when you mention something that a statement does not apply to. **Besides** means 'in addition to'.

What languages do you know besides Arabic and English?

⇨ See **Usage** entry at **beside - besides**.

Unless is used to introduce the only situation in which something takes place or is true.

In the 1940s, unless she wore gloves a woman was not properly dressed.
You must not give compliments unless you mean them.

⇨ See **Usage** entry at **unless**.

2 'but'

After **all** or a word beginning with '**every-**' or '**any-**' you can use **but** instead of 'except'.

All but two of the dead, including six children, were holidaymakers on a bus from Argentina.
It is no longer respectable to marry for anything but love.

3 used with a verb

You cannot use **except** immediately in front of a finite verb. You can, however, use it in front of a 'to'-infinitive.

I never wanted anything except to be an actress.
She seldom goes out except to go to Mass.

After 'do', you can use **except** in front of an infinitive without 'to'.

There was little I could <u>do except wait</u>.
She <u>did nothing except make</u> empty conversation.

4   **used with a finite clause**

You can use **except** in front of a finite clause, but only when the clause is introduced by **when**, **while**, **where**, **what**, or **that**.

He no longer went out, <u>except when Jeannie forced him</u>.
I have every confidence in your wisdom <u>except where this sort of thing is concerned</u>.
I knew nothing about Judith <u>except what I'd heard at second hand</u>.
I can scarcely remember what we ate, <u>except that it was plentiful and simple</u>.

5   **'except for'**

You use **except for** in front of a noun group when you are mentioning something that prevents a statement from being completely true.

The classroom was silent, <u>except for the busy scratching of pens on paper</u>.
The room was very cold and, <u>except for Morris</u>, entirely empty.

⇨ See **Usage** entry at **accept**.

exception

1   **'exception'**

An **exception** is something or someone that a general statement does not apply to.

The troops had the support of the local population, the <u>exception</u> being some environmentalist groups who protested at the noise.
With a few <u>exceptions,</u> the writing is good.

2   **'with the exception of'**

When you are mentioning an exception, you often use the expression **with the exception of**.

We all went, <u>with the exception of</u> Otto, who complained of feeling unwell.
They are all, <u>with the exception of</u> one Swedish coin, of Portuguese origin.

3   **'no exception'**

If you want to emphasize that a general statement applies to a particular person or thing, you can say that they are **no exception**.

We've mentioned the joys of many Greek islands in springtime, and Paxos is <u>no exception</u>.
The Monday following an outing often brings some absentees from school, and today was <u>no exception</u>.

4   **'without exception'**

If you want to emphasize that a statement applies to all the people or things in a group, you can say that it applies to all of them **without exception**.

Every country <u>without exception</u> is committed to economic growth.
<u>Without exception</u> all our youngsters wanted to leave school and start work.

exchange

When people **exchange** things, they give them to each other at the same time.

We <u>exchanged</u> addresses.
They <u>exchanged</u> glances.

If you **exchange** one thing **for** another, you give the first thing to someone and they give the second thing to you.

She <u>exchanged</u> the jewels <u>for</u> money.
Leather goods made in the camp were <u>exchanged for</u> bread and clothing.

excited - exciting

1   **'excited'**

Excited is used to describe how a person feels when they are looking forward eagerly to an enjoyable or special event.

He was so <u>excited</u> he could hardly sleep.
There were hundreds of <u>excited</u> children to meet us.

You say that someone is **excited about** something.

I'm very <u>excited about</u> the possibility of playing for England's first team.

You can say that someone is **excited about doing** something.

Kendra was especially <u>excited about seeing</u> him after so many years.

(*i*) Note that when someone is looking forward to doing something, you do not say that they are 'excited to do' it.

2   'exciting'

Do not confuse **excited** with **exciting**. You use **exciting** to describe something which is enjoyable, special, or unusual and which makes you feel excited.

Growing up in the heart of London was very <u>exciting.</u>
It did not seem a very <u>exciting</u> idea.

excursion

⇨ See **Usage** entry at **journey.**

excuse

Excuse can be a noun or a verb. When it is a noun, it is pronounced /ɪkskjuːs/. When it is a verb, it is pronounced /ɪkskjuːz/.

1   used as a noun

An **excuse** is a reason that you give in order to explain why something has been done, has not been done, or will not be done.

It might be used as an <u>excuse</u> for evading our responsibilities.
There is no <u>excuse</u> for this happening in a new building.

You say that someone **makes** an excuse.

I <u>made</u> an <u>excuse</u> and left.
You don't have to <u>make</u> any <u>excuses</u> to me.

(*i*) Note that you do not say that someone 'says' an excuse.

2   used as a verb

If someone **is excused** from doing something, they are officially allowed not to do it.

She <u>is usually excused</u> from her duties during the school holidays.
You can apply to <u>be excused</u> payment if your earnings are low.

In conversation, if you say you must **excuse** yourself or if you ask someone to **excuse** you, you are indicating politely that you must leave.

Now I must <u>excuse</u> myself, ladies.
You'll have to <u>excuse</u> me; I ought to be saying goodnight.

If you **excuse** someone for something wrong they have done, you decide not to criticize them or be angry with them.

Such delays cannot <u>be excused.</u>

3   'forgive'

Forgive is used in a similar way. However, when you say that you **forgive** someone, you usually mean that you have already been angry with them or quarrelled with them. You cannot use **excuse** in this way.

I <u>forgave</u> him everything.

4   'apologize'

When people say they are sorry for something they have done, you do not say that they 'excuse themselves'. You say that they **apologize**.

In her first letter she <u>had apologized</u> for being so mean to Rudolph.

5 **'excuse me'**
People often say **'Excuse me'** as a way of apologizing.
⇨ For more information, see **Topic** entry at **Apologizing**.

exhausted - exhausting - exhaustive

1 **'exhausted'**
If you are **exhausted**, you are very tired indeed.
At the end of the day I felt <u>exhausted.</u>
All three men were hot, dirty and <u>exhausted.</u>

You do not use words such as 'rather' or 'very' in front of **exhausted**. You can, however, use words such as **completely, absolutely**, or **utterly**.
'And how are you feeling?'–'Exhausted. <u>Completely exhausted.</u>'
The guest speaker looked <u>absolutely exhausted.</u>
<u>Utterly exhausted,</u> he fell into a deep sleep.

2 **'exhausting'**
If an activity is **exhausting,** it is very tiring.
…a difficult and <u>exhausting</u> job.
Carrying bags is <u>exhausting.</u>

3 **'exhaustive'**
An **exhaustive** study or description is thorough and complete.
He studied the problem in <u>exhaustive</u> detail.
For a more <u>exhaustive</u> treatment you should read Margaret Boden's 'Artificial Intelligence and Natural Man'.

exist

If something **exists,** it is actually present in the world.
National differences do seem to <u>exist.</u>
Tendencies towards sadistic behaviour <u>exist</u> in all human beings.
They walked through my bedroom as if I didn't <u>exist.</u>

When **exist** has this meaning, you do not use it in a continuous tense. You do not say, for example, 'Tendencies towards sadistic behaviour are existing in all human beings'.
You also use **exist** to say that someone manages to live under difficult conditions or with very little food or money.
How we are to <u>exist</u> out here I don't know.
The whole band <u>exist</u> on a diet of cup-a-soup and crisps.

When **exist** has this meaning, it can be used in a continuous tense.
People <u>were existing</u> on a hundred grams of bread a day.

expect

1 **'expect'**
If you **expect** that something will happen, you believe that it will happen.
I <u>expect</u> you'll be glad when I get on the bus this afternoon.
They <u>expect</u> that about 1,500 of the existing force will take up the chance to go to sea.

You can sometimes use a 'to'-infinitive after **expect** instead of a 'that'-clause. For example, instead of saying 'I expect Johnson will come to the meeting', you can say 'I **expect Johnson to come** to the meeting'. However, the meaning is not quite the same. If you say 'I expect Johnson will come to the meeting', you are expressing a simple belief. If you say 'I expect Johnson to come to the meeting', you are indicating that you want Johnson to come to the meeting and that you will be annoyed or disappointed if he does not come.
The horse is on tremendous form and I <u>expect him to win.</u>
Nobody <u>expected the strike to succeed.</u>

USAGE

The talks are expected to last two or three days.

Instead of saying you 'expect something will not' happen, you usually say you **do not expect it will** happen or **do not expect it to** happen.

I don't expect it will be necessary.
I did not expect to find detectives waiting at home.
I did not expect to be acknowledged.

If you say that you **expect** something is the case, you mean that you are fairly confident that it is the case.

I expect they've gone.
I expect they even play cricket on Christmas Day.

Instead of saying you 'expect something is not' the case, you usually say you **do not expect it is** the case.

I do not expect such parties are given now.

If someone asks if something is the case, you can say **'I expect so'**.

'Will Joe be here at Christmas?' – 'I expect so.'
'Did you say anything when I first came up to you?'–'Well, I expect so, but how on earth can I remember now?'

(*i*) Note that you do not say 'I expect it'.

If you **are expecting** someone or something, you believe that they are going to arrive or happen.

They were expecting Wendy and the children.
Rodin was expecting an important letter from France.
We are expecting rain.

(*i*) Note that when **expect** is used like this, you do not use a preposition after it.

2 **'wait for'**

Do not confuse **expect** with **wait for**. If you **are waiting for** someone or something, you are remaining in the same place or delaying doing something until they arrive or happen.

Whisky was served while we waited for Vorster.
He sat on the bench and waited for his coffee.
Stop waiting for things to happen. Make them happen.

⇨ See **Usage** entry at **wait**.

3 **'look forward to'**

When you **look forward to** something that is going to happen, you feel happy because you think you will enjoy it.

I'll bet you're looking forward to your holidays.
I always looked forward to seeing her.

⇨ See **Usage** entry at **look forward to**.

expensive

If something is **expensive**, it costs a lot of money.

I get very nervous because I'm using a lot of expensive equipment.
'Vogue' was more expensive than the other magazines.

You do not say that the price of something is 'expensive'. You say that it is **high**.

The price is much too high.
This must result in consumers paying higher prices.

experience - experiment

1 **'experience'**

If you have **experience** of something, you have seen it, done it, or felt it.

I had no military experience.
The new countries have no experience of democracy.

An **experience** is something that happens to you or something that you do.

Moving house can be a traumatic experience.

You say that someone **has** an experience.

I had a peculiar experience tonight.

(*i*) Note that you do not say that someone 'makes' an experience.

2 **'experiment'**
You do not use 'experience' to refer to a scientific test which is carried out in order to discover or prove something. The word you use is **experiment**.

... experiments in physics.
You try it out in an experiment in a laboratory.

You usually say that someone **does** an experiment.

You don't really need to do an experiment.
It's like working out what's happening when you're doing an experiment.

(*i*) Note that you do not say that someone 'makes' an experiment.

explain

If you **explain** something, you give details about it so that it can be understood.

The Head should be able to explain the school's teaching policy.

You say that you explain something **to** someone.

Let me explain to you about Jackie.
It was explained to him that he would not be expected to enter the chapel.

(*i*) Note that you must use **to** in sentences like these. You do not say, for example, 'Let me explain you about Jackie'.

You can use **explain** with a 'that'-clause to say that someone tells someone else the reason for something.

I explained that I was trying to write a book.

explode - blow up

1 **'explode'**
When a bomb **explodes**, it bursts loudly and with great force, often causing a lot of damage.

A bomb had exploded in the next street.

You can say that someone **explodes** a bomb.

They exploded a nuclear device.

2 **'blow up'**
However, if someone destroys a building with a bomb, you do not say that they 'explode' the building. You say that they **blow** it **up**.

He was going to blow the place up.

extended - extensive

1 **'extended'**
You use **extended** to describe things which last longer than usual.

... extended news bulletins on TV.
If smoked in large doses for an extended period, marijuana can be physically addictive.

2 **'extensive'**
If something is **extensive**, it covers a large area.

...an extensive Roman settlement in north-west England.

An **extensive** effect is very great.

Many buildings suffered <u>extensive</u> damage in the blast.

Extensive also means 'covering many details'.

We had fairly <u>extensive</u> discussions.

exterior - external

1 **'exterior'**

The **exterior** of a building or vehicle is the outside part of it.

The church is famous for its <u>exterior.</u>

You're supposed to keep your car <u>exterior</u> in good condition.

Exterior is often used as an adjective in front of a noun to refer to an outside part of a building or vehicle.

The aerial can be fixed to an <u>exterior</u> wall.

…the <u>exterior</u> bodywork.

2 **'external'**

External can be used in front of a noun to refer to an outside part of a building.

… <u>external</u> walls.

… <u>external</u> doorways.

External can be used in front of other nouns to refer to things which happen, come from, or exist outside a place or area of activity.

Kindly observers may suggest that Novar is being hit by <u>external</u> factors outside its control.

They did it in response to <u>external</u> pressures.

You cannot use **exterior** in this way.

extreme

Extreme means 'very great in degree or intensity'.

He died in <u>extreme</u> poverty.

When her granddaughter Mary was ill, she endured <u>extreme</u> anxiety.

You must proceed with <u>extreme</u> caution.

Extreme opinions are unacceptably severe or unreasonable.

…a far-Right Conservative group with <u>extreme</u> views on immigration.

He had written to Marcus Garvey rejecting his <u>extreme</u> black nationalism.

You do not use **extreme** in front of nouns that refer to events or changes. Instead you use adjectives such as **major**, **great**, or **considerable**.

…the need for <u>major</u> expansion of the University.

This would give <u>great</u> encouragement to the freedom fighters.

F f

fabric

Fabric is cloth or other material produced by weaving cotton, nylon, wool, silk, or other threads together.

A piece of white <u>fabric</u> was thrown out of the window.
…silks and other soft <u>fabrics</u>.

You do not use **fabric** to refer to a building where machines are used to make things. A building like this is usually called a **factory**.

⇨ See **Usage** entry at **factory**.

fact

1 **'fact'**

A **fact** is an item of knowledge or information that is true.

It may help you to know the full <u>facts</u> of the case.
The report is several pages long and full of <u>facts</u> and figures.

⚠ **WARNING:** You never talk about 'true facts' or say, for example, ~~'These facts are true'~~.

2 **'the fact that'**

You can refer to a whole situation by using a clause beginning with **the fact that**.

<u>The fact that quick results are unlikely</u> is no excuse for delay.
<u>The fact that the centre is overcrowded</u> is the major issue with the local opponents.

(*i*) Note that you must use **that** in clauses like these. You do not say, for example, ~~'The fact quick results are unlikely is no excuse for delay'~~.

factory - works - mill - plant

1 **'factory'**

A building where machines are used to make things is usually called a **factory**.

…a carpet <u>factory</u>.
… <u>factories</u> producing domestic electrical goods.

2 **'works'**

A place where things are made or where an industrial process takes place can also be called a **works**. A **works** can consist of several buildings and may include outdoor equipment and machinery.

…an old iron <u>works</u>.

After **works** you can use either a singular or plural form of a verb.

The sewage works <u>was</u> like a closed fort.
…a district where engineering works <u>are</u> planned.

3 **'mill'**

A building where a particular material is made is often called a **mill**.

…a cotton <u>mill</u>.
…a steel <u>mill</u>.

4 **'plant'**

A building where chemicals are produced is called a chemical **plant**.

…the Rhone-Poulenc chemical <u>plant</u> in Dagenham.

A power station can also be referred to as a **plant**.

…the re-opening of a nuclear <u>plant</u>.

USAGE

fair - carnival

1 'fair'

In British English, a **fair** is an event held in a park or field at which people pay to ride on various machines for amusement or try to win prizes in games.

…all of the fun of the <u>fair</u>, with dodgem cars, stalls, candy floss and children's rides.

2 'carnival'

 In American English, an event like this is called a **carnival**.

It reminds me of when the <u>carnival</u> came to Hudson Falls, N.Y., when I was a boy.

In British English, a **carnival** is an outdoor public festival which is held every year in a particular place. During a carnival, music is played and people sometimes dance in the streets.

The Notting Hill <u>Carnival</u> in August is the largest street festival in Europe.

fair - fairly

1 'fair'

You say that behaviour or a decision is **fair** when it is reasonable, right, or just.

It wouldn't be <u>fair</u> to disturb the children's education at this stage.
A work dress code must be <u>fair</u> to both sexes, otherwise it is likely to be ruled discriminatory.

2 'fairly'

You do not use **fair** as an adverb, except in the expression **play fair**. If you want to say that something is done in a reasonable or just way, the word you use is **fairly**.

We want it to be <u>fairly</u> distributed.
He had not put the defence case <u>fairly</u> to the jury.

Fairly also means 'to quite a large degree'.

The information was <u>fairly</u> accurate.
I wrote the first part <u>fairly</u> quickly.

⚠ **WARNING:** You do not use **fairly** in front of a comparative form. You do not say, for example, '~~The train is fairly quicker than the bus~~'. In conversation, you say 'The train is **a bit** quicker than the bus'.

Golf's <u>a bit</u> more expensive.
I began to understand her <u>a bit</u> better.

In writing, you use **rather** or **somewhat**.

In short, the problems now look <u>rather</u> worse than they did a year ago.
The results were <u>somewhat</u> lower than analysts' estimates.

Many other words and expressions can be used to indicate degree.

⇨ For graded lists, see section on **degree** in **Grammar** entry at **Adjuncts** and section on **grading adverbs** in **Grammar** entry at **Adverbs**.

fair - fare

These words are both pronounced /feə/.

1 'fair'

Fair can be an adjective or a noun. If something is **fair**, it is reasonable, right, or just.
⇨ See **Usage** entry at **fair - fairly**.

If someone is **fair** or has **fair** hair, they have light coloured hair.

My daughter has three children, and they're all <u>fair.</u>

A **fair** is an event held in a park or field for people's amusement.
⇨ See **Usage** entry at **fair - carnival**.

USAGE

☐2 **'fare'**

Fare can be a noun or a verb. Your **fare** is the money you pay for a journey by bus, taxi, train, boat, or plane.

Coach fares are cheaper than rail fares.

The **fare** at a restaurant is the food served there. This is an old-fashioned use. It is more common nowadays to simply talk about the **food** in a restaurant.

Army kitchens serve better fare than some hotels.

Fare is used as a verb to say how well or badly someone is treated or how successful they are at something. This use occurs mainly in writing. In conversation, you usually use the verb **do** instead.

They fared badly in the 1978 elections.
How would an 8-stone boxer fare against a 14-stone boxer?
They do badly in elections held at such times.

fall

Fall can be a verb or a noun.

☐1 **used as a verb**

You use **fall** as a verb to talk about a quick downward movement onto or towards the ground.

Drizzle was beginning to fall.
…when the leaves start to fall.

The past tense of **fall** is **fell**, not 'falled'. The past participle is **fallen.**

The china fell from her hand and shattered.
…table napkins that had fallen to the floor.

⚠ **WARNING: Fall** is an intransitive verb. You cannot say that someone 'falls' something. You do not say, for example, 'She screamed and fell the tray'. You say 'She screamed and **dropped** the tray'.

He bumped into a chair and dropped his cigar.
Careful! Don't drop it!

Similarly, you do not say that someone 'falls' a person. You do not say, for example, 'He bumped into the old lady and fell her'. You say 'He bumped into the old lady and **knocked** her **down** ' or 'He bumped into the old lady and **knocked** her **over** '.

I nearly knocked down a person at the bus stop.
I got knocked over by a car when I was six.

When someone who is standing or walking **falls,** they drop downwards so that they are kneeling or lying on the ground.

He tottered and fell full-length.
She lost her balance and would have fallen if she hadn't supported herself.

In conversation, you do not usually say that someone 'falls'. You say that they **fall down** or **fall over.**

He fell down in the mud.
He fell over backwards and lay as if struck by lightning.

You can also say that a tall object **falls down** or **falls over.**

The pile of hymn books fell down and scattered all over the floor.
A tree fell over in a storm.

☐2 **used as a noun**

Fall can also be a noun. If you have a **fall,** you lose your balance and drop on to the ground, hurting yourself.

He read that his mother had had a bad fall.

In American English, **fall** is the season between summer and winter.
In the <u>fall,</u> there is nowhere I would rather be than Vermont.

British speakers call this season **autumn.**
⇨ See **Usage** entry at **autumn.**

familiar

1 'familiar'
If someone or something is **familiar,** you recognize them because you have seen, heard, or experienced them before.
There was something <u>familiar</u> about him.
Gradually I began to recognize <u>familiar</u> faces.

2 'familiar to'
If something is **familiar to** you, you know it well.
My name was now <u>familiar to</u> millions of people.
The things Etta spoke of were <u>familiar to</u> Judy only from magazines.

3 'familiar with'
If you know or understand something well, you can say that you are **familiar with** it.
I am of course <u>familiar with</u> your work.
…statements which I am sure you are <u>familiar with.</u>

⇨ See **Usage** entry at **aware - familiar.**

famous - well-known - notorious - infamous

1 'famous'
If someone or something is **famous,** very many people know about them.
Have you ever dreamed of becoming a <u>famous</u> writer?
…the world's most <u>famous</u> picture.

2 'well-known'
Well-known has a similar meaning to **famous.** However, a **well-known** person or thing is usually known to fewer people or in a smaller area than a **famous** one.
…a club run by Paul Ross, a <u>well-known</u> Lakeland climber.
…his two <u>well-known</u> books on modern art.

Well-known can be spelled with or without a hyphen. You usually spell it with a hyphen in front of a noun and without a hyphen after a verb.
I took him to a <u>well-known</u> doctor in Harley Street.
The building became very <u>well known.</u>

3 'notorious'
Someone or something that is **notorious** is well known for something that is bad or undesirable.
The area was <u>notorious</u> for murders.
…his <u>notorious</u> arrogance.

3 'infamous'
People and things are described as **infamous** when they are well known because they are connected with wicked or cruel behaviour.
…the <u>infamous</u> serial killer known as 'the Boston Strangler'.
…the <u>infamous</u> shower scene from Psycho.

ⓘ **Infamous** is a rather literary word. Note that it is not the opposite of 'famous'.

far

1 distance
You use **how far** when you are asking about a distance.

How far is it to Charles City?
How far is Amity from here?
He asks us how far we have come.

However, you do not use 'far' when you are stating a distance. You do not say, for example, that something is 10 kilometres 'far' from a place. You say that it is 10 kilometres **from** the place or 10 kilometres **away from** it.

The property was a mere fifty miles from the ocean.
I was about five miles away from some hills.

You use **far** in questions and negative sentences to mean 'a long distance'. For example, if you say that it is **not far** to a place, you mean that the place is not a long distance from where you are.

Do tell us more about it, Lee. Is it far?
It isn't far now.
I don't live far from here.

You do not use 'far' like this in positive sentences. You do not say, for example, that a place is 'far'. You say that it is **far away** or **a long way away**.

The lightning was far away.
He is far away in Australia.
That's up in the Cairngorms, which is quite a long way away.

⇨ See **Usage** entry at **away**.

In modern English, 'far' is not used in front of a noun. You do not, for example, talk about 'far hills'. Instead you use **distant** or **faraway**.

…a distant blue plain.
…the faraway sound of a waterfall.

2 | **degree or extent**
You also use **far** in questions and negative sentences to talk about the degree or extent to which something happens.

How far have you got in developing this?
Prices will not come down very far.
None of us would trust them very far.

3 | **used as an intensifier**
You use **far** in front of comparatives to say that something has very much more of a quality than something else. For example, if you say that one thing is **far bigger** than another, you mean that it is very much bigger than the other thing.

It is a far better picture than the other one.
The situation was far more dangerous than Woodward realized.

Far more in front of a noun means 'very much more' or 'very many more'.

He had to process far more information than before.
Professional training was provided in far more forms than in Europe.

You can also use **far** in front of **too**. For example, if you say that something is **far too big**, you mean that it is very much bigger than it should be.

I was far too polite.
It is far too early to judge.

You can use **far** in front of **too much** or **too many**. For example, if you say that there is **far too much** of something, you mean that there is a very much greater quantity than is necessary or desirable.

Teachers are being bombarded with far too much new information.
Every middle-class child gets far too many toys.

⇨ See also **Usage** entry at **farther - further**.

USAGE

fare

⇨ See **Usage** entry at **fair - fare.**

farther - further

Farther and **further** are both comparative forms of **far. Farthest** and **furthest** are the superlative forms. When you are talking about distance, you can use any of these forms.

Birds were able to find food by flying <u>farther</u> and <u>farther.</u>
He must have found a window open <u>further</u> along the balcony.
Gus was in the <u>farthest</u> corner of the room.
The sun is then at its <u>furthest</u> point to the south.

However, when you are talking about the degree or extent of something, you can only use **further** or **furthest.**

He needed to develop his reading <u>further.</u>
The <u>furthest</u> you can get on a farm is foreman, and you won't be this until it's time to retire.

fascinated

If you are **fascinated by** something or **fascinated with** it, you find it very interesting.

He was <u>fascinated by</u> films as a child.
He became <u>fascinated with</u> their whole way of life.

You can also say that you are **fascinated by** a person.

At first Rita was <u>fascinated by</u> him.

You do not use words such as 'very' or 'extremely' in front of **fascinated.** If you find something very interesting indeed, you can say that you are **absolutely fascinated** or **deeply fascinated** by it.

Dr Shaw had been <u>absolutely fascinated</u> by a print on her wall.
He was <u>deeply fascinated</u> by war.

fatness

The following words can all be used to describe someone who has a lot of flesh on their body:

beefy	chunky	fleshy	plump	stocky
big	corpulent	gross	podgy	stout
broad	cuddly	heavy	portly	thick-set
bulky	dumpy	heavyset (*Am*)	pudgy	tubby
buxom	fat	obese	solid	well-built
chubby	flabby	overweight	squat	

1 neutral words

Big, broad, bulky, chunky, corpulent, fleshy, heavy, heavyset, plump, stocky, stout, and **thick-set** are fairly neutral words.

How tall was he? Thin or <u>heavyset</u>?
<u>Stout</u> prosperous men converged on the hotel.
…the portrait of a <u>plump</u>, dark girl, the Colonel's daughter.

2 'big' and 'stocky'

You use **big** to describe someone who is tall and has quite a lot of flesh.

Zabeth was a <u>big</u> woman with a dark complexion.

You use **stocky** to describe someone who is fairly short and has quite a lot of flesh.

His friend was a <u>stocky,</u> bald man in his late forties.

3 polite words

Beefy, buxom, chubby, cuddly, portly, solid, tubby, and **well-built** are words that you use when you like the person you are describing and think their shape is quite attractive. **Beefy, cuddly,** and **tubby** are used in conversation.

His relatives were all <u>solid, well-built</u> people with dark or gray curly hair.

Buxom is used only to describe women.

…the <u>buxom</u> ladies in Rubens' paintings.

Chubby is used mainly of babies and children. **Portly** is used mainly of people who are middle-aged and rather dignified.

Janice was a <u>chubby</u> child but she really started to pile on weight at 12.
…a <u>portly</u> gentleman in his late fifties.

4 **impolite words**
Dumpy, fat, flabby, gross, obese, overweight, podgy, pudgy, and **squat** are considered impolite and should not be used when speaking to the person you are describing, or to someone who knows and likes them.

He'll get <u>fat,</u> the way he eats.
He doesn't do anything physical. So he must be <u>flabby</u> and unfit.
Laura was hugely <u>overweight</u>.

Obese and **overweight** are also used in more technical contexts.

Really <u>obese</u> children tend to grow up into <u>obese</u> men and women.
<u>Overweight</u> people run a slightly higher risk of cancer than people of average weight.

People who are **dumpy** or **squat** are both short and fat.

She was a little woman, and would probably, one day, be a <u>dumpy</u> one.

⚠ **WARNING: Wide** is used to describe things, not people.

…the <u>wide</u> staircase leading down to the hall.

However, it can be used to describe parts of the body.

Her features were coarse – a <u>wide</u> forehead, a large nose, prominent cheekbones.
She had a <u>wide</u> mouth that smiled a great deal.

---

fault
⇨ See **Usage** entry at **blame - fault**.

---

favourite
Your **favourite** thing or person of a particular type is the one you like most.

What is your <u>favourite</u> television programme?
Her <u>favourite</u> writer is Hans Christian Andersen.

You do not usually use 'most' with **favourite**. You do not say, for example, 'This is my most favourite book'. You say 'This is my **favourite** book'.

 The American spelling of **favourite** is **favorite**.

---

fear
Fear can be a noun or a verb.

1 **used as a noun**
Fear is an unpleasant feeling that you have when you think you are in danger.

They huddled together, quaking with <u>fear</u>.
She was brought up with no <u>fear</u> of animals.

You do not say that someone 'feels fear'. You say that they **are afraid** or **are frightened**.

They <u>were afraid</u> of you. They knew you had killed many men.
Everyone here <u>is frightened</u> of the volcano.

⇨ See **Usage** entry at **afraid - frightened**.

2 **used as a verb**

If you **fear** someone or something, you are afraid of them.

…a woman whom he disliked and <u>feared</u>.
He <u>fears</u> nothing.

(*i*) Note that you do not use **fear** as a verb in conversation.

feel

Feel is a common verb which has several meanings. Its past tense and past participle is **felt**, not 'feeled'.

1 **awareness**

If you **can feel** something, you are aware of it because of your sense of touch, or you are aware of it in your body.

I <u>can feel</u> the heat of the sun on my face.
I wonder if he <u>can feel</u> pain.

(*i*) Note that you usually use **can** in sentences like these. You say, for example, 'I **can feel** a pain in my foot'. You do not say 'I feel a pain in my foot'. You also do not use a continuous tense. You do not say 'I am feeling a pain in my foot'.

If you want to say that someone was aware of something in the past, you use **felt** or **could feel.**

They <u>felt</u> the wind on their damp faces.
Through several layers of clothes I <u>could feel</u> his muscles.

However, if you want to say that someone suddenly became aware of something, you must use **felt.**

He <u>felt</u> a sting on his elbow.

You can use an '-ing' form after **felt** or **could feel** to indicate that someone was aware of something that was continuing to take place.

He <u>felt</u> moisture <u>creeping</u> through to his skin.
He <u>could feel</u> the warm blood <u>pouring</u> down his face.

You can use an infinitive without 'to' after **felt** to indicate that someone became aware of a single action.

She <u>felt</u> his hand <u>pat</u> hers.

2 **touching**

When you **feel** an object, you touch it deliberately in order to find out what it is like.

Eric <u>felt</u> his face. 'I'm all rough. Am I bleeding?'

3 **impressions**

The way something **feels** is the way it seems to you when you hold it or touch it.

His fork <u>felt</u> heavy.
How does it <u>feel</u>? Warm or cold?
It looks and <u>feels</u> like a normal fabric.

When you use **feel** like this, you do not use a continuous tense. You do not say, for example, 'His fork was feeling heavy'.

4 **emotions and sensations**

You can use **feel** with an adjective to say that someone is or was experiencing an emotion or sensation. When you use **feel** like this, you use either a simple tense or a continuous tense.

I <u>feel</u> lonely.
I 'm feeling terrible.
She <u>felt</u> happy.
I <u>was feeling</u> hungry.

You can also use **feel** with a noun group to say that someone experiences an emotion or

sensation. When you use **feel** with a noun group, you use a simple tense.
Mrs Oliver felt a sudden desire to burst out crying.

⚠ **WARNING:** When you use **feel** to say that someone experiences an emotion or sensation, you do not use a reflexive pronoun. You do not say, for example, 'I felt myself uncomfortable'. You say 'I **felt** uncomfortable'.

5 **'feel like'**
If you **feel like** a particular type of person or thing, you are aware of having some of the qualities or feelings of that person or thing.
If you want to feel like a star, travel like a star.
I feel like a hamster stuck on a treadmill.

If you **feel like doing** something, you want to do it.
Whenever I felt like talking, they were ready to listen.
Are there days when you don't feel like writing?

In sentences like these, you can sometimes use a noun group instead of an '-ing' form. For example, instead of saying 'I feel like going for a walk', you can say 'I **feel like** a walk'.
I feel like a stroll.
I feel like a drink.

(*i*) Note that you never say that you 'feel like to do' something.

6 **beliefs**
If you **feel** that something is the case or that something should be done, you believe it.
I feel I'm neglecting my duty.
Does this make you feel we ought to become as independent as possible?

For emphasis, you can use 'strongly' or 'very strongly' after **feel.**
We feel very strongly that traditional family values must be maintained.

⚠ **WARNING:** You do not use a continuous tense of **feel** in sentences like these. You do not say, for example, 'I am feeling I ought to go'. You say 'I **feel** I ought to go'.

Instead of saying that you 'feel that something is not' the case, you can say that you **do not feel that it is** the case.
She did not feel that she was entitled to join this group.
He still did not feel that he could trust anyone.

---

female - feminine - effeminate

1 **'female'**
Female means 'relating to the sex that can have babies'. You can use **female** as an adjective to talk about either people or animals.
…pay claims from female employees.
A female toad may lay 20,000 eggs each season.

You can also use **female** as a noun, but only to talk about animals.
The male fertilizes the female's eggs.
He came upon a family of lions – a big male, a beautiful female, and two half grown cubs.

🇺🇸 In American English, however, young people sometimes use **female** to talk about young women, to avoid using 'woman' or 'girl'.
I cannot say for certain, as she is a female.

2 **'feminine'**
Feminine means 'typical of women, rather than men'.
The bedroom has a light, feminine look.
…a good, calm, reasonable and deeply feminine woman.

You do not use **feminine** to talk about animals.

USAGE

3 **'effeminate'**

Effeminate is only used to describe men and boys. People say that a man or boy is **effeminate** if he behaves, looks, or sounds like a woman or girl. It is best not to use this word, as many people find it offensive.

They find European men slightly <u>effeminate.</u>

fetch

⇨ See **Usage** entry at **bring - take - fetch.**

few - a few

1 **used in front of nouns**

Few and **a few** are both used in front of nouns, but they do not have the same meaning. You use **a few** simply to indicate that you are talking about a small number of people or things. When you use **few** without 'a', you are emphasizing that there are only a small number of people or things of a particular kind. So, for example, if you say 'I have **a few** friends', you are simply saying that you have some friends. However, if you say 'I have **few** friends', you are saying that you do not have many friends.

They may have <u>a few</u> books on the shelf.
There were <u>few</u> books in Grandfather's study.

2 **used as pronouns**

Few and **a few** can be used in a similar way as pronouns.

Each volunteer spent one night a week in the cathedral. <u>A few</u> spent two.
Many are invited but <u>few</u> are chosen.

3 **'not many'**

In conversation, people do not usually use **few** without 'a'. Instead they use **not many.** For example, instead of saying 'I have few friends', people usually say 'I **haven't got many** friends' or 'I **don't have many** friends'.

They <u>haven't got many</u> good players in their side.
I <u>don't have many</u> visitors.

⚠ **WARNING:** You do not use 'few' or 'a few' with an uncount noun when you are talking about a small amount of something. You do not say, for example, 'Would you like a few more milk in your tea?' You say 'Would you like **a little** more milk in your tea?'

fewer

⇨ See **Usage** entry at **less.**

fictional - fictitious

1 **'fictional'**

A **fictional** character, thing, or event occurs in a story, play, or film, and has never actually existed or happened.

I had to put myself into the position of lots of <u>fictional</u> characters.
…a musical about a <u>fictional</u> composer called Moony Shapiro.

Fictional also means 'relating to fiction and the telling of stories'.

James Joyce's final <u>fictional</u> experiment was a novel composed entirely of mathematical equations.

2 **'fictitious'**

Something that is **fictitious** is false and is intended to deceive people.

They bought the materials under <u>fictitious</u> names.

film

A **film** consists of moving pictures shown on a screen, especially one shown to an audience in a building built for this purpose.

The film is based on the bestselling novel by Scott B Smith, who also wrote the script.

 Films are sometimes referred to as **pictures.** In the United States, films are often called **movies.**

We worked together in the last picture I made.
His last book was made into a movie.

 When British people go to see a film, they say that they are going to the **cinema** or to the **pictures.** American speakers talk about going to the **movies.**

Everyone has gone to the cinema.
She went twice a week to the pictures.
Some friends and I were driving home from the movies.

 In Britain, a building where films are shown is usually called a **cinema.** In the United States, it is called a **movie theater** or **movie house.**

finally
⇨ See **Usage** entry at **eventually - finally.**

find

1 **result of a search**
If you **find** something you have been looking for, you see it or learn where it is.

The mill will not be easy to find.

The past tense and past participle of 'find' is **found,** not 'finded'.

I eventually found what I was looking for.
His body has not been found.

(*i*) Note that when **find** has this meaning, you do not use 'out' after it.

2 **'discover'**
Discover is sometimes used instead of 'find'. **Discover** is a rather formal word.

The bodies of the family were discovered by police officers on Tuesday.

If you cannot see the thing you are looking for, you say that you **cannot find** it.

I think I'm lost – I can't find the bridge.

However, you do not say that you 'cannot discover' something.

3 **noticing something**
You can use **find** or **discover** to say that someone notices an object somewhere.

She found a drawing on her bed.
Look what I 've found!
A bomb could well be discovered and that would ruin everything.

Come across has a similar meaning.

They came across something that looked like the skull of a large monkey.

4 **obtaining information**
If you **find, find out,** or **discover** that something is the case, you learn that it is the case.

The observers found that the same rules applied here.
It was such a relief to find out that the boy was normal.
He has since discovered that his statement was wrong.

In clauses beginning with **when, before,** or **as soon as,** you can omit the object after **find out.** You cannot do this with **find** or **discover.**

When mother finds out, she'll divorce you.
You want it to end before anyone finds out.
As soon as I found out, I jumped into the car.

USAGE

USAGE

If you **find out** or **discover** some information that is difficult to obtain, you succeed in obtaining it.

Have you <u>found out</u> who killed my husband?
MI6 <u>had discovered</u> that Saten was working for the Nazis.

You can also say that someone **finds out** facts that are easy to obtain.

I <u>found out</u> the train times.

(*i*) Note that you do not say that someone 'discovers' facts that are easy to obtain.

5 **another meaning of 'discover'**

If you **discover** a place, substance, fact, or method which nobody knew about before, you are the first person to find it or know it.

Columbus <u>discovered</u> the largest island in the Caribbean.
Penicillin <u>was discovered</u> by Alexander Fleming.

6 **another meaning of 'find'**

You can use **find** followed by **it** and an adjective to say whether it is difficult or easy for someone to do something. For example, if you have difficulty doing something, you can say that you **find it difficult to do** it.

The 87 girls in the survey said they <u>found it difficult to show</u> how clever they were.
I also <u>find it difficult to chat</u> to the other parents.

(*i*) Note that you must use **it** in sentences like these. You do not say, for example, 'She found impossible to believe that I meant it'. You say 'She found **it** impossible to believe that I meant it'.

fine - finely

Fine is usually an adjective, but in conversation you can also use it as an adverb. **Fine** has three main meanings.

1 **used to mean 'very good'**

You can use it to say that something is very good or impressive.

Paul Scofield gave a <u>fine</u> performance.
From the top there is a <u>fine</u> view.

When you use **fine** like this, you can use words such as **very** or **extremely** in front of it.

He's interested and he'd do a <u>very fine</u> job.
…an <u>unusually fine</u> piece of work.

You cannot use **fine** as an adverb with this meaning, but you can use the adverb **finely** in front of a past participle.

… <u>finely</u> written novels.

2 **used to mean 'satisfactory'**

You can also use **fine** to say that something is satisfactory or acceptable.

'Do you want it stronger than that?'–'No, that's <u>fine.</u>'

If you say that you are **fine,** you mean that your health is satisfactory.

'How are you?'–'<u>Fine</u>, thanks.'

When you use **fine** to mean 'satisfactory', you do not use 'very' in front of it, but you can use **just**.

Everything is <u>just fine.</u>
'Is she settling down nicely in England?'–'Oh, she's <u>just fine.</u>'

In conversation, you can use **fine** as an adverb to mean 'satisfactorily' or 'well'.

We got on <u>fine.</u>
I was doing <u>fine.</u>

(*i*) Note that you do not use 'finely' in sentences like these. You do not say, for example, 'We got on finely'.

3 used to mean 'small' or 'narrow'

You can also use **fine** to say that something is very narrow, or consists of very small or narrow parts.

… *fine* hair.

…handfuls of *fine* sand.

When you use **fine** like this, you can use words such as **very** in front of it.

These pins are very fine and won't split the wood.

You can use **finely** as an adverb with this meaning.

… *finely* chopped meat.

finish

When you **finish** what you are doing, you reach the end of it.

Aren't you ever going to finish the ironing?

When he had finished, he closed the file.

You can say that someone **finishes doing** something.

Jonathan finished studying at the West Surrey college three years ago.

I've finished reading your book.

ⓘ Note that you do not say that someone 'finishes to do' something.

first - firstly

1 'first' used as an adjective

The **first** thing, event, or person of a particular kind is the one that comes before all the others.

She lost 16 pounds in the first month of her diet.

…the *first* man in space.

If you want to emphasize that a thing, event, or person is the first one of their kind, you can put **very** in front of **first**.

The very first thing that happened was that I got ravenously hungry.

2 'first' used as an adverb

If an event happens before other events, you say that it happens **first**.

Ralph spoke first.

When people get their newspaper, which page do they read first?

ⓘ Note that you do not say that something happens 'firstly'.

3 used as sentence adverbs

You can use **first** or **firstly** to introduce the first point in a discussion, the first of a series of questions or instructions, or the first item in a list.

Four tendencies began to converge. First, there was a growing awareness of the true dimensions of the threat.

There are two reasons. Firstly I have no evidence that the original document has been destroyed.

If you want to emphasize that an item is the first one you are going to mention, you can say **first of all**.

…*our long-term commitment, first of all to Afghanistan, and secondly to this region.*

First of all dig a little hole.

ⓘ Note that you do not say 'firstly of all'.

4 'at first'

When you are contrasting feelings or actions at the beginning of an event with ones that came later, you say **at first**.

USAGE

At first I was reluctant.
At first I thought it was moonlight, but then realized it was snow.

ⓘ Note that you do not use 'firstly' in sentences like these.

first floor

⇨ See **Usage** entry at **ground floor**.

first name

⇨ See **Usage** entry at **Christian name - first name - forename - given name**.

fish

Fish can be a count noun or an uncount noun.

1 used as a count noun

A **fish** is a creature that lives in water and has a tail and fins.
…an islander who had just caught a <u>fish</u>.

In modern English, the plural of **fish** is **fish**, not 'fishes'.
My sister was singing happily because we'd caught so many <u>fish</u>.

2 used as an uncount noun

Fish is the flesh of a fish which you eat as food.
Fresh <u>fish</u> is expensive.

fit - suit

1 'fit'

If clothes **fit** you, they are the right size, neither too big nor too small.
…a dress of purple silk that <u>fits</u> her snugly.
He was wearing pyjamas which did not <u>fit</u> him.

 When **fit** has this meaning, its usual past tense is **fitted.** However, many American speakers use **fit** as the past tense.
The boots <u>fitted</u> Rudolph perfectly.
The pants <u>fit</u> him well and looked like men's slacks.

2 'suit'

If clothes make you look attractive, you do not say that they 'fit' you. You say that they **suit** you.
I love you in that dress, it really <u>suits</u> you.

flammable - inflammable

Both **flammable** and **inflammable** are used to describe materials or chemicals that burn easily.
A window had been smashed and <u>flammable</u> liquid poured in.
…commercial centres, holding large stocks of <u>inflammable</u> materials.

⚠ **WARNING: Inflammable** is not the opposite of **flammable**. The opposite is **non-flammable**.
The fuel is recyclable, clean and <u>non-flammable</u>.

flat - apartment

1 'flat'

In British English, a **flat** is a set of rooms for living in, usually on one floor of a large building. You can rent a flat or you can own it yourself.
She went to live in a tiny furnished <u>flat</u> near Sloane Square.

2 '**apartment**'

 In American English, a set of rooms like this is usually called an **apartment**. When it is owned by the person or people who live there, it is sometimes called a **condominium** or, in conversation, a **condo**.

It is a six-storey building with 20 luxury two- and three-bedroom apartments.
He urged me to buy a condominium.

3 '**block of flats**'

In British English, a large building containing flats is called a **block of flats**.

 In American English, it is called an **apartment house**, an **apartment building**, or an **apartment block**.

The building was pulled down to make way for a block of flats.
The next night police rushed to an apartment house on Charlesgate East.
Several apartment buildings were destroyed.

---

flat - flatly

Flat is usually a noun or an adjective, but it is sometimes an adverb.

1 '**flat**' used as a noun

In British English, a **flat** is a set of rooms for living in, usually on one floor of a large building.

...a ground floor flat.

⇨ See **Usage** entry at **flat - apartment**.

2 '**flat**' used as an adjective or adverb

Something that is **flat** is not sloping, curved, or pointed.

Every flat surface in our house is covered with junk.
Use a saucepan with a flat base.

If something lies or rests **flat** against a surface, all of it is touching the surface.

He was lying flat on his back.
She let the blade of her oar rest flat upon the water.

(*i*) Note that you do not say that something lies or rests 'flatly' against a surface.

A **flat** refusal, denial, or rejection is definite and firm, and not likely to be changed.

He has issued a flat denial of these allegations.

3 '**flatly**'

The adverb corresponding to this meaning of **flat** is **flatly**, not 'flat'.

She has flatly refused to go.
The Norwegians and Danes flatly rejected the evidence.

Flatly goes in front of **refuse** and **deny**, but you put it after **say**, **state** and **tell**.

He flatly refused to accept it.
Many scientists flatly denied the possibility.
I could use some money, Sarah told him flatly.

---

floor - ground

1 '**floor**'

The **floor** of a room is the flat part you walk on.

The book fell to the floor.

A **floor** of a building is all the rooms on a particular level.

...the stairs leading to the ground floor.
18 prisoners seized control of the top floor.

You say that something is **on** a particular floor.
My office is <u>on the second floor.</u>

(i) Not that you do not say that something is 'in' a particular floor.

⇨ See also **Usage** entry at **ground floor**.

[2] **'ground'**

You do not normally refer to the surface of the earth as the 'floor'. You call it the **ground**.
He set down his bundle carefully on the <u>ground.</u>
The <u>ground</u> all round was very wet and marshy.

However, the surface of the earth in a forest is sometimes referred to as the **forest floor**, and the land under the sea is sometimes called the **sea floor** or the **ocean floor**.
The <u>forest floor</u> is not rich in vegetation.
Some species take rests at night and slumber on the <u>sea floor.</u>

---

folk - folks

Folk and **folks** are sometimes used to refer to particular groups of people. Both these words are plural nouns. You always use a plural form of a verb with them.

[1] **'folk'**

Folk is sometimes used with a modifier to refer to all the people who have a particular characteristic.
<u>Country folk</u> are a suspicious lot.
She was like all the <u>old folk,</u> she did everything in strict rotation.

However, this is not a common use. You usually say **country people** or **old people**, rather than 'country folk' or 'old folk'.

[2] **'folks'**

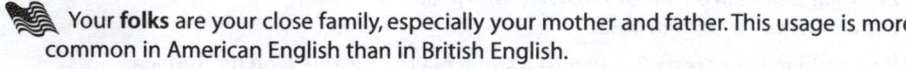 Your **folks** are your close family, especially your mother and father. This usage is more common in American English than in British English.
I don't even have time to write letters to my <u>folks.</u>
Vera's visiting her <u>folks</u> up in Paducah.

Some people use **folks** when addressing a group of people in an informal way. This use is more common in American English than in British English.
That's all for tonight, <u>folks.</u>
They saw me drive out of town taking you <u>folks</u> up to McCaslin.

---

following

Following is most commonly used in expressions like **the following day** and **the following week**.

⇨ For an explanation of this use, see **Usage** entry at **next**.

Following can also be a preposition. It is usually used to indicate that one event happens after another and to some extent as a result of it.
<u>Following</u> that outburst, the general was banished.
Durga Lal died on February 1, <u>following</u> a heart attack.

Sometimes **following** is used simply to say that one event happens after another.
<u>Following</u> your introduction you will be issued with an authorised user card.
<u>Following</u> a day of medical research, the conference focused on educational practices.

This use is fairly common, but some people think that it is incorrect. In sentences like these, you can also use **after**, rather than 'following'.
…the under-funding of community care <u>after</u> the closure of mental hospitals.
He flew into a rage when he returned to his hotel <u>after</u> Algeria's 1-0 defeat by Egypt.

fond
⇨ See **Usage** entry at **like - dislike**.

foot

1 **part of the body**

Your **foot** is the part of your body at the end of your leg. Your foot includes your toes.

He kept on running despite the pain in his <u>foot</u>.

When you use **foot** with this meaning, its plural is **feet**.

She's got very small <u>feet</u>.

If someone goes somewhere **on foot**, they walk, rather than using some form of transport.

The city should be explored <u>on foot</u>.

2 **measurements**

A **foot** is also a unit for measuring length, equal to 12 inches or 30.48 centimetres. When **foot** has this meaning, its usual plural is **feet**.

We were only a few <u>feet</u> away from the edge of the cliff.
The planes flew at 65,000 <u>feet</u>.

However, you can use **foot** as the plural in front of words like **high**, **tall**, and **long**.

She's five <u>foot</u> eight inches tall.

(i) Note that you always use **foot** as the plural in front of another noun. For example, if a gap is twenty feet wide, you refer to it as a 'twenty **foot** gap'. You do not refer to it as a 'twenty feet gap'.

…a forty <u>foot</u> wall.

football

1 **'football'**

In Britain, **football** is a game played between two teams who kick a round ball around a field in an attempt to score goals. In America, this game is called **soccer**.

Italian <u>football</u> fans.
The pressure will not let up for the US <u>soccer</u> team.

2 **'American football'**

In America, **football** is a game played between two teams who throw or run with an oval ball in an attempt to score points. In Britain, this game is called **American football**.

This year's national college <u>football</u> championship was won by Princeton.
In youth he was a minor <u>American football</u> star.

3 **'match'**

In Britain, two teams play a football **match**. In America, they play a football **game**.

Paul Scholes will miss United's away <u>match</u> with Wimbledon through suspension.
Why are you watching the football <u>game</u>, Daddy?

footprint
⇨ See **Usage** entry at **pace**.

footstep
⇨ See **Usage** entry at **pace**.

for

1 **'for'**

If something is **for** someone, they are intended to have it or benefit from it.

USAGE

He left a note for her on the table.
She held out the flowers and said, 'They're for you.'
I am doing everything I can for you.

You use **for** in front of a noun group or '-ing' form when you are mentioning the use to which an object is put.

I had two knives with me, one for leather work and one for skinning animals.
The mug had been used for mixing flour and water.

You use **for** in front of a noun group when you are saying why someone does something.

We stopped for lunch by the roadside.
I walked two miles for a couple of pails of water.

⚠ **WARNING:** You do not use 'for' with an '-ing' form when you saying why someone does something. You do not say, for example, 'He went to the city for finding work'. You say 'He went to the city **to find** work' or 'He went to the city **in order to find** work'.
People would stroll down the path to admire the garden.
He had to hurry in order to reach the next place on his schedule.

2 duration

You use **for** to say how long something lasts or continues.
I'm staying with Bob DeWeese for a few days.
The five nations agreed not to build any new battleships for a ten-year period.

You also use **for** to say how long something has been the case.
I have known you for a long time.
He has been missing for three weeks.
...artists who have been famous for years.
He hadn't had a proper night's sleep for a month.

⚠ **WARNING:** When you use 'for' to say how long something has been the case, you must use a perfect tense. You cannot say, for example, 'I am living here for five years'. You must say 'I **have lived** here for five years'.

3 'since'

Do not confuse **for** with **since**. You use **since** to say that something has been the case from a particular time in the past until now.
Exam results have improved rapidly since 1999...
We had been travelling since dawn.
I had known her since she was twelve.

⇨ See **Usage** entry at **since**.

4 used to mean 'because'

In stories, **for** is sometimes used to mean 'because'.
This is where he spent a good deal of his free time, for he had nowhere else to go.

⇨ See **Usage** entry at **because**.

forcefulness

The following words can all be used to describe a person who speaks and acts in a strong, determined, and confident way:

aggressive	forceful	positive	strong-willed
assertive	in-your-face	pushy	tyrannical
domineering	overbearing	self-confident	

1 **complimentary words**
Assertive, forceful, positive, self-confident, and **strong-willed** are complimentary words.
Women have become more <u>assertive</u> in the past decade.
He was a man of <u>forceful</u> character, with considerable insight and diplomatic skills.
She'd blossomed into a <u>self-confident</u> young woman.

2 **negative words**
Aggressive, domineering, in-your-face, overbearing, pushy, and **tyrannical** are used to show disapproval of someone's behaviour. **Pushy** is used mainly in conversation.
Many of her women friends also had <u>domineering</u> husbands.
Teddy abandoned subtlety and tried the <u>in-your-face</u> approach.
We worry about being <u>pushy</u> parents.

forename
⇨ See **Usage** entry at **Christian name - first name - forename - given name.**

forever
Something that will last or continue **forever** will always last or continue.
She would remember his name <u>forever.</u>
They thought that their empire would last <u>forever.</u>

Something that has gone **forever** has gone and will never reappear.
This innocence is lost <u>forever.</u>
They will vanish <u>forever</u> into the grey twilight.

For the above two meanings, you can use the alternative spelling **for ever** in British English.
My fate had been sealed <u>for ever.</u>
We'll be married soon and then these lonesome nights will be over <u>for ever.</u>

Other words and expressions can be used to say how long something lasts.
⇨ For a graded list, see section on **duration** in **Grammar** entry at **Adjuncts.**

If you say that someone **is forever doing** something, you mean that they do it very often.
Babbage <u>was forever spotting</u> errors in their calculations.

For this meaning, the only acceptable spelling is **forever.**

forget

1 **'forget'**
If you **forget** something, you stop thinking about it. The past tense of this verb is **forgot,** not 'forgetted'. The past participle is **forgotten.**
Tim <u>forgot</u> his troubles.
Ash, having <u>forgotten</u> his fear, had become bored and restless.

If you **have forgotten** something that you knew, you can no longer remember it.
I <u>have forgotten</u> where it is.
…a Grand Duke whose name I <u>have forgotten.</u>

If you **forget** something such as a key or an umbrella, you do not remember to take it with you when you go somewhere.
Sorry to disturb you – I <u>forgot</u> my key.

⚠ **WARNING:** Note that you cannot use the verb 'forget' to say that you have put something somewhere and left it there. Instead you use the verb **leave.**
I <u>left</u> my bag on the bus.

2 **'forget to'**
If you **forget to do** something which you had intended to do, you do not do it because you do not remember it at the right time.

USAGE

She forgot to lock her door one day and two men got in.
Don't forget to send your entries by Wednesday to this address.

(i) Note that you do not say that someone 'forgets doing' something.

form

⇨ See **Usage** entry at **class - form - grade.**

former - late

1 **'former'**
You use **former** in front of a noun to indicate that the person you are talking about is no longer the thing referred to by the noun. For example, the **former chairman** of a company used to be the chairman, but is not the chairman now.

... former President Gerald Ford.
...William Nickerson, a former Treasury official.

2 **'late'**
You use **late** in front of a name or noun to indicate that the person you are talking about has recently died.

...the late Mr Parkin.
I'd like to talk to you about your late husband.

⇨ For another meaning of **former,** see **Usage** entry at **latter.**

fortnight

In British English, two weeks is often called a **fortnight.**
I went to Rothesay for a fortnight.
He borrowed it a fortnight ago.

 American speakers do not usually use this word.

fortune

Good fortune is good luck.
He has since had the good fortune to be promoted.
He could hardly believe his good fortune.

(i) Note that you do not say that something good that happens is 'a good fortune'. You do not say, for example, ~~'It's a good fortune I remembered to bring my umbrella'~~. You say 'It's **lucky** I remembered to bring my umbrella' or 'It's **a good job** I remembered to bring my umbrella'.

It's lucky that I'm going abroad.
It's a good job you were there.

 Note that in American English, you use **a good thing,** rather than **a good job.**

It's a good thing you didn't call me that night.

forward - forwards

1 **'forward' and 'forwards'**
If you move or look **forward** or **forwards,** you move or look in a direction that is in front of you.

Salesmen rushed forward to serve her.
John peered forward through the twilight.
Ralph walked forwards a couple of steps.

Forwards is only used as an adverb.

2 **'look forward to'**
If you **are looking forward to** something that is going to happen, you want it to happen because you think you will enjoy it.

He's <u>looking forward to</u> going home.

(*i*) Note that you do not say that someone is 'looking forwards to' something.

⇨ For more information about this use, see **Usage** entry at **look forward to.**

3 **'forward' used as an adjective**

Forward is also an adjective. A **forward** movement is one in which someone or something moves forwards.

Slow <u>forward</u> movement was made possible by pivoting his body with his shoulders.
He points out that flapping wings provide <u>forward</u> thrust as well as upward lift.

When **forward** has this meaning, it can only be used in front of a noun.

4 **'forward' used as a verb**

Forward is also a verb. If you **forward** a letter to someone, you send it on to them when they have moved to a different address.

Would you mind <u>forwarding</u> my mail to this address?

found

Found is the past tense and past participle of **find.**

I <u>found</u> a five-pound note in the gutter.
His body <u>has not been found.</u>

⇨ See **Usage** entry at **find.**

Found is also a verb. If someone **founds** a town or an organization, they cause it to be built or to exist. The past tense and past participle of **found** is **founded.**

Tyndall <u>founded</u> his own publishing company.

free - freely

1 **no controls**

You use **free** as an adjective to describe activities which are not controlled or limited.

The <u>free</u> movement of peoples within the EU is a principle I applaud.
The elections were <u>free</u> and fair.

You do not use **free** as an adverb with this meaning. Instead you use **freely.**

We are all comrades here and I may talk <u>freely</u>.

2 **no payment**

If something is **free**, you can have it or use it without paying for it.

The coffee was <u>free.</u>
… <u>free</u> school meals.

The adverb you use with this meaning is **free**, not 'freely'. For example, you say 'Pensioners can travel **free** on the buses'. You do not say ~~'Pensioners can travel freely on the buses'.~~

Children can get into the museum <u>free.</u>

3 **releasing**

If something is cut or pulled **free**, it is cut or pulled so that it is no longer attached to something or no longer trapped.

She tugged to get it <u>free.</u>
I shook my jacket <u>free</u> and hurried off.

(*i*) Note that you do not say that something is cut or pulled 'freely'.

frequently

⇨ See section on **frequency** in **Grammar** entry at **Adjuncts.**

friend

1 **'friend'**

Your **friends** are people you know well and like spending time with. You can refer to a friend who you know very well as a **good friend**, a **great friend**, or a **close friend**.

He's a good friend of mine.

She later married Shaw's great friend Harley Granville-Barker.

A close friend told me about it.

If someone has been your friend for a long time, you can refer to them as an **old friend**.

I was brought up by an old friend of mother's called Lucy Nye.

2 **'be friends with'**

If someone is your friend, you can say that you are **friends with** them.

Dolley continued to be friends with Theodosia.

You used to be great friends with him, didn't you?

I also became friends with Melanie.

friendly

A **friendly** person is kind and pleasant.

Malawians seemed to be the friendliest people in the world.

If you are **friendly to** someone or **friendly towards** someone, you are kind and pleasant to them.

The women had been friendly to Lyn.

I have noticed that your father is not as friendly towards me as he used to be.

If you are **friendly with** someone, you like each other and enjoy spending time together.

I became friendly with a young engineer.

Friendly is never an adverb. You do not say, for example, 'He behaved friendly'. You say 'He behaved **in a friendly way**'.

We talk to them in a friendly way.

She looked up at Bal, smiling at him in such a friendly way.

⚠ **WARNING:** Do not confuse **friendly** and **sympathetic**. If you have a problem and someone is **sympathetic** or shows a **sympathetic** attitude, they show that they care and would like to help you.

My boyfriend was very sympathetic.

⇨ See **Usage** entry at **sympathetic**.

fries

⇨ See **Usage** entry at **chips**.

frighten - frightened

1 **'frighten' and 'frightened'**

If something **frightens** you, it makes you feel afraid.

Rats and mice don't frighten me.

Frighten is almost always a transitive verb. You never say that someone 'frightens'. If you want to say that someone is afraid because of something that has happened or that might happen, you say that they **are frightened**.

Miriam was too frightened to tell her family what had happened.

He told the audience not to be frightened.

⇨ For more information about **frightened**, see **Usage** entry at **afraid - frightened**.

2 **'frightening'**

Do not confuse **frightened** with **frightening**. Something that is **frightening** causes you to feel fear.

It was a very <u>frightening</u> experience.
It is <u>frightening</u> to think what damage could be done.

from

1 source or origin

You use **from** to say what the source, origin, or starting point of something is.

…wisps of smoke <u>from</u> a small fire.
Get the leaflet <u>from</u> a post office.
The shafts were cut <u>from</u> heavy planks of wood.

When you are talking about the person who has written you a letter or sent a message to you, you say that the letter or message is **from** that person.

He received a message <u>from</u> Vito Corleone.

If you **come from** a particular place, you were born there, or it is your home.

I <u>come from</u> Scotland.

⇨ See **Usage** entry at **come from**.

2 time

If something happens **from** a particular time, it begins to happen at that time.

<u>From</u> November 1980, the amount of money you receive may be less.
We had no rain <u>from</u> March to October.

You do not use **from** to say that something began to be the case at a particular time in the past and is still the case now. You do not say, for example, 'I have lived here from 1984'. You say 'I have lived here **since** 1984'.

He has been vice-chairman <u>since</u> 1998.

⇨ See **Usage** entry at **since.**

⚠ **WARNING:** You do not use 'from' to say who wrote a book, play, or piece of music. You do not say, for example, 'Have you seen any plays from Ibsen?' You say 'Have you seen any plays **by** Ibsen?'

…the latest book <u>by</u> Hilda Offen.
…a collection of pieces <u>by</u> Mozart.

front

1 'front'

The **front** of a building is the part that faces the street or that has the building's main entrance.

Attached to the <u>front</u> of the house, there was a large veranda.

2 'in front of'

If you are between the front of a building and the street, you say that you are **in front of** the building.

A crowd had assembled <u>in front of</u> the courthouse.
A soldier was taking snapshots of his friends <u>in front of</u> the National Assembly.

ⓘ Note that you do not say that you are 'in the front of' a building.

3 'opposite'

If there is a street between you and the front of a building, you do not say that you are 'in front of' the building. You say that you are **opposite** it.

The hotel is <u>opposite</u> a railway station.
<u>Opposite</u> is St Paul's Church.
There was a banner on the building <u>opposite</u>.

USAGE

 Note that speakers of American English usually say **across from** rather than **opposite**.

Stinson has rented a home <u>across from</u> his parents.

frontier

⇨ See **Usage** entry at **border - frontier - boundary**.

fruit

Fruit is usually an uncount noun. Oranges, bananas, grapes, and apples are all **fruit**.

I have eaten <u>fruit</u> all my life.

… <u>fruit</u> imported from Australia.

You can refer to an individual orange, banana, etc as a **fruit**, but this use is not common.

Each <u>fruit</u> contains many juicy seeds.

You do not use a plural form of **fruit** to refer to several oranges, bananas, etc. Instead you use **fruit** as an uncount noun. For example, you say 'I'm going to the market to buy some **fruit**'. You do not say ~~'I'm going to the market to buy some fruits'~~.

…a table with some <u>fruit</u> on it.

They gave me <u>fruit</u> and cake and wine.

full

If something is **full of** things or people, it contains a very large number of them.

…a long garden <u>full of</u> pear and apple trees.

His office was <u>full of</u> people.

ⓘ Note that you do not use any preposition except **of** after **full** in sentences like these.

fun - funny

1 'fun'

If something is **fun**, it is pleasant, enjoyable, and not serious.

It's <u>fun</u> working for him.

If you have **fun**, you enjoy yourself.

We had great <u>fun</u> sleeping rough on the beaches.

She wanted a bit more <u>fun</u> out of life.

Fun is an uncount noun. You do not say that someone 'has funs' or 'has a great fun'.

2 'funny'

You say that something is **funny** when it is strange, surprising, or puzzling.

The <u>funny</u> thing is, we went to Arthur's house just yesterday.

'I always thought of him as very ordinary.'–'That's <u>funny</u>. So did I.'

Have you noticed anything <u>funny</u> about this plane?

Several other words can be used to mean 'strange' or 'surprising'.

⇨ For more information, see **Usage** entry at **unusual**.

You also say that something is **funny** when it is amusing and makes you smile or laugh.

He told <u>funny</u> stories.

It did look <u>funny</u> upside down.

furniture

Furniture consists of the large moveable objects in a room, such as tables and chairs.

She arranged the <u>furniture.</u>

All the <u>furniture</u> is painted green to balance the red walls.

Furniture is an uncount noun. You do not talk about 'furnitures'.

further

⇨ See **Usage** entry at **farther - further**.

G g

---

gain - earn

1 **'gain'**

If you **gain** something such as an ability or quality, you gradually get more of it.

After a nervous start, the speaker began to gain confidence.

This gives you a chance to gain experience.

2 **'earn'**

You do not say that someone 'gains' wages or a salary. The word you use is **earn**.

She earns sixty pounds a week.

---

garbage

⇨ See **Usage** entry at **rubbish**.

---

gas - petrol

1 **'gas'**

The air-like substance that burns easily and that is used for cooking and heating is called **gas**.

Coal is usually cheaper than gas.

 In American English, the liquid that is used as fuel for motor vehicles is also called **gas**, or sometimes **gasoline**.

I'm sorry I'm late. I had to stop for gas.

2 **'petrol'**

In British English, this liquid is called **petrol**.

Petrol only costs 30p per gallon there.

---

gay

In modern English, if you say that a person is **gay**, you mean that they are homosexual.

I told them I was gay.

A homosexual man can be referred to as a **gay**.

Many gays were worried about the new system.

Gay is sometimes used to describe colours, places, or pieces of music which make people feel cheerful because they are bright or lively. This is a rather old-fashioned use.

Pauline wore a gay yellow scarf.

---

gaze - stare

The verbs **gaze** and **stare** are both used to talk about looking at something for a long time. If you **gaze** at something, it is often because you think it is marvellous or impressive.

A fresh-faced little girl gazes in wonder at the bright fairground lights.

If you **stare** at something or someone, it is often because you think they are strange or shocking.

Various families came out and stared at us.

---

generally - mainly

1 **'generally'**

Generally means 'usually', 'in most cases', or 'on the whole'.

Wool and cotton blankets are <u>generally</u> cheapest.
His account was <u>generally</u> accurate.

2 'mainly'

You do not use 'generally' to say that something is true about most of something, or about most of the people or things in a group. The word you use is **mainly.**

The spacious main bedroom is <u>mainly</u> blue.
The African half of the audience was <u>mainly</u> from Senegal or Mali.

gently - politely

1 'gently'

If you do something **gently,** you do it carefully and without using force, in order to avoid hurting someone or damaging something.

I shook her <u>gently</u> and she opened her eyes.

2 'politely'

You do not use 'gently' to say that someone behaves with good manners. The word you use is **politely.**

He thanked me <u>politely</u>.

geographical

The physical features of an area are often referred to as its **geographical** features.

…the <u>geographical</u> features which make the coast so attractive.
… <u>geographical</u> and climatic conditions.

A **geographical** area is one which is determined by its physical features, rather than, for example, by administrative or political boundaries.

The country stretches over three very different <u>geographical</u> areas.
There was gradual change over a broad <u>geographical</u> region.

Geographical and **Geographic** occur in the names of some organizations and publications concerned with the subject of geography.

…the Royal <u>Geographical</u> Society of Oslo.
…the latest issue of National <u>Geographic</u>.

If you want to say that something relates to the teaching of geography, you use **geography** in front of another noun. You do not use 'geographical' or 'geographic'.

…a <u>geography</u> book.
…my <u>geography</u> course.

get

Get is a very common verb which has several different meanings. Its past tense is **got**, not 'getted'. In British English and formal American English, its past participle is also **got**. However, many American speakers use **gotten** as the past participle.

⇨ See **Usage** entry at **gotten.**

1 used to mean 'become'

Get is very often used to mean 'become'.

The sun shone and I <u>got</u> very brown.
I <u>was getting</u> quite hungry.

⇨ See **Usage** entry at **become.**

2 used to form passives

In conversation, you often use **get** instead of 'be' to form passives.

My husband <u>got</u> fined in Germany for crossing a road.
Our car <u>gets</u> cleaned about once every two months.

(*i*) Note that you only use **get** like this to refer to an event which is not planned or intended, or which happens later or less often than intended.

You do not use **get** to form passives in formal English.

3 | **used to describe movement**
You use **get** instead of 'go' when you are describing a movement that involves difficulty.
We got along the street as best we could.
I don't imagine we can get over that wall.

Get is also used in front of **in**, **into**, **on**, and **out** to describe acts of entering and leaving vehicles and buildings.
Sometimes I would get into my car and drive into San Diego.
I got out of there as fast as possible.

⇨ See **Usage** entries at **go into** and **go out.**

4 | **'get to'**
When you **get to** a place, you arrive there.
When we got to Firle Beacon we had a rest.

Get to is also used in front of a verb to say that someone gradually acquires a particular attitude, gradually becomes aware of something, or gradually becomes acquainted with someone or something.
I got to hate surprises.
I got to know Shrewsbury.

⇨ See **Usage** entry at **get to - grow to.**

5 | **transitive uses of 'get'**
If you **get** something, you obtain or receive it.
He's trying to get a flat.
I got the anorak for Christmas.

If you **get** a meal, you prepare it.
He was in the galley getting supper.
She was getting breakfast as usual.

⇨ See **Usage** entry at **cook.**

6 | **'have got'**
Got is also used in the expression **have got.**
⇨ See **Usage** entry at **have got.**

get away
⇨ See **Usage** entries at **escape** and **leave.**

get to - grow to
You use **get to** or **grow to** in front of another verb to say that someone gradually acquires a particular attitude. **Grow to** is more formal than **get to.**
I got to like the whole idea.
I grew to dislike working for the cinema.

You also use **get to** to say that someone gradually becomes aware of something, or gradually becomes acquainted with someone or something.
I got to realize it more as I grew older.
I got to know a few people.

If you **get to** do something, you have the opportunity to do it, and you do it.
I got to do a little work in Cuba.
They get to stay in nice hotels.

USAGE

get up
⇨ See **Usage** entry at **rise - raise**.

girl

1 **'girl'**

Girl is used in two different ways.
It is used to refer to a female child.

…*a girl of eleven.*

It is also used to refer to a young woman up to the age of about 30.

We'd been invited to the wedding of a girl we knew.
At the next table was a pretty girl waiting for someone.

2 **'little girl'**

You can refer to a girl up to the age of 10 as a **little girl**.

She's a very well behaved little girl.

3 **'young woman'**

Many young women object to being referred to as **girls**. Instead they prefer to be referred to as **women**. In formal writing, the expression **young woman** is used, instead of 'girl'.

The Society aims to serve the needs of young women.

 In American English, young people sometimes use **female** to talk about young women, to avoid using **woman** or **girl**.

I cannot say for certain, as she is a female.

give

1 **form and word order**

Give is a very common verb which has several meanings. Its past tense is **gave**, not 'gived'. Its past participle is **given**.

Give usually takes an indirect object. For some meanings of **give,** the indirect object must go in front of the direct object. For other meanings, it can go either in front of the direct object or after it.

2 **physical actions**

Give is often used to describe physical actions. When you use **give** like this, you put the indirect object in front of the direct object. For example, you say 'He **gave the ball a kick** '. You do not say 'He gave a kick to the ball'.

He gave the door a push.
Judy gave Bal's hand a squeeze.

3 **expressions and gestures**

Give is also used to describe expressions and gestures. When **give** is used like this, the indirect object goes in front of the direct object.

He gave her a fond smile.
As he passed me, he gave me a wink.

4 **effects**

You can also use **give** to describe an effect produced by someone or something. Again, you put the indirect object in front of the direct object.

I thought I'd give you a surprise.
That noise gives me a headache.

5 **things**

If you **give** someone something, you offer it to them and they take it. When you use **give** like this, the indirect object can go either in front of the direct object or after it. When you put the direct object first, you put 'to' in front of the indirect object.

She <u>gave Minnie</u> the keys.
He <u>gave</u> the letter <u>to the platoon commander.</u>

However, when the direct object is a pronoun and the indirect object is not a pronoun, you must put the direct object first. You say 'He **gave it to his father** '. You do not say '~~He gave his father it~~'.

He poured some whisky and <u>gave it to Atkinson.</u>

6 | **information**

You also say that you **give** someone information, advice, a warning, or an order. When **give** is used like this, the indirect object can go either in front of the direct object or after it.

Castle <u>gave the porter</u> the message.
Dad <u>gave</u> a final warning <u>to them</u> not to look at the sun.
He <u>gave</u> an order <u>to his subordinates</u>.

given name

⇨ See **Usage** entry at **Christian name - first name - forename - given name.**

glad - happy - pleased

1 | **'glad'**

If you are **glad** about something, you are pleased about it.

I'm so <u>glad</u> that Dr. Herenton won.
She seemed <u>glad</u> of the chance to get rid of the responsibility.

⇨ For a graded list of words indicating how pleased someone is, see **Usage** entry at **pleased - disappointed.**

2 | **'happy'**

You do not use 'glad' in front of a noun, and you do not use it to describe someone's mental state at a particular time in their life. If you want to say that someone is contented and enjoys life, you say that they are **happy**, not 'glad'.

She always seemed such a <u>happy</u> woman.

3 | **'cheerful'**

If someone shows that they are happy by smiling and laughing a lot, you say that they are **cheerful.**

She had remained <u>cheerful</u> and energetic throughout the trip.

⇨ For a graded list of words indicating how happy someone is, see **Usage** entry at **happy - sad.**

glasses

A person's **glasses** are two lenses in a frame which they wear to help them to see better.

He took off his <u>glasses.</u>
...a girl with red hair and <u>glasses.</u>

Glasses is a plural noun. You do not talk about 'a glasses'. Instead you talk about **a pair of glasses.**

Gretchen took <u>a pair of glasses</u> off the desk.

After **glasses** you use a plural form of a verb. After **a pair of glasses** you use a singular form.

My glasses <u>are</u> misted up.
A pair of glasses <u>costs</u> more than a pair of tights.

go

1 | **describing movement**

When you are describing movement from one place to another, or movement past or

USAGE

through a place, you usually use the verb **go**.

⇨ See, however, Usage entry at **come**.

The past tense of **go** is **went**. The past participle is **gone**.

I <u>went</u> to Stockholm.
A girl <u>went</u> past, smiling to herself.
Celia <u>had gone</u> to school.

2 using 'get'

If a movement involves difficulty, you often use **get,** rather than 'go'. For example, you say 'We managed to **get** over the wall'. You do not say 'We managed to go over the wall'.

It used to take them three days to <u>get</u> to school.
Nobody can <u>get</u> past.
Frankie and Clive were trying to <u>get</u> through the window.

⇨ See Usage entry at **get.**

3 leaving

Go is sometimes used to say that someone or something leaves a place.

'I must <u>go</u>,' she said.
Our train <u>went</u> at 2.25.

⇨ See Usage entry at **leave.**

4 'let go'

If you **let** a person or animal **go,** you release them.

<u>Let</u> me <u>go</u>!
I'm quite happy really to net a fish and then <u>let</u> it <u>go.</u>

⇨ See Usage entry at **release - let go.**

5 'have gone' and 'have been'

If someone is visiting a place or now lives there, you can say that they **have gone** there.

He <u>has gone</u> to Argentina.
Someone said she <u>'d gone</u> to Wales.

If someone has visited a place and has now returned, American speakers say that they **have gone** there. British speakers say that they **have been** there.

I <u>'ve</u> never <u>gone</u> to Italy.
I <u>'ve been</u> to Santander many times.

6 talking about activities

You can use **go** with an '-ing' form to talk about activities.

Let's <u>go shopping</u>!
We <u>went exploring</u> together in the fields.

You can also use **go** with **for** and a noun group to talk about activities.

He <u>went for a hike.</u>
She said you <u>were going for a swim.</u>

⚠ **WARNING:** You do not use **go** with a 'to'-infinitive to talk about activities. You do not say, for example, 'They went to fish below the falls' or 'He went to hike'.

7 'go and'

To **go and** do something means to move from one place to another in order to do it.

I'll <u>go and</u> see him in the morning.
Let's <u>go and</u> have a drink somewhere.
I <u>went and</u> fetched another glass.

8 'be going to'

You use **be going to** to talk about the future. For example, if you say that something **is**

going to happen, you mean that it will happen, or that you intend it to happen.
She told him she was going to leave her job.
I 'm not going to be made a scapegoat.

⇨ See **Grammar** entry at **The Future.**

9 **used to mean 'become'**
Go is sometimes used to mean 'become'.
The water had gone cold.
I 'm going bald.

⇨ See **Usage** entry at **become.**

go away
⇨ See **Usage** entry at **leave.**

go into

1 **'get into'**
When you enter a building or room, you usually say that you **go into** it or **go in.**
One day I went into the church.
She took him into a small room, switching on the light as she went in.

2 **'get into'**
However, you say that you **get into** a car or **get in.**
I saw him get into a cab.
I walked to the van, got in and drove away.

You also say that you **get into** a lift, a small boat, or a small plane.

3 **'get on' and 'board'**
When you enter a bus, train, large plane, or ship, you say that you **get on** it or **board** it.
George got on the bus with us.
Griffiths took a taxi to the Town station and boarded a train there.

4 **'embark'**
You can also say that someone **embarks on** a ship.
She had embarked on the S.S. Gordon Castle at Tilbury.

⚠ **WARNING:** You never say that someone 'goes into' any kind of vehicle.

5 **entering with difficulty**
If you enter a building or room with difficulty, you say that you **get into** it or **get in.**
We tried to get into the dormitory unnoticed.
It cost three pounds to get in.

good - well

1 **'good'**
Something that is **good** is pleasant, acceptable, or satisfactory. The comparative form of **good** is **better,** not 'gooder'. The superlative form is **best.**
Your French is probably better than mine.
Some of our best English actors have gone to live in Hollywood.

2 **'well'**
'Good' is never an adverb. If you want to say that something is done to a high standard or to a great extent, you use **well,** not 'good'.
She speaks French well.
You say you don't know this man very well?

⇨ See **Usage** entry at **well.**

The comparative form of **well** is **better,** not 'more well'. The superlative form is **best.**

good-looking

People are <u>better</u> housed than ever before.
The film works <u>best</u> as a marital drama.

⇨ See **Usage** entry at **better**.

good-looking

⇨ See **Usage** entry at **beautiful**.

goods - possessions

1 **'goods'**

Goods are things that are made to be sold. **Goods** is a plural noun. You do not use 'a' in front of it, and you use the plural form of a verb after it.

...a wide range of electrical <u>goods.</u>
You are responsible for seeing that your <u>goods are</u> insured.

2 **'possessions'**

You do not refer to the things that someone owns as their 'goods'. The word you use is **possessions**.

He had few <u>possessions.</u>
I kept one room locked, with my most treasured <u>possessions</u> inside.

go on

The phrasal verb **go on** can be followed by either an '-ing' form or a 'to'-infinitive, but with different meanings.

If you **go on doing** something, you continue to do it.

But I just <u>went on eating</u> like I hadn't heard a thing.
I'll <u>go on trying</u> to persuade him.

If you **go on to do** something, you do it after doing something else.

She <u>went on to talk</u> about the political consequences.
He later <u>went on to</u> form a successful computer company.

go out

1 **'go out'**

When you leave a building or room, you usually say that you **go out** of it or **go out**.

He threw down his napkin and <u>went out</u> of the room.
I <u>went out</u> into the garden.
He bowed and <u>went out.</u>

2 **'get out'**

However, you say that you **get out** of a car or **get out**.

We <u>got out</u> of the car.
I <u>got out</u> and examined the right rear wheel.

You also say that you **get out** of a lift, plane, or small boat.

3 **'get off'**

When you leave a bus or train, you say that you **get off**.

When the train stopped, he <u>got off.</u>
Get off</u> at Mayfield Church.

You can also say that you **get off** a plane.

⚠ **WARNING:** You never say that someone 'goes out' of any kind of vehicle.

4 **leaving with difficulty**

If you leave a building or room with difficulty, you say that you **get out** of it or **get out**.

I <u>got out</u> of the room somehow and made for the bathroom.

got

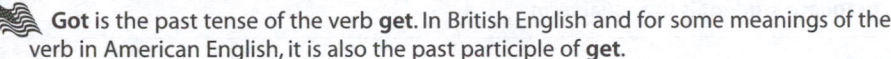 **Got** is the past tense of the verb **get**. In British English and for some meanings of the verb in American English, it is also the past participle of **get**.

⇨ See **Usage** entry at **get**.

Got is also used in the expression **have got**.

⇨ See **Usage** entry at **have got**.

gotten

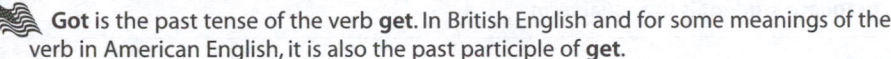 In American English, **gotten** is usually the past participle of **get**. It is used to mean 'obtained', 'received', 'become', or 'caused to be'.

He could have gotten his boots without anyone seeing him.
He'd gotten some tear gas in his eyes.
His leg may have gotten tangled in a harpoon line.
I had gone to work and gotten quite a lot done.

It is also used in many phrasal verbs and phrases.

No one had gotten around to cleaning up the mess.
He must have gotten up at dawn.
We should have gotten rid of him.
She had gotten married and given birth to a child.

⚠ **WARNING:** You do not use **have gotten** to mean 'possess'. For example, you do not say 'I have gotten a headache' or 'He has gotten two sisters'.
You also do not use **have gotten** to mean 'must'. For example, 'I had gotten to see the President' does not mean 'It was necessary for me to see the President'. It means 'I had succeeded in seeing the President'.

⇨ See **Usage** entry at **get to - grow to**.

In British English, the past participle of **get** is **got**, not 'gotten'.

government

The **government** of a country is the group of people responsible for ruling it. After **government** you can use either a singular or plural form of a verb.

The government has had to cut back on public expenditure.
The government have made up their minds that they are going to win no matter what.

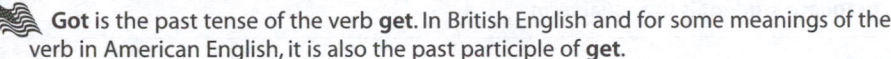 Note that in American English, a singular form of the verb is usually used with **government**. Note also that when talking about the US president and the people he appoints to help him govern, speakers of American English use the word **administration**.

He pledged that his administration will consult with allies and Congress.

go with

⇨ See **Usage** entry at **accompany**.

grade

⇨ See **Usage** entry at **class - form -grade**.

graduate

A **graduate** is someone who has successfully completed a first degree at a university or college.

 In America, a **high school graduate** is someone who has completed a course at a high school.

⇨ See **Usage** entry at **high school**.

 Someone who already has a first degree and who is studying for a higher degree can

USAGE

be called a **graduate student,** a **postgraduate student,** or a **postgraduate.** In America, **graduate student** is the usual term.

great

⇨ See **Usage** entry at **big - large - great.**

greatly

⇨ See section on **degree** in **Grammar** entry at **Adjuncts.**

grill

⇨ See **Usage** entry at **cook.**

ground floor

In British English, the floor of a building which is level with the ground is called the **ground floor.** The floor above it is called the **first floor,** the floor above that is the **second floor,** and so on.

 In American English, the floor which is level with the ground is called the **first floor,** the floor above it is the **second floor,** and so on.

So, for example, the highest floor of a three-storey building is called the **second floor** in British English and the **third floor** in American English.

grow

1 **'grow'**

When children or young animals **grow,** they become bigger or taller. The past tense of **grow** is **grew,** not 'growed'. The past participle is **grown.**

Babies who are small at birth grow faster.
The animal grew to a height of over a metre.
Has he grown any taller?

2 **'grow up'**

When someone **grows up,** they gradually change from a child into an adult. People often talk about the place where they **grew up** or the period during which they **grew up.**

He grew up in Cambridge.
They grew up in the early days of television.

⚠ **WARNING:** Be careful not to confuse the verbs **grow up** and **bring up. Bring up** is a transitive verb, and describes the process of looking after and socializing a child.

...we both felt the town was the perfect place to bring up a family.

Note then, that parents do not 'grow up' their children, they **bring** them **up.**

⇨ See **Usage** entry at **bring up - raise - educate.**

3 **used to mean 'become'**

Grow is also used to mean 'become'.
He's growing old.

⇨ See **Usage** entry at **become.**

4 **'grow to'**

Grow to is used to say that someone gradually acquires a particular attitude.
I grew to hate those smiling faces.

⇨ See **Usage** entry at **get to - grow to.**

guardian - guard

1 **'guardian'**

A young person's **guardian** is someone who is legally appointed to look after their affairs, usually because their parents are dead.

Geldof has plenty of money to care for Tiger Lily himself as her legal <u>guardian</u>.

 'guard'

You do not use 'guardian' to refer to a railway official who travels on a train and makes sure that it arrives and leaves at the correct time. This official is called the **guard** or **conductor** in British English.

In American English, he or she is called the **conductor**.

If anybody has lost anything, please contact the <u>guard</u> at the back of the train.
The <u>conductor</u> stopped the train, and Union Pacific called 911 to report the fire.

guess

 'guess'

If you **guess** that something is the case, you decide that it is probably the case.

By this time they'<u>d guessed</u> that something was gravely wrong.
I should have <u>guessed</u> that you were a detective.

You also use **guess** to say that someone finds the correct answer to a problem or question without knowing that it is correct.

I <u>had guessed</u> the identity of her lover.

2 **'I guess'**

People sometimes say **I guess** to indicate that they think that something is true or likely.

I <u>guess</u> I got the news a day or so late.
'What's that?'–'Some sort of blackbird, I <u>guess</u>.'

People also sometimes reply to a question in an affirmative way by saying **'I guess so'**. Note that they do not say 'I~~ guess it~~'.

'You think you can find out something about Larry's partners?'–'I <u>guess so</u>.'
'Does that answer your question?'–'Yeah, I <u>guess so</u>.'

People sometimes show agreement with a negative statement, or reply to a negative question in an affirmative way, by saying **'I guess not'**.

'So no one actually saw this shark.'–'No, I <u>guess not</u>.'

 All of these expressions are more common in American English than in British English.

guilty

If you feel unhappy because you think you have done something wrong, you can say that you **feel guilty about doing** it.

Some people <u>feel guilty about being</u> so much richer than the rest of the world.
I <u>feel guilty about using</u> all that water.

ⓘ Note that you do not use a 'to'-infinitive after **feel guilty**. You do not say, for example, '~~Some people feel guilty to be so much richer than the rest of the world~~'.

gymnasium

A **gymnasium** is a building or large room used for physical exercise, with equipment such as bars, mats, and ropes in it. In conversation, people often refer to a gymnasium as a **gym**.

⚠ **WARNING:** You do not use **gymnasium** to refer to a British or American school for older pupils. In Britain, the general term for a school of this kind is **secondary school**.

In America, it is **high school**.

⇨ See **Usage** entry at **high school**.

H h

habit - custom

1 'habit'

A **habit** is something that an individual person does often or regularly, usually for no particular reason.

He had a nervous <u>habit</u> of biting his nails.
I wish I could get out of this <u>habit</u>.

2 'custom'

A **custom** is something done by the people in a society in particular circumstances or at a particular time of the year.

It is the <u>custom</u> to take chocolates or fruit when visiting a patient in hospital.
My wife likes all the old English <u>customs</u>.

hair

Hair can be a count noun or an uncount noun.

1 used as a count noun

Each of the thread-like things growing on your head and body is a **hair.** You can refer to several of these things as **hairs.**

…two strands of high-purity glass, each thinner than a human <u>hair</u>.
…the black <u>hairs</u> on the back of his hands.

2 used as an uncount noun

However, you do not refer to all the hairs on your head as your 'hairs'. You refer to them as your **hair.**

I washed my hands and combed my <u>hair</u>.
…a young woman with long blonde <u>hair</u>.

half - half of

1 used in front of noun groups

Half or **half of** an amount or object is one of the two equal parts that together make up the whole amount or object.
You use **half** or **half of** in front of a noun group beginning with a determiner. **Half** is more common.

He had finished about <u>half his drink</u>.
She is allowed to keep <u>half of her tips</u>.
She'd known me <u>half her life</u>.
For <u>half of her adult life</u> she has been pregnant.

(i) Note that in standard English you do not say 'the half of'.

In front of measurement words like **metre**, **kilogram**, or **hour**, you always use **half**, not 'half of'.

They were nearly <u>half a mile</u> away.
The fault was fixed in <u>half an hour</u>.
They had been friends for about <u>half a century</u>.

You use **half of** in front of pronouns. You do not use 'half'.

The waitress brought the drink she had ordered, and Ellen drank <u>half of it</u> immediately.
More than <u>half of them</u> have gone back to their home towns.

(i) Note that you do not use 'they' or 'we' after **half of**. Instead you use **them** or **us**.

Half of them have had no education at all.
If production goes down by half, half of us lose our jobs.

When you use **half** or **half of** in front of a singular noun or pronoun, you use a singular form of a verb after the noun or pronoun.

Half her property belongs to him.
Half of it was exposed above water.

When you use **half** or **half of** in front of a plural noun or pronoun, you use a plural form of a verb after the noun or pronoun.

Half my friends have jobs and wives and children.
Half of them were still married.

2. **used as a pronoun**
Half can itself be a pronoun.

Roughly half are French and roughly half are from North America.
…some of the money for you, half for me.

3. **used as a noun**
You can also use **half** as a noun to talk about a particular part of something.

… the first half of the eighteenth century.
Philip Swallow rented an apartment in the top half of a two-storey house.

hand

Your **hand** is the part of your body at the end of your arm. It includes your fingers and your thumb.

You do not usually refer to a particular person's hand as 'the hand'. You say **his hand** or **her hand**. You refer to your own hand as **my hand**.

The young man held a letter in his hand.
Louise stood shading her eyes with her hand.
I raised my hand.
Some passengers had their hands bound.

However, if you say that someone does something to someone else's hand, you usually use **the**.

I grabbed Rick by the hand.
Father took his wife by the hand.

handicapped
⇨ See **Usage** entry at **crippled**.

handsome
⇨ See **Usage** entry at **beautiful**.

hang

1. **'hang' something somewhere**
If you **hang** something somewhere, you place it so that its highest part is supported and the rest is not. When **hang** has this meaning, its past tense and past participle is **hung**.

She hung the kettle on the iron post.
He had hung the coat where he could see it.

2. **'hang' a person**
To **hang** a person means to kill them by tying a rope around their neck and taking away the support from under their feet so that they hang in the air. When **hang** has this meaning, its past tense and past participle is **hanged**.

He went off and hanged himself.
Rebecca Smith was hanged in 1849.

USAGE

happen

3 other meanings

Hang has several other meanings and is used in some phrasal verbs. For all these other meanings, the past tense and past participle is **hung.**

Her long hair <u>hung</u> over her face.
The smell of paint <u>hung</u> in the air.
'Good night.' He <u>hung up</u> the phone.

happen

1 'happen'

When something **happens,** it takes place without being planned.

Then a strange thing <u>happened.</u>
I dare say there'll be an investigation into what <u>happened</u> and why.

Happen does not have a passive form. You do not say, for example, that something 'was happened'.

2 'take place', 'occur'

Happen is usually used after vague words like **something, thing, what,** or **this.** After words with a more precise meaning, you usually use **take place** or **occur.**

The incident <u>had taken place</u> many years ago.
Mrs Weaver had been in the milking shed when the explosion <u>occurred.</u>

You do not say that a planned event 'happens'. You say that it **takes place.**

The first meeting of the committee <u>took place</u> on 9 January.
The election <u>took place</u> in June.

3 'happen to'

When something **happens to** someone or something, it takes place and affects them.

I wonder what <u>'s happened to</u> Jeremy?
I'm sure something <u>has happened to</u> Molly.
If anything <u>happens to</u> the car, you'll have to pay for it.

(i) Note that in sentences like these you do not use any preposition except **to** after **happen.**

You use **happen** in front of a 'to'-infinitive to indicate that something happens or is the case by chance. For example, instead of saying 'The two people he wanted to speak to lived in the same street', you can say 'The two people he wanted to speak to **happened to live** in the same street'.

I just <u>happened to be</u> in the wrong place at the wrong time.
If you <u>happen to see</u> Jane, ask her to phone me.

You often use **happen to be** in sentences beginning with **there.** For example, instead of saying 'A post office happened to be in the next street', you say '**There happened to be** a post office in the next street'.

There <u>happened to be</u> a policeman on the corner, so I asked him the way.

(i) Note that in sentences like these you must use **there.** You do not say, for example, ~~'Happened to be a post office in the next street'.~~

happy - sad

There are a number of adjectives which are used to indicate how happy or sad someone is. The adjectives in the following list are arranged from 'most happy' to 'least happy':

● **ecstatic, elated, euphoric**

His wife gave birth to their first child, and he was <u>ecstatic</u> about it.
'That was one of the best races of my life,' said an <u>elated</u> Hakkinen.
It had received <u>euphoric</u> support from the public.

● **joyful, radiant, jubilant**

A wedding is a <u>joyful</u> celebration of love.

On her wedding day the bride looked truly radiant.
Hogg was jubilant after winning the men's doubles for the 10th time.

● **happy, cheerful, jolly**

Marina was a confident, happy child.
They are both very cheerful in spite of their colds.
She was a jolly, kindhearted woman.

● **light-hearted**

They were light-hearted and prepared to enjoy life.

● **contented, fulfilled**

She was gazing at him with a soft, contented smile on her face.
I feel more fulfilled doing this than I've ever done.

● **dissatisfied, moody, discontented**

82% of voters are dissatisfied with the way their country is being governed.
David's mother was unstable and moody.
The government tried to appease discontented workers.

● **sad, unhappy, depressed, gloomy, glum, dejected, despondent, dispirited**

I'd grown fond of our little house and felt sad to leave it.
Her marriage is in trouble and she is desperately unhappy.
She's been very depressed and upset about this whole situation.
Do you tend to be over-serious or gloomy?
She was very glum and was obviously missing her children.
Everyone has days when they feel dejected or down.
I feel despondent when my work is rejected.
I left eventually at six o'clock feeling utterly dispirited and depressed.

● **miserable, wretched**

I took a series of badly paid secretarial jobs which made me really miserable.
I feel really confused and wretched.

hard - hardly

[1] **'hard'**

Hard can be an adjective or an adverb, often with a similar meaning.

Coping with three babies is very hard work.
Many old people have worked hard all their lives.

[2] **'hardly'**

Hardly is an adverb. It has a totally different meaning from **hard**. You use **hardly** to say that something is only just true.

I hardly knew him.
Nick, on the sofa, hardly slept.

If you use an auxiliary or modal with **hardly,** you put the auxiliary or modal first. You say, for example, 'I **can hardly** see'. You do not say 'I hardly can see'.

Two years before, the wall had hardly existed.
She can hardly wait to begin.
We could hardly move.

⚠ **WARNING:** You do not use 'not' with **hardly.** You do not say, for example, 'I did not hardly know him'. You say 'I **hardly** knew him'.

Hardly is sometimes used in longer structures to say that one thing happened immediately after another.

The local police had hardly finished their examination when the CID arrived.

ⓘ Note that in structures like these you use **when,** not 'than'. You do not say, for example,

USAGE

'The local police had hardly finished their examination than the CID arrived'.

In stories, **hardly** is sometimes put at the beginning of a sentence, followed by 'had' or the verb 'to be' and the subject.

Hardly had he uttered the words when he began laughing.

3 | 'hardly ever'

If something **hardly ever** happens, it almost never happens.

I hardly ever spoke to them.
Daisy had women friends whom Tim hardly ever met.

⇨ Many other words and expressions can be used to say how frequently something happens. For a graded list, see section on **frequency** in **Grammar** entry at **Adjuncts**.

harm

⇨ See **Usage** entry at **damage**.

harmful

If something is **harmful to** someone or **harmful for** them, it has a bad effect on them.

Too much salt can be harmful to a young baby.
Potassium could be harmful for those with impaired kidneys.

You can also say that something is **harmful to** a thing.

Excessive amounts may be harmful to the skin.

ⓘ Note that you do not say that something is 'harmful for' a thing.

hate

⇨ See **Usage** entry at **like - dislike**.

have

Have is one of the most common verbs in English. It is used in many different ways. Its other forms are **has, having, had**.

1 | used as an auxiliary

Have is often an auxiliary.

They have just bought a new car.
She has never been to Rome.
Having been warned beforehand, I knew how to react.

⇨ See **Grammar** entries at **Auxiliaries** and **Tenses**.

Have, has, and **had** are not usually pronounced in full when they come after a pronoun or noun. When you write down what someone says, you usually represent **have, has**, and **had** as **'ve, 's**, and **'d** after a pronoun. You can also represent **has** as **'s** after a noun.

I've changed my mind.
She's become a very interesting young woman.
I do wish you'd met Guy.
Ralph's told you often enough.

⇨ See **Usage** entry at **Contractions**.

2 | 'have to'

Have to is often used to say that someone must do something.

I have to speak to your father.
He had to sit down because he felt dizzy.

⇨ See **Usage** entry at **must**.

3 | actions and activities

Have is often used in front of a noun group to say that someone performs an action or takes part in an activity.

Did you <u>have</u> a look at the shop when you were there?
I'm going to <u>have</u> a bath.

⇨ See **Usage** entry at **have - take.**

4 | causing something to be done

Have can also be used to say that someone arranges for something to be done. When **have** is used like this, it is followed by a noun group and a past participle.

We 've just <u>had the house decorated.</u>
They <u>had him killed.</u>

You can also use **have** to say that someone causes another person to do something or to be in a particular state. When **have** is used like this, it is followed by a noun group and either an '-ing' form or a past participle.

Alan <u>had me looking</u> for that book all day.
He <u>had me</u> utterly <u>confused.</u>

5 | possession

Have is often used to indicate possession.

He <u>had</u> a small hotel.
There is no point in <u>having</u> a mobile phone if you cannot hear your calls clearly.

In spoken British English, **have got** is usually used instead of 'have' to indicate possession.

She <u>'s got</u> two sisters.
<u>Have</u> you <u>got</u> any brochures on Holland, please?

⇨ See **Usage** entry at **have got.**

6 | using a simple tense

Note especially that you do not use a continuous tense in any of the following ways:

● You do not use a continuous tense when you are talking about ownership. For example, you do not say 'I am having a collection of old coins'. You say 'I **have** a collection of old coins' or 'I **'ve got** a collection of old coins'. Similarly, you do not use a continuous tense when you are talking about relationships. You do not say 'I am having three sisters' or 'I am having a lot of friends'.

We <u>haven't got</u> a car.
They <u>have</u> one daughter.
I <u>'ve got</u> loads of friends.

● You do not use a continuous tense to say that someone or something has a particular feature. For example, you do not say 'He is having a beard'.

He <u>has</u> nice eyes.
He <u>had</u> beautiful manners.
…toys which roll or <u>have</u> wheels.
The door <u>'s got</u> a lock on it.

● You do not use a continuous tense to say that someone has an illness or disease. For example, you do not say 'She is having a bad cold'.

He <u>had</u> a headache.
Sam <u>'s got</u> measles.

● You do not use a continuous tense to say how much time someone has in which to do something. For example, you do not say 'He is having plenty of time to get to the airport'.

I <u>haven't got</u> time to go to the library.
He <u>had</u> only a short time to live.
I hope I <u>'ll have</u> time to finish it.

7 | using a continuous tense

Here are some ways in which you do use a continuous tense of **have:**

● You use a continuous tense to say that an activity is taking place. For example, you say 'He **is having** a bath at the moment'. You do not say 'He has a bath at the moment'.

USAGE

The children are having a party.
I was having a chat with an old friend.

● You use a continuous tense to say that an activity will take place at a particular time in the future. For example, you can say 'I'**m having** lunch with Barbara tomorrow'.

We 're having a party tonight.
She 's having a baby next month.

● You also use a continuous tense to talk about continuous or repeated actions, events, or experiences. For example, you can say 'I **am having** driving lessons'.

I 'm having an affair with Bernard.
I was already having problems.
Neither of us was having any luck.
You 're having a very busy time.

have - take

1 'have' and 'take' to talk about actions

Have and **take** are both commonly used with nouns as their objects to indicate that someone performs an action or takes part in an activity. With some nouns, you can use either **have** or **take** with the same meaning. For example, you can say '**Have** a look at this' or '**Take** a look at this'. Similarly, you can say 'We **have** our holidays in August' or 'We **take** our holidays in August'.

 There is often a difference between British and American usage. For example, British speakers usually say 'He **had** a bath', while American speakers say 'He **took** a bath'.

I'm going to have a bath.
I took a bath, my second that day.

 When talking about activities such as walking and swimming, American speakers often use **take.** For example, they say 'He **took** a walk' or 'She **took** a swim'. British speakers sometimes use **have,** but it is much more common in British English to say 'He **went for** a walk' or 'She **went for** a swim'.

Brody decided to take a walk.
I went down to the ocean and took a swim.
After dinner we went for a walk.
She's going for a swim.

2 meals

In modern English, you use **have** to say that someone eats a meal.

He has his meals at home.
We might have dinner together.

In the past, **take** was sometimes used instead of 'have', but this use now sounds very formal.

I always took my meals at White's.

⇨ For more information about verbs used in connection with meals, see **Topic** entry at **Meals**.

have got

1 form and basic uses

Have got is often used in spoken English with the same meaning as 'have'.

I have got two cats and a dog.
You have got a problem.

Have got, has got, and **had got** are not usually pronounced in full. When you write down what someone says, you usually write '**ve got, 's got,** or '**d got.**

I 've got her address.

He 's got a beard now.
They' d got a special grant from the Institute.

 Have got is not used in formal written English, and is less common in American English than British English.

You cannot use **have got** for all meanings of **have**. You use it when you are talking about a situation or state, but not when you are talking about an event or action. For example, you say 'I **'ve got** a new car', but not ~~'I've got a bath every morning'~~.

2 possession
Have got is most commonly used to talk about possession, relationships, and qualities or features.

I 've got a rather curious table.
She 's got two sisters.
He 's got a lovely smile.
It's a nice town. It 's got very nice shops.

3 illness
You often use **have got** to talk about illnesses.

Sam 's got measles.
I 've got an awful headache.

4 availability
You also use **have got** to talk about the availability of something.

Come in and have a chat when you 've got time.
I think we 've got an enormous amount to offer.

5 future events
You can use **have got** with a noun group to mention a future event that you will be involved in.

I 've got a date.
I 've got an appointment with two Americans.

You can use **have got** with a noun group and an '-ing' form to mention an event that you have arranged or that will affect you.

I 've got two directors flying out first class.
I 've got some more people coming.

You use **have got** with a noun group and a 'to'-infinitive to say that there is some work that you must do.

I 've got some work to do.
She 's got the house to clean.

6 negatives
In negative sentences, **not** goes between **have** and **got**, and is almost always shortened to **n't**.

He hasn't got a moustache.
I haven't got any graph paper.

 American speakers do not usually use this form. Instead they use the auxiliary **do**, followed by **not** and **have**. **Not** is usually shortened to **n't**.

I don't have a boyfriend.
I'm bored. I don't have anything to do.

7 questions
In questions, you put the subject between **have** and **got**.

Have you got enough money for a taxi?
I need a drink. What have you got?

 American speakers do not usually use this form. Instead they use the auxiliary **do**,

USAGE

followed by the subject and **have**. Some British speakers also use **do** and **have**.

Do you <u>have</u> her address?
What kind of animals <u>do</u> you <u>have?</u>

8 past tense
The past tense form of **have got** is quite common in spoken British English.

He '<u>d got</u> this interview at Oxford.
I didn't tell them I '<u>d got</u> some other pearls.

9 future tense
The future tense of **have got** is hardly ever used. Instead you use the future tense of **have**.

I'm hoping he '<u>ll have</u> more positive opinions at some point.
We '<u>ll have</u> all morning to get them.

10 infinitives and participles
Similarly, if you use an infinitive or a participle, you use **have** rather than 'have got'.

People with dishwashers always seem <u>to have</u> tidy kitchens.
I'd like <u>to have</u> a room like yours.
He dreamed of <u>having</u> a car.

---

have got to
⇨ See **Usage** entry at **must**.

---

have to
⇨ See **Usage** entry at **must**.

---

he

He is the subject of a verb. You use **he** to refer to a man, boy, or male animal that has already been mentioned, or whose identity is known.

<u>He</u> had a nervous habit of biting his nails.
Bill had flown back from New York and <u>he</u> and his wife took me out to dinner.

When the subject of a sentence is followed by a relative clause, you do not use **he** in front of the main verb. For example, you do not say ~~'The man who is going to buy my car, he lives in Norwich'~~. You say 'The man who is going to buy my car lives in Norwich'.

The man who came into the room was small and slender.
Professor Marvin, who was always early, was there already.

---

he - she - they

1 'he'
He, **him**, **his**, and **himself** are sometimes used to refer back to an indefinite pronoun or to a word such as 'person', 'child', or 'student'.

If anybody complained about this, <u>he</u> was told that things would soon get back to normal.
It won't hurt a child to have <u>his</u> meals at a different time.

Many people object to this use because it suggests that the person referred to is male.

2 'he or she'
You can sometimes use **he or she**, **him or her**, **his or her**, or **himself or herself**.

Teach a child to dial 999 and read out the telephone number from which <u>he or she</u> is speaking.
New species are usually given the name of their finder, but there is nothing to prevent <u>him or her</u> waiving this right.
Nothing excuses the child from <u>his or her</u> own responsibilities.
Anyone can call <u>himself or herself</u> a psychologist, even if untrained and unqualified.

Many people avoid these expressions because they think they sound clumsy and unnatural, especially when more than one of them is used in the same sentence.

In writing, some people use **s/he** to mean 'he or she'.

It is worth asking your doctor if s/he knows of anyone locally.

3 **'they'**

In conversation, most speakers use **they, them,** and **their.**

Nearly everybody thinks they 're middle class.

If I think someone may attempt to take an overdose, I will spend hours talking to them.

Don't hope to change anyone or their attitudes.

This use used to be considered incorrect, but it is becoming more common in writing as well as in speech. In this book, we usually use **they, them,** and **their.**

It is often possible to avoid all the above uses. You can sometimes do this by using plurals. For example, instead of saying 'Every student has his own room', you can say '**All** the students have **their** own rooms'. Instead of saying 'Anyone who goes inside must take off his shoes', you can say '**People** who go inside must take off **their** shoes'.

headache

If you have a **headache,** you have a pain in your head.

I told Derek I had a headache.

Headache is a count noun. You do not say that someone 'has headache'.

headline

⇨ See **Usage** entry at **title.**

headmaster - principal

 In Britain, the teacher in charge of a school is called the **headmaster** or **headmistress.** In the United States, these terms refer only to teachers in charge of private schools. The teacher in charge of any other kind of school is called the **principal.**

 In Britain, the person in charge of a college is often called a principal. In the United States, the person in charge of a college is usually called a **president.**

Dr Susan Danby, Principal of the College of the Royal Academy of Dancing, 1979-99.

…a high-profile team of business people and educators, including former Yale president Benno Schmidt.

heap - stack - pile

1 **'heap'**

A **heap** of things is usually untidy, and often has the shape of a hill or mound.

Now, the house is a heap of rubble.

2 **'stack'**

A **stack** is usually tidy, and often consists of flat objects placed directly on top of each other.

…a neat stack of dishes.

3 **'pile'**

A **pile** of things can be tidy or untidy.

…a neat pile of clothes.

hear

1 **'hear' in the present**

If you **can hear** a sound, you are aware of it because it has reached your ears.

I can hear a car.

(i) Note that you usually use **can** in sentences like these. You say, for example, 'I **can hear** a

USAGE

radio'. You do not say 'I hear a radio'. You also do not use a continuous tense. You do not say 'I am hearing a radio'.

The past tense and past participle of **hear** is **heard** /hɜːrd/. If you want to say that someone was aware of something in the past, you use **heard** or **could hear.**

She heard no further sounds.
Below me I could hear the roar of a waterfall.

2 'hear' in the past

However, if you want to say that someone suddenly became aware of something, you must use **heard.**

I heard a shout.

You can use an '-ing' form after **heard** or **could hear** to indicate that someone was aware of something that was continuing to take place.

He heard Alan shouting and laughing.
I could hear him crying.

You can use an infinitive without 'to' after **heard** to indicate that someone was aware of a complete event or action.

I heard him dash into the bathroom.
I heard Amy O'Shea cry out in fright.

⚠ **WARNING:** You do not use a 'to'-infinitive with an active form of **hear.** You do not say, for example, 'I heard him to open the door'.

3 passive use

You can use a passive form of **hear,** followed by either a 'to'-infinitive or an '-ing' form. You use a 'to'-infinitive after a passive form when you are talking about a complete event or action.

He was heard to say 'We're not going to have any more of this.'

You use an '-ing' form when you are talking about an event or action that was continuing to take place.

Her companions could be heard playing games.

⇨ See also **Usage** entry at **listen to.**

heat

In informal English, if you want to emphasize how hot the weather is, you can say that it is **boiling** or **scorching.**

'It's boiling in here', complained Miriam.
That race was run in scorching weather.

In winter, if the temperature is above average, you can say that it is **mild.** In general, **hot** suggests a higher temperature than **warm,** and **warm** things are usually pleasant.

The area is famous for its mild winter climate.
It was too hot even for a gentle stroll.
…a warm evening.

help

1 'help' as a transitive verb

If you **help** someone, you make something easier for them. When **help** has this meaning, it can be followed by an infinitive, with or without 'to'. For example, you can say 'I **helped him to move** the desk' or 'I **helped him move** the desk'. There is no difference in meaning.

We must try to help students to have confidence in their ability.
Something went wrong with his machine so I helped him fix it.

2 'help' as an intransitive verb

You can also use **help** as an intransitive verb, followed by an infinitive with or without 'to'. If someone **helps do** something or **helps to do** it, they help other people to do it.

My mum used to help cook the meals for the children.
Dora helped to carry the wounded off the battlefield.

If something **helps do** something or **helps to do** it, it makes it easier for that thing to be done.

The money helped keep me off the streets for a while.
This helped to improve the competitiveness of American exports.

⚠ **WARNING:** You do not use an '-ing' form after **help.** You do not say, for example, 'I helped moving the desk' or 'I helped him moving the desk'.

3 'cannot help'

If you **cannot help** doing something, you are unable to prevent yourself from doing it.

I couldn't help teasing him a little.

⚠ **WARNING:** You do not use a 'to'-infinitive after **cannot help.** You do not say, for example, 'I couldn't help to tease him a little'.

her

Her can be the object of a verb or preposition. You use **her** to refer to a woman, girl, or female animal that has already been mentioned, or whose identity is known.

They gave her the job.
I knew your mother. I was at school with her.

⚠ **WARNING:** You do not use 'her' as the indirect object of a sentence when you are referring to the same person as the subject. Instead you use **herself.**

Rose bought herself a piece of cheese for lunch.

here

1 'here'

Here refers to the place where you are.

I'm glad you'll still be here next year.
We're allowed to come here at any time.

⚠ **WARNING:** You never use 'to' in front of **here.** You do not say, for example, 'We're allowed to come to here at any time'.

2 'here is' and 'here are'

You can use **here is** or **here are** at the beginning of a sentence when you want to draw attention to something or to introduce something. In standard English, you use **here is** in front of a singular noun group and **here are** in front of a plural noun group.

Here is a summer soup that is almost a meal in itself.
Here are the addresses to which you should apply.

here - hear

These words are both pronounced /hɪə/.

1 'here'

You use **here** to refer to the place where you are.

Come here.
She left here at eight o'clock.

⇨ See **Usage** entry at **here.**

USAGE

2 **'hear'**

When you **hear** a sound, you are aware of it through your ears.

Did you <u>hear</u> anything unusual?

⇨ See **Usage** entry at **hear**.

high - tall

1 **'high'**

You use **high** to describe things which measure a larger distance than usual from the bottom to the top. For example, you talk about a **high hill** or a **high fence**.

…the <u>high</u> mountains of northern Japan.

…the <u>high</u> walls of the prison.

2 **'tall'**

You use **tall** to describe things which are higher than usual, but which are also much higher than they are wide. So, for example, you talk about a **tall tree** or a **tall chimney**.

…a lawn of <u>tall</u> waving grass.

…a <u>tall</u> heron standing on one leg.

You always use **tall** when you are talking about people.

…a <u>tall</u> handsome man.

She was a young woman, fairly <u>tall</u> and slim.

(*i*) Note that when talking about babies, you use **long**, not **tall**.

Baby Megan McDonald was 22 inches <u>long</u> when she was born.

3 **another meaning of 'high'**

High also means 'a long way above the ground'. For example, you talk about a **high window** or a **high shelf**.

…a large room with a <u>high</u> ceiling.

high school

 In America, a **high school** is a school for older pupils up to the age of 18. In Britain, the general term for a school of this kind is **secondary school**.

him

Him can be the object of a verb or preposition. You use **him** to refer to a man, boy, or male animal that has already been mentioned, or whose identity is known.

He asked if you'd ring <u>him</u> when you got in.

There's no need for <u>him</u> to worry.

⚠ **WARNING:** You do not use 'him' as the indirect object of a sentence when you are referring to the same person as the subject. Instead you use **himself**.

He poured <u>himself</u> a whisky.

hire - rent - let

1 **'hire' and 'rent'**

 If you pay a sum of money in order to use something for a short period of time, you can say that you **hire** it or **rent** it. **Hire** is more common in British English and **rent** is more common in American English.

We <u>hired</u> a car from a local car agency and drove across the island.

He <u>rented</u> a car for the weekend.

If you make a series of payments in order to use something for a long period, you say that you **rent** it. You do not usually say that you 'hire' it.

A month's deposit may be required before you can <u>rent</u> the house.

2 **'hire out'**

If you hire something from someone, you can say that they **hire** it **out** to you.

Companies <u>hiring out</u> narrow boats report full order books.

3 **'rent out'**

If you rent something from someone, you can say that they **rent** it **out** to you.

They had to <u>rent out</u> the upstairs room.

4 **'let' and 'let out'**

If you rent a building or piece of land from someone, you can say that they **let** it to you or **let** it **out** to you. The past tense and past participle of **let** is **let**, not 'letted'.

The cottage <u>was let</u> to an actress from London.
I couldn't sell the London flat, so I <u>let</u> it <u>out</u>.

Note that this usage is more common in British English than American English. The usual American terms are **rent** and **rent out**.

The house was <u>rented</u> to a tenant farmer.
He repaired the boat and <u>rented</u> it <u>out</u> for $150.

historic - historical

1 **'historic'**

You use **historic** to say that something was important in history, or that it will be regarded as important in the future.

…their <u>historic</u> struggle for emancipation.
…a <u>historic</u> decision.

2 **'historical'**

You use **historical** to say that someone or something really existed or happened in the past, rather than being invented by a writer.

Which <u>historical</u> figure would be guest of honour at your house-warming party?

Historical novels, plays, and films deal with real or imaginary events in the past.

…Richard of Bordeaux, a <u>historical</u> play by Gordon Daviot.

Historical occurs in the names of some organizations concerned with the subject of history.

…the German <u>Historical</u> Institute.

However, if you want to say that something relates to the teaching of history, you use **history** in front of another noun. You do not use 'historic' or 'historical'.

…a <u>history</u> book.
…a <u>history</u> lesson.

hit

To **hit** someone or something means to touch them quickly with a lot of force. The past tense and past participle of **hit** is **hit**, not 'hitted'.

He <u>hit</u> the burglar with a candlestick.
The truck <u>had hit</u> a wall.

hold

1 **'hold' used to mean carry**

When you **hold** something, you carry or support it using your hands or arms. The past tense and past participle of **hold** is **held**, not 'holded'.

I <u>held</u> the picture up to the light.
A baby should <u>be held</u> for feedings and comforting, and at other times.

2 **used to mean 'have'**

Hold is sometimes used with the meaning 'have' or 'possess'. It is used, for example, with words like **licence** and **passport**.

You need to <u>hold</u> a work permit.

It is also used with words like **opinion**.

He <u>held</u> firm opinions which usually conflicted with my own.
This soon dispelled any foolish notions they might <u>hold</u> about Baldwin's ability.

Both of these uses are rather formal, and in conversation you normally use **have,** not 'hold'.

He doesn't need to <u>have</u> a licence.
I <u>have</u> very strong opinions about electoral reform.

holiday - vacation

1   'holiday'

In British English, you refer to a period of time which you are allowed to spend away from work or school as the **holiday** or the **holidays.**

The school had undergone repairs during the <u>holiday</u>.
One day after the Christmas <u>holidays</u> I rang her up.

You refer to a period of time spent away from home enjoying yourself as a **holiday.**

He thought that Vita needed a <u>holiday</u>.
I went to Marrakesh for a <u>holiday</u>.

When you spend a long period of time like this each year, you refer to it as your **holidays.**

Where are you going for your <u>holidays</u>?

(*i*) Note that you usually use a determiner or a possessive in front of **holiday** or **holidays.** You do not say, for example, '~~I went to Marrakesh for holidays~~'.

If you are **on holiday,** you are spending a period of time away from work or school, or you are spending some time away from home enjoying yourself.

Remember to turn off the gas when you go <u>on holiday</u>.

In American English, a **holiday** is a single day when people do not work, often to commemorate an important event.

In British English, a day like this is called a **bank holiday.**

When Americans talk about **the holidays,** they mean the period at the end of the year that includes Christmas and the New Year; sometimes Thanksgiving (at the end of November) is also included in this.

Now that <u>the holidays</u> are over, Christmas trees on sidewalk curbs are a familiar sight.

2   'vacation'

The usual American word for a longer period of time spent away from work or school, or for a period of time spent away from home enjoying yourself, is **vacation.**

Harold used to take a <u>vacation</u> at that time.

At a British university or college, the **vacation** is one of the periods of several weeks when the university or college is officially closed for teaching.

I've a lot of reading to do over the <u>vacation.</u>

3   'vac'

In conversation, British students often refer to one of these periods as the **vac.**

Think ahead to exams, orals, long <u>vac</u> courses.

home

1   'home'

Your **home** is the place where you live and feel that you belong. **Home** is most commonly used to refer to a person's house, but it can also be used to refer to a town, a

region, or a country.
His father worked away from <u>home</u> for much of Jim's first five years.
Jack dreamed of <u>home</u> from his prisoner-of-war camp.

You do not refer to a particular person's home as 'the home'. You say **his home, her home,** or just **home.**

The biographer Victoria Glendinning is selling <u>her home</u> in Ireland.
Their children have left <u>home.</u>

⚠ **WARNING:** You never use 'to' immediately in front of **home.** You do not say, for example, '~~We went to home~~'. You say 'We went **home** '.

Come <u>home</u> with me.
The policeman escorted her <u>home.</u>

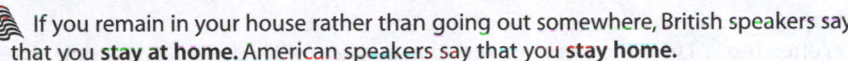 If you remain in your house rather than going out somewhere, British speakers say that you **stay at home.** American speakers say that you **stay home.**

Oh, we'll just have to <u>stay at home</u> for the weekend.
What was Cindy supposed to do? <u>Stay home</u> all day and dust the house?

2 'the home' and 'a home'

You use **the home** or **a home** when you are talking about homes in general.

Their view of women is that their place is in <u>the home.</u>
<u>A home</u> should be as clean as you can get it.

You also use **a home** when you are describing a situation in which someone does not have a place of their own where they can live.

I want <u>a home</u> and children.
I had never had <u>a home</u> of my own.

You use **a** with an adjective to talk about a particular kind of home. For example, you can say 'She has **a pleasant home** '.

I long for <u>a happy home</u> but my daughters are so difficult.
He has <u>a nice home</u> in Bradford.

homely

 In American English, if you say that a person is **homely,** you mean that they are not attractive to look at.

He was presumably Caporelli's neighbor, this meek-looking, <u>homely</u> man in the tweed jacket.
A broad grin spread across his <u>homely</u> features.

You cannot use **homely** in this way in British English. If you want to say that someone is not attractive to look at, you say that they are **plain.**

…a <u>plain</u> plump girl with pigtails.

In British English, if you say that someone is **homely,** you mean that they behave kindly and in a simple, unsophisticated way.

He greeted us in his usual <u>homely</u> manner.

homework - housework

1 'homework'

Homework is work that pupils are given to do at home. You say that pupils **do** homework. You do not say that they 'make' homework.

He never did any <u>homework.</u>

2 'housework'

Housework is work such as cleaning or washing that is done in a house.

She relied on him to do most of the <u>housework.</u>

homework • house

USAGE

> ⚠ **WARNING:** Both **homework** and **housework** are uncount nouns. You do not talk about 'a homework' or 'houseworks'.

hood

⇨ See **Usage** entry at **bonnet - hood**.

hope

Hope can be a verb or a noun.

1 **used as a verb**

If you **hope** that something is true or will happen, you want it to be true or to happen.

She hoped she wasn't going to cry.
I sat down, hoping to remain unnoticed.

2 **'I hope'**

You often use '**...I hope**' to express a wish that someone will have a pleasant time. After **hope** you can use either the future tense or the simple present tense. For example, you can say '**I hope you'll enjoy** the film' or '**I hope you enjoy** the film'.

I hope you'll enjoy your stay in Roehampton.
I hope you get well very soon.

ⓘ Note that if you say to someone that you **hope they are going to do** something, you are usually asking or reminding them to do something that they may not want to do.

I hope you're going to show me what you're working on.
Next time I come I hope you're going to be a lot more entertaining.

3 **'I hope so'**

If someone says that something is the case, or asks you whether something is the case, you can express your wish that it is the case by saying '**I hope so**'.

'I will see you in the church.'– 'I hope so.'
'You'll be home at six?'– 'I hope so.'

ⓘ Note that you do not say 'I hope it'.

4 **'I hope not'**

Similarly, you can express your wish that something is not the case by saying '**I hope not**'.

'You haven't lost the ticket, have you?'– 'I hope not.'

ⓘ Note that you do not say 'I don't hope so'.

5 **'hope' used as a noun**

Hope is a feeling of confidence that what you want to happen might happen.

The government ignored the problem in the hope that it would go away.
She never completely gave up hope.

If you think that it is impossible that something will happen, you can say that there is **no hope of** it happening.

There seemed to be no hope of winning.
The infantry had no hope of keeping up with the tanks.

ⓘ Note that you do not use any preposition except **of** after **no hope**.

hopefully

1 **used after a verb**

If you do something **hopefully**, you do it hoping that a particular thing will happen.

She continued to gaze hopefully in their direction.
For the first time in a long time, she smiles hopefully.

This use of **hopefully** occurs mainly in books, rather than in conversation.

2   **used as a sentence adverb**

Hopefully is much more commonly a sentence adverb. You add **hopefully** to a statement to indicate that you hope that what you are saying is true or will be true.

Hopefully, future fossil-hunters will unearth some evidence to resolve this question.
They've learnt a few lessons which, hopefully, will put them back on track.

This use of **hopefully** is fairly new in British English, and some people object to it. However, it is now very common in conversation and writing. No other English adverb can be used with the same meaning.

horrible - horrid - horrific - horrifying - horrendous

1   **describing unpleasant events or experiences**

All of these words except **horrid** can be used to describe a very unpleasant and shocking event, experience, or story.

Still the horrible shrieking came out of his mouth.
It was one of the most horrific experiences of my life.
…the horrifying descriptions of life in the trenches.
…the horrendous murder of a prostitute.

2   **expressing dislike**

In conversation, people use **horrible** and **horrid** to show their dislike for someone or something. These words can be used to describe almost anything which is unpleasant, ugly, disgusting, or depressing.

The hotel was horrible.
His suit was a horrible colour.
We had to live in a horrid little flat.

3   **for emphasis**

Horrible is also used in front of a noun to emphasize how bad something is. For example, you can say 'I've made a **horrible** mistake'.

Everything's in a horrible muddle.

4   **'horrendous'**

Horrendous is usually used to describe something which is extremely difficult to deal with.

… horrendous problems.
The cost can be horrendous.

hospital

A **hospital** is a place where sick people are looked after by doctors and nurses. In British English, if you want to say that someone is in a hospital without mentioning which hospital they are in, you say they are **in hospital.**

I used to visit him in hospital.
The mother broke down completely and had to go into hospital.

American speakers do not say 'in hospital'. They say **in the hospital.**

She will be better off in the hospital.
She broke a bone in her back and spent some time in the hospital.

In both British and American English, if you want to say that something happened in a particular hospital, you usually say **at the hospital.**

I was working at the hospital.

house

Your **house** is the building where you live and which you own or rent. You do not usually say 'I am going to my house' or 'She was in her house'. You say 'I am going **home**' or 'She was at **home**'.

Brody arrived <u>home</u> a little before five.
I'll finish the script at <u>home.</u>

⇨ See **Usage** entry at **home.**

housework

⇨ See **Usage** entry at **homework - housework.**

how

1 ways of doing things

You use **how** in questions and explanations when you are talking about the way something is done.

<u>How</u> do you get rid of a nasty smell?
Tell me <u>how</u> to get there.
This is <u>how</u> I make a vegetable curry.

⚠ **WARNING:** You do not use 'how' to mean 'in the way that'. For example, you do not say ~~'He walks to work every day, how his father did'.~~ Instead you use **like, as,** or **the way.**

⇨ See **Usage** entry at **like - as - the way.**

2 asking about someone's health

You use **how** with **be** to ask about someone's health.

<u>How</u> are you?
<u>How</u> is she? All right?
<u>How</u> is your son this morning?

⚠ **WARNING:** You do not use 'how' to ask what kind of person someone is. For example, if you are asking someone for a description of their boss, you do not say ~~'How is your boss?'.~~ You say ' **What** is your boss **like?'**

<u>What</u>'s his mother <u>like?</u>

3 asking about impressions

You use **how** with **be** to ask about someone's impressions of something.

<u>How</u> was your trip?
<u>How</u> was the smoked trout?

⚠ **WARNING:** You do not use 'how' to ask for a description of a thing or place. For example, if you say 'How is Birmingham?', you are not asking someone what kind of place Birmingham is; you are asking them if they are enjoying living or working there. If you want them to give you a description of Birmingham, you say **'What** is Birmingham **like?'**

<u>What</u> is Fiji <u>like?</u>

You also do not say ~~'How do you think of Birmingham?'~~ You say **'What do you think of** Birmingham?'

<u>What do you think of</u> his writing style?
<u>What did you think of</u> Holland?

4 commenting on a quality

In the past, people used to use **how** in front of adjectives to remark about the extent to which someone or something had a quality. For example, they said things like 'How clever he is!' Note the word order here: they did not say ~~'How he is clever!'~~

Sentences like these are not usually used in modern English. Instead of 'How clever he is!', people usually say **'He's so clever', 'Isn't he clever?',** or **'What a clever man!'**

They're so childish.

Aren't they amazing?
What a beautiful girl!

People often use **how** with an adjective and nothing else, when they are commenting on what someone has just said.

'She has a flat there as well.' – 'How nice!'
'To my surprise, I found her waiting for me at the station.' – 'How kind!'
The paper listed me as dead? How strange.

⇨ For other ways of commenting on what someone has just said, see **Topic** entry at **Reactions**.

however

1 **'however'**

You use **however** when you are adding a comment which contrasts with what has just been said.

The more I talked, the more silent Eliot became. However, I left thinking that I had created quite an impression.
Losing at games doesn't matter to some women. Most men, however, can't stand it.

You also use **however** to say that it makes no difference how something is done.

You can do it however you want.
However we add that up, it does not make a dozen.

2 **'how ever'**

Sometimes people use **ever** after **how** at the beginning of a question. They do this to express surprise at something that has happened. For example, instead of saying 'How did you get here?', they say '**How ever** did you get here?'

How ever did you find me?

How ever is always written as two separate words. You do not write, for example, 'However did you find me?'

how much

You use **how much** when you are asking about the price of something. For example, you say '**How much** is that T-shirt?'

I like that dress – how much is it?

ⓘ Note that you do not say 'How much is the price of that T-shirt?'

You only use **how much** with **be** when you are asking about the price of something. You do not use it to ask about other amounts of money. You do not say, for example, 'How much is his income?' You say '**What is his income?**', '**What does he earn?**', or '**How much does he earn?**'

Similarly, you do not say 'How much is the temperature outside?' or 'How much is the population of Tokyo?' You say '**What** is the temperature outside?' or '**What** is the population of Tokyo?'

What is the basic rate of income tax?
What is the lowest temperature it's possible to reach?

huge

⇨ See **Usage** entry at **small - large**.

hundred

A hundred or **one hundred** is the number 100.
You can say that there are **a hundred** things or **one hundred** things.

She must have had a hundred cats at least.
The group claimed the support of over one hundred MPs.

ⓘ Note that you do not say that there are 'hundred' things.

You do not add '-s' to the word **hundred** when you put another number in front of it.

There are more than two hundred languages spoken in Nigeria.

For numbers greater than 100, most speakers add **and** before pronouncing the second part of the number, but speakers of American English sometimes leave out the **and.** For example, 370 is expressed as **three hundred and seventy** in British English and sometimes as **three hundred seventy** in American English.

… nine hundred and eighty-three votes.

… a hundred fifty pounds.

hunting - shooting

In American English, **hunting** is the killing of wild animals or birds as a sport or for food, using guns.

… the shotgun the President used when he went deer hunting.

In British English, **hunting** usually refers to the chasing and killing of foxes by dogs, followed by people on horseback. The killing of animals and birds with guns is referred to in British English as **shooting.**

Fox hunting with hounds was voted illegal in Scotland.
Grouse shooting begins in August.

hurt

Hurt can be a verb or an adjective.

1 used as a verb

If you **hurt** yourself or **hurt** a part of your body, you accidentally injure yourself. The past tense and past participle of **hurt** is **hurt,** not 'hurted'.

…a young boy who had fallen down and hurt himself.
How did you hurt your finger?

If a part of your body **hurts,** you feel pain there.

My leg was beginning to hurt.

In American English, you can also say that a person **hurts.**

When that anesthetic wears off, you're going to hurt a bit.

Some British speakers also use **hurt** like this, but this use is not generally accepted in British English.

2 used as an adjective

You can use **hurt** as an adjective to describe an injured person.

Nobody in the bunker seemed to be hurt.
His comrades asked him if he was hurt.

If someone has a bad injury, you do not say that they are 'very hurt'. You say that they are **badly hurt** or **seriously hurt.**

The soldier was badly hurt.
Last year 107 child pedestrians were killed and 5,000 seriously hurt in car accidents.

You do not usually use 'hurt' in front of a noun. You do not, for example, talk about 'a hurt soldier'. You say 'an **injured** soldier'.

⇨ See **Usage** entry at **injure.**

hyphen

⇨ See **Topic** entries at **Punctuation** and **Spelling.**

I i

I

A speaker or writer uses **I** to refer to himself or herself. **I** is the subject of a verb. It is always written as a capital letter.

I shall be leaving soon.
I like your dress.

You can also use **I** as part of the subject of a verb. For example, you can say '**My friend and I** are going to Sicily'. Note that you mention the other person first. You do not say '~~I and my friend are going to Sicily~~'.

My mother and I stood beside the road and waited.
My brothers and I are musicians.

(i) Note that you do not use 'I' after **is**.

⇨ See **Usage** entry at **me**.

identical

If two or more things are **identical**, they are exactly the same in every detail.

...twenty or thirty suitcases with identical blue labels.

You can say that one thing is **identical with** another thing or **identical to** it. There is no difference in meaning.

Chemically, it is almost identical to limestone.
Is creativity identical with intelligence?

i.e.

⇨ See **Usage** entry at **namely - i.e.**

if

1 possible situations

You use **if** to introduce a conditional clause in which you mention a possible situation.

If a tap is dripping, it needs a new washer.
If you can thread a needle, you can mend a fuse.

You can use **if** to mention a situation that might exist in the future. In the conditional clause, you use the simple present tense. You do not use the future tense.

If all goes well, Voyager II will head on to Uranus.
If nuclear weapons are employed in a world war, the world will be destroyed.

You sometimes use **if** in a conditional clause to suggest that someone does something. You usually use the simple present tense in the conditional clause.

If you look in the middle of the picture, you'll see Mrs Galsworthy.

You can use **if** to mention a situation that sometimes existed in the past.

They sat on the grass if it was fine.
If it was raining, we usually stayed indoors.

You can also use **if** to mention something that might have happened in the past, but did not in fact happen. In the conditional clause, you use the past perfect tense. You do not use the simple past tense.

If he had realized that, he would have run away.
If she had not married, she would probably have become something special in her field.

USAGE

ill - sick

2 | **unlikely situations**

You also use **if** in conditional clauses to mention situations that do not exist, or events that are unlikely to happen. In the conditional clause, you use the simple past tense. You do not use a present tense.

The older men would find it difficult to get a job if they <u>left</u> the farm.
If I <u>frightened</u> them, they might take off and I would never see them again.

When the subject of the conditional clause is **I**, **he**, **she**, **it**, **there**, or a singular noun, it is generally considered correct to use **were** in the clause instead of was'.

If I <u>were</u> in his circumstances, I would do the same thing.
Mr Fatchett said that if the policy <u>were</u> to be dropped, it would be better to do it in October.
If education <u>were</u> even better organized, there would be no complaint about the content or level of work required.

However, in conversation people usually use **was** (except in the expression '**If I were you**').

If I <u>was</u> an architect, I'd re-design this house.
There is no quarantine at the stud so if it <u>was</u> there the virus would have spread by now.
This would still be true if Britain <u>was</u> out of the Community.

You can use **was** or **were** in conversation, but you should use **were** in formal writing.

3 | **in reported questions**

If is also used in reported questions.

I asked her <u>if</u> I could help her.
He inquired <u>if</u> her hair had always been that colour.
I wonder <u>if</u> you'd give the children a bath.

⇨ See **Grammar** entry at **Reporting**.

ill - sick

1 | **'ill' and 'sick'**

Ill and **sick** are both used to say that someone has a disease or some other problem with their health.

Davis is <u>ill.</u>
...a <u>sick</u> child.
Your uncle is very <u>sick.</u>

Most British speakers do not use **ill** in front of a noun unless they are also using an adverb. For example, they do not talk about 'an ill woman', but they might talk about 'a **seriously ill** woman'.

...a terminally <u>ill</u> patient.

 American and Scottish speakers sometimes use **ill** in front of a noun without using an adverb.

We had to get medical help for our <u>ill</u> sisters.

⚠ **WARNING:** You do not say that someone becomes 'iller' or 'more ill'. You say that they become **worse**.

Each day Kunta felt a little <u>worse.</u>

2 | **'be sick'**

To **be sick** means to bring up food from your stomach.
⇨ See **Usage** entry at **sick**.

⚠ **WARNING:** You do not use **ill** or **sick** to say that someone has received an injury. You say that they are **injured** or **hurt**.

⇨ See **Usage** entries at **injure** and **hurt**.

illness - disease

1 **'illness'**

If you have an **illness,** there is something wrong with your health, so that you cannot work or live normally. An illness can affect several parts of your body. It can last for a long time or a short time, and its effects can be serious or not serious.

Most members believed that Stephen's illness was due to overwork.

You can use adjectives like **long**, **short**, **serious**, and **mild** in front of **illness.**

He died at the age of 66 after a long illness.
He was still not properly on his feet after a serious illness.

2 **'disease'**

A **disease** is a particular kind of illness caused by bacteria or an infection. Diseases can often be passed from one person to another.

I have a rare eye disease.
Whooping cough is a dangerous disease for babies.

Animals and plants can also have diseases.

...cattle disease.
...Dutch Elm disease.

illusion - delusion

You can use either of these words to say that someone has a wrong belief.

They have the illusion that every contingency can be worked out in advance.
One patient had the delusion that he was Trotsky.

You say that someone is **under** an illusion or delusion.

Finally, I think he wanted me because he was under the illusion that I was loaded with money.
I still laboured under the nice middle-class delusion that everyone was a good guy at heart.

You can also say that someone **suffers from** an illusion or delusion.

A man who has had a leg amputated often suffers from the delusion that the leg is still there.

If you have an **illusion of** something, you believe that it exists when in fact it does not.

We have an illusion of freedom.
In return they are allowed the illusion of a guiltless life.

An **illusion** is also something that looks or sounds like one thing, but is either something else or is not there at all.

It might be an optical illusion but he actually seems to lift some horses in races when they are tired.
I fancy I can hear her voice, but that must be an illusion.

You do not use **delusion** with this meaning.

imaginary - imaginative

1 **'imaginary'**

Something that is **imaginary** exists only in someone's imagination, and not in real life.

Many children develop fears of imaginary dangers.
...pictures of completely imaginary plants.

2 **'imaginative'**

Imaginative people are good at forming ideas of new and exciting things.

...an imaginative schoolteacher.

You can also describe someone's ideas as **imaginative.**

...an imaginative scheme.

imagine

If you **imagine** a situation, you think about it and your mind forms a picture or idea of it.
It is difficult to imagine anyone wanting to run the marathon in this summer smog.
Try to imagine you're sitting on a cloud.

You can use an '-ing' form after **imagine.**
She could not imagine living with Daniel.
It is hard to imagine anyone starting a war.

(*i*) Note that you do not use a 'to'-infinitive after **imagine.** You do not say, for example, 'She could not imagine to live with Daniel'.

If you say that you **imagine** something is true, you mean that you think it is probably true.
I imagine there would be difficulties if you were expected to make a profit.
I imagine that sooner or later he'll ask you to join him there.

If someone asks you if something is true, you can say **'I imagine so'** or **'I would imagine so'** to indicate that you think it is probably true.
'Can he bite through that?'– 'I imagine so.'
'Was that the point of it all?'– 'I would imagine so.'

(*i*) Note that you do not say 'I imagine it'.

Instead of saying that you 'imagine something is not' true, you usually say that you **don't imagine it is** true.
I don't imagine we'll have a problem, anyway.

immediately

1 **used as an adverb**
Immediately is usually an adverb. If something happens **immediately,** it happens without delay.
I have to go down to Brighton immediately. It's very urgent.
She finished her cigarette, then lit another one immediately.

If something happens **immediately after** something else, it happens as soon as the other thing is finished.
He had to see a client immediately after lunch.
They must have contacted him immediately after my meeting with them last Tuesday.

If something is **immediately above** something else, it is above it and very close to it. You can use **immediately** in a similar way with other prepositions such as **under, opposite,** and **behind.**
…a window on the second floor immediately above the entrance.
The first layer of fat is immediately under the skin.
This man had seated himself immediately behind me.

2 **used as a conjunction**
In British English (but not American English), **immediately** is also a conjunction. You use **immediately** to say that something happens or is done as soon as something else has happened.
Immediately I finish the show I get changed and go home.
Contact can be made immediately the door is opened.

In sentences like these, you do not use a future tense after **immediately.** You do not say, for example, 'I will do it immediately I will arrive'. You say 'I will do it immediately I **arrive**'.

immigrant
⇨ See **Usage** entry at **emigration - immigration - migration.**

immigration
⇨ See **Usage** entry at **emigration - immigration - migration**.

imply - infer

1 **'imply'**

If you **imply** that something is the case, you suggest that it is the case without actually saying so.

Somehow he implied that he was the one who had done all the work.
Her tone implied that her time and her patience were limited.

2 **'infer'**

If you **infer** that something is the case, you decide that it is the case on the basis of the information that you have.

I inferred from what she said that you have not been well.
It is only from doing experiments that cause-and-effect relationships can be inferred.

important

Important is an adjective. Something that is **important** is very significant, valuable, or necessary.

This is the most important part of the job.
It is important to get on with your employer and his wife.

⚠ **WARNING:** You do not use 'important' to say that an amount or quantity is very large. You do not talk, for example, about 'an important sum of money'. Instead you use a word such as **considerable** or **substantial**.

He claimed he had been paid a substantial sum for working for MI5.
A considerable amount of rain had fallen.

in

1 **used to say where something is**

You use **in** as a preposition to say where someone or something is, or where something happens.

Colin was in the bath.
I wanted to play in the garden.
How much is the hat in the window?
In Hamburg the girls split up.

In is sometimes used with superlatives. For example, you can say that a particular building is 'the tallest building in Tokyo'.

Hakodate is the oldest port in Hokkaido.
…the biggest lizards in the world.

2 **used to say where something goes**

You use **in** as an adverb to say that someone goes into a place, or that something is put into a container.

There was a knock at Howard's door. 'Come in ,' he shouted.
She opened her bag and put her diary in.

In is sometimes a preposition meaning 'into'.

She threw both letters in the bin.

⇨ See **Usage** entry at **into**.

3 **used with expressions of time**

In is often used with expressions of time.
You use **in** to say how long something takes.

He learned to drive in six months.
He was dead in a few seconds.

USAGE

You also use **in** to say how long it will be before something happens in the future.
In another few minutes it will be dark.

You use **in** to say that something happens during a particular year, month, or season.
In 1872, Chicago was burned to the ground.
In April we prepared to make our first trip to Europe.
It'll be warmer in the spring.

You use **in** with **the** to say that something happens regularly each morning, afternoon, or evening.
I have stopped reading the papers. I go swimming instead in the morning.
You could sit there in the evening and listen to the radio.

⇨ See **Usage** entries at **morning, afternoon,** and **evening.**

However, you do not use 'in' to say that something happens regularly each night. Instead you use **at** without 'the'.
There were no lights in the street at night.

⇨ See **Usage** entry at **night.**

⚠ **WARNING:** You do not say that something happens 'in' a particular day or date. You say that it happens **on** that day or date.
On Tuesday they went shopping again.
Caro was born on April 10th.

 American speakers sometimes omit the **on.**

I've got a party Wednesday.
Friday we had promised that we would have dinner at his house.

ⓘ Note that you do not say that something lasts or continues 'in' a period of time. You say that it lasts or continues **for** that time.
I have known you for a long time.
I had been with my company for ten years.

⇨ See **Usage** entry at **for.**

4 used to mean 'wearing'
In is sometimes used to mention what someone is wearing.
The bar was full of men in cloth caps.

⇨ See **Usage** entry at **wear.**

⚠ **WARNING:** You do not use 'in' when you are talking about someone's ability to speak a foreign language. You do not say, for example, 'She speaks in Russian'. You say 'She speaks Russian'.

⇨ See **Usage** entry at **speak - talk.**

incapable
If someone is **incapable of doing** something, they are unable to do it.
He was incapable of enjoying himself.
This woman sounds as if she is totally incapable of loving anyone.

You do not say that someone is 'incapable to do' something.

in case
⇨ See **Usage** entry at **case.**

include

If one thing **includes** another, it has that thing as one of its parts.

He is a former president of the Campania region, which <u>includes</u> Naples.
A good British breakfast always <u>includes</u> sausages.

⚠ **WARNING:** You do not use 'include' when mentioning all the parts of something. Instead, you use a word such as **comprise**.
⇨ See **Usage** entry at **comprise**.

---

indeed

[1] **used after an adjective or adverb**

When you are using **very** with an adjective or adverb, you can put **indeed** after the adjective or adverb, for extra emphasis.

I think it's <u>very good indeed</u>.
She had got <u>very angry indeed</u>.
They can run <u>very fast indeed</u>.

⚠ **WARNING:** You do not use **indeed** after an adjective or adverb unless you have put **very** in front of it. You do not say, for example, 'I think it's good indeed'.

[2] **used after a noun**

If you use **very** with an adjective in front of a noun, you can put **indeed** after the noun.

That's <u>a very good answer indeed</u>.
It is <u>a very rare bird indeed</u>.

ⓘ Note that you do not say 'That's a good answer indeed' or 'It is a rare bird indeed'.

People often say **'Thank you very much indeed'**.

'I will confirm that by phone or by telex.'– '<u>Thank you very much indeed</u>.'
<u>Thank you very much indeed</u> for having us here.

ⓘ Note that you do not say 'Thank you indeed'.

---

indicate - show

[1] **talking about evidence and results**

Indicate has the general meaning 'show', and you can sometimes use **indicate** and **show** in a similar way, for example when you are talking about evidence or the results of research.

Evidence <u>indicates</u> that the experiments were unsuccessful.
Evidence <u>shows</u> that doctors are working harder.

[2] **used with a person as subject**

However, **indicate** and **show** are not always used in the same way when they have a person as their subject.

If someone **indicates** an object, they show someone else where it is, usually by pointing or nodding towards it. **Indicate** is only used like this in stories.

'The car's just down there,' she said, <u>indicating</u> it with a nod of her head.
She sat down in the armchair that Mrs Jones <u>indicated</u>.

When **indicate** has this meaning, it is sometimes used with an indirect object, although this use is not common. The indirect object always has **to** in front of it.

Without speaking, he <u>indicated to him</u> the inside of the hut.

If you **show** an object to someone, you hold it up or give or take it to them, so that they can see it and examine it. When **show** has this meaning, it always takes an indirect object. When the indirect object comes after the direct object, you put **to** in front of the indirect object.

I showed William what I had written.
Fetch that drawing you did and show it to the doctor.

indoors - indoor

1 'indoors'

Indoors is an adverb. If you go **indoors,** you go into a building.

Let's go indoors.

If something happens **indoors,** it happens inside a building.

I spent all the evenings indoors.
Since she was indoors, she had not been wearing a coat.

2 'indoor'

Indoor is an adjective used in front of a noun. You use it to describe objects or activities that exist or take place inside a building.

… indoor swimming pools.
… indoor games.

industrious - industrial

1 'industrious'

An **industrious** person works very hard.

He was industrious and strove to improve himself.
The people were industrious and very thrifty.

2 'industrial'

You do not use 'industrious' to refer to the work and processes involved in making things in factories. The word you use is **industrial.**

They have increased their industrial production in recent years.
…the future of industrial relations in Britain.

infamous

⇨ See **Usage** entry at **famous - well-known - notorious - infamous.**

infer

⇨ See **Usage** entry at **imply - infer.**

inferior

If one thing is **inferior to** another, it is of poorer quality than the other thing.

His photographs were inferior to those taken by Ernie.
Tolstoy's thinking was vastly inferior to his fiction.

(i) Note that you do not use any preposition except **to** after **inferior.**

inflammable

⇨ See **Usage** entry at **flammable - inflammable - non-flammable.**

inflate - blow up

1 'inflate'

If you **inflate** something such as a tyre, balloon, or airbed, you fill it full of air or gas.

…a rubber dinghy that took half an hour to inflate.

2 'blow up'

Inflate is a formal or technical word. In conversation, you usually say that you **blow up** a tyre, balloon, or airbed.

She blew up the airbed.
She would buy her son a dinghy and a pump to blow it up.

influence

1 used as a noun

You use **influence** as a noun to refer to the power that someone or something has to affect people's behaviour or decisions.

His wife had a lot of influence.
His teachings still exert a strong influence.

If you want to mention the person or thing affected, you use **on**.

He was a bad influence on the children.
We shall be looking at the influence of religion on society.

⚠ **WARNING:** You do not use 'influence' to refer to a change or event that is the result of something. The word you use is **effect.**

The incident had a great effect on Serge. He was very shocked by it.
The intense heat had no effect on the spacecraft.

⇨ See **Usage** entry at **affect - effect.**

2 used as a verb

You can use **influence** as a verb. You say that one person or thing **influences** another.

I didn't want him to influence me in my choice.
There was little opportunity to influence foreign policy.

ⓘ Note that when you use **influence** as a verb, you do not use 'on' after it.

inform

If you **inform** someone **of** something, you tell them about it.

He intended to inform her of his objections.

Inform is often followed by a 'that'-clause.

I informed her that I was unwell.
She informed me that she had not changed her plans.

You do not usually omit **that** after **inform.** You do not say, for example, 'I informed her I was unwell'.

Inform is a fairly formal word. In conversation, you usually use **tell.**
⇨ See **Usage** entry at **tell.**

information - news

1 'information'

Information consists of facts that you obtain or receive.

You can obtain information about support groups from your physician.
I wanted information on washable nappies and where to buy them from.

Information is an uncount noun. You do not use 'an' in front of it, and you do not talk about 'informations'. However, you can talk about a **piece of information.**

I kept wondering what use I could make of this piece of information.

You say that you **give** people information.

He thought I'd given them the information.

You do not say that you 'tell' people information.

You refer to information **about** something or **on** something.

I'd like some information about trains, please.
I'm afraid that I have no information on that.

2 'news'

You do not use **information** to refer to descriptions of recent events in newspapers or on television or radio. The word you use is **news.**

He's recently been in the <u>news.</u>
It was on the <u>news</u> at 8.30.

⇨ See **Usage** entry at **news.**

in front of
⇨ See **Usage** entry at **front.**

injure

1 **'injure' used as a verb**

To **injure** someone means to damage a part of their body.

The earthquake killed 24,000 people and <u>injured</u> 77,000.
A number of bombs have exploded seriously <u>injuring</u> at least five people.

If you accidentally damage a part of your body, you can say that you **injure** yourself or **injure** that part of your body.

He's going to <u>injure</u> himself if he isn't careful.
Peter recently <u>injured</u> his right hand in a training accident.

⚠ **WARNING: Injure** cannot be an intransitive verb. You do not say, for example, 'He ~~injured in a car accident~~'. You say 'He **was injured** in a car accident'.
Seventy policemen <u>were injured</u> in the fighting.

A number of other verbs are used to refer to damage done to a person's body.
⇨ For more information, see **Usage** entry at **damage.**

2 **'injured' used as an adjective**

Injured is often an adjective.

Thousands of <u>injured</u> people still lay among the ruins.
East Grinstead won 3-1 without van Asselt, who was <u>injured.</u>

Adverbs such as **badly**, **seriously**, and **critically** are often used in front of **injured.**

She was not <u>badly injured.</u>
A man lay <u>critically injured</u> for eight hours after his car skidded off a road and smashed into trees.

⇨ See also **Usage** entry at **hurt.**

inquire - enquire - ask

1 **'inquire' and 'enquire'**

If you **inquire** or **enquire** about something, you ask for information about it. There is no difference in meaning between these words. **Inquire** is more common, especially in American English.

We <u>inquired</u> about the precise circumstances surrounding the arrest.
I <u>enquired</u> about the scenery and Beaumont told me it was being built in a carpenter's shop in Waterloo.

You can use **inquire** or **enquire** with a 'wh'-clause.

She <u>inquired how Ibrahim was getting on.</u>
I <u>enquired what kind of aircraft he had commanded</u> before returning home.

In writing, **inquire** and **enquire** are sometimes used in quote structures.

'Anything you need?' <u>inquired</u> the girl.
'Who compiles these reports?' Philip <u>enquired.</u>

⚠ **WARNING:** You do not use these verbs with a direct object. You do not say, for example, 'He ~~inquired her if she was well~~'.

2 **'ask'**

Inquire and **enquire** are fairly formal words. In conversation, people usually use **ask**. **Ask** can be used with or without a direct object.

She asked about his work.
I asked him what he wanted.

insane

⇨ See **Usage** entry at **mad**.

insensible

If you are **insensible to** a physical sensation, you are unable to feel it. **Insensible** is a formal word.

We believe that all animals should be rendered insensible to pain before slaughter.

Insensible is not the opposite of **sensible**. If someone behaves in a way that is not sensible, you do not say that they are 'insensible'. You say, for example, that they or their actions are **silly** or **foolish.**

You're a silly little boy.
It would be foolish to tell such things to a total stranger.

inside

1 **used as a preposition**

When someone or something is in a building or vehicle, you can say that they are **inside** it.

The policemen inside the building opened fire on the crowd.
Two minutes later we were safely inside the taxi.

(i) Note that you do not say that someone is 'inside of' a building or vehicle.

2 **used as an adverb**

Inside can also be an adverb.

My main concern was to get the man away from the house because my wife and children were inside.
'I have been expecting you,' she said, inviting him inside.

insist

If someone **insists on doing** something, they say very firmly that they will do it, and they do it.

He insisted on paying for the meal.
He insists on getting paid a hundred dollars just to appear on the talk show.

(i) Note that you do not say that someone 'insists to do' something.

in spite of - despite

1 **'in spite of'**

You use **in spite of** when you are mentioning circumstances which surprisingly do not prevent something from happening or being true. Note that the spelling is **in spite of**, not 'inspite of'.

The morning air was still clear and fresh, in spite of all the traffic and the crowd.
In spite of poor health, my father was always cheerful.

⚠ **WARNING:** You do not use 'in spite of' to say that something will not be affected by any circumstances. You do not say, for example, 'Everyone can take part, in spite of their ability'. You say 'Everyone can take part **regardless of** their ability' or 'Everyone can take part **whatever** their ability'.

If they are determined to strike, they will do so <u>regardless of</u> what the law says.
Bridgemere – ideal for a visit <u>whatever</u> the weather or time of year.

You also do not use 'in spite of' as a conjunction. You do not say, for example, 'In spite of we protested, they took him away'. You say '**Although** we protested, they took him away'.

<u>Although</u> he was late, he stopped to buy a sandwich.
Gretchen kept her coat on, <u>although</u> it was warm in the room.

2 **'despite'**

Despite means the same as **in spite of.** You do not use 'of' after **despite.**

<u>Despite</u> the differences in their ages they were close friends.
The cost of public services has risen steeply <u>despite</u> a general decline in their quality.

---

instead - instead of

1 **'instead'**

Instead is an adverb. You use it when you are saying that someone does something rather than doing something else that you have just mentioned.

Judy did not answer. <u>Instead</u> she looked out of the taxi window.
Robert had a great desire to turn away, but <u>instead</u> he led her towards the house.

2 **'instead of'**

Instead of is a preposition. You use it to introduce something which is not done, not used, or not true when you are contrasting it with something which is done, is used, or is true.

We have had many converts when we offer people a free juice <u>instead of</u> their usual coffee.
If you want to have your meal at seven o'clock <u>instead of</u> five o'clock, you can.

You can say that someone does something **instead of doing** something else.

You could always write this <u>instead of using</u> your word processor.
I went up the tributary <u>instead of sticking</u> to the river.

ⓘ Note that you do not say that someone does something 'instead to do' something else.

---

instruct

If you **instruct** someone to do something, you tell them to do it. When **instruct** has this meaning, it is followed by an object and a 'to'-infinitive.

The judge <u>instructed them to keep</u> silent.
General Geldenhuys <u>has instructed me to take</u> a full statement from you.

You do not use 'instruct' like this without an object. You do not say, for example, 'He instructed to take the prisoners away'. Instead you can say 'He **gave instructions for** the prisoners **to be taken away**' or 'He **gave instructions that** the prisoners **should be taken away**'.

She <u>gave instructions for</u> Lady Illingworth <u>to be cremated.</u>
You <u>had given instructions that</u> physical force <u>should</u> if necessary <u>be used.</u>

---

insure

⇨ See **Usage** entry at **assure - ensure - insure.**

intense - intensive

1 **'intense'**

Intense means 'very great or strong'.

… _intense_ heat.
I could not help feeling _intense_ discomfort.

2 **'intensive'**

Intensive activities involve using a lot of energy or effort in order to achieve something in a short time.

Intensive training courses are provided by the local authority.
…my last _intensive_ preparations for my Ph.D.

intention

1 **'intention to' and 'intention of'**

When someone intends to do something, you can talk about their **intention to do** it or their **intention of doing** it.

To date, seven candidates have declared their _intention to run_ for president.
They announced their _intention of cutting_ down all the trees.

You can say that **it is** someone's **intention to do** something.

It had been her intention to walk around Ougadougou.
_It is_ still _my intention to resign._

(i) Note that you do not say that 'it is someone's intention of doing' something.

2 **'with the intention'**

When someone does something because they intend to do something else, you can say that they do the first thing **with the intention of doing** the second thing.

The troops had come _with the intention of firing_ on the crowd.

(i) Note that you do not say that someone does something 'with the intention to do' something else.

3 **'no intention'**

You can say that someone **has no intention of doing** something.

She _had no intention of spending_ the rest of her life working as a waitress.

(i) Note that you do not say that someone 'has no intention to do' something.

interested - interesting

1 **'interested'**

If you want to know more about something or someone, you can say that you are **interested in** them.

I am very _interested in_ politics.
Ellen seemed genuinely _interested in_ him and his work.

(i) Note that you do not use any preposition except **in** after **interested.**

⇨ For more information about other words which can be used to say that you want to know more about a person, see **Usage** at **curiosity.**

If you want to do something, you can say that you are **interested in doing** it.

I was _interested in seeing_ different kinds of theatre.
I'm only _interested in finding out_ what the facts are.

(i) Note that you do not say that you are 'interested to do' something.

2 **'interesting'**

Do not confuse **interested** with **interesting.** You say that someone or something is **interesting** when they have qualities or features which make you want to know more about them.

I've met some very <u>interesting</u> people.
…some <u>interesting</u> old coins.

⚠ **WARNING:** You do not use 'interesting' to describe things which result in your receiving a lot of money. For example, if you earn a large salary, you do not say that your job is 'interesting'. You say that it is **well-paid.**
They go on to get university degrees and <u>well-paid</u> careers in business.
Sylvia found herself a series of quite <u>well-paid</u> secretarial jobs.

interior - internal

1 'interior'

The **interior** of a building or vehicle is the inside part of it.
…the fire that destroyed the <u>interior</u> of the Savoy Theatre.
The car's <u>interior</u> was becoming stuffy.

Interior is often used as an adjective in front of a noun to refer to an inside part of a building or vehicle.
The <u>interior</u> walls were coated with green mould.
I put the <u>interior</u> light on and looked at her.

2 'internal'

You do not usually use 'interior' to refer to the inside parts of other things. Instead you use **internal.**
A pig's <u>internal</u> organs match our own in size and weight.

into

The preposition **into** is usually used in connection with movement of some kind. You use **into** to say where someone or something goes, or where something is put.
I went <u>into</u> the church.
He shook a little dust <u>into</u> the basin.

However, in front of **here** and **there**, you use **in,** not 'into'.
Come <u>in</u> here.
She went <u>in</u> there and stood at the foot of his bed.

After verbs meaning **put, throw, drop,** or **fall,** you can use **into** or **in** with the same meaning.
William put the letter <u>into</u> his pocket.
He locked the bag and put the key <u>in</u> his pocket.
He crumpled the envelope up and threw it <u>into</u> his wastebasket.
She threw both letters <u>in</u> the bin.
He fell <u>into</u> an ornamental pond.
The dog slipped and fell <u>in</u> the water.

intolerable - intolerant

1 'intolerable'

If a situation is **intolerable,** it is so bad that you cannot bear it.
They find this situation <u>intolerable.</u>
…the things that made his life <u>intolerable.</u>

2 'intolerant'

Someone who is **intolerant** tries to prevent people from behaving in ways that they do not approve of, or from expressing opinions that they do not agree with.
She is <u>intolerant</u> by nature.
… <u>intolerant</u> attitudes toward non-Catholics.

USAGE

invaluable

If you say that someone or something is **invaluable**, you mean that they are extremely useful.

He was an <u>invaluable</u> source of information.
This experience proved <u>invaluable</u> later on.

Invaluable is not the opposite of **valuable**. If you want to say that an object has no value at all, you can say that it is **worthless** or **not worth anything**.

The goods are often <u>worthless</u> by the time they arrive.
I started collecting his pictures when they <u>weren't worth anything</u>.

invent - discover

1 'invent'

If someone **invents** something new, they are the first person to think of it or make it.

Walter Hunt and Elias Howe <u>invented</u> the sewing machine.

2 'discover'

You do not use 'invent' to say that someone finds out about something which exists but which was not previously known. The word you use is **discover**.

Herschel <u>discovered</u> a new planet.
Having found these fragments, the team of researchers <u>discovered</u> a way to date them.

invite

If you **invite** someone to a party or a meal, you ask them to come to it.

The Hogans <u>invited</u> me to a cocktail party.
He <u>invited</u> Alexander to dinner.

(*i*) Note that you must use **to** in sentences like these. You do not say '~~I invited her my party~~'.

When you ask someone to do something which you think they will enjoy, you can say that you **invite** them **to do** it.

He <u>invited</u> Axel <u>to come</u> with him.
Dr Kiryushin <u>invited</u> Medvedev and his son <u>to visit</u> him.

(*i*) Note that you do not say that you invite someone 'for doing' something.

involved

1 used after a link verb

The adjective **involved** is usually used after a link verb such as **be** or **get**.
If you are **involved in** an activity, you are taking part in it.

Should religious leaders get <u>involved in</u> politics?
In all, 6000 companies are <u>involved in</u> producing the parts that are needed for these aircraft.

2 used after a noun

Involved can also be used immediately after a noun. The people **involved** in something are the people affected by it or taking part in it.

We never managed to get anything done, simply because of the large number of people <u>involved</u>.
None of the parents or students <u>involved</u> came to the hearing.

You also use **involved** immediately after a noun when you are mentioning an important aspect of something that is being discussed.

There is quite a lot of work <u>involved</u>.
She had no real understanding of the problems <u>involved</u>.

3 another meaning

Involved has another meaning. If you say that a process or situation is **involved**, you mean that it is very complicated. When **involved** has this meaning, it can only go after a verb or in front of a noun.

USAGE

The problem's a little bit more <u>involved</u> than I suggested.
We had long, <u>involved</u> discussions.

irritated

⇨ See **Usage** entry at **nervous**.

issue

If something **is issued to** you, it is officially given to you.

Radios <u>were issued to</u> the troops.
The boots <u>issued to</u> them had fallen to bits.

In British English, you can also say that someone **is issued with** something.

She <u>was issued with</u> travel documents.
Staff <u>will be issued with</u> new grey-and-yellow designer uniforms.

 American speakers do not say that someone 'is issued with' something.

it

1 used to refer to things

You use **it** to refer to an object, animal, or other thing that has just been mentioned.

...a tray with glasses on <u>it</u>.
The horse must have been thirsty, because <u>it</u> went straight to the fountain and drank.
The strike went on for a year before <u>it</u> was settled.

⚠ **WARNING:** When the subject of a sentence is followed by a relative clause, you do not use 'it' in front of the main verb. You do not say, for example, ~~The town where I work, it is near London~~. You say 'The town where I work **is** near London'.

The bitter fighting which has split the Party in recent years <u>has</u> finally reached the General Council.
The message that indiscriminate use of insecticides does not produce higher yields <u>seems</u> to be getting through.
The cave, which Ralph Solecki has been excavating, <u>has yielded</u> a rich selection of Neanderthal remains.

2 used to refer to situations

You can also use **it** to refer to a situation, fact, or experience.

I like <u>it</u> here.
She was frightened, but tried not to show <u>it</u>.

⚠ **WARNING:** You often refer to something such as an experience or wish using an '-ing' form or 'to'-infinitive after a verb such as **like**. When you do this, you do not use 'it' in front of the '-ing' form or infinitive.

For example, you do not say '~~I like it, walking in the park~~'. You say 'I like walking in the park'. Similarly, you do not say '~~I prefer it, to make my own bread~~'. You say 'I prefer to make my own bread'.

I <u>like being</u> in your house.
I <u>enjoy working</u> with women.
I <u>want to be</u> a successful solo artist.

3 used with link verbs

It is often the subject of a link verb such as **be**. Usually **it** refers to something that has just been mentioned.

I like your Hungarian accent. I think <u>it's</u> quite attractive.
So you don't like them? <u>It's</u> a pity.

You can also use **it** as the subject of 'be' to say what the time, day, or date is.

It's seven o'clock.
It's Sunday morning.

You can also use **it** as the subject of a link verb to describe the weather or the light.

It was terribly cold.
It was a windy afternoon.
It's getting dark.

4 **used to describe an experience**

You can use **it** with a link verb and an adjective to describe an experience. After the adjective, you use an '-ing' form or a 'to'-infinitive. For example, instead of saying 'Walking by the lake was nice', people usually say '**It was** nice walking by the lake'.

It's nice hearing your voice again.
It was sad to see her the victim of continual pain.

You can use **it** with a link verb and an adjective to describe the experience of being in a particular place. After the adjective, you use an adjunct such as **here** or **on the beach**.

It is very quiet and pleasant here.
It was warm in the restaurant.
It was cosy in the car.

5 **used to comment on a situation**

You can use **it** with an adjective or noun group to comment on a whole situation. After the adjective or noun group, you use a 'that'-clause.

It is lucky that I am going abroad.
It's a pity you didn't stay.

After an adjective, you can sometimes use a 'wh'-clause instead of a 'that'-clause.

It's funny how people change.
Get a carpet cleaner to do your carpets. It's amazing what they can do.

⚠ **WARNING:** You do not use 'it' with a link verb and a noun group to say that something exists or is present. You do not say, for example, '~~It's a lot of traffic on this road tonight~~'. You say ' **There's** a lot of traffic on this road tonight'.

There's a lecturer in the Law Faculty called Hodgson.
There was no room in the cottage.
There will be no one to help you.

⇨ See **Usage** entry at **there**.

its - it's

1 **'its'**

Its is a possessive determiner. You use **its** to indicate that something belongs or relates to a thing, place, animal, or child.

He discovered the river had lost its beauty.
The pig managed to keep its balance.
She hoisted the child on her shoulder and started patting its back.

2 **'it's'**

It's is a shortened form of **it is** or **it has**.

It's just like riding a bike – you never forget.
It's been very nice talking to you.

J j

jam
⇨ See **Usage** entry at **marmalade - jam - jelly.**

job
⇨ See **Usage** entry at **work.**

joke

A **joke** is something which you say or do in order to make people laugh. There are three kinds of joke.

When someone **makes** or **cracks** a joke, they make a witty remark.

He debated about whether to <u>make</u> a joke about shooting rabbits.
He even <u>cracked</u> the odd joke about my drinking too much.

A **joke** is also something clever or funny which you have heard, read, or invented at an earlier time and which you repeat to amuse people. When **joke** has this meaning, you say that someone **tells** a joke.

<u>Tell</u> Uncle Henry the joke you <u>told</u> us.
He has a way of screwing up his face when he is <u>telling</u> a joke.

A **joke** is also something that is done to make someone appear foolish. When **joke** has this meaning, you say that someone **plays** a joke **on** someone else.

They're <u>playing</u> a joke <u>on</u> you.

⚠ **WARNING:** You never say that someone 'says' or 'does' a joke.

jolly
⇨ See **Usage** entry at **happy - sad.**

journal

A **journal** is a magazine for people with a particular interest. Many magazines have **Journal** as part of their name.

…the British Medical <u>Journal</u>.

Journal is also an old-fashioned or literary word for a diary.

He had been keeping a <u>journal</u> of his travels.

⚠ **WARNING:** You do not refer to a newspaper as a 'journal'.

journey - trip -voyage - excursion

1 'journey'

A **journey** is the process of travelling from one place to another by land, air, or sea.

…a <u>journey</u> of over 2,000 miles.

When you **make** a **journey,** you travel from one place to another.

He <u>made</u> the <u>journey</u> to Mardan.

You can also say that someone **goes on** a **journey.**

He <u>went on</u> a <u>journey</u> to London.

ⓘ Note that you do not say that someone 'does' a journey.

If you **journey** to a place, you travel there. This is a literary use.

The nights became colder as they <u>journeyed</u> north.

2 **'trip'**
A **trip** is the process of travelling from one place to another, staying there, usually for a short time, and coming back again..
...*a business trip to Milan.*

(i) Note that the verb 'trip' is not used with this meaning.

3 **'voyage'**
A **voyage** is a long journey from one place to another in a ship or spacecraft.
The ship's voyage is over.
...*the voyage to the moon in 1972.*

4 **'excursion'**
An **excursion** is a short trip made either as a tourist or in order to do a particular thing.
The tourist office organizes excursions to the palace of Knossos.

just

You use **just** to say that something happened a very short time ago. British speakers usually use the present perfect tense with **just.** For example, they say 'I **'ve just** arrived'.
I've just bought a new house.

American speakers usually use the simple past tense. Instead of saying 'I've just arrived', they say 'I **just** arrived'.
He just died.
I just broke the pink bowl.

Some British speakers also use the simple past tense, but in Britain this use is usually regarded as incorrect.

⚠ **WARNING:** You do not use 'just' with adverbs such as **partly** to give the meaning 'not completely'. You do not say, for example, 'The job is just partly done'. You say 'The job is **only partly** done'.
This is only partly true.
He was only partially successful.
Dazed and only half awake, he was still in his underwear.

just now
⇨ See **Usage** entry at **now**.

K k

keep

1 used as a transitive verb

To **keep** someone or something in a particular state or place means to cause them to remain in that state or place. The past tense and past participle of **keep** is **kept**, not 'keeped'.

She kept her arm around her husband as she spoke.
They had been kept awake by nightingales.

2 used as an intransitive verb

To **keep** in a particular state means to remain in that state.

They've got to hunt for food to keep alive.

If a sign says **'Keep Out'**, it is warning you not to go somewhere.

3 used with an '-ing' form

Keep can be used in two different ways with an '-ing' form.
You can use it to say that something is repeated many times.

The phone keeps ringing.
My mother keeps asking questions.

You can also use it to say that something continues to happen and does not stop.

I turned back after a while, but he kept walking.
The bonfire is still burning. I think it'll keep going all night.

For emphasis, you can use **keep on** instead of 'keep'.

Did he give up or keep on trying?

⚠ **WARNING:** You never say that someone or something 'keeps to do' something.

kerb

⇨ See **Usage** entry at **curb - kerb**.

killing

There are several words which mean similar things to **kill**.
To **murder** someone means to kill them deliberately.

… the body of a murdered religious and political leader.

Assassinate is used to talk about the murder of an important person, often for political reasons.

The plot to assassinate Martin Luther King.

If a large number of people are murdered, the words **slaughter** or **massacre** are sometimes used.

Thirty four people were slaughtered while queuing up to cast their votes.
300 civilians are believed to have been massacred by the rebels.

Slaughter can also be used to talk about killing animals for their meat.

Chicken farms are having to slaughter their stock.

kind

Kind can be a noun or an adjective.

1 used as a noun

You use it as a noun to talk about a class of people or things. **Kind** is a count noun. After

words like **all** and **many**, you use **kinds,** not 'kind'.
It will give you an opportunity to meet all _kinds_ of people.
Soil derives from many _kinds_ of rock.
The trees were filled with birds of all _kinds._

After **kinds of** you can use either the plural or singular form of a noun. For example, you can say 'I like most kinds of **cars**' or 'I like most kinds of **car**'. The singular form is more formal.
I met all different kinds of _people._
People have been working hard to produce the kinds of _courses_ that we need.
I've seen this in several kinds of _profession._
There will be two kinds of _certificate._

After **kind of** you use the singular form of a noun.
I'm not the kind of _person_ to get married.
He gave me the fleshy leaf of a kind of _cactus._
She makes the same kind of _point_ in another essay.

In conversation, **these** and **those** are often used with **kind.** For example, people say 'I don't like these kind of films' or 'I don't like those kind of films'. This use is generally thought to be incorrect, and it is best to avoid it. Instead you should say 'I don't like **this kind of film**' or 'I don't like **that kind of film**'.
There are problems with _this kind of explanation._
We're always equipped to handle _that kind of question._

You can also say 'I don't like films **of this kind**'.
This appears to be the natural way of interpreting data _of this kind._

In conversation, people often say **like this, like that,** or **like these.**
I hope we see many more enterprises _like this._
I'd read a few books _like that._
I'm sure they don't have chairs _like these._

Some people use **kind of** when they are describing something in a vague or uncertain way.
⇨ For more information about this use, see **Usage** entry at **sort of - kind of.**

2 **used as an adjective**
When **kind** is an adjective, it has a totally different meaning. You use it to describe gentle, caring behaviour.
Gertrude had been immensely _kind._
'Need some help?' he asked in a _kind_ voice.

You also use it to describe people who always behave in this way.
He was a thoroughly _kind_ and generous man.
I find them all very pleasant and extremely _kind_ and helpful.

You say that someone is **kind to** someone else.
She's been very _kind to_ you.
He was so _kind to_ young people.

ⓘ Note that when **kind** has this meaning, you do not use any preposition except **to** after it.

kindly

Kindly can be an adverb or an adjective.
1 **used as an adverb**
If you do something **kindly,** you do it in a kind way.
Priscilla played with Edal _kindly_ and patiently.
She smiled very _kindly._

You can use **kindly** to show that you are grateful to someone.

They <u>kindly</u> contributed to our funds.
Manfred and Mrs Mount are very <u>kindly</u> taking me back.

Some people use **kindly** when they are asking someone to do something in an annoyed way. This is a rather old-fashioned use.

<u>Kindly</u> stand back a minute, please.

2 'take kindly'

If you do not **take kindly to** something, you are very unwilling to accept it.

He doesn't <u>take too kindly to</u> discipline.
It is hard to imagine her <u>taking kindly to</u> too much interference.

3 used as an adjective

Kindly is sometimes an adjective with the same meaning as 'kind'. This is a rather old-fashioned use.

They are <u>kindly</u> people.
He had been given shelter by a <u>kindly</u> villager.

---

know

1 awareness of facts

If you **know** that something is the case, you are aware that it is the case. The past tense of **know** is **knew,** not 'knowed'. The past participle is **known.**

I <u>knew</u> that she had recently graduated from law school.
I <u>should have known</u> that something was seriously wrong.

⚠ **WARNING:** You never use a continuous tense with **know.** You do not say, for example, 'I am knowing that this is true'. You say 'I **know** that this is true'.

2 'I know'

In British English, if someone tells you a fact that you already know, you do not say 'I know it'. You say 'I **know** '.

'The stuff's very good.'–'<u>I know</u> .'
'That's not their fault, Peter.'–'Yes, <u>I know</u> .'

3 'want to know'

You use **want to know** in front of a 'wh'-clause to say that someone requires some information.

Mrs Fleming <u>wants to know</u> what you feel about it.
Celia <u>wants to know</u> what really happened.

4 'let...know'

If you say that you will **let** someone **know** something, you mean that you will give them some information when you receive it, or if you receive it.

I'll find out about the car and <u>let</u> you <u>know</u> what's happened.
You will <u>let</u> me <u>know</u> if she turns up again, won't you?

5 acquaintance and familiarity

If you **know** a person, place, or thing, you are acquainted with them or are familiar with them.

Do you <u>know</u> David?
He <u>knew</u> London well.
Do you <u>know</u> the poem 'Kubla Khan'?

6 'get to know'

If you want to say that someone gradually becomes acquainted with a person or gradually becomes familiar with a place, you say that they **get to know** the person or place.

I got to know some of the staff quite well.
I really wanted to get to know America.

⚠ **WARNING:** You do not use **know** without **get to** to mean 'become acquainted with'.

7 **'know how to'**
If you **know how to** do something, you have the necessary knowledge to do it.
No one knew how to repair it.
Do you know how to drive?

ⓘ Note that you do not say that someone 'knows to' do something.

knowledge

Knowledge is information and understanding about a subject, which people have in their minds.

…advances in scientific knowledge.
All knowledge comes to us through our senses.

Knowledge is an uncount noun. You do not talk about 'knowledges' or 'a knowledge'. You talk about someone's **knowledge of** a subject.

Her knowledge of French and Italian was good.
My knowledge of the play was a great help.

ⓘ Note that you do not use any preposition except **of** after **knowledge**.

L l

lack

Lack can be a noun or a verb.

1 used as a noun

If there is a **lack of** something, there is not enough of it, or it does not exist at all.

I hated the <u>lack of</u> privacy in the dormitory.

2 used as a verb

If someone or something **lacks** a quality, they do not have it.

I don't believe the club <u>lacks</u> ambition.

It <u>lacked</u> the power of the Italian cars.

(i) Note that you do not say that someone or something 'lacks of' a quality.

lady

⇨ See **Usage** entry at **woman - lady**.

landscape

⇨ See **Usage** entry at **scene - sight - view - landscape - scenery**.

lane - path

1 'lane'

A **lane** is a narrow road which can be used by vehicles, especially in the country.

A **lane** is also a part of a main road which is marked by the edge of the road and painted line, or by two painted lines.

The lorry was travelling at 20mph in the slow <u>lane.</u>

2 'path'

You do not use 'lane' to refer to a strip of ground which people walk along and which vehicles cannot use. The word you use is **path** or **footpath**.

Feet had worn a <u>path</u> in the rock.

Can a landowner keep a bull in a field crossed by a public <u>footpath</u>?

large

⇨ See entries at **big - large - great** and **small - large**.

last - lastly

Last can be an adjective or an adverb.

1 'last' used as an adjective

The **last** thing, event, or person of a particular kind is the one that comes after all the others.

He missed the <u>last</u> bus.

They met for the <u>last</u> time just before the war.

He was the <u>last</u> man out of Esseph at the time of its earthquake.

If you want to emphasize that someone or something is the last one of their kind, you can put **very** in front of **last**.

Those were his <u>very last</u> words.

I decided at the <u>very last</u> minute to go.

Latest is sometimes used in a similar way.

⇨ See **Usage** entry at **latest - last**.

2 **'last' used as an adverb**

If something **last** happened on a particular occasion, it has not happened since then.

They last saw their homeland nine years ago.
It's a long time since we met last.

If an event is the final one in a series of similar events, you can say that it happens **last**. You put **last** at the end of a clause.

He added the milk last.
Mr Ross was meant to have gone first, but in fact went last.

3 **'lastly'**

You can also use **lastly** to say that an event is the final one in a series. You put **lastly** at the beginning of a clause.

They wash their hands, arms and faces, and lastly, they wash their feet.

However, **last** and **lastly** are not always used in the same way. You usually use **last** to say that an event is the final one in a series of similar events. You use **lastly** when you are talking about events which are not similar.
For example, if you say 'George rang his aunt **last** ', you usually mean that George had rung several people and that his aunt was the last person he rang. If you say '**Lastly** George rang his aunt', you mean that George had done several things and that the last thing he did was to ring his aunt.

Lastly has a much more common use. You use it to introduce a final point in a discussion, ask a final question, give a final instruction, or mention a final item in a list.

Lastly, no description of German biscuits would be complete without mentioning wafers.
Lastly I would like to ask about your future plans.

4 **'at last'**

At last and **at long last** are used to indicate that something that you have been waiting for or expecting for a long time has happened. These expressions usually go at the beginning or end of a clause.

I'm free at last.
At long last I've found a girl who really loves me.

5 **'last' with time expressions**

You use **last** in front of a word such as **week** or **month** to say when something happened. For example, if it is August and something happened in July, you say that it happened **last month**.

He opened up another shop last month.
The group held its first meeting last week.

(i) Note that you do not say that something happened 'the last month' or 'the last week'.

Last can be used in a similar way in front of the names of festivals, seasons, months, or days of the week.

Last Christmas he insisted on dressing up as Santa Claus.
She died last autumn.
Police seized other documents at his home last March.
We saw a rare sight last Saturday.

However, you do not use **last** like this in front of **decade** or **century**. You do not say, for example, that something happened 'last decade'. You say that something happened **in the last decade** or **during the last decade**.

This was well known during the last century.

You also do not say 'last morning' or 'last afternoon'. You say **yesterday morning** or **yesterday afternoon**.

It's not so warm this morning as it was yesterday morning.
Yesterday afternoon we drove down the road from Wells Summit.

USAGE

ⓘ Note that you do not say 'last evening'. You say **yesterday evening** or **last night**.

Yesterday evening another British soldier was killed by gunmen in Lichfield.
I've been thinking about what we said last night.

6 **'previous' and 'before'**

When you are describing something that happened in the past and you want to refer to an earlier period of time, you use **previous** or **before** instead of 'last'. For example, if you are talking about events that happened in 1983 and you want to mention something that happened in 1982, you say that it happened **the previous year** or **the year before**.

We had had a row the previous night.
His village had been destroyed the previous summer.
The two had met in Bonn the weekend before.
The quarrel of the night before seemed forgotten.

7 **'before last'**

You use **before last** to refer to the period of time immediately before the most recent one of its kind. For example, **the year before last** means 'the year before last year'.

Eileen was visiting friends made on a camping holiday the year before last.
I have not slept since the night before last.

8 **'the last'**

You can also use **last** to refer to any period of time measured back from the present. For example, if it is July 16th and you want to refer to the period from July 2nd to the present, you refer to it as **the last fortnight**. Note that you must use **the**. If you want to say that something happened during this period, you say that it happened **in the last fortnight** or **during the last fortnight**.

How many passports issued in the last hundred days remain to be checked?
All this has happened during the last few years.

ⓘ Note the order of words in these examples. You do not say 'the hundred last days' or 'the few last years'.

last-named

⇨ See **Usage** entry at **latter**.

late - lately

1 **'late'**

Late can be an adjective or an adverb.

If you are **late** for something, you arrive after the time that was arranged.

I was ten minutes late for my appointment.

You can also say that someone arrives **late**.

Etta arrived late.

ⓘ Note that you do not say that someone arrives 'lately'.

⇨ For another meaning of **late**, see **Usage** entry at **former - late**.

2 **'lately'**

You use **lately** to say that something has been happening since a short time ago.

As you know, I've lately been dabbling in psychology.

⇨ For more information about this use, see **Usage** entry at **recently - newly - lately**.

later

⇨ See **Usage** entry at **after - later**.

latest - last

You use **latest** or **last** to talk about one of a series of events which is continuing to happen, or one of a series of things which someone is continuing to have or produce.

1 **events**

If one of a series of events is happening now or has just happened, you refer to it as the **latest** one.

The latest closure marks yet another chapter in the history of Gebeit.

You refer to the event before the latest one as the **last** one. If no event of the kind you are talking about has happened recently, you refer to the most recent one as the **last** one.

…the weeds that had grown since the last harvest.

2 **things you have or produce**

If someone keeps having or producing a series of things, you refer to the one they have now or the one they have produced most recently as their **latest** one.

…her latest boyfriend.

…her latest book.

You refer to the one before their latest one as their **last** one. If they have not had or produced one recently, you refer to their most recent one as their **last** one.

Loach has not been idle since Family Life, his last film for the cinema.

You can talk about more than one thing in this way by putting **last** in front of a number. For example, you can talk about 'his **last three** books'.

Her last two pictures have been disasters.

---

latter

The latter should only be used to refer to the second of two items which have already been mentioned:

Given the choice between working for someone else and being on call day and night for the family business, she'd prefer the latter.

The last of three or more items can be referred to as **the last-named.**

Sunsail has three yacht charter centres in the UK, at Port Solent, Plymouth and Largs, in Scotland. The last-named is a great place from which to begin a tour of Arran, Kintyre and Bute.

Compare this with **the former** which is used to talk about the first of two things already mentioned.

These two firms are in direct competition, with the former trying to cut costs and increase profits.

---

lawful

⇨ See **Usage** entry at **legal - lawful - legitimate.**

lawyer

1 **'lawyer'**

Lawyer is a general term for a person who is qualified to advise people about the law and represent them in court.

Her lawyer was presenting closing arguments to the jury.

2 **'barrister'**

In Britain, a **barrister** is a lawyer who speaks in the higher courts of law on behalf of either the prosecution or the defence.

… the barrister who had represented Reed at the criminal trial.

3 **'advocate'**

In Scotland, a barrister is usually called an **advocate.**

… the defence teams, consisting of one Scottish advocate, one Scottish solicitor, and one Libyan lawyer each.

USAGE

4 'solicitor'

In Britain, a **solicitor** is a lawyer who gives legal advice to clients, prepares legal documents and cases, and in certain limited circumstances may represent a client in court.

Anyone with a legal problem had to consult a solicitor.

5 'attorney'

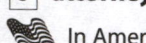 In America, an **attorney** is a lawyer who acts for someone in a legal matter and is qualified to represent them in court.

Blagg has not met with an attorney since his arrest late Wednesday evening.

---

lay - lie

1 'lay'

Lay is a transitive verb, and it is also a past tense of another verb, **lie**.

To **lay** something somewhere means to put it there carefully.

Lay a sheet of newspaper on the floor.

The other forms of **lay** are **lays, laying, laid.**

Michael lays the box on the sand gently and looks at me.
'I couldn't get a taxi,' she said, laying her hand on Nick's sleeve.
She laid the cigarette in the ash-tray.

2 'lie' used as a verb

Lie is an intransitive verb with two different meanings.

To **lie** somewhere means to be there in a horizontal position, or to get into that position.

She would lie on the floor in her overalls.

When **lie** is used like this, its other forms are **lies, lying, lay, lain.** The past participle **lain** is rarely used.

A dress lies on the floor.
The baby was lying on the table.
I lay in bed in the dormitory.

To **lie** means to say or write something which you know is untrue. When **lie** is used like this, its other forms are **lies, lying, lied.**

Why should he lie to me?
Rudolph was sure that Thomas was lying.
He had lied about never going back.

3 'lie' used as a noun

Lie is also a noun. A **lie** is something that someone says or writes which they know is untrue.

He knew that all these statements were lies.

You say that someone **tells** a lie.

I have never told a lie to my pupils.

ⓘ Note that you do not say that someone 'says' a lie.

---

lead

Lead is used with various related meanings as a verb, singular noun, or count noun, and with a totally different meaning and pronunciation as an uncount noun.

1 used as a verb

If you **lead** /liːd/ someone somewhere, you show them the way by going in front of them, or by walking beside them holding their hand or arm. The past tense and past participle of **lead** is **led** /lɛd/, not 'leaded'.

My mother took me by the hand and led me downstairs.
I had led her to the armchair and she sat down.

2 **'drive' and 'take'**

You do not say that you 'lead' someone somewhere in a car. You say that you **drive** or **take** them there.

Ginny <u>drove</u> Mrs Yancy to the airport.

It's his turn to <u>take</u> the children to school.

3 **used as a singular noun**

The person who has the **lead** in a race or competition is the one who is winning.

This win gave him the overall <u>lead.</u>

You often say that someone is **in the lead.**

Hammond was well <u>in the lead</u> for the first 40 minutes.

4 **used as a count noun**

A dog's **lead** is a chain or long piece of leather or plastic which is attached to the dog's collar so that you can control the dog.

Always keep your dog on a <u>lead</u> in the street.

 Note that the American word for this item is **leash.**

Dog owners say they have to exercise their dogs without a <u>leash.</u>

5 **used as an uncount noun**

Lead /l<u>e</u>d/ is a soft, grey, heavy metal.

…pipes made of <u>lead.</u>

learn

1 **knowledge and skills**

When you **learn** something, you obtain knowledge or a skill as a result of studying or training.

 The past tense and past participle of **learn** can be either **learned** or **learnt**, though note that **learnt** is rarely used in American English.

We first <u>learned</u> to cross-country ski at les Rousses.

He <u>had</u> never <u>learnt</u> to read and write.

2 **'teach'**

You do not say that you 'learn' someone something or 'learn' them how to do something. The word you use is **teach.**

Mother <u>taught</u> me how to read.

⇨ See **Usage** entry at **teach.**

3 **learning from experience**

You can use **learn** to say that someone becomes wiser or better able to do something as the result of an experience.

Industry and commerce <u>have learned</u> a lot in the last few years.

You say that someone **learns** something **from** an experience.

They <u>had learned</u> nothing <u>from</u> their early victories.

ⓘ Note that you do not use any preposition except **from** in a sentence like this.

4 **information**

Learn can also be used to say that someone receives some information. After **learn**, you use **of** and a noun group, or you use a 'that'-clause.

He <u>had learned of his father's death in Australia.</u>

She <u>learned that her mother had been a nurse with the US Red Cross.</u>

leave

1 **movement from a place**

You use **leave** to say that someone moves away from a place in order to go somewhere else. The past tense and past participle of **leave** is **left**, not 'leaved'.

They <u>left</u> the house to go for a walk after tea.
I <u>'d left</u> Pretoria in a hurry.

(i) Note that you do not say that someone 'leaves from' a place.

2 'get away from' and 'depart from'

You can say that someone **gets away from** or **departs from** a place. **Get away from** usually indicates that someone is eager or anxious to leave a place. **Depart** is a formal word.

You've got to <u>get away from</u> home.
When you <u>depart from</u> the airport, you will be driven to Paris.

3 intransitive uses

You can use **leave** as an intransitive verb.

He stood up to <u>leave</u>.

You can also say that someone **goes, gets away, goes away,** or **departs.**

'I must <u>go</u>,' she said.
She wanted to <u>get away</u>.
I told him to <u>go away</u>.
They watched the visitor <u>depart</u> as quietly as he had come.

Get away and **go away** are often used to say that someone leaves a place and spends a period of time somewhere else, especially as a holiday.

It's nice to <u>get away</u> in the autumn.
What did you do over the summer? Did you <u>go away</u>?

4 transport

You can say that a train, ship, or other means of transport **leaves, goes,** or **departs** at a particular time or from a place.

My train <u>leaves</u> Euston at 11.30.
Our train <u>went</u> at 2.25.
Ships carrying toys and books were preparing to <u>depart</u> from Dover.

(i) Note that you do not say that a train or ship 'goes away'.

5 movement to a place

When a person or vehicle moves away from a place in order to go to another place, you can say that they **leave for** or **depart for** the second place.

She <u>left for</u> Geneva on May 5th.
He would breakfast with his staff and then <u>depart for</u> Germany.

(i) Note that you do not use any preposition except 'for' in sentences like these.

6 movement from a person

You can say that someone **leaves** or **gets away from** a person or group of people. You use **get away from** to indicate that someone is eager or anxious to move away from the person or group.

I <u>left</u> Conrad and joined the Count at his table.
I wish you could <u>get away from</u> all those people.

(i) Note that you do not say that someone 'departs from' a person or group of people.

If someone tells you to **go away,** they are telling you firmly that they do not want to speak to you or to spend any more time in your company.

There was a knock at the door. 'Go away!' Stroganov called.
<u>Go away</u> now and leave me alone.

left hand - left-handed

1 'left hand'

The **left hand** part of something is the part which is towards your left.

We were on the <u>left hand</u> side of the road.

2 **'left-handed'**

Left-handed people use their left hand rather than their right hand for activities such as writing.

There is a place in London that supplies practically everything for <u>left handed</u> people.

legal - lawful - legitimate

1 **'legal' and 'lawful'**

Legal and **lawful** both mean 'allowed by law'. **Lawful** is a formal word.

A breath test showed he had drunk more than twice the <u>legal</u> limit for driving.
Capital punishment is <u>legal</u> in many countries.
Hunting is a <u>lawful</u> activity.
All his activities had been perfectly <u>lawful</u>.

2 **'legitimate'**

Legitimate means 'correct or acceptable according to a law or rule'.

...a <u>legitimate</u> business transaction.

Legitimate can also mean 'justifiable under the circumstances'.

Religious leaders have a <u>legitimate</u> reason to be concerned.

If someone is **legitimate,** their parents were married at the time they were born.

...evidence that he was his father's <u>legitimate</u> son.

3 **another meaning of 'legal'**

Legal also means 'relating to the law'. You cannot use 'lawful' or 'legitimate' with this meaning.

...the British <u>legal</u> system.
... <u>legal</u> language.

4 **'law' in front of nouns**

You use **law**, not 'legal', in front of a noun when you are talking about someone or something connected with the study of law.

...a <u>law</u> student.
He had only just received his <u>law</u> degree.

Law also appears in the names of some places and institutions connected with the law.

...the <u>Law Courts.</u>
...the <u>Law Society.</u>

legible

⇨ See **Usage** entry at **readable**.

lend

⇨ See **Usage** entry at **borrow - lend**.

less

1 **used in front of nouns**

You use **less** in front of an uncount noun to say that one quantity is not as big as another, or that a quantity is not as big as it was before.

A shower uses <u>less</u> water than a bath.
His work gets <u>less</u> attention than it deserves.
They wanted me to take much <u>less</u> money.

Less is sometimes used in front of plural nouns.

This proposal will mean <u>less</u> jobs and a dwindling rail network.
<u>Less</u> people are going to university than usual.

Some people object to this use. They say that you should use **fewer** in front of plural nouns, not 'less'.

There are <u>fewer</u> trees here.
The new technology allows products to be made with <u>fewer</u> components than before.

However, **fewer** sounds formal when used in conversation. As an alternative to 'less' or 'fewer', you can use **not as many** or **not so many** in front of plural nouns. These expressions are acceptable in both conversation and writing.

There are <u>not as many</u> cottages as there were.
There are <u>n't so many</u> trees there.

(i) Note that after **not as many** and **not so many** you use **as**, not 'than'.

2 **'less than' and 'fewer than'**
You use **less than** in front of a noun group to say that an amount or measurement is below a particular point or level.

It's hard to find a house in Beverly Hills for <u>less than</u> a million dollars.
I travelled <u>less than</u> 3000 miles.

Less than is sometimes used in front of a noun group referring to a number of people or things.

The whole of Switzerland has <u>less than</u> six million inhabitants.
The country's standing army consisted of <u>less than</u> a hundred soldiers.

Some people object to this use. They say that you should use **fewer than,** not 'less than', in front of a noun group referring to people or things.

He had never been in a class with <u>fewer than</u> forty children.
In 1900 there were <u>fewer than</u> one thousand university teachers.

You can use **less than** in conversation, but you should use **fewer than** in formal writing. However, **fewer than** can only be used when the following noun group refers to a number of people or things. You do not use 'fewer than' when the noun group refers to an amount or measurement.

3 **'no less than'**
You use **no less than** or **no fewer than** in front of a number to show that you think that it is surprisingly large.

By 1880, there were <u>no less than</u> fifty-six coal mines.
<u>No fewer than</u> five cameramen lost their lives.

In formal writing, you should use **no fewer than,** rather than 'no less than'.

4 **'less' used in front of adjectives**
Less can be used in front of an adjective to say that someone or something has a smaller amount of a quality than they had before, or a smaller amount than someone or something else has.

From this time on, I felt <u>less</u> guilty.
Most of the other plays were <u>less</u> successful.

⚠ **WARNING:** You do not use **less** in front of the comparative form of an adjective. You do not say, for example, 'It is less colder than it was yesterday'. You say 'It is **less cold** than it was yesterday'.

5 **'not as ... as'**
In conversation, people do not usually use 'less' in front of adjectives. They do not say, for example, 'It is less cold than it was yesterday'. They say 'It is **not as cold as** it was yesterday'.

No 14 Sumatra Road was <u>not as pretty as</u> Walnut Cottage.

Not so is also sometimes used, but this is less common.

The officers here are <u>not so young as</u> the lieutenants.

(i) Note that after **not as** and **not so**, you use **as**, not 'than'.

let

1 'let'

Let is used to say that someone allows someone else to do something. After the object, you use an infinitive without 'to'.

The farmer <u>lets</u> me <u>live</u> in a caravan behind his barn.
She never <u>lets</u> her <u>leave</u> home.
They sit back and <u>let</u> everyone else <u>do</u> the work.

ⓘ Note that you do not use a 'to'-infinitive or an '-ing' form after **let**. You do not say, for example, '~~He lets me to use his telephone~~' or '~~He lets me using his telephone~~'.

The past tense and past participle of **let** is **let,** not 'letted'.

He <u>let</u> Jack lead the way.
She <u>had let</u> him go off with her papers.

⚠ **WARNING:** There is no passive form of **let.** You do not say, for example, '~~He was let go~~' or '~~He was let to go~~'. If you want to use a passive form, you use a different verb, such as **allow** or **permit.**
Perhaps when he grew up he would <u>be allowed to</u> do as he pleased.
She was the only prisoner <u>permitted to</u> enter my cell.

2 'let ... know'

If you **let** someone **know** something, you tell them about it.

I'll find out about the car and <u>let</u> you <u>know</u> what happened.
It doesn't matter so long as she <u>lets</u> her doctor <u>know.</u>

3 'let me'

People often use **let me** when they are offering to do something for someone.

<u>Let me</u> show you.
<u>Let me</u> help you off with your coat.

⇨ For other ways of making an offer, see **Usage** entry at **Offers.**

4 another meaning

Let has another meaning. If you **let** your house or land to someone, you allow them to use it in exchange for regular payments.

⇨ See **Usage** entry at **hire - rent - let.**

let go

⇨ See **Usage** entry at **release - let go.**

let's - let us

1 making a suggestion

You use **let's** when you are suggesting that you and someone else should do something. **Let's** is short for **let us.** It is followed by an infinitive without 'to'.

<u>Let's go</u> outside.
<u>Let's decide</u> what we want.

The full form **let us** is used with this meaning only in formal English.

<u>Let us</u> postpone the matter.

If you are suggesting that you and someone else should not do something, you say **let's not.**

<u>Let's not</u> talk about that.
<u>Let's not</u> waste time.

Some British speakers say **don't let's.**

<u>Don't let's</u> tell anyone.

 In informal American English, the expression **let's don't** is sometimes used.
<u>Let's don't</u> talk about it.

⇨ For other ways of making suggestions, see **Topic** entry at **Suggestions**.

2 **making a request**

You can use **let us** when you are making a request on behalf of yourself and someone else. In sentences like these, you do not shorten **let us** to 'let's'.

Let us know what progress has been made.

Please, don't let us be frightened of making mistakes.

lettuce

⇨ See **Usage** entry at **salad - lettuce**.

level

A **level** is a point on a scale, for example a scale of amount or importance.

The noise levels were too high.

We now have a high level of unemployment.

These decisions are made well below the level of top management.

You say that something is **at** a particular level.

Mammals maintain their body temperature at a constant level.

Corruption is rampant at all levels of government.

ⓘ Note that you do not use any preposition except **at** in sentences like these.

library - bookshop

1 **'library'**

A **library** is a building where books are kept which people can look at or borrow.

A **library** is also a private collection of books, or a room in a large house where books are kept.

… the local library.

I once stayed in one of his houses and saw his library.

2 **'bookshop'**

You do not refer to a shop where you can buy books as a 'library'. In Britain, a shop like this is called a **bookshop**. In America, it is called a **bookstore**.

… bookshop window displays.

My wife's sister Laura works in a bookstore.

licence - license

1 **'licence'**

In British English, a **licence** is an official document which gives you permission to do, use, or own something.

I haven't got a television licence.

Keep your driving licence on you.

2 **'license' used as a noun**

In American English, this word is spelled **license**.

A photo identification, such as a driver's license, is required.

3 **'license' used as a verb**

In both British and American English, if you **are licensed** to do something, you have official permission to do it.

These men are licensed to carry firearms.

lie

⇨ See **Usage** entry at **lay - lie**.

lift - elevator

1 'lift'

If you give someone a **lift**, you drive them in your car from one place to another.

She offered me a lift home.

In British English, a **lift** is also a device that moves up and down inside a tall building and carries people from one floor to another.

I took the lift to the eighth floor.

2 'elevator'

In American English, a device like this is called an **elevator**.

The elevator descended to the lobby.

⇨ For information on **lift** as a verb, see **Usage** entry at **carry - take.**

light

If you **light** something such as a cigarette or candle, you make it start burning. The past tense and past participle of **light** is either **lit** or **lighted. Lit** is more common.

He lit a cigarette.
I lighted a candle.

You can say that a street, building, or room **is lit** or **is lighted** by a particular kind of light, for example electricity.

…a room lit by candles.
The room was lighted by a very small, dim bulb.

For both meanings of **light**, you use **lighted**, not 'lit', in front of a noun.

Mitchell took the lighted cigarette from his lips.
I noticed a lighted window across the street.

However, after an adverb you use **lit.**

…a freshly lit cigarette.
…the dimly lit department store.

like

Like is used with one meaning as a preposition or conjunction, and with another meaning as a verb.

1 used as a preposition

If one person or thing is **like** another, they have similar characteristics or behave in a similar way.

He looks like Father Christmas.
His voice was like dripping honey.

If you ask someone what something is **like**, you are asking them to describe it.

What was Essex like?
What did they taste like?

2 used as a conjunction

In conversation, you can say that something is **like** you remembered it or **like** you imagined it.

Is it like you remembered it?

In writing, it is better to say that something is **how** you remembered or imagined it.

You can use **like** with **do** when you are comparing someone's behaviour or appearance to another person's. For example, you can say 'She swims in the lake every day, **like** her mother **did**'.

⇨ For more information about this use, see **Usage** entry at **like - as - the way.**

Some speakers use **like** with other verbs to describe how someone or something looks,

USAGE

or how someone behaves.

He did it like he was used to it.

This use is generally regarded as incorrect. Instead of 'like', it is better to use **as if** or **as though**.

⇨ See **Usage** entry at **as if**.

3 | used as a verb

If you **like** someone or something, you find them pleasant or attractive.

She's a nice girl, I like her.
Very few of the women liked Saigon.

⇨ For a graded list of verbs and expressions used to express liking or dislike, see **Usage** entry at **like - dislike**.

⚠ **WARNING:** You do not use a continuous tense of **like**. You do not say, for example, 'I am liking peanuts'. You say 'I **like** peanuts'.

You can use **like** in front of an '-ing' form to say that you enjoy an activity.

I like reading.
I just don't like being in crowds.

You can add **very much** to emphasize how much you like someone or something, or how much you enjoy an activity.

I like him very much.
I like driving very much.

⚠ **WARNING:** Note that you put **very much** after the object, not after **like**. You do not say, for example, 'I like very much driving'.

If someone asks you if you like something, you can say 'Yes, I **do**.' You do not say 'Yes, I like.'

'Do you like walking?'–'Yes I do , I love it.'

⚠ **WARNING:** You do not use **like** immediately in front of a clause beginning with **when** or **if**. For example, you do not say 'I like when I can go home early'. You say 'I **like it** when I can go home early'.

The guests don't like it when they can't use the pool.
I'd like it if you fell in love with Michael.

4 | 'would like'

You say **'Would you like…?'** when you are offering something to someone.

Would you like some coffee?

ⓘ Note that you do not say 'Do you like some coffee?'

You say **'Would you like…'** followed by a 'to'-infinitive when you are inviting someone to do something.

Would you like to meet him?

ⓘ Note that you do not use an '-ing' form after **'Would you like…'** . You do not say, for example, 'Would you like meeting him?'

⇨ For more information about making invitations, see **Topic** entry at **Invitations**.

You can say **'I'd like…'** when asking for something in a shop or café.

I'd like some apples, please.

⇨ For more information about asking for something, see section on **asking as a customer** in **Topic** entry at **Requests, orders, and instructions**.

You say **'I'd like you to…'** when you are telling someone to do something in a fairly polite way.

I'd like you to tell them where I am.

⇨ For more information about ways of telling people to do something, see section on **orders and instructions** in **Topic** entry at **Requests, orders, and instructions.**

like - as - the way

1 used as conjunctions

You can use **like, as,** or **the way** as conjunctions when you are comparing one person's behaviour or appearance to another's. In the clause which follows the conjunction, the verb is usually **do.**

For example, you can say 'He walked to work every day, **like** his father had done', 'He walked to work every day, **as** his father had done', or 'He walked to work every day, **the way** his father had done'.

How can you live like she does?
They were people who spoke and thought as he did.
Start lending things, the way people did in the war.

Learners used to be taught that only **as** was correct in sentences like these, but this use now sounds rather formal or literary. In conversation, people usually use **like** or **the way.**

2 used as prepositions

Like and **as** can be prepositions, but their meaning is not usually the same. For example, if you do something **like** a particular kind of person, you do it the way that kind of person would do it, although you are not that kind of person.

We worked like slaves.

If you do something **as** a particular kind of person, you are that kind of person.

Over the summer she worked as a waitress.
I can only speak as a married man without children.

like - dislike

The verbs and expressions in the following list are all used to indicate how much someone likes or dislikes something. They are arranged from 'like most' to 'dislike most':

● **adore**

She adored her parents and would do anything to please them.

● **love, be crazy about, be mad about, be a great fan of**

We loved the food so much, especially the fish dishes.
He's still crazy about both his work and his hobbies.
She's not as mad about sport as I am.
I am a great fan of rave music.

● **like, be fond of, be keen on**

What music do you like best?
She was especially fond of a little girl named Betsy.
Both companies were keen on a merger.

● **don't mind**

I hope you don't mind me calling in like this, without an appointment.

● **dislike**

We don't serve liver often because so many people dislike it.

● **hate**

She hated hospitals and didn't like the idea of having an operation.

● **abhor, can't bear, can't stand, detest, loathe**

He was a man who abhorred violence and was deeply committed to reconciliation.

I <u>can't bear</u> people who make judgements and label me.
I <u>can't stand</u> that man and his arrogance.
Jean <u>detested</u> being photographed.
The two men <u>loathe</u> each other.

likely

1 used as an adjective

Likely is usually an adjective. You say, for example, that something is **likely to** happen.

These services are <u>likely to</u> be available to us all before long.

You can also say that **it is likely that** something will happen.

It is likely that his symptoms will disappear of their own accord.
If this is your first baby, it's far more <u>likely that</u> you'll get to the hospital too early.

2 used as an adverb

In conversation, **likely** is sometimes an adverb with **most**, **more than**, or **very** in front of it, or as part of the phrase **more likely than not**. You do not use it as an adverb on its own.

One pupil will have been taught, <u>most likely,</u> by five people.
<u>More than likely,</u> the cause is a root rot fungus.
<u>More likely than not</u> he will realize he is beaten.

listen to

If you **listen to** a sound or **listen to** a person who is talking, you pay attention to the sound or to what the person is saying.

I do my ironing while <u>listening to</u> the radio.
<u>Listen</u> carefully <u>to</u> what he says.
They wouldn't <u>listen to</u> me.

⚠ **WARNING: Listen** is not a transitive verb. You do not say that someone 'listens' a sound or 'listens' a person.

If you have been to a musical performance, you do not usually say that you 'listened to' the music or 'listened to' the performer. You say that you **heard** them.

That was the first time I ever <u>heard</u> Jimi Hendrix.
She can <u>hear</u> it played by a professional orchestra.

⇨ See also **Usage** entry at **hear**.

literal - literary - literate

1 'literal'

The **literal** meaning of a word is its most basic meaning.

She was older than I was, and not only in the <u>literal</u> sense.
The <u>literal</u> meaning of the Greek word hamartia, translated as sin, is 'missing the mark'.

2 'literary'

Literary words and expressions are used to create a special effect in poems or novels, and are not usually used in ordinary speech or writing.

'Awaken' and 'waken' are old-fashioned or <u>literary</u> words.

Literary also means 'connected with literature'.

... <u>literary</u> critics.
... <u>literary</u> magazines.

3 'literate'

A **literate** person is able to read and write.

Only half the children are <u>literate.</u>

little - a little

1 **'little' used as an adjective**

Little is usually an adjective. You use it to talk about the size of something.

…*a little table with a glass top.*

⇨ See **Usage** entry at **small - little**.

2 **'a little' used as an adverb**

A little is usually an adverb. You use it after a verb, or in front of an adjective or another adverb. It means 'to a small extent or degree'.

They get paid for it. Not much. Just a little.
Trading is thought to have been a little disappointing.
The local football team is doing a little better.
The celebrations began a little earlier than expected.

(*i*) Note that you do not use 'a little' in front of an adjective when the adjective comes in front of a noun.

⇨ Several other words and expressions can be used to express degree. For a graded list, see section on **degree** in **Grammar** entry at **Adjuncts**. See also section on **grading adverbs** in **Grammar** entry at **Adverbs**.

3 **used in front of nouns**

Little and **a little** are also used in front of nouns to talk about quantities. When they are used like this, they do not have the same meaning.

You use **a little** simply to indicate that you are talking about a small quantity or amount of something. When you use **little** without 'a', you are emphasizing that there is only a small quantity or amount of something.

So, for example, if you say 'I have **a little** money', you are simply saying that you have some money. However, if you say 'I have **little** money', you mean that you do not have enough money.

I had made a little progress.
It is clear that little progress was made.
He started a new business with a little help from his friends.
Having an independent allowance will be little help.

4 **used as pronouns**

Little and **a little** can be used in similar ways as pronouns.

Beat in the eggs, a little at a time.
Little has changed.

5 **'not much'**

In conversation, people do not usually use **little** without **a**. Instead they use **not much**. For example, instead of saying 'I have little money', they say 'I **haven't got much** money' or 'I **don't have much** money'.

I haven't got much appetite.
You haven't got much to say to me, have you?
We probably don't have much time.
When you're 16 you don't have much experience.

⚠ **WARNING:** You do not use 'little' or 'a little' with a count noun when you are talking about a small number of people or things. You do not say, for example, 'She has a little hens'. You say 'She has **a few** hens'. Similarly, you do not say 'Little people attended his lectures'. You say 'Few people attended his lectures', or '**Not many** people attended his lectures'.

⇨ See **Usage** entry at **few - a few**.

USAGE

live - leave

1 'live'

If you **live** in a particular place, it is your home.

I have some friends who <u>live</u> in Wandsworth.
I <u>live</u> in a flat just down the road from you.

When you are simply saying that a place is someone's home, you do not use a continuous tense. You only use a continuous tense when you are saying that someone has just moved to a place, or that it is their home for a temporary period.

Her husband had been released from prison and <u>was</u> now <u>living</u> at the house.
Remember that you <u>are living</u> in someone else's home.
We have to leave Ziatur, the town where we <u>have been living</u>.

If you want to say how long you have been living in a place, you use **for** or **since**. You say, for example, 'I have been living here **for** four years', 'I have been living here **since** 1988', or 'I have lived here **since** 1988'. You do not say 'I am living here for four years' or 'I am living here since 1988'.

He has been living in France now <u>for</u> almost two years.
The Fayed brothers have been living in Britain <u>since</u> the 1960s.
She has lived there <u>since</u> she was six.

⇨ See **Usage** entries at **for** and **since**.

2 'leave'

Do not confuse **live** /lɪv/ with **leave** /liːv/. If you **leave** a place, you go away from it.

We will <u>leave</u> the town by the old road.

⇨ See **Usage** entry at **leave.**

---

lonely - lonesome

1 'lonely'

In British English, someone who is **lonely** is unhappy because they are alone.

Since he left India he had been <u>lonely</u> and homesick.

2 'lonesome'

 American speakers sometimes say **lonesome,** not 'lonely'.

I bet you told her how <u>lonesome</u> you were.

---

long

1 used to talk about length

You use **long** when you are talking about the length of something.

…an area up to 3000 feet <u>long</u> and 900 feet wide.
How <u>long</u> is that side of the triangle?

2 talking about distance

You use **a long way** to talk about the distance from one place to another. You say, for example, 'It's **a long way** from here to Birmingham'.

I'm <u>a long way</u> from London.

ⓘ Note that you do not say 'It's long from here to Birmingham' or 'I'm long from London'. In negative sentences, you use **far.** You say, for example, 'It's **not far** from here to Birmingham'.

They had rented a villa <u>not far</u> from the Hotel Miranda.

You also use **far** in questions. You say, for example, 'How **far** is it from here to Birmingham?'

How <u>far</u> is Amity from here?

ⓘ Note that you do not use 'long' in negative sentences and questions like these.

When you are talking about the extent of a journey, you use **as far as**, not 'as long as'. You say, for example, 'We walked **as far as** the church'.
Vita and Rosamund went with Harold as far as Bologna.

3 **used to talk about time**
In a negative sentence or a question, you can use **long** as an adverb to mean 'a long time'.
Wilkins hasn't been with us long.
Are you staying long?

You can also use **long** to mean 'a long time' after **too** or in front of **enough**.
He's been here too long.
You've been here long enough to know what we're like.

However, you do not use **long** with this meaning in any other kind of positive sentence. Instead you use **a long time**.
We may be here a long time.
It may seem a long time to wait.

The comparative and superlative forms **longer** and **longest** can be used with this meaning in any kind of positive sentence.
Reform in Europe always takes longer than expected.
Korda's performance will linger longest in the memory.

⇨ Several other words and expressions can be used to say how long something lasts. For a graded list, see section on **duration** in **Grammar** entry at **Adjuncts**.

4 **'no longer'**
When something that happened in the past does not happen now, you can say that it **no longer** happens or that it does not happen **any longer**.
We no longer feed our infants in this way.
I noticed that he wasn't sitting by the door any longer.

⇨ For more information, see section on **any longer** in **Usage** entry at **any more**.

look

1 **'look at'**
If someone directs their eyes towards something, you say that they **look at** it.
Lang looked at his watch.
She looked at the people around her.

When **look** has this meaning, it must be followed by **at**. You do not say, for example, 'Lang looked his watch'.

⚠ **WARNING:** Do not confuse **look** with **see** or **watch**.
⇨ For an explanation of the differences, see **Usage** entry at **see - look at - watch**.

If you want to say that someone shows a particular feeling when they look at someone or something, you indicate this using an adverb, not an adjective. For example, you say 'She looked **sadly** at her husband'. You do not say 'She looked sad at her husband'.
Jack looked uncertainly at Ralph.
When he saw me, he looked adoringly at me!

2 **'look and see'**
If you intend to use your eyes to find out if something is the case, you say that you will **see** or **look and see** if it is the case.
Have a look at your wife's face to see if she's blushing.
Now let's look and see whether that's true or not.

ⓘ Note that you do not say that you will 'look' if something is the case.

You can use **see** to say that you will find out about something, even if you are not talking

USAGE

about using your eyes. For example, you can say 'I'll **see** if George is in his office', and then find out whether George is in his office by making a phone call there.

I'll just see if he's at home.
I'll see if I can borrow a car for the weekend.

3 used to mean 'seem'
Look can also be used to mean 'seem' or 'appear'. When you use **look** like this, you use an adjective after it, not an adverb. For example, you say 'She looked **sad** '. You do not say 'She looked sadly'.

You look very pale.
The place looked a bit bare.

⚠ **WARNING:** You only use **look** to mean 'seem' when talking about the appearance of something.

look after - look for

1 'look after'
If you **look after** someone or something, you take care of them.

She will look after the children during their holidays.
It doesn't worry me who owns the club so long as it is looked after.

2 'look for'
If you **look for** someone or something, you try to find them.

Were you looking for me, Miss Nicandra?
He looked for his shoes under the bed.

look forward to

1 used with a noun
If you **are looking forward to** something that you are going to experience, you are pleased or excited about it.

They 're so much looking forward to the opportunity to watch our programmes.
Is there any particular thing you are looking forward to next year?

⚠ **WARNING:** You do not use this expression without **to**. You do not say, for example, 'I am looking forward the party'. You also do not say that someone 'is looking forwards to' something.

2 used with an '-ing' form
You can use an '-ing' form after **look forward to**.

I was so much looking forward to talking to you.
I look forward to seeing you in Washington.

⚠ **WARNING:** You do not use an infinitive after **look forward to**. You do not say, for example, 'He's looking forward to go home'.

loose - lose

1 'loose'
Loose /luːs/ is an adjective. It means 'not firmly fixed', or 'not tight'.

The doorknob is loose.
Mary wore loose clothes.

2 'lose'
Lose /luːz/ is a verb. If you **lose** something, you no longer have it, or you cannot find it.

I do not want to lose my job.
… a toll-free phone number to call if you lose your pet.

The other forms of **lose** are **loses, losing, lost.**
They were willing to risk losing their jobs.
He had lost his passport somewhere.

lorry - truck

1 **'lorry'**

In British English, a **lorry** is a large motor vehicle used for transporting goods by road.
… a seven-ton lorry.

2 **'truck'**

In American English, a vehicle like this is called a **truck.** In British English, small open lorries are sometimes called **trucks.**
A blue truck drives up and delivers some boxes.

In British English, open vehicles used for transporting goods by rail are sometimes called **trucks.**

⇨ See **Usage** entry at **carriage - car - truck - wagon.**

lose

⇨ See **Usage** entry at **loose - lose.**

lot

1 **'a lot of' and 'lots of'**

You use **a lot of** or **lots of** in front of a noun when you are talking about a large number of people or things, or a large quantity or amount of something. For example, you can talk about 'a lot of money' or 'lots of money'. **Lots of** is only used in conversation.
A lot of people thought it was funny.
We have quite a lot of newspapers.
There's a lot of research to be done.
You've got lots of time.

When you use **a lot of** or **lots of** in front of a plural count noun, you use a plural form of a verb with it.
A lot of people come to our classes.
There are lots of things that affect people's livelihoods.

When you use **a lot of** or **lots of** in front of an uncount noun, you use a singular form of a verb with it.
A lot of time is spent talking on the phone.
There is lots of money to be made in advertising.

2 **'a lot' and 'lots'**

You use **a lot** to refer to a large quantity or amount of something.
I'd learnt a lot.
I feel that we have a lot to offer.

You use **a lot** as an adverb to mean 'to a great extent' or 'often'.
You like Ralph a lot, don't you?
They talk a lot about equality.

⇨ Many other words and expressions can be used to say that something is the case to a smaller or greater extent. For a graded list, see section on **degree** in **Grammar** entry at **Adjuncts.**

You also use **a lot** in front of comparatives. For example, if you want to emphasize the difference in age between two things, you can say that one thing is **a lot older** than the other.
The weather's a lot warmer there.
I've known people who were in a lot more serious trouble than you.

USAGE

You also use **a lot** or **lots** with **more** to emphasize the difference between two quantities or amounts. **Lots** is only used in conversation.

He had gained a lot more sleep than the others.
She meets lots more people than I do.

Far is used in a similar way.

Far more research has been done on finding a cure for the problem in men than in women.
Workplaces today have far more women employed than in the past.

loudly

⇨ See **Usage** entry at **aloud - loudly**.

love

The verb **love** is usually used to express a strong feeling of affection for a person or place.

She loved her husband deeply.
He had loved his aunt very much.
He loved his country above all else.

If you want to say that something gives you pleasure, or that you enjoy a person's company, you usually say **like**, not 'love'.

I like reading.
We liked him very much.

In conversation, people sometimes use **love** to emphasize that they like a thing or activity very much.

I love your new hairdo.
I love reading his plays.

⇨ For a graded list of words and expressions used to express liking, see **Usage** entry at **like - dislike**.

low - lowly

1 **'low'**

Low can be an adjective or an adverb.
Something that is **low** measures a short distance from the bottom to the top.

…a low brick wall.
… low hills.

You also say that something is **low** when it is very close to the ground.

She made a low curtsey.
He bumped his head on the low beams.

You can use **low** as an adverb to say that something moves close to the ground. For example, you can say 'He bowed **low** '.

I asked him to fly low over the beach.

ⓘ Note that you do not say 'He bowed lowly' or 'I asked him to fly lowly over the beach'.

Low also means 'small in amount, value, or degree'.

…workers on low incomes.
… low expectations.

Low is not an adverb with this meaning, except in front of **paid**.

We must make low -paid work more attractive than welfare.

Like the adjective, the adverb **low** has the comparative and superlative forms **lower, lowest**.

In a series of quick, jerky movements he bent lower and lower.
…the lowest paid workers in the country.

2 **'lowly'**

Lowly is an adjective. It is a literary word meaning 'low in rank, status, or importance'.

…a lowly employee.
…his lowly social origins.
The comparative and superlative forms of **lowly** are **lowlier** and **lowliest**.

luck

Luck is success that comes to you by accident rather than by your own efforts.
I had some wonderful luck.
All he did was shake hands and wish me luck.

Luck is an uncount noun. You do not talk about 'lucks' or 'a luck'.

lucky - happy

1 **'lucky'**
You say that someone is **lucky** when something nice happens to them, or when they always seem to have good luck.
You're a lucky girl.
He was the luckiest man in the world.

2 **'happy'**
You do not use 'lucky' to say that someone has feelings of pleasure and contentment. The word you use is **happy**.
Sarah's such a happy person.
Barbara felt tremendously happy.

luggage - baggage

In British English, both these words refer to the bags and suitcases that you take with you when you travel, together with their contents. **Luggage** is more common than **baggage**.
Leave your luggage in the hotel.

 In American English, **luggage** usually refers to empty bags and suitcases. **Baggage** refers to bags and suitcases with their contents.
… a decline in sales of hand-sized luggage.
The passengers went through immigration control and collected their baggage.

Both these words are uncount nouns. You do not talk about 'luggages' or 'a baggage'.

lunch

⇨ See **Usage** entry at **dinner - lunch - luncheon**.

luxury - luxurious

1 **'luxury'**
Luxury is great comfort among beautiful and expensive surroundings.
We lived in great luxury.
…a life of luxury.

Luxury is often used as an adjective in front of a noun. You use it to talk about a class of comfortable, expensive things, or to identify something as belonging to such a class.
He could not afford luxury food on his pay.
…a luxury car for the President.

(*i*) Note that although you can talk about **luxury goods**, you do not talk about 'luxury things'. Instead you say **luxuries**.
We are not able to afford luxuries.

2 **'luxurious'**
You use **luxurious** to describe something as being comfortable and expensive, without identifying it as belonging to a particular class. You can use words like **very** and **more** in front of **luxurious**.
He let himself fall into the most luxurious of the armchairs.

M m

machine - motor - engine

1 'machine'

A **machine** is a piece of equipment which uses electricity or some other form of power to perform a particular task.

…*a washing machine.*
I put the coin in the machine and pulled the lever.

2 'motor'

When a machine operates by electricity, you refer to the part of the machine that converts power into movement as the **motor**.

…*a malfunctioning fan motor in the attic space of the building.*

3 'engine'

You do not use 'machine' to refer to the part of a vehicle that provides the power that makes the vehicle move. This part of a car, bus, lorry, or plane is usually called the **engine**.

He couldn't get his engine started.
The starboard engines were already running.

You talk about the **engine** of a ship, but the **motor** of a small boat.

Black smoke belched from the engine into the cabin.
We patched leaks, overhauled the motor, and refitted her.

machinery

You can refer to machines in general as **machinery**.

Farmers import most of their machinery and materials.
…*a manufacturer of farm machinery.*

Machinery is an uncount noun. You do not talk about 'machineries' or 'a machinery'. However, you can talk about a **piece of machinery**.

He was called out to do some work on a piece of machinery that had broken down.

mad

1 'mad' and 'insane'

In the past, when someone had a mental illness which made them behave in strange ways, people used to say that they were **mad** or **insane**. Nowadays these words are not usually used about living people, as they are thought to be offensive. People usually say that someone is **mentally ill**.

They were found to be mentally ill.
…*the treatment of mentally ill patients.*

A number of other words are used to talk about people who have a mental illness.

⇨ See **Usage** entry at **madness**.

2 other meanings of 'mad'

It is fairly common to describe a foolish action or proposal as **mad** or **insane**.

Anyone could see it was a mad idea.
…*the Community's insane agricultural policy.*

In conversation, **mad** is sometimes used to mean 'angry'. If you are **mad at** someone, you are angry with them.

People wanted to make money out of him and when he said no to them, they got mad.
I guess that they're mad at me for getting them up so early.

3 **'mad about'**

If you are **mad about** something that has happened, you are angry about it.

I'm pretty mad about it, I can tell you.

If you are **mad about** something such as an activity, you like or enjoy it very much.

How is Rosalind? Still mad about ponies?

She loved dancing and was mad about the cinema.

(i) Note that you do not use 'mad' in any of these ways in formal writing.

made from - made of - made out of

Made is the past tense and past participle of the verb **make**.

⇨ See **Usage** entry at **make**.

If one thing has been produced from another in such a way that the original thing is completely changed, you can say that the first thing is **made from, made out of,** or **made of** the second thing.

Our rope was made from ordinary hemp.

…artificial meat made out of soya-bean protein.

…cloth made of goats' hair.

If you want to indicate that one thing has been produced from another in an unusual or surprising way, you usually use **made out of.**

…a loincloth made out of a kitchen towel.

If you are mentioning the parts or materials from which something is constructed, you use **made of** or **made out of.** You do not use 'made from'.

My cabin was made of logs.

madness

You should be careful which words you use to refer to someone who has an abnormal mental condition. The adjectives **mad, insane, crazy, demented,** and **deranged,** and the nouns **lunatic, maniac,** and **madman** are usually avoided nowadays in serious speech and writing because they are thought to be offensive.

Instead, you can say that someone is **mentally ill.** If their condition is less severe, you can say that they are **mentally disturbed** or **unbalanced,** or that they have **psychological problems.**

At least ninety percent of the men and women who kill themselves are mentally ill.

…an institution for mentally disturbed children.

…the area of the jail reserved for women with psychological problems.

magazine - shop

1 **'magazine'**

A **magazine** is a weekly or monthly publication containing articles, photographs, and advertisements.

Her face is on the cover of a dozen or more magazines.

2 **'shop'**

You do not use 'magazine' to refer to a building or part of a building where things are sold. The word you use is **shop.**

…health food shops.

magic - magical

1 **'magic' used as a noun**

Magic is a special power that occurs in children's stories and that some people believe exists. It can make apparently impossible things happen.

Janoo-Bai was suspected of practising magic.

USAGE

2 'magic' used as an adjective

You use **magic** in front of a noun to indicate that an object or utterance does things or appears to do things by magic.

...a _magic_ potion.
...the _magic_ password.

3 'magical'

Magical can be used with a similar meaning.

... _magical_ garments.
...a _magical_ car.

You also use **magical** to say that something involves magic or is produced by magic.

...medieval _magical_ practices.
...a little boy who has _magical_ powers.

4 another meaning

Magic and **magical** can also be used to say that something is wonderful and exciting.

...a truly _magic_ moment.
The journey had lost its _magical_ quality.

---

mail

⇨ See **Usage** entry at **post - mail.**

majority

1 'majority'

If something is true of **the majority** of the people or things in a group, it is true of more than half of them.

The majority of young mothers are totally dependent on their husbands' salaries.
This is true in _the majority_ of cases.

When **the majority** is not followed by 'of', you can use either a singular or plural form of a verb after it.

This tax will soon be abolished as far as the majority _is_ concerned.
The majority _feel_ threatened by change.

However, when you use **the majority of** followed by a plural noun or pronoun, you must use a plural form of a verb after it.

The majority of birds _have_ much to gain from remaining inconspicuous.

2 'most of'

You do not use 'the majority' when you are talking about an amount of something or part of something. You do not say, for example, ~~'The majority of the forest has been cut down'.~~ You say '**Most of** the forest has been cut down'.

Most of the wood was rotten.
Mrs Leonard did _most of_ the work.

⇨ See **Usage** entry at **most.**

---

make

Make is a very common verb which is used in many different ways. The past tense and past participle of **make** is **made.**

1 performing an action

Make is most commonly used to say that someone performs an action. For example, if someone suggests something, you can say that they **make** a suggestion. If someone promises something, you can say that they **make** a promise.

I think that I _made_ the wrong decision.
He _made_ the shortest speech I have ever heard.
In 1978 he _made_ his first visit to Australia.

Here is a list of common nouns that you can use with **make** in this way:

arrangement	decision	noise	promise	speech	trip
choice	enquiry	plan	remark	suggestion	visit
comment	journey	point	sound	tour	

You do not use 'make' when you are talking generally about action, rather than mentioning a particular action. Instead you use **do**. For example, if someone is unsure what action to take, you do not say they do not know what to 'make'. You say that they do not know what to **do**.

What have you done?
You've done a lot to help us.
We'll see what can be done.

2 making an object or substance

If you **make** an object or substance, you construct or produce it.

Sheila makes all her own clothes.
You can make petroleum out of coal.

You can also say that someone **makes** a meal or a drink.

I made his breakfast.

⇨ See **Usage** entry at **cook**.

When **make** is used to talk about constructing or producing something, it can have an indirect object. You say that you **make** someone something, or **make** something **for** them.

I have made you a drink.
We made collars for the horses.
I shall have a copy made for you.

3 making someone do something

If someone forces you to do something, you can say that they **make you do** it.

You've got to make him listen.
Mama made him clean up the plate.

ⓘ Note that in active sentences like these, you do not use a 'to'-infinitive after **make**. You do not say, for example, ~~'You've got to make them to listen'~~.
However, in passive sentences you must use a 'to'-infinitive.

They were made to pay $8.8 million in taxes.
One old woman was made to wait more than an hour.

4 used to mean 'be'

Make is sometimes used instead of 'be' to say how successful someone is in a particular job or role. For example, instead of saying 'He will be a good prime minister', you can say 'He will **make** a good prime minister'.

You really mean it when you say he'll make a good president?
They make a good team.

5 used as a noun

Make is sometimes a noun. The **make** of something such as a car or radio is the name of the company that made it.

My own boots were a different make.

Make is usually followed by **of** and another noun. After **makes of** you use either the plural or singular form of a noun. For example, you can say 'We sell all makes of **cars**' or 'We sell all makes of **car**'. The singular form is more formal.

There are now over a hundred makes of micro-computers for sale.
…tests on well-known makes of car.

After **make of** you use the singular form of a noun.

…a certain make of wristwatch.

USAGE

make up
⇨ See **Usage** entry at **comprise**.

---

male - masculine

1 'male'
Male means 'relating to the sex that cannot have babies'. You can use **male** as an adjective to talk about either people or animals.

… _male nurses._
…_a young male chimpanzee._

You can use **male** as a noun to talk about an animal.

The _males establish a breeding territory._

(i) Note that you do not usually use 'male' as a noun to talk about men or boys.

2 'masculine'
Masculine means 'typical of men, rather than women'.

Perhaps some kind of masculine pride was involved.
The Duke's study was very masculine, with deep red wall-covering and oak shelves.

(i) Note that you do not use 'masculine' to talk about animals.

---

man

1 'man'
A **man** is an adult male human being. The plural of **man** is **men,** not 'mans'.
Larry was a handsome man in his early fifties.
He was visited by two men in the morning.

Man is sometimes used to refer to human beings in general. For example, instead of saying 'Human beings are destroying the environment', you can say ' **Man** is destroying the environment'. Note that when **man** has this meaning, you do not use 'the' in front of it.
Man is not inherently violent.
…_the most dangerous substance known to man._

Men is sometimes used to refer to all human beings, considered as individuals.
All men are born equal.
Darwin concluded that men were descended from apes.

2 'mankind'
Mankind is used to refer to all human beings, considered as a group.
You have performed a valuable service to mankind.

Some people object to the use of **man, men,** and **mankind** to refer to human beings of both sexes, because they think it suggests that men are more important than women.

3 another meaning of 'man'
In conversation, a woman's boyfriend or the man she is married to can be referred to humorously as her **man.**
The two women have abandoned their men and are going to spend an evening in town.

4 'husband'
However, you do not usually refer to the man a woman is married to as her 'man'. You refer to him as her **husband.**

---

manage - arrange

1 'manage'
If you **manage to do** something, you succeed in doing it.
Manuelito managed to avoid capture.
How did you manage to do that?

(*i*) Note that you use a 'to'-infinitive, not an '-ing' form, after **manage**.

2 **'arrange'**

You do not use a 'that'-clause after 'manage'. You do not say, for example, that you ~~'manage that something is done'~~. You say that you **arrange for it to be done.**

He had arranged for roadblocks to be erected.

You also do not say that you ~~'manage that someone does something'~~. You say that you **arrange for them to do it.**

I had arranged for a photographer to take pictures of the body.

manifestation - demonstration

1 **'manifestation'**

A **manifestation** of something is a sign that it is happening or that it exists.

…the first manifestations of student unrest in Britain.

2 **'demonstration'**

You do not use 'manifestation' to refer to a public meeting or march held to show opposition to something or support for something. The word you use is **demonstration.**

The opposition staged a huge demonstration.

⇨ See **Usage** entry at **demonstration.**

mankind

⇨ See **Usage** entry at **man.**

manufacture - factory

1 **'manufacture'**

Manufacture refers to the making of a product using machinery. **Manufacture** is an uncount noun.

…the manufacture of nuclear weapons.

2 **'factory'**

You do not use 'manufacture' to refer to a building where machines are used to make things. A building like this is usually called a **factory.**

⇨ See **Usage** entry at **factory - works - mill - plant.**

many

1 **'many' used in front of a plural noun**

You use **many** immediately in front of the plural form of a noun to talk about a large number of people or things.

Many girls report that the experience is unpleasant.
Capital punishment is legal in many countries.

2 **'many of'**

When you want to talk about a large number of the people or things belonging to a particular group, you use **many of** in front of a plural pronoun, or in front of a plural noun group beginning with **the, these, those,** or a possessive.

Many of them are being forced to give up.
Many of the inhabitants had fair skins.
Many of these caves are perfect for long-term occupation.
Many of his books are still available.
This enables scientists to confirm many of Einstein's ideas about relativity.

3 **'many' used as a pronoun**

Many is sometimes used as a pronoun to refer to a large group of people or things. This is a fairly formal use.

Many were still lying where they had been injured.

> ⚠ **WARNING:** You do not use 'many' or 'many of' to talk about a large quantity or amount of something. Instead you use **much** or **much of**.
> ⇨ See **Usage** entry at **much**.

4 'many more'

You can use **many** with **more** to emphasize the difference in size between two groups of people or things.

I know <u>many more</u> country people than I do town people.
Why does man seem to have <u>many more</u> diseases than animals have?

---

mark - make

1 'mark'

A **mark** is a small stain or damaged area on a surface.

…grease <u>marks.</u>
There seems to be a dirty <u>mark</u> on it.

A **mark** is also a number or letter which indicates your score in a test or examination.

You need 120 <u>marks</u> out of 200 to pass.

 Note that in American English, the word for this is usually **points**.

I got 30 <u>points</u> on the test out of 60.

Mark sometimes appears in the name of a vehicle or machine, followed by a number.

…his <u>Mark II</u> Ford Cortina.

2 'make'

However, you do not refer to a type of product as a 'mark'. If you want to indicate which company makes a product, you use the noun **make**.

She couldn't tell what <u>make</u> of car he was driving.

⇨ See **Usage** entry at **make**.

marmalade - jam - jelly

1 'marmalade'

Marmalade is a sweet food made from oranges, lemons, limes, or grapefruit. In Britain, people spread it on bread or toast and eat it as part of their breakfast.

Harrod's Seville Orange <u>Marmalade</u>.

2 'jam' and 'jelly'

 Note that in English **marmalade** refers only to a food made from oranges, lemons, limes, or grapefruit. You do not use it to refer to a similar food made from some other fruit, for example blackberries, strawberries, or apricots. A food like this is called **jam** in British English, and **jam** or **jelly** in American English.

My wife sent you this gooseberry <u>jam</u> of hers.
…homemade raspberry <u>jelly</u> sandwiches.

---

marriage - wedding

1 'marriage'

Marriage refers to the state of being married, or to the relationship between a husband and wife.

<u>Marriage</u> might not suit you.
It has been a happy <u>marriage.</u>

You can also use **marriage** to refer to the act of getting married.

Victoria's <u>marriage</u> to her cousin was not welcomed by her family.

2 **'wedding'**
However, you do not usually use 'marriage' to refer to the ceremony in which two people get married. The word you use is **wedding.**
He had been invited to the wedding.

married - marry

1 **'married to'**
If you are **married to** someone, they are your husband or wife.
Her daughter was married to a Frenchman.

2 **'marry'**
When you **marry** someone, you become their husband or wife during a special ceremony.
I wanted to marry him.
(*i*) Note that you do not say that someone 'marries to' someone else.

3 **'get married'**
You do not usually use 'marry' without an object. You do not say, for example, that a person 'marries' or that two people 'marry'. You say that they **get married.**
I'm getting married next month.
They got married in October 1994.

In stories, **marry** is sometimes used without an object. This is an old-fashioned use.
Your sister and I have every right to marry if we wish to.

masculine
⇨ See **Usage** entry at **male - masculine.**

match
If one thing has the same colour or design as another thing, you say that the first thing **matches** the other thing.
The lampshades matched the curtains.
But when the suite arrived the chair didn't match the rest – it had different trimmings.
(*i*) Note that you do not say that one thing 'matches to' another thing.

mathematics
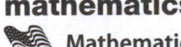 **Mathematics** is the study of numbers, quantities, and shapes. When mathematics is taught as a subject at school, it is usually called **maths** in British English, and **math** in American English.
I enjoyed maths and that was my best subject.
...methods for teaching English or Math.

When you are talking about mathematics as a science, rather than as a subject taught at school, you call it **mathematics,** not 'maths' or 'math'.
...the laws of mathematics.

All these words are uncount nouns and are used with a singular form of a verb. So, for example, you say 'Maths **is** my favourite subject'. You do not say 'Maths are my favourite subject'.

matter
1 **talking about a problem**
The matter is used after **what, something, anything,** or **nothing** to talk about a problem or difficulty. You use **the matter** as if it was an adjective like 'wrong'. For example, instead of saying 'Is something wrong?' you can say 'Is something **the matter**?'

USAGE

What's <u>the matter?</u>
There's something <u>the matter</u> with your eyes.
Is anything <u>the matter?</u>
They told me there was nothing <u>the matter.</u>

(*i*) Note that you do not use 'the matter' with this meaning in other types of sentence. You do not say, for example, '~~The matter is that we don't know where she is~~'. Instead you say **the problem** or **the trouble.**

<u>The problem</u> is that she can't cook.
<u>The trouble</u> is there's a shortage of prime property.

2 **'It doesn't matter'**

When someone apologizes to you, you can say **'It doesn't matter.'** You do not say '~~No matter~~'.

'I've only got dried milk.' – <u>'It doesn't matter.'</u>

⇨ For other ways of replying to an apology, see **Topic** entry at **Apologizing.**

3 **'no matter'**

You use **no matter** in expressions such as **no matter what** and **no matter how** to indicate that something happens or is true in all circumstances.

They smiled almost continuously, <u>no matter what</u> was said.
I told him to report to me after the job was completed, <u>no matter how</u> late it was.

You do not use 'no matter' to mention something which makes your main statement seem surprising. You do not say, for example, '~~No matter the rain, we carried on with the game~~'. You say ' **In spite of** the rain, we carried on with the game'.

<u>In spite of</u> poor health, my father was always cheerful.
The morning air was still clear and fresh <u>in spite of</u> all the traffic.

4 **used as a count noun**

A **matter** is a situation that someone has to deal with.

It was a purely personal <u>matter.</u>
She's very honest in money <u>matters.</u>
This is a <u>matter</u> for the police.

You can use the plural form **matters** to refer to a situation that has just been discussed.

There is only one applicant, which simplifies <u>matters.</u>
The murder of Jean-Marie will not help <u>matters.</u>

When **matters** has this meaning, you do not put 'the' in front of it.

may

⇨ See **Usage** entry at **might - may.**

maybe - perhaps

You use **maybe** or **perhaps** to indicate that something is possible, although you are not certain about it. There is no difference in meaning between these words.

<u>Maybe</u> he was wrong.
<u>Perhaps</u> Andrew is right after all.

Maybe is normally used only at the beginning of a clause.

<u>Maybe</u> he'll be prime minister one day.
I do think about having children, <u>maybe</u> when I'm 40.

Perhaps can be used in other positions in a clause.

If you live in the country, you can, <u>perhaps,</u> profit by buying and freezing local produce.
The Allies had better luck, <u>perhaps,</u> than they deserved.
It was <u>perhaps</u> Ellen's unconventional approach to life that made her such a great actress.

⇨ Many other words can be used to indicate how certain you are about something. For a graded list, see section on **probability** in **Grammar** entry at **Adjuncts.**

⚠ **WARNING:** Do not confuse **maybe** /ˈmeɪbiː/ with **may be** /meɪ biː/. **May be** is used in sentences such as 'He **may be** the best person for the job'.
⇨ See **Usage** entry at **might - may**.

me

1 'me'

Me can be the object of a verb or preposition. You use **me** to refer to yourself.
He told me about it.
He looked at me reproachfully.

⚠ **WARNING:** In standard English, you do not use 'me' as the indirect object of a sentence when **I** is the subject. You do not say, for example, 'I~~got me a drink~~'. You say 'I got **myself** a drink'.
I poured myself a small drink.
I had set myself a time limit of two years.

In standard English, you do not use 'me' as part of the subject of a sentence. You do not say, for example, '~~Me and my friend are leaving~~'. You say ' **My friend and I** are leaving'.
My sister and I were a bit worried.
Father and I both saw him.

2 'it's me'

If you are asked 'Who is it?', you can say '**It's me** ', or just '**Me**'.
'Who is it?' – ' It's me, Frank Rogers.'

In conversation, if you want to emphasize that something applies to you rather than to anyone else, you can say '**it's me...**' followed by a relative clause. For example, instead of saying 'She wants me', you can say ' **It's me** she wants'. Note that you do not say '~~It's I she wants~~'.
As long as it's me who's doing it, then it's all right.

In sentences like this, you can say '**I'm the one...**' instead of 'it's me...'.
I'm always the one who's got to do the talking.
I'm the one who introduced them.

If someone asks who did something, you can say '**Me**' or '**I did**'. You do not say '**I**'.
'Who said that?' snapped Sid. - ' I did, ' said Mike.

mean

1 'mean' used as a verb

Mean is usually a verb. Its past tense and past participle is **meant** /ment/, not 'meaned'. You use **mean** when you are talking about the meaning of a word or expression. For example, you might say 'What does "promissory" **mean** ?'
What does 'imperialism' mean ?
'Pandemonium' means 'the place of all devils'.

ⓘ Note that you must use the auxiliary **does** in questions like these. You do not say, for example, '~~What means "promissory"?~~'

You can use **mean** with an '-ing' form to say what an attitude or type of behaviour implies or involves.
Healthy living means being physically, spiritually and mentally healthy.
Some people will buy them even if it means defying the law.

What someone **means** is what they are referring to or are intending to say.
I know the guy you mean.
I thought you meant you wanted to take your own car.

⚠ **WARNING:** You do not use 'mean' when you are talking about people's opinions or beliefs. You do not say, for example, 'Most of the directors mean he should resign'. You say 'Most of the directors **think** he should resign'. Similarly, you do not say 'His subjects mean that he is descended from God'. You say 'His subjects **believe** that he is descended from God'.

I think a woman has as much right to work as a man.
Most scientists believe the atmosphere of Jupiter is too unstable for life.

2 **'means' used as a noun**

A **means** of doing something is a method or thing that makes it possible.

Scientists are working to devise a means of storing this type of power.
The essential means of transport for the islanders remains the donkey.

The plural of **means** is also **means.**

An attempt was made to sabotage the ceremony by violent means.

3 **'by means of'**

If you do something **by means of** a particular method or object, you do it using that method or object.

The rig is anchored in place by means of steel cables.

4 **'by all means'**

You can say **by all means** to indicate that you are very willing to allow something to be done.

If you feel you need to ask any questions, by all means do so.
'Would it be all right if I left a bit early?' – 'Yes, yes, by all means.'

⚠ **WARNING:** You do not use 'by all means' to mean 'using whatever methods are necessary'. You do not say, for example, 'He was determined to become leader by all means'. You say 'He was determined to become leader **by any means** ' or 'He was determined to become leader **by whatever means** '.

We want justice and we will get it by any means necessary.
The prime minister wants to stay in power by whatever means and at whatever cost.

5 **'mean' used as an adjective**

 In American English, and sometimes in British English, a **mean** person or action is cruel.

The meanest fighter in the world.

In British English, someone who is **mean** is unwilling to spend much money or to use much of something. **Mean** is used to express disapproval.

Become a regular customer and don't be mean with the tips.

 Note that 'mean' is not usually used in American English in this way.

---

meaning - intention - opinion

1 **'meaning'**

The **meaning** of a word, expression, or gesture is the thing or idea that it refers to or represents.

The word 'guide' is used with various meanings.
This gesture has the same meaning throughout Italy.

The **meaning** of what someone says is what they intend to express.

The meaning of the remark was clear.

2 **'intention'**

You do not use 'meaning' to refer to what someone intends to do. You do not say, for example, 'His meaning was to reach the border before nightfall'. You say 'His **intention** was to reach the border before nightfall'.

Their intention was to make the trip inconspicuous.

3 'opinion'

You also do not use 'meaning' to refer to what someone thinks about a particular matter. You do not say, for example, 'I think he should resign. What's your meaning?' You say 'I think he should resign. What's your **opinion** ?'

My opinion is that this is an absolute disaster for the club.
If you want my honest opinion, I don't think it will work.

meanness

The following adjectives can be used in both British and American English to describe someone who does not spend much money:

economical	miserly	penny-pinching	thrifty	tight-fisted
frugal	parsimonious	stingy	tight	

1 neutral words

Economical and **frugal** are neutral words.

Spaghetti, ravioli, and noodles have for years been the staple dishes of economical Italian countryfolk.
Make some stringent economies, be as frugal as a monk.

2 'thrifty'

Thrifty is a complimentary word.

The people were industrious and very thrifty.

3 words showing disapproval

Miserly, parsimonious, penny-pinching, stingy, tight, and **tight-fisted** are used to show disapproval. **Parsimonious** is a formal word.

He was a bit showy with money and overtipped for fear of being thought stingy.
At home he was churlish, parsimonious, and unloving to his daughters.

Penny-pinching is used mainly by journalists and public speakers.

He said the Government's penny-pinching policies were causing loss of life.

measurement - measure

1 'measurement'

A **measurement** is a result obtained by measuring something.

Check the measurements carefully.
Every measurement was exact.

2 'measure'

You do not use 'measurement' to refer to an action taken by a government. The word you use is **measure.**

Measures had been taken to limit the economic decline.
Day nurseries were started as a war-time measure to allow mothers to work.

media

Media is a noun, and it is also a plural form of another noun, **medium.**

1 'the media'

You can refer to television, radio, and newspapers as **the media.**

I don't think he will want to say anything to the media.

It is usually regarded as correct to use a plural form of a verb with **the media,** but some people use a singular form.

USAGE

The media <u>have</u> generally refrained from comment.
The media <u>is</u> full of pictures of tearful, anxious families.

You can use a singular or plural form in conversation, but you should use a plural form in formal writing.

2 'medium'

A **medium** is a way of expressing your ideas or communicating with people. The plural of **medium** is either **mediums** or **media.**

He would prefer to be remembered for his talents in other <u>mediums</u> besides photography.
Marketeers are keener on using a range of different <u>media</u> – radio, billboards, direct mail.

---

meet

Meet is usually a verb. Its past tense and past participle is **met,** not 'meeted'.
When you **meet** someone, you happen to be in the same place and you start talking to each other.

I <u>met</u> a Swedish girl on the train.
I <u>have met</u> you here before.

When this meeting is intentional, you can say that you **meet** or **meet with** the other person.

 Meet with is especially common in American English.

I went with Mrs Mellish to <u>meet</u> some of the teachers.
We can <u>meet with</u> the professor Monday night.

---

memoirs - memories

1 'memoirs'

When someone writes their **memoirs,** they write a book about people and events that they remember.

He was busy writing his <u>memoirs.</u>
They're making a movie of his war <u>memoirs.</u>

2 'memories'

You do not use 'memoirs' to refer to things that you remember about the past. The word you use is **memories.**

My <u>memories</u> of a London childhood are happy ones.
One of my earliest <u>memories</u> is of a total eclipse of the sun.

---

memory

⇨ See **Usage** entry at **souvenir - memory.**

---

mention

⇨ See **Usage** entry at **comment - mention - remark.**

---

merry-go-round

⇨ See **Usage** entry at **roundabout.**

---

metre - meter

1 'metre'

In British English, a **metre** is a unit of length equal to 39.37 inches.
The blue whale grows to over 30 <u>metres</u> long.

2 'meter'

 In American English, this word is spelled **meter.**
I stopped about fifty <u>meters</u> down the road.

In both British and American English, some kinds of measuring devices are also called **meters.**

…a parking <u>meter</u>.
He'd come to read the gas <u>meter</u>.

middle - centre

1. **'middle'**
The **middle** of a two-dimensional shape or area is the part that is furthest from its sides, edges, or boundaries.
In the <u>middle</u> of the lawn was a great cedar tree.
Foster was standing in the <u>middle</u> of the room.

2. **'centre'**
Centre is used in a similar way, but it usually refers to a more precise point or position. For example, in mathematics you talk about the **centre** of a circle, not the 'middle'.
…the <u>centre</u> of the cyclone.

 In American English, this word is spelled **center**.
At the <u>center</u> of the monument was a photograph.

3. **other meanings of 'middle'**
The **middle** of a road or river is the part that is furthest from its sides or banks.
…white lines painted along the <u>middle</u> of the highway.
We managed to pull on to a sandbank in the <u>middle</u> of the river.

(*i*) Note that you do not talk about the 'centre' of a road or river.

The **middle** of an event or period of time is a period which is halfway between its beginning and its end.
We landed at Canton in the <u>middle</u> of a torrential storm.
…the <u>middle</u> of December.

(*i*) Note that you do not talk about the 'centre' of an event or period of time.

Middle Ages - middle age

1. **'Middle Ages'**
In European history, **the Middle Ages** were the period between approximately 1000 AD and 1400 AD.
This practice was common throughout <u>the Middle Ages</u>.

2. **'middle age'**
Middle age is the period in a person's life when they are no longer young but are not yet old.
…the onset of <u>middle age</u>.
Men tend to put on weight in <u>middle age</u>.

3. **'middle-aged'**
When someone has reached this period of their life, you can say that they are **middle-aged**.
The boss was a <u>middle-aged</u> woman.
… <u>middle-aged</u>, married businessmen.

might - may

Might and **may** are used mainly to talk about possibility. They can also be used to make a request, to ask permission, or to make a suggestion. When **might** and **may** can be used with the same meaning, **may** is more formal than **might**. **Might** and **may** are called **modals**.

⇨ See **Grammar** entry at **Modals**.

In conversation, the negative form **mightn't** is often used. The form **mayn't** is much less common. People usually use the full form **may not**.

USAGE

He mightn't have time for such things.
It may not be quite so depressing as you think.

1 possibility: the present and the future

You can use **might** or **may** to say that it is possible that something is true or that something will happen in the future.

His route from the bus stop might be the same as yours.
This may be why women enjoy going back to work.
They might be able to remember what he said.
Clerical work may be available for two students who want to learn about publishing.

You can use **could** in a similar way, but only in positive sentences.

Don't eat it. It could be a toadstool.

⇨ See **Usage** entry at **can - could - be able to.**

You can use **might well** or **may well** to indicate that it is fairly likely that something is the case.

You might well be right.
I think that may well have been the intention.

You use **might not** or **may not** to say that it is possible that something is not the case.

He might not be in England at all.
That mightn't be true.
That may not seem like a lot.

⚠ **WARNING:** You do not use 'might not' or 'may not' to say that it is impossible that something is the case. Instead you use **could not, cannot,** or **can't.**

...knowledge which could not have been gained in any other way.
The court cannot know what you intended if it is not stated legally.
You can't talk to the dead.

You never use 'may' when you are asking if something is possible. You do not say, for example, 'May he be right?' You say '**Might** he be right?' or, more usually, '**Could** he be right?'

Might it be even earlier?
Could this be true?
Could he remember having seen the picture before?

Similarly, you do not say 'What may happen?' You usually say 'What **is likely to** happen?'

What are likely to be the ecological effects of intensive agricultural production?

2 possibility: the past

You use **might** or **may** with **have** to say that it is possible that something happened in the past, but you do not know whether it happened or not.

Grandpapa might have secretly married Pepita.
I may have seemed to be overreacting.

Could have can be used in a similar way.

It is just possible that such a small creature could have preyed on dinosaur eggs.

However, if something did not happen and you want to say that there was a possibility of it happening, you can only use **might have** or **could have.** You do not use 'may have'. For example, you say 'If he hadn't hurt his ankle, he **might have** won the race.' You do not say 'If he hadn't hurt his ankle, he may have won the race'.

A lot of men died who might have been saved.

You use **might not** or **may not** with **have** to say that it is possible that something did not happen or was not the case.

They might not have considered me as their friend.
My father mightn't have been to blame.
The parents may not have been ready for this pregnancy.

⚠ **WARNING:** You do not use 'might not' or 'may not' with 'have' to say that it is impossible that something happened or was the case. Instead you use **could not have** or (in British English) **cannot have**.
The measurement <u>couldn't have</u> been wrong.
The girls <u>cannot have</u> been seriously affected by the system.
An attack of this magnitude <u>cannot have</u> been planned in two weeks.

3 | requests and permission
May and **might** are sometimes used when someone is making a request, or asking or giving permission. These are formal uses.
<u>May</u> I look round?
<u>Might</u> we leave our bags here for a moment?
You <u>may</u> leave the table.

⇨ For more information, see **Topic** entries at **Requests, orders, and instructions** and **Permission.**

4 | suggestions
Might is often used in polite suggestions.
You <u>might</u> like to comment on his latest proposal.
I think it <u>might</u> be a good idea to stop the recording now.

⇨ For more information about ways of making a suggestion, see **Topic** entry at **Suggestions.**

migrate - migration - migrant
⇨ See **Topic** entry at **emigration - immigration - migration.**

mill
⇨ See **Usage** entry at **factory - works - mill - plant.**

million
A **million** or **one million** is the number 1,000,000.

ⓘ Note that you do not add '-s' to the word **million** when you put another number in front of it. You do not say, for example, 'five millions people'. You say 'five **million** people'.
…130 <u>million</u> litres.

mind
Mind can be a noun or a verb.

1 | used as a noun
Your **mind** is your ability to think.
…the evolution of the human <u>mind.</u>
Studying stretched my <u>mind</u> and got me thinking about things.

2 | 'make up one's mind'
When someone decides to do something, you can say that they **make up their mind** to do it.
Egged on by Iago, Othello <u>makes up his mind</u> to kill Desdemona.
She <u>made up her mind</u> to write to Teddy Boylan.

ⓘ Note that you use a 'to'-infinitive, not an '-ing' form, after this expression.

3 | used as a verb
If you have no objection to doing something, you can say that you **don't mind doing** it.
I <u>don't mind walking.</u>

ⓘ Note that you do not say that you 'do not mind to do' something.

USAGE

You can indicate that you do not object to a situation or proposal by saying **'I don't mind'.**

'Do you want me to go and do it?' – ' I don't mind, if you want to.'
I want to play for a top club and I don't mind where it is.
It was raining, but he didn't mind.

(i) Note that you do not use 'it' after **mind** in sentences like these.

minority

If something is true of **a minority** of the people or things in a group, it is true of less than half of the whole group.

Only a minority of cable and satellite viewers are shocked by what they see on television.

You can talk about **a small minority** (for example 8%) or **a large minority** (for example 40%).

Only a small minority of children get a chance to benefit from the system.
The incomes of a large minority of tenants are inadequate to enable them to pay their rents.

When **a minority** is not followed by 'of', you can use either a plural or singular form of a verb after it. The plural form is more common.

Only a minority were active in pursuing their beliefs.

When you use **a minority of** followed by a plural noun, you must use a plural form of a verb after it.

Only a minority of people ever become actively engaged on any issue.

miserable

⇨ See **Usage** entry at **happy - sad**.

mistake

1 **'mistake'**

A **mistake** is something incorrect or unfortunate that someone does, such as spelling a word wrongly. You say that someone **makes** a mistake.

He had made a terrible mistake.
We made the mistake of leaving our bedroom window open.

(i) Note that you do not say that someone 'does' a mistake.

2 **'fault'**

You do not use **mistake** to refer to something wrong in a machine or structure. The word you use is **fault**.

There's usually a fault in one of the appliances.
The machine has developed a fault.

3 **'in mistake for'**

If someone has taken something when they intended to take something else, you say that they took the first thing **in mistake for** the second thing.

I had taken Ewen Waite's gun in mistake for my own.

You can use **in mistake for** in a similar way with several other verbs.

It may mean that Brigid was killed in mistake for Lauren.

4 **'by mistake'**

However, you do not say that someone does something 'in mistake'. You say that they do it **by mistake**.

I once burst into his bedroom by mistake.
Griffiths thought he had been sent there by mistake.

misused
⇨ See **Usage** entry at **disused - unused - misused.**

modern
⇨ See **Usage** entry at **new.**

moment

1 **'moment'**

A **moment** is a very short period of time.

She hesitated for only a moment.
A few moments later he heard footsteps.

2 **'the moment'**

The moment is often used as a conjunction to say that something happens or is done at the same time as something else, or immediately after it.

The moment I saw this, it appealed to me.

When you use **the moment** like this to talk about the future, you use the simple present tense after it. You do not use a future tense.

The moment he shows up I want to see him.

momentarily

Something that happens **momentarily** happens for only a short time.

She paused momentarily when she saw them.
He had momentarily forgotten that the Captain couldn't see.

 In American English, **momentarily** is also used to mean 'very soon indeed', especially in announcements about the arrival or departure of planes. 'Momentarily' is not used like this in British English.

We will arrive momentarily in Paris.

money

Money is the coins or bank notes that you use to buy things. **Money** is an uncount noun. You do not talk about 'moneys' or 'a money'.

I spent all my money on sweets.
I had very little money left.

After **money** you use a singular form of a verb.

My money has been returned to me.
Money isn't everything.

moral - morality - morale

1 **'moral'**

Moral /mɒrəl/ can be an adjective, a count noun, or a plural noun.
When you use it as an adjective, it means 'relating to right and wrong behaviour'.

I have noticed a fall in moral standards.
It is our moral duty to stay.

The **moral** of a story is what it teaches you about how you should or should not behave.

The moral is clear: you must never marry for money.

Morals are principles of behaviour.

There can be no doubt about the excellence of his morals.
We agreed that business morals nowadays were very low.

2 **'morality'**

Morality /məræləti/ is the idea that some forms of behaviour are right and others are wrong.

Punishment always involves the idea of <u>morality</u>.
…standards of <u>morality</u> and justice in society.

3 **'morale'**
Your **morale** /mərɑːl/ is the amount of confidence you have when you are in a difficult or dangerous situation.
The <u>morale</u> of the men was good.

more

1 **talking about a greater number or amount**
You use **more** or **more of** to indicate that you are talking about a greater number of people or things, or a greater amount of something.
You use **more** in front of a noun which does not have a determiner or possessive noun in front of it.
There are <u>more people</u> getting a better education than ever.
Better management may enable one man to milk <u>more cows.</u>
They are offered <u>more food</u> than they need.

You use **more of** in front of a pronoun, or in front of a noun which has a determiner or possessive noun in front of it.
There are <u>more of them</u> seeking jobs than ever.
I suppose I've read <u>more of his novels</u> than anybody else's.
He knew <u>more of Mr Profumo's statement</u> than he had hitherto admitted.

2 **talking about an additional number or amount**
You also use **more** or **more of** to talk about an additional number of people or things, or an additional amount of something.
<u>More officers</u> will be brought in.
We need <u>more information.</u>
<u>More of the land</u> is needed to grow crops.
I sipped a little <u>more of Otto's scotch.</u>

3 **used with modifiers**
You can use words such as **some** and **any** and expressions such as **a lot** in front of **more** and **more of.**
Bond promised he would buy her <u>some more</u> diamonds.
I don't want to hear <u>any more of</u> this crazy talk.
It will give us <u>a lot more</u> freedom.
People are concerned about crime because there is <u>much more of</u> it.

These words and expressions can be used in front of **more** and **more of** when they are followed by a plural form:

any	many	some	a great many
far	no	a few	a lot
lots	several	a good many	

These words and expressions can be used in front of **more** and **more of** when they are followed by an uncount noun or a singular pronoun:

any	much	some	a great deal
far	no	a bit	a little
lots	rather	a good deal	a lot

ⓘ Note that you do not use 'many', 'several', 'a few', 'a good many', or 'a great many' in front of **more** or **more of** when they are followed by an uncount noun or a singular pronoun.

4 **'more than'**

If you want to say that the number of people or things in a group is greater than a particular number, you use **more than** in front of the number.

Police arrested <u>more than 70</u> people.
By the age of five, the child had a vocabulary of <u>more than 2,000</u> words.
He had been awake for <u>more than forty-eight</u> hours.

When you use **more than** in front of a number and a plural noun, you use a plural form of a verb after it.

More than 17,000 children <u>are</u> said to have written to Richard.
More than 100 people <u>were</u> arrested.

5 **used as an adverb**

More can be an adverb meaning 'to a greater extent or degree'.

What impressed me <u>more</u> was that she knew Tennessee Williams.
I couldn't have agreed <u>more.</u>

6 **used in comparatives**

More is also used in front of adjectives and adverbs to form comparatives.

Your child's health is <u>more important</u> than the doctor's feelings.
Next time, I will choose <u>more carefully.</u>

⇨ See **Grammar** entries at **Comparative and superlative adjectives** and **Comparative and superlative adverbs**.

morning

The **morning** is the part of each day which begins when you get up or when it becomes light outside, and which ends at noon or lunchtime.

1 **the present day**

You refer to the morning of the present day as **this morning**.

His plane left <u>this morning.</u>
'When did it come?' – '<u>This morning.</u>'

You refer to the morning of the previous day as **yesterday morning**.

<u>Yesterday morning</u> there were more than 1,500 boats waiting in the harbour for the weather to improve.

If you want to say that something will happen during the morning of the next day, you say that it will happen **tomorrow morning** or **in the morning**.

You've got to be in court <u>tomorrow morning.</u>
Phone him <u>in the morning.</u>

2 **single events in the past**

If you want to say that something happened during a particular morning in the past, you use **on**.

She left after breakfast <u>on Saturday morning.</u>
<u>On the morning of our departure,</u> an old man came up and spoke to him.

If you have been describing what happened during a particular day, you can then say that something happened **that morning** or **in the morning**.

<u>That morning</u> I flew from East London to Johannesburg.
The tracks told me what had happened <u>in the morning.</u>

If you are talking about a day in the past and you want to mention that something had happened during the morning of the day before, you say that it had happened **the previous morning**.

My head felt clear, as it had been <u>the previous morning.</u>

If you want to say that something happened during the morning of the next day, you say that it happened **the next morning**, **in the morning**, **next morning**, or **the following morning**.

USAGE

The next morning I got up early and ate my breakfast.
In the morning Bernard wanted to go out for fresh milk.
Next morning we drove over to Leysin.
The ship was due to sail the following morning.

In stories, if you want to say that something happened during a morning in the past, without saying which morning, you say that it happened **one morning**.

One morning there was a fire in the prison camp.
Dennis Sheldon awoke one morning to discover that one-third of his plants had been stolen.

You can also say, for example, that something happened **one January morning** or **on a January morning**.

We travelled overnight from Paris and arrived in London one cold February morning.
One morning in 1936 I accompanied Bertha to church.
On a fine May morning Washington reviewed the troops.

3 talking about the future

If you want to say that something will happen during a particular morning in the future, you use **on**.

They're coming to see me on Friday morning.

If you are already talking about a day in the future, you can say that something will happen **in the morning**.

The teams will arrive at Orpington on Sunday, when the South of England will play Vermont in the morning.

If you are talking about a day in the future and you want to say that something will happen during the morning of the next day, you say that it will happen **the following morning**.

We will arrive in Delhi on Friday evening and set off for Nepal the following morning.

4 regular events

If something happens or happened regularly every morning, you say that it happens or happened **in the morning** or **in the mornings**.

I have stopped reading the papers. I go swimming instead in the morning.
The museums may open only in the mornings.
I had to get up very early in the morning.
She stayed in bed in the mornings.

If you want to say that something happens or happened once a week during a particular morning, you use **on** followed by the name of a day of the week and **mornings**.

You can deposit and withdraw money on Saturday mornings.
My father mended shoes on Sunday mornings.

Note that in American English, **mornings** can be used in this sense as an adverb, without a preposition.

The land I toured mornings on a bike was flat and fertile.

5 exact times

If you have mentioned an exact time and you want to make it clear that you are talking about the period between midnight and noon rather than the period between noon and midnight, you add **in the morning**.

They often hold policy meetings at seven in the morning.
It was five o'clock in the morning.

most

1 used to mean 'the majority' or 'the largest part'

You use **most** or **most of** to indicate that you are talking about the majority of a group of

things or people, or the largest part of something.
You use **most** in front of a plural noun which does not have a determiner or possessive noun in front of it.

Most people don't enjoy their own parties.
In most schools, sports are compulsory.

You use **most of** in front of a pronoun, or in front of a noun which has a determiner or possessive noun in front of it.

Most of us have strong views on politics.
The trees cut out most of the light.
He used to spend most of his time in the library.
Most of the region's timber is imported.

(i) Note that when you use **most** like this, you do not use a determiner in front of it. You also do not talk about 'the most part' of something. You do not say, for example, 'She had drunk the most part of the wine'. You say 'She had drunk **most of** the wine'.

2 | **used to form superlatives**
Most is used in front of adjectives and adverbs to form superlatives.

The head is the most sensitive part of the body.
These are the works I respond to most strongly.

⇨ See **Grammar** entries at **Comparative and superlative adjectives** and **Comparative and superlative adverbs**.

3 | **used to mean 'very'**
Some people use **most** in front of adjectives and adverbs to mean 'very'. They do this when they are expressing their opinion of something. They do not use 'most' in front of very common words like **good** or **big**.

That's most kind of you, Mr President.
He always acted most graciously.

4 | **'really'**
Most is more emphatic than **very**, but it sounds rather formal and old-fashioned. In conversation, if you want to use a stronger word than **very**, you usually use **really**. **Really** can be used with any graded adjective.

It was really good, wasn't it, Andy?
They were really nice people.
We're doing really well actually.

---

motor
⇨ See **Usage** entry at **machine**.

---

movie
⇨ See **Usage** entry at **film**.

---

much

1 | **'very much'**
You use **very much** to say that something is true to a great extent.

I enjoyed it very much.

When **very much** is used with a transitive verb, it usually goes after the object. You do not use it immediately after the verb. You do not say, for example, 'I enjoyed very much the party'. You say 'I enjoyed the party **very much**'.

When **very much** is used with an intransitive verb followed by a 'that'-clause or a 'to'-infinitive, you can put **very much** either in front of the verb or after it. For example, you can say 'She **very much wants** to come' or 'She **wants very much** to come'.

We very much hope he'll continue to be able to represent you.

USAGE

I hope very much you will be coming on Saturday.
We 'd very much like to give you a present.
He would like very much to write to Dennis himself.

⚠ **WARNING:** In positive sentences, you do not use **much** without **very**. You do not say, for example, 'I enjoyed it much' or 'We'd much like to give you a present'. In negative sentences, you can use **much** without 'very'.
I didn't like him much.
The situation isn't likely to change much.

You can also use **much** in negative sentences and questions to mean 'often'.
She doesn't talk about them much.
Does he come here much?

⚠ **WARNING:** You do not use 'much' in positive sentences to mean 'often'. You do not say, for example, 'He comes here much'.

Many other words and expressions can be used to indicate degree.
⇨ For a graded list, see section on **degree** in **Grammar** entry at **Adjuncts**.

2 used with adjectives
Much and **very much** are used in front of comparatives (see below), but are not usually used in front of other adjectives. However, you can use them in front of '-ed' words.
Education is a much debated subject.
If anything on this list were to be served measurably below its best, I would be very much surprised.

You can use **very much** in front of **afraid**, **alike**, **alive**, and **awake**.
I'm very much afraid that someone else has been killed.
Dolly and Molly were very much alike.
The animal was not dead but very much alive.
The children were very much awake.

3 used with comparatives
You often use **much** or **very much** in front of comparative adjectives and adverbs. For example, if you want to emphasize the difference in size between two things, you can say that one thing is **much bigger** or **very much bigger** than the other.
She was much older than me.
Now I feel much more confident.
The new machine was very much bigger and very much more complicated.
This could all be done very much more quickly.

Much more and **very much more** can be used in front of a noun to emphasize the difference between two quantities or amounts.
She ought to have been allowed much more time.
Children, whose bones are growing, need much more calcium than adults.
We get very much more value for money.

4 used with superlatives
Much is sometimes used in front of superlative adjectives.
I thought he was much the best speaker.
…the Svalbard group of islands, of which Spitzbergen is much the largest.

5 used with adjuncts and noun groups
You use **very much** in front of adjuncts. You do not use 'very'.
She does things very much her own way.
Battle damage and fatigue left the eventual outcome of the fighting very much in doubt.

Very much is sometimes used in front of noun groups. You use it to emphasize that someone or something has all the qualities you would expect a particular kind of person or thing to have.

He was very much a seaman.
He was very much a man of the people.

6 **'much too'**
You use **much too** in front of an adjective to say that something cannot be done or achieved because someone or something has too much of a quality.

I knew where it was, but was much too polite to say.
The rooms were much too cold for comfort.
The price is much too high.

(i) Note that in sentences like these you put **much** in front of **too**, not after it. You do not say, for example, ~~The rooms were too much cold for comfort~~.

If there is very much more of something than is necessary or desirable, you can say that there is **much too much** of it.

Eating much too much salt can be dangerous during pregnancy.

However, if there is a very much larger number of people or things than is necessary or desirable, you do not usually say that there are 'much too many' of them. You say that there are **far too many** of them.

Every middle-class child gets far too many toys.

7 **used as a determiner**
You use **much** in front of an uncount noun when you are talking about a large quantity or amount of something. **Much** is usually used like this in negative sentences, in questions, or after **too**, **so**, or **as**.

I don't think there is much danger.
Is this going to make much difference?
It gave the President too much power.
There is so much financial hardship.
My only ambition in boxing is to make as much money as possible.

8 **'much of'**
In front of **it**, **this**, or **that**, you use **much of**, not 'much'.

I still remember much of it in some detail.
Much of this is already possible.

You also use **much of** in front of a noun group which begins with a determiner or a possessive.

Much of the recent trouble has come from outside.
Caroline devoted much of her life to education.

9 **used as a pronoun**
You can use **much** as a pronoun to refer to a large quantity or amount of something.

There wasn't much to do.
Much has been gained from our discussions.

(i) Note that you do not usually use 'much' as an object pronoun in positive sentences. Instead you use **a lot**. For example, instead of saying '~~He knows much about butterflies~~', you say 'He knows **a lot** about butterflies'.

She knows a lot about music.
I suppose they learned a lot by doing it.

⇨ See **Usage** entry at **lot**.

10 **'how much'**
You use **how much** when you are asking about the price of something.

I like that dress – how much is it?

USAGE

⇨ See **Usage** entry at **how much**.

⚠ **WARNING:** You do not use 'much' or 'much of' to talk about a large number of people or things. Instead you use **many** or **many of**.
⇨ See **Usage** entry at **many**.

music - musical

1 'music'
Music is the sound that people make when they sing or play instruments. **Music** is an uncount noun. You use the singular form of a verb after it.
Their music is uplifting and fun.

You do not call a musical composition a 'music'. You call it a **piece of music**.
The only pieces of music he knew were the songs in the school's songbook.

2 'musical' used as an adjective
Musical can be an adjective or a noun. You use it as an adjective to describe things which are connected with the playing or studying of music.
… musical instruments.
…a musical career.
…one of London's most important musical events.

Someone who is **musical** has a natural ability and interest in music.
He came from a musical family.

However, a student who studies music is called a **music student**, not a 'musical student'. Someone who teaches music is a **music teacher**, not a 'musical teacher'. Here is a list of nouns in front of which you use **music**, not 'musical':

business	department	industry	library	shop	teacher
critic	festival	lesson	room	student	video

3 'musical' used as a noun
A **musical** is a play or film that uses singing and sometimes dancing as part of the story.
She appeared in the musical 'Oklahoma'.

must
Must is usually used to say that something is necessary. It can also be used to say that you believe that something is true. **Must** is called a **modal**.
⇨ See **Grammar** entry at **Modals**.

1 'must', 'have to', 'have got to', 'need to'
The expressions **have to, have got to,** and **need to** can sometimes be used with the same meaning as **must**.

 Have got to is not used in formal English or American English.

The negative form of **must** is **must not** or **mustn't**. The negative forms of **have to** and **have got to** are **don't have to** and **haven't got to**. The negative form of **need to** is **need not, needn't** or **don't need to**. However, these negative forms do not all have the same meaning. This is explained below under **negative necessity**.

2 necessity in the present
Must, have to, have got to, and **need to** are all used to say that it is necessary that something is done.
I must leave fairly soon.
It must be protected at all costs.
You have to find some compromise.
We 've got to get up early tomorrow.

A number of points <u>need to</u> be made about this.

After **must** you use an infinitive without 'to'. You do not use a 'to'-infinitive.

If you want to say that someone is required to do something regularly, for example because it is part of their job, you use **have to.** You do not use 'must'.
She <u>has to</u> do the housework while her brother reads.
Every year she <u>has to</u> do battle with city and state officials to keep the funds in place.

If you want to say that someone is required to do something on a particular occasion, you use **have got to.**
I 've got to report to the office.
We 've got to get in touch with the builders.

In formal English, **must** is used to say that someone is required to do something by a rule or law.
People who qualify <u>must</u> apply within six months.

3 necessity in the past

If you want to say that something was necessary in the past, you use **had to.** You do not use 'must'.
She <u>had to</u> go to work immediately.
We <u>had to</u> keep still for about four minutes.

4 necessity in the future

If you want to say that something will be necessary in the future, you use **will have to.**
He <u>'ll have to</u> go to the casualty department.

5 negative necessity

You use **must not** or **mustn't** to say that it is important that something is not done.
You <u>must not</u> accept it.
We <u>mustn't</u> forget the paraffin.

If you want to say that it is not necessary that something is done, you use **don't have to, haven't got to, needn't,** or **don't need to.**
I <u>don't have to</u> do it any longer.
It's all right if you <u>haven't got to</u> work.
You <u>needn't</u> be a Dickens scholar to get something out of Giannetti's ballet.
You <u>don't need to</u> go into all the details.

⚠ **WARNING:** You do not use 'must not', 'mustn't', or 'have not to' to say that it is not necessary that something is done.

If you are talking about the past and you want to say that it was not necessary for something to be done on a particular occasion, you use **didn't have to** or **didn't need to.**
Fortunately, she <u>didn't have to</u> choose.
I <u>didn't need to</u> say anything at all.

⇨ See **Usage** entry at **need.**

6 strong belief

You use **must** to say that you strongly believe that something is the case, because of particular facts or circumstances.
There <u>must</u> be some mistake.
Oh, you <u>must</u> be Sylvia's husband.

Have to and **have got to** can also be used in this way, but not when the subject is **you.**
There <u>has to</u> be some kind of way out.
Money <u>has got to</u> be the reason.

You can use **must** with **be** and an '-ing' form to say that you believe something is happening.

She must be exaggerating.
You must be getting a little tired of having people in your house.

⚠ **WARNING:** You do not use **must** with an infinitive to say that you believe something is happening. You do not say, for example, 'He isn't in his office. He must work at home'. You say 'He isn't in his office. He **must be working** at home'.

If you want to say that you believe something is not the case, you use **cannot** or **can't**. You do not use 'must' or 'have to' with **not**.
The two messages cannot both be true.
You can't have forgotten me.

⇨ See **Usage** entry at **can - could - be able to.**

mutual

You describe a feeling as **mutual** when two people or groups feel it about each other.
I didn't like him and I was sure the feeling was mutual.
There had been a great measure of mutual respect.

You describe behaviour as **mutual** when two people or groups behave in the same way towards each other.
Single parents can join self-help groups for social life and mutual help.
They are in danger of mutual destruction.

Mutual is also used to indicate that two people have the same feeling about something, are interested in the same thing, or know the same person.
…their mutual indifference to children.
We discovered we had mutual interests in cricket and music.
They had no mutual acquaintances.

This last use is very common in written and spoken English, but some people consider it to be incorrect. You can avoid it by using other expressions. For example, instead of saying 'We discovered we had mutual friends' you can say 'We discovered we had **some of the same** friends'. Instead of talking about 'our mutual love of music' you can say 'the love **we both had** for music'.

N n

name

1 **'name'**

If you **name** someone or something, you give them a name.

She wanted to <u>name</u> the baby Colleen.
He <u>named</u> his horse Circuit.

2 **'name after'**

In British English, if you intentionally give someone or something the same name as a particular person or thing, you say that you **name** them **after** that person or thing.

She was <u>named after</u> her mother.
I was very surprised when I was asked if I would have a rose <u>named</u> after me.

3 **'name for'**

American speakers also say that you **name** someone or something **for** a person or thing.

They had a son, James, <u>named for</u> me.
They also <u>named</u> a locomotive <u>for</u> him.

named

⇨ See **Usage** entry at **called - named**.

namely - i.e.

Namely and **i.e.** are both used to give more information about something that you have just mentioned.

1 **'namely'**

You use **namely** to say exactly what you mean when you have just referred to something in a general or indirect way.

One group of people seems to be forgotten, <u>namely</u> pensioners.
This virus was shown to be responsible for causing a very common illness, <u>namely</u> glandular fever.

2 **'i.e.'**

You use **i.e.** when you are giving an explanation of a word or expression that you have just used.

You must be an amateur, <u>i.e.</u> someone who has never competed for prize money in athletics.
A good pass in French (<u>i.e.</u> at least grade B) is desirable.

nation

You use **nation** to refer to a country, together with its social and political structures.

For a great part of the 19th century, Britain was the richest and most powerful <u>nation</u> on earth.

You can also use **nation** to refer to the inhabitants of a country.

He appealed to the <u>nation</u> for self-restraint.

(i) Note that **nation** can also to refer to a group of people who are part of the same linguistic or historical group, even if they do not constitute an independent state.

…the traditions and culture of the Great Sioux <u>Nation.</u>

However, you do not use 'nation' simply to refer to a place. You do not say, for example, 'What nation do you come from?' When you are referring to a place, you use **country**, not 'nation'.

There are over a hundred edible species growing in this <u>country</u>.
Mexico is a large and diverse <u>country</u>.

national - nationalist - nationalistic - patriotic

1 **'national'**

National is used to describe something that belongs to or is typical of a particular country or nation.

…the <u>national</u> economy.
…changes in the <u>national</u> diet.

2 **'nationalist'**

Nationalist is usually a noun. A **nationalist** is someone who tries to obtain political independence for his or her country.

…Basque <u>nationalists</u>.

You can also use **nationalist** as an adjective to describe people, movements, or ideas.

<u>Nationalist</u> leaders demanded the extension of democratic rights.
…the <u>nationalist</u> movements of French West Africa.

3 **'nationalistic'**

If someone is very proud of their country and thinks it is better than other countries, you can say that they or their views are **nationalistic**. This word is always used to indicate disapproval of someone's views.

…an attempt to arouse <u>nationalistic</u> passions against the foreigner.

4 **'patriotic'**

Normally, if someone is proud of their country, you say that they or their feelings are **patriotic**. This word is usually used to indicate approval of someone's feelings.

…an earnest wish to enlist the <u>patriotic</u> spirit of the nation.
I believe that this is the only way that an ordinary person can inspire others to be <u>patriotic</u>.

nationality

You use **nationality** to say what country someone legally belongs to. For example, you say that someone 'has Belgian **nationality**'.

He's got British <u>nationality</u>.
They have the right to claim Hungarian <u>nationality</u>.

(i) Note that you do not use 'nationality' to talk about things. You do not say, for example, that something 'has Swedish nationality'. You say that it **comes from** Sweden or **was made in** Sweden.

Most of the bauxite <u>comes from</u> Jamaica.
They use parts <u>made in</u> Britain to assemble their tractors.

nature

1 **'nature'**

Nature is used to talk about all living things and natural processes.

The most amazing thing about <u>nature</u> is its infinite variety.
…the ecological balance of <u>nature</u>.

When **nature** has this meaning, you do not use 'the' in front of it.

2 **'the country'**

You do not use 'nature' to refer to land which is situated away from towns and cities. You refer to this land as **the country** or **the countryside**.

We live in <u>the country</u>.
We longed for <u>the English countryside</u>.

near - close

If something is **near**, **near to**, or **close to** a place or thing, it is a short distance from it. When **close** has this meaning, it is pronounced /kləʊs/.

I live now in Reinfeld, which is <u>near</u> Lübeck.
I stood very <u>near to</u> them.
They owned a sheep station <u>close to</u> the sea.

1 'nearby'

When 'near' and 'close' have this meaning, you do not use them immediately in front of a noun. Instead you use **nearby.**

He was taken to a <u>nearby</u> building to recuperate.
He took the bag and tossed it into some <u>nearby</u> bushes.

However, the superlative form **nearest** can be used immediately in front of a noun.

They rush, stumbling, for the <u>nearest</u> exit.

2 other meanings

You can use **near** immediately in front of a noun to say that something is almost a particular thing.

…a state of <u>near chaos</u>.
The right and left arms of the sea wall formed a <u>near circle</u>.

You can also use **near** immediately in front of an adjective and a noun to say that something almost has the quality described by the adjective.

…a <u>near fatal accident.</u>
The Government faces a <u>near impossible dilemma.</u>

You can use **near**, **near to**, or **close to** immediately in front of a noun to say that someone or something is almost in a particular state.

Her father was angry, her mother <u>near tears.</u>
…her anxiety on finding him again <u>near to death.</u>
She was <u>close to tears.</u>

You can refer to someone you know well as a '**close** friend'.

His father was a <u>close</u> friend of Peter Thorneycroft.

You do not refer to someone as a 'near' friend.
You can refer to someone who is directly related to you as a '**close** relative'.

She had no very <u>close</u> relatives.

You can also refer to someone as a '**near** relative', but this is less common.

> ⚠ **WARNING:** Do not confuse the adjective **close** with the verb **close** /kləʊz/. If you **close** something, you move it so that it fills a hole or gap.
> ⇨ See **Usage** entry at **close - closed - shut.**

nearly

⇨ See **Usage** entry at **almost - nearly.**

necessary

1 used with an infinitive

If **it is necessary to do** a particular thing, that thing must be done.

It is <u>necessary to act</u> fast.
It is <u>necessary to examine</u> this claim before we proceed any further.

2 used with 'for'

You can say that it is necessary **for someone** to do something.

It was necessary <u>for me</u> to keep active and not think about Sally.
In the early years, it is necessary <u>for governments</u> to directly subsidize rents.

USAGE

(i) Note that if you use **necessary** in sentences like these, the subject must be **it**. You do not say, for example, ~~'She was necessary to make several calls'~~. You say '**It was necessary for her** to make several calls'. However, in conversation people would normally say '**She had to** make several calls'.

⇨ For more information on this use of **have to,** see Usage entry at **must.**

If one thing is **necessary for** another, the second thing can only happen or exist if the first one happens or exists.

Dreams are <u>necessary for</u> mental well-being.
The drink-driving laws are <u>necessary for</u> safety on our roads.

3 | used with 'to'

If something is **necessary to** someone, they must have it.

Solitude, no doubt, is <u>necessary to</u> the poet and the philosopher.
An active social life was as <u>necessary to</u> her as meat and drink.

---

need

Need can be a verb or a noun.

The verb has the negative forms **need not** and **do not need.** The contracted forms **needn't** and **don't need** are also used. However, you cannot use all these forms for all meanings of **need.** This is explained below.

1 | used as a transitive verb

If you **need** something, it is necessary for you to have it.

These animals <u>need</u> food throughout the winter.
I don't <u>need</u> any help, thank you.

For this meaning of **need,** the negative form is **do not need.**

You <u>do not need</u> special clothes to meditate or even a special chair.
I <u>didn't need</u> any further encouragement.

⚠ **WARNING:** You do not use a continuous form of **need.** You do not say, for example, ~~'We are needing some milk'~~. You say 'We **need** some milk'.

2 | used as an intransitive verb or modal

If you **need to do** something, it is necessary for you to do it.

To pass examinations you <u>need to work</u> effectively.
For an answer to these problems we <u>need to look</u> elsewhere.

(i) Note that you must use **to** in sentences like these. You do not say, for example, ~~'To pass examinations you need work effectively'~~.

However, in negative statements and questions, you can use either **need to** or **need.** You can say, for example, 'He **doesn't need to** go' or 'He **needn't** go'. Note that you do not say ~~'He doesn't need go'~~ or ~~'He needn't to go'~~.

You <u>don't need to shout.</u>
You <u>needn't talk</u> about it unless you feel like it.
'Congratulations, Mrs Taylor.' – 'What on?' – '<u>Do I need to say?</u>'
<u>Need I remind</u> you that you owe the company twelve-and-a-half thousand pounds?

3 | 'must not'

Note that if you say that someone **doesn't need to** do something or **need not** do something, you are saying that it is not necessary for them to do it. If you want to say that it is necessary for someone **not** to do something, you do not use 'need'. Instead you use **must not** or **mustn't.**

You <u>must not</u> accept it.
We <u>mustn't</u> forget the paraffin.

⇨ See Usage entry at **must.**

4 **talking about the past**

If you are talking about the past and you want to say that it was not necessary for someone to do something on a particular occasion, you say that they **didn't need to** do it or they **didn't have to** do it. You do not say that they 'needn't' do it.

I didn't need to say anything at all.
Fortunately, she didn't have to choose.

However, in a reporting clause you can use **needn't**.

They knew they needn't bother about me.

If someone has done something and you want to say that it was not necessary, you can say that they **needn't have** done it.

I was wondering whether you were getting properly fed and looked after, but I needn't have worried, need I?

5 **'need' with '-ing' forms**

You can use **need** with an '-ing' form to say that something ought to have something done to it. For example, you usually say 'The cooker **needs cleaning**', rather than 'The cooker needs to be cleaned'.

The scheme needs improving.
…things that needed doing.

6 **used as a noun**

When someone needs something, you can talk about their **need for** it or their **need of** it. **Need for** is more common.

…the centre's need for fresh supplies.
…his need for forgiveness.
It was a matter of recognizing my need of others.

You can also say that someone is **in need of** something. You do not say that someone is 'in need for' something.

He felt in need of a rest.
The blackboards are in need of repair.

7 **'no need'**

If you want to say that it is unnecessary to do something, you can say **there is no need to** do it.

There is no need to worry.
There was no need to awaken him because he knew exactly what was going on.

You do not say 'it is no need to' do something.

negligent - negligible

1 **'negligent'**

If someone has been **negligent**, they have not performed their duties carefully enough.

The jury determined that the airline was negligent in training and supervising the crew.

2 **'negligible'**

If something is **negligible**, it is so small or unimportant that it is not worth considering.

The damage appears to have had a negligible effect on the yacht's speed.
They can make extra copies of videotapes at a negligible cost.

neither

1 **'neither' and 'neither of'**

You use **neither** or **neither of** to make a negative statement about two people or things. You use **neither** in front of the singular form of a count noun. You use **neither of** in front of a plural pronoun or a plural noun group beginning with **the, these, those**, or a possessive.

USAGE

So, for example, you can say 'Neither child was hurt' or 'Neither of the children was hurt'. There is no difference in meaning.

Neither man spoke or moved.
Neither of them spoke for several moments.

⚠ **WARNING:** You do not use **neither** without **of** in front of a plural form. You do not say, for example, 'Neither the children was hurt'. You also do not use 'not' after **neither.** You do not say, for example, 'Neither of the children wasn't hurt'.

People sometimes use a plural form of a verb after **neither of** and a noun group. For example, they say 'Neither of the children **were** hurt'.

Neither of them are employees of the White House.
…in those moments when neither of you are speaking.

This use is acceptable in conversation, but in formal writing you should always use a singular form of a verb after **neither of.**

2 **used as a pronoun**
Neither can be used on its own as a pronoun. This is a fairly formal use.

Neither was suffering pain.
She chose first one, then another, but neither was to her satisfaction.

3 **adding a clause**
When a negative statement has been made, you can use **neither** to indicate that this statement also applies to another person or thing. You put **neither** at the beginning of the clause, followed by an auxiliary, a modal, or **be**, then the subject.

'I didn't invite them.' – 'Neither did I.'
He'll never forget it, and neither will we.

neither ... nor

In writing and formal speech, **neither** and **nor** are used to link two words or expressions of the same type in order to make a negative statement about two people, things, qualities, or actions. You put **neither** in front of the first word or expression and **nor** in front of the second one.

For example, instead of saying 'The President did not come and the Vice-President did not come' you can say ' **Neither** the President **nor** the Vice-President came'.

Neither he nor Melanie owe me any explanation.
He neither drinks nor smokes.

⚠ **WARNING:** You do not use 'or' after **neither.** You do not say, for example, 'He neither drinks or smokes'.

You always put **neither** immediately in front of the first of the words or expressions linked by **nor.** You do not put it any earlier in the sentence. You do not say, for example, 'She neither ate meat nor fish'. You say 'She ate **neither** meat **nor** fish'.

In conversation, people do not usually use **neither** and 'nor'. Instead of saying 'Neither the President nor the Vice-President came', you would normally say 'The President didn't come and **neither did** the Vice-President'.

Margaret didn't talk about her mother and neither did Rosa.
I won't give in to their threats, and neither will my colleagues.

Instead of saying 'She ate neither meat nor fish', you would normally say 'She **didn't** eat meat **or** fish'. Instead of saying 'She neither smokes nor drinks', you would say 'She **doesn't** smoke **or** drink'.

Karin's from abroad and hasn't any relatives or friends here.
You can't run or climb in shoes like that.

nervous - anxious - irritated

1 **'nervous'**

If you are **nervous,** you are rather frightened about something that you are going to do or experience.

…*the child who is* <u>nervous</u> *about starting school.*

2 **'anxious'**

If you are worried about something that might happen to someone else, you do not say that you are 'nervous'. You say that you are **anxious.**

It's time to be going home – your mother will be <u>anxious.</u>
I had to deal with calls from <u>anxious</u> *relatives.*

⇨ See **Usage** entry at **anxious.**

3 **'irritated'**

If something annoys you because you cannot stop it continuing, you do not say that it makes you 'nervous'. You say that you are **irritated** by it.

Perhaps they were <u>irritated</u> *by the sound of crying.*

---

never

1 **uses**

You use **never** to say that something did not, does not, or will not happen at any time.

She <u>never</u> *asked him to lend her any money.*
I will <u>never</u> *give up.*

⚠ **WARNING:** You do not use 'do' in front of **never.** You do not say, for example, 'He does never write to me'. You say 'He **never writes** to me'.

He <u>never complains.</u>
He <u>never speaks</u> *to you, does he?*

However, for emphasis, people sometimes use **do** after **never.** They say, for example, 'He **never does write** to me'.

I <u>never do</u> *discover what happens next.*
I <u>never did want</u> *a council house.*

⚠ **WARNING:** You do not usually use another negative word with **never.** You do not say, for example, 'I haven't never been there' or 'They never said nothing'. You say 'I have **never** been there' or 'They **never** said **anything**'.

It was an experience I will <u>never</u> *forget.*
I've <u>never</u> *seen* <u>anything</u> *like it.*

Similarly, you do not use 'never' if the subject of a clause is a negative word such as **nothing** or **no one.** Instead you use **ever.** You say, for example, 'Nothing will **ever** happen'. You do not say 'Nothing will never happen'.

<u>Nothing ever</u> *changes.*
<u>No one</u> *will* <u>ever</u> *know.*
<u>Nobody ever</u> *mentioned this to me.*

2 **position in clause**

If you are not using an auxiliary or modal, you put **never** in front of the verb, unless the verb is **be.**

He <u>never allowed</u> *himself to lose control.*
They <u>never take</u> *risks.*

USAGE

- If the verb is **be**, you usually put **never** after it.
The road alongside the river was never quiet.

- If you are using an auxiliary or modal, you put **never** after it.
I have never known a year quite like this.
My husband says he will never retire.
He could never overtake his opponent.

- However, if you are using **do** for emphasis, you put **never** in front of it (see above).

- If you are using more than one auxiliary or modal, you put **never** after the first one.
He was one of the few people there who had never been arrested.
The answers to such questions would never be known with certainty.

- If you are using an auxiliary on its own, you put **never** in front of it.
I do not want to marry you. I never did. I never will.

- In stories, **never** is sometimes put first for emphasis, followed by an auxiliary and the subject of the clause.
Never had Dixon been so glad to see Margaret.
Never had two hours gone so slowly.

3 **'never' with an imperative**
You can use **never** with an imperative instead of 'do not'. You do this when you want to emphasize that something should not be done at any time.
Never attempt to apply eyeliner while driving a car.
Never use a natural fibre such as string to hang pictures.

newness

1 **'new'**
You use **new** to describe things which were created, made, built, or begun a short time ago.
I recently bought a copy of the new book by Simon Singh.
… new methods of medical care.
…smart new houses.

You also use **new** to describe something which has replaced something else.
They would have to decorate and get new furniture.
He loved his new job.

There are several other words which have a similar meaning to **new**:

2 **'recent'**
Recent is used to describe events and periods of time that occurred a short time ago.
…the recent kidnapping of a British judge.
The energy conservation budget has been substantially reduced in recent years.

You do not usually use **recent** to describe objects, but you can use it to describe things such as newspaper articles and photographs.
…a recent report from the Food and Agriculture Organization.
You will need to take with you your passport and two recent black and white photographs.

You can also use **recent** to describe governments and people with particular jobs.
…one of the most poorly drafted pieces of legislation produced by any recent government.
Many recent composers have been less imaginative.

3 **'modern' and 'present-day'**
You use **modern** or **present-day** to describe things that exist now, when you want to emphasize that they are different from earlier things of the same kind.
… modern power stations.
…the stresses of modern life.
By present-day standards, its technology was, of course, cumbersome and limited.

4 **'contemporary'**

Contemporary has the same meaning as **modern** and **present-day**, but it is usually used only to describe abstract things or things relating to the arts.

What is women's situation in <u>contemporary</u> society?
<u>Contemporary</u> music is played there now.

You also use **contemporary** to indicate that something existed in the past at the same time as something else that you have been talking about.

<u>Contemporary</u> records of the case do not, however, mention these two items.

5 **'current'**

Current is used to describe things that exist now, but that might end or change soon.

…the root causes of our <u>current</u> crisis.
…Kitty King, Boyd Stuart's <u>current</u> girlfriend.

newly

⇨ See **Usage** entry at **recently - newly - lately**.

news

News is information that you give to someone about a recent event or a recently changed situation.

I've got some good <u>news</u> for you.
Maureen was at home when she heard <u>news</u> of the Paddington disaster.

You also use **news** to refer to descriptions of recent events on television or radio or in a newspaper.

They continued to broadcast up-to-date <u>news</u> and pictures of these events.

News looks like a plural noun but is in fact an uncount noun. You use a singular form of a verb after it.

The news <u>is</u> likely to be received with apprehension.
I was still lying helpless in bed when the news <u>was</u> brought to me.

You talk about **this news**, not 'these news'.

I had been waiting at Camp 3 for <u>this news.</u>

You do not talk about 'a news'. You refer to a piece of information as **some news, a bit of news,** or **a piece of news.**

I've got <u>some good news</u> for you.
I've had <u>a bit of bad news.</u>
A respectful silence greeted <u>this piece of news.</u>

You refer to a description of an event on television or in a newspaper as **a news item** or **an item of news.**

… <u>a small news item</u> in The Times last Friday.
<u>An item of news</u> in the Sunday paper caught my attention.

next

Next is usually used to say when something will happen. It can also be used to talk about the physical position of something, or the position that something has in a list or series.

1 **talking about the future**

You use **next** in front of words such as **week, month,** or **year** to say when something will happen. For example, if it is Wednesday and something is going to happen on Monday, you can say that it will happen **next week.**

I'm getting married <u>next month.</u>
I don't know where I will be <u>next year.</u>

USAGE

(i) Note that you do not use 'the' or a preposition in front of **next.** You do not say, for example, that something will happen 'the next week' or 'in the next week'.

You can also use **next** without 'the' or a preposition in front of **weekend** or in front of the name of a season, month, or day of the week.

Next weekend there is a by-election in Marseilles.
You must come and see us next autumn.
He said he would be seventy-five next April.
Let's have lunch together next Wednesday.

However, you do not use **next** like this in front of **decade** or **century.** You do not say, for example, that something will happen 'next decade'. You say that it will happen **in the next decade** or **during the next decade.**

In the next decade, tourism is expected to create more than 200,000 jobs.
Local leaders predict that another 10,000 to 20,000 new jobs will be created in the borough during the next decade.

(i) Note that you do not say that something will happen 'next day'. You say that it will happen **tomorrow.** Similarly, you do not say that something will happen 'next morning', 'next afternoon', 'next evening', or 'next night'. You say that it will happen **tomorrow morning, tomorrow afternoon, tomorrow evening,** or **tomorrow night.**

Can we meet tomorrow at five?
I'm going down there tomorrow morning.
We're all having dinner together tomorrow night.

⚠ **WARNING:** You do not usually use 'next' to refer to a day in the same week. For example, if it is Monday and you intend to ring someone in four days' time, you do not say 'I will ring you next Friday'. You say 'I will ring you **on Friday** '.
He's going off to scout camp on Friday.

If you want to make it completely clear that you are talking about a day in the same week, you use **this.**
The film opens this Thursday at various ABC Cinemas in London.

Similarly, you can say that something will happen **this weekend.**
I might be able to go skiing this weekend.

You use **the next** to refer to any period of time measured forward from the present. For example, if it is July 2nd and you want to say that something will happen between now and July 23rd, you say that it will happen **in the next three weeks** or **during the next three weeks.**

Mr John MacGregor will make the announcement in the next two weeks.
Caravan retailers fear a further slump in business during the next ten years.

2 **talking about the past**

When you are talking about the past and you want to say that something happened on the day after events that you have been describing, you say that it happened **the next day** or **the following day.**

I telephoned the next day and protested to the receptionist.
The following day I went to speak at a conference in Scotland.

In stories, **next day** is sometimes used, especially at the beginning of a clause.
Next day we all got up rather early.

Next, the next, and **the following** can also be used in front of **morning.**
Next morning he began to work but felt uninspired.
The next morning, as I left for the office, a letter arrived for me.
The following morning he checked out of the hotel and took the express to Paris.

However, in front of **afternoon**, **evening**, or the name of a day of the week you normally only use **the following**.

I arrived at the village <u>the following afternoon</u>.
He was due to start <u>the following Friday</u>.

3 | **talking about physical position**

You use **next to** to say that someone or something is by the side of a person or object.

She went and sat <u>next to</u> him.
There was a bowl of goldfish <u>next to</u> the bed.

If you talk about **the next room**, you are referring to a room that is separated by a wall from the one you are in.

I can hear my husband in <u>the next room</u>, typing away.

Similarly, if you are in a theatre or a bus, **the next seat** is a seat which is by the side of the one you are sitting in.

He became aware that the girl in <u>the next seat</u> was studying him with interest.

You can use **next** like this with a few other nouns, for example **desk, bed**, or **compartment**.

> ⚠ **WARNING:** However, you do not use 'next' simply to say that a particular thing is closer than anything else of its kind. You do not say, for example, ~~They took him to the next hospital~~. You say 'They took him to **the nearest hospital**'.
> *<u>The nearest town</u> is Brompton.*
> *<u>The nearest beach</u> is 15 minutes' walk away.*

4 | **talking about a list or series**

The **next** one in a list or series is the one that comes immediately after the one you have been talking about.

Let's go on to the <u>next</u> item of business – Harry's report on the situation in Central America.

In British English, the **next** thing **but one** in a list or series is the one that comes after the next one.

The <u>next</u> entry <u>but one</u> is another recipe.

---

nice

1 | **basic meaning**

Nice is a very common adjective. You use it to show that you like someone or something, or that something gives you pleasure.

He has <u>nice</u> eyes.
It's a very <u>nice</u> town.
I got a <u>nice</u> hat and a green dress.

Some people object to the use of **nice** because they say it does not have a clear meaning. This is only partly true.

2 | **talking about people**

When you use **nice** to talk about people or their behaviour, its meaning is clear. If you say that someone is 'a **nice** man' or 'a **nice** woman', you mean that they are kind and thoughtful.

They seemed very <u>nice</u> men.
We've got very <u>nice</u> neighbours.

You can say that it is **nice of** someone to do something. This is a way of showing gratitude when someone has behaved in a kind and thoughtful way.

It's <u>nice of</u> you to say that.
How <u>nice of</u> you to come.

If someone is **being nice to** someone else, they are behaving in a pleasant and friendly way towards them, even though they may not like them.

Promise you'll <u>be nice to</u> her when she comes back.

3 talking about enjoyment

You can use **nice** with some nouns to talk about spending time in a pleasant way. This is a very common use. For example, if you say 'Have a **nice** evening', you are saying to someone that you hope they will spend the evening in a pleasant way. Similarly, if you say 'Did you have a **nice** holiday?', you are asking someone if they enjoyed their recent holiday.

They were having a <u>nice</u> time.
'Have a <u>nice</u> weekend.' – 'You too.'

4 talking about things and places

In conversation, you can use **nice** to say that you like a thing or place. However, in formal writing it is better to find another adjective which expresses your meaning more exactly.

…a <u>delightful</u> room.
…a bottle of nail polish in an <u>attractive</u> shade.
It is one of the <u>pleasantest</u> places I know.

5 'nice' with other adjectives

In conversation, **nice** is often used with other adjectives. For example, you can say that a room is **nice and warm** or describe it as a **nice, warm** room. When you use **nice** like this, you are saying that the room is nice because it is warm.

The room is <u>nice and clean.</u>
It's <u>nice and peaceful</u> here.
I want a <u>nice, warm, comfortable</u> bed.

night

1 'night', 'at night'

Night is the period during each twenty-four hours when it is dark. If something happens regularly during this period, you say that it happens **at night**.

The veranda was equipped with heavy wooden rain doors that were kept closed <u>at night</u>.
I used to lie awake <u>at night</u> watching the rain seep through the ceiling.

A **night** is one of these periods of darkness. You usually refer to a particular period as **the night**.

He was at the hotel and intended to spend <u>the night</u> there.
Is that what you've come out here in the middle of <u>the night</u> to tell me?

2 the previous night

If you want to say that something happened during the night before the present day, you say that it happened **in the night, during the night,** or **last night**.

I didn't hear Sheila <u>in the night</u>.
I had the strangest dream <u>last night</u>.

You can also say that a situation existed **last night**.

I didn't manage to sleep much <u>last night</u>.

(*i*) Note that **last night** is also used to say that something happened during the previous evening.

I met your husband <u>last night</u>.

If you are talking about a day in the past and you want to say that something happened the night before that day, you say that it happened **in the night, during the night,** or **the previous night**.

His father had died <u>in the night</u>.
There had been sporadic gunfire <u>during the night</u>.
…the hill they had climbed <u>the previous night</u>.

3 **exact times**
If you have mentioned an exact time and you want to make it clear that you are talking about the early part of the night rather than the morning, you add **at night**.
This took place at eleven o'clock <u>at night</u> on our second day of travel.
However, if you are talking about a time after midnight and you want to make it clear that you are talking about the night and not the afternoon, you say **in the morning**.
It was five o'clock <u>in the morning</u>.

no

1 **used as a reply**
No can be a negative reply.
'Is he down there already?' – ' <u>No</u>, he's not there.'
'Did you come alone?' – ' <u>No</u>. John's here with me.'

(*i*) Note that **no** is a negative reply to negative questions. For example, if you are Spanish and someone says to you 'You aren't Italian, are you?', you say **'No'**. You do not say ~~'Yes'~~.
'You don't smoke, do you?' – '<u>No.</u>'
'It won't take you more than ten minutes, will it?' – '<u>No.</u>'

2 **used as a determiner**
No is used in front of nouns as a negative determiner. It means 'not any'. For example, instead of saying 'She doesn't have any friends', you can say 'She has **no friends**'.
I have <u>no complaints.</u>
My children are hungry. We have <u>no food.</u>

3 **used with comparatives**
No is used in front of comparative adjectives instead of 'not'. For example, instead of saying 'She isn't taller than her sister', you say 'She is **no taller** than her sister'.
The woman was <u>no older</u> than Kate.
…shells <u>no bigger</u> than a little fingernail.
However, you do not use 'no' and a comparative in front of a noun. You do not talk, for example, about 'a no older woman' or 'a no bigger shell'.

4 **used with 'different'**
No is used in front of **different** instead of 'not'.
Kilkenny is <u>no different</u> from other towns, say locals.

5 **used to forbid things**
No is often used on notices to tell you that something is not allowed. **No** is followed by an '-ing' form or a noun.
<u>No</u> smoking.
<u>No</u> entry.
<u>No</u> wheeled vehicles beyond this point.

nobody
⇨ See **Usage** entry at **no-one**.

noise
⇨ See **Usage** entry at **sound - noise**.

no longer
⇨ See **Usage** entry at **any more**.

none

1 **'none of'**
You use **none of** in front of a plural noun group to make a negative statement about every thing or person in a particular group.

USAGE

None of these suggestions is very helpful.
None of his rivals could mount a challenge.

You use **none of** in front of a noun group containing an uncount noun to make a negative statement about every part of something.

None of the furniture appeared out of place.

You can use **none of** in front of a singular or plural pronoun.

None of this seems to have made any impression on him.
We had none of these at home.

You do not use 'we' or 'they' after **none of**. Instead you use **us** or **them**.

None of us had been responsible for the reports.
None of them had learned anything about the teaching of reading.

When you use **none of** in front of a plural noun or pronoun, you can use either a plural or singular form of a verb after it. The singular form is more formal.

None of his books have been published in England.
None of their matches has been staged at Old Trafford.
None of them are real.
None of them is impressed.

When you use **none of** in front of an uncount noun or a singular pronoun, you use a singular form of a verb after it.

None of the wheat was ruined.
Yet none of this has seriously affected shares.

2 **used as a pronoun**
None can be used on its own as a pronoun.

There were none left.
He asked for some documentary proof. I told him that I had none.

⚠ **WARNING:** You do not usually use any other negative word after **none of** or **none**. You do not say, for example, 'None of them weren't ready'. You say 'None of them **were** ready'. Similarly, you do not use 'none of' or 'none' as the object of a sentence which already has a negative word in it. You do not say, for example, 'I didn't want none of them'. You say 'I didn't want **any** of them'.

ⓘ Note that you only use **none of** or **none** to talk about a group of three or more things or people. If you want to talk about two things or people, you use **neither of** or **neither**.
⇨ See **Usage** entry at **neither**.

---

no one

No one or **nobody** means 'not a single person', or 'not a single member of a particular group'. There is no difference in meaning between **no one** and **nobody**. In British English, **no one** can also be written **no-one**. **Nobody** is always written as one word.
You use a singular form of a verb with **no one** or **nobody**.

Everyone wants to be a hero, but no one wants to die.
Nobody knows where he is.

⚠ **WARNING:** You do not usually use any other negative word after **no one** or **nobody**. You do not say, for example, 'No one didn't come'. You say 'No one **came** '.
Similarly, you do not use 'no one' or 'nobody' as the object of a sentence which already has a negative word in it. You do not say, for example, 'We didn't see no one'. You say 'We didn't see **anyone**' or 'We didn't see **anybody**'.

You mustn't tell anyone.
He didn't trust anybody.

ⓘ Note that you do not use **of** after 'no one' or 'nobody'. You do not say, for example, 'No one of the children could speak French'. You say '**None of** the children could speak French'.

None of the women will talk to me.

It was something none of us could possibly have guessed.

⇨ See **Usage** entry at **none**.

nor

1 **'neither...nor'**

You can use **nor** with **neither** to make a negative statement about two people or things.

Neither Margaret nor John was there.

He spoke neither English nor French.

⇨ For a full explanation, see **Usage** entry at **neither ... nor**.

2 **used to link clauses**

Nor is also used to link negative clauses. You put **nor** at the beginning of the second clause, followed by an auxiliary, a modal, or **be**, followed by the subject and the main verb, if there is one.

The officer didn't believe me, nor did the girls when they came back.

North does not explain what 'blame' he is speaking of, nor does he explain what the 'blame' is for.

You can put **and** or **but** in front of **nor**.

I would have nothing to do with it, and nor would most of us.

Prices are not going up, but nor are they falling.

You do not normally begin a sentence with **nor**, but you can sometimes do so when you want to make the sentence seem more dramatic or forceful.

The overall ratings are virtually unchanged from earlier surveys. Nor has there been much change in the sense of job security.

I do not want these letters. Nor do I even want any copies.

3 **'nor' in replies**

You can reply to a negative statement using **nor**. You do this to indicate that what has just been said also applies to another person or thing.

'I don't like him.' – ' Nor do I.'

'I can't stand much more of this.' – ' Nor can I.'

normally

⇨ See section on **frequency** in **Grammar** entry at **Adjuncts**.

north - northern

1 **'north'**

The **north** is the direction which is on your left when you are looking towards the direction where the sun rises.

The land to the north and east was low-lying.

There is a possibility of colder weather and winds from the north.

A **north** wind blows from the north.

The north wind was blowing straight into her face.

The **north** of a place is the part that is towards the north.

Poaching started in the north of the country.

The best asparagus comes from the Calvados region in the north of France.

North occurs in the names of some countries, states, and regions.

They have hopes for business in North Korea.

USAGE

...the mountains of <u>North Carolina.</u>
...ecological damage in <u>North America.</u>

2 'northern'

However, you do not usually talk about a 'north' part of a country or region. You talk about a **northern** part.

...Soya, the <u>northern</u> cape of Japan.
...the <u>northern</u> tip of Caithness.

Similarly, you do not talk about 'north Europe' or 'north England'. You say **northern** Europe or **northern** England.

Bowman had flown over <u>northern</u> Canada.

---

northerly

If something moves in a **northerly** direction, it moves towards the north.

We continued in a <u>northerly</u> direction.

However, a **northerly** wind blows **from** the north.

...a <u>northerly</u> wind blowing off the sea.

The most **northerly** of a group of things is the one that is furthest to the north. The form **northernmost** is also used with the same meaning

...the Summer solstice, when the sun reaches its most <u>northerly</u> point.
...the <u>northernmost</u> tip of the British Isles.

---

northwards

1 'northwards'

If you move or look **northwards,** you move or look towards the north.

Morning Rose moved off slowly <u>northwards</u> from the jetty.

Northwards is only used as an adverb.

2 'northward'

In American English and old-fashioned British English, **northward** is often used instead of 'northwards'.

Tropical storm Marco is pushing <u>northward</u> up Florida's coast.

In both British and American English, **northward** is sometimes used as an adjective in front of a noun.

The <u>northward</u> journey from Jalalabad was no more than 120 miles.

---

no sooner

⇨ See **Usage** entry at **soon.**

---

not

Not is used with verbs to form negative sentences.

1 position and form of 'not'

You put **not** after the first auxiliary or modal, if there is one.

They <u>are not seen</u> as major problems.
They <u>might not even notice.</u>
Most people suffering from the disease <u>have not been exposed</u> unduly to radiation.

If there is no other auxiliary, you use **do** as the auxiliary. After **not** you use the base form of a verb.

The girl <u>did not answer.</u>
He <u>does not speak</u> English very well.

In conversation, when **not** is used after **be, have, do,** or a modal, it is not usually pronounced in full. When you write down what someone says, you usually represent **not**

as **n't** and add it to the verb in front of it. In some cases, the verb also changes its form.
⇨ For an explanation of these changes, see **Grammar** entry at **Contractions**.

(i) Note that with almost all verbs you do not use **not** without an auxiliary. You do not say, for example, 'I not liked it' or 'I liked not it'. You say 'I **didn't like** it'.

There are two exceptions to this. When you use **not** with **be**, you do not use an auxiliary. You simply put **not** after **be**.

I 'm not sure about this.
The program was not a success.

When **have** is a main verb with **not**, it is sometimes used without an auxiliary, but only in the contracted forms **hasn't**, **haven't**, and **hadn't**.

You haven't any choice.
The sky hadn't a cloud in it.

However, it is more common to use the forms **doesn't have**, **don't have**, and **didn't have**.

This question doesn't have a proper answer.
We don't have any direct control of the rents.
I didn't have a cheque book.

⚠ **WARNING:** When you use **not** to make what you are saying negative, you do not usually use another negative word such as 'nothing', 'never', or 'none'. You do not say, for example, 'I don't know nothing about it'. You say 'I don't know **anything** about it'.

2 **'not really'**
You can make a negative statement more polite or less strong by using **really** after **not**.

Winning or losing is not really important.
It doesn't really matter.
I don't really want to be part of it.

You can reply to some questions by saying **'Not really'**.

⇨ See **Topic** entry at **Replies**.

3 **'not very'**
When you make a negative statement using **not** and an adjective, you can make the statement less strong by putting **very** in front of the adjective.

The fees are not very high.
I'm not very interested in the subject.
That's not a very good arrangement.

⚠ **WARNING:** Although you can say that something is **not very good**, you do not use **not** in front of other words meaning 'very good'. You do not say, for example, that something is 'not excellent' or 'not marvellous'.

4 **used with negative adjectives**
You can make a positive statement by using **not** in front of an adjective that already has a negative meaning. For example, if you say that something is **not unreasonable**, you mean that it is quite reasonable.

Frost and snow are not uncommon during these months.
It's not impossible that he'll succeed.

When you use **a** and a short adjective in statements like these, you put **not** in front of **a**. With long adjectives, you can put **not** either in front of **a** or after it.

It's not a bad idea.
It is not an unpleasant feeling.
This is a not unreasonable interpretation.

USAGE

5 | used with 'to'-infinitives

You can use **not** with a 'to'-infinitive. You put **not** in front of **to**, not after it.

The Prime Minister has asked his ministers <u>not to discuss</u> the issue publicly any more.
I decided <u>not to go</u> in.
Be careful <u>not to overdo</u> it.

6 | 'not' in contrasts

You can use **not** to link two words or expressions. You do this to point out that something is the case, and to contrast it with what is not the case.

The plaque confirmed that the paintings were a gift, <u>not</u> a bequest.
The world can only be grasped by action, <u>not</u> by contemplation.

You can make a similar contrast by changing the order of the words or expressions. When you do this, you put **not** in front of the first word or expression and **but** in front of the second one.

A passport was now <u>not</u> a right <u>but</u> a privilege.
He was caught, <u>not</u> by the police, <u>but</u> by a mob who beat him to death.

7 | used with sentence adverbs

You can use **not** with **surprisingly**, **unexpectedly**, or **unusually** to make a negative comment on a statement.

<u>Not surprisingly,</u> the Council rejected the suggestion.
<u>Not unexpectedly,</u> the revelation caused enormous interest.
I find that <u>not unusually</u> a patient feels trapped or victimized by life.

8 | 'not all'

Not is sometimes used with **all** and with words beginning with **every-** to form the subject of a sentence. For example, instead of saying 'Some snakes are not poisonous', you can say ' **Not all** snakes are poisonous'.

<u>Not all</u> the houses we get offered have central heating.
<u>Not everyone</u> agrees with me.

9 | 'not only'

Not only is often used with **but** or **but also** to link two words or word groups.
⇨ For an explanation of this use, see **Usage** entry at **not only**.

notable

⇨ See **Usage** entry at **noticeable - notable**.

nothing

1 | 'nothing'

Nothing means 'not a single thing', or 'not a single part of something'.
You use a singular form of a verb with **nothing**.

Nothing <u>is</u> happening.
Nothing <u>has</u> been discussed.

⚠ **WARNING:** You do not usually use any other negative word such as 'not' after **nothing**. You do not say, for example, 'N̶o̶t̶h̶i̶n̶g̶ ̶d̶i̶d̶n̶'̶t̶ ̶h̶a̶p̶p̶e̶n̶'. You say 'Nothing **happened**'. Similarly, you do not use 'nothing' as the object of a sentence which already has a negative word in it. You do not say, for example, 'I̶ ̶c̶o̶u̶l̶d̶n̶'̶t̶ ̶h̶e̶a̶r̶ ̶n̶o̶t̶h̶i̶n̶g̶'. You say 'I couldn't hear **anything**.'

I did not say <u>anything</u>.
He never seemed to do <u>anything</u> at all.

2 | 'nothing but'

Nothing but is used in front of a noun group or an infinitive without 'to' to mean 'only'. For example, instead of saying 'In the fridge there was only a piece of cheese', you can say 'In the fridge there was **nothing but** a piece of cheese'.

For a few months I thought and talked of <u>nothing but</u> Jeremy.
He did <u>nothing but</u> complain.

notice

Notice can be a noun or a verb.

1 used as a noun

A **notice** is a sign in a public place which gives information or instructions.

There was a <u>notice</u> on the lift saying it was out of order.

2 'note'

You do not use **notice** to refer to a short, informal letter. The word you use is **note**.

I shall have to write a <u>note</u> to Eileen's mother to explain her hurt arm.

3 'take notice'

If you **take notice of** someone or something, you pay attention to them.

I'll make her <u>take notice of</u> me.
Police officers taught residents to <u>take notice of</u> suspicious activities and unfamiliar cars and faces.

When someone does not pay any attention to someone or something, you can say that they **take no notice** of them or **do not take any notice** of them.

Her mother <u>took no notice of</u> her weeping.
They refused to <u>take any notice of</u> one another.

4 'notice' used as a verb

If someone becomes aware of something, you do not say that they 'take notice of' it. You say that they **notice** it.

I've <u>noticed</u> your hostility towards him.
He <u>noticed</u> two grey trucks parked near his house.

noticeable - notable

1 'noticeable'

Something that is **noticeable** is large enough or clear enough to be noticed.

There has also been a <u>noticeable</u> increase in the number of people seeking counselling and psychotherapy.
I experienced no <u>noticeable</u> ill effects.

2 'notable'

Something that is **notable** is important or remarkable. **Notable** is a fairly formal word.

His most <u>notable</u> journalistic achievement was to bring out his own paper.
With a few <u>notable</u> exceptions, doctors are a pretty sensible lot.

not only

1 used with 'but' or 'but also'

You use **not only** to link two words or word groups referring to things, actions, or situations. You put **not only** in front of the first word or group, and **but** or **but also** in front of the second one. The second thing mentioned is usually more surprising, informative, or important than the first one.

The government radio <u>not only</u> reported the demonstration, <u>but</u> announced it in advance.
Some parents are <u>not only</u> concerned with safety <u>but also</u> sceptical of the educational value of such trips.
We are interested in assessing <u>not only</u> what the children have learnt <u>but</u> how they have learnt it.

2 used with a pronoun

When you are linking word groups that begin with a verb, you can omit 'but' or 'but also' and use a personal pronoun instead. For example, instead of saying 'Margaret not only came to the party but brought her aunt as well', you can say 'Margaret not only came to the party, **she** brought her aunt as well'.

Imported taps <u>not only</u> provide more variation, <u>they</u> are often more attractively designed.
Her interest in your work has <u>not only</u> continued, <u>it</u> has increased.

3 **putting 'not only' first**

For emphasis, you can put **not only** first, followed by an auxiliary or **be**, then the subject, then the main verb.

<u>Not only did they send</u> home substantial earnings, but they also saved money.
<u>Not only do they rarely go</u> on school outings, they rarely, if ever, leave Brooklyn.

Not only must come first when you are linking two clauses which have different subjects.

Not only were <u>the locals</u> all old, but <u>the women</u> still dressed in long black dresses.
Not only were <u>the instruments</u> unreliable, <u>the crew</u> had not flown together before.

4 **'not just'**

Not just is sometimes used instead of **not only**.

It is <u>not just</u> the most fashionable but also one of the best restaurants in the West End.
I want to see more and more people <u>not just</u> voting in polling stations, but formulating the policies of the political parties.

Not just is used only in front of adjectives, nouns, phrases, and participles. You do not use it in front of verbs.

notorious

⇨ See **Usage** entry at **famous - well-known - notorious - infamous.**

now

1 **'now'**

Now is usually used to contrast a situation in the present with an earlier situation.

She gradually built up energy and is <u>now</u> back to normal.
He knew <u>now</u> that he could rely completely on Paul Irving.
<u>Now</u> he felt safe.

2 **'right now' and 'just now'**

In conversation, you use **right now** or **just now** to say that a situation exists at present, although it may change in the future.

The new car market is in chaos <u>right now</u>.
I'm awfully busy <u>just now</u>.

You also use **right now** to emphasize that something is happening now.

The crisis for forests in many countries is occurring <u>right now</u>.

If you say that something happened **just now,** you mean that it happened a very short time ago.

Did you feel the ship move <u>just now</u>?
I told you a lie <u>just now</u>.

If something is going to be done **now** or **right now,** it is going to be done immediately, without any delay.

He wants you to come and see him <u>now,</u> in his room.
I guess we'd better do it <u>right now</u>.

ⓘ Note that you do not use 'right now' or 'just now' in formal writing.

nowadays

Nowadays means 'at the present time, in contrast with the past'.

Life is so complicated <u>nowadays</u>.
Why don't we ever see Jim <u>nowadays</u>?

(*i*) Note that **nowadays** is an adverb, not an adjective. You do not use it in front of a noun. You do not talk, for example, about 'nowadays children'. However, you can use **nowadays** immediately after a noun. You can say, for example, 'Children **nowadays** have much more money'.

Kids nowadays are lazy.
People nowadays have much greater expectations about their rights.

nowhere

You use **nowhere** to say that there is no place where something happens or can happen.
There's nowhere for either of us to go.
There was nowhere to hide.

Nowhere is sometimes put first for emphasis, followed by **be** or an auxiliary and the subject of the clause.
Nowhere is language a more serious issue than in Hawaii.
Nowhere have I seen any serious mention of this.

⚠ **WARNING:** You do not usually use another negative word with 'nowhere'. You do not say, for example, 'I couldn't find her nowhere'. You say 'I couldn't find her **anywhere** '.
I changed my mind and decided not to go anywhere.

number

1 'a number of'
A number of things or people means several things or people. You use a plural form of a verb after **a number of**.
A number of key issues remain unresolved.
An increasing number of women are taking up self-defence.

2 'the number of'
When you talk about **the number of** people or things of a particular kind, you are talking about an actual number. After **the number of** you use a singular form of a verb.
In the last 30 years, the number of electricity consumers has risen by 50 per cent.

When you use **number** in either of these ways, you can use **large** or **small** with it.
His private papers revealed little of interest except a large number of unpaid bills.
The small number of samples involved precludes drawing any strong statistical correlation from the results.

However, you do not use 'big' or 'little' with **number** in sentences like these.

O o

obedience

The following words can all be used to describe someone who does what they are told and can be controlled easily:

acquiescent	docile	servile	submissive	tame
compliant	obedient	slavish	subservient	

1 indicating approval

Obedient usually shows approval, especially when you are talking about children or people who are under strict authority.

She was, on the whole, an <u>obedient</u> little girl.

Everyone ought to do military training. It would do them good and make them <u>obedient</u>.

Acquiescent, compliant, docile and **submissive** often show approval but are also sometimes used to indicate mild disapproval.

The soldiers were grateful and <u>docile,</u> and did not pester her.

…men who preferred their women to be <u>submissive.</u>

Acquiescent and **compliant** are formal words.

Some children seem to be totally <u>acquiescent,</u> always agreeing with the adult's view.

She was fed up with being eternally <u>compliant.</u>

2 indicating disapproval

Subservient and **tame** show mild disapproval.

His gesture of respect seemed old-fashioned and <u>subservient.</u>

I was too dull and ordinary a fellow, too <u>tame</u> for you.

Servile and **slavish** show strong disapproval.

For a student job he waited at table, but was demoted to washing up because his manner was not sufficiently <u>servile.</u>

…a <u>slavish</u> conformity to the styles of their classmates.

3 animals

(*i*) Note that **tame** is more commonly used to describe an animal of a kind that usually lives in the wild which has been born in captivity or has become used to people.

He sometimes let her play with his <u>tame</u> gazelle.

Docile and **obedient** are also used to describe animals. When used like this, they show approval.

We call them wild horses, but they are <u>docile</u>, gentle creatures.

You cannot begin show jumping until your horse is <u>obedient</u> and supple.

obey

If you **obey** someone who has authority over you, you do what they tell you to do.

She wanted her daughter to <u>obey</u> her.

Alfonsin issued the same order three times, but he <u>was not obeyed.</u>

You can also **obey** an order or instruction.

In all 198 NCOs and men refused to <u>obey</u> orders.

Be careful to <u>obey</u> the manufacturer's washing instructions.

(*i*) Note that you do not say that someone 'obeys to' a person, order, or instruction.

object

Object can be a noun or a verb. When it is a noun, it is pronounced /ɒbdʒekt/. When it is a verb, it is pronounced /ɒbdʒekt/.

1 used as a noun

You can refer to anything which has a fixed shape and which is not alive as an **object**.

…the shabby, black object he was carrying.
The icon is an object of great beauty.

A person's **object** is their aim or purpose.

My object was to publish a scholarly work on Peter Mourne.
The object, of course, is to persuade people to remain at their jobs.

2 used as a verb

If you **object to** something that is proposed or being done, you do not approve of it, or you say that you do not approve of it.

He does not object to loans in principle.
People have the opportunity to object to proposed developments in their neighbourhood.

If you **object to doing** something that you have been asked to do, you say that you do not think you should do it.

The women objected to cooking in the midday sun.
This group did not object to returning.

(*i*) Note that you use an '-ing' form, not an infinitive, after **object to**.

If it is clear what you are referring to, you can use **object** without 'to'.

The men objected and the women supported their protest.
Other authorities will still have the right to object.

If you want to say why someone does not approve of something or does not agree with something, you can use **object** with a 'that'-clause. For example, you can say 'They wanted me to do some extra work, but I **objected that** I had too much to do already'. This is a fairly formal use.

The others quite rightly object that he is holding back the work.
It can be objected that the private sector will serve a different market.

obligation - duty

1 'obligation' and 'duty'

If you say that someone has an **obligation to do** something or a **duty to do** something, you mean that they ought to do it, because it is their responsibility. When **obligation** and **duty** are used like this, they have the same meaning.

The Government has an obligation to reverse the decline of this important industry.
Perhaps it was his duty to inform the police of what he had seen.

2 'duties'

Your **duties** are the things that you do as part of your job.

She has been given a reasonable time to learn her duties.
They also have to carry out many administrative duties.

(*i*) Note that you do not refer to the things that you do as part of your job as 'obligations'.

oblige

If something **obliges** you **to do** something, it makes it necessary for you to do it.

This decree obliges unions to delay strikes.
Security requirements obliged her to stop.

If someone feels that they must do something, for example in order to be polite or because they think it is their duty, you can say that they **feel obliged** to do it.

He looked at me so blankly that I felt obliged to explain.

USAGE

> ⚠ **WARNING:** You do not use **oblige** in impersonal structures. You do not say, for example, ~~'He looked at me so blankly that it obliged me to explain'~~.

observance - observation

1 **'observance'**

The **observance** of a rule or custom is the practice of obeying it or following it. **Observance** is a fairly formal word.

Local councils should use their powers to ensure strict <u>observance</u> of laws.

2 **'observation'**

You do not use **observance** to refer to the activity of watching someone or something carefully. The word you use is **observation.**

Stephens had crashed and was taken to hospital for <u>observation</u>.

By far the greatest part of his work is careful <u>observation</u> and precise thinking.

obstinate

⇨ See **Usage** entry at **stubborn.**

obtain

1 **'obtain'**

If you **obtain** something that you want or need, you get it.

…my attempt to <u>obtain</u> employment.

He <u>had obtained</u> the papers during occasional visits to Berlin.

2 **'get'**

'Obtain' is a formal word. You do not usually use it in conversation. Instead you use **get.**

I <u>got</u> a job at the sawmill.

He had been having trouble <u>getting</u> a hotel room.

In writing, **obtain** is often used in the passive.

All the above items <u>can be obtained</u> from Selfridges.

You need to know where this kind of information <u>can be obtained.</u>

ⓘ Note that you do not usually use 'get' in the passive. You do not say, for example, ~~'Maps can be got from the Tourist Office'~~. You say 'Maps **can be obtained** from the Tourist Office' or, in conversation, '**You can get** maps from the Tourist Office'.

obvious

If something is **obvious,** you can easily see it or understand it.

It was painfully <u>obvious</u> that I knew very little about it.

For <u>obvious</u> reasons, I preferred my house to his.

You can say that something is **obvious to** someone.

The reasons are <u>obvious to</u> all of us.

It must have been <u>obvious to</u> everyone in Bristol what was happening.

ⓘ Note that you do not use any preposition except **to** after **obvious** in sentences like these.

occasion - opportunity - chance

1 **'occasion'**

An **occasion** is a time when a particular event happens or a particular situation arises.

I remember the <u>occasion</u> vividly.

There are <u>occasions</u> when you must refuse.

You often say that something happens **on** a particular occasion.

I think it would be better if I went alone <u>on this occasion.</u>

I met him only <u>on one occasion.</u>

An **occasion** is also an important event, ceremony, or celebration.

It was a fitting conclusion to a memorable <u>occasion.</u>
They have the date fixed for the big <u>occasion.</u>

2 **'opportunity' and 'chance'**

You do not use **occasion** to refer to a situation in which it is possible for someone to do something. Instead you use **opportunity** or **chance**.

I am very grateful to have had the <u>opportunity</u> of working with Paul.
She put the phone down before I had a <u>chance</u> to reply.

⇨ See **Usage** entries at **opportunity** and **chance**.

occasionally

⇨ See section on **frequency** in **Grammar** entry at **Adjuncts**.

occupation

⇨ See **Usage** entry at **work**.

occur

You can say that an event **occurs**.

The accident <u>occurred</u> at 8:40 a.m.
There is a revolution <u>occurring</u> in how people manage their money.
Mistakes are bound to <u>occur.</u>

However, you only use **occur** to talk about events which are not planned. **Occur** is a fairly formal word. In conversation, you usually say that an event **happens**.

You might have noticed what <u>happened</u> on Tuesday.
A curious thing <u>has happened.</u>

⇨ See **Usage** entry at **happen**.

(*i*) Note that you do not say that a planned event 'occurs' or 'happens'. You say that it **takes place**.

The first meeting of this committee <u>took place</u> on 9 January.
These lessons <u>took place</u> twice a week.

You do not use 'occur to' to say that someone is affected by an event. You do not say, for example, 'I wonder what's occurred to Jane'. You say 'I wonder what **'s happened to** Jane'.

She no longer cared what <u>happened to</u> her.
It couldn't <u>have happened to</u> a nicer man.

If an idea **occurs to** you, you suddenly think of it.

The idea <u>had</u> never even <u>occurred to</u> him before.
The thought <u>had</u> just <u>occurred to</u> him.

If you want to say what the idea is, you usually use **it** as the subject of **occur** and mention the idea in a 'that'-clause or a 'to'-infinitive clause.

It occurred to him <u>that he hadn't eaten anything since the night before.</u>
It occurred to him <u>to tell the colonel of the problem.</u>

of

1 **possession and other relationships**

Of is used to indicate possession. It can also be used to indicate other kinds of relationship between people or things.

…the home <u>of a sociology professor.</u>
…the sister <u>of the Duke of Urbino.</u>
At the top <u>of the hill</u> Hilary Jackson paused for breath.

You can use **of** in front of a possessive pronoun such as **mine**, **his**, or **theirs**. You do this to indicate that someone is one of a group of people or things connected with a particular

USAGE

person. For example, instead of saying 'He is one of my friends', you can say 'He is a friend **of mine.**'

He's _a very good friend of mine._
I talked to _a colleague of yours_ recently.

You can use **of** like this in front of other possessives.

… _a friend of my mother's._
She was _a great friend of Lorna Cook's._

 The 's is sometimes omitted, especially in American English.

… _a close friend of the President._

Of is also sometimes used with a possessive after a noun group beginning with **this**, **that**, **these**, or **those**.

… _this experiment of mine._
… _those brilliant shining eyes of hers._

⚠ **WARNING:** You do not use 'of' in front of a personal pronoun such as 'me', 'him', or 'them'. You do not say, for example, 'the sister of me'. Instead you use a **possessive determiner** such as **my**, **his**, or **their**.

_My_ sister came down the other week.
He had _his_ hands in _his_ pockets.
…the future of _our_ society.

⇨ See **Grammar** entry at **Possessive determiners.**

You do not usually use 'of' in front of short noun groups. Instead you use **'s** or the apostrophe '. For example, instead of saying 'the car of my friend', you say '**my friend's** car'.

… _Ralph's_ voice.
… _Mr Duffield's_ sister.
… _my colleagues'_ offices.

⇨ See **Usage** entry at **'s.**

⇨ For more information about possession, see **Topic** entry at **Possession and other relationships.**

2 **descriptions**

You can sometimes use **of** and a noun group to describe something, instead of using an adjective and a grading adverb. For example, instead of saying that something is 'very interesting', you can say that it is **of great interest.** This is a rather formal use.

It will be _of great interest_ to you.
The result is _of little importance._

When you use an adjective to comment on an action, you can put **of** and a pronoun after the adjective. The pronoun refers to the person who has performed the action. For example, you can say 'That was **stupid of you**'.

It was _brave of them._
I'm sorry, that was _silly of me._

3 **authorship**

You do not talk about a book 'of' a particular author, or a piece of music 'of' a particular composer. Instead you use **by.**

…the latest book _by_ Hilda Offen.
…a collection of pieces _by_ Mozart.

Similarly, you use **by** to indicate who painted a picture. A picture **of** a particular person shows that person as the subject of the picture.

…the famous painting _by_ Rubens, The Straw Hat.
…a 16th century painting _of_ Henry VIII.

4 | location

You can talk about the capital **of** a country, state, or province.

…Ulan Bator, the capital *of* Mongolia.

However, you do not talk about a town or village 'of' a particular country or area. Instead you use **in.**

…an old Spanish colonial town *in* Southern Ecuador.
My favourite town *in* Shropshire is Ludlow.

You also use **in,** rather than 'of', after superlatives. For example, you talk about 'the tallest building **in** Tokyo'. You do not say 'the tallest building of Tokyo'.

Hakodate is the oldest port *in* Hokkaido.
…the biggest lizards *in* the world.

5 | materials

In literary or old-fashioned writing, **of** is sometimes used with a noun group to mention the material from which something has been made.

The walls were *of bare plaster.*
…houses *of brick and stone.*

off

You use **off** as a preposition or adverb to say that something is removed from an object or surface.

He took his hand *off* her arm.
I knocked the clock *off* the bedside table.
The paint was peeling *off.*

Off is also used as an adverb to say that someone leaves a place.

The sailors ran *off.*
He started the motor and drove *off* immediately.

offer - give - invite

1 | 'offer'

If you **offer** something to someone, you ask them if they would like to have it or use it.

He *offered* me a cigarette. I shook my head.

2 | 'give'

If you put something in someone's hand expecting them to take it, and they do take it, you do not say that you 'offer' it to them. You say that you **give** it to them.

She *gave* Minnie the keys.
He *gave* me a red jewellery box.

3 | 'offer to'

If you **offer to do** something, you say that you are willing to do it.

He *offered to take* her home in a taxi.
I *offered to answer* any questions they might have.

4 | 'invite'

If someone asks you to do something that they think you will want to do, you do not say that they 'offer' you to do it. You say that they **invite** you to do it.

I *was invited* to attend future meetings.
She never once *invited* him to sit with them.

officer - official - office worker

1 | 'officer'

An **officer** is a person who has a position of authority in the armed forces.

…a retired army *officer.*

USAGE

Officer is also used in the name of some people's jobs.

He was arrested and charged with assaulting a <u>police officer</u>.
Suddenly the <u>press officer</u> came out and announced the result.

2 **'official'**

An **official** is a person who holds a position of authority in an organization, especially a government department or a trade union.

Government <u>officials</u> have rejected calls for international intervention.
Management and union <u>officials</u> agreed to go to the Labour Relations Commission today.

3 **'office worker'**

You do not use 'officer' or 'official' to refer to someone who works in an office. A person like this is called an **office worker.**

<u>Office workers</u> have been found to make more mistakes when distracted by traffic noise.

often

If something happens **often,** it happens many times.

1 **position in clause**

● If there is no auxiliary, you put **often** in front of the verb, unless the verb is **be.** If the verb is **be,** you put **often** after it.

We <u>often get</u> very cold winters here.
They <u>were often</u> hungry.

● If there is an auxiliary, you put **often** after it.

She <u>has often spoken</u> of the individual's 'right to choose'.
He <u>had often pointed</u> this out to Lucy.

● If there is more than one auxiliary, you put **often** after the first one.

The facts <u>had often been distorted.</u>
It's a word you <u>must often have come across.</u>

● If a sentence is fairly short, you can put **often** at the end of it.

He's in London <u>often.</u>
He could see Gertrude <u>often.</u>

● In writing, **often** is sometimes put at the beginning of a long sentence.

<u>Often</u> in the evening the little girl would be clutching at my knees while I held the baby.

⚠ **WARNING:** You do not use 'often' to talk about something that happens several times within a short period of time. You do not say, for example, 'I often phoned her yesterday'. You say 'I phoned her **several times** yesterday' or 'I **kept phoning** her yesterday'.

That fear was expressed <u>several times</u> last week.
Rather than correct her, I <u>kept trying</u> to change the subject.

⇨ For a graded list of words used to say how frequently something happens, see section on **frequency** in **Grammar** entry at **Adjuncts.**

2 **other uses of 'often'**

You use **often** with **how** when you are asking about the number of times that something happens or happened.

<u>How often</u> do you need to weigh the baby?
<u>How often</u> have you done this programme?

Often can also be used to say that something is done just once by many people, or that something is true about many people.

People <u>often</u> asked me why I didn't ride more during the trip.
Old people <u>often</u> don't like raw cabbage.

old

1 'old'

Old is most commonly used to state the age of a person or thing. For example, you say that someone 'is forty years **old**'.

The Law required witnesses to <u>be</u> at least <u>fourteen years old.</u>
…bone fragments which <u>are three-and-a-half million years old.</u>

You can also describe someone as, for example, 'a **forty-year-old** man'. Note that you do not say 'a forty-years-old man'.

… <u>a sixty-year-old man.</u>
Sue lives with <u>her five-year-old son</u> John in the West Country.

You can also say that someone is 'a man **of forty**'. However, you do not say 'a man of forty years old'.

Mary is <u>a tall, strong woman of thirty.</u>
Actually, he doesn't look bad for <u>a man of 62.</u>

⇨ For a discussion of the different ways of expressing age, see **Topic** entry at **Age**.

2 asking about age

You use **old** after **how** when you are asking about the age of a person or thing.

'<u>How old</u> are you?' – 'I'll be eight next year.'
'<u>How old</u> is the Taj Mahal?' – 'It was built about 1640, I think.'

3 'older' and 'oldest'

The usual comparative and superlative forms of **old** are **older** and **oldest**.

Harriet was ten years <u>older</u> than I was.
It claims to be the <u>oldest</u> insurance company in the world.

However, the forms **elder** and **eldest** are sometimes used.

⇨ For a full explanation, see **Usage** entry at **elder**.

4 another meaning of 'old'

You can also use **old** to describe someone who has lived a very long time.

…a little <u>old</u> lady.
He was emaciated and he looked really <u>old.</u>

5 'elderly' and 'aged'

This use of **old** can sometimes sound impolite. **Elderly** is a more polite word.

I keep house for my <u>elderly</u> mother.
Like many <u>elderly</u> people, Mrs Carstairs could remember voices better than she did faces.

Old people are often referred to as **the elderly** or **the aged**.

…organizations which help <u>the elderly.</u>
Hospital food seldom caters for the special needs of <u>the aged.</u>

ⓘ Note that **aged** is pronounced /ˈeɪdʒɪd/ when it is used like this. Its usual pronunciation, for example when talking about 'children aged five', is /eɪdʒd/.

6 old friends and enemies

An **old** friend or **old** enemy is someone who has been your friend or enemy for a long time. He or she is not necessarily an old person.

Some of the lads had taken the opportunity to visit <u>old</u> friends.
He realized that the leader was an <u>old</u> enemy of his.

7 'old' used to describe objects

An **old** building or other object was built or made a long time ago.

…a massive <u>old</u> building of crumbling red brick.
…wardrobes full of <u>old</u> clothes.

8 'ancient'

You can describe a very old building or object as **ancient**.

…the restoration of their <u>ancient</u> halls and manors.
They discovered an <u>ancient</u> manuscript hidden in a chimney.

Ancient is also used to describe people who lived a very long time ago.

The number zero was unknown to the <u>ancient</u> Greeks and Romans.
We know the <u>ancient</u> Egyptians were keen flower arrangers.

9 'old' used to mean 'former'

Old is sometimes used to mean 'former'.

Mark was heartbroken when Jane returned to her <u>old</u> boyfriend.
I still have affection for my <u>old</u> school.

on

1 used to say where something is

On is usually a preposition. You use **on** to say where someone or something is by mentioning the object or surface that is supporting them.

When I came back, she was just sitting <u>on</u> the stairs.
There was a photograph of a beautiful girl <u>on</u> Daintry's desk.

On is used in some other ways to say where someone or something is. For example, you use it to mention an area of land where someone works or lives, such as a farm, building site, or housing estate.

Not many girls today want to live <u>on</u> a farm.
…a labourer who worked <u>on</u> my father's building site.

You also use **on** to mention an island where something exists or happens.

This plant is now found only <u>on</u> Lundy in the Bristol Channel.
I was born <u>on</u> Honshu, the main island.

⇨ You usually use **in** or **at** to say where something is. See **Usage** entries at **in** and **at**.

2 used to say where something goes

You can use **on** to say where someone or something falls or is put.

He fell <u>on</u> the floor.
I put a hand <u>on</u> his shoulder.

Onto is used in a similar way.

⇨ See **Usage** entry at **onto**.

You use **on** after **get** to say that someone enters a bus, train, or ship.

George <u>got on</u> the bus with us.

⇨ For more information, see **Usage** entry at **go into**.

3 used to talk about time

You say that something happens **on** a particular day or date.

She intended to come to see the play <u>on</u> the following Friday.
Caro was born <u>on</u> April 10th.

⇨ For more information, see **Topic** entry at **Days and dates**.

You can use **on** to say that one thing immediately after another. For example, if something happens **on** someone's arrival, it happens immediately after they arrive.

'It's so unfair,' Clarissa said <u>on</u> her return.

4 the subject of a book

You use **on** or **about** to say what the subject of a book is.

…a book <u>on</u> astronomy.
…his book <u>about</u> the First World War.

⚠️ **WARNING:** However, you do not use 'on' to say what a work of fiction such as a novel or play deals with. You do not say, for example, 'The Coral Island is on three boys on a desert island'. You say 'The Coral Island is **about** three boys on a desert island'.
Ultimately, this is a novel <u>about</u> ethics.
…a story <u>about</u> growing up.

5 **used as an adverb**
On is sometimes an adverb, usually indicating that something continues to happen or be done.
His spirit lives <u>on.</u>
She plodded <u>on,</u> silently thinking.
I flew <u>on</u> to California.

once

1 **used to mean 'only one time'**
If something happens **once**, it happens only one time.
I've been out with him <u>once,</u> that's all.
I have never forgotten her, though I saw her only <u>once.</u>

When **once** is used with this meaning, it usually goes at the end of a clause.

2 **used to talk about the past**
You also use **once** to indicate that something happened at an unspecified time in the past.
I <u>once</u> investigated this story and it seems to be wholly untrue.
'<u>Once</u> I saw a shooting star here,' Jeffrey says.

When **once** is used with this meaning, it usually goes in front of a verb or at the beginning of a clause.

You also use **once** to say that something was the case in the past, although it is no longer the case.
He had <u>once</u> been a big star but now he was finished.
These carvings were <u>once</u> brightly coloured.
She was in the trade herself <u>once.</u>

When **once** is used with this meaning, it usually goes after **be** or an auxiliary, or at the end of a clause.

⚠️ **WARNING:** You do not use 'once' to indicate that something will happen at some time in the future. Instead you use **one day** for events in the distant future, or **sometime** for events in the fairly near future.
<u>One day,</u> you'll be very glad we stopped you.
I'll give you a ring <u>sometime.</u>

3 **'at once'**
If you do something **at once**, you do it immediately.
She stopped playing <u>at once.</u>
I knew <u>at once</u> that something was wrong.

one

1 **used in front of a noun**
One is the number 1. You use **one** in front of a noun to emphasize that you are talking about a single thing or person.
He balanced himself on <u>one</u> foot.
The two friends share <u>one</u> job.

USAGE

(i) Note that **one** is used like this for emphasis only. Normally, you use **a** or **an** to talk about a single thing or person.

2 **used instead of a noun group**

You can use **one** instead of a noun group beginning with **a** when it is clear what sort of thing you are talking about. For example, instead of saying 'If you want a drink, I'll get you a drink', you say 'If you want a drink, I'll get you **one**'.

Although she wasn't a rich customer, she looked and acted like <u>one.</u>
The cupboards were empty except for <u>one</u> at the top of the bookshelves.

(i) You cannot use a plural form of 'one' in this kind of sentence. You do not say, for example, 'If you like grapes, I'll get you ones'. You say 'If you like grapes, I'll get you **some**'.

The shelves contained Daisy's books, mostly novels but <u>some</u> on occult or mystical subjects.
We need more anti-tank helicopters. There are <u>some,</u> but we need more.

3 **used instead of a noun**

You can use **one** or **ones** instead of a count noun when the noun comes after an adjective. For example, instead of saying 'I've had this car a long time, and I'm thinking of getting a new car', you say 'I've had this car a long time, and I'm thinking of getting **a new one**'.

I got this trumpet for thirty pounds. It's quite <u>a good one.</u>
This idea has become <u>a very influential one.</u>
…buying old houses and building <u>new ones.</u>

You can also use **one** or **ones** instead of a count noun in front of a relative clause or a prepositional phrase.

…a slightly higher class than <u>the one you were born into.</u>
Could I see that map again – <u>the one with lines across it?</u>

You can use **one** instead of a singular count noun when the noun comes immediately after any determiner except 'a'. For example, instead of saying 'I bought these masks when I was in Africa. That mask came from Kenya', you say 'I bought these masks when I was in Africa. **That one** came from Kenya'.

We'll have to have a small fire. <u>This one's</u> too big.
He took the steel tubes and wrapped <u>each one</u> carefully in the sacking.
She had a plateful, then went back for <u>another one.</u>

⚠ **WARNING:** You do not use 'the one' in front of 'of' and a name. You do not say, for example, 'This is my mug. That's the one of Jane'. You say 'This is my mug. That's **Jane's**'.
…a northern accent like <u>Brian's.</u>

4 **'one of'**

You use **one of** in front of a plural noun group to talk about one member of a group of people or things.

<u>One of my students</u> sold me her ticket.
The Institute of Directors (IOD) was <u>one of the few business groups</u> to back the move.

After the noun group you use a singular form of a verb.

One of Mirella Freni's first records <u>was</u> a collection of Puccini arias.
One of them <u>was</u> also a mountain climber.

One of is often used with superlatives.

…Mr Gordon Getty, <u>one of the world's richest men.</u>
It's <u>one of the slowest cars</u> on the market.

5 **used as an impersonal pronoun**

One is sometimes an impersonal pronoun indicating that something is generally done or should generally be done. This is a fairly formal use.

I'm a socialist but <u>one</u> doesn't talk about politics at the club.

Occasionally, you may hear a speaker use **one** instead of 'I' or 'me' simply to refer to himself or herself. This is also a fairly formal use.

One tries to take an interest in what is going on.

The possessive determiner and reflexive pronoun corresponding to this use of **one** are **one's** and **oneself.**

Naturally, one wanted only the best for <u>one's</u> children.
…the fear of making a fool of <u>oneself.</u>

However, when **one** has already been used as the subject of the sentence, some speakers use **his** and **himself** instead of 'one's' and 'oneself'. This use is more common in American English than British English.

In these situations, one has to do <u>his</u> best.

Most British and American speakers do not use 'one' like this at all. Here are some other ways in which you can say that something is generally done or should be done:

6 **'you'**
You can use **you.** This is a fairly common use, especially in conversation. In this book, we usually use **you.**

There are things that have to be done and <u>you</u> do them and <u>you</u> never talk about them.
Instead of saying 'on their arrival', <u>you</u> can just say 'on arrival'.

7 **'people'**
You can use **people.** This is also a fairly common use.

<u>People</u> shouldn't leave jobs unfinished.
I don't think <u>people</u> should make promises they don't mean to keep.

8 **'we'**
You can use **we** to say that something is generally done by a group of people that includes yourself.

If you are not known to the Bank, <u>we</u> usually require someone to speak for you.
<u>We</u> say things in the heat of an argument that <u>we</u> don't really mean.

9 **'they'**
They is sometimes used to refer to people in general, or to a group of people whose identity is not actually stated.

Isn't that what <u>they</u> call love?
<u>They</u> found the body in a dustbin.

Some people use **they** when they are mentioning a saying or repeating a piece of gossip.

<u>They</u> say that the camera never lies – but it doesn't always show the full picture.
He marketed some of his compounds and made a fortune, <u>they say.</u>

10 **the passive**
Instead of using one of these words and an active verb, you can sometimes use a passive verb. This is a fairly common use in formal writing.

If there is swelling and increasing pain, medical advice <u>should be taken.</u>
Bookings <u>must be made</u> by the end of December.

one another
⇨ See **Usage** entry at **each other - one another.**

only
Only can be an adjective or an adverb.

1 **used as an adjective**
You use **only** in front of a noun or **one** to say that something is true about one person, thing, or group and not true about anyone or anything else. In front of **only** you put **the** or a possessive.

USAGE

Grace was the only survivor.
I was the only one smoking.
'Have you a spare one?' – 'No, it's my only copy unfortunately.'

When **only** has this meaning, you must use a noun or **one** after it. You cannot say, for example, 'He was the only to escape'. If you do not want to use a more precise noun, you can use **person** or **thing**. You can say, for example, 'He was **the only person** to escape'.

He was the only person authorized to issue documents of that sort.
It was the only thing they could do.

(i) Note that if you use another adjective or a number, you put **only** in front of it.

The only English city he enjoyed working in was Manchester.
So I probably have the only three copies of the album in existence.

'Only' is not normally used after **an**. There is one common exception: if you say that someone is **an only child,** you mean that they have no brothers or sisters.

As an only child she is accustomed to adult company.

2   used as an adverb

Only is used as an adverb to say that something is the one thing that is done, that happens, or that is relevant in a particular situation, in contrast to all the other things that are not done, do not happen, or are not relevant.

● If **only** applies to the subject of a clause, you put it in front of the subject.

Only his close friends knew how much he idolized his daughters.
…the belief that only a completely different approach will be effective.

● If the verb is **be**, you put **only** after it.

There is only one train that goes from Denmark to Sweden by night.

● If the verb is not 'be' and **only** does not apply to the subject, you usually put it in front of the verb or after the first auxiliary, regardless of what it applies to. For example, instead of saying 'I see my brother only at weekends', you usually say 'I **only** see my brother at weekends'.

The motorist only encounters serious traffic jams in the city centre.
We could only choose two of them.
New technology will only be introduced by mutual agreement.

3   emphatic uses

However, if you want to be quite clear or emphatic, you put **only** immediately in front of the word, word group, or clause it applies to.

He played only instrumental music.
You may borrow only one item at a time.
We excavate only when something interesting is found.

For extra emphasis, you can put **only** after the word or word group that it applies to.

We insisted on being interviewed by women journalists only.
This strategy was used once only.

In writing and formal speech, you can put **only** at the beginning of a sentence, followed by the word, word group, or clause it applies to. After this word, word group, or clause, you put an auxiliary or **be** followed by the subject of the main clause.

Only here was it safe to prepare and handle hot drinks.
Only then did Ginny realize that she still hadn't phoned her mother.
Only when drugs become unavailable will young people become drug-free.

An alternative way of emphasizing is to start with '**It is only**…' or '**It was only**…' and the word or words that you want to emphasize. You put the rest of the sentence in a 'that'-clause.

It is only now that his virtues are beginning to be more widely appreciated.
It was only when he started to take photographs that Defra officials stopped him.

4 **'not only'**

You use **not only** with **but** or **but also** as a way of linking words or word groups.
⇨ For a full explanation, see **Usage** entry at **not only.**

onto

You usually use the preposition **onto** to say where someone or something falls or is put.

He slumped down back onto his pillow.
Place the bread onto a large piece of clean white cloth.

After many verbs you can use either **onto** or **on** with the same meaning.

I fell with a crash onto a sandy bank.
He fell on the floor with a thud.
Stuart put the reel of film onto the bench.
I put a hand on his shoulder.

However, after verbs meaning **climb** or **lift** you should use **onto,** rather than 'on'.

She climbed up onto his lap.
The little boy was hoisted onto a piano stool.

If you hold **onto** something, you put your hand round it or against it in order to prevent yourself from falling. After verbs meaning **hold,** you use **onto** as a preposition and **on** as an adverb.

She had to hold onto the edge of the table.
I couldn't put up my umbrella and hold on at the same time.
We were both hanging onto the side of the boat.
He had to hang on to avoid being washed overboard.

(i) Note that **onto** is sometimes written as two words **on to.**

She sank on to a chair.

open

Open can be a verb or an adjective.

1 **used as a verb**

If you **open** something such as a door, you move it so that it no longer covers a hole or gap.

She opened the door with her key.
He opened the window and looked out.

⚠ **WARNING:** When you use **open** with a person as the subject, you must put an object after it. You do not say, for example, 'I went to the door and opened'. You say 'I went to the door and **opened it** '.

I went to the starboard door, opened it, and looked out.

When you are telling a story, you can use **open** as an intransitive verb, with a noun group such as **the door** or **the window** as the subject.

The door opened and a staff officer hurried in.
The gates opened and the procession began.

2 **used as an adjective**

When a door or window is not covering the hole or gap it is intended to cover, you say that it is **open.**

The door was open.
He was sitting by the open window of the office.

⚠ **WARNING:** When a door or window is in this position, you do not say that it is 'opened'. **Opened** is the past tense or past participle of the verb **open.** You only use it when you are describing the action of opening a door or window.

The front door was opened, then slammed shut.

USAGE

3 | used after other verbs

Open can be used after other verbs of position besides 'be'.

The doors of the ninth-floor rooms hung open.
The front door gaped open.

You can also use **open** after verbs of movement such as **push**.

Buller pushed the door fully open.
He noticed the way in which the drawer slid open.

(i) Note that **open** is one of several words that can be used after verbs of position or movement like this. Others are **closed, shut, free, loose, straight**, and **upright**. These words are sometimes considered to be adverbs and sometimes adjectives.

⚠ **WARNING:** You do not use **open** as a verb or adjective to talk about electrical devices. For example, if someone causes an electrical device to work by pressing a switch or turning a knob, you do not say that they 'open' it. You say that they **put it on, switch it on**, or **turn it on**.

Do you mind if I put the light on?
I went across and switched on the TV.
I turned on the radio as I always did upon waking.

opinion

Your **opinion** of something is what you think about it.

We would like to have your opinion.
The students were eager to express their opinions.

When you want to indicate whose opinion you are giving, you can use an expression such as '**in my opinion…**', '**in Sarah's opinion…**', or '**in the opinion of the voters…**'.

In my opinion, there are four key problems that have to be addressed.
In King's opinion, rioting was 'absolutely wrong' as a form of protest.
In the opinion of the Court of Appeal the sentence was too lenient.

In formal speech or writing, people sometimes say '**It is my opinion that…**' or '**It is our opinion that…**'

It is my opinion that high school students should have the vote.

(i) Note that you do not say 'To my opinion…' or 'According to my opinion…'.

⇨ See **Usage** entry at **point of view - view - opinion**.

opportunity

1 | 'opportunity'

An **opportunity** is a situation in which it is possible for something to be done. You talk about an **opportunity for** something or an **opportunity to do** something.

They must regard it as an opportunity for a genuine new start.
They don't even give them the opportunity to become better.

(i) Note that you can use either **the** or **an** in front of **opportunity** in sentences like these.

You can also talk about an **opportunity for doing** something, especially if you use an adjective such as **perfect** or **excellent** in front of **opportunity**.

This was a marvellous opportunity for exchanging gossip with the other girls.
This provides an excellent opportunity for bird-watching.

You can also talk about **the opportunity of doing** something.

This gave him the opportunity of developing his talent as a teacher.

(i) Note that you do not use 'an' in front of **opportunity** when it is followed by **of**.

2 | 'no opportunity'

You can say there is **no opportunity to do** something.

I suppose you had <u>no opportunity to bring</u> it.
For some reason he had had <u>no opportunity to eat</u> the day before.

(*i*) Note that you do not say that there is 'no opportunity of doing' something.

3 **'chance'**
Chance is used in a similar way to **opportunity**.

⇨ See **Usage** entry at **chance**.

opposite

Opposite can be a preposition, a noun, or an adjective.

1 **used as a preposition**
If one building or room is **opposite** another, they are separated from each other by a street or corridor.

The hotel is <u>opposite</u> a railway station.
The bathroom was located <u>opposite</u> my room.

If two people are **opposite** each other, they are facing each other, for example when they are sitting at the same table.

Lynn was sitting <u>opposite</u> him.
He drank off half <u>his</u> beer, still eyeing the Englishman <u>opposite</u> him.

Note that speakers of American English usually say **across from** rather than 'opposite' in both of the above senses.

Stinson has rented a home <u>across from</u> his parents.
He took a seat on one side of the table, and Judy sat <u>across from</u> him.

2 **used as a noun**
If two things or people are totally different from each other in some way, you can say that one is **the opposite of** the other.

The <u>opposite of</u> right is wrong.
He was <u>the exact opposite of</u> Herbert, of course.

You can use **the opposite** without 'of', if it is clear what you are making a contrast with.

Well, whatever he says you can bet he's thinking <u>the opposite</u>.
They take the statement as true because <u>the opposite</u> is inconceivable.

⚠ **WARNING**: You do not express difference by saying that one thing or person is 'opposite' another.

3 **used as an adjective**
Opposite can be an adjective either in front of a noun or after a noun, but with different meanings.

You use **opposite** in front of a noun when you are mentioning one of two sides of something.

I was moved to a room on the <u>opposite</u> side of the corridor.
On the <u>opposite</u> side of the room a telephone rang.

You also use **opposite** in front of a noun when you are talking about something which is totally different from something else in some way.

Holmes took the <u>opposite</u> point of view.
Such a policy would not promote human rights, it would achieve the <u>opposite</u> result.

You use **opposite** after a noun when you are mentioning someone or something that is on the other side of a street, corridor, room, or table from yourself.

The elderly woman <u>opposite</u> glanced up at the ventilation window.
In one of the smart new houses <u>opposite</u>, a party was in progress.

(*i*) Note that the same building can be referred to as 'the house on **the opposite** side of the street' or 'the house **opposite**'. You do not refer to it as 'the opposite house'.

USAGE

4 'opposed'

Do not confuse **opposite** with **opposed**. If someone is **opposed to** something, they disagree with it or disapprove of it.

I am opposed to capital punishment.

---

or

1 basic uses

You use **or** when you are mentioning two or more alternatives or possibilities. You use **or** to link nouns, noun groups, adjectives, adjuncts, verbs, or clauses.

Would you like some coffee or tea, Dr Floyd?
A bad tax or an unjust law can be changed.
It is better to defer planting if the ground is very wet or frosty.
Girls may do some work with their mothers in the fields or help in the house.

2 used with negative words

You use **or** instead of 'and' after using a negative word. For example, you say 'I do not like coffee or tea'. You do not say 'I do not like coffee and tea'.

The situation is just not fair on the children or their parents.
I am not detached or remote.

3 verb agreement

When you link two or more nouns using **or**, you use a plural verb after plural count nouns, and a singular verb after singular count nouns or uncount nouns.

Even minor amendments or innovations were given heavy publicity.
If your son or daughter is taking drugs, it is no use being angry.

4 'either ... or'

You use **either** with **or** when you are mentioning two alternatives and you want to indicate that no other alternatives are possible. **Either** goes in front of the first alternative and **or** goes in front of the second one.

Most of the fuel rods were either wholly melted down or substantially damaged.

⇨ See **Usage** entry at **either ... or.**

⚠ **WARNING:** You do not use 'or' after **neither.** You use **nor** instead.

He speaks neither English nor German.

⇨ See **Usage** entry at **neither ... nor.**

5 linking more than two items

When you link more than two items, you usually only put **or** in front of the last one. After each of the others you put a comma. Often the comma is omitted in front of **or.**

...flying from Heathrow, Manchester, Gatwick, or Glasgow.
The costs of progress are all too often ignored, concealed or written off.

6 used to begin a sentence

You do not normally put **or** at the beginning of a sentence, but you can sometimes do so when you are reporting what someone says or thinks.

I may go home and have a steak. Or I may have some spaghetti.
They say dogs grow to be like their masters. Or is it the other way round?

7 used for correcting

You can use **or** when you are correcting a mistake you have made, or when you think of a more appropriate word or expression than the one you have just used.

The man was a fool, he thought, or at least incompetent.

When you use **or** like this, you often put **rather** after it.

He explained what the Crux is, or rather, what it was.

oral
⇨ See **Usage** entry at **aural - oral**.

ordinary
⇨ See **Usage** entry at **usual - usually**.

or else
⇨ See **Usage** entry at **else**.

other

1 **'the other'**

When you are talking about two people or things and have already referred to one of them, you refer to the second one as **the other** or **the other one**.

They had two little daughters, one a baby, <u>the other</u> a girl of twelve.
He blew out one of his candles and moved <u>the other one.</u>

2 **'the others'**

When you are talking about several people or things and have already referred to one or more of them, you usually refer to the remaining ones as **the others**.

Jack and <u>the others</u> paid no attention.
First, concentrate only on the important tasks, then move on to <u>the others.</u>

3 **'others'**

When you have been talking about some people or things of a particular type, you refer to more people or things of this type as **others**.

Some players are better than <u>others</u> in varied weather conditions.
One policeman was stabbed and three <u>others</u> received minor injuries.

ⓘ Note that you do not use 'the' with **others** in sentences like these. You do not say, for example, '~~Some writers are greater than the others~~'.

4 **'another'**

When you have been talking about people or things of a particular type, you refer to one more person or thing of this type as **another** or **another one**.

I saw one girl whispering to <u>another.</u>
She had one plateful and then went back for <u>another one.</u>

⇨ See **Usage** entry at **another**.

5 **used in front of nouns**

The other, other, and **another** can be used in a similar way in front of count nouns.

I was happy there, in spite of not getting on all that well with <u>the other girls.</u>
The roof was covered with straw and <u>other materials.</u>
He opened <u>another shop</u> last month.

otherwise

1 **use and position in clause**

You use **otherwise** when you are mentioning an undesirable situation which would occur if something did not happen. You usually put **otherwise** at the beginning of a clause.

Well you've got to laugh, haven't you? <u>Otherwise</u>, you'd cry.
I'm lucky that I'm interested in school work, <u>otherwise</u> I'd go mad.

⚠ **WARNING:** You do not use 'or' in front of **otherwise**.

2 **used in relative clauses**

Otherwise is sometimes used in a relative clause that contains a modal. You put **otherwise** after the modal or at the end of the clause.

They support services which would <u>otherwise</u> be uneconomic.
He was lured into a crime he would not <u>otherwise</u> have committed.
We have met interesting people over the years, people we wouldn't have met <u>otherwise.</u>

ought to

⇨ See **Usage** entry at **should - ought to.**

out

1 **'out of'**

When you go **out** of a place or get **out of** something such as a vehicle, you leave it, so that you are no longer inside it.

She rushed <u>out of</u> the house.
He got <u>out of</u> the car.
She's just got <u>out of</u> bed.

(*i*) Note that in standard English you must use **of** in sentences like these. You do not say, for example, 'He got out the car'.

⇨ For more information about **go out** and **get out**, see **Usage** entry at **go out.**

You do not usually use 'from' after **out**. However, you use **from** in front of another preposition such as **behind** or **under**.

He came <u>out from behind</u> the table.

2 **'out' used as an adverb**

You can use **out** as an adverb to say that someone leaves a place.

I ran <u>out</u> and slammed the door.
Why don't we go <u>out</u> into the garden?

If someone is **out**, they are not at home.

He came when I was <u>out.</u>

outdoors - outdoor

1 **'outdoors'**

Outdoors is an adverb. If something happens **outdoors**, it does not happen inside any building.

He spent a good deal of his time <u>outdoors.</u>
School classes were held <u>outdoors.</u>

When someone goes out of a building, you do not usually say that they go 'outdoors'. You say that they go **outside**.

⇨ See **Usage** entry at **outside.**

2 **'outdoor'**

Outdoor is an adjective used in front of a noun. You use it to describe things or activities that exist or take place in the open air, rather than inside a building.

…an <u>outdoor</u> play area.
If you enjoy <u>outdoor</u> activities, this is the trip for you.

outside

Outside can be a preposition or an adverb.

1 **used as a preposition**

When someone or something is close to a building but not actually inside it, you say that they are **outside** the building.

I parked <u>outside</u> the hotel.
There are queues for jobs <u>outside</u> the shipping offices.

(*i*) Note that in standard English you do not say that someone is 'outside of' a building.

2 **used as an adverb**

You can also say that someone or something is **outside** or that something is happening **outside**.

The shouting <u>outside</u> grew louder.
Please could you come and fetch me in 20 mins, I'll be waiting <u>outside</u>.

When you go **outside**, you leave a building and go into the open air, but stay quite close to the building.

When they went <u>outside</u>, a light snow was falling.
Go <u>outside</u> and play for a bit.

If you leave a building in order to go some distance from it, you do not say that you go 'outside'. You say that you go **out**.

Towards dark he went <u>out</u>.
I have to go <u>out</u>. I'll be back late tonight.

You can also say that someone is **outside** when they are close to a room, for example in a hallway or corridor.

I'd better wait <u>outside</u> in the corridor.
Your father's lawyer is waiting <u>outside</u>.

3 **another meaning of 'outside'**

You can also talk about someone or something being **outside** a country. When **outside** is used like this, it does not have 'near' as part of its meaning. If you are **outside** a country, you can be near to the country or a long way away from it.

…if you have lived <u>outside</u> Britain.

---

over

Over is a preposition used in several different ways.

1 **position**

If one thing is **over** another thing, it is directly above it.

I had reached the little bridge <u>over</u> the stream.
…the monument <u>over</u> the west door.

2 **movement**

If you go **over** something, you cross it and get to the other side.

Castle stepped <u>over</u> the dog.
…on the way back <u>over</u> the Channel.

3 **age**

If someone is **over** a particular age, they are older than that age.

She was well <u>over</u> fifty.

4 **time**

If something happens **over** a period of time, it happens during that time.

He'd had flu <u>over</u> Christmas.
Many strikes <u>over</u> the last few years have not ended successfully.

If you do something **over** a meal, you do it while you are eating the meal.

It's often easier to discuss difficult ideas <u>over</u> lunch.

⇨ For more information on **over**, see **Usage** entry at **above - over**.

---

overseas

Overseas can be an adverb or an adjective.

1 **used as an adverb**

If you go **overseas**, you visit a foreign country which is separated from your own country by sea.

Roughly 4 million Americans travel <u>overseas</u> each year.

USAGE

2 used as an adjective

Overseas is used in front of a noun to describe things relating to countries across the sea from your own country. **Overseas** has a similar meaning to 'foreign', but is more formal. You use it especially when talking about trade, finance, and travel.

...major programmes of <u>overseas</u> aid.
...on a recent <u>overseas</u> visit.

(*i*) Note that you do not use **overseas** after **be** with this meaning. If you say that someone **is overseas,** you do not mean that they are foreign; you mean that they are visiting a foreign country.

Mr Barton <u>is overseas</u> and was unavailable for comment last night.

overweight

⇨ See **Usage** entry at **fatness.**

owing to

⇨ See **Usage** entry at **due to.**

own

1 used after a possessive

If you want to emphasize that something belongs or relates to a particular person or thing, you use **own** after a possessive.

I took no notice till I heard <u>my own</u> name mentioned.
These people have total confidence in <u>their own</u> ability.
How far it also influenced <u>the King's own</u> beliefs, we cannot now be certain.
Now <u>the nuclear industry's own</u> experts support these claims.

2 'own' with a number

If you are also using a number, you put the number after **own.** You say, for example, 'She had given the same advice to her **own three** children'. You do not say 'She had given the same advice to her three own children'.

She was younger than my <u>own two</u> daughters.

3 'of your own'

You do not use **own** after 'an'. You do not say, for example, 'I've got an own place'. You say 'I've got **my own** place' or 'I've got a place **of my own**'.

By this time Laura had got <u>her own</u> radio.
She says we cannot have <u>our own</u> key to the apartment.
What you need is a dry, clear, sparkling lemonade with little flavour <u>of its own.</u>

4 emphasizing 'own'

You can use **very** in front of **own** for emphasis.

...the aptly-named Inside Out, the prison's <u>very own</u> pop group.
Accountants have a language of their <u>very own.</u>

5 'own' without a noun

You can use **own** without a noun after it, when it is clear what you are talking about. However, there must always be a possessive in front of it.

...people whose principles and values they had thought were the same as <u>their own.</u>
I refused to clean the cell unless I was given clothes other than <u>my own</u> to wear.

6 'on your own'

If you are **on your own,** you are alone.

She lived <u>on her own.</u>

If you do something **on your own,** you do it without any help from anyone else.

We can't solve this problem <u>on our own.</u>

P p

pace - footstep - footprint

1 'pace'

A **pace** is a step of normal length that you take when you walk.

He'd only gone a few paces before he stopped again.
The waiter stepped back a pace, watching his customer carefully.

2 'footstep'

You do not use 'pace' to refer to the sound made by a person's step. The word you use is **footstep.**

They heard footsteps and turned round.

3 'footprint'

You also do not use 'pace' to refer to a mark in the ground made by a person's foot. The word you use is **footprint.**

There were no footprints or any signs of how the burglars got in.

package

⇨ See **Usage** entry at **parcel - package - packet.**

packet

⇨ See **Usage** entry at **parcel - package - packet.**

painful

1 'painful'

You say that something is **painful** when it makes you feel pain.

My boots are still painful.
…a long and painful illness.

If a part of your body is **painful,** it hurts.

My back is so painful that I cannot stand upright.
My legs are stiff but not painful.

2 'in pain'

When someone feels pain, you do not say that they are 'painful'. You say that they are **in pain.**

He was in pain and could not move into a comfortable position.

pair - couple

1 'a pair of'

A **pair of** things are two things of the same size and shape that are used together, such as shoes.

… a pair of new gloves.
He bought a pair of hiking boots.

When you use **a pair of** like this, you can use either a singular or a plural form of a verb with it.

He put on a pair of brown shoes which were waiting there for him.
Not a single pair of shoes was on display.

You also use **a pair of** when you are referring to something which has two main parts of the same size and shape, such as trousers, glasses, or scissors.

USAGE

She put on <u>a pair of</u> glasses.
There would be a razor in the bathroom or <u>a pair of</u> scissors.

When you use **a pair of** like this, you use a singular form of a verb with it.

On a hook behind the door <u>was</u> an old pair of grey trousers.
A good pair of binoculars <u>is</u> essential if you want to spot these birds.

2 'a couple of'

A couple of people or things are two people or things.

They've been helped by <u>a couple of</u> newspaper reporters.
We'd had <u>a couple of</u> dances.

You use a plural form of a verb with **a couple of.**

There <u>were</u> a couple of tables littered with saucepans.
On the hallstand <u>were</u> a couple of periodicals.

(i) Note that you do not use 'a couple of' in formal writing.

3 referring to two people as a 'pair'

Two people who do something together or are involved in a relationship together can be referred to as a **pair.** This is a slightly humorous use.

They'd always been a devoted <u>pair.</u>
They were a somewhat sinister <u>pair.</u>

When **pair** is used like this, you use a plural form of a verb with it.

The pair <u>were</u> wanted for the theft of certain jewellery.

4 referring to two people as a 'couple'

You refer to two people as a **couple** when they have an intimate relationship such as that of husband and wife or boyfriend and girlfriend.

In Venice we met a South African <u>couple.</u>
This would raise pensions for married <u>couples</u> considerably.

You usually use a plural form of a verb with **couple.**

Behind me a couple <u>were</u> pushing a pram.

pants - shorts

In British English, **pants** are a piece of clothing worn by men, women, or children under their other clothes. Pants have two holes to put your legs through and elastic round the waist or hips to keep them up.

Men's pants are sometimes referred to as **underpants.** Women's pants are sometimes referred to as **panties** or **knickers.**

I put on my bra and <u>pants.</u>

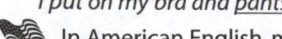 In American English, men's pants are usually referred to as **shorts** or **underpants.** Women's pants are usually referred to as **panties.**

In American English, **pants** are men's or women's trousers.

He wore brown corduroy <u>pants</u> and a white cotton shirt.

In both British and American English, **shorts** are also short trousers that leave your knees and part of your thighs bare.

Both **pants** and **shorts** are plural nouns. You use a plural form of a verb with them.

The pants <u>were</u> big in the waist.
His grey shorts <u>were</u> sticking to him with sweat.

⚠ **WARNING:** You do not talk about 'a pants' or 'a shorts'. You say **a pair of pants** or **a pair of shorts.**

It doesn't take long to choose <u>a pair of pants.</u>
He is wearing <u>a pair of shorts</u> and a thin sweater.

You usually use a singular form of a verb with **a pair of pants** or **a pair of shorts**.
I like a pair of pants that fits well.

---

paper

Paper is the material that you write things on or wrap things in.
The students will all be equipped with pencils and paper.

You can refer to several sheets of paper with information on them as **papers**.
He consulted the papers on his knee.

However, you do not refer to a single sheet of paper as a 'paper'. You refer to it as a **sheet of paper** or, if it is small, as a **piece of paper.**
He wrote his name at the top of a blank sheet of paper.
Rudolph picked up the piece of paper and gave it to her.

Newspapers are often referred to as **papers**.
I read about the riots in the papers.
… The Daily News, the country's largest daily paper.

---

parcel - package - packet

1 **'parcel' and 'package'**

A **parcel** or **package** is an object or group of objects wrapped in paper that can be carried somewhere or sent by post. There is very little difference in meaning between these two words. A **parcel** usually has a more regular shape than a **package.**
International charities sent parcels of food and clothes to the refugees.
I am taking this package to the post office.

 In American English, **package** is more common than **parcel.**

2 **'packet'**

A **packet** is a small container in which a quantity of something is sold. Packets are either small boxes made of thin cardboard, or bags or envelopes made of paper or plastic.
The room was littered with cups and cigarette packets.
Check the washing instructions on the packet.

 In American English, containers like these are usually called **packages** or **packs**.

You can use **a packet of** or **a package of** to refer either to a packet or package and its contents, or to the contents only.
He took a package of cigarettes out of his pocket.
All I've had to eat today is a packet of crisps.

---

pardon

In old-fashioned English, if you **pardon** someone's behaviour or attitudes, you forgive them for them.
She asked him to pardon her rudeness.

You can apologize to someone by saying **'I beg your pardon'.**

 Some American speakers say **'Pardon me'.**

⇨ See **Topic** entry at **Apologizing.**

---

parking - car park

 Note that you do not use the word 'parking' to refer to a place where cars are parked. Instead, you talk about a **car park** in British English and a **parking lot** in American English.
A multi-storey car park with room for 300 cars has already opened.
The high school parking lot was filled with police cars.

part 356

USAGE

Parking is used only to refer to the action of parking your car, or to the state of being parked.

...a 'No Parking ' sign.

part

Part can be a noun or a verb.

1 **used as a noun**

Part of or **a part of** something is one of the pieces or elements that it consists of. You use **part of** or **a part of** in front of the singular form of a count noun, or in front of an uncount noun.

Economic measures must form part of any solution to this crisis.
Conducting business online has become a part of everyday life.

2 **'some of'**

You do not use 'part of' or 'a part of' in front of a plural noun group. You do not say, for example, 'Part of the soldiers have no rifles'. You say '**Some of** the soldiers have no rifles'.

Some of the singers were having trouble getting to the theatre.
Some of them went up north.

Similarly, you do not say 'A large part of the houses have flat roofs'. You say '**Many of** the houses have flat roofs'.

Many of the old people were blind.

⇨ See **Usage** entries at **some** and **many**.

3 **used as a verb**

When **part** is a verb, it is usually followed by **from** or **with**.

If you **part from** someone, you leave them, or you stop having a relationship with them. This is a formal or literary use.

He has confirmed he is parting from his Swedish-born wife Eva.

If you **are parted from** someone or something, you cannot be with them, although you would like to be.

He had never been parted from her before.
It's natural that a mother should not wish to be parted from her children.

If you **part with** something that is valuable or that you would prefer to keep, you give it or sell it to someone else.

She didn't want to part with the money.
I took the book, thanked her, and told her I would never part with it.

partly

⇨ See section on **extent** in **Grammar** entry at **Adjuncts.**

party

A **party** is a social event at which people enjoy themselves by eating, drinking, dancing, talking, or playing games. When someone organizes a party, you say that they **have, give,** or **throw** it. **Throw** is informal.

We are having a party on the beach.
She and Tim were giving a party.
We threw a huge birthday party.

ⓘ Note that you do not say that someone 'makes' a party.

pass

The verb **pass** is used with several different meanings.

1 **movement**

If you **pass** someone or something, you go past them.

We passed the New Hotel.
Please let us pass.

 In American English, **pass** is used if you go past a vehicle which is ahead of you and moving in the same direction. In British English, the word **overtake** is used in this meaning.

The getaway car passed another car at an estimated 100 mph.
When he eventually overtook the last truck, he pulled over to the inside lane.

If you **pass** something to someone, you take it in your hand and give it to them.

She passed me her glass.
Pass me Philip's card, would you?

2 time

If you **pass** time in a particular way, you spend it that way.

We passed a pleasant afternoon together.
Am I to pass all my life abroad?

⇨ For more information about this use of **pass,** see **Usage** entry at **spend - pass.**

3 tests and exams

If you **pass** a test or exam, you are successful in it.

I passed my driving test in Holland.
She told me that I had passed.

> ⚠ **WARNING:** If you want to say that someone has completed a test or exam, without mentioning the result, you do not say that they have 'passed' the test or exam. You say that they have **taken** it.
>
> *She 's not yet taken her driving test.*
> *She took her degree last year.*

past

1 time before the present

Past can be a noun or adjective referring to a period of time before the present.

He never discussed his past.
I've spent most of the past eight years at sea.

2 telling the time

In British English, when you are telling the time, you use **past** to say how many minutes it is after a particular hour.

It's ten past eleven.
I went back to bed and slept until quarter past eight.

 American speakers usually say **after.**

It's ten after eleven.
I arrived back in my room around a quarter after twelve.

⇨ For other ways of telling the time, see **Topic** entry at **Time.**

3 going near something

Past is also used as a preposition or adverb to say that someone goes near something when they are moving in a particular direction.

He walked past Lock's hat shop.
People ran past laughing.

4 'passed'

You do not use 'past' as the past tense or past participle of the verb **pass.** The word you use is **passed.**

As she passed the library door, the telephone began to ring.
The Act was passed at the end of last year.

USAGE

patriotic
⇨ See **Usage** entry at **national - nationalist - nationalistic - patriotic.**

pay

Pay can be a verb or noun used to talk about money. The past tense and past participle of the verb is **paid,** not 'payed'.

1 used as a verb

If you **pay for** something which has been done or provided, you give money to the person doing or providing it.

Pupils would be <u>paid for</u> any work they did.
Willie <u>paid for</u> the drinks.

(i) Note that you must use **for** after **pay** in sentences like these.

⚠ **WARNING:** If you pay for a drink that is drunk by someone else, you do not say that you 'pay' them the drink. You say that you **buy** them the drink.

Let me <u>buy</u> you a drink.
Monty <u>bought</u> Kaspar at least half-a-dozen whiskies.

If you pay for a meal that is eaten by someone else, you do not say that you 'pay' them the meal. You say that you **buy** them the meal or **treat** them **to** it.

I'll <u>buy</u> you lunch.
She offered to <u>treat</u> them <u>to</u> dinner.

2 used as a noun

A person's **pay** is their wages or salary.

She lost three weeks' <u>pay</u>.
They paid 6.5 per cent of their <u>pay</u> to the National Insurance Fund.

(i) Note that you do not use 'a' with **pay.** You do not say, for example, 'It is a good pay'. You say 'The **pay** is good'.

The <u>pay</u> is dreadful.

3 other meanings

You can say that someone **pays** a call or a visit.

We went to <u>pay</u> a call on some people I used to know.
It would be nice if you <u>paid</u> me a visit.

⇨ See **Usage** entries at **call** and **visit.**

You can also say that someone **pays** attention to something.

Look, <u>pay</u> attention to what I'm saying.

⇨ See **Usage** entry at **attention.**

penny

Pennies usually refers to a number of individual coins.

He took two <u>pennies</u> out of his pocket.

You use **pence** or **p** when you are talking about a sum of money.

It only cost fifty <u>pence</u>.
Admission for children is 50<u>p</u>.

⇨ See **Topic** entry at **Money.**

people - person

1 'people'

People is a plural noun. You use a plural form of a verb after it.
People is most commonly used to refer to a particular group of men and women.

There were 120 people at the lecture.
We'll talk to the people concerned and see how they feel.

People can also be used to refer to a group of men, women, and children.

…the Great Fire of Chicago, when 250 people were killed.

You often use **people** to refer to all the men, women, and children of a particular country, tribe, or race.

The British people deserve a lot better.

2 'peoples'

When you are referring to the men, women, and children of several countries, tribes, or races, you can use the plural form **peoples.**

Mediterranean peoples gesticulate more freely than northern Europeans.

3 another use of 'people'

People can also be used to say that something is generally done.

I don't think people should make promises they don't mean to keep.
She could not resist being unkind to people.

(*i*) Note that there are several ways of saying that something is generally done.

⇨ For more information, see **Usage** entry at **one.**

4 'person'

Person is a count noun. A **person** is an individual man, woman, or child.

There was far too much meat for one person.
They think you are a suitable person to join the church.

The usual plural of **person** is **people,** but in formal English **persons** is sometimes used.

The bomb exploded killing 111 persons.

percentage - per cent

When you express an amount as a **percentage** of a whole, you say how many parts the amount would have if the whole had 100 equal parts. You write a percentage as a number followed by **per cent** or by the symbol **%.** So, for example, if there are 1000 people living in a village and 250 of them are children, you say that **25 per cent (25%)** of the people in the village are children.

What is the percentage of nitrogen in air?
He won 28.3 per cent of the vote.

 Per cent is sometimes written as one word, especially in American English.

Remember that 90 percent of most food is water.

You also use **percentage** to indicate roughly how large or small an amount is as a proportion of a whole. For example, you can say that an amount is **a large percentage** or **a small percentage** of a whole.

It's a tiny percentage of the total income.
A high percentage of the share capital is held by Scottish institutions.

When **percentage** is used like this in front of the plural form of a noun, you use a plural form of a verb after it.

A good percentage of the people were his own age.

When **percentage** is used in front of a singular form, you use a singular form of a verb after it.

A high percentage of the pet population has been adopted off the streets.

perfect

1 'perfect'

Something that is **perfect** is as good as it can possibly be.

She speaks perfect English.
I've got the perfect solution.

In conversation, some people use **perfect** to mean 'very good indeed'. It is fairly common for people to say that one thing is **more perfect** than another, or that something is the **most perfect** thing of its kind.

The resulting film is more perfect than a genuine live broadcast.
Some claim its acoustics to be the most perfect in the world.

2 'perfectly'

You do not use 'perfect' as an adverb. You do not say, for example, 'She did it perfect'. You say 'She did it **perfectly**'.

The plan worked perfectly.
He was dressed perfectly.

perhaps
⇨ See **Usage** entry at **maybe - perhaps**.

permissible - permissive

1 'permissible'

If something is **permissible,** you are allowed to have it or do it, because it does not break any rules, laws, or conventions.

Towing caravans up to 2.30m wide are permissible in Norway.
I understood that it was permissible to ask a question.

2 'permissive'

A **permissive** society or person tolerates things which some people disapprove of, especially freedom of sexual behaviour.

We live in a permissive age.
Baby-boomers are realising that their permissive approach didn't work.

permission

If someone gives you **permission** to do something, they say they will allow you to do it.

He gave me permission to go.
You can't do it without permission.

Permission is an uncount noun. You do not talk about 'permissions' or 'a permission'.

When you ask for permission to do something and are given it, you say that you **get** or **obtain** permission to do it.

I went as often as I could get permission.
Consul-General Lee obtained permission for an autopsy.

ⓘ Note that you do not say that someone 'takes' permission to do something.

When you have been given permission to do something, you say that you **have** or **have got** permission to do it.

I have permission to tell you how things went in Bonn.
We 've got permission to climb the Tower.

permissive
⇨ See **Usage** entry at **permissible - permissive**.

permit
⇨ See **Usage** entry at **allow - permit - let**.

persecute - prosecute

1 'persecute'

To **persecute** someone means to continually treat them badly and make them suffer, for example because of their political or religious beliefs.

Members of these sects <u>are</u> ruthlessly <u>persecuted</u>.
They claim that nobody <u>is persecuted</u> for religious belief.

2 **'prosecute'**

To **prosecute** someone means to accuse them of a crime and bring criminal charges against them.

He <u>was prosecuted</u> for drunken driving.
Trespassers <u>will be prosecuted.</u>

person
⇨ See **Usage** entry at **people - person.**

personal - personnel

1 **'personal'**

Personal /pɜːʳsənəl/ is an adjective. You use it to say that something belongs or relates to a particular person.

This is my <u>personal</u> opinion.
…books, furniture, and other <u>personal</u> belongings.

2 **'personnel'**

Personnel /pɜːʳsənel/ is a noun. The **personnel** of a company or organization are the people who work for it.

We've advertised for extra security <u>personnel</u>.
There has been very little renewal of <u>personnel</u> in higher education.

Personnel is a plural noun. You do not talk about 'personnels' or 'a personnel'.

persuade
⇨ See **Usage** entry at **convince - persuade.**

petrol
⇨ See **Usage** entry at **gas - petrol.**

pharmacist
⇨ See **Usage** entry at **chemist - pharmacist.**

pharmacy
⇨ See **Usage** entry at **chemist's - drugstore - pharmacy.**

phenomenon

A **phenomenon** is something that happens or exists and that can be seen or experienced.

We are witnessing a very significant <u>phenomenon</u>.
Many theories have been put forward to explain this <u>phenomenon</u>.

The plural of **phenomenon** is **phenomena,** not 'phenomenons'.

…scientific explanations of natural <u>phenomena</u>.
All of these <u>phenomena</u> required explanation.

⚠ **WARNING: Phenomena** is only a plural form. You do not talk about 'a phenomena' or 'this phenomena'.

phone

When you **phone** someone, you dial their phone number and speak to them by phone.

I went back to the motel to <u>phone</u> Jenny.
I <u>phoned</u> him and offered him a large salary.

USAGE

You can also **phone** a place.

He phoned the police station and spoke to the officer in charge.
Each day we phoned Geneva Airport for a weather forecast.

(i) Note that you do not use 'to' after **phone**.

physician - physicist

1 **'physician'**

A **physician** is a doctor, especially one who treats illnesses or injuries using medicine rather than surgery. **Physician** is a formal or old-fashioned word.

…a highly respected Victorian physician and surgeon .

2 **'physicist'**

A **physicist** is a person who studies physics or does research connected with physics.

…a nuclear physicist.

physique - physics

1 **'physique'**

Your **physique** /fɪziːk/ is the shape and size of your body.

…a good-looking lad with a fine physique.

2 **'physics'**

You do not use 'physique' to refer to the scientific study of such things as heat, light, sound, and electricity. The word you use is **physics** /fɪzɪks/.

…nuclear physics.

pick

⇨ See **Usage** entry at **choose**.

picture

⇨ See **Usage** entry at **film**.

pile

⇨ See **Usage** entry at **heap - stack - pile**.

place

Place is usually a noun.

1 **used in descriptions**

You can use it after an adjective when you are describing a building, room, town, or area of land. For example, instead of saying 'Richmond is nice', you can say 'Richmond is a nice **place**'.

It's a beautiful place.
He's building himself a really comfortable place to live in.

2 **saying where something is**

You can say where something is using **the place** followed by a clause beginning with **where**. For example, you can say 'This is **the place where** I parked my car'.

He reached the place where I was standing.
He said he would walk with me to the place where I had been knocked down.

⚠ **WARNING:** You do not use 'where' with a 'to'-infinitive after **place**. You do not say, for example, 'I'm looking for a place where to park my car'. You say 'I'm looking for **a place to park** my car' or 'I'm looking for **a place where I can park** my car'. You can also say 'I'm looking for **somewhere to park** my car'.

I always tried to find a place to hide.
It was a place where they could go swimming or surfing.
We had to find somewhere to stop for lunch.

3 **'anywhere'**
In British English, you do not usually use 'place' after 'any' in questions or negative statements. You do not say, for example, 'She never goes to any place without her sister'. You say 'She never goes **anywhere** without her sister'.
I changed my mind and decided not to go anywhere.
Is there an ashtray anywhere?

In American English, **anyplace** is sometimes used (without 'to') instead of **anywhere**.
He doesn't stay anyplace for very long.

4 **'there'**
You do not use 'that place' to refer to somewhere that has just been mentioned. You do not say, for example, 'I drove my car into a field and left it in that place'. You say 'I drove my car into a field and left it **there**'.
I decided to try Newmarket. I soon found a job there.
I must get home. Bill's there on his own.

5 **'seat'**
You can use **place** or, more often, **seat** to refer to somewhere where someone can sit.
There was only one seat free on the train.

6 **'room'**
You do not use 'place' as an uncount noun to refer to an open or empty area. You should use **room** or **space** instead. **Room** is more likely to be used when you are talking about space inside an enclosed area.
There's not enough room in the bathroom for both of us.
Leave plenty of space between you and the car in front.

7 **'place' used as a verb**
Place is sometimes a verb with the same meaning as 'put'.
Some of the women lit candles and placed them carefully among the flowers.

⇨ See **Usage** entry at **place - put.**

8 **'take place'**
When something **takes place**, it happens.
The talks will take place in Vienna.
...the changes which are taking place at the moment.

⇨ See **Usage** entry at **take place.**

place - put

1 **'place' and 'put'**
The verbs **place** and **put** are often used with the same meaning. **Place** is more formal than **put,** and is mainly used in writing.
If you **place** something somewhere, you put it there. You often use **place** to say that someone puts something somewhere neatly or carefully.
She placed the music on the piano and sat down.
Each piece of furniture is carefully placed, as in a gallery.

2 **pressure**
If you **place** or **put** pressure on someone, you urge them to do something.
Renewed pressure will be placed on the Government this week.
He may have put pressure on her to agree.

3 **adverts**
If you **place** or **put** an advert in a newspaper, you pay for the advert to be printed in the newspaper.
We placed an advert in an evening paper.
You could put an advert in the 'Mail'.

USAGE

plain
⇨ See **Usage** entry at **homely.**

play

1 **children's games**
When children **play,** they spend time amusing themselves with their toys or taking part in games.
The kids went off to play on the swings.

2 **sports and games**
If you **play** a particular sport or game, you take part in it regularly.
Ray and I play squash at least three times a week.
Do you play chess?

You use **play** with **in** to say that someone takes part in a game, match, or competition on a particular occasion.
I hope to play in many more matches for Celtic.

3 **'game'**
You do not use 'play' as a noun to refer to a sport or other activity in which two or more people compete against each other. The word you usually use is **game.**
You need two people to play this game.
In a game like tennis, the score is kept by the umpire.

4 **tapes and records**
If you **play** a tape, record, or compact disc, you put it in or onto a piece of equipment and listen to it.
I'll play you the tape in a minute.
She played her CDs too loudly.

However, you do not say that someone 'plays' a film or a television programme. You say that they **show** it.
One evening the school showed a cowboy film.
The BBC World Service television news showed the same film clip.

5 **musical instruments**
If you **play** a musical instrument, you produce music from it.
He sometimes played the organ in the cathedral.

If you want to say that someone is able to play a particular instrument, you use **the.** For example, you say 'She **plays the piano**' or 'He **plays the flute**'.
Uncle Rudi played the cello.

However, rock and jazz musicians usually omit the 'the'. They say 'She **plays piano**' or 'He **plays guitar**'.
There was one kid who played sax.

6 **used as a noun**
A **play** is a piece of writing which is performed in a theatre, on the radio, or on television.
It's my favourite Shakespeare play.

pleased - disappointed
The following adjectives can be used to indicate how pleased or disappointed someone is. They are arranged from 'most pleased' to 'most disappointed':

● **thrilled, overjoyed**
I was so thrilled to get a good report from him.
He was overjoyed at his son's return.

● **delighted**
I know Frank will be delighted to see you.

● **glad, pleased**

The people seem genuinely glad to see you.
They're pleased to be going home.

● **satisfied**

We are not satisfied with these results.

● **resigned, philosophical**

Pauline was already resigned to losing her home.
I was always philosophical about being ill.

● **disappointed**

I was disappointed that Kluge was not there.

● **upset**

After she died I felt very, very upset.

● **shattered, devastated**

It is desperately sad news and I am absolutely shattered to hear it.
Teresa was devastated, her dreams shattered.

pleasure

Pleasure is a feeling of happiness, satisfaction, or enjoyment.

McPherson could scarcely conceal his pleasure at my resignation.
I can't understand how people can kill for pleasure.

Pleasure is usually an uncount noun. You say, for example, that something gives you **pleasure.** You do not say that it gives you 'a pleasure'.

I don't think any other book I have written has given me such great pleasure.
The event gave enormous pleasure to a lot of people.

You can talk about the **pleasure of doing** something.

I'd travel a thousand miles just for the pleasure of meeting you.
The soil has been tended here not for profit or prestige but for the pleasure of growing and caring for living things.

(*i*) Note that you do not talk about the 'pleasure to do' something.

point

1 **'point'**

A **point** is something you say which expresses an idea, opinion, or fact.

That's a very good point.
I want to make several quick points.

A **point** is also an aspect or detail of something, or a part of a person's character.

The two books have some interesting points in common.
His best point was his communication, from the players to the catering staff.

2 **'the point'**

The point is the most important fact in a situation.

The point is that everyone's got something to offer.
Philip, I may as well come straight to the point. I'm pregnant.
You've all missed the point.

The **point of doing** something is the reason for doing it.

What was the point of attempting to live together?
I didn't see the point of boring you with all this.

3 **'no point'**

If you say that **there is no point in doing** something, you mean that it has no purpose or will not achieve anything.

There's no point in talking to you.
There was not much point in thinking about it.

(i) Note that you do not say 'there is no point to do' something. You also do not say 'it is no point in doing' something.

4 'full stop'

You do not refer to the punctuation mark (.) which comes at the end of a sentence as a 'point'. In British English, it is called a **full stop**. In American English, it is called a **period**.

⇨ For more information, see **Topic** entries at **Punctuation** and **Numbers and fractions**.

point of view - view - opinion

1 'point of view'

When you are considering one aspect of a situation, you can say that you are considering it from a particular **point of view**.

From a practical point of view it is quite irrelevant.
From the commercial point of view they have little to lose.

A person's **point of view** is their general attitude to something, or the way they feel about something that affects or concerns them.

We understand your point of view.
I tried to see things from Frank's point of view.

2 'view' and 'opinion'

You do not refer to what someone thinks or believes about a particular matter as their 'point of view'. You refer to it as their **view** or **opinion**.

Mr Carr's view is that the Bill is not anti-trade union.
If you want my honest opinion, I don't think it will work.

View is most commonly used in the plural.

Your views have always been respected here.
He was sent to jail for his political views.

You talk about someone's opinions or views **on** or **about** a particular matter.

He always asked for her opinions on every aspect of his work.
I have strong views about politics and the Church.

You can add expressions such as **in my opinion** or **in his view** to a statement to indicate that what you are saying is only what someone thinks, and is not necessarily a fact.

Well he's not making a very good job of it in my opinion.
Such a proposal in his view would do nothing but harm.

police

The police are the official organization responsible for making sure that people obey the law. They also protect people and property and arrest criminals.

He had called the police.
Contact the police as soon as possible after a burglary.

Police is a plural noun. You use a plural form of a verb after it.

The police were called to the scene of the crime.

(i) Note that you do not refer to an individual member of the police force as a 'police'. You refer to him or her as a **police officer**, a **policeman**, or a **policewoman**.

You have made a very serious allegation against a police officer.
He had been a policeman for six years.
Many of the younger policewomen resented not being allowed to take part in tougher assignments.

politics - policy - political

1 **'politics'**
The noun **politics** is used in two ways. It is usually used to refer to the methods by which people acquire, retain, and use power in a country or society.

They are reluctant to take part in politics.
I have no idea what his politics are.

When **politics** is used like this, you can use either a singular or plural form of a verb with it. Most people use a singular form.

Politics is by no means the only arena in which women are excelling.
I have no idea what his politics are.

Politics can also refer to the study of the ways in which countries are governed, and of the ways in which power is acquired and used in them. When you use **politics** like this, you must use a singular form of a verb with it.

Politics is a wide subject.

2 **'policy'**
Note that there is no noun 'politic'. If you want to refer to a course of action or plan that has been agreed upon by a government or political party, the word you use is **policy.**

There is no change in our policy.
He was criticized for pursuing a policy of reconciliation.

3 **'political'**
You also do not use 'politic' to mean 'relating to politics'. The word you use is **political.**

The Canadian government is facing another political crisis.
...the major political parties.

pollution

When there is **pollution,** the water or air in a place is dirty, impure, and dangerous, usually because poisonous chemicals have got into it.

...changes in the climate due to pollution of the atmosphere.

Pollution is an uncount noun. You do not talk about 'pollutions' or 'a pollution'.

pore - pour

These words are pronounced /pɔːʳ/.

1 **'pore'**
A **pore** is a small hole in the skin of a person or animal.

There was dirt in the pores around his nose.

2 **'pore over'**
If you **pore over** something such as a piece of writing or a map, you examine it carefully.

We spent hours poring over travel brochures.

3 **'pour'**
If you **pour** a liquid, you cause it to flow out of a container.

The waiter poured the wine into her glass.

If it **is pouring,** it is raining very heavily.

It was absolutely pouring.

4 **'poor'**
Note that the adjective **poor** /pʊəʳ/ is sometimes pronounced /pɔːʳ/.

position - post - job

1 **'position' and 'post'**
When someone has a regular job, it is referred to in formal English as their **position** or **post.** When a job is advertised, it is often described as a **position** or **post,** and a person applying for a job usually uses one of these words.

USAGE

…*top management* *positions*.
She is well qualified for the *post*.

2 **'job'**

In conversation, you do not use 'position' or 'post' with this meaning. You simply use **job**.
He's afraid of losing his *job*.

There are a number of other nouns which refer to activities which people are paid to do.
⇨ For information on these words, see **Usage** entry at **work**.

possess

The verb **possess** is usually used to say that someone or something has a quality, ability, or feature.

Energetic and sagacious, Snodgrass *possessed* *the very qualities needed.*
For hundreds of years London *possessed* *only one bridge.*

This is a fairly formal use. In conversation, you do not use 'possess'. Instead you use **have** or **have got**.
⇨ See **Usage** entries at **have** and **have got**.

In legal English, if you **possess** an object or substance, you own it or have it with you.
They were found guilty of *possessing* *petrol bombs.*
…the arrest of the mayor on charges of *possessing* *cocaine.*

possibility - opportunity

1 **'possibility'**

If there is a **possibility** of something happening or being the case, it might happen or be the case.

There was just a *possibility* *that they had taken the wrong road.*
We must accept the *possibility* *that we might be wrong.*

If there is **no possibility** of something happening or being the case, it cannot happen or be the case.

There was now *no possibility* *of success.*
There was *no possibility* *that she hadn't heard Jane.*

When people are talking or thinking about the **possibility of doing** something, they are considering whether to do it.

He began talking about the *possibility of living* *together as a family.*

(i) Note that you do not say that someone talks or thinks about the 'possibility to do' something.

2 **'opportunity'**

When a situation occurs in which it is possible for someone to do something, you do not say that they have the 'possibility to do' it. You say that they have the **opportunity to do** it or the **opportunity of doing** it.
⇨ See **Usage** entry at **opportunity**.

possible - possibly

1 **'possible'**

Possible is an adjective. If something is **possible**, it can be done or achieved.

It is *possible* *for us to measure his progress.*
A breakthrough may be *possible* *next year.*

Possible is often used in expressions such as **as soon as possible** and **as much as possible**. If you do something **as soon as possible**, you do it as soon as you can.

Go *as soon as possible.*
I like to know *as much as possible* *about my patients.*
He sat *as far* *away from the others* *as possible.*

ⓘ Note that you do not say that someone does something 'as soon as possibly' or 'as much as possibly'.

You also use **possible** to say that something may be true or correct.

It is possible that he said these things.

That's one possible answer.

2 **'possibly'**

Possibly is an adverb. You use **possibly** to indicate that you are not sure about something.

Television is possibly to blame for this.

That explained why his flat had been searched, and possibly why he'd been killed.

⇨ For a graded list of words used to say how sure you are about something, see section on **probability** in **Grammar** entry at **Adjuncts**.

You also use **possibly** when you are asking someone to do something in a very polite way. For example, you say '**Could you possibly** give me a lift to town?'

Could you possibly check if a Mr Keith Dayton was on the aircraft?

⇨ For more information about requests, see **Topic** entry at **Requests, orders, and instructions**.

post - mail

1 **'post' and 'mail'**

The public service by which letters and parcels are collected and delivered is usually called the **post** in British English and the **mail** in American English. **Mail** is also sometimes used in British English, for example in the name **Royal Mail**.

There is a cheque for you in the post.

Winners will be notified by post.

Your reply must have been lost in the mail.

British speakers usually refer to the letters and parcels delivered to them on a particular occasion as their **post**. American speakers refer to these letters and parcels as their **mail**. Some British speakers also talk about their **mail**.

They read their bosses' post.

I started to read my mail.

British speakers talk about **posting** a letter or parcel. Americans usually say that they **mail** it.

Some of the letters had been posted.

…the magazine that her friend had mailed to her.

2 **'postage'**

Note that you do not use 'post' or 'mail' to refer to the amount of money that you pay to send a letter or parcel. In both British and American English, this money is called **postage**.

Send 25p extra for postage and packing.

postgraduate
⇨ See **Usage** entry at **graduate**.

postpone
⇨ See **Usage** entry at **delay - cancel - postpone - put off**.

pour
⇨ See **Usage** entry at **pore - pour**.

USAGE

power - strength

1 'power'

If someone has **power,** they are able to control other people and their activities.

…*people in positions of <u>power</u>.*

It gave the President too much <u>power</u>.

2 'strength'

You do not use 'power' to refer to someone's physical energy, or their ability to move heavy objects. The word you use is **strength.**

They were recovering their <u>strength</u> before setting off again.

I admired his immense physical <u>strength</u>.

practically

⇨ See section on **extent** in **Grammar** entry at **Adjuncts.**

practice - practise

In British English, **practice** is a noun and **practise** is a verb.

1 used as an uncount noun

Practice involves doing something regularly in order to improve your ability at it.

Skating's just a matter of <u>practice</u>.

I help them with their music <u>practice</u>.

2 used as a count noun

A **practice** is something that is done regularly, for example as a custom.

Benn began the <u>practice</u> of holding regular meetings.

…the ancient Japanese <u>practice</u> of binding the feet from birth.

3 used as a verb

If you **practise** something, you do it or take part in it regularly.

I played the piece I <u>had been practising</u> for months.

He was brought up in a family which <u>practised</u> traditional Judaism.

In American English, the spelling 'practise' is not normally used. The verb is spelled **practice,** like the noun.

I <u>practiced</u> and learned the headstand.

precede

⇨ See **Usage** entry at **proceed - precede.**

prefer

If you **prefer** one person or thing **to** another, you like the first one better.

I <u>prefer</u> Barber <u>to</u> his deputy.

I became a teacher because I <u>preferred</u> books and people <u>to</u> politics.

ⓘ Note that you do not use any preposition except **to** in sentences like these. Note also that **prefer** can often sound rather formal in ordinary conversation. Verbal expressions such as **like…better** and **would rather** are used more frequently. For example, instead of saying 'I prefer football to tennis', you can say 'I **like** football **better** than tennis', instead of 'I'd prefer an apple', you can say 'I**'d rather** have an apple', and instead of 'I'd prefer to walk', you can say 'I**'d rather** walk'.

preferable

If one thing is **preferable to** another, it is more desirable or suitable than the other thing.

Knowledge is always <u>preferable to</u> ignorance.

Gradual change is <u>preferable to</u> sudden, large-scale change.

ⓘ Note that you do not use any preposition except **to** after **preferable.** You also do not say that one thing is 'more preferable than' another.

prepare

If you **prepare** a meal, you produce it by mixing foods together. **Prepare** is one of several verbs which can be used to say that someone produces a meal.

⇨ For more information, see **Usage** entry at **cook.**

present

You use **present** as an adjective in front of a noun to indicate that you are talking about something which exists now, rather than about something in the past or future.

…the government's *present* economic difficulties.
The *present* system has many failings.

You also use **present** in front of a noun to indicate that you are talking about the person who has a job, role, or title now, rather than someone who had it in the past or will have it in the future.

The *present* chairperson is a woman.
The author has the full support of the *present* Lord Montgomery.

When **present** is used after **be**, it has a different meaning. If someone **is present** at an event, they are there.

He *had been present at* the dance.
I *was* once *present at* a meeting in the Ministry of Education.

(*i*) Note that you do not use any preposition except **at** in sentences like these.

If it is clear what event you are talking about, you can just say that someone **is present.**
The Lord Mayor and Lady Mayoress of Westminster *were present.*

You can also use **present** with this meaning immediately after a noun.

There was a photographer *present.*
I had more to lose than any other person *present.*

presently

1. **used to mean 'soon'**

If something will happen **presently,** it will happen quite soon.

He will be here *presently.*
I shall have more to say *presently.*

If you are talking about the past, you use **presently** to say that something happened quite soon after something else.

Presently all was quiet again.
He was shown to a small office. *Presently,* a young woman in a white coat came in.

Both these uses of **presently** are slightly old-fashioned.

2. **used to mean 'now'**

Some people use **presently** after **be** to mean 'now'.

…the oil and gas rigs that are *presently* in operation.
She is *presently* developing a number of projects.

This use of **presently** is fairly new in British English, and some speakers find it unacceptable. Instead of 'presently', you can say **at present.**

He is *at present* serving a life sentence.
The comet is *at present* between the constellations of Pegasus and Delphinius.

You can put **at present** at the beginning or end of a clause. You cannot do this with 'presently' when it means 'now'.

At present there is a world energy shortage.
We're short of staff *at present.*

USAGE

press

The **press** are the newspapers in a particular place, or the journalists who write them. In British English, you can use either a singular or plural form of a verb with **press.**

Small wonder the press is hostile to the prime minister.

…a number of cases where the press have been very aggressive.

 Note that in American English, a singular verb form is preferred.

The Supreme Court will consider whether the press is protected from being sued by someone promised confidentiality.

pretty

⇨ See **Usage** entry at **beauty.**

prevent - protect

1 **'prevent'**

If someone or something **prevents** you **from doing** something, they do not allow you to do it.

My only idea was to prevent him from speaking.

Cotton mittens will prevent the baby from scratching his own face.

ⓘ Note that you do not say that someone 'prevents you to do' something.

2 **'protect'**

You do not use 'prevent' to say that something keeps you safe from something unpleasant or harmful. The word you use is **protect.**

Babies are protected against diseases like measles by their mother's milk.

She had his umbrella to protect her from the rain.

previous

⇨ See **Usage** entry at **last - lastly.**

previously

1 **'previously' and 'before'**

If you are talking about a period measured back from some earlier time, you use **before** or **previously.**

He had died a month before.

She had rented the flat some fourteen months previously.

⇨ See **Usage** entry at **before.**

2 **'ago'**

You only use **ago** when you are talking about a period of time measured back from the present.

We met two years ago.

⇨ See **Usage** entry at **ago.**

3 **'for'**

You use **for** to say how long a period lasts in the past, present, or future, or how much time passes without something happening.

She slept for eight hours.

He will be away for three weeks.

I hadn't seen him for four years.

⇨ See **Usage** entry at **for.**

4 **'since'**

You use **since** to say when a period of time started.

She has been with the group <u>since</u> it began.
...the first civilian president <u>since</u> the coup 17 years ago.

You also use **since** to refer to the last time that something happened, or to how much time passes without something happening.

She hadn't eaten <u>since</u> breakfast.
It was a long time <u>since</u> she had been to church.

⇨ See **Usage** entry at **since**.

price - cost

[1] **'price' and 'cost'**

The **price** or **cost** of something is the amount of money you must pay to buy it.

...the <u>price</u> of sugar.
...an increase in the <u>cost</u> of fertilizer.

(*i*) Note that you do not use any preposition except **of** after **price** or **cost** in sentences like these.

You can also use **cost** to refer to the amount of money needed to do or make something.

The building was recently restored at a <u>cost</u> of £500,000.
They are now manufactured by the billion at a <u>cost</u> of a few pence each.

You do not use 'price' in this way.

[2] **'costs'**

You use the plural noun **costs** when you are referring to the total amount of money needed to run something such as a business.

She decided she needed to cut her <u>costs</u> by half.
Moulton's have had to raise their prices still higher to cover increased <u>costs</u>.

[3] **'cost' used as a verb**

You use **cost** as a verb to talk about the amount of money that you must pay for something.

The dress <u>costs $200.</u>
How much do they <u>cost?</u>

You can use **cost** with two objects to say how much money someone actually pays for something on a particular occasion. Note that the past tense and past participle of **cost** is **cost**, not 'costed'.

A two-day stay there <u>cost me $125.</u>

(*i*) Note that you do not use 'to' after **cost** in a sentence like this.

price - prize

[1] **'price'**

The **price** /praɪs/ of something is the amount of money that you must pay to buy it.

The <u>price</u> is still only five dollars.

⇨ See **Usage** entry at **price - cost**.

[2] **'prize'**

A **prize** /praɪz/ is something given to someone for winning a competition or game, or for doing good work.

He won a <u>prize</u> in a crossword competition.
...the Nobel <u>Prize</u> for Peace.

pride

The following words can all be used to describe someone who has a high opinion of themselves:

USAGE

arrogant	haughty	self-respecting	smug	vain
conceited	proud	self-satisfied	supercilious	

1 words used to show approval

Proud and **self-respecting** are used in a complimentary way.

…with millions of decent, <u>proud</u>, hard-working people.
…so that they grow into responsible and <u>self-respecting</u> citizens.

However, **proud** is also sometimes used to show disapproval.

She was too <u>proud</u> to apologize.

2 words used to show disapproval

Arrogant, conceited, haughty, self-satisfied, smug, and **supercilious** are all used to describe someone who thinks they are better than other people. These words show disapproval.

I hope I didn't sound like a <u>conceited</u> know-it-all.
…his smooth, <u>smug</u> brother-in-law.
They were standing by themselves looking <u>supercilious</u> and remote.

Arrogant is used to describe people who behave in an unpleasant way towards other people.

My husband was an <u>arrogant</u>, bullying little drunkard.

Haughty is used in writing, not in conversation.

He spoke in a <u>haughty</u> tone.

Vain also shows disapproval. It is used to describe someone who thinks they are very good-looking, or very clever or talented.

I think he is shallow, <u>vain</u> and untrustworthy.

principal - principle

1 'principal'

Principal can be an adjective or a noun.
The **principal** thing or person in a group is the most important one.

His <u>principal</u> interest in life was to be the richest man in Britain.
…the <u>principal</u> character in James Bernard Fagan's play.

The **principal** of a school or college is the person in charge of it.

Complaints from the students began arriving at the <u>principal's</u> office.
…Mr Patrick Miller, <u>principal</u> of Esher College.

⇨ See **Usage** entry at **headmaster - principal.**

2 'principle'

Principle is always a noun. A **principle** is a general rule that someone tries to obey in the way they behave.

…a man of high <u>principles</u>.
The <u>principle</u> of equality in recruitment deserves to be highly prized.

print - publish

1 'print'

To **print** a book or newspaper means to produce many copies of it using machinery.

The book <u>is printed</u> on fine acid-free paper.

2 'publish'

To **publish** a book or newspaper means to produce and distribute it for sale to the public.

Dr Johnson's dictionary <u>was published</u> in 1755.

prison

1 used as a count noun

A **prison** is a building where criminals or other people are officially kept and prevented from leaving.

The prison 's inmates are being kept in their cells.

2 used as an uncount noun

If you want to say that someone is in a prison without mentioning which prison they are in, you say they are **in prison**.

He died in prison.

Similarly, you say that someone is sent **to prison** or that they are released **from prison**.

He was eventually sent to prison for a very long time.

(i) Note that you do not use 'the' in front of **prison** unless you are referring to a particular prison.

prize

⇨ See **Usage** entry at **price - prize**.

probably

You use **probably** to indicate that a statement is very likely to be true.

● If you are using a verb group consisting of an auxiliary and a main verb, you put **probably** after the auxiliary. For example, you say 'He **will probably come** soon'. You do not say 'He probably will come soon'.

He 's probably telling the truth.
Chaucer was probably born in this area.

● If you are using more than one auxiliary, you put **probably** after the first auxiliary.

Next year I shall probably be looking for a job.
I 'll probably be sent back to London.

● When there is no auxiliary, you put **probably** in front of the verb unless the verb is **be**.

He probably misses the children.
He probably kept your examination papers.

● If the verb is **be**, you put **probably** after it.

You 're probably right.
The owner is probably a salesman.

● In a negative sentence, if you are using a contracted form such as **won't** or **can't**, you put **probably** in front of the contracted form.

They probably won't help.
They probably don't want us to have it.

● You can also put **probably** at the beginning of a clause.

Probably it was just my imagination.
400 children go to registered child-minders, and probably thousands more spend their day with illegal minders.

(i) Note that you do not put **probably** at the end of a clause.

⇨ For a graded list of words used to say how certain someone is about something, see section on **probability** in **Grammar** entry at **Adjuncts**.

problem

The noun **problem** has two common meanings.

1 an unsatisfactory situation

A **problem** is an unsatisfactory situation that needs to be dealt with.

…the problem of refugees.

You can say that someone **has a problem** or **has problems**.

I think we may have a problem here.

They have financial problems.

You can also say that someone **has problems doing** something.

They have such problems paying back debts that private credit is drying up.

Already Third World countries have desperate problems feeding, educating, and clothing their people.

(*i*) Note that you do not say that someone 'has problems to do' something.

2 **'reason'**

You do not use 'problem' with **why** when you are explaining why a situation has occurred. You do not say, for example, 'The problem why he couldn't come is that he is ill'. You say 'The **reason** why he couldn't come is that he is ill'.

The reason why tents were useless was that the build-up of snow simply crushed them.

⇨ For more information, see **Usage** entry at **reason**.

3 **a puzzle**

A **problem** is also a puzzle that requires logical thought or mathematics to solve it.

With mathematical problems, you can save time by approximating.

…his friends, one of whom solved a difficult chess problem.

proceed - precede

1 **'proceed'**

If you **proceed** /prəsiːd/ to do something, you do it after you have finished doing something else.

He proceeded to explain.

She proceeded to hand over the key to my room.

In stories and formal English, if someone **proceeds** in a particular direction, they go in that direction.

He proceeded downstairs.

…as we were proceeding along Chiswick High Street.

2 **'precede'**

To **precede** /prɪsiːd/ an event means to happen before it. **Precede** is a formal word.

The children's dinner was preceded by party games.

produce - product

1 **'produce' used as a verb**

Produce is usually a verb and pronounced /prədjuːs/.

To **produce** a result or effect means to cause it to happen.

His comments produced an angry response.

All our efforts have not produced an agreement.

To **produce** goods or food means to make or grow them in large quantities.

…factories producing domestic electrical goods.

Farmers must produce a good deal more than they need.

2 **'produce' used as a noun**

Food that is grown in large quantities is called **produce** (pronounced /prɒdjuːs/).

Sugar became the chief produce of the Caribbean.

3 **'product'**

Goods that are made and sold in large quantities are called **products**.

Manufacturers spend huge sums of money advertising their products.

USAGE

profession
⇨ See **Usage** entry at **work**.

professor - teacher

1 **'professor'**

In a British university, a **professor** is the most senior teacher in a department.

… *Professor Cole.*
He was Professor of English at Strathclyde University.

 In an American or Canadian university or college, a **professor** is a senior teacher. He or she is not necessarily the most senior teacher in a department.

2 **'teacher'**

You do not use 'professor' to refer to a person who teaches at a school or similar institution. The word you use is **teacher**.

I'm a qualified French teacher.
…her chemistry teacher.

programme - program

A **programme** is a plan which has been developed for a particular purpose.

 This word is spelled **program** in American English.

The company has major programmes of research and development.
There has been a lot of criticism of the new nuclear power program.

A television or radio **programme** is a single broadcast, for example a play, discussion, or show. This word, too, is spelled **program** in American English.

…the last programme in our series on education.
Then Mr. Gill watched a British television program.

A computer **program** is a set of instructions that a computer uses to perform a particular operation. This word is spelled **program** in both British and American English.

Whatever you do, you must run an anti-virus program on your computer at all times.
…the chances of an error occurring in a computer program.

progress

You say that there is **progress** when something improves gradually, or when someone gets nearer to achieving or completing something.

…technological progress.
They came in from time to time to check on my progress.

Progress is an uncount noun. You do not talk about 'progresses' or 'a progress'.
You can say that someone or something **makes progress.**

She is making good progress with her German.
The offensive had got off well and was making progress.

ⓘ Note that you do not say that someone or something 'does progress'.

prohibit

To **prohibit** something means to forbid it or make it illegal.

We prohibit air guns and other weapons that might wound someone.
She believes that nuclear weapons should be totally prohibited.

You can say that someone **is prohibited from doing** something.

Guests were once prohibited from entering the kitchen.
The country has a law prohibiting employees from striking.

ⓘ Note that you do not say that someone 'is prohibited to do' something.

USAGE

proper

The adjective **proper** is used with several different meanings.

1 used to mean 'real'

You use it in front of a noun to indicate that someone or something really is the thing referred to by the noun.

Have you been to a proper doctor?
He's never had a proper job.

2 used to mean 'correct'

You also use **proper** in front of a noun to say that something is correct or suitable.

Everything was in its proper place.
What's the proper word for those things?

3 used to mean 'acceptable'

If a way of behaving is **proper,** it is correct or acceptable. This is an old-fashioned use.

It wasn't proper for a man to show his emotions.

4 used to mean 'main'

Proper is sometimes used after a noun to refer to the main or central part of a place.

By the time I got to the village proper everyone was out to meet me.

property

If something is someone's **property,** it belongs to them.

The field is the University's property.
Eventually the piano became my property.

You can also refer to all the things that a person owns as their **property.**

Her property passes to her next of kin.
Their property was confiscated and they were driven back to the ghettos.

When **property** is used in either of these ways, it is an uncount noun. You do not talk about a person's 'properties'.

propose

1 suggestions

If someone **proposes** a plan or idea, they suggest it so that other people can think about it and decide on it.

British Airways has proposed a one-way surcharge of $57.
This would help them to become accustomed to the methods we proposed.

You can say that someone **proposes** that something **should be done** or **proposes** that something **be done.**

They proposed that political strikes should be made illegal.
The staff association proposed that a mediator be nominated.

(i) Note that you do not use a 'to'-infinitive in sentences like these. You do not say, for example, 'The staff association proposed a mediator to be nominated'.

2 intentions

However, if you intend to do something yourself, you can say that you **propose to do** it.

I propose to focus attention on one type of resource.
I propose to undertake a further and thorough review of the documentary evidence.

You can also say that you **propose doing** something.

So what do you propose doing now?

(i) Note that you do not say that you 'propose to not do' something. You say that you **do not propose to do** it.

I do not propose to get deeply involved in it.
I do not propose to discuss this matter.

prosecute

⇨ See **Usage** entry at **persecute - prosecute**.

protest

Protest can be a verb or a noun, but with different pronunciations.

1 used as a verb

Protest /prɒˈtest/ is used as a verb to say that someone shows publicly that they do not approve of something. You can say that someone **protests about** something or **protests against** something.

He was criticized for protesting about Gerald Brooke's imprisonment.
Groups of women took to the streets to protest against the arrests.

 Some speakers of American English use **protest** as a transitive verb. They say that someone **protests** something.

He protested the action in a telephone call to the President.

'Protest' is not used like this in British English.

Protest can also be a reporting verb. If you **protest** that something is the case, you insist that it is the case, when someone has said or suggested the opposite.

They protested that they had never heard of him.
'You're wrong,' I protested.

2 used as a noun

When people show publicly that they do not approve of something, you can describe their behaviour as a **protest** /ˈprəʊtest/.

They joined in the protests against the government's proposals.
…a letter of protest.

proud

You can say that someone is **proud of** something they have or something they have done. This means that they think it is good and are glad about it.

He was proud of his son-in-law.
We were all tired but proud of our efforts.

If someone is **proud to do** something, they feel pleased about doing it.

She's proud to work with you.

prove - test

1 'prove'

If you **prove** that something is true or correct, you provide evidence which shows that it is definitely true or correct.

He was able to prove that he was an American.
The autopsy proved that she had drowned.

2 'test'

When you use a practical method to try to find out how good or bad someone or something is, you do not say that you 'prove' the person or thing. You say that you **test** them.

I will test you on your knowledge of French.
A number of new techniques were tested.

provide

1 'provide with'

To **provide** something that someone needs or wants means to give it to them or make it available to them. You can say that you **provide** someone **with** what they want.

USAGE

The embassy had provided him with cash to buy new clothes.
The government cannot provide all young people with a job.

(*i*) Note that you must use **with** in sentences like these. You do not say that you 'provide someone' what they want.

2 'provide for'

You can also say that you **provide** something **for** someone.

Most animals provide food for their young.
One player wants to provide nursing care for his mother-in-law.

(*i*) Note that you do not use any preposition except **for** in sentences like these.

If you regularly give someone the things they need, such as money, food, or clothing, you say that you **provide for** them.

Parents are expected to provide for their children.
I just want to be sure you 're provided for.

You must use **for** in sentences like these. You do not say that you 'provide' someone.

pub

In Britain, a **pub** or **public house** is a building where people meet their friends and have drinks, especially alcoholic drinks. **Pub** is the word people usually use. **Public house** is only used in formal speech and writing.

He was in the pub most evenings and always offered us drinks.

 In American English, a place where you can buy and drink alcoholic drinks is usually called a **bar.**

…the city's most popular country-western bar.

⇨ See **Usage** entry at **bar.**

public

You can refer to people in general as **the public.** In British English, after **the public** you can use either a singular or plural form of a verb.

I think that the public has learnt that we have to wait for news.
The public are entitled to know what happened.

 In American English, a singular verb form is preferred.

public house

⇨ See **Usage** entry at **pub.**

public school - state school

In England and Wales, a **public school** is a private school that provides secondary education which parents have to pay special fees for.

He then won a scholarship to a local public school.

 In Scotland and the United States, a **public school** is a school that is supported financially by the government. In England and Wales, this kind of school is called a **state school.**

…a government-operated public school.
Our state schools are doing nothing to address that problem.
Oxford still enrols the lowest percentage of state-school pupils of all UK universities.

publish

⇨ See **Usage** entry at **print - publish.**

pupil

⇨ See **Usage** entry at **student.**

purposefully - purposely

1 'purposefully'

If someone does something **purposefully,** they do it in a way that suggests that they have a definite purpose and a strong desire to achieve this purpose.

He strode <u>purposefully</u> towards the barn.
He walked <u>purposefully</u> out through the secretary's office.

2 'purposely'

If someone does something **purposely,** they do it deliberately, rather than by accident or chance.

They are <u>purposely</u> withholding information.
Her voice was <u>purposely</u> low.

purse

A **purse** is a very small bag that people, especially women, keep their money in.

My <u>purse</u> disappeared from my bag during a bus journey.

 In American English, a **purse** is also a woman's handbag.

She looked at me and then reached in her <u>purse</u> for cigarettes.

put

If you **put** something in a particular place or position, you move it into that place or position. The past tense and past participle of **put** is **put,** not 'putted'.

She <u>put</u> her hand on his arm
I <u>put</u> her suitcase on the table.

Put has several other meanings. For some of its meanings, you can use **place** instead of 'put'.

⇨ For more information about this, see **Usage** entry at **place - put.**

put off

⇨ See **Usage** entry at **delay - cancel - postpone - put off.**

put up with

⇨ See **Usage** entry at **bear.**

Q q

quality

When you are talking about things that have been made or produced, you can use **quality** to say how good or bad they are.

The quality of the photograph was poor.
Over the years they have received many awards for the high quality of their products.

You can say that something is **of good quality** or **of poor quality**.

The dresses – all of good quality – had had their labels removed.
The treatment and care provided were also of poor quality.
Television ensures that films of high quality are exhibited to large audiences.

You can also use expressions such as **good quality** and **high quality** in front of nouns.

I've got some good quality paper.
Teaching is backed up by the highest quality research.

You can also use **quality** on its own in front of a noun. When you do this, you are indicating that something is of a high standard.

… quality Australian fiction.
The employers don't want quality work any more.

quarrel - fight

1 'quarrel'

A **quarrel** is an angry argument or series of arguments between two or more people.

He got in a quarrel with that wild Wainright boy.
There wasn't any evidence of quarrels between them.

2 'fight'

You do not use 'quarrel' to refer to an incident in which people try to hurt each other using their fists or weapons. The word you use is **fight**.

He had had a fight with Smith and bloodied his nose.

question

1 'out of the question'

If you say that something is **out of the question**, you mean that it cannot be done, and is therefore not worth considering.

She knew that a holiday this year was out of the question.
It has been so cold that gardening has been out of the question.

2 'beyond question'

You do not use 'out of the question' to say that there is no doubt about something. The expression you use is **beyond question**.

She knew beyond question that I was a person who could be trusted.
It remains, beyond question, one of the premier races in the international calendar.

quick

⇨ See **Usage** entry at **speed**.

quiet - quite

1 'quiet'

Quiet is an adjective. Someone or something that is **quiet** makes only a small amount of noise.

Bal said in a quiet voice, 'I have resigned.'
Such submarines are very quiet and almost impossible to detect.

If a place is **quiet,** there is very little noise there.

It was very quiet there; you could just hear the wind moving in the trees.

2 **'quite'**

Do not confuse **quiet** /kwaɪət/ with **quite** /kwaɪt/. You use **quite** to indicate that something is the case to a fairly great extent.

quite

1 **used in front of an adjective, adverb and noun**

You use **quite** in front of an adjective or adverb to indicate that something is the case to a fairly great extent but not to a very great extent.

He was quite young.
The end of the story can be told quite quickly.

Note that in American English, this use of **quite** is not as common as it is in British English. Speakers of American English tend to use **fairly** or **somewhat** instead.

This is a fairly typical example.
Homes have become somewhat more affordable in recent months.

You can also use **quite** in front of **a**, an adjective, and a noun. For example, instead of saying 'It was quite cold', you can say 'It was **quite a cold day'.**

It's quite a good job.
She was quite a pretty girl.

(*i*) Note that in sentences like these you put **quite** in front of **a**, not after it. You do not say, for example, 'It was a quite cold day'.

⚠ **WARNING:** You do not use 'quite' in front of comparative adjectives or adverbs. You do not say, for example, 'The train is quite quicker than the bus'. Instead you use **a bit, a little,** or **slightly.**

I ought to do something a bit more ambitious.
He arrived at their bungalow a little earlier than he expected.
The risk of epidemics may be slightly higher in crowded urban areas.

⇨ **Quite** is one of several words and expressions which can be used to indicate degree or extent. For graded lists, see sections on **degree** and **extent** in **Grammar** entry at **Adjuncts.**

2 **used for emphasis**

Quite can be used with a different meaning. You can use it in front of an adjective, adverb, or verb to emphasize that something is completely the case or very much the case.

You're quite right.
I saw its driver quite clearly.
I quite understand.

⇨ For a list of adverbs used to emphasize a verb, see section on **emphasis** in **Grammar** entry at **Adjuncts.**

R r

raise

⇨ See **Usage** entry at **rise - raise**.

rapid

⇨ See **Usage** entry at **fast**.

rarely

⇨ See section on **frequency** in **Grammar** entry at **Adjuncts**.

rather

1 **used as adverb of degree**

Rather means 'to a small extent'. However, it is often used without any real meaning, but simply to soften the effect of the word or expression that follows it. For example, if someone asks you to do something, you might say 'I'm **rather** busy'. You mean that you are busy, but **rather** makes your reply seem more polite.

I'm rather puzzled by this question.
He did it rather badly.

Rather usually goes in front of an adjective or an adverb, but it can also be used in front of a singular noun group.

I'm in rather a hurry.
He was rather a silent young man.

(*i*) Note that you can say either 'He was **rather a** silent young man' or 'He was **a rather** silent young man'. **Rather a** is more common.

You can use **rather** in front of **like** when you are using **like** as a preposition.

This animal looks and behaves rather like a squirrel.
The food, rather like that provided by motorway cafes, has become a bit of a joke.

You can also use **rather** in front of verbs such as **think** and **hope**.

I rather think it was three hundred and fifty pounds.
I rather hoped that one day you would get married.

(*i*) Note that several words and expressions can be used to say that something is the case to a smaller or greater extent.

⇨ For graded lists, see section on **degree** in **Grammar** entry at **Adjuncts** and section on **grading adverbs** in **Grammar** entry at **Adverbs**.

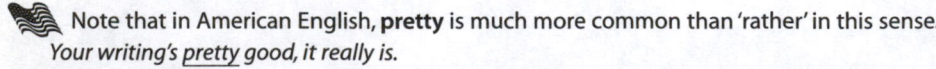 Note also that **rather** is more common in British than American English in the above senses.

2 **used as an emphasizer**

Rather has a different meaning when you use it in front of words such as **good** and **well**. If you say that something is **rather** good, you are emphasizing that it is good.

There's a teashop near here that does rather good toasted muffins.
The company thought I did rather well.

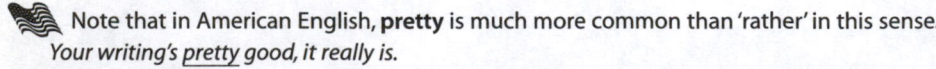 Note that in American English, **pretty** is much more common than 'rather' in this sense.

Your writing's pretty good, it really is.

3 **'would rather'**

If you say that you **would rather do** something, you mean that you would prefer to do it.

I'll order tea. Or perhaps you would rather have coffee.
'What was all that about?' – 'I'm sorry, I 'd rather not say.'

ⓘ Note that in sentences like these you use an infinitive without 'to' after **would rather.** You can also use **would rather** followed by a clause to say that you would prefer something to happen or be done. In the clause you use the simple past tense.

Would you <u>rather</u> she <u>came</u> to see me?

'May I go on?' – '<u>I'd rather</u> you <u>didn't.</u>'

4 **'rather than'**

Rather than is used like a conjunction to link words or expressions of the same type. You use **rather than** when you have said what is the case and you want to compare it with what is not the case.

I have used familiar English names <u>rather than</u> scientific Latin ones.

It made him frightened <u>rather than</u> angry.

Gambling was a way of redistributing wealth <u>rather than</u> acquiring it.

5 **correcting a mistake**

You can also use **rather** when you are correcting a mistake you have made, or when you think of a more appropriate word than the one you have just used.

Suddenly there stood before him, or <u>rather</u> above him, a gigantic woman.

He explained what the Crux is, or <u>rather,</u> what it was.

rational

⇨ See **Usage** entry at **reasonable - rational.**

reach

⇨ See **Usage** entry at **arrive - reach.**

read

1 **reading to yourself**

When you **read** /riːd/ a piece of writing, you look at it and understand what it says.

Why don't you <u>read</u> your letter?

The past tense and past participle of **read** is **read** /rɛd/, not 'readed'.

I <u>read</u> through the whole paper.

<u>Have</u> you <u>read</u> that article I gave you?

2 **reading to someone else**

If you **read** something such as a book to someone, you say the words aloud so that the other person can hear them. When you use **read** like this, it has two objects. If the indirect object is a pronoun, it usually goes in front of the direct object.

I'm going to read <u>him</u> some of my poems.

If the indirect object is not a pronoun, it usually goes after the direct object. When this happens, you put **to** in front of the indirect object.

Read books <u>to your baby</u> - this helps to develop language and listening skills.

You also put the indirect object after the direct object when the direct object is a pronoun.

You will have to read it <u>to him.</u>

⇨ See section on **ditransitive verbs** in **Grammar** entry at **Verbs.**

ⓘ Note that you can also omit the direct object.

I'll go up and <u>read to Sam</u> for five minutes.

3 **reading a subject**

In British English, if you **read** a subject at university, you study it.

He went up to Magdalen College to <u>read</u> history.

 Read is not used like this in American English.

USAGE

readable - legible

1 'readable'

If you say that a book or article is **readable**, you mean that it is interesting and not boring or difficult to understand.

He has written a most readable and entertaining autobiography.

2 'legible'

If you can recognize the letters and words that a piece of writing consists of, you do not say that the writing is 'readable'. You say that it is **legible**.

The inscription is still perfectly legible.

ready

1 used after a verb

If you are **ready**, you have prepared yourself for something.

Are you ready now? I'll take you back to your flat.
We were getting ready for bed.

If something is **ready**, it has been prepared and you can use it.

Lunch is ready.
Go and get the boat ready.

(*i*) Note that you cannot use **ready** with either of these meanings in front of a noun.

2 used in front of a noun

You use **ready** in front of a noun to indicate that something is available to be used very quickly and easily.

His calves are healthy and there is a ready market for his veal abroad.
I have no ready explanation for this fact.

Ready money is in the form of notes and coins rather than cheques, and so can be used immediately.

…people who performed services for ready money.
…£3000 in ready cash.

real

Real is used to say that something actually exists.

… real or imagined feelings of inferiority.
Robert squealed in mock terror, then in real pain.

You also use **real** to say that a substance or object is genuine and not artificial.

I would never wear real fur.
Rudolph couldn't tell whether the jewellery was real or not.

Some American speakers use **real** in front of an adjective or adverb for emphasis.

That suit looks real nice.
I'm being looked after real well.

This use is generally regarded as incorrect, both in British and American English. Instead of 'real', you should use **really**.

It was really good.
He did it really carefully.

⇨ See **Usage** entry at **really**.

realize

⇨ See **Usage** entry at **understand**.

really

You use **really** in conversation to emphasize something that you are saying.
Really usually goes in front of a verb, or in front of an adjective or adverb.

I really enjoyed that.
It was really good.
He did it really carefully.

You can put **really** in front of or after an auxiliary verb. For example, you can say 'He **really is** coming' or 'He **is really** coming'. There is no difference in meaning.

We really are expecting it to be a best-seller.
It would really be too much trouble.

When you use **really** in front of an adjective or adverb, it has a similar meaning to 'very'. Note that you can say either 'Gilbert **is really** clever' or 'Gilbert **really is** clever'. The meaning is almost the same. In both cases you are saying that Gilbert is very clever, but when you say 'Gilbert **really is** clever', you are expressing surprise that Gilbert is clever, or trying to convince someone else that he is.

This is really serious.
He really is famous.

⚠ **WARNING:** You do not use 'really' in formal writing. Words such as **very** or **extremely** are usually used instead.

reason

The **reason for** something is the fact or situation which explains why it happens, exists, or is done.

I asked the reason for the decision.
The reason for this relationship is clear.

ⓘ Note that you do not use any preposition except **for** after **reason** in sentences like these.

You can talk about a person's **reason for doing** something.

One of the reasons for coming to England is to make money.
The women's reasons for wearing wigs are various.

You can also talk about the **reason why** something happens or is done.

There are several reasons why we can't do that.

However, if you are actually stating the reason, you do not use 'why'. Instead you use a 'that'-clause.

The reason that Daniel had come under suspicion was that he'd gone to work for Bob.
The reason I'm calling you is that I know Larry talked with you earlier.

ⓘ Note that the second clause in these sentences is also a 'that'-clause. Instead of a 'that'-clause, some speakers use a clause beginning with **because.**

The reason they are not like other boys is because they have been brought up differently.

This use of **because** is fairly common in spoken English. However, some people think that it is incorrect, and you should avoid it.

reasonable - rational

1 'reasonable'

When someone is **reasonable**, they behave in a fair and sensible way.

Our mother was always very reasonable.
I can't do that, Morris. Be reasonable.

If something such as a proposal or judgement is **reasonable**, it is acceptable because it is fair or sensible.

Rules and procedures need to be accepted as reasonable by those who operate them.
There was no reasonable explanation for her decision.

2 'rational'

You say that someone is **rational** when they are able to think clearly and make decisions and judgements based on reason rather than emotion.

Let's talk about this like two rational people.

USAGE

You can also describe people's behaviour as **rational.**
This was a totally <u>rational</u> response to a set of complex problems.

receipt - recipe

1 **'receipt'**

A **receipt** /rɪˈsiːt/ is a piece of paper that confirms that money or goods have been received.
We've got <u>receipts</u> for each thing we've bought.

2 **'recipe'**

You do not use **receipt** to refer to a set of instructions telling you how to cook something. The word you use is **recipe** /ˈrɛsəpi/.
…an old Polish <u>recipe</u> for beetroot soup.

receive

When you **receive** something, someone gives it to you, or it arrives after it has been sent to you. **Get** is used in a similar way. You use **receive** in formal writing and **get** in conversation.

For example, in a business letter you might write 'I **received** a letter from Mr Jones', but in conversation you would say 'I **got** a letter from Mr Jones'.

The police <u>received</u> a call from the house at about 4.50 a.m.
I <u>got</u> a call from the President.

You can say that someone **receives** or **gets** a wage, salary, or pension.

His mother <u>received</u> no pension or compensation.
He <u>was getting</u> a very low salary.

You can also say that someone **receives** or **gets** help or advice.

She is said to <u>have received</u> help from Lord Cowper.
<u>Get</u> advice from your local health department.

recent

⇨ See **Usage** entry at **newness.**

recently - newly - lately

Recently and **newly** are both used to indicate that something happened only a short time ago. There is no difference in meaning, but **newly** can only be used with an '-ed' form, usually in front of a noun.

…the <u>newly elected</u> Government.
On the <u>newly painted</u> white wall was a photograph of the President.

Recently can be used in several positions in a sentence.

… his <u>recently</u> established Internet business.
<u>Recently</u> a performance of Macbeth was given there.
There was <u>recently</u> a formal inquiry.
I have <u>recently</u> re-read all his books.

You can use **recently** or **lately** to say that something started happening a short time ago and is continuing to happen. You cannot use **newly** with this meaning.

They have <u>recently</u> been taking German lessons.
<u>Lately</u> he's been going around with Miranda Watkins.

recognize - realize

1 **'recognize'**

If you **recognize** someone or something, you know who or what they are because you have seen them before, or because they have been described to you.

She didn't <u>recognize</u> me at first.
They are trained to <u>recognize</u> the symptoms of radiation-sickness.

If you **recognize** something such as a problem, you accept that it exists.

Governments are beginning to <u>recognize</u> the problem.
We <u>recognize</u> this as a genuine need.

2 'realize'

If you become aware of a fact, you do not say that you 'recognize' it. You say that you **realize** it.

I <u>realized</u> that this man wasn't going to hurt me.
She <u>realized</u> that she could not reach the shore.

recommend

If you **recommend** someone or something, you praise them and advise other people to use them or buy them.

I asked my friends to <u>recommend</u> a doctor who is good with children.
We strongly <u>recommend</u> the publications listed on the back page of this leaflet.

You can say that you **recommend** someone or something **for** a particular job or purpose.

Nell was <u>recommended for</u> a job as a nursery governess.
I <u>recommend</u> hill running <u>for</u> strengthening thighs.

If you **recommend** a particular action, you say that it is the best thing to do in the circumstances.

They <u>recommended</u> a merger of the two biggest supermarket groups.
The doctor may <u>recommend</u> limiting the amount of fat in your diet.

You can **recommend that someone does** something or **recommend that someone should do** something.

It is not <u>recommended that students pay</u> in advance.
The Committee must decide whether or not to <u>recommend that the President should resign.</u>

You can also **recommend someone to do** something.

Although they have eight children, they do not <u>recommend other couples to have</u> families of this size.

(i) Note that some people consider this usage to be incorrect and say that you should say 'Although they have eight children, they do not **recommend that other couples should have** families of this size.

⚠ **WARNING:** You do not say that you 'recommend someone' a particular action. You do not say, for example, 'I recommend you a visit to Paris'. You say 'I **recommend a visit** to Paris', 'I **recommend visiting** Paris', or 'I **recommend that you visit** Paris'.

recover

If you **recover**, you become well again after an illness or injury.

It was weeks before he fully <u>recovered.</u>

Recover is a fairly formal word. In conversation, you usually say that someone **gets better**.

He soon <u>got better</u> after a few days in bed.

You can say that someone **recovers from** an illness.

How long do people take to <u>recover from</u> sickness of this kind?

(i) Note that you do not say that someone 'gets better from' an illness.

referee

⇨ See **Usage** entry at **umpire - referee**.

USAGE

refuse

Refuse can be a verb or a noun. When it is a verb, it is pronounced /rɪfjuːz/. When it is a noun, it is pronounced /ˈrefjuːs/.

1 used as a verb

If you **refuse** to do something, you deliberately do not do it, or you say firmly that you will not do it.

He refused to accept their advice.
Three employees were dismissed for refusing to join a union.

2 'reject'

If you do not agree with an idea or belief, you do not say that you 'refuse' it. You say that you **reject** it.

Some people reject the idea of a mixed economy.
It was hard for me to reject my family's religious beliefs.

3 used as a noun

Refuse is a noun used to refer to things that you throw away.

…a dump for refuse.
This department is also responsible for refuse collection.

Several other words are used to refer to things that are thrown away.

⇨ For more information, see **Usage** entry at **rubbish.**

regard

If you **regard** someone or something **as** a particular thing, you believe that they are that thing.

I regard it as one of my masterpieces.
Kenworthy did not regard himself as an expert on language.

You can also say that someone or something **is regarded as being** a particular thing or **is regarded as having** a particular quality.

The play was regarded as being of mixed merits.
The couple are regarded as having one of the strongest marriages in showbiz.

ⓘ Note that you do not say that someone or something 'is regarded to be' a particular thing or 'is regarded to have' a particular quality.

regret - be sorry

1 sadness and disappointment

Regret and **be sorry** are both used to say that someone feels sadness or disappointment about something that has happened, or about something they have done. **Regret** is more formal than **be sorry**.

You can say that you **regret** something or **are sorry about** it.

I immediately regretted my decision.
I'm more sorry about losing Pat.

You can also say that you **regret** or **are sorry** that something has happened.

Pisarev regretted that no real changes had occurred.
He was sorry he had agreed to stay.

You can also say that you **regret doing** something.

None of the women I spoke to regretted making this change.

ⓘ Note that you do not say that you 'are sorry doing' something.

2 apologizing

When you are apologizing to someone for something that has happened, you can say that you **are sorry about** it.

She was very sorry about all the trouble she'd caused.

ⓘ Note that you do not say that you are 'sorry for' something.

In conversation, you do not apologize by saying that you 'regret' something. **Regret** is only used in formal letters and announcements.

London Transport regrets any inconvenience caused by these delays.

⇨ For information on other ways of apologizing, see **Topic** entry at **Apologizing**.

3 **giving bad news**
When you are giving someone some bad news, you can begin by saying 'I'**m sorry to** tell you…'. In a formal letter, you say 'I **regret to** tell you…'.

I 'm sorry to tell you this, but the Board have changed their opinion of you.
I regret to inform you that your application has not been successful.

reject
⇨ See **Usage** entry at **refuse**.

related
If something is **related to** something else, the two things are connected in some way.

This species is related to the familiar grass snake Natrix natrix.
Physics is closely related to mathematics.

ⓘ Note that you do not use any preposition except **to** in sentences like these.

relation - relative - relationship
These words are used to refer to people or to connections between people.

1 **'relation' and 'relative'**
Your **relations** or **relatives** are the members of your family.

I said that I was a relation of her first husband.
His wife had to visit some of her relatives.

The **relations** between people or groups are the contacts between them and the way they behave towards each other.

Apparently relations between husband and wife had not improved.
The unions should have close relations with management.

2 **'relationship'**
You can talk in a similar way about the **relationship** between two people or groups.

The old relationship between the friends was quickly re-established.
Pakistan's relationship with India has changed dramatically.

A **relationship** is also a close friendship between two people, especially one involving sexual or romantic feelings.

When the relationship ended two months ago, he said he wanted to die.

relax
When you **relax,** you make yourself calmer and less worried or tense.

Make the room dark, get into bed, close your eyes, and relax.
Some people can't even relax when they are at home.

ⓘ Note that **relax** is not a reflexive verb. You do not say that you 'relax yourself'.

release - let go
Release and **let go** are used in similar ways. **Release** is more formal than **let go.**
If you **release** a person or animal or **let** them **go,** you allow them to leave or escape.

They had just been released from prison.
Eventually I let the frog go.

To **release** or **let go of** something or someone also means to stop holding them.

He released her hand quickly.
'Let go of me,' she said.

USAGE

relieve - relief

1 'relieve'

Relieve /rɪliːv/ is a verb. If something **relieves** an unpleasant feeling, it makes it less unpleasant.

Anxiety may <u>be relieved</u> by talking to a friend.
The passengers in the plane swallow to <u>relieve</u> the pressure on their eardrums.

If someone or something **relieves** you **of** an unpleasant feeling or difficulty, you no longer have it.

The news <u>relieved</u> him <u>of</u> some of his embarrassment.

2 'relief'

Relief /rɪliːf/ is a noun. If you feel **relief**, you feel glad because something unpleasant has stopped or has not happened.

I breathed a sigh of <u>relief.</u>
To my <u>relief,</u> he found the suggestion acceptable.

Relief is also money, food, or clothing that is provided for people who are very poor or hungry.

We are providing <u>relief</u> to vulnerable refugees, especially those who are sick.

remain - stay

Remain and **stay** are often used with the same meaning. **Remain** is more formal than **stay**. To **remain** or **stay** in a particular state means to continue to be in that state.

Oliver <u>remained</u> silent.
I <u>stayed</u> awake.

If you **remain** or **stay** in a place, you do not leave it.

I was allowed to <u>remain</u> at home.
Fewer women these days <u>stay</u> at home to look after their children.

If something still exists, you can say that it **remains**. You do not say that it 'stays'.

Even today remnants of this practice <u>remain.</u>
He was cut off from what <u>remained</u> of his family.

If you **stay** in a town, hotel, or house, you live there for a short time.

How long can you <u>stay</u> in Brussels?
She <u>was staying</u> in the same hotel as I was.

ⓘ Note that you do not use **remain** with this meaning.

remark

⇨ See **Usage** entry at **comment - mention - remark**.

remember - remind

1 'remember'

If you **remember** people or events from the past, your mind still has an impression of them and you are able to think about them.

I <u>remember</u> the look on Gary's face as he walked out the door.
He <u>remembered</u> the man well.

ⓘ Note that you do not usually use a continuous tense of **remember**. You do not say, for example, 'I am remembering the look on Gary's face as he walked out the door'.

You can use either an '-ing' form or a 'to'-infinitive after **remember,** but with different meanings. If your mind has an impression of something you did in the past, you say that you **remember doing** it.

I <u>remember asking</u> one of my sons about this.

If you do something you had intended to do, you can say that you **remember to do** it.
He remembered to turn the gas off.

2 **'remind'**

If you mention to someone that they had intended to do something, you do not say that you 'remember' them to do it. You say that you **remind** them to do it.
⇨ See **Usage** entry at **remind**.

remind

If you **remind** someone **of** a fact or event that they already know about, you say something which causes them to think about it.
She reminded him of two appointments.
You do not need to remind people of their mistakes.

You can **remind** someone **that** something is the case.
I reminded him that we had a wedding to go to on Saturday.

If you **remind** someone **to do** something, you tell them again that they should do it, or you mention to them that they had intended to do it.
She reminded me to wear the visitor's badge at all times.
Remind me to speak to you about Davis.

(i) Note that you do not say that you remind someone 'of doing' something.

If someone or something **reminds** you **of** another person or thing, they are similar to that other person or thing and make you think about them.
Your son reminds me of you at his age.

(i) Note that you must use **of** in a sentence like this.

remove - move

1 **'remove'**

If you **remove** something, you take it away.
The tea-ladies came in to remove the cups.
He removed his hand from the man's collar.

2 **'move'**

If you go to live in a different house taking your possessions with you, you do not say that you 'remove'. You say that you **move**.
Send me your new address if you move.
Last year my parents moved from Hyde to Stepney.

In British English, you can also say that you **move house**.
Cats sometimes get lost when families move house.

rent
⇨ See **Usage** entry at **hire - rent - let**.

repair
⇨ See **Usage** entry at **restore - repair**.

request

Request can be a noun or a verb.

1 **used as a noun**

When someone asks for something to be done or provided, you can say that they make a **request**.
My friend made a polite request.
The Minister had granted the request.

USAGE

You say that someone makes a **request for** something.
He agreed to my request for psychiatric help.

2 used as a verb

When someone **requests** something, they ask for it.
The President requested an emergency session of the United Nations.
Mr Dennis said he had requested access to a telephone.

(i) Note that when **request** is a verb, you do not use 'for' after it.

require

If you **require** something, you need it or want it.
Is there anything you require?
We cannot guarantee that any particular item will be available when you require it.

Require is a formal word. You do not usually use it in conversation. Instead, you use **need** or **want**.

I won't need that book any more.
All they want is a holiday.

If something **is required,** it must be obtained in order that something else can be done.
Parliamentary approval would be required for any scheme.
An increase in funds might well be required.

If you **are required to** do something, you have to do it, for example because of a rule or law.
All the boys were required to study religion.

research - search

1 'research'

Research is work that involves studying something and trying to discover facts about it. You say that someone **does research.**
I had come to India to do some research into Anglo-Indian literature.

You can refer to the research that someone is doing as their **research** or their **researches.** You normally only use **researches** after a possessive form such as **my**, **his**, or **Gordon's.**
Soon after, Faraday began his researches into electricity.
… Kinsey's research on sexual behavior.

2 'search'

You do not use **research** to refer to an attempt to find something by looking for it carefully. The word you use is **search.**
A huge search for the missing documents was mounted.
A quick search of the boat revealed nothing.

resign - retire

1 'resign'

If someone **resigns** from their job, they leave it after saying that they do not want to do it any more. You can **resign** from your job at any age, and perhaps start another job soon afterwards.
A hospital administrator has resigned over claims he lied to get the job.

2 'retire'

When someone **retires,** they leave their job and stop working, often because they have reached the age when they can get a pension. When professional sportsmen and women stop playing sport as their job, you can also say that they **retire,** even if they are fairly young.

At the age when most people <u>retire</u>, he is ready to face a new career.
I have decided to <u>retire</u> from Formula One racing at the end of the season.

respectable - respectful

1 **'respectable'**
Someone or something that is **respectable** is approved of by people and considered to be morally correct.
He came from a perfectly <u>respectable</u> middle-class family.

2 **'respectful'**
If your behaviour is **respectful,** you show respect for someone or something.
The woman kept a <u>respectful</u> silence.
The Security Officer was standing at a <u>respectful</u> distance holding a plastic cup of coffee.

responsible

1 **'responsible for'**
If you are **responsible for doing** something, it is your job or duty to do it.
The children were <u>responsible for cleaning</u> their own rooms.

(i) Note that you do not say that someone is 'responsible to do' something.

If you are **responsible for** something bad that has happened, it is your fault.
They were charged with being <u>responsible for</u> the death of two policemen.

(i) You do not use any preposition except **for** after **responsible** in a sentence like this.

2 **used after a noun**
Responsible can also be used after a noun. If you talk about 'the person **responsible**', you mean 'the person who is responsible for what has happened'.
I hope they get the man <u>responsible</u>.
The company <u>responsible</u> refused to say what happened.

3 **used in front of a noun**
However, if you use **responsible** in front of a noun, it has a completely different meaning.
A **responsible** person is someone who can be relied on to behave properly and sensibly without needing to be controlled by anyone else.
… <u>responsible</u> members of the local community.

Responsible behaviour is sensible and correct.
I thought it was a very <u>responsible</u> decision.

rest

If you are talking about something that cannot be counted, the verb following **rest** is singular.
The rest of the <u>food was</u> delicious.

If you are talking about several people or things, the verb is plural.
The rest of the <u>boys were</u> delighted.

restful - restless

1 **'restful'**
Something that is **restful** helps you to feel calm and relaxed.
The lighting is <u>restful</u>.

2 **'restless'**
A **restless** child cannot keep still or quiet.
Some babies are tense and <u>restless</u> during the early weeks.

You also say that someone is **restless** when they are bored with what they are doing and

USAGE

want to do something else.

I knew within a fortnight I should feel restless again.

restore - repair

1 **'restore'**

To **restore** an old building, painting, or piece of furniture means to repair and clean it, so that it returns to its original condition.

Several million pounds will be required to restore the theatre.

I asked whether the pictures could be restored.

2 **'repair'**

To **repair** something that has been damaged or that is not working properly means to mend it.

No one knew how to repair the engine.

result - effect

1 **'result'**

A **result** of something is an event or situation that happens or exists because of it.

The result of this was months of anguish and guilt.

I nearly missed the flight as a result of going to Havana.

Twice he followed his own advice, with disastrous results.

2 **'effect'**

When something produces a change in a thing or person, you do not refer to this change as a 'result' on the thing or person. The word you use is **effect.**

Road transport has a considerable effect on our daily lives.

retarded

In the past, when a child had a mental condition that made learning difficult, people used to say that he or she was **retarded, backward, simple,** or **educationally subnormal.** Nowadays these words are avoided because they are considered offensive. The adjective **mentally handicapped** is sometimes used to describe children who have a mental condition of this kind. However, the most sensitive ways of referring to such children are to call them **children with special needs** or **children with learning difficulties.**

…a school for children with special needs.

Food supplements may help children with learning difficulties to make big improvements.

(i) Note that children with physical handicaps are also called **children with special needs.**

⇨ See **Usage** entry at **crippled.**

retire - retiring

1 **'retire'**

When someone **retires,** they leave their job and stop working, usually because they have reached the age when they can get a pension.

Gladys retired at the age of sixty-eight.

They had decided to retire from farming.

⇨ See **Usage** entry at **resign - retire.**

2 **'retiring'**

The adjective **retiring** has two meanings.

You use it in front of a noun such as **MP** or **chairman** to indicate that someone will soon give up their present job and be replaced by someone else.

…Jim Dacre, the retiring Labour MP.

The retiring President of the Methodist Conference.

You also use it to describe someone who is very quiet and avoids meeting other people.
She was a shy, <u>retiring</u> girl.

return

1 going back
When someone **returns** to a place, they go back there after they have been somewhere else.
I <u>returned</u> to my hotel.
Mr Platt <u>returned</u> from Canada in 1995.

(i) Note that you do not say that someone 'returns back' to a place.

Return is a fairly formal word. In conversation, you usually use **go back, come back,** or **get back.**
I <u>went back</u> to the kitchen and poured my coffee.
I have just <u>come back</u> from a holiday in the Highlands.
I've got to <u>get back</u> to London.

Return is also a noun. When someone goes back to a place, you can refer to their arrival there as their **return.**
It was published only after his <u>return</u> to Russia in 1917.

In writing, if you want to say that something happens immediately after someone returns to a place, you can use a phrase beginning with **on**. For example, you can say ' **On his return** to London, he was offered a post at the Foreign Office'.
<u>On his return</u> to Paris he painted a series of portraits.
<u>On her return</u> she wrote the last paragraph of her autobiography.

2 giving or putting something back
When someone **returns** something they have taken or borrowed, they give it back or put it back.
He borrowed my best suit and didn't <u>return</u> it.
We <u>returned</u> the books to the shelf.

(i) Note that you do not say that someone 'returns something back'.

3 'bring back'
When people start using a practice or method that was used in the past, you do not say that they 'return' the practice or method. You say that they **bring** it **back** or **reintroduce** it.
He was all for <u>bringing back</u> the cane as a punishment in schools.
They <u>reintroduced</u> a scheme to provide housing for refugees.

review
⇨ See **Usage** entry at **critic - critical - critique.**

reward - award
Both these nouns are used to refer to something you receive because you have done something useful or good.

1 'reward'
A **reward** is usually something valuable, such as money.
Hearst announced a <u>reward</u> of £ 50,000 for information.

2 'award'
An **award** is something such as a prize, certificate, or medal.
The only <u>award</u> he had ever won was the Toplady Prize for Divinity.

rid

1 'get rid of'
Rid is usually used in the expression **get rid of.** If you **get rid of** something or someone

USAGE

that you do not want, you take action so that you no longer have them.

She bathed thoroughly to get rid of the last traces of make-up.

We had to get rid of the director.

2 **'rid' used as a verb**

You can also use **rid** as a verb. If you **rid** a place or yourself **of** something unpleasant or annoying, you take action so that it no longer exists or no longer affects you. Note that the past tense and past participle of **rid** is **rid,** not 'ridded'.

We must rid the country of this wickedness.

He had rid himself of his illusions.

---

ride

1 **'ride'**

When you **ride** an animal, bicycle, or motorcycle, you control and travel on it.

Every morning he used to ride his mare across the fields.

They overcome their fears and learn to swim or ride a bike.

The past tense of **ride** is **rode,** not 'rided'. The past participle is **ridden.**

Niall MacKenzie rode a Suzuki, ahead of Sito Pons, who rode a Honda.

He was the best horse I have ever ridden.

2 **'ride on'**

You can also say that someone **rides on** an animal, bicycle, or motorcycle.

At the end of the film Gregory Peck rode off with Ingrid Bergman on a horse.

He rode around the campus on a bicycle.

3 **'drive'**

When someone controls a car, lorry, or train, you do not say that they 'ride' it. You say that they **drive** it.

It was her turn to drive the car.

Dennis has never learned to drive.

However, if you are a passenger in a vehicle, you can say that you **ride in** it.

We rode back in a taxi.

He prefers travelling on the tube to riding in a limousine.

---

right

If you say that something is **right,** you mean that it is correct or appropriate.

You've got the pronunciation right.

You must do things in the right order.

In conversation, **right** is sometimes an adverb. For example, someone might say 'He did it **right**'. In writing, it is better to avoid this use. You should say 'He did it **the right way**' or 'He did it **in the right way**'.

I assured him that he was playing exactly the right way.

I thought I handled it in the right way.

---

ring

When you **ring** someone, you dial their phone number and speak to them by phone. The past tense of **ring** is **rang,** not 'ringed' or 'rung'.

I rang Aunt Jane this evening.

The past participle is **rung.**

Mr Carlin said he had rung Mr Macalister at Glasgow CID.

You can say that someone **rings** a place.

You must ring the hospital at once.

In conversation, people often use **ring up,** instead of 'ring'. There is no difference in meaning.

He <u>had rung up</u> Emily and told her all about it.

 Note that you do not use 'to' after **ring** or **ring up.**

American speakers do not say that one person 'rings' another. The word they use is **call.** Some British speakers also say **call.**

He promised to <u>call</u> me soon.
He <u>called</u> Colonel Ocker at regimental headquarters.

rise - raise

Rise and **raise** are usually verbs.

1 'rise'

Rise is an intransitive verb. If something **rises,** it moves upwards.

Thick columns of smoke <u>rise</u> from the houses

The other forms of **rise** are **rises, rising, rose, risen.**

The birds <u>rose</u> screaming around them.
The sun <u>had risen</u> behind them.

If an amount **rises,** it increases.

Commission rates are expected to <u>rise.</u>
Prices <u>rose</u> by more than 10% per annum.

When someone who is sitting **rises,** they raise their body until they are standing. This use of **rise** occurs mainly in stories.

Dr Willoughby <u>rose</u> to greet them.

In conversation, you do not usually say that someone 'rises'. You say that they **stand up.**

I put down my glass and <u>stood up.</u>

You can also use **rise** to say that someone gets out of bed in the morning. This use of **rise** also occurs mainly in stories, especially when the author is mentioning the time at which someone gets out of bed.

They <u>had risen</u> at dawn.

In conversation, you do not usually use 'rise' to say that someone gets out of bed. You say that they **get up.**

Mike decided it was time to <u>get up.</u>

 Note that you never say that someone 'gets up out of bed'.

2 'raise'

Raise is a transitive verb. If you **raise** something, you move it to a higher position.

He tried to <u>raise</u> the window, but the sash cord was broken.
She <u>raised</u> her eyebrows in surprise.

⇨ For another meaning of **raise,** see Usage entry at **bring up - raise - educate.**

3 used as nouns

Rise and **raise** can also be nouns. A **rise** is an increase in an amount or quantity.

The price <u>rises</u> are expected to continue.
…the <u>rise</u> in crime.

In British English, a **rise** is also an increase in someone's wages or salary.

He went to ask for a <u>rise.</u>

 In American English, this is called a **raise.**

He thought about asking his boss for a <u>raise.</u>

USAGE

risk

Risk can be a noun or a verb.

1 used as a noun

If there is a **risk** of something unpleasant, there is a possibility that it will happen.

There is very little risk of infection.
There's a serious risk that the main issues will be forgotten.

2 used as a verb

If someone **risks doing** something, it may happen as a result of some other action they take.

They were unwilling to risk bombing their own troops.

You can also say that someone **risks doing** something when they do it even though they know it might have unpleasant consequences.

If you have an expensive rug, don't risk washing it yourself.

(i) Note that you do not say that someone 'risks to do' something.

rob - steal

1 'rob'

The verb **rob** is often used in stories and newspaper reports.

If someone takes something that belongs to you without intending to return it, you can say that they **rob you of** it.

Pirates boarded the vessels and robbed the crew of money and valuables.
The two men were robbed of more than £700.

If something that belongs to you has been stolen, you can say that you have **been robbed.**

He was kicked to death after being robbed near a cashpoint machine.

If someone takes several things from a building without intending to return them, you say that they **rob** the building.

The only way I can get money is to rob a few banks.

2 'steal'

When the object of the verb is a person, you use **rob**. However, when you are talking about the thing which has been stolen, you use **steal**.

My first offence was stealing a pair of binoculars.

⇨ See **Usage** entry at **steal.**

robber

⇨ See **Usage** entry at **thief - robber - burglar.**

rock

⇨ See **Usage** entry at **stone.**

role - roll

These words are both pronounced /rəʊl/.

1 'role'

Your **role** is your position and function in a situation or society.

What is the role of the University in modern society?
He had played a major role in the formation of the United Nations.

A **role** is also one of the characters that an actor or singer plays in a film, play, opera, or musical.

She played the leading role in The Winter's Tale.

2 **'roll'**

A **roll** is a very small loaf.

…*a roll and butter.*

A **roll** of something such as cloth or paper is a long piece of it wrapped many times around itself or around a tube.

… *a roll of wallpaper.*

rotary

⇨ See **Usage** entry at **roundabout.**

round

⇨ See **Usage** entry at **around - round - about.**

roundabout

In British English, a **roundabout** or **merry-go-round** is a large mechanical device which rotates horizontally. It has plastic or wooden cars or animals on it which children sit in or on.

The children's roundabout was £1 a ride.

 In American English, a device like this is usually called a **carousel.**

…*a 1903 fairground carousel is being restored.*

In British English, a **roundabout** is also a circular area at a place where several roads meet. You drive round it until you come to the road you want.

The turning is off the roundabout where the A140 meets Norwich's ring road.

 In American English, an area like this is called a **traffic circle** or a **rotary.**

Staff said the traffic circle has successfully slowed down vehicle traffic.

rubbish

In British English, waste food and other unwanted things that you throw away are called **rubbish.**

…*unwanted household rubbish.*

 In American English, waste food is called **garbage** and other things that are thrown away are called **trash.**

…*rotting piles of garbage.*
They dumped their trash on the street.

A more formal word for all things that you throw away is **refuse** /rɛfjuːs/. **Refuse** is used in both British and American English.

The District Council made a weekly collection of refuse.

rude

If someone is **rude to** you, their behaviour towards you is not polite.

Gertrude felt she had been rude to Sylvia.
I was rather rude to a young nurse.

(*i*) Note that you do not use any preposition except **to** after **rude.**

run

When you **run,** you move in a similar way to walking, but faster and taking longer strides. The past tense of **run** is **ran,** not 'runned' or 'run'. The past participle is **run.**

Karl ran over to see if he could help.
Two men had run out of the wood.

⇨ For another meaning of **run,** see **Usage** entry at **stand.**

S s

's

1 used to form possessives

When a singular noun refers to a person or animal, you form the possessive by adding **'s.**

... _Ralph's_ voice.

...the _President's_ conduct.

...the _princess's_ aides.

...the _horse's_ eyes.

When a plural noun ends in 's', you form the possessive by adding an apostrophe (').

..._my colleagues'_ offices.

...their _parents'_ activities.

When a plural noun does not end in 's', you form the possessive by adding **'s.**

... _women's_ rights.

... _children's_ games.

When a name ends in 's', you usually form the possessive by adding **'s.**

... _Charles's_ Christmas present.

... _Mrs Jones's_ dressing-table.

In formal writing, the possessive of a name ending in 's' is sometimes formed by adding an apostrophe (').

..._a statue of Prince Charles'_ grandfather King George VI.

You do not usually add **'s** to nouns that refer to things. For example, you do not say 'the building's front'; you say 'the front **of the building**'. Similarly, you do not say 'my bicycle's bell'; you say 'the bell **on my bicycle**'.

...the bottom _of the hill._

...the end _of August._

2 pronouns

You can add **'s** to the following pronouns:

another	anyone	everyone	no-one	other	someone
anybody	everybody	nobody	one	somebody	

It puts _one's_ problems in perspective.
One side gives in too easily and accepts the other's demands.

The possessive forms of other pronouns are called **possessive determiners**.

⇨ For more information about these, see **Grammar** entry at **Possessive determiners**.

3 other uses of possessives

In British English, you can add **'s** to a person's name to refer to the house where they live. For example, 'I met him at **Gwyneth's**' means 'I met him at Gwyneth's house'.

Afterward Gene invited her to a party at Ford's.

British speakers also use words ending in **'s** to refer to shops. For example, they talk about a **chemist's**, a **tobacconist's**, or a **greengrocer's**.

Louise went back to the chemist's to get the rest of the prescription.

In Sydney, he had run a newsagent's.

You can use **be** and a short noun group ending in **'s** to say who something belongs to. For example, if someone says 'Whose is this coat?', you might say 'It's **my mother's**'.

One of the cars was his wife's.

(i) Note that you do not use this construction in formal writing. Instead you use **belong to**. You also use **belong to** when you are using several words to refer to someone. For example, you say 'It **belongs to** the man next door'. You do not say 'It is the man next door's'.

The painting belongs to a man living in Norfolk.

4 other uses of 's
Apart from its use in possessives, **'s** has three other uses:

● It can be a shortened form of **is**, especially after pronouns.

He's a novelist.
It's fantastic.
There's no hurry.

● It can be a shortened form of **has** when **has** is an auxiliary verb.

He's got a problem.
She's gone home.

● It can be a shortened form of **us** after **let**.

Let's go outside.

⇨ For more information about this use, see **Usage** entry at **let's - let us**.

sack

A **sack** is a large container made of rough woven material. Sacks are used to carry and store things such as potatoes and coal.

1 'bag' and 'sack'
In British English, you do not use **sack** to refer to a small container made of paper, or to a container with handles for putting shopping or personal possessions in. Containers like these are called **bags**.

⇨ See **Usage** entry at **bag**.

 However, in American English, **sack** is used to describe a small container made of paper.

The woman gave Kelly the total and put all her purchases in a paper sack.

2 'pocket'
You also do not use **sack** to refer to the parts of your clothes in which you carry money and other small articles. These parts are called **pockets**.

The man stood with his hands in his pockets.

sad
⇨ See **Usage** entry at **happy - sad**.

safe
⇨ See **Usage** entry at **save - safe**.

salad - lettuce

1 'salad'
A **salad** is a mixture of uncooked vegetables. You can eat it on its own or with other foods.

A salad of tomato, onion and cucumber.

2 'lettuce'
A salad usually includes the large green leaves of a vegetable called a **lettuce** /ˈletɪs/. Note that you do not refer to this vegetable as a 'salad'.

Tear the lettuce into bite-sized pieces.

salary - wages

Salary and **wages** are both used to refer to the money paid to someone regularly for the work they do.

1 'salary'

Professional people such as teachers are usually paid a **salary**. Their **salary** is the amount of money which they are paid each year, although they actually get a certain amount each month.

She earns a high salary as an accountant.

2 'wages'

If someone gets money each week for the work they do, you refer to this money as their **wages**.

His wages will double to £15,000 a week at Ipswich.

3 'wage'

You can refer in a general way to the amount that someone earns as a **wage**.

They're campaigning for a legal minimum wage.
… the problems of bringing up children on a low wage.

sale

1 'sale'

The **sale** of something is the act of selling it, or the occasion on which it is sold.

One such measure was stricter control of the sale of dynamite.
…the sale of the Elliotdale property.

A **sale** is an event in which a shop sells things at a reduced price.

Debenhams are having a sale.

2 'for sale'

If something is **for sale** or **up for sale**, its owner is trying to sell it.

I enquired if the horse was for sale.
Their house is up for sale.

3 'on sale'

A product that is **on sale** is available for people to buy.

The only English newspaper on sale was the Morning Star.
The jackets had only been on sale a week.

In American English, if you buy something **on sale**, you buy it at a reduced price, for example in a sale.

On sale. Slacks marked down from $39.95 to $20.00.

salute - greet

1 'salute'

When members of the armed forces **salute** someone, they raise their right hand as a formal sign of greeting or respect.

One of the company stepped out and saluted the General.

2 'greet'

Note that this is the only way in which the verb **salute** is used in modern English. You do not use **salute** to say that someone expresses friendliness or pleasure when they meet someone else. The word you use is **greet**.

He greeted his mother with a hug.
He hurried to greet his guests.

same - similar

Same is almost always used with **the**.

1 'the same'

If two or more things are **the same,** they are exactly alike.

Both categories may be present and both may look <u>the same.</u>

In essence, all computers are <u>the same.</u>

2 'the same as'

You say that one thing is **the same as** another thing.

It is really just <u>the same as</u> any other police work.

24 Springburn Terrace was <u>the same as</u> its neighbours.

(*i*) You do not use any preposition except **as** after **the same** in sentences like these.

You can put a noun between **the same** and **as.** You can say, for example, 'She works in **the same office as** her sister'.

It was <u>the same colour as</u> the wall.

They're not in <u>the same position as</u> the other universities.

You can also use **the same as** to compare actions. For example, you can say 'She did **the same as** her sister did', or just 'She did **the same as** her sister'.

He did exactly <u>the same as</u> John did.

They've got to do their housekeeping <u>the same as</u> anybody else.

3 'the same...that'

You can also use a 'that'-clause after **the same** and a noun.

They made exactly <u>the same recommendations that</u> are now finally being implemented.

That was <u>the same year that</u> he won the British Open.

4 modifiers used with 'the same'

You can use words like **exactly** and **nearly** in front of **the same.**

I had the impression that on the far side the view would be <u>exactly the same.</u>

This is <u>practically the same as</u> on the previous sheet.

5 'similar'

If two people or things are **similar,** each one has some features which the other one has.

The two men were remarkably <u>similar.</u>

The letters are basically very <u>similar.</u>

You say that one thing is **similar to** another thing.

It is <u>similar to</u> the rest of the field.

Do you run programmes <u>similar to</u> that overseas?

You can use **similar** in front of a noun when you are comparing a person or thing to someone or something else that has just been mentioned.

Many of today's adults have had a <u>similar</u> experience.

6 modifiers used with 'similar'

You can use words like **rather** and **very** with **similar.**

His own background was <u>rather similar to</u> my own.

My problems are <u>very similar to</u> yours.

satisfactory - satisfying

1 'satisfactory'

You say that something is **satisfactory** when it is acceptable or fulfils a particular need or purpose.

His doctor described his state of health as fairly <u>satisfactory.</u>

It's not a <u>satisfactory</u> system.

2 'satisfying'

You do not use **satisfactory** to describe something that gives you a feeling of pleasure and fulfilment. The word you use is **satisfying.**

USAGE

There's nothing more <u>satisfying</u> than doing the work you love.
It's wonderful to have a <u>satisfying</u> hobby.

satisfied

If you are **satisfied with** something, you are pleased with it, because it is what you wanted.

Children at this age are <u>satisfied with</u> simple answers.
Are you <u>satisfied with</u> the pay structure in your company?

(i) Note that you do not use any preposition except **with** in sentences like these.

You can use adverbs such as **well** and **completely** in front of **satisfied.**

He was <u>well satisfied with</u> the progress that had been made so far.
We were <u>quite satisfied with</u> the catalogue.

⇨ Several other words can be used to show how pleased or disappointed someone is with something. For a graded list, see **Usage** entry at **pleased - disappointed.**

save - safe

1 **'save'**

Save /seɪv/ is a verb. If you **save** someone, you rescue them from danger or death.

He risked death to <u>save</u> his small daughter from a fire.

If you **save** money, you gradually collect it by not spending it.

They had managed to <u>save</u> enough to buy a house.

2 **'safe'**

Safe /seɪf/ is an adjective. If you are **safe** from something, you cannot be harmed by it.

We're <u>safe</u> now. They've gone.

(i) Note that when **safe** is used to describe people, you do not use it in front of a noun.

savings

⇨ See **Usage** entry at **economics.**

say

1 **'say'**

When you **say** something, you use your voice to produce words. The past tense and past participle of **say** is **said** /sed/, not 'sayed'.

You use **say** when you are quoting directly the words that someone has spoken.

'I've never felt so relaxed,' she <u>said.</u>
'Listen, Rudy,' he <u>said</u> , 'I'm not getting any younger.'
He <u>said</u> , 'Gertrude, I'm an awful liar.'

⇨ In writing, you can use many other verbs instead of **say** when you are quoting someone's words. See **Grammar** entry at **Reporting.**

However, in speech you always use **say**. In speech, you mention the person whose words you are quoting first.

She <u>said</u> , 'Just drop me a postcard when you're coming.'

You can use **it** after **said** to refer to the words a person used when they said something. For example, you can say 'Jane said, "I'm going now." She **said it** very quietly'.

He hadn't <u>said it</u> very nicely.
I just <u>said it</u> for something to say.

However, if you are referring to what someone has expressed rather than their actual words, you use **so**, not 'it'. For example, you say 'I didn't agree with him and I **said so**'. You do not say 'I didn't agree with him and I said it'.

Why didn't you <u>say so</u> earlier?
If you <u>say so,</u> I suppose I'll have to accept it.

You can report what someone has said without mentioning their exact words using **say** and a 'that'-clause.

Officials <u>said</u> that at least one soldier had been killed.

⚠ **WARNING:** Note that you do not use 'say' with an indirect object. For example, you do not say ~~The woman said me that Mr Calthrop had left some days before~~. You say 'The woman **said** that Mr Calthrop had left some days before' or 'The woman **told me** that Mr Calthrop had left some days before'.

2 **'tell'**

If you are mentioning the hearer as well as the speaker, you usually use **tell,** rather than 'say'. The past tense and past participle of **tell** is **told.** So, for example, instead of saying 'I said to him that his mother had arrived', you say 'I **told** him that his mother had arrived'.

He <u>told</u> me that he had once studied chemistry.

'He has the ability to run a business,' one financial analyst <u>told</u> me.

Similarly, if you want to mention who an order or instruction was given to, you use **tell,** not 'say'.

She <u>told</u> me to be careful.

I <u>was told</u> to sit on the front bench.

You say that someone **tells** a story, lie, or joke.

You <u>'re telling</u> lies now.

Mr Crosby, the organist, <u>told</u> jokes and stories.

ⓘ Note that you can also say that someone **makes** or **cracks** a joke. However, the meaning is not the same.

⇨ See **Usage** entry at **joke.**

You do not say that someone 'says' a story, lie, or joke.

3 **'ask'**

You do not say that someone 'says' a question. You say that they **ask** a question.

Jill began to <u>ask</u> Fred a lot of questions about his childhood.

I wasn't the only one <u>asking</u> questions.

4 **'give'**

You do not say that someone 'says' an order or instruction. You say that they **give** an order or instruction.

He <u>gave</u> an order for special food to be brought to Harold.

He <u>had given</u> instructions that a peaceful protest could go ahead.

5 **'call'**

If you want to say that someone describes someone else in a particular way, you can use **say** followed by a 'that'-clause. For example, you can say 'He **said** that I was a liar'. A simpler way is to use **call.** You say 'He **called** me a liar'.

She <u>calls</u> me lazy and selfish.

6 **'talk about'**

You do not use **say** to mention what someone is discussing. You do not say, for example, '~~He said about the customs of the Incas~~'. You say 'He **talked about** the customs of the Incas'.

He <u>talked about</u> the pleasures and problems of adopting children.

scarce - scarcely

1 **'scarce'**

Scarce is an adjective. If something that people use is **scarce,** very little of it is available.

Good quality land is <u>scarce.</u>

…a place where water is <u>scarce.</u>

[2] **'rare'**

You do not use **scarce** to say that something is not common, and is therefore interesting. The adjective you use is **rare**.

…a flower so <u>rare</u> that few botanists have ever seen it.
Diane's hobby is collecting <u>rare</u> books.

[3] **'scarcely'**

Scarcely is an adverb. It has a totally different meaning from **scarce**. You use **scarcely** to say that something is only just the case. **Scarcely** is a fairly formal word.

…a denim jacket <u>scarcely</u> warm enough for mid-winter.
It was a very young man who had said this, <u>scarcely</u> more than a boy.

⚠ **WARNING:** You do not use 'not' with **scarcely**. You do not say, for example, 'I am not scarcely able to earn a living'. You say 'I am **scarcely** able to earn a living'.

If you use an auxiliary or modal with **scarcely,** you put the auxiliary or modal first. You say, for example, 'I **could scarcely** stand'. You do not say 'I scarcely could stand'.

I <u>can scarcely</u> remember what we ate.
The two characters <u>could scarcely</u> be more different.

Scarcely is sometimes used in longer structures to say that one thing happened immediately after another.

The noise had <u>scarcely</u> died away when someone started to laugh again.

ⓘ Note that you use **when,** not 'than', in sentences like these. You do not say, for example, 'The noise had scarcely died away than someone started to laugh again'.

In stories, **scarcely** is sometimes put at the beginning of a sentence, followed by **had** or the verb **be** and the subject.

<u>Scarcely had the car</u> drawn to a halt when armed police surrounded it.
<u>Scarcely was the letter bomb case</u> cleared up when more bombs went off in the capital.

scene - sight - view - landscape - scenery

[1] **'scene'**

The noun **scene** has several meanings.
It can refer to a part of a play, film, or novel.

…the balcony <u>scene</u> from 'Romeo and Juliet'.
It was like some <u>scene</u> from a Victorian novel.

The **scene** of an accident or crime is the place where it happened.

They were only a few miles from the <u>scene</u> of the crime.

You can indicate your impression of the things that are happening in a place at a particular time by referring to them as a **scene** of a particular kind.

…a <u>scene</u> of domestic tranquillity.
The moon rose over a <u>scene</u> of extraordinary destruction.

[2] **'sight'**

If you want to indicate your impression of the appearance of a particular thing or person, you use **sight**.

The room was a remarkable <u>sight</u>.
He was an awful <u>sight</u>.

Here are some other nouns that are commonly used to refer to things that people see:

[3] **'view'**

If you want to refer to what you can see from a window or high place, the word you use is **view**.

The window of her flat looked out on to a superb <u>view</u> of London.
From the top there is a fine <u>view</u>.

4 **'landscape'**

If you want to describe what you can see around you when you are travelling through an area of land, the word you use is **landscape.** You can use this word whether the area is attractive or not.

The landscape seemed desolate.

…the industrial landscape of eastern Massachusetts.

5 **'scenery'**

If you want to refer to what you see around you in an attractive part of the countryside, the word you use is **scenery.**

We had time to admire the scenery.

(i) Note that **scenery** is an uncount noun. You do not talk about 'sceneries' or 'a scenery'.

sceptic - sceptical

1 **'sceptic'**

Sceptic is a noun. A **sceptic** is someone who has doubts about things that other people believe.

The sceptic may argue that there are no grounds for such optimism.

He will need to polish his arguments if he is to convince the sceptics.

2 **'sceptical'**

Sceptical is an adjective. If you are **sceptical** about something, you have doubts about it.

Robert's father was sceptical about hypnotism.

At first Meyer had been sceptical.

 The usual American spellings of 'sceptic' and 'sceptical' are **skeptic** and **skeptical.**

scholar

A **scholar** is a child or student who has obtained a **scholarship,** by which they obtain money for their studies from their school or university, or from some other organization.

…a Rhodes scholar.

A person who studies an academic subject and knows a lot about it is sometimes referred to as a **scholar.** This is a rather old-fashioned use.

…Benjamin Jowett, the theologian and Greek scholar.

⇨ See **Usage** entry at **student.**

school - university

1 **used as count nouns**

In both British and American English, a **school** is a place where children are educated, and a **university** is a place where students study for degrees.

2 **used as uncount nouns**

In American English, **school** (without 'a' or 'the') is used to refer to both schools and universities. If someone is attending a school or university, Americans say that they are **in school.**

All the children were in school.

She is doing well in school.

Note that when speakers of American English ask an adult 'Where did you go to school?', they mean 'What college or university did you study in?'.

In British English, **school** refers only to schools. If someone is attending a school, British speakers say they are **at school.** If they are attending a university, British speakers say they are **at university.**

I was <u>at school</u> with her.
Her one aim in life is to go to <u>university</u>.

⇨ See also **Usage** entry at **student.**

scissors

Scissors are a small tool consisting of two sharp blades joined together. You use **scissors** for cutting things such as paper, cloth, or hair.

Scissors is a plural noun. You do not talk about 'a scissors'. Instead you talk about **some scissors** or **a pair of scissors.**

I wish I'd brought <u>some scissors.</u>
She took <u>a pair of scissors</u> and cut his hair.

search

Search can be a verb or a noun.

1 **used as a verb**

If you **search** a place or person, you examine them thoroughly because you are trying to find something.

Armed troops <u>searched</u> the hospital yesterday.
He stood with his arms outstretched while Fassler <u>searched</u> him.

ⓘ Note that you do not say that you 'search' the thing you are trying to find. You can say that you **search for** it, but you usually say that you **look for** it.

He'<u>s looking for</u> his keys.

2 **used as a noun**

A **search** is an attempt to find something by looking for it carefully.

I found the keys after a long <u>search.</u>
…the <u>search</u> for oil.

seat

⇨ See **Usage** entry at **sit.**

see

The verb **see** is used with several different meanings. Its past tense is **saw,** not 'seed'. Its past participle is **seen.**

1 **using your eyes**

If you **can see** something, you are aware of it through your eyes.

We <u>can see</u> the horizon now.

ⓘ Note that you usually use **can** in sentences like these. You say, for example, 'I **can see** the sea'. You do not say 'I see the sea'. You also do not use a continuous tense. You do not say 'I am seeing the sea'.

If you want to say that someone was aware of something in this way in the past, you usually use **could see.**

He <u>could see</u> Wilson's face in the mirror.

If you want to say that someone became aware of something, you use **saw.**

We suddenly <u>saw</u> a vessel through a gap in the fog.

You can use an '-ing' form after **saw** or **could see** to indicate that someone was aware of something that was continuing to take place.

I <u>saw</u> Benjamin <u>standing</u> there patiently.
They <u>could see</u> the planes <u>coming in</u> over the fields.

You can use an infinitive without 'to' after **saw** to indicate that someone was aware of a complete event or action.

He <u>saw</u> the tears <u>come</u> to her eyes.
I <u>saw</u> Bogeslavski <u>get</u> to his feet.

⚠ **WARNING:** You do not use a 'to'-infinitive with an active form of **see.** You do not say, for example, '~~I saw him to take the book~~'.

2 | **passive use**
You can use a passive form of **see,** followed by either a 'to'-infinitive or an '-ing' form. You use a 'to'-infinitive after a passive form when you are talking about a complete event or action.

One pilot <u>was seen to bail out.</u>

You use an '-ing' form when you are talking about an event or action that was continuing to take place.

A man <u>was seen walking</u> into the sea.

⚠ **WARNING:** Do not confuse **see** with **look at** or **watch.**
⇨ For an explanation of the differences, see **Usage** entry at **see - look at - watch.**

3 | **meeting someone**
See is often used to mean 'visit' or 'meet by arrangement'.
It would be a good idea for you to <u>see</u> a doctor.

If two people are meeting each other regularly, for example because they are in love, you can say that they **are seeing** each other. When **see** has this meaning, it is usually used in a continuous tense.
Does he know we <u>are seeing</u> each other?

4 | **understanding**
See is very commonly used to mean 'understand'.
I don't quite <u>see</u> how they can argue that.
He didn't seem to notice much, if you <u>see</u> what I mean.

People often say **'I see'** to show that they have understood something.
'Humbert is Dolly's real father.' – '<u>I see.</u>'

When **see** means 'understand', you can use **can** or **could** with it.
I <u>can see</u> why Mr Smith is worried.
I <u>could see</u> his point.

ⓘ Note that you do not use a continuous tense when **see** means 'understand'. You do not say, for example, '~~I am seeing what you mean~~'.

5 | **attending to something**
If you **see** that something is done or **see to it** that it is done, you make sure that it is done, by getting someone else to do it or by doing it yourself.
<u>See</u> that everything is marked with your initials.
I'll <u>see to it</u> that there is some action.

When someone attends to something that needs attention, you can say that they **see to** it or **see about** it.
A man was there to <u>see to</u> our luggage.
Rudolph went into the station to <u>see about</u> Thomas's ticket.

see - look at - watch

1 | **'see'**
When you **see** something, you are aware of it through your eyes, or you notice it.
We <u>saw</u> the black smoke rising over the barbed wire.

⇨ See **Usage** entry at **see.**

USAGE

2 'look at'

When you **look at** something, you direct your eyes towards it.

He _looked at_ the food on his plate.
People _looked at_ her in astonishment.

⇨ See **Usage** entry at **look.**

3 'watch'

When you **watch** something, you pay attention to it using your eyes, because you are interested in what it is doing, or in what may happen.

We stopped and refuelled at Ti Tree and _watched_ the sunset.

After **watch** you can use an infinitive without 'to' or you can use an '-ing' form. You use an infinitive without 'to' when you are referring to a complete event or action.

He _watched_ her _climb_ into a compartment.

You use an '-ing' form to refer to an action that was continuing to take place.

They _watched_ Sheila _driving around_ in her yellow car.

4 sightseeing

If you go somewhere in order to look at something or watch something, you can say that you **go to see** it.

He _went_ to India _to see_ the Taj Mahal.
We _went_ to the zoo _to see_ the giant pandas.

5 entertainment and sport

Both **see** and **watch** are used when you are talking about entertainment or sport. When you go to the theatre or cinema, you say that you **see** a play or film.

I _saw_ my first stage play here in London, at the age of 12.
We _saw_ Greta Garbo in 'Queen Christina'.

You do not say that someone 'looks at' or 'watches' a play or film.

You say that someone **watches** television. However, you can say that someone **watches** or **sees** a particular programme.

He spends several hours _watching_ television.
…a rugby match he _watched_ on television.
I _saw_ it on television after the news.

Similarly you say that someone **watches** a sport such as football, but that they **watch** or **see** a particular match.

More people _are watching_ cricket than ever before.
Did you _watch_ the match against Romania, Garry?
…those of us who _saw_ England's defeat at Wrexham.

---

seek

If you **seek** something such as help, advice, or the solution to a problem, you try to obtain it.

I _was seeking_ the help of someone who spoke French.
Always _seek_ professional legal advice before entering into any agreement.

(ⁱ) Note that you do not say that someone 'seeks for' something.

The past tense and past participle of **seek** is **sought,** not 'seeked'.

Some units and formations _sought_ the earliest opportunity to surrender.
His views on the war _were sought_ by the American press.

Seek is often used in writing, but you do not normally use it in conversation. Instead of saying that someone 'seeks' something, you usually say that they **try to get** it or **try to find** it.

I _tried to get_ their support for a trade union.
They _tried to find_ other work.

In modern English, you never say that someone **seeks** a person or an object. You say that they **look for** the person or object.

I've been <u>looking for</u> you all over.
I <u>looked for</u> it for ages before I found it.

seem

You use **seem** to say that someone or something gives a particular impression.

1 used with adjectives

Seem is usually followed by an adjective. If someone gives the impression of being happy, you can say that they **seem** happy. You can also say that they **seem to be** happy. There is no difference in meaning.

Even minor problems <u>seem</u> important.
You <u>seem to be</u> very interested.

However, if the adjective is a ungraded adjective, you usually use **seem to be.** For example, you say 'He **seemed to be** alone'. You do not say '~~He seemed alone~~'.
She <u>seemed to be</u> asleep.

⇨ For an explanation of ungraded adjectives, see **Grammar** entry at **Adjectives.**

If you want to indicate who has an impression of someone or something, you use **seem** followed by an adjective and the preposition **to.**
He always <u>seemed old to me.</u>
This attitude <u>seemed nonsensical to the general public.</u>

2 used with noun groups

Instead of an adjective, you can use a noun group after **seem** or **seem to be.** For example, instead of saying 'She seemed nice', you can say 'She **seemed a nice person**' or 'She **seemed to be a nice person**'. In conversation, people often say 'She **seemed like a nice person**'.

It <u>seemed a long time</u> before the food came.
She <u>seems to be a very nice girl.</u>
It <u>seemed like a good idea.</u>

ⓘ Note that you do not use 'as' after **seem.** You do not say, for example, '~~It seemed as a good idea~~'.

If the noun group contains a determiner but not an adjective, you must use **seemed to be.** For example, you say 'He **seemed to be the owner** of the car'. You do not say '~~He seemed the owner of the car~~'.

The parcel <u>seemed to be a gift</u> for our children.
What <u>seems to be the trouble?</u>

3 used with verbs

You can use other 'to'-infinitives besides 'to be' after **seem.** For example, you can say 'He **seemed to need** help'. You can also say ' It **seemed that he needed** help' or ' It **seemed as though he needed** help'.

The experiments <u>seem to prove</u> that sugar is not very good for you.
It <u>did seem</u> to me <u>that she was</u> far too romantic.
It <u>seemed as though the war had ended.</u>

seldom

Seldom is a formal or literary word. It is used to say that something happens only occasionally.

1 position in clause

● If there is no auxiliary, **seldom** usually goes in front of the verb, unless the verb is **be.**
He <u>seldom bathed.</u>
It <u>seldom rains</u> there.

● **Seldom** goes after **be**.

The waiting time was seldom less than four hours.

● If there are auxiliaries, **seldom** goes after the first one.

That is why these dishes are seldom served at state banquets.
I can seldom use these reports as nobody would believe them.

● **Seldom** is sometimes put at the beginning of a sentence, followed by an auxiliary and the subject.

Seldom did a week pass without a request for information.
Seldom can there have been such a happy meeting.

2 **'hardly ever'**

Seldom is not normally used in conversation. Instead people say **hardly ever**.

People are hardly ever fooled by that.
I must confess that I've hardly ever been to the British Museum.

⇨ For a graded list of words and expressions which are used to say how often something happens, see section on **frequency** in **Grammar** entry at **Adjuncts**.

select

⇨ See **Usage** entry at **choose**.

self-conscious - confident

1 **'self-conscious'**

Someone who is **self-conscious** is easily embarrassed and worries about what other people think of them.

I stood there, feeling self-conscious.
Patrick is self-conscious about his thinness.

2 **'confident'**

If someone is sure of their own abilities, qualities, or ideas, you do not say that they are 'self-conscious'. You say that they are **confident, self-confident,** or **self-assured**.

…a witty, young and confident lawyer.
She was remarkably self-confident for her age.
His comments were firm and self-assured.

semester

⇨ See **Usage** entry at **term - semester**.

send - sent

1 **'send'**

Send and **sent** are different forms of the same verb. Because they sound similar, they are sometimes confused. **Send** /send/ is the base form. If you **send** something to someone, you arrange for it to be taken and delivered to them, for example by post.

The children used to send me a card at Christmas.

2 **'sent'**

Sent /sent/ is the past tense and past participle of **send**.

I drafted a letter and sent it to the President.
He had sent Axel a telegram.

sensible - sensitive

1 **'sensible'**

A **sensible** person makes good decisions and judgements based on reason rather than emotion.

She was a sensible girl and did not panic.

2 **'sensitive'**

Sensitive has two meanings.

A **sensitive** person is easily upset or offended by other people's remarks or behaviour.

You really must stop being <u>sensitive</u> about your accent.

This may make a <u>sensitive</u> child tense and apprehensive.

However, if you say that someone is **sensitive to** other people's problems or feelings, you mean that they show understanding and awareness of them.

We're trying to make people more <u>sensitive to</u> the difficulties faced by working mothers.

Picasso was courteous and <u>sensitive to</u> my feelings.

serious

1 **'serious'**

You say that a problem or situation is **serious** when it is bad enough to make people worried or afraid.

Bad housing is one of the most <u>serious</u> problems in the inner cities.

...a <u>serious</u> illness.

Serious matters are important and deserve careful consideration.

It's time to get down to the <u>serious</u> business of the meeting.

I think this is a <u>serious</u> point.

People who are **serious** are thoughtful and quiet and do not often make jokes.

...a rather <u>serious</u> girl.

You can also describe someone's expression as **serious**.

She had a <u>serious,</u> thoughtful face.

Don't look so <u>serious</u>!

2 **'serious about'**

If someone is **serious about** doing something that they have talked about doing, they really intend to do it.

This would prove that we were <u>serious about</u> overcoming the obstacles.

If the government is <u>serious about</u> encouraging us to save, it should overhaul the system.

(i) Note that you do not use any preposition except **about** in sentences like these.

sew

⇨ See **Usage** entry at **sow - sew**.

shadow - shade

1 **'shadow'**

A **shadow** is a dark shape made on a surface when something stands between a light and the surface.

An oak tree cast its <u>shadow</u> over a tiny round pool.

If a place is dark because something prevents light from reaching it, you can say that it is **in shadow.**

The whole canyon is <u>in shadow</u>.

2 **'shade'**

You refer to an area which is dark and cool because the sun cannot reach it as **the shade.**

They sat in <u>the shade</u> between the palms.

I moved my chair into <u>the shade</u>.

shall - will

1 **'shall' and 'will'**

Shall and **will** are used to make statements and ask questions about the future.

Shall and **will** are not usually pronounced in full when they come after a pronoun. When you write down what someone says, you usually represent **shall** or **will** as **'ll** and add it to the end of the pronoun.

He'll come back.
They'll spoil our picnic.

Shall and **will** have the negative forms **shall not** and **will not**. In speech, these are usually shortened to **shan't** /ʃɑːnt/ and **won't** /wəʊnt/. **Shan't** is rather old-fashioned, and is rarely used in American English.

I shan't ever do it again.
You won't hear much about it.

It used to be considered correct to write **shall** after **I** or **we**, and **will** after any other pronoun or noun group. However, most people now write **will** after **I** and **we**, and this is not regarded as incorrect, although **shall** is still sometimes used after **I** and **we**.

But I hope some day I will meet you.
We will be able to defend them.
I shall not be travelling to Blackpool for the Labour Party conference.

There are a few special cases in which you use **shall**, rather than 'will':

2 suggestions

You can make a suggestion about what you and someone else should do by asking a question beginning with '**Shall we...**'.

Shall we go and see a film?

You can also suggest what you and someone else should do by using a sentence which begins with '**Let's...**' and ends with '**...shall we?**'

Let's try out one for size, shall we?

3 asking for advice

You can use **shall I** or **shall we** when you are asking for suggestions or advice.

What shall I give them for dinner?
Where shall we go for our drink?

4 offering

You can say '**Shall I...**' when you are offering to do something.

Shall I shut the door?

Will also has some special uses:

5 requests

You can use **will you** to make a request.

Will you please destroy all my papers.
Don't let this out, will you, Dixon?

⇨ See **Topic** entry at **Requests, orders, and instructions**.

6 invitations

You can also use **will you** or the negative form **won't you** to make an invitation. **Won't you** is very polite.

Will you stay to lunch?
Won't you sit down, Inspector?

⇨ See **Topic** entry at **Invitations**.

7 ability

Will is sometimes used to say that someone or something is able to do something.

This will cure anything.
The car won't start.

> ⚠ **WARNING:** You do not normally use **shall** or **will** in clauses beginning with words and expressions such as **when, before,** or **as soon as.** You do not say, for example, ~~'I'll ring as soon as I shall get home'~~. Instead you use the simple present tense. You say 'I'll ring as soon as I **get** home'.

shave

When a man **shaves,** he cuts hair from his face using a razor.

When he <u>had shaved</u> and dressed, he went down to the kitchen.

Shave is not usually a reflexive verb. You do not normally say that a man 'shaves himself'. In conversation, you usually say that a man **has a shave,** rather than that he 'shaves'.

I can't remember when I last <u>had a shave.</u>

she

1. **used as the subject of a verb**

She can be the subject of a verb. You use **she** to refer to a woman, girl, or female animal that has already been mentioned, or whose identity is known.

'So long,' Mary said as <u>she</u> passed Miss Saunders.

The eggs of the female mosquito can only mature if <u>she</u> has a meal of human blood.

When the subject of a sentence is followed by a relative clause, you do not use **she** in front of the main verb. You do not say, for example, ~~'The woman who lives next door, she is a doctor'~~. You say 'The woman who lives next door is a doctor'.

The woman who owns this cabin will come back in the autumn.

2. **used to refer to things**

She is sometimes used instead of 'it' to refer to a country, ship, or car.

Now Britain needs new leadership if <u>she</u> is to play a significant role shaping Europe's future.

When the repairs had been done <u>she</u> was a fine and beautiful ship.

sheep - lamb

1. **'sheep'**

A **sheep** is a farm animal with a thick woolly coat. The plural of **sheep** is **sheep,** not 'sheeps'.

…six hundred <u>sheep.</u>

…grassland on which a flock of <u>sheep</u> were grazing.

2. **'lamb'**

The meat of a sheep is called **lamb.** The meat of an adult sheep used to be called **mutton,** but this word is no longer widely used.

ship

⇨ See **Usage** entry at **boat - ship.**

shooting

⇨ See **Usage** entry at **hunting - shooting.**

shops

When you want to refer to a particular type of shop, you can often simply use the word for the person who owns or manages the shop.

Down the road there is another <u>greengrocer.</u>

Bring me back a paper from the <u>newsagent.</u>

Alternatively, you can use the possessive form with **'s,** without a following noun.

…items which can be purchased at the <u>greengrocer's.</u>

She also cleans offices and serves in a local <u>newsagent's.</u>

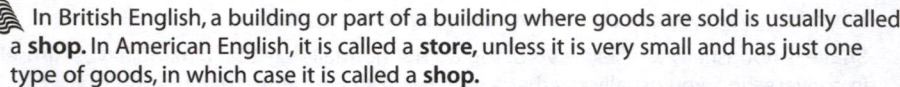

You can also use the same pattern with other words that refer to a person or business that provides a service, such as **hairdresser** or **dentist**.

Three or four times a week they'll go to the <u>hairdresser.</u>
It's worse than being at the <u>dentist's.</u>

shop - store

1 'shop'

In British English, a building or part of a building where goods are sold is usually called a **shop**. In American English, it is called a **store**, unless it is very small and has just one type of goods, in which case it is called a **shop**.

In British English, very large shops are sometimes called **stores**.

...a record <u>shop</u>.
...a local record <u>store</u>.

In both British and American English, a large shop which has separate departments selling different types of goods is called a **department store**.

The furnishings department of a large <u>department store</u>.

2 'shop' used as a verb

Shop can also be a verb. When people **shop**, they go to shops and buy things.

I usually <u>shop</u> on Saturdays.

However, you usually say that someone **goes shopping**, rather than that they 'shop'.

They <u>went shopping</u> after lunch.

3 'shopping'

Shopping is often a noun. It has two meanings. It can refer to the activity of buying things from shops.

I don't like <u>shopping</u>.

It can also refer to the things that someone has just bought from a shop or shops.

She put her <u>shopping</u> away in the kitchen.

Shopping is an uncount noun. You do not talk about 'a shopping' or someone's 'shoppings'.

When someone goes to the shops to buy things that they need regularly such as food, you say that they **do the shopping** or **do their shopping**.

Who's going to <u>do the shopping</u>?
She went to the next town to <u>do her shopping</u>.

shore

⇨ See **Usage** entry at **beach - shore - coast**.

short - shortly - briefly

1 'short'

Short is an adjective. You usually use it to indicate that something does not last for a long time.

...a <u>short</u> holiday.
He uttered a <u>short</u> cry of surprise.

2 'shortly'

Shortly is an adverb. If something is going to happen **shortly**, it is going to happen soon. This is a slightly old-fashioned use.

They should be returning <u>shortly</u>.

If something happened **shortly** after something else, it happened soon after it.

She died <u>shortly</u> afterwards.
Very <u>shortly</u> after I joined the church, I became a preacher.

3 **'briefly'**

You do not use **shortly** to say that something lasts or is done for a short time. You do not say, for example, ~~'She told them shortly what had happened'~~. The word you use is **briefly**.

She told them <u>briefly</u> what had happened.

shorts

⇨ See **Usage** entry at **pants - shorts**.

should

1 **basic uses**

Should is sometimes used with a similar meaning to 'ought to' and sometimes with a similar meaning to 'would'.

⇨ See separate **Usage** entry at **should - ought to**.

Should has the negative form **should not**. The **not** is not usually pronounced in full. When you write down what somebody says, you write **shouldn't**.

The following are some less common uses of **should**. When **should** is used in any of these ways, you pronounce it in full and you do not write it as "d".

2 **'should' in subordinate clauses**

Should is sometimes used in subordinate clauses, especially in writing. You use it in 'that'-clauses after verbs like **propose** and **suggest**.

He proposes that the Government <u>should</u> hold an inquiry.
His vets advised that the horse <u>should</u> be put down.

ⓘ Note that you can omit **should** and use the base form of the verb on its own. This is a rather formal use.

Someone suggested that they <u>break</u> into small groups.

In formal English, **should** is sometimes used in conditional clauses.

We worry about them having to suffer taunts and ridicule if anyone <u>should</u> find out.

In a sentence like this, **should** can be put at the beginning of the clause, followed by the subject.

<u>Should</u> ministers decide to instigate an inquiry, we would welcome it.

In conversation and most kinds of writing, it is not necessary to use **should** in this kind of clause. You just use the simple present tense. For example, instead of saying 'If he should come, we will talk to him', you say 'If he **comes**, we will talk to him'.

3 **requests and offers**

When you are making a formal request or offer, you can use **should** in a conditional sentence.

I <u>should</u> be obliged if you would send them to me.
If you know of a better method, I <u>should</u> be delighted to try it.

You can also make a request by using **I should like**.

I <u>should like</u> a large cutlet, please.

ⓘ Note that **would** is preferred in both of these senses.

If I could help, I <u>would</u> be delighted to do anything I can.
I <u>would like</u> to ask you one question please.

4 **announcements**

You can use **should** with **like** when you are formally announcing that you are going to do something.

We <u>should like</u> to make the following proposals.

ⓘ Note that **would** is preferred in this sense.

I <u>would like</u> to make some general observations.

USAGE

USAGE

5 **purpose clauses**

Should can be used after **I** or **we** in a purpose clause.

He left the dirty things in his bedroom on purpose so that I should see them.

(i) Note that **would** is preferred in this sense.

6 **wishes and requests**

You can express a wish by using **I should like.**

I should like to live in the country.

You can say what you do not want by using **I shouldn't like.**

I shouldn't like Amanda to see more of him than is absolutely unavoidable.

(i) Note that **would** is preferred for both of these uses.

I would like to be able to help.
I wouldn't like to live in the city.

7 **possible situations**

You use **should** after **I** or **we** to say that something is certain to happen in particular circumstances.

I should be very unhappy on the continent.

(i) Note that **would** is preferred for this use. Note also that after other pronouns you must use **would.** You do not use **should.**

We would be glad to have money of our own.

---

should - ought to

1 **forms and pronunciation**

Should and **ought to** are sometimes used with similar meanings. When **should** has a similar meaning to **ought to,** you pronounce it in full and you do not write it as "d".

⇨ See **Usage** entry at **should - would.**

Should and **ought to** have the negative forms **should not** and **ought not to.** The **not** is not usually pronounced in full. When you write down what someone says, you write **shouldn't** or **oughtn't to.**

2 **expectation**

You use **should** or **ought to** to say that you expect something to happen.

We should be there by dinner time.
It ought to get better as it goes along.

You use **should** or **ought to** with **have** to say that you expect something to have happened already.

Dear Mom, you should have heard by now that I'm O.K.

You also use **should** or **ought to** with **have** to say that something was expected to happen, but did not happen.

Two bags which should have gone to Rome were loaded aboard a flight to Milwaukee.
The brandy I'd swallowed ought to have knocked me silly.

(i) Note that you must use **have** and a past participle in sentences like these. You do not say, for example, 'The brandy I'd swallowed ought to knock me silly'.

3 **moral rightness**

You use **should** or **ought to** to say that something is morally right.

Crimes should be punished.
This should not be allowed to continue.
I ought to call the police.
We ought to be doing something about it.

4 **giving advice**

You can say **you should** or **you ought to** when you are giving someone advice.

I think you should get in touch with your solicitor.
I think you ought to try a different approach.

shout

1 **'shout'**

When you **shout,** you speak as loudly as you can.

The children on the sand were shouting with excitement.
'Stop it!' he shouted.

2 **'shout to'**

If you **shout to** someone who is a long way away, you speak very loudly so that they can hear you.

'What are you doing down there?' he shouted to Robin.
Our sergeant shouted to a battalion of soldiers carrying guns: 'The war's over!'

3 **'shout at'**

If you speak very loudly to someone who is near to you, for example because you are angry with them, you do not say that you 'shout to' them. You say that you **shout at** them.

Jefferson shouted at him, 'Get in! Get in!'
She shouted at us for spoiling her lovely evening.

You can use a 'to'-infinitive with **shout to** or **shout at.** If you **shout to** someone **to do** something, or **shout at** them **to do** it, you tell them to do it by shouting at them.

An officer shouted to us to stop all the noise.
She shouted at him to speak up.

show

⇨ See **Usage** entry at **indicate - show.**

shrink

1 **'shrink'**

If something **shrinks,** it becomes smaller.

Sometimes the rains fail and the rivers shrink or dry up.
Be generous, as the tomatoes will shrink as they cook.

2 **'shrank'**

The past tense of **shrink** is **shrank,** not 'shrinked' or 'shrunk'. The past participle is **shrunk.**

Last year the economy shrank by 7 per cent.
Their workforce of 25,000 has shrunk to 8,000.

3 **'shrunken'**

Shrunken is an adjective, used in front of a noun. A **shrunken** thing or person has become smaller.

…old women selling shrunken baboon heads.
…a shrunken old man.

shut

⇨ See **Usage** entry at **close - closed - shut.**

sick

1 **'sick'**

A **sick** person has an illness or some other problem with their health.

…a sick baby.
He still looked sick.

⇨ See **Usage** entry at **ill - sick.**

USAGE

2 **'be sick'**

To **be sick** means to bring up food through your mouth from your stomach.

I think I'm going to be sick.

He was kneeling by the lavatory being violently sick.

ⓘ Note that 'George is being sick' means 'George is bringing up food from his stomach'; 'George is sick' means 'George is ill'. However, 'George was sick' can mean either 'George brought up food from his stomach' or 'George was ill'.

3 **'vomit' and 'throw up'**

Vomit has the same meaning as 'be sick'. **Vomit** is a fairly formal word. In conversation, some people say **throw up** instead of 'be sick'.

She was stricken with pain and began to vomit.

I think I'm going to throw up.

4 **'feel sick'**

To **feel sick** means to feel that you want to be sick.

Flying always makes me feel sick.

sight

⇨ See **Usage** entry at **scene - sight - view - landscape - scenery.**

sightseeing

Sightseeing is the activity of travelling around a city or region to see the interesting places that tourists usually visit.

...a two-week tour, allowing some time in all the major cities for sightseeing.

Sightseeing is an uncount noun. You do not talk about 'sightseeings' or 'a sightseeing'. However, you can talk about a **sightseeing trip.**

I took a sightseeing trip on one of those tourist buses.

You can also say that someone **goes sightseeing** or **does some sightseeing.**

Vita and Violet went sightseeing.

I decided to do some sightseeing.

sign - signature

1 **'sign'**

When you **sign** a document, you write your name on it. You do this to show, for example, that you have written the document or that you agree with what it says.

I was in the act of signing a traveller's cheque.

...an order signed by the Home Secretary.

You can also say that someone **signs** their name.

Sign your name in the book each time you use the photocopier.

2 **'signature'**

However, when you write your name, you do not refer to what you write as your 'sign'. You call it your **signature.**

Nino scrawled his signature on the bottom of the slip.

... petitions bearing thousands of signatures.

similar

⇨ See **Usage** entry at **same - similar.**

since

1 **'since'**

You use **since** to say that something has been the case from a particular time in the past until now.

Exam results have improved rapidly <u>since</u> 1999.
I've been wearing glasses <u>since</u> I was three.

ⓘ Note that in these sentences you use a perfect tense with **since**. You do not say '~~It is on my desk since 1959~~' or '~~I am wearing glasses since I was three~~'.

You can also use **since** to say how long ago something happened. When you use **since** like this, you use a simple tense. For example, instead of saying 'I last saw him five years ago', you can say 'It's five years **since** I last saw him'.

It's three months <u>since</u> you were here last.
It's years <u>since</u> I saw a photo of him.

2 'for'

However, if you want to say how long something has been the case, you use **for**, not 'since'.

We've been married <u>for</u> seven years.

⇨ See **Usage** entry at **for**.

3 'during' and 'over'

If you want to mention how long something has been happening, you use **during** or **over**.

A considerable amount of rain has fallen <u>during</u> the past two years.
Things have become noticeably worse <u>over</u> the past two or three months.

⇨ See **Usage** entries at **during** and **over**.

4 'from ... to'

If you want to mention when something began and finished, you use **from** and **to**.

Lord Charteris of Amisfield was private secretary to the Queen <u>from</u> 1972 <u>to</u> 1977.

Instead of 'to', you can use **till** or **until**.

... <u>from</u> nine in the morning <u>till</u> 5 p.m.

ⓘ Note that you do not use **since** and **to**. You do not say, for example, '~~...private secretary to the Queen since 1972 to 1977~~'.

5 used to mean 'because'

Since can also be used to mean 'because'.

Aircraft noise is a particular problem here <u>since</u> we're close to Heathrow Airport.

⇨ See **Usage** entry at **because**.

sink

1 'sink'

If something **sinks**, it moves slowly downwards. **Sink** is especially used to say that something moves downwards below the surface of water.

The boat <u>was sinking</u>.

To **sink** a ship means to cause it to sink.

The Confederates managed to <u>sink</u> one ship and damage another.

2 'sank' and 'sunk'

The past tense of **sink** is **sank**, not 'sunk' or 'sinked'. The past participle is **sunk**.

The boat <u>sank</u> to the bottom of the lake.
The leading craft <u>was sunk</u> almost immediately by the artillery.

3 'sunken'

Sunken is an adjective, used in front of a noun. You use it to describe things which have sunk to the bottom of the sea or a lake.

...the remains of a <u>sunken</u> battleship.

USAGE

sit

1 describing a movement

When you **sit** or **sit down,** you lower your body until your bottom is resting on something. The past tense and past participle of **sit** is **sat,** not 'sitted'.

You usually use **sit** rather than 'sit down' when you mention the place where someone gets into this position.

A strange woman came and <u>sat next to her.</u>
<u>Sit on this chair,</u> please.

If you are not mentioning the place, you use **sit down.**

She <u>sat down</u> and poured herself a cup of tea.

2 saying where someone is

If you **are sitting** somewhere, your bottom is resting on something such as a chair. Note that in standard English you do not say that someone 'is sat' somewhere.

They <u>are sitting</u> at their desks.
She <u>was sitting</u> on the edge of the bed.

3 prepositions used with 'sit'

You usually say that someone **sits on** something.

We <u>were sitting on</u> hard little chairs.

However, you say that someone **sits in** an armchair.

He <u>was sitting</u> quietly <u>in</u> his armchair, smoking a pipe.

When someone is sitting close to a desk or table, for example because they are writing or eating, you say that they are **sitting at** the desk or table.

I <u>was sitting at</u> my desk reading.

4 another meaning of 'sit'

In British English, if you **sit** an exam, you take part in it.

June and July are the traditional months for <u>sitting</u> exams.

⇨ See **Usage** entry at **exam - examination.**

5 'seat'

Do not confuse **sit** /sɪt/ with **seat** /siːt/. A **seat** is an object that you can sit on.

The girl in the next <u>seat</u> was watching him.
I had a reserved <u>seat</u> from Holland to Denmark.

In stories, **seat** is sometimes a reflexive verb. If you **seat yourself** somewhere, you sit down.

'Thank you,' she said, <u>seating herself</u> on the sofa.

If you **are seated** somewhere, you are sitting there.

General Tomkins <u>was seated</u> behind his desk.

size

⇨ For information on describing **size**, see **Topic** entry at **Measurements.**

skeptic - skeptical

⇨ See **Usage** entry at **sceptic - sceptical.**

skid

⇨ See **Usage** entry at **slide.**

skilful - skilled - talented

1 'skilful'

Someone who is **skilful** at something does it very well.

...a great team with a lot of <u>skilful</u> players.
The girl had grown more <u>skilful</u> with the sewing-machine.

Skilful is spelled **skillful** in American English.

2 **'skilled'**

You use **skilled** in front of a noun to describe someone who has been trained to do a particular kind of work and does it very well.

A skilled engineer takes four years to train.

You also use **skilled** in front of a noun to describe work that can only be done by a skilled person.

Wood turning is skilled work.
Weaving was a highly skilled job, requiring a five-year apprenticeship.

3 **'talented'**

You use **talented** to describe someone who has a natural ability to do something.

…a talented writer.

You can also use **talented** to describe someone who is naturally good at doing several things.

… talented children.
The whole family was so talented.

skinny

⇨ See **Usage** entry at **thinness**.

sleep - asleep

1 **'sleep'**

Sleep can be a noun or a verb. The past tense and past participle of the verb is **slept,** not 'sleeped'.

Sleep is the natural state of rest in which you are unconscious with your eyes closed.

I haven't been getting enough sleep recently.

To **sleep** means to be in this state of rest.

He was so excited he could hardly sleep.
I had not slept or eaten for three days.

2 **'asleep'**

You do not usually use the verb **sleep** simply to say that someone is in this state. You do not say, for example, 'Gordon sleeps' or 'Gordon is sleeping'. You say 'Gordon **is asleep**'.

She was asleep in the guest room when we walked in.

You use **sleep** in more complex statements, for example to say how long someone was in this state, or to talk about a regular occurrence.

She slept till ten in the morning.
He slept on the kitchen floor.

⚠ **WARNING:** **Asleep** is only used after a verb. You do not use it in front of a noun. You do not, for example, talk about an 'asleep child'. Instead you use **sleeping.**
I glanced down at the sleeping figure.

You do not say that someone is 'very asleep' or 'completely asleep'. Instead you say that they are **sound asleep, fast asleep,** or **deeply asleep.**

Chris is still sound asleep in the other bed.
Colette had been fast asleep when he left her.
Miss Haynes was very deeply asleep.

3 **'go to sleep'**

When someone changes from being awake to being asleep, you say that they **go to sleep.**

They <u>had</u> both <u>gone to sleep.</u>
Now <u>go to sleep</u> and stop worrying about it.

4 'fall asleep'

When someone goes to sleep suddenly or unexpectedly, you say that they **fall asleep.**
The moment my head touched the pillow I <u>fell asleep.</u>

5 'get to sleep'

When someone goes to sleep with difficulty, for example because they are in a noisy place or because they are worried about something, you say that they **get to sleep.**
Could you turn that radio down – I'm trying to <u>get to sleep.</u>
I couldn't <u>get to sleep</u> until six in the morning.

6 'go back to sleep'

When someone goes to sleep again after waking up, you say that they **go back to sleep.**
She turned over, hugged her pillow, and <u>went back to sleep.</u>

7 'send...to sleep'

If something causes you to sleep, you say that it **sends** you **to sleep.**
I brought him a hot drink, hoping it would <u>send</u> him <u>to sleep.</u>

slide - skid

1 'slide'

When something **slides,** it moves smoothly over a surface.
Tears were <u>sliding</u> down his cheeks.

The past tense and past participle of **slide** is **slid,** not 'slided'.
The gate <u>slid</u> open at the push of a button.

2 'skid'

You do not use **slide** to describe the movement of a vehicle when its wheels move sideways on a wet or icy road. The word you use is **skid.**
The car moved forward, <u>skidding</u> on the loose snow.
We <u>skidded</u> into the ditch.

slightly

⇨ See section on **degree** in **Grammar** entry at **Adjuncts,** and section on **grading adverbs** in **Grammar** entry at **Adverbs.**

slim

⇨ See **Usage** entry at **thin.**

small - large

The following adjectives are used to indicate how small or large something is. They are arranged from 'smallest' to 'largest'.

● **microscopic, infinitesimal**

... <u>microscopic</u> fibres of protein.
...mineral substances present in <u>infinitesimal</u> amounts in the soil.

● **tiny, minute, miniature, diminutive, minuscule**

Though she was <u>tiny,</u> she had a very loud voice.
Only a <u>minute</u> amount is needed.
He looked like a <u>miniature</u> version of his handsome and elegant big brother.
She noticed a <u>diminutive</u> figure standing at the entrance.
While Rolls Royce are still British-owned their sales are <u>minuscule.</u>

● **small, little**

The window was far too <u>small</u> for him to get through.
We sat around a <u>little</u> table, eating and drinking wine.

● **medium-sized, average-sized**

…a <u>medium-sized</u> saucepan.
Most <u>average-sized</u> women just aren't born to be ultra tiny.

● **large, big, great**

He was a <u>large</u> man with thick dark hair.
The car was too <u>big</u> to fit into our garage.
…a <u>great</u> hall as long and high as a church.

● **huge, enormous, massive**

…a tiny little woman with <u>huge</u> black glasses.
The main bedroom is <u>enormous.</u>
There was evidence of <u>massive</u> fraud.

● **vast, immense, gigantic, colossal**

…farmers who own <u>vast</u> stretches of land.
…an <u>immense</u> cloud of smoke.
Britain faces a <u>gigantic</u> problem over the disease.
There has been a <u>colossal</u> waste of public money.

ⓘ Note that the adjective **minute** is pronounced /maɪnjuːt/.

⇨ See also **Usage** entries at **small - little** and **big - large - great**.

small - little

Small and little are both used to say that someone or something is not large. There are some important differences in the ways these words are used.

1 **position in clause**

Small can be used in front of a noun, or after a verb such as **be**.

They escaped in <u>small boats.</u>
She <u>is small</u> for her age.

Little is normally used only in front of nouns. You can talk about 'a **little** town', but you do not say ~~'The town is little'~~.

…a <u>little table</u> with a glass top.
…a <u>little piece</u> of rock.

2 **used with grading adverbs**

You can use words like **quite** and **rather** in front of **small**.

… <u>quite small</u> changes in climate.
…a <u>rather small</u> paper knife.

⇨ See section on **grading adverbs** in **Grammar** entry at **Adverbs**.

You do not use these words in front of **little.**

You can use **very** and **too** in front of **small**.

The trees are full of <u>very small</u> birds.
…houses which are <u>too small.</u>

You do not use **very** or **too** in front of **little** when you use it as an adjective. You do not say, for example, ~~'I have a very little car'~~ or ~~'Our house is very little'~~.

3 **comparatives and superlatives**

Small has the comparative and superlative forms **smaller** and **smallest**.

They are <u>smaller,</u> darker birds.
…the <u>smallest</u> yachts in the fleet.

The comparative form **littler,** and the superlative form **littlest** are less common and are mostly used in spoken English.

The <u>littler</u> boy spoke rapidly.
You used to be the <u>littlest</u> boy in the school.

4 **used with other adjectives**

You can use other adjectives in front of **little**.

…*a nice little man.*

…*a historic little ship.*

(i) Note that you do not normally use other adjectives in front of **small**.

⇒ For a graded list of adjectives which are used to describe how small or large something is, see **Usage** entry at **small - large**. See also **Usage** entry at **little - a little**.

smell

Smell can be a noun or a verb. The past tense and past participle of the verb is **smelled** , but **smelt** is also used in British English.

1 **used as a noun**

The **smell** of something is a quality it has which you are aware of through your nose.

…*the smell of fresh bread.*

What's that smell?

2 **used as an intransitive verb**

If you say that something **smells,** you mean that people are aware of it because of its unpleasant smell.

The fridge is beginning to smell.

You can say that a place or object **smells of** a particular thing.

The room smelled of cigars.

Her clothes smelt of smoke.

(i) You must use **of** in sentences like these. You do not say ~~'The room smelled cigars'~~.

You can say that one place or thing **smells like** another.

Our kitchen smelt like a rubber factory.

The tutor's breath smelled like a full ashtray.

You can also use **smell** with an adjective to say that something has a pleasant or unpleasant smell.

What is it? It smells delicious.

The papers smelt musty and stale.

(i) Note that you do not use an adverb after **smell**. You do not say, for example, that something 'smells deliciously'.

3 **used as a transitive verb**

If you **can smell** something, you are aware of it through your nose.

I can smell the aroma from the frying trout in the kitchen.

He could smell the rich fragrance of bamboo freshly chopped.

(i) Note that you usually use **can** or **could** in sentences like these. You say, for example, 'I **can smell** gas'. You do not say ~~'I smell gas'~~. Note also that you do not use a continuous tense. You do not say ~~'I am smelling gas'~~.

If you want to say that someone became aware of a smell on a particular occasion in the past, you use the simple past tense, **smelled** or **smelt.**

He smelled the smell of burning fat.

I smelt smoke, so I got up and came out.

smile

Smile can be a verb or a noun.

1 **used as a verb**

When you **smile,** the corners of your mouth curve outwards and slightly upwards, for example because you are pleased or amused.

When he saw me, he smiled and waved.

If someone looks at you and smiles, for example to show kindness or friendliness, you say that they **smile at** you.

The girl was smiling at me.

(*i*) Note that you do not use any preposition except **at** in a sentence like this.

2 used as a noun

A **smile** is the expression that you have on your face when you smile.

Barber welcomed me with a smile.
He's got a nice smile, hasn't he?

You can say that someone **gives** you a **smile**.

'How nice to see you.' He gave me a smile.

SO

So is used in several different ways.

1 referring back

You can use **so** after **do** to refer back to an action that has just been mentioned. For example, instead of saying 'He crossed the street. As he crossed the street, he hummed a tune', you say 'He crossed the street. As he **did so**, he hummed a tune'.

He went to close the door, tripping as he did so over a pair of boots.
A signal which should have turned red failed to do so.

You can use **so** after **if** to form a conditional clause. For example, instead of saying 'Have you been to Chesterfield? If you have been to Chesterfield, you will remember the twisted spire on the church', you say 'Have you been to Chesterfield? **If so**, you will remember the twisted spire on the church'.

Do you enjoy romantic films? If so, you should watch the film on ITV tonight.
Will that be enough? If so, do not ask for more.

You often use **so** after a reporting verb, especially when you are replying to what someone has said. For example, if someone says 'Is Alice at home?', you can say 'I **think so**', meaning 'I think Alice is at home'.

'Are you all right?' – 'I think so. '
'Is there anything else you want to tell me?' – 'I don't think so. '
'Is it to rent?' – 'I believe so. '
'Will you be able to take driving lessons at your new school?' - 'I expect so. '

The reporting verbs most commonly used with **so** are **believe**, **expect**, **hope**, **say**, **suppose**, **tell**, and **think**.

⇨ See separate **Usage** entries at these words.

So is also used in a similar way after **I'm afraid**.

'So you think you could lose?' – 'I'm afraid so. '

You can also use **so** to say that something which has just been said about one person or thing is true about another. You put **so** at the beginning of a clause, followed by **be**, **have**, an auxiliary, or a modal, and then the subject of the clause.

His shoes are brightly polished; so is his briefcase.
Etta laughed heartily, and so did he.
'He looks very hot and dry.' – ' So would you if you had a temperature of 103.'

2 used for emphasis

You can use **so** to emphasize an adjective. For example, you can say 'It's **so cold** today'.

I was so busy.
These games are so boring.

However, if the adjective is in front of a noun, you use **such**, not 'so'. You say, for example, 'It's **such a cold day** today'.

She was so nice.

USAGE

She was <u>such a nice girl.</u>
The children seemed <u>so happy.</u>
She seemed <u>such a happy woman.</u>

⇨ See **Usage** entry at **such**.

If the adjective comes after **the, this, that, these, those,** or a possessive, you do not use **so** or **such.** You do not say, for example 'It was our first visit to this so old town'. You say 'It was our first visit to **this very old town**'.

He had recovered from <u>his very low state</u> of the previous evening.
I sincerely hope that <u>these very unfortunate people</u> will not be forgotten.

You can also use **so** to emphasize an adverb.

I sleep <u>so soundly.</u>
Time seems to have passed <u>so quickly.</u>

3 'ever so'

In conversation, you can use **ever so** as an emphatic form of 'so'.

I am <u>ever so grateful</u> to you for talking to me.
She's <u>ever so serious.</u>

4 'so ... that' used to mention a result

You use **so** in front of an adjective when you are saying that something happens because someone or something has a quality to an unusually large extent. After the adjective, you use a 'that'-clause.

The crowd was <u>so large that it overflowed the auditorium.</u>
We were <u>so angry we asked to see the manager.</u>

ⓘ Note that you do not use 'so' in the second clause. You do not say, for example, 'We were so angry so we asked to see the manager'.

You can use **so** in a similar way in front of an adverb.

He dressed <u>so quickly that he put his boots on the wrong feet.</u>
She had fallen down <u>so often that she was covered in mud.</u>

Instead of using **so** in front of an adjective, you can use **such** in front of a noun group containing the adjective. For example, instead of saying 'The house was **so big** that we decided to sell it', you can say 'It was **such a big house** that we decided to sell it'.

The change was <u>so gradual</u> that it escaped the tourists' notice.
This can be <u>such a gradual process</u> that you are not aware of it happening.

When you use **so** with **that,** you can change the order of the words in the first clause for greater emphasis. You put **so** and the adjective at the beginning of the clause, followed by **be,** an auxiliary, or a modal, and then the subject.

<u>So rapid is the rate of progress</u> that advance seems to be following advance on almost a monthly basis.
<u>So successful have they been</u> that they are moving to Bond Street.

This kind of construction is only used in writing and broadcasts. You do not use it in conversation.

You can use **so, and so,** or **so that** to introduce the result of a situation that you have just mentioned.

He speaks very little English, <u>so</u> I talked to him through an interpreter.
My offer met with no response <u>and so</u> I tried again.
My suitcase had become damaged, <u>so that</u> the lid would not stay closed.

5 'so that' in purpose clauses

You also use **so that** to say that something is done for a particular purpose.

He has to earn lots of money <u>so that</u> he can buy his children nice food and clothes.

so - very - too

So, very, and too can all be used to intensify the meaning of an adjective, an adverb, or a word like much or many. However, they are not used in the same way.

1 'very' and 'so'

Very is the simplest intensifier. It has no other meaning beyond that. So can suggest an emotional reaction on the part of the speaker, such as pleasure, surprise, or disappointment.

John makes me so angry!
Oh thank you so much!

So can also refer forward to a result clause introduced by that.

The procession was forced to move so slowly that he arrived three hours late.

⇨ See Usage entry at so.

2 'too'

Too suggests an excessive or undesirable amount, often so much that a particular result does not or cannot happen.

She does wear too much make-up at times.
He was too late to save her.

⇨ See Usage entry at too.

soccer

⇨ See Usage entry at football.

social - sociable - socialist

1 'social'

The adjective social is used in front of a noun. Its usual meaning is 'relating to society'.

…statistics on crime and other social problems.
…the government's social and economic policy.

You can also use social to indicate that something relates to a leisure activity which involves people meeting each other.

We've met at social and business functions.
Social interaction and social contacts are an important need for every human being.

2 'sociable'

You do not use social to describe people who are friendly and enjoy talking to other people. The word you use is sociable.

Adler was an outgoing, sociable kind of man.

You also use sociable to describe someone's behaviour on a particular occasion. If someone is sociable at an event, they talk to a lot of people in a friendly way.

Kitty had tried to be sociable to everyone.

3 'socialist'

You do not use social to mean 'relating to socialism' or to describe people who believe in socialism. The word you use is socialist.

… socialist policies.
…the socialist leader, Felipe Gonzalez.

society

1 used as an uncount noun

You refer to people in general as society when you are thinking of them as belonging to a large organized group.

Women must have equal status in society.
We are going to have to change the whole structure of society.

When society has this meaning, you do not use 'a' or 'the' in front of it.

USAGE

2 used as a count noun
You refer to the people of a particular country as a **society** when you are thinking of them as an organized group.
We live in a multi-racial society.
…the increasing complexity of industrial societies.

A **society** is also an organization for people who have the same interest or aim.
…the Royal Horticultural Society.
…the Society of African Culture.

solicitor
⇨ See **Usage** entry at **lawyer**.

some

1 used as a determiner
You use **some** in front of the plural form of a noun to talk about a number of people or things, without saying who or what they are, or how many of them there are.
Some children were barefoot.
I have some important things to tell them.

You can also use **some** in front of an uncount noun to talk about a quantity of something, without saying how much of it there is.
She had a piece of pie and some coffee.
But some caution is advised.

When you use **some** in front of the plural form of a noun, you use a plural form of a verb with it.
Some hunting lodges were also manor houses.
If you are doing it yourself, here are some suggestions.

When you use **some** in front of an uncount noun, you use a singular form of a verb with it.
Some action is necessary.
There 's some pizza left from dinner.

2 used as a quantifier
You use **some of** in front of a plural noun group beginning with **the**, **these**, **those**, or a possessive. You do this to talk about a number of people or things belonging to a particular group.
… some of the large airlines.
… some of these people have young children.
… some of those ideas we'd talked about.
… some of Edgar Allen Poe's stories.

Similarly, you use **some of** in front of a singular noun group beginning with **the**, **this**, **that**, or a possessive to talk about a part of something.
We did some of the journey by night.
Somebody might take some of his money away.

You can use **some of** like this in front of plural or singular pronouns.
Some of these are included in this leaflet.
Some of it is very beautiful.

You do not use 'we' or 'they' after **some of**. Instead you use **us** or **them**.
I think some of us find it a bit intrusive.
They spread out and some of them went up north.

3 used as a pronoun
Some can itself be a plural or singular pronoun.

Some activities are very dangerous and <u>some</u> are not so dangerous.
'You'll need some graph paper.' – 'Yeah, I've got <u>some</u> at home.'

⚠ **WARNING:** You do not use **some** as part of the object of a negative sentence. You do not say, for example, '~~I don't have some money~~'. You say 'I don't have **any** money'.
I hadn't had <u>any</u> breakfast.
It won't do <u>any</u> good.

4 used in questions

In questions, you can use either **some** or **any** as part of an object. You use **some** when you are asking someone to confirm that something is true. For example, if you think someone wants to ask you some questions, you might say to them 'Do you have **some** questions?' or 'You have **some** questions?' But if you do not know whether they want to ask you any questions or not, you would say 'Do you have **any** questions?'
Sorry – have I missed out <u>some</u> questions?
Were you in <u>any</u> danger?

5 duration

You use **some** with **time** or with a word such as **hours** or **months** to indicate that something lasts for a fairly long time.
You will be unable to restart the car for <u>some time.</u>
I did not meet her again for <u>some years.</u>

If you want to indicate that a period of time is fairly short, you do not use **some**. You talk about **a short time** or you use **a few** in front of a word such as **hours** or **months**.
The chiefs would be there in <u>a short time.</u>
Patey and I were due to arrive only <u>a few days</u> before the transmission.

someone - somebody

1 used in statements

You use **someone** or **somebody** to refer to a person without saying who you mean. There is no difference in meaning between **someone** and **somebody.**
Carson sent <u>someone</u> to see me.
There was an accident and <u>somebody</u> got killed.

⚠ **WARNING:** You do not usually use **someone** or **somebody** as part of the object of a negative sentence. You do not say, for example, '~~I don't know someone who lives in Nottingham~~'. You say 'I don't know **anyone** who lives in Nottingham'.
There wasn't <u>anyone</u> there.
There wasn't much room for <u>anybody</u> else.

2 used in questions

In questions, you can use **someone, somebody, anyone,** or **anybody** as part of the object. You use **someone** or **somebody** when you are asking someone to confirm that something is true. For example, if you think I met someone in the park, you might say to me 'Did you meet **someone** in the park?' If you do not know whether I met someone in the park or not, you would say 'Did you meet **anyone** in the park?'
Marit, did you have <u>someone</u> in your room last night?
Was there <u>anyone</u> behind you?

⚠ **WARNING:** You do not use **someone** or **somebody** with 'of' in front of the plural form of a noun. You do not say, for example, '~~Someone of my friends is a sculptor~~'. You say 'One of my friends is a sculptor'.
<u>One of his friends</u> made a radio from spare parts.
'Where have you been?' <u>one of them</u> asked.

3 **'some people'**

Someone and somebody do not have plural forms. If you want to refer to a group of people without saying who you mean, you say **some people**.

Some people attempted to dash across the bridge.
The law may be held to be unsatisfactory by some people.

someplace

⇨ See **Usage** entry at **somewhere**.

something

1 **used in statements**

You use **something** to refer to an object, situation, etc without saying exactly what it is.

Hendricks saw something ahead of him.
It's something that has often puzzled me.

⚠ **WARNING:** You do not usually use **something** as part of the object of a negative sentence. You do not say, for example, 'We haven't had something to eat'. You say 'We haven't had **anything** to eat'.

I did not say anything.
He never seemed to do anything at all.

2 **used in questions**

In questions, you can use **something** or **anything** as part of the object.
If you are asking for confirmation that something is true, you use **something**. For example, if you think I found something in the cupboard, you might say 'Did you find **something** in the cupboard?' If you do not know whether I found something in the cupboard or not, you would say 'Did you find **anything** in the cupboard?'

Has something happened?
Did you buy anything?

sometimes - sometime

1 **'sometimes'**

You use **sometimes** to say that something happens on certain occasions, rather than all the time.

Queues were sometimes a quarter of a mile long.
Sometimes I wish I was back in Africa.

⇨ Many other words and expressions can be used to say how often something happens. For a graded list, see section on **frequency** in **Grammar** entry at **Adjuncts**.

2 **'sometime'**

Do not confuse **sometimes** with **sometime**. **Sometime** means 'at a time in the past or future that is unknown or has not yet been fixed'.

Can I come and see you sometime?

Sometime is often written as **some time**.

He died some time last year.

somewhat

⇨ See **Usage** entry at **fair - fairly**.

somewhere

You use **somewhere** to talk about a place without saying exactly where you mean.

I was somewhere in Greenwich Village.
They lived somewhere near Bournemouth.
I'm not going home yet. I have to go somewhere else first.

⚠ **WARNING:** You do not usually use **somewhere** in negative sentences. You do not say, for example, 'I can't find my hat somewhere'. You say 'I can't find my hat **anywhere**'.
I changed my mind and decided not to go anywhere.
I haven't got anywhere to live.

In questions, you can use **somewhere** or **anywhere**. If you are expecting the answer 'yes', you usually use **somewhere**. If you do not know whether the answer will be 'yes' or 'no', you can use either **somewhere** or **anywhere**.
Are you taking a trip somewhere?
Is there an ashtray anywhere?

 Some American speakers say **someplace** instead of 'somewhere'.
She had seen it someplace before.
Why don't you boys sit someplace else?

Someplace is sometimes written as **some place**.
Why don't we go some place where it's quieter?

soon

1 talking about the future
You use **soon** to say that something will happen in a short time from now.
It should be ready soon.
We may very soon reach the limit of what we can cram on to a silicon chip.

2 talking about the past
When you are talking about the past, you use **soon** to say that something happened a short time after something else.
The mistake was very soon spotted.
The glum faces soon changed to smiles.

3 position in sentence
● **Soon** is often put at the beginning or end of a sentence.
Soon unemployment will start rising.
I will see you soon.

● You can also put **soon** after the first auxiliary in a verb group. For example, you can say 'We **will soon** be home'. You do not say 'We soon will be home'.
It will soon be Christmas.
Herbert was soon taking part in numerous plays.

● If there is no auxiliary, you put **soon** in front of the verb, unless the verb is **be**.
I soon forgot about our conversation.
I soon discovered that this was only partly true.

● If the verb is **be**, you put **soon** after it.
She was soon asleep.

4 'how soon'
You use **how soon** when you are asking how long it will be before something happens.
How soon do I have to make a decision?
How soon are you returning to Paris?

5 'as soon as'
You use **as soon as** to say that one event happens immediately after another.
As soon as she got out of bed, the telephone stopped ringing.
As soon as we get the tickets, we'll send them to you.

6 'no sooner'
No sooner is also used, especially in writing, to say that one event happens immediately

after another. **No sooner** usually goes in front of the main verb in the first clause. The second clause begins with **than**.

You <u>no sooner</u> pour your aperitif <u>than</u> the bell goes.

In stories, **no sooner** is sometimes put at the beginning of a sentence, followed by an auxiliary and the subject.

<u>No sooner did I</u> reach the surface than I was pulled back again.

sorry

You say **'Sorry'** or **'I'm sorry'** as a way of apologizing for something you have done.

'You're giving me a headache with all that noise.' – '<u>Sorry.</u>'
<u>I'm sorry</u> I'm so late.

i Note that **sorry** is an adjective, not a verb. You do not say '~~I sorry~~'.

⇨ For more information about apologies, see **Topic** entry at **Apologizing**. See also **Usage** entry at **regret - be sorry**.

sort

Sort is used as a noun to talk about a class of people or things. **Sort** is a count noun. After words like **all** and **several**, you use **sorts**, not 'sort'.

There are all <u>sorts</u> of reasons why this is true.
There are several <u>sorts</u> of stitching.

After **sorts of** you can use either the plural or singular form of a noun. For example, you can say 'They sell most sorts of **shoes**' or 'They sell most sorts of **shoe**'. The singular form is more formal.

There were five different sorts of <u>biscuits.</u>
There are two sorts of <u>double star.</u>

After **sort of** you use the singular form of a noun.

I know you're interested in this sort of <u>thing.</u>
'What sort of <u>iron</u> did she get?' – 'A steam iron.'

In conversation, **these** and **those** are often used with **sort**. For example, people say 'I don't like these sort of jobs' or 'I don't like those sort of jobs'. This use is generally thought to be incorrect, and it is best to avoid it. Instead, you should say 'I don't like **this sort of job**' or 'I don't like **that sort of job**'.

They never fly in <u>this sort of weather.</u>
I've had <u>that sort of experience</u> with other photographers.

You can also say 'I don't like jobs **of this sort**'.

A device <u>of this sort</u> costs a good deal of money.

In conversation, people often say **like this, like that,** or **like these**.

I want to know what evidence people are using when they make statements <u>like this.</u>
I haven't studied any subjects <u>like that.</u>
Scenes <u>like these</u> are found in every city in Britain.

sort of - kind of

In conversation, people use **sort of** or **kind of** in front of a noun to indicate that something has some of the features of a particular kind of thing.

There's a <u>sort of</u> ridge. Do you see?
I'm a <u>kind of</u> anarchist, I suppose.

Some people also use **sort of** in front of adjectives, verbs, and other types of word. When **sort of** is used like this, it has very little meaning.

I'm <u>sort of</u> fond of him.
I've <u>sort of</u> heard of him, but I don't know who he is.
He was <u>sort of</u> banging his head against a window.

Some speakers, especially in American English, use **kind of** in a similar way, especially in front of adjectives.

I felt <u>kind of</u> sorry for him.

sound

Sound can be a noun, a verb, or an adjective.

1 used as a noun

A **sound** is a particular thing that you hear.

He heard the <u>sound</u> of footsteps in the hall.
He opened the door without a <u>sound.</u>

Sound is everything that can be heard.

<u>Sound</u> travels more slowly through cold water than through warm water.

⚠ **WARNING:** Do not confuse **sound** with **noise.**
⇨ For an explanation of the difference, see **Usage** entry at **sound - noise.**

2 used as a verb

You use **sound** as a verb in front of an adjective group when you are describing something that you hear.

The deep foghorn <u>sounded alarmingly close.</u>

You can also use **sound** in front of an adjective group to describe the impression you have of someone when they speak.

'Ah,' Piper said. He <u>sounded a little discouraged.</u>

You also use **sound** to describe the impression you have of someone or something that you have just heard about or read about.

'They've got a small farm down in Devon.' – 'That <u>sounds nice.</u> '
That <u>sounds a bit complicated.</u>

ⓘ Note that you do not use a continuous tense. You do not say, for example, 'That is sounding nice'.
Note also that **sound** is followed by an adjective, not an adverb. You do not say 'That sounds nicely'.

3 'sound like'

You can use **sound like** and a noun group to to say that something has a similar sound to something else.

One of this animal's commonest calls <u>sounds like the miaow of a cat.</u>
Her footsteps <u>sounded like pistol shots.</u>

You can use **sound like** and a noun group to say that someone is talking the way someone else usually talks.

He <u>sounded like a small boy boasting.</u>
You <u>sound</u> just <u>like an insurance salesman.</u>

You can use **sound like** and a noun group to say that you think you can recognize what something is, because of its sound.

They were playing a symphony that <u>sounded like Haydn or Mozart.</u>

You can also use **sound like** and a noun group to express an opinion about something which someone has just described to you.

That <u>sounds like a good idea.</u>

4 'sound' used as an adjective

When **sound** is an adjective, it has a completely different meaning. If something is **sound**, it is healthy or in good condition.

My heart is basically <u>sound.</u>

If something such as an argument or piece of advice is **sound,** it is sensible and based on reason.

Cook met every objection with <u>sound</u> arguments.

5 **'sound asleep'**

If someone is **sound asleep,** they are sleeping deeply and peacefully.

Chris is still <u>sound asleep</u> in the other bed.

sound - noise

1 **used as count nouns**

A **sound** is something that you can hear. If it is unpleasant or unexpected, you refer to it as a **noise.** You say that machinery makes a **noise.** People and animals can also make **noises.**

A sudden <u>noise</u> made Brody jump.

Dolphins produce a great variety of <u>noises.</u>

2 **used as uncount nouns**

Sound and **noise** can both be uncount nouns.

Sound is the general term for what you hear as a result of vibrations travelling through the air, water, etc.

…the speed of <u>sound.</u>

(i) Note that when you use **sound** with this meaning, you do not talk about 'the sound'.

You do not use expressions such as 'much' or 'a lot of' with **sound.** You do not say, for example, ~~'There was a lot of sound'.~~ You say 'There was **a lot of noise'.**

Is that the wind making <u>all that noise?</u>

Try not to make <u>so much noise.</u>

south

1 **'south'**

The **south** /sauθ/ is the direction which is on your right when you are looking towards the direction where the sun rises.

Most of the house overlooks the city to the <u>south.</u>

To the <u>south,</u> an hour's drive away, lay Benidorm.

A **south** wind blows from the south.

The bigger islands gave some shelter from the <u>south</u> wind.

The **south** of a place is the part that is towards the south.

He died at his home in Antibes in the <u>south</u> of France.

South occurs in the names of some countries, states, and regions.

…the Republic of <u>South Korea.</u>

…a senator from <u>South Carolina.</u>

…the rivers of <u>South America.</u>

2 **'southern'**

However, you do not usually talk about a 'south' part of a country or region. You talk about a **southern** /sʌðən/ part.

…the <u>southern</u> tip of South America.

…the <u>southern</u> half of England.

Similarly, you do not talk about 'south England' or 'south Europe'. You say **southern** England or **southern** Europe.

…the cities of <u>southern</u> Spain.

southerly

If something moves in a **southerly** /sʌðəli/ direction, it moves towards the south.

Peter headed in a <u>southerly</u> direction.

However, a **southerly** wind blows **from** the south.
The dunes afford the house some shelter from the <u>southerly</u> gales.

The **most southerly** of a group of things is the one that is furthest to the south. The form **southernmost** is also used with the same meaning.
…the <u>most southerly</u> tip of Bear Island.
…Aswan, Egypt's <u>southernmost</u> city.

southwards - southward

1 **'southwards'**

If you move or look **southwards,** you move or look towards the south.
He took the road <u>southwards</u> into the hills.
The Duke turned to stare <u>southwards.</u>

Southwards is always an adverb.

2 **'southward'**

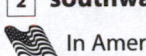 In American English and old-fashioned British English, **southward** is often used instead of 'southwards'.
We headed <u>southward</u> on Route 95.

In both British and American English, **southward** is sometimes used as an adjective in front of a noun.
While I was sitting there I observed a large flying object coming from a <u>southward</u> direction.

souvenir - memory

1 **'souvenir'**

A **souvenir** /su:vənɪə/ is an object which you buy or keep to remind you of a holiday, place, or event.
He kept a spoon as a <u>souvenir</u> of his journey.

2 **'memory'**

You do not use 'souvenir' to talk about something that you remember. The word you use is memory.
Her earliest <u>memory</u> is of singing at the age of four to wounded soldiers.
She had no <u>memory</u> of what had happened.

Your **memory** is your ability to remember things.
You've got a wonderful <u>memory</u>.
A few things stand out in my <u>memory</u>.

sow - sew

The verbs **sow** and **sew** are both pronounced /səʊ/.

1 **'sow'**

If you **sow** seeds, you plant them in the ground. The past tense of **sow** is **sowed**. The past participle can be either **sown** or **sowed**. **Sown** is more common.
An enemy came and <u>sowed</u> weeds among the wheat.
Spring wheat should <u>be sown</u> as early as you can get the land ready.

2 **'sew'**

If you **sew**, you join pieces of cloth together by passing thread through them with a needle. The past tense of **sew** is **sewed**. The past participle can be either **sewn** or **sewed**. **Sewn** is more common.
She <u>sewed</u> all her own dresses.
Before I went to Alice Springs I <u>had</u> never <u>sewn</u> a dress or mended a sock.

USAGE

speak - say - tell

1 'speak'

When you **speak,** you use your voice to produce words. The past tense of **speak** is **spoke,** not 'speaked'. The past participle is **spoken.**

Both leaders spoke warmly of the frankness of their discussions.
A lot of women I've spoken to agree with me.

2 'say'

You do not use **speak** to report what someone says. You do not say, for example, 'He spoke that the doctor had arrived'. You say 'He **said** that the doctor had arrived'.

I said that I would like to teach English.
He said it was an accident.

3 'tell'

If you mention the person who is being spoken to, you use **tell.**

He told me that he was a farmer.
I told her what the doctor had said.

⇨ See **Usage** entries at **say** and **tell.**

4 'talk'

⇨ Do not confuse **speak** with **talk.** For an explanation of the differences, see **Usage** entry at **speak - talk.**

speak - talk

Speak and **talk** have very similar meanings, but there are some differences in the ways in which they are used.

1 'speaking' and 'talking'

When you mention that someone is using his or her voice to produce words, you usually say that they **are speaking.**

He hadn't looked at me once when I was speaking.
'So we won't waste any time,' he said, speaking rapidly.

However, if two or more people are having a conversation, you usually say that they **are talking.** You do not say that they 'are speaking'.

The old man was sitting near us as we were talking.
They sat in the kitchen drinking and talking.

2 used with 'to' and 'with'

If you **speak to** someone or **talk to** them, you have a conversation with them.

I saw you speaking to him just now.
I enjoyed talking to Anne.

Some American speakers say **speak with** or **talk with.**

When he spoke with his friends, he told them what had happened.
I talked with his mother many times.

When you make a telephone call, you ask if you can **speak to** someone. You do not ask if you can 'talk to' them.

Hello. Could I speak to Sue, please?

3 used with 'about'

If you **speak about** something, you describe it to a group of people, for example in a lecture.

I spoke about my experiences at University.

In conversation, you can refer to the thing someone is discussing as the thing they **are talking about.**

You know the book I'm talking about.

You can refer in a general way to what someone is saying as **what** they **are talking about.**

What are you talking about?

If two or more people are discussing something, you say they **are talking about** it. You do not say they 'are speaking about' it.

The men were talking about some medical problem.
Everybody will be talking about it at school tomorrow.

4 **languages**

You say that someone **speaks** or **can speak** a foreign language.

They spoke fluent English.
How many languages can you speak?

You do not say that someone 'talks' a foreign language.

⚠ **WARNING:** You do not use 'in' when you are talking about someone's ability to speak a foreign language, and you do not use a continuous tense. For example, if someone is able to speak Dutch, you do not say ~~'She speaks in Dutch'~~ or ~~'She is speaking Dutch'~~. However, if you hear some people talking, you can say 'Those people **are speaking in** Dutch' or 'Those people **are talking in** Dutch'.

She heard two voices talking in French.
They are speaking in Arabic.

5 **other transitive uses**

Speak and **talk** have some other transitive uses.
You can **speak** particular words.

He spoke the words firmly and clearly.

You cannot 'talk' words.
You can say that someone **talks sense** or **talks nonsense**. Similarly, a group of people can **talk politics** or **talk sport**.

He was talking sense for once.
Don't talk nonsense.
We used to sit down and talk politics all evening.
The guests were mostly middle-aged men talking business.

You cannot use **speak** in any of these ways.

6 **reflexive use**

You can say that a person **is talking to** himself or herself.

She seemed to be talking to herself.
I'm always daydreaming and talking to myself.

ⓘ Note that you do not say that someone 'is speaking to' himself or herself.

specially

⇨ See **Usage** entry at **especially - specially**.

spectacle - spectacles

1 **'spectacle'**

A **spectacle** is a sight or view which is remarkable or impressive.

I was confronted with an appalling spectacle.
She stood at the head of the stairs and surveyed the spectacle.

2 **'spectacles'**

A person's **spectacles** are their glasses. **Spectacles** is a formal or old-fashioned word.

...a schoolteacher in horn-rimmed spectacles.

speech - talk

If you make a **speech** or give a **talk,** you speak for a period of time to an audience, usually saying things which you have prepared in advance.

USAGE

1 'speech'

A **speech** is made on a formal occasion, for example at a dinner, wedding, or public meeting.

We listened to an excellent speech by the President.

Mr Macmillan presented the prizes and made a speech on the importance of education.

2 'talk'

A **talk** is more informal, and is intended to give information.

Angus Wilson came here and gave a talk last week.

That's what you said in your talk this lunchtime.

---

speed

Fast, quick, rapid, and **swift** are all used to say that something moves or happens with great speed. **Rapid** and **swift** are not usually used in conversation.

1 'fast'

Fast is used both as an adjective and an adverb. There is no adverb 'fastly'.

… fast communications.

I ran as fast as I could.

2 'quick'

Quick is an adjective. You do not usually use it as an adverb. Instead you use the adverb **quickly**.

It is this muscle which gives us our quick, springing movements.

I walked quickly up the passage.

In conversation, you can use the comparative form **quicker** as an adverb.

I swam on a bit quicker.

Goats could ruin a farmer's field quicker than baboons.

In writing, you usually use **more quickly.**

He began to speak more quickly.

You can use the superlative form **quickest** as an adverb in speech or writing.

… and Freedman reacted quickest to head the ball into the net.

3 'rapid' and 'swift'

Rapid and **swift** are adjectives. The corresponding adverbs are **rapidly** and **swiftly.**

Jobs tend to be plentiful at a time of rapid economic growth.

They walked rapidly past the churchyard.

…a swift decision.

He walked swiftly towards home.

4 asking about speed

Fast is the word you usually use when you are asking about the speed of something.

How fast is the fish swimming?

…looking out of the windows to see how fast we were going.

5 vehicles

You use **fast** to say that a vehicle is capable of moving with great speed.

…a fast car.

6 people

You do not usually use **fast** to talk about people, but you can use it in front of words like **driver** and **runner** to say that someone drives quickly or is capable of running quickly.

Not being a fast runner, I was glad I had parked close to the hall.

7 changes

When you are talking about the speed at which something increases or decreases, you usually use **rapid**.

People are worried about the rapid and massive increase in military spending.

8 **no delay**

Fast, **immediate**, **quick**, **rapid**, and **swift** are all used to say that something happens without any delay.

I only got a fast return on my investment once.
My immediate reaction was just disgust.
They are pressing for a quick resumption of arms negotiations.
…managers plagued by demands for rapid decisions.
The response was swift and intense.

9 **short duration**

You can use **quick**, **rapid**, or **swift** to say that something lasts only a short time.

…a quick visit.
You are likely to make a rapid recovery.
…the swift descent from gentility to near-poverty.

speed - speed up

Speed can be a noun or a verb.

1 **used as a noun**

The **speed** of someone or something is the rate at which they move.

He increased his speed to 115mph.
…the speed of light.

Speed is often used in prepositional phrases beginning with **at** or **with**.
You can say that someone or something moves **at** a particular **speed**.

He goes on driving at the same speed.
The bullets hit Ilie Popescu at a speed of 1,350 feet per second.

If you want to emphasize how fast something is moving, you can use **at** and an adjective in front of **speed**.

I drove at great speed to West Bank.
A plane flew low over the ship at lightning speed.

If you want to emphasize how quickly something happens or is done, you use **with** and an adjective in front of **speed**.

The shape of their bodies changes with astonishing speed.
They have succeeded in expanding their industries with remarkable speed.

2 **used as a verb**

In stories, if someone **speeds** somewhere, they move or travel there quickly. When **speed** has this meaning, its past tense and past participle is **sped**.

They sped along Main Street towards the highway.
They drove through Port Philip and sped on down south.

3 **'speed up'**

If something **speeds up** or if you **speed** it **up**, it moves, happens, or is done more quickly.

They're way ahead of us. Speed up!

The past tense and past participle of **speed up** is **speeded up**.

Tom speeded up and overtook them.
The process is now being speeded up.

spend

You usually use the verb **spend** when you are talking about money or time. The past tense and past participle of **spend** is **spent**, not 'spended'.

1 **money**

When you **spend** money, you use it to pay for things.

I had no very clear idea how much I had spent.
Her husband had spent all her money.

You say that someone spends money **on** something.

We always spend a lot of money <u>on</u> parties.
The buildings need a lot of money spent <u>on</u> them.

(*i*) Note that you do not use any preposition except **on** in sentences like these.

2 time

If you **spend** a period of time doing something, you do it from the beginning to the end of that time.

I <u>spent all day</u> typing information into a computer.
They <u>spent the night</u> chatting intimately.

⇨ For more information about this use, see **Usage** entry at **spend - pass**.

spend - pass

1 'spend' and 'pass'

These verbs are used in a similar way to talk about time.
If someone does something from the beginning to the end of a period of time, you say that they **spend** the time doing it.

We <u>spent the evening</u> talking about art and the theatre.
She woke early, meaning to <u>spend all day</u> writing.

(*i*) Note that you do not say that someone spends a period of time 'in doing', 'on doing', or 'to do' something.

If someone is in a place from the beginning to the end of a period of time, you can say that they **spend** the time there.

He <u>spent most of his time</u> in the library.
We found a hotel where we could <u>spend the night</u>.

You can say that someone **spends** or **passes** a period of time in another person's company. This use of **pass** is rather old-fashioned.

I <u>spent an evening</u> with Davis.
We <u>passed a pleasant afternoon</u> together.

2 'to pass the time'

If you do something to occupy yourself while you are waiting for something, you say that you do it **to pass the time**.

He had brought a book along <u>to pass the time</u>.
<u>To pass the time</u> they played Scrabble.

3 'have'

If you enjoy yourself while you are doing something, you do not say that you 'pass' or 'spend' a good time. You say that you **have** a good time.

We're just having a good time being boyfriend and girlfriend right now.
A lot of my friends <u>had a marvellous time</u> over New Year.

spite

⇨ See **Usage** entry at **in spite of - despite**.

spoil

⇨ See **Usage** entry at **destroy - spoil - ruin**.

spokesman

1 'spokesman'

A **spokesman** is someone who is asked to speak as the representative of an organization or group of people.

A <u>spokesman</u> for the school said the expulsions were a precautionary measure.

'We regret the heavy loss of life and call upon all involved to show respect for the rule of law,' a White House <u>spokesman</u> said.

2 'spokeswoman'

In the past, **spokesman** was used to refer to both men and women, but it is now hardly ever used to refer to women. A female representative is now usually referred to as a **spokeswoman.**

A <u>spokeswoman</u> said official grant figures might need to be revised.
A police <u>spokeswoman</u> said 'This man is extremely dangerous.'

3 'spokesperson'

Spokesperson is a fairly new word which can refer to either a man or a woman.

A <u>spokesperson</u> for the regime said that there was an explosion in an ammunition depot.

spring

Spring can be a noun or a verb.

1 used as a noun

Spring is the season between winter and summer.
If you want to say that something happens every year during this season, you say that it happens **in spring** or **in the spring.**

<u>In spring</u> birds nest there.
…a huge flower bed which is full of tulips <u>in the spring.</u>

ⓘ Note that you do not say that something happens 'in the springs'.

2 used as a verb

When a person or animal **springs,** they suddenly move upwards or forwards. The past tense of **spring** is **sprang,** not 'springed'. The past participle is **sprung.**

She <u>sprang</u> to her feet.
The lions <u>had sprung</u> out to kill passing antelope.

 In American English, **sprung** is sometimes the past tense.

She <u>sprung</u> at him, and aimed a wild blow at his face.

stack

⇨ See **Usage** entry at **heap - stack - pile.**

staff

The people who work for an organization can be referred to as its **staff.**

She was invited to join the <u>staff</u> of the BBC.
The police questioned me and all the <u>staff.</u>

You can use a plural or singular form of a verb after **staff.** The plural form is more common.

The staff <u>are</u> very helpful.
The teaching staff <u>is</u> well-qualified and experienced.

⚠ **WARNING:** You do not refer to an individual person who works for an organization as a 'staff'. You refer to him or her as a **member of staff.**

There are two students to every <u>member of staff.</u>
At times <u>members of HQ staff</u> adopted a secretive attitude.

stair

⇨ See **Usage** entry at **step - stairs.**

stand

Stand is usually a verb. Its past tense and past participle is **stood,** not 'standed'.

USAGE

stare

1 saying where someone is

When you **are standing** somewhere, your body is upright, your legs are straight, and your weight is supported by your feet. Note that in standard English you do not say that someone 'is stood' somewhere.

He <u>is standing</u> in the middle of the road.
She <u>was standing</u> at the bus stop.

2 saying where someone goes

Stand is also used to say that someone moves to a different place and remains standing there.

She told the girls to <u>stand</u> aside and let her pass.
She came and <u>stood</u> close to him.

3 'stand up'

Stand is sometimes used to say that someone raises their body to a standing position when they have been sitting.

The children <u>stood</u> and applauded.

However, you normally say that someone **stands up.**

Lewis Jones refused to <u>stand up</u> when I came into the room.
I put down my glass and <u>stood up.</u>

4 'cannot stand'

If you **cannot stand** someone or something, you do not like them at all.

She <u>can't stand</u> children.

5 'stand' in an election

In British English, if you **stand** in an election, you are a candidate in it.

She was invited to <u>stand</u> as the Liberal candidate.
He <u>has stood</u> for Parliament 21 times.

 American speakers say **run,** not 'stand'.

He then <u>ran</u> for Governor of New York.

---

stare

⇨ See **Usage** entry at **gaze - stare.**

---

start - begin - commence

1 used with noun groups

If you **start, begin,** or **commence** something, you do it from a particular time.

My father <u>started</u> work when he was ten.
The US is prepared to <u>begin</u> talks immediately.
I <u>commenced</u> a round of visits.

There is no difference in meaning between these words, but **commence** is a formal word. You do not use it in conversation.

The past tense of **begin** is **began,** not 'beginned' or 'begun'. The past participle is **begun.**

Strathclyde Police <u>began</u> a search for the boy's parents.
The company <u>has begun</u> a programme of rationalization.

2 used with other verbs

You can use a 'to'-infinitive or an '-ing' form after **start** and **begin.**

Ralph <u>started to run.</u>
He <u>started laughing.</u>
I was <u>beginning to feel</u> better.
We <u>began chattering</u> and <u>laughing</u> together.

ⓘ Note that you do not use an '-ing' form after **starting** or **beginning.** You do not say, for example, 'Now that I feel better, I'm beginning eating more'. You must say 'Now that I feel better, I'm beginning to eat more'.

After **commence,** you use an '-ing' form. You do not use a 'to'-infinitive.

He let his oars sink into the water and <u>commenced pulling</u> with long strokes.

3 **used as intransitive verbs**

Start, begin, and **commence** can all be intransitive verbs to say that something happens from a particular time.

His meeting <u>starts</u> at 7.

My career as a journalist was about to <u>begin</u>.

He had been held for 9 months when his trial <u>commenced</u>.

4 **special uses of 'start'**

Start has some special meanings. You do not use **begin** or **commence** with any of these meanings.

You use **start** to say that someone makes a machine or engine start to work.

He couldn't get his engine <u>started</u>.

He <u>started</u> the car and drove off.

You use **start** to say that someone creates a business or other organization.

He scraped up the money to <u>start</u> a restaurant.

Now is probably as good a time as any to <u>start</u> a business.

stationary - stationery - stationer

Stationary and **stationery** are both pronounced /steɪʃənri/. However, their meanings are completely different.

1 **'stationary'**

Stationary is an adjective. If a vehicle is **stationary,** it is not moving.

…a <u>stationary</u> car.

Only use the handbrake when your vehicle is <u>stationary</u>.

2 **'stationery'**

Stationery is a noun. It refers to paper, envelopes, pens, and other equipment used for writing.

The same number said it was acceptable to steal small items, such as <u>stationery</u> from work.

…the office <u>stationery</u> cupboard.

3 **'stationer'**

A shop where you buy these things is called a **stationer** or a **stationer's.** It is not called a 'stationery'.

…a high street <u>stationer</u>.

…a <u>stationer's</u> in Islington.

 Stationer's is not normally used in American English.

statistics - statistical

1 **'statistics'**

Statistics are numerical facts obtained from analysing information.

I happen to have the official <u>statistics</u> with me.

…the difference in road accident <u>statistics</u> between north and south Europe.

When **statistics** is used with this meaning, it is a plural noun. You use the plural form of a verb with it.

The same statistics <u>are</u> fed into the computer.

Statistics never <u>prove</u> anything.

Statistics is also the branch of mathematics dealing with these facts.

…a Professor of <u>Statistics</u>.

When you use **statistics** with this meaning, it is an uncount noun. You use a singular form of a verb with it.

Statistics <u>has</u> never been taught here before.

2 **'statistical'**

You do not use **statistic** as an adjective to mean 'relating to statistics'. The word you use is **statistical.**

<u>Statistical</u> techniques are regularly employed.
The report contains a great deal of <u>statistical</u> information.

---

stay

⇨ See **Usage** entry at **remain - stay.**

---

steal

When someone **steals** something, they take it without permission and without intending to return it.

He tried to <u>steal</u> a caravan from a caravan site.
My first offence was <u>stealing</u> a pair of binoculars.

The past tense of **steal** is **stole,** not 'stealed'. The past participle is **stolen.**

Armed raiders disguised as postmen <u>stole</u> 50 bags of mail.
My car <u>was stolen</u> on Friday evening.
He was sentenced to probation for receiving <u>stolen</u> property.

⚠ **WARNING:** When you are speaking about the object which has been stolen, you use **steal** or **take**. However, when the object of the verb is a person, you use **rob.**

I <u>had stolen my father's money.</u>
I know you 've <u>taken my stamps.</u>
They <u>robbed</u> me and stole my car.

---

step - stairs

1 **'step'**

A **step** is a raised flat surface which you put your feet on to move to a different level.

Mind the <u>step.</u>
She was sitting on the top <u>step.</u>

A series of steps, for example on a steep slope or on the outside of a building, is called a **flight** of steps.

…a <u>flight</u> of concrete steps.
We walked in silence up a <u>flight</u> of stairs.

2 **'stairs'**

A series of steps inside a building which you use to get from one floor to another is called **stairs** or a **staircase.**

I was running up and down the <u>stairs.</u>
There was a large hall with a big <u>staircase</u> winding up from it.

---

still

Still is most commonly used to say that a situation continues to exist.

1 **position in sentence**

● You usually put **still** after the first auxiliary in a verb group. For example, you say 'He **was still** waiting'. You do not say 'He still was waiting'.

He <u>could still</u> get into serious trouble.
I <u>'ve still</u> got three left.
Individual payments <u>had still</u> not been calculated.

● If there is no auxiliary, you put **still** in front of the verb, unless the verb is **be**.
She still lives in London.

● If the verb is **be**, you put **still** after it.
She was still beautiful.
There is still a chance the plan could collapse.

● In conversation, **still** is sometimes put at the end of a sentence.
We have a lot to do still.

However, you do not use **still** with this meaning at the beginning of a sentence.

2 used with 'even if'
Still is often used in sentences which begin with **even if** or **even though**.
But even if they do change the system, they've still got an economic crisis on their hands.

⇨ For more information about this use, see **Usage** entry at **even**.

3 used in negative clauses
You can use **still** in a negative clause for emphasis. **Still** goes in front of the first auxiliary in the clause.
I still don't understand.
Pollard still did not know Uzi's last name.

However, you do not use **still** in a negative clause simply to say that something has not happened up to the present time. The word you use is **yet**. **Yet** goes after **not** or at the end of the clause.
I haven't yet met Davis.
It isn't dark yet.

⇨ See **Usage** entry at **yet**.

sting - bite

1 'sting'
Sting is usually a verb. Its past tense and past participle is **stung,** not 'stang' or 'stinged'. If a creature such as a bee, wasp, or scorpion **stings** you, it pricks your skin and pushes poison into your body.
Bees do not normally sting without being provoked.
Perry was taken to hospital, stung by a wasp inside the mouth.

2 'bite'
You do not say that a mosquito or ant 'stings' you. You say that it **bites** you. The past tense and past participle of **bite** are **bit** and **bitten.**
The mosquitoes always made her swell up when they bit her.
A mosquito had bitten her on the wrist.

You also say that a snake **bites** you.
In Britain you are more likely to be struck by lightning than bitten by a snake.

stone

1 'stone' and 'rock'
Stone is the hard, solid substance which is found in the ground and is often used for building.
The bits of stone are joined together with cement.
…a stone wall.

In British English, a **stone** is a small piece of stone which you can pick up in your hand.
Roger picked up a stone and threw it.

In American English, a small piece of stone like this may also be called a **rock.**
She bent down, picked up a rock and threw it into the trees.

USAGE

In both British and American English, a **rock** is also a large piece of stone that sticks up out of the ground or the sea, or that has broken away from a mountain.

2 'stone' and 'pit'

In British English, the large, hard seed in a fruit such as a cherry, date, or apricot is called the **stone**.

...a cherry stone.

 In American English, this seed is called the **pit**.

stop

You usually use the verb **stop** to say that someone no longer does something. After **stop**, you can use either an '-ing' form or a 'to'-infinitive, but with different meanings.

1 'stop doing'

If you **stop doing** something at a particular time, you no longer do it after that time.

We all stopped talking.
He couldn't stop crying.

2 'stop to do'

If you **stop to do** something, you interrupt what you are doing in order to do something else. For example, if you are talking about someone who is walking somewhere, you can say 'She **stopped to admire** the view'; this means that she stopped walking and admired the view before starting to walk again.

Several of the men he passed recognized him and stopped to speak.
I stopped to tie my shoelace.

3 'stop somebody doing something'

If you are prevented from doing something, you can say that something **stops you doing** it or **stops you from doing** it.

Did any of them try to stop you coming?
How do you stop a tap dripping?
Nothing was going to stop Sandy from being a writer.

You do not say that something 'stops you to do' something.

4 'stop' and 'stay'

In conversation, British speakers sometimes use **stop** to say that someone is staying somewhere for a short time.

They 're stopping a couple of nights.
I can go and stop with my brother for a couple of days.

 In writing, and in American English, you use **stay,** not 'stop'.
The children were staying with Betty's stepmother in Glasgow.

store

⇨ See **Usage** entry at **shop - store**.

storey - floor

1 'storey'

You refer to the different levels in a building as its **storeys** or **floors.** If you are saying how many levels a building has, you usually use **storeys.** For example, you say 'The new hospital is **five storeys** high' or 'I work in a **six-storey** building'.

...a house with four storeys.
...a single-storey building.

 'Storey' is spelled **story** in American English. The plural of **story** is **stories.**

...a four-story building.
...three hotel towers, each 30 stories high.

2 **'floor'**

If you are talking about a particular level in a building, you usually use **floor**, not 'storey'. You do not say that something is on a particular 'storey'. You say that it is on a particular **floor**.

My office is on the second <u>floor</u>.
…a ground <u>floor</u> flat.

story - storey

1 **'story'**

A **story** is a description of imaginary people and events, written or told in order to entertain people. The plural of **story** is **stories**.

Tell me a <u>story</u>.
Her <u>stories</u> about the boy wizard have sold 27.5 million copies.

(*i*) Note that a description of a series of real events can also be called a **story**.

We had succeeded in selling the <u>story</u> of the expedition to the Daily Express.

 In American English, a **story** is also one of the floors or levels in a building.
The house was four <u>stories</u> high.

2 **'storey'**

In British English, one of these floors is called a **storey**.

The house was three <u>storeys</u> high.

⇨ See **Usage** entry at **storey - floor**.

strange - unusual

1 **'strange'**

You use **strange** to say that something is unfamiliar or unexpected in a way that makes you puzzled, uneasy, or afraid.

It was <u>strange</u> to hear her voice again.
I had a <u>strange</u> dream last night.

2 **'unusual'**

If you just want to say that something is not common, you use **unusual**, not 'strange'.

He had an <u>unusual</u> name.
The California race is over the <u>unusual</u> distance of one mile and a half.

⇨ For a list of words which can be used to describe someone who is unusual, see **Usage** entry at **unusual**.

strangeness

The following words can all be used to describe someone whose character or appearance is different from that of most other people:

bizarre	extraordinary	interesting	peculiar	strange	unusual
curious	funny	odd	queer	striking	weird

If you say, for example, 'She's odd' or 'She's an odd woman', you are talking about someone's character. If you say 'She looks odd' or 'She has an odd face', you are describing her appearance.

1 **'unusual'**

Unusual is a neutral word which does not show approval or disapproval.

I was not prepared for this <u>unusual</u> man.
They have replanted many areas with rare and <u>unusual</u> plants.

2 **'interesting' and 'striking'**

Interesting and **striking** are used to indicate approval. **Striking** is only used to describe

USAGE

someone's appearance, not their character.

...filling your life up with <u>interesting</u> new acquaintances.
You've got a very interesting face. <u>Striking.</u>

3 'extraordinary'

When **extraordinary** is used to describe someone's character, it usually indicates approval.

She was an <u>extraordinary</u>, fascinating woman.

4 other words

Bizarre, curious, funny, odd, peculiar, queer, strange, and **weird** indicate amusement or disapproval when they are used to describe people.

His old school tie and blazer looked distinctly <u>bizarre.</u>
There was something a bit <u>odd</u> about this woman.
The girl was wearing a very <u>peculiar</u> trouser suit.
He's different. He's <u>weird.</u>

stranger

A **stranger** is someone who you have never met before.

A <u>stranger</u> appeared.
Antonio was a <u>stranger</u> to all of us.

⚠ **WARNING:** You do not use **stranger** to talk about someone who comes from a country which is not your own. You can refer to him or her as a **foreigner,** but this word can sound rather impolite. It is better to talk, for example, about 'someone **from abroad**' or 'a person **from overseas**'.

… <u>visitors from abroad.</u>
…a very large rise in postgraduate <u>students from overseas.</u>

street

A **street** is a road in a town or large village, usually with houses or other buildings built alongside it.

The two men walked slowly down the <u>street.</u>
They went into the café across the <u>street.</u>

You do not use **street** to refer to a road in the countryside.

strike

If you **strike** someone or something, you hit them with your hand, a stick, or something else. This is a formal use.

He <u>was striking</u> his dog with his whip.

The past tense and past participle of **strike** is **struck,** not 'striked'.

The young man <u>struck</u> his father.
He <u>had struck</u> her only in self-defence.

Strike is also used in the following ways to describe the effect something has on a person's mind:

If an idea or thought **strikes** you, it comes into your mind suddenly.

It <u>struck</u> him how foolish his behaviour had been.

If something **strikes** you in a particular way, it gives you a particular impression.

Gertie <u>strikes</u> me as a very silly girl.
How did London <u>strike</u> you?

If you **are struck by** something, you are very impressed with it.

I <u>was struck by</u> his good manners.

strong

The adjective **strong** is used in a number of different ways to describe people. When you say that someone is **strong,** you usually mean that they have powerful muscles and the ability to lift or carry heavy objects.

Claudia was young, strong, and healthy.
The little boy has grown into a tall, strong man.

A **strong** personality is someone who is very confident and not easily influenced by other people.

But Alan is a strong personality with leadership qualities that are fantastic for this club.

A **strong believer in** something is convinced that it is very good or desirable.
The Secretary of State is a strong believer in parental involvement in classrooms.

A **strong supporter of** a person or organization supports them in an enthusiastic way.
I'm still a strong supporter of the NHS.

⚠ **WARNING:** If someone smokes a lot or drinks a lot of alcohol, you do not say that they are a 'strong smoker' or a 'strong drinker'. You say that they are a **heavy smoker** or a **heavy drinker.**

strongly

You use **strongly** when you are talking about people's feelings or attitudes. For example, if you are **strongly** in favour of something, you are very much in favour of it.
I feel this very strongly.
He remains strongly opposed to commercial radio.

If you are urging someone to do something that will be to their advantage, you can say that you **strongly advise** them to do it.
I strongly advise you to get someone to help you.

⚠ **WARNING:** You do not use **strongly** to describe the way someone holds something. Instead, you use **tightly** or **firmly.**
…the rifle which he gripped tightly in his right hand.
He held her arm firmly.

You do not say that a person works 'strongly'. You say that they work **hard.**
He had worked hard all his life.

stubbornness

The following words can all be used to describe someone who is determined to do what they want to do, and refuses to change their mind:

firm	obstinate	pig-headed	steadfast
intransigent	ornery (*Am*)	rigid	stubborn

1 **positive words**
You use **firm** or **steadfast** to show that you approve of someone's behaviour. **Steadfast** is a rather literary word.
If parents are firm, children accept discipline.
He relied on the calm and steadfast Kathy.

2 **negative words**
Stubborn, obstinate, pig-headed, rigid, and **intransigent** are all used to show disapproval. **Intransigent** is a formal word.
He and his officials remained as stubborn as ever.

…an <u>obstinate</u> and rebellious child.
They can be stupid and <u>pig-headed.</u>
My father is very <u>rigid</u> in his thinking.
He told them how <u>intransigent</u> the racists in his country had been.

student

1 **'student'**

In British English, a **student** is someone who is studying or training at a university or college.

…medical <u>students.</u>
…the <u>students</u> of Edinburgh University.

 In American English, anyone who studies at a school, college, or university can be referred to as a **student.**

…high school <u>students.</u>

2 **'schoolchildren'**

In British English, children attending schools are referred to generally as **schoolchildren, schoolboys,** or **schoolgirls.**

Each year the sanctuary is visited by thousands of <u>schoolchildren.</u>
…when I was still a <u>schoolboy.</u>
…the number of <u>schoolgirls</u> attracted to engineering.

3 **'pupils'**

In Britain, the children attending a particular school are officially referred to as its **pupils.**

…a school with more than 1300 <u>pupils.</u>

 Pupil is sometimes used in this way in American English, but more often it refers to someone who is receiving private instruction.

I try to teach a <u>pupil</u> to swing the club correctly.

4 **'children'**

However, in conversation you talk about the **children** at a school, not its 'pupils'.

We have forty-three <u>children</u> in Fairacre School.

subconscious - unconscious

1 **used as a noun**

Your **subconscious** is the part of your mind that can influence you or affect your behaviour without your being aware of it.

The memory of it all was locked deep in my <u>subconscious.</u>

2 **used as an adjective**

You can also use **subconscious** as an adjective in front of a noun.

The <u>subconscious</u> mind forgets nothing.
He was urged on by some <u>subconscious</u> desire to punish himself.

3 **'unconscious'**

You do not say that a person is 'subconscious'. If someone is not conscious, you say that they are **unconscious.**

The blow knocked him <u>unconscious.</u>

subject

The **subject** of something such as a book or talk is the thing that is discussed in it.

He knew what the <u>subject</u> of the meeting was.
What was the <u>subject</u> of the opera you planned to write?

ⓘ Note that you do not say that the subject of a book or talk 'is about' something.

subway - underground

1 **'subway'**
A **subway** is a path for pedestrians under a busy road.
You feel worried if you walk through a subway.

In some American cities, the **subway** is also a railway system in which electric trains travel below the ground in tunnels.
I don't ride the subway late at night.

2 **'Underground'**
In Britain, a railway system like this is not called the 'subway'. The London and Glasgow systems are both called the **Underground.** The London system is also called the **tube.**
He crossed London by Underground.
I took the tube and then the train.

succeed

If you **succeed in doing** something that involves difficulty or effort, you do it.
I succeeded in getting the job.

(i) Note that you do not say that you 'succeed to do' something,

successful

If something is **successful,** it achieves what it was intended to achieve.
…a successful attempt to land on the moon.
If this method is not successful, consult your health visitor or doctor.

You can also say that a person **is successful in doing** something.
On finishing his training, he was successful in obtaining a post at Halifax.

You do not say that someone 'is successful to do' something.

such

1 **referring back**
Such a thing or person means a thing or person like the one that has just been described, mentioned, or experienced.
We could not believe such a thing.

When **such** is used like this in front of a noun group, **as this** or **as these** is sometimes added after the noun group. This is a fairly formal use.
How can we make sense of such a story as this?
It's the only way to behave at such times as these.

In sentences like these, the word order is often changed. For example, instead of saying 'such times as these', people say **times such as these.** You can also say **times like these.**
They were not involved in issues such as this.
There is nothing wrong in having thoughts like these.

⚠ **WARNING:** You do not use **such** when you are talking about something that is present, or about the place where you are. For example, if you are admiring someone's watch, you do not say 'I'd like such a watch'. You say 'I'd like a watch **like that**'. Similarly, you do not say about the town where you are living 'There's not much to do in such a town'. You say 'There's not much to do in a town **like this**'.
I would have thought I was free in a place like this.
I'm sure they don't have chairs like these.

2 **'such as'**
You use **such as** between two noun groups when you are giving an example of something.
…a game of chance such as roulette.

The first noun group is sometimes put between **such** and **as**.

We talked about <u>such</u> subjects <u>as</u> the weather.

3 | 'such' used for emphasis

Such is sometimes used to emphasize the adjective in a noun group. For example, instead of saying 'He's a nice man', you can say 'He's **such a nice man**'.

She was <u>such a nice girl</u>.
She seemed <u>such a happy woman</u>.

(i) Note that you must use **a** when the noun group is singular. You do not say, for example, '~~She was such nice girl~~'. You also do not say '~~She was a such nice girl~~'.

For greater emphasis, some people say **ever such** instead of 'such'.

I think that's <u>ever such a nice photo</u>.

(i) Note that you do not use **ever such** in writing.

You can use **such** to refer to something or someone that has just been described or mentioned and to emphasize some quality that they have. For example, instead of saying 'It was a very dull place. I was surprised to see her there', you can say 'I was surprised to see her in **such a dull place**'.

I was, of course, impressed to meet <u>such a famous actress</u>.
You really shouldn't tell <u>such obvious lies</u>.

4 | 'such ... that': mentioning a result

You can also use **such** in front of a noun group when you are saying that something happens because someone or something has a quality to an unusually large extent. After the noun group, you use a 'that'-clause.

A few boas grow to <u>such a length</u> that they can tackle creatures as big as goats.
This can be <u>such a gradual process</u> that you are not aware of it happening.

---

suffer - put up with - stand - bear

1 | 'suffer'

You can say that someone **suffers** pain or an unpleasant experience.

He <u>suffered</u> a lot of discomfort.
Young <u>suffered</u> imprisonment and intimidation.

2 | 'put up with'

You do not use **suffer** to say that someone tolerates an unpleasant person. You say that they **put up with** the person.

The local people have to <u>put up with</u> gaping tourists.

3 | 'stand' and 'bear'

If you do not like someone at all, you do not say that you 'can't suffer' them. You say that you **can't stand** them or **can't bear** them.

She said she <u>couldn't stand</u> him.
I <u>can't bear</u> kids.

---

suggest

When you **suggest** something, you mention it as a plan or idea for someone to consider.

Your bank manager will probably <u>suggest</u> a personal loan.
We have to <u>suggest</u> a list of possible topics for next term's seminars.

(i) Note that **suggest** cannot usually be followed directly by a noun or pronoun referring to a person. You generally have to put the preposition **to** in front of it. You do not 'suggest someone something', you 'suggest something to someone'.

John Caskey first <u>suggested this idea to me</u>.

Nor do you 'suggest someone to do something' unless **suggest** means 'recommend'. You 'suggest **that** someone **does** something'.

Beatrice <u>suggested that he spend the summer at their place</u>.

In sentences like these, you usually use a simple tense in the 'that'-clause. However, it is possible to use an infinitive without 'to'. This is a formal use.

The committee suggest that even greater emphasis <u>be placed</u> upon this effort.

The modals **might** and **should** are also sometimes used. This is also a formal use.

Sometimes he would suggest that the destitute <u>might</u> turn to their own families for support.

It's unfair of you to suggest that I <u>should</u> remain faithful to a dead man.

⚠ **WARNING:** Do not confuse **suggest** and **advise**. If you **suggest** something, you mention it as an idea or plan for someone to think about. If you **advise** someone to do something, you tell them what you think they should do.

I <u>advised him to leave</u> as soon as possible

⇨ See **Usage** entry at **advise**, and **Topic** entries at **Advising someone** and **Suggestions**.

suit - suite

1 **'suit'**

Suit /suːt/ can be a verb or a noun.

If something **suits** you, it is convenient, acceptable, or appropriate for you.

Would Monday <u>suit</u> you?

A job where I was indoors all day wouldn't <u>suit</u> me.

ⓘ Note that you do not say that something 'suits to' you.

A **suit** is a set of clothes made from the same material.

He arrived at the office in a <u>suit</u> and tie.

2 **'suite'**

Suite /swiːt/ is a noun.

A **suite** is a set of rooms in a hotel.

They always stayed in a <u>suite</u> at the Ritz.

A **suite** is also a set of matching furniture for a sitting room or bathroom.

I need a three-piece <u>suite</u> for the lounge.

suitable

Someone or something that is **suitable for** a particular person or purpose is right or acceptable for them.

These flats are not really <u>suitable for</u> families with children.

Farm tractors are not <u>suitable for</u> small plots of land.

ⓘ Note that you do not use any preposition except **for** in sentences like these.

suitcase

⇨ See **Usage** entry at **bag**.

summer

Summer is the season between spring and autumn.

If you want to say that something happens every year during this season, you say that it happens **in summer** or **in the summer**.

Auckland is sub-tropical, with sweltering noon temperatures <u>in summer.</u>

Mist is common here even <u>in the summer.</u>

ⓘ Note that you do not say that something happens 'in the summers'.

sunk - sunken

⇨ See **Usage** entry at **sink**.

USAGE

superior

If one person or thing is **superior to** another, they are better than the other person or thing.

I secretly felt superior to him.
The film is vastly superior to the book.

(*i*) Note that you do not use any preposition except **to** after **superior**. You also do not say that one person or thing is 'more superior to' another.

supper

Some people call a large meal they eat in the early part of the evening their **supper**.
Other people use **supper** to refer to a small meal eaten just before going to bed at night.

⇨ For more information, see **Topic** entry at **Meals**.

supply

If you **supply** someone **with** something, you provide them with it.

I can supply you with food and drink.
The Baird Co. supplies Hollywood with everything from decorative wall posters to fictional police badges.

(*i*) Note that you must use **with** in sentences like these. You do not say, for example, 'I can supply you food and drink'.

You can also say that something **is supplied to** someone.

This system ensures that heat is supplied to all customers at an adequate temperature.
Much of the material supplied to the army was faulty.

support

If you **support** someone or **support** their aims, you agree with their aims and try to help them to succeed.

We supported the nurses by taking industrial action.
A lot of building workers supported the campaign.

If you **support** a sports team, you want them to win.

He has supported Oldham Athletic all his life.

If you **support** someone, you provide them with money or the things they need.

He has a wife and three children to support.

⚠ **WARNING:** You do not use 'support' in any of the following ways:
You do not use 'support' to say that someone accepts pain or an unpleasant situation.
You say that they **bear** it, **put up with** it, or **tolerate** it.

It was painful of course but I bore it.
You have to put up with these inconveniences.
She can no longer tolerate the position that she's in.

You do not use 'support' to say that someone allows something that they do not approve of. You say that they **put up with** it or **tolerate** it. If they do not allow it, you can say that they **won't stand for** it.

I've put up with more than enough from you already.
...the tendency to tolerate the extremes of human behaviour.
I won't stand for any more of your disobedience.

If you do not like something at all, you do not say that you 'can't support' it. You say that you **can't bear** it or **can't stand** it.

I can't bear the thought of being without him.
She can't stand children.

suppose - assume

1 'suppose'

If you **suppose** that something is the case, you think it is probably the case.

I suppose it was bound to happen.
I suppose he left fairly recently.

2 'assume'

If you **assume** that something is the case, you are fairly sure that it is the case, and act as if it were the case.

I assumed that he had started working as soon as he left.
When you have a language degree, people assume that you speak the language fluently.

You do not say that someone supposes or assumes 'something to be' the case.

3 'don't suppose'

Instead of saying that you **suppose** something is **not** the case, you usually say that you **don't suppose that it is** the case.

I don't suppose you would be prepared to stay in Edinburgh?

4 'I suppose so'

If someone says that something is the case, or asks you whether something is the case, you can say 'I **suppose so**' as a way of agreeing with them or saying 'yes'. When you say 'I **suppose so**', you are indicating that you are uncertain or unenthusiastic about something.

'So it was worth doing?' – 'I suppose so.'

(i) Note that you do not say 'I suppose it'.

5 'I suppose not'

Similarly, you can agree with a negative statement or question by saying 'I **suppose not**'.

'It doesn't often happen.' – 'No, I suppose not.'

6 'suppose' used as a conjunction

You can use **suppose** as a conjunction when you are considering a possible situation or action and trying to think what effects it would have.

Suppose we don't say a word, and somebody else finds out about it.

Supposing can be used in a similar way.

Supposing something should go wrong, what would you do then?

7 'be supposed to'

If something **is supposed to** be done, it should be done because of a rule, instruction, or custom.

You are supposed to report it to the police as soon as possible.
I 'm not supposed to talk to you about this.

If something **is supposed to** be true, people generally think that it is true.

The hill was supposed to be haunted by a ghost.
She was supposed to be very good as an actress.

(i) Note that you do not say that something 'is suppose to' be done or be true.

sure

⇨ See **Usage** entry at **certain - sure**.

surely - definitely - certainly - naturally

1 'surely'

You use **surely** for emphasis when you are objecting to something that has been said or done.

Prince Charles speaks of becoming a multi-faith king. Surely, what we really need in the 21st century is a no-faith king.

USAGE

Their lawyers and advisers assured us that they have not broken the rules, but <u>surely</u> this is not good practice.

2 'definitely' and 'certainly'

You do not use 'surely' simply to give strong emphasis to a statement. The word you use is **definitely.**

They were <u>definitely</u> not for sale.
The call <u>definitely</u> came from your phone.

In British English, you also do not use 'surely' when you are agreeing with something that has been said, or confirming that something is true. The word you use is **certainly.**

Ellie was <u>certainly</u> a student at the university but I'm not sure about her brother.
'You keep out of their way, don't you?' – 'I <u>certainly</u> do'.

 American speakers use both **surely** and **certainly** to agree with requests and statements.

'It is still a difficult world for women.' – 'Oh, <u>certainly</u>.'
<u>Surely</u>, yes, I agree entirely with that.

You do not use 'surely' to say emphatically that something will happen in the future. Instead you use **definitely** or **certainly.**

The Conference will <u>definitely</u> be postponed.
If nothing is done, there will <u>certainly</u> be an economic crisis.

3 'naturally'

You do not use **surely** to emphasize that someone is behaving in the way you would expect in particular circumstances. The word you use is **naturally.**

Dina was crying, so <u>naturally</u> Hannah was upset.

---

surgery

1 used as an uncount noun

In both British and American English, **surgery** is medical treatment in which a person's body is cut open so that a surgeon can deal with a diseased or damaged part.

He underwent <u>surgery</u> at Queen's Medical Centre.

2 used as a count noun

In British English, a doctor's or dentist's **surgery** is the building or room where he or she works and where people go to receive advice and minor treatment.

His <u>surgery</u> was rebuilt three years ago.

 In American English, a building or room like this is called the doctor's or dentist's **office.**

Dr Peabody's <u>office</u> was just across the street.

---

surprise

Surprise can be a verb or a noun.

1 used as a verb

If something **surprises** you, you did not expect it.

Dad's reply <u>surprised</u> me.
Her sudden death <u>had surprised</u> everybody.

You do not use a continuous form of **surprise.** You do not say, for example, '~~What you say is surprising me~~'.

2 used as a noun

If something is a **surprise,** it surprises someone.

The ruling came as a <u>surprise</u> to everyone.
It was a great <u>surprise</u> to find out I had won something.

In stories, expressions such as **to my surprise** and **to her surprise** are sometimes used.

They indicate that someone is surprised at something that happens.
To her surprise he sat down.

ⓘ Note that you do not use any preposition except **to** in expressions like these.

3 **'surprised'**
Surprised is an adjective. If you are **surprised to see** something or **surprised to hear** something, you did not expect to see it or hear it.
I was surprised to see her return home so soon.
You'll be surprised to learn that Charles Boon is living here.

⚠ **WARNING:** You do not say that someone is 'surprised at seeing' or 'surprised at hearing' something. You also do not say that someone is 'surprise to' see or hear something.

suspicious
⇨ See **Usage** entry at doubtful - dubious - suspicious.

sweetcorn
⇨ See **Usage** entry at **corn**.

sweets - candy
1 **'sweets'**
In British English, small, sweet things that you eat, such as toffees and chocolates, are called **sweets.**
She urged her children not to eat too many sweets.

2 **'candy'**
In American English, sweet things like these are called **candy. Candy** is an uncount noun.
You eat too much candy. It's bad for your teeth.

swift
⇨ See **Usage** entry at **speed**.

sympathetic - nice - likeable
1 **'sympathetic'**
You say that someone is being **sympathetic** when they are kind to someone who has problems, and show that they understand their feelings.
My boyfriend was very sympathetic and it did make me feel better.

ⓘ Note that people sometimes refer to characters in a play or novel who are easy to like as **sympathetic**.
There were no sympathetic characters in my book.

2 **'nice' and 'likeable'**
You do not say that someone is 'sympathetic' when they are very pleasant and easy to like. The word you use is **nice** or **likeable**.
He was a terribly nice man.
…a very likeable and attractive young man.

⇨ See **Usage** entry at **nice**.

T t

take

Take is one of the commonest verbs in English. It is used in many different ways. Its other forms are **takes, taking, took, taken.**

1 actions and activities

Take is most commonly used with a noun referring to an action to say that someone performs that action.

She took a shower.
He formed the habit of taking long, solitary walks.

⇨ For more information about this use, see **Usage** entry at **have - take.**

2 moving things

If you **take** something from one place to another, you carry it there.

Don't forget to take your umbrella.
He has to take the boxes to the office every morning.

⇨ For more information about this use, see **Usage** entry at **carry - take.**

⚠ **WARNING:** Do not confuse **take** with **bring** or **fetch.**
⇨ For an explanation of some of the differences, see **Usage** entry at **bring - take - fetch.**

3 exams and tests

When someone completes an exam or test, you say that they **take** the exam or test.

She 's not yet taken her driving test.
She took her degree last year.

4 time

If something **takes** a certain amount of time, you need that amount of time to do it.

How long will it take?
It may take them several weeks to get back.

take place

You say that an event **takes place.**

The wedding took place on the stage of the Sydney Opera House.
A second revolution in fashion took place just after World War I.

Happen and **occur** have a similar meaning, but they can only be used to talk about events which were not planned. You can use **take place** to talk about either planned or unplanned events.

The talks will take place in Vienna.
The accident took place on Saturday morning in the village of Whiston.

ⓘ Note that **take place** is intransitive. You do not say that something 'was taken place'.

talented

⇨ See **Usage** entry at **skilful - skilled - talented.**

talk

Talk can be a verb or a noun.

1 used as a verb

When you **talk,** you say things.

Nancy's throat was so sore that she could not talk.

You do not use **talk** to report what someone says. You do not say, for example, 'He talked that the taxi had arrived'. You say 'He **said** that the taxi had arrived'.
I said that I would like to teach English.

If you mention the person who is being spoken to, you use **tell**.
He told me that Sheldon would be over to see me in a few days.

⇨ See **Usage** entries at **say** and **tell**.

Do not confuse **talk** with **speak**.

⇨ For an explanation of the differences, see **Usage** entry at **speak - talk**.

2 **used as a noun**
If you give a **talk**, you speak for a period of time to an audience.
Colin Blakemore came here and gave a talk a couple of years ago.

⇨ For more information about this use, see **Usage** entry at **speech - talk**.

tall
⇨ See **Usage** entry at **high - tall**.

tasteful - tasty - delicious

1 **'tasteful'**
Something that is **tasteful** is attractive and elegant. You can use **tasteful** to talk about things such as furniture, ornaments, and clothes.
The bedroom was simple but tasteful.
He always sent the most tasteful Christmas cards.

2 **'tasty'**
Food that is **tasty** has a pleasant flavour.
Try this tasty dish for supper with a crispy salad.
The seeds, when toasted, are tasty and nutritious.

3 **'delicious'**
Note that you do not usually describe sweet foods as 'tasty'. Instead, you can say that they are **delicious**.
Martha makes the most delicious chocolate pudding.

tasteless - distasteful

1 **'tasteless'**
Something that is **tasteless** is vulgar and unattractive.
…a flat crammed with spectacularly tasteless objets d'art.
Apart from a few tasteless remarks, he was reasonably well-behaved.

Tasteless food has very little flavour.
…cold, tasteless pizzas.

2 **'distasteful'**
If something is **distasteful** to you, you dislike it or disapprove of it.
Unnecessary slaughter of animals is distasteful to most people.

ⓘ Note that **distasteful** is not the opposite of 'tasteful'.

tasty
⇨ See **Usage** entry at **tasteful - tasty**.

tea

1 **the drink**
Tea is a drink made by pouring boiling water onto the dried leaves of the tea bush. In Britain, **tea** is usually drunk with milk.

She poured herself another cup of <u>tea.</u>
She went into the kitchen to make a fresh pot of <u>tea.</u>

2 **meals**

Tea is also used to refer to two different types of meal.

Some people use it to refer to a light meal eaten in the afternoon. This meal usually consists of sandwiches and cakes, with tea to drink. It is sometimes called **afternoon tea.**

Some British people use **tea** to refer to a main meal eaten in the early evening.

⇨ For more information, see **Topic** entry at **Meals.**

teach

1 **teaching a subject**

If you **teach** a subject, you explain it to people so that they know about it or understand it. The past tense and past participle of **teach** is **taught,** not 'teached'.

I <u>taught</u> history for many years.
English <u>will be taught</u> in primary schools.

When **teach** has this meaning, it often has an indirect object. The indirect object can go either in front of the direct object or after it. If it goes after the direct object, you put **to** in front of it.

…the guy that taught <u>us English</u> at school.
I found a job teaching <u>English to a group of adults</u> in Paris.

2 **teaching a skill**

If you **teach** someone **to do** something, you give them instructions so that they know how to do it.

He <u>taught</u> me <u>to sing</u> a song.
Boylan <u>had taught</u> him <u>to drive.</u>

When **teach** is used with a 'to'-infinitive like this, it must have a direct object. You do not say, for example, 'Boylan had taught to drive'.

Instead of using a 'to'-infinitive, you can sometimes use an '-ing' form. For example, instead of saying 'I taught them to ski', you can say 'I taught them **skiing**'. You can also say 'I taught them **how to ski**'.

She taught them <u>singing</u> because she enjoyed it herself.
My mother taught me <u>how to cook.</u>

team

A **team** is a group of people who play against another group in a game.

He got into the New Zealand rugby <u>team</u> in 1978.

After **team** you can use either a singular or plural form of a verb.

The team <u>has</u> qualified again for Italy next summer.
Redknapp's team <u>have</u> lost their last five away games.

technique - technology

1 **'technique'**

A **technique** is a method of doing something.

…the <u>techniques</u> of film-making.
…modern management <u>techniques.</u>

Technique is skill and ability which you develop through training and practice.

He went off to the Amsterdam Academy to improve his <u>technique.</u>

2 **'technology'**

Technology is the use of scientific knowledge for practical purposes, for example in industry.

…our belief in the power of modern <u>technology</u>.
Computer <u>technology</u> can be expected to change.

telegram
⇨ See **Usage** entry at **wire**.

tell

Tell is a common verb which is used in several different ways. Its past tense and past participle is **told**, not 'telled'.

1 information

If someone **tells** you something, they give you some information. You usually refer to this information by using a 'that'-clause or a 'wh'-clause.

Tell Father <u>the carpenter has come.</u>
I told her <u>what the doctor had said.</u>

You can sometimes refer to the information that is given by using a noun group as the direct object of **tell**. When the direct object is not a pronoun, you put the indirect object first.

She told <u>him the news.</u>
I never told <u>her a thing.</u>

When the direct object is a pronoun, you usually put it first. You put **to** in front of the indirect object.

I've never told <u>this to anyone else</u> in my whole life.

When you are referring back to information that has already been mentioned, you use **so** after **tell**. For example, you say 'I didn't agree with him and I **told him so**'. You do not say 'I didn't agree with him and I told him it'.

She knows that you and I adore each other. I have <u>told her so.</u>
'Then how do you know she's well?' – 'She <u>told me so.</u>'

2 stories, jokes, lies

You say that someone **tells** a story or a joke.

She <u>told</u> me the story of her life.
How often do you see a woman <u>telling</u> a joke in a pub?

You can also say that someone **makes** or **cracks** a joke.
⇨ For more information, see **Usage** entry at **joke**.

You say that someone **tells** a lie.

We <u>told</u> a lot of lies.

If someone is not lying, you say that they are **telling the truth.**

We knew that he was <u>telling the truth.</u>
I wondered why I <u>hadn't told</u> Mary <u>the truth.</u>

When you use **tell** to talk about stories, jokes, or lies, the indirect object can go either after the direct object or in front of it.

His friend <u>told me this story.</u>
Many hours had passed when Karen finished <u>telling her story to Kitty.</u>

3 orders

If you **tell** someone **to do** something, you order or instruct them to do it. When **tell** has this meaning, it is followed by an object and a 'to'-infinitive.

<u>Tell Martha to build</u> a fire.
They <u>told us to put</u> on our seat-belts.

⚠ **WARNING:** You do not use **tell** like this without an object. You do not say, for example, 'They told to put on our seat-belts'.

4 recognizing the truth

If you **can tell** what is happening or what is true, you are able to judge correctly what is happening or what is true.

I _can usually tell_ when I'm being lied to.
I _couldn't tell_ what they were thinking.

(*i*) Note that when **tell** has this meaning, you usually use **can**, **could**, or **be able to** with it.

temperature

⇨ See section on **temperature** in **Topic** entry at **Measurements**.

term - semester

1 'term'

At a British school, each year is divided into three **terms**. At an American school, it is divided into four **terms**.

…_the summer term_.

2 'semester'

At a British college or university, each year is also divided into three **terms**.

 At an American college or university, it is divided into two **semesters**, three **trimesters**, or four **quarters**.

The first semester starts in three weeks.

terrible - terribly

1 'terrible'

The adjective **terrible** is used in two ways. In conversation, you use it to say that something is very unpleasant or of very poor quality.

I know this has been a _terrible_ shock to you.
His eyesight was _terrible._

In writing or conversation, you use **terrible** to say that something is very shocking or distressing.

That was a terrible air crash last week.

2 'terribly'

The adverb **terribly** is sometimes used to emphasize how shocking or distressing something is.

My son has suffered _terribly_. He has lost his best friend.
The wound bled _terribly._

However, **terribly** is much more commonly used to emphasize that someone or something has a feeling or quality to a great extent.

I'm _terribly_ sorry.
We all miss him _terribly_ and are desperate for him to come home.
It's a _terribly_ dull place.

You do not use **terribly** like this in formal writing.

test

A **test** is a series of questions which you answer to show how much you know about a subject. You say that someone **takes** or **does** a test of this kind.

All candidates will be required to _take_ an English language _test._
We _did_ another _test._

A **test** is also a series of actions which you do to show how well you are able to do something. You say that someone **takes** a test of this kind.

She _'s_ not yet _taken_ her driving _test._

(*i*) Note that you never say that someone 'makes' a test.

If someone is successful in a test of either kind, you say that they **pass** it.
I passed my driving test in Holland.

⚠ **WARNING:** To **pass** a test always means to succeed in it. It does not have the same meaning as **take** or **do**.

If someone is unsuccessful in a test, you say that they **fail** it.
I told her I thought I'd failed the test.

text - article

1 'text'
The **text** of a book or magazine is the main written part of it, rather than the introduction, pictures, or index.
The illustrations and text were beautifully produced.

2 'article'
You do not refer to a piece of writing written for a newspaper or magazine as a 'text'. You call it an **article**.
Four years ago Clive Norling wrote an article in the Times.

than

1 'than' used with comparatives
Than is mainly used after comparative adjectives and adverbs. After **than** you use a noun group, a clause, or an adjunct.
The cataloguing is more difficult than the other part of the work.
I am happier than I have ever been.
They had to work harder than expected.
Last year, terrorist activities were worse than in any of the previous twelve years.

If you use a personal pronoun on its own after **than**, it must be an object pronoun such as **me** or **him**.
My brother is younger than me.
Lamin was shorter than her.

However, if the pronoun is the subject of a clause, you use a subject pronoun.
They knew my past much better than she did.
He's taller than I am.

You can use **than** after a noun group which contains a comparative adjective. For example, instead of saying 'Suzanne was more contented than her brother', you can say 'Suzanne was **a more contented baby than** her brother'.
Kairi was a more satisfactory pet than Tuku had been.
Willy owned a larger collection of books than anyone else I have ever met.

You can also use a comparative adjective immediately after a noun, followed by **than**. For example, instead of saying 'I wouldn't like to live in a town which is larger than Lichfield', you can say 'I wouldn't like to live in a town **larger than** Lichfield'.
We were then living in a house bigger than we required.
…packs of cards larger than he was used to.

You can use an infinitive with or without **to** after **than**.
He is more likely to continue his crimes than to stop.
The number of seats is more likely to rise to 151 than fall to 149.

You can also use an '-ing' form after **than**.
Putting a good product on the market involves more than just producing it.

2 'than ever'
You can also use **ever** or **ever before** after **than**. For example, if you say that something is

'bigger **than ever**' or 'bigger **than ever before**', you are emphasizing that it has never been as big as it is now, although it has always been big.

Bill worked harder <u>than ever.</u>

He was now farming a bigger area <u>than ever before.</u>

⚠ **WARNING:** You do not use **than** when you are making comparisons using **not as** or **not so**. You do not say, for example, '~~He is not as tall than his sister~~'. You say 'He is not as tall **as** his sister'.

⇨ See **Usage** entry at **as … as.**

⇨ For more information about comparatives, see **Grammar** entries at **Comparative and superlative adjectives** and **Comparative and superlative adverbs.**

3 **'more than'**

You use **more than** to say that the number of people or things in a group is greater than a particular number.

…in a city of <u>more than</u> a million people.

There are <u>more than</u> two hundred and fifty species of shark.

⇨ For more information about this use, see **Usage** entry at **more.**

You can also use **more than** in front of some adjectives as a way of emphasizing them. For example, instead of saying 'If you can come, I shall be very pleased', you can say 'If you can come, I shall be **more than** pleased'. This is a fairly formal use.

I am <u>more than satisfied</u> with my achievements in Australia.

You would be <u>more than welcome.</u>

4 **'more…than'**

You can use **more** and **than** to say that something is one type of thing rather than another. You put **more** in front of the first of two noun groups and **than** in front of the second one.

This is <u>more</u> a war movie <u>than</u> a western.

5 **'less than' and 'fewer than'**

You use **less than** to say that an amount or measurement is below a particular level.

The formerly robust war hero weighed <u>less than</u> a hundred pounds.

You use **less than** or **fewer than** to say that the number of people or things in a group is smaller than a particular number.

In 1900 there were <u>fewer than</u> one thousand university teachers in the United Kingdom.

⇨ For more information about these uses, see **Usage** entry at **less.**

6 **'rather than'**

You use **rather than** when you have said what is the case and you want to compare it with what is not the case.

Its interests lay in London <u>rather than</u> in Nottingham.

She was angry <u>rather than</u> afraid.

⇨ See **Usage** entry at **rather.**

7 **'no sooner… than'**

In stories, **than** is often used after **no sooner**. If you say **no sooner** did one thing happen **than** another thing happened, you mean that the second thing happened immediately after the first.

<u>No sooner</u> had he closed his eyes <u>than</u> he fell asleep.

⇨ For more information about this use, see **Usage** entry at **soon.**

⚠ **WARNING:** You do not use 'than' after **barely, hardly,** or **scarcely.** You do not say, for example, '~~He had barely got in than the telephone rang~~'. You say 'He had barely got in **when** the telephone rang'.
⇨ See **Usage** entries at **bare - barely, hard - hardly,** and **scarce - scarcely.**

8 **'different than'**

 Some American speakers use **than** after **different.**
I love the English style of football. It's so <u>different than</u> ours.
⇨ See **Usage** entry at **different.**

thank

1 **'thank you'**
Thank is mainly used in the expressions **Thank you** and **Thanks.**
⇨ For an explanation of these uses, see **Topic** entry at **Thanking someone.**

2 **'thank' used as a verb**
Thank is also a verb. If you **thank** someone, you express gratitude for something they have done or something they have given you.
She smiled at him, <u>thanked</u> him, and drove off.

You say that you **thank** someone **for** something.
I <u>thanked</u> Jenny <u>for</u> her time, patience and sense of humour.
He <u>thanked</u> me <u>for</u> what I had done.

You can also **thank** someone **for doing** something.
He <u>thanked</u> the miners <u>for coming.</u>

ⓘ Note that you do not say that you thank someone 'to do' something.

that

That has three main uses:

1 **used to refer back**
You use it in various ways to refer to something which has already been mentioned or which is already known about. When **that** is used like this, it is always pronounced /ðæt/.
<u>That</u> car was my pride and joy.
How about natural gas? Is <u>that</u> an alternative?
⇨ See **Usage** entry at **that - those.**

2 **used in 'that'-clauses**
That is used at the beginning of a special type of clause called a **'that'-clause.** In 'that'-clauses, **that** is usually pronounced /ðət/.
He said <u>that the police had directed him to the wrong room.</u>
Mrs Kaul announced <u>that the lecture would now begin.</u>
⇨ See **Grammar** entries at **'That'-clauses** and **Reporting.**

3 **used in relative clauses**
That is also used at the beginning of another type of clause called a **defining relative clause.** In defining relative clauses, **that** is usually pronounced /ðət/.
I reached the gate <u>that</u> opened onto the lake.
⇨ See **Grammar** entry at **Relative clauses.**

USAGE

> ⚠ **WARNING:** You do not use 'that' to introduce a reason clause. You do not say, for example, ~~'Jane was worried because Tom was late, especially that it was snowing so heavily'~~. You say '…especially **as** it was snowing so heavily' or '…especially **since** it was snowing so heavily'.
> *I do feel isolated, especially <u>as</u> we're not active in our community.*
> *I'm forever on a diet, <u>since</u> I put on weight easily.*
> ⇨ See section on **'as' and 'since'** in **Usage** entry at **because**.

---

that - those

That and **those** are used in a number of different ways when you are referring to people, things, events, or periods of time. They can both be determiners or pronouns. **Those** is the plural form of **that**.

1 referring back

You can use **that** or **those** to refer to people, things, or events which have already been mentioned or which are already known about.
I knew <u>that</u> meeting would be difficult.
'Did you see him?' – 'No.' – ' <u>That</u>'s a pity.'
Not all crimes are committed for <u>those</u> reasons.
One problem is you're going to get oxides of nitrogen, but one can remove <u>those,</u> I think.

2 things you can see

You can also use **that** or **those** to refer to people or things that you can see but that are not close to you.
Look at <u>that</u> bird!
Don't be afraid of <u>those</u> people.

3 'that' used to refer to a person

However, you do not usually use **that** as a pronoun to refer to a person. You only use it when you are identifying someone or asking about their identity.
'Who's the woman with the handkerchief?' – ' <u>That</u>'s my wife.'
Who's <u>that?</u>

⇨ For information on the use of **that** when telephoning, see **Topic** entry at **Telephoning**.

4 saying when something happened

When you have been describing an event, you can use **that** with a word like **day**, **morning**, or **afternoon** to indicate that something else happened during the same day.
There were no services <u>that day,</u> and the church was empty.
Paula had been shopping in Sapele <u>that morning.</u>

You can also use **that** with **week**, **month**, or **year** to indicate that something happened during the same week, month, or year.
There was a lot of extra work to do <u>that week.</u>
Later <u>that month</u> 11,000 attended another party at Maidenhead.

5 talking about a part of something

When you are talking about a particular part of a place or thing, you can use **that** instead of 'the' in front of words like **part**. This is a rather formal use.
The company mines ore in <u>that part of northeastern Minnesota</u> known as the Iron Range.

Similarly, you can use **those** instead of 'the' in front of a plural noun to talk about a group of people or things which is part of a larger group.
… <u>those</u> firms with the most progressive policies.

Those can be used in a similar way as a pronoun.
Many were finding it difficult to make ends meet, especially <u>those</u> with young children.

⑥ **'this' and 'these'**
This and **these** are used in some similar ways to **that** and **those**.
⇨ For an explanation of the differences, see **Usage** entry at **this - that**.

the

① **basic uses**
The is called the **definite article**. You use **the** at the beginning of a noun group to refer to someone or something that has already been mentioned or that is already known to the hearer or reader.
A man and a woman were struggling up <u>the dune</u>. <u>The man</u> wore shorts, a T-shirt, and basketball sneakers. <u>The woman</u> wore a print dress.

You add a qualifier, such as a prepositional phrase or a relative clause, when you need to indicate which person or thing you are talking about.
I've no idea about <u>the geography of Scotland</u>.
That is a different man to <u>the man that I knew</u>.

You use **the** with a singular noun to refer to something of which there is only one.
They all sat in <u>the sun</u>.
<u>The sky</u> was a brilliant blue.

② **types of thing or person**
You can use **the** with the singular form of a count noun when you want to make a general statement about all things of a particular type.
<u>The computer</u> allows us to deal with a lot of data very quickly.
My father's favourite flower is <u>the rose</u>.

ⓘ Note that you can make a similar statement using a plural form. If you do this, you do not use 'the'.
It is then that <u>computers</u> will have their most important social effects.
If you like <u>movies high on machismo and low on credibility,</u> this is for you.

Similarly, you do not use 'the' with an uncount noun when it is used with a general meaning. For example, if you are talking about pollution in general, you say '**Pollution** is a serious problem'. You do not say '~~The pollution is a serious problem~~'.
...victims of <u>crime</u>.
Alcoholism causes <u>disease</u> and <u>death</u>.

You can use **the** with words such as **rich, poor, young, old,** or **unemployed** to refer to all people of a particular type.
Only <u>the rich</u> could afford his firm's products.
They were discussing the problem of <u>the unemployed</u>.

ⓘ Note that when you use one of these words like this, you do not add '-s' or '-es' to it. You do not talk, for example, about 'the unemployeds'.

③ **nationalities**
You can use **the** with some nationality adjectives to refer to the people who live in a particular country, or to a group of people who come from that country.
They will be increasingly dependent on the support of <u>the French</u>.

⇨ See **Topic** entry at **Nationality words**.

④ **systems and services**
You use **the** with a singular count noun to refer to a system or service.
I don't like using <u>the phone</u>.
How long does it take on <u>the train</u>?

⑤ **musical instruments**
You usually use **the** with the name of a musical instrument when you are talking about someone's ability to play it.

USAGE

You play <u>the guitar</u>, I see.
I can't play <u>the piano</u>.

However, rock and jazz musicians omit the 'the'.

...the night spot where John played <u>guitar</u>.

6 professions

The is sometimes used at the beginning of a noun group in which you mention a well-known person's profession as well as their name. For example, you can talk about '**the singer** Jill Gomez'.

... <u>the Russian poet</u> Yevtushenko.

If the person has two professions, you can mention both of them. For example, you can talk about '**the pianist and conductor** Daniel Barenboim'.

(i) Note that you only use **the** once; you do not say 'the pianist and the conductor Daniel Barenboim'.

... <u>the Irish writer and critic</u> Maeve Binchy.

Journalists and broadcasters sometimes omit the 'the'.

...an event chaired by <u>writer and critic</u> Hermione Lee.

7 institutions

You do not usually use 'the' between a preposition and a word like **church**, **college**, **home**, **hospital**, **prison**, **school**, or **university**.

Will we see you <u>in church</u> tomorrow?
I was <u>at school</u> with her.

⇨ See separate **Usage** entries at these words.

8 meals

You do not usually use 'the' in front of the names of meals.

I open the mail immediately after <u>breakfast</u>.
I haven't had <u>dinner</u> yet.

⇨ See **Topic** entry at **Meals**.

9 used instead of a possessive

You sometimes use **the** instead of a possessive determiner, particularly when you are talking about something being done to a part of a person's body.

She hit him smartly and swiftly on <u>the head</u>.
He took her by <u>the arm</u> and began drawing her firmly but gently away.

⇨ See **Grammar** entry at **Possessive determiners**.

10 used with superlatives and comparatives

You usually use **the** in front of superlative adjectives.

... <u>the smallest</u> church in England.

You do not usually use 'the' in front of superlative adverbs.

...the language they know <u>best</u>.

You do not usually use 'the' in front of comparative adjectives or adverbs.

The model will probably be <u>smaller</u>.
I wish we could get it done <u>quicker</u>.

However, there are a few exceptions to this.

⇨ For more information, see **Grammar** entries at **Comparative and superlative adjectives** and **Comparative and superlative adverbs**.

their

⇨ See **Usage** entry at **there**.

them

1 used to refer to a plural noun

Them can be the object of a verb or preposition. You use **them** to refer to people or things that have just been mentioned or whose identity is known.

Those children are now getting ready for kindergarten; some of them may be disappointed.
She gathered the last few apples and stuffed them into a bag.

⚠ **WARNING:** You do not use 'them' as the object of a clause when you are referring to the same people as the subject. Instead you use **themselves.**
Imagine if you had never taught your children how to dress themselves.

2 used to mean 'him or her'

You can use **them** instead of 'him or her' to refer to a person whose sex is not known or not stated. Some people consider this use to be incorrect.

If anyone phones, tell them I'm out.

⇨ See **Usage** entry at **he - she - they.**

there

There has two main uses. You use it in front of a verb such as **be**, or you use it as an adverb to refer to a place.

1 used in front of 'be'

You use **there** in front of **be** to say that something exists or happens, or that something is in a particular place. When **there** is used like this, it is usually pronounced /ðe/ or /ðə/. In slow or careful speech, it is pronounced /ðeə/.

There must be a reason.
There was an accident and somebody got killed.
There was a new cushion on one of the settees.

After **there,** you use a singular form of **be** in front of a singular noun group, and a plural form in front of a plural noun group.

There is a fire on the fourth floor.
' There are people who want to kill me right now,' he said.

In conversation, some people use **there's** in front of a plural noun group. For example, they say 'If it's foggy, **there's** more **collisions**.' This use is generally regarded as incorrect.

⚠ **WARNING:** You do not use 'there is' or 'there are' with **since** to say how long ago something happened. You do not say, for example, ~~There are four days since she arrived in London~~. You say '**It's** four days since she arrived in London' or 'She arrived in London four days **ago**'.
It's three months since you were here last.
Her husband died four years ago.

2 'there seems to be…'

You can use **there** in front of **seems to be** to say that you have the impression that something exists, or that something is in a particular place. For example, you can say 'There seems to be a misunderstanding'. You do not say '~~There seems a misunderstanding~~'.

There seems to be a problem.
I'm sorry, there seems to be a dirty mark on it.

3 'there happens to be…'

You can also use **there** in front of **happens to be** to say that something is in a particular place by chance. For example, you can say '**There happened to be** a post office in the next street'. You do not say '~~There happened a post office in the next street~~'.

There happened to be a roll of thin nylon tubing lying on the desk.

USAGE

4 **used with other verbs**

In formal English, **there** is sometimes used with other verbs to say that something exists or is in a particular place.

But there still remains a major puzzle.
There follow two examples of Tarot stories, written by the authors.

In stories, **there** is sometimes used with **was** or **came** to say that something happened suddenly.

There was a tremendous explosion and the boat disintegrated.
There came the crack of a shot.

5 **used as an adverb**

In its other main use, **there** is used to refer to a place which has just been mentioned. When **there** is used like this, it is always pronounced /ðeə/.

I must get home. Bill's there on his own.
Come into the kitchen. I spend most of my time there now.

⚠ **WARNING:** You do not use 'to' in front of **there**. You do not say, for example, 'I like going to there'. You say 'I like going **there**'.
My family live in India. I still go there often.

You also do not use 'there' to introduce a subordinate clause. You do not say, for example, 'I went back to the park, there my sister was waiting'. You say 'I went back to the park, **where** my sister was waiting'.
There was still fear in closed communities, where everyone knew everyone else's business.

6 **'their'**

Do not confuse **there** with **their**, which is also pronounced /ðeə/. You use **their** to show that something belongs or relates to particular people, animals, or things.

I looked at their faces.
What would they do when they lost their jobs?

these

⇨ See **Usage** entry at **this - these**.

they

They can be the subject of a verb. You use **they** to refer to people or things that have just been mentioned or whose identity is known.

All universities have chancellors. They are always rather senior people.
The women had not expected a visitor and they were in their everyday clothes.

ⓘ Note that when the subject of a sentence is followed by a relative clause, you do not use **they** in front of the main verb. You do not say, for example, 'The people who live next door, they keep pigs'. You say 'The people who live next door keep pigs'.
Two children who were rescued by their father from a fire are in a critical condition.
Two girls who had been following him came to a halt.

They is sometimes used to refer to people in general, or to a group of people whose identity is not actually stated.

They say that a former nurse makes the worst patient.
In Bradford, they put special teachers in areas with a high percentage of immigrants.

⇨ See **Usage** entry at **one**.

You can also use **they** instead of 'he or she' to refer to an individual person whose sex is not known or not stated.

I was going to stay with a friend, but they were ill.

⇨ See **Usage** entry at **he - she - they**.

⚠ **WARNING:** You do not use 'they' with **are** to say that a number of things exist or are in a particular place. You do not say, for example, ~~'They are two bottles of wine in the fridge'.~~ You say ' **There are** two bottles of wine in the fridge'.
There are always plenty of jobs to be done.

⇨ See **Usage** entry at **there**.

thief - robber - burglar

Anyone who steals can be called a **thief**. A **robber** often uses violence or the threat of violence to steal things from places such as banks or shops.

…an armed <u>robber</u> who raided an off-licence.

A **burglar** breaks into houses or other buildings and steals things.

The average <u>burglar</u> spends just 2 minutes inside your house.

think

The verb **think** is used in several different ways. Its past tense and past participle is **thought,** not 'thinked'.

1 **used with a 'that'-clause**

You can use **think** with a 'that'-clause when you are giving your opinion about something or mentioning a decision that you have made.

I <u>think</u> you should go.
I <u>thought</u> I'd wait.

When you use **think** like this, you do not use a continuous tense. You do not say, for example, '~~I am thinking you should go~~'.

Instead of saying that you think something is not the case, you usually say that you **don't think** it **is** the case.

I <u>don't think</u> they really represent the people.
I <u>don't think</u> there is any doubt about that.

2 **'I think so'**

If someone asks you whether something is the case, you can express your opinion that it is probably the case by saying **'I think so'.** You do not say '~~I think it~~'.

'Do you think my mother will be all right?' – '<u>I think so.</u>'

If you want to reply that something is probably not the case, you usually say **'I don't think so'.** You can also say **'I think not'**, but this is rather formal.

'I have another friend, Barbara Robson. Do you know her?' – '<u>I don't think so.</u>'
'She doesn't want a real investigation, does she?' – '<u>I think not.</u>'

3 **using a continuous tense**

When someone **is thinking,** they are considering something. When you use **think** with this meaning, you often use a continuous tense.

I'll fix us both a gin-and-tonic while I '<u>m thinking.</u>
You <u>have been thinking,</u> haven't you?

You also use a continuous tense when you are talking about what is in someone's mind at a particular time.

That's what I <u>was thinking.</u>
It's very difficult to determine what the other people <u>are thinking.</u>

You can say that someone **is thinking about** something or someone, or **is thinking of** something or someone.

I spent hours in the warmth of the bathtub <u>thinking about</u> China.
She <u>was thinking of</u> her husband.

If you are considering doing something, you can say that you **are thinking of doing** it.

I was thinking of voting Conservative this time.

ⓘ Note that you do not say that you 'are thinking to do' something.

thinness

The following words can all be used to describe someone who has very little flesh on their body:

bony	lean	slender	spare	underweight
emaciated	scrawny	slight	thin	willowy
lanky	skinny	slim	trim	

1 neutral words

Thin is used to describe someone's appearance in a neutral way.

She was tall and thin, with fairish hair.

2 words used for approval

Lean, slender, slim, slight, spare, and **trim** are all used to show approval of someone's appearance. **Slim** is the commonest of these words. The others are used mainly in stories.

She used to be pretty and slim.

The door sprang open and a lean, well-tailored man stepped out.

…a beautiful slender girl with a strong American accent.

3 words used for disapproval

Bony, scrawny, and **skinny** are used to show disapproval.

She was rather ugly and skinny.

…a scrawny woman with dyed black hair.

If you say that someone is **underweight,** you mean that they are too thin, because they have not eaten enough or are ill. When they are very thin indeed, you can say that they are **emaciated.**

Many people who are underweight are happy with their size.

… emaciated kids begging for milk.

4 'lanky' and 'willowy'

Lanky and **willowy** are used to say that someone is tall and thin. **Lanky** is a slightly humorous word. **Willowy** is used to show approval.

Quentin was a lanky boy with long skinny legs.

…looking so much more slender and willowy than in her photo.

---

this - that

This and **that** are determiners or pronouns. The plural form of **this** is **these**. The plural form of **that** is **those**.

⇨ See **Usage** entries at **this - these** and **that - those**.

This entry deals with the similarities and differences between the ways in which these words are used.

1 referring back

This, these, that, and **those** are all used to refer to people, things, events, etc that have already been mentioned. It is more common to use **this** and **these** than **that** and **those**.

New machines are of course more expensive and this is something one has to consider.

So, for all these reasons, my advice is to be very, very careful.

You use **that** or **those** when you are referring to something for the second time in a sentence, using the same noun.

You haven't shown any interest in the identity of the person who's been poisoned or how ill that person is.

Staff suggest books for the library, and normally we're quite happy to get those books.

You usually use **that,** rather than 'this', to refer to a statement that someone has just made.

'She was terribly afraid of offending anyone.' – 'That's right.'
'That's a good point,' he said to reporters over and over in response to various demands.

2 present and past

You can use **this** or **that** to talk about events or situations.

You use **this** to refer to a situation that is continuing to exist, or to an event that is continuing to take place.

'My God,' I said, 'This is awful.'
I'm sorry to barge in on you like this.
This whole business has gone on too long.

You use **that** to refer to an event or situation that has taken place recently.

I knew that meeting would be difficult.
That was a terrible air crash last week.

3 closeness

You use **this** or **these** to refer to people or things that are very near to you. For example, you use **this** to refer to an object when you are holding it in your hand, or when it is on a desk or table in front of you.

'What is this?' said a policeman, holding up a canister of shaving cream.
This coffee tastes like tea.
Wait a minute. I just have to sort these books out.

You use **that** or **those** to refer to people or things that you can see or hear, but that are not very near to you, so that, for example, you cannot put out your hand and touch them.

Look at that bird!
Can you move those books off there?

When you are comparing two things and one of them is nearer to you than the other, you can use **this** to refer to the one which is nearer and **that** to refer to the one which is further away.

This one's nice but I don't like that one much.
This side of the street doesn't get the sun in the afternoon.

this - these

This and these are used in a number of different ways when you are referring to people, things, situations, events, or periods of time. They can both be determiners or pronouns. **These** is the plural form of **this.**

1 referring back

You can use **this** or **these** to refer to people, things, or events that have just been mentioned.

He's from the Institute of English Language in Bangkok. This institute has been set up to serve language teachers in the area.
Tax increases may be needed next year to do this.
These particular students are extremely bright.
Where once it had been surrounded by other villas, these had long since made way for hotels.

You do not use 'this' as a pronoun to refer to a person who has just been mentioned. Instead you use **he** or **she.**

He was known to all as Eddie.
'So long,' Mary said as she passed Miss Saunders.

In conversation, many people use **this** and **these** as determiners even when they are mentioning people or things for the first time.

USAGE

Then <u>this</u> guy came to the door of the class and he said, 'Mary Tinker, you're wanted out here.'
At school we had to wear <u>these</u> awful white cotton hats.

2 **closeness**
You can use **this** or **these** to refer to people or things that are very near to you. For example, if you are holding a book, you refer to it as '**this** book'.

<u>This</u> book is sensational.
The colonel handed him the bag. '<u>This</u> is for you,' he said.
Get <u>these</u> kids out of here.
I'm sure they don't have chairs like <u>these.</u>

'This' is not usually used as a pronoun to refer to a person. You only use it when you are identifying someone or asking them about their identity. For example, you use **this** when you are introducing someone. Note that when you are introducing more than one person, you use **this,** not 'these'.

<u>This</u> is Bernadette, Mr Zapp.
<u>This</u> is my brother Andrew and his wife Claire.

You also use **this** to say who you are when you phone someone.

Sally? <u>This</u> is Martin Brody.

3 **present situations**
You can use **this** to refer to a situation that exists at present or to an event that is happening now.

You know a lot about <u>this</u> situation.
<u>This</u> is an opportunity to put into practice thoughts I have had for some time.

4 **'this' and 'these' in time expressions**
This is used in the following ways in time expressions:
You use it with **morning**, **afternoon**, or **evening** to refer to the morning, afternoon, or evening of the present day.

I've got to go to the University <u>this morning</u>.
I was here <u>this afternoon</u>. Have you forgotten?
Come and have a drink with me <u>this evening</u>.

However, you do not say 'this day'. You say **today**.

I had a letter <u>today</u> from my solicitor.

You also do not say 'this night'. You refer to the previous night as **last night**. You refer to the night of the present day as **tonight**.

We left our bedroom window open <u>last night</u>.
I think I'll go to bed early <u>tonight</u>.

This week, **month**, or **year** means the present week, month, or year.

They're talking about going on strike <u>this week</u>.
The Congress was held in Portoviejo earlier <u>this month</u>.

You usually use **this** with **weekend** or with the name of a day, month, or season to refer to the next weekend or to the next day, month, or season with that name.

Come down there with me <u>this weekend</u>.
Let's fix a time. <u>This Sunday</u>. Four o'clock.

However, you can also use **this** with one of these words to refer to the previous weekend, or the previous day, month, or season with that name.

His presence <u>this weekend</u> was especially ominous.
<u>This summer</u> he also authorised £15 million to provide emergency shelters for the homeless.

These days means 'at the present time'. You usually use **these days** as an adjunct, but it can also be qualified and used as an ordinary noun group.

The prices <u>these days</u> are absolutely astronomical.
Kids are less attentive in <u>these days of instant gratification</u>.

5 **'that' and 'those'**

That and **those** are used in some similar ways to **this** and **these**.

⇨ For an explanation of the differences, see **Usage** entry at **this - that**.

those
⇨ See **Usage** entry at **that - those**.

though
⇨ See **Usage** entry at **although - though**.

thousand

A thousand or **one thousand** is the number 1,000.

You can say that there are **a thousand** things or **one thousand** things.

We'll give you a thousand dollars for the story.
…a ship about one thousand yards off shore.

You do not say that there are 'thousand' things.

You do not change the word **thousand** when you put another number in front of it. You do not say, for example, 'five thousands'. You say 'five **thousand**'.

…seven thousand dollars.
…five thousand acres.

threaten

If you **threaten to do** something that will harm or upset someone, you warn them that you may do it.

The police threatened to imprison me.
He threatened to resign.

ⓘ Note that you do not say that you 'threaten doing' something.

You can **threaten** someone **with** an action that will harm them.

The group's members were threatened with imprisonment.
The 21-year-old claimed she was threatened with death.

ⓘ Note that you do not use any preposition except **with** in sentences like these.

till
⇨ See **Usage** entry at **until - till**.

time

⇨ This entry deals with uses of the word **time**. For information on telling the time, and on prepositions and adverbs used to talk about time, see **Topic** entry at **Time**.

1 **'time'**

Time is what we measure in hours, days, years, etc.

…a period of time.
More time passed.

You do not usually use **time** when you are saying how long something takes or lasts. You do not say, for example, 'The course took two years' time' or 'Each song lasts ten minutes' time'. You say 'The course took **two years**' or 'Each song lasts **ten minutes**'.

The whole process probably takes twenty-five years.
The Mount Vernon tour lasts 4 hours.

You can, however, use **time** when you are saying how long it will be before something happens. For example, you can say 'We are getting married **in two years' time**'.

The exchange ends officially in a month's time.
In a few days' time, she may change her mind.

Time is usually an uncount noun, so you do not use 'a' with it. You do not say, for

USAGE

example, 'I haven't got a time to go shopping'. You say 'I haven't got **time** to go shopping'.
I didn't know if we'd have time for tea.

2 'a...time'

However, you can use **a** with an adjective and **time** when you are indicating how long
something takes or lasts. You can say, for example, that something takes **a long time** or
takes **a short time.**

The proposal would take quite a long time to discuss in detail.
After a short time one of them said 'It's all right, we're all friends here.'

You can also use expressions like these, with or without **for**, as adjuncts.

They had been camped there for a long time.
He's going to have to wait a very long time.
They worked together for a short time.
You've only been in the firm quite a short time.

If you are enjoying yourself while you are doing something, you can say, for example,
that you **are having a good time.**

Downstairs, Eva was having a wonderful time.
Did you have a good time up in Edinburgh?

ⓘ Note that you must use **a** in sentences like these. You do not say, for example, 'Eva was
having wonderful time'.

3 'a time'

You use **a time** after **for** or **after** to mean 'a fairly long time'.

She sat down for a time on a rush-seated chair.
After a time the pain passed.

You also use **a time** with a qualifier to refer to a period of time when something was or
will be the case.

The ancient microfossils may date from a time before there were genes.
*I cannot remember a time when a Prime Minister allowed so much freedom for the
expression of dissent.*

4 used to mean 'occasion'

Time is used with **the** or **that** and a qualifier to refer to the occasion when something
happened or will happen.

By the time the waiter brought their coffee, she was drunk.
Do you remember that time when Adrian phoned up?

When **time** has this meaning, you can use words like **first** or **last** in front of it.

It was the first time she spoke.
When was the last time I saw you?

Expressions such as **the first time** and **the next time** are often adjuncts.

The next time he would offer to fight.
The second time I hired a specialist firm.

Next time (without 'the') is also an adjunct.

You'll see a difference next time.
Next time you will do everything right.

5 'on time'

If something happens **on time,** it happens at the right time or punctually.

He turned up regularly on time for guard duty.
He might play poker until dawn but he was always on time.

6 'in time'

Do not confuse **on time** with **in time**. If you are **in time** for a particular event, you are not
late for it.

We're just in time.
He returned to his hotel in time for a late supper.

If something such as a job or task is finished **in time,** it is finished at or before the time when it should be finished.

I can't do it in time.

In time has another meaning. You use it to say that something happens eventually, after a lot of time has passed.

In time the costs will decrease.
In time I came to see how important this was.

tiny
⇨ See **Usage** entry at **small - large.**

tiresome - tiring

1 **'tiresome'**

You say that someone or something is **tiresome** when they make you feel annoyed, irritated, or bored.

She can be a very tiresome child at times.
I really came to ask you some rather tiresome questions.

2 **'tiring'**

Something which is **tiring** makes you feel tired.

We should have an early night after such a tiring day.

title - headline

1 **'title'**

The **title** of a book, play, painting, or piece of music is its name.

He wrote a book with the title 'The Castle'.
'Walk under Ladders' is the title of her new play.

2 **'headline'**

You do not refer to the words printed in large letters at the top of a newspaper report as a 'title'. You call them a **headline.**

All the headlines are about the Ridley affair.

to

To is used in several different ways as a preposition. Its usual pronunciation is /tə/. However, when it is followed by a word beginning with a vowel sound, it is pronounced /tu/ and when it comes at the end of a clause, it is pronounced /tuː/.

1 **destination**

You use **to** when you mention the place where someone goes.

I'm going with her to Australia.
The children have gone to school.
I made my way back to my seat.

You do not use 'to' in front of **here** or **there**. You do not say, for example, 'We go to there every year'. You say 'We go **there** every year'.

Before I came here, there were a few offers from other clubs.
His mother was from New Orleans and he went there every summer.

You also do not use 'to' in front of **home.**

I want to go home.
I'll pick the parcels up on my way home.

2 **direction**

You can use **to** to indicate the place that a person is intending to arrive at.

We're sailing to Europe.
We used to go through Yugoslavia on our way to Greece.

However, you do not use 'to' to indicate the general direction in which someone or something is moving. You do not say, for example, 'The boat was drifting to the shore'. You say 'The boat was drifting **towards** the shore'.

He saw his mother running towards him.
We started to walk back towards Heathrow.

Toward is sometimes used instead of 'towards'.

They walked along the pathway toward the house.

You also say that someone looks **towards** or **toward** something.

She glanced towards the mirror.
He stood looking toward the rear of the restaurant.

You can use **to, towards,** or **toward** to indicate what someone or something is pointing at or facing.

He was pointing to an oil tanker somewhere on the horizon.
The window faced towards Paris.
'Turn in here,' he said, pointing toward a footpath.

3 position

You can use **to** to indicate the position of something. For example, if something is **to** your left, it is nearer your left side than your right side.

My father was in the middle, with me to his left carrying the umbrella.
To the west lies Gloucester.

You can also use **to** to indicate where something is tied or attached, or what it is touching.

I was planning to tie him to a tree.
He clutched the parcel to his chest.

4 time

To is sometimes used with a similar meaning to 'until'.

Breakfast was from 9 to 10.
Only ten shopping days to Christmas.

5 indirect objects

You put **to** in front of the indirect object of some verbs when the indirect object comes after the direct object.

He showed the letter to Barbara.
She had given German lessons to a leading industrialist.

⇨ See section on **ditransitive verbs** in **Grammar** entry at **Verbs.**

6 used in infinitives

To is used to introduce a special kind of clause called a **'to'-infinitive clause.**

He was doing this to make me more relaxed.
The rocket soon begins to accelerate upwards.

⇨ See **Grammar** entry at **'To'-infinitive clauses.**

⚠ **WARNING:** Do not confuse **to** with **too** or **two,** both of which are pronounced /tuː/. You use **too** to indicate that what has just been said applies to someone or something else.

I'm on your side. Seibert is too.

You also use **too** when you want to say that an amount or degree of something is more than is desirable or acceptable.

Eggs shouldn't be kept in the fridge, it's too cold.

⇨ See **Usage** entry at **too.**

Two is the number 2.

The <u>two</u> boys glanced at each other.

today

Today means the day on which you are speaking or writing.

I had a letter <u>today</u> from my solicitor.
<u>Today</u> is Thursday.

You do not use 'today' in front of **morning, afternoon,** or **evening.** Instead, you use **this.**

His plane left <u>this morning</u>.
Can I take it with me <u>this afternoon?</u>
Come and have a drink with me <u>this evening</u>.

toilet

1 **'toilet'**

A **toilet** is a large bowl connected to the plumbing and used by people to get rid of waste from their bodies.

British speakers also use **toilet** to refer to a room containing a toilet. When this room is in a house, they might also refer to it as the **lavatory,** the **loo,** the **cloakroom,** or the **WC. Lavatory** and **WC** are rather old-fashioned words. **Loo** is only used in conversation.

Annette ran and locked herself in the <u>toilet</u>.

 In American English, the room in a house containing a toilet is called the **bathroom. Washroom** and **john** are also used. **John** is only used in conversation.

She had gone in to use the <u>bathroom</u>.

2 **'conveniences'**

In British English, a group of toilets in a public place can be referred to as **conveniences** or **public conveniences.** They can also be referred to as **the ladies** and **the gents.**

…a row of porcelain <u>conveniences</u>.
…a quick visit to the <u>the ladies'</u> to re-apply lipstick.

 In American English, a group of toilets in a public place can be referred to as a **rest room,** a **comfort station,** or a **washroom.** They can also be referred to as **the ladies' room** and **the men's room.**

He walked into the men's <u>rest room</u> and looked at himself in the mirrror.

tolerate

⇨ See **Usage** entry at **bear.**

too

Too can be an adverb or a grading adverb.

1 **used as an adverb**

You use **too** as an adverb to indicate that what has just been said applies to or includes someone or something else.

Of course, you know Africa <u>too</u>, don't you?
Hey, where are you from? Brooklyn? Me <u>too!</u>

⇨ See **Usage** entry at **also - too - as well.**

2 **used as a grading adverb**

You use **too** in front of an adjective or adverb to say that an amount or degree of a quality is more than is desirable or acceptable.

By then he was far <u>too large</u> to sleep in a crib.
I realized my mistake <u>too late</u>.

USAGE

You do not use 'very' in front of **too.** You do not say, for example, ~~The slipper was very too small for her~~'. You say 'The slipper was **much** too small for her' or 'The slipper was **far** too small for her'.

That may well seem <u>much too dramatic</u>.
The eyes were <u>far too deeply</u> set.

You can use **rather, slightly,** or **a bit** in front of **too.**

The dress was <u>rather too small</u> for her.
They sat round a table that was <u>slightly too long and shiny</u> for the simple meal it carried.
My sister's boots were <u>a bit too small</u> for her long feet.

(*i*) Note that you do not use 'fairly', 'quite', or 'pretty' in front of **too.**

You do not normally use **too** with an adjective in front of a noun. You do not say, for example, ~~These are too big boots~~'. You say 'These boots **are too big**'.

However, **too** is sometimes used with an adjective in front of a noun in formal or literary English. **A** or **an** is put after the adjective. For example, you can say 'This is **too complex a problem** to be dealt with here'. You do not say '~~This is a too complex problem to be dealt with here~~'.

That's <u>too easy an answer</u>.
Somehow, Francis seems <u>too nice a man</u> for the job.

3 **used as an intensifier**
Some people use **too** in front of words like **kind** to express their gratitude for something that someone has done.

You're <u>too kind</u>.

However, you do not usually use 'too' in front of an adjective or adverb simply to emphasize it. You do not say, for example, '~~I am too pleased with my new car~~'. The word you use is **very.**

She was upset and <u>very angry</u>.
Think <u>very carefully</u>.

⇨ See **Usage** entry at **very.**

4 **'too much' and 'too many'**
You can use **too much** with an uncount noun to say that there is more of something than is necessary or desirable.

There is <u>too much chance</u> of error.
They said I was earning <u>too much money</u>.

You can also say that there is **too little** of something.

<u>Too little money</u> was made available.
There would be <u>too little moisture</u> for plants to get started again.

You can use **too many** with a count noun to say that there are more people or things than are necessary or desirable.

I was making <u>too many mistakes</u>.

You can also say that there are **too few** people or things.

<u>Too few people</u> nowadays are interested in literature.

You can use **much too much** or **far too much** an uncount noun to say that there is very much more of something than is necessary or desirable.

This would leave <u>much too much power</u> in the hands of the judges.
There's <u>far too much attention</u> being paid to these people.

You can use **far too many** with a count noun to say that there is a very much larger number of people or things than is necessary or desirable. You do not say that there are 'much too many' of them.

Every middle-class child gets <u>far too many toys</u>.

You can also say that there are **far too few** people or things.

There were far too few lifeboats.

⚠ **WARNING:** You do not use **too much** or **much too much** in front of an adjective which is not followed by a noun. You do not say, for example, '~~It's too much hot to play football~~'. You say 'It's **too hot** to play football' or 'It's **much too hot** to play football'.

tools

The following are general words used to refer to objects or pieces of equipment that you use to help you to do a particular kind of job:

appliance	gadget	instrument	tool
device	implement	machine	utensil

1 'tool'

A **tool** is usually a simple object that you use to make, shape, or mend something, for example a hammer, saw, spade, or spanner.

Remember to put all your tools away safely.

…a glass-cutting tool.

Tools that operate by electricity are called **power tools.**

Keep power tools out of children's reach.

Other things which are used to achieve something can also be referred to as **tools.** This is a fairly formal use.

Textbooks became the essential tools of the teacher.

2 'implement'

An **implement** is a simple tool used for digging or cooking. **Implement** is a formal word.

The earliest wooden implements known are spears, clubs and sharpened sticks.

Don't use metal implements such as spoons when using non-stick pans.

3 'instrument'

An **instrument** is an object used for a scientific or medical purpose, or for measuring something.

…surgical and dental instruments.

A **musical instrument** is an object from which music is produced, for example a violin, a drum, or a flute.

The drum is one of the oldest musical instruments.

4 'utensil'

A **utensil** is usually a container or small object used for cooking, such as a saucepan or a spoon. **Utensil** is a formal word.

Students usually provide their own crockery, cutlery, cooking utensils and bedding.

5 'device' and 'gadget'

A **device** or **gadget** is usually a fairly small object, often a complicated or unusual one. Some devices and gadgets are powered by electricity. **Gadget** is an informal word, and is often used showing disapproval.

…a tiny 'pacemaker' – a device that sends pulses of electricity to activate the heart.

A dangerous new gadget will make it easy for bosses to spy on their staff.

6 'machine'

A **machine** is a piece of equipment which uses electricity or some other form of power to perform a task. It can be quite large.

…when Walter Hunt and Elias Howe invented the sewing machine.

Employers have to provide workplaces, machines and methods of work that are safe.

USAGE

7 'appliance'

An **appliance** is usually a machine that is used in people's homes, such as a washing machine or cooker. **Appliance** is a formal word.

…household *appliances.*

touch - affect

1 'touch'

If you **touch** something, you gently put your fingers or hand on it.

The metal is so hot I can't touch it.
Madeleine stretched out her hand to touch his.

If you **are touched** by something, it makes you feel sad, sympathetic, or grateful.

I was touched that he should remember the party where he had kissed me for the first time.
I was touched by his thoughtfulness.

2 'affect'

You do not use 'touch' to say that something changes or influences a person or thing. You do not say, for example, 'We wanted to know how these proposals would touch our town'. The word you use is **affect**.

…the ways in which computers can affect our lives.
The disease affected Jane's lungs.

toward - towards

⇨ See section on **direction** in **Usage** entry at **to**.

traffic

You use **traffic** to refer to all the vehicles moving along a road.

In many areas rush-hour traffic lasted until 11am.

Traffic is an uncount noun. You do not talk about 'traffics' or 'a traffic'.

traffic circle

⇨ See **Usage** entry at **roundabout**.

translate

If you **translate** something that has been said or written, you say or write it in a different language.

These jokes would be far too difficult to translate.

You say that someone translates something from one language **into** another.

An interpreter was going to translate his words into English.
My books have been translated into many languages.

ⓘ Note that you do not use any preposition except **into** in sentences like these.

transport - transportation

1 'transport'

In British English, vehicles that you travel in are referred to generally as **transport**.

It's easier to travel if you have your own transport.
The new museum must be accessible by public transport.

Transport is an uncount noun. You do not refer to a single vehicle as 'a transport'.

British speakers also use **transport** to refer to the moving of goods or people from one place to another.

The goods were ready for transport and distribution.
High transport costs make foreign goods too expensive.

2 **'transportation'**

 American speakers usually use **transportation** to refer both to vehicles and to the moving of goods or people.

Do you two children have <u>transportation</u> home?

…long-distance <u>transportation</u>.

trash

⇨ See **Usage** entry at **rubbish**.

travel

 Travel can be a verb or a noun. The other forms of the verb are **travels, travelling, travelled** in British English, and **travels, traveling, traveled** in American English.

1 **used as a verb**

If you make a journey to a place, you can say that you **travel** there.

I <u>travelled</u> to work by train.

When you **travel**, you go to several places, especially in foreign countries.

They brought news from faraway places in which they <u>travelled.</u>

You have to have a passport to <u>travel</u> abroad.

2 **used as a noun**

Travel is the act of travelling. When **travel** has this meaning, it is an uncount noun.

They arrived after four days of hard <u>travel.</u>

…air <u>travel</u>.

3 **'travels'**

When someone has made several journeys to different places, especially places a long way from their home, you can refer to these journeys as their **travels**.

Marsha told us all about her <u>travels.</u>

…rare plants and trees collected during lengthy <u>travels</u> in the Far East.

(*i*) Note that you do not talk about 'a travel'. Instead you talk about a **journey**, a **trip**, or a **voyage.**

⇨ See **Usage** entry at **journey - trip - voyage - excursion.**

trip

⇨ See **Usage** entry at **journey - trip - voyage - excursion.**

trouble

1 **used as an uncount noun**

Trouble is most commonly an uncount noun. If something causes you **trouble**, you have difficulty dealing with it.

The obstacles were causing more <u>trouble</u> than the enemy.

This would save everyone a lot of <u>trouble.</u>

You can say that someone **has trouble doing** something.

Did you <u>have any trouble finding</u> your way here?

(*i*) Note that you do not say that someone 'has trouble to do' something.

2 **'troubles'**

Your **troubles** are the problems in your life.

It helps me forget my <u>troubles</u> and relax.

(*i*) Note that you do not usually refer to a single problem as 'a trouble'.

3 **'the trouble'**

If a particular aspect of something is causing problems, you can refer to this aspect as **the trouble.**

USAGE

It's getting a bit expensive now, that's <u>the trouble.</u>
<u>The trouble</u> is there's a shortage of prime property.

trousers

Trousers are a piece of clothing that covers your body from the waist downwards, and covers each leg separately. **Trousers** is a plural noun. You use a plural form of a verb with it.

His trousers <u>were</u> covered in mud.

You do not talk about 'a trousers'. You say **some trousers** or **a pair of trousers**.

It's time I bought myself <u>some new trousers.</u>
Claud was dressed in <u>a pair of black trousers.</u>

You usually use a singular form of a verb with **a pair of trousers**.

There <u>was</u> a pair of trousers in his carrier-bag.

The form **trouser** is often used in front of another noun.

The waiter took a handkerchief from his <u>trouser pocket.</u>
Hamo was rolling up his <u>trouser leg.</u>

 Note that in American English, **trousers** is used mainly in technical contexts. More common words for this garment are **pants** or **slacks**.

truck

⇨ See **Usage** entries at **carriage -car - truck - wagon** and **lorry - truck**.

true - come true

1 'true'

A **true** story or statement is based on facts, and is not invented or imagined.

The story about the murder is <u>true.</u>
Unfortunately it was <u>true</u> about Sylvie.

2 'come true'

If a dream, wish, or prediction **comes true**, it actually happens.

Remember that some dreams <u>come true.</u>
The worst of the predictions might <u>come true.</u>

(*i*) Note that you do not say that something 'becomes true'.

trunk

⇨ See **Usage** entry at **boot - trunk**.

try - attempt

Both these words can be verbs or nouns. The other forms of **try** are **tries, trying, tried**.

1 'try' used as a verb

If you **try to do** something, you make an effort to do it.

My sister <u>tried to cheer</u> me up.
He <u>was trying</u> his best <u>to understand.</u>

You can also **try and do** something. There is no difference in meaning.

<u>Try and see</u> how many of these questions you can answer.
We must <u>try and understand.</u>

(*i*) Note that you can only use **and** after the base form of **try** – that is, when you are using it as an imperative or infinitive, or after a modal. You cannot say, for example, 'I was trying and help her' or 'I was trying and helping her'.

If you **try doing** something, you do it in order to find out how useful, effective, or enjoyable it is.

He <u>tried changing</u> the subject.
Have you ever <u>tried painting,</u> Humbert?

2 **'attempt' used as a verb**

If you **attempt to do** something, you try to do it. **Attempt** is a more formal word than **try.**

Some of the crowd <u>attempted to break</u> through police cordons.
Rescue workers <u>attempted to cut</u> him from the wreckage.

(*i*) Note that you do not say that you 'attempt and do' something or 'attempt doing' something.

3 **'try' and 'attempt' used as nouns**

When someone tries to do something, you can refer to what they do as a **try** or an **attempt. Try** is normally used only in conversation. In writing, you usually talk about an **attempt.**

After a few <u>tries</u> they gave up.
The young birds manage to fly several kilometres at their first <u>attempt.</u>

You say that someone **has a try at** something or **gives** something **a try.**

You've had a good <u>try at</u> it.
'I'll go and see him in the morning.' – 'Yes, <u>give</u> it <u>a try.</u>'

You say that someone **makes an attempt to do** something.

He <u>made an attempt to call</u> Courtney; she wasn't in.
Two recent reports <u>made an attempt to assess</u> the success rate of the project.

4 **'trying'**

The adjective **trying** is not related to the verb 'try'. You say that someone or something is **trying** when they make you feel impatient or annoyed.

I find him very <u>trying.</u>
It had been a most <u>trying</u> experience for them.

type

Type is a noun used to talk about a class of people or things. **Type** is a count noun. After words like **all** and **many,** you use **types,** not 'type'.

…hundreds of ships of every size and <u>type.</u>
…in hospitals of <u>all types.</u>
… <u>many types</u> of public service.

After **types of** you can use either the plural or singular form of a noun. You can say 'He eats most types of **vegetables**' or 'He eats most types of **vegetable**'. The singular form is more formal.

How many types of <u>people</u> live in these households?
This only happens with certain types of <u>school.</u>

If you use a number in front of **types of,** you should use a singular form after it.

There are three types of <u>muscle</u> in the body.
…two types of <u>playgroup.</u>

After **type of** you use the singular form of a noun.

He was an unusual type of <u>actor.</u>
This type of <u>problem</u> is common in families.

In conversation, **these** and **those** are often used with **type.** For example, people say 'These type of books are boring' or 'Those type of books are boring'. This use is generally thought to be incorrect, and it is best to avoid it. Instead you should say '**This type of book** is boring' or '**That type of book** is boring'.

<u>This type of person</u> has very little happiness.
I could not be happy in <u>that type of household.</u>

You can also say '**Books of this type** are boring'.

<u>Conferences of this type</u> have already been held.

U u

ultimately - lately

1 'ultimately'

You use **ultimately** to indicate that something is the final result of a series of events.

The discovery may ultimately lead to the development of new contraceptives.

The rebels hoped to create bad feeling and ultimately war between Spain and the United States.

You also use **ultimately** when you are drawing attention to a basic fact about a situation.

Ultimately, the problems are not scientific but moral.

It is ultimately the fault of the universities.

2 'lately'

You do not use 'ultimately' to say that something has been happening since a short time ago. You do not say, for example, 'Ultimately I have been feeling rather unwell'. You say 'I have been feeling rather unwell **lately**'.

⇨ See **Usage** entry at **recently - newly - lately**.

umpire - referee

An **umpire** or **referee** is an official whose job is to make sure that a game is played fairly and that the rules are not broken.

1 'umpire'

These games have an **umpire** or **umpires**:

badminton	cricket	tennis
baseball	table tennis	volleyball

2 'referee'

These games have a **referee**:

basketball	boxing	rugby football	wrestling
billiards	football	snooker	

The official in charge of a hockey match is sometimes called an **umpire** and sometimes a **referee**.

unconscious

⇨ See **Usage** entry at **subconscious**.

under - below - beneath

1 'under'

Under is almost always a preposition. You use **under** to say that one thing is at a lower level than another, and that the other thing is directly above it. For example, you might say that an object on the floor is **under** a table or chair.

There was a cask of beer under the bench.

A path runs under the trees.

2 'underneath'

Underneath can be a preposition or adverb with a similar meaning to **under**.

The tortoise was underneath the table.

There was a portrait with an inscription underneath.

3 **'below'**

Below is usually an adverb. You normally use it to say that one thing is at a much lower level than another. For example, if you are at the top of a mountain, you can talk about a valley **below**.

You can see the town spread out below.
Down below in the valley the chimneys were smoking.

4 **'beneath'**

Beneath can be a preposition or an adverb. It has a similar meaning to **under** or **below**. **Beneath** is a rather formal word.

…the feel of the soft ground beneath his feet.
The Minister stared out of the window into the circular courtyard beneath.

understand - realize

1 **'understand'**

If you can **understand** someone or can **understand** what they are saying, you know what they mean.

His lecture was confusing; no one could understand the terminology.
…listening to stories that are hard to understand.

If you say that you **understand** that something is the case, you mean that you have been told that it is the case.

I understand he's had several wives.
There was no definite evidence, I understand, which could be brought against her.

2 **'realize'**

You do not use 'understand' to say that someone becomes aware of something. You do not say, for example, '~~Until he stopped working he hadn't understood how late it was~~'. You say 'Until he stopped working he **hadn't realized** how late it was'.

As soon as I saw him, I realized that I'd seen him before.

understanding

⇨ See **Usage** entry at **comprehension - understanding**.

underweight

⇨ See **Usage** entry at **thinness**.

unhappy

⇨ See **Usage** entry at **happy - sad**.

uninterested

⇨ See **Usage** entry at **disinterested - uninterested**.

unique

1 **used to mean 'the only one'**

If something is **unique**, it is the only thing of its kind.

This is a unique opportunity.
Humans are unique because they have the capacity to choose what they do.

For emphasis, you can use words such as **totally** or **absolutely** in front of **unique**.

By the late 1930's the country had full employment – an absolutely unique achievement.

You can say that something is **almost unique**.

You suffer from an almost unique mental condition.

2 **used to mean 'unusual'**

Some people use **unique** to mean 'unusual'. They say, for example, that something is **very unique** or **rather unique**.

USAGE

Oh, I say, that's <u>rather unique, isn't it?</u>
I realized I had hit on something <u>pretty unique.</u>

These uses of **unique** are generally thought to be incorrect.

university

⇨ See **Usage** entry at **school - university.**

unless

You usually use **unless** to say that something can only happen or be true in particular circumstances. For example, instead of saying 'I will go to France only if the firm pays my expenses', you can say 'I will **not** go to France **unless** the firm pays my expenses'.

In Scotland you have no right to keep people off your land <u>unless</u> they are doing damage.

(i) Note that in the subordinate clause you use the simple present tense. You do not say, for example, 'I will not go to France unless the firm will pay my expenses'.

When you are talking about a situation in the past, you use the simple past tense after **unless.**

She wouldn't go with him <u>unless</u> I <u>came</u> too.

You also use **unless** to mention the only circumstances in which something will not happen or be true. For example, instead of saying 'If we are not told to stop, we will carry on selling the furniture', you can say 'We will carry on selling the furniture **unless** we are told to stop'.

The mail will go by air <u>unless</u> it is quicker by other means.
We might as well stop <u>unless</u> you've got something else you want to talk about.

⚠ **WARNING:** You do not use 'unless' to say that something would happen or be true if particular circumstances did not exist. For example, if you have a cold, you do not say 'I would go to the party unless I had this cold'. You say 'I would go to the party **if I didn't have** this cold'.

She'd be pretty <u>if she didn't wear</u> so much make-up.

unqualified - disqualified

1. **'unqualified'**

Unqualified people have not passed or taken the exams which relate to their work.

…some <u>unqualified</u> member of the teaching staff.

2. **'disqualified'**

When someone **is disqualified,** they are officially told they cannot do something, because they have broken a law or rule.

They <u>were disqualified</u> from driving.
If convicted, she could <u>be disqualified</u> from public office for up to seven years.

unsatisfied - dissatisfied

1. **'unsatisfied'**

If something such as a demand is **unsatisfied,** there is not enough of what is wanted.

There is already an <u>unsatisfied</u> demand for timber products.

2. **'dissatisfied'**

If a person is **dissatisfied,** they are not contented and want changes in a situation or in their lives.

People are utterly <u>dissatisfied</u> with the economic situation.
The universities produced a number of <u>dissatisfied</u> idealists.

unsociable

⇨ See **Usage** entry at **anti-social - unsociable.**

until - till

Until and **till** are common words which are prepositions or conjunctions. There is no difference in meaning between **until** and **till**. **Till** is more common in conversation, and is not used in formal writing.

1 used as prepositions

If you do something **until** or **till** a particular time, you stop doing it at that time.

He continued to practise as a vet <u>until</u> 1960.
I said I'd work <u>till</u> 4 p.m.

If you want to emphasize that something does not stop before the time you mention, you can use **up until, up till,** or **up to.**

<u>Up until</u> 1950 coal provided over 90% of our energy needs.
Etta had not <u>up till</u> then taken a very active part in the discussion.
<u>Up to</u> now they've had very little say.

If something does not happen **until** or **till** a particular time, it does not happen before that time.

Details will not be available <u>until</u> January.
We didn't get back <u>till</u> two.

2 used with 'after'

You can use **until** or **till** with phrases beginning with **after**.

The Count had resolved to wait <u>until after Christmas</u> to propose to Gertrude.
We didn't get home <u>till after midnight</u>.

⚠ **WARNING:** You do not use 'until' or 'till' to say that something will have happened before a particular time. You do not say, for example, ~~The work will be finished until four o'clock~~. You say 'The work will be finished **by** four o'clock'.

<u>By</u> 8.05 the groups were ready.
Total sales in these countries reached 1 million <u>by</u> 1980.

3 used with 'from'

From is often used with **until** or **till** to say when something finishes and ends.

The ticket office will be open <u>from</u> 10.00am <u>until</u> 1.00pm.
They seem to be working <u>from</u> dawn <u>till</u> dusk.

In sentences like these, you can use **to** instead of 'until' or 'till'. Some American speakers also use **through**.

Open daily 1000-1700 <u>from</u> 23rd March <u>to</u> 3rd November.
I was in college <u>from</u> 1927 <u>through</u> 1932.

4 saying how much time there is

If you want to say how much time there is before a particular event, you usually use **to,** rather than 'until' or 'till'.

Only ten shopping days <u>to</u> Christmas.

⚠ **WARNING:** You only use **until** or **till** when you are talking about time. You do not use these words to talk about position. You do not say, for example, '~~She walked until the post office~~'. You say 'She walked **as far as** the post office'.

I walked <u>as far as</u> her office.
They have gone <u>as far as</u> the Cantabrian mountains.

5 used as conjunctions

Instead of a noun group, you can use a subordinate clause after **until** or **till**.

Stay here with me <u>until</u> help comes.
They concentrate on one language <u>till</u> they go to university.

ⓘ Note that you use the simple present tense in the subordinate clause. You do not say, for example 'Stay here with me until help will come'.

You can also use the present perfect tense in the subordinate clause. For example, you can say 'I'll wait here until you **have had** your breakfast'. You do not say 'I'll wait here until you will have had your breakfast'.

Tell him I won't discuss anything <u>until</u> I <u>'ve spoken</u> to my wife.

When you are talking about events in the past, you use the simple past tense or the past perfect tense after **until** or **till**.

The Geneva visit remained secret <u>until</u> it <u>was exposed</u> by the Sunday Times.
He continued watching <u>until</u> I <u>had driven off</u> in my car.

unused

⇨ See **Usage** entry at **disused - unused - misused**.

up

1 **'up'**

Up can be a preposition or an adverb. You usually use it to indicate that someone or something moves towards a higher place or position.

I carried my suitcase <u>up</u> the stairs behind her.
The coffee was sent <u>up</u> from the kitchen below.
Bill put <u>up</u> his hand.

You also use **up** as an adverb to indicate that someone or something is in a high place.

He was <u>up</u> in his bedroom.
…comfortable houses <u>up</u> in the hills.

2 **'up to'**

You can say that someone goes **up to** a higher place.

I went <u>up to</u> the top floor.

You also say that someone goes **up to** a place when it is further north than the place they started from.

I thought of going <u>up to</u> Yorkshire.
Why did you come <u>up to</u> Edinburgh?

British speakers sometimes use **up to** instead of 'to' for no special reason.

The other day I went <u>up to</u> the supermarket.
We all went <u>up to</u> the pub.

upset

⇨ See **Usage** entry at **pleased - disappointed**.

upstairs

If you go **upstairs** in a building, you go up a staircase towards a higher floor.

He went <u>upstairs</u> and pulled down the blind.

If you say that someone or something is **upstairs**, you mean that they are on a higher floor than the one you are on.

…the student who lived <u>upstairs</u>.
He had a revolver <u>upstairs</u> in a drawer beside his bed.

ⓘ Note that you do not use 'to', 'at', or 'in' in front of **upstairs**.

upwards - upward

1 **'upwards'**

In British English, if you move or look **upwards**, you move or look towards a place that is higher than the place where you are.

She stretched upwards to the curtain pole.
He had happened to look upwards.

Upwards is always an adverb.

2 'upward'

 Speakers of American English usually say **upward** instead of 'upwards'.
I began to climb upward over the steepest ground.

In both British and American English, **upward** is an adjective. An **upward** movement or look is one in which someone or something moves or looks upwards.

…a quick upward flick of the arm.
He would steal upward glances at the clock.

When **upward** is an adjective, you can only use it in front of a noun.

urge

If you **urge** someone **to do** something, you try hard to persuade them to do it.
I urged him to take a year off to study drawing.
Father Swiebel urged him to talk.

(*i*) Note that **urge** must be followed by an object when you use it with a 'to'-infinitive. You say, for example, 'He **urged them to stay**'. You do not say 'He urged to stay'.

In writing, you can use a 'that'-clause after **urge**. In the 'that'-clause, you use **should** or the base form of a verb.
The Press Commission urged that the ownership of the press and broadcasting should be kept separate.
Sir Fred urged that Britain join the European Monetary System.

In writing, **urge** can also be used with an object referring to a course of action.
US officials urged restraint.
The report urged a more positive role for local government.

us

Us can be the object of a verb or preposition. You use **us** to refer to yourself and one or more other people.
Why didn't you tell us?
There wasn't room for us all.

> ⚠ **WARNING:** In standard English, you do not use 'us' as the object of a sentence when **we** is the subject. You do not say, for example, 'We bought us some drinks'. You say 'We bought **ourselves** some drinks'.
> *After the meeting we introduced ourselves.*

use - used - used to

1 'use'

If you **use** /juːz/ something, you do something with it in order to achieve a particular result.
They used the money to buy foreign technology.
It is better not to use a knife.

The **use** /juːs/ of something is the act of using it.
…the dangers of the large-scale use of fertilisers and insecticides.

2 'used'

Used /juːzd/ can be used as an adjective in front of a noun. You use it to indicate that something has been owned by someone else, or is dirty as a result of being used before.

…a _used_ glass on the coffee table.
Would you buy a _used_ car from this man?

3 **'used to'**

If something **used to** /juːs tuː, juːs tə/ happen, it happened regularly in the past. Similarly, if something **used to** be the case, it was the case in the past.

She used to tell me stories about people in India and Egypt.
I used to be told I looked quite handsome.
I used to be afraid of you.

4 **'used to' in negative structures**

In conversation, you can say that something **didn't use to** happen or **didn't use to** be the case.

The house didn't use to be so clean.

⚠ **WARNING:** Note that many people use the form **didn't used to** instead of **didn't use to.** However, some people consider that this use is incorrect.
They didn't used to mind what we did.

You can also say that something **never used to** happen or be the case.
Where I was before, we never used to have posters on the walls.
Snooker and darts never used to be televised sports.

You can also say that something **used not to** happen or be the case. This is a fairly formal use.
It used not to be taxable, but now it will be subject to tax.

ⓘ Note that in standard English you do not say that something 'usedn't to' happen or be the case.

5 **'used to' in questions**

You form 'yes/no'-questions with **used to** by putting **did** in front of the subject, followed by **use to.**

Did you use to do that, when you were a kid?

⚠ **WARNING:** Note that many people use the form **used to** instead of **use to** in questions. However, some people consider that this use is incorrect.
Did you used to play with your trains?

Used to can also be used in 'wh'-questions. If the 'wh'-word is the subject of the clause, or part of the subject, you put **used to** after it, without an auxiliary.
What used to annoy you most about him?

If the 'wh'-word is the object of the clause, or part of the object, you use the auxiliary **do** after it, followed by the subject and **used to.**
What did you used to do on Sundays?

6 **familiarity**

Used to has another meaning. If you are **used to** something, you have become familiar with it and you accept it.

It doesn't frighten them. They're used to it.
I'm used to having my sleep interrupted.

⚠ **WARNING:** Note that with this sense, **used to** is always preceded by the verb **be**, and is always followed by a noun or an '-ing' form. When **used to** refers to regular events in the past, it is always followed by an infinitive, and is not preceded by the verb **be**.
⇨ See **Usage** entry at **accustomed to.**

usual - usually

1 'usual'

Usual is used to describe the thing that happens most often, or that is done or used most often, in a particular situation.

They are not taking the <u>usual</u> amount of exercise.
He sat in his <u>usual</u> chair.

Usual normally comes after **the** or a possessive. You do not use it after 'a'.
You can say that it is **usual for** a person or animal **to do** something.

It is <u>usual for</u> union representatives <u>to meet</u> regularly.
It was quite <u>usual for</u> the ponies <u>to wander</u> short distances.

(*i*) Note that you do not say that it is 'usual that' a person or animal 'does' something.

2 'ordinary'

You do not use 'usual' to say something is not of a special kind. You do not say, for example, 'I haven't got any chocolate biscuits, only usual ones'. You say 'I haven't got any chocolate biscuits, only **ordinary** ones'.

These children should be educated in an <u>ordinary</u> school.
It was furnished with <u>ordinary</u> office furniture.

3 'usually'

You use the adverb **usually** when you are mentioning the thing that most often happens in a particular situation.

She <u>usually</u> found it easy to go to sleep at night.
He realized he was talking more freely than he <u>usually</u> did with strangers.

4 'as usual'

When something happens on a particular occasion and it is the thing that most often happens in that situation, you can say that it happens **as usual.**

Nino sounded a little drunk, <u>as usual.</u>
She wore, <u>as usual,</u> her black dress.

(*i*) Note that you do not say that something happens 'as usually'.

V v

vacation

⇨ See **Usage** entry at **holiday - vacation**.

variety

1 'a variety of'

If there are **a variety of** things or people, there are several different kinds of them.

West Hampstead has <u>a variety of</u> good shops and supermarkets.
These were not easy aims to achieve, for <u>a variety of</u> reasons.

After **a variety of** you use a plural form of a verb.

A variety of treatment methods <u>exist.</u>

If you want to emphasize how many different kinds of people or things there are, you can use **great** or **wide** in front of **variety.**

A <u>great variety of</u> animals survive there.
The college library had <u>a wide variety of</u> books.

2 used as a count noun

You can refer to a type of plant or animal as a **variety of** that plant or animal.

The courgettes were from Spain, as was one <u>variety of</u> lettuce.
There are numerous <u>varieties of</u> fish to choose from.

After **varieties of** you can use either the plural or singular form of a noun. The singular form is more formal.

Dozens of varieties of <u>roses</u> are carefully cultivated.
There are many varieties of <u>water turbine</u> on the market.

After **variety of** you use a singular form.

Each variety of <u>tree</u> has its own name.

very

1 basic use

You use **very** to emphasize an adjective or adverb.

…a <u>very small</u> child.
That's <u>very nice</u> of you.
Think <u>very carefully.</u>

2 used with '-ed' words

You can use **very** to emphasize adjectives ending in '-ed', especially when they refer to a state of mind or emotional condition. For example, you can say 'I was **very bored**' or 'She was **very frightened**'.

He seemed <u>very interested</u> in everything.
Joe must have been <u>very worried</u> about her.

However, you do not use 'very' to emphasize '-ed' words when they are part of a passive construction. You do not say, for example, 'He was very liked'. You say 'He was **well liked**'. Similarly, you do not say 'She was very admired'. You say 'She was **much admired**', 'She was **very much admired**', or 'She was **greatly admired**'.

Argentina were <u>well beaten</u> by Italy in the first round.
I was <u>much influenced</u> by many writers.
He is <u>very much resented</u> by the unions.
She was <u>greatly changed</u> in appearance.

You do not say someone is 'very awake'. You say that they are **wide awake** or **fully awake**.

He was wide awake by the time we reached my flat.
He was not fully awake.

You also do not say that someone is 'very asleep'. You say that they are **sound asleep, fast asleep,** or **deeply asleep.**

Chris is still sound asleep in the other bed.
Charlotte had been fast asleep when he left her.
Miss Haynes was very deeply asleep.

You do not say that two things are 'very apart'. You say that they are **far apart.**

His two hands were far apart.

You also do not use 'very' with adjectives which already describe an extreme quality. You do not say, for example, that something is 'very enormous'. Here is a list of adjectives of this kind:

absurd	delighted	excellent	massive	terrible
awful	enormous	furious	perfect	wonderful
brilliant	essential	huge	splendid	

3 comparatives and superlatives

You do not use 'very' with comparatives. You do not say, for example, ~~Tom was very quicker than I was~~. You say 'Tom was **much quicker** than I was' or 'Tom was **far quicker** than I was'.

It was much colder than before.
It is a far better picture than the other one.

You can use **very** in front of **best, worst,** or any superlative which ends in '-est'.

It's one of Shaw's very best plays.
…the very worst crimes.
…the very latest photographs.

However, you do not use 'very' with superlatives that begin with **the most**. Instead you use **much, by far,** or **far and away.**

He is much the most likely winner.
He insists that, of all his novels, 'The Hammer of God' was by far the most difficult to write.
This is far and away the most important point.

4 used with 'first', 'next', and 'last'

You can use **very** in front of **first, next,** or **last** to emphasize that something is the first, next, or last thing of its kind.

Last week, I was their very first guest.
The very next day we held a jumble sale in the village hall.
Those were his very last words.

⚠️ **WARNING:** You do not use 'very' to say that something happens because someone or something has a quality to an unusually large extent. You do not say, for example, '~~He looked very funny that we couldn't help laughing~~'. You say 'He looked **so** funny that we couldn't help laughing'.

He found the girl so attractive that he fell in love.
He had shouted so hard that he had no voice left.

⇨ See **Usage** entry at **so.**

5 prepositions

You do not use 'very' in front of prepositions such as **ahead of** or **behind**. Instead you use **well** or **far.**

USAGE

Applications are <u>well ahead of</u> last year's.
Davids was not <u>far behind</u> Zinedine Zidane as one of the outstanding talents of the World Cup.

6 prepositional phrases

You also do not use 'very' in front of prepositional phrases. You do not say, for example, ~~'He was very in love with Kate'~~. Instead, you use **very much** or **greatly**.

The findings were <u>very much in line with</u> previous medical thinking.
I was <u>greatly in awe of</u> Jane at first.

very much

⇨ See **Usage** entry at **much**.

vest

In British English, a **vest** is a piece of clothing which you wear on the top half of your body underneath a shirt, blouse, or dress in order to keep warm.

He wore a <u>vest</u> under his shirt.

 In American English, a piece of clothing like this is called an **undershirt**.

…a v-necked jersey cut to reveal a flannel <u>undershirt</u>.

 In American English, a **vest** is a piece of clothing with buttons and no sleeves, which a man wears over his shirt and under his jacket. In British English, a piece of clothing like this is called a **waistcoat**.

…a navy blue <u>vest</u> with black buttons.
…an Indian <u>waistcoat</u> embroidered with mirrors.

victim - casualty

1 'victim'

You refer to someone as a **victim** when they have suffered as the result of a crime, natural disaster, or serious illness.

…a rape <u>victim.</u>
We have been the <u>victims</u> of a monumental swindle.
After about two weeks, the <u>victim's</u> hair starts to fall out.

2 'casualty'

You do not usually use 'victim' to refer to someone who has been injured or killed in a war or accident. The word you use is **casualty**.

There were heavy <u>casualties</u> on both sides.
The <u>casualty</u> figure has increased.
The <u>casualties</u> were taken to the nearest hospital.

In Britain, **casualty** or **the casualty ward** is the part of a hospital where people are taken for emergency treatment when they have been hurt in an accident or have suddenly become ill.

I was taken to <u>casualty</u> at St Thomas's Hospital.

 Note that this department is also called **Accident and Emergency** or **A and E**. In American English the term is the **Emergency Room** or the **ER**.

view

1 'view'

A **view** is a belief or opinion that you have on a particular subject.

He was sent to jail for his political <u>views.</u>
I have strong <u>views</u> about politics and the Church.

⇨ See **Usage** entry at **point of view - view - opinion**.

You also use **view** to refer to what you can see from a window or high place.

From the top there is a fine <u>view</u>.
The window of her flat looked out on to a superb <u>view</u> of London.

2 'in view of'

You use **in view of** when you are mentioning a reason why something has been done or should be done.

The folder was marked 'Very Secret', not surprisingly, <u>in view of</u> the contents.
<u>In view of</u> the fact that all the other members of the group are going, I think you should go too.

3 'with a view to'

If you do something **with a view to** doing something else, you do it with the aim of eventually doing the second thing.

We have exchanged letters <u>with a view to</u> meeting to discuss these problems.
They entered into talks <u>with a view to</u> amalgamation.

visit

1 used as a verb

If you **visit** a place, you go to see it because you are interested in it.

He had arranged to <u>visit</u> a number of museums in Paris.
I could <u>visit</u> Blackpool next.

If you **visit** someone, you go to see them at their home, or you stay with them there for a short time.

I <u>visited</u> the newly-married couple.
She <u>visited</u> some of her relatives for a few days.

You can also **visit** a professional person such as a doctor or lawyer, in order to get treatment or advice.

He persuaded me to <u>visit</u> a doctor.
You might need to <u>visit</u> a solicitor before thinking seriously about divorce.

 Some American speakers use **visit with** instead of 'visit'.

She wanted to <u>visit with</u> her family for a few weeks.

 However, in American English, to **visit with** someone usually means to chat to them.

You and I could <u>visit with</u> each other undisturbed.

2 used as a noun

Visit is also a noun. You can **make** a visit to a place or **pay** a visit to someone.

He <u>made</u> a <u>visit</u> to the prison that day.
It was after nine o'clock, too late to <u>pay</u> a <u>visit</u> to Sally.

(i) Note that you do not say that someone 'does' a visit.

visual - visible

1 'visual'

Visual means 'relating to sight'.

<u>Visual</u> jokes are an increasing part of modern fashion.
…exhibitions of the <u>visual</u> arts.

2 'visible'

Something that is **visible** is large enough to be seen, or is in a position where it can be seen.

These tiny creatures are hardly <u>visible</u> to the naked eye.
Beyond them the volcano's peak, just <u>visible</u> from this angle, shone gold tinged with pink.

voyage

⇨ See **Usage** entry at **journey - trip - voyage - excursion**.

W w

wages
⇨ See **Usage** entry at **salary - wages**.

wagon
⇨ See **Usage** entry at **carriage - car - truck - wagon**.

waist - waste
These words are both pronounced /weɪst/.

1 **'waist'**

Waist is a noun. Your **waist** is the middle part of your body, above your hips.

She tied an apron around her waist.
He was naked from the waist up.

2 **'waste' used as a verb**

Waste is most commonly a verb. If you **waste** time, money, or energy, you use it on something that is unimportant or unnecessary.

You 're wasting your time.
Let's not waste money on a court case.

3 **'waste' used as a noun**

You can also say that something is **a waste of** time, money, or energy.

I'll never do that again. It's a waste of time.
It's a waste of money hiring skis.

Waste has another meaning. You use it to refer to material which has been used and is no longer wanted, for example because the useful part of it has been removed.

The river was thick with industrial waste.

waistcoat
⇨ See **Usage** entry at **vest**.

wait

1 **'wait'**

You use the verb **wait** to say that someone remains in the same place, or avoids doing something, until something happens or someone arrives.

I waited in a reception room until a secretary came for me.
She had been waiting in the queue to buy some stamps.
The man waited, and said nothing.

2 **'wait for'**

You can say that someone **waits for** something or someone.

I'm staying here and I'll wait for her call.
And if he's not there yet, then stick around and wait for him.

You can also say that someone **waits for** a person or thing **to do** something.

She waited for me to say something.
I waited for Donald to come home.

⚠ **WARNING: Wait** is never a transitive verb. You do not say that someone 'waits' someone or something. You must use **wait for**.

⇨ See also **Usage** entry at **await**.

wake - waken
⇨ See **Usage** entry at **awake**.

wallet

A **wallet** is a small, flat case made of leather or plastic, in which someone, especially a man, keeps banknotes and other small things such as credit cards.

In American English, a man's wallet is sometimes called a **billfold,** and a woman's wallet is sometimes called a **pocketbook.**

⇨ See **Usage** entry at **purse**.

want

1 | basic use

If you **want** something, you feel a need for it or a desire to have it.

Do you <u>want</u> a cup of coffee?
All they <u>want</u> is a holiday.

ⓘ Note that you do not normally use a continuous tense of **want**. You do not say, for example, 'All they are wanting is a holiday'.

2 | used with a 'to'-infinitive

You can say that someone **wants to do** something.

They <u>wanted to go</u> shopping.
I <u>want to ask</u> a favour of you, Anna.

ⓘ Note that you do not say that someone 'wants to not do' something or 'wants not to do' something. You say that they **don't want to do** it.

I <u>don't want to discuss</u> this.
He <u>didn't want to come.</u>

Instead of using a 'to'-infinitive clause, you can sometimes use **to** on its own after **don't want**. For example, instead of saying 'I was invited to go, but I didn't want to go', you would normally say 'I was invited to go, but I **didn't want to**'. Note that you do not say 'I was invited to go, but I didn't want it'.

I could finish it by October, but I just <u>don't want to.</u>
I think that it is very wrong to force people to work if they <u>don't want to.</u>

You can say that you **want** someone else **to do** something.

I <u>want</u> him <u>to learn</u> to read.
The little girl <u>wanted</u> me <u>to come</u> and play with her.

You do not use a 'that'-clause after **want**. You do not say, for example, 'I want that he should learn to read'.

3 | 'wish'

Note that **want** and **wish** have similar meanings, but are used differently. If you use **wish** with a 'to-' infinitive, this has the same meaning as **want** but is more formal.

She <u>wished to consult</u> him about her future.

⇨ See **Usage** entry at **wish**.

4 | requests

You do not normally use 'want' when you are making a request. It is not polite, for example, to walk into a shop and say 'I want a box of matches, please'. You should say 'Could I have a box of matches, please?' or just 'A box of matches, please.'

⇨ See **Topic** entry at **Requests, orders, and instructions**.

5 | another meaning of 'want'

Want has another meaning. If something **wants doing,** there is a need for it to be done.

We've got a couple of jobs that want doing in the garden.
The windows wanted cleaning.

(i) Note that you do not use a 'to'-infinitive in sentences like these. You do not say, for example, 'We've got a couple of jobs that want to be done in the garden'.

6 **'be about to'**

You do not use 'want to' to say that someone is going to do something very soon. You do not say, for example, 'I had put on my coat, and was just wanting to leave when the telephone rang'. The expression you use is **be about to**.

Her father is about to retire soon.
He was just about to go on stage again.

wardrobe

⇨ See **Usage** entry at **cupboard - wardrobe - closet**.

wash

1 **used as a transitive verb**

If you **wash** something, you clean it with water and usually with soap or detergent.

He got a job washing dishes in a pizza parlour.
She washes and irons his clothes.

You can **wash** a part of your body.

First wash your hands.
She combed her hair and washed her face.

2 **used as an intransitive verb**

If someone **washes,** they wash parts of their body, especially their hands and face. **Wash** is used like this mainly in stories.

She got up and washed.

3 **'have a wash'**

In conversation, you usually say that someone **has a wash.**

He was having a wash.
They look as if they haven't had a wash.

4 **'wash up'**

In American English, if someone **washes up,** they wash parts of their body, especially their hands and face.

He headed to the bathroom to wash up.

Wash up is not used with this meaning in British English. In British English, if you **wash up,** you wash the pans, plates, cups, and cutlery which have been used in cooking and eating a meal.

We washed up in the kitchen while the coffee heated on the stove.

5 **'wash your hands'**

In British English, if someone asks where they can **wash their hands,** they may be asking politely where the toilet is.

washroom

⇨ See **Usage** entry at **toilet**.

waste

⇨ See **Usage** entry at **waist - waste**.

way

1 **'way'**

You use **way** to refer to the thing or series of things that someone does in order to achieve a particular result. You can talk about a **way of doing** something or a **way to do** it. There is no difference in meaning.

…the most effective *way of helping* the unemployed.
…the best *way to help* a fourteen-year-old with reading problems.

ⓘ Note that if you use a possessive with **way,** you must use **of** and an '-ing' form after it. You do not use a 'to'-infinitive.

…a nurse who is willing to fit in with *your way of doing* things.
They are part of *the author's way of telling* his story.

2 'means'

You do not usually use a noun after 'way of' when you are saying how something is done or achieved. For example, you do not refer to an animal or vehicle as a 'way of transport'. The word you use is **means.**

The essential *means of transport* for the islanders was the donkey.
…the use of drums as a *means of communication.*

3 used in adjuncts of manner

You can say that something is done **in** a particular **way.**

It was done *in a very civilized way.*
She smiled *in a friendly way.*
We have to describe this *in some other way.*

When you use **this** or **that** with **way,** you usually omit the 'in'.

I can do it *this way.*
It might be done *that way.*

You can also omit 'in' when you are using **the** or a possessive.

We don't look at things *the same way.*
I'm going to handle this *my way.*

4 used with relative clauses

When **the way** is followed by a defining relative clause, this clause can be either a 'that'-clause or a clause beginning with **in which.** For example, you can say '**the way** she told the story', '**the way that** she told the story', or '**the way in which** she told the story'. There is no difference in meaning.

It's *the way* they used to do it.
He didn't like *the way that* his father spoke to his mother.
… *the way in which* we treat our juveniles.

5 'in the way'

If someone or something is **in the way** or **in your way,** they are preventing you from moving freely or from seeing clearly.

A large tree was *in the way.*
Why did you stand *in the way?*
Get *out of my way.*

6 'on the way'

If something happens to you during a journey, you do not say that it happens to you 'in the way' or 'in your way'. You say that it happens **on the way** or **on your way.**

On the way she went into the sweet shop.
Lynn was *on her way* home.

7 used as a grading adverb

Way can also be a grading adverb to emphasize, for example, that something is a great distance away, or is very much below or above a particular level or amount.

Way down in the valley to the west is the town of Freiburg.
These exam results are *way* above average.

USAGE

we

we

You use **we** to refer to yourself together with one or more other people. **We** is the subject of a verb.

We could hear the birds singing.
We both sat down.

You can use **we** to include the person or people you are speaking or writing to.

If you had to stay in town we might have dinner together.

ⓘ Note that you never say 'you and we' or 'we and you'. Instead of saying 'You and we must go and see John', you say ' **We** must go and see John'.

wear

1 **'wear'**

When you **wear** something, you have it on your body. You can **wear** clothes, shoes, a hat, gloves, jewellery, make-up, or a pair of glasses. The past tense of **wear** is **wore**, not 'weared'. The past participle is **worn**.

...a girl who wore spectacles.
I 've worn the same suit for five years.

2 **'dressed in'**

You can also say that someone is **dressed in** particular clothes.

...a man dressed in a grey suit.

However, you do not say that someone is 'dressed in' a hat, shoes, gloves, jewellery, make-up, or glasses.

⇨ See also **Usage** entry at **dress**.

3 **'in'**

You can also use **in** to mention the clothes, shoes, hat, or gloves someone is wearing. **In** usually goes immediately after a noun group.

...a small girl in a blue dress watching a cricket match.
The bar was full of men in cloth caps.

You can use **in** as part of an adjunct.

...when I see you walking along in your light-blue suit.
I stood all alone in my Sunday dress.

ⓘ Note that you do not usually use 'in' after 'be' when you are mentioning what someone is wearing. You do not say, for example, 'Mary was in a red dress'. You say 'Mary **was wearing** a red dress'.

However, you can use **in** after **be** when you are using a possessive determiner such as **his** or **my**. You can say, for example, 'Mary was **in her red dress**'.

I was in my dark suit and my university tie.
Hilary was in her nightdress and dressing gown.

In is sometimes used to mean 'wearing only'. For example, 'George was **in** his underpants' means 'George was wearing only his underpants'.

He was standing in the hall in his underpants.
He opened the door in his pyjamas.

If you say that a man is **in shirtsleeves** or **in his shirtsleeves**, you mean that he is wearing a shirt but not a jacket, usually because it is hot or he is working hard.

I started coming to work in shirtsleeves.
I lay on the bed in my shirtsleeves.

If you say that someone is **in their stockinged feet**, you mean that they are wearing socks, stockings, or tights, but no shoes.

I stood five-and-a-half feet tall in my stockinged feet.

weather - whether

1 'weather'

If you are talking about the **weather,** you are saying, for example, that it is raining, cloudy, sunny, hot, or cold.

The weather was good for the time of year.
…bad weather conditions.

Weather is an uncount noun. You do not use 'a' with it. You do not say, for example, 'We can expect a bad weather in the next few days'. You say 'We can expect **bad weather** in the next few days'.

They remained on the move for seventeen days, in appalling weather.
The journey to Fyn, in perfect May weather, was beautiful.

You do not tell someone what the weather is like by saying, for example, 'It's lovely weather'. You say 'The weather **is lovely**'.

And the weather was awful. It hardly ever stopped raining.

2 'whether'

Do not confuse **weather** with **whether.** You use **whether** when you are talking about two or more alternatives. You say, for example, 'I don't know **whether** to go out or stay at home'.

⇨ See **Usage** entry at **whether.**

weave

When people **weave** cloth, they make it by crossing threads over and under each other using a machine called a loom. When you use **weave** with this meaning, its past tense is **wove,** not 'weaved'. Its past participle is **woven.**

They were famous for the brilliant patterns of cloth they wove.
'Broadloom' just means that the cloth was woven on a loom over 6 feet wide.

Weave has another meaning. If you **weave your way** somewhere, you keep changing direction while you go there, in order to avoid hitting things. When you use **weave** with this meaning, its past tense and past participle is **weaved,** not 'wove'.

A stout woman weaved her way along the edge of the pool.

wedding

⇨ See **Usage** entry at **marriage - wedding.**

week

A **week** is a period of seven days. A week is sometimes regarded as beginning on a Sunday, and sometimes on a Monday.

That was a terrible air crash last week.
She won't be back till next week.

If something happens **in the week** or **during the week,** it happens on weekdays, rather than at the weekend.

In the week, we get up at seven.
I can never be bothered to cook much during the week.

⇨ See **Usage** entries at **last, next,** and **this.** See also **Topic** entry at **Days and dates.**

weekday

A **weekday** is any of the days of the week except Saturday or Sunday.

She spent every weekday at meetings.
If you want to avoid the crowds, it's best to come on a weekday.

Saturday is also sometimes considered to be a weekday.

The Tower is open 9.30 to 6.30 on weekdays and 2.00 to 6.00 on Sundays.

You can say that something happens **on weekdays.**

USAGE

I visited them <u>on weekdays</u> for lunch.
Commercials are limited to 12 minutes per hour <u>on weekdays.</u>

 American speakers sometimes omit the 'on'.
<u>Weekdays</u> after six, I'd go fetch him for dinner.

weekend

1 **'weekend'**

A **weekend** consists of a Saturday and the Sunday that comes after it. Sometimes Friday evening is also considered to be part of the weekend. The weekend is the time when most people in Europe, North America, and Australia do not go to work or school.
I spent the <u>weekend</u> at home.
Traffic was normal for an August <u>weekend.</u>

2 **regular events**

British speakers say that something takes place **at weekends.**
The tower is often open to the public <u>at weekends.</u>

 American and Australian speakers usually say that something takes place **on weekends.**
<u>On weekends</u> I rarely work more than 8 hours.

 American speakers sometimes omit the 'on'.
I stayed in the city <u>weekends</u> and did errands.

3 **single events**

You can say that an event takes place **during** a particular weekend.
Air and sea travel seems certain to be disrupted <u>during the Bank Holiday weekend</u> by industrial action.

On a weekday, **the weekend** or **this weekend** can refer either to the previous weekend or the following weekend. You can use **at**, **during** or **over** in front of **the weekend.** You do not use any preposition in front of **this weekend.**
Nine people were killed in road accidents <u>at the weekend.</u>
I may well call you <u>over the weekend.</u>
His first film, The Producers, was shown on television <u>this weekend.</u>
We might be able to go skiing <u>this weekend.</u>

weep

⇨ See **Usage** entry at **cry - weep.**

welcome

Welcome can be a verb, a noun, or an adjective. It can also be a greeting.

1 **used as a verb**

If you **welcome** someone, you greet them in a friendly way when they arrive at the place where you are.
He moved eagerly towards the door to <u>welcome</u> his visitor.

2 **used as a noun**

If you want to describe the way in which someone is welcomed to a place, you can use **welcome** as a noun. For example, you can say that someone is given 'a warm welcome'.
He was given <u>a warm welcome</u> by the President of Harvard himself.
We always receive <u>a wonderful welcome</u> from the warm and friendly staff.

3 **used as an adjective**

If you are **welcome** in a place, the people there are glad that you have come.
All members of the public are <u>welcome.</u>
I was a <u>welcome</u> visitor in both camps.

(i) Note that the adjective is **welcome**, not 'welcomed'. You do not say, for example, 'I was a welcomed visitor in both camps'.
If something is **welcome**, people are pleased to get it, or pleased that it happens.
The money was <u>welcome</u>, of course.
…a <u>welcome</u> cup of cocoa.

4 used as a greeting
When someone arrives at the place where you are, you can greet them in a rather formal way by saying '**Welcome**' to them.
<u>Welcome</u> to Peking
<u>Welcome</u> home, Marsha.
<u>Welcome</u> back.

---

well

1 used before a statement
People sometimes say **well** when they are about to make a statement. There is often no special reason for this, but sometimes **well** can indicate hesitation or uncertainty.
'Is that right?' – '<u>Well,</u> I think so.'

People also use **well** when they are correcting something they have just said.
We walked along in silence for a bit; <u>well</u>, not really silence, because she was humming.
It took me years, <u>well</u> months at least, to realise that he'd lied to me.

2 used as an adverb
Well is very commonly an adverb.
You use **well** to say that something is done to a high standard or to a great extent.
He handled it <u>well.</u>
The strategy has worked very <u>well</u> in the past.
They did not look after my family very <u>well.</u>

You use **well** to emphasize some past participles when they are part of a passive construction.
You seem to be <u>well liked</u> everywhere.
Argentina were <u>well beaten</u> by Italy in the first round.

You also use **well** in front of some prepositions such as **ahead of** and **behind**.
Applications are <u>well ahead of</u> last year's.
The border now lay <u>well behind</u> them.

When **well** is an adverb, its comparative and superlative forms are **better** and **best**.
People are <u>better</u> housed than ever before.
What works <u>best</u> is a balanced, sensible diet.

3 used as an adjective
Well is also an adjective. If you are **well**, you are healthy and not ill.
She looked <u>well.</u>
I am very <u>well</u>, thank you.

Note that most British speakers do not use **well** in front of a noun. They do not say, for example, 'He's a well man'. They say 'He's **well**'. However, American and Scottish speakers sometimes use **well** in front of a noun.

When **well** is an adjective, it does not have a comparative form. However, you can use **better** to say that the health of a sick person has improved. When **better** is used like this, it means 'less ill'.
He seems <u>better</u> today.
He is much <u>better</u> now. He's fine.

Better is more commonly used to say that someone has completely recovered from an illness or injury.

I hope you'll be <u>better</u> soon.
Her cold was <u>better.</u>

4 'as well'

You use **as well** when you are giving more information about something.

Filter coffee is definitely better for your health than boiled coffee. And it tastes nicer <u>as well.</u>
They will have a difficult year next year <u>as well.</u>

⇨ See **Usage** entry at **also - too - as well.**

well-known

⇨ See **Usage** entry at **famous - well-known - notorious - infamous.**

were

1 used to talk about the past

Were is the plural form and the second person singular form of the past tense of **be**.

They <u>were</u> only fifty miles from the coast.
We <u>were</u> quite busy that week.
You <u>were</u> only twelve at the time.

2 used in conditional clauses

Were has a special use in conditional clauses when these clauses are used to mention situations that do not exist, or events that are unlikely to happen. When the subject of the clause is **I, he, she, it, there**, or a singular noun, it is generally considered correct to use **were** instead of 'was'.

If I <u>were</u> in his circumstances, I would go his way too.
Mr Fatchett said that if the policy <u>were</u> to be dropped, it would be better to do it in October.

However, in conversation people usually use **was** (except in the expression 'If I **were** you').

If I <u>was</u> an architect, I'd re-design this house.
'If the country <u>was</u> properly run there wouldn't be needy people,' Kitty said.

You can use **was** or **were** in conversation, but you should use **were** in formal writing.

⚠ **WARNING:** Do not confuse **were** /wə/ with **where** /weə, weə/. You use **where** to make statements or ask questions about place or position.

<u>Where</u> can I get my book published?

⇨ See **Usage** entry at **where.**

west

1 'west'

The **west** is the direction which you look towards in order to see the sun set.

The next settlement is two hundred miles to the <u>west.</u>
Jupiter and Saturn will be low in the <u>west.</u>

A **west** wind blows from the west.

A warm <u>west</u> wind rushed to us across the downs.

The **west** of a place is the part that is towards the west.

...in remote rural areas of the <u>west</u> of Ireland.

West occurs in the names of some states and regions.

... <u>West Virginia.</u>
...a town in <u>West Sumatra.</u>

2 'western'

You do not usually talk about a 'west' part of a country or region. You talk about a **western** part.

...the northern and <u>western</u> parts of the United Kingdom.

Similarly, you do not talk about 'west Europe' or 'west France'. You say **western** Europe or **western** France.

…*the peoples of* <u>western</u> *Europe.*

… <u>western</u> *Nigeria.*

You can use **Western** to describe people and things connected with the United States, Canada, the countries of western Europe, and sometimes other industrialized countries.

… *pressure from* <u>Western</u> *governments.*

…*the defects of* <u>Western</u> *society.*

westerly

If something moves in a **westerly** direction, it moves towards the west.

…*a* <u>westerly</u> *journey.*

However, a **westerly** wind blows **from** the west.

The ship was driven by the incessant <u>westerly</u> *gales.*

The **most westerly** of a group of things is the one that is furthest to the west. The form **westernmost** is also used with the same meaning

…*the* <u>most westerly</u> *of the Falkland islands.*

…*the extreme isolation of living in the* <u>westernmost</u> *part of the province.*

westwards - westward

1. **'westwards'**

If you move or look **westwards,** you move or look towards the west.

The reef stretches <u>westwards</u> *from the tip of Florida.*

Ten minutes later we were flying <u>westwards</u> *over the great marshes.*

Westwards is always an adverb.

2. **'westward'**

In American English and old-fashioned British English, **westward** is often used instead of 'westwards'.

He sailed <u>westward</u> *from Palos de la Frontera.*

In both British and American English, **westward** is sometimes used as an adjective in front of a noun.

…*the* <u>westward</u> *expansion of the city.*

what

1. **asking for information**

You use **what** when you are asking for information about something. You can use **what** as a pronoun or a determiner.

When you use **what** as a pronoun, it can be the subject, object, or complement of a verb. It can also be the object of a preposition.

<u>What</u> *happened to the crew?*

<u>What</u> *did she say then?*

<u>What</u> *is your name?*

<u>What</u> *did he die of?*

ⓘ Note that when **what** is the object of a verb, it is followed by an auxiliary verb, the subject, and then the main verb. Note also that when **what** is the object of a preposition, the preposition usually goes at the end of the question.

2. **used as a determiner**

When you use **what** as a determiner, it usually forms part of the object of a verb.

<u>What books</u> *can I read on the subject?*

USAGE

What qualifications do you have?
What car did you hire?

⚠ **WARNING:** You do not use **what** when your question involves a choice from a limited number of people or things. For example, if someone has hurt their finger, you do not say to them 'What finger have you hurt?' You say '**Which** finger have you hurt?'

When you get your daily paper, which page do you read first?
Which department do you want?

You use **what** when you are asking about the time.

What time is it?
What time does the coach get in?

3 **used in reported clauses**

What is often used in reported clauses.

I asked her what had happened,
I don't know what to do.
I find it difficult to understand what people are saying.

⇨ See **Grammar** entry at **Reporting.**

4 **'what...for'**

You use **what** with **for** when you are asking about the purpose of something. You put **what** at the beginning of the question and **for** at the end of it. For example, '**What** is this handle **for**?' means 'What is the purpose of this handle?'

What are those lights for?

Some people use **what** with **for** when they are asking about the reason for something. They say, for example, '**What** are you staring **for** ?' This means 'Why are you staring?'

What are you going for?

5 **'what if'**

You use **what if** to ask what should be done if a particular difficulty occurs. For example, '**What if** the bus doesn't come?' means 'What shall we do if the bus doesn't come?'

What if it's really bad weather?
What if this doesn't work out?

6 **'what about'**

You use **what about** to remind someone of something, or to draw their attention to something. **What about** is followed by a noun group.

What about the others on the list?
What about your breakfast?

ⓘ Note that when you ask someone a question beginning with **what about** you are often expecting them to do something, rather than answer your question.

7 **used in relative clauses**

What is sometimes used at the beginning of a special kind of relative clause called a **nominal relative clause.** This kind of clause functions like a noun group; it can be the subject, object, or complement of a verb, or the object of a preposition. In a nominal relative clause, **what** means 'the thing which' or 'the things which'.

What he said was perfectly true.
They did not like what he wrote.
I'm what's generally called a traitor.
That is a very good account of what happened.

People often use a nominal relative clause in front of **is** or **was** to focus attention on the thing they are about to mention.

What I need is a lawyer.

What we as a nation want is not words but deeds.
What impressed me most was their sincerity.

A similar type of clause consists of **what** followed by the subject and **do**. After a clause like this, you use **be** and an infinitive structure with or without **to**. For example, instead of saying 'I wrote to George immediately', you can say '**What I did** was to write to George immediately'.

What Stephen did was to interview a lot of old people.
What you need to do is to choose five companies to invest in.

⚠ **WARNING:** You do not use 'what' in defining or non-defining relative clauses. You do not say, for example, ~~The man what you met is my brother~~' or ~~The book what you lent me is very good~~'. In sentences like these, you use **who, which,** or **that,** or you do not use a relative pronoun at all.
⇨ See **Grammar** entry at **Relative clauses.**

8 used to mean 'whatever'
What can be used with the same meaning as 'whatever', both as a pronoun and a determiner.

Do what you like.
People survived by sharing out what money they could get from cattle work.

⇨ See **Usage** entry at **whatever.**

9 used in exclamations
What is often used in exclamations.

What a marvellous idea!
What fun!

⇨ See **Topic** entry at **Reactions.**

whatever

Whatever can be a pronoun, a determiner, or an adverb.

1 used as a pronoun or determiner
You use **whatever** as a pronoun or determiner to refer to anything or everything of a particular kind.

I went to the library and read whatever I could find about Robert Owen.
She was doing whatever she could to stay alive.
She had to rely on whatever books were lying around.

You can also use **whatever** to say that something is the case in all possible circumstances.

I will come back. Whatever happens, I'll find a way.
Whatever brand you use, you will need four times as many teaspoonfuls as before.

2 used as an adverb
You use **whatever** after **nothing** or after a noun group beginning with 'no' to emphasize that there is nothing of a particular kind.

He knew nothing whatever about it.
There is no scientific evidence whatever to support such a view.

3 used in questions
When you are asking a question, you can use **ever** after **what** to express surprise.

What ever does it mean?

What ever is sometimes written **whatever.**

Whatever is the matter?
Whatever do you want to go up there for?

However, many people consider this form to be incorrect, and it is better to write **what ever** as two separate words.

USAGE

when

1 used in questions

You use **when** to ask about the time that something happened or will happen.

When did you arrive?

When are you getting married?

'I have to go to Germany.' – 'When?' – 'Now.'

2 used in time clauses

You use **when** in time clauses to say that something happened, happens, or will happen at a particular time.

He left school when he was eleven.

When I have free time, I always spend it fishing.

If you are talking about the future, you use the simple present tense in the time clause, not a future tense.

When you arrive in Britain, you will have to pass through immigration control.

Stop when you feel that your muscles have had enough.

3 'when' and 'if'

Do not confuse **when** with **if**. You use **if** to mention an event or situation that might happen. You use **when** to mention something that you expect to happen.

For example, if you say '**When** we buy a new car, you must come for a drive', you have decided that you are going to buy a new car. If you say '**If** we buy a new car, you must come for a drive', you are still undecided about whether or not to buy a car.

4 'when', 'as', and 'while'

If you want to say what was happening at the time that an event occurred, you can begin by saying what was happening, then add a clause beginning with **when.**

I was just going out when there was a knock at the door.

I was dancing when I felt the floor collapsing.

You can also use **as** or **while** to say what was happening when an event occurred. However, when you use one of these words, you describe the event in the main clause and say what was happening in the clause beginning with **as** or **while**.

As I was walking one day in Hyde Park, I noticed two elderly ladies.

While I was standing outside Woolworth's, I saw Jeremy.

If you want to say that two events are continuing to happen at the same time, you usually use **while**.

What were you thinking about while I was getting the drinks?

I disliked the noise of football while I was working.

5 used in non-finite clauses

When is sometimes used in non-finite clauses – that is, in clauses containing an infinitive or participle, rather than a finite verb.

You can use a clause containing **when** and a 'to'-infinitive to report an order or instruction.

You need to know when to buy the right wines at the right price.

In writing, people often use a clause containing **when** and a participle. For example, instead of writing 'I often read a book when I am travelling by train', they write 'I often read a book **when travelling by train**.'

Adults sometimes do not realize their own strength when dealing with children.

Two other important matters must be considered by anglers when deciding where to fish.

Similarly, instead of writing 'When he is interrupted, he gets very angry', someone might write '**When interrupted,** he gets very angry'.

Michael used to look hurt and surprised when scolded.

When asked whether he was from Britain or France, he said he was Jamaican.

6 used with prepositional phrases and adjectives

In writing, **when** is sometimes not followed by a clause at all, but by a prepositional phrase or an adjective such as **necessary** or **possible**. For example, instead of writing 'When you are in Paris, you should visit the Louvre', you might write '**When in Paris,** you should visit the Louvre'.

When under stress, he took one bath after another.
She had spoken only when necessary.
Fresh yeast can be used when available.

7 used in relative clauses

When is often used in non-defining relative clauses.

I want to see you at 12 o'clock, when you go to lunch.
The Fleishers arrived on a Wednesday, when I was alone.

When can also be used in defining relative clauses after **time** or after a word such as **day** or **year**.

There had been a time when she thought they were wonderful.
This is the year when the profits should start.

⇨ See **Grammar** entry at **Relative clauses**.

8 used with 'why'

When has a special use which is not related to time. You can add a clause beginning with **when** to a question which begins with **why**. You do this as a way of expressing surprise or disagreement at something that someone has said. The 'when'-clause indicates the reason for your surprise or disagreement.

Why should he do me an injury when he has already saved my life?
Why worry her when it's all over?

whenever

1 used in time clauses

You use **whenever** in time clauses to say that something always happens or is always the case when something else happens or is the case.

Whenever she had a cold, she only ate fruit.
She always called at the vicarage whenever she was in the area.

If you are talking about the future, you use the simple present tense in the time clause, not a future tense.

Come and see me whenever you feel depressed.

Every time and **each time** can be used in a similar way to 'whenever'.

Every time I go to that class I panic.
He flinched each time she spoke.

2 used with 'possible'

You can use **whenever** with **possible** instead of using a time clause. For example, instead of saying 'She met him whenever it was possible for her to meet him', you simply say 'She met him **whenever possible**'.

I avoided conflict whenever possible.
It paid to speak the truth whenever possible.

where

1 used in questions

You use **where** to ask questions about place or position.

Where's Jane?
Where does she live?
Where is the station?

You also use **where** to ask about the place that someone or something is coming from or going to.

Where does all this energy come from?
Where are you going?
Where do you want to fly to?

2 **used in place clauses**
You use **where** in place clauses when you are talking about the place or position in which someone or something is.

He said he was happy where he was.
He left it where it lay.
...an official policy which encouraged people to stay where they were.

A place clause usually goes after the main clause. However, in stories, the place clause can be put first.

Where Kate had stood last night, Maureen now stood.
Where the pink cliffs rose out of the ground there were often narrow tracks winding upwards.

3 **used in reported clauses**
Where is often used in reported clauses.

I think I know where we are.
I asked someone where the cheapest accommodation was.

After some reporting verbs, **where** can be used in a non-finite clause containing a 'to'-infinitive.

How did you know where to find me?

⇨ See **Grammar** entry at **Reporting.**

4 **used in relative clauses**
Where is often used in non-defining relative clauses.

He came from Herne Bay, where Lally had once spent a holiday.
She carried them upstairs to the art room, where the brushes and paint had been set out.

Where can also be used in defining relative clauses after **place** or after a word such as **room** or **street**.

... the place where they work.
... the room where I did my homework.
... the street where my grandmother had lived.

Where can also be used in defining clauses after words such as **situation** and **stage**.

We have a situation where people feel afraid of going out.
You get to a stage where you need a new challenge.
I've reached the point where I'm about ready to retire.

⇨ See **Grammar** entry at **Relative clauses.**

5 **used with 'possible' and 'necessary'**
Where is sometimes used in front of adjectives such as **possible** and **necessary**. When it is used like this, it has a similar meaning to 'when' or 'whenever'.

Where possible, prisoners with long sentences were put in the same blocks.
Help must be given where necessary.

wherever

1 **used in place clauses**
You use **wherever** in place clauses to say that something happens or is the case in every place where something else happens or is the case.

Soft-stemmed herbs and ferns spread across the ground wherever there was enough light.
In Bali, wherever you go, you come across ceremonies.
Wherever I looked, enemies lurked.

You can also use **wherever** to say that something is the case and that it does not matter what place is involved.

Wherever it is, you aren't going.

2 **used with 'possible'**

Wherever is sometimes used in front of adjectives such as **possible** and **practicable**. When it is used like this, it has a similar meaning to 'when' or 'whenever'.

All experts agree that, wherever possible, children should learn to read in their own way.

3 **used in questions**

When you are asking a question, you can use **ever** after **where** to express surprise.

Where ever did you get that hat?

Where ever is sometimes written **wherever**.

Wherever did you get that idea?
Wherever have you been?

However, many people consider this form to be incorrect, and it is better to write **where ever** as two separate words.

---

whether

Whether is used in reported clauses and conditional clauses.

1 **used in reported clauses**

You can use a clause beginning with **whether** after a reporting verb such as **know, ask,** or **wonder.** You use **whether** when you are mentioning two or more alternatives. You put **whether** in front of the first alternative, and **or** in front of the second one.

I don't know whether he's in or out.
I was asked whether I wanted to stay at a hotel or at his home.

When the two alternatives are opposites, you do not need to mention both of them. For example, instead of saying 'I don't know whether he's in or out', you can simply say 'I don't know **whether he's in**'.

Lucy wondered whether Rita had been happy.
She didn't say whether he was still alive.
I asked Professor Fred Bailey whether he agreed.

2 **'whether…or not'**

You can also mention the second alternative using **or not.** You put **or not** either at the end of the sentence or immediately after **whether.**

I didn't know whether to believe him or not.
The barman didn't ask whether or not they were over eighteen.

3 **'if'**

If can be used instead of 'whether', especially when the second alternative is not mentioned.

I asked her if I could help her.
I rang up to see if I could get seats.

4 **reporting uncertainty**

If someone is uncertain about taking a particular course of action, or uncertain how to respond to a situation, you can report this using a clause consisting of **whether** and a 'to'-infinitive.

I've been wondering whether to retire.
He didn't know whether to feel glad or sorry at his dismissal.

5 **used in conditional clauses**

You can add a clause containing **whether** and **or not** to a sentence to indicate that something is true in any of the circumstances you mention.

He's going to buy a house whether he gets married or not.

USAGE

6 'weather'

Do not confuse **whether** with **weather,** which is pronounced the same way. If you say that it is raining, windy, hot, or cold, you are talking about the **weather.**

...the wet <u>weather</u> which persisted through the holiday.

⇨ See **Usage** entry at **weather - whether.**

which

Which can be a determiner or a pronoun.

1 asking for information

You use **which** when you are asking for information about one of a limited number of things or people. A noun group beginning with **which** or consisting of the pronoun **which** can be the subject, object, or complement of a verb. It can also be the object of a preposition.

<u>Which mattress</u> is best?
<u>Which</u> came first?
<u>Which hotel</u> did you want?
<u>Which</u> do you fancy?
<u>Which one</u> is the robber?
<u>Which</u> is her room?
<u>Which station</u> did you come from?
Using a dishwasher or washing up by hand - <u>which</u> do you opt for?

(*i*) Note that when the noun group is the object of a verb or preposition, you put an auxiliary verb after the object, followed by the subject and the main verb. Note also that when the noun group is the object of a preposition, the preposition usually goes at the end of the clause.

2 used in reported clauses

Which is often used in reported clauses.

Do you know <u>which country he played for?</u>
I don't know <u>which to believe.</u>

⇨ See **Grammar** entry at **Reporting.**

3 used in relative clauses

Which can be a relative pronoun in both defining and non-defining relative clauses. In relative clauses, **which** always refers to things, never to people.

Last week we heard about the awful conditions <u>which exist in British prisons.</u>
I'm teaching at the Selly Oak Centre, <u>which is just over the road.</u>

In relative clauses, you can use either **which** or **who** after a collective noun such as **family, committee,** or **group.** After **which** you use a singular verb. After **who** you usually use a plural verb.

He is chairing a scientific group <u>which has</u> set itself the task of preventing liver cancer.
...a separate ethnic group <u>who have</u> their own language.
...the importance of a family <u>who loves</u> you.

⚠ **WARNING:** When **which** is the subject of a non-defining clause, you do not use another pronoun after it. You do not say, for example, 'He stared at the painting, which it was completely ruined'. You say 'He stared at the painting, **which** was completely ruined'.

⇨ See **Grammar** entry at **Relative clauses.**

whichever

Whichever can be a determiner or a pronoun. It is used in two different ways.

You can use it to say that it does not matter which of a range of alternatives happens or is chosen.

The United States would be safe <u>whichever side won.</u>
<u>Whichever way you look at it,</u> neutrality is folly.
We will immediately refund your money in full, or replace the item, <u>whichever you prefer.</u>

You can also use **whichever** when you are indicating which of a range of things is the right one or the one you mean.

Use <u>whichever soap powder is recommended by the manufacturer.</u>
Use <u>whichever of the forms is appropriate.</u>

while

1 used in time clauses

If one thing happens **while** another thing is happening, the two things happen at the same time.

He stayed with me <u>while Dad talked with Dr Leon.</u>
<u>While I was overseas</u> she was in Maritzburg studying.

2 used in non-finite clauses

In writing, people often use a non-finite clause beginning with **while.** For example, instead of writing 'I often knit while I am watching television', they write 'I often knit **while watching** television'.

Mark watched us <u>while pretending not to.</u>
Working without a desk, he tends to interview visitors <u>while hunched at the edge of his chair.</u>

3 used with prepositional phrases

In writing, **while** is sometimes not followed by a clause at all, but by a prepositional phrase. For example, instead of writing 'I heard the news while I was on holiday', you might write 'I heard the news **while on holiday**'.

They wanted a place to stay <u>while in Paris.</u>

4 'while' in concessive clauses

While has a special use which is not related to time. You use it to introduce a clause that contrasts with something else that you are saying.

Fred gambled his money away <u>while Julia spent all hers on dresses.</u>
<u>While I have some sympathy for these fellows,</u> I think they went too far.

5 'a while'

A while is a period of time.

After <u>a while,</u> my eyes became accustomed to the darkness.

⇨ See **Usage** entry at **awhile - a while.**

whilst

Whilst is a formal word which has the same meaning as 'while'. It is used in both time clauses and concessive clauses.

Her sister had fallen <u>whilst walking in her sleep at night.</u>
Raspberries have a matt, spongy surface <u>whilst blackberries have a taut, shiny skin.</u>

 You do not use **whilst** in conversation, and it is not used in American English.

who - whom

Who and **whom** are pronouns.

1 asking for information

You use **who** when you are asking about someone's identity. **Who** can be the subject, object, or complement of a verb. It can also be the object of a preposition.

<u>Who</u> invited you?
<u>Who</u> are you going to invite?
<u>Who</u> are you?
<u>Who</u> did you dance with?

USAGE

(i) Note that when **who** is the object of a verb or preposition, it is followed by an auxiliary verb, the subject, and then the main verb. Note also that when **who** is the object of a preposition, the preposition must go at the end of the clause. You do not use it in front of **who**.

Whom is a formal word which is sometimes used instead of 'who'. **Whom** can only be the object of a verb or preposition.

Whom shall we call?
By whom are they elected?

(i) Note that when **whom** is the object of a preposition, the preposition must go in front of **whom**. You do not use it at the end of a clause.

2 used in reported clauses

Who is often used in reported clauses.

She didn't know who I was.
We have to find out who did this.

⇨ See **Grammar** entry at **Reporting**.

3 used in relative clauses

Who and **whom** are used in both defining and non-defining relative clauses.

He's the man who I saw last night.
Joe, who was always early, was there already.
…two girls whom I met in Edinburgh.
…Lord Scarman, for whom I have immense respect.

In relative clauses, you can use either **who** or **which** after a collective noun such as **family**, **committee**, or **group**. After **who** you usually use a plural verb. After **which** you use a singular verb.

…a separate ethnic group who have their own language.
…the importance of a family who loves you.
He is chairing a scientific group which has set itself the task of preventing liver cancer.

⚠ **WARNING:** When **who** is the subject of a non-defining clause, you do not use another pronoun after it. You do not say, for example, 'He told his mother, ~~who she was very shocked~~'. You say 'He told his mother, **who** was very shocked'.

---

whoever

1 used in statements

You use **whoever** to refer to any person involved in the kind of situation you are describing.

If death occurs at home, whoever discovers the body should contact the family doctor.
You can have whoever you like to visit you.

You also use **whoever** to refer to someone whose identity you do not know.

Whoever answered the telephone was a very charming woman.

You also use **whoever** to say that the identity of someone will not affect a situation.

Whoever wins this civil war, there will be little rejoicing at the victory.
Whoever you vote for, prices will go on rising.

2 used in questions

When you are asking a question, you can use **ever** after **who** to express surprise.

Who ever told you that?

Who ever is sometimes written **whoever**.

Whoever could that be at this time of night?

However, many people consider this form to be incorrect, and it is better to write **who ever** as two separate words.

whole

1 'the whole of ' and 'whole'

When you talk about **the whole of** something, you mean all of it.

… the whole of July.
… the whole of Europe.
I was cold throughout the whole of my body.

Instead of using **the whole of** in front of a noun group beginning with **the**, you can simply use **whole** after **the**. For example, instead of saying 'The whole of the house was on fire', you can say ' **The whole house** was on fire'.

I spent the whole day in the Prado.
They're the best in the whole world.

You can use **whole** in a similar way after **this**, **that**, or a possessive.

I just want to say how sorry I am about this whole business.
I've never told this to anyone else in my whole life.

You use **whole** after **a** to emphasize that you mean all of something of a particular kind.

I played Macbeth for a whole year.
You can easily devote a whole morning to it.

You can also use **whole** like this in front of the plural form of a noun.

There were whole speeches I did not understand.

ⓘ Note that in front of plurals **whole** does not have the same meaning as **all**. If you say '**All** the buildings have been destroyed', you mean that every building has been destroyed. If you say '**Whole** buildings have been destroyed', you mean that some buildings have been destroyed completely.

2 'as a whole'

You use **as a whole** after a noun to emphasize that you are talking about all of something and regarding it as a single unit.

Is this true just in India, or in the world as a whole?
In the country as a whole, she reckons, average house prices will jump by 19%.

3 'on the whole'

You add **on the whole** to a statement to indicate that what you are saying is only true in general and may not be true in every case.

One or two were all right, but on the whole I used to hate going to lectures.
I don't pretend that housework is fun because on the whole it isn't.

---

whom

⇨ See **Usage** entry at **who - whom**.

---

whose

1 used in relative clauses

You use a noun group containing **whose** /huːz/ at the beginning of a relative clause to show who or what something belongs to or is connected with. **Whose** is used in both defining and non-defining clauses.

A noun group containing **whose** can be the subject or object of a verb, or the object of a preposition. When it is the object of a preposition, the preposition can come at the beginning or end of the clause.

…a woman whose husband had deserted her.
…Martin Browne, whose autobiography I have been reading.
…the governments in whose territories they operate.
…some strange fragment of thought whose origin I have no idea of.

2 used in questions

You use **whose** in questions when you are asking who something belongs to or is connected with. **Whose** can be a determiner or a pronoun.

USAGE

Whose fault is it?
Whose car were they in?
Whose is this?

3 used in reported clauses

Whose is also used in reported clauses.

It would be interesting to know whose idea it was.
Do you know whose fault it is?
It's hard to say whose dog it is.

⇨ See **Grammar** entry at **Reporting**.

⚠ **WARNING:** Note that **who is** and **who has** are also sometimes pronounced /huːz/.
When you write down what someone says, you can write 'who is' or 'who has' as **who's**.
You do not write them as 'whose'.

'Edward drove me here.' – 'Who's Edward?'
…an American author who's settled in London.

---

why

1 used in questions

You use **why** when you are asking a question about the reason for something.

'I had to say no.' – 'Why?'
Why did you do it, Martin?

2 used when no answer is expected

You sometimes use **why** in questions without expecting an answer. For example, you can
make a suggestion by asking a question beginning with **Why don't**.

Why don't we all go?
Why don't you write to her yourself?

You can emphasize that there is no reason for something to be done by asking a
question beginning with **Why should**.

Why should I be angry with you?
'Will you come?' – 'No, why should I?'

You can emphasize that there is no reason why something should not be done by asking
a question beginning with **Why shouldn't**.

Why shouldn't he go to college?

You can suggest that an action is pointless by using **why** followed by an infinitive
without 'to'.

Why ring the police? It wouldn't do any good.

3 used in reported clauses

Why is often used in reported clauses.

I knew why Solly had been killed.
He wondered why she had come.
You never really told me why you and Dad got divorced.

Why can be used on its own instead of a reported clause, if it is clear what you mean. For
example, instead of saying 'She doesn't like him. I don't know why she doesn't like him',
you can say 'She doesn't like him, I don't know **why**'.

They won't call me David – I don't know why.
He's certainly cheerful, though I can't think why.

4 used in relative clauses

Why is used in defining relative clauses after the word **reason**.

That is a major reason why they were such poor countries.
There are several good reasons why I have a freezer.

When you use **the** in front of **reason**, you can use **that** instead of 'why' in the defining clause, or you can use no pronoun at all. For example, instead of saying 'the reason why I came', you can say 'the reason **that** I came' or 'the reason I came'.

The reason that consumption went down was because real incomes were plunging.

That's the reason I'm checking it now.

wide - broad

Something that is **wide** or **broad** measures a large distance from one side to the other. You can say that something such as a street or river is **wide** or **broad**. **Wide** is more common in conversation.

There were no shops on this wide street.

The streets of this town are broad.

In front of them was a long, wide river.

He thought of the prisoners peering out at the broad river.

When you are talking about objects, you usually say that they are **wide**, rather than 'broad'.

...a wide bed.

Six men came stumbling out through a wide doorway.

When you are talking about people's physical characteristics, you usually use **broad**, rather than 'wide'.

He was tall, with broad shoulders.

...a broad, hefty Irish nurse.

widow - widower

1 **'widow'**

You say that a woman is a **widow** when her husband has died and she has not married again.

I had been a widow for five years.

When a man has died, you can refer to his wife as **his widow.**

His savings had been left to his widow.

...Coretta Scott King, widow of Martin Luther King.

2 **'widower'**

You say that a man is a **widower** when his wife has died and he has not married again.

I'm a widower in my late forties.

However, when a woman has died, you do not refer to her husband as 'her widower'.

will

⇨ See **Usage** entry at **shall - will.**

win - defeat - beat

1 **'win'**

If you **win** a war, fight, game, or contest, you defeat your opponent. The past tense and past participle of **win** is **won** /wʌn/, not 'winned'.

The Party won a convincing victory at the polls.

They had won a great victory.

2 **'defeat' and 'beat'**

You do not say that someone 'wins' an enemy or opponent. In a war or battle, you say that one side **defeats** the other.

The French defeated the English troops.

In a game or contest, you say that one person or side **defeats** or **beats** the other.

Hampstead defeated Bath 18-9.

They were playing draughts and she beat him.

USAGE

wind

Wind can be a noun or a verb.

1 used as a noun

The **wind** /wɪnd/ is a current of air moving across the earth's surface.

…an icy <u>wind</u> blowing clouds of snow.
…a leaf blown on the <u>wind</u>.

2 used as a verb

The verb **wind** /wɪnd/ is usually used in the passive. If you **are winded** by something such as a blow, the air is suddenly forced out of your lungs so that you have difficulty in breathing for a short time. The past tense and past participle of this verb is **winded.**

If you go too fast, you get <u>winded</u>.
I fell with a crash onto a sandy bank, <u>winded</u> but not hurt.

The verb **wind** /waɪnd/ has a completely different meaning. If a road or river **winds** in a particular direction, it goes in that direction with a lot of bends.

The Moselle <u>winds</u> through some 160 miles of tranquil countryside.

The past tense and past participle of this verb is **wound,** pronounced /waʊnd/.

The road <u>wound</u> through the desolate salt ranges.

You can also **wind** /waɪnd/ something round something else. For example, you can **wind** a wire round a stick. This means that you wrap the wire round the stick several times.

She started to <u>wind</u> the bandages around her arm.
He had a long green woollen scarf <u>wound</u> about his neck.

When you **wind** /waɪnd/ a watch or a clock, you turn a knob or handle several times in order to make the watch or clock operate.

I still hadn't <u>wound</u> my watch so I didn't know the time.

Wound can also be pronounced /wuːnd/. When it is pronounced like this, it is a noun or a verb, and it has a completely different meaning.

⇨ See **Usage** entry at **wound.**

winter

Winter is the season between autumn and spring. In winter, the weather is cold.

It was a terrible <u>winter</u>.
…a dark <u>winter's</u> night.

If you want to say that something happens every year during this season, you say that it happens **in winter** or **in the winter.**

<u>In winter</u>, the Tower closes an hour earlier.
<u>In the winter</u>, the path is uneven, it can be icy.

ⓘ Note that you do not say that something happens 'in the winters'.

wire - telegram

1 'wire'

A **wire** is a long, thin piece of metal used for fastening things, or for carrying electricity or electrical signals.

 In American English, a **wire** is also a message sent by telegraph and then printed and delivered to your house or office.

2 'telegram'

In British English, a message like this is usually called a **telegram.**

wish

Wish can be a noun or a verb.

1 used as a noun

A **wish** is a longing or desire for something, often something that is difficult to obtain or achieve.

She told me of her <u>wish</u> to leave the convent.
They are driven on partly by a <u>wish</u> for democracy.

2 **used as a verb**

When **wish** is a verb, it is usually followed by a 'that'-clause. If you **wish** that something was the case, you would like it to be the case, although you know it is unlikely or impossible.

I <u>wish</u> I lived nearer London.
They never have enough resources and they <u>wish</u> they had more.

(*i*) Note that you use a past tense in the 'that'-clause, not a present tense. You do not say, for example, 'I wish I have more friends'. You say 'I wish **had** more friends'. Similarly, you do not say 'I wish I have sold my car'. You say 'I wish I **had sold** my car'.

I wish I <u>had</u> more time for it.
I wish I <u>had asked</u> her more about her stage career.
I envy you. I wish I <u>was going</u> away too.

When you are talking about the past, you use the same tense in the 'that'-clause that you would use if you were talking about the present. For example, you say 'She wished she **lived** in Tuscany' as well as 'She wishes she **lived** in Tuscany'.

The inspector wished he <u>carried</u> a gun.
He wished he <u>had phoned</u> for a cab.
There were some days when Johnnie wished that he <u>was working</u> for the Americans.

When the subject of the 'that'-clause is a singular pronoun such as **I** or **he** or a singular noun group, you can use either **was** or **were** after it. This use of **were** is rather formal, especially in British English.

Sometimes, I wish I <u>was</u> back in Africa.
I often wish I <u>were</u> really wealthy.
He wished it <u>was</u> time for Lamin to return.
My sister occasionally wished that she <u>were</u> a boy.

You can also use **could** in the 'that'-clause.

I wish I <u>could</u> paint.
He wished he <u>could</u> believe her.

You can also use **would** in the 'that'-clause. If you **wish** that something **would** happen, you want it to happen, and you are angry, worried, or frustrated because it has not happened already.

I wish he <u>would</u> come!
I wish she <u>would</u> explain it to me.

If you say to someone that you **wish** they **would** do something, you are indicating that you want them to do it, and you are annoyed or disappointed because they have not done it already.

I wish you <u>would</u> try to understand.
I wish you <u>would</u> get your facts right before you get into such a state.

You can also use a 'to'-infinitive after **wish**. If you **wish to do** something, you want to do it.

They are in love and <u>wish to marry</u>.
We do not <u>wish to waste</u> our money.

However, this is a formal use. The word you normally use is **want**.

I <u>want to be</u> an actress.
He <u>doesn't want to get up</u>.

⚠ **WARNING:** You do not use 'wish' with a 'that'-clause simply to express a wish for the future. You do not say, for example, 'I wish you'll have a nice time in Finland'. You say 'I **hope you'll have** a nice time in Finland' or 'I **hope you have** a nice time in Finland'.

I hope I'll <u>see</u> you before you go.
I hope you <u>like</u> this village.

USAGE

However, you can sometimes express a wish for the future using **wish** as a transitive verb with two objects.

May I wish you luck in writing your book.
I wish you every possible happiness.
She shook hands with Alix and wished her a happy vacation.

with

1 basic uses

If one person or thing is **with** another, they are together in one place.

I stayed with her until dusk.
He spent several seasons there with a man called Cartwright.
Put the knives with the other cutlery.

If you do something **with** a tool or object, you do it using that tool or object.

Clean mirrors with a mop.
He brushed back his hair with his hand.

2 used to mention an opponent

You use **with** after verbs like **fight** or **quarrel**. For example, if two people are fighting, you can say that one person is fighting **with** the other.

He was always fighting with his brother.
Judy was quarrelling with Bal.

Similarly, you can use **with** after nouns like **fight** or **quarrel**.

…my quarrel with Greenberg.
…a naval war with France.

3 used in descriptions

You can use **with** immediately after a noun group to mention a physical feature that someone or something has.

…an old man with a beard.
…an old house with steep stairs and dark corridors.

(*i*) Note that you can use **with** like this to identify someone or something. For example, you can refer to someone as 'the tall man **with** red hair'.

… the man with the bright, staring eyes.
… the house with the blue shutters.

You do not usually use 'with' to mention something that someone is wearing. Instead you use **in**.

…an old peasant woman in a black dress.
The bar was full of men in cloth caps.

⇨ See **Usage** entry at **wear.**

within

1 location

If you are **within** something, you are inside it or surrounded by it.

The prisoners demanded the freedom to congregate within the prison.
The central shrine was a huge copper dome within a railing.

This is a fairly formal use. Instead of 'within', you usually use **inside**.

Ibrahim waited inside the house for a few moments.
She couldn't see whether all four men were sitting inside the car.

⇨ See **Usage** entry at **inside.**

2 limits

If something is **within** a particular limit, it does not go beyond that limit, or is not more than what is allowed.

Within these limitations there were a number of options open to me.
We must ask the schools to keep within their budget.

3 time

If something happens **within** a particular length of time, it happens before that length of time has passed.

Within six years a fifty-mile canal was cut.
The population doubled within a few hundred years.

4 'by'

Do not confuse **within** with **by.** If you do something **by** a particular time, you have done it at or before that time.

By two in the morning I had come to a conclusion.
By 8.05 the group were in position.

⇨ See **Usage** entry at **by.**

without

If someone or something is **without** something, they do not have it.

I have never allowed my husband to see me without any clothes on.
…city slums without lights, roads or water.

If you do one thing **without** doing another thing, you do not do the second thing.

They drove into town without talking to each other.
'Goodbye, dear,' Mrs Saunders said, without looking up.

ⓘ Note that in sentences like these you use an '-ing' form after **without,** not an infinitive. You do not say, for example, 'I could go out at night without to disturb anyone'.

woman - lady

1 used as a noun

You usually refer to an adult female person as a **woman** /wʊmən/.

…a tall, dark-eyed woman in a simple brown dress.

The plural of **woman** is **women** /wɪmɪn/, not 'womans' or 'womens'.

There were men and women working in the fields.

You can use **lady** as a polite way of referring to a woman, especially if the woman is present.

…a rich American lady.
There is a Japanese lady here, looking for someone who looks like you.

ⓘ Note that it is almost always better to refer to someone as an **old lady** or an **elderly lady,** rather than an 'old woman'.

There's a little old lady who drives a horse and buggy around town.
… elderly ladies living on their own.

If you are addressing a group of women, you call them **ladies,** not 'women'.

Ladies, could I have your attention, please?
Good evening, ladies and gentlemen.

2 used as modifiers

Woman and **lady** are sometimes used in front of other nouns.

…a woman politician.
…a lady novelist.

You use **women** in front of plural nouns, not 'woman'.

… women drivers.
… women candidates.

However, you use **lady** in front of plural nouns, not 'ladies'.

… lady traffic wardens.
The two most important lady guests were Karen Blixen and Edith Sitwell.

⚠ **WARNING:** Many women object to being referred to as 'lady doctors', 'lady teachers', etc. They prefer being referred to just as **doctors** or **teachers**, but if it is necessary to indicate their sex, they usually prefer to be called **women doctors, women teachers,** and so on.

⇨ See **Usage** entries at **female - feminine - effeminate** and **girl,** and **Topic** entry at **Male and female.**

wonder

1 basic use

The verb **wonder** is usually used to say that someone thinks about something and tries to guess or understand more about it.

And I keep <u>wondering</u> about the parents whose kids never come back.

2 used with 'wh'-clauses

Wonder is often used with 'wh'-clauses.

I <u>wonder what she'll look like.</u>
I <u>wonder which hotel it was.</u>

3 used with 'if' and 'whether'

Wonder is also used with **if** or **whether.** If you **wonder if** something is the case, you think about it and try to decide whether it is the case.

He <u>wondered if Dominic was going to give him a signal.</u>
He was beginning to <u>wonder whether Gertrude was there at all.</u>

ⓘ Note that you do not use a 'that'-clause in sentences like these. You do not say, for example, '~~He wondered that Dominic was going to give him a signal~~'.

Wonder is sometimes used with **if** to make an invitation.

⇨ See section on **casual invitations** in **Topic** entry at **Invitations.**

4 used to express surprise

Wonder has another meaning. If you **wonder at** something, you are surprised and amazed about it. This use of **wonder** occurs mainly in writing.

He liked to sit and <u>wonder at all that had happened.</u>

When **wonder** has this meaning, you can use a 'that'-clause after it.

She only wondered <u>that she could have been so blind for so long.</u>

wood

1 used as an uncount noun

Wood is the material which forms the trunks and branches of trees, and which is used to make things such as furniture.

...a piece of <u>wood.</u>
The screws are very fine and won't split the <u>wood.</u>

ⓘ Note that you do not refer to a piece of wood as 'a wood'.

2 'wooden'

You do not usually use 'wood' in front of a noun to say that something is made of wood. The word you use is **wooden.**

...a <u>wooden</u> box with instructions on the lid.
They were all sitting at a long <u>wooden</u> table.

3 'wood' used as a count noun

A **wood** is a large area of trees growing close to each other.

...the big <u>wood</u> where the pheasants lived.

People sometimes refer to a very large wood as **the woods.**

They walked through <u>the woods</u> towards the main house.

USAGE

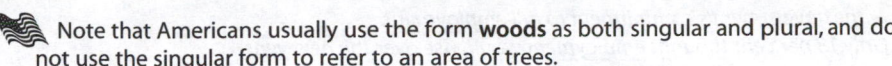 Note that Americans usually use the form **woods** as both singular and plural, and do not use the singular form to refer to an area of trees.

4 **'forest'**

An extremely large area of trees is called a **forest.**

They had their picnic in a clearing in the <u>forest.</u>
…Sherwood <u>Forest.</u>

---

work

Work can be a verb or a noun.

1 **used as a verb**

People who **work** have a job which they are paid to do.

I'm not working any more.
I used to <u>work</u> in a hotel.

You can use **as** with **work** to say what a person's job is.

Pam <u>works as</u> a careers officer.

(i) Note that the verb **work** has a different meaning in the continuous tenses than it does in the simple tenses. You use the continuous tenses, with the '-ing' form, to talk about a temporary job, but the simple tenses to talk about a permanent job. For example, if you say '**I'm working** in London', this suggests that the situation is temporary and you may soon move to a different place. If you say '**I work** in London', this suggests that London is your permanent place of work.

2 **used as an uncount noun**

If you have **work,** you have a job which you are paid to do.

…people who can't find <u>work.</u>
…different types of <u>work.</u>

When someone has a job, you can say that they are **in work.**

Fewer and fewer people are <u>in work.</u>

When someone does not have a job, you can say that they are **out of work.**

There are one and a half million people <u>out of work</u> in this country.

Work is also used to talk about the place where someone works. When **work** has this meaning, you do not use a determiner in front of it.

He too drives to <u>work</u> by car.
I can't leave <u>work</u> till five.

3 **'works'**

A place where things are made is sometimes called a **works.**

⇨ See **Usage** entry at **factory - works - mill - plant.**

4 **nouns with a similar meaning**

The following nouns all refer generally to activities which people are paid to do:

business	job	position	profession
employment	occupation	post	trade

5 **'employment'**

Employment is a formal word with a similar meaning to 'work'. Like 'work', it is an uncount noun.

Of those who had paid jobs, perhaps only half were in full-time <u>employment.</u>
There is no hope of regular <u>employment</u> as an agricultural labourer.

Employment is also used to talk about the number of people in a country or area who have jobs.

…the government's commitment to full <u>employment</u>.
Only 18 per cent thought <u>employment</u> would rise over the next year.

6 **'job'**

A person's **job** is a particular set of duties which they are paid to do. **Job** is a count noun.

Her mother had a cleaning <u>job</u>.
Well, congratulations on your new <u>job</u>.

You can also use **job** to refer to one particular thing that needs to be done.

It will be a long <u>job</u>, I'm afraid.
It's always better to concentrate on the <u>job</u> in hand.

7 **'piece of work' and 'task'**

You can also call this a **piece of work.** If it is difficult or unpleasant, you can call it a **task.** **Task** is a fairly formal word.

…a means of doing an essential <u>piece of work</u>.
The first <u>task</u> is to raise educational levels.

8 **'position' and 'post'**

In formal English, **position** and **post** are used instead of 'job'. When a job is advertised, it is often described as a **position** or **post.** A person applying for a job usually uses one of these words.

I have today resigned my <u>position</u> as director and chief executive of Rangers.
Today the Foreign Ministry announced that the Ambassador to Cuba is retiring from his <u>post</u>.

9 **'occupation'**

Your **occupation** is your job. **Occupation** is often used on official forms.

The Judge asked his <u>occupation</u>. 'Security consultant,' he replied.
…men preparing to switch to a new <u>occupation</u>.

(i) Note that if you are asked to write your occupation on a form, you can put 'student', 'housewife', 'unemployed', or 'retired' if you do not have a paid job.

10 **'profession' and 'trade'**

Profession and **trade** are both used to refer to types of job which require special training.

A **profession** is a type of job which requires formal training and which has fairly high status, for example the job of a doctor, teacher, or lawyer.

Both her parents had been school teachers and after college she entered the same <u>profession</u>.

You can also use **profession** to refer to all the people in a particular profession. For example, you can talk about 'the teaching **profession**' or 'the medical **profession**'.

There would be an outcry from <u>the legal profession</u> if these proposals were seriously put forward.

A **trade** is a type of skilled job, usually one which involves making or repairing something.

Learning a <u>trade</u> such as plumbing does not take as long as earning a four-year degree.
He was the son of a newspaperman and he never thought there was any other <u>trade</u> to follow.

You also use **trade** to refer to work that involves buying and selling things, or catering for tourists.

More than other businesses, the antiques <u>trade</u> depends on confidence.
The absence of a tourist <u>trade</u> will bring more economic hardships.

11 **'business'**

Business is used to refer to work that involves making, buying, or selling things.

You were in the film <u>business</u>?
You'd better go into the oil <u>business</u> or become a banker.

worse

Worse is the comparative form of **bad** and the usual comparative form of **badly.**

⇨ See **Usage** entry at **bad - badly.**

worst

Worst is the superlative form of **bad** and the usual superlative form of **badly**.
⇨ See **Usage** entry at **bad - badly**.

worth

Worth can be a preposition or a noun.

1 used as a preposition

If something is **worth** an amount of money, that is the amount you would get for it if you sold it.

His yacht is <u>worth</u> $1.7 million.
…a two-bedroom house <u>worth</u> $550,000.

ⓘ Note that **worth** is not a verb. You do not say ~~'His yacht worths $1.7 million'~~.

2 used as a noun

You use **worth** as a noun after words like **pounds** or **dollars** to indicate how much money you would get for an amount of something if you sold it.

…about fifty pence <u>worth</u> of chocolate.
…12 million pounds <u>worth</u> of gold and jewels.

You do not talk about the 'worth' of something that someone owns. You do not say, for example, ~~'The worth of his house has greatly increased'~~. You say 'The **value** of his house has greatly increased'.

What will happen to the <u>value</u> of my property?
The <u>value</u> of the horse is now in excess of £500,000.

worthless

⇨ See **Usage** entry at **invaluable**.

would

1 form and pronunciation

Would is a modal. It is used in a number of different ways.
When **would** comes after a pronoun, it is not usually pronounced in full. When you write down what someone says, you represent 'would' as **'d** and add it to the end of the pronoun. **Would** has the negative form **would not**. The **not** is not usually pronounced in full. When you write down what someone says, you usually write **wouldn't**.

2 'should'

Would is sometimes used with a similar meaning to 'should'.
⇨ See **Usage** entry at **should**.

The following are some other ways in which you can use **would**. You cannot use 'should' in any of these ways.

3 talking about the past

You can use **would** to talk about something which happened regularly in the past but which no longer happens.

We <u>would</u> normally spend the winter in Miami.
She <u>would</u> often hear him grumbling.

ⓘ Note that **used to** is used in a similar way.

She <u>used to</u> get quite cross with Lally.
In the afternoons, I <u>used to</u> hide and read.

However, **used to** can also be used to talk about states and situations that existed in the past but no longer exist. You cannot use **would** like this.

I'm not quite as sure as I <u>used to</u> be.

You use **would have** to talk about actions and events that were possible in the past, although they did not in fact happen.

It would have been unfair if we had won.
I would have said yes, but Julie talked us into staying at home.

When **would not** is used to talk about something that happened in the past, it has a special meaning. It is used to say that someone was unwilling to do something, or refused to do something.

They just would not believe what we told them.

Would is sometimes used in stories to talk about someone's thoughts about the future.

He thought to himself how wonderful it would taste.
Would he always be like this?

4 used in conditional sentences

You use **would** in a conditional sentence when you are talking about a situation which you know does not exist. You use **would** in the main clause; in the conditional clause, you use the simple past tense, the past continuous tense, or **could**.

If I had enough money, I would buy the car.
If he was coming, he would ring.
If I could afford it, I would buy a boat.

⚠ **WARNING:** You do not use 'would' in the conditional clause in sentences like these. You do not say, for example, 'If I would have enough money, I would buy the car'.

When you are talking about the past, you use **would have** in a conditional sentence to mention an event that might have happened but did not in fact happen. In this kind of sentence, you use the past perfect tense in the conditional clause and **would have** in the main clause.

Perhaps if he had realized, he would have run away while there was still time.
If he had been beaten, he would have been unlucky.

5 used in reported clauses

Would is also used in reported clauses.

He asked if I would answer some questions.
He made me promise that I would never break the law.
I felt confident that everything would be all right.

⇨ See **Grammar** entry at **Reporting**.

6 requests, orders, and instructions

You can use **would** to make a request.

Would you do me a favour?

You can also use **would** to give an order or instruction.

Put the light on, Bryan, would you?
Would you ask them to leave, please?

⇨ See **Topic** entry at **Requests, orders, and instructions**.

7 offers and invitations

You can say '**Would you...?**' when you are offering something to someone, or making an invitation.

Would you like a drink?
Would you care to stay with us?

⇨ See **Topic** entries at **Offers** and **Invitations**.

🇺🇸 Note that speakers of American English use **would** in some cases where speakers of British English sometimes use **should**.

⇨ See **Usage** entry at **should**.

wound

1 **form and pronunciation**
Wound is pronounced /waʊnd/ or /wuːnd/.
When it is pronounced /waʊnd/, it is a past tense and past participle of the verb **wind**.
⇨ See **Usage** entry at **wind**.

When **wound** is pronounced /wuːnd/, it is a noun or a verb.

2 **used as a noun**
A **wound** is damage to part of your body, caused by a gun, knife, or other weapon.
…a soldier with a leg wound.
The wound is healing nicely.

3 **used as a verb**
If someone **wounds** you, they damage your body using a weapon.
He had been badly wounded in the fighting.
He was wounded in the leg.

4 **'injury'**
When someone is hurt in an accident, such as a car crash or a natural disaster, you do not
say that they receive a 'wound' or that they 'are wounded'. You say that they receive an
injury or **are injured**.
A fall on the head is a common injury for a baby.
12 people died and 40 were injured in the crash.

⇨ See **Usage** entry at **injure**.

write

1 **'write' and 'write down'**
When you **write** something or **write** it **down,** you use a pen or pencil to make words, letters,
or numbers on a surface. The past tense of **write** is **wrote**. The past participle is **written**.
I wrote down what the boy said.
…the page on which the words are written.

2 **writing a letter**
When you **write** a letter to someone, you write information or other things in a letter and
send it to the person. When you use **write** like this, it has two objects. If the indirect
object is a pronoun, it usually goes in front of the direct object.
We wrote them a threatening letter.
I wrote him a very nice letter.

If the indirect object is not a pronoun, it usually goes after the direct object. When this
happens, you put **to** in front of the indirect object.
I wrote to my sister asked her to come up to my house.
Once a week, on Tuesdays, she wrote a letter to her husband.

You can also omit the direct object. If you **write to** someone, you write a letter to them.
She wrote to me last summer.
I wrote to Kettles and we arranged a number of successful meetings.

 American speakers often omit the 'to'.
If there is anything you want, write me.
I had a letter from a friend. He wrote me I'd better be careful in Russia.

You can write **'I am writing…'** at the beginning of a letter to introduce the topic you are
writing about.
*Dear Morris, I am writing to ask whether you would care to come and visit us during the
Easter vacation.*

ⓘ Note that you do not write 'I write to ask…'.

Y y

yard

The noun **yard** has two main meanings.

1 measurement

A **yard** is a unit of length in the imperial system of measurement. It is equal to thirty-six inches, or approximately 91.4 centimetres.

Jack was standing under a tree about ten yards away.

(*i*) Note that in Britain it is becoming more common to give measurements in metres, rather than yards.

⇨ See **Topic** entry at **Measurements**.

2 area behind a house

In both British and American English, a **yard** or **back yard** is an area of ground attached to a house. In British English, it is a small area behind a house, with a hard surface and usually a wall round it. In American English, it is a fairly large area, on any side of a house, usually with grass growing on it. In British English, a fairly large area like this is called a **garden** or **back garden**.

year

A **year** is a period of 365 or 366 days, especially one beginning on the first day of January and ending on the last day of December.

...at the end of next year.
The school has been empty for ten years.

You can use **year** when you are mentioning the age of a person or thing.

She is now seventy-four years old.
A friend of mine has just bought a house which is about 300 years old.

When you use **year** to talk about age, you must use **old** after it. You do not say, for example, 'She is now seventy-four years'.

⇨ See **Topic** entry at **Age** and **Usage** entry at **old.**

yes

You use **yes** to agree with someone, to say that something is true, or to accept something.

'There's always tomorrow, sir.' – 'Yes, you're right.'
'Is that true?' – 'Yes.'
'Tea?' – 'Yes, thanks.'

⚠ **WARNING:** When someone asks a negative question, you must say **yes** if you want to give a positive answer. For example, if someone says 'Aren't you going out this evening?', you say ' **Yes,** I am'. You do not say 'No, I am'. Similarly, if someone says 'Haven't you met John?', you say, ' **Yes,** I have'.

'Haven't you any socks or anything with you?' – 'Yes, in that suitcase.'
'Didn't you get a dictionary from him?' – 'Yes, I did.'

Similarly, you say **yes** if you want to disagree with a negative statement. For example, if someone says 'He doesn't want to come', you can say '**Yes,** he does'.

'That isn't true.' – 'Oh yes, it is.'

yesterday

Yesterday means the day before today.

It was hot yesterday.
We spent yesterday in Glasgow.

You refer to the morning and afternoon of the day before today as **yesterday morning** and **yesterday afternoon**.

Yesterday morning there were more than 1500 boats waiting in the harbour for the weather to improve.
Heavy rain fell here yesterday afternoon.

You can also talk about **yesterday evening,** but it is more common to refer to the previous evening as **last night.**

I met your husband last night.
I've been thinking about what we said last night.

You can also use **last night** to refer to the previous night.

We left our bedroom window open last night.
He never made it home at all last night.

(i) Note that you do not talk about 'yesterday night'.

In writing, **yesterday** is sometimes used to refer to the past, especially the recent past.

The worker of today is different from the worker of yesterday.

yet

1 **used in negative sentences**

You use **yet** in negative sentences to say that something has not happened up to the present time. In conversation, you usually put **yet** at the end of a clause.

It isn't dark yet.
I haven't decided yet.

In writing, you can put **yet** immediately after **not**.

Computer technology has not yet reached its peak.
The city had not yet been bombed.

2 **'have yet to'**

Instead of saying that something 'has not yet happened', you can say that it **has yet to happen.** People often use this structure to indicate that they do not expect something to happen.

I have yet to meet a man I can trust.
How it will work has yet to be seen.

3 **used in questions**

You often use **yet** in questions when you are asking if something has happened. You put **yet** at the end of the clause.

Have you done that yet?
Have you had your lunch yet?

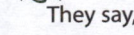 Note that some American speakers use the simple past tense in questions like these. They say, for example,' **Did** you **have** your lunch yet?'

4 **'already'**

Do not confuse **yet** with **already.** You use **already** at the end of a question to express surprise that something has happened sooner than expected.

Is he down there already?
You mean you've been there already?

⇨ See **Usage** entry at **already.**

5 **'still'**

You do not use 'yet' to say that something is continuing to happen. You do not say, for example, 'I am yet waiting for my luggage'. The word you use is **still**.

He still doesn't understand.
Brian's toe is still badly swollen.

⇨ See **Usage** entry at **still**.

6 **'just yet'**

If you do not intend to do something **just yet,** you do not intend to do it immediately.

It is too risky to announce an increase in our charges just yet.
There may be other reasons not to panic just yet.

you

You use **you** to refer to the person or people that you are speaking or writing to. **You** can be the subject or object of a verb, or the object of a preposition.

Have you got any money?
I have nothing to give you.
I want to come with you.

You can also be used to refer to people in general, rather than to a particular person or group. **You** is often used like this in this book.

⇨ See **Usage** entry at **one**.

your - you're

1 **'your'**

You use **your** /jə/ or /jɔː/ to indicate that something belongs or relates to the person or people that you are speaking to.

Will you pick your clothes up off the floor?
Where's your father?

2 **'you're'**

Note that **you are** is also sometimes pronounced /jɔː/. When you write down what someone says, you write this as **you're**. You do not write it as 'your'.

You're quite right.
You're not an expert.

yourself - yourselves

When **you** is the subject of a verb and refers to one person, you use **yourself** as the object of the verb or of a preposition in the clause to refer to the same person.

Are you feeding yourself properly?
You might be making a fool of yourself.

When **you** refers to more than one person, you use **yourselves** as the object of the verb or preposition.

I hope you both behaved yourselves.
Don't you boys ever think for yourselves?

Yourself and **yourselves** are often used in imperative structures.

Control yourself.
Please help yourselves to another drink.

Yourself and **yourselves** can also be used to emphasize the subject of a clause.

You don't even know it yourself.
Neither Andy Sutcliffe nor his team can do anything about it directly, but you yourselves can.

If you do something **yourself,** you do it without any help from anyone else.

You didn't do this yourself, did you?

youth

1 **used as an uncount noun**

Someone's **youth** is the period of their life when they are a child or an adolescent.

We change and learn from youth to old age.

When **youth** has this meaning, it is an uncount noun. You use a singular form of verb with it.

Youth has always been the time for rebellion.

2 **used as a count noun**

A **youth** is a boy or a young man, especially a teenager. This use occurs mainly in writing.

The road was occupied by a long line of youths and young girls carrying black flags.

3 **used as a plural noun**

The youth of a place or country are the young people there. This is a formal use.

… the youth of America.

You can also talk about **the youth of** a particular period.

… the youth of today.

When **youth** has either of these meanings, it is a plural noun. You use a plural form of a verb with it.

The youth of the country are too often uncouth, unfit, and uncivilised.

Today's youth are very cynical.

Z z

z

The letter **z** is called **zed** /z<u>e</u>d/ in British English and **zee** /z<u>i:</u>/ in American English.

zero

 Zero is the number 0. American speakers use **zero** in both conversation and writing.

Why are we so crazy about getting the thing down to <u>zero</u>?
There we stood, five men holding infants between <u>zero</u> and three.

In British English, **zero** is normally used only in scientific writing.

…a scale ranging from <u>zero</u> to seven.
*The gravitational pull would grow weaker until we reached the very centre of the planet,
when it would be <u>zero</u>.*

In conversation, British speakers usually say **nought** or **oh**.

… <u>nought</u> point nine.
…linguistic development between the ages of <u>nought</u> and one.
You arrive at Palma at <u>oh</u> two thirty-five.

⇨ See section on **zero** in **Topic** entry at **Numbers and fractions**.

Grammar Section

Grammar section

Adjectives

An **adjective** is a word that is used to describe someone or something or give information about them.

1 form

The form of an adjective does not change: the same form is used for singular and plural and for male and female.

We were looking for a good place to camp.
Good places to fish were hard to find.

2 graded adjectives

Graded adjectives are adjectives that indicate that someone or something has a particular quality. For example, **sad**, **pretty**, **happy**, and **wise** are graded adjectives.

…a sad story.
…a small child.

Graded means that the person or thing described can have more or less of the quality mentioned. One way of indicating the amount of a quality that something or someone has is by using **grading adverbs** such as **very** and **rather**.

⇨ See **Grammar** entry at **Adverbs**.

…a very pretty girl.
…a rather clumsy person.

3 comparatives and superlatives

Another way in which adjectives can be graded is by the use of the **comparative** and **superlative** forms '-er' and '-est' and the comparatives **more** and **most**. The comparative is used to say that something has more of a quality than something else, or more than it used to have. The superlative is used to say that something has more of a quality than anything else of its kind, or more than anything else in a particular group or place.

⇨ See **Grammar** entry at **Comparative and superlative adjectives**.

4 ungraded adjectives

Ungraded adjectives are adjectives that are used to indicate that something is of a particular type. For example, if you say 'financial help', you are using the adjective 'financial' to classify the noun 'help'. There are many different kinds of help: 'financial help' is one of them. These adjectives cannot be graded and do not have comparative or superlative forms.

…my daily shower.
… Victorian houses.
… civil engineering.

GRAMMAR

5 **colour adjectives**

Colour adjectives are used to indicate what colour something is.

...*a small <u>blue</u> car.*
Her eyes are <u>green.</u>

To specify a colour more precisely, a word such as **light, pale, dark,** or **bright** is put in front of the adjective.

... *<u>light brown</u> hair.*
...*a <u>bright green</u> suit.*
...*a <u>dark blue</u> dress.*

Colour words are also nouns. When they are nouns, they are typically used in the singular with no determiner.

I like <u>blue.</u>
Christina always wore <u>red.</u>
<u>Yellow</u> is my favourite colour.

The more frequent colour words can be used in the plural, or in the singular with a determiner, to refer to the different shades of a colour.

They blended in well with the <u>greens</u> of the landscape.
The shadows had turned <u>a deep blue</u>.

6 **emphasizing adjectives**

Emphasizing adjectives are used in front of a noun to emphasize your description of something or the degree of something.

He made me feel like a <u>complete</u> idiot.
Some of it was <u>absolute</u> rubbish.
World Cup tickets are <u>dead</u> expensive you know.
The redundancy of skilled workers is a <u>terrible</u> waste.
It was the <u>supreme</u> arrogance of the killer that dismayed him.

The following adjectives are emphasizing adjectives:

absolute	dead	outright	pure	simple	total
awful	entire	perfect	real	supreme	true
complete	mere	positive	sheer	terrible	utter

7 **specifying adjectives**

There is a small group of adjectives, sometimes called **postdeterminers,** which you use to indicate precisely what you are referring to. These adjectives come after a determiner and in front of any other adjectives.

...*the <u>following</u> brief description.*
He wore his <u>usual</u> old white coat.

They also come in front of numbers.

What has gone wrong during the <u>last</u> ten years?

The following adjectives are used in this way:

additional	first	next	past	same
certain	following	only	present	specific
chief	further	opposite	previous	usual
entire	last	other	principal	whole
existing	main	particular	remaining	

8 **adjectives with special endings**

A large number of adjectives end in '**-ed**' or '**-ing**'.

⇨ See **Grammar** entries at '**-ed' adjectives** and '**-ing' adjectives.**

⇨ For information on adjectives ending in '**-ic**' and '**-ical**', see **Grammar** entry at '**-ic' and '-ical' words.**

⇨ For information on adjectives ending in '**-ly**', see **Grammar** entry at '**-ly' words.**

9 compound adjectives

Compound adjectives are made up of two or more words, usually written with hyphens between them. They may be graded, ungraded, or colour adjectives.

He was giving a very light-hearted talk.
Olivia was driving a long, low-slung, bottle-green car.
…a good-looking girl.
…a part-time job.

10 position of adjectives

Most adjectives can be used in front of nouns to give more information about something that is mentioned.

She bought a loaf of white bread.
There was no clear evidence.

⚠ **WARNING:** Adjectives cannot usually be used after a determiner without being followed by either a noun or **one**. You cannot say, for example, 'He showed me all of them, but I preferred the large'. You have to say 'He showed me all of them, but I preferred the large one'.

⇨ See **Usage** entry at **one.**

⇨ For information on the use of **the** with an adjective to refer to a group of people, as in **the rich**, see **Usage** entry at **the.**

Most adjectives can also be used after a link verb such as **be**, **become**, **get**, **seem**, or **feel**.

The room was large and square.
I felt angry.
Nobody seemed amused.
He was so exhausted that he could hardly keep awake.

Some adjectives are normally used only as the complement of link verbs, not in front of nouns, when used with a particular meaning. For example, you can say '**She was alone**' but you cannot say 'an alone girl'. The following adjectives are only used after link verbs:

afraid	alive	ashamed	awake	ill	sorry	well
alike	alone	asleep	glad	ready	sure	

There are many other adjectives that are only used after a link verb in one or more of their meanings.
Instead of using these adjectives in front of a noun, you can sometimes use an alternative word or expression. For example, instead of 'the afraid child' you can say '**the frightened child**'.

11 coordination of adjectives

When two adjectives are used as the complement of a link verb, a conjunction (usually **and**) is used to link them. With three or more adjectives, the last two are linked with a conjunction, and commas are put after the others.

The day was hot and dusty.
The house was old, damp and smelly.

When more than one adjective is used in front of a noun, the adjectives are not usually separated by 'and'. You do not normally say 'a short, fat and old man'.

⇨ For more information on how to link adjectives, see **Usage** entry at **and.**

12 order of adjectives

When more than one adjective is used in front of a noun, the usual order is as follows:

GRAMMAR

graded adjective – colour adjective – ungraded adjective

…*a little white wooden house.*
… *rapid technological advance.*
…*a large circular pool of water.*
…*a necklace of blue Venetian beads.*

However, ungraded adjectives indicating shape, such as **circular** and **rectangular**, often come in front of colour adjectives, even though they are ungraded.

…*the rectangular grey stones.*
…*the circular yellow patch on the lawn.*

13 order of graded adjectives

The order of graded adjectives is normally as follows:
opinions – size – quality – age – shape

We shall have a nice big garden with two apple trees.
It had beautiful thick fur.
… *big, shiny beetles.*
He had long curly red hair.
She put on her dirty old fur coat.

(i) Note that when you refer to '**a nice big garden**' or '**a lovely big garden**', you usually mean that the garden is nice because it is big, not nice in some other way.

⇨ See **Usage** entry at **nice**.

14 order of ungraded adjectives

If there is more than one ungraded adjective in front of a noun, the normal order is:
age – shape – nationality – material

…*a medieval French village.*
…*a rectangular plastic box.*
…*an Italian silk jacket.*

Other types of ungraded adjective usually come after a nationality adjective.

…*the Chinese artistic tradition.*
…*the American political system.*

15 comparatives and superlatives

Comparatives and superlatives normally come in front of all other adjectives in a noun group.

Some of the better English actors have gone to live in Hollywood.
These are the highest monthly figures on record.

16 noun modifiers

When a noun group contains both an adjective and a **noun modifier** (a noun used in front of another noun), the adjective is placed in front of the noun modifier.

He works in the French film industry.
He receives a large weekly cash payment.

17 adjectives after a noun

You do not usually put adjectives after nouns. However, there are some exceptions, which are explained below.

You can put an adjective after a noun if the adjective is followed by a prepositional phrase or a 'to'-infinitive clause.

…*a warning to people eager for a quick cure.*
…*the sort of weapons likely to be deployed against it.*

The adjectives **alive** and **awake** can be put after a noun which is preceded by a superlative, an adverb, or **first**, **last**, **only**, **every**, or **any**.

Is Phil Morgan the only man only man alive who knows all the words to that song?
She sat at the window, until she was the last person awake.

A few formal adjectives are only used after a noun:

designate	emeritus	incarnate	par excellence
elect	extraordinaire	manqué	

…*British Rail's* <u>*chairman designate*</u>, *Mr Robert Reid.*
She was now the <u>*president elect.*</u>
Doctors, lawyers and engineers are <u>*professionals par excellence.*</u>

18 adjectives before or after a noun

Some adjectives can be used in front of or after a noun without any change of meaning:

affected	deluxe	payable	suggested
available	enough	required	

Newspapers were the only <u>*available*</u> *source of information.*
…the number of teachers <u>*available.*</u>
I'll do it by <u>*next*</u> *Friday.*
Your account will be posted to you on Thursday <u>*next.*</u>

A few adjectives can be used in front of or after a noun which is preceded by a superlative or **first**, **last**, **only**, **every**, or **any**:

free	necessary	possible	visible
imaginable	open	vacant	

…the best <u>*possible*</u> *environment.*
I said you'd assist him in every way <u>*possible.*</u>

A few adjectives have a different meaning depending on whether they come in front of a noun or after it. For example, '**the concerned mother**' describes a mother who is worried, but '**the mother concerned**' simply refers to a mother who has been mentioned.

…the approval of interested and <u>*concerned*</u> *parents.*
The idea needs to come from the individuals <u>*concerned.*</u>

The following adjectives have different meanings in different positions:

concerned	involved	present	proper	responsible

⇨ For more information, see separate **Usage** entries at these words.

19 adjectives after measurements

Some adjectives that describe size can come after a noun group consisting of a number or determiner and a noun that indicates the unit of measurement. The following adjectives can be used like this:

deep	high	long	square	tall	thick	wide

He was about <u>*six feet tall.*</u>
The island is only <u>*29 miles long.*</u>

Some of these adjectives can also be used after words like **knee**, **ankle** and **waist**:

The grass was <u>*knee high.*</u>
The track ahead was <u>*ankle deep*</u> *in mud.*

⇨ See **Topic** entry at **Measurements.**

'Old' is used after noun groups in a similar way.
⇨ See **Topic** entry at **Age.**

GRAMMAR

20 adjectives with prepositions and other structures

Some adjectives are usually followed by a particular preposition, a 'to'-infinitive, or a 'that'-clause, because otherwise their meaning would be unclear or incomplete. For example, you cannot simply say that someone is 'fond'. You have to say that they are **fond of** something.

They are very <u>fond of</u> each other.
The sky is <u>filled with</u> clouds.

The following lists show some of the adjectives which must be followed by the preposition given when used immediately after a link verb.

accustomed to	conducive to	proportional to	subservient to
adapted to	devoted to	proportionate to	susceptible to
allergic to	impervious to	reconciled to	unaccustomed to
attributable to	injurious to	resigned to	
attuned to	integral to	resistant to	
averse to	prone to	subject to	

He seemed to be becoming <u>accustomed to</u> my presence.
For all her experience, she was still <u>prone to</u> nerves.

aware of	desirous of	illustrative of	reminiscent of
bereft of	devoid of	incapable of	representative of
capable of	fond of	indicative of	
characteristic of	heedless of	mindful of	

Smokers are well <u>aware of</u> the dangers to their own health.
We must be <u>mindful of</u> the consequences of selfishness.

unhampered by	rooted in	conversant with	tinged with
descended from	steeped in	filled with	
inherent in	swathed in	fraught with	
lacking in	contingent on	riddled with	

…the dangers <u>inherent in</u> an outbreak of war.
Her homecoming was <u>tinged with</u> sadness.

In some cases, there is a choice between two prepositions. The following adjectives are usually or always used immediately after a link verb and can be followed by either of the prepositions indicated:

burdened by/with	inclined to/towards	parallel to/with
dependent on/upon	incumbent on/upon	reliant on/upon
immune from/to	intent on/upon	stricken by/with

We are in no way <u>immune from</u> this danger.
He was curiously <u>immune to</u> teasing.

⇨ For lists of adjectives followed by a 'to'-infinitive clause or a 'that'-clause, see **Grammar** entries at '**To'-infinitive clauses** and '**That'-clauses**.

Adjuncts

1	adjuncts and adverbs	11	emphasis
2	manner	12	focus
3	aspect	13	probability
4	opinion	14	position: manner, place, time
5	place	15	putting the adjunct first
6	time	16	position: frequency, probability
7	frequency	17	position: degree, extent
8	duration	18	position: emphasizing
9	degree	19	position: focusing
10	extent		

1 adjuncts and adverbs

It is important to know the difference between **adjuncts** and **adverbs**. **Adjuncts** are words or phrases which give information about when, how, where, or in what circumstances something happens. They have a functional role in a clause. An **adverb**, on the other hand, is a single word that may be used as an adjunct. In fact an adjunct is very often an adverb, but it may also be an adverb group or a prepositional phrase. A few noun groups can also be used as adjuncts.

The main types of adjuncts indicate manner, aspect, opinion, place, time, frequency, duration, degree, extent, emphasis, focus, and probability. These are explained below, and then information is given on the position of adjuncts in a clause.

⇨ For information on adjuncts such as **moreover**, **however**, and **at the same time**, which are used to indicate connections between clauses, see **Grammar** entry at **Linking adjuncts**.

2 manner

Adjuncts of manner are used to describe the way in which something happens or is done. They may be adverbs, adverb groups, or prepositional phrases.

They looked <u>anxiously</u> at each other.
He did not play <u>well enough</u> to win.
She listened <u>with great patience</u> as he told his story.

Adjuncts of manner are usually adverbs of manner. Most of these are formed by adding '**-ly**' to an adjective. For example, the adverbs **quietly** and **badly** are formed by adding '-ly' to the adjectives 'quiet' and 'bad'.

⇨ See **Grammar** entry at **'-ly' words**.

I didn't play <u>badly.</u>
He reported <u>accurately</u> what they had said.

Some adverbs of manner have the same form as adjectives and have similar meanings. These are the ones most commonly used:

direct	hard	loud	right	solo	tight
fast	late	quick	slow	straight	wrong

I've always been interested in <u>fast</u> cars.
The driver was driving too <u>fast.</u>

GRAMMAR

The adverb of manner related to the adjective **good** is **well**.

He is a good dancer.
He dances well.

(i) Note that **well** can also be an adjective describing someone's health.

'How are you?'–'I am very well, thank you.'

3 **aspect**

Not all adverbs ending in **-ly** are adverbs of manner. You use '-ly' adverbs formed from classifying adjectives to make it clear what aspect of something you are talking about. For example, if you want to say that something is important in the field of politics or from a political point of view, you can say that it is '**politically important**'. Here is a list of the most common of these adverbs:

biologically	geographically	politically	statistically
commercially	intellectually	psychologically	technically
economically	logically	racially	visually
emotionally	morally	scientifically	
financially	outwardly	socially	

It would have been politically damaging for him to retreat.
We had a very bad year last year financially.

Speaking is sometimes added to these adverbs. For example, '**technically speaking**' can be used to mean 'from a technical point of view'.

He's not a doctor, technically speaking.
There are some signs of spring, economically speaking, in the latest figures.

4 **opinion**

Other '-ly' adverbs are used as adjuncts to indicate your reaction to, or your opinion of, the fact or event you are talking about. These are sometimes called **sentence adverbs**.

Surprisingly, most of my help came from the technicians.
Luckily, I had seen the play before so I knew what it was about.

⇨ For a list of these adverbs, see **Topic** entry at **Opinions**.

⇨ For information about other small groups of '-ly' adverbs, see **Grammar** entry at **'-ly' words**.

⚠ **WARNING:** Some '-ly' adverbs have a different meaning from adjectives to which they seem to be related. For example, 'hardly' has a different meaning from 'hard'.

This has been a long hard day.
Her bedroom was so small she could hardly move in it.

⇨ For more information, see **Usage** entries at **awful - awfully, bare - barely, hard - hardly, late - lately, scarce - scarcely, short - shortly - briefly,** and **terrible - terribly.**

5 **place**

Adjuncts of place are used to say where something happens or where something goes. Again they are usually adverbs or prepositional phrases.

A plane flew overhead.
The children were playing in the park.
No birds or animals came near the body.

⇨ For information on adjuncts of place, see **Topic** entry at **Places** or **Usage** entries at the individual adverbs and prepositions.

6 **time**

Adjuncts of time are used to say when something happens.

GRAMMAR

She will be here <u>soon.</u>
He was born <u>on 3 April 1925.</u>
Come and see me <u>next week.</u>

⇨ For information on adjuncts of time, see **Topic** entries at **Days and dates** and **Time,** or **Usage** entries at the individual words.

7 **frequency**

Adjuncts of frequency are used to say how often something happens.

Here is a list of adjuncts of frequency, arranged from 'least often' to 'most often':

● **never**

That was a mistake. We'll <u>never</u> do it again.

● **rarely, seldom, hardly ever, not much, infrequently**

I very <u>rarely</u> wear a raincoat because I spend most of my time in a car.
We were <u>seldom</u> at home.
We ate chips every night, but <u>hardly ever</u> had fish.
'Can you hear it where you live?' He shook his head. ' <u>Not much.</u> '
The bridge is used <u>infrequently.</u>

● **occasionally, periodically, intermittently, sporadically, from time to time, now and then, once in a while, every so often**

He still misbehaves <u>occasionally.</u>
Meetings are held <u>periodically</u> to monitor progress on the case.
The talks went on <u>intermittently</u> for three years.
The distant thunder from the coast continued <u>sporadically.</u>
Her daughters visited him <u>from time to time</u> when he was ill.
My father has a collection of magazines to which I return every <u>now and then.</u>
<u>Once in a while</u> she phoned him.
<u>Every so often</u> the horse's heart and lungs are checked.

● **sometimes**

You must have noticed how tired he <u>sometimes</u> looks.

● **often, frequently, regularly, a lot**

They <u>often</u> spent Christmas at Prescott Hill.
Iron and folic acid supplements are <u>frequently</u> given to pregnant women.
He also writes <u>regularly</u> for 'International Management' magazine.
They went out <u>a lot,</u> to the Cafe Royal or the The Ivy.

● **usually, generally, normally**

They ate, as they <u>usually</u> did, in the kitchen.
It is <u>generally</u> true that the darker the fruit the higher its iron content.
<u>Normally,</u> the transportation system in Paris carries 950,000 passengers a day.

● **nearly always**

They <u>nearly always</u> ate outside.

● **always, all the time, constantly, continually**

She's <u>always</u> late for everything.
He was looking at me <u>all the time.</u>
The direction of the wind is <u>constantly</u> changing.
She cried almost <u>continually.</u>

ⓘ Note that **regularly** and **periodically** indicate that something happens at fairly regular intervals. **Intermittently** and **sporadically** indicate that something happens at irregular intervals.

He writes <u>regularly</u> for 'International Management' magazine.
The talks went on <u>intermittently</u> for three years.

GRAMMAR

GRAMMAR

8 duration

Adjuncts of duration are used to say how long something takes or lasts.

Here is a list of adverbs used as adjuncts of duration, arranged from 'least long' to 'longest':

● **briefly**

Guerillas captured and <u>briefly</u> held an important provincial capital.

● **temporarily**

The peace agreement has at least <u>temporarily</u> halted the civil war.

● **long**

Repairs to the cable did not take too <u>long</u>.

● **indefinitely**

I couldn't stay there <u>indefinitely</u>.

● **always, permanently, forever**

We will <u>always</u> remember his generous hospitality.
The only way to lose weight <u>permanently</u> is to completely change your attitudes toward food.
I think that we will live together <u>forever</u>.

(*i*) Note that **long** is normally used only in questions and negative sentences.

Have you known her <u>long</u>?
I can't stay <u>long</u>.

9 degree

Adjuncts of degree are used to indicate the degree or intensity of a state or action.

The following is a list of adverbs which are used as adjuncts of degree and are used with verbs. They are arranged from 'very low degree' to 'very high degree'.

● **little**

On their way back to Marseille, they spoke very <u>little</u>.

● **a bit, a little, slightly**

This girl was <u>a bit</u> strange.
He complained <u>a little</u> of a nagging pain between his shoulder blades.
Each person learns in a <u>slightly</u> different way.

● **rather, fairly, quite, somewhat, sufficiently, adequately, moderately, pretty**

I'm afraid it's <u>rather</u> a long story.
Both ships are <u>fairly</u> new.
I was <u>quite</u> a long way away, on the terrace.
A recent public opinion survey has come up with <u>somewhat</u> surprising results.
She recovered <u>sufficiently</u> to accompany Chou on his tour of Africa in 1964.
I speak the language <u>adequately</u>.
…a <u>moderately</u> attractive woman.
I had a <u>pretty</u> good idea what she was going to do.

● **significantly, noticeably**

The number of MPs now supporting him had increased <u>significantly</u>.
Standards of living were deteriorating rather <u>noticeably</u>.

● **very much, a lot, a great deal, really, heavily, greatly, strongly, considerably, extensively, badly, dearly, deeply, hard, soundly, well**

I love my family <u>very much</u>.
I like you <u>a lot</u>.
He depended <u>a great deal</u> on his wife for support.
They were <u>really</u> nice people.
It has been raining <u>heavily</u> all day.
People would benefit <u>greatly</u> from a pollution-free vehicle.
He is <u>strongly</u> influenced by Spanish painters such as Goya and El Greco.

Children vary <u>considerably</u> in the rate at which they learn these lessons.
All these issues have been <u>extensively</u> researched in recent years.
The bomb destroyed a police station and <u>badly</u> damaged a church.
I would <u>dearly</u> love to marry.
Our meetings and conversations left me <u>deeply</u> depressed.
It was snowing <u>hard</u> by then.
Duke was <u>soundly</u> defeated in this month's Louisiana governor's race.
Wash your hands <u>well</u> with soap.

● **remarkably, enormously, intensely, profoundly, immensely, tremendously, hugely, severely, radically, drastically**

For his age, he was in <u>remarkably</u> good shape.
Blackwell is 59, strong looking and <u>enormously</u> energetic.
The fast-food business is <u>intensely</u> competitive.
This has <u>profoundly</u> affected my life.
I enjoyed this movie <u>immensely</u>.
The business is <u>tremendously</u> profitable.
…a <u>hugely</u> successful businessman.
The UN wants to send food aid to 10 countries in Africa <u>severely</u> affected by the drought.
…two large groups of people with <u>radically</u> different beliefs and cultures.
As a result, services have been <u>drastically</u> reduced.

ⓘ Note that **quite** can also be used to indicate completeness or to emphasize a verb.

⇨ See **Usage** entry at **quite.**

Some of these adverbs are used with only one verb or with a restricted set of verbs, as shown in the examples below.

We <u>love</u> him <u>dearly</u>.
I should <u>dearly like</u> to meet her.
The corn ration was <u>drastically reduced</u>.
Our attitude to the land itself must be <u>radically changed</u>.
He protested that he had not touched it, but was disbelieved and <u>soundly beaten</u>.

⇨ For information on the use of adverbs of degree in front of adjectives and other adverbs, see section at **grading adverbs** in **Grammar** entry at **Adverbs.**

10 **extent**
Adjuncts of extent are used to indicate the extent to which something happens or is true.
The following is a list of adverbs which are used as adjuncts of extent and are used with verbs. They are arranged from 'smallest extent' to 'greatest extent'.

● **partly, partially**
It's <u>partly</u> my fault.
Lisa is deaf in one ear and <u>partially</u> blind.

● **largely**
His appeals have been <u>largely</u> ignored.

● **almost, nearly, practically, virtually**
The couple have been dating for <u>almost</u> three years.
The beach was <u>nearly</u> empty.
He'd known the old man <u>practically</u> all his life.
It would have been <u>virtually</u> impossible to research all the information.

● **completely, entirely, totally, quite, fully, perfectly, altogether, utterly**
Dozens of flats had been <u>completely</u> destroyed.
…an <u>entirely</u> new approach.
The fire <u>totally</u> destroyed the top floor.

Her sense of humour is <u>quite</u> different from her mother's.
I don't <u>fully</u> agree with that.
They are <u>perfectly</u> safe to eat.
When Artie stopped calling <u>altogether</u>, Julie found a new man.
The new laws coming in are <u>utterly</u> ridiculous.

11 emphasis

Emphasizing adjuncts add emphasis to the action described by a verb. They are always adverbs. The following adverbs are used to add emphasis:

absolutely	just	quite	simply
certainly	positively	really	totally

I <u>quite</u> agree.
I <u>simply</u> adore this flat.

Some emphasizing adverbs are used to emphasize adjectives.
⇨ See **Grammar** entry at **Adverbs.**

12 focus

Focusing adjuncts are used to indicate the main thing involved in a situation. They are always adverbs. The following is a list of adverbs that can be used like this:

chiefly	mostly	predominantly	specially
especially	notably	primarily	specifically
mainly	particularly	principally	

I'm <u>particularly</u> interested in classical music.
We want <u>especially</u> to thank the numerous friends who encouraged us.

Some focusing adverbs can be used to emphasize that only one thing is involved in what you are saying. The following adverbs can be used like this:

alone	just	purely	solely
exclusively	only	simply	

This is <u>solely</u> a matter of money.
It's a large canvas covered with <u>just</u> one colour.

The adverbs of extent **largely, partly**, and **entirely** can be used to focus on additional information.
The house was cheap <u>partly</u> because it was falling down.

Adverbs of frequency such as **usually** and **often** can also be used like this.
They often fought each other, <u>usually</u> as a result of arguments over money.

13 probability

Adjuncts of probability are used to indicate how certain you are about something.
The following adverbs and adverb groups are used to indicate probability or certainty. They are arranged from 'least certain' to 'most certain'.

● **conceivably**
The mission could <u>conceivably</u> be accomplished within a week.

● **possibly**
Exercise will not only lower blood pressure but <u>possibly</u> protect against heart attacks.

● **perhaps, maybe**
Millson regarded her thoughtfully. <u>Perhaps</u> she was right.
<u>Maybe</u> she is in love.

● **hopefully**

Hopefully, you won't have any problems after reading this.

● **probably**

Van Gogh is probably the best-known painter in the world.

● **presumably**

He had gone to the reception desk, presumably to check out.

● **almost certainly**

The bombs are almost certainly part of a much bigger conspiracy.

● **no doubt, doubtless**

She's a very sweet woman, as you no doubt know by now.
He will doubtless try and persuade his colleagues to change their minds.

● **definitely**

I'm definitely going to get in touch with these people.

14 **position: manner, place, time**

Adjuncts of manner, place, and time usually come after the main verb. If the verb has an object, the adjunct comes after the object.

She sang beautifully.
Thomas made his decision immediately.

If more than one of these adjuncts is used in a clause, the usual order is manner, then place, then time.

They were sitting quite happily in the car.
She spoke very well at the village hall last night.

If the object of the verb is a long one, the adjunct is sometimes put in front of it.

He could picture all too easily the consequences of being found by the owners.
Later I discovered in a shop in Monmouth a weekly magazine about horse-riding.

You can also put an adverb of manner in front of the main verb.

He carefully wrapped each component in several layers of foam rubber.
Dixon swiftly decided to back down.
He silently counted four, then put the receiver down.

Adverbs of manner are rarely put in front of the verb if the verb would then be the last word in the clause. For example, you would say, 'She listened carefully'. You would not say 'She carefully listened'. However, sentences such as 'Smith gladly obliged', where the adverb describes the attitude of the subject, are possible in stories and formal speech.

I gladly gave in.
His uncle readily agreed.

If the verb group contains one or more auxiliaries, you can put the adverb of manner in front of the main verb or after the first auxiliary, especially if that auxiliary is a modal.

I felt that the historical background had been very carefully researched.
She had carefully measured out his dose of medicine.
Still, Brody thought, one death would probably be quickly forgotten.
Provided you are known to us, arrangements can quickly be made to reimburse you.

ⓘ Note that adverbs which indicate how well something is done go after the object of the verb if there is one. If there is no object, they go after the verb.

Teddy did everything perfectly.
You played well.

If the verb is in the passive voice, the adverb can also go in front of the verb, after any auxiliaries.

I had been well conditioned by the world in which I grew up.
In the sharp blacks and whites from the midday sun Bond was well camouflaged.

GRAMMAR

Most adverbs of manner which do not end in '-ly', for example **hard** and **loud**, are only used after verbs or the objects of verbs.

You work <u>too hard.</u>

The exception is **fast**, which is also used in front of the present participles of verbs in continuous tenses.

We are <u>fast</u> becoming a nation fed entirely on canned and processed food.

If the adjunct is a prepositional phrase, it is usually put at the end of the clause, not in front of the verb. For example, you say 'He looked at her in a strange way'. You do not say 'He in a strange way looked at her'.

One consequence is that the horse's incisor teeth become worn down <u>in an unusual way.</u>
He had been brought up through each level <u>in the proper manner.</u>
It just fell out <u>by accident.</u>

15 putting the adjunct first

In stories and descriptive accounts, adjuncts of manner are sometimes put at the beginning of a sentence. This position gives the adjunct more emphasis.

<u>Gently</u> I took hold of Mary's wrists to ease her arms away.
<u>Slowly</u> people began to desert the campaign.
<u>With a sigh,</u> he rose and walked away.

Similarly, adjuncts of time and duration are often placed first in accounts of events.

<u>At eight o'clock</u> I went down for my breakfast.
<u>In 1937</u> he retired.
<u>For years</u> I'd had to hide what I was thinking.

Adjuncts of place are often put first when describing a scene or telling a story, or when contrasting what happens in one place with what happens in another.

<u>In the kitchen</u> there was a message for him from his son.
<u>In Paris</u> there was a massive wave of student riots.

ⓘ Note that in the following two examples, inversion occurs: that is, the verb is put in front of the subject.

<u>At the very top of the steps</u> was a bust of Shakespeare on a pedestal.
She rang the bell for Sylvia. <u>In</u> came a girl she had not seen before.

Inversion does not occur when the subject is a pronoun.

Off <u>they ran.</u>

⚠ **WARNING:** You cannot use a pronoun and 'be' after an adjunct. For example, you cannot say 'At the top of the steps it was'. You say 'It was at the top of the steps'. When negative adjuncts are put first, inversion occurs even when the subject is a pronoun.

<u>Never</u> have so few been commanded by so many.
<u>On no account</u> must they be let in.

⇨ See **Grammar** entry at **Inversion.**

Adjuncts which indicate your opinion are sentence adverbs. They are usually put first in a sentence.

⇨ See **Topic** entry at **Opinions.**

16 position: frequency, probability

Adjuncts of frequency and probability are often put after the first auxiliary, if there is one, or in front of the main verb. They are usually adverbs.

Landlords have <u>usually</u> been able to evade land reform.
Women are <u>often</u> encouraged to do the jobs that don't particularly interest men.
They can <u>probably</u> afford another one.
This <u>sometimes</u> led to trouble.

GRAMMAR

They can also be put first in a clause.

Sometimes people expect you to do more than is reasonable.
Presumably they'd brought him home and he'd invited them in.

They are put after the link verb **be** when there is no auxiliary.

They are usually right.
He was definitely scared.

(i) Note that adverbs of probability are put in front of negative contractions such as **don't** and **won't**.

They definitely don't want their girls breaking the rules.
He probably doesn't really want them at all.
It probably won't be that bad.

Maybe and **perhaps** are usually put first in a clause.

Maybe I ought to go back there.
Perhaps they just wanted to warn us off.

17 position: degree, extent

Some adverbs of degree and extent usually come in front of the main verb. If there are auxiliaries, they can come after the first auxiliary or in front of the main verb. The following adverbs are used like this:

almost	nearly	really	virtually
largely	rather	quite	

He almost crashed into a lorry.
She really enjoyed the party.
So far we have largely been looking at the new societies from the inside.
This finding has been largely ignored.

Other adverbs of degree and extent can come in front of the main verb, after the main verb, or after the object (if there is one). The following adverbs are used like this:

badly	greatly	little	severely	totally
completely	heavily	seriously	strongly	

Mr Brooke strongly criticized the Bank of England.
I disagree completely with John Taylor.
That argument doesn't convince me totally.

Some adjuncts of degree are always or nearly always used after a verb or the object of a verb. They are usually adverbs. The following adverbs and adverb groups are used like this:

a bit	a lot	immensely	terribly
a great deal	hard	moderately	tremendously
a little	hugely	remarkably	

The audience enjoyed it hugely.
I missed you terribly.
Annual budgets varied tremendously.

18 position: emphasizing

Emphasizing adjuncts usually come after the subject, after an auxiliary, or after **be**. They are always adverbs.

I absolutely agree.
I would just hate to have a daughter like her.
That kind of money is simply not available.

GRAMMAR

ⓘ Note that they are put in front of negative contractions such as **don't** and **won't**.

It just can't be done.
That simply isn't true.

19 position: focusing

Focusing adjuncts are generally put after the first auxiliary or in front of the main verb, or in front of the words you are focusing on. They are always adverbs.

Up to now, the law has mainly had a negative role in this area.
This at least told him what he chiefly wanted to know.
I survive mainly by pleasing others.

If the verb is **be**, the focusing adverb is put after **be** if there is no auxiliary.

Economic development is primarily a question of getting more work done.

The focusing adverbs **alone** and **only** can be put in other positions in a clause.

⇨ See **Usage** entries at **alone- lonely** and **only**.

⚠ **WARNING:** You do not usually use an adjunct to separate a verb from its object. You do not say, for example, 'I like very much English'. You say 'I like English very much'.

Adverbs

An adverb is a word that gives information about how, when, where, or in what circumstances something happens. For example, **quickly**, **well**, **now**, and **here** are adverbs.

Sit there quietly, and listen to this music.
Everything we used was bought locally.

⇨ For full information on the different types of adverbs used to give information about events and situations, see **Grammar** entry at **Adjuncts**.

1 grading adverbs

Some **adverbs of degree** can be used in front of adjectives and other adverbs. When adverbs of degree are used in this way they are called **grading adverbs.**

…a rather clumsy person.
…an extremely disappointed young man.
He prepared his speech very carefully.
We were able to hear everything pretty clearly.

Grading adverbs which are used in front of an adjective to reinforce it and make it more emphatic are sometimes called **intensifiers.** The following adverbs are intensifiers:

awfully	extremely	horribly	remarkably
dreadfully	greatly	incredibly	terribly
exceptionally	highly	really	very

They're awfully brave.
The other girls were dreadfully dull.

ⓘ Note that **greatly** is only used in front of adjectives ending in **-ed** and the adjectives **different** and **superior**.

He was not greatly surprised to learn that she had left.

The following grading adverbs indicate a small or moderate degree of a quality. They are arranged from 'low degree' to 'higher degree'.

● **faintly**

She felt faintly ridiculous.

● **a bit, a little, slightly**

I think people feel a bit more confident.

GRAMMAR

We were a little late.
I couldn't help feeling slightly disappointed.

● **rather, quite, fairly, somewhat, relatively, moderately**

I'm afraid it's rather a long story.
I felt quite bitter about it at the time.
Both ships are fairly new.
He explained somewhat unconvincingly that the company was paying for everything.
I like to think I'm relatively easy to get along with.
…a moderately attractive woman.

● **reasonably**

I can dance reasonably well.

● **pretty**

I had a pretty good idea what she was going to do.

ⓘ Note that **quite** can also be used to emphasize adjectives.

⇨ See **Usage** entry at **quite**.

A bit and **a little** can only be used in front of an adjective when the adjective is being used after a verb such as **be**. You cannot use them with an adjective that is in front of a noun. For example, you say 'It was a bit unpleasant', but you do not say 'It was a bit unpleasant experience'.

⇨ See **Usage** entries at **bit** and **little - a little**.

You use emphasizing adverbs to modify adjectives such as **astonishing**, **furious**, and **wonderful** which indicate an extreme degree of a quality.

…a quite astonishing ignorance of human nature.
I think he's absolutely wonderful.

The following emphasizing adverbs are used in front of adjectives:

absolutely	completely	perfectly	simply	utterly
altogether	entirely	quite	totally	

Purely is used in front of ungraded adjectives and noun group complements to indicate that something is of only one kind. It is not used in front of graded adjectives.

The action had been purely instinctive.
…something that appears at first glimpse to be a purely local issue.

2 **adding to a description**

In writing, adverbs formed from graded adjectives can be used in front of an adjective to add to a description of someone or something. For example, if someone is confident and cool, you can describe them as **coolly confident**.

…her nervously polite manner.
…these proudly individual characters.
…a beautifully sunny day.

Auxiliaries

1 **forms and uses**

An **auxiliary** or **auxiliary verb** is a verb that is used with a main verb to form a verb group. The auxiliaries **be** and **have** are used to form tenses. **Be** is also used to form passive verb groups. The auxiliary **do** is most commonly used in questions and negative clauses.

I am feeling reckless tonight.
They have been looking for you.
Thirteen people were killed.

GRAMMAR

Did you see him?
I do not remember her.

⇒ See **Grammar** entries at **Tenses** and **Questions**, and **Usage** entry at **not**.

⇒ See **Usage** entry at **do** for the use of **do** to emphasize or focus on an action.

You put the auxiliaries you want to use in the following order: **have** (for perfect tenses), **be** (for continuous tenses), **be** (for the passive voice).

Twenty-eight flights have been cancelled.
Three broad strategies are being adopted.

⚠ **WARNING:** You do not use the auxiliary **do** in combination with other auxiliaries.

Auxiliaries are often used without a main verb when the verb has already been used.

I didn't want to go but a friend of mine did.
'Have you been there before?'–'Yes, I have. '

⇒ See **Grammar** entry at **Ellipsis** and **Topic** entry at **Replies**.

The different forms of the auxiliaries **be**, **have**, and **do** are shown in the following table.

	be	have	do
Simple present:			
with **I**	am	have	do
with **you**, **we**, **they** and plural noun groups	are		
with **he**, **she**, **it** and singular noun groups	is	has	does
Simple past:			
with **I**, **he**, **she**, **it** and singular noun groups	was	had	did
with **you**, **we**, **they** and plural noun groups	were		
Participles:			
present participle	being	having	doing
past participle	been	had	done

2 modals

Modals, such as **can**, **should**, **might**, and **may**, are also auxiliary verbs. You put them in front of all other auxiliaries.

The law will be changed.
She must have been dozing.

⇒ For more information, see **Grammar** entry at **Modals**.

3 contractions

⇒ For information on the contracted forms of auxiliaries, see **Grammar** entry at **Contractions**.

Broad negatives

1 broad negatives

A **broad negative** is one of a small group of words which are used to make a statement almost negative.

We were scarcely able to move.
Fathers and sons very seldom now go together to football matches.

The five broad negatives are:

barely	hardly	rarely	scarcely	seldom

GRAMMAR

The position of broad negatives within a clause is similar to that of 'never'.

⇒ See **Usage** entry at **never**.

2 with 'any' words

If you want to say that there is very little of something, you can use a broad negative with **any** or with a word which begins with 'any-'.

There is <u>rarely any</u> difficulty in finding enough food.
<u>Hardly anybody</u> came.

3 'almost'

Instead of using a broad negative, you can use **almost** followed by a negative word such as **no** or **never**. For example, 'There was almost no food left' means the same as 'There was hardly any food left'.

They've <u>almost no</u> money for anything.
Some men <u>almost never</u> begin conversations.

⇒ For information on other uses of **almost**, see **Usage** entry at **almost - nearly**.

4 tag questions

If you make a **tag question** out of a statement that contains a broad negative, the tag at the end of the statement is normally positive, as it is with other negatives.

She's hardly the right person for the job, <u>is she?</u>
You seldom see that sort of thing these days, <u>do you?</u>

⇒ For more information on the meanings and use of some of these broad negatives, see **Usage** entries at **bare - barely, hard - hardly, scarce - scarcely,** and **seldom**.

Clauses

A **clause** is a group of words containing a verb. A **simple sentence** has one clause.

I waited.
She married a young engineer.

1 main clauses

A **compound sentence** has two or more **main clauses** – that is, clauses which refer to two separate actions or situations which are equally important. Clauses in compound sentences are joined with **a coordinating conjunction** such as **and, but**, and **or**.

He met Jane at the station <u>and</u> they went shopping.
I wanted to go <u>but</u> I felt too ill.
You can come now <u>or</u> you can meet us there later.

(*i*) Note that the subject of the second clause can be omitted if it is the same as that of the first clause.

I wrote to him but received no reply.

2 subordinate clauses

A **complex sentence** contains a **subordinate clause** and at least one main clause. A subordinate clause gives more information about a main clause, and is introduced by a conjunction such as **because, if, whereas that,** or a **wh**-word. Subordinate clauses can come in front of, after, or inside the main clause.

<u>When he stopped,</u> no one said anything.
They were going by car <u>because it was more comfortable.</u>
I said <u>that I should like to come.</u>
My brother, <u>who lives in New York,</u> is visiting us next week.

⇒ See **Grammar** entries at **Subordinate clauses** and **Relative clauses**.
⇒ For more information on 'that'-clauses and 'wh'-clauses used after reporting verbs, see **Grammar** entry at **Reporting**.

3 finite clauses

Finite clause always indicate the time at which something happened; they have a tense.

I <u>went</u> there last year.
<u>Did</u> you see him?

4 non-finite clauses
A **non-finite clause** is a subordinate clause which is based on a participle or an infinitive. Non-finite clauses do not show the time at which something happened; they have no tense.

Quite often <u>while talking to you</u> they'd stand on one foot.
He pranced about <u>feeling very important indeed.</u>
I wanted <u>to talk to her.</u>

⇨ See **Grammar** entries at **'-ing' forms, Past participles**, and **'To'-infinitive clauses.**

Comparative and superlative adjectives

1 comparative adjectives	**11** another use of 'most'
2 superlative adjectives	**12** 'more or less'
3 forming comparative and superlative adjectives	**13** using comparatives
	14 comparatives with 'than'
4 two syllables	**15** linked comparatives
5 three or more syllables	**16** using superlatives
6 irregular forms	**17** indicating group or place
7 'little'	**18** 'of all'
8 'ill'	**19** with ordinal numbers
9 colour adjectives	**20** comparison with 'less' and 'least'
10 compound adjectives	

1 comparative adjectives
Comparative adjectives are used to indicate that something has more of a quality than something else, or more than it used to have. The comparative of an adjective is formed by adding '**-er**', as in 'smaller', or by putting **more** in front of the adjective, as in 'more interesting'.

…the battle for <u>safer</u> and <u>healthier</u> working environments.
Current diesel engines are <u>more efficient</u> than petrol engines in terms of miles per gallon.

2 superlative adjectives
Superlative adjectives are used to indicate that something has more of a quality than anything else of its kind, or more than anything else in a particular group or place. The superlative of an adjective is formed by adding '**-est**', as in 'smallest', or by putting **most** in front of the adjective, as in 'most interesting'. Superlatives are usually preceded by **the**.

…the <u>oldest</u> building in the city.
A house or a self-contained flat is the <u>most suitable</u> type of accommodation for a family.

⚠ **WARNING:** In conversation, people often use a superlative rather than a comparative when they are comparing just two things. For example, someone might say 'The train is quickest' rather than 'The train is quicker' when comparing a train service with a bus service. However, you should not use a superlative like this in formal writing.

3 forming comparative and superlative adjectives
The choice between adding '**-er**' and '**-est**' or using **more** and **most** usually depends on the number of syllables in the adjective.

With one-syllable adjectives, you usually add '**-er**' and '**-est**' to the end of the adjective.

tall → **taller** → **tallest**   **quick** → **quicker** → **quickest**

If the adjective ends in a single vowel letter and a single consonant letter, you double the consonant letter (unless the consonant is 'w').

big → **bigger** → **biggest**   **fat** → **fatter** → **fattest**

If the adjective ends in 'e', you remove the 'e'.

rare → **rarer** → **rarest**   **wide** → **wider** → **widest**

Dry usually has the comparative **drier** and the superlative **driest**. However, with the other one-syllable adjectives ending in 'y' (**shy**, **sly**, and **spry**), you do not change the 'y' to 'i' before adding '-er' and '-est'.

4 two syllables

You also add '**-er**' and '**-est**' to two-syllable adjectives ending in 'y', such as **angry**, **dirty**, and **silly**. You change the 'y' to 'i'.

dirty → **dirtier** → **dirtiest**   **happy** → **happier** → **happiest**
easy → **easier** → **easiest**

Other two-syllable adjectives usually have comparatives and superlatives formed with **more** and **most**. However, **clever** and **quiet** have comparatives and superlatives formed by adding '**-er**' and '**-est**'.
Some two-syllable adjectives have both kinds of comparative and superlative.
I can think of many <u>pleasanter</u> subjects.
It was <u>more pleasant</u> here than in the lecture room.
Exposure to sunlight is one of the <u>commonest</u> causes of cancer.
…five hundred of the <u>most common</u> words.

Here is a list of common adjectives which have both kinds of comparative and superlative:

angry	cruel	likely	pleasant	shallow
busy	gentle	mature	polite	simple
clever	handsome	narrow	quiet	stupid
common	hungry	obscure	remote	subtle

Bitter has the superlative form **bitterest** as well as **most bitter**. **Tender** has the superlative form **tenderest** as well as **most tender**.

5 three or more syllables

Adjectives which have three or more syllables usually have comparatives and superlatives with **more** and **most**.

dangerous → **more dangerous** → **most dangerous**
ridiculous → **more ridiculous** → **most ridiculous**

However, this does not apply to three-syllable adjectives formed by adding '**un-**' to the beginning of other adjectives, for example **unhappy** and **unlucky**. These adjectives have comparatives and superlatives formed by adding '-er' and '-est' as well as ones formed by using **more** and **most**.
He felt crosser and <u>unhappier</u> than ever.
He may be <u>more unhappy</u> seeing you occasionally.

6 irregular forms

A few common adjectives have irregular comparative and superlative forms.

bad → **worse** → **worst**   **far** → **farther/further** → **farthest/furthest**
good → **better** → **best**   **old** → **older/elder** → **oldest/eldest**

GRAMMAR

⇨ See **Usage** entries at **farther - further** and **elder- eldest - older - oldest** for more information on the forms of **far** and **old**.

7 'little'

There is no comparative or superlative of **little** in standard English. To make a comparison, **smaller** and **smallest** are used.

8 'ill'

Ill does not have a comparative or superlative form. When you want to use a comparative, you use **worse**.

Each day Kunta felt a little <u>worse.</u>

9 colour adjectives

Usually only graded adjectives have comparatives and superlatives, but a few basic colour adjectives also have these forms.

His face was <u>redder</u> than usual.
…some of the <u>greenest</u> scenery in America.

10 compound adjectives

The comparatives and superlatives of compound adjectives are usually formed by putting **more** and **most** in front of the adjective.

nerve-racking → more nerve-racking → most nerve-racking

Some compound adjectives have as their first part adjectives or adverbs with single-word comparatives and superlatives. The comparatives and superlatives of these compounds sometimes use these single-word forms, rather than 'more' and 'most'.

good-looking → better-looking → best-looking
well-known → better-known → best-known

The following compound adjectives have comparatives or superlatives using single-word forms:

good-looking	long-lasting	low-paid	well-behaved	well-known
high-paid	long-standing	short-lived	well-dressed	well-off

11 another use of 'most'

Most can also be used in front of some adjectives to mean 'very'.

This book was <u>most interesting.</u>
My grandfather was a <u>most extraordinary</u> man.

⇨ See **Usage** entry at **most**.

12 'more or less'

The expression **more or less** is used in front of adjectives (and other words) to indicate that something is almost the case. It does not indicate a comparison.

The basic federal organization remained <u>more or less intact.</u>
I had gradually become <u>more or less immune</u> to feeling of every kind.

13 using comparatives

Comparatives can be used in front of nouns or as complements after link verbs.

Their demands for a <u>bigger</u> defence budget were refused.
To the <u>brighter, more advanced</u> child, they will be challenging.
Be <u>more careful</u> next time.
His breath became <u>quieter.</u>

Comparatives normally come in front of all other adjectives in a noun group.

Some of the <u>better</u> English actors have gone to live in Hollywood.

Comparative and superlative adjectives

14 **comparatives with 'than'**

Comparatives are often followed by **than** and a noun group or clause, to specify the other thing involved in the comparison.

My brother is younger <u>than me.</u>
I was a better writer <u>than he was.</u>
I would have done a better job <u>than he did.</u>

15 **linked comparatives**

You can indicate that the amount of one quality or thing is linked to the amount of another quality or thing by using two comparatives preceded by **the**.

<u>The larger</u> the organization, <u>the less</u> scope there is for decision.
<u>The earlier</u> you detect a problem, <u>the easier</u> it is to cure.

(i) Note that you can use comparative adjectives or adverbs in this structure. You can also use **more**, **less**, and **fewer**.

16 **using superlatives**

Superlatives can be used in front of nouns, or as complements after link verbs.

He was the <u>cleverest</u> man I ever knew.
Now we come to the <u>most important</u> thing.
He was the <u>youngest.</u>

Superlatives normally come in front of all other adjectives in a noun group.

These are the <u>highest</u> monthly figures on record.

You usually put **the** in front of a superlative. However, 'the' is omitted after a link verb when the comparison does not involve a group of things. It is also sometimes omitted in conversation or informal writing when comparing a group of things.

Beef is <u>nicest</u> slightly underdone.
Wool and cotton blankets are generally <u>cheapest.</u>

⚠ **WARNING:** You cannot omit **the** when the superlative is followed by a structure indicating what group of things you are comparing. For example, you cannot say 'Amanda was youngest of our group'. You must say 'Amanda was **the** youngest of our group'. You can use possessive determiners and nouns with **'s** instead of 'the' in front of a superlative.

… <u>the school's</u> most famous headmaster.
… <u>my</u> newest assistant.

17 **indicating group or place**

You can use a superlative on its own if it is clear what is being compared. However, if you need to indicate the group or place involved, you use:

● a prepositional phrase, normally beginning with **of** for a group or **in** for a place

Henry was the biggest <u>of them.</u>
These cakes are probably the best <u>in the world.</u>
…one of the worst deserts <u>in Australia.</u>

● a relative clause

The visiting room was the worst <u>I had seen.</u>
That's the most convincing answer <u>that you've given me.</u>

● an adjective ending in '**-ible**' or '**-able**'

…the longest <u>possible</u> gap.
…the most beautiful scenery <u>imaginable.</u>

18 **'of all'**

If you want to emphasize that something has more of a quality than anything else of its kind or in its group, you can use **of all** after a superlative adjective.

GRAMMAR

The third requirement is the most important <u>of all.</u>
We are unlikely yet to have discovered the oldest fossils <u>of all.</u>

19 **with ordinal numbers**

Ordinal numbers, such as **second**, are used with superlatives to say that something has more of a quality than nearly all other things of its kind or in its group. For example, if you say that a mountain is 'the second highest mountain in the world', you mean that it is higher than any other mountain except the highest one.

…Mobil, the <u>second biggest</u> industrial company in the United States.
It is Japan's <u>third largest</u> city.

20 **comparison with 'less' and 'least'**

To indicate that something does not have as much of a quality as something else or as it had before, you can use **less** in front of an adjective.

⇨ See **Usage** entry at **less**.

The cliffs here were <u>less high</u>.
As the days went by, Sita became <u>less anxious.</u>

To indicate that something has less of a quality than anything else or less than anything in a particular group or place, you use **least** in front of an adjective.

This is the <u>least popular</u> branch of medicine.

Comparative and superlative adverbs

Comparative and superlative adverbs are used to say how something happens or is done compared with how it happened or was done on a different occasion. They are also used to say how something is done by one person or thing compared with how it is done by someone or something else.

1 **forming comparative and superlative adverbs**

The comparative of an adverb is usually formed by putting **more** in front of the adverb.

He began to speak <u>more quickly</u>.
The people needed business skills so that they could manage themselves <u>more effectively.</u>

The superlative of an adverb is usually formed by putting **most** in front of the adverb.

You are likely to have bills which can <u>most easily</u> be paid by post.
The country <u>most severely</u> affected was Holland.

2 **single-word forms**

Some very common adverbs have comparatives and superlatives that are single words and are not formed using 'more' and 'most'. The comparative and superlative forms of **well** are **better** and **best**.

…when I got to know him <u>better.</u>
Why don't you go back to doing what you do <u>best</u>?

The usual comparative and superlative forms of **badly** are **worse** and **worst**.

Socially, my wife fares <u>worse</u> than I do.
Those in the poorest groups are <u>worst</u> hit.

However, **badly** has a special meaning for which the comparative and superlative are **more badly** and **most badly**.

⇨ See **Usage** entry at **bad - badly**.

Adverbs which have the same form as adjectives have the same comparatives and superlatives as the adjectives. The following words have the same comparative and superlative forms whether they are used as adverbs or adjectives:

close	far	long	near	straight
deep	fast	loud	quick	tight
early	hard	low	slow	wide

GRAMMAR

They worked <u>harder,</u> they were more honest.
The person who sang <u>loudest</u> took the rest of us with him.

The adverb **late** has the comparative form **later**, and the adverb **soon** has the comparative form **sooner**. The superlative forms are **latest** and **soonest**.

3 **'the' with superlatives**

It is possible to use **the** with single-word superlative adverbs, but this use is not common.

The old people work <u>the hardest.</u>
Sports in general are about who can run <u>the fastest.</u>

Comparison

You can use **comparative adjectives** or **comparative adverbs** to say that something has more of a quality than something else, or more than it used to have.

The climbing became <u>more difficult.</u>
I thought I could deal with it <u>better than Ivan.</u>

⇨ See **Grammar** entries at **Comparative and superlative adjectives** and **Comparative and superlative adverbs**.

It is also possible to make comparisons using words and structures which indicate that something is the same as something else or is done in the same way.

Once she returned to Woodland, life went on very much <u>as</u> before.
You're just <u>as bad as</u> your sister.
He looked <u>like</u> an actor.
Their life expectancy is about <u>the same as</u> ours.

⇨ See **Usage** entries at **as, as … as, like - as - the way**, and **same - similar**.

Complements

A **complement** is an adjective or noun group which comes after a link verb such as **be**, and gives more information about the subject of the clause.

The children seemed <u>frightened.</u>
He is <u>a geologist.</u>

⇨ There are also complements which describe the object of a clause: see the section below on **object complements**.

1 **adjectives as complements**

Adjectives or **adjective groups** can be used as complements after the following link verbs:

appear	come	get	keep	prove	smell	taste
be	feel	go	look	remain	sound	turn
become	find	grow	pass	seem	stay	

We were <u>very happy.</u>
The other child looked <u>a bit neglected.</u>
Their hall was <u>larger than his whole flat.</u>
She looked <u>worried.</u>
It smells <u>nice.</u>

⚠ **WARNING:** You do not use an adverb after a link verb. For example, you say 'We felt very happy', not 'We felt very happily'.

Come, go, and **turn** are used with a restricted range of adjectives.

⇨ For more information on this, and on the use of **get** and **grow**, see **Usage** entry at **become**.

2 noun groups as complements

Noun groups can be used as complements after the following link verbs:

be	constitute	look	remain	sound
become	feel	make	represent	
comprise	form	prove	seem	

He always seemed _a controlled sort of man._
He'll make _a good president._
I feel _a bit of a fraud._

(_i_) Note that when you are saying what someone's job is, you use **a** or **an**. You do not just use the noun. For example, you say 'She's **a** journalist'. You do not say ~~'She's journalist'~~.

3 pronouns as complements

Pronouns are sometimes used as complements to indicate identity or to describe something.

It's _me_ again.
This one is _yours._
You're _someone who does what she wants._

4 'to'-infinitive clauses

⇨ For information on the use of 'to'-infinitives after complements, as in 'It's an easy mistake to make', see **Grammar** entry at **'To'-infinitive clauses.**

5 other verbs with complements

A small number of verbs which refer to actions and processes can be followed by complements. For example, instead of saying 'He returned. He had not been harmed', you can say 'He returned unharmed'. The following verbs can be used with a complement like this:

arrive	die	escape	hang	return	stand	survive
be born	emerge	grow up	lie	sit	stare	watch

George _stood motionless_ for at least a minute.
I used to _lie awake_ watching the rain seep through the roof.
He _died young._

A lot of adjectives with negative meanings are used as complements in this way, especially those with the prefix '**un-**' like **unannounced**, **unhurt** and **untouched**.
I considered arriving _unannounced_ at his front door, but rejected the idea.
The man's car was hit by rifle fire but he escaped _unhurt._

6 object complements

Some transitive verbs have a complement after their object when they are used with a particular meaning. This complement describes the object, and is often called the **object complement.** The following transitive verbs are used with an adjective as object complement:

believe	count	judge	presume	render
call	declare	keep	pronounce	serve
certify	eat	label	prove	term
colour	find	leave	rate	think
consider	hold	make	reckon	

Willie's jokes _made_ her _uneasy._
He had _proved_ them all _wrong._

GRAMMAR

The journal 'Nature' _called_ this book _dangerous._
They _held_ him _responsible_ for the brutal treatment they had endured.

Some verbs are used with a very restricted range of object complements:

to drive someone crazy/mad	to rub something dry/smooth
to burn someone alive	to scare someone stiff/silly
to get someone drunk/pregnant	to send someone mad
to keep someone awake	to shoot someone dead
to knock someone unconscious	to set someone free
to open something wide	to squash something flat
to paint something red, blue, etc	to sweep something clean
to pat something dry	to turn something white, black, etc
to pick something clean	to wipe something clean/dry
to plane something flat/smooth	

She _painted_ her eyelids _deep blue._
Waves of insecurity _kept_ him _awake_ at night.
He _wiped_ the bottle _dry_ with a dishcloth.

The following transitive verbs are used with a noun group as object complement:

appoint	consider	find	nominate	term
believe	crown	hold	presume	think
brand	declare	judge	proclaim	
bring up	designate	label	prove	
call	elect	make	reckon	

They _brought_ him up _a Christian._
If you _elect_ me _president,_ you'll be better off four years from now.
In 1910 Asquith _made_ him _a junior minister._

The following transitive verbs are used with a name as object complement:

call	christen	dub	name	nickname

Everyone _called_ her _Molly._

Conjunctions

A **conjunction** is a word which links two clauses, groups, or words. There are two kinds of conjunction: coordinating conjunctions and subordinating conjunctions.

1 coordinating conjunctions

Coordinating conjunctions link clauses, groups, or words of the same grammatical type, for example two main clauses or two adjectives.

The coordinating conjunctions are:

and	but	nor	or	then	yet

Anna had to go into town _and_ she wanted to go to Bride Street.
I asked if I could borrow her bicycle _but_ she refused.
Her manner was hurried _yet_ painstakingly courteous.

Nor, then, and **yet** can be used after **and. Nor** and **then** can be used after **but.**
Eric moaned something _and then_ lay still.
It is a simple game _and yet_ interesting enough to be played with skill.
Institutions of learning are not taxed _but nor_ are they much respected.

When coordinating conjunctions are used to link clauses that have the same subject, the subject is not usually repeated in the second clause.

She was born in Budapest <u>and</u> raised in Manhattan.
He didn't yell <u>or</u> scream.
When she saw Morris she went pale, <u>then</u> blushed.

⇨ For more detailed information, see **Usage** entries at **and, but, nor,** and **or.**

2 subordinating conjunctions

Subordinating conjunctions introduce **subordinate clauses.** A subordinating conjunction does not have to come between two clauses. It can introduce the first clause in a sentence.

He only kept thinking about it <u>because</u> there was nothing else to think about.
<u>When</u> the jar was full, he turned the water off.
<u>Although</u> she was eighteen, her mother didn't like her to stay out late.

Some of the most frequent subordinating conjunctions are:

although	despite	though	when
as	if	unless	whenever
because	in spite of	whereas	while

⇨ For information on subordinating conjunctions and the conjunctions that are used to introduce the various types of subordinate clause, see **Grammar** entry at **Subordinate clauses.**

Continuous tenses

1 continuous tenses

A **continuous tense** contains a form of the verb **be** and a present participle. Continuous tenses are used when talking about temporary situations at a particular point in time.

⇨ See **Grammar** entry at **Tenses.**

Verbs which are used in continuous tenses are sometimes called **dynamic verbs.**
The video industry <u>has been developing</u> rapidly.
He '<u>ll be working</u> nights next week.

2 stative verbs

There are a number of verbs which are not normally used in continuous tenses. Verbs of this kind are sometimes called **stative verbs.**

The verbs in the following list are not normally used in continuous tenses when they are used with their commonest or basic meaning.

admire	despise	include	owe	seem
adore	detest	interest	own	sound
appear	dislike	involve	please	stop
astonish	envy	keep	possess	suppose
be	exist	know	prefer	surprise
believe	fit	lack	reach	survive
belong to	forget	last	realize	suspect
concern	hate	like	recognize	understand
consist of	have	look like	remember	want
contain	hear	love	resemble	wish
deserve	imagine	matter	satisfy	
desire	impress	mean	see	

GRAMMAR

3 **'be'**

Be is not usually used as a main verb in continuous tenses. However, you use it in continuous tenses when you are describing someone's behaviour at a particular time.

You 're being naughty.

4 **'have'**

Have is not used in continuous tenses to talk about possession. However, you can use it in continuous tenses to indicate that someone is doing something.

We were just having a philosophical discussion.

⇨ See **Usage** entry at **have**.

5 **other verbs**

Some verbs have very specific senses in which they are not used in continuous tenses. For example, **smell** is sometimes used in continuous tenses when it means 'to smell something deliberately', but not when it means 'to smell of something'.

She was smelling her bunch of flowers.
The air smelled sweet.

The following verbs are not used in continuous tenses when they have the meanings indicated:

depend (be related to)	taste (of something)
feel (have an opinion)	think (have an opinion)
measure (have length)	weigh (have weight)
smell (of something)	

Contractions

1 **basic forms**

A **contraction** is a shortened form in which a subject and an auxiliary verb, or an auxiliary verb and **not**, are combined to form one word.

I'm getting desperate.
She wouldn't believe me.

You use contractions when you are writing down what someone says, or when you are writing in a conversational style, for example in letters to friends.

The contracted forms of **be** are used when **be** is a main verb as well as when it is an auxiliary. The contracted forms of **have** are not usually used when **have** is a main verb.

The following table shows contractions of personal pronouns and **be**, **have**, **will**, **shall**, and **would**.

be — simple present		
I am	**I'm**	/aɪm/
you are	**you're**	/jɔː/, /jʊə/
he is	**he's**	/hiːz/
she is	**she's**	/ʃiːz/
it is	**it's**	/ɪts/
we are	**we're**	/wɪə/
they are	**they're**	/ðeə/
Also: **'s** added to names, singular nouns, and 'wh-' words		
there's, here's, that's		

GRAMMAR

GRAMMAR

have — simple present

I have	**I've**	/aɪv/
you have	**you've**	/juːv/
he has	**he's**	/hiːz/
she has	**she's**	/ʃiːz/
it has	**it's**	/ɪts/
we have	**we've**	/wiːv/
they have	**they've**	/ðeɪv/

Also: **'s** added to names, singular nouns, and 'wh-' words
there's, there've (not common), **that's**

have — simple past

I had	**I'd**	/aɪd/
you had	**you'd**	/juːd/
he had	**he'd**	/hiːd/
she had	**she'd**	/ʃiːd/
it had	**it'd**	/ɪtəd/
we had	**we'd**	/wiːd/
they had	**they'd**	/ðeɪd/

Also: **there'd, who'd**

will/shall

I shall/will	**I'll**	/aɪl/
you will	**you'll**	/juːl/
he will	**he'll**	/hiːl/
she will	**she'll**	/ʃiːl/
it will	**it'll**	/ɪtəl/
we will	**we'll**	/wiːl/
they will	**they'll**	/ðeɪl/

Also: **'ll** added to names and nouns (in speech)
there'll, who'll, what'll, that'll

would

I would	**I'd**	/aɪd/
you would	**you'd**	/juːd/
he would	**he'd**	/hiːd/
she would	**she'd**	/ʃiːd/
it would	**it'd**	/ɪtəd/
we would	**we'd**	/wiːd/
they would	**they'd**	/ðeɪd/

Also: **there'd, who'd, that'd**

⚠ **WARNING:** You cannot use any of the above contractions at the end of a clause. You must use the full form instead. For example, you say 'I said I would', not 'I said I'd'.

2 **negative contractions**

The following table shows contractions of **be**, **do**, **have**, modals, and semi-modals with **not**.

be		
are not	**aren't**	/ɑːnt/
is not	**isn't**	/ɪznt/
was not	**wasn't**	/wɒznt/
were not	**weren't**	/wɜːnt/
do		
do not	**don't**	/dəʊnt/
does not	**doesn't**	/dʌznt/
did not	**didn't**	/dɪdnt/
have		
have	**haven't**	/hævnt/
has	**hasn't**	/hæznt/
modals		
cannot	**can't**	/kɑːnt/
could not	**couldn't**	/kʊdnt/
might not	**mightn't**	/maɪtnt/
must not	**mustn't**	/mʌsnt/
ought not	**oughtn't**	/ɔːtnt/
shall not	**shan't**	/ʃɑːnt/
should not	**shouldn't**	/ʃʊdnt/
will not	**won't**	/wəʊnt/
would not	**wouldn't**	/wʊdnt/
semi-modals		
dare not	**daren't**	/deənt/
need not	**needn't**	/niːdnt/

⚠ **WARNING:** There is no contracted form of 'am not' in standard English. In conversation and informal writing, '**I'm not**' is used. However, '**aren't I?**' is used in questions and question tags.

Aren't I brave?

I'm right, aren't I?

In very informal English **ain't** is sometimes used with this meaning. However, many people consider this usage incorrect.

I certainly ain't going to retire.

In standard English, a pronoun followed by a negative contraction of a modal or **have** is more commonly used than a contraction followed by 'not'. For example, **I won't**, **I wouldn't**, and **I haven't** are more common than 'I'll not', 'I'd not', and 'I've not'. However, in the case of **be**, both types of contraction are equally common. For example, **you're not** and **he's not** are used as commonly as **you aren't** and **he isn't**.

You aren't responsible.

You're not responsible.

GRAMMAR

3 **modals and 'have'**

The auxiliary **have** is not usually pronounced in full after **could**, **might**, **must**, **should**, and **would**. The contractions **could've**, **might've**, **must've**, **should've**, and **would've** are occasionally used in writing when reporting a conversation.

I <u>must've</u> fallen asleep.
You <u>should've</u> come to see us.

Determiners

A **determiner** is a word used in front of a noun to indicate whether you are referring to a specific thing or just to something of a particular type. There are two types of determiners: specific determiners and general determiners.

1 **specific determiners**

You use **specific determiners** when the person you are talking to will know which person or thing you are referring to. The specific determiners are:

● **the definite article: the**

<u>The</u> man began to run towards <u>the</u> boy.

● **demonstratives: this, that, these, those**

How much is it for <u>that</u> big box?
Young people don't like <u>these</u> operas.

● **possessive determiners: my, your, his, her, its, our, their**

I'd been waiting a long time to park <u>my</u> car.
<u>Her</u> face was very red.

⇨ See **Usage** entries at the individual words and **Grammar** entry at **Possessive determiners**.

2 **general determiners**

You use **general determiners** when you are mentioning people or things for the first time, or talking about them generally without saying exactly which ones you mean. The general determiners are:

a	an	each	few	many	neither	some
a few	another	either	fewer	more	no	
a little	any	enough	less	most	other	
all	both	every	little	much	several	

There was <u>a</u> man in the lift.
You can stop at <u>any</u> time you like.
There were <u>several</u> reasons for this.

⇨ See **Usage** entries at the individual words, and **Grammar** entry at **Quantity**.

3 **related pronouns**

Most words used as determiners are also used as pronouns.

<u>This</u> is a very complex issue.
Have you got <u>any</u> that I could borrow?
There is <u>enough</u> for all of us.

However, **the**, **a**, **an**, **every**, **no**, **other**, and the possessive determiners cannot be used as pronouns. You use **one** as a pronoun instead of 'a' or 'an', **each** instead of 'every', **none** instead of 'no', and **others** instead of 'other'.

Have you got <u>one</u>?
<u>Each</u> has a separate box and number.
There are <u>none</u> left.
Some stretches of road are more dangerous than <u>others</u>.

'-ed' adjectives

A large number of adjectives end in '-**ed**'.

1 | **related to verbs**

Many of them have the same form as the past participle of a transitive verb, and have a passive meaning. For example, a **frightened** person is a person who has been frightened by something.

When I saw my face in the mirror, I was <u>astonished</u> at the change.
Soak <u>dried</u> fruit in water before cooking it.

Some past participles which do not end in '-ed' are also used as adjectives. They are still sometimes called '-ed' adjectives.

It is a good idea to get at least two <u>written</u> estimates.
…searching for a <u>lost</u> ball.

A few '-ed' adjectives are related to intransitive verbs and have an active meaning. For example, an **escaped** prisoner is a prisoner who has escaped. The following '-ed' adjectives have an active meaning:

accumulated	escaped	fallen	swollen
dated	faded	retired	wilted

She is the daughter of a <u>retired</u> army officer.
…a tall woman with a <u>swollen</u> leg.

2 | **related to verbs but different in meaning**

Some '-ed' adjectives are related to verbs in form, but have a different meaning from the usual meaning of the verb. For example, to **attach** something to something else means to join or fasten it on, but a person who is **attached** to someone or something is very fond of them.

The following adjectives have a different meaning from the usual or commonest meaning of the related verb:

advanced	disposed	marked
attached	disturbed	mixed
determined	guarded	noted

The tiles <u>had been attached</u> with an inferior adhesive material and were already beginning to fall off.
'Oh, yes,' says Howard, 'I'm quite <u>attached</u> to Henry. I've known him for ages.'

3 | **related to nouns**

Many adjectives are formed by adding '-**ed**' to a noun. They indicate that a person or thing has the thing that the noun refers to. For example, a **bearded** man has a beard. The following adjectives are formed by adding '-**ed**' to a noun:

armoured	flowered	pointed	striped
barbed	freckled	principled	turbaned
beaded	gifted	salaried	veiled
bearded	gloved	skilled	walled
detailed	hooded	spotted	winged

The visitor was a <u>bearded</u> man with mean and unreliable eyes.
Every <u>skilled</u> adult reader takes all of this for granted.

4 | **not related to verbs or nouns**

There are a few '-ed' adjectives that are not related to verbs or nouns in the ways described above. For example, the adjective **antiquated** is not related to a verb, because there is no such verb as 'antiquate'. The following adjectives are not directly related to verbs or nouns:

antiquated	beloved	crazed	rugged
ashamed	bloated	deceased	sophisticated
assorted	concerted	indebted	

It was not until the 1970s that a <u>concerted</u> effort was made to import the game of pool into Britain.
Without language, complex social systems and <u>sophisticated</u> technology would be impossible.

Ellipsis

1	used in place of a verb group	
2	'be'	
3	'have' used as a main verb	
4	'have' used as an auxiliary	
5	'to-' infinitive clauses	
6	'dare' and 'need'	
7	'would rather'	
8	'had better'	
9	in conversation	
10	in coordinate clauses	

GRAMMAR

1

used in place of a verb group

Ellipsis involves leaving out words which are obvious from the context. In many cases you use an auxiliary in place of a full verb group, or in place of a verb group and its object. For example, you say 'John won't like it but Rachel will' instead of 'John won't like it but Rachel will like it'.

They would stop it if they <u>could</u>.
I never did go to Stratford, although I probably <u>should have</u>.
...a topic which should have attracted far more attention from philosophers than it <u>has</u>.

A full clause would sound unnatural in these examples.

You use **do**, **does**, or **did**, when the auxiliary already occurs in the first verb group or when the verb group is simple present or simple past:

Do farmers still warrant a ministry all to themselves? I think they <u>do</u>.
I think we want it more than they <u>do</u>.
He went shopping yesterday; at least, I think he <u>did</u>.

2 **'be'**

You do not, however, use the auxiliary 'do' to stand for the link verb **be**. You just use a form of **be**. You also use a form of **be** when it is used as an auxiliary in the first verb group:

'I think you're right.'–'I'm sure I <u>am</u>.'
'He was driving too fast.'– 'Yes, I know he <u>was</u>.'

If the second verb group contains a modal, you usually put **be** after the modal.

'He thought that the condition was hereditary in his case.'–'Well, it <u>might be</u>.'

Be is sometimes used after a modal in the second clause to contrast with another link verb such as **seem**, **look**, or **sound**.

'It <u>looks</u> like tea to me.'–'Yes, it <u>could be</u>.'

With passives, **be** is often, but not always, kept after a modal.

He argued that if tissues could be marketed, then anything <u>could be</u>.

3 **'have' used as a main verb**

When you are using **have** as a main verb, for example to indicate possession, you can use a form of **have** or a form of **do** to refer back to it.

 American speakers usually use a form of **do**.

She probably has a temperature – she certainly looks as if she <u>has.</u>
…since the Earth has a greater diameter than the Moon <u>does.</u>

ⓘ Note that in the second example you do not need to use any verb after **than**. You can just say 'since the Earth has a greater diameter than the Moon'.

4 **'have' used as an auxiliary**
When **have** is used as an auxiliary in the first verb group in a perfect tense, you repeat it in the second verb group and omit the main verb:

'Have you visited Rome? I <u>have.</u>'

When you use the auxiliary **have** to stand for a perfect passive, you do not usually add 'been'. For example, you say, 'Have you been interviewed yet? I have.'

However, when **have** is used after a modal, **been** cannot be omitted.

I'm sure it was repeated in the media. It <u>must have been.</u>
Priller noticed that they were not flying in tight formation as they <u>should have been.</u>

5 **'to'-infinitive clauses**
Instead of using a full 'to'-infinitive clause after a verb, you can just use **to**, if the action or state has already been mentioned.

Don't tell me if you don't want <u>to.</u>
At last he agreed to do what I asked him <u>to.</u>

6 **'dare' and 'need'**
You can omit a verb after **dare** and **need**, but only when they are used in the negative.

'I don't mind telling you what I know.'–'You <u>needn't.</u> I'm not asking you to.'
'You must tell her the truth.'–'But, Neill, I <u>daren't.</u>'

 Note that speakers of American English do not use the contraction 'daren't'. Instead, they say **don't dare**.

I hear her screaming and I <u>don't dare</u> open the door.

7 **'would rather'**
Similarly, the verb is only omitted after **would rather** when it is used in a negative clause or an 'if'-clause.

It's just that I <u>'d rather not.</u>
We could go to your place, if you <u>'d rather.</u>

8 **'had better'**
The verb is sometimes omitted after **had better**, even when it is used affirmatively.

'I can't tell you.'–'You<u>'d better.</u>'

However, you do not usually omit **be**.

'He'll be out of town by nightfall.'– 'He<u>'d better be.</u>'

9 **in conversation**
Ellipsis often occurs in conversation in replies and questions.

⇨ See **Topic** entries at **Agreeing and disagreeing**, **Reactions**, and **Replies**, and **Grammar** entry at **Questions**.

10 **in coordinate clauses**
Words are often left out of the second of two coordinate clauses, for example after **and** or **or**.

⇨ See **Usage** entry at **and**.

The Future
⇨ For the formation of future tenses, see **Grammar** entry at **Tenses**.

GRAMMAR

GRAMMAR

1 **talking about the future**

You can talk about future events in a variety of ways. You use **will** or **shall** when making predictions about the future, though **shall** is not used very often to form the future.

⇨ See **Usage** entry at **shall-will**.

The weather tomorrow <u>will be</u> warm and sunny.
I'm sure you <u>will enjoy</u> your visit to the zoo.

You can also use the future continuous tense when you are referring to something that will happen in the normal course of events.

You'll <u>be starting</u> school soon, I suppose.
Once the war is over, they'<u>ll be cutting down</u> on staff.

If you are certain that an event will happen, you can use **be bound to** in conversation.

Marion<u>'s bound to be</u> back soon.
The parade <u>'s bound to be cancelled</u> now.

Be sure to and **be certain to** are also sometimes used.

She<u>'s sure to find out</u> sooner or later.
He<u>'s certain to be</u> elected.

You use **be going to** when referring to an event that you think will happen fairly soon.

It<u>'s going to rain</u>.
I<u>'m going to be</u> late.

You use **be about to** when referring to an event that you think will happen very soon.

Another 385 people <u>are about to lose</u> their jobs.
She seemed to sense that something terrible <u>was about to happen.</u>
I <u>was just about to serve</u> dinner when there was a knock on the door.

You can also refer to events in the very near future using **be on the point of**. You use an '-ing' form after it.

She <u>was on the point of bursting</u> into tears.
You may remember that I <u>was on the point of asking</u> you something else when we were interrupted by Doctor Smithers.

2 **intentions and plans**

When you are talking about your own intentions, you use **will** or **be going to**. When you are talking about someone else's intentions, you use **be going to**.

I'<u>ll ring</u> you tonight.
I'<u>m going to stay</u> at home.
They'<u>re going to have</u> a party.

⚠ **WARNING:** People tend to avoid using 'be going to' with the verb 'go'. For example, they would probably say 'I'm going away next week' rather than 'I'm going to go away next week'.

⇨ For more information on how to express intentions, see **Topic** entry at **Intentions.**

You can also talk about people's plans or arrangements for the future using the present continuous tense.

I'<u>m meeting</u> Bill next week.
They'<u>re getting married</u> in June.

The future continuous tense is also sometimes used.

I'<u>ll be seeing</u> them when I've finished with you.

Be due to is used in writing and more formal speech to indicate that an event is intended to happen at a particular time in the future.

He <u>is due to start</u> as a courier shortly.
The centre <u>'s due to be completed</u> in 1996.

The simple present tense is used to talk about an event which is planned to happen soon, or which happens regularly, in accordance with a timetable or schedule.

My flight <u>leaves</u> in half an hour.
Our next lesson <u>is</u> on Thursday.

In writing and broadcasting, 'to'-infinitive clauses are used after **be** to indicate that something is planned to happen.

A national centre to promote the efficient use of energy <u>is to be set up</u>.
The Prime Minister <u>is to visit</u> Hungary and Czechoslovakia in the autumn.

3 using the future perfect

When you want to talk about something that will happen before a particular time in the future, you use the future perfect tense.

By the time we phone he <u>'ll</u> already <u>have started</u>.
By 2002, he <u>will have worked</u> for twelve years.

4 present tenses in subordinate clauses

In some subordinate clauses, you use a present tense when referring to a future event. For example, in conditional clauses and time clauses, you normally use the simple present tense or present perfect tense when talking about the future.

<u>If he comes,</u> I'll let you know.
Please start <u>when you are ready.</u>
We won't start <u>until everyone arrives.</u>
I'll let you know <u>when I have arranged everything.</u>

You also use a present tense in reason clauses introduced by **in case**.

It would be better if you could arrive back here a day early, <u>just in case there are some last minute details to talk over.</u>

⇨ For further information on tenses used in subordinate clauses, see **Usage** entry at **if** and **Grammar** entry at **Subordinate clauses.**

In a defining relative clause, you use the simple present tense, not 'will', when you are clearly referring to the future in the main clause.

Any decision <u>that you make</u> will need her approval.
Give my love to any friends <u>you meet.</u>
The next woman <u>I marry</u> is not going to be so damned smart.

However, you use **will** in the relative clause when you need to make it clear that you are referring to the future, or when the relative clause refers to an even later time.

Thousands of dollars can be spent on something <u>that will be worn for only a few minutes.</u>
The only people <u>who will be killed</u> are those who have knowledge which is dangerous to our cause.
I send my boys to a good public school so that they will meet people <u>who will be useful to them later on.</u>

You use a present tense in reported questions and similar clauses which refer to a future event when the event will happen at about the same time as the reporting or knowing.

I'll telephone you. If I say it's Hugh, you'll know <u>who it is.</u>

However, if the future event is going to happen after the reporting, you use **will** in the reported question.

I'll tell you <u>what I will do.</u>

In a 'that'-clause after the verb **hope**, you often use the simple present tense to refer to the future.

I hope you <u>enjoy</u> your holiday.

⇨ For information on tenses in other 'that'-clauses, see **Grammar** entry at **Reporting.**

'-ic' and '-ical' adjectives

Many adjectives end in **'-ic'** or **'-ical'**.

1 adjectives related to '-ic' nouns

Sometimes an adjective ending in '-ical' is related to a noun ending in '-ic'.
The words in the following two lists are nouns ending in '-ic' which have related adjectives ending in '-ical'.

● These nouns refer to things:

arithmetic	comic	logic	magic	music	tactic

The finance for <u>musical</u> performances comes from the audiences.
It's simpy a <u>tactical</u> move.

● These nouns refer to people:

comic	critic	cynic	fanatic	mystic	sceptic

…a <u>cynical</u> contempt for truth and decency.
…a <u>fanatical</u> supporter of the government.

(i) Note that **comic**, **fanatic**, **magic**, and **mystic** can themselves be used as adjectives. Many other nouns end in '-ic', for example **fabric**, **panic**, and **relic**, but they do not have related adjectives ending in '-ical'.

2 adjectives related to '-ics' nouns

Many nouns end in '-ics'. Sometimes the adjective related to them ends in '-ic' and sometimes it ends in '-ical'. The following nouns have related adjectives ending in '-ic':

acoustics	athletics	graphics	linguistics
acrobatics	basics	gymnastics	obstetrics
aerobatics	economics	heroics	specifics
aerobics	electronics	histrionics	thermodynamics
aerodynamics	genetics	italics	

…the rapid progress being made in the field of <u>genetic</u> research.
…students with <u>linguistic</u> ability.

● The following nouns have related adjectives ending in '-ical':

aeronautics	ethics	mathematics	statistics
classics	hysterics	physics	tropics

…the kinds of <u>ethical</u> and moral problems that will arise.
It's nothing to get <u>hysterical</u> about, darling.

(i) Note that **logistics** has two related adjectives: **logistic** and **logistical**.

3 '-ic' and '-ical' adjectives

A number of adjectives have forms ending in '-ic' and '-ical', with no great difference in meaning.
The following pairs of adjectives have similar meanings:

cyclic - cyclical	ironic - ironical
egoistic - egoistical	logistic - logistical
egotistic - egotistical	mystic - mystical
fanatic - fanatical	problematic - problematical
geographic - geographical	rhythmic - rhythmical
geometric - geometrical	syntactic - syntactical

There was some scattered <u>ironic</u> applause from the crowd.

He smiled a friendly, slightly <u>ironical</u> smile.
The whole business becomes <u>problematic,</u> tinged with anxiety.
The relationship between private business and government remains <u>problematical.</u>

Sometimes there is a difference in meaning or use between pairs of adjectives ending in '**-ic**' and '**-ical**'.

⇨ See **Usage** entries at **classic - classical, comic - comical, electric - electrical, historic - historical,** and **magic - magical.**

⇨ See also **Usage** entry at **economics** for the difference between **economic** and **economical.**

4 **other '-ic' adjectives**

Some adjectives not mentioned above consist of a noun with '**-ic**' on the end. The adjective indicates that something is connected with the thing referred to by the noun. For example, if a drink is **alcoholic**, it contains alcohol, something that is **magnetic** is like a magnet and causes metal objects to stick to it.

He took a carving knife from a <u>magnetic</u> board on the wall.
I was getting more and more <u>journalistic</u> work.
…distributing <u>photographic</u> products to retailers.

Sometimes it may not be very clear what noun an '**-ic**' adjective is related to. For example, **ironic** is related to 'irony', not to 'iron' and **organic** means 'relating to organisms' (living things), not 'relating to an organ'.

Imperatives

You use an **imperative** clause when you are telling someone to do something or not to do something. An imperative clause usually has no subject.

1 **form**

The imperative form of a verb is the same as its base form.

<u>Come</u> here.
<u>Take</u> two tablets every four hours.

For a **negative imperative,** you use **don't** and the base form of the verb. In formal English, you use **do not** and the base form.

<u>Don't touch</u> that wire!
<u>Don't be</u> afraid of them.
<u>Do not forget</u> to leave the key on the desk.

2 **emphasis and politeness**

An imperative form usually comes at the beginning of a sentence. However, you can put **always** or **never** first for emphasis.

<u>Always</u> check that you have enough money first.
<u>Never</u> believe what he tells you.

You can also use **do** to add emphasis.

<u>Do</u> be careful!

You can add **please** to the beginning or end of the clause in order to be more polite.

<u>Please</u> don't do that.
Follow me, <u>please.</u>

Question tags are sometimes added after imperative clauses to make them sound more like requests, or to express impatience or anger.

Post that letter for me, <u>will you</u>?
Hurry up, <u>can't you</u>?

⇨ See **Topic** entry at **Requests, orders, and instructions.**

The subject **you** is sometimes used when people want to indicate which person they are talking to, or want to add emphasis or express anger.

<u>You</u> get in the car this minute!

GRAMMAR

> ⚠️ **WARNING:** An imperative can often sound rude or abrupt.
> ⇨ See **Topic** entries at **Advising someone, Invitations, Requests, orders, and instructions, Suggestions,** and **Warning someone** for detailed information on alternatives to imperatives.

3 conditional use

Sometimes, when an imperative is followed by **and** or **or**, it has a meaning similar to a conditional clause beginning 'If you…'. For example, 'Take that piece away, and the whole lot falls down' means 'If you take that piece away, the whole lot falls down'. 'Go away or I'll call the police' means 'If you don't go away, I'll call the police'.

Say that again, <u>and</u> I'll hit you.
Hurry up, <u>or</u> you'll be late for school.

Infinitives

1 infinitives with and without 'to'

There are two kinds of infinitive. One kind is called the **'to'-infinitive.** It consists of **to** and the base form of a verb.

I wanted <u>to escape</u> from here.
I asked Don Card <u>to go</u> with me.

⇨ See **Grammar** entry at **'To'-infinitive clauses.**

The other kind of infinitive is sometimes called the **infinitive without 'to'** or the **bare infinitive.** It is the same as the base form of a verb. Its uses are explained in this entry.

They helped me <u>get</u> settled here.

2 used after other verbs

You use a bare infinitive to refer to a completed action that someone sees, hears, or notices.

She heard him <u>fall</u> down the stairs.
The kids at the Youth Club just don't want to listen to anybody <u>speak.</u>

A bare infinitive is used in this way after the object of the following verbs:

| feel | hear | listen to | notice | see | watch |

I <u>felt her touch</u> my hand.
Chandler did not <u>notice him enter.</u>

These verbs can also have an '-ing' form after their object.
⇨ See **Grammar** entry at **'-ing' forms.**

3 'have', 'let', and 'make'

You use a bare infinitive after the object of **have, let,** and **make** when it means 'cause or force someone to do something'.

Have him <u>recommend a club that best fits your needs.</u>
Don't let Tim <u>go</u> by himself!
They made me <u>write</u> all the details down again.

4 'know'

 In British English, a bare infinitive can be used after the object of **know** in negative, simple past clauses or in perfect clauses, but American English uses a 'to-' infinitive.

I never knew him <u>smoke</u> before breakfast.
Have you ever known him <u>buy</u> a round?
I've never known him <u>to be</u> unkind.

5 **'help'**

You can also use a bare infinitive with **help**. You can leave out the object if you do not think it is necessary to mention the person who is being helped.

John helped the old lady carry the bags upstairs.
We got up and helped clear up the debris of the party.

Help can also be used with a 'to'-infinitive.
⇨ See **Usage** entry at **help**.

⚠ **WARNING:** When you are using the verbs mentioned above in passive clauses, you do not use a bare infinitive after them. You use a 'to'-infinitive instead.

…magazines which nobody was ever seen to buy.
I resent being made to feel guilty.
…if people are helped to liberate themselves.

6 **used after modals**

You use a bare infinitive after all modals except 'ought'.

I must go.
Can you see him?

⇨ See **Grammar** entry at **Modals**.

You use a bare infinitive after the expressions **had better** and **would rather**.

I had better go.
Would you rather do it yourself?

You sometimes use a bare infinitive after **dare** and **need**.

I daren't leave before six.
Need you pay him right now?

⇨ See **Usage** entries at **dare** and **need**.

7 **other uses**

You can use a bare infinitive after **Why** to indicate that you think that an action is foolish or pointless.

Why wait until then?

You can use a bare infinitive after **Why not** to suggest what someone should do.

Why not come with us?

You can use a bare infinitive after **be** when you are explaining what someone or something does or should do. The subject must be a clause beginning with **all** or **what**.

All he did was open the door.
What it does is cool the engine.

⚠ **WARNING:** You cannot use bare infinitives after prepositions. You can, however, use an '-ing' form.
⇨ See **Grammar** entry at **'-ing' forms**.

'-ing' adjectives

A large number of adjectives end in '-ing'.

1 **related to transitive verbs**

Many '-ing' adjectives have the same form as the present participle of a transitive verb, and are similar in meaning. For example, **an astonishing fact** is a fact that astonishes you.

…her annoying habit of repeating what I had just said.
…a brilliantly amusing novel.

ⓘ Note that '-ing' adjectives of this kind often describe the person or thing causing a

GRAMMAR

feeling, as in **a boring lecture**, whereas '-ed' adjectives describe the person or thing affected by a feeling, as in **a bored student**.

⇨ See **Grammar** entry at **'-ed' adjectives**.

When the present participle of a transitive verb does not refer to causing a feeling, you can often put the object of the verb in front of the '-ing' form to form a compound adjective.

The news was listened to by at least half the <u>German-speaking</u> population.
Each colony would be completely <u>self-governing</u>.

2 related to intransitive verbs

Some '-ing' adjectives are related to intransitive verbs. They describe processes, changes, or states. For example, if there is a **decreasing** number of things, the number of things is getting smaller; an **existing** law is one which already exists. When an '-ing' word of this kind is used after **be**, it forms part of a continuous tense.

When she cried she looked old and vulnerable, like an <u>ageing</u> monkey.
Much of the world's tanker fleet <u>is ageing</u>.
…an <u>increasing</u> amount of leisure time.
Efficiency and productivity <u>are increasing</u>.

Here is a list of common '-ing' adjectives related to intransitive verbs:

ageing	decreasing	existing	recurring	rising
bleeding	diminishing	increasing	reigning	sleeping
booming	dwindling	living	remaining	
bursting	dying	prevailing	resounding	

3 related to verbs but different in meaning

A few '-ing' adjectives are related to verbs in form, but have a different meaning from the usual or commonest meaning of the verb. For example, the verb **dash** usually means 'move quickly', but someone or something that is **dashing** is stylish and attractive. The following adjectives have a different meaning from the verb they appear to be related to:

becoming	disarming	fetching	promising	trying
dashing	engaging	halting	retiring	

She kept <u>dashing</u> out of the kitchen to give him a kiss.
I used to be told I looked quite <u>dashing</u>.

4 not related to verbs

A few '-ing' adjectives are not related to verbs at all. For example, there are no verbs 'to appetize', 'to bald', or 'to scathe'. The following '-ing' adjectives are not related to verbs:

appetizing	cunning	excruciating	neighbouring	unwitting
balding	enterprising	impending	scathing	

…the <u>appetizing</u> aromas of the dishes I produced for myself.
Pitman glanced at the fat, <u>balding</u> man sitting beside him.
He launched into a <u>scathing</u> attack on Gates.

5 used for emphasis in informal speech

A small group of '-ing' adjectives are used in informal speech for emphasis:

blinking	blooming	flipping	stinking
blithering	flaming	raving	

These adjectives are always used in front of a noun, never after a link verb.

If you plan to join the others, you might tell your <u>blinking</u> brother.

Several of these adjectives are usually used with a particular noun, as shown in the examples below.

He's in America, according to that <u>blithering idiot</u> Pete.
I knew that I was carrying on a dialogue with a <u>raving lunatic.</u>

ⓘ Note that you are advised not to use any of these adjectives, because they would sound inappropriate from someone who is not a native speaker.

⚠ **WARNING:** The '-ing' adjectives **fucking** and **sodding** are also used in very informal speech for emphasis. However these words are considered very offensive by many people and should therefore be avoided.

'-ing' forms

1 form	**7** separate '-ing' clauses
2 continuous tenses	**8** active meaning
3 after verbs	**9** passive meaning
4 choice of '-ing' form and 'to'-infinitive	**10** subject and '-ing' form
5 after the object of a verb	**11** after a noun
6 '-ing' forms after conjunctions	**12** used like nouns
	13 other uses

GRAMMAR

1 form

'-ing' forms are also called **present participles.** Most '-ing' forms are formed by adding **-ing** to the base form of a verb, for example **asking**, **eating**, and **passing**. Sometimes there is a change in spelling, as in **dying**, **making**, and **putting**.

⇨ For a table showing these changes, see **Grammar** entry at **Verbs.**

⇨ For information about '-ing' forms used as adjectives, see **Grammar** entry at **'-ing' adjectives.**

⇨ For the use of '-ing' forms in sentences such as 'It was difficult saying goodbye', see **Usage** entry at **it.**

2 continuous tenses

One common use of '-ing' forms is as part of continuous tenses of verbs.

He <u>was sleeping</u> in the other room.
Cathy <u>has been looking</u> at the results.

⇨ See **Grammar** entries at **Tenses** and **Continuous tenses.**

3 after verbs

When you are talking about someone's behaviour in relation to an action, or their attitude towards doing it, you often use a verb followed by a clause beginning with an '-ing' form (an '**-ing' clause.**) The following verbs can be followed by an '-ing' clause:

admit	delay	enjoy	keep	resent
adore	deny	escape	mind	resist
avoid	describe	fancy	miss	risk
chance	detest	finish	postpone	stop
commence	dislike	imagine	practise	suggest
consider	dread	involve	recall	

He wisely <u>avoided mentioning the incident to his boss.</u>
They <u>enjoy working together.</u>
You must <u>keep trying.</u>

Need, require, and **want** can be followed by an '-ing' form which has a passive meaning. For example, if you say that something **needs doing**, you mean that it needs to be done. These constructions are less common in American English, where a passive 'to-' infinitive is commonly used.

It <u>needs dusting.</u>
The beans <u>want picking.</u>
The room <u>needs to be cleaned.</u>

Deserve and **merit** are also sometimes used in this way.

4 choice of '-ing' form and 'to'-infinitive

After some verbs, you can use an '-ing' clause or a 'to'-infinitive clause without greatly changing the meaning.

It <u>started raining</u> soon after we set off.
Then it <u>started to rain.</u>

Here are some common verbs which can be followed by an '-ing' clause or a 'to'-infinitive clause:

begin	cease	deserve	intend	love	prefer
bother	continue	hate	like	omit	start

After the verbs **go on, regret, remember**, and **try**, an '-ing' form has a different meaning from a 'to'-infinitive.

⇨ See **Usage** entries at **go on, regret - be sorry, remember - remind,** and **try - attempt.**

5 after the object of a verb

Some verbs, many of which are verbs of perception, are used with an object and an '-ing' clause. The '-ing' clause indicates what the person or thing referred to by the object is doing.

I <u>saw him looking at me.</u>
A blast <u>brought her home crashing down on top of her.</u>

The following verbs are commonly used with an object and an '-ing' clause:

bring	find	keep	notice	picture	see	show
catch	have	leave	observe	prevent	send	spot
feel	hear	listen to	photograph	save	set	watch

Some of these verbs can also be used with an object and an infinitive without 'to'.
⇨ See **Grammar** entry at **Infinitives.**

6 '-ing' forms after conjunctions

You can use '-ing' forms after some subordinating conjunctions, with no subject or auxiliary. Note that you can only do this when the subject would be the same as the one in the main clause, or when it is not specific.

I deliberately didn't read the book <u>before going to see the film.</u>
<u>When buying a new car,</u> it is best to seek expert advice.

⇨ See **Grammar** entry at **Subordinate clauses.**

7 separate '-ing' clauses

When you are describing two actions done by the same person at about the same time, you can use an '-ing' clause in front of the main clause. You can also put the '-ing' clause after the main clause, if it is clear who the subject is.

Walking down Newbury Street, they spotted the same man again.
He looked at me, suddenly realising that he was talking to a stranger.

If you want to indicate that someone did one thing immediately after another, you can mention the first thing they did in an '-ing' clause in front of the main clause.

Leaping out of bed, he dressed so quickly that he put his boots on the wrong feet.

⚠ **WARNING:** You should not use an '-ing' clause in front of a main clause when the subject of the '-ing' clause is not the same as the subject of the main clause. If you say 'Driving home later that night, the streets were deserted', you are suggesting that the streets were driving. However, if the verb in the main clause is transitive and active, you can use an '-ing' clause which relates to the object after the main clause. For example, you could say 'They spotted the same man again, walking down Newbury Street', meaning that the man was walking down Newbury Street. You should try to avoid making your sentence ambiguous.

8 active meaning

When an '-ing' form is used to begin a clause, it has an active meaning.

'You could play me a tune,' said Simon, sitting down.
Glancing at my clock, I saw that it was midnight.

Combinations beginning with **having** are sometimes used, especially in writing. For example, instead of writing 'John, who had already eaten, left early', you could write 'John, having already eaten, left early'.

Ash, having forgotten his fear, had become bored and restless.
Having beaten Rangers the previous week, Aberdeen were entitled to be confident about their ability to cope with Celtic.

9 passive meaning

'-ing' clauses beginning with **having been** and a past participle have a passive meaning.

Having been declared insane, he was confined for four months in a prison hospital.

10 subject and '-ing' form

In writing, you can use a clause containing a subject and an '-ing' form when you want to mention a fact or situation that is relevant to the fact stated in the main clause, or is the reason for it.

Bats are surprisingly long-lived creatures, some having a life-expectancy of around 20 years.
Her eyes glistening with tears, she stood up and asked the Council: 'What am I to do?'
Ashton being dead, the whole affair must now be laid before Colonel Browne.
The subject having been opened, he had to go on with it.

You do this when the subject of the '-ing' clause is closely connected with the subject of the main clause, or when the '-ing' form is **being** or **having**. **With** is sometimes added at the beginning of clauses of this type.

The old man stood up with tears running down his face.

With is always used when the two subjects are not closely connected and the '-ing' form is not 'being' or 'having'.

With the conditions increasing from breezy to windy, she had plenty of chances to show off her control.
Our correspondent said it resembled a frontline city, with helicopters patrolling overhead.

11 after a noun

You can use an '-ing' clause after a noun, **those**, or an indefinite pronoun to identify or describe someone by saying what they do or are doing.

GRAMMAR

She is now a British citizen <u>working for the Medical Research Council</u>.
Many of those <u>crossing the river</u> had brought books.
Anyone <u>following this advice</u> could find himself in trouble.

The '-ing' clause has a similar function to a relative clause.

12 **used like nouns**

You can use '-ing' forms like nouns. When used like this, they are sometimes called **gerunds** or **verbal nouns**. They can be the subject, object, or complement of a clause.

Does slow <u>talking</u> point to slow mental development?
Most men regarded <u>shopping</u> as women's work.
His hobby was <u>collecting</u> old coins.

They can be used after prepositions, including **to**.

They get a thrill <u>from taking</u> it home and <u>showing</u> it to their parents.
Local corner shops object <u>to seeing</u> their more expensive personal service undermined <u>by</u> cut-price supermarket-style <u>selling</u>.

When you are not using a determiner in front of an '-ing' form, the '-ing' form can have a direct object. When you are using a determiner, you use **of** to introduce the object.

I somehow didn't get round to <u>taking the examination</u>.
…an interview recorded during <u>the making of Karel Reisz's film</u>.

The object of the verb is put in front of the '-ing' form to form a compound noun if you are referring to a common type of activity, such as a type of job or hobby.

He regarded <u>film-making</u> as the most glamorous job on earth.
As a child, his interests were drawing and <u>stamp collecting</u>.

(i) Note that you use a singular form for the object. For example, you refer to **stamp collecting**, not 'stamps collecting'. You can use an '-ing' form with a possessive. This is rather formal.

<u>Your being</u> in the English department means that you must have chosen English as your main subject.
'I think <u>my mother's being</u> American had considerable advantage,' says Lady Astor's son.

You can use an '-ing' form in a similar way with a pronoun or noun. This is less formal.

What do you reckon on the prospects of <u>him being</u> re-elected?

A few nouns ending in '-ing', particularly ones referring to leisure activities, are not related to verbs but are formed from other nouns, or are much commoner than the related verbs.

ballooning	hang-gliding	power-boating	skydiving
caravanning	pot-holing	skateboarding	tobogganing

Camping and <u>caravanning</u> are increasingly cost-attractive.
<u>Skateboarding</u> has come back with a vengeance.

13 **other uses**

A few '-ing' forms are used as subordinating conjunctions:

assuming	considering	presuming	providing	supposing

The payments would gradually increase to £1,298, <u>assuming</u> interest rates stayed the same.
<u>Supposing</u> you heard that I'd died in the night, what would you feel?

A few '-ing' forms are used as prepositions or in compound prepositions:

according to	considering	excluding	owing to
barring	depending on	following	regarding
concerning	excepting	including	

The property tax would be set <u>according to</u> the capital value of the home.
There seems no reason why, <u>barring</u> accidents, Carson should not surpass the late Doug Smith's total.
We had already closed the party down shortly after midnight, <u>following</u> complaints from residents.

Inversion

Inversion means changing the normal word order in a sentence by putting part or all of the verb group in front of the subject. Usually an auxiliary is put in front of the subject, and the rest of the verb group is put after the subject. If no other auxiliary is used, a form of **do** is used, unless the verb is **be**.

1 in questions

Inversion is normal in questions.

<u>Are you</u> ready?
<u>Can John</u> swim?
<u>Did he</u> go to the fair?
Why <u>did you</u> fire him?
How many <u>are there?</u>

You do not need to use inversion when you are expecting someone to confirm what you are saying, or when you want to express a reaction such as surprise, interest, doubt, or anger about what has just been said.

<u>You've</u> been having trouble?
<u>She's</u> not going to do it?
'She's gone home.'–' <u>She's</u> gone back to Montrose?'

⚠ **WARNING:** You must use inversion in a question that begins with a 'wh'-word, unless the 'wh'-word is the subject. For example, you must say 'What did she think?', not '~~What she thought?~~' If the wh-word is the subject, there is no need for inversion. For example, you say 'Who was there?' Inversion is not used in reported questions. You do not say, for example, '~~She asked what was I doing~~'. You say 'She asked what I was doing'.
⇨ See **Grammar** entry at **Reporting**.

2 after place adjuncts

Inversion occurs in descriptions of a place or scene when an adjunct of place is put at the beginning of a clause. This type of structure is found mainly in writing.

On the ceiling <u>hung dustpans and brushes.</u>
Beyond them <u>lay the fields.</u>
Behind the desk <u>was a middle-aged woman.</u>

ⓘ Note that in this kind of inversion the main verb is put in front of the subject.

Inversion is used in speech after **here** and **there** when you are drawing attention to something.

<u>Here's the money,</u> go and buy yourself a watch.
Here <u>comes the cloud of smoke.</u>
There<u>'s another one!</u>

GRAMMAR

> ⚠ **WARNING:** You do not use inversion when the subject is a personal pronoun.
> *Here <u>he comes.</u>*
> *There <u>she is.</u>*

3 after negative adjuncts

Inversion occurs when broad negative adverbs or other negative adjuncts are put at the beginning of a clause for emphasis. This structure is used in formal speech and writing.

Never <u>have I</u> experienced such agony.
Seldom <u>have enterprise and personal responsibility</u> been more needed.
Rarely <u>has so much time</u> been wasted by so many people.
The police said the man was extremely dangerous and that on no account <u>should he</u> be approached.

ⓘ Note that inversion also occurs in formal speech and writing after adjuncts preceded by **only**.

Only then <u>would I</u> ponder the contradictions inherent in my own personality.

⇨ See **Usage** entry at **only**.

4 after 'neither' and 'nor'

You use inversion after **neither** and **nor** when you are saying that the previous negative statement also applies to another person or group.

'I can't remember.'–'Neither <u>can I.</u>'
Research assistants don't know how to do it, and nor <u>do qualified tutors.</u>

5 after 'so'

You use inversion after **so** when you are saying that the previous positive statement also applies to another person or group.

'I've been through the Ford works at Dagenham.'–'So <u>have I.</u>'
'I hate KB.'–'So <u>do I.</u> A most unsociable place, isn't it?'
'Skating's just a matter of practice.'–'Yes, well, so <u>is skiing.</u>'
Bioff went to jail. So <u>did the national president.</u>

ⓘ Note that when **so** is used to express surprise or to emphasize that someone should do something, inversion does not occur.

'It's on the table behind you.'–'So <u>it is!</u>'
'I feel very guilty about it.'–'So <u>you should.</u>'

6 other uses

Inversion occurs in conditional clauses that are not introduced by a conjunction. This structure is formal.

<u>Had the two tied,</u> victory would have gone to Todd.

Inversion can occur in comparisons after **as**.

The piece was well and confidently played, as <u>was Peter Maxwell Davies' 'Revelation and Fall'.</u>
Their father, George Churchill, also made jewellery, as <u>did their grandfather.</u>

Inversion is often used after a quote.

⇨ See **Grammar** entry at **Reporting**.

Irregular verbs

An **irregular verb** has a past form or a past participle which is not formed by adding '-ed'. A few irregular verbs have regular past forms, but two past participle forms, one of which is irregular. The commoner one is given first.

base form	past form	past participle
mow	mowed	mowed, mown
prove	proved	proved, proven
sew	sewed	sewed, sewn
show	showed	showed, shown
sow	sowed	sowed, sown
swell	swelled	swelled, swollen

Some irregular verbs have two past forms and two past participle forms. The form more commonly used is given first in the following table; note that some of the verbs have no regular forms, only irregular ones.

base form	past form	past participle
bid	bid, bade	bid, bidden
burn	burned, burnt	burned, burnt
bust	busted, bust	busted, bust
dream	dreamed, dreamt	dreamed, dreamt
dwell	dwelled, dwelt	dwelled, dwelt
hang	hanged, hung	hanged, hung
kneel	kneeled, knelt	kneeled, knelt
lean	leaned, leant	leaned, leant
leap	leaped, leapt	leaped, leapt
lie	lied, lay	lied, lain
light	lit, lighted	lit, lighted
smell	smelled, smelt	smelled, smelt
speed	sped, speeded	sped, speeded
spell	spelled, spelt	spelled, spelt
spill	spilled, spilt	spilled, spilt
spoil	spoiled, spoilt	spoiled, spoilt
weave	wove, weaved	woven, weaved
wet	wetted, wet	wetted, wet
wind	wound, winded	wound, winded

Note that **burnt**, **leant**, **learnt**, **smelt**, **spelt**, **spilt**, and **spoilt** are not used as verb forms in American English, and the verbs connected with them are regarded as regular. **Burnt** and **spilt** are sometimes used as adjectives in American English. With a few verbs, different forms are used for different meanings. For example, the past form and the past participle of the verb **hang** is **hung** for most of its meanings. However, **hanged** is used when it means 'executed by hanging'.

⇨ See **Usage** entries at **bid**, **hang**, **lay - lie**, **speed - speed up**, **weave**, and **wind**.

The following table shows verbs which have irregular past forms and past participles.

GRAMMAR

GRAMMAR

base form	past form	past participle	base form	past form	past participle
arise	arose	arisen	hide	hid	hidden
awake	awoke	awoken	hit	hit	hit
bear	bore	born	hold	held	held
beat	beat	beaten	hurt	hurt	hurt
become	became	become	keep	kept	kept
begin	began	begun	know	knew	known
bend	bent	bent	lay	laid	laid
bet	bet	bet	lead	led	led
bind	bound	bound	leave	left	left
bite	bit	bitten	lend	lent	lent
bleed	bled	bled	let	let	let
blow	blew	blown	lose	lost	lost
break	broke	broken	make	made	made
breed	bred	bred	mean	meant	meant
bring	brought	brought	meet	met	met
build	built	built	pay	paid	paid
burst	burst	burst	plead	pled	pled
buy	bought	bought	put	put	put
cast	cast	cast	quit	quit	quit
catch	caught	caught	read	read	read
choose	chose	chosen	rend	rent	rent
cling	clung	clung	ride	rode	ridden
come	came	come	ring	rang	rung
cost	cost	cost	rise	rose	risen
creep	crept	crept	run	ran	run
cut	cut	cut	saw	sawed	sawn
deal	dealt	dealt	say	said	said
dig	dug	dug	see	saw	seen
draw	drew	drawn	seek	sought	sought
drink	drank	drunk	sell	sold	sold
drive	drove	driven	send	sent	sent
eat	ate	eaten	set	set	set
fall	fell	fallen	shake	shook	shaken
feed	fed	fed	shed	shed	shed
feel	felt	felt	shine	shone	shone
fight	fought	fought	shoe	shod	shod
find	found	found	shoot	shot	shot
flee	fled	fled	shrink	shrank	shrunk
fling	flung	flung	shut	shut	shut
fly	flew	flown	sing	sang	sung
forbear	forbore	forborne	sink	sank	sunk
forbid	forbade	forbidden	sit	sat	sat
forget	forgot	forgotten	slay	slew	slain
forgive	forgave	forgiven	sleep	slept	slept
forsake	forsook	forsaken	slide	slid	slid
forswear	forswore	forsworn	sling	slung	slung
freeze	froze	frozen	slink	slunk	slunk
get	got	gotten	speak	spoke	spoken
give	gave	given	spend	spent	spent
go	went	gone	spin	spun	spun
grind	ground	ground	spread	spread	spread
grow	grew	grown	spring	sprang	sprung
hear	heard	heard	stand	stood	stood

base form	past form	past participle	base form	past form	past participle
steal	stole	stolen	teach	taught	taught
stick	stuck	stuck	tear	tore	torn
sting	stung	stung	tell	told	told
stink	stank	stunk	think	thought	thought
strew	strewed	strewn	throw	threw	thrown
stride	strode	stridden	thrust	thrust	thrust
strike	struck	struck	tread	trod	trodden
string	strung	strung	understand	understood	understood
strive	strove	striven	wake	woke	woken
swear	swore	sworn	wear	wore	worn
sweep	swept	swept	weep	wept	wept
swim	swam	swum	win	won	won
swing	swung	swung	wring	wrung	wrung
take	took	taken	write	wrote	written

Note that **gotten** is often used instead of 'got' as the past participle of **get** in American English.

⇨ See **Usage** entry at **gotten**.

Linking adjuncts

1 position

Linking adjuncts are words and phrases which indicate a connection between one clause or sentence and another. They are usually put at the beginning of the clause, or after the subject or the first auxiliary.

It will never be possible to release these criminals. Moreover, as the years go by, there are bound to be other similar cases.

Many species have survived. The effect on wild flowers, however, has been enormous.

He has seen it all before and has consequently developed a feeling for what will happen next.

2 adding information

Some linking adjuncts are used to indicate that you are adding an extra point or piece of information.

also	at the same time	furthermore	on top of that
as well	besides	moreover	too

His first book was published in 1932, and it was followed by a series of novels. He also wrote a book on British pubs.

This limits both their reliability and their scope. The smaller nations, moreover, cannot afford them.

⇨ See also **Usage** entry at **also - too - as well**.

3 giving a parallel

Other linking adjuncts are used to indicate that you are giving another example of the same point, or are using the same argument in two different cases.

again	equally	likewise
by the same token	in the same way	similarly

Retaining nuclear weapons may be significantly different from acquiring them, and, by the same token, relinquishing them may be different from refraining from acquiring them.

GRAMMAR

I still remember clearly the time and place where I first saw a morning glory in full bloom.
<u>Similarly,</u> I remember the first occasion when I saw a peacock spread its tail.

4 contrasting

Another group of linking adjuncts are used to indicate that you are making a contrast or giving an alternative.

all the same	even so	nonetheless	still
alternatively	however	on the contrary	then again
by contrast	instead	on the other hand	though
conversely	nevertheless	rather	

They were too good to allow us to score, but <u>all the same</u> they didn't play that well.
I would not have been surprised if he had smashed the bottle in my face. <u>Instead,</u> he sank back in his chair, gasping for breath.
He always had good manners. He was very quiet, <u>though.</u>

⇨ See **Usage** entry at **although - though** for information on the position of **though**.

5 indicating a result

Some linking adjuncts are used to indicate that the situation you are about to mention exists because of the fact you have just mentioned.

accordingly	consequently	so	therefore
as a result	hence	thereby	thus

Sales are still running at a lower rate than a year ago. <u>Consequently</u> stocks, with their attendant cost, have grown.
The terrain was more thickly wooded here, and <u>thus</u> more favourable to the defenders.

So is always put at the beginning of the clause.

His father had been a Member of Parliament and Chairman of the Isle of Wight County Council. <u>So,</u> as with so many of his famous family, Sir Charles Baring's own life was dominated by public service.

6 indicating sequence

Adjuncts of time are often used to link two sentences by indicating that one event took place after another.

afterwards	finally	next	suddenly
at last	immediately	presently	then
at once	instantly	since	within minutes
before long	last	soon	within the hour
eventually	later	soon after	
ever since	later on	subsequently	

Philip had a shrimp salad sandwich with Sy Gootblatt in the Silver Steer restaurant on campus. <u>Afterwards,</u> Sy went back to his office.

⇨ See **Usage** entries at **after - afterwards - later, eventually - finally, last - lastly, presently,** and **soon.**

Some adjuncts of time are used to indicate that one event took place or will take place before another.

beforehand	first	meanwhile
earlier	in the meantime	previously

Then he went out to Long Beach to thank his benefactor. Arrangements had been made <u>*beforehand,*</u> *of course.*
Ask the doctor to come as soon as possible. <u>*Meanwhile,*</u> *give first-aid treatment.*

⇨ See also **Usage** entry at **first - firstly.**
A few adjuncts are used to indicate that an event took place at the same time as another event.

at the same time	meanwhile	simultaneously	throughout

Barrie and John very unselfishly offered to go back down. <u>*Meanwhile,*</u> *the Italians were just coming into sight.*

'-ly' words

1 adverbs related to adjectives

Most **'-ly' words** are adverbs of manner, aspect, opinion, degree, or extent. They are formed from adjectives and have a similar meaning to the adjective.

They were hoping to bring a <u>*quick*</u> *end to the civil war.*
…tasks that I would ordinarily have expected to finish <u>*quickly*</u> *and easily.*
She succeeded in retaining her <u>*political*</u> *independence.*
…where societies remained <u>*politically*</u> *independent of their neighbours.*
This is hardly <u>*surprising.*</u>
<u>*Surprisingly,*</u> *I was not dismissed.*
It is very easy to do <u>*severe*</u> *damage to your eyes.*
The roots are <u>*severely*</u> *damaged.*

Usually you just add **-ly** to the end of an adjective when forming an adverb.

bad → **badly**   beautiful → **beautifully**   quiet → **quietly**   safe → **safely**

Sometimes a spelling change has to be made, depending on the ending of the adjective.

	adjective	adverb
'**-le**' changes to '**-ly**'	gentle	gently
'**-y**' changes to '**-ily**'	easy	easily
'**-ic**' changes to '**-ically**'	automatic	automatically
'**-ue**' changes to '**-uly**'	true	truly
'**-ll**' changes to '**-lly**'	full	fully

ⓘ Note that:
- the adverb related to **whole** is spelled **wholly**
- one-syllable adjectives ending in '-y' usually have '-ly' added in the normal way: **wryly, shyly**
- the adverb related to **dry** can be spelled **drily** or **dryly**
- the adverb formed from **public** is **publicly**

⇨ For more information about '-ly' adverbs of manner, aspect, opinion, degree, and extent, see **Grammar** entry at **Adjuncts.**

2 adverbs related to nouns

The adverbs in the following examples are formed from nouns, not from adjectives.

The other change, <u>*namely*</u> *the increase in electronic equipment, has slowed down.*
Here the problem is <u>*partly*</u> *economic.*
I am <u>*purposely*</u> *picking out examples of children with mixed rates of development.*

GRAMMAR

3 **adverbs not related to adjectives or nouns**

A few '-ly' adverbs are not directly related to any adjective or noun.

accordingly	exceedingly	manfully	mostly	presumably

You have a clear picture of how much you have to repay and can plan <u>accordingly</u>.
I could just see Simon <u>manfully</u> wielding a shovel.

4 **'-ly' adjectives**

Some '-ly' words are adjectives, not adverbs.

Current solar cells are too <u>costly</u> for commercial use.
...an <u>elderly</u> man with bushy eyebrows.
My husband said how <u>lonely</u> he had been while I was away.
I mustn't ask <u>silly</u> questions any more.

⚠ **WARNING:** You cannot form adverbs from these adjectives. However, you can use them in prepositional phrases with nouns such as **way**, **manner**, or **fashion**. For example, you can say 'He smiled in a friendly way'. Note that **kindly** is used as an adjective and an adverb.
⇨ See **Usage** entries at **kindly** and **homely**.

5 **adjectives related to nouns**

Many adjectives ending in '-ly' are formed from nouns referring to people, and indicate a quality that those people typically have or should have.

brotherly	friendly	miserly	saintly	soldierly
cowardly	gentlemanly	motherly	scholarly	womanly
fatherly	manly	neighbourly	sisterly	

Tell them how <u>cowardly</u> you were as a boy at school.
She treated him in a cordial, <u>sisterly</u> way.

6 **adjectives and adverbs**

Some '-ly' words are both adjectives and adverbs. They are related to nouns and describe things that happen at regular intervals.

daily	hourly	quarterly	yearly
fortnightly	monthly	weekly	

... <u>daily</u> or <u>weekly</u> visits to a children's clinic.
Maids were usually paid <u>monthly</u>.

Modals

1 **word order and form**

Modals are a type of auxiliary verb. They are used, for example, to indicate the possibility or necessity of an event, and to make requests, offers, and suggestions. They can also be used to make what you are saying more tactful or polite. The following words are modals:

can	dare	might	need	should	would
could	may	must	shall	will	

A modal is always the first word in a verb group. All modals are followed by the base form of a verb (the infinitive without 'to'), unless the verb has already been mentioned.

I must leave fairly soon.
Things might have been so different.
People may be watching.

⇨ See **Grammar** entry at **Ellipsis**.

The modals **dare** and **need** also occur as main verbs. In 'He doesn't dare climb the tree', **dare** is a main verb, but in 'He dare not climb the tree', **dare** is a modal.

⇨ See **Usage** entries at **dare** and **need**.

Modals have only one form. There is no '-s' form for the third person singular of the present tense, and there are no '-ing' or '-ed' forms.

There's nothing I can do about it.
I'm sure he can do it.

2 **short forms**

Shall, **will**, and **would** are not usually pronounced in full. When you write down what someone says, or write in a conversational style, you usually represent 'shall' and 'will' using **'ll**, and 'would' using **'d**, after pronouns.

⇨ See **Grammar** entry at **Contractions**.

I'll see you tomorrow.
Posy said she'd love to stay.

You can also represent 'will' as **'ll** after a noun.

My car'll be outside.

⚠ **WARNING:** Shall, **will**, and **would** are never shortened if they come at the end of a sentence.

Paul said he'd come, and I hope he will.

In questions, too, you use the full form of **shall**, **will**, and **would**.

Shall I open the door for you?
Will you hurry up!
Would you like an apple?

Remember that **'d** is also the short form of the auxiliary **had**.

I'd heard it many times.

The auxiliary **have** is not usually pronounced in full after **could**, **might**, **must**, **should**, and **would**. The contractions **could've**, **might've**, **must've**, **should've**, and **would've** are occasionally used in writing when reporting a conversation.

I must've fallen asleep.
You should've come to see us.

Not is not usually pronounced in full after a modal. You usually represent what someone says using **'nt** after the modal.

⇨ See **Grammar** entry at **Contractions**.

⇨ For information about modals that consist of more than one word, like **ought to** and **had better**, see **Grammar** entry at **Phrasal modals**.

⇨ For more information about the uses of modals, see the individual **Usage** entries for each word. See also **Topic** entries at **Advising someone, Invitations, Offers, Opinions, Permission**, and **Suggestions**.

⇨ For information on the use of **will** to talk about the future and **would** to talk about the past, see **Grammar** entries at **The Future** and **The Past**.

Modifiers

A **modifier** is a word or group of words which comes in front of a noun and adds information about the thing which the noun refers to. Modifiers can be:

● **adjectives**

This is the main bedroom.

After the crossroads look out for the <u>large white</u> building.
A <u>harder</u> mattress often helps with back injuries.

⇨ See **Grammar** entry at **Adjectives**.

- **nouns**

…the <u>music</u> industry.
… <u>tennis</u> lessons.

⇨ See **Grammar** entry at **Noun modifiers** and **Topic** entry at **Possession and other relationships**.

- **place names**

…a <u>London</u> hotel.
… <u>Arctic</u> explorers.

⇨ See **Topic** entry at **Places**.

- **place and direction adverbs**

…the <u>downstairs</u> television room.
The <u>overhead</u> light went on.

⇨ See **Topic** entry at **Places**.

- **times**

Castle was usually able to catch the <u>six thirty-five</u> train from Euston.
Every morning he would set off right after the <u>eight o'clock</u> news.

⇨ See **Topic** entry at **Time**.

Noun groups

A **noun group,** which is sometimes called a **noun phrase,** is a group of words which acts as the subject, object, complement, or adjunct of a clause, or as the object of a preposition.

<u>*Strawberries*</u> *are very expensive now.*
<u>He</u> was eating <u>an apple.</u>
That 's <u>a good idea.</u>
I swam <u>the other day.</u>
<u>*She*</u> *wanted <u>a job</u> in <u>the oil industry.</u>*

A noun group can consist of a noun by itself, or it can also contain a determiner, adjective, or other modifier or qualifier.

…picking <u>apples</u> on an autumn afternoon.
Peel, core, and slice <u>the apples.</u>
She noticed the two apple trees, already bearing a crop of <u>small green apples.</u>
<u>The apples hanging above us</u> were tinged with pink.

A noun group can also be a pronoun.

<u>I</u> 've got two boys, and <u>they</u> both enjoy playing football.
<u>Someone</u> is coming to mend <u>it</u> tomorrow.

⇨ See also **Grammar** entries at **Adjectives, Determiners, Modifiers, Nouns, Pronouns,** and **Qualifiers**.

Noun modifiers

A **noun modifier** is a noun that is used in front of another noun to give more specific information about someone or something. It is nearly always singular.

…the <u>car</u> door.
…a <u>football</u> player.
…a <u>surprise</u> announcement.

A few plural nouns remain plural when used as modifiers.

⇨ See section on **plural nouns** in **Grammar** entry at **Nouns**.

The use of noun modifiers is very common in English. You can use noun modifiers to indicate a wide range of relationships between two nouns. For example, you can indicate:

- what something is made of, as in **cotton socks**
- what is made in a particular place, as in **a glass factory**
- what someone does, as in **a football player**
- where something is, as in **my bedroom curtains** and **Brighton Technical College**
- when something happens, as in **the morning mist** and **her wartime activities**
- the nature or size of something, as in **a surprise attack** and **a pocket chess-set**

⇨ See also **Topic** entry at **Possession and other relationships.**

Noun modifiers can be used together.

… _car body repair_ kits.
…a _family dinner_ party.
…a _Careers Information_ Officer.

Adjectives can be put in front of a noun modifier.

…a _long_ car journey.
…a _new scarlet_ silk handkerchief.
… _complex_ business deals.

Nouns

1 **count nouns**	7 **collective nouns**
2 **uncount nouns**	8 **proper nouns**
3 **variable nouns**	9 **compoud nouns**
4 **mass nouns**	10 **abstract and concrete nouns**
5 **singular nouns**	11 **nouns followed by prepositions**
6 **plural nouns**	

A **noun** is used to identify a person or thing. Nouns can be classified into eight main grammatical types: count nouns, uncount nouns, variable nouns, mass nouns, singular nouns, plural nouns, collective nouns, and proper nouns.

1 count nouns

Nouns referring to things which can be counted are called **count nouns.** They have two forms, singular and plural. The plural form usually ends in 's'.

⇨ For full information on how to form plurals, see **Grammar** entry at **Plural forms of nouns.**

The singular form of a count noun is usually preceded by a determiner such as **a**, **another**, **every**, or **the**.

They left _the house_ to go for _a walk_ after tea.

When you use a singular form as the subject of a verb, you use a singular verb form.

My son _likes_ playing football.
The address on the letter _was_ wrong.

The plural form of a count noun can be used with or without a determiner. You do not use a determiner if you are referring to a type of thing in general. You use a determiner such as **the** or **my** if you are referring to a particular group of things. You use a determiner such as **many** or **several** when you are indicating how many things there are.

Does the hotel have large _rooms?_
The rooms at Watermouth are all like this.
The house had _many rooms_ and a terrace with a view of Etna.

When you use a plural form as the subject of a verb, you use a plural verb form.

These cakes _are_ delicious.

GRAMMAR

Count nouns can be used after numbers.

… _one_ table.
… _two_ cats.
… _three hundred_ pounds.

2 **uncount nouns**

Nouns which refer to things such as substances, qualities, feelings, and types of activity, rather than to individual objects or events, are called **uncount nouns.** These nouns have only one form.

I needed <u>help</u> with my <u>homework.</u>
The children had great <u>fun</u> playing with the puppets.

⚠ **WARNING:** Some nouns which are uncount nouns in English are count nouns or plural nouns in other languages.

advice	furniture	knowledge	money
baggage	homework	luggage	news
equipment	information	machinery	traffic

Uncount nouns are not used with 'a' or 'an'. They are used with **the** or possessive determiners when they refer to something that is specified or known.

I liked <u>the music,</u> but the words were boring.
Eva clambered over the side of the boat into <u>the water.</u>
She admired <u>his vitality.</u>

When you use an uncount noun as the subject of a verb, you use a singular verb form.

Electricity <u>is</u> dangerous.
Food <u>was</u> expensive in those days.

Uncount nouns are not used after numbers. It is possible to refer to a quantity of something which is expressed by an uncount noun by using a word like **some**, or a phrase like **a piece of**.

⇨ See **Grammar** entry at **Quantity.**

I want <u>some privacy.</u>
I pulled <u>the two pieces of paper</u> from my pocket.

⚠ **WARNING:** Some uncount nouns end in '**-ics**' or '**-s**' and therefore look like plural count nouns.

<u>Mathematics</u> is too difficult for me.
<u>Measles</u> is in most cases a harmless illness.

These nouns usually refer to:

● subjects of study and activities

acoustics	athletics	ethics	logistics	physics
aerobics	classics	genetics	mathematics	politics
aerodynamics	economics	gymnastics	mechanics	statistics
aeronautics	electronics	linguistics	obstetrics	thermodynamics

● games

billiards	cards	darts	skittles
bowls	checkers	draughts	tiddlywinks

GRAMMAR

● illnesses

| diabetes | measles | mumps | rabies | rickets |

3 | variable nouns

Variable nouns are nouns which combine the behaviour of count and uncount nouns. They are like count nouns when they refer to an instance or more than one instance of something, for example **an injustice; injustices** or to individual members of a class, for example **a cake; cakes.** Otherwise they behave like uncount nouns, referring to something in more general terms.

He has been in <u>prison</u> for ten years.
Staff were called in from <u>a prison</u> nearby to help stop the violence.
… the problems of British <u>prisons.</u>
They ate all their chicken and nearly all the stewed <u>apple.</u>
She brought in a tray on which were toast, butter, <u>an apple,</u> and some marmalade.
There was a bowl of red <u>apples</u> on the window sill.

4 | mass nouns

Mass nouns are nouns which behave like uncount nouns when they refer to a substance, for example '**Use detergent**', and like count nouns when they refer to types or brands of substance, for example '**Use a strong detergent**'; '**More detergents are now available**'.

I pass the lighted window of a shop where <u>perfume</u> is sold.
I found <u>an</u> interesting new <u>perfume</u> last week.
Department stores are finding that French <u>perfumes</u> are selling slowly.
The roast chicken is filled with <u>cheese</u> and spinach.
I was looking for <u>a cheese</u> which was soft and creamy.
There are plenty of delicious <u>cheeses</u> made in the area.

5 | singular nouns

There are some nouns, and some particular meanings of nouns, which are only used in the singular form. **Singular nouns** are always used with a determiner and take a singular verb.

<u>The sun</u> was shining.
He's always thinking about <u>the past</u> and worrying about <u>the future.</u>
They were beginning to find Griffiths' visits rather <u>a strain.</u>
There was <u>a note</u> of satisfaction in his voice.

6 | plural nouns

Some nouns have only a plural form. For example, you can buy **goods**, but not 'a good'. Other nouns have only a plural form when they are used with a particular meaning. They take a plural verb.

Take care of your <u>clothes.</u>
The weather <u>conditions</u> were the same.

⚠ **WARNING:** Plural nouns are not usually used after numbers. For example, you do not say 'two clothes' or 'two goods'.

Some plural nouns refer to single items that have two linked parts. These plural nouns are:

● things that people wear

| glasses | knickers | pants | shorts | trousers |
| jeans | panties | pyjamas | tights | |

GRAMMAR

GRAMMAR

- tools that people use

binoculars	pliers	scissors	tweezers
pincers	scales	shears	

You use **some** in front of these words when talking about one item.
I wish I'd brought <u>some scissors.</u>

You can also use **a pair of** when talking about one item, and **two pairs of**, **three pairs of**, and so on when talking about more than one item.
I was sent out to buy <u>a pair of scissors.</u>
Liza had given me <u>three pairs of jeans.</u>

Many plural nouns lose their '-s' and '-es' endings when they are used in front of other nouns.
…my <u>trouser</u> pocket.
… <u>pyjama</u> trousers.

However, some plural nouns keep the same form when used in front of other nouns.

arms	clothes	jeans
binoculars	glasses	sunglasses

… <u>arms</u> control.
… <u>clothes</u> pegs.

7 collective nouns
Some nouns, called **collective nouns,** refer to a group of people or things.

army	company	family	government	navy	staff
audience	crew	flock	group	press	team
committee	enemy	gang	herd	public	

The singular form of these nouns can be used with a singular or plural verb form, depending on whether the group is seen as one thing or as several things. It is more common to use a plural form in British English. The singular form of the verb is nearly always preferred in American English.
Our <u>family isn't</u> poor any more.
My <u>family are</u> perfectly normal.

When referring back to a collective noun, you usually use a singular pronoun or determiner if you have used a singular verb. You use a plural pronoun or determiner if you have used a plural verb.
The government <u>has</u> said <u>it</u> would wish to do this only if there was no alternative.
The government <u>have</u> made up <u>their</u> minds that <u>they</u> 're going to win.

However, plural pronouns and determiners are sometimes used to refer back to a collective noun even when a singular verb has been used. This is done especially in a separate clause.
The team <u>was</u> not always successful but <u>their</u> rate of success far exceeded expectations.
His family <u>was</u> waiting in the next room, but <u>they</u> had not yet been informed.

Names of organizations and groups such as football teams also behave like collective nouns in British English, but in American English they are usually regarded as singular.
<u>Liverpool is</u> leading 1-0.
<u>Liverpool are</u> attacking again.
<u>Sears is</u> struggling to attract shoppers.

⚠️ **WARNING:** Although you can use a plural verb after the singular form of a collective noun, these singular forms do not behave exactly like plural count nouns. Numbers cannot be used in front of them. For example, you cannot say ~~'Three crew were killed'~~. You have to say 'Three of the crew were killed' or 'Three members of the crew were killed'.

Most of the collective nouns listed above have ordinary plural forms, which refer to more than one group. However, **press** (meaning 'newspapers' or 'journalists') and **public** (meaning 'the people of a country') do not have plural forms.

8 proper nouns

Names of people, places, organizations, institutions, ships, magazines, books, plays, paintings, and other unique things are **proper nouns** and are spelled with initial capital letters. A proper noun is sometimes used with a determiner but normally has no plural.

⇨ See **Topic** entries at **Names and titles** and **Places**.

...Mozart.
...Romeo and Juliet.
...the President of the United States.
...the United Nations.
...the Seine.

9 compound nouns

Compound nouns are made up of two or more words. Some are written as separate words, some are written with hyphens between the words, and some have a hyphen between the first two words.

His luggage came sliding towards him on the <u>conveyor belt.</u>
There are many <u>cross-references</u> to help you find what you want.
It can be cleaned with a spot of <u>washing-up liquid.</u>

Some compound nouns are written in several ways. A Cobuild dictionary will tell you how you should write each compound noun.

⇨ For information on compound nouns ending in 'ing', see **Grammar** entry at **'-ing' forms**.

⇨ For information on the plurals of compound nouns, see **Grammar** entry at **Plural forms of nouns**.

10 abstract and concrete nouns

An **abstract noun** is a noun which refers to a quality, idea, or experience rather than something that can be seen or touched.

...a boy or girl with <u>intelligence.</u>
We found Alan weeping with <u>relief</u> and <u>joy.</u>
I am stimulated by <u>conflict.</u>

Abstract nouns are often variable nouns. They behave like count nouns when they refer to a particular instance of something. Otherwise they behave like uncount nouns, referring to something in more general terms.

⇨ See section above on **variable nouns.**

Russia had been successful in previous <u>conflicts.</u>

A **concrete noun** is a noun which refers to something that can be seen or touched. Nouns referring to objects, animals, and people are usually countable.

...a broad <u>highway</u> with shady <u>trees.</u>

A few nouns that refer to groups of objects, such as **furniture** and **equipment**, are uncount.

⇨ See section above on **uncount nouns.**

Nouns referring to substances are usually uncount.

There is not enough <u>water.</u>

GRAMMAR

However, when they refer to a particular type or brand of a substance, they behave like count nouns.

⇨ See section above on **mass nouns**.

11 nouns followed by prepositions

Some nouns, especially abstract nouns, are often followed by a prepositional phrase to show what they relate to. There is often little or no choice about which preposition to use after a particular noun.

I demanded <u>access to</u> a telephone.
…his <u>authority over</u> them.
…the <u>solution to</u> our energy problem.

● The following nouns usually or often have **to** after them:

access	alternative	devotion	preface	return
addiction	answer	disloyalty	prelude	sequel
adherence	antidote	exception	recourse	solution
affront	approach	fidelity	reference	susceptibility
allegiance	aversion	immunity	relevance	threat
allergy	contribution	incitement	relevance	vulnerability
allusion	damage	introduction	resistance	witness

● The following nouns usually or often have **for** after them:

admiration	cure	disrespect	recipe	substitute
appetite	demand	hunger	regard	sympathy
aptitude	desire	love	remedy	synonym
bid	disdain	need	respect	taste
craving	dislike	provision	responsibility	thirst
credit	disregard	quest	room	

● The following nouns usually or often have **on** or **upon** after them:

assault	concentration	dependence	insistence	stance
attack	constraint	effect	reflection	tax
ban	crackdown	embargo	reliance	
comment	curb	hold	restriction	

● The following nouns usually or often have **with** after them:

affinity	dealings	familiarity	intersection
collusion	dissatisfaction	identification	sympathy

● The following nouns usually or often have **with** or **between** after them:

collision	contrast	encounter	link	quarrel
connection	correspondence	intimacy	parity	relationship

Many other nouns are usually or often followed by a particular preposition. The following list indicates which preposition follows each noun.

authority over	foray into	reaction against
control over	freedom from	relapse into
departure from	grudge against	safeguard against
escape from	insurance against	
excerpt from	quotation from	

As you can see from the lists given above, it is often the case that words with a similar meaning are typically followed by the same preposition. For example, **appetite**, **craving**, **desire**, **hunger**, and **thirst** are all followed by **for**. **Acceleration**, **decline**, **fall**, **drop**, and **rise** are all followed by **in**.

Objects

1 direct objects

The **object** of a verb or clause is a noun group which refers to the person or thing that is involved in an action but does not perform the action. The object comes after the verb. It is sometimes called the **direct object**.

He closed the door.
It was dark by the time they reached their house.
Some of the women noticed me.

2 indirect objects

Some verbs have two objects. For example in the sentence 'I gave John the book', 'the book' is the direct object, and 'John' is the **indirect object**. The indirect object usually refers to the person who benefits from an action or receives something as a result of it. You can put an indirect object in front of the direct object or in a prepositional phrase after the direct object.

Dad gave me a car.
He handed his room key to the receptionist.

⇨ For more information, see section on **ditransitive verbs** in **Grammar** entry at **Verbs**.

3 prepositional objects

Prepositions also have objects. The noun group after a preposition is sometimes called the **prepositional object**.

I climbed up the tree.
Miss Burns looked calmly at Marianne.
Woodward finished the second page and passed it to the editor.

⇨ See **Grammar** entry at **Prepositions**.

The Passive

1 form and usage

The **passive** refers to verb groups whose subject is the person or thing that is affected by an action. For example, 'He was helped by his brother' contains a passive verb. With **active** verb groups, the subject is the person or thing doing the action, as in 'His brother helped him'.

You use the passive when you are more interested in the person or thing affected by the action than in the person or thing doing the action, or when you do not know who performed the action. When you use the passive, you do not have to mention the performer of the action, as in 'He was helped'.

Passive verb groups consist of a tense of **be**, followed by the past participle of the main verb. For example, if you want to use the passive of the simple past of 'eat', you use the simple past of 'be' (**was** or **were**) and the past participle of 'eat' (**eaten**). You can have passive infinitives, such as **to be eaten** and passive '-ing' forms, such as **being eaten**.

⇨ For full information, see **Grammar** entry at **Tenses**.

Nearly all transitive verbs (verbs which can have an object) can be used in the passive.

The room <u>has been cleaned.</u>
Some very interesting work <u>is being done</u> on this.
The name of the winner <u>will be announced</u> tomorrow.

⚠ **WARNING:** A few transitive verbs are rarely or never used in the passive:

elude	flee	have	like	resemble
escape	get	let	race	suit

Many phrasal verbs which consist of an intransitive verb and a preposition can also be used in the passive.

In some households, the man <u>was referred to</u> as the master.
Sanders asked if such men could <u>be relied on</u> to keep their mouths shut.

ⓘ Note that the preposition is still put after the verb, but it is not followed by a noun group because the noun group it applies to is being used as the subject.

2 'by' and 'with'

In a passive sentence, if you want to mention the person or thing that performs an action, you use the preposition **by**.

He had been poisoned <u>by his girlfriend.</u>
He was brought up <u>by an aunt.</u>

If you want to mention the thing that is used to perform an action, you use the preposition **with**.

A circle was drawn in the dirt <u>with a stick.</u>
Moisture must be drawn out first <u>with salt.</u>

3 object complements

Some verbs can have a complement after their object. The complement is an adjective or noun group which describes the object.

⇨ See section on **object complements** in **Grammar** entry at **Complements**.

When these verbs are used in the passive, the complement is put immediately after the verb.

In August he <u>was elected Vice President of the Senate.</u>
If a person today talks about ghosts, he <u>is considered ignorant or mad.</u>

4 'get'

In conversation, **get** is sometimes used instead of 'be' to form the passive.

Our car <u>gets cleaned</u> about once every two months.
My husband <u>got fined</u> in Germany for crossing the road.

5 in report structures

⇨ For information on the use of reporting verbs in the passive, see **Grammar** entry at **Reporting**.

The Past

⇨ For the formation of past tenses, see **Grammar** entry at **Tenses**.

1 talking about the past

The **simple past** tense is used to refer to an event in the past.

She <u>opened</u> the door.

GRAMMAR

One other factor <u>influenced</u> him.

In order to indicate exactly when something happened, or to indicate that something happened for a period of time or took place regularly, it is necessary to use additional words and expressions.

The Prime Minister <u>flew</u> to New York <u>yesterday.</u>
He <u>thought for a few minutes.</u>
They <u>went</u> for picnics <u>most weekends.</u>

When you want to talk about something which had been happening for some time when an event occurred, or which continued to happen after the event, you use the **past continuous** tense.

We <u>were driving</u> towards the racetrack when a policeman stepped in front of our car to ask for identification.
While they <u>were approaching</u> the convent, a couple of girls ran out of the gate.

You also use the past continuous to talk about a temporary state of affairs in the past.

Our team <u>were losing</u> 2-1 at the time.
We <u>were staying</u> with friends in Italy.

2 **regular events**
Would or **used to** can be used instead of the simple past to talk about something which occurred regularly in the past.

We <u>would</u> normally <u>spend</u> the winter in Miami.
She <u>used to get</u> quite cross with Lally.

Used to is also used to talk about situations that no longer exist.

People <u>used to believe</u> that the earth was flat.

Would is not used like this.

3 **perfect tenses**
When you are concerned with the present effects of something which happened at some time in the past, you use the **present perfect** tense.

I'm afraid I <u>'ve forgotten</u> my book, so I don't know.
<u>Have</u> you <u>heard</u> from Jill recently? How is she?

You also use the present perfect when you are talking about a situation which started in the past and still continues.

I <u>have known</u> him for years.
He <u>has been</u> here since six o'clock.

You use the **present perfect continuous** tense when you want to emphasize the fact that a recent event continued to happen for some time.

She <u>'s been crying.</u>
I <u>'ve been working</u> hard all day.

When you are looking back to a point in the past, and you are concerned with the effects of something which happened at an even earlier time in the past, you use the **past perfect** tense.

I apologized because I <u>had left</u> my wallet at home.
He learned that the fence between the two properties <u>had been removed.</u>

You use the **past perfect continuous** tense when referring to a situation or event which started at an earlier time and continued for some time, or was still continuing.

I was about twenty. I <u>had been studying</u> French for a couple of years.
He <u>had been working</u> there for ten years when the trouble started.

4 **future in the past**
When you want to talk about something that was in the future at a particular moment in the past, you can use **would**, **was/were going to**, or the past continuous tense.

He thought to himself how wonderful it <u>would taste.</u>

Her daughter <u>was going to do</u> the cooking.
Mike <u>was taking</u> his test the week after.

Past participles

1 basic uses

The **past participle** of a verb is used to form perfect tenses, passives, and, in some cases, adjectives. It is also called the **'-ed' form,** especially when it is used as an adjective.

Advances have <u>continued,</u> though actual productivity has <u>fallen.</u>
Jobs are still being <u>lost.</u>
We cannot refuse to teach children the <u>required</u> subjects.

⇨ See **Grammar** entries at **Tenses** and **'-ed' adjectives.**

The past participle is usually the same as the past form of the verb, except in the case of irregular verbs.

⇨ See **Grammar** entry at **Irregular verbs.**

2 in non-finite clauses

In writing, a past participle can be used to begin a non-finite clause, with a passive meaning. For example, instead of writing 'She was saddened by their betrayal and resigned', you could write 'Saddened by their betrayal, she resigned'. The main clause can refer to a consequence of the situation mentioned in the past participle clause, or just to a related event that followed it.

<u>Stunned by the swiftness of the assault,</u> the enemy were overwhelmed.
<u>Granted an amnesty and prematurely released,</u> she rallied her followers and continued the struggle.

This structure is used especially with past participles which indicate feelings. Alternative structures are **having been, after having been**, or **after being** followed by a past participle.

<u>Having been left fatherless in early childhood</u> he was brought up by his uncle.
…the prints of two hands pressed on the stone <u>after having been dipped in red paint.</u>
<u>After being left for an hour in the shower room,</u> we were placed in separate cells.

Past participles can be used in clauses introduced by a subordinating conjunction, with no subject or auxiliary, when the subject would be the same as the one in the main clause.

Dogs, <u>when threatened,</u> make themselves smaller and whimper like puppies.
<u>Although now recognised as an important habitat for birds,</u> the area of Dorset heathland has been cut in half since 1962.

3 after nouns

You can use a clause beginning with a past participle after a noun, **those**, or an indefinite pronoun to identify or describe someone by saying what happens or has happened to them.

…a successful method of bringing up children <u>rejected by their natural parents.</u>
Many of those <u>questioned in the poll</u> agreed with the party's policy on defence.
It doesn't have to be someone <u>appointed by the government.</u>

Phrasal modals

A **phrasal modal** is a phrase which forms a single verb group with another verb and which affects the meaning of that verb in the same way that a modal verb does.

Some phrasal modals begin with **be** or **have**, for example **be able to, be bound to, be going to, have got to**, and **have to**. The first word in these phrases changes its form depending on the subject and the tense, in the way that 'be' and 'have' normally do. You say 'I am bound to fall asleep', 'She is bound to fall asleep', 'We have to leave tonight' and 'They had to leave last night'. The other phrasal modals do not change in this way. You say 'I would rather go by bus' and 'He would rather go by bus'. The phrasal modals are:

be able to	have got to	would rather	be unable to
had best	have to	would just as soon	used to
had better	be liable to	would sooner	would do well to
be bound to	be meant to	be supposed to	
be going to	ought to	be sure to	

It <u>was supposed to</u> last for a year and actually lasted eight.
We <u>would do well not to</u> add salt to our diet at all.
The deep sea diving <u>is bound to</u> take me away from home a good deal.
She <u>is able to</u> sit up in a wheelchair.
He <u>used to</u> shout at people.
I <u>would sooner</u> give up sleep than miss my evening class.

Phrasal verbs

1 | **phrasal verbs**

A **phrasal verb** is a combination of a verb and an adverb, a verb and a preposition, or a verb, an adverb, and a preposition, which together have a single meaning. The adverb or preposition is also called a **particle**. Phrasal verbs extend the usual meaning of the verb or create a new meaning.

The pain gradually <u>wore off.</u>
I had to <u>look after</u> the kids.
They <u>broke out of</u> prison.
Kroop tried to <u>talk</u> her <u>out of</u> it.

2 | **position of objects**

● With phrasal verbs consisting of a transitive verb and an adverb, the object of the verb can usually be put in front of the adverb or after it.

Don't give <u>the story</u> away, silly!
I wouldn't want to give away <u>any secrets.</u>

● However, when the object of the verb is a pronoun, the pronoun must go in front of the adverb.

He cleaned <u>it</u> up.
I answered <u>him</u> back and took my chances.

● With phrasal verbs consisting of a transitive verb and a preposition, the object of the verb is put after the verb, and the object of the preposition is put after the preposition.

They agreed to let <u>him</u> into <u>their little secret.</u>
The farmer threatened to set <u>his dogs</u> on <u>them.</u>

● With phrasal verbs where a verb and a preposition act as one transitive unit, the object is put after the verb and the preposition.

I love looking after <u>the children.</u>
Elaine wouldn't let him provide for <u>her.</u>
…friends who stuck by <u>me</u> during the difficult times.

● With phrasal verbs consisting of a transitive verb, an adverb, and a preposition, the object of the verb is usually put in front of the adverb, not after it.

Multinational companies can play <u>individual markets</u> off against each other.
I'll take <u>you</u> up on that generous invitation.

● With phrasal verbs where a verb, an adverb, and a preposition act as one transitive unit, The object is put after the verb, adverb, and preposition.

They had to put up with <u>their son's bad behaviour.</u>
He was looking forward to <u>life after retirement.</u>
Look out for <u>the symptoms of influenza.</u>

GRAMMAR

3 **passives**

With transitive phrasal verbs which can be used in the passive, the verb and the preposition or adverb stay together.

She died a year later, and I was taken in by her only relative.
I was dropped off in front of my house.
The factory was closed down last year.

Plural forms of nouns

The following table shows the basic ways of forming the plurals of count nouns.

	singular form	plural form
		add '-s' (/s/ or /z/)
regular	hat	hats
	tree	trees
		add '-s' (/ɪz/)
ending in '-se'	rose	roses
ending in '-ze'	prize	prizes
ending in '-ce'	service	services
ending in '-ge'	age	ages
		add '-es' (/ɪz/)
ending in '-sh'	bush	bushes
ending in '-ch'	speech	speeches
ending in '-ss'	glass	glasses
ending in '-x'	box	boxes
ending in '-s'	bus	buses
		change '-y' to '-ies'
ending in consonant + '-y'	country	countries
	lady	ladies
		add '-s'
ending in vowel + '-y'	boy	boys
	valley	valleys

Nouns ending with a long vowel sound and the sound /θ/ have their plural forms pronounced as ending in /ðz/. For example, the plural of **path** is pronounced /pɑːðz/ and the plural of **mouth** is pronounced /maʊðz/.

House is pronounced /haʊs/, but its plural form **houses** is pronounced /haʊzɪz/.

ⓘ Note that, if the '-ch' at the end of a noun is pronounced as /k/ , you add '-s', not '-es', to form the plural. For example, the plural of **stomach** /stʌmək/ is **stomachs**.

> stomach → stomachs   monarch → monarchs

1 **nouns with no change in form**

Some nouns have the same form for both singular and plural.

…a sheep.
…nine sheep.

Many of these nouns refer to animals or fish.

bison	fish	grouse	mullet	sheep	whitebait
cod	goldfish	halibut	reindeer	shellfish	
deer	greenfly	moose	salmon	trout	

(*i*) Note that even when a noun referring to an animal has a plural form ending in '-s', it is quite common to use the form without '-s' to refer to a group of the animals in the context of hunting.

Zebra are a more difficult prey.

Similarly, when you are referring to a large number of trees or plants growing together, you can use the form without '-s'. However, this is used like an uncount noun, not a plural form.

…the rows of willow and cypress which lined the creek.

The following nouns also have the same form for singular and plural:

aircraft	gallows	insignia	series
crossroads	grapefruit	mews	spacecraft
dice	hovercraft	offspring	species

2 nouns ending in '-f' or '-fe'

There are several nouns ending in '-f' or '-fe' where you form the plural by substituting '-**ves**' for '-f' or '-fe'.

calf → calves	elf → elves	half → halves	knife → knives
leaf → leaves	life → lives	loaf → loaves	scarf → scarves
sheaf → sheaves	shelf → shelves	thief → thieves	turf → turves
wharf → wharves	wife → wives	wolf → wolves	

The plural of **hoof** can be **hoofs** or **hooves**.

3 nouns ending in '-o'

With many nouns ending in '-o', you just add '-s' to form the plural.

photo → photos	radio → radios

However, the following nouns have plurals ending in '-**oes**':

domino	embargo	negro	tomato
echo	hero	potato	veto

The following nouns ending in '-o' can have plurals ending in either '-**os**' or '-**oes**':

buffalo	ghetto	memento	stiletto
cargo	innuendo	mosquito	tornado
flamingo	mango	motto	torpedo
fresco	manifesto	salvo	volcano

4 irregular plurals

A few nouns have special plural forms, as shown below:

child	→ children	foot	→ feet	goose	→ geese	louse	→ lice
man	→ men	mouse	→ mice	ox	→ oxen	tooth	→ teeth
woman	→ women						

GRAMMAR

(i) Note that the first syllable of **women** /wɪmɪn/ is pronounced differently from that of **woman** /wʊmən/.

Most nouns which refer to people and which end with '**-man**','**-woman**', or '**-child**' have plural forms ending with '**-men**','**-women**', or '**-children**'.

Englishwoman	→	Englishwomen
grandchild	→	grandchildren
postman	→	postmen

However, the plural forms of **German, human, Norman,** and **Roman** are **Germans, humans, Normans,** and **Romans**.

5 | plurals of compound nouns

Most compound nouns have plurals formed by adding '**-s**' to the end of the last word.

down-and-out	→	down-and-outs
swimming pool	→	swimming pools
tape recorder	→	tape recorders

However, in the case of compound nouns which consist of a noun ending in '**-er**' and an adverb such as **on** or **by** and which refer to a person, you add '**-s**' to the first word to form the plural.

passer-by	→ passers-by	hanger-on → hangers-on

Compound nouns consisting of three or more words have plurals formed by adding '**-s**' to the first word when the first word is a noun identifying the type of person or thing you are talking about.

brother-in-law → brothers-in-law	bird of prey → birds of prey

6 | plurals of foreign words

There are words in English which are borrowed from other languages, especially Latin, and which still form their plurals according to the rules of those languages. Many of them are technical or formal, and some are also used with a regular '**-s**' or '**-es**' plural ending in non-technical or informal contexts. You may need to check these in a dictionary.

● Some nouns ending in '**-us**' have plurals ending in '**-i**'.

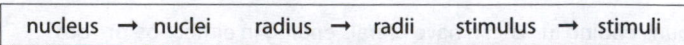

nucleus → nuclei	radius → radii	stimulus → stimuli

● However, other nouns ending in '**-us**' have different plurals.

corpus → corpora	genus → genera

● Nouns ending in '**-um**' often have plurals ending in '**-a**'.

aquarium → aquaria	memorandum → memoranda

● Some nouns ending in '**-a**' have plurals formed by adding '**-e**'.

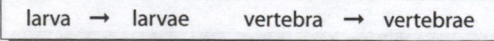

larva → larvae	vertebra → vertebrae

- Nouns ending in '**-is**' have plurals in which the '**-is**' is replaced by '**-es**'.

analysis → analyses	crisis → crises	hypothesis → hypotheses

- Some nouns ending in '**-ix**' or '**-ex**' have plurals ending in '**-ices**'.

appendix → appendices	index → indices	matrix → matrices

- Nouns borrowed from Greek which end in '**-on**' have plurals in which the '**-on**' is replaced by '**-a**'.

criterion → criteria	phenomenon → phenomena

- The following words borrowed from French have the same written form for the plural as for the singular. The '**-s**' at the end is not pronounced for the singular but is pronounced /z/ for the plural.

bourgeois	chassis	corps	patois	précis	rendezvous

Possessive determiners

1 **possessive determiners**

Possessive determiners show who or what something belongs to or is connected with. The possessive determiners are:

	singular	plural
1st person	my	our
2nd person	your	
3rd person	his her its	their

You choose a possessive determiner according to the identity of the person or thing who has the thing you are talking about. For example, if you are talking about a pen belonging to a woman, you say '**her** pen', but if the pen belongs to a man, you say '**his** pen'.

Soon after five that day the vicar called at <u>my house</u>.
Sir Thomas More built <u>his house</u> there.
I walked out of <u>her house</u> and collided with a pillar box.
Sometimes I would sleep in <u>their house</u> all night.

The same determiner is used whether the noun after the possessive determiner is singular or plural, or refers to a person or a thing.

I just went on writing in <u>my notebook</u>.
<u>*My parents*</u> *don't trust me.*

⚠ **WARNING:** You do not use another determiner with a possessive determiner. For example, you do not say 'I took off the my shoes'. You say 'I took off my shoes'.

2 **'the' instead of possessive**

Sometimes the determiner **the** is used when there is an obvious possessive meaning, particularly when you are talking about someone doing something to a part of someone else's body.

GRAMMAR

They hit him over <u>the head</u> with a stick.
He took his daughters by <u>the hand</u> and led them away.

You can also use **the** when referring to one of your possessions. For example, you can say 'I'll go and get **the** car' instead of 'I'll go and get my car'.
I went back to <u>the</u> house.
The noise from <u>the</u> washing-machine is getting worse.

However, you cannot use 'the' like this when referring to something that someone is wearing. For example, you say 'My watch is slow'. You do not say '~~The watch is slow~~'. It is not usual to use 'the' with a possessive meaning when referring to a relative such as an uncle or a sister. However, people often refer to their children as '**the** children' or '**the** kids'.
When <u>the children</u> had gone to bed I said, 'I'm going out for a while'.

(i) Note that possessive determiners are more commonly used to indicate that something belongs to a person than to a thing. For example, it is more usual to say '**the** door' than to say 'its door' when referring to the door of a room.

⇨ For more information on when to use a possessive determiner, see **Topic** entry at **Possession and other relationships**.

Prepositions

1 with a following noun group

A **preposition** is a word like **at**, **in**, **on**, or **with** which is normally followed by a noun group, forming a **prepositional phrase**. The noun group after a preposition is sometimes called the **prepositional object**.
Prepositions are often used in phrases which indicate place and time.

She waited <u>at</u> the bus stop <u>for</u> twenty minutes.
Tell me if you're coming <u>to</u> my party <u>on</u> Saturday.
They arrived <u>at</u> Scunthorpe <u>in</u> the morning.

⇨ See **Topic** entries at **Places** and **Time**.

Prepositions are also used after nouns, adjectives, and verbs to introduce phrases which give more information about a thing, quality, or action.

⇨ See **Grammar** entries at **Nouns**, **Adjectives**, **Verbs**, and **Qualifiers**.

2 without a following noun group

There are some cases where a preposition is not followed by a noun group. The noun group it relates to comes earlier in the sentence. These cases are:

● **questions and reported questions**
<u>What</u> will you talk <u>about</u>?
She doesn't know <u>what</u> we were talking <u>about</u>.

⇨ See **Grammar** entries at **Questions** and **Reporting**.

● **relative clauses**
...the job <u>which</u> I'd been training <u>for</u>.

⇨ See **Grammar** entry at **Relative clauses**.

● **passive structures**
<u>Amateur theatricals</u> have already been referred <u>to</u>.

⇨ See **Grammar** entry at **The Passive**.

● **after a complement and 'to'-infinitive**
<u>She</u>'s very difficult to get on <u>with</u>.
<u>The whole thing</u> was just too awful to think <u>about</u>.

⇨ See **Grammar** entry at **'To'-infinitive clauses**.

3 complex prepositional object

After a preposition, you can sometimes use another prepositional phrase or a 'wh'-clause.

I had taken his drinking bowl <u>from beneath the kitchen table.</u>
I threw down my book and walked across the room <u>to where she was sitting.</u>
…the question <u>of who should be President of the Board of Trade.</u>

4 prepositions and adverbs

Some words that are used as prepositions are also used with a similar meaning as adverbs (that is, without a noun group after them).

I looked <u>underneath the bed,</u> but the box had gone.
Always put a sheet of paper <u>underneath.</u>
The door was <u>opposite the window.</u>
The kitchen was <u>opposite,</u> across a little landing.

The following words can be used as prepositions or adverbs with a similar meaning:

aboard	alongside	by	on	since
about	before	down	on board	through
above	behind	in	opposite	throughout
across	below	in between	outside	under
after	beneath	inside	over	underneath
against	beside	near	past	up
along	beyond	off	round	within

The Present

⇨ For the formation of present tenses, see **Grammar** entry at **Tenses.**

The **simple present** tense is usually used for talking about long-term situations that exist at the present time, regular or habitual actions currently taking place, and general truths.

My dad <u>works</u> in Saudi Arabia.
I <u>wake</u> up early and <u>eat</u> my breakfast in bed.
Water <u>boils</u> at 100 degrees centigrade.

The **present continuous** tense is used to talk about something which is regarded as temporary or something which is happening at the present moment.

I'm <u>working</u> as a British Council officer.
Wait a moment. I'm <u>listening</u> to the news.

⚠ **WARNING:** There are a number of verbs which are not used in the present continuous tense, even when talking about the present moment.
⇨ See **Grammar** entry at **Continuous tenses.**

ⓘ Note that present tenses are sometimes used to talk about future events.
⇨ See **Grammar** entry at **The Future.**
⇨ For the use of **present perfect** tenses, see **Grammar** entry at **The Past.**

Pronouns

1 pronouns

Pronouns are words such as **it**, **this**, and **nobody** which are used in a sentence like noun groups containing a noun. Some pronouns are used in order to avoid repeating nouns. For example, you would not say 'My mother said my mother would phone me this evening'. You would say 'My mother said **she** would phone me this evening'.

⚠ **WARNING:** You use a pronoun instead of a noun group containing a noun, not in addition to a noun group. For example, you do not say 'My mother she wants to see you'. You say either 'My mother wants to see you' or 'She wants to see you'.

In this entry, information is given on **personal pronouns, possessive pronouns, reflexive pronouns,** and **indefinite pronouns.**

GRAMMAR

⇨ For information on **demonstrative pronouns**, see **Usage** entry at **this - that**.

⇨ For information on **reciprocal pronouns**, see **Usage** entry at **each other - one another**.

⇨ Some **'wh'-words** are pronouns; see **Grammar** entry at **'Wh'-words**.

Words such as **many** and **some** which are used to refer to quantities of people or things can also be used as pronouns.

⇨ See section on **pronoun use** in **Grammar** entry at **Quantity**.

One can be used to replace a noun group, but can also be used to replace a noun within a noun group.

⇨ See **Usage** entry at **one**.

2 personal pronouns

Personal pronouns are used to refer to something or someone that has already been mentioned, or to the speaker or hearer. There are two sets of personal pronouns: **subject pronouns** and **object pronouns**.

Subject pronouns are used as the subject of a verb. The subject pronouns are:

	singular	plural
1st person	I	we
2nd person	you	
3rd person	he she it	they

I do the washing; he does the cooking; we share the washing-up.
My father is fat – he weighs over fifteen stone.

Object pronouns are used as the direct or indirect object of a verb, or after a preposition. The object pronouns are:

	singular	plural
1st person	me	us
2nd person	you	
3rd person	him her it	them

The nurse washed me with cold water.
I'm going to read him some of my poems.

ⓘ Note that you do not use an object pronoun as the indirect object of a verb when you are referring to the same person as the subject. Instead you use a **reflexive pronoun**.
He cooked himself an omelette.

ⓘ Note that **me**, not 'I', is used after **it's** in modern English.
'Who is it?'–'It's me.'

⇨ See **Usage** entry at **me**.

We and **us** can be used either to include the person you are talking to or not to include the person you are talking to. For example, you can say 'We must meet more often', meaning that you and the person you are talking to must meet each other more often. You can also say 'We don't meet very often now', meaning that you and someone else do not meet very often.

You and **they** can be used to refer to people in general.
You have to drive on the other side of the road on the continent.
They say she's very clever.

⇨ See **Usage** entry at **one.**

They and **them** are sometimes used to refer back to indefinite pronouns referring to people.

⇨ See **Usage** entry at **he - they.**

It is used as an impersonal pronoun in general statements about the time, the date, the weather, or a situation.

⇨ See **Usage** entry at **it.**

3 possessive pronouns

Possessive pronouns show who the person or thing you are referring to belongs to or is connected with. The possessive pronouns are:

	singular	plural
1st person	mine	ours
2nd person	yours	
3rd person	his hers	theirs

Is that coffee yours or mine?
It was his fault, not theirs.
'What's your name?'–'Frank.'–' Mine 's Laura.'

⚠ **WARNING:** There is no possessive pronoun 'its'.

Possessive pronouns are sometimes confused with **possessive determiners**, which are quite similar in form.

⇨ See **Grammar** entry at **Possessive determiners.**
Possessive pronouns can be used after **of**.

⇨ See **Usage** entry at **of.**
He was an old friend of mine.

4 reflexive pronouns

Reflexive pronouns are used as the object of a verb or preposition when the person or thing affected by an action is the same as the person or thing doing it. The reflexive pronouns are:

	singular	plural
1st person	myself	ourselves
2nd person	yourself	yourselves
3rd person	himself herself itself	themselves

She stretched herself out on the sofa.
The men formed themselves into a line.

⇨ For more information about this use of reflexive pronouns, see section on **reflexive verbs** in **Grammar** entry at **Verbs.**

Reflexive pronouns are also used after nouns or pronouns to emphasize them.
I myself have never read the book.
The town itself was so small that it didn't have a bank.

They are also used at the end of a clause to emphasize the subject.
I find it a bit odd myself.

Reflexive pronouns are also used at the end of a clause to say that someone did something without any help from anyone else.
Did you make those yourself?

You can also indicate that someone did something without any help, or that someone was alone, by using a reflexive pronoun after **by** at the end of a clause.
Did you put those shelves up all by yourself?
He went off to sit by himself.

5 **indefinite pronouns**
Indefinite pronouns are used to refer to people or things without indicating exactly who or what they are. The indefinite pronouns are:

anybody	anything	everyone	nobody	nothing
anyone	everybody	everything	no one	somebody

Everyone knows that.
Jane said nothing for a moment.
Is anybody there?

You always use singular verbs with indefinite pronouns.
Is anyone here?
Everything was ready.

However, the plural pronouns **they**, **them**, or **themselves** are often used to refer back to an indefinite pronoun referring to a person.
⇨ See **Usage** entry at **he - she - they.**

You can use adjectives immediately after indefinite pronouns.
Choose someone quiet.
There is nothing extraordinary about this.

Qualifiers

A **qualifier** is a word or group of words which comes after a noun and gives more information about the person or thing referred to. Qualifiers can be:

● **prepositional phrases**
...a girl with red hair.
...the man in the dark glasses.

● **place adverbs** or **time adverbs**
...down in the dungeon beneath.
...a reflection of life today in England.
⇨ See **Topic** entries at **Places** and **Time.**

● **adjectives** followed by phrases or clauses
...machinery capable of clearing rubble off the main roads.
...the sort of weapons likely to be deployed against it.

● **adjectives** such as **concerned** and **available**
The idea needs to come from the individuals concerned.
...the person responsible for his death.
⇨ See **Grammar** entry at **Adjectives.**

GRAMMAR

- **relative clauses**

The man <u>who had done it</u> was arrested.
…the town <u>that John came from.</u>

- **non-finite clauses**

…two of the problems <u>mentioned above.</u>
…a simple device <u>to test lung function.</u>

⇨ See **Grammar** entries at **'-ing' forms, Past participles,** and **'To'-infinitive clauses.**

Quantity

1 numbers	**12** with specific plural noun groups
2 general determiners	**13** with all singular noun groups
3 with singular nouns	**14** with all uncount noun groups
4 with plural and uncount nouns	**15** with all plural noun groups
5 with plural count nouns	**16** pronoun use
6 with uncount nouns	**17** fractions
7 with all types of noun	**18** quantifiers used with abstract nouns
8 words used in front of determiners	**19** partitives
9 quantifiers	**20** measurement nouns
10 with specific or general noun groups	**21** containers
	22 '-ful'
11 with specific uncount nouns	**23** count nouns

1 **numbers**
Quantities and amounts of things are often referred to using **numbers.**
⇨ See **Topic** entries at **Numbers and fractions** and **Measurements.**

2 **general determiners**
You can use **general determiners** such as **some, any, all, every,** and **much** to talk about quantities and amounts of things.
There is <u>some</u> chocolate cake over there.
He spoke <u>many</u> different languages.
<u>Most</u> farmers are still using the old methods.

3 **with singular nouns**
The following general determiners can only be used in front of singular count nouns:

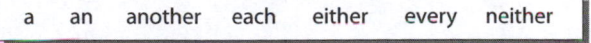

a	an	another	each	either	every	neither

Could I have <u>another cup</u> of coffee?
I agree with <u>every word</u> Peter says.

4 **with plural and uncount nouns**
The following general determiners are used with plural forms of nouns and with uncount nouns:

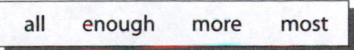

all	enough	more	most

He does <u>more hours</u> than I do.
It had <u>enough room</u> to store all the information.

5 **with plural count nouns**
The following general determiners are only used with plural forms of nouns:

a few	fewer	many	several
few	fewest	other	

The town has <u>few monuments</u>.
He wrote <u>many novels</u>.

6 with uncount nouns

Much, **little**, and **a little** are only used with uncount nouns.

Do you watch <u>much television?</u>
We've made <u>little progress</u>.

⚠ **WARNING:** There are restrictions on using **much** in positive statements.
⇨ See **Usage** entry at **much**.

Some people think that **less** and **least** should only be used with uncount nouns, not with plural forms of nouns.

⇨ See **Usage** entry at **less**.

7 with all types of noun

Any, **no**, and **some** are used with all types of noun.

Cars can be rented at almost <u>any US airport</u>.
He had <u>no money</u>.
They've had <u>some experience</u> of fighting.

ⓘ Note that **any** is not generally used in positive statements.

⇨ See **Usage** entry at **any**.

8 words used in front of determiners

A few words used to indicate amounts or quantities can come in front of specific determiners such as **the, these**, and **my**. These are also called **predeterminers.**

all	both	double	half	twice

<u>All the boys</u> started to giggle.
I invited <u>both the boys</u>.
She paid <u>double the sum</u> they asked for.

Half can also come in front of **a** or **an**.

I read for <u>half an hour</u>.

What is a predeterminer that can only be used before **a** or **an**.

<u>What a lovely day!</u>
<u>What an awful thing to do</u>.

⇨ See **Usage** entries at **all, both,** and **half - half of**.

9 quantifiers

Quantities and amounts are also referred to using a word or phrase such as **several, most**, or **a number** linked with **of** to the following noun group. These words and phrases followed by **of** are called **quantifiers.**

I am sure <u>both of</u> you agree with me.
I make <u>a lot of</u> mistakes.
In Tunis there are <u>a number of</u> art galleries.

When you use a quantifier as the subject of a verb, you use a singular verb form if the noun group after **of** is singular or uncount, and a plural verb form if the noun group after **of** is plural.

Some of the information <u>has</u> already been analysed.
Some of my best friends <u>are</u> policemen.

10 **with specific or general noun groups**

Quantifiers are often used to refer to part of a particular amount, group, or thing. The noun group after **of** begins with a specific determiner such as **the**, **these**, or **my**, or consists of a pronoun such as **us**, **them**, or **these**.

Nearly <u>all of the increase</u> has been caused by inflation.
<u>Very few of my classes</u> were stimulating.
<u>Several of them</u> died.

Sometimes quantifiers are used to refer to part of something of a particular kind. The noun group after **of** is a singular count noun preceded by a general determiner such as **a**, **an**, or **another**.

It had taken him <u>the whole of an evening</u> to get her to admit that she still had a grievance.

Often quantifiers are used simply to indicate how many or how much of a type of thing you are talking about. In this case, the noun group after **of** is a general plural or uncount noun group, without a determiner.

I would like to ask you <u>a couple of questions.</u>
There's <u>a great deal of money</u> involved.

11 **with specific uncount nouns**

The following quantifiers are used with specific uncount noun groups, but not general ones:

all of	less of	most of	part of	the remainder of
any of	little of	much of	some of	the rest of
enough of	more of	none of	a little of	the whole of

<u>Most of my hair</u> had to be cut off.
Ken and Tony did <u>much of the work.</u>

12 **with specific plural noun groups**

The following quantifiers are used with specific plural noun groups, but not general ones:

all of	each of	many of	one of	a little of
another of	either of	more of	several of	a good many of
any of	enough of	most of	some of	a great many of
both of	few of	neither of	various of	the remainder of
certain of	fewer of	none of	a few of	the rest of

Start by looking through their papers for <u>either of the two documents.</u>
<u>Few of these organizations</u> survive for long.

13 **with all singular noun groups**

The following quantifiers are used with specific and general singular noun groups:

all of	more of	some of	a great deal of	the majority of
any of	most of	traces of	a little bit of	the remainder of
enough of	much of	an abundance of	a little of	the rest of
less of	none of	an amount of	a lot of	the whole of
little of	part of	a bit of	a quantity of	
lots of	plenty of	a good deal of	a trace of	

<u>Part of the farm</u> lay close to the river bank.
<u>Much of the day</u> was taken up with classes.
Meetings are quarterly and take up <u>most of a day.</u>
Would you know what to do if someone accidentally swallowed <u>some of a chemical</u> you work with?

GRAMMAR

Quantity

14 with all uncount noun groups

The following quantifiers are used with specific and general uncount noun groups:

heaps of	plenty of	an abundance of	a good deal of	a quantity of
loads of	quantities of	an amount of	a great deal of	a trace of
lots of	tons of	a bit of	a lot of	
masses of	traces of	a little bit of	the majority of	

These creatures spend <u>a great deal of their time</u> on the ground.
<u>A lot of the energy</u> that is wasted in negotiations could be directed into industry.
There had been <u>plenty of action</u> that day.
There was <u>a good deal of smoke.</u>

15 with all plural noun groups

The following quantifiers are used with specific and general plural noun groups:

heaps of	numbers of	an abundance of	a minority of
loads of	plenty of	a couple of	the majority of
lots of	quantities of	a lot of	a number of
masses of	tons of	a majority of	a quantity of

I picked up <u>a couple of the pamphlets.</u>
<u>A lot of them</u> were middle-aged ladies.
They had <u>loads of things to say to each other.</u>
Very large <u>quantities of aid</u> were needed.

(*i*) Note that **numbers of** and **quantities of** are very often preceded by adjectives such as **large** and **small**.

The report contained <u>large numbers of</u> inaccuracies.
Chemical batteries are used to store <u>relatively small quantities of</u> electricity.

⚠ **WARNING:** Heaps of, loads of, lots of, masses of, and tons of are used only in conversation. Note that when these quantifiers are used with an uncount noun or a singular noun group as the subject of a verb, the verb is singular, even though the quantifier sounds plural.

<u>Masses of evidence has</u> been accumulated.
<u>Lots of it isn't</u> relevant, of course.

16 pronoun use

Most of the words and expressions listed so far in this entry can be used as pronouns when it is clear who or what you are referring to.

<u>Many</u> are themselves shareholders in companies.
<u>A few</u> crossed over the bridge.
I have four bins. I keep one in the kitchen and <u>the rest</u> in the dustbin area.

However, **a**, **an**, **every**, **no**, and **other** are not used as pronouns.

17 fractions

Fractions such as **a fifth** and **two-thirds** can be used with **of** in the same way as quantifiers such as **all of** and **some of**.

⇨ See **Topic** entry at **Numbers and fractions**.

18 quantifiers used with abstract nouns

The following quantifiers are used only or mainly when referring to qualities or emotions:

| an element of | a hint of | a measure of | a modicum of | a touch of |

There was <u>an element of danger</u> in using the two runways together.
Women have gained <u>a measure of independence.</u>
I must admit to <u>a tiny touch of envy</u> when I heard about his success.

A trace of is also often used when referring to an emotion.
She spoke without <u>a trace of embarrassment</u> about the problems that she had.

19 partitives

You can refer to a particular quantity of something using a **partitive** such as **piece** or
group linked by **of** to a noun. Partitives are all count nouns. Often a partitive indicates
the shape or nature of the amount or group.

Some partitives are used with **of** and an uncount noun.
Who owns this <u>bit of land?</u>
… <u>portions of mashed potato.</u>

Some are used with **of** and a plural noun.
…a huge <u>heap of stones.</u>
It was evaluated by an independent <u>team of inspectors.</u>

⇨ For more information about partitives used with uncount nouns, see **Topic** entry at
Pieces and amounts.

⇨ For more information about partitives used with plural nouns, see **Topic** entry at **Groups
of things, animals, and people.**

When you use a singular partitive as the subject, you use a singular verb form if the noun
after **of** is an uncount noun.
A <u>piece of paper is</u> lifeless.

If the noun after **of** is a plural count noun, you can use a plural verb form or a singular
verb form. A plural verb form is more commonly used.
The second <u>group of animals were</u> brought up in a stimulating environment.
Each small <u>group of workers is</u> responsible for their own production targets.

When you use a plural partitive, you use a plural verb form.
Two <u>pieces of metal were</u> being rubbed together.

20 measurement nouns

Nouns referring to units of measurement are often used as partitives.
He owns only five hundred <u>square metres of</u> land.
I drink a <u>pint of</u> milk a day.

⇨ See section on **measurement nouns before 'of'** in **Topic** entry at **Measurements.**

21 containers

You can use the names of containers as partitives when you want to refer to the contents
of a container, or to a container and its contents.
They drank another <u>bottle of</u> champagne.
I went to buy a <u>bag of</u> chips.

22 '-ful'

You can add '-**ful**' to partitives referring to containers.
He brought me a <u>bagful of</u> sweets.
Pour a <u>bucketful of</u> cold water on the ash.

When people want to make a noun ending in '-**ful**' plural, they usually add an '-**s**' to the
end of the word, as in **bucketfuls**. However, some people put the '-**s**' in front of '-**ful**', as in
bucketsful.
She ladled three <u>spoonfuls of</u> sugar into my tea.
…two <u>teaspoonsful of</u> milk.

GRAMMAR

You can also add '-ful' to some parts of the body to form partitives. The commonest partitives of this kind are **armful**, **fistful**, **handful**, and **mouthful**.

Eleanor was holding an <u>armful of</u> roses.
He took another <u>mouthful of</u> whisky.

23 **count nouns**

Instead of using a partitive and **of**, you can sometimes use a noun that is usually uncount as a count noun. For example, **two teas** means the same as 'two cups of tea', and **two sugars** means 'two spoonfuls of sugar'.

We drank a couple of <u>beers.</u>
I asked for two <u>coffees</u> with milk.

⇨ See section on **count nouns** in **Grammar** entry at **Nouns**.

Questions

1	'yes/no'-questions	**6**	'wh'-questions
2	'be'	**7**	'wh'-word as subject
3	'have'	**8**	'wh'-word as object or adverb
4	negative 'yes/no'-questions	**9**	questions in reply
5	answers to 'yes/no'-questions	**10**	indirect ways of asking questions

There are two main types of question: **'yes/no'-questions** and **'wh'-questions'**.

1 **'yes/no'-questions**

Questions which can be answered by 'yes' or 'no' are called **'yes/no'-questions.**

'Are you ready?'–'Yes.'
'Have you read this magazine?'–'No.'

'Yes/no'-questions are formed by changing the order of the subject and the verb group. If the verb group consists a main verb and one or more **auxiliaries,** you put the first auxiliary at the beginning of the sentence, in front of the subject. You put the rest of the verb group after the subject.

<u>Will you</u> have finished by lunchtime?
<u>Has he</u> been working?

If you are using a simple tense (present simple or past simple), you use an appropriate form of the auxiliary **do** in front of the subject. You put the base form of the main verb after the subject.

<u>Do the British take</u> sport seriously?
<u>Does David do</u> this sort of thing often?
<u>Did you meet</u> George in France?

2 **'be'**

However, if the main verb is **be**, you put a form of **be** at the beginning of the clause, followed by the subject. You do not use 'do'.

<u>Are you</u> okay?
<u>Was it</u> lonely without us?

3 **'have'**

You can use a structure such as **Have you got…?** or a structure such as **Do you have…?**

⇨ See **Usage** entry at **have got**.

People no longer say 'Have you…?' when using **have** as the main verb.

⚠ **WARNING:** If you want to ask a 'yes/no'-question, you do not usually use the normal word order of a statement. However, you can use the normal word order of a statement if you want to express surprise, or to check that something is true.

You've flown this machine before?
You've got two thousand already?

4 │ negative 'yes/no'-questions

You use a negative 'yes/no'-question when you think the answer will be, or should be, 'Yes'. For example, you say 'Didn't we see Daphne last weekend?' if you think you saw Daphne last weekend. You say 'Haven't you got a pen?' if you think the person you are speaking to should have a pen.

'Can't the trade unionists do something about this?'–'Yes, but they can't solve the problem by themselves.'
'Wasn't he French?'–'Yes.'
'Didn't you say you'd done it?'–'Yes.'

5 │ answers to 'yes/no'-questions

When you answer a 'yes/no'-questions, you can just say '**Yes**' or '**No**', or you can follow '**Yes**' or '**No**' with a subject and auxiliary. For example, if you are asked a question like 'Have you finished?', you can say '**Yes, I have**' or '**No, I haven't**'. You use the auxiliary that was used in the question. However, if the main verb is **be** you can use the same form of **be** in your answer.

'Did you enjoy the film?'–'Yes I did'.
'Have you met him yet?'–'No I haven't.'
'Were you late?'–'Yes I was.'

6 │ 'wh'-questions

'**Wh'-questions** are used to ask about the identity of the people or things involved in an action, or about the circumstances of an action. 'Wh'-questions begin with a '**wh'-word**. The 'wh'-words are:

- the adverbs **how, when, where**, and **why**
- the pronouns **who, whom, what, which**, and **whose**
- the determiners **what, which**, and **whose**

(*i*) Note that **whom** is only used as the object of a verb or preposition, not as a subject.

⇨ See **Usage** entry at **who - whom.**

7 │ 'wh'-word as subject

When a 'wh'-word is the subject of a question, the 'wh'-word comes first, followed by the verb group. The word order of the clause is the same as that of an ordinary statement.

What happened?
Who could have done it?

The form of a question is similar when the 'wh'-word is part of the subject.

Which men had been ill?

8 │ 'wh'-word as object or adverb

When a 'wh'-word is the object of a verb or preposition, or when it is an adverb, the 'wh'-word comes first. The formation of the rest of the clause is the same as for 'yes/no'-questions; that is, the subject is put after the first auxiliary in the verb group, and the auxiliary **do** is used for simple tenses.

Which do you like best?
When would you be coming down?

The form of a question is similar when the 'wh'-word is part of the object.

Which graph are you going to use?

If there is a preposition, it usually comes at the end of the clause.

What are they looking for?
Which country do you come from?

However, if a phrase such as **at what time** or **in what way** is being used, the preposition is put at the beginning.

In what way are they different?

GRAMMAR

If **whom** is used, the preposition is always put first. **Whom** is only used in formal speech and writing.

With whom were you talking?

9 **questions in reply**

When you are asking a question in reply to what someone has said, you can often just use a 'wh'-word, not a whole clause, because it is clear what you mean.

'There's someone coming.'– 'Who?'
'Maria! We won't discuss that here.'– 'Why not?'

10 **indirect ways of asking questions**

When you ask someone for information, it is more polite to use the expressions '**Could you tell me…?**' or '**Do you know…?**'

Could you tell me how far it is to the bank?
Do you know where Jane is?

(i) Note that the second part of the question has the form of a reported question.

⇨ See **Grammar** entry at **Reporting**.

People sometimes use expressions like '**May I ask…?**' and '**Might I ask…?**' to ask a question indirectly. However, it is best not to use this way of asking a question, as it can sound hostile or aggressive.

May I ask what your name is?
Might I inquire if you are the owner?

Question tags

A **question tag** is a short phrase that you add to the end of a statement to turn it into a 'yes/no'-question. You usually do this when you expect the other person to agree with the statement. For example, if you say 'It's cold, **isn't it?**', you expect the other person to say 'Yes'. If you say 'It isn't very warm, **is it?**', you expect the other person to say 'No'.

You form a question tag by using the same auxiliary verb or form of **be** as in the statement, followed by a personal pronoun. The pronoun refers to the subject of the statement.

You've never been to Benidorm, have you?
David's school is quite nice, isn't it?

If the statement is in a simple tense, that is, it does not contain an auxiliary or **be**, the verb **do** is used in the question tag.

You like it here, don't you?
He played for Ireland, didn't he?

(i) Note that you usually add a negative tag to a positive statement, and a positive tag to a negative statement. However, you add a positive tag to a positive statement when checking that you have guessed something correctly, or to show interest, surprise, or anger.

You've been to North America before, have you?
Oh, he wants us to make films as well, does he?

If you add a tag to a statement that contains a broad negative such as **hardly**, **rarely**, or **seldom**, the tag is normally positive, as it is with other negatives.

She's hardly the right person for the job, is she?
You seldom see that sort of thing these days, do you?

If you are making a statement about yourself and you want to check if the person you are talking to has the same opinion or feeling, you can put a tag with **you** after your statement.

I think this is the best thing, don't you?
I love tea, don't you?

GRAMMAR

⇨ For examples of the use of question tags, see **Topic** entries at **Agreeing and disagreeing; Invitations; Requests, orders, and instructions;** and **Suggestions.**

Relative clauses

1 relative pronouns	9 referring to a situation
2 defining relative clauses	10 prepositions with relative pronouns
3 referring to people	
4 referring to things	11 'of whom' and 'of which'
5 not using a relative pronoun	12 'whose' in relative clauses
6 non-defining relative clauses	13 'when', 'where', and 'why'
7 referring to people	14 referring to the future
8 referring to things	

A **relative clause** is a subordinate clause which gives more information about someone or something mentioned in the main clause. The relative clause comes immediately after the noun which refers to the person or thing being talked about.

The man <u>who came into the room</u> was small and slender.
Opposite is St. Paul's Church, <u>where you can hear some lovely music.</u>

1 relative pronouns
Many relative clauses begin with a **relative pronoun**. The relative pronouns are:

that	which	who	whom

The relative pronoun usually acts as the subject or object of a verb in the relative clause.
…a girl <u>who wanted</u> to go to college.
There was so much <u>that</u> she wanted to <u>ask.</u>

There are two kinds of relative clause: **defining relative clauses** and **non-defining relative clauses.**

2 defining relative clauses
Defining relative clauses give information that helps to identify the person or thing being spoken about. For example, in the sentence 'The woman who owned the shop was away', the defining relative clause 'who owned the shop' makes it clear which particular woman is being referred to.

The man <u>who you met yesterday</u> was my brother.
The car <u>which crashed into me</u> belonged to Paul.

Defining relative clauses are sometimes called **identifying relative clauses.**

3 referring to people
When you are referring to a person or group of people in a defining relative clause, you use **who** or **that** as the subject of the defining clause.

The man <u>who</u> employed me would transport anything anywhere.
…the people <u>who</u> live in the cottage.
He was the man <u>that</u> bought my house.

You use **who**, **that**, or **whom** as the object of a defining clause.
…someone <u>who</u> I haven't seen for a long time.
…a woman <u>that</u> I dislike.
…distant relatives <u>whom</u> he had never seen.

ⓘ Note that **whom** is a formal word.
⇨ See **Usage** entry at **who - whom.**

GRAMMAR

4 referring to things

When you are referring to a thing or group of things, you use **which** or **that** as the subject or object of a defining clause.

…pasta <u>which</u> came from Milan.
There are a lot of things <u>that</u> are wrong.
…shells <u>which</u> my sister has collected.
The thing <u>that</u> I really liked about it was its size.

In general, **that** is more common in American English, in defining relative clauses of this type, but both forms are found in both dialects.

5 not using a relative pronoun

You do not have to use a relative pronoun as the object of the verb in a defining relative clause. For example, instead of saying 'a woman that I dislike', you can say 'a woman I dislike'.

The woman <u>you met yesterday</u> lives next door.
The car <u>I wanted to buy</u> was not for sale.

However, when the relative pronoun is the subject of the verb in a defining relative clause, the relative pronoun cannot be omitted.

The man <u>who did this</u> was a criminal.

⚠ **WARNING:** The relative pronoun in a relative clause acts as the subject or object of the clause. This means that you should not add another pronoun as the subject or object. For example, you say 'There are a lot of people that want to be rich'. You do not say ~~'There are a lot of people that they want to be rich'~~. Similarly, you say 'This is the book which I bought yesterday'. You do not say ~~'This is the book which I bought it yesterday'~~. Even if you do not use a relative pronoun, as in 'This is the book I bought yesterday', you do not put in another pronoun.

6 non-defining relative clauses

Non-defining relative clauses are used to give further information about someone or something, not to identify them. For example, in 'I'm writing to my mother, who's in hospital', the relative clause 'who's in hospital' gives more information about 'my mother' and is not used to indicate which mother you mean.

He was waving to the girl, <u>who was running along the platform.</u>
He walked down to Broadway, the main street of the town, <u>which ran parallel to the river.</u>

ⓘ Note that you put a comma in front of a non-defining relative clause.

7 referring to people

When a non-defining clause relates to a person or group of people, you use **who** as the subject of the clause, or **who** or **whom** as the object of the clause.

Heath Robinson, <u>who died in 1944</u>, was a graphic artist and cartoonist.
I was in the same group as Janice, <u>who</u> I like a lot.
She was engaged to a sailor, <u>whom</u> she had met at Dartmouth.

8 referring to things

When a non-defining clause relates to a thing or a group of things, you use **which** as the subject or object.

I am teaching at the Selly Oak Centre, <u>which</u> is just over the road.
He was a man of considerable inherited wealth, <u>which</u> he ultimately spent on his experiments.

GRAMMAR

⚠ **WARNING:** You cannot use 'that' to begin a non-defining relative clause. For example, you cannot say ~~'She sold her car, that she had bought the year before'~~. You must say 'She sold her car, which she had bought the year before'. Non-defining clauses cannot be used without a relative pronoun. For example, you cannot say ~~'She sold her car, she had bought the year before'~~.

9 **referring to a situation**

Non-defining relative clauses beginning with **which** can be used to say something about the whole situation described in the main clause.

I never met Brando again, <u>which</u> was a pity.
Small computers need only small amounts of power, <u>which</u> means that they will run on small batteries.

10 **prepositions with relative pronouns**

In both types of relative clause, a relative pronoun can be the object of a preposition. In conversation, the preposition usually comes at the end of the clause, with no noun group after it.

I wanted to do the job <u>which</u> I'd been trained <u>for</u>.
…the world <u>that</u> you are interacting <u>with</u>.

Often, in a defining relative clause, no relative pronoun is used.

…the pages she was looking <u>at</u>.
I'd be wary of anything Matt Davis is involved <u>with</u>.

In formal English, the preposition comes in front of the relative pronoun **whom** or **which**.

I have at last met John Parr's tenant, <u>about whom</u> I have heard so much.
He was asking questions <u>to which</u> there were no answers.

⚠ **WARNING:** If the verb in a relative clause is a **phrasal verb** ending with a preposition, you cannot move the preposition to the beginning of the clause. For example, you cannot say ~~'all the things with which I have had to put up'~~. You have to say 'all the things I've had to put up with'.

…the delegates she had been <u>looking after</u>.
Everyone I <u>came across</u> seemed to know about it.

ⓘ Note that a non-defining relative clause can begin with a preposition, **which**, and a noun. The only common expressions of this kind are **in which case**, **by which time**, and **at which point**.

It may be that your circumstances are different or unusual, <u>in which case</u> we can ensure that you have taken the right action.
Leave the whole thing to cool down for two hours, <u>by which time</u> the spices should have thoroughly flavoured the vinegar.

11 **'of whom' and 'of which'**

Words such as **some**, **many**, and **most** can be put in front of **of whom** or **of which** at the beginning of a non-defining relative clause. You do this to give information about part of the group just mentioned.

At the school we were greeted by the teachers, <u>most of whom</u> were middle-aged.
It is a language shared by several quite diverse cultures, <u>each of which</u> uses it differently.

Numbers can be put in front of **of whom** or **of which** or, more formally, after these phrases.

They act mostly on suggestions from present members (<u>four of whom</u> are women).
Altogether 1,888 people were prosecuted, <u>of whom 1,628</u> were convicted.

12 **'whose' in relative clauses**

When you want to talk about something belonging or relating to a person, thing, or group, you use a defining or non-defining relative clause beginning with **whose** and a noun.

…workers <u>whose bargaining power</u> is weak.
According to Cook, <u>whose book</u> is published on Thursday, most disasters are avoidable.

Some people think it is incorrect to use **whose** to indicate that something belongs or relates to a thing.

⇨ See **Usage** entry at **whose**.

13 'when', 'where', and 'why'

When, **where**, and **why** can be used in defining relative clauses after certain nouns. **When** is used after **time** and other time words, **where** is used after **place** or place words, and **why** is used after **reason**.

This is one of <u>those occasions when</u> I regret not being able to drive.
That was <u>the room where</u> I did my homework.
There are <u>several reasons why</u> we can't do that.

When and **where** can be used in non-defining relative clauses after expressions of time and place.

This happened in 1957, <u>when</u> I was still a baby.
She has just come back from a holiday in Crete, <u>where</u> Alex and I went last year.

14 referring to the future

In a defining relative clause, you sometimes use the simple present tense and sometimes use **will** when referring to the future.

⇨ See section on **present tenses in subordinate clauses** in **Grammar** entry at **The Future**.

Reporting

1	direct speech	14	with past reporting verb
2	report structures	15	referring to the future
3	reporting verbs	16	modals in reported clauses
4	reporting verbs with a negative	17	with past reporting verb
5	reported clauses	18	ability
6	'that'-clauses	19	possibility
7	mentioning the hearer	20	permission
8	use of the passive	21	the future
9	'to'-infinitive clauses	22	'can', 'may', 'will'
10	'-ing' clauses	23	obligation
11	reported questions	24	prohibiting
12	tense of reporting verb	25	using reporting verbs for politeness
13	tense of verb in reported clause		

1 direct speech

One way of reporting what someone has said is to repeat their actual words. When you do this, you use a **reporting verb** such as **say**.

I said, 'Where are we?'
'I don't know much about music,' Judy said.

Sentences like these are called **direct speech** or **quote structures**. Direct speech is used more in stories than in conversation.

⇨ See **Topic** entry at **Punctuation** for information on how to punctuate.

In stories, you can put the reporting verb after the quote. The subject is often put after the verb.

'I see', <u>said John.</u>

> ⚠ **WARNING:** However, when the subject is a pronoun, it must go in front of the verb.
> *'Hi there!' <u>he said.</u>*

The only reporting verb you typically use in conversation is **say**. Recently, however, people have begun to use **go** or **be like** in very informal situations when they are quoting what someone said.

…and he <u>went</u> 'What's the matter with you?'
'I'<u>m like</u> 'What happened?' and he'<u>s like</u> 'I reversed into a lamp-post.'

In stories you can indicate what kind of statement someone made using reporting verbs such as **ask**, **explain**, or **suggest**.

'What have you been up to?' he <u>asked.</u>
'It's a disease of the blood,' <u>explained</u> Kowalski.
'Perhaps,' he <u>suggested,</u> 'it was just an impulse.'

You can also use verbs such as **add**, **begin**, **continue**, and **reply** to show when one statement occurred in relation to another.

'I want it to be a surprise,' I <u>added.</u>
'Anyway,' she <u>continued,</u> 'it's quite out of the question.'
She <u>replied,</u> 'My first thought was to protect him.'

In a story, if you want to indicate the way in which something was said, you can use a reporting verb such as **shout**, **wail**, or **scream**.

'Jump!' <u>shouted</u> the oldest woman.
'Get out of there,' I <u>screamed.</u>

The following verbs indicate the way in which something is said:

babble	drawl	mumble	shout	storm
bellow	exclaim	murmur	shriek	thunder
call	growl	mutter	sing	wail
chant	hiss	purr	splutter	whine
chorus	howl	roar	squeal	whisper
cry	lisp	scream	stammer	yell

You can use a verb such as **smile**, **grin**, or **frown** to indicate the expression on someone's face while they are speaking.

'I'm awfully sorry.'–'Not at all,' I <u>smiled.</u>
'Hardly worth turning up for,' he <u>grinned.</u>

2 **report structures**

In conversation, you normally give an idea of what someone said using your own words in a **report structure,** rather than quoting them directly. You also use report structures to report people's thoughts.

She said it was quite an expensive one.
They thought that he should have been locked up.

Report structures are also often used in writing.
A report structure consists of two parts: a **reporting clause** and a **reported clause**.

3 **reporting verbs**

The **reporting clause** contains the **reporting verb** and usually comes first.

<u>I told him</u> that nothing was going to happen to me.
<u>I asked</u> what was going on.

The reporting verb with the widest meaning and use is **say**. You use **say** when you are

GRAMMAR

simply reporting what someone said and do not want to imply anything about their statement.

He _said_ that you knew his family.
They _said_ the prison was surrounded by police.

⇨ See **Usage** entry at **say** for more information on its use, and the difference between it and other verbs referring to speaking.

You can use a reporting verb such as **answer**, **explain**, and **suggest** to indicate what kind of statement you think the person was making.

She _explained_ that a friend of her husband's had been arrested.
I _suggested_ that it was time to leave.

You can also indicate your own personal opinion of what someone said by using a reporting verb such as **claim** or **admit**. For example, if you say that someone **claimed** that they did something, you are implying that you think they may not be telling the truth. If you say that someone **admitted** something, you are implying that they are telling the truth.

He _claims_ he knows more about the business now.
She _admitted_ she was very much in love with you once.

4 reporting verbs with a negative

With a small number of reporting verbs, you usually make the reporting clause negative rather than the reported clause. For example, you would usually say 'I don't think Mary is at home' rather than 'I think Mary is not at home'.

I _don't think_ I will be able to afford it.
I _don't believe_ we can enforce a total ban.

The following reporting verbs are often used with a negative in this way:

believe	feel	propose	think
expect	imagine	suppose	

5 reported clauses

The second part of a report structure is the **reported clause**.

She said _that she had been to Belgium._
The man in the shop told me _how much it would cost._

There are several types of reported clause. The type used depends on whether a statement, order, suggestion, or question is being reported.

6 'that'-clauses

A report clause beginning with the conjunction **that** is used after a reporting verb to report a statement or someone's thoughts.

He said _that the police had directed him to the wrong room._
He thought _that Vita needed a holiday._

Some common reporting verbs used in front of a 'that'-clause are:

accept	comment	explain	mention	report
admit	complain	feel	notice	reveal
agree	concede	guarantee	observe	say
allege	conclude	guess	point out	stress
announce	confess	hint	predict	suggest
answer	decide	hope	promise	swear
argue	declare	imagine	realize	think
assert	deny	imply	recommend	warn
assume	discover	insist	remark	
believe	emphasize	joke	remember	
claim	expect	know	reply	

That is often omitted from a 'that'-clause.

They <u>said</u> I had to see a doctor first.

I <u>think</u> there's something wrong.

However, **that** is nearly always used after some verbs, for example **answer**, **argue**, **complain**, **explain**, **recommend**, and **reply**.

He <u>answered that</u> the price would be three pounds.

A 'that'-clause can contain a modal, especially when someone makes a suggestion about what someone else should do.

He proposes that the Government <u>should</u> hold an enquiry.

7 mentioning the hearer

After some reporting verbs that refer to speech, the hearer must be mentioned as the direct object. **Tell** is the most common of these verbs.

He <u>told me</u> that he was a farmer.

I <u>informed her</u> that I could not come.

The following verbs must have the hearer as direct object:

assure	inform	persuade	remind
convince	notify	reassure	tell

You can also choose to mention the hearer as object with **promise**, **teach** and **warn**.

I <u>promised</u> that I would try to phone her.

I <u>reminded Myra</u> I'd be home at seven.

With many other reporting verbs, if you want to mention the hearer, you do so in a prepositional phrase beginning with **to**.

I explained <u>to her</u> that I had to go home.

I mentioned <u>to Tom</u> that I was thinking of working for George McGovern.

The following verbs need the preposition **to** if you mention the hearer:

admit	confess	mention	suggest
announce	explain	reply	swear
boast	hint	report	whisper
complain	lie	reveal	

8 use of the passive

Verbs such as **tell** and **inform** can be used in the passive, with the hearer as the subject.

<u>She was told</u> that there were no tickets left.

A passive form of other reporting verbs is sometimes used to avoid saying whose opinion or statement is being reported, or to imply that it is an opinion that is generally held. This use of the passive is formal. You can use **it** as the subject with a 'that'-clause, or you can use an ordinary subject with a 'to'-infinitive clause.

<u>It is now believed</u> that foreign languages are most easily taught to young children.

<u>He is said</u> to have died a natural death.

9 'to'-infinitive clauses

You use a **'to'-infinitive clause** after a reporting verb such as **tell**, **ask**, or **advise** to report an order, a request, or a piece of advice. The person being addressed, who is going to perform the action, is mentioned as the object of the reporting verb.

Johnson <u>told her to wake him up.</u>

He <u>ordered me to fetch the books.</u>

He <u>asked her to marry him.</u>

Some common reporting verbs used after an object in front of a 'to'-infinitive clause are:

GRAMMAR

advise	command	forbid	nag	request
ask	dare	implore	order	tell
beg	direct	instruct	persuade	urge
challenge	encourage	invite	remind	warn

The following verbs referring to saying, thinking, or discovering are always or usually used in the passive when followed by a 'to'-infinitive.

allege	consider	find	reckon	see
assume	discover	know	report	think
believe	estimate	learn	rumour	understand
claim	feel	prove	say	

The 'to'-infinitive that follows them is most commonly **be** or **have**.

The house <u>was believed to be haunted</u>.
Over a third of the population <u>was estimated to have no access to the health service</u>.
…the primitive molecules which <u>are believed to have given rise to life on Earth</u>.

You can also use a 'to'-infinitive after some reporting verbs which are not used with an object. The person who speaks is also the person who will perform the action.

agree	consent	offer	refuse	volunteer
ask	demand	promise	swear	vow
beg	guarantee	propose	threaten	

They <u>offered to show me the way</u>.
He <u>threatened to arrest me</u>.

(i) Note that when you are reporting an action that the speaker intends to perform, you can sometimes use either a 'to'-infinitive or a 'that'-clause.

I promised <u>to come back</u>.
She promised <u>that she would not leave hospital until she was better</u>.

You do not use a 'to'-infinitive if the hearer is being mentioned.

I promised <u>her</u> I would send her the money.
I swore <u>to him</u> that I would not publish the pamphlet.

Claim and **pretend** can also be used with these two structures. For example, 'He claimed to be a genius' has the same meaning as 'He claimed that he was a genius'.

He claimed <u>to have witnessed the accident</u>.
He pretended <u>that he had found the money in the forest</u>.

Several verbs which indicate someone's intentions, wishes, or decisions, such as **intend**, **want**, and **decide**, are used with a 'to'-infinitive clause.

⇨ See Grammar entry at **'To'-infinitive clauses**.

10 '-ing' clauses

When reporting a suggestion about doing something, it is possible to use one of the reporting verbs **suggest**, **advise**, **propose**, or **recommend** followed by an **'-ing' clause**.

Barbara <u>suggested going to another coffee house</u>.
The committee <u>recommended abandoning the original plan</u>.

(i) Note that you only **propose doing** actions that you yourself will be involved in.

Daisy <u>proposed moving to New York</u>.

11 reported questions

You use the reporting verb **ask** when reporting a question. You can mention the hearer as the direct object if you need to or want to.

He <u>asked</u> if I had a message for Cartwright.
I <u>asked her</u> if she wanted them.

Inquire and **enquire** also mean 'ask', but these are fairly formal words. You cannot mention the hearer as the object of these verbs.

An **'if'-clause** or a **'whether'-clause** is used when reporting **'yes/no' questions. Whether** is used especially if there is a choice of possibilities.
She asked him <u>if his parents spoke French.</u>
I was asked <u>whether I wanted to stay at a hotel or at his home.</u>

A reported clause beginning with a **'wh'-word** is used to report a **'wh'-question.**
He asked <u>where I was going.</u>
She enquired <u>why I was so late.</u>

⚠ **WARNING:** The word order in a reported question is the same as that of a statement, not that of a question. For example, you say 'She asked me what I had been doing'. You do not say ~~'She asked me what had I been doing'.~~
You do not use a question mark when you write reported questions.

If the 'wh'-word in a reported question is the object of a preposition, the preposition comes at the end of the clause, with no noun after it.
She asked <u>what</u> they were looking <u>for.</u>
He asked <u>what</u> we lived <u>on.</u>

Other verbs which refer to speech or thought about uncertain things can be used in front of clauses beginning with 'wh'-words or with **if** or **whether**.
She doesn't <u>know</u> what we were talking about.
They couldn't <u>see</u> how they would manage without her.

A 'to'-infinitive clause beginning with a 'wh'-word or **whether** can be used to refer to an action that someone is uncertain about doing.
I asked him <u>what to do.</u>
I've been wondering <u>whether to retire.</u>

12 tense of reporting verb
You usually use a past tense of the reporting verb when you are reporting something said in the past.
She <u>said</u> you threw away her sweets.
Brody <u>asked</u> what happened.

However, you can use a present tense of the reporting verb, especially if you are reporting something that is still true.
She <u>says</u> she wants to see you this afternoon.
My doctor <u>says</u> it's nothing to worry about.

13 tense of verb in reported clause
If you are using a present tense of the reporting verb, you use the same tense in the reported clause as you would use for an ordinary, direct statement. For example, if a woman says 'He hasn't arrived yet', you could report this by saying 'She says he hasn't arrived yet'.
He knows he <u>'s being watched.</u>
He says he <u>has</u> never <u>seen</u> a live shark in his life.
He says he <u>was</u> very worried.

14 with past reporting verb
If you are using a past tense of the reporting verb, you usually put the verb in the reported clause into a tense that is appropriate at the time that you are speaking. If the event or situation described in the reported clause was in the past when the statement was made, you use the past perfect tense. You can sometimes use the simple

past tense instead when you do not need to relate the event to the time that the statement was made.

Minnie said she <u>had given</u> it to Ben.
A Western diplomat said he <u>saw</u> about 250 foreigners at the airport trying to get on flights out of the country.

You can also use the present perfect tense if the event or situation is recent or relevant to the present situation.

He said there <u>has been</u> a 56 per cent rise in bankruptcies in the past 12 months.

When reporting a habitual past action or a situation that no longer exists, you can use **used to**.

He said he <u>used to go</u> canoeing on rivers and lakes.

If the event or situation described in the reported clause was happening at the time when it was mentioned, you use the simple past tense or the past continuous tense.

Dad explained that he <u>had</u> no money.
She added that she <u>was smoking</u> too much.

(i) Note that a past tense is usually used for the verb in the reported clause even if the reported situation still exists. For example, you say 'I told him I was eighteen' even if you are still eighteen. You are concentrating on the situation at the past time that you are talking about.

He said he <u>was</u> English.
I said I <u>liked</u> sleeping on the ground.

A present tense is sometimes used, however, to emphasize that the situation still exists or to mention a situation that often occurs among a group of people.

I told him that I <u>don't drink</u> more than anyone else.
A social worker at the Society explained that some children <u>live</u> in three or four different foster homes in one year.

15 referring to the future

If the event or situation was in the future at the time of the statement or is still in the future, you usually use a **modal**. See the section below on **modals in reported clauses**. However, you use a present tense in reported questions and similar 'wh'-clauses referring to a future event when the event will happen at about the same time as the statement or thought.

I'll telephone you. If I say it's Hugh, you'll know <u>who it is.</u>

If the future event will happen after the statement, you use **will** in the reported question.

I'll tell you <u>what I will do.</u>

16 modals in reported clauses

If the verb in the reporting clause is in a present tense, you use modals as you would use them in an ordinary, direct statement.

Helen says I <u>can</u> share her flat.
I think some of the sheep <u>may</u> die this year.
I don't believe he <u>will</u> come.
I believe that I <u>could</u> live very comfortably here.

⇨ See the individual **Usage** entries for modals for information on their uses.

17 with past reporting verb

If the verb in the reporting clause is in a past tense or has **could** or **would** as an auxiliary, you usually use **could**, **might**, or **would** in the reported clause, rather than **can**, **may**, or **will**, in the ways explained below.

18 ability

When you want to report a statement (or question) about someone's ability to do something, you normally use **could**.

They believed that war <u>could</u> be avoided.
Nell would not admit that she <u>could</u> not cope.

19 **possibility**
When you want to report a statement about possibility, you normally use **might**.
They told me it <u>might</u> flood here.
He said you <u>might</u> need money.

If the possibility is a strong one, you use **must**.
I told her she <u>must</u> be out of her mind.

20 **permission**
When you want to report a statement giving permission or a request for permission, you normally use **could**. **Might** is used in more formal English.
I told him he <u>couldn't</u> have it.
Madeleine asked if she <u>might</u> borrow a pen and some paper.

21 **the future**
When you want to report a prediction, promise, or expectation, or a question about the future, you normally use **would**.
She said they <u>would</u> all miss us.
He insisted that reforms <u>would</u> save the system, not destroy it.

22 **'can', 'may', 'will'**

ⓘ Note that you can use **can**, **may**, **will**, and **shall** when you are using a past tense of the reporting verb, if you want to emphasize that the situation still exists or is still in the future.
It was claimed that Pires <u>may</u> not need surgery.
A spokesman said that the board <u>will</u> meet tomorrow.

23 **obligation**
When you want to report a statement in the past about obligation, it is possible to use **must**, but the expression **had to** is more common.
He said he really <u>had to</u> go back inside.
Sita told him that he <u>must</u> be especially kind to the little girl.

You use **have to**, **has to**, or **must** if the reported situation still exists or is in the future.
He said the Government <u>must</u> come clean on the issue.
A spokesman said that all bomb threats <u>have to</u> be taken seriously.

When you want to report a statement or thought about what is morally right, you can use **ought to** or **should**.
He knew he <u>ought to</u> be helping Harold.
I felt I <u>should</u> consult my family.

24 **prohibiting**
When you want to report a statement prohibiting something, you normally use **mustn't**.
He said they <u>mustn't</u> get us into trouble.

25 **using reporting verbs for politeness**
Reporting verbs are often used to say something in a polite way. For example, if you want to contradict someone or to say something which might be unwelcome to them, you can avoid sounding rude by using a reporting verb such as **think** or **believe**.
<u>I think</u> it's time we stopped.
<u>I don't think</u> that will be necessary.
<u>I believe</u> you ought to leave now.

Sentences

1 **simple and command sentences**
A **sentence** is a group of words which expresses a statement, question, or order. A

sentence usually has a verb and a subject. A **simple sentence** has one clause. A **compound sentence** or **complex sentence** has two or more clauses.

⇨ See **Grammar** entry at **Clauses.**

Did you believe him?
I packed my gear and walked outside.
If it's four o'clock in the morning, don't expect them to be pleased to see you.

In writing, a sentence has a capital letter at the beginning and a full stop, question mark, or exclamation mark at the end.

⇨ For more information, see **Topic** entry at **Punctuation.**

2 incomplete sentences

In speech, it is possible to say something using a subordinate clause on its own, or a group of words which does not contain a verb. For example, if someone asks you when you are going home, you can say 'When I've finished' or 'This afternoon'. Subordinate clauses and verbless groups of words are sometimes written as if they were sentences in informal letters, novels, and advertisements. However, in any other kind of writing you should avoid writing these clauses and groups of words as if they were sentences.

Singular and plural

The **singular** is the form of a count noun or a verb which you use when referring to one person or thing. The **plural** is the form which you use when referring to more than one person or thing.

⇨ See **Grammar** entries at **Plural forms of nouns** and **Verbs.**

There are also singular and plural pronouns.

⇨ See **Grammar** entry at **Pronouns.**

1 agreement within noun group

A possessive determiner or an adjective in a noun group has the same form whether the noun is singular or plural. However, the determiner **this** has the plural form **these** and the determiner **that** has the plural form **those.**

Some progress has already been made toward alleviating <u>this problem.</u>
I thought about <u>these problems</u> all the way home.
<u>That person</u> has been following us all day.
For <u>those people,</u> however, there was no going back.

Some general determiners, such as **each**, are only used with singular count nouns; some, such as **all**, are only used with uncount nouns or plural forms of nouns; and some, such as **several**, are only used with plural forms of nouns.

⇨ See **Grammar** entry at **Quantity.**

2 agreement of verb with noun group

When you use a verb in a statement or question, you must choose a singular verb form or a plural verb form to agree with the subject.

<u>My mother hates</u> her.
<u>They hate</u> each other.

However, with all verbs except **be**, only one form is used for the simple past tense, and modals only have one form, so in these cases no choice needs to be made.

<u>Rudolph walked</u> slowly back towards the store.
<u>They walked</u> towards the gate.
<u>Power must</u> be shared.
<u>All these questions must</u> be given answers.

You also have to choose an appropriate verb form when using **there** followed by **be**. The verb form agrees with the noun group after **be**.

<u>There was a car</u> parked there.
<u>There were no cars</u> outside.

GRAMMAR

However, when you are talking about two people or things joined by **and**, you use the singular form of **be**.

There was a computer and a printer on the table.

3 **use of singular verb form**

The singular form of a verb is used with:

● the singular form of count nouns uncount nouns **he**, **she**, and **it**

● **this** and **that**

● indefinite pronouns such as **anybody**, **no-one**, and **something**

● noun groups referring to a single quantity of something, such as **a lump of sugar** or **a kilo of coffee**.

Note that when you are referring to a period of time or an amount of something, you use a singular verb, even though you are using the plural form of a noun.

Twenty years is a long time.

Three hundred pounds is missing from club funds.

4 **use of plural verb form**

The plural form of a verb is used with:

● the plural form of count nouns

● plural nouns such as **clothes** and **goods**

● **we** and **they**

● **you**, even when referring to just one person

● **these** and **those**

● pronouns such as **several** and **many**

● quantifiers such as **a couple of** and **few of**.

⇨ See **Grammar** entry at **Quantity** for information on quantifiers and other words indicating quantity.

ⓘ Note that the form of a verb used with I is usually the same as the plural form. However, if the verb is **be**, you use **am** for the simple present tense and **was** for the simple past tense.

I like working.

I have a lot of sympathy for them.

I am not ashamed of that.

I was so cold.

⚠ **WARNING:** Some plural forms of count nouns do not look plural because they do not end in 's'. However, they are still used with a plural verb form.

⇨ See **Grammar** entry at **Plural forms of nouns**.

All men are equal.

On the other hand, some nouns that end in 's' and look plural are uncount nouns and are used with a singular verb form.

⇨ See section on **uncount nouns** in **Grammar** entry at **Nouns**.

Mathematics is too difficult for me.

A small group of plural nouns refer to single items that have two linked parts, such as **jeans**, **trousers**, and **scissors**. They are used with the plural form of a verb.

⇨ See section on **plural nouns** in **Grammar** entry at **Nouns**.

These scissors are sharp.

However, when you want to refer to one of these items using **a pair of** you can use a singular or plural verb form.

⇨ See **Usage** entry at **pair - couple**.

GRAMMAR

In the case of **collective nouns** such as **family** and **government**, you can use a singular or a plural verb form after the singular form of the noun.

⇨ See section on **collective nouns** in **Grammar** entry at **Nouns**.

Split infinitives

A **split infinitive** is a 'to'-infinitive which has the **to** separated from the base form by an adjunct.

There are enough nuclear arms <u>to utterly destroy</u> all civilization.

Some people think this structure is not acceptable and believe that the adjunct should be put elsewhere in the clause.

However, when an adjunct can be put in front of a verb in an ordinary clause, it sometimes seems natural to put the same adjunct in front of the base form in a 'to'-infinitive clause. For example, you say 'You must really make an effort', so it seems natural to say 'I told them to really make an effort'.

Use that opening <u>to really establish</u> contact with the other actors.
The directors of companies in this position often own some of the shares, but rarely enough <u>to actually control</u> a majority.
Then in front of me I saw two cars placing themselves in such a manner as <u>to completely block</u> my way.

● With an intransitive 'to'-infinitive, you can put the adjunct after the 'to'-infinitive or at the end of the clause.

They seemed <u>to have disappeared completely.</u>
Do you think it is right for you and your family <u>to rely completely</u> on the State?
Nancy wanted <u>to go back to China immediately.</u>

● With transitive 'to'-infinitives, it is often possible to put an adjunct after the object or at the end of the clause.

The treatment is <u>to remove these foods completely</u> from the diet.
Uncle Nick was tactful enough not <u>to shatter this illusion immediately.</u>
It's better <u>to introduce him to school gradually.</u>

● However, if the clause is very long, it is better to put the adjunct after the **to** (if it is not possible to rephrase the sentence).

…an incomes policy which aimed <u>to gradually reduce</u> wage settlements in the public sector.
When several injections are given they stimulate the body <u>to slowly build</u> its own, long-lasting protection against tetanus.

Subjects

1 **subjects**

In an active clause, the **subject** is the part of the clause that refers to the person or thing that does the action indicated by the verb, or that is in the state indicated by the verb. The subject is usually a noun group.

<u>Our computers</u> *can give you all the relevant details.*
<u>They</u> *need help badly.*

In a passive clause, the subject refers to the person or thing that is affected by an action or involved in someone's thoughts.

<u>She</u> *had been taught logic by an uncle.*
<u>The examination</u> *is regarded as an arbitrary, unnecessary barrier.*

ⓘ Note that you do not usually add a pronoun after the subject in a clause. For example, you do not say 'My sister ~~she came to see me yesterday~~'. You say 'My sister came to see me yesterday'. However, in very informal speech this is sometimes possible. You can also use an '-ing' clause, a clause beginning with **what**, a 'wh'-clause, or a 'to'-infinitive clause as the subject of a verb.

Measuring the water correctly is most important.
What I saw was unforgettably horrifying.
Whether they believed me or not didn't matter.
To generalize would be wrong.

⇨ See **Grammar** entries at **'-ing' forms, 'Wh'-clauses,** and **'To'-infinitive clauses** and **Usage** entry at **what.**

2 agreement
The verb in a clause should agree with the subject. This means it should have an appropriate form depending on whether the subject is singular, uncount, or plural.
He wears striped shirts.
People wear woollen clothing here even on hot days.

⇨ For detailed information, see **Grammar** entry at **Singular and plural.**

3 position
In a statement, the subject usually comes in front of the verb.
I want to talk to Mr Castle.
Gertrude looked at Ann.

⇨ See **Grammar** entry at **Inversion** for information on when the subject comes after all or part of a verb group.

In questions, the subject comes after an auxiliary verb or after the verb **be**, unless the subject is a 'wh'-word or begins with a 'wh'-word.
Did you give him my letter?
Where is my father?
Who taught you to read?
Which library has the book?

In an imperative clause, there is usually no subject.
Give him a good book.
Show me the complete manuscript.

The Subjunctive
The **subjunctive** is a structure which is not very common in English and which is usually regarded as formal or old-fashioned. Using the subjunctive involves using the base form of a verb instead of a present or past tense, or instead of 'should' and a base form.

1 'whether' and 'though'
The subjunctive can be used instead of a present tense in a conditional clause beginning with **whether** or a clause containing **though.**
The new world must be welcomed, if only because it will come whether it be welcomed or not.
The church absorbs these monuments, large though they be, in its own immense scope.

2 'that'
The subjunctive can be used in a 'that'-clause when making a suggestion or giving an order.
Someone suggested that they break into small groups.
It was his doctor who suggested that he change his job.
He ordered that the books be burnt.

3 'lest'
Lest is sometimes used with a subjunctive verb form in a purpose clause to say what an action is intended to prevent.
He was put in a cell with no clothes and shoes lest he injure himself.

4 subjunctive use of 'were'
In writing and sometimes in conversation, **were** is used instead of 'was' in conditional

GRAMMAR

clauses referring to a situation that does not exist or that is unlikely. This use of **were** is also a type of subjunctive use.

If I were you I'd see a doctor.
He would be persecuted if he were sent back.
If I were asked to define my condition, I'd say 'bored'.

Were is also often used instead of 'was' in clauses beginning with **as though** and **as if**.
You talk as though he were already condemned.
Margaret looked at me as if I were crazy.

Subordinate clauses

1	subordinate clauses	11	less common conjunctions
2	position of adjunct clauses	12	manner clauses
3	concessive clauses	13	place clauses
4	omitting the subject	14	purpose clauses
5	words in front of 'though'	15	reason clauses
6	'much as'	16	result clauses
7	'despite' and 'in spite of'	17	time clauses
8	conditional clauses	18	tenses in time clauses
9	inversion	19	omitting the subject
10	imperatives	20	regular occurrences

1 subordinate clauses

A **subordinate clause** is a clause which adds to or completes the information given in a main clause. Most subordinate clauses begin with a **subordinating conjunction** such as **because, if,** or **that**.

Many subordinate clauses are **adjunct clauses.** These clauses give information about the circumstances of an event. The different types of adjunct clause are described in detail below.

⇨ For information about other kinds of subordinate clause, see **Grammar** entry at **Relative clauses** and section on **report structures** in **Grammar** entry at **Reporting.**

⇨ See also **Grammar** entries at **'-ing' forms, Past participles,** and **'To'-infinitive clauses.**

2 position of adjunct clauses

The usual position for an adjunct clause is just after the main clause.
Her father died when she was young.
They were going by car because it was more comfortable.

However, most types of adjunct clause can be put in front of the main clause when you want to draw attention to the adjunct clause.
When the city is dark, we can move around easily.
Although crocodiles are inactive for long periods, on occasion they can run very fast indeed.

Occasionally, an adjunct clause is put in the middle of another clause, especially a relative clause.
They make allegations which, when you analyse them, do not have too many facts behind them.

3 concessive clauses

Concessive clauses contain a fact that contrasts with the main clause. These are the main conjunctions used to introduce concessive clauses:

although	though	while
even though	whereas	whilst

I used to read a lot <u>although I don't get much time for books now.</u>
<u>While I did well in class,</u> I was a poor performer at games.

 Whilst is a formal word, and is not used at all in American English, which uses only **while**.

4 omitting the subject

The subject of a concessive clause beginning with **although**, **though**, **while**, or **whilst** is sometimes omitted when it is the same as the main subject, and a participle is used as the verb. For example, instead of saying 'Whilst he liked cats, he never let them come into his house', you might say 'Whilst liking cats, he never let them come into his house'. This is a rather formal use.

…some of my colleagues who, <u>whilst not voting for the Tories,</u> had abstained.
Both the journalists, <u>though greeted as heroes on their return from prison,</u> not long afterwards quietly disappeared from their newspapers.

These four conjunctions can also be used in front of a noun group, an adjective group, or an adjunct.

It was an unequal marriage, <u>although a stable and long-lasting one.</u>
<u>Though not very attractive physically,</u> she possessed a sense of humour.

5 words in front of 'though'

You can put a complement in front of **though** for emphasis in formal English. For example, instead of saying 'Though he was ill, he insisted on coming to the meeting', you can say 'Ill though he was, he insisted on coming to the meeting'.

<u>Astute businessman though he was,</u> Philip was capable at times of extreme recklessness.
I had to accept the fact, <u>improbable though it was.</u>
<u>Tempting though it may be to follow this point through,</u> it is not really relevant and we had better move on.

When the complement is an adjective, you can use **as** instead of **though**.

<u>Stupid as it sounds,</u> I was so in love with her that I believed her.

You can also put an adverb such as **hard**, **bravely**, or **valiantly** in front of **though**.

Some members of the staff couldn't handle Murray's condition, <u>hard though they tried.</u>

6 'much as'

When you are talking about a strong feeling or desire, you can use **much as** instead of using 'although' and 'very much'. For example, instead of saying 'Although I like Venice very much, I couldn't live there', you can say 'Much as I like Venice, I couldn't live there'.

<u>Much as they admired her looks and her manners,</u> they had no wish to marry her.

7 'despite' and 'in spite of'

Despite and **in spite of** are also used to introduce a contrast, but they are used as prepositions in front of noun groups or '-ing' clauses, not as conjunctions.

These mothers still play a big part in their children's lives, <u>despite working and having a full-time nanny.</u>
<u>In spite of his mildness</u> he was tremendously enthusiastic about his subject.

However, you can say '**despite the fact that…**' or '**in spite of the fact that…**'.

<u>Despite the fact that it sounds like science fiction,</u> most of it is technically realizable at this moment.

⇨ See also **Usage** entry at **in spite of - despite**.

GRAMMAR

8   conditional clauses

Conditional clauses are used to talk about possible situations. The event described in the main clause depends on the condition described in the subordinate clause. Conditional clauses usually begin with **if** or **unless**.

⇨ See **Usage** entries at **if** and **unless**.

When using a conditional clause, you often use a **modal** in the main clause. You always use a modal in the main clause when talking about a situation which does not exist.

If you weren't here, she <u>would</u> get rid of me in no time.
If anybody had asked me, I <u>could</u> have told them what happened.

9   inversion

Instead of using 'if' or 'unless', you can use **inversion** in formal speech and writing. For example, instead of saying 'If I'd been there, I would have stopped them', you can say 'Had I been there, I would have stopped them'.

<u>Had I been found innocent,</u> I would have been accepted as innocent by society.

10   imperatives

People sometimes use an imperative clause followed by **and** or **or** instead of a conditional clause. For example, instead of saying 'If you keep quiet, you won't get hurt', they say 'Keep quiet and you won't get hurt'.

⇨ See **Topic** entries at **Advising someone** and **Warning someone**.

11   less common conjunctions

You use **provided**, **providing**, **as long as**, or **only if** to begin a conditional clause referring to a situation that is a necessary condition for the situation referred to in the main clause.

A child will learn what is right and what is wrong in good time <u>provided he is not pressured.</u>
<u>As long as you print fairly clearly</u> you don't have to learn any new typing skills.

When you use **only if**, the subject and verb in the main clause are inverted.

Only if oil is very scarce <u>is it</u> likely that there will be a major use of coal to make oil.

To indicate that a situation is not affected by another possible situation, you use **even if**.

<u>Even if you've never been taught to mend a fuse,</u> you don't have to sit in the dark.
I would have married her <u>even if she had been penniless.</u>

To indicate that a situation is not affected by any of several possibilities, you use **whether** and **or**.

If the lawyer made a long, oratorical speech, the client was happy <u>whether he won or lost.</u>
Some children start with a huge appetite at birth and never lose it afterwards, <u>whether they're well or sick, calm or worried.</u>

To indicate that a situation is not affected by either of two opposite possibilities, you use **whether or not**.

A parent shouldn't hesitate to talk over the child's problems with the teacher, <u>whether or not they are connected with school.</u>
He will have to foot at least part of the bill <u>whether he likes it or not.</u>

12   manner clauses

Manner clauses describe someone's behaviour or the way that something is done. The following conjunctions are used to introduce manner clauses:

as	as if	as though	like	the way

I don't understand why he behaves <u>as he does.</u>
Is she often rude and cross <u>like she's been this last month?</u>
Joyce looked at her <u>the way a lot of girls did.</u>

⇨ See **Usage** entry at **like - as - the way**.

As if and **as though** are used to say that something is done as it would be done if something else were the case. Note that a past tense is used in the subordinate clause.

Presidents can't dispose of companies <u>as if people didn't exist.</u>
She treats him <u>as though he was her own son.</u>

The subjunctive form **were** is often used instead of 'was'.

He swallowed a little of his whisky <u>as if it were nasty medicine.</u>

13 place clauses

Place clauses indicate the location or position of something. Place clauses usually begin with **where**.

He said he was happy <u>where he was.</u>
He left it <u>where it lay.</u>

You use **wherever** to say that something happens in every place where something else happens.

Soft-stemmed herbs and ferns spread across the ground <u>wherever there was enough light.</u>
<u>Wherever I looked,</u> I found patterns.

Everywhere can be used instead of 'wherever'.

<u>Everywhere I went,</u> people were angry or suspicious.

 Informally, speakers of American English also use **everyplace** instead of 'everywhere'.

<u>Everyplace</u> her body touched the seat began to itch.

14 purpose clauses

Purpose clauses indicate the intention someone has when they do something. The most common type of purpose clause is a 'to'-infinitive clause.

All information in this brochure has been checked as carefully as possible <u>to ensure that it is accurate.</u>
Carol had brought the subject up simply <u>to annoy Sandra.</u>

In formal writing and speech, **in order** followed by a 'to'-infinitive clause is often used instead of a simple 'to'-infinitive clause.

They had to take some of his land <u>in order to extend the church.</u>

You can also use **so as** followed by a 'to'-infinitive clause.

The best thing to do is to fix up a screen <u>so as to let in the fresh air and keep out the flies.</u>

⚠ **WARNING:** You cannot use 'not' with a simple 'to'-infinitive clause when indicating a negative purpose. For example, you cannot say '~~He slammed on his brakes to not hit it~~'. Instead, you must use **to avoid** followed by an '-ing' form, or **in order** or **so as** followed by **not** and a 'to'-infinitive.

He had to hang on <u>to avoid being washed overboard.</u>
I would have to give myself something to do <u>in order not to be bored.</u>
They went on foot, <u>so as not to be heard.</u>

Other purpose clauses are introduced by **so**, **so that**, or **in order that**.

She said she wanted to be ready at six <u>so she could be out by eight.</u>
I have drawn a diagram <u>so that my explanation will be clearer.</u>
…people who are learning English <u>in order that they can study a particular subject.</u>

ⓘ Note that you usually use a modal in these purpose clauses.

15 reason clauses

Reason clauses explain why something happens or is done. They are usually introduced by **because**, **since**, or **as**.

I couldn't feel anger against him <u>because I liked him too much.</u>
I didn't know that she had been married, <u>since she seldom talked about herself.</u>

GRAMMAR

You use **in case** or **just in case** when you are mentioning a possible future situation which is someone's reason for doing something. In the reason clause, you use the simple present tense.

Mr Woods, I am here just in case anything out of the ordinary happens.

When you are talking about someone's reason for doing something in the past, you use the simple past tense in the reason clause.

Sam had consented to take an overcoat in case the wind rose.

16 result clauses

Result clauses indicate the result of an event or situation. Result clauses are introduced by the conjunctions **so that** or **so**. They always come after the main clause.

He persuaded Nichols to turn it into a film so that he could play the lead.
The young do not have the money to save and the old are consuming their savings, so it is mainly the middle-aged who are saving.

'That'-clauses (with or without **that**) can also be used as result clauses when **so** or **such** has been used in the main clause.

They were so surprised they didn't try to stop him.
These birds have such small wings that they cannot get into the air even if they try.

⇨ See **Usage** entry at **so**.

17 time clauses

Time clauses indicate the time of an event. The following conjunctions are used to introduce time clauses:

after	before	the minute	until	whilst
as	once	the moment	when	
as soon as	since	till	while	

We arrived as they were leaving.
When the jar was full, he turned the water off.

⇨ More information on the uses of the words listed above can be found in the entry for each word.

18 tenses in time clauses

When talking about the past or the present, the verb in a time clause has the same tense that it would have in a main clause or a simple sentence. However, if the time clause refers to the future, you use the simple present tense. You do not use 'will'.

As soon as I get back, I'm going to call my lawyer.
He wants to see you before he dies.

When mentioning an event in a time clause which will happen before an event referred to in the main clause, you use the present perfect tense in the time clause. You do not use 'will have'.

We won't be getting married until we 've saved enough money.
Tell the DHSS as soon as you have retired.

When reporting a statement or thought about such an event, you use the simple past tense or the past perfect tense in the time clause.

I knew he would come back as soon as I was gone.
He constantly emphasised that violence would continue until political oppression had ended.

⇨ For information on the use of tenses with **since** in a time clause, see **Usage** entry at **since**.

19 omitting the subject

If the subject of the main clause and the time clause are the same, the subject in the time clause is sometimes omitted and a participle is used as the verb. This is done especially in formal English.

I read the book <u>before going to see the film.</u>
The car was stolen <u>while parked in a London street.</u>

When, **while**, **once**, **until**, or **till** can be used in front of a noun group, an adjective group, or an adjunct.

<u>When in Venice,</u> we booked a table at the 'historic' Harry's Bar.
He had read of her elopement <u>while at Oxford.</u>
Steam or boil them <u>until just tender.</u>

20 **regular occurrences**

If you want to say that something always happens or happened in particular circumstances, you use a clause beginning with **when** or, more emphatically, **whenever**, **every time**, or **each time**.

<u>When he talks about the Church,</u> he does sound like an outsider.
<u>Whenever she had a cold,</u> she ate only fruit.
<u>Every time I go to that class</u> I panic.
He flinched <u>each time she spoke to him.</u>

Tenses

1 **uses**

Tenses are the different verb forms and verb groups that indicate roughly what time you are referring to. **Simple tenses** are used to refer to situations, habitual actions, and single completed actions.

I <u>like</u> him very much.
He always <u>gives</u> both points of view.
He <u>walked</u> out of the kitchen.

Continuous tenses are used when talking about temporary situations at a particular point in time.

Inflation <u>is rising.</u>
We believed we <u>were fighting</u> for a good cause.

Some verbs are not used in continuous tenses.

⇨ See section on **stative verbs** in **Grammar** entry at **Continuous tenses.**

Perfect tenses are used when relating an action or situation to the present or to a moment in the past.

Football <u>has become</u> international.
She did not know how long she <u>had been lying</u> there.

The passive voice is used when the subject of a clause is the person or thing affected by an action. Tenses in the passive voice are formed by using an appropriate tense of **be** and the past participle of the main verb.

The earth <u>is baked</u> by the sun into a hard, brittle layer.
They <u>had been taught</u> to be critical.

⇨ See **Grammar** entry at **The Passive.**

⇨ For more information on the uses of tenses, see **Grammar** entries at **The Future, The Past,** and **The Present.**

⇨ Sometimes the tense used in a subordinate clause is not what you would expect: see **Grammar** entries at **The Future, Reporting,** and **Subordinate clauses.**

2 **present and past tenses**

The following table shows how to form present and past tenses.

Active	Passive
simple present	
base form *I want a breath of air.* (3rd person singular) '-s' form *Flora laughs again.*	simple present of **be** + past participle *It is boiled before use.*
present continuous	
simple present of **be** + '-ing' form *Things are changing.*	present continuous of **be** + past participle *My advice is being ignored.*
present perfect	
simple present of **have** + past participle *I have seen this before.*	present perfect of **be** + past participle *You have been warned.*
present perfect continuous	
present perfect of **be** + '-ing' form *Howard has been working hard.*	present perfect continuous of **be** + past participle (not common)
simple past	
past form *I resented his attitude.*	simple past of **be** + past participle *He was murdered.*
past continuous	
simple past of **be** + '-ing' form *I was sitting on the rug.*	past continuous of **be** + past participle *We were being watched.*
past perfect	
had + past participle *Everyone had liked her.*	past perfect of **be** + past participle *Raymond had been rejected.*
past perfect continuous	
had been + '-ing' form *Miss Gulliver had been lying.*	past perfect continuous of **be** + past participle (not common)

GRAMMAR

3 | **future tenses**

There are several ways of referring to the future in English. The commonest way is to use the modal **will** or **shall**.

⇨ See **Usage** entry at **shall - will.**

Verb groups in which **will** and **shall** are used to talk about the future are sometimes called **future tenses.**

The following table shows future tenses.

Active	Passive
future	
will or **shall** + base form *They will arrive tomorrow.*	**will be** or **shall be** + past participle *More land will be destroyed.*
future continuous	
will be or **shall be** + '-ing' form *I shall be leaving soon.*	**will be being** or **shall be being** + past participle (not common)
future perfect	
will have or **shall have** + past participle *They will have forgotten you.*	**will have been** or **shall have been** + past participle *By the end of the year, ten projects will have been approved.*
future perfect continuous	
will have been or **shall have been** + '-ing' form *By March, I will have been doing this job for six years.*	**will have been being** or **shall have been being** + past participle (very rare)

⇨ For other ways of referring to the future, see **Grammar** entry at **The Future.**

'That'-clauses

A **'that'-clause** is a clause beginning with **that** which is used to refer to a fact or idea.

1 | **reporting**

'That'-clauses are commonly used to report something that is said.

She said that she'd been married for about two months.
Sir Peter recently announced that he is to retire at the end of the year.

⇨ See **Grammar** entry at **Reporting.**

2 | **after adjectives**

You can use a 'that'-clause after adjectives which indicate someone's feelings or beliefs to say what fact those feelings or beliefs relate to.

She was <u>sure that he meant it.</u>
He was <u>frightened that something terrible might be said.</u>

The following adjectives often have a 'that'-clause after them:

afraid	conscious	frightened	optimistic	sure
amazed	convinced	furious	pessimistic	surprised
angry	definite	glad	pleased	suspicious
annoyed	determined	grateful	positive	terrified
anxious	disappointed	happy	proud	thankful
ashamed	disgusted	hopeful	puzzled	unaware
astonished	dismayed	horrified	relieved	uncertain
astounded	doubtful	insistent	sad	unconvinced
aware	eager	jealous	satisfied	unhappy
certain	envious	keen	scared	unlucky
concerned	fearful	lucky	shocked	upset
confident	fortunate	nervous	sorry	worried

You can use a 'that'-clause after **it is** and an adjective to comment on a situation or fact.
It is <u>extraordinary that we should ever have met.</u>

⇨ See **Usage** entry at **it**.

3 **after nouns**

Nouns such as **assumption**, **feeling**, and **rumour**, which refer to what someone says or thinks, can be followed by a 'that'-clause.

Our strategy has been based on <u>the assumption that our adversary is just one man.</u>
I had <u>a feeling that no-one thought I was good enough.</u>
There is no truth in <u>the rumour that the delay was due to a judge falling asleep.</u>

The following nouns are often followed by a 'that'-clause:

accusation	conclusion	guess	opinion	saying
admission	contention	hint	point	sense
advice	conviction	hope	prediction	statement
agreement	criticism	hypothesis	principle	suggestion
allegation	decision	idea	promise	superstition
announcement	declaration	illusion	proposal	theory
argument	demand	impression	question	thought
assertion	denial	information	realization	threat
assumption	excuse	insistence	recognition	view
assurance	expectation	judgement	remark	warning
belief	explanation	knowledge	reminder	wish
charge	fear	message	report	
claim	feeling	news	request	
comment	generalization	notion	rule	
concept	guarantee	observation	rumour	

4 **after 'be'**

A 'that'-clause can be used as a complement after **be**.
Our hope is <u>that this time all parties will co-operate.</u>
The important thing is <u>that we love each other.</u>

5 **omitting 'that'**

'That' is sometimes omitted in all of the above cases, especially in spoken English.
He knew <u>the attempt was hopeless.</u>
She is sure <u>Harold doesn't mind.</u>
I'd just walk in and have the feeling <u>I'd seen some of it before.</u>
All I hope is <u>I can hang back when we have to attack.</u>

6 **'the fact that'**

In very formal English, a 'that'-clause is sometimes used as the subject of a sentence.

That man can aspire to and achieve goodness is evident through all of history.

However, if the main verb is a reporting verb or **be**, it is much more usual to have **it** as the subject, with the 'that'-clause coming later.

It cannot be denied that this view is abundantly justified by history.

In other cases, it is more usual to use a structure consisting of **the fact** and a 'that'-clause as the subject.

The fact that your boss is actually offering to do your job for you should certainly prompt you to question his motives.

Structures beginning with **the fact that** are also used as the object of prepositions and of verbs which cannot be followed by a simple 'that'-clause.

…acknowledgement of the fact that we have no intrinsic right to receive answers to all our questions.
We overlooked the fact that the children's emotional development had been retarded.

'To'-infinitive clauses

1	forms	**7**	as purpose clauses
2	negative 'to'-infinitives	**8**	after adjectives
3	linking 'to'-infinitive clauses	**9**	with 'too' and 'enough'
4	after verbs	**10**	after a noun group
5	after 'be'	**11**	used as subject
6	after 'be' in questions		

GRAMMAR

1 **forms**

A **'to'-infinitive clause** is a subordinate clause beginning with a 'to'-infinitive – that is, **to** and the base form of a verb.

She began to laugh.
Christopher and I went to see him.
I wanted to be popular.

A 'to'-infinitive clause can include auxiliaries.

Only two are known to have defected.
I seem to have been eating all evening.
I didn't want to be caught off guard.

2 **negative 'to'-infinitives**

When you use **not** with a 'to'-infinitive, you put **not** in front of the **to**.

I told him not to be late.

⇨ For information on the position of adverbs in relation to 'to'-infinitives, see **Grammar** entry at **Split infinitives.**

3 **linking 'to'-infinitive clauses**

When two infinitives are linked by **and, or, rather than**, or **than**, the second infinitive can be used without 'to'.

I told Dave to wait and watch.
I'd far prefer to drive than go by train.

4 **after verbs**

When a verb is followed by a 'to'-infinitive clause, the subject of the verb is also the subject of the 'to'-infinitive clause. The following verbs are often followed by a 'to'-infinitive clause:

aim	deserve	hope	opt	start
appear	endeavour	intend	plan	tend
arrange	expect	learn	prefer	try
attempt	fail	like	prepare	venture
begin	fear	long	pretend	want
cease	fight	love	prove	wish
choose	forget	manage	remember	
continue	happen	mean	resolve	
dare	hate	need	seek	
decide	hesitate	neglect	seem	

They <u>decided to wait.</u>
England <u>failed to win a place in the finals.</u>
She <u>seemed to like me.</u>

Some verbs, such as **begin**, **continue**, and **prefer** can be followed by a 'to'-infinitive or an '-ing' form.

Marcus <u>began to scream.</u>
They all <u>began screaming.</u>

⇨ See **Grammar** entry at **'-ing' forms** for a list of these verbs.

A 'to'-infinitive clause is also used after reporting verbs such as **agree**, **ask** and **threaten**.

⇨ See **Grammar** entry at **Reporting**.

Sometimes you use a 'to'-infinitive clause after the object of a verb. The object is the subject of the 'to'-infinitive clause. The following verbs are often used with an object and a 'to'-infinitive:

allow	defy	induce	love	prefer	tempt
cause	enable	inspire	mean	prepare	train
choose	expect	intend	oblige	programme	want
compel	force	lead	pay	prompt	will
condemn	get	like	permit	teach	wish

Higher productivity <u>has enabled companies to earn higher profits.</u>
…until ill health <u>forced him to retire.</u>

ⓘ Note that **help** can be followed by a 'to'-infinitive or an infinitive without 'to'.

⇨ See **Usage** entry at **help**.

A 'to'-infinitive clause is also used after an object with reporting verbs such as **advise**, **persuade**, and **promise**.

⇨ See **Grammar** entry at **Reporting**.

5 **after 'be'**

In formal English, newspapers, and broadcasting, 'to'-infinitive clauses are used after **be** to indicate that something is planned to happen.

After dinner they <u>were to go to a movie.</u>
A clean coal-fired power plant <u>is to be built at Bilsthorpe Colliery.</u>

You can also use a 'to'-infinitive clause after **be** when specifying something such as a task, aim, or method.

Our job is <u>to work out what the rules are.</u>
Their aim is <u>to help countries achieve an independent judiciary.</u>
The simplest way is <u>to smuggle the cash out of the country and invest it in tax havens.</u>

You can also say that it is someone's job 'to do something'.

It is my job <u>to keep the players confident.</u>

GRAMMAR

6 **after 'be' in questions**

A 'to'-infinitive clause can be used in questions after **who** or **what** and **be** to ask what should happen or be done in a particular situation.

Who is to question him?
What is to be done with the wastelands of old industry?

⇨ For information on the use of 'to'-infinitives in reported questions, see **Grammar** entry at **Reporting**.

7 **as purpose clauses**

People often use 'to'-infinitive clauses to show the purpose of an action.

They locked the door to stop us from getting in.
He patted his breast pocket to make sure his wallet was in place.

⇨ For other ways of indicating purpose, see section on **purpose clauses** in **Grammar** entry at **Subordinate clauses**.

8 **after adjectives**

Some adjectives need to be followed by a 'to'-infinitive clause to complete their meaning. For example, you cannot say 'He is unable'. You have to say 'He is unable to come', 'He is unable to cope', etc.

They were unable to help her.
I am willing to try.

The following adjectives are usually or always followed by a 'to'-infinitive clause:

able	doomed	fit	likely	prepared	unwilling
bound	due	inclined	loath	unable	willing
destined	fated	liable	obliged	unfit	

You can put a 'to'-infinitive clause after other adjectives when you want to give information about the action that a feeling relates to.

afraid	determined	happy	reluctant	unafraid
amused	disappointed	impatient	sad	unhappy
angry	dismayed	interested	scared	upset
anxious	eager	keen	sorry	willing
ashamed	frightened	pleased	surprised	
astonished	furious	proud	terrified	
delighted	glad	puzzled	thankful	
desperate	grateful	relieved	thrilled	

I was afraid to go home.
He was anxious to leave before it got dark.
They were terribly pleased to see you.

You use a 'to'-infinitive clause after adjectives such as **easy** or **nice** when you want to say how easy, difficult, or pleasant it is to do something to a person or thing.

She had been easy to deceive.
The windows will be almost impossible to open.
They're quite nice to look at.

ⓘ Note that you use a transitive verb or a verb followed by a preposition in this structure. The subject of the main clause is the object of the 'to'-infinitive clause.

You can also use this structure with a complement consisting of a noun group.

They're a pleasure to have in the class.

You can use a 'to'-infinitive clause after the following adjectives which describe someone, as a way of commenting on how sensible or right an action is.

GRAMMAR

clever	daft	mad	sensible	stupid	wrong
correct	foolish	naive	silly	unwise	
crazy	insane	right	smart	wise	

Am I <u>wrong to stay here?</u>
I have been extremely <u>stupid</u> and <u>foolish to leave it there tonight</u>.

You can use **it** with a link verb and an adjective followed by a 'to'-infinitive clause as a way of describing an experience or action.

It's <u>nice to be made a fuss of!</u>
It would be <u>interesting to hear the Government explain this</u>.
It's <u>impossible to say when I'll finish this</u>.

⇨ See also **Usage** entry at **it**.

9 with 'too' and 'enough'

When you are using **too**, you can use a 'to'-infinitive clause to indicate the action that is not possible. Similarly, you can use a 'to'-infinitive clause after **enough** to indicate the action that is possible.

He was <u>too proud to apologise</u>.
She spoke <u>too quickly</u> for me <u>to understand</u>.
He was <u>old enough to understand</u>.
I could see <u>well enough to know we were losing</u>.

10 after a noun group

You can use a 'to'-infinitive clause after a noun group to indicate the aim or purpose of something.

We arranged <u>a meeting to discuss the new rules</u>.

You can also use a 'to'-infinitive clause after a noun group to indicate that something needs to have something done to it, or can have something done to it.

I gave him <u>several things to mend</u>.
I have <u>work to do.</u>
He now had <u>plenty to eat</u> and <u>clean clothes to wear</u>.

You can also use a 'to'-infinitive clause after a noun group that includes an ordinal number, a superlative, or for example, the words **next**, **last**, **best**, **right**, or **only**.

She was <u>the first woman to be elected to the council</u>.
Mr Holmes was <u>the oldest person to be chosen</u>.
<u>The only person to speak</u> was James.
He was not <u>the right person to lead us into the next decade</u>.

Sometimes a noun is used with **the** but without an adjective to mean 'the right one'.
We think he is <u>the man to lead Chelsea into the next century</u>.

A 'to'-infinitive clause is used after some abstract nouns to indicate the action that they relate to.

All it takes is <u>a willingness to learn</u>.
He'd lost <u>the ability to communicate with people</u>.

The following abstract nouns are often followed by a 'to'-infinitive clause:

ability	desire	inability	permission	urge
aim	determination	inclination	promise	willingness
ambition	eagerness	intention	reluctance	wish
attempt	effort	longing	resolve	
chance	failure	need	suggestion	
concern	freedom	offer	tendency	
decision	impatience	opportunity	unwillingness	

GRAMMAR

11 **used as subject**

In formal writing and speech, a 'to'-infinitive clause is sometimes used as the subject of a clause.

To impose these reforms on the trade union movement would be folly.
To enjoy mischief is surely a long way from being wicked.

Verbless clauses

Most clauses contain a verb. However, some groups of words have the same function as a main clause or a subordinate clause, but do not contain a verb. These groups of words are called **verbless clauses**. The following examples show verbless clauses used as exclamations and questions.

What a pleasant surprise!
What about your breakfast?
Well, professor?
Drink, Ted?

In writing, verbless subordinate clauses are sometimes used. These clauses can be based on an adjective, or on a subordinating conjunction and an adjective.

Surprised at my reaction, she tried to console me.
Weak with laughter, they lumbered off.
Though not very attractive physically, she possessed a good sense of humour.
Fry the fritters on both sides *until golden brown.*

⇨ For information on the conjunctions that can be used in this way with an adjective and no verb, see **Grammar** entry at **Subordinate clauses**.

Other verbless subordinate clauses are based on a noun group and an adjective or adjunct describing a state. These clauses are used to describe people in stories.

'What do you mean by that?' said Hugh, his face pale.
I became aware that Otto was standing close by, his eyes wide, his mouth slightly open.
Marie Pennington sat in her study, her head in her hands.

(*i*) Note that **with** is often used in front of groups of words like these.

She walked on, with her eyes straight ahead.

Verbs

1 verb forms	**9** reciprocal verbs
2 uses of verb forms	**10** verbs with object or prepositional
3 intransitive verbs	phrase
4 transitive verbs	**11** ditransitive verbs
5 reflexive verbs	**12** link verbs
6 delexical verbs	**13** compound verbs
7 transitive or intransitive	**14** other verbs
8 ergative verbs	

A **verb** is a word which is used with a subject to say what someone or something does, what they are, or what happens to them. This entry explains the different verb forms and then gives information about different types of verbs.

1 **verb forms**

Regular verbs have the following forms:

- a base form, for example **walk**
- an '-s' form, for example **walks**

- an '-ing' form or present participle, for example **walking**
- a past form, for example **walked**

In the case of regular verbs, the past form is used for the past tense and is also used as the past participle. However, with many **irregular verbs** there are two past forms:

- a past tense form, for example **stole**
- a past participle form, for example **stolen**

⇨ See **Grammar** entry at **Irregular verbs**.

⇨ The forms of the common irregular verbs **be**, **have**, and **do** are given in the **Grammar** entry at **Auxiliaries**.

Sometimes there is a spelling change when the '**-s**', '**-ing**', and '**-ed**' endings are added, as shown in the table on the next page.

	base form	'-s' form	'-ing' form or present participle	past form and past participle
		add '-s'	add '-ing'	add '-ed'
	join	joins	joining	joined
		add '-es'		
ending in '-sh'	finish	finishes	finishing	finished
ending in '-ch'	reach	reaches	reaching	reached
ending in '-ss'	pass	passes	passing	passed
ending in '-x'	mix	mixes	mixing	mixed
ending in '-z'	buzz	buzzes	buzzing	buzzed
ending in '-o'	echo	echoes	echoing	echoed
			omit '-e' before adding '-ing' or '-ed'	
ending in '-e'	dance	dances	dancing	danced
			change '-ie' to '-y' before adding '-ing'	omit '-e' before adding '-ed'
ending in '-ie'	tie	ties	tying	tied
ending in consonant + '-y'		change '-y' to '-ies'		change '-y' to '-ied'
	cry	cries	crying	cried
one syllable ending in single vowel + consonant			double final consonant before adding '-ing' or '-ed'	
	dip	dips	dipping	dipped
last syllable stressed			double final consonant before adding '-ing' or '-ed'	
	refer	refers	referring	referred
ending in '-ic'			add '-k' before adding '-ing' or '-ed'	
	panic	panics	panicking	panicked

GRAMMAR

(i) Note that in the case of the following verbs ending in '**-e**', you just add '**-ing**' in the normal way to form the '-ing' form. For example, the '-ing' form of **age** is **ageing**.

age	disagree	eye	hoe	referee	tiptoe
agree	dye	free	knee	singe	

You do not double the final consonant of verbs ending in '**-w**','**-x**', or '**-y**' when forming the '-ing' form or past form.

row → rowing → rowing	box → boxing → boxed	play → playing → played

In British English, you double the final '**l**' of verbs like **travel** and **quarrel**, even though the last syllable is not stressed.

travel → travelling → travelled	quarrel → quarrelling → quarrelled

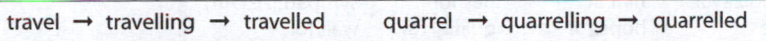 You do not double the final 'l' in American English. In British English, and sometimes in American English, the final consonant of the following verbs is doubled, even though the last syllable is not stressed.

handicap	hiccup	kidnap	program	worship

2 **uses of verb forms**
The base form is used for the simple present tense, the imperative, and the infinitive, and is used after modals.

I hate him.
Go away.
He asked me to send it to him.
He asked if he could take a picture.

The '**-s**' form is used for the third person singular of the simple present.

She likes you.

The '**-ing**' form or present participle is used for continuous tenses, '-ing' adjectives, verbal nouns, and some non-finite clauses.

⇨ See **Grammar** entries at '**-ing' adjectives** and '**-ing' forms**.

The attacks are getting worse.
…the increasing complexity of industrial societies.
She preferred swimming to tennis.
'So you're quite recovered now?' she said, smiling at me.

The past form is used for the simple past tense, and for the past participle of regular verbs.

I walked down the garden with him.
She had walked out without speaking.

The past participle is used for perfect tenses, the passive voice, '-ed' adjectives, and some non-finite clauses.

⇨ See **Grammar** entries at '**-ed' adjectives** and **Past participles**.

Two countries have refused to sign the document.
It was stolen weeks ago.
He became quite annoyed.
The cargo, purchased all over Europe, included ten thousand rifles.

⇨ See also **Grammar** entry at **Tenses**.

3 intransitive verbs

Some verbs do not have an object. These verbs are called **intransitive verbs.** Intransitive verbs often describe actions or events which do not involve anyone or anything other than the subject.

Her whole body ached.
The gate squeaked.

Some intransitive verbs always or typically have a preposition after them.

I'm relying on Bill.
The land belongs to a rich family.

These are some of the commonest:

amount to	depend on	object to	resort to
apologize for	hint at	pay for	sympathize with
aspire to	hope for	qualify for	wait for
believe in	insist on	refer to	
belong to	lead to	relate to	
consist of	listen to	rely on	

You will find information on what preposition to use after a particular verb in many of the entries for individual words in this book.

4 transitive verbs

Some verbs describe events that must, in addition to the subject, involve someone or something else. These verbs are called **transitive verbs.** They have an **object,** that is, a noun group which is put after the verb.

He closed the door.
Some of the women noticed me.

Some transitive verbs always or typically have a particular preposition after their object.

The police accused him of murder.
He just prevented the bottle from toppling.

These are some of the commonest:

accuse of	deprive of	pelt with	return to	trust with
attribute to	entitle to	prevent from	rob of	view as
base on	mistake for	regard as	subject to	
dedicate to	owe to	remind of	swap for	

Some transitive verbs have a complement after their object when used with a particular meaning, as in 'They make me angry'.

⇨ See section on **object complements** in **Grammar** entry at **Complements.**

Most transitive verbs can be used in the passive. However, a few, such as **have**, **get**, and **let**, are rarely or never used in the passive.

⇨ See **Grammar** entry at **The Passive.**

5 reflexive verbs

A **reflexive verb** is a transitive verb which is normally or often used with a **reflexive pronoun** such as **myself, himself,** or **themselves** as its object. The following verbs are often reflexive verbs:

GRAMMAR

amuse	cut	excel	hurt	restrict
apply	distance	exert	introduce	strain
blame	dry	express	kill	teach
compose	enjoy	help	prepare	

Sam amused himself by throwing branches into the fire.
'Can I borrow a pencil?'–'Yes, help yourself.'

The verbs **busy, content,** and **pride** must be used with a reflexive pronoun.

He had busied himself in the laboratory.
He prides himself on his tidiness.

⚠ **WARNING:** Reflexive pronouns are not used as much in English as in some other languages when talking about actions that you normally do to yourself. You only use a reflexive pronoun to emphasize that a person is doing the action himself or herself.

She washed very quickly and rushed downstairs.
Children were encouraged to wash themselves.

6 | delexical verbs

A number of very common verbs can be used with an object referring to an action simply to indicate that the action takes place. They are called **delexical verbs.** The verbs most commonly used in this way are:

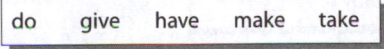

| do | give | have | make | take |

The noun which is the object of the delexical verb is usually countable and singular, although it can sometimes be plural.

We were having a joke.
She gave an amused laugh.
They took regular walks along cart-tracks.

In a few cases, an uncount noun is used after a delexical verb.

We have made progress in both science and art.
A nurse is taking care of him.

⇨ For information on the nouns used with delexical verbs, see **Usage** entries at **do, give, have - take,** and **make.**

7 | transitive or intransitive

Many verbs are transitive when used with one meaning and intransitive when used with another meaning.

She runs a hotel.
The hare runs at enormous speed.

It is often possible to use a verb intransitively because the object is known or has already been mentioned.

I don't own a car. I can't drive.
Both dresses are beautiful. I can't choose.
Come and eat.

ⓘ Note that even verbs which are almost always followed by a direct object can occasionally be used intransitively, when you are making a very general statement.

Some people build while others destroy.
She was anxious to please.

8 **ergative verbs**

An **ergative verb** can be used either transitively to focus on the person who performs an action, or intransitively to focus on the thing affected by an action.

When I <u>opened the door,</u> there was Laverne.
Suddenly <u>the door opened.</u>
The driver <u>stopped the car.</u>
<u>The big car stopped.</u>
He slammed the door with such force that <u>a window broke.</u>
They threw stones and <u>broke the windows of buses.</u>

Many ergative verbs refer to change or movement:

age	crack	fade	rot	stick
alter	crash	fill	shake	stop
balance	crumble	finish	shatter	stretch
begin	darken	freeze	shrink	swing
bend	decrease	grow	shut	tear
bleach	diminish	heal	slow	thicken
break	disperse	improve	snap	turn
bruise	dissolve	increase	spin	vary
burn	double	move	split	widen
burst	drop	open	spoil	worsen
change	drown	quicken	spread	
close	dry	rest	stand	
continue	empty	ripen	start	
cool	end	rock	steady	

I <u>shattered the glass.</u>
<u>Wine bottles had shattered</u> all over the pavement.
Jefferson <u>spun the globe</u> slowly on its axis.
<u>The wheels of the car spun</u> furiously.

Verbs which refer to cooking are usually ergative verbs.

bake	brown	freeze	melt	steam
boil	cook	marinate	simmer	thaw

While the water <u>boiled,</u> I put the shopping away.
Residents have been advised to <u>boil their tap water</u> or drink bottled water.

So are verbs which refer to driving or controlling vehicles.

anchor	capsize	reverse	sink	stop
back	halt	sail	start	swerve

The boys <u>reversed their car</u> and set off down the road we had just climbed.
<u>The jeep reversed</u> at full speed.

The following verbs are used ergatively with one or two nouns only:

- **catch** (an article of clothing)
- **fire** (a gun, rifle, pistol)
- **play** (music)
- **ring** (a bell, the alarm)
- **show** (an emotion such as fear, anger)
- **sound** (a horn, the alarm)

GRAMMAR

He had caught his sleeve on a splinter of wood.
The hat caught on a bolt and tore.

The following ergative verbs usually have an adjunct after them when they are used intransitively:

clean	handle	polish	stain
freeze	mark	sell	wash

I like the new Range Rover. It handles beautifully.
Wool washes well if you treat it carefully.

9 **reciprocal verbs**

A **reciprocal verb** describes an action or process which involves two or more people doing the same thing to each other, having a relationship, or linked because they are participating jointly in an action or event. Reciprocal verbs have two basic patterns:

● They can be used with a plural subject - that is, a subject consisting of a plural noun group. When they are used with this plural subject, the meaning is that the people, groups, or things involved are interacting with each other. For example, two people can **quarrel**, can **have a chat**, or can **meet**.

Their children are always quarrelling.
He came out and we hugged.
Their eyes met.

● They can be used with a subject which refers to one of the participants, and an object, prepositional object, or adjunct which refers to the other participant, as in 'She agreed with her sister', 'I had a chat with him' and 'I met him at university'.

He quarrelled with his father.
I hugged him.
His eyes met hers.

To emphasize that the participants are equally involved in the action, **each other** or **one another** can be put after the verb group.

We embraced each other.
It was the first time they had touched one another.

The following reciprocal verbs can be followed by **each other** or **one another**:

cuddle	divorce	engage	hug	marry	meet
date	embrace	fight	kiss	match	touch

With some verbs it is necessary to use a preposition, usually **with**, in front of **each other** and **one another**.

You've got to be able to communicate with each other.
Third World countries are competing with one another for a restricted market.

The following reciprocal verbs can be used with a plural subject or can be followed by **with**:

agree	collide	contrast	engage	mix
alternate	combine	converse	fight	negotiate
argue	communicate	co-operate	flirt	quarrel
bicker	compete	correspond	gossip	row
chat	conflict	dance	integrate	speak
clash	connect	differ	joke	struggle
coincide	consult	disagree	mate	talk
collaborate	contend	draw	merge	wrangle

Her parents never argued.
He was arguing with his girlfriend and she hit him with a frying pan.
Owens and his boss are still negotiating.
She believed that no country should negotiate with terrorists. .

You can also use **against** after **compete** and **fight**, and **to** after **correspond** and **talk**. You use **from** after **part** and **separate**. You use **to** after **relate**.

(i) Note that **engage** and **fight** can be used either transitively or with a preposition.

10 verbs with object or prepositional phrase

A small group of verbs can be followed by either an object or a prepositional phrase. For example, you can say either 'He tugged her sleeve' or 'He tugged at her sleeve'. There is usually little difference in meaning between using the verb on its own and using a preposition after it.

Her arm brushed my cheek.
Something brushed against the back of the shelter.
We climbed the mountain.
I climbed up the tree.

The following verbs can be used with an object or a prepositional phrase:

boo (at)	gnaw (at)	play (against)
brush (against)	hiss (at)	rule (over)
check (on)	infiltrate (into)	sip (at)
distinguish (between)	jeer (at)	sniff (at)
enter (for)	juggle (with)	tug (at)
fight (against)	mock (at)	twiddle (with)
fight (with)	mourn (for)	
gain (in)	nibble (at)	

11 ditransitive verbs

Some verbs can have two objects: a **direct object** and an **indirect object.** These verbs are called **ditransitive verbs.** The indirect object usually refers to the person who benefits from the action or receives something as a result. When the indirect object is a short noun group such as a pronoun, or **the** and a noun, you often put it in front of the direct object.

I gave him the money.
Sheila showed the boy her new bike.
I taught myself French.

(i) Note that you do not usually put a preposition in front of the indirect object when it is in this position. For example, you do not say 'I gave to him the money'.

Instead of putting the indirect object in front of the direct object, it is possible to put the indirect object in a prepositional phrase that comes after the direct object.

He handed his driving licence to the policeman.

It is normal to use this prepositional structure when the indirect object is long, or when you want to emphasize it.

I've given the key to the woman who lives in the house next door to the garage.
I bought that for you.

You must use a preposition when the direct object is a personal pronoun and the indirect object is not. You do not say, for example 'He bought his wife it.'

He got a glass from the cupboard, filled it and gave it to Atkinson.
Then Stephen Jumel bought it for his wife.

If both the direct object and the indirect object are personal pronouns, you should use a preposition in writing. A preposition is also often used in conversation.

He gave it to me.
Save it for me.

However, some people do not use a preposition in conversation. Sometimes the direct object follows the indirect object, and sometimes the indirect object follows the direct object. For example, someone might say either 'My mother bought me it' or, in British English 'My mother bought it me'.

With the following verbs, you use **to** to introduce the indirect object.

accord	donate	lease	pass	repay
advance	export	leave	pay	sell
award	feed	lend	post	send
bequeath	forward	loan	present	serve
bring	give	mail	quote	show
deal	grant	offer	read	supply
deliver	hand	owe	rent	teach

He lent my apartment to a friend for the weekend.
We picked up shells and showed them to each other.

You can sometimes use **to** to introduce the indirect object of **tell**.
⇨ See **Usage** entry at **tell**.

With the following verbs, you use **for** to introduce the indirect object.

book	cut	guarantee	paint	secure
build	design	keep	pick	set
buy	fetch	knit	pour	spare
cash	find	make	prepare	win
collect	fix	mix	reserve	
cook	get	order	save	

They booked a place for me.
She painted a picture for her father.

With the following verbs, you can use either **to** or **for** to introduce the indirect object, depending on the meaning you want to express.

bring	play	take
leave	sing	write

Mr Schell wrote a letter the other day to the New York Times.
Once, I wrote a play for the children.

With a few ditransitive verbs, the indirect object almost always comes in front of the direct object rather than being introduced by 'to' or 'for'.

allow	bet	cost	envy	promise
ask	cause	deny	forgive	refuse
begrudge	charge	draw	grudge	

The radio cost me three quid.
It was time for one of them to go and meet a man who had promised him a job.

ⓘ Note that in passive sentences either the direct object or the indirect object can become the subject. For example, you can say either 'The books will be sent to you next week' or 'You will be sent the books next week'.

A seat had been booked for him on the 6 o'clock flight.
I was given two free tickets.

Most of the verbs listed above as ditransitive verbs can be used with the same meaning with just a direct object.

He left <u>a note.</u>
She fetched <u>a jug</u> from the kitchen.

A few verbs can be used with a direct object referring to the person who benefits from the action, or receives something.

ask	feed	pay
envy	forgive	teach

I <u>fed the baby</u> when she awoke.
I <u>forgive you.</u>

12 link verbs

A **link verb** is a verb that is followed by a **complement** rather than an object. The complement gives more information about the subject, and can be an adjective or a noun group. The link verbs are:

appear	equal	keep	remain	taste
be	feel	look	represent	total
become	form	measure	seem	turn
come	get	pass	smell	weigh
comprise	go	prove	sound	
constitute	grow	rank	stay	

I <u>am</u> proud of these people.
She <u>was getting</u> too old to play tennis.

⇨ For information on which link verbs are used with which kind of complement, see **Grammar** entry at **Complements**.

Some link verbs are often followed by **to be** and an adjective, instead of immediately by an adjective.

appear	get	look	seem
come	grow	prove	

Mary was breathing quietly and <u>seemed to be asleep.</u>
The task of inspecting it <u>proved to be exacting and interesting.</u>

13 compound verbs

Compound verbs consist of two words which are normally linked by a hyphen.

It may soon become economically attractive to <u>mass-produce</u> hepatitis vaccines.
Somebody <u>had short-changed</u> him.
Send it to the laundry. Don't <u>dry-clean</u> it.
He <u>chain-smoked</u> cheap cigars.

Only the second part of a compound verb changes to show tense and number.

dry-clean	→	dry-cleans	→	dry-cleaning	→	dry-cleaned
force-feed	→	force-feeds	→	force-feeding	→	force-fed

GRAMMAR

14 **other verbs**

⇨ For information on verbs followed by a reported clause, see section on **report structures** in **Grammar** entry at **Reporting**.

⇨ For information on verbs followed by an '-ing' form or an infinitive, see **Grammar** entries at '-ing' forms, **Infinitives**, and 'To'-infinitive clauses.

⇨ See also **Grammar** entry at **Phrasal verbs**.

'Wh'-clauses

A 'wh'-clause is a clause beginning with a 'wh'-word such as **who** or **what**, or with **whether**. 'Wh'-clauses are used to refer to matters that are uncertain or about which a choice has to be made.

'Wh'-clauses are used after some verbs referring to speaking and thinking, for example in reported questions.

She wanted to know <u>where you were.</u>
She asked <u>whether my baby had recovered.</u>

⇨ See section on **reported questions** in **Grammar** entry at **Reporting**.

You can also use 'wh'-clauses after prepositions, and as the subject of verbs such as **be**, **depend**, and **matter**.

The State is desperately uncertain about <u>what it wants artists to do.</u>
<u>What you get</u> depends on <u>how badly you were injured.</u>
<u>Whether I went twice or not</u> doesn't matter.

Structures consisting of a 'wh'-word plus a 'to'-infinitive clause, which refer to a possible course of action, are used after verbs and prepositions. However, they are not usually used as subjects.

He couldn't decide <u>what to do.</u>
…the problem of <u>where to eat dinner.</u>

'Why' is not usually used in this kind of structure.

⚠ **WARNING**: Note that 'if'-clauses, which are used for reported questions, cannot be used after prepositions or as the subject of a verb. For example, you can say 'Whether she likes it or not is irrelevant', but you cannot say 'If she likes it is irrelevant'.

'Wh'-words

'Wh'-words are a set of adverbs, pronouns, and determiners which all, with the exception of **how**, begin with 'wh'. They are:

- the adverbs **how, when, where**, and **why**
- the pronouns **who, whom, what, which**, and **whose**
- the determiners **what, which**, and **whose**
- 'Wh'-words are used in questions.

<u>Why</u> are you smiling?

⇨ See **Grammar** entry at **Questions**.

They are also used in reported questions.

He asked me <u>where</u> I was going.

⇨ See **Grammar** entry at **Reporting**.

With the exception of 'how' and 'what', 'wh'-words can be used to begin relative clauses.

…nurses <u>who</u> have trained for two years.

That is also used to begin relative clauses, although it is not used for questions and reported questions.

⇨ See **Grammar** entry at **Relative clauses.**

⇨ See **Grammar** entry at **'Wh'-clauses** for information on the use of 'wh'-words to begin clauses used as subjects and prepositional objects.

⇨ You will find information on how to use each 'wh'-word in the **Usage** entry for that word.

Topics Section

Abbreviations

An **abbreviation** is a shortened form of a word, compound, or phrase, made by leaving out some of the letters or by using only the first letter of each word. For example, **g** is an abbreviation for **gram** in an expression such as **25g**, and **BBC** is an abbreviation for **British Broadcasting Corporation**. Some abbreviations are more commonly used than the full form.

You have to follow the accepted way of abbreviating, although with certain words there can be more than one way. For example, you can use either **cont.** or **contd.** as an abbreviation for **continued**.

In general, if a word begins with a capital letter, its abbreviation also begins with a capital letter. For example, the title **Captain** is written with a capital letter when used in front of a name, so the abbreviation **Capt** is also written with a capital letter.

There are five basic types of abbreviation.

1 **abbreviating one word**
The first three types of abbreviation are used for abbreviating a single word.

● The first type consists of the first letter of the word. When read aloud, the abbreviation is usually pronounced like the full word.

m = metre
p. = page
F = Fahrenheit
N = North

● The second type consists of the first few letters of the word. When read aloud, the abbreviation is usually pronounced like the full word.

cont. = continued
usu. = usually
vol. = volume
Brit. = British
Thurs. = Thursday

● The third type consists of the word with several letters missed out. When read aloud, the abbreviation is pronounced like the full word.

asst. = assistant
dept. = department
km = kilometre
tbsp. = tablespoonful
Sgt = sergeant

ⓘ Note that that the abbreviations for **headquarters**, **television**, and **tuberculosis** are of this type but consist of capital letters: **HQ**, **TV**, and **TB**. You say each letter separately. In the case of some units of measurement, the second letter is a capital. For example, the abbreviation for **kilowatt** or **kilowatts** is **kW**.

2 **abbreviating more than one word**
The fourth and fifth types of abbreviation are used for abbreviating a compound noun or a phrase.

● The fourth type consists of the first letter of each word. You usually say each letter separately, with the main stress on the last letter.

MP = Member of Parliament
CD = compact disc
USA = United States of America
VIP = very important person
rpm = revolutions per minute

The choice of **a** or **an** before an abbreviation of this type depends on the pronunciation of the first letter of the abbreviation. For example, you say **an MP** not 'a MP' because the pronunciation of 'M' begins with a vowel sound: /em/.

(*i*) Note that abbreviations of compound nouns usually consist of capital letters even when the full words do not begin with capital letters. However, abbreviations of phrases usually consist of small letters.

A few abbreviations of this type also include the second letter of one of the words, which is not written as a capital. For example, the abbreviation for **Bachelor of Science** (someone who has a science degree) is **BSc**.

● The fifth type of abbreviation uses the first letter of each word to form a new word. This type of abbreviation is called an **acronym**. You pronounce an acronym as a word, rather than saying each letter.

OPEC /ˈəʊpek/ = Organization of Petroleum-Exporting Countries
SARS /sɑːrz/ = severe acute respiratory syndrome
TEFL /ˈtefl/ = teaching English as a foreign language

Most acronyms consist of capital letters. When an acronym is written with small letters, for example **laser** (= light amplification by stimulated emission of radiation), it is regarded as an ordinary word.

3 full stops with abbreviations

You can put a full stop at the end of the first three types of abbreviation, or after each letter of the fourth kind of abbreviation. However, people often do not put in full stops nowadays, especially between capital letters.

b. = born
Apr. = April
St. = Saint
D.J. = disc jockey

Full stops are more commonly put at the end of abbreviations in American writing than in British writing. The abbreviations commonly used before a person's name (**Mr.**, **Mrs.**, **Ms.** and **Dr.**) always have full stops in American English.

Full stops are not usually used when writing abbreviations that are pronounced as words.

NATO /ˈneɪtəʊ/ = North Atlantic Treaty Organization
AIDS /eɪdz/ = acquired immune deficiency syndrome

4 plurals of abbreviations

If you want to make an abbreviation plural, you usually add a small '**s**' to the singular abbreviation.

hr → hrs
MP → MPs
UFO → UFOs

However, the plural of **p** (= page) is **pp**, and the plural of **St** (= Saint) is **SS**.

⚠ **WARNING:** With words which refer to units of measurement, you usually use the same abbreviation for the singular and the plural. For example, **ml** is the abbreviation for both **millilitre** and **millilitres**.

TOPICS

Addressing someone

1	position of vocatives	5	addressing relatives
2	writing vocatives	6	addressing a group of people
3	addressing someone you do not know	7	vocatives showing dislike
		8	vocatives showing affection
4	addressing someone you know	9	other vocatives

When you talk to someone, you sometimes use their name. You can sometimes use their title, if they have one. Sometimes you use a word that shows how you feel about them, for example **darling** or **idiot**. Words used to address people are called **vocatives**.

Vocatives are not as common in English as in some other languages. They are less common in British English than in American English.

1 position of vocatives

If you use a vocative, you usually use it at the end of a sentence.

I told you he was okay, Phil.
Where are you staying, Mr Swallow?

When you want to get someone's attention, you use a vocative at the beginning of a sentence.

John, how long have you been at the university?
Dad, why have you got that suit on?

A vocative can also be used between clauses or after the first group of words in a clause. People often do this to emphasize the importance of what they are saying.

I regret to inform you, Mrs West, that Miss Sadler is dead.
Don't you think, John, it would be wiser to wait?

2 writing vocatives

When you are writing speech down, you separate a vocative from words in front of it or after it using a comma.

Don't leave me, Jenny.
John, do you think that there are dangers associated with this policy?

3 addressing someone you do not know

In British English, if you want to say something to someone you do not know, for example in the street or in a shop, you do not usually use a vocative at all. You say '**Excuse me**' if you need to attract their attention.

⇨ For more information about the use of '**Excuse me**', see **Topic** entry at **Apologizing**.

⚠ **WARNING:** In modern British English, the titles **Mr, Mrs, Miss**, and **Ms** are only used in front of names. You should not use them on their own to address people you do not know, nor should you use 'gentleman' or 'lady'.

In British English, you should not use 'sir' or 'madam'; these words are normally only used by people who work in shops to address customers politely.
However, in American English, some people use **Sir** and **ma'am** when speaking politely to a man or woman whose name they do not know.

What does your father do, sir?
Do you need assistance getting that to your car, ma'am?

In British English, it is usually considered old-fashioned to use a word that indicates the person's job, such as **officer** (to a policeman). However, this is commonly used in American English. **Doctor** and **nurse** can be used in this way in British and American English.

Is he all right, doctor?

TOPICS

Some people use **you** to address someone whose name they do not know, but this is very impolite.

4 addressing someone you know

If you know the surname of the person you are talking to, you can address them using their title (usually **Mr, Mrs, Miss,** or **Ms**) and surname.

Thank you, Ms Jones.
Goodbye, Dr Kirk.

Titles showing a person's rank can be used without a surname after them.

I'm sure you have nothing to worry about, Professor.
Is that clear, Sergeant?

Mr and **Madam** are sometimes used in front of the titles **President, Chairman, Chairwoman,** and **Chairperson.**

No, Mr President.

⇨ See **Topic** entry at **Names and titles** for information on titles that are used with names.

⚠ **WARNING:** People do not usually address other people using their first name and surname.

If you know someone well, you can address them using their first name. However, people do not usually do this in the course of an ordinary conversation, unless they want to make it clear who they are talking to.

What do you think, John?
Shut up, Simon!

Short, informal forms of people's names, such as **Jenny** and **Mike**, are sometimes used as vocatives. However, you should not use a form like this unless you are sure that the person does not object to it.

5 addressing relatives

People usually address their parents and grandparents using a noun that shows their relationship to them.

Someone's got to do it, mum.
Sorry, Grandma.

The following list shows the commonest nouns that people use to address their parents and grandparents:

mother:
in British English, **Mum, Mummy, Mother**
in American English, **Mom, Mommy,** and especially for young children, **Mama** or **Momma**.
father:
in British English, **Dad, Daddy, Father**
in American English, **Dad, Daddy,** and sometimes **Pop**
grandmother:
in British English, **Gran, Grannie, Grandma, Nan, Nanna**
in American English, **Granny** or **Grandma**
grandfather:
in British English, **Grandad, Grandpa**
in American English, **Grandad** or **Grandpa**

Aunt and **Uncle** are also used as vocatives, usually in front of the person's first name.

This is Ginny, Aunt Bernice.
Goodbye, Uncle Harry.

⚠ **WARNING:** Nouns indicating other family relationships, such as 'daughter', 'brother', and 'cousin' are not used as vocatives.

TOPICS

6 **addressing a group of people**

If you want to address a group of people formally, for example at a meeting, you say **ladies and gentlemen** (or **ladies** or **gentlemen**, if the group is not mixed).

Good evening, <u>ladies and gentlemen.</u>

If you want to address a group of people informally, you can use **everyone** or **everybody**, although it is not necessary to use any vocative. You can also use **guys** to address a group of people informally, whether they are male or female.

I'm so terribly sorry, <u>everybody.</u>
Hi <u>guys,</u> how are you doing?

If you want to address a group of children or young people, you can use **kids**. You can use **boys** or **girls** if the group is not mixed.

Come and say 'How do you do?' to our guest, <u>kids.</u>
Give Mr Hooper a chance, <u>boys.</u>

The use of **children** as a vocative is formal.

7 **vocatives showing dislike**

People show dislike, contempt, or impatience using nouns and combinations of nouns and adjectives as vocatives, usually with **you** in front of them.

Shut your big mouth, <u>you stupid idiot.</u>
Give it to me, <u>you silly girl.</u>

8 **vocatives showing affection**

Vocatives showing affection are usually used by themselves.

Goodbye, <u>darling.</u>
Come on, <u>love.</u>

⚠ **WARNING:** Some people use **my** or the person's name in front of affectionate vocatives, but this usually sounds old-fashioned or humorous.

We've got to go, <u>my dear.</u>
Oh <u>Harold darling,</u> why did he die?

9 **other vocatives**

People who are serving in shops, or providing a service to the public, sometimes politely call male customers or clients **sir** and female ones **madam**.

 In American English the abbreviation **ma'am** is used.

A liqueur of any kind, <u>sir?</u>
'Thank you very much.' – 'You're welcome, <u>madam.</u>'
Do you need assistance getting that to your car, <u>ma'am?</u>

A number of words, such as **love**, **dear**, and **mate**, are used by people in informal situations to address other people, including people they do not know. These vocatives are often characteristic of a region or a social group, or both.

 In American English, the words **buddy** and **dude** are also used in this way.

She'll be all right, <u>mate.</u>
Trust me, <u>kid.</u>
How's it going, <u>buddy?</u>

⚠ **WARNING:** You are advised not to use any of these vocatives, because they would sound inappropriate from someone who is not a native speaker from a particular region.

Advising someone

1 **general advice**

There are many ways of giving someone advice.

In conversation, or in informal writing such as letters to friends, you can use **I would**, or **I'd**.

I would try to restrain him gently by saying 'It isn't polite.'
I'd buy tins of one vegetable rather than mixtures.

People often emphasize these expressions with **if I were you**.

If I were you, I'd just take the black one.
I should let it go if I were you.

You can also say '**You ought to…**' or '**You should…**'. People often say '**I think**' first, in order not to sound too forceful.

You should explain this to him at the outset.
I think maybe you ought to try a different approach.

You can indicate to someone which course of action or choice is likely to be most successful by using the informal expression '**Your best bet is…**' or '**…is your best bet**'.

Well, your best bet is to go to Thomas Cook in the High Street.
I think Boston's going to be your best bet.

2 firm advice

If you want to give advice firmly, especially if you are in a position of authority, you can say '**You'd better…**'. This way of giving advice can also be used as a kind way of telling someone to do something that will benefit them.

You'd better write it down.
Perhaps you'd better listen to him.
I think you'd better go in and have a sit down.

When you are talking to someone you know well, you can use an imperative form.

Make sure you note that down.
Take no notice of him, Mr Swallow.

People sometimes add **and** followed by a good consequence of taking the advice, or **or** followed by a bad consequence. These structures are similar in meaning to conditional sentences.

Stick with me and you'll be okay.
Now hold onto the chain, or you'll hurt yourself.

(i) Note that **and** and **or** are also used like this in threats.

Just try – and you'll have a real fight on your hands.
Drop that gun! Drop it or I'll kill you!

⇨ Imperative forms are also used by experts to give advice: see section 4 on **professional advice**.

3 serious advice

A more formal and serious way of giving advice is to say '**I advise you to…**'.

'What shall I do about it?' – 'I advise you to consult a doctor, Mrs Smedley.'
I strongly advise you to get somebody to come and help you the first time.

A very strong way of giving advice is to say '**You must…**'.

You must tell the pupils what it is you want to do, so that they feel involved.
You must maintain control of the vehicle at all times.

You can also use '**You've got to…**' or '**You have to…**' with the same meaning.

If somebody makes a mistake you've got to say so.
You have to put all these things behind you.

4 professional advice

There are other ways of giving advice which are used mainly in books, articles, and broadcasts.

TOPICS

One common way is to use an imperative form.

<u>Clean</u> one room at a time.
If you don't have a freezer, <u>keep</u> bread in a dry, cool, well-ventilated bin.
<u>Make sure</u> you get out all weed roots and grass.

Another way of advising that is used mainly in writing and broadcasting is to say '**It's a good idea to…**'.

<u>It's a good idea to</u> spread your savings between several building societies.
<u>It's a good idea to</u> get a local estate agent to come and value your house.

Another expression that is used is '**My advice is…**' or '**My advice would be…**'. Again, this is used especially by professionals or experts, who have knowledge on which to base their advice.

<u>My advice is</u> to look at all the options before you buy.
<u>My advice would always be</u>: find out what the local people consider good to eat in your locality and eat that.

The expression '**A word of advice…**' is sometimes used to introduce a piece of advice.

<u>A word of advice</u> – never be put off by those who suggest that practising is somehow un-British.

⇨ See also **Topic** entry at **Suggestions**.
⇨ For information on how to advise someone not to do something, see **Topic** entry at **Warning someone**.

Age

1	asking about age	4	similar ages
2	exact age	5	age when something happens
3	approximate age	6	indicating the age of a thing

1 asking about age

When you want to ask about the age of a person or thing, you use **How old** and the verb **be**.

'<u>How old are</u> you?' – 'Thirteen.'
'<u>How old is</u> he?' – 'About sixty-five.'
'<u>How old's</u> your house?' – 'I think it was built about 1950.'

There are several ways in which you can say how old someone or something is. You can be exact, or you can be less precise and indicate their approximate age.

2 exact age

When you want to say how old someone is, you use the verb **be** followed by a number.

I <u>was nineteen,</u> and he <u>was twenty-one.</u>
I <u>'m only 63.</u>

You can put **years old** after the number if you want to be more emphatic.

She <u>is twenty-five years old.</u>
I <u>am forty years old.</u>

You can also put **years of age** after the number, but this is more formal and is more usual in written English.

He <u>is 28 years of age.</u>

⚠ **WARNING:** You never use 'have' to talk about age. For example, you do not say '~~He has thirteen years~~'. You say 'He **is thirteen**' or 'He **is thirteen years old**'.

 When you are mentioning someone, you can indicate their exact age using **of** or **aged**,

TOPICS

or, in American English, **age** after the noun which refers to them, followed by a number.

...*a man of thirty.*
...*two little boys aged nine and eleven.*
They have twin daughters, age 18.

You can also mention someone's age using a compound adjective in front of a noun. For example, you can refer to a **five-year-old boy**. Note that the noun referring to the period of time, such as **year**, is always singular, even though it comes after a number. The compound adjective is usually hyphenated.

...*a twenty-two-year-old student.*
...*a five-month-old baby.*

You can also refer to someone using a compound noun such as **ten-year-old**. The compound noun is usually hyphenated.

All the six-year-olds are taught by one teacher.
...*Melvin Kalkhoven, a tall, thin thirty-five-year-old.*

3 | **approximate age**

If you are not sure exactly how old someone is, or you do not want to state their exact age, you can use the verb **be** followed by **about**, **almost**, **nearly**, **over**, or **under**, and a number.

I think he's about 60.
He must be nearly thirty.
She was only a little over forty years old.
There weren't enough people who were under 25.

You can also use a number with the suffix '**-ish**' to give an approximate age.

The nurse was fiftyish.

You can also use **above the age of** or **below the age of** followed by a number. This is more formal.

55 percent of them were below the age of twenty-one.

You can indicate that someone's age is between 20 and 29 by saying '**He's in his twenties**' or '**She's in her twenties**'. You can use **thirties**, **forties**, and so on in the same way. Young people aged 13 to 19 are said to be **in their teens**.

(i) Note that you use **in** and a possessive determiner in these structures.

He was in his sixties.
...*when I was in my teens.*

Another way of showing approximate age is to use **something** after a number that ends in zero.

...*table of thirty-something guys.*
She was twenty-something.
...*a group of 20 and 30-somethings.*

You can use **early**, **mid-**, **middle**, or **late** to indicate approximately where someone's age comes in a particular ten-year period (or eight-year period in the case of **teens**).

Jane is only in her early forties.
She was in her mid-twenties.
He was then in his late seventies.

You can put most of the above structures after a noun such as **man** or **woman** to indicate someone's approximate age.

...*help for ladies over 65.*
She had four children under the age of five.
... *a woman in her early thirties.*

In British English, however, you cannot use **about**, **almost**, or **nearly** immediately after a noun. For example, you cannot say '~~he is a man about 60~~'. You say 'he is a man **of** about 60'.

In British English, you can refer to a group of people whose age is more or less than a particular number using a compound noun which consists of **over** or **under** followed by the plural form of the number. This usage is understood but not used in American English.

The <u>over-sixties</u> do not want to be turned out of their homes.
Schooling for the <u>under-fives</u> should be expanded.

4 **similar ages**

If you want to indicate that someone's age is similar to someone else's, you can use the verb **be** followed by expressions such as **my age**, **his own age**, and **her parents' age**.

I wasn't allowed to do that when I <u>was her age.</u>
He guessed the policeman <u>was about his own age.</u>

To indicate the age of a person you are mentioning, you can use these expressions after the noun which refers to the person, or after the noun and **of**.

I just happen to know a bit more literature than <u>most girls my age.</u>
It's easy to make friends because you're with <u>people of your own age.</u>

5 **age when something happens**

There are several ways of indicating how old someone was when something happened.

You can use a clause beginning with **when**.

I left school <u>when I was thirteen.</u>
Even <u>when I was a child</u> I was frightened of her.

You can use **at the age of** or **at**, followed by a number showing the person's age.

She had finished college <u>at the age of 20.</u>
All they want to do is leave school <u>at sixteen</u> and get a job.

Aged followed by a number is also used, mainly in writing, especially when talking about someone's death.

Her husband died three days ago, <u>aged only forty-five.</u>

A structure with an ordinal is sometimes used in writing, especially to emphasize that someone did something when they were old. For example, instead of saying that someone did something 'at the age of 79', you can say that they did it 'in their eightieth year'.

He died in 1951, <u>in his eighty-ninth year.</u>

As is used with a noun group such as **a girl** or **a young man** to indicate that someone did something when they were young. This structure occurs mainly in writing.

She suffered from bronchitis <u>as a child.</u>
<u>As teenagers</u> we used to stroll round London during lunchtime.

If you want to indicate that someone does something before they reach a particular age, you can say that they do it, for example, **before the age of four** or **by the age of four**.

He maintained that children are not ready to read <u>before the age of six.</u>
It set out the things he wanted to achieve <u>by the age of 31.</u>

If you want to indicate that something happens to people after they reach a particular age, you can say that it happens, for example, **after the age of four**.

<u>After the age of five</u>, your child will be at school full time.

6 **indicating the age of a thing**

If you want to say how old something is, you use the verb **be** followed by a number, followed by **years old**.

Most of the coral <u>is some 2 million years old.</u>
The house <u>was about thirty years old.</u>

ⓘ Note that you cannot just use 'be' and a number, as you can when stating the age of a person. You cannot say, for example, 'The house was about thirty'.

TOPICS

The usual way of indicating the age of something you are mentioning is to use a compound adjective in front of the noun referring to it. For example, you can refer to a **thirty-year-old** house. As with compound adjectives indicating the age of a person, the noun **year** is always singular and the adjective is usually hyphenated.

…Mr Watt's rattling, <u>ten-year-old</u> car.
…a violation of a <u>six-year-old</u> agreement.

You can also use a number, especially a large number, and **years old** after a noun referring to a thing.

…rocks <u>200 million years old.</u>

You can indicate the approximate age of something by using an adjective indicating the period in history in which it existed or was made.

…a splendid <u>Victorian</u> building.
…a <u>medieval</u> castle.

You can indicate the century when something existed or was made by using a modifier consisting of an ordinal number and **century**.

…a <u>sixth-century</u> church.
…life in <u>fifth-century</u> Athens.

Agreeing and disagreeing

1	asking for agreement	5	expresssing ignorance or uncertainty
2	expressing agreement		
3	strong agreement	6	expressing disagreement
4	partial agreement	7	strong disagreement

1 asking for agreement

You can ask someone if they agree with your opinion of something or someone by using a question tag. When you do this, you usually expect them to agree with you.

That's an extremely interesting point, <u>isn't it?</u>
It was really good, <u>wasn't it,</u> Andy?

(i) Note that people sometimes use question tags like this and carry on talking because they think a reply is unnecessary. You can also use a question tag to ask someone if they agree that something is a fact.

Property in France is quite expensive, <u>isn't it?</u>
That's right, <u>isn't it?</u>
You don't have a television, <u>do you?</u>

You can also indicate that you want someone to express agreement by using a negative 'yes/no'-question, or by saying a statement as if it were a question.

Wasn't it marvellous?
So there's no way you could go back to work?
He's got a scholarship?

You can use the tag **don't you?** after a clause in which you say that you like or dislike something, or think it is good or bad. The pronoun **you** is stressed.

I adore it, <u>don't you?</u>
I think this is one of the best things, <u>don't you?</u>

In formal situations, people sometimes use expressions such as '**Don't you agree…?**' and '**Would you agree…?**'

<u>Don't you agree</u> with me that it is rather an impossible thing to do after all this time?
<u>Would you agree</u> with that analysis?

TOPICS

2 **expressing agreement**
When you want to indicate that you agree with someone or something, the simplest way is to say **yes**. People often say something further, especially in more formal discussions.
'That was probably the border.' – 'Yes.'
'It's quite a nice school, isn't it?' – 'Yes, it's well decorated and there's a nice atmosphere there.'

You can add an appropriate tag such as **I do** or **it is** to **Yes**. This tag is often followed by a question tag.
'That's fantastic!' – 'Yes, it is, isn't it?'
'I was really rude to you at that party.' – 'Yes, you were. But I deserved it.'

You can also just add a question tag to **Yes**, or use a question tag by itself. You do not expect a reply.
'He's a completely changed man.' – 'Yes, isn't he?'
'What a lovely evening!' – 'Isn't it?'

⚠ **WARNING:** If you want to express agreement with a negative statement, you say **No**, not 'Yes'.
'She's not an easy person to live with.' – 'No.'
'I don't think it's as good now.' – 'No, it isn't really.'
'That's not very healthy, is it?' – 'No.'

You can also express agreement using expressions such as **'That's right', 'That's true'**, or **'True'**, when agreeing that something is a fact. You say **'That's true'** or **'True'** when you think a good point has been made.
'Most teenagers are perfectly all right.' – 'That's right, yes.'
'You don't have to be poor to be lonely.' – 'That's true.'
'They're a long way away.' – 'True.'

People sometimes say **'Sure'** when accepting what someone has said in a discussion.
'You can earn some money as well.' – 'Sure, sure, you can make quite a bit.'

The expression **'I agree'** is quite formal.
'It's a catastrophe.' – 'I agree.'

When someone has made a statement about what they like or think, you can indicate that you share their opinion by saying **'So do I'** or **'I do too'**.
'I find that amazing.' – 'So do I.'
'I like baked beans.' – 'Yes, I do too.'

When you want to indicate that you share someone's negative opinion, you can say **'Nor do I', 'Neither do I'**, or **'I don't either'**.
'I don't like him.' – 'Nor do I.'
'Oh, I don't mind where I go as long as it's a break.' – 'No, I don't either.'

3 **strong agreement**
You can show strong agreement by using expressions such as the ones shown in the examples below. Most of these sound rather formal. **'Absolutely'** and **'Exactly'** are less formal.
'I thought June Barry's performance was the performance of the evening.' – 'Absolutely. I thought she was wonderful.'
'It's good practice and it's good fun.' – 'Exactly.'
'There's far too much attention being paid to these hoodlums.' – 'Yes, I couldn't agree more.'
'We reckon that this is what he would have wanted us to do.' – 'I think you're absolutely right.'

🌊 The expressions that use **quite** are used in British English, but would not be used in American English.
'I feel I ought to give her a hand.' – 'Oh, quite, quite.'
'I must do something, though.' – 'Yes, I quite agree.'
'The public showed that by the way it voted in the General Election.' – 'That's quite true.'

TOPICS

You can show that you agree strongly with someone's description of something by repeating the adjective they have used and using **very** in front of it. You usually use **indeed** after the adjective.

'It was very tragic, wasn't it.' – 'Very tragic indeed. '
'The pacing in all these performances is subtle, isn't it?' – 'Oh, very subtle indeed.'

4 | partial agreement

If you agree with someone, but not entirely or with reluctance, you can reply '**I suppose so**'.

'I must have a job.' – 'Yes, I suppose so.'
'That's the way to save lives, and save ourselves a lot of trouble.' – 'I suppose so.'

If you are replying to a negative statement, you say '**I suppose not**'.

'Some of these places haven't changed a bit.' – 'I suppose not.'

5 | expressing ignorance or uncertainty

If you do not know enough to agree or disagree with a statement, you say '**I don't know**'.

'He was the first four-minute miler, wasn't he?' – 'Perhaps. I don't know.'

If you are not sure of a particular fact, you say '**I'm not sure**'.

'He was world champion one year, wasn't he?' – 'I'm not sure.'

6 | expressing disagreement

Rather than simply expressing complete disagreement, people usually try to disagree politely using expressions which soften the contradictory opinion they are giving. '**I don't think so**' and '**Not really**' are the commonest of these expressions.

'You'll change your mind one day.' – 'Well, I don't think so. But I won't argue with you.'
'It was a lot of money in those days.' – 'Well, not really.'

The expressions shown below are also used.

'You'll need bolts,' he said – 'Actually, no' I said.
'He will forgive you.' – 'Do you really think so?'
'I know he loves you.' – 'I don't know about that.'
'It's all over now, anyway.' – 'No, I'm afraid I can't agree with you there.'

People often say '**Yes**' or '**I see what you mean**', to indicate partial agreement, and then go on to mention a point of disagreement, introduced by **but**.

'It's a very clever film.' – 'Yes, perhaps, but I didn't like it.'
'They ruined the whole thing.' – 'I see what you mean, but they didn't know.'

7 | strong disagreement

The following examples show stronger ways of expressing disagreement. You should be very careful when using them, in order to avoid offending people.

'That's very funny.' – 'No it isn't.'
'It might be a couple of years.' – 'No! Surely not as long as that!'
'He killed himself.' – 'That's not right. I'm sure that's not right. Tell me what happened.'
'You were the one who wanted to buy it.' – 'I'm sorry, dear, but you're wrong.'

The expressions shown in the following examples are more formal.

'University education does divide families in a way.' – 'I can't go along with that.'
'There would be less of the guilt which characterized societies of earlier generations.' – 'Well, I think I would take issue with that.'
'When it comes to the state of this country, he should keep his mouth shut.' – 'I wholly and totally disagree.'

In formal situations, you can use '**With respect…**' to make your disagreement seem more polite.

'We ought to be asking the teachers some tough questions.' – 'With respect, Mr Graveson, you should be asking pupils some questions as well, shouldn't you?'

TOPICS

When people are angry, they use very strong, impolite words and expressions to disagree.

'He's absolutely right.' – 'Oh, <u>come off it!</u> He doesn't know what he's talking about.'
'They'll be killed.' – '<u>Nonsense.</u>'
'He wants it, and I suppose he has a right to it.' – '<u>Rubbish</u> .'
'You're ashamed of me.' – '<u>Don't talk rubbish.</u>'
'He said you plotted to get him removed.' – '<u>That's ridiculous!</u>'
'He's very good at his job, isn't he?' – '<u>You must be joking!</u> He's absolutely useless!'

With people you know well, you can use expressions like these in a casual, light-hearted way.

 Note that the word 'rubbish' is not used in American English.

Apologizing

1 saying sorry	**4** saying something wrong
2 interrupting, approaching, or leaving someone	**5** formal apologies
	6 apologies on notices
3 doing something embarrassing	**7** accepting an apology

1 saying sorry

There are several ways of apologizing and accepting apologies. You apologize when you have upset someone or caused trouble for them in some way.

The commonest way of apologizing is to say '**Sorry**' or '**I'm sorry**'. When using '**I'm sorry**', you can use adverbs such as **very**, **so**, **terribly**, and **extremely** to be more emphatic.

'Stop that, please. You're giving me a headache.' – '<u>Sorry.</u>'
<u>Sorry</u> I'm late.
<u>I'm sorry</u> about this morning.
<u>I'm sorry</u> if I've distressed you by asking all this.
<u>I'm very sorry,</u> but these are vital.
<u>I'm so sorry</u> to keep on coughing.
<u>I'm terribly sorry</u> – we shouldn't have left.

Some people use **awfully** to modify **sorry** but this sounds rather formal or old-fashioned.

<u>I'm awfully sorry</u> to give you this trouble at a time like this.

When apologizing for accidentally doing something, for example stepping on someone's foot, some people say '**I beg your pardon**' or '**I do beg your pardon**' instead of '**Sorry**'. This is rather old-fashioned.

She bumped into someone behind her. '<u>I beg your pardon,</u>' she said.

 Speakers of American English usually say '**Excuse me**' in the above situations.

2 interrupting, approaching, or leaving someone

You use '**Excuse me**' to apologize politely to someone when you are disturbing or interrupting them, or when you want to get past them. This is also the expression to use when you want to speak to a stranger.

<u>Excuse me</u> for disturbing you at home.
<u>Excuse me</u> butting in.
<u>Excuse me,</u> but is there a fairly cheap restaurant near here?
<u>Excuse me,</u> do you mind if I move your bag slightly?

 The expression '**Pardon me**' is used by some speakers of American English.

<u>Pardon me,</u> Sergeant, I wonder if you'd do me a favour?

When you are disturbing or interrupting someone, you can also say '**I'm sorry to disturb you**' or **I'm sorry to interrupt**'.

TOPICS

I'm sorry to disturb you again but we need some more details on this fellow Wilt.
Sorry to interrupt, but I've some forms to fill in.

You also say '**Excuse me**' when you have to leave someone for a short time in order to do something.

Excuse me. I have to make a telephone call.
Will you excuse me a second?

3 doing something embarrassing

You can use '**Excuse me**' or '**I beg your pardon**' to apologize when you have done something slightly embarrassing or impolite, such as burping, hiccupping, or sneezing.

4 saying something wrong

You say '**I beg your pardon**' to apologize for making a mistake in what you are saying, or for using the wrong word. You can also say **sorry**.

It is treated in a sentence as a noun – I beg your pardon – as an adjective.
It's in the southeast, sorry, southwest corner of the USA.

5 formal apologies

When you want to apologize in a formal way, you can say explicitly '**I apologize**'.

I apologize for my late arrival.
How silly of me. I do apologize.
I really must apologize for bothering you with this.

Another formal expression, used especially in writing, is '**Please accept my apologies**'.

Please accept my apologies for this unfortunate incident.

Some people say '**Forgive me**'.

Forgive me, Mr Turner. I am a little disorganized this morning.

You can use **forgive** in polite expressions like '**Forgive me**' and '**Forgive my ignorance**' to reduce the directness of what you are saying, and to apologize in a mild way for saying something that might seem rude or silly.

Look, forgive me, but I thought we were going to talk about my book.
Forgive my ignorance, but who is Jennifer Lopez?

6 apologies on notices

Regret is often used in public notices and formal announcements.

London Transport regrets any inconvenience caused by these repairs.
The notice said: 'Dr.Beamish has a cold and regrets he cannot meet his classes today.'

7 accepting an apology

To accept an apology, you normally use a short fixed expression such as '**That's okay**', '**That's all right**', '**Forget it**', '**Don't worry about it**', or '**It doesn't matter**'.

'I'm sorry about this, sir.' – 'That's all right. Don't let it happen again.'
'I apologize for my outburst just now.' – 'Forget it.'
She spilt his drink and said 'I'm sorry.' 'Don't worry about it, ' he said, 'no harm done.'
'I'm sorry to ring at this late hour.' – 'I'm still up. It doesn't matter.'

⚠ **WARNING:** Some words and expressions that are used to apologize are also used to ask someone to repeat something that they just said.
⇨ See **Topic** entry at **Asking for repetition**.

Asking for repetition

You ask someone to repeat what they have said when you have not heard them or when you have not understood them. You can also ask someone to repeat what they have said when you feel that what they have said is surprising or impolite.

1 asking informally

In an informal situation, you usually ask someone to repeat what they have said using a short fixed expression such as '**Sorry?**', '**I'm sorry?**', or '**Pardon?**'

'Have you seen the health guide book anywhere?' – '<u>Sorry?</u>' – 'Seen the health guide book?'
'Well, what about it?' – '<u>I'm sorry?</u>' – 'What about it?'
'How old is she?' – '<u>Pardon?</u>' – 'I said how old is she?'

Some people say '**Come again?**' This is very informal.

'It's on Monday.' – '<u>Come again?</u>' – 'Monday.'

In American English, '**Excuse me?**' is also used in this way. Some people say '**Pardon me?**'

'You do see him once in a while, don't you?' – '<u>Excuse me?</u>' – 'I thought you saw him sometimes.'

Some people use '**What?**', '**You what?**', or '**Eh?**' to ask someone to repeat something, but these expressions are impolite.

'Do you want another coffee?' – '<u>What?</u>' – 'Do you want another coffee?'
'Well, I still have a cheque book.' – '<u>Eh?</u>' – 'I said I still have a cheque book.'

You can use a 'wh'-word to check part of what someone has said.

'Can I speak to Nikki, please?' – '<u>Who?</u>' – 'Nikki.'
'We've got a special offer in April for Majorca.' – 'For <u>where?</u>' – 'Majorca.'
'I don't like the tinkling.' – 'The <u>what?</u>' – 'The tinkling.'

If you think you heard what someone said but are not sure, or are surprised, you can repeat it, or repeat part of it, making it sound like a question.

'I just told her that rain's good for her complexion.' – '<u>Rain?</u>'
'I have a message for you?' – '<u>A message?</u>'

You add **again** to the end of a question when you are asking someone to repeat something that they told you a little while ago and which you have forgotten.

What's his name <u>again?</u>
Where are we going <u>again?</u>

2 asking more formally

When talking to someone you do not know well, for example on the phone, you use longer expressions such as '**Sorry, what did you say?**', '**I'm sorry, I didn't quite catch that**', '**I'm sorry, I didn't hear what you said**', '**I'm sorry, would you mind repeating that again?**', and '**Would you repeat that, please?**'

'What about tomorrow at three?' – '<u>Sorry, what did you say?</u>' – 'I said, What about meeting tomorrow at three?'
<u>Would you repeat that, I didn't quite catch it.</u>

The expressions '**Beg your pardon?**' and '**I beg your pardon?**' are sometimes used, but they are fairly formal and old-fashioned.

'Did he listen to you?' – '<u>Beg your pardon?</u>' – 'Did he listen to you?'
'Did they have a dog?' – '<u>I beg your pardon?</u>' – 'I said did they have a dog?'

ⓘ Note that '**I beg your pardon?**' (but not '**Beg your pardon?**') is also used to indicate that you find what someone says surprising or offensive. The word **beg** is stressed.

'Where the devil did you get her?' – '<u>I beg your pardon?</u>'

Speakers of American English also use '**Excuse me**' in this way, but it is important that you strongly stress the second syllable of **excuse** to make the meaning clear.

Capital letters

1 obligatory capital letter

You must use a capital letter for the first word of a sentence or a piece of direct speech.

⇨ See **Topic** entry at **Punctuation**.

You must also start the following words and word groups with a capital letter:

● names of people, organizations, books, films, and plays (except for short, common words like **of**, **the**, and **and**)

…Miss Helen Perkins, head of management development at Price Waterhouse.
Troilus and Coriolanus are the greatest political plays that Shakespeare wrote.

(*i*) Note that you spell even short, common words with a capital letter when they come at the beginning of the title of a book, film, or play.

…his new book, 'A Future for Socialism'.

● names of places

Dempster was born in India in 1941.
The strongest gust was recorded at Berry Head, Brixham, Devon.

● names of days, months, and festivals

The trial continues on Monday.
It was mid- December and she was going home for Christmas.

● nouns referring to people of a particular nationality

The Germans and the French move more of their freight by rail or water than the British.
I had to interview two authors – one an American, one an Indian.

● names of people used to refer to art, music, and literature created by them

In those days you could buy a Picasso for £300.
I listened to Mozart.
I stayed in the dressing-room until lunchtime, reading my latest Jeffrey Archer.

● nouns referring to products produced by a particular company

I bought a second-hand Volkswagen.
…a cleansing powder which contains bleach (such as Vim).

● titles used in front of someone's name

There has been no statement so far from President Bush.
The tower was built by King Henry II in the 12th century.

● adjectives indicating nationality or place

…a French poet.
…the Californian earthquake.

● adjectives indicating that something is associated with or resembles a particular person

…his favourite Shakespearean sonnet.
…in Victorian times.

2 **'I'**

The personal pronoun I is always written as a capital letter.
I thought I was alone.

⚠ **WARNING:** The words **me**, **my**, **mine**, and **myself** are not written with a capital letter, unless they come at the beginning of a sentence.

3 **optional capital letter**

You can use either a small letter or a capital letter at the beginning of:

● words referring to directions such as **North** and **South**

We shall be safe in the north.
The home-ownership rate in the South East of England is higher than in the North.

● words referring to decades

Adult literacy work became in the seventies a kind of call for emergency troops.
Most of it was done in the Seventies.

TOPICS

● names of seasons
I planted it last <u>autumn</u>.
In the <u>Autumn</u> of 1948 Caroline returned to the United States.

 Note that in American English, a small letter is used unless the word is part of a title.
Construction is expected to begin next <u>spring</u>.
…Rachel Carson's seminal book 'Silent <u>Spring</u>'.

● titles of people (especially when used to refer to a type of person)
…the great <u>prime ministers</u> of the past.
…one of the greatest <u>Prime Ministers</u> who ever held office.
…portraits of the <u>president</u>.
…the brother of the <u>President</u>.

4 referring to God
Some people write **he**, **him**, and **his** with a capital letter when they are referring to God or Jesus.
Some said they saw the Son of God; others did not see <u>Him</u>.

Complimenting and congratulating someone

1 clothes and appearance	**4** achievements
2 meals	**5** accepting compliments and
3 skills	congratulations

1 clothes and appearance
If you know someone quite well, or are talking to someone in an informal situation, you can compliment them on their clothes or appearance using an expression such as '**That's a nice coat**', '**What a lovely dress**', or '**I like your jacket**.'
That's a nice dress.
What a pretty dress.
I like your haircut.
I love your shoes. Are they new?

You can also say something like '**You look nice**' or '**You're looking very smart today**'. If you want to be more emphatic, you can use adjectives such as **great** or **terrific**.
You're looking very glamorous.
You look terrific.

You can also compliment someone on their appearance by saying that what they are wearing suits them.
I love you in that dress, it really suits you.

2 meals
You can compliment someone on a meal by saying something like '**This is delicious**' during the meal or '**That was delicious**' after the meal.
This is delicious, Ginny.
He took a bite of meat, chewed it, savoured it, and said, 'Fantastic!'
Mm, that was lovely.

3 skills
You can compliment someone on doing something skilfully or well using an exclamation.
What a marvellous memory you've got!
Oh, that's true. Yes, what a good answer!
'Look – there's a boat.' – 'Oh yes – well spotted!'

A teacher might praise a pupil who has given a correct answer by saying '**Good**'.

'What sort of soil do they prefer?' – 'Acid soil.' – '<u>Good.</u>'

4 achievements

You can say '**Congratulations**' to someone to congratulate them on achieving something.

Well, <u>congratulations,</u> Ginny. You've done it.
<u>Congratulations</u> to all three winners.

ⓘ Note that you can also say '**Congratulations**' to someone when something nice has happened to them.

'I'm being discharged tomorrow.' – 'That is good news. <u>Congratulations.</u>'
'<u>Congratulations,</u> ' the doctor said. 'You have a son.'

⇨ For other ways of expressing your reaction to good news, see the section on **expressing pleasure** in the **Topic** entry at **Reactions**.

There are several more formal ways of congratulating someone.

<u>I must congratulate you</u> on your new job.
<u>Let me offer you my congratulations</u> on your success.
<u>Let me be the first to congratulate you</u> on a wise decision, Mr Dorf.
<u>May I congratulate you</u> again on your excellent performance.
Very good. <u>I congratulate you.</u> A beautiful piece of work.

You can congratulate someone informally by saying '**Well done**'.

'You did very well today. <u>Well done</u>.'

5 accepting compliments and congratulations

You can accept compliments with several different expressions.

Oh, thanks!
It's very nice of you to say so.
I'm glad you think so.

If someone compliments you on something you are wearing, you can also say something like '**It is nice, isn't it?**'

'I do like your dress.' – 'Yes, <u>it is nice, isn't it?</u>'

You can also respond by saying how old it is, or how or where you got it.

'That's a nice blouse.' – 'Have you not seen this before? <u>I've had it for years.</u>'
'That's a nice piece of jewellery.' – 'Yeah, <u>my ex-husband bought it for me.</u>'

If someone compliments you on your skill, you can say something modest that implies that what you did was not very difficult or skilful.

Oh, <u>there's nothing to it.</u>
'Terrific job.' – 'Well, <u>I don't know about that.</u>'

When someone congratulates you, you usually say **Thanks** or **Thank you**.

'Congratulations on publication.' – '<u>Thanks</u> very much.'
'Congratulations to both of you.' – '<u>Thank you.</u>'

Criticizing someone

1 mild criticism

People do not usually express criticism strongly unless they know the person they are criticizing well.

If you want to criticize someone for doing something badly, you can say something like '**That's not very good**' or '**I think that's not quite right**'.

What answer have you got? Oh dear. Thirty-three. <u>That's not very good.</u>
<u>I think your answer's wrong.</u>

A teacher might criticize a pupil's work by saying '**You can do better than this**'.

2 **stronger criticism**

If you want to criticize someone for doing something wrong or stupid, you can use a question beginning '**Why did you…?**' or '**Why didn't you…?**' Questions like this can be used to express great anger or distress, or merely exasperation.

Why did you send him? Why Ben?
Why did you lie to me?
Why did you do it?
Why didn't you tell me?

You can be more direct and say '**You shouldn't have…**' or '**You should have…**'.

You shouldn't have given him money.
You should have asked me.

Some people say '**How could you?**' when they feel very strongly that someone has been thoughtless.

How could you? You knew I didn't want anyone to know!
How could you be so stupid?

3 **very strong criticism**

There are other ways of expressing criticism which are even more direct or impolite. If you use expressions like the ones below, you will probably offend the other person.

That's no good.
That won't do.
This is wrong. These are all wrong.
You're hopeless.
'He told me he was going straight to you.' – 'But he didn't.' – 'You liar.'

Days and dates

1 days		**9** decades and centuries	
2 special days		**10** part of a decade or century	
3 months		**11** using prepositions	
4 saying years		**12** using other adjuncts	
5 'AD' and 'BC'		**13** indefinite dates	
6 writing dates		**14** modifying nouns	
7 saying dates		**15** regular events	
8 seasons			

⇨ For information on how to indicate the time or part of the day when something happens, see **Topic** entry at **Time**.

1 **days**

These are the days of the week:

Monday	Wednesday	Friday	Sunday
Tuesday	Thursday	Saturday	

Days of the week are always written with a capital letter. They are usually used without a determiner.

I'll send the cheque round on Monday.

However, if you are referring generally to any day with a particular name, you put **a** in front of the day.

It is unlucky to cut your nails on a Friday.

If you want to say that something happened or will happen on a particular day of a particular week, especially when making a contrast with other days of that week, you put **the** in front of the day.

He died on the Friday and was buried on the Sunday.
We'll come and see you on the Sunday.

⇨ See also section 15 on 'regular events'.

Saturday and Sunday are often referred to as **the weekend**, and the other days as **weekdays**.

I went down and fetched her back at the weekend.
The Tower is open 9.30 to 6.00 on weekdays.
They are open weekdays and Saturday mornings.

ⓘ Note that in Britain Saturday is sometimes considered to be a weekday.

When people say that something happens **during the week**, they mean that it happens on weekdays, not on Saturday or Sunday.

They used to spend the whole Sunday at chapel but most of them behaved shockingly during the week.

2 special days

A few days in the year have special names, for example:

New Year's Day (1st January)
Valentine's Day (14th February)
April Fool's Day (1st April)
Good Friday (not fixed)
Easter Sunday (not fixed)
Easter Monday (not fixed; not used in the USA)
May Day (1st May)

Hallowe'en (31st October)
Guy Fawkes Night (5th November)
Christmas Eve (24th December)
Christmas Day (25th December)
Boxing Day (26th; not used in the USA)
New Year's Eve (31st December)

3 months

These are the months of the year:

January	April	July	October
February	May	August	November
March	June	September	December

Months are always written with a capital letter. They are usually used without a determiner.

I wanted to leave in September.

In a date, months can be represented by a number. January is represented by 1, February by 2, and so on. You can use **early**, **mid**, and **late** to specify part of a month.

ⓘ Note that you cannot use 'middle' like this, although you can use **the middle of**.

I should very much like to come to California in late September or early October.
We must have five copies by mid February.
By the middle of June the Campaign already had more than 1000 members.

4 saying years

You normally say a year in two parts. For example, '1970' is said as **nineteen seventy**, and '1820' is said as **eighteen twenty**.
In the case of years ending in '00', you say the second part as **hundred**. For example, '1900' is said as **nineteen hundred**.

ⓘ Note that people often write **the year 2000**, not just '2000'. They usually say **the year two thousand**.

There are two ways of saying years ending in '01' to '09'. For example, '1901' can be said as **nineteen oh one** or **nineteen hundred and one**. However, for dates after 2000, people usually say **two thousand and one, two thousand and two**, and so on.

TOPICS

5 **'AD' and 'BC'**

To be more specific, for example when talking about early history, **AD** is added in front of a year or after it to show that it occurred a particular number of years after the time when Christ is believed to have been born. **AD** is an abbreviation for the Latin expression **anno Domini**, which means 'in the year of our Lord'.

…the eruption of Vesuvius in <u>AD 79.</u>
The earliest record of an animal becoming extinct dates from about <u>800 AD.</u>

BC (meaning **before Christ**) is added after a year to show that it occurred before Christ is believed to have been born.

The figurine was found near a sandal dated at <u>6925 BC.</u>

Some people, especially people who are not Christians, prefer to use the abbreviations **CE** (**Common Era**) and **BCE** (**before the Common Era**) instead of **AD** and **BC**. They are used in the same way as **BC** and **AD**.

The New Testament was written from approximately <u>50 CE</u> to <u>the early or middle 100s CE.</u>

6 **writing dates**

When writing a date, you use a number to indicate which day of the month you are talking about. There are several different ways of writing a date:

20 April   20th April   April 20   April 20th   the twentieth of April

If you want to give the year as well as the day and the month, you put it last.

I was born on <u>December 15th, 1933.</u>

You can write a date entirely in figures:

20/4/03   20.4.03

Note that Americans put the month in front of the day when writing the date in figures, so the date above would be written **4/20/03** or **4.20.03**.

This way of writing dates is often used for the date at the top of a letter, and for dates on forms. Dates within a piece of writing are not usually written entirely in figures.

7 **saying dates**

You say the day as an ordinal number, even when it is written in figures as a cardinal number. Speakers of British English say **the** in front of the number. For example, 'April 20' is said as **April the twentieth**.

Speakers of American English usually say **April twentieth**.
When the month comes after the number, you use **of** in front of the month. For example, '20 April' would be said as **the twentieth of April**.
You can omit the month when it is clear which month you are referring to.

So Monday will be <u>the seventeenth.</u>
Valentine's Day is on <u>the fourteenth.</u>

When you want to tell someone today's date, you use **It's.**

'What's the date?' – '<u>It's</u> the twelfth.'

8 **seasons**

These are the four seasons of the year:

spring	summer	autumn	winter

Seasons are sometimes written with a capital letter in British English, but it is more usual to use a small letter.

I was supposed to go last <u>summer.</u>
I think it's nice to get away in the <u>autumn.</u>

In American English, **fall** is usually used instead of 'autumn'.
They usually give a party in the <u>fall</u> and in the <u>spring.</u>

TOPICS

Springtime, **summertime**, and **wintertime** are also used to refer generally to particular times of year.

It was springtime and we were able to grow some food.
We tell people in the summertime, they always need to wear sunscreen.

(*i*) Note that there is no word 'autumntime'.

⇨ For information on using these words, see **Usage** entries at **spring, summer, autumn,** and **winter**.

9 decades and centuries

A decade is a period of ten years. A century is a period of a hundred years. Decades are usually thought of as starting with a year ending in zero and finishing with a year ending in nine. For example, the decade from 1960 to 1969 is referred to as **the 1960s**.

In the 1950s, synthetic hair was invented.
In the 1840s it was still possible for working-class newspapers to be profitable.

When you are talking about a decade in the twentieth century, you do not have to indicate the century. For example, you can refer to the 1920s as **the 20s**, **the 20s**, **the twenties**, or **the Twenties**.

...the depression of the twenties and thirties.
Most of it was done in the Seventies.

⚠ **WARNING:** You cannot refer to the first or second decade of a century in the way described above. Instead you can say, for example, **the early 1800s** or **the early nineteenth century**. Some people refer to the first decade of the twenty-first century as **the noughties**.

Centuries are considered by many people to start with a year ending in 00 and finish with a year ending in 99. They are calculated from the birth of Christ and referred to using ordinals. For example, the years 1400–1499 are referred to as **the fifteenth century**, and we are currently in **the twenty-first century** (2000–2099). Centuries can also be written using figures, for example **the 21st century**.

And then, in the eighteenth century, dawned the age of the French Salon.
That practice continued right through the 19th century.

(*i*) Note that some people think that centuries start with a year ending in 01, so, for example, the twenty-first century is 2001–2100. You can, if necessary, indicate whether you are referring to a century before or after the birth of Christ using **BC** or **AD**, or **CE** or **BCE**.

The great age of Greek sport was the fifth century BC.
the fall of Jerusalem to the Babylonians in 586 BCE.

You can also refer to a century using the plural form of its first year. For example, you can refer to the eighteenth century as **the 1700s** or **the seventeen hundreds**.

The building goes back to the 1600s.
...furniture in the heavy style of the early eighteen hundreds.

10 part of a decade or century

You can use **early**, **mid**, and **late** to specify part of a decade or century. Note that you cannot use 'middle' like this, although you can use **the middle of**.

His most important writing was done in the late 1920s and early 1930s.
...the wars of the late nineteenth century.
In the mid 1970s forecasting techniques became more sophisticated.
The next major upset came in the middle of the nineteenth century.

11 using prepositions

You use particular prepositions when mentioning the day, date, or time of year of an event.

TOPICS

● You use **at** with:

religious festivals: at Christmas, at Easter
short periods: at the weekend, at the beginning of March

In American English you say 'on the weekend' not 'at the weekend'.

● You use **in** with:

months: in July, in December
seasons: in autumn, in the spring
long periods: in wartime, in the holidays
years: in 1985, in the year 2000
decades: in the thirties
centuries: in the nineteenth century

● You use **on** with:

days: on Monday, on weekdays, on Christmas Day, on the weekend

In British English you say **at the weekend** not 'on the weekend'.

dates: on the twentieth of July, on June 21st, on the twelfth

Note that American speakers sometimes omit 'on' with days and dates.
Can you come Tuesday?

To indicate that something happened at some time in a particular period, or throughout
a period, you can use **during** or **over**.
There were 1.4 million enquiries during 1988 and 1989 alone.
More than 1,800 government soldiers were killed in fighting over Christmas.

12 **using other adjuncts**
You can indicate when something happens using the adverbs **today**, **tomorrow**, and
yesterday.
One of my children wrote to me today.

You can also use a noun group consisting of a word like **last**, **this**, or **next** combined with
a word like **week**, **year**, or **month**. Note that you do not use prepositions with these time
expressions.
They're coming next week.

⇨ See **Usage** entries at **last - lastly**, **this - these**, and **next** for detailed information on the
use of these expressions.

If you say that you did something **the week before last**, you mean that you did it in the
week just before the week that has just passed.
Eileen went to visit friends made on a camping trip the year before last in Spain.
I saw her the Tuesday before last.

If you say that something happened **a week ago last Tuesday**, you mean that it
happened exactly one week before the previous Tuesday.
If you say that you will do something **the week after next**, you mean that you will do it
in the week after the week that comes next.
I was appointed a week ago last Friday.
He wants us to go the week after next.

In British English, if you say that something is going to happen **Thursday week**, you
mean that it is going to happen exactly one week after the next Thursday.
'When is it to open?' – 'Monday week.'

This construction is not used in American English, where you have to say **a week
from Thursday**.
…a week from Wednesday.

If you say that something will happen **three weeks on Thursday**, you mean that it will
happen exactly three weeks after the next Thursday.
England's first game takes place five weeks on Sunday.

TOPICS

13 indefinite dates

⇨ For information on how to indicate an indefinite date, see **Topic** entry at **Time**.

14 modifying nouns

If you want to indicate that you are referring to something that occurred or will occur on a particular day or in a particular period, you use **-'s** after a noun group referring to that day or period.

How many of you were at Tuesday's lecture?
… yesterday's triumphs.
… next week's game.
… one of this century's most controversial leaders.

You can use the name of a day or period of the year as a modifier if you are referring to a type of thing.

Some of the people in the Tuesday class had already done a ten or twelve hour day.
I had summer clothes and winter clothes.
Ash had spent the Christmas holidays at Pelham Abbas.

When indicating what season a day occurs in, you use the name of the season as a noun modifier. You can also use **-'s** with **summer** and **winter**.

… a clear spring morning.
… wet winter days.
… a summer's day.

15 regular events

If something happens regularly, you can say that it happens **every day**, **every week**, and so on.

The nurse came in and washed him every day.
I used to go every Sunday.
Every week we sang 'Lord of the Dance'.

You can also use an adverb such as **daily** or **monthly**. This is more formal and less common.

We give each child an allowance yearly or monthly to cover all he or she spends.

If you want to say that something happens regularly on a particular day of the week, you can use **on** and the plural form of the day instead of using 'every' and the singular form of the day. You do this when you are simply saying when something happens, rather than emphasizing that it is a regular event.

He went there on Mondays and Fridays.

Note that in American English, the 'on' is often omitted in this meaning.

My father came out to the farm Saturdays to help his father.

If something happens at intervals of two days, two weeks, and so on, you can say that it happens **every other day**, **every other week**, and so on.

We wrote every other day.

A less common way of indicating an interval is to say that something happens **on alternate days**, **in alternate weeks**, and so on.

Just do some exercises on alternate days at first.

You can also indicate an interval by saying that something happens **every two weeks**, **every three years**, and so on.

World Veteran Championships are staged every two years.
… an antidote of serum renewed every six months.

You can also indicate that something happens regularly by saying that it happens, for example, **once a week**, **once every six months**, or **twice a year**.

The group met <u>once a week.</u>
…in areas where it only rains <u>once every five or ten years.</u>
You only have a meal <u>three times a day.</u>

Fixed pairs

There are a number of pairs of words which are joined by **and** or **or** which always or nearly always occur in the same order. For example, you always say **bread and butter.** You do not say 'butter and bread'. The following lists show some of the most common pairs for nouns, adjectives, adverbs and verbs.

1 Nouns

bits and pieces	food and water	knife and fork	pen and paper
board and lodging	friend or foe	land and sea	peace and quiet
(BRIT)	give and take	law and order	pros and cons
body and soul	hands and knees	nearest and	room and board
bread and butter	health and safety	dearest	(AM)
cup and saucer	heart and soul	north and south	salt and pepper
fish and chips	heaven and earth	nuts and bolts	trial and error
flesh and blood	kith and kin	odds and ends	ups and downs

Together, he and I shovelled all the <u>bits and pieces</u> back in the tin box.
Tim crawled on <u>hands and knees</u> out of the water.

2 Adjectives

alive and well	good or bad	right or wrong
black and white	hot and bothered	safe and sound
born and bred	hot and cold	sick and tired
drunk and disorderly	ready and waiting	

It's nice to know he is <u>alive and well.</u>
I'm <u>sick and tired</u> of being pushed around.

3 Adverbs

back and forth	cut and dried	in and out	short and sweet
backwards and	far and wide	loud and clear	to and fro
forwards	few and far between	now and then	up and down
black and blue	first and foremost	out and about	well and truly
bright and early	here and now	really and truly	
by and large	high and low	rightly or wrongly	

The plough is drawn <u>backwards and forwards</u> across the field.
They began jumping <u>up and down.</u>

4 Verbs

come and go	forgive and forget	twist and turn	wine and dine
ebb and flow	huff and puff	wait and see	
fetch and carry	rant and rave	wax and wane	

People are ceaselessly <u>coming and going.</u>
Fish react to the state of the tide as it <u>ebbs and flows.</u>

TOPICS

Greetings and goodbyes

1 greetings		**5** greetings on special days	
2 informal greetings		**6** goodbyes	
3 formal greetings		**7** informal goodbyes	
4 replying to a greeting		**8** formal goodbyes	

This entry deals with ways of greeting someone when you meet them, and with ways of saying goodbye.

⇨ For information on what to say when meeting someone for the first time, see **Topic** entry at **Introducing yourself and other people**.

⇨ For information on beginning and ending a telephone conversation, see **Topic** entry at **Telephoning**.

1 **greetings**

The usual way of greeting someone is to say '**Hello**'. You can add '**How are you?**' or another comment or question.

Hello there, Richard, how are you today?
Hello, Luce. Had a good day?

ⓘ Note that the greeting '**How do you do?**' is used only by people who are meeting each other for the first time.

⇨ See **Topic** entry at **Introducing yourself and other people**.

2 **informal greetings**

A more informal way of greeting someone is to say '**Hi**' or '**Hiya**'. In American English, '**Hey**' is also sometimes used in this way.

'Hi,' said Brody.'Come in.'
'Hey! How are ya?'

You can use other informal expressions to greet friends when you meet them unexpectedly after not seeing them for a long time.

Well, look who's here!
Well, well, it is nice to see you again.

If you meet someone in a place where you did not expect to see them, you can say '**Fancy seeing you here**'.

'Well I never, Mr Delfont! Fancy seeing you here!'

3 **formal greetings**

When you greet someone formally, the greeting you use depends on what time of day it is. You say '**Good morning**' until about noon. '**Good afternoon**' is normal from about noon until about six o'clock, or until it is dark in the winter. After six o'clock, or after dark, you say '**Good evening**'.

Good morning. I can give you three minutes. I have to go out.
Good evening. I'd like a table for four, please.

These greetings are often used by people who are making formal telephone calls, or introducing a television programme or other event.

'Good afternoon. William Foux and Company.' – 'Good afternoon. Could I speak to Mr Duff, please?'
Good evening. I am Brian Smith and this is the second of a series of programmes about the University of Sussex.

You can make these expressions less formal by omitting '**Good**'.

Morning, Alan.
Afternoon, Jimmy.

TOPICS

⚠️ **WARNING:** You only say '**Goodnight**' when you are leaving someone in the evening or going to bed. You do not use 'Goodnight' to greet someone.

'**Good day**' is old-fashioned and rather formal in British and American English, although it is more common in Australian English.

🏴 '**Welcome**' can be used to greet someone who has just arrived. It is quite formal in British English, but is normal in American English.

Welcome to Peking.
Welcome home, Marsha.
Welcome back.

4 replying to a greeting

The usual way of replying to a greeting is to use the same word or expression.

'*Hello, Sydney.*' – '*Hello, Yakov! It's good to see you.*'
'*Good afternoon, Superintendent. Please sit down.*' – '*Good afternoon, sir.*'

If the other person has also asked you a question, you can just answer the question.

'*Hello, Barbara, did you have a good shopping trip?*' – '*Yes, thanks.*'
'*Hello. May I help you?*' – '*Yes, I'd like a table, please.*'
'*Good morning. And how are you this fine day?*' – '*Very well, thank you.*'

ⓘ Note that if someone says '**How are you?**' to you, you say something brief like '**Fine, thanks**', unless they are a close friend and you know they will be interested in details of your life and health. It is polite to add '**How are you?**' or '**And you?**'

'*Hello John. How are you?*' – '*All right. And you?*' – '*Yeah, fine.*'
'*How are you?*' – '*Good. You?*' – '*So-so.*'

5 greetings on special days

There are particular expressions which you use to give someone your good wishes on special occasions such as Christmas, Easter, or their birthday.

At Christmas, you say '**Happy Christmas**' or '**Merry Christmas**'. At New Year, you say '**Happy New Year**'. At Easter, you say '**Happy Easter**'. You reply by repeating the greeting, or saying something like '**And a happy Christmas to you too**' or '**And you!**'

If it is someone's birthday, you can say '**Happy Birthday**' to them, or '**Many happy returns**'. When someone says this to you, you reply by saying '**Thank you**'.

6 goodbyes

You say '**Goodbye**' to someone when you or they are leaving.

'*Goodbye, dear,*' *Miss Saunders said.*

At night, you can say '**Goodnight**' or, more informally, '**Night**'.

'*Well, I must be off.*' – '*Goodnight, Moses dear.*'
'*Night, Jim.*' – '*Night, Rita.*'

People also say '**Goodnight**' to people in the same house before they go to bed.

⚠️ **WARNING:** In modern English, '**Good morning**', '**Good afternoon**', and '**Good evening**' are not used to say goodbye.

7 informal goodbyes

'**Bye**' is commonly used as an informal way of saying goodbye.

See you about seven. Bye.

'**Bye-bye**' is even more informal. It is used between close relatives and friends, and to children.

Bye-bye, dear; see you tomorrow.

If you expect to meet the other person again soon, you can say things like '**See you**', '**See you later**', '**See you soon**', '**See you around**', or '**I'll be seeing you**'.

TOPICS

See you later maybe.
Must go in now. See you tomorrow.
See you in the morning, Quent.

Some people say '**So long**'.

'Well. So long.' He turned and walked back to the car.

You can say '**Take care**', '**Take care of yourself**', or '**Look after yourself**' when you are saying goodbye to a friend or relative.

'Take care.' – 'Bye-bye.'
'Look after yourself, Ginny dear.' – 'You, too, Mother.'

Many speakers of American English use the expression '**Have a nice day**' to say goodbye to people they do not know as friends. For example, employees in some shops and restaurants say it to customers.

'Have a nice day.' – 'Thank you.'

'**Cheers**' and '**Cheerio**' are used by speakers of British English.

See you at six, then. Cheers!
I'll give Brigadier Sutherland your regards. Cheerio.

8 formal goodbyes

When you are saying goodbye to someone you do not know very well, you can use a more formal expression such as '**I look forward to seeing you again soon**' or '**It was nice meeting you**'.

I look forward to seeing you in Washington. Goodbye.
It was nice meeting you, Dimitri. Hope you have a good trip back.
It was nice seeing you again.

Groups of things, animals, and people

There are many words which are used in front of **of** and a plural noun to refer to a group of things, animals, or people. The commonest ones are given here.

1 indicating range

Some words can be used to refer to a wide range of things or people:

assortment	cluster	group	set
batch	collection	host	variety
battery	crop	selection	

She joined a group of gossiping villagers in the street.
She may have a collection of old toys left from the time her children were young.

Some words are usually used to refer to people or animals, rather than things:

army	crowd	horde	party	throng
band	gathering	knot	swarm	

A large crowd of students gathered to watch the parade.
An army of ants crossed the flagstones in two close columns.

2 indicating shape

Some words indicate the shape of a group of things or people:

circle	jumble	mountain	row	sprinkling
column	line	pile	scatter	stack
heap	mound	ring	scattering	string

He sat down in the middle of the front row of chairs and waited.
The circle of boys broke into applause.

3 | indicating movement or occurrence

Some words indicate the movement or occurrence of a group of things or people:

hail	rash	spate	tide
barrage	series	stream	trickle
flood	shower	string	volley

Throughout the evening an unbroken <u>stream</u> of people came in.
After a <u>spate</u> of protests the authorities reacted by bringing many of them to trial.

4 | typical groups

The following table shows which word is typically used to refer to a group of animals of a particular kind.

ants	→ an army of ants	goats	→ a herd/flock of goats
bees	→ a swarm of bees	hounds	→ a pack of hounds
birds	→ a flock/flight of birds	insects	→ a swarm/colony of insects
cattle	→ a herd of cattle	kittens	→ a litter of kittens
cubs	→ a litter of cubs	lions	→ a pride of lions
deer	→ a herd of deer	monkeys	→ a troop of monkeys
dolphins	→ a school of dolphins	puppies	→ a litter of puppies
elephants	→ a herd of elephants	sheep	→ a flock of sheep
fish	→ a shoal of fish	wolves	→ a pack of wolves
geese	→ a gaggle of geese		

The following table shows which word is typically used to refer to a group of people or things of a particular kind.

actors	→ a company/troupe of actors	papers	→ a sheaf/bundle of papers
		reporters	→ a team of reporters
banknotes	→ a wad/roll of banknotes	ships	→ a fleet of ships
bullets	→ a hail of bullets	steps	→ a flight of steps
cards	→ a pack/deck of cards	terrorists	→ a gang of terrorists
experts	→ a team/panel of experts	thieves	→ a gang/band/pack of thieves
faces	→ a sea of faces		
flowers	→ a bunch/bouquet of flowers	tourists	→ a party of tourists
grapes	→ a bunch of grapes	trees	→ a clump of trees
keys	→ a bunch of keys	volunteers	→ an army of volunteers

Intentions

1	general intentions	4	expressing intentions formally
2	vague intentions	5	involuntary actions
3	firm intentions		

1 | general intentions

When you want to express an intention, especially one relating to an immediate action, you can say '**I'm going to…**'.

<u>I'm going to</u> call my father.
<u>I'm going to</u> have a bath.

You can also say '**I think I'll…**'.

<u>I think I'll</u> do some more typing.
<u>I think I'll</u> go to sleep now.

TOPICS

You can use the present continuous tense when you regard your intention as a fixed plan or have already made the necessary arrangements.

I'm taking it back to the library soon.
I'm going away.

The future continuous tense is also sometimes used.

I'll be waiting.

You can also express an intention by saying '**I've decided to…**'.

I've decided to clear this place out.
I've decided to go there.

To express a negative intention, you say '**I'm not going to…**' or '**I've decided not to…**'.

I'm not going to make it easy for them.
I've decided not to take it.

2 vague intentions

If your intention is not a firm one, you can say '**I'm thinking of…**'.

I'm thinking of going to the theatre next week.
I'm thinking of writing a play.

You can also say '**I might…**' or '**I may…**'.

I might stay a day or two.
I may come back to Britain, I'm not sure.

If you feel that your intention might surprise the person you are talking to, or are not sure that they will approve of it, you say '**I thought I might…**'.

I thought I might buy a house next year.
I thought I might get him over to dinner one evening.

To express a vague negative intention, you can say '**I might not…**'.

I might not go.

3 firm intentions

You use '**I'll…**' to express a firm intention, especially when making arrangements or reassuring someone.

I'll do it this afternoon and ring you back.
I'll explain its function in a minute.

To express a firm negative intention, you can say '**I won't…**'.

I won't go.
I won't let my family suffer.

4 expressing intentions formally

A more formal way of expressing an intention is to say '**I intend to…**'.

I intend to carry on with it.
I intend to go into this in rather more detail this term.

I intend is also occasionally followed by an '-ing' form.

I intend retiring to Florence.

The emphatic expression '**I have every intention of…**' is also sometimes used.

I have every intention of buying it.

Even more formal expressions are '**My intention is to…**' and '**It is my intention to…**'.

My intention is to provide a reconstruction of this largely discredited ideology.
It is still my intention to resign if they wilfully fail to print the story.

To express a negative intention formally, you can say '**I don't intend to…**'.

I don't intend to investigate that at this time.
I don't intend to stay too long.

TOPICS

You can also say '**I have no intention of…**'. This is more emphatic.

I have no intention of retiring.
I've no intention of marrying again.

5 **involuntary actions**

Note that **be going to**, **might**, **may**, and **will** are also used to make statements about involuntary future actions.

If you keep chattering I'm going to make a mistake.
I might not be able to find it.
I may have to stay there awhile.
If I don't have lunch, I'll faint.

Introducing yourself and other people

1 introducing yourself	**4** more casual introductions
2 introducing other people	**5** responding to an introduction
3 more formal introductions	

1 **introducing yourself**

When you meet someone for the first time, and they do not already know who you are, you can introduce yourself by saying who you are. You may need to say '**Hello**' or make a remark first.

'I'm Helmut,' said the boy. 'I'm Edmond Dorf,' I said.
I had better introduce myself. I am Colonel Marc Rodin.
May I introduce myself? The Reverend John Hunt.
You must be the Kirks. My name's Macintosh.

In formal situations, people sometimes say '**How do you do?**' when introducing themselves.

I'm Nigel Jessop. How do you do?

2 **introducing other people**

If you are introducing people who have not met each other before, you say '**This is…**'. You introduce each person, unless you have already told one of them who they are going to meet.

'This is Bernadette, Mr Zapp,' said O'Shea.

You use an appropriate form of each person's name, depending on how formal the occasion is.

⇨ See **Topic** entry at **Names and titles.**

(i) Note that 'these' is rarely used, although you might say, for example, '**These are my children**' or '**These are my parents**'. When you are introducing a couple, you can use **this** once instead of repeating it.

This is Mr Dixon and Miss Peel.

You can just say the name of the person or people you are introducing, indicating with your hand which one you mean.

3 **more formal introductions**

If you need to be more formal, you first say something like '**May I introduce my brother**', '**Let me introduce you to my brother**', or '**I'd like to introduce my brother**'.

By the way, may I introduce my wife? Karin – Mrs Stannard, an old friend.
Bill, I'd like to introduce Charlie Citrine.

You can also say '**I'd like you to meet…**'.

Officer O'Malley, I'd like you to meet Ted Peachum.

TOPICS

4 **more casual introductions**

A more casual way of introducing someone is to say something like 'You haven't met John Smith, have you?', 'You don't know John, do you?', or 'I don't think you know John, do you?'

'I don't think you know Colonel Daintry.' – 'No. I don't think we've met. How do you do?'

If you are not quite sure whether an introduction is necessary, you can say something like 'Have you met…?' or 'Do you two know each other?'

'Do you know my husband, Ken?' – 'Hello. I don't think I do.'

If you are fairly sure that the people have met each other before, you say something like 'You know John, don't you?' or 'You've met John, haven't you?'

Hello, come in. You've met Paul.

5 **responding to an introduction**

When you have been introduced to someone, you both say 'Hello'. If you are both young and in an informal situation, you can say 'Hi'. If you are in a formal situation, you can say 'How do you do?'

'Francis, this is Father Sebastian.' – 'Hello, Francis,' Father Sebastian said, offering his hand. How do you do? Elizabeth has spoken such a lot about you.

People sometimes say 'Pleased to meet you' or 'Nice to meet you'.

Pleased to meet you, Doctor Floyd.
It's so nice to meet you, Edna. Ginny's told us so much about you.

Invitations

1	polite invitations	**6**	indirect invitations
2	informal invitations	**7**	inviting someone to ask you for
3	persuasive invitations		something
4	very emphatic invitations	**8**	responding to an invitation
5	casual invitations		

There are several ways of inviting someone to do something or to come to a place.

1 **polite invitations**

The usual polite way to invite someone to do something is to say 'Would you like to…?'

<u>Would you like to</u> come up here on Sunday?
<u>Would you like to</u> look at it, Ian?

Another polite form of invitation is **please** with an imperative. This form of invitation is used mainly by people who are in charge of a situation.

<u>Please</u> help yourselves to another drink.
Sit down, <u>please</u>.

2 **informal invitations**

In informal situations, you can use an imperative form without 'please'. However, you should only do this if it is clear that you are giving an invitation rather than an order.

<u>Come and have</u> a drink, Max.
<u>Sit down, sit down.</u> I'll order tea.
<u>Stay</u> as long as you like.

3 **persuasive invitations**

You can make your invitation more persuasive or firm by putting **do** in front of the imperative. You do this especially when the other person seems reluctant to do what you are inviting them to do.

<u>Do</u> sit down.
What you said just now about Seaford sounds most intriguing. <u>Do</u> tell me more.

You can also say '**Wouldn't you like to...?**' when you want to be persuasive.
Wouldn't you like to come with me?

When you want to be very polite and persuasive, you can say '**Won't you...?**'
Won't you take off your coat?
Won't you sit down, Mary, and have a bite to eat?

4   very emphatic invitations

If you know the person you are inviting well, and you want to make your invitation very emphatic, you can say '**You must...**', or '**You have to...**' or '**You've got to...**'. You use this form of invitation when inviting someone to do something in the future, rather than immediately.
You must come and stay.
You have to come down to the office and see all the technology we have.

5   casual invitations

A casual, non-emphatic way of inviting someone to do something is to say '**You can...**' or '**You could...**'. You can add '**if you like**'.
Well, when I get my flat, you can come and stay with me.
You can tell me about your people, if you like.

'**You're welcome to...**' is another way of starting a casual invitation, but is more friendly.
You're welcome to live with us for as long as you like.
The cottage is about fifty miles away. But you're very welcome to use it.

Another way of making an invitation seem casual is to say '**I was wondering if...**'.
I was wondering if you'd care to come over next weekend.
I was wondering if you're free for lunch.

6   indirect invitations

An invitation can be indirect. For example, you can invite someone to do something in the future by saying '**I hope you'll...**'. You use this form of invitation especially when you are not confident that the other person will accept your invitation.
I hope you'll be able to stay the night. We'll gladly put you up.
I hope, Kathy, you'll come and see me again.

You can also invite someone indirectly using '**How would you like to...?**' or '**Why don't you...?**'
How would you like to come and work for me?
Why don't you come to the States with us in November?

You can also use a question beginning with '**How about**' followed by an '-ing' form or a noun.
Now, how about coming to stay with me, at my house?
How about a spot of lunch with me, Mrs Sharpe?

You can also use a statement that begins with '**You'll...**' and ends with the tag '**...won't you?**' This implies that you are expecting the other person to accept.
You'll bring Angela up for the wedding, won't you?

7   inviting someone to ask you for something

You can invite someone else to ask you for something by saying '**Don't hesitate to...**'. This form of invitation is polite and emphatic, and is usually used between people who do not know each other well. It is often used in formal or business correspondence.
Should you have any further problems, please do not hesitate to telephone.
When you want more, don't hesitate to ask me.

8   responding to an invitation

If you want to accept an invitation, you say '**Thank you**' or, more informally, '**Thanks**'. You can also say something like '**Yes, I'd love to**' or '**I'd like that very much**'.
'We have a swimming pool. Come over and use it any time.' – 'Thank you. I'll come round sometime.'

TOPICS

'You could come and tutor me in physics and maths.' – 'Yes, I'd love to.'
'Won't you join me and the girls for lunch, Mr Jordache?' – 'Thanks, Larsen. I'd like that very much.'

If you want to decline an invitation to visit someone or go somewhere with them, you can say something like **'I'm sorry, I can't'**, **'I'm afraid I'm busy then'**, or **'I'd like to, but…'**.

'I'm phoning in the hope of persuading you to spend the day with me.' – 'Oh, I'm sorry, I can't.'
'I would like it very much if you could come on Sunday.' – 'I'm afraid I'm busy.'
'Would you like to stay for dinner?' – 'I'd like to, but I can't.'

You can also decline an invitation by saying **'No, thanks'**, **'Thanks, but…'**, or **'I'm all right, thanks'**.

'Come home with me.' – 'No thanks. I don't want to intrude on your family.'
'Eat with us.' – 'Thanks, but I've eaten.'
'Would you like to lie down?' – 'No, I'm all right.'

Letter writing

1	formal letters	**6**	address and date
2	address and date	**7**	beginning an informal letter
3	beginning a formal letter	**8**	ending an informal letter
4	ending a formal letter	**9**	addressing an envelope
5	informal letters		

When you are writing a letter, the language you use and the layout of the letter will depend on how formal the letter is.

1 formal letters

If you are writing a formal letter, such as a business letter or an application for a job, you use formal language, as in the example below.

> 80 Green Road
> Moseley
> Birmingham
> B13 9PL
>
> 29/4/04
>
> The Personnel Manager
> Cratex Ltd.
> 21 Fireside Road
> Birmingham
> B15 2RX
>
> Dear Sir
>
> I am writing in response to your advertisement for the position of Team Leader in *The Times* (28/4/04). Could you please send me an application form and details about the position. I have recently graduated from Southampton University in Mechanical Engineering.
> I look forward to hearing from you soon.
>
> Yours faithfully
> *James Laker*
> James Laker

TOPICS

2 **address and date**
You put your address in the top right-hand corner. You can put a comma at the end of each line, and a full stop at the end of the last one, but this is not necessary. You do not put your name above the address.

You put the date under your address. If you are using headed notepaper, you put the date above the address of the person you are writing to or at the right-hand side of the page. You can write the date in several different ways, for example **29.4.04**, **29/4/04**, **29 April 2004**, or **April 29th, 2004**.

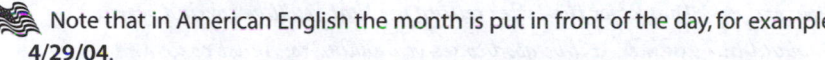 Note that in American English the month is put in front of the day, for example **4/29/04**.

You put the name or job title and the address of the person you are writing to on the left-hand side of the page, usually starting on the line below the date.

3 **beginning a formal letter**
You begin a formal letter with the person's title and surname, for example **Dear Mr Jenkins**, **Dear Mrs Carstairs**, or **Dear Miss Stephenson**.

⇨ See **Topic** entry at **Names and titles** for information on titles.

If you do not know whether the woman you are writing to is married or not, you can use the title **Ms**. Some younger women prefer **Ms** to 'Mrs' and 'Miss', especially if they have married but not changed their surname. However, some older women do not like this title.

In less formal letters, people sometimes use the person's first name and surname after **Dear**, for example **Dear Fiona Smart**.

If you are writing a very formal letter, or do not know the person's name, you use **Dear Sir** or **Dear Madam**. If you are not sure whether the person you are writing to is a man or a woman, it is safest to write **Dear Sir or Madam**.

When writing to a company, **Dear Sirs** is used in British English and **Gentlemen** in American English. It is also acceptable in American English to address a company as if it were a person when you do not have a name or person to send your letter to: **Dear AT&T**.

People writing in formal American style put a colon after the '**Dear...**' expression, for example **Dear Mr. Jones:**. If you are writing in the British style, you can either use a comma or have no punctuation.

4 **ending a formal letter**
If you begin the letter using the person's title and surname (for example **Dear Mrs Carstairs**), you finish with **Yours sincerely**. If you want to be less formal, you can finish with **Yours**. If you begin your letter with **Dear Sir**, **Dear Madam**, or **Dear Sirs**, you finish with **Yours faithfully**.

In American English, the usual way of finishing a letter is with the expression **Sincerely yours** or, more formally, **Very truly yours**. You write your signature underneath the expression you finish with. You can type your name (or write it in capitals) underneath your signature. If you are writing a business letter, you can also put your job title.

5 **informal letters**
If you are writing a letter to a friend or relative, you use informal language, as in the example on the next page.

TOPICS

63 Pottery Row
Birmingham
B13 8AS
18/4/04

Dear Mario

How are you? Thanks for the letter telling me that you'll be coming over to England this summer. It'll be good to see you again. You must come and stay with me in Birmingham.

I'll be on holiday when you're here as the University will be closed, so we can have some days out together. Write or phone me to tell me when you want to come and stay.

All the best,

Dave

6   address and date

You put your address and the date, or just the date, in the top right-hand corner. You do not put the address of the person you are writing to at the top of the letter.

7   beginning an informal letter

You normally begin an informal letter to a friend using **Dear** and the person's first name, for example **Dear Louise**. When people are writing to a relative, they use the person's 'relative' title, for example **Dear Mum**, **Dear Grandpa**, or **Dear Grandma**. If you are very fond of the friend or relative you are writing to, you can begin your letter with something like **My dearest Sara** or **Darling Alison**.

8   ending an informal letter

There are various ways in which you can end an informal letter. You can use **Love** or **Lots of love** when writing to close friends or relatives. When writing to someone you know less well, you can use **Yours**, **Best wishes**, or **All the best**. Men generally tend to use more formal expressions than women.

9   addressing an envelope

The example below shows how to write the name and address on an envelope. In British English, some people put a comma at the end of each line, and a full stop after the county or country.

Miss S. Wilkins
13 Magpie Close
Guildford
Surrey
GL4 2PX

TOPICS

You usually use the title, initial or initials, and surname of the person you are writing to.

You can also use the person's title, first name, and surname: **Miss Sarah Wilkins**. When the letter is informal, you can just use their first name and surname, or their initial (or initials) and surname: **Sarah Wilkins** or **S Wilkins**.

If you are writing to someone who is temporarily staying with someone else or staying in a particular place, you put their name first and then, on the line below, put **c/o** in front of the name of the other person or the place, as in the example below. **c/o** stands for **care of**.

> Mr JL Martin
> c/o Mrs P Roberts
> 28 Fish Street
> Cambridge
> CB2 8AS

 When sending a letter to a place in Britain, you should put the **postcode** (the set of letters and numbers at the end of the address) on a separate line. The American equivalent is a **zip code**, and needn't be on a separate line.

Male and female

1 pronouns and determiners	**7** men and women with a particular job
2 'she' and 'her' for things	
3 modifiers	**8** other male people
4 nouns referring to males or females	**9** other female people
	10 '-man' and '-person'
5 male relatives	**11** nationality words
6 female relatives	**12** nouns referring to animals

1 pronouns and determiners

The fact that you are referring to a male person or a female person makes a difference grammatically only when you are using personal pronouns, reflexive pronouns, possessive pronouns, or possessive determiners.

She sat twisting her hands together.
She managed to free herself.

⇨ See **Grammar** entries at **Possessive determiners** and **Pronouns**.

If you are referring to more than one person, there is only one pronoun or determiner of each type to use. For example, the subject pronoun you use to refer to a group of men, a group of women, a group of men and women, or one man and one woman together is **they**.

Boys are taught that they mustn't show their feelings.
People were looking to me as though they thought I might know the secret.
They had been married for forty-seven years.

2 'she' and 'her' for things

Although **it** and **its** are generally used when referring to a thing, **she** and **her** are sometimes used when referring to countries, ships, and cars.

Mr Putin has a high regard for Britain and <u>her</u> role in Europe.
When the repairs had been done <u>she</u> was a fine and beautiful ship.

3 modifiers

If you need to indicate someone's sex when using a noun to refer to them, you can use **woman**, **female**, or **male** in front of the noun. You do not usually use 'man' in front of a noun.

We went to the home of a <u>woman factory worker</u> named Liang.
A <u>female employee</u> was dismissed.
He asked some other <u>male relatives</u> for help.

ⓘ Note that **women**, not 'woman', is used in front of a plural noun.

I did a survey on <u>women lawyers</u>.

4 nouns referring to males or females

English nouns are not generally masculine, feminine, or neuter. Some nouns, however, are used to refer only to males and others only to females.

He announced that he was a <u>policeman</u>.
The <u>bride</u> was very young.

Words that refer only to women often end in '**-ess**', for example **actress**, **waitress**, and **hostess**. Another ending is '**-woman**', as in **policewoman**.

She told me she intended to be an <u>actress</u>.
…Margaret Downes, who is this year's <u>chairwoman</u> of the examination committee.

Fewer words ending in '**-ess**' are used in modern English than were used in the past. For example, people nowadays refer to a woman who writes books as an **author**, not an 'authoress', and **actor** is used for both men and women appearing in plays and films. Words ending in '**-man**', such as **chairman**, which were previously used to refer to both men and women, are now often replaced by words ending in '**-person**', or by gender-neutral alternatives.

An association was formed, with Ron as <u>chairperson</u>.
…Ross McGinn, <u>chair</u> of the local community council.

5 male relatives

The following words are used to refer to male relatives:

brother	godfather	husband	stepbrother
brother-in-law	godson	nephew	stepfather
father	grandfather	son	stepson
father-in-law	grandson	son-in-law	uncle

6 female relatives

The following words are used to refer to female relatives:

aunt	godmother	mother-in-law	stepdaughter
daughter	grandmother	niece	stepsister
daughter-in-law	granddaughter	sister	stepmother
goddaughter	mother	sister-in-law	wife

ⓘ Note that **cousin** is used to refer to both males and females.

7 men and women with a particular job

The following table shows some common words used to refer to men and women who have a particular job. Where possible, a gender-neutral alternative is shown in the third column, and is often preferred nowadays.

Men	Women	Gender—neutral
actor	actress	actor
air steward	air hostess, stewardess	flight attendant
ambulanceman	ambulancewoman	paramedic
(male) ballet dancer	ballerina	ballet dancer
barman	barmaid	bar tender
businessman	businesswoman	businessperson
cameraman	camerawoman	camera operator
chairman	chairwoman	chairperson, chair
—	chambermaid, maid	(in hotel) cleaner
clergyman	clergywoman	member of the clergy
comedian	comedienne	comedian
congressman (AM)	congresswoman	congressperson
conman	conwoman	con artist
fireman	firewoman	firefighter
foreman	forewoman	supervisor
headmaster	headmistress	headteacher, principal
house-husband	housewife	homemaker
host	hostess	host
male nurse	nurse	nurse
manager	manageress	manager
master	mistress	—
monk	nun	—
poet	poetess	poet
policeman	policewoman	police officer
postman, postmaster, mailman (AM)	postwoman, postmistress, mailwoman (AM)	postal worker
priest	priestess	—
repairman	repairwoman	repair person, repairer
salesman	saleswoman	salesperson, sales assistant, sales executive, sales agent
schoolmaster	schoolmistress	schoolteacher
serviceman	servicewoman	—
spokesman	spokeswoman	spokesperson, representative
sportsman	sportswoman	—
statesman	stateswoman	official, diplomat
tradesman	—	shopkeeper, salesperson, trader
waiter	waitress	wait staff
weatherman	weathergirl	(weather) forecaster
workman	—	labourer, worker

8 other male people

These words are also used to refer only to men or boys:

bachelor	bridegroom	gentleman	man
bloke	buddy	groom	schoolboy
boy	chap	guy	suitor
boyfriend	fiancé	lad	widower

ⓘ Note that you do not usually refer to a man or boy as a 'male'.

9 other female people

These words are also used to refer only to women or girls:

blonde	fiancée	heiress	schoolgirl
bride	girl	lady	spinster
bridesmaid	girlfriend	lass	widow
brunette	goddess	mistress	woman

i Note that you do not usually refer to a woman as a 'female'.

10 **'-man' and '-person'**

Words ending in '**-man**' are used either to refer only to men or to refer to both men and women. For example, a **workman** is a man, but a **spokesman** can be a man or a woman. The words ending in '**-man**' in the lists of male words above are generally used to refer only to men. When women begin to do a job that used to be done only by men, the word ending in '**-man**' is sometimes still used. Sometimes a new word is invented to refer to women doing the job, for example **policewoman**. However, it is becoming more common to use terms which do not indicate the sex of the person who has a particular job. For example, **police officer** is used instead of 'policeman' or 'policewoman', and **head teacher** is used instead of 'headmaster' or 'headmistress'. Words ending in '**-person**' are also sometimes used.

⇨ See **Usage** entries at **chairman** and **spokesman.**

11 **nationality words**

A few nouns which refer to a person of a particular nationality are used only for a man or only for a woman, for example **Englishman** and **Englishwoman**.

⇨ See **Topic** entry at **Nationality words.**

12 **nouns referring to animals**

Most names of animals are used to refer to both male and female animals, such as **cat**, **elephant**, and **sheep**.

In some cases there are different words that refer specifically to male animals or female animals. For example, a **ram** is a male sheep and a **ewe** is a female sheep. However, most of these words are rarely used, or are used mainly by people who have a special interest in animals, such as farmers or vets. The ones most commonly used are **bull** (for a male cow) and **hen** (for a female chicken).

Meals

1 'breakfast'	6 'for' and 'to'
2 'dinner', 'lunch', 'luncheon'	7 'have'
3 'tea' and 'supper'	8 'make'
4 more formal terms	9 'a' with meals
5 'at' and 'over'	10 meal times

The meanings of words referring to meals, and the ways that these words are used, are explained below. Some words for meals are used by different people to refer to different meals.

1 **'breakfast'**

Breakfast is the first meal of the day. You eat it in the morning, just after you get up.

Every morning, the four of them met up for breakfast.

2 **'dinner', 'lunch', 'luncheon'**

Dinner, for most people, is the name of the main evening meal. However, in some regions, the word **dinner** is used for the meal people have in the middle of the day. These people call their evening meal **tea** or **supper**, depending on where they come from.

TOPICS

People who call their evening meal **dinner** usually refer to a meal eaten in the middle of the day as **lunch. Luncheon** is a formal and rather old-fashioned word for 'lunch'.

The grateful foreigner had taken him out to <u>dinner</u> on Tuesday night.
Workers started at 9am and finished at 5pm with an hour for <u>lunch</u>.
An annual <u>luncheon</u> is held in his honour.

3 'tea' and 'supper'

Tea can be a light meal eaten in the afternoon, usually consisting of sandwiches and cakes, with tea to drink. This meaning of **tea** is used mainly in Britain, by middle-class people. The expression **afternoon tea** is often used in hotels and restaurants.

I invited him for <u>tea</u> that afternon.
Traditional <u>afternoon tea</u> is served.

Tea can also be a main meal that is eaten in the early evening. This meaning of **tea** is often used by working-class people in Britain. It is also more common in northern parts of Britain, and in Australia and New Zealand. The expression **high tea** is also used in Britain, but it is now rather old-fashioned.

I bought four rashers of bacon for <u>tea</u>.

 Tea is not used to talk about meals in American English.

Some people call a large meal they eat in the early part of the evening **supper.** Other people use **supper** to refer to a small meal eaten just before going to bed at night.

We had eaten a light <u>supper</u> at six.
He just has <u>supper</u>, watches telly, and goes to bed.

4 more formal terms

You can refer to a meal that you eat in the middle of the day as a **midday meal.** Similarly, you can refer to a meal that you eat in the evening as an **evening meal.** However, these terms are not normally used in conversation to refer to meals eaten at home, only to meals provided for you, for example at school or in lodgings.

5 'at' and 'over'

You indicate that someone does something while they are having a meal using the preposition **at.**

He had told her <u>at</u> lunch that he couldn't take her to the game tomorrow.
Mrs Zapp was seated next to me <u>at</u> dinner.

However, you usually use **over** when talking about an event that takes some time, especially when saying that people discuss something while having a meal.

It's often easier to discuss difficult ideas <u>over</u> lunch.
He said he wanted to reread it <u>over</u> lunch.

6 'for' and 'to'

When you talk about what a meal consists of, you say what you have **for** breakfast, lunch, and so on.

They had hard-boiled eggs <u>for</u> breakfast.
What's <u>for</u> dinner?

When you invite someone to have a meal with you, for example at your house, you say that you ask them **for** the meal or **to** the meal.

Why don't you join me and the girls <u>for</u> lunch, Mr Jordache?
Stanley Openshaw invited him <u>to</u> lunch once.

7 'have'

You often use **have** to say that someone eats a meal. You can say, for example, that someone **has breakfast** or **has their breakfast.**

When we've <u>had breakfast,</u> you can phone for a taxi.
That Tuesday, Lo <u>had her dinner</u> in her room.

(i) Note that you do not say that someone 'has a breakfast' or 'has the breakfast'.

8 **'make'**

When someone prepares a meal, you can say, for example, that they **make breakfast,** **make the breakfast,** or **make their breakfast.**

I'll go and <u>make dinner.</u>
He <u>makes the breakfast</u> every morning.
She <u>had been making her lunch</u> when he arrived.

(i) Note that you do not say that someone 'makes a breakfast'.

9 **'a' with meals**

Words referring to meals can be used either as uncount nouns or as count nouns. However, these words are not generally used with 'a'. For example, you do not say 'I had a lunch with Deborah' or 'I had a dinner early'. You say 'I had **lunch** with Deborah' or 'I had **dinner** early'. You can, however, use **a** when you are describing a meal.

They had <u>a quiet dinner</u> together.
He was a big man and needed <u>a big breakfast.</u>

10 **meal times**

When you want to refer to the period of the day when a particular meal is eaten, you can use a compound noun consisting of a word referring to a meal and the word **time**. The compound noun can be hyphenated or written as two separate words.

I shall be back by <u>dinner-time.</u>
It was almost <u>lunch time.</u>

 The forms **dinnertime, lunchtime, suppertime,** and **teatime** are also used, and are preferred in American English. **Breakfast time** is never written as one word.

He had a great deal to do before <u>lunchtime.</u>

Measurements

1	metric and imperial measurements	**9**	weight
2	size	**10**	temperature
3	size of circular objects and areas	**11**	speed, rates, and ratios
4	size by dimensions	**12**	measurements used as modifiers
5	area	**13**	and qualifiers
6	volume	**14**	size of something abstract
7	distance	**15**	measurement nouns before 'of'
8	distance and position		

You can refer to a size, area, volume, weight, distance, speed, or temperature by using a number or general determiner in front of a **measurement noun**.

…blocks of stone weighing up to a hundred <u>tons.</u>
They may travel as far as 70 <u>kilometres</u> in their search for fruit.
Reduce the temperature by a few <u>degrees.</u>

1 **metric and imperial measurements**

In Britain, two systems of measurement are used – the **metric system** and the **imperial system.** The metric system is now commonly used for most purposes, but the imperial system is still used for people's heights and weights, drinks in pubs, distances on road signs, and sports such as cricket, football, and horseracing.
Each system has its own measurement nouns, as shown in the table below. Their abbreviations are shown in brackets.

TOPICS

	metric units	**imperial units**
size/distance	millimetre (mm) centimetre (cm) metre (m) kilometre (km)	inch (in or ") foot (ft or ') yard (yd) mile (m)
area	hectare (ha)	acre (a)
volume	millilitre (ml) centilitre (cl) litre (l)	fluid ounce (fl oz) pint (pt) quart (q) gallon (gal)
weight	milligram (mg) gram (g) kilogram (kg) tonne (t)	ounce (oz) pound (lb) stone (st) hundredweight (cwt) ton (t)

If you are using metric units, you use decimal numbers. For example, you say that something is **1.68 metres long** or weighs **4.8 kilograms**. With imperial units, fractions are often used instead, for example **six and three-quarter inches** or **one and a half tons of wheat**.

Kilo is sometimes used instead of 'kilogram', and **metric ton** instead of 'tonne'.

In the United States, the metric system is not commonly used, except for military, medical, and scientific purposes. The spellings **meter** and **liter** are used instead of 'metre' and 'litre'. The terms 'stone' and 'hundredweight' are very rarely used. Note that U.S. **pints**, **quarts**, and **gallons** are slightly smaller than British ones.

2 **size**

When you want to state the size of something, you usually use a number, a measurement noun, and an adjective. The verb you use is **be**.

The water was fifteen feet deep.
One of the layers is six metres thick.

As well as the plural form **feet**, the singular form **foot** can be used with numbers.

The spears were about six foot long.

If you are expressing size using feet and inches, you do not have to say 'inches'. For example, you can say that something is **two foot six long**. However, you do not say 'two feet six' or 'two foot six inches'.

He's Italian, and immensely tall, six feet six inches.

When the context makes it clear that you are talking about measurement, you do not need to use the measurement words at all; it will be understood that you mean feet and inches.

At six two he's not exactly inconspicuous.

The following adjectives can be used after measurement nouns indicating size:

deep	high	long	tall	thick	wide

TOPICS

ⓘ Note that you do not use adjectives such as 'narrow', 'shallow', 'low', or 'thin'. When mentioning someone's height, you can use the adjective **tall** or leave it out.

She was six feet tall.
He was six foot six.

ⓘ Note that you do not use the adjective 'high' for people, and that you use **long** for babies, not 'tall'.

When describing how wide something is, you can use **across** instead of 'wide'.

…a squid that was 21 metres long with eyes 40 centimetres across.

Instead of using an adjective when stating size, you can use one of the following prepositional phrases after the measurement noun.

in depth	in height	in length	in thickness	in width

They are thirty centimetres in length.
He was five feet seven inches in height.

When asking a question about the size of something, you use **how** and the adjectives listed earlier. You can also use the less specific adjective **big**.

How tall is he?
How big is it going to be?

3 size of circular objects and areas

If you are talking about the size of a circular object or area, you can give its circumference (edge measurement) or diameter (width) using **in circumference** or **in diameter**. You can also say that something has a **radius** (half the diameter) of a particular length. However, you do not say 'in radius'.

Some of its artificial lakes are ten or twenty kilometres in circumference.
They are about nine inches in diameter.
It had a radius of fifteen kilometres.

4 size by dimensions

If you want to describe the size of an object or area fully, you can give its **dimensions**; that is, you can give the measurements for its length and width, or length, width, and depth. When you give the dimensions of an object or area, you separate the figures using **and**, **by**, or the multiplication sign **x** (pronounced 'by'). You use the verb **be** or **measure**. You can use adjectives such as **long** and **wide** or leave them out.

Each frame was was four metres tall and sixty-six centimetres wide.
The island measures about 25 miles by 12 miles.
The box measures approximately 26 inches wide x 25 inches deep x 16 inches high.

You can add **in size** after the dimensions if you want to be precise.

…two sections, each 2 x 2 x 1 metres in size.

5 area

Area is often expressed by using **square** in front of units of length. For example, a **square metre** has the same area as a square whose sides are one metre long.

He had cleared away about three square inches.
They are said to be as little as 300 sq cm.

You can add **in area** if you want to be precise.

These hot spots are often hundreds of square miles in area.

If you are talking about a square object or area, you can give the length of each side followed by the word **square**.

Each family has only one room eight or ten feet square.
…an area that is 25 km square.

⚠ **WARNING:** Do not confuse the two uses of **square**. A room five metres square has an area of twenty-five square metres.

When talking about large areas of land, the words **hectare** and **acre** are often used.
In 1975 there were <u>1,240 million hectares</u> under cultivation.
His land covers <u>twenty acres</u>.

6 **volume**

The volume of an object is the amount of space it occupies or contains.
Volume is usually expressed by using **cubic** in front of units of length. For example, you can say **10 cubic centimetres** or **200 cubic feet**.
Its brain was close to <u>500 cubic centimetres (49 cubic inches)</u>.

Units of volume such as **litre** and **gallon** are used to refer to quantities of liquids and gases.
Wine production is expected to reach <u>4.1 billion gallons</u> this year.
The amount of air being expelled is about <u>1,000 to 1,500 mls</u>.

ⓘ Note that, in Britain, **a pint** by itself often refers to a pint of beer.
A lorry driver came into the pub for <u>a pint</u>.

7 **distance**

You can indicate the distance from one thing to another by using a number and measurement noun in front of **from**, **away from**, or **away**.
…when the fish are <u>60 yds from the beach</u>.
These offices were approximately <u>nine kilometres away from the centre</u>.
She sat down about <u>a hundred metres away</u>.

Distance can also be indicated by stating the time taken to travel it.
It is <u>half an hour from the Pinewood Studios</u> and <u>forty-five minutes from London</u>.
They lived only <u>two or three days away from Juffure</u>.

The method of travelling can be stated to be more precise.
It is less than <u>an hour's drive from here</u>.
It's about <u>five minutes' walk from the bus stop</u>.

If you want to know the distance to a place, you use **how far**, usually with **from**, or with impersonal **it** and **to**.
<u>How far</u> is Chester <u>from here</u>?
<u>How far is it to</u> Charles City?

ⓘ Note that 'far' is not used when stating distances.

⇨ See **Usage** entry at **far**.

8 **distance and position**

To indicate both the distance and the position of something in relation to another place or object, the distance can be stated in front of the following prepositions:

above	below	inside	outside	underneath
across	beneath	into	over	up
along	beyond	off	past	
behind	down	out of	under	

He guessed that he was about <u>ten miles above the surface</u>.
Maurice was only <u>a few yards behind him</u>.

All the words in the list above, except 'across', 'into', 'over', and 'past', can be used as adverbs after the distance. The adverbs **apart**, **in**, **inland**, **offshore**, **on**, and **out** can also be used.
These two fossils had been lying about <u>50 feet apart</u> in the sand.

TOPICS

We were now <u>forty miles inland</u>.
<u>A few metres further on</u> were other unmistakable traces of disaster.

The distance can also be stated in front of phrases such as **north of**, **to the east of**, and **to the left**.

He was <u>some miles north of Ayr</u>.
The low crest <u>1,000 metres away to the east</u> was dimly visible.
The maker's name was engraved <u>a millimetre to the right of the '2'</u>.
It had exploded <u>100 yards to their right</u>.

9 **weight**

When you want to state how much an object or animal weighs, you use the verb **weigh**.

The statue <u>weighs</u> fifty or more kilos.
The calf <u>weighs</u> 50 lbs.

When you want to state how much a person weighs, you can use **weigh** or **be**. In Britain, you usually use the singular form **stone**.

He <u>weighs</u> about nine and a half <u>stone</u>.
You <u>'re</u> about ten and a half <u>stone</u>.

If you express weight using stones and pounds, you can leave out the word 'pounds'. For example, you can say that someone weighs **twelve stone four**.

(i) Note that you do not usually say '~~twelve stones four~~' or '~~twelve stone four pounds~~'.

You do not say '~~two pounds heavy~~', but you can say 'two pounds in weight'.
I put on nearly a stone <u>in weight</u>.

🌊 In the United States, all weights are normally expressed in **pounds** or **tons**. 'Stone' and 'hundredweight' are very rarely used.
Philip Swallow weighs about <u>140 pounds</u>.

🌊 Americans often omit the words 'hundred' and 'pounds' when talking about a person's weight.
I bet he weighs <u>one seventy</u>, at least.

When asking about the weight of something or someone, you can use **how much** and **weigh**.

<u>How much</u> does the whole thing <u>weigh</u>?

You can also use **how heavy**.

<u>How heavy</u> are they?

10 **temperature**

You express temperature using either degrees centigrade (often written **°C**), or degrees Fahrenheit (often written **°F**). In everyday language the metric term **centigrade** is used, whereas in scientific language **Celsius** is used to refer to the same scale of measurement.

The temperature was still <u>23 degrees centigrade</u>.
…about <u>30 degrees Celsius</u>.
It was <u>9°C</u>, and felt much colder.
The temperature was probably <u>50°F</u>.

If the scale is known, **degrees** can be used by itself.

It's <u>72 degrees</u> down here and we've had a dry week.

🌊 In cold weather, temperatures are often stated as **degrees below freezing** or **degrees below zero**. Note that in Britain **below zero** usually means below zero celsius, but in the US **below zero** means below zero farenheit, which is much colder.

…when the temperature is <u>fifteen degrees below freezing</u>.
It's amazingly cold: must be <u>twenty degrees below zero</u>.

11 **speed, rates, and ratios**

You talk about the speed of something by saying how far it travels in a particular unit of time. To do this, you use a noun such as **kilometre** or **mile**, followed by **per**, **a**, or **an**, and a noun referring to a length of time.

Wind speeds at the airport were 160 kilometres per hour.
He'd been driving at 10 miles an hour.

When writing about speeds, rates, or pressures, you can use the symbol '/' instead of 'per' between abbreviations for the units of measurement.

…a velocity of 160 km/sec.

Per, **a**, and **an** are also used when talking about other rates and ratios.

…a heart rate of 70 beats per minute.
He earns two rupees a day collecting rags and scrap paper.
A quarter of the annual rainfall comes in showers of sixty millimetres an hour.

Per can also be used in front of a word that does not refer to a length of time or a unit of measurement.

In Indonesia there are 18,100 people per doctor.
I think we have more paper per employee in this department than in any other.

ⓘ Note that **per head** or **a head** are often used instead of 'per person' or 'a person'.

The average cereal consumption per head per year in the U.S.A. is 900 kg.

You can also use **to the** when you are talking about rates and ratios.

The exchange rate would soon be $2 to the pound.
Those German Fords got forty-three miles to the gallon.

12 **measurements used as modifiers and qualifiers**

Expressions indicating size, area, volume, distance, and weight can be used as modifiers in front of a noun.

…a 5 foot 9 inch bed.
15 cm x 10 cm posts would be ideal.
…a 2-litre engine.
…a 20-mile journey that took two-and-a-half hours.
The 4,700 pound bomb was dropped on a single target.

ⓘ Note that you can use adjectives like **long** and **high**.

If the expression consists simply of a number and a measurement noun, it is often hyphenated.

…a five-pound bag of lentils.
We finished our 500-mile journey at 4.30 p.m. on the 25th September.

⚠ **WARNING:** The measurement noun is singular, not plural, even though it comes after a number. For example, you do not say 'a ten-miles walk'. You say **a ten-mile walk**. However, the plural form is used in athletics, because the measurement is really the name of a race. For example, 'the 100 metres record' means 'the record for the 100 metres (race)'.

…winning the 100 metres breaststroke.

You can use measurement expressions, usually ending in an adjective or **in** phrase, after a noun.

There were seven main bedrooms and a sitting-room fifty feet long.
…a giant planet over 30,000 miles in diameter.

You can also indicate the area or weight of something using '-ing' forms such as **covering**, **measuring**, or **weighing**.

…a largish park covering 40,000 square feet.
…a square area measuring 900 metres on each side.
…an iron bar weighing fifteen pounds.

You can also indicate the area or volume of something using a phrase beginning with **of**.

TOPICS

...industrial units of less than 15,000 sq ft.
...an empire of 13 million square miles and 360 million people.
...vessels of 100 litres.

13 size of something abstract

If you want to indicate how great something abstract such as an area, speed, or increase is, you use **of**.

There were fires burning over a total area of about 600 square miles.
...speeds of nearly 100 mph.
...an increase of 10 per cent.

You can also sometimes use a modifier, for example when talking about percentages or salaries.

...a 71 per cent increase in earnings.
...his £ 25,000-a-year salary.

14 measurement nouns before 'of'

Measurement nouns are often used in front of **of** to refer to an amount of something which is a particular length, area, volume, or weight.

...20 yds of nylon.
Americans consume about 1.1 billion pounds of turkey and 81 million gallons of hard liquor at this time.

In addition to units of measurement, people often use **a half** by itself when referring to half a pint of a drink in a pub, and **a quarter** when referring to a quarter of a pound of something such as vegetables.

I'll have a half of lager.
A quarter of mushrooms, please.

⇨ For information on other ways of referring to amounts, see **Grammar** entry at **Quantity** and **Topic** entry **Pieces and amounts**.

Money

1 writing amounts of money	5 expressing a rate
2 saying amounts of money	6 expressing quantity by cost
3 asking and stating the cost of something	7 American currency
4 notes and coins	8 other currencies

British currency consists of **pounds** and **pence**. There are a hundred pence in a pound.

1 writing amounts of money

When you write amounts of money in figures, the pound symbol **£** is shown in front of the figures. For example, **two hundred pounds** is written as **£200**. **Million** is sometimes abbreviated to **m**, and **billion** to **bn**. **k** and **K** are sometimes used as abbreviations for **thousand** when people's salaries are being mentioned.

About £20m was invested in the effort.
...generating revenues of £6bn.
...Market Manager, £30K + bonus + car.

If an amount of money consists only of pence, you put the letter **p** after the figures. For example, **fifty pence** is written as **50p**.
If an amount of money consists of both pounds and pence, you write the pound symbol and separate the pounds and the pence with a full stop. You do not write 'p' after the pence. For example, **two pounds fifty pence** is written as **£2.50**.

2 saying amounts of money

When saying aloud an amount of money that consists only of pence, you say the word

pence or the letter **p** (pronounced like 'pea') after the number.
When saying aloud an amount of money that consists of pounds and pence, you do not usually say the word 'pence'. For example, you say **two pounds fifty**.

⚠️ **WARNING:** In conversation, people sometimes say **pound** not 'pounds'. For example, 'I get ten **pound** a week'. However, many people regard this as incorrect, so you should say **pounds**.

The words 'pounds' and 'pence' are often left out when it is clear which you are referring to.

At the moment they're paying £2 for their meal, and it costs us <u>three</u>.
'I've come to pay an account.' – 'All right then, fine, that's <u>four seventy-eight sixty</u> then, please.'

In very informal speech, **quid** is often used instead of 'pound' or 'pounds'.

'How much did you have to pay?' – 'Eight <u>quid</u> .'

3 **asking and stating the cost of something**
When you ask or state the cost of something, you use the verb **be**. You begin a question about cost with '**How much…**'.

How much <u>is</u> that?
The cheapest <u>is</u> about eight pounds.

You can also use the verb **cost**. This is slightly more formal.

How much will it <u>cost</u>?
They <u>cost</u> several hundred pounds.

You can mention the person buying something by adding a pronoun or other noun group after **cost**.

It would cost <u>me</u> around six hundred.

4 **notes and coins**
You use **notes** to refer to paper money. In British currency, there are notes worth five, ten, twenty, and fifty pounds.

You didn't have a five-pound <u>note,</u> did you?
Several paid on the spot in <u>notes.</u>

ⓘ Note that you do not say 'a~~five-pounds note~~'.

You use **coins** to refer to metal money. In British currency, there are coins worth one, two, five, ten, twenty, and fifty pence, one pound and two pounds.

You should make sure that you have a ready supply of <u>coins</u> for telephoning.

If you want to refer to a coin that is worth a particular amount, you usually use the word **piece**.

That fifty pence <u>piece</u> has been there all day.
The machine wouldn't take 10p <u>pieces.</u>

You can refer to coins that you have with you as **change**.

He rattled the loose <u>change</u> in his pocket.

5 **expressing a rate**
When you want to express the rate at which money is spent or received, you use **a** or **per** after the amount. **Per** is more formal.

He gets £180 <u>a week.</u>
Farmers spend more than half a billion pounds <u>per year</u> on pesticides.

Per annum is sometimes used instead of 'per year'.

…staff earning less than £11,500 <u>per annum.</u>

6 **expressing quantity by cost**
You can talk about a quantity of something by saying how much it costs using **worth of**.

You've got to buy <u>thousands of pounds worth of stamps</u> before you get a decent one.
He owns some <u>20 million pounds worth of property</u> in Mayfair.

TOPICS

7 American currency

American currency consists of **dollars** and **cents.** There are a hundred cents in a dollar. Americans use the word **bill** to refer to paper money. There are bills worth one, two, five, ten, twenty, fifty, and a hundred dollars. Bills larger than this are used only between banks.

Ellen put a five-dollar <u>bill</u> and three ones on the counter.

There are coins worth one, five, ten, twenty-five and fifty cents. These are often referred to by the special words **penny, nickel, dime, quarter,** and **half-dollar.**

I had just that - a dollar bill, a <u>quarter,</u> two <u>dimes</u> and a <u>nickel,</u> and three <u>pennies.</u>

In very informal speech, **buck** is often used instead of 'dollar'.

I got 500 <u>bucks</u> for it.

When writing amounts of money, you use the dollar symbol **$**, or **¢** for cents. For example, **two hundred dollars** is written as **$200**, **fifty cents** is written as **50¢**, and **two dollars fifty cents** is written as **$2.50**.

(i) Note that when saying aloud an amount of money that consists of dollars and cents, you do not usually say the word 'cents'. For example, you say **two dollars fifty** or simply **two fifty.**

8 other currencies

Many countries use the same units for their currencies. If you need to indicate which country's currency you are talking about, you use a nationality adjective.

…a contract worth 200 million <u>Canadian dollars.</u>
It cost me about thirteen hundred <u>Swiss francs.</u>

(i) Note that some currencies have some units in common, but also have some different units. For example, Britain uses **pounds** and **pence**, but Egypt uses **pounds** and **piastres.**

When talking about exchange rates, you say how many units of one currency there are **to the** other unit of currency.

The rate of exchange while I was there was 1.40 euros <u>to the</u> pound.

Names and titles

1	kinds of names	**8**	referring to a family
2	short forms	**9**	using a determiner with names
3	nicknames	**10**	titles
4	spelling	**11**	titles of relatives
5	initials	**12**	titles before 'of'
6	referring to someone	**13**	plurals of titles
7	referring to relatives	**14**	very formal titles

This entry gives basic information about names and titles, and explains how you use them when talking or writing about people.
You also use a person's name or title when you talk or write to them.

⇨ For information on using names and titles when talking to someone, see **Topic** entry at **Addressing someone.**

⇨ For information on using names and titles when writing to someone, see **Topic** entry at **Letter writing.**

1 kinds of names

People in English-speaking countries have a **first name,** (also called a **given name**) which is chosen by their parents, and a **surname,** (also called a **family name** or **last name**), which is the last name of their parents or one of their parents.

TOPICS

Many people also have a **middle name,** which is also chosen by their parents. This name is not generally used in full, but the initial (first letter) is sometimes given, especially in the United States.

…the assassination of John F. Kennedy.

Christians use the term **Christian name** to refer to the names they choose for their children. On official forms, the term **first name** or **forename** is used.

In the past, married women always used their husband's surname. Nowadays, some women continue to use their own surname after getting married.

2 short forms

People often use an informal and usually shorter form of someone's first name, especially in conversation. Many names have traditional short forms. For example, if someone's first name is **James**, people may call him **Jim** or **Jimmy**.

3 nicknames

Sometimes a person's friends invent a name for him or her, for example a name that describes them in some way, such as **Lofty** (meaning 'tall'). This kind of name is called a **nickname**.

4 spelling

People's names begin with a capital letter.

…John Bacon.
…Jenny.
…Smith.

In names beginning with **Mac**, **Mc**, or **O'**, the next letter is often a capital.

Elliott is the first athlete to be coached by <u>McDonald.</u>
…the author of the article, Mr Manus <u>O'Riordan.</u>

In Britain, some people's surnames consist of two names joined by a hyphen or written separately.

…John <u>Heath-Stubbs.</u>
…Ralph <u>Vaughan Williams.</u>

5 initials

Someone's **initials** are the capital letters that begin their first name, middle name, and surname, or just their first name and middle name. For example, if someone's full name is 'Elizabeth Margaret White', you can say that her initials are **EMW**, or that her surname is 'White' and her initials are **EM**. Sometimes a dot is put after each initial: **E.M.W.**

6 referring to someone

When you refer to someone, you use their first name if the person you are talking to knows who you mean.

<u>John</u> and I have discussed the situation.
Have you seen <u>Sarah</u>?

If you need to make it clear who you are referring to, or do not know them well, you usually use both their first name and their surname.

If <u>Matthew Davis</u> is unsatisfactory, I shall try <u>Sam Billings.</u>

You use their **title** and their surname if you do not know them as a friend and want to be polite. People also sometimes refer to people much older than themselves in this more polite way.

<u>Mr Nichols</u> can see you now.
We'd better not let <u>Mrs Townsend</u> know.

Information on **titles** is given later in this entry.

You do not generally use someone's title and full name in conversation. However, people are sometimes referred to in this way in broadcasting and formal writing.

TOPICS

An even more ambitious reading machine has been developed by <u>Professor Jonathan Allen</u> at the Massachusetts Institute of Technology.

In general, you only use someone's initials and surname in writing, not in conversation. However, some well-known people (especially writers) are known by their initials rather than their first name, for example **T.S. Eliot** and **J.G. Ballard**.
You refer to famous writers, composers, and artists using just their surname.
…the works of <u>Shakespeare.</u>

Other famous people are also sometimes referred to in this way. Men are more often referred to by their surnames than women.

7 **referring to relatives**
Nouns such as **father**, **mum**, **grandpa**, and **granny**, which refer to your parents or grandparents, are also used as names.
<u>Mum</u> will be pleased.
You can stay with <u>Grandma</u> and <u>Grandpa.</u>

8 **referring to a family**
You can refer to a family or a married couple with the same surname by using **the** and the plural form of that name.
…some friends of hers called <u>the Hochstadts.</u>

9 **using a determiner with names**
When you use a person's name, you usually use it without a determiner. However, in formal or business situations, you can put **a** in front of someone's name when you do not know them or have not heard of them before.
You don't know <u>a Mrs Burton-Cox,</u> do you?
Just over two years ago, <u>a Mr Peter Walker</u> agreed to buy a house from <u>a Mrs Dorothy Boyle.</u>

You can use a famous person's name with **another** in front of it to mean someone like that person.
He dreamed of becoming <u>another Joseph Conrad.</u>
What we need is <u>another Churchill.</u>

You can check that someone actually means a well-known person, or simply express surprise, using **the** /ðiː/ emphatically.
You actually met <u>the George Harrison?</u>

10 **titles**
A person's **title** shows their social status or job.
You use a person's title and surname, or their title, first name, and surname, as explained above. The titles that are most commonly used are **Mr** for a man, **Mrs** for a married woman, and **Miss** for an unmarried woman. **Ms** /məz/ or /mɪz/ can be used for both married and unmarried women. Many women prefer **Ms** to 'Mrs' or 'Miss', especially if they have married but not changed their surname, but some women, especially older women, do not like this title. The following titles are also used in front of someone's surname, or first name and surname:

Ambassador	Bishop	Doctor	Justice	Rabbi
Archbishop	Canon	Father	Nurse	Superintendent
Archdeacon	Cardinal	Governor	Police Constable	Viscount
Baron	Constable	Inspector	President	Viscountess
Baroness	Councillor	Judge	Professor	

<u>Inspector Flint</u> thinks I murdered her.
…representatives of <u>President Anatolijs Gorbunovs</u> of Latvia.

Titles indicating rank in the armed forces, such as **Captain** and **Sergeant**, are also used in front of someone's surname, or first name and surname.

TOPICS

General Haven-Hurst wanted to know what you planned to do.
…his nephew and heir, Colonel Richard Airey.

11 titles of relatives

The only words which are generally used in modern English in front of names when referring to relatives are **Uncle**, **Aunt**, **Auntie**, **Great Uncle**, and **Great Aunt**. You use them in front of the person's first name. People who have two living grandmothers or grandfathers may distinguish them by using a name after them.

…Aunt Jane.
She's named after my granny Kathryn.

Father is used as the title of a priest, **Brother** as the title of a monk, and **Mother** or **Sister** as the title of a nun, but these words are not used in front of the names of relatives.

Mother Teresa spent her life caring for the poor.
Sister Joseann is from a large Catholic family.

12 titles before 'of'

A title can sometimes be followed by **of** to show what place, organization, or part of an organization the person with the title has authority over.

…the President of the United States.
…the Prince of Wales.
…the Bishop of Birmingham.

The following titles can be used after **the** and in front of **of**:

Archbishop	Duchess	Governor	Mayoress	Queen
Bishop	Duke	King	President	
Chief Constable	Earl	Marchioness	Prime Minister	
Countess	Emperor	Marquis	Prince	
Dean	Empress	Mayor	Princess	

13 plurals of titles

You can use plurals of titles. However, they are rather formal, especially when used in front of a name rather than in front of 'of'.

…the Presidents of Colombia, Venezuela and Panama.
…Presidents Carter and Thompson.

⚠ **WARNING:** There is no plural of **Ms**. People hardly ever use the plural of **Mrs**. **Messrs**, the plural of **Mr**, and **Misses**, the plural of **Miss**, are used only in very formal English or in humorous writing and speech. **Misses** is usually preceded by **the**.

…your solicitors, Messrs Levy and McRae.
The Misses Seeley had signed the petition.

14 very formal titles

When you refer formally to someone important such as a king or queen, an ambassador, or a judge, you use a title consisting of a possessive determiner in front of a noun. For example, if you want to refer to the Queen, you can say **Her Majesty the Queen** or **Her Majesty**. The possessive determiner is usually spelled with a capital letter.

Her Majesty must do an enormous amount of travelling each year.
His Excellency is occupied.

TOPICS

Nationality words

1 basic forms	5 combining nationality adjectives
2 referring to a person	6 language
3 referring to the people	7 cities, regions, and states
4 country as modifier	

1 basic forms

When talking about people and things from a particular country, you use one of three types of words:

● an adjective indicating the country, such as **French** in **French wine**

● a noun referring to a person from the country, such as **Frenchman**

● a noun preceded by **the** which refers to all the people of the country, such as **the French**

In many cases, the word for a person who comes from a particular country is the same as the adjective, and the word for all the people of the country is the plural form of this. Here are some examples:

country	adjective	person	people
America	American	an American	the Americans
Australia	Australian	an Australian	the Australians
Belgium	Belgian	a Belgian	the Belgians
Canada	Canadian	a Canadian	the Canadians
Chile	Chilean	a Chilean	the Chileans
Germany	German	a German	the Germans
Greece	Greek	a Greek	the Greeks
India	Indian	an Indian	the Indians
Italy	Italian	an Italian	the Italians
Mexico	Mexican	a Mexican	the Mexicans
Norway	Norwegian	a Norwegian	the Norwegians
Pakistan	Pakistani	a Pakistani	the Pakistanis

All nationality adjectives that end in '**-an**' follow this pattern. All nationality adjectives that end in '**-ese**' also follow this pattern. However, the plural form of these words is the same as the singular form. For example:

country	adjective	person	people
China	Chinese	a Chinese	the Chinese
Portugal	Portuguese	a Portuguese	the Portuguese
Vietnam	Vietnamese	a Vietnamese	the Vietnamese

A form ending in '**-ese**' is in fact not commonly used to refer to one person. For example, people tend to say **a Portuguese man** or **a Portuguese woman** rather than 'a Portuguese'.

(i) Note that **Swiss** also follows this pattern.

There is a group of nationality words where the word for all the people of a country is the plural of the word for a person from that country, but the adjective is different. Here are some examples:

TOPICS

country	adjective	person	people
Czech Republic	Czech	a Czech	the Czechs
Denmark	Danish	a Dane	the Danes
Finland	Finnish	a Finn	the Finns
Iceland	Icelandic	an Icelander	the Icelanders
New Zealand	New Zealand	a New Zealander	the New Zealanders
Poland	Polish	a Pole	the Poles
Slovakia	Slovak	a Slovak	the Slovaks
Sweden	Swedish	a Swede	the Swedes
Turkey	Turkish	a Turk	the Turks

Another group of nationality words have a special word for the person who comes from the country, but the adjective and the word for the people are the same. Here are some examples:

country	adjective	person	people
Britain	British	a Briton	the British
England	English	an Englishman	the English
		an Englishwoman	
France	French	a Frenchman	the French
		a Frenchwoman	
Holland	Dutch	a Dutchman	the Dutch
		a Dutchwoman	
Ireland	Irish	an Irishman	the Irish
		an Irishwoman	
Spain	Spanish	a Spaniard	the Spanish
Wales	Welsh	a Welshman	the Welsh
		a Welshwoman	

Briton is used only in writing, and is not common in British English, but is the standard term for someone from the UK in American English.

The adjective relating to **Scotland** is usually **Scottish**. **Scotch** is old-fashioned. A person from Scotland is **a Scot**, **a Scotsman**, or **a Scotswoman**. You usually refer to all the people in Scotland as **the Scots**.

2 **referring to a person**

Instead of using a nationality noun to refer to a person from a particular country, you can use a nationality adjective followed by a noun such as **man**, **gentleman**, **woman**, or **lady**.

…*an Indian gentleman.*

…*a French lady.*

If someone uses a nationality noun in the singular, they are more likely to be referring to a man of a particular nationality than a woman. When people want to refer to a woman of a particular nationality, they tend to use a nationality adjective followed by a noun such as **woman** or **girl**.

He had married a Spanish girl.

An American woman in her sixties told me that this was her first trip abroad.

People usually use nationality adjectives rather than nouns after **be**. For example, you would say **He's Polish** rather than 'He's a Pole'.

Spike is American. You can tell from the accent.

Plural nationality nouns ending in '**-men**' sometimes refer to both men and women. Similarly, singular nouns ending in '**-man**' are sometimes used to refer in a general way to a person of a particular nationality.

…advice that has strongly antagonized many ordinary <u>Frenchmen.</u>

…if you're a <u>Frenchman</u> or a <u>German.</u>

3 referring to the people

When you are saying something about a nation, you use a plural form of the verb, even when the nationality word you are using does not end in '-s'.

The British <u>are</u> worried about the prospect of cheap imports.

You can use plural nouns ending in '**-s**' on their own to refer to the people of a particular country.

There is no way in which <u>Italians,</u> for example, can be prevented from entering Germany or France to seek jobs.

You can use a general determiner, a number, or an adjective in front of a plural noun to refer to some of the people of a particular country.

<u>Many Americans</u> assume that the British are stiff and formal.

There were <u>four Germans</u> with Dougal.

Increasing numbers of <u>young Swedes</u> choose to live together rather than to marry.

⚠ **WARNING:** You cannot use nationality words which do not end in '-s' like this. For example, you cannot say 'many French', 'four French', or 'young French'.

You can also use the name of a country to mean the people who belong to it or who are representing it officially. You use a singular form of a verb with it.

…the fact that <u>Britain has</u> been excluded from these talks.

American Indian tribes and nations usually use a single form for the adjective and noun. It can designate a person or group.

Was this man a <u>Navajo</u>?

Tourism has undermined the traditions of the <u>Hopi.</u>

…the lives and gatherings of the <u>Lakota</u> people.

4 country as modifier

If there is no adjective that indicates what country someone or something belongs to, you can use the name of the country as a modifier.

…the <u>New Zealand</u> government.

5 combining nationality adjectives

You can usually combine nationality adjectives by putting a hyphen between them when you want to indicate that something involves two countries.

…joint <u>German-American</u> tactical exercises.

…the <u>Italian-Swiss</u> border.

There are a few special adjectives which are only used in this sort of combination, in front of the hyphen.

- Anglo- (England or Britain)
- Euro- (Europe)
- Franco- (France)
- Indo- (India)
- Italo- (Italy)
- Russo- (Russia)
- Sino- (China)

… <u>Anglo-American</u> trade relations.

People with US citizenship but with origins in another country usually use a

TOPICS

hyphenated form to identify themselves.
… *German-Americans.*
a *Latvian-American* lawyer.

African American is used only for Americans whose ancestors were slaves, not for people who have come recently from Africa. It is not usually hyphenated when it is a noun or predicative adjective.

African Americans are the largest minority group in the United States.
Both men are African American.
She was the only African-American woman there.

A more specific term is used for more recent immigrants from Africa.
…an outspoken Egyptian-American professor of sociology.
Tyson had been scheduled to fight Nigerian American David Izon.

6 language
Many nationality adjectives can be used to refer to the language that is spoken in a particular country or that was originally spoken in a particular country.
She speaks French so well.
There's something written here in Greek.

7 cities, regions, and states
There are a number of nouns which are used to refer to a person from a particular city, region, or state.
…a 23-year-old New Yorker.
Perhaps Londoners have simply got used to it.
Captain Cook was a hard-headed Yorkshireman.
Their children are now indistinguishable from other Californians.

Similarly, there are a number of adjectives which show that a person or thing comes from or exists in a particular city or state.
…a Glaswegian accent.
…a Californian beach.

Numbers and fractions

1 numbers	**12** ordinals as modifiers
2 expressing numbers	**13** ordinals as pronouns
3 position	**14** fractions
4 agreement	**15** agreement of fractions
5 numbers as pronouns	**16** fractions as pronouns
6 numbers in compound adjectives	**17** decimals
7 'one'	**18** percentages
8 'zero'	**19** approximate numbers
9 Roman numerals	**20** minimum numbers
10 ordinal numbers	**21** maximum numbers
11 written forms	**22** indicating a range of numbers

TOPICS

1 numbers
The following table shows the names of numbers. These numbers are sometimes called **cardinal numbers.** You can see from the numbers in this table how to form all the other numbers.

0	zero, nought, nothing, oh	26	twenty-six
1	one	27	twenty-seven
2	two	28	twenty-eight
3	three	29	twenty-nine
4	four	30	thirty
5	five	40	forty
6	six	50	fifty
7	seven	60	sixty
8	eight	70	seventy
9	nine	80	eighty
10	ten	90	ninety
11	eleven	100	a hundred
12	twelve	101	a hundred and one
13	thirteen	110	a hundred and ten
14	fourteen	120	a hundred and twenty
15	fifteen	200	two hundred
16	sixteen	1000	a thousand
17	seventeen	1001	a thousand and one
18	eighteen	1010	a thousand and ten
19	nineteen	2000	two thousand
20	twenty	10,000	ten thousand
21	twenty-one	100,000	a hundred thousand
22	twenty-two	1,000,000	a million
23	twenty-three	2,000,000	two million
24	twenty-four	1,000,000,000	a billion
25	twenty-five		

In the past, British speakers used **billion** to mean a million million. However, nowadays they usually use it to mean a thousand million, like American speakers.

⚠ **WARNING:** When you use **hundred, thousand, million,** or **billion,** they remain singular even when the number in front of them is greater than one.

... _six hundred_ miles.

Most of the coral is some 2 million years old.

You do not use 'of' after these words when referring to an exact number. For example, you do not say 'five hundred of people'; you say 'five **hundred** people'.

⇨ For information on using these words to refer to less exact numbers, see the section on **approximate numbers** later in this entry.

Dozen is used in a similar way to these words. It is used to refer to twelve things.

⇨ See **Usage** entry at **dozen.**

2 expressing numbers

Numbers over 100 are generally written in figures. However, if you want to say them aloud, or want to write them in words rather than figures, you put **and** in front of the number expressed by the last two figures. For example, **203** is said or written as **two hundred and three** and **2840** is said or written as **two thousand, eight hundred and forty.**

Four hundred and eighteen men were killed and _a hundred and seventeen_ wounded.

'And' is usually omitted in American English.

... _one hundred fifty_ dollars.

If you want to say or write in words a number between 1000 and 1,000,000, there are various ways of doing it. For example, the number **1872** is usually said or written in words as **one thousand, eight hundred and seventy-two** when it is being used to refer to a quantity of things.

Four-figure numbers ending in 00 can also be said or written as a number of hundreds. For example, **1800** can be said or written as **eighteen hundred**.

If the number **1872** is being used to identify something, it is said as **one eight seven two**. You always say each figure separately like this with telephone numbers.

In British English, if a telephone number contains a double number, you use the word **double**. For example, **1882** is said as **one double eight two**. In American English, it is more common to repeat the number: **one eight eight two**'.

If you are mentioning the year **1872**, you usually say **eighteen seventy-two**.

⇨ See **Topic** entry at **Days and dates.**

When numbers over 9999 are written in figures, a comma is usually put after the fourth figure from the end, the seventh figure from the end, and so on, dividing the figures into groups of three, for example **15,000** or **1,982,000**. With numbers between 1000 and 9999, a comma is sometimes put after the first figure, for example **1,526**.

3 position

When you use a determiner and a number in front of a noun, you put the determiner in front of the number.

… _the three young men._

All three candidates are coming to Blackpool later this week.

When you put a number and an adjective in front of a noun, you usually put the number in front of the adjective.

… _two small children._

… _fifteen hundred local residents._

… _three beautiful young girls._

However, you can put a few adjectives such as **following** and **only** after numbers.

⇨ See the section on **specifying adjectives** in the **Grammar** entry at **Adjectives.**

4 agreement

When you use any number except 'one' in front of a noun, you use a plural noun and a plural verb.

…_a hundred years._

Seven guerrillas were wounded.

There were ten people there, all men.

However, when you are talking about an amount of money, a period of time, or a distance, speed, or weight, you usually use a singular verb.

Three hundred pounds is a lot of money.

Ten years is a long time.

90 miles an hour is much too fast.

5 numbers as pronouns

When it is clear what sort of thing you are referring to, you can use a number without a noun following it. Numbers can be used on their own or with a determiner.

They bought eight companies and sold off five.

These two are quite different.

You use **of** to indicate the group that a number of people or things belong to.

I saw four of these programmes.

All four of us wanted to get away from the Earl's Court area.

6 numbers in compound adjectives

Numbers can be used as part of **compound adjectives**. These adjectives are usually hyphenated.

He took out a five-dollar bill.

I wrote a five-page summary.

ⓘ Note that the noun remains singular even when the number is two or more and that compound adjectives formed like this cannot be used as complements. For example, you cannot say 'My essay is ~~five-hundred-word~~'. Instead you would probably say 'My essay is five hundred **words long**'.

7 'one'

One is used as a number in front of a noun to emphasize that there is only one thing or to show that you are being precise. It is also used when you are talking about a particular member of a group. **One** is followed by a singular noun and is used with a singular verb.

There was only <u>one</u> gate into the palace.
<u>One</u> member declared that he would never vote for such a proposal.

When no emphasis or precision is wanted, you use **a** instead.

<u>A</u> car came slowly up the road.

8 'zero'

The number 0 is not used in ordinary English to indicate that the number of things you are talking about is zero. Instead the determiner **no** or the pronoun **none** is used, or **any** is used with a negative.

She had <u>no</u> children.
Sixteen people were injured but luckily <u>none</u> were killed.
There <u>weren't any</u> seats.

⇨ See **Usage** entries at **no** and **none**.

There are several ways of expressing the number 0:

● as **zero**, when expressing some numerical values, for example temperatures, taxes, and interest rates

It was fourteen below <u>zero</u> when they woke up.
… <u>zero</u> tax liability.
…lending capital to their customers at low or <u>zero</u> rates of interest.

● as **nought**, when expressing some numerical values in British English. For example, 0.89 is said as **nought point eight nine**.

 American English uses **zero** for this kind of number.

x equals <u>nought.</u>
…linguistic development between the ages of <u>nought</u> and one.
…babies from ages <u>zero</u> to five years.

● as **nothing**, when talking informally about calculations

Subtract <u>nothing</u> from that and you get a line on the graph like that.
'What's the difference between this voltage and that voltage?' – 'Nothing .'

● like **oh** or the letter O, when reading out numbers figure by figure. For example, the telephone number **021 4620** is said as **oh two one, four six two oh**; and the decimal number **.089** is said as **point oh eight nine**.

● as **nil**, in sports scores and informal speech and writing.

 This word is not commonly used in American English, which uses **nothing** in sports scores and **zero** otherwise.

The England Women's XI beat them by one goal to <u>nil.</u>
It used to be a community of 700 souls. Now the population is precisely <u>nil.</u>
Harvard won thirty-six to <u>nothing.</u>

9 Roman numerals

In a few situations, numbers are expressed in Roman numerals. Roman numerals are in fact letters:

I = 1
V = 5

TOPICS

X = 10
L = 50
C = 100
M = 1000

These letters are used in combination to express all numbers. A smaller Roman numeral is subtracted from a larger one if put in front of it. It is added to a larger numeral if put after it. For example, **IV** is 4 and **VI** is 6.

Roman numerals are used after the name of a king or queen when other kings or queens have had the same name.

...*Queen Elizabeth II.*

This would be said as **Queen Elizabeth the Second**.

In American English, roman numerals are sometimes used after a man's name to show that he has the same name as his father or grandfather.

...*Marshall Field IV.*

This would be said as **Marshall Field the fourth**.

Roman numerals are often used to number chapters and sections of books, plays, or other pieces of writing.

Chapter IV: Summary and Conclusion.
...*stalking upstage as the curtain fell on Act I.*

Roman numerals are also sometimes used to express dates formally, for example at the end of films and television programmes. For example, **1992** can be written as **MCMXCII**.

10 ordinal numbers

If you want to identify or describe something by indicating where it comes in a series or sequence, you use an **ordinal number**.

Quietly they took their seats in the <u>first</u> three rows.
Flora's flat is on the <u>fourth</u> floor of this five-storey block.

The following table shows the ordinal numbers.

1st	first	26th	twenty-sixth
2nd	second	27th	twenty-seventh
3rd	third	28th	twenty-eighth
4th	fourth	29th	twenty-ninth
5th	fifth	30th	thirtieth
6th	sixth	31st	thirty-first
7th	seventh	40th	fortieth
8th	eighth	41st	forty-first
9th	ninth	50th	fiftieth
10th	tenth	51st	fifty-first
11th	eleventh	60th	sixtieth
12th	twelfth	61st	sixty-first
13th	thirteenth	70th	seventieth
14th	fourteenth	71st	seventy-first
15th	fifteenth	80th	eightieth
16th	sixteenth	81st	eighty-first
17th	seventeenth	90th	ninetieth
18th	eighteenth	91st	ninety-first
19th	nineteenth	100th	hundredth
20th	twentieth	101st	hundred and first
21st	twenty-first	200th	two hundredth
22nd	twenty-second	1000th	thousandth
23rd	twenty-third	1,000,000th	millionth
24th	twenty-fourth	1,000,000,000th	billionth
25th	twenty-fifth		

11 **written forms**

As shown in the table, ordinals can be written in abbreviated form, especially in dates.

He lost his job on January 7th.

Write to HPT, 2nd floor, 59 Picadilly, Manchester.

12 **ordinals as modifiers**

Ordinals are used in front of nouns, preceded by a determiner. They are not usually used as complements after link verbs like 'be'.

He took the lift to the sixteenth floor.

...on her twenty-first birthday.

They are used after verbs such as **come** or **finish** when giving the results of a race or competition.

An Italian came second.

He was third in the 100m and 200m.

Ordinals are included in the small group of adjectives that are put in front of cardinal numbers, not after them.

The first two years have been very successful.

Your second three minutes are up, caller.

13 **ordinals as pronouns**

When it is clear what sort of thing you are referring to, you can use an ordinal number without a noun following it. Note that you must use a determiner.

A second pheasant flew up. Then a third and a fourth.

There are two questions to be answered. The first is 'Who should do what?' The second is 'To whom should he be accountable?'

You use **of** to indicate the group that the person or thing belongs to.

This is the third of a series of programmes from the University of Sussex.

Tony was the second of four sons.

14 **fractions**

When you want to indicate how large a part of something is compared to the whole of it, you use a **fraction,** such as **a third** or **two fifths,** followed by **of** and a noun group referring to the whole thing. Most fractions are based on ordinal numbers. The exceptions are the words **half** (one of two equal parts) and **quarter** (one of four equal parts).

You can write a fraction in figures. For example, 'a half' can be written as $^1/_2$, 'a quarter' as $^1/_4$, 'three-quarters' as $^3/_4$, and 'two thirds' as $^2/_3$.

When referring to one part of something, you usually use **a.** You only use **one** in formal speech and writing or when you want to emphasize the amount.

This state produces a third of the nation's oil.

... one quarter of the total population.

Plural fractions are often written with a hyphen.

More than two-thirds of the globe's surface is water.

He was not due at the office for another three-quarters of an hour.

You can put an adjective in front of a fraction, after **the.**

... the southern half of England.

... the first two-thirds of this century.

When you use **a half** and **a quarter** in combination with whole numbers, they come in front of the plural noun you are using.

... one and a half acres of land.

... five and a quarter days.

However, if you are using **a** instead of the number 'one', the noun modified by **a** is singular and comes in front of the fraction word.

TOPICS

… *an acre and a half* of woodland.
… *a mile and a quarter* of motorway.

15 agreement of fractions

When you talk about part of a single thing, you use a singular form of a verb.

Half of our work is to design programmes.
Two fifths of the forest was removed.

However, when you talk about part of a group of things, you use a plural form of the verb.

Two fifths of the dwellings have more than six people per room.
A quarter of the students were seen individually.

16 fractions as pronouns

When it is clear who or what you are referring to, you can use fractions without 'of' and a noun group.

Most were women and about half were young with small children.
One fifth are appointed by the Regional Health Authority.

17 decimals

Decimals are a way of expressing fractions. For example, 0.5 is the same as ½ and 1.4 is the same as 1⅖.

…an increase of 16.4 per cent.
The library contains over 1.3 million books.

You say the dot as **point**. For example, **1.4** is said as **one point four**.

⚠ **WARNING:** You do not use a comma in decimal numbers in English.

Numbers which look like decimal numbers are used when referring to one of a number of sections, tables, or illustrations that are closely connected.

Domestic refuse can be dried and burnt to provide heat (see section 3.3).
The normal engineering drawing is quite unsuitable (figure 3.4).

18 percentages

Fractions are often given a special form as a number of hundredths. This type of fraction is called a **percentage**. For example, 'three hundredths', expressed as a percentage, is **three per cent**. This is often written as **3%**.

About 20 per cent of student accountants are women.
…interest at 10% per annum.

 In American English, 'per cent' is written as a single word **percent**.

In 1980, only 29 per cent of Americans were Republicans.

19 approximate numbers

You can refer to a large number imprecisely by using **several**, **a few**, or **a couple of** in front of **dozen**, **hundred**, **thousand**, **million**, or **billion**.

… several hundred people.
A few thousand cars have gone.

You can be even more imprecise, and emphasize how large the number is, by using **dozens**, **hundreds**, **thousands**, **millions**, or **billions**, followed by **of**.

That's going to take hundreds of years.
We travelled thousands of miles across Europe.

People often use plural forms when they are exaggerating.

I was meeting thousands of people.
Do you have to fill in hundreds of forms before you go?

The following expressions are used to indicate that a number is approximate and that the actual figure could be larger or smaller:

TOPICS

about	around	or so		roughly	something like
approximately	odd	or thereabouts		some	

You put **about**, **approximately**, **around**, **roughly**, **some**, and **something like** in front of a number.

About 85 students were there.
It costs roughly $10,000 a year to educate an undergraduate.
I found out where this man lived, and drove some four miles inland to see him.

ⓘ Note that this use of **some** is quite formal.

You put **odd**, **or so**, and **or thereabouts** after a number or the noun that follows a number.

… a hundred odd acres.
The car should be here in ten minutes or so.
Get the temperature to 30°C or thereabouts.

20 **minimum numbers**

The following expressions indicate that a number is a minimum figure and that the actual figure may be larger:

a minimum of	from	more than	over
at least	minimum	or more	plus

You put **a minimum of**, **from**, **more than**, and **over** in front of a number.

He needed a minimum of 26 Democratic votes.
…3 course dinner from £15.
…a school with more than 1300 pupils.
The British have been on the island for over a thousand years.

You put **or more**, **plus**, and **minimum** after a number or after the noun that follows a number.

…a choice of three or more possibilities.
This is the worst disaster I can remember in my 25 years plus as a police officer.
They should be getting £180 a week minimum.

Plus is sometimes written as the symbol '+', for example in job advertisements.

2+ years' experience of market research required.

You usually put **at least** in front of a number.

She had at least a dozen brandies.
It was a drop of at least two hundred feet.

However, this expression is sometimes put after a number or noun. This position is more emphatic.

I must have slept twelve hours at least.
He was fifty-five at least.

21 **maximum numbers**

The following expressions indicate that a number is a maximum figure and that the actual figure is or may be smaller:

almost	at the maximum	less than	no more than	under
a maximum of	at the most	maximum	or less	up to
at most	fewer than	nearly	or under	

You put **almost**, **a maximum of**, **fewer than**, **less than**, **nearly**, **no more than**, **under**, and **up to** in front of a number.

The company now supplies <u>almost 100</u> of Paris's restaurants.
We managed to finish the entire job in <u>under three</u> months.

You put **at the maximum, at most, at the most, maximum, or less**, and **or under** after a number or the noun that follows a number.

They might have IQs of 10, or <u>50 at the maximum.</u>
The area would yield only <u>200 pounds of rice or less.</u>

22 **indicating a range of numbers**

You can indicate a range of numbers using **between** and **and**, or **from** and **to**, or just **to**.

Most of the farms are <u>between four and five hundred</u> years old.
My hospital groups contain <u>from ten to twenty</u> patients.
…peasants owning <u>two to five</u> acres of land.

Anything is used in front of **between** and **from** to emphasize how great a range is.

An average rate of <u>anything between 25 and 60</u> per cent is usual.
It is a job that takes <u>anything from two to five</u> weeks.

A hyphen is used between two figures to indicate a range. It is said as **to**.

Allow to cool for <u>10–15</u> minutes.
In <u>1965–9,</u> people drank a little more, namely 6.0 litres of alcohol.
…the Tate Gallery (open <u>10 a.m.–6 p.m.,</u> Sundays, <u>2–6</u>).

When mentioning two numbers that follow each other in a range or sequence, you can use the symbol '/' (said aloud as **stroke** (mainly *BRIT*), **slash**, or **to**).

The top ten per cent of income earners gained 25.8 per cent of all earned income in <u>1975/6.</u>
Write for details to <u>41/42</u> Berners Street, London.

Offers

> | **1** offering something to someone | **5** less confident or firm offers |
> | **2** other ways of offering something | **6** offers to a customer |
> | **3** offering to help or do something | **7** replying to an offer |
> | **4** confident offers | |

1 **offering something to someone**

There are several ways of offering something to someone.

A polite way of offering something is to say '**Would you like…?**'

<u>Would you like</u> another biscuit or something?
I was just making myself some tea. <u>Would you like</u> some?

When talking to someone you know well, you can use the less polite form '**Do you want…?**'

<u>Do you want</u> a biscuit?
<u>Do you want</u> a coffee?

If you know the other person well, and you want to be persuasive, you can use the imperative form **have**.

<u>Have</u> some more tea.
<u>Have</u> a chocolate biscuit.

You can also use just a noun group, making it sound like a question.

'<u>Tea?</u>' – 'Yes, thanks.'
<u>Ginger biscuit?</u>

2 **other ways of offering something**

If what you are offering is not immediately available, you can say something like '**Can I get you something?**' or '**Let me get you something to eat**'.

TOPICS

Can I get you anything?
Sit down and let me get you a cup of tea or a drink or something.

If you want the other person to take what they need, you say '**Help yourself**'.

Help yourself to sugar.
'Do you suppose I could have a drink?' – 'Of course. You know where everything is. Help yourself.'

A casual, non-emphatic way of offering something is to say '**You can have…**' or, if appropriate, '**You can borrow…**'.

You can borrow my pen if you like.

(i) Note that a British person might say '**Fancy some coffee?**' or '**Fancy a biscuit?**' as a way of informally offering something.

3 offering to help or do something

If you want to offer to help someone or to do something for them, you say '**Shall I…?**' You can use this kind of question whether you are offering to do something immediately or at some time in the future.

Shall I fetch another doctor?
'What's the name?' – 'Khulaifi. Shall I spell that for you?'

4 confident offers

If you are fairly sure that the other person wants to have something done for them at that moment, you can say '**Let me…**'.

Let me buy you a drink.
Let me help.

If you want to make an offer in a firm but friendly way, you say '**I'll…**'.

Leave everything, I'll clean up.
Come on out with me. I'll buy you a beer.

5 less confident or firm offers

If you are not sure whether the other person wants you to do something, you can say '**Do you want me to…?**', '**Should I…?**' or, more politely, '**Would you like me to…?**' However, this can sound as if you are rather reluctant to do what you are offering to do.

Do you want me to check his records?
Should I go in?
Would you like me to read to you tonight?

You can also say '**Do you want…?**', '**Do you need…?**', or, more politely, '**Would you like…?**', followed by a noun referring to an action. Although you do not say directly that you are offering to do something, that is what you are implying.

Do you want a lift?
Are you all right, Alan? Need any help?

'**Can I…?**' is also sometimes used, by people who know each other slightly or have just met.

Can I give you a lift anywhere?

Another way of making an offer when you are not sure that it is necessary is to add '**…if you want**' or '**…if you like**' after using '**I'll…**' or '**I can…**'.

I'll drive it back if you want.
I can show it to you now if you like.

6 offers to a customer

Employees of a shop or company sometimes say '**Can I…**' or '**May I…**' when they are politely offering to help a customer on the phone or in person.

Flight information, can I help you?
Morgan Brown, Janine speaking, how may I help you?

7 replying to an offer

The usual way of accepting an offer is to say '**Yes, please**'. You can also say '**Thank you**' or, informally, '**Thanks**'.

'Shall I read to you?' – '*Yes, please.*'
'Have a cup of coffee.' – '*Thank you very much.*'
'You can take the jeep.' – '*Thanks.*'

If you want to show that you are very grateful for an offer, especially an unexpected one, you can say something like '**Oh, thank you, that would be great**' or '**That would be lovely**'. You can also say '**That's very kind of you**', which is more formal.

'Shall I run you a bath?' – '*Oh, yes, please! That would be lovely.*'
'I'll have a word with him and see if he can help.' – '*That's very kind of you.*'

The usual way of refusing an offer is to say '**No, thank you**' or, informally, '**No, thanks**'.

'Would you like some coffee?' – '*No, thank you.*'
'Do you want a biscuit?' – '*No, thanks.*'

You can also say things like '**No, I'm fine, thank you**', '**I'm all right, thanks**', or '**No, it's all right**'.

'Is the sun bothering you? Shall I pull the curtain?' – '*No, no, I'm fine, thank you.*'
'Do you want a lift?' – '*No, it's all right, thanks, I don't mind walking.*'

(*i*) Note that you do not refuse an offer by just saying '~~Thank you~~'.

If someone says they will do something for you, you can refuse their offer politely by saying '**Please don't bother**'.

'I'll get you some sheets.' – '*Please – don't bother.*'

Opinions

1	indicating type of opinion	**7**	indicating honesty
2	being cautious	**8**	indicating form of statement
3	indicating degree of certainty	**9**	explicitly labelling a thought
4	indicating that something is obvious	**10**	explicitly labelling a statement
5	emphasizing truth	**11**	drawing attention to what you are about to say
6	indicating personal opinion		

People often use expressions which show their attitude to what they are saying.
If you want to show how certain you are that what you are saying is true, you can use a **modal**.

⇨ See **Usage** entries at **can - could - be able to, might - may, must, shall - will**, and **should**.

There are many adverbs which are used to show your attitude to what you are saying. These adverbs, which are sometimes called **sentence adverbs**, are explained below. Most of them are usually put first in a clause. They can also come at the end of a clause, or within a clause.

1 **indicating type of opinion**
There are many sentence adverbs which you can use to indicate your opinion of the fact or event you are talking about, for example whether you think it is surprising or is a good thing or not. The following adverbs are commonly used in this way:

absurdly	incredibly	oddly	surprisingly
astonishingly	interestingly	of course	typically
characteristically	ironically	paradoxically	unbelievably
coincidentally	luckily	predictably	understandably
conveniently	mercifully	remarkably	unexpectedly
curiously	miraculously	sadly	unfortunately
fortunately	mysteriously	significantly	unhappily
happily	naturally	strangely	

TOPICS

Luckily, I had seen the play before so I knew what it was about.
It is fortunately not a bad bump, and Henry is only slightly hurt.

A small number of adverbs are often used in front of **enough**.

curiously	funnily	interestingly	oddly	strangely

Funnily enough, old people seem to love bingo.
Interestingly enough, this proportion has not increased.

You can show what you think of someone's action using one of the following adverbs:

bravely	cleverly	foolishly	kindly	wisely
carelessly	correctly	generously	rightly	wrongly

She very kindly arranged a beautiful lunch.
Paul Gayner is rightly famed for his menu for vegetarians.
Foolishly, we had said we would do the decorating.

(i) Note that these adverbs typically come after the subject or the first auxiliary of the clause. They can be put in other positions for emphasis.

2 being cautious

You can use one of the following adverbs and adjuncts to indicate that you are making a general, basic, or approximate statement:

all in all	basically	generally	overall
all things	broadly	in essence	ultimately
considered	by and large	in general	
altogether	essentially	on average	
as a rule	for the most part	on balance	
at a rough estimate	fundamentally	on the whole	

Basically, the more craters a surface has, the older it is.
I think on the whole we don't do too badly.

You can also use the expressions **broadly speaking**, **generally speaking**, and **roughly speaking**.

We are all, broadly speaking, middle class.
Roughly speaking, the problem appears to be confined to the tropics.

You can use one of the following adverbs and adjuncts to show that your statement is not completely true, or only true in some ways:

almost	so to speak
in a manner of speaking	to all intents and purposes
in a way	to some extent
in effect	up to a point
more or less	virtually
practically	

It was almost a relief when the race was over.
In a way I liked her better than Mark.
Rats eat practically anything.

(i) Note that **almost**, **practically**, and **virtually** are not used at the beginning of a clause, unless they relate to a subject beginning with a word like **all**, **any**, or **every**.
Practically all schools make pupils take examinations.

TOPICS

3 **indicating degree of certainty**

You can indicate how certain or definite you are about what you are saying by using one of the following adverbs and adjuncts. They are arranged from 'least certain' to 'most certain'.

- conceivably
- possibly
- perhaps, maybe
- hopefully
- probably
- presumably
- almost certainly
- no doubt, doubtless, undoubtedly
- definitely, surely

She is probably right.
Perhaps they looked in the wrong place.
He knew that under the surgeon's knife, he would surely die.

Maybe is normally used at the beginning of a sentence.
Maybe you ought to try a different approach.

Definitely is hardly ever used at the beginning of a sentence.
I'm definitely going to get in touch with these people.

You can imply that you do not have personal knowledge of something, or responsibility for it, by using **it seems that** or **it appears that**.
I'm so sorry. It seems that we're fully booked tonight.
It appears that he followed my advice.

You can also use the adverb **apparently**.
Apparently they had a row.

4 **indicating that something is obvious**

You can use the following adverbs and adjuncts to indicate that you think it is obvious that what you are saying is right:

clearly	naturally	obviously	of course	plainly

Obviously I can't do the whole lot myself.
Price, of course, is a critical factor.

You can also use expressions such as '**I need hardly say…**' and '**I need hardly tell you…**'.
I need hardly say that none of those involved saw fit to declare their latest acquisitions to the proper authorities.
I need hardly tell you what a delight it would be to serve under you again.
This, it need hardly be said, is a fantastic improvement.

5 **emphasizing truth**

You can emphasize the truth of your statement using the following adverbs and adjuncts:

actually	certainly	indeed	truly
believe me	honestly	really	

Sometimes we actually dared to penetrate their territory.
Believe me, if you get robbed, the best thing to do is forget about it.
I don't mind, honestly.

TOPICS

Eight years was <u>indeed</u> a short span of time.
I <u>really</u> am sorry.

(i) Note that you use **indeed** at the end of a clause only when you have used **very** in front of an adjective or adverb.

I think she is a <u>very stupid person indeed.</u>

⇨ See **Usage** entry at **indeed**.

You can use **exactly**, **just**, and **precisely** to emphasize the correctness of your statement.

They'd always treated her <u>exactly</u> as if she were their own daughter.
I know <u>just</u> how you feel.
It is <u>precisely</u> his sensitivity to injustice which is presented as a sick deviation.

6 indicating personal opinion

If you want to emphasize that you are expressing an opinion, you can use one of the following adverbs and adjuncts:

as far as I'm concerned	in my view
for my money (*informal*)	personally
in my opinion	to my mind

The city itself is brilliant. <u>For my money,</u> it's better than Manchester.
<u>In my opinion</u> it was probably a mistake.
There hasn't, <u>in my view,</u> been enough research done on mob violence.
<u>Personally,</u> I'm against capital punishment for murder.
She succeeded, <u>to my mind,</u> in living up to her legend.
<u>As far as I'm concerned,</u> it would be a moral duty.

7 indicating honesty

You can indicate that you are making an honest statement using **frankly** or **in all honesty**.

<u>Frankly,</u> the more I hear about him, the less I like him.
<u>In all honesty,</u> I would prefer Madison.

Another way of indicating this is to use **to be** followed by **frank**, **honest**, or **truthful**.

I don't really know, <u>to be honest.</u>
<u>To be perfectly honest,</u> he was a tiny bit frightened of them.
'How do you rate him as a photographer?' – 'Not particularly highly, <u>to be frank.</u>'

These types of adjuncts often act as a kind of warning or apology that you are going to say something rather impolite or controversial.

8 indicating form of statement

You can use **to put it** followed by an adverb to draw attention to the fact that you are making your statement in a particular way.

<u>To put it crudely,</u> all unions have got the responsibility of looking after their members.
Other social classes, <u>to put it simply,</u> are either not there or are only in process of formation.

You can use **to put it mildly** or **to say the least** to indicate that what you are saying is an understatement.

A majority of college students have, <u>to put it mildly,</u> misgivings about military service.
The history of these decisions is, <u>to say the least,</u> disquieting.

9 explicitly labelling a thought

You can use **I** with a verb which refers to having an opinion or belief to indicate how strongly you hold an opinion. If you just say **I think** or **I reckon**, this often has the effect of softening your statement and making it less definite. By using **I suppose**, you often imply that you are not really convinced about what you are saying. The following verbs are used like this:

TOPICS

agree	fancy	imagine	reckon	trust
assume	guess	presume	suppose	understand
believe	hope	realize	think	

A lot of that goes on, I imagine.
He was, I think, in his early sixties when I first encountered him.
I reckon you're right.
I suppose she could have shot the two of them, but I don't really see why.

You can use **I'm** with the following adjectives in a similar way.

certain	convinced	positive	sure

I'm sure he'll win.
I'm convinced that it is a viable way of teaching.
I'm quite certain they would have made a search and found him.

10 explicitly labelling a statement

You can explicitly indicate what kind of thing you are saying by using **I** and one of the following verbs:

acknowledge	confess	maintain	submit	warn
admit	contend	pledge	suggest	
assure	demand	predict	swear	
claim	deny	promise	tell	
concede	guarantee	propose	vow	

I admit there are problems about removing these safeguards.
It was all in order, I assure you.
I guarantee you'll like my work.

(i) Note that **I can't deny** and **I don't deny** are used much more often than **I deny**.

I can't deny that you're upsetting me.

People often use **say**, for example with modals, to show that they are thinking carefully about what they are saying, or to show that they are only giving a personal opinion.

I must say I have a good deal of sympathy with Dr Pyke.
All I can say is that it's extraordinary how similar they are.
What I'm really saying is, I'm delighted they've got it.
I would even go so far as to say that we are on the brink of a revolution.

Let me, **May I**, and **I would like** are used with various verbs to introduce explicitly a point or question.

Let me give you an example.
May I make one other point.
I would like to ask you one question.

11 drawing attention to what you are about to say

You can use a structure consisting of **the**, a noun (or adjective and noun), and **is** to classify what you are about to say, in a way that draws attention to it and shows that you think it is important. The nouns most commonly used in this structure are:

answer	point	rule	tragedy
conclusion	problem	solution	trouble
fact	question	thing	truth

The fact is they were probably right.

TOPICS

The point is, why should we let these people do this to us?
The only trouble is it's rather noisy.
Well, you see, the thing is she's gone away.
The crazy thing is, most of us were here with him on that day.

(*i*) Note that **that** can be used after **is**, unless the next clause is a question.

The important thing is that she's eating normally.
The problem is that the demand for health care is unlimited.

You can also use a clause beginning with **what** as the subject.

What's particularly impressive, though, is that they use electronics so well.
But what's happening is that each year our old machinery becomes less adequate.

Permission

There are several ways of asking, giving, and refusing permission.

1 asking permission

If you want to ask permission to do something, you can use '**Can I…?**' or '**Could I…?**' (You use **we** instead of **I** if you are speaking on behalf of a group.) '**Could I…?**' is more polite.

Can I light the fire? I'm cold.
Could we put this fire on?
Could I stay at your place for a bit, Rob?

You can add **please** to be more polite.

David, can I look at your notes please?
Good afternoon. Could I speak to Mr Duff, please.
Could you ask for them to be taken out, please.

You can also make your request very polite by adding **perhaps** or **possibly** after '**Could I…**' or '**May I…**'.

Could I perhaps bring a friend with me?
May I possibly have a word with you?

You can ask permission in a stronger way by using **can't** or **couldn't** instead of **can** or **could**. You do this if you think you may not be given the permission you want.

Can't I come?
Couldn't we stay here?

Another way of requesting permission is to say '**Let me…**'. However, if you use a firm tone, this can sound like an order.

Oh, let me come with you.
Please let me do it, Cyril!

(*i*) Note that '**Let me…**' is also used as a way of offering to do something for someone.

Anne, let me drive you home. You don't look at all well.

⇨ See **Topic** entry at **Offers**.

2 indirect ways

There are other, more indirect, ways of asking for permission to do something. You can use expressions such as '**Would it be all right if I…?**' and, more informally, '**Is it okay if I…?**'

Would it be all right if I used your phone?
Is it all right if I go to the bathroom?
Is it okay if I go home now?

In very informal situations, these expressions are often shortened so that they start with the adjective. This sounds more casual, as if you are assuming the other person will give their permission.

Okay if I smoke?

TOPICS

An even more indirect way is to say something like '**Would it be all right to…?**', using a 'to'-infinitive.

Would it be all right to take this?

A more polite way is to say '**Do you mind if I…?**' or '**Would you mind if I…?**'
Do you mind if we speak a bit of German?
Would you mind if I just ask you some routine questions?

Again, these expressions are shortened in very informal situations.
Mind if I bring my bike in?

You can also say '**I was wondering if I could…**' or '**I wonder if I could…**'.
I was wondering if I could go home now.
I wonder if I could have a few words with you.

(i) Note that, in formal situations, you can add **if I may** after stating your intention to do something. You do this when you do not think it is really necessary to ask permission but want to appear polite.
I'll take a seat if I may.
Switching, if I may, from the Victorian novelist to more contemporary novelists, who do you think are the good novelists of today?

3 giving someone permission
There are many words and expressions that you can use to give someone permission to do something when they have just asked you for it.
In informal situations, you can say '**OK**' or '**All right**'.
'Could I have a word with him?' – 'OK.'
'I'll be back in a couple of minutes, okay?' – 'All right.'

'**Sure**' is slightly more emphatic, and is used especially by American speakers.
'Can I go with you?' – 'Sure.'

'**Of course**', '**Yes, do**', and '**By all means**' are more formal, and emphatic.
'Could I make a telephone call?' – 'Of course.'
'Do you mind if I look in your cupboard? There are some hot water bottles somewhere.' – 'Yes, do.'
'May I come too?' – 'By all means.'

If you are not very certain or enthusiastic about giving permission, you can say '**I don't see why not**'.
'Can I take it with me this afternoon?' – 'I don't see why not.'

You can give someone permission to do something when they have not asked for it by saying '**You can…**'. If you want to be more formal, you say '**You may…**'.
You can go off duty now.
You may use my wardrobe.

4 refusing permission
The commonest way of refusing someone permission is to use an expression such as '**Sorry**', '**I'm sorry**', or '**I'm afraid not**', and give an explanation.
'I was wondering if I could borrow a book for the evening.' – 'Sorry, I haven't got any with me.'
'Could I see him – just for a few minutes?' – 'No, I'm sorry, you can't. He's very ill.'
'I wonder if I might see him.' – 'I'm afraid not, sir. Mr Wilt is still helping us with our enquiries.'

If you know the other person very well, you can simply say '**No**' or '**No, you can't**', but this is impolite. In informal situations, people sometimes use even more impolite and emphatic expressions to refuse permission, such as '**No way**' and '**No chance**'.
You can indicate that you do not really want someone to do something by saying '**I'd rather you didn't**'. You say this when you cannot in fact prevent them from doing it.
'May I go on?' – 'I'd rather you didn't.'

In British English, you can refuse someone permission to do something when they have not asked for it by saying 'You can't...' or 'You mustn't...'.

You can't go.
You mustn't open it until you have it in the right place.

Note that speakers of American English do not usually use 'You mustn't...' and say 'Don't...' instead.

Don't eat all the cookies.

You can also use 'You're not...' and an '-ing' form. This is informal and emphatic.

You're not putting that thing on my boat.

Pieces and amounts

1 substances	**4** typical pieces and amounts
2 liquids	**5** measurements and containers
3 food	

There are many words which are used in front of **of** and an uncount noun to refer to a piece of something or a particular amount of something. The most common words are given here.

1 substances
Some words can be used to refer to a piece or amount of many kinds of substance:

atom	dollop	mound	roll	splinter
ball	flake	mountain	scrap	stick
bit	fragment	patch	sheet	strip
block	heap	particle	shred	trace
chunk	hunk	piece	slab	tuft
crumb	lump	pile	slice	wad
dab	mass	pinch	sliver	wedge
dash	molecule	ring	speck	wodge

Always kneel on a <u>bit</u> of sponge rubber.
...a big comforting soup, with <u>lumps</u> of bacon, and <u>chunks</u> of potato and cabbage.

2 liquids
Some words are used to refer to an amount of a liquid:

dash	drop	jet	puddle	spot
dribble	globule	pool	splash	trickle

Rub a <u>drop</u> of vinegar into the spot where you were stung.
One fireman was kneeling down in a great <u>pool</u> of oil.

3 food
Helping, portion, and **serving** are used when talking about the amount of a particular kind of food that you are given at a meal.

He had two <u>helpings</u> of ice-cream.
I chose a hefty <u>portion</u> of local salmon.

You can refer to a very small piece of food as a **morsel** of food.

He had a <u>morsel</u> of food caught between one tooth and another.

4 typical pieces and amounts
The following table shows you which word is typically used to refer to a piece or amount of something of a particular kind. Where more than one word is given, the meanings are often very different. Use a Cobuild dictionary if you are unsure of the differences.

TOPICS

bread	a loaf/slice of bread
butter	a knob (BRIT)/pat (AM) of butter
cake	a slice/piece of cake
chocolate	a bar/piece/square of chocolate
cloth	a bolt/length/piece of cloth
coal	a lump of coal
corn	an ear/sheaf of corn
dust	a speck/particle/cloud of dust
fog	a wisp/bank/patch of fog
glass	a sliver/splinter/pane of glass
grass	a blade of grass
hair	a lock/strand/wisp/tuft/mop/shock of hair
hay	a bale of hay
land	a piece/area of land
light	a ray/beam/shaft of light
medicine	a dose of medicine
money	a sum of money
paper	a piece/sheet/scrap of paper
rice	a grain of rice
rope	a coil/length/piece of rope
salt	a grain/pinch of salt
sand	a grain of sand
smoke	a cloud/blanket/column/puff/wisp of smoke
snow	a flake/blanket of snow
soap	a bar/cake of soap
stone	a slab/block of stone
string	a ball/piece/length of string
sugar	a grain/lump of sugar
sweat	a bead/drop/trickle of sweat
thread	a reel/strand of thread
wheat	a grain/sheaf of wheat
wire	a strand/piece/length of wire
wool	a ball of wool

5 **measurements and containers**

You can also refer to an amount of something using a measurement noun such as **pound** or **metre**, or a noun referring to a container such as **bottle** or **box**.

⇨ See **Topic** entry at **Measurements** and section on **containers** in **Grammar** entry at **Quantity.**

Places

1	asking about someone's home	8	qualifier use
2	place names	9	prepositions with parts and areas
3	modifier use	10	adverbs: position
4	adjuncts	11	adverbs: direction or destination
5	prepositions: position	12	qualifier use
6	prepositions: destination and	13	modifier use
7	direction	14	indefinite place adverbs

TOPICS

1 **asking about someone's home**

If you want to know where someone's home is, you say '**Where do you live?**' or
'**Whereabouts do you live?**'

'Where do you live?' – 'I have a little studio flat, in Chiswick.'
'I actually live near Chester.' – '<u>Whereabouts?</u>'

If you want to know where someone spent their early life, you can say '**What part of the
country are you from?**' You can also say, '**Where do you come from?**' or '**Where are you
from?**', especially if you think they spent their early life in a different country.

'Where do you come from?' – 'India.'

2 **place names**

Place names such as **Italy** and **Amsterdam** are a type of proper noun and are spelled
with a capital letter and are not preceded by an article.

The table on this page and the following page shows ways of referring to different types
of places. Those marked with a star are less common.

Continents	proper noun	Africa Asia
Areas and regions	**the** + proper noun	the Arctic the Midlands
	adjective + proper noun	Eastern Europe North London
	the + **North, South, East, West**	the East the South of France
Oceans, seas, deserts	**the** + modifier + **Ocean, Sea, Desert**	the Indian Ocean the Gobi Desert
	the + proper noun	the Pacific the Sahara
Countries	proper noun	France Italy
	****the** + type of country	the United States the United Kingdom the Netherlands
Counties and states	proper noun	Surrey California
	*proper noun + **County** (AM)	Butler County
Islands	proper noun	Malta
	proper noun + **Island**	Easter Island
	the Isle of + proper noun	the Isle of Wight
Groups of islands	**the** + modifier + **Islands**	the Channel Islands the Scilly Isles
	the + plural proper noun	the Bahamas
Mountains	**Mount** + proper noun	Mount Everest
	proper noun	Everest
	****the** + proper noun	the Matterhorn
Mountain ranges	**the** + plural proper noun	the Andes
	the + modifier + **Mountains**	the Rocky Mountains

TOPICS

Rivers	the + **River** + proper noun	the River Thames
	the + proper noun	the Thames
	*the + proper noun + **River** (not British)	the Colorado River
Lakes	**Lake** + proper noun	Lake Michigan
Capes	**Cape** + proper noun	Cape Horn
	*the + **Cape** + proper noun	the Cape of Good Hope
Other natural places	the + modifier + place noun	the Grand Canyon
	modifier + place noun	the Bering Strait
		Sherwood Forest
	the + place noun + **of** + proper noun	Beachy Head
		the Gulf of Mexico
		the Bay of Biscay
Towns	proper noun	London
Buildings and structures	proper noun + place noun	Durham Cathedral
		London Zoo
	the + modifier + place noun	the Severn Bridge
		the Tate Gallery
	the + place noun + **of** + proper noun/ noun	the Church of St. Mary
		the Museum of Modern Art
Cinemas, theatres, pubs, hotels	the + proper noun	the Odeon
		the Bull
Railway stations	proper noun	Paddington
	proper noun + **station**	Paddington Station
Streets	modifier + **Road**, **Street**, **Drive**, etc	Downing Street
	*the + proper noun	the Strand
	*the + modifier + **Street** or **Road**	the High Street

Most place names are used with a singular verb form. Even place names that look like plural nouns, for example **The United States** and **The Netherlands**, are used with a singular verb form.

Canada still has large natural forests.
Milan is the most interesting city in the world.
…when the United States was prospering.

However, the names of groups of islands or mountains are usually used with a plural verb form.

…one of the tiny Comoro Islands that lie in the Indian Ocean midway between Madagascar and Tanzania.
The Andes split the country down the middle.

TOPICS

The name of a country or its capital city is often used to refer to the government of that country.

Britain and France jointly suggested a plan.
Washington had put a great deal of pressure on Tokyo.

You can also sometimes use the name of a place to refer to the people who live there. You use a singular verb form even though you are talking about a group of people.

Europe was sick of war.
…to pay for additional imports that Poland needs.

⇨ For other ways of referring to the people of a country, see **Topic** entry at **Nationality words.**
Place names can also be used to refer to a well-known event that occurred in that place, such as a battle or a disaster.

After Waterloo, trade and industry surged again.
…the effect of Chernobyl on British agriculture.

3 **modifier use**
You can use a place name as a modifier to indicate that something is in a particular place, or that something comes from or is characteristic of a particular place.

…a London hotel.
She has a Midlands accent.

4 **adjuncts**
Many adjuncts – that is, prepositional phrases and adverbs – are used to talk about place.
⇨ For information on where to put these adverbs and adjuncts in a clause, see **Grammar** entry at **Adjuncts.**

5 **prepositions: position**
The main prepositions used to indicate position are **at**, **in**, and **on**.

Sometimes we went to concerts at the Albert Hall.
I am back in Rome.
We sat on the floor.

⇨ For more information, see **Usage** entries at **at**, **in**, and **on.**
⇨ See also **Usage** entry at **arrive - reach.**
⇨ For the difference in use between **by** and **near**, see **Usage** entry at **by.**

Here is a full list of prepositions which are used to indicate position:

aboard	among	between	near	past
about	around	beyond	near to	through
above	astride	by	next to	throughout
across	at	close by	off	under
against	away from	close to	on	underneath
ahead of	before	down	on top of	up
all over	behind	in	opposite	upon
along	below	in between	out of	with
alongside	beneath	in front of	outside	within
amidst (AM amid)	beside	inside	over	

6 **prepositions: destination and direction**
The main preposition used to indicate a destination is **to**.

I went to the door.
She went to Australia in 1970.

ⓘ Note that **at** is not usually used to indicate a person's destination. It is used to indicate what someone is looking towards, or what they cause an object to move towards.

They were staring at a garage roof.
Supporters threw petals at his car.

⇨ See also **Usage** entries at **into** and **onto**. See also **Usage** entry at **go into** for information on how to talk about entering vehicles.

Here is a full list of prepositions which are used to indicate where something goes:

aboard	at	by	near	past
about	away from	down	near to	round (AM around)
across	behind	from	off	through
ahead of	below	in	on	to
all over	beneath	in between	onto	towards (AM toward)
along	beside	in front of	out of	under
alongside	between	inside	outside	underneath
around	beyond	into	over	up

As you can see from the above lists, many prepositions can be used to indicate both place and direction.

The bank is just <u>across</u> the High Street.
I walked <u>across</u> the room.
We live in the house <u>over</u> the road.
I stole his keys and escaped <u>over</u> the wall.

7 **qualifier use**

Prepositional phrases are used after nouns as qualifiers to indicate the location of the thing or person referred to by the noun.

The table <u>in the kitchen</u> had a tablecloth over it.
The driver <u>behind me</u> began hooting.

8 **prepositions with parts and areas**

If you want to say explicitly which part of something else an object is nearest to, or exactly which part of an area it is in, you can use **at**, **by**, **in**, **near**, or **on**. **To** and **towards** (**toward** in American English), which are usually used to indicate direction, are used to express position in a more approximate way.

You use **at**, **near**, and **towards** with the following nouns:

back	centre	foot	side
base	edge	front	top
bottom	end	rear	

<u>At the bottom</u> of the stairs you will find a rough patch of mosaic paving.
The old building of University College is <u>near the top</u> of the street.
He was sitting <u>towards the rear.</u>

You can also use **to** with **rear** and **side**.

A company of infantry was swiftly redeployed in a stronger position <u>to the rear.</u>
There was one sprinkler in front of the statue and one <u>to the side</u> of it.

You use **on** or **to** with **left** and **right**, and **in** with **middle**. You can also use **on** instead of **at** with **edge**.

The church is <u>on the left</u> and the town hall and police station are <u>on the right.</u>
<u>To the left</u> were the kitchens and staff quarters.
My mother stood <u>in the middle</u> of the road, watching.
He lives <u>on the edge</u> of Sefton Park.

You use **to** or **in** with the following nouns:

east	south
north	south-east (AM southeast)
north-east (AM northeast)	south-west (AM southwest)
north-west (AM northwest)	west

TOPICS

To the south-west lay the city.
The National Liberation Front forces were still active in the north.

You use **at** or **by** with the following nouns:

bedside	lakeside	roadside
dockside	poolside	seaside
fireside	quayside	waterside
graveside	ringside	
kerbside (AM curbside)	riverside	

…sobbing bitterly at the graveside.
We found him sitting by the fireside.

(i) Note that you generally use **the** with the nouns in the three previous lists.
I ran inside and bounded up the stairs. Wendy was standing at the top.
To the north are the main gardens.

However, you can also use a possessive determiner with the nouns in the first list above (**back, base**, etc), and with **left, right,** and **bedside**.
We reached another cliff face, with trees and bushes growing at its base.
There was a gate on our left leading into a field.
I was at his bedside at the very last.

(i) Note that **in front of** and **on top of** are fixed phrases, without a determiner. They are compound prepositions.
She stood in front of the mirror.
I fell on top of him.

9 | **adverbs: position**

There are many adverbs which indicate position. Many of these indicate that something is near a place, object, or person that has already been mentioned.
Seagulls were circling overhead.
Nearby, there is another restaurant.
This information is summarized below.

Here is a list of the main adverbs which are used to indicate position:

aboard	below	here	offshore	throughout
about	beneath	in	opposite	underfoot
above	beside	in between	out of doors	underground
abroad	beyond	indoors	outdoors	underneath
ahead	close by	inland	outside	underwater
aloft	close to	inside	over	up
alongside	down	near	overhead	upstairs
ashore	downstairs	nearby	overseas	upstream
away	downstream	next door	round (AM around)	upwind
behind	downwind	off	there	

A small group of adverbs of position are used to indicate how wide an area something exists in:

globally	locally	nationally	widely
internationally	regionally	universally	worldwide

Everything we used was bought locally.
Western culture was not universally accepted.

Unlike most other adverbs of position, these adverbs (with the exception of **worldwide**) cannot be used after 'be' to state the position of something.
The adverbs **deep, far, high,** and **low,** which indicate distance as well as position, are

usually followed by another adverb or phrase indicating position, or are modified or qualified in some other way.

Many of the eggs remain buried <u>deep among the sand grains.</u>
One plane, flying <u>very low,</u> swept back and forth.

Deep down, **far away**, **high up**, and **low down** are often used instead of the adverbs on their own.

The window was <u>high up,</u> miles above the rocks.
Sita scraped a shallow cavity <u>low down</u> in the wall.

10 **adverbs: direction or destination**

There are also many adverbs which indicate direction or destination.

They went <u>downstairs</u> hand in hand.
Go <u>north</u> from Leicester Square up Wardour Street.
She walked <u>away.</u>

Here is a list of the main ones:

aboard	downtown	left	skyward
abroad	downwards	near	south
ahead	east	next door	southwards
along	eastwards	north	there
anti-clockwise (AM	forwards	northwards	underground
counterclockwise)	heavenward	on	up
around	here	onward	upstairs
ashore	home	out of doors	uptown
back	homeward	outdoors	upwards
backwards	in	outside	west
clockwise	indoors	overseas	westwards
close	inland	right	
down	inside	round (AM around)	
downstairs	inwards	sideways	

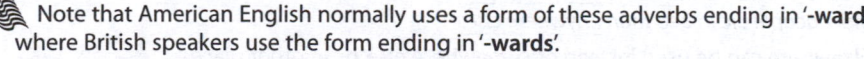 Note that American English normally uses a form of these adverbs ending in '**-ward**' where British speakers use the form ending in '**-wards**'.

You move <u>forward</u> and <u>backward</u> by leaning slightly in those directions.
We were drifting <u>backwards</u> and <u>forwards.</u>
Millions of people moved <u>westward</u> across the American continent.
The war in the North moved <u>westwards.</u>

11 **qualifier use**

Place adverbs can be used after nouns as qualifiers.

…a small stream that runs through the sand to the ocean <u>beyond.</u>
My suitcase had become damaged on the journey <u>home.</u>

12 **modifier use**

Some place adverbs can be used in front of nouns as modifiers.

Gradually the <u>underground</u> caverns fill up with deposits.
There will be some variations in your heart rate as you encounter <u>uphill</u> stretches or increase your pace on <u>downhill</u> sections.

The following place adverbs can be used as modifiers:

anti-clockwise (AM	downstairs	northward	underground
counterclockwise)	eastward	outside	underwater
backward	inland	overhead	uphill
clockwise	inside	overseas	upstairs
downhill	nearby	southward	westward

TOPICS

13 **indefinite place adverbs**

There are four indefinite adverbs of position and direction: **anywhere**, **everywhere**, **nowhere**, and **somewhere**.

In informal American English **someplace** and **anyplace** are also used, as well as **no place** and **every place**.

No-one can find Howard or Barbara anywhere.
There were bicycles everywhere.
I thought I'd seen you somewhere.
I suggested they stay someplace else.

⇨ For information on when to use **anywhere** and when to use **somewhere**, see **Usage** entry at **somewhere**.

Nowhere makes a clause negative.

I was to go nowhere without an escort.

In writing, you can put **nowhere** at the beginning of a clause for emphasis. You put the subject of the verb after an auxiliary or a form of **be**.

Nowhere have I seen any serious mention of this.
Nowhere are they overwhelmingly numerous.

ⓘ Note that you can put a 'to'-infinitive clause after **anywhere**, **somewhere**, or **nowhere** to indicate what you want to do in a place.

I couldn't find anywhere to put it.
We mentioned that we were looking for somewhere to live.
There was nowhere for us to go.

You can also put a relative clause after these adverbs. Note that you do not usually use a relative pronoun.

I could go anywhere I wanted.
Everywhere I went, people were angry or suspicious.

You can use **else** after an indefinite place adverb to indicate a different or additional place.

We could hold the meeting somewhere else.
More people die in bed than anywhere else.

Elsewhere can be used instead of 'somewhere else' or 'in other places'.

It was obvious that he would rather be elsewhere.
Elsewhere in the tropics, rainfall is notoriously variable and unreliable.

Possession and other relationships

1	something belonging to a person	**11**	person who controls something
2	quality possessed by a person	**12**	person or thing of a particular type
3	quality possessed by a thing	**13**	object made of a particular material
4	something associated with a thing	**14**	quantity of a substance
5	part of a person or animal	**15**	person with a particular job
6	part of a thing	**16**	something that lasts a particular time
7	action done by a person or thing		
8	something done to a person	**17**	other uses
9	something done to a thing		
10	person or thing from a particular place		

TOPICS

This entry explains how to show that something belongs to or is related to something else.

There are six basic ways of doing this:

- using a **possessive determiner** such as **my** or **their** in front of the main noun
- adding **apostrophe s** (**'s**) to the end of a noun and putting it in front of the main noun
- using the preposition **of** after the main noun
- using another **preposition** after the main noun
- using a **noun modifier** in front of the main noun
- using an **adjective** in front of the main noun

An apostrophe ('), not 's, is added to plural nouns ending in 's'.

⇨ See **Usage** entry at **'s** for more information.

A noun modifier is a noun that is used in front of another noun. It is nearly always singular.

⇨ See **Grammar** entry at **Noun modifiers**.

1 something belonging to a person

If you want to indicate who something belongs to or is associated with, you can use a possessive determiner. If you are using a short noun group to refer to the person, you add 's to the noun group and put it in front of the main noun. If you are using a long noun group, you put **of** in front of it and put it after the main noun.

… _his_ car.
… _her_ home.
… _Hogan's_ car.
… _a woman's_ voice.
… _Mr Heseltine's_ views.
…the son _of the chairman of Prudential Insurance._
…the dog _of the prosperous junk dealer next door._

2 quality possessed by a person

If you are referring to a quality possessed by a particular person or animal, you use a possessive determiner, **'s**, or **of**.

… _his_ bravery.
… _the woman's_ abruptness.
…the zeal and courage _of the workers._

3 quality possessed by a thing

If you are referring to a quality possessed by a particular thing, you use **of** or a possessive determiner. People sometimes also use **'s**.

…the efficiency _of the teaching processes._
…the speed _of the car travelling in front._
… _its_ speed.
… _the plane's_ speed.

4 something associated with a thing

If you want to indicate that something is associated with an object or with an abstract thing, you use **of** or a possessive determiner.

…the design _of the engine._
…the impact _of inflation._
… _its_ impact.

People sometime use **'s** when indicating association with an object.

… _the car's_ location.

5 part of a person or animal

If you are referring to part of a person or animal, you use a possessive determiner or **'s** with a short noun group, and **of** with a long noun group.

… _your_ leg.

TOPICS

… *a hummingbird's wings.*

…*the bare feet of the young girls.*

In the case of an animal, you can also use **of** with a short noun group beginning with **a**.

…*the wings of a humming-bird.*

6 part of a thing

If you are referring to part of a thing, you generally use **of**. You always use **of** with words like **top**, **middle**, and **end**.

…*the top of the hill.*

…*the leg of the chair.*

If you are referring to one of the parts that an object consists of, you can sometimes also use **'s** or a possessive determiner.

… *the car's engine.*

… *its doors.*

If the part is considered to be a type of thing, you use a noun modifier.

…*the kitchen floor.*

…*a car door.*

7 action done by a person or thing

If you are referring to an action done by a particular person or thing, you can use a possessive determiner or **'s**.

… *her death.*

… *Mr Lawson's resignation.*

… *the Government's refusal to increase its basic 6.5 per cent pay offer.*

You can also use **of** in front of a noun group referring to the person or thing that performs an action. This is done especially when the noun group is a long one.

…*the death of a prisoner last December.*

…*the arrival of powerful processing computers.*

…*the refusal of certain large grain suppliers to continue supplies until they are paid.*

You can also use **by** when mentioning an action that affects someone or something else.

…*the rejection of pay offers of up to 7.8 per cent by union leaders.*

…*the defeat of James II by William III.*

8 something done to a person

If you are referring to something that is done to a particular person, you use a possessive determiner or **'s**. You can also use **of**, especially for longer noun groups or when the agent is mentioned too.

… *his appointment as managing director.*

… *Agassi's last defeat.*

…*the murder of his colleague.*

…*England's defeat of the West Indies.*

Similarly, if you are referring to someone who does something to a person, or has a particular attitude towards them, you can use a possessive determiner, **'s**, or **of**.

… *their supporters.*

… *the Prime Minister's supporters.*

…*supporters of Dr Eames.*

(*i*) Note that if you are referring to a type of action or person that affects people of a particular kind, you use a noun modifier.

… *staff training.*

… *child abuse.*

… *child killers.*

9 something done to a thing

If you are referring to something that is done to a particular thing, you use **of**.

TOPICS

...*his handling of the economy.*
...*the introduction of new crops.*
...*the creation of a modern banking system.*

However, if you are referring to a person who does something to a particular thing, you can use a possessive determiner, **'s**, or **of**.

... *its owner.*
... *the vessel's owner.*
...*the owner of the house rented by the bombers.*

(*i*) Note that if you are referring to a type of action or person that affects things of a particular kind, you use a noun modifier.

... *crime prevention.*
... *home owners.*

However, you can also sometimes use **of**.

...*the prevention of accidents.*
...*owners of hotels and guest houses.*
...*lovers of poetry.*

10 **person or thing from a particular place**
If you want to indicate what place a particular person or thing comes from or is associated with:

● you add **'s** to general nouns like **city** and **country**
... *the country's roads.*
... *the city's population.*
... *the world's finest wines.*

● you use an adjective indicating a particular country (or occasionally a state or city)
...*an Australian film.*
... *Swiss climbers.*
...*a strong Glaswegian accent.*

● you use the name of a county or town (or occasionally country) as a noun modifier
...*a London hotel.*
...*a Yorkshire chemist.*
...*the New Zealand government.*

● you use a preposition such as **in** or **from**. **In** is used especially after a superlative has been used.
...*the largest department store in the world.*
...*students from Britain.*

11 **person who controls something**
If you want to indicate the country or organization that someone controls, you use **of**.
...*the President of Iceland.*
...*the head of the Secret Service.*

Reporters and broadcasters also use an adjective or noun modifier, or **'s**.
...*the Nicaraguan President.*
...*the CBI President.*
... *Lithuania's President.*

12 **person or thing of a particular type**
If you want to indicate what a type of thing or person is suitable for or connected with, you can use a noun modifier.
... *bedroom slippers.*
...*a milk bottle.*
... *car owners.*
... *man management.*

If an appropriate adjective exists, you can use that adjective, especially in formal or technical contexts.

... *industrial* output.

...a *political* analyst.

... *abdominal* wounds.

You may also be able to use an appropriate preposition.

...a degree *in Classics.*

...a book *on Chinese regional cookery.*

(i) Note that there are sometimes two ways of referring to something. For example, you can talk about **a heart attack** (using a noun modifier) or, in formal or medical contexts, **a cardiac arrest** (using an adjective). You can talk about **a History degree** (using a noun modifier) or **a degree in History** (using a preposition).

You use **'s** to indicate that a type of thing is suitable for or used by a type of person.

...a *man's* black suit.

...a *knight's* helmet.

When you are talking about a number of things that are suitable for a particular type of person, you usually make the noun with **'s** plural. For example, you talk about **children's shoes**, not 'child's shoes'.

... *men's* hats.

You also make the noun with **'s** plural when referring to a type of thing that is used by more than one person.

...a *men's* prison.

...a *children's* book.

You also use **'s** when referring to a type of thing that is produced by a type of animal. Note that whether you use a determiner or not depends on the main noun, not the noun with **'s**. For example, you do not need to use a determiner with an uncount noun such as **milk**.

...a *hen's* egg.

... *cow's* milk.

13 **object made of a particular material**

If you want to indicate what something is made of, you usually use a noun modifier. Sometimes there is an adjective you can use.

...a *plastic* bucket.

... *cotton* socks.

...a *wooden* spoon.

Of is used only in literary or old-fashioned writing.

...roofs *of iron.*

14 **quantity of a substance**

If you want to indicate how much of a substance there is, or what shape it is, you use **of**.

...a bottle *of milk.*

...a kilo *of fruit.*

...a drop *of blood.*

⇨ See also **Topic** entry at **Pieces and amounts** and **Grammar** entry at **Quantity**.

⚠ **WARNING:** When you want to refer to a full container, or to its contents, you must use **of**. For example, you would buy or eat **a packet of cereal**. When you want to refer just to a container, especially an empty one, you use a noun modifier, as in **a cereal packet**.

Occasionally, you can use a noun modifier with words indicating the shape of a quantity of a substance.

TOPICS

…a <u>wax</u> block.
…an <u>ice</u> cube.

15 person with a particular job

If you want to indicate what job someone does as well as the relationship they have with someone, you can use a noun modifier.

…her <u>soldier</u> husband.
…my <u>geologist</u> friend.

You can also put another noun group after the main noun and a comma.

…his friend, <u>a football player.</u>

16 something that lasts a particular time

If you want to indicate that something lasts a particular length of time, you use **'s** in front of uncount nouns and a noun modifier in front of count nouns. Note that the noun modifier is usually hyphenated.

… <u>two years'</u> imprisonment.
…a <u>two-year</u> course.

When you are talking about something that lasts one week, one month, or one year, you can use a noun modifier with **one**. You can also use **week-long**, **month-long**, or **year-long**, which emphasizes the length of time.

…a <u>one-year</u> contract.
…a <u>year-long</u> experiment.

If you are talking about an amount, you use **'s**.

… <u>a year's</u> supply of cat food.
… <u>a month's</u> salary.

17 other uses

Noun modifiers, **'s**, and **of** are also used to indicate the age, day, size, or time of something.

⇨ See **Topic** entries at **Days and dates, Measurements,** and **Time.**
⇨ See **Usage** entry at **of** for information on other uses of **of**.

Punctuation

1	full stop	10	brackets
2	question mark	11	square brackets
3	exclamation mark	12	apostrophe
4	comma	13	hyphen
5	optional comma	14	slash or stroke
6	no comma	15	direct speech
7	semi-colon	16	titles and quoted phrases
8	colon	17	italics
9	dash	18	other uses of punctuation

The first section of this entry deals with the punctuation of ordinary sentences.

⇨ For information on how to punctuate direct speech and how to mention titles and other words, see the sections on **direct speech** and **titles and quoted phrases** later in this entry.

1 full stop (.)

You start a sentence with a capital letter. You put a **full stop** at the end of a sentence, unless it is a question or an exclamation.

It's not your fault.
Cook the rice in salted water until just tender.

TOPICS

🏴 In American English, the punctuation mark (.) is called a **period.**

2 question mark (?)

If a sentence is a question, you put a **question mark** at the end.

Why did you do that?
Does any of this matter?
He's certain be be elected, isn't he?

ⓘ Note that you put a question mark at the end of a question, even if the words in the sentence are not in the normal question order.

You know he doesn't live here any longer?

People occasionally do not put a question mark at the end of a sentence in question form if, for example, it is really a request.

Would you please call my office and ask them to collect the car.

⚠ **WARNING:** You put a full stop, not a question mark, after a reported question or an indirect question.

He asked me where I was going.
I wonder what's happened.

3 exclamation mark (!)

If a sentence is an exclamation, that is, something said with strong emotion, you put an **exclamation mark** at the end. In informal writing, people also put an exclamation mark at the end of a sentence which they feel is exciting, surprising, or very interesting.

How awful!
What an aroma! It's tremendous!
Your family and children must always come first!
We actually heard her talking to them!

🏴 In American English, the punctuation mark (!) is called an **exclamation point.**

4 comma (,)

You must put a **comma**

● after or in front of a vocative

Jenny, I'm sorry.
Thank you, Adam.
Look, Jenny, can we just forget it?

● between items in a list, except ones separated by **and** or **or**

We ate fish, steaks and fruit.
The men hunted and fished, kept cattle and sheep, forged weapons and occasionally fought amongst themselves.
…educational courses in accountancy, science, maths or engineering.

ⓘ Note that when items are in a list, some writers also place a comma after the last item, before **and** or **or**.

…political, social, and ecomomic equality.

● between three or more descriptive adjectives in front of a noun, without **and**

…in a cool, light, insolent voice.
Eventually the galleries tapered to a long, narrow, twisting corridor.

● after a name or noun group, before a description or further information

…Carlos Barral, the Spanish publisher and writer.
…a broad-backed man, baldish, in a fawn coat and brown trousers.

● between the name of a place and the county, state, or country it is in. Note that a comma is usually put after the county, state, or country as well, unless it is at the end of a sentence.

She was born in Richmond, Surrey, in 1913.
There he met a young woman from Cincinnati, Ohio.

● after or in front of an adjective which is separate from the main part of the sentence, or after a separate participle

She nodded, speechless.
I left them abruptly, unwilling to let them have anything to do with my project.
Shaking, I crept downstairs.

● before a relative clause which does not specify someone or something

She wasn't like David, who cried about everything.
The only decent room is the living room, which is rather small.
He told us he was sleeping in the wood, which seemed to me a good idea.

● before a question tag

That's what you want, isn't it?
You've noticed, haven't you?

5 optional comma

You can put a comma, for emphasis or precision,

● after the first of two qualitative adjectives used in front of a noun

We had long, involved discussions.
...a tall, slim girl with long, straight hair.

(i) Note that **young, old,** and **little** do not usually have commas in front of them.

...a huge, silent young man.
...a sentimental old lady.
...a charming little town.

● after or in front of a word or group of words which adds something to the main part of the sentence. Note that if you put a comma in front of the word or group, you should also put one after it, unless it comes at the end of the sentence.

In 1880, John Benn founded a furniture design trades journal called 'The Cabinetmaker'.
Obviously, it is not always possible.
There are indeed stylistic links between my work and William Turnbull's, for instance.
They were, in many ways, very similar in character and outlook.
The ink, surprisingly, washed out easily.

(i) Note that long groups of words are usually separated with commas.

He is, with the possible exception of Robert de Niro, the greatest screen actor in the world.

A comma is put after or in front of an adverb or adjunct if its meaning is otherwise likely to be misunderstood.

'No,' she said, surprisingly.
Mothers, particularly, don't like it.

● in front of **and, or, but,** or **yet,** when giving a list or adding a clause

...a dress-designer, some musicians, and half a dozen artists.
...if you are prey to fear, stress, or anxiety.
This would allow the two countries to end hostilities, but neither of them seems in a mood to give way.
...remarks which shocked audiences, yet also enhanced her reputation as a woman of courage.

● after a subordinate clause

When the fish is cooked, strain off the liquid and add this to the flour and margarine.
Even if the boxer survives surgery, he may be disabled permanently.

TOPICS

Although the law of the land made education compulsory for all European children, François's father decided not to send him to school.

It is usually best to put a comma after a subordinate clause, although many people do not put commas after short subordinate clauses.

(*i*) Note that you do not normally put a comma in front of a subordinate clause, unless it contains something such as an afterthought, contrast, or exception.

Don't be afraid of asking for simple practical help when it is needed.
Switch that thing off if it annoys you.
The poor man was no threat to her any longer, if he ever really had been.
He was discharged from hospital, although he was homeless and had nowhere to go.

If you do put a comma in front of a clause, you should also put a comma after it if it does not come at the end of the sentence.

This is obviously one further incentive, if an incentive is needed, for anybody who needs to take slimming a little more seriously.

● in front of a participle which is separate from the main part of the sentence
Maurice followed, laughing.
Marcus stood up, muttering incoherently.

● after a noun being used in front of someone's name
…that marvellous singer, Jessye Norman.
She had married the gifted composer and writer, Paul Bowles.

6 no comma
You do not put a comma

● in front of **and**, **or**, **but**, and **yet** when these words are being used to link just two nouns, adjectives, or verbs
Eventually they had a lunch of <u>fruit and cheese.</u>
…when they are <u>tired or unhappy.</u>

● between a qualitative adjective and a classifying adjective, or between two classifying adjectives
…a <u>large Victorian</u> building.
…a <u>medieval French</u> poet.

● after the subject of a clause, even if it is long
<u>Even this part of the Government's plan for a better National Health Service</u> has its risks and potential complications.
Indeed, <u>the degree of backing for the principle of the community charge</u> surprised ministers.

● in front of a 'that'-clause or a reported question
His brother complained <u>that the office was not business-like.</u>
Georgina said <u>she was going to bed.</u>
She asked <u>why he was so silent all the time.</u>

● in front of a relative clause which specifies someone or something
I seem to be the only one <u>who can get close enough to him.</u>
Happiness is all <u>that matters.</u>
The country can now begin to fashion a foreign policy <u>which serves national interests.</u>

7 semi-colon (;)
The **semi-colon** is used

● in formal writing to separate clauses that are closely related and could be written as separate sentences, or that are linked by **and**, **or**, **but**, or **yet**.
I can see no remedy for this; one can't order him to do it.
He knew everything about me; I knew nothing about his recent life.

TOPICS

He cannot easily reverse direction and bring interest rates down; yet a failure to do so would almost certainly push the economy into recession.

● between items in a list, especially if the list items are phrases or clauses, or if they contain internal punctuation.

…when working with the things he seemed to like: their horse, Bonnie; the cart he brought the empty bottles home in; bits of old harness; tools and things.

8 colon (:)
The **colon** is used

● in front of a list or explanation

To be authentic these garments must be of natural materials: cotton, silk, wool and leather.
Nevertheless, the main problem remained: what should be done with the two murderers?

● between two main clauses that are connected, mainly in more formal writing
It made me feel claustrophobic: what, I wonder, would happen to someone who was really unable to tolerate being locked into such a tiny space?
Be patient: this particular cruise has not yet been advertised.

● after introductory headings
Cooking time: About 5 minutes.

● in front of the second part of a book title
…a volume entitled Farming and Wildlife: A Study in Compromise.

A colon is also sometimes used in front of quotes. See below at **direct speech.**

9 dash (–)
The **dash** is used

● in front of a list or explanation
The poor need simple things – building materials, clothing, household goods, and agricultural implements.
The Labour Government had just nationalised the basic industries – coal, rail and road transport.
…another of Man's most basic motives – commercialism.

● after and in front of a group of words or a clause which adds something to the main sentence but could be removed
Many species will take a wide variety of food – insects, eggs, nestlings and fruit – but others will only take the leaves of particular trees.
Number seventeen was – of all things – underground.

● in front of an adjunct, clause, or other group of words, for emphasis
I think Rothko was right – in theory and practice.
Let Tess help her – if she wants help.
I'm beginning to regret I ever made the offer – but I didn't seem to have much option at the time.
My family didn't even know about it – I didn't want anyone to know.
Mrs O'Shea, that's wonderful – really it is.

⚠ **WARNING:** Dashes are not used in very formal writing.

10 brackets ( )
Brackets, also called **parentheses,** are used after and in front of a word, group of words, or clause which adds something to the main sentence, or explains it, but could be removed.
This is a process which Hayek (a writer who came to rather different conclusions) also observed.

TOPICS

Normally he had the last word (at least in the early days).
A goat should give from three to six pints (1.7 to 3.4 litres) of milk a day.
This is more economical than providing heat and power separately (see section 3.2 below).

(*i*) Note that full stops, question marks, exclamation marks, and commas go after the second bracket, unless they apply only to the words in the brackets.

I ordered two coffees and an ice cream (for her).
We had sandwiches (pastrami on rye and so on), salami, coleslaw, fried chicken, and potato salad.
In the face of unbelievable odds (the least being a full-time job!) Gladys took the six-hour exam – and passed.

11 square brackets [ ]

Square brackets are used, usually in books and articles, when supplying words that make a quotation clearer or comment on it, although they were not originally said or written.

Mr Runcie concluded: 'The novel is at its strongest when describing the dignity of Cambridge [a slave] and the education of Emily [the daughter of an absentee landlord].'

12 apostrophe (')

You use an **apostrophe**

● in front of an **'s'** added to a noun or pronoun, or after a plural noun ending in **'s'**, to show a relationship such as possession.

…my friend's house.
… someone's house.
… friends' houses.

⇨ See **Usage** entry at **'s** and **Topic** entry at **Possession and other relationships.**

● in front of contracted forms of **be**, **have**, and modals, and between **'n'** and **'t'** in contracted forms with **not**.

I'm terribly sorry.
I can't see a thing.

⇨ See **Grammar** entry at **Contractions.**

● in front of **'s'** for the plurals of letters and, sometimes, numbers

Rod asked me what grades I got. I said airily, 'All A's, of course.'
There is a time in people's lives, usually in their 40's and 50's, when they find themselves benefiting from financial windfalls.

● in front of two figures referring to a year or decade

…souvenirs from the '68 campaign.
…the grim subject that obsessed him throughout the '60s and the early '70s.

An apostrophe sometimes indicates that letters are missing from a word. Often the word is never written in full in modern English. For example, **o'clock** has been reduced from 'of the clock', but it is never written in full.

She left here at eight o'clock this morning.
Martin had only recently recovered from a bout of 'flu.

Often people stop using an apostrophe at the beginning of a shortened word. For example, people nowadays usually write **phone**, not "phone'.

⚠ **WARNING:** You do not use an apostrophe in front of the 's' of a plural word like **apples** or **cars**. Also, you do not use an apostrophe in front of the 's' of the possessive pronouns **yours**, **hers**, **ours**, and **theirs**, or the possessive determiner **its**.

13 hyphen (-)

When you cannot fit the whole of a word at the end of a line, you can put part of the word and a **hyphen** on one line and the rest of the word on the next line. If the word is

TOPICS

clearly made up of two or more smaller words or elements, you put the hyphen after the first of these parts. For example, you would write **wheel-** on one line and **barrow** on the next, **inter-** on one line and **national** on the next, **listen-** on one line and **ing** on the next. Otherwise, you put the hyphen at the end of a syllable. For example, you could write **compli-** on one line and **mentary** on the next, and **infor-** on one line and **mation** on the next.

⚠ **WARNING:** It is best not to break a word if the word is a short one, or if it would mean writing just one or two letters at the end or beginning of a line. For example, it would be better to write **unnatural** on the next line rather than writing 'un-' on one line and 'natural' on the next.

If the word already has a hyphen, because it is a compound, put the second part of the word on the next line. For example, with **short-tempered** and **self-control**, you would put **tempered** and **control** on the next line.

⇨ For information on the use of the hyphen in compound words, see **Topic** entry at **Spelling**.

14 **slash or stroke (/)**
A **slash**, **stroke**, or **oblique** is used

● between two words or numbers that are alternatives
Write here, and/or on a card near your telephone, the number of the nearest hospital with a casualty ward.
…the London Hotels Information Service (telephone 629 5414/6).

● between two words describing something that is in fact two things, as in **a washer/drier** or **a clock/radio**
Each apartment includes a sizeable lounge/diner with colour TV.

A slash or stroke is also sometimes used to mark where a line of poetry ends when you are quoting part of a poem without putting each line on a separate line.
'Sweet and low, sweet and low,/Wind of the western sea.'

15 **direct speech (' ' or " ")**
You put **inverted commas**, also called **quotation marks** or **quotes,** at the beginning and end of direct speech. You start the direct speech with a capital letter.
'Thank you,' I said.
"What happened?"

🏴 Note that British writers use both single and double inverted commas (' ' and " "), but American writers tend to use double inverted commas (" ").

If you put something like **he said** after the direct speech, you put a comma in front of the second inverted comma, not a full stop. However, if the direct speech is a question or an exclamation, you put a question mark or an exclamation mark instead.
'We have to go home,' she told him.
'What are you doing?' Sarah asked.
'Of course it's awful!' shouted Clarissa.

If you then give another piece of direct speech said by the same person, you start it with a capital letter and put inverted commas round it.
'Yes, yes,' he replied. 'He'll be all right.'

If you put something like **he said** within a sentence in direct speech, you put a comma after the first piece of direct speech and after **he said**, and you start the continuation of the direct speech with inverted commas. Note that you do not give the first word of the continuation a capital letter, unless it would have one anyway.
'Frankly darling,' he murmured, 'it's none of your business.'
'Margaret,' I said to her, 'I'm so glad you came.'

TOPICS

If you put something like **he said** in front of the direct speech, you put a comma in front of the direct speech and a full stop, question mark, or exclamation mark at the end of it.

She added, 'But it's totally up to you.'
He smiled and asked, 'Are you her grandson?'

People sometimes put a colon in front of the direct speech, especially to indicate that what follows is important.

I said: 'Perhaps your father was right.'

A dash is used to indicate that someone who is speaking hesitates or is interrupted.

'Why don't I – ' He paused a moment, thinking.
'It's just that – circumstances are not quite right for you to come up just now.'
'Oliver, will you stop babbling and – ' 'Jennifer,' Mr Cavilleri interrupted, 'the man is a guest!'

A line of dots (usually three) is used to show that someone hesitates or pauses.

'I think they may come soon. I…' He hesitated, reluctant to add to her trouble.
'Mother was going to join us but she left it too late…'

(*i*) Note that sometimes what a person thinks is directly quoted in front of a comma or after it, rather than in inverted commas.

My goodness, I thought, Tony was right.
I thought, what an extraordinary childhood.

When you are writing a conversation, for example in a story, you start a new line for each new piece of direct speech.

⚠ **WARNING:** When the direct speech takes up more than one line, you do not put an opening inverted comma at the beginning of each line, only at the beginning of the direct speech. If you are giving more than one paragraph of direct speech, you put inverted commas at the beginning of each paragraph but not at the end of any paragraph except the last one.

16 titles and quoted phrases

When you are mentioning the title of a book, play, film, etc, you can put inverted commas round it, although people quite often do not, especially in informal writing. In books and articles, titles are often written without inverted commas, or in **italics** (sloping letters). The titles of newspapers, especially, are not usually written in inverted commas.

…Robin Cook's novel 'Coma'.
…Follett's most recent novel, Hornet Flight.

When you are mentioning a word, or quoting a few words that someone said, you put the word or words in inverted commas.

The Great Britain team manager later described the incident as 'unfortunate'.
Bragg says that all 'post-16 students' – she dislikes the term 'sixth-formers' – will follow a course of study designed to equip them with 'core skills'.
He has always claimed that the programme 'sets the agenda for the day'.

(*i*) Note that in British English you do not usually put the punctuation of your sentence within the inverted commas.

Mr Wilson described the price as 'fair'.
What do you mean by 'boyfriend'?

However, when people are quoting a whole sentence, they often put a full stop in front of the closing inverted comma, rather than after it.

You have a saying, 'Four more months and then the harvest.'

If they want to put a comma after the quote, the comma comes after the closing inverted comma.

The old saying, 'A teacher can learn from a student', happens to be literally true.

In American English, a full-stop or comma is put in front of the closing inverted comma, not after it.

The judge said the man had "richly earned a sentence of incarceration."
There was a time when people were divided roughly into children, "young persons," and adults.

If you are quoting someone who is also quoting, you need to use a second set of inverted commas. If you begin with a single inverted comma, you use double inverted commas for the second quote. If you begin with double inverted commas, you use single inverted commas for the second quote.

'What do they mean,' she demanded, 'by a "population problem"?'
"One of the reasons we wanted to make the programme," Raspiengeas explains, "is that the word 'hostage' had been used so often that it had lost any sense or meaning."

(*i*) Note that people sometimes put inverted commas round a word or expression which they think is inappropriate.

The chest of one fourteen-year-old was a mass of scar tissue where a 'friend' had jokingly poured petrol over him and set fire to it.

A line of dots (usually three) is used to show that you are giving an incomplete quotation, for example from a review.

'A creation of singular beauty…magnificent.' Washington Post.

17 italics

You will see **italics** (sloping letters) used in printed books and articles, for example to mention titles or foreign words, and emphasize or highlight other words. Italics are not used in this way in handwriting. When mentioning titles, use inverted commas, or have no special punctuation at all. When mentioning foreign words, use inverted commas. In informal writing, you can underline words to emphasize them.

18 other uses of punctuation

⇨ For the use of punctuation marks in writing abbreviations, dates, numbers, measurements, and times, see **Topic** entries at **Abbreviations, Days and dates, Numbers and fractions, Measurements,** and **Time.**

Reactions

1 exclamations	7 expressing relief
2 'how'	8 expressing annoyance
3 'what'	9 expressing disappointment or
4 exclamations in question form	distress
5 expressing surprise or interest	10 expressing sympathy
6 expressing pleasure	

There are several ways of expressing your reaction to something you have been told or something you see.

1 exclamations

You often use an **exclamation** to express your reaction to something. An exclamation may consist of a word, a group of words, or a clause.

Wonderful!
Oh dear!
That's awful!

In speech, you say an exclamation emphatically. When you write down an exclamation, you usually put an exclamation mark (!) at the end of it.

TOPICS

2 'how'

How and **what** are sometimes used to begin exclamations. **How** is normally used with an adjective and nothing else after it.

'They've got free hotels run by the state specially for tourists.' – *'How marvellous!'*
'There was no attempt made to set things out – they were just piled in the tomb higgledy-piggledy.' – *'How strange!'*

The use of **how** to begin a clause in an exclamation, as in **'How clever he is!'**, is now regarded as old-fashioned.

⇨ See **Usage** section on **commenting on a quality** in entry at **how**.

3 'what'

What is used in front of a noun group.

'I'd have loved to have gone.' – *'What a shame!'*
'…and then she died in poverty.' – *'Oh dear, what a tragic story.'*
What a marvellous idea!
What rubbish!

⚠ **WARNING:** You must use **what** and **a** (or **an**) if you are using a singular count noun. For example, you say **'What an** extraordinary experience!' You do not say 'What extraordinary experience!'

You can put a 'to'-infinitive such as **to say** or **to do** after the noun group, if it is appropriate.

'If music dies, we'll die.' – *'What an awful thing to say !'*
What a terrible thing to do!

4 exclamations in question form

You can express a reaction by using an exclamation in the form of a question beginning with **'Isn't that…'**.

'University teachers seem to me far bolder here than they are over there.' – *'Isn't that interesting.'*
'It's one they don't make any more.' – *'Oh, isn't that sad!'*
'It was a big week for me. I got a letter from Paris.' – *'Oh, isn't that nice!'*

A few common exclamations have the same form as positive questions.

Alan! Am I glad to see you!
Well, would you believe it. They got their motor fixed.
'How much?' – *'A hundred million.'* – *'Are you crazy?'*

5 expressing surprise or interest

You can express surprise or interest by saying **'Really?'** or **'What?'**, or by using a short fixed expression such as **'Good heavens'** or **'Good grief'**.

'It only takes 35 minutes from my house.' – *'Really? To Oxford Street?'*
'He's gone to borrow John Powell's gun.' – *'What?'*
Good heavens, is that the time?
'What's happened?' – *'Good grief! You mean you don't know anything about it?'*

'Good Lord', **'Goodness'**, **'My goodness'**, and **'Good gracious'** are rather old-fashioned expressions which are still used by some people.

My goodness, this is a difficult one.

'Good God' and **'My God'** are also used to express surprise or interest. However, you should not use them if you are with religious people who might be offended by them.

'I haven't set eyes on him for seven years.' – *'Good God.'*
My God, what are you doing here?

You can also express surprise or interest using a short question with the form of a question tag.

'He gets free meals.' – *'Does he?'*
'They're starting up a new arts centre there.' – *'Are they?'*
'I had a short story in Varsity last week.' – *'Did you? Good for you.'*

To express very great surprise, you can use a short statement that contradicts what you have just heard, although you do in fact believe it.

'I just left him there and went home.' – *'You didn't!'*

You can also express surprise, and perhaps annoyance, by repeating part of what has just been said, or checking that you have understood it.

'Could you please come to Ira's right now and help me out?' – *'Now? Tonight?'*
'We haven't found your man.' – *'You haven't?'*

You can also use **That's** or **How** with an adjective such as **strange** or **interesting** to express surprise or interest.

'Is it a special sort of brain?' – *'Probably.'* – *'Well, that's interesting.'*
'He said he hated the place.' – *'How strange! I wonder why.'*
'They sound somehow familiar.' – *'They do? How interesting.'*

You can say '**Strange**', '**Odd**', '**Funny**', '**Extraordinary**', or '**Interesting**' to express your reaction to something.

'You falsify your results?' – *'If necessary, yes.'* – *'Extraordinary.'*
'They both say they saw it.' – *'Mmm. Interesting.'*

You can also say '**What a surprise!**'

Tim! Why, what a surprise!
'Flick? How are you?' – *'Oh, Alan! What a surprise to hear you! Where are you?'*

In informal situations, you can use expressions such as '**No!**', '**You're joking!**', or '**I don't believe it!**' to show that you find what someone has said very surprising. '**You're kidding**' is a more informal way of saying '**You're joking**'.

'Gertrude's got a new boyfriend!' – *'No! Who is he?'* – *'Tim Reede!'* – *'You mean the little painter chap? You're joking!'*
You've never sold the house? I don't believe it!
'They'll be allowed to mess about with it.' – *'You're kidding!'*

In very informal English, some people use expressions like '**Bloody Hell!**' to express surprise. However, this may cause offence, and should be avoided.

Some people use expressions beginning with '**Fancy…**' and an '-ing' form to express surprise.

Fancy seeing you here!
Fancy choosing that!

6 **expressing pleasure**

You can show that you are pleased about a situation or about what someone has said by saying something like '**That's great**' or '**That's wonderful**', or just using the adjective.

'I've arranged the flights.' – *'Oh, that's great.'*
'Today we had the final signing. We can drink champagne morning, noon, and night for the rest of our lives.' – *'That's wonderful.'*
'We can give you an idea of what the prices are.' – *'Great.'*

You can also say things like '**How marvellous**' or '**How wonderful**'.

'I'll be able to stay for a week.' – *'How marvellous!'*
'I've just spent six months in Italy.' – *'How lovely!'*
Oh, Robert, how wonderful to see you.

However, you do not say '*How great*'.

You can also say things like '**Isn't that nice**' or '**Isn't that wonderful**'.

'The children always do the washing up. They love to.' – *'Well, isn't that nice.'*
'And he can see me?' – *'Perfectly.'* – *'Isn't that marvellous.'*

TOPICS

In a formal situation, you can say '**I'm glad to hear it**', '**I'm pleased to hear it**', or '**I'm delighted to hear it**' when someone tells you something.

'He saw me home, so I was well looked after.' – *'<u>I'm glad to hear it.</u>'*

(i) Note that these expressions are often used to indicate in a humorous way that you would have been annoyed if something had not been the case.

'I have a great deal of respect for you.' – *'<u>I'm delighted to hear it!</u>'*

You can also show that you are pleased about something by saying something like '**That is good news**' or '**That's wonderful news**'.

'My contract's been extended for a year.' – *'<u>That is good news.</u>'*

7 expressing relief

You can express relief when you are told something by saying '**Oh good**' or '**That's all right then**'.

'I think he will understand.' – *'<u>Oh good.</u>'*
'They're all right?' – *'They're perfect.'* – *'<u>Good, that's all right then.</u>'*

You can also say '**That's a relief**' or '**What a relief!**'

'He didn't seem to notice much.' – *'Well, <u>that's a relief,</u> I must say.'*
'It's nothing like as bad as that.' – *'<u>What a relief!</u>'*

When you are very relieved, you can say '**Thank God**', '**Thank goodness**', '**Thank God for that**', or '**Thank heavens for that**'.

'He's arrived safely in Moscow.' – *'<u>Thank God.</u>'*
<u>Thank God you're safe!</u>
'You've found all my treasures?' – *'They were in the trunk.'* – *'<u>Thank goodness.</u>'*
'I won't bore you with my views on smoking.' – *'<u>Thank heavens for that!</u>'*

In formal situations, you should say something like '**I'm relieved to hear it**'.

'Is that the truth?' – *'Yes.'* – *'<u>I am relieved to hear it!</u>'*
'I certainly did not support Captain Shays.' – *'<u>I am relieved to hear you say that.</u>'*

People sometimes use sounds rather than words to express relief. In writing, this is usually represented by the words **phew** (in British English) or **whew** (American English).

<u>Phew,</u> I'm glad that's sorted out.
<u>Whew,</u> what a relief!

8 expressing annoyance

You can express annoyance by saying '**Oh no**' or '**Bother**'. '**Bother**' is slightly old-fashioned.

'We're going to have one of those awful scrambles to get to the airport.' – *'<u>Oh no!</u>'*
<u>Bother.</u> I forgot to eat my sandwiches before I came here.

People often use swear words to express annoyance. **Blast, damn**, and **hell** are mild swear words used in this way. However, you should not use even these words when you are with people you do not know well. Words like **fuck** and **shit** are stronger swear words, and you should avoid using them, as they may cause offence.

<u>Damn.</u> It's nearly ten. I have to get down to the hospital.
'It's broken.' – *'<u>Oh, hell!</u>'*

Some people use words such as **sugar** or **flipping** in British English, and **darn, dang** or **shoot** in American English, to avoid using swear words in situations where they might cause offence.

I can't <u>flipping</u> believe it.
Oh <u>shoot,</u> I don't have a can opener.

You can also say '**What a nuisance**' or '**That's a nuisance**.'

He'd just gone. <u>What a nuisance!</u>

(i) Note that people often say things like '**Great**' or '**Oh, that's marvellous**' to express annoyance in a sarcastic way. Usually the way they say these things makes it clear that

they are annoyed, not pleased.

'I phoned up about it and they said it's a mistake.' – '*Marvellous.*'

9 **expressing disappointment or distress**

You can show that you are disappointed or upset at something by saying '**Oh dear**'.

'We haven't got any results for you yet.' – '*Oh dear.*'
Oh dear, I wonder what's happened.

You can also say '**That's a pity**', '**That's a shame**', '**What a pity**', or '**What a shame**'.

'They're going to demolish it.' – '*That's a shame. It's a nice place.*'
'Perhaps we might meet tomorrow?' – 'I have to leave Copenhagen tomorrow, I'm afraid.
What a pity!'
'Why, Ginny! I haven't seen you in years.' – 'I haven't been home much lately.' – '*What a shame.*'

People often just say '**Pity**'.

'Do you play the violin by any chance?' – 'No.' – '*Pity. We could have tried some duets.*'

You can also say '**That's too bad**'.

'We don't play that kind of music any more.' – '*That's too bad. David said you were terrific.*'

You can express great disappointment or distress by saying '**Oh no!**'

'Johnnie Frampton has had a nasty accident.' – '*Oh no! What happened?*'

10 **expressing sympathy**

When someone has just told you about something bad that has happened to them, you can express sympathy by saying '**Oh dear**'.

'First of all, it was pouring with rain.' – '*Oh dear.*'

You can also say things like '**How awful**' or '**How annoying**'.

'He's ill.' – '*How awful. So you aren't coming home?*'
'We couldn't even see the stage.' – 'Oh, *how annoying.*'
'We never did find the rest of it.' – 'Oh, *how dreadful!*'

You can also say '**What a pity**' or '**What a shame**'.

'It took four hours, there and back.' – 'Oh, *what a shame.*'

You can express sympathy more formally by saying '**I'm sorry to hear that**'.

'I was ill on Monday.' – 'Oh, *I'm sorry to hear that.*'
'I haven't heard from him for over a week.' – '*I'm sorry to hear that. Maybe he's away from his base and out of touch.*'

If what has happened is very serious, for example if a relative of the other person has died, you can express strong sympathy by saying '**I'm so sorry**' or, more informally, '**That's terrible**'.

'You remember Gracie, my sister? She died last autumn.' – 'Oh, *I'm so sorry.*'
'My wife's just been sacked.' – '*That's terrible.*'

If someone has failed to achieve something, you can say '**Bad luck**' or '**Hard luck**', which implies that the failure was not their fault. If they can make a second attempt, you can say '**Better luck next time**'.

'I've definitely missed out there.' – 'Oh, then *hard luck.*'
Well, there we are, we lost this time, but better luck next time.

Replies

This entry explains how to reply to 'yes/no'-questions and 'wh'-questions which are being used to ask for information.

⇨ Other ways of replying to things that people say are explained in the **Topic** entries at **Agreeing and disagreeing**; **Apologizing**; **Complimenting and congratulating someone**; **Greetings and goodbyes**; **Invitations**; **Offers**; **Requests, orders, and instructions**; **Suggestions**; and **Thanking someone**.

1 replying to 'yes/no'-questions

When you reply to a positive 'yes/no'-question, you say '**Yes**' if the situation referred to exists and '**No**' if the situation does not exist.

'*Did you enjoy it?*' – '*Yes, it was very good.*'
'*Have you tried Woolworth's?*' – '*Yes, I think we've tried them all.*'
'*Have you decided what to do?*' – '*Not yet, no.*'
'*Did he lose his job?*' – '*No. They sent him home.*'

You can add an appropriate tag such as **I have** or **it isn't**. Sometimes the tag is said first.

'*Are they very complicated?*' – '*Yes, they are. They have quite a number of elements.*'
'*Have you ever been hypnotised by anyone?*' – '*No, no I haven't.*'
'*Did you have a look at the shop when you were there?*' – '*I didn't, no.*'

Some speakers, particularly Irish and some Americans, answer with a tag question only, without using 'yes' or 'no'.

'*You do believe me?*' – '*I do.*'

Some people say '**Yeah**' /jeə/ instead of 'Yes' when speaking informally.

'*Have you got one?*' – '*Yeah.*'

People sometimes make the sound '**Mm**' instead of saying 'Yes'.

'*Is it very expensive?*' – '*Mm, it's quite pricey.*'

Sometimes you can answer a question with an adverb of degree.

'*Did she like it?*' – '*Oh, very much, said it was marvellous.*'
'*Has he talked to you?*' – '*A little. Not much.*'

If you feel a 'No' answer is not quite accurate, you can say **not really** or **not exactly** instead or as well.

'*Right, is that any clearer now?*' – '*Not really, no.*'
'*Have you thought at all about what you might do?*' – '*No, not really.*'
'*Has Davis suggested that?*' – '*Not exactly, but I think he'd be glad to get away.*'

If the question has **or** in it, you reply with a word or group of words that indicates what the situation is. You only use a whole clause for emphasis or if you want to make your answer really clear.

'*Do you want traveller's cheques or currency?*' – '*Traveller's cheques.*'
'*Are they undergraduate courses or postgraduate courses?*' – '*Mainly postgraduate.*'
'*Are cultured pearls synthetic or are they real pearls?*' – '*They are real pearls, but a tiny piece of mother-of-pearl has been inserted in each oyster.*'

Often when people ask a question, they do not want just a 'Yes' or 'No' answer; they want detailed information of some kind. In reply to questions like this, people sometimes do not say 'Yes' or 'No' but just give the information, often after **well**.

'*Do you have any plans yourself for any more research in this area?*' – '*Well, I hope to look more at mixed ability teaching.*'
'*Did you find any difficulties when you were interviewing people from the University?*' – '*Well, most of them are very articulate, and in fact the problem on occasions was actually shutting them up!*'

2 replying to negative 'yes/no'-questions

Negative 'yes/no'-questions are usually used when the speaker thinks the answer will be, or should be, 'Yes'.

You should reply to questions of this kind with '**Yes**' if the situation does exist and '**No**' if the situation does not exist, just as you would reply to a positive question. For example, if someone says '**Hasn't James phoned?**', you reply '**No**' if he hasn't phoned.

'*Haven't they just had a conference or something?*' – '*Yes.*'
'*Haven't you any socks or anything with you?*' – '*Well – oh, yes – in that suitcase.*'
'*Didn't he comment on your research, or your style, or anything?*' – '*No. He just called it good.*'
'*Didn't you like it, then?*' – '*Not much.*'

If you are replying to a negative statement which is said as a question, you reply '**No**' if the statement is true.

'*So you've never been guilty of physical violence?*' – '<u>No.</u>'
'*You didn't mind me coming in?*' – '<u>No,</u> *don't be daft.*'

If you are replying to a positive statement said as a question, you reply '**Yes**' if the statement is true.

'*He liked it?*' – '<u>Yes,</u> *he did.*'
'*You've heard me speak of Angela?*' – '*Oh,* <u>yes.</u>'

3 **replying when uncertain**

If you do not know the answer to a 'yes/no'-question, you say '**I don't know**' or '**I'm not sure**'.

'*Did they print the list?*' – '<u>I don't know.</u>'
'*Is there any chance of you getting away this summer?*' – '<u>I'm not sure.</u>'

You can also sometimes use **could**, **might**, or **may**.

'*Is it yours?*' – '*It <u>could</u> be.*'
'*Is there a file on me somewhere?*' – '*Well, there <u>might</u> be.*'
'*Did you drive down that road towards Egletons on Friday morning?*' – '*I <u>might</u> have done.*'

If you think the situation probably exists, you say '**I think so**'.

'*Do you understand?*' – '<u>I think so.</u>'
'*Will he be all right?*' – '*Yes,* <u>I think so.</u>'

American speakers often say '**I guess so**'.

'*Can we go inside?*' – '<u>I guess so.</u>'

If you are making a guess, you can also say '**I should think so**', '**I would think so**', '**I expect so**', or '**I imagine so**'.

'*Will Sarah be going?*' – '<u>I would think so,</u> *yes.*'
'*Did you say anything when I first came up to you?*' – '*Well,* <u>I expect so,</u> *but how on earth can I remember now?*'

If you are rather unenthusiastic or unhappy about the situation, you say '**I suppose so**'.

'*Are you on speaking terms with them now?*' – '<u>I suppose so.</u>'

If you think the situation probably does not exist, you say '**I don't think so**'.

'*Was there any paper in the safe?*' – '<u>I don't think so.</u>'
'*Did you ever meet Mr Innes?*' – '*No,* <u>I don't think so.</u>'

If you are making a guess, you can also say '**I shouldn't think so**', '**I wouldn't think so**', or '**I don't expect so**'.

'*Would Nick mind, do you think?*' – '*No,* <u>I shouldn't think so.</u>'
'*Is my skull fractured?*' – '<u>I shouldn't think so.</u>'

4 **replying to 'wh'-questions**

In replying to 'wh'-questions, people usually use one word or a group of words instead of a full sentence.

'*How old are you?*' – '<u>Thirteen.</u>'
'*How do you feel?*' – '<u>Strange.</u>'
'*What sort of iron did she get?*' – '<u>A steam iron.</u>'
'*Where are we going?*' – '<u>Up the coast.</u>'
'*Why did you run away?*' – '<u>Because Michael lied to me.</u>'

Sometimes, however, a full sentence is used, for example when giving the reason for something.

'*Why did you quarrel with your wife?*' – '<u>She disapproved of what I'm doing.</u>'

If you do not know the answer, you say '**I don't know**' or '**I'm not sure**'.

'*What shall we do?*' – '<u>I don't know.</u>'
'*How old were you then?*' – '<u>I'm not sure.</u>'

Requests, orders, and instructions

1	asking for something	**6**	signs and notices
2	asking as a customer	**7**	instructions on how to do
3	asking someone to do something		something
4	orders and instructions	**8**	replying to a request or order
5	emphatic orders		

When you make a **request,** you ask someone for something or ask them to do something. If you have authority over someone or know them well, you give them an **order** or an **instruction,** that is you tell them to do something rather than asking them to do something. You can also give someone **instructions** on how to do something or what to do in a particular situation.

⇨ For information on how to request permission to do something, see **Topic** entry at **Permission.**

Information on how to reply to a request or order is given at the end of this entry.

1 asking for something
The simplest way to ask for something is to say '**Can I have...?**' (You use **we** instead of **I** if you are speaking on behalf of a group.) You can add **please** in order to be more polite.

Can I have a light?
Can I have some tomatoes?
Can I have my hat back, please?
Can we have something to wipe our hands on, please?

It is more polite to use **could.**

Could I have another cup of coffee?

Requests with **may** sound very polite and formal, and requests with **might** sound old-fashioned.

May we have something to eat?

You use **can't** or **couldn't** instead of 'can' or 'could' to make a request sound more persuasive, if you think you may not get what you are asking for.

Can't we have some music?

You can use '**Have you got...?**', or '**You haven't got...**' and a question tag, to ask for something in an informal, indirect way.

Have you got a piece of paper or something I could write it on?
You haven't got that 20 pence, have you?

An indirect way of asking for something you think you might not get is to say '**Any chance of...?**' This is very informal and casual.

Any chance of a bit more cash in the New Year?

2 asking as a customer
If you want to ask for something in a shop, bar, café, or hotel, you can simply use a noun group followed by **please.**

A packet of crisps, please.
Scotch and water, please.

You can also say '**I'd like...**'.

As I'm here, doctor, I'd like a prescription for some aspirins.
I'd like a room, please. For one night.

If you are not sure whether a particular thing is available, you say '**Have you got...?**'. In American English, '**Do you have...?**' is used in the same way.

Have you got any brochures on Holland?
Do you have any information on that?

When you are in a restaurant or bar, you can say '**I'll have…**'. You can also say this when you are offered something to eat or drink in someone's house. You can also say '**I'd like…**'.

The waitress brought their drinks and said, 'Ready?' 'Yes,' said Ellen. 'I'll have the shrimp cocktail and the chicken.'
'Well, here at last, Mr Adamson! Now what'll you have?' – 'I'll have a glass of beer, thanks, Mr Crike.'
I'd like some tea.

3 asking someone to do something

You can ask someone to do something by saying '**Could you…?**' or '**Would you…?**' This is fairly polite. You can add **please** to be more polite.

Could you just switch the projector on behind you?
Could you make out our bill, please?
Could you tell me, please, what time the flight arrives?
Would you tell her that Adrian phoned?
Would you take the call for him, please?

You can make a request even more polite by adding **perhaps** or **possibly** after '**Could you**'.

Morris, could you possibly take me to the railroad station on your way to work this morning?

If you want to be very polite, you can say '**Do you think you could…?**' or '**I wonder if you could…?**'

Do you think you could help me?
I wonder if you could look after my cat for me while I'm away?

You can also use '**Would you mind…?**' and an '-ing' form.

Would you mind doing the washing up?
Would you mind waiting a moment?

In formal letters and speech, you use very polite expressions such as '**I would be grateful if…**', '**I would appreciate it if…**', or '**Would you kindly…**'.

I would be grateful if you could let me know.
I would appreciate it if you could do anything to bring all that happened into the open.
Would you kindly call to see us next Tuesday at eleven o'clock?

(i) Note that these very polite expressions are in fact sometimes used as indirect ways of telling someone to do something.

In informal situations, you can say '**Can you…?**' or '**Will you…?**'

Can you give us a hand?
Can you make me a copy of that?
Will you post this for me on your way to work?
Will you turn on the light, please, Henry?

If you think it is unlikely that the person you are asking will agree to your request, you use '**You wouldn't…would you?**', or '**You couldn't…could you?**' You also use these structures when you realize that you are asking them to do something which is difficult or will involve a lot of work.

You wouldn't sell it to me, would you?
You wouldn't lend me a bit of your greeny eyeshadow too, would you?
You couldn't give me a lift, could you?

You can also use '**I suppose you couldn't…**' or '**I don't suppose you would…**'.

I suppose you couldn't just stay an hour or two longer?
I don't suppose you'd be prepared to stay in Edinburgh?

People sometimes use expressions such as '**Would you do me a favour?**' and '**I wonder if**

TOPICS

you could do me a favour' to indicate that they are about to ask you to do something for them.

'Oh, Bill, I wonder if you could do me a favour.' – 'Depends what it is.' – 'Could you ring me at this number about eleven on Sunday morning?'

'I wonder if you'd do me a favour.' – 'Of course.' – 'In that bag there's something I'd like your opinion on.'

'Will you do me a favour?' – 'Depends.' – 'Be nice to him.'

'Do me a favour, Grace. Don't say anything about a shark to Sally.' – 'All right, Martin.'

4 orders and instructions

People often ask someone to do something, rather than telling them to do it, even when they have authority over them, because this is more polite. More direct ways of telling someone to do something are explained below.

In an informal situation, you can use an imperative clause. This is a direct and forceful way of giving an order.

Pass the salt.
Let me see it.
Don't touch that!
Hurry up!
Look out! There's a car coming.

(i) Note that it is not very polite to use imperative clauses like this in speech and you only commonly use them when talking to people you know well, or in situations of danger or urgency.

However, imperative forms are quite often used to invite someone to do something, in phrases such as '**Come in**' and '**Take a seat**'.

⇨ See **Topic** entry at **Invitations**.

You can use **please** to make orders more polite.

Go and get the file, please.
Wear rubber gloves, please.

You can use the question tag **will you?** to make an order sound less forceful and more like a request.

Come into the kitchen, will you?
Don't mention them, will you?

(i) Note that people also use **will you?** to make an order more forceful when they are angry.

⇨ See section below on **emphatic orders**.

You can also use the tag **won't you?** to make an order more like a request, unless you are giving a negative order.

See that she gets safely back, won't you?

You can say '**I would like you to…**' or '**I'd like you to…**' as an indirect, polite way of telling someone to do something, especially someone you have authority over.

John, I would like you to get us the files.
I'd like you to read this.
I shall be away tomorrow, so I'd like you to chair the weekly meeting.

5 emphatic orders

You use **do** in front of an imperative form to add emphasis when you are telling someone to do something that will be for their own benefit, or when you are friendly with them.

Do be careful.
Do remember to tell William about the change of plan.

You use '**You must…**' to emphasize the importance and necessity of the action.

You must come at once.
You mustn't tell anyone.

TOPICS

You can also use 'You have to…' or 'You can't…' for this usage, and these forms are preferred in American English.

You have to come and register now.
You can't tell anyone about this place.

You can also add emphasis to an order by putting **you** in front of an imperative form. However, this is very informal and sometimes shows impatience.

You take it.
You get in the car.

You use 'Will you…?' to give an order in a forceful and direct way, either to someone you have authority over or when you are angry or impatient.

Will you pack everything, please, Maria.
Will you stop yelling!

People also add the tag **will you?** to an imperative clause when they are angry.

Just listen to me a minute, will you?

People say 'Can't you…?' when they are very angry. This is very impolite.

Really, can't you show a bit more consideration?
Look, can't you shut up about it?
For God's sake, can't you leave me alone?

Adding the question tag **can't you?'** to an imperative clause is also impolite and shows annoyance.

Do it quietly, can't you?

People use 'You will…', with stress on **will**, to emphasize the fact that the other person has no choice but to carry out the order. This is a very strong form of order, and is only used by people who have unquestionable authority.

You will go and get one of your parents immediately.
You will give me those now.

6 **signs and notices**

On signs and notices, negative orders are sometimes expressed by **no** and an '-ing' form.

No Smoking.

Must be is sometimes used for positive orders.

Dogs must be kept on a lead at all times.

7 **instructions on how to do something**

You can use an imperative clause to give instructions on how to do something. This is not impolite.

Turn right off Broadway into Caxton Street.
In emergency, dial 999 for police, fire or ambulance.
Fry the chopped onion and pepper in the oil.

Imperative clauses are especially common in written instructions. Note that verbs which usually have an object are often not given an object in instructions, when it is clear what the instructions refer to. For example, you might see **Store in a dry place** on a packet of food, rather than 'Store this food in a dry place'. Similarly, determiners are often left out. You might read in a recipe **Peel and core apples** rather than 'Peel and core the apples'. **Must be** is used to indicate what you should do with something. **Should be** is used in a similar way, but is less strong.

Mussels must be bought fresh and cooked on the same day.
No cake should be stored before it is quite cold.

⇨ See **Topic** entry at **Advising someone.**

In conversation and informal writing, you can also use **you** and the simple present tense to give instructions. We use **you** like this in this book.

First you take a few raisins and soak them overnight in water.

TOPICS

You take an underblanket and put it on the bed, and you tuck in the four corners. And then
you take the sheet and lay it in the centre of the bed.
Note that in sentences like these *you use* an infinitive without 'to' after 'would rather'.

8 **replying to a request or order**
You can agree to someone's request informally by saying '**OK**', '**All right**', or '**Sure**'.

'Do them as fast as you can.' – 'Yes, OK.'
'Don't do that.' – 'All right, I won't.'
'Could you give me lift?' – 'Sure.'

If you want to be more polite, you can say '**Certainly**'.

'Could you make out my bill, please?' – 'Certainly, sir.'

You can refuse someone's request by saying something like '**I'm sorry, I'm afraid I can't**'
or by giving the reason why you are unable to do what they want.

'Put it on the bill.' – 'I'm afraid I can't do that.'
'Do me this favour. This once.' – 'I'm sorry, Larry, I can't.'
'Could you phone me back later?' – 'No, I'm going out in five minutes.'
'Could you do me a taxi from 1 Updale Close to the station?' – 'I'm afraid there's nothing
available at the moment.'

(*i*) Note that it is impolite just to say 'No'.

Spelling

1	short vowel or long vowel	**15**	'-oul' and '-ol'
2	doubling final consonants	**16**	'-re' and '-er'
3	omitting final 'e'	**17**	'ae' or 'oe' and 'e'
4	changing final 'y' to 'i'	**18**	'-ise' and '-ize'
5	'ie' or 'ei'	**19**	small groups
6	'-ically'	**20**	individual words
7	'-ful'	**21**	two words or one word
8	'-ible'	**22**	hyphens: compound nouns
9	'-able'	**23**	compound adjectives
10	'-ent' and '-ant'	**24**	compound verbs
11	silent consonants	**25**	phrasal verbs
12	difficult words	**26**	numbers
13	doubling consonants	**27**	other points
14	'-our' and '-or'		

Some spellings are explained in more detail at other entries in this book.
⇨ See **Topic** entries at **Abbreviations; Capital letters** and **Names and titles**, and **Grammar**
entries at **Comparative and superlative adjectives; Contractions; Irregular verbs; '-ly'**
words; Plural forms of nouns, and **Verbs**.
⇨ See also **Topic** entries at **Words with alternative spellings** and **Words with the same**
pronunciation.

1 **short vowel or long vowel**
If a one-syllable word has a short vowel, it usually does not have '**e**' at the end. The most
common exceptions to this rule are the words **have** and **give**. If it has a long vowel
represented by a single letter, the word usually does have an '**e**' at the end. For example:
/fæt/ is spelled **fat** and /feɪt/ is spelled **fate** /bɪt/ is spelled **bit** and /baɪt/ is spelled **bite**
/rɒd/ is spelled **rod** and /rəʊd/ is spelled **rode**.

TOPICS

2 doubling final consonants

If a one-syllable word ends in a single vowel and consonant, you double the final consonant before adding a suffix that begins with a vowel.

run – ru<u>nn</u>er
set – se<u>tt</u>ing
stop – sto<u>pp</u>ed
wet – we<u>tt</u>est

If the word has more than one syllable, you usually only double the final consonant if the final syllable is stressed.

admit – admi<u>tt</u>ed
begin – begi<u>nn</u>er
refer – refe<u>rr</u>ing
motor – m<u>o</u>toring
open – <u>o</u>pener
suffer – s<u>u</u>ffered

However, in British English, you double the final 'l' of verbs like **travel** and **quarrel**, even though the last syllable is not stressed.

travel – tr<u>a</u>velling
quarrel – qu<u>a</u>rrelled

In British English, and sometimes in American English, the final consonant of the following verbs is doubled, even though the last syllable is not stressed.

| hiccup | kidnap | program | worship |

(*i*) Note that the final 'p' of **handicap** is also doubled.

3 omitting final 'e'

If a final 'e' is silent, you omit it before adding a suffix beginning with a vowel.
bake – baked
blame – blaming
fame – famous
late – later
nice – nicest
secure – security

You do not omit the final 'e' of words like **courage** or **notice** when forming words like **courageous** /kəreɪdʒəs/ and **noticeable** /nəʊtɪsəbl/, because the 'e' indicates that the preceding 'g' is pronounced /dʒ/ and the preceding 'c' is pronounced /s/. Compare **analogous** /ənæləgəs/ and **practicable** /præktɪkəbl/. You sometimes omit the silent final 'e' in front of suffixes that begin with a consonant. For example **awful** is formed from **awe** and **truly** is formed from **true**. However, you do not always omit the 'e': **useful** is formed from **use**, and **surely** is formed from **sure**.

4 changing final 'y' to 'i'

If a word ends in a consonant and 'y', you usually change 'y' to 'i' before adding a suffix.
carry – carries
early – earlier
lovely – loveliest
try – tried

However, you do not change 'y' to 'i' when adding 'ing'.
carry – carrying
try – trying

You do not usually change the final 'y' of one-syllable adjectives like **dry** and **shy**.
dry – dryness
shy – shyly

TOPICS

5 'ie' or 'ei'

When the sound is /iː/, the spelling is often '**ie**'. Here is a list of the commonest words in which /iː/ is spelled '**ie**':

achieve	chief	niece	relieve	siege
belief	field	piece	reprieve	thief
believe	grief	priest	retrieve	wield
brief	grieve	relief	shield	yield

(*i*) Note that in **mischief** and **sieve** the '**ie**' is pronounced /ɪ/.

After '**c**', when the sound is /s/, the spelling is usually '**ei**'.

ceiling	conceive	deceive	receipt
conceit	deceit	perceive	receive

In some words, '**c**' is followed by '**ie**', but the sound of '**ie**' is not /iː/; for example, **efficient** /ɪfɪʃnt/, **science** /saɪəns/, and **financier** /fɪnænsɪə/.
In the following words '**ei**' is pronounced /eɪ/:

beige	feign	reign	veil	weight
deign	freight	rein	vein	
eight	neighbour	sleigh	weigh	

The '**ei**' in **either** and **neither** can be pronounced /aɪ/ or /iː/. Note also the pronunciation of '**ei**' in **height** /haɪt/, **foreign** /fɒrɪn/, and **sovereign** /sɒvrɪn/.

6 '-ically'

With adjectives ending in '**ic**', you add '**ally**' to form adverbs, for example, **artistically**, **automatically**, **democratically**, **specifically**, and **sympathetically**. You do not add '**ly**', although the '**ally**' ending is often pronounced like '**ly**'. However, **publicly** is an exception.
⇨ See **Grammar** entry at '**-ly**' words for full information on forming adverbs.

7 '-ful'

You form some adjectives by adding '**ful**' to a noun, for example, **careful, harmful, useful**, and **wonderful**. You do not add '**full**'.

6 '-ible'

Many adjectives end in '**ible**', but there is a fixed set of them, and new words are not formed by adding '**ible**'. Here is a list of the most common adjectives ending in '**ible**':

accessible	defensible	inadmissible	irrepressible	responsible
admissible	digestible	incorrigible	irresistible	reversible
audible	discernible	incorruptible	legible	sensible
collapsible	edible	indelible	negligible	susceptible
combustible	eligible	indestructible	ostensible	tangible
compatible	fallible	indivisible	perceptible	terrible
comprehensible	feasible	inexhaustible	permissible	visible
contemptible	flexible	inexpressible	plausible	
convertible	forcible	intelligible	possible	
credible	gullible	invincible	reducible	
crucible	horrible	irascible	reprehensible	

Negative forms are only included in the above list if the positive form is rarely used. You can add a negative prefix to many of the positive forms in the list, for example, **illegible, impossible, invisible, irresponsible**, and **unintelligible**.
⇨ See point 27 below.

TOPICS

9 '-able'

Many adjectives end in '**able**'. There is no fixed set of them, and new words are often formed by adding '**able**' to verbs. Here is a list of the most common adjectives ending in '**able**':

acceptable	desirable	miserable	respectable
available	fashionable	probable	suitable
capable	formidable	profitable	valuable
comfortable	inevitable	reasonable	
comparable	invaluable	reliable	
considerable	liable	remarkable	

You can add a negative prefix to most of the positive forms in the list, for example, **incapable** and **uncomfortable**.

⇨ See point 27 below.

10 '-ent' and '-ant'

You cannot usually tell from the sound of a word whether it ends in '**ent**' or '**ant**'. These are the commonest adjectives ending in '**ent**':

absent	different	intelligent	silent
confident	efficient	magnificent	sufficient
consistent	evident	patient	urgent
convenient	frequent	permanent	violent
current	independent	present	
decent	innocent	prominent	

These are the commonest adjectives ending in '**ant**':

abundant	expectant	militant	resistant
arrogant	extravagant	poignant	resonant
brilliant	exuberant	predominant	self-reliant
buoyant	fragrant	pregnant	significant
defiant	hesitant	radiant	tolerant
distant	ignorant	redundant	vacant
dominant	important	relevant	vigilant
elegant	intolerant	reluctant	

These are the commonest nouns ending in '**ent**':

accident	development	government	present
achievement	element	investment	president
agent	employment	management	punishment
agreement	environment	moment	statement
apartment	equipment	movement	student
argument	establishment	parent	treatment
department	excitement	parliament	unemployment

(*i*) Note that nouns referring to actions and processes, such as **assessment** and **improvement**, end in '**ment**', not '**mant**'.

These are the commonest nouns ending in '**ant**':

accountant	defendant	instant	participant	tenant
applicant	descendant	lieutenant	peasant	tyrant
attendant	giant	merchant	pheasant	
commandant	immigrant	migrant	protestant	
confidant	infant	occupant	sergeant	
consultant	informant	pageant	servant	

(i) Note that many of these words refer to people.

⇨ See also **Usage** entry at **currant - current**.

Adjectives ending in '**ent**' have related nouns ending in '**ence**' or '**ency**'. Here are some other common nouns ending in '**ence**' or '**ency**':

agency	consequence	essence	licence	science
audience	constituency	existence	preference	sentence
coincidence	currency	experience	presidency	sequence
conference	deterrence	incidence	reference	subsistence
conscience	emergency	influence	residence	tendency

Adjectives ending in '**ant**' have related nouns ending in '**ance**' or '**ancy**'. Here are some other common nouns ending in '**ance**' or '**ancy**':

acceptance	assistance	guidance	maintenance	tenancy
acquaintance	assurance	infancy	nuisance	
alliance	balance	inheritance	performance	
allowance	disturbance	instance	resemblance	
appearance	entrance	insurance	substance	

11 silent consonants

Many words are spelled with consonants that are not pronounced. Here are the main rules about silent consonants.

silent 'b' (followed by 't' in the same syllable)	debt doubt subtle	/dɛt/ /daʊt/ /sʌtl/
silent b (after 'm' at end of syllable)	bomb climb lamb	/bɒm/ /klaɪm/ /læm/
silent d	sandwich	/sænwɪdʒ/
silent g (in front of 'm' or 'n' at start/end of syllable)	foreign gnat phlegm sign	/fɒrɪn/ /næt/ /flɛm/ /saɪn/
silent h (at start of word)*	heir honest honour hour	/eə/ /ɒnɪst/ /ɒnə/ /aʊə/
silent h (after vowel at the end of word)	hurrah oh	/hərɑː/ /oʊ/
silent h (between vowels)	annihilate vehicle	/ənaɪəleɪt/ /viːɪkl/
silent h (after 'r')	rhythm rhubarb	/rɪðəm/ /ruːbɑːb/
silent k (at start of word followed by 'n')	knee know	/niː/ /nəʊ/
silent l (between 'a' and 'f', 'k', or 'm')	half talk palm	/hɑːf/ /tɔːk/ /pɑːm/

TOPICS

silent l (between 'ou' and 'd')	should would	/ʃʊd/ /wʊd/
silent n (at end of word, after 'm')	column hymn	/kɒləm/ /hɪm/
silent p (in front of 'n', 's', or 't' at start of words of Greek origin)	pneumatic psychology pterodactyl	/njuːmætɪk/ /saɪkɒlədʒi/ /terədæktɪl/
silent r (in standard British, when followed by a consonant or a silent 'e', or at the end of a word)**	farm more stir	/fɑːm/ /mɔː/ /stɜː/
silent s	island	/aɪlənd/
silent s (in many words of French origin)	debris viscount	/debri/ /vaɪkaʊnt/
silent t	listen thistle	/lɪsn/ /θɪsl/
silent t (at the end of words of French origin)	buffet chalet	/bʊfeɪ/ /ʃæleɪ/
silent w (at the start of words, in front of 'r')	wreck write	/rek/ /raɪt/
silent w	answer sword two	/ɑːnsə/ /sɔːd/ /tuː/

*For a list of these words, see **Usage** entry at **a - an.**

Note also the pronunciation of **iron /aɪən/.

12 difficult words

Many people find some words especially hard to spell. Here is a list of some common problem words:

accommodation	exceed	medicine	referred
acknowledge	February	necessary	science
across	fluorescent	occasion	secretary
address	foreign	occurred	separate
allege	gauge	parallel	skilful (AM skillful)
argument	government	parliament	succeed
awkward	harass	precede	supersede
beautiful	inoculate	privilege	surprise
bureau	instalment (AM	proceed	suspicious
bureaucracy	installment)	professor	threshold
calendar	language	pronunciation	tomorrow
cemetery	library	psychiatrist	vegetable
committee	manoeuvre (AM	pursue	vehicle
conscience	maneuver)	recommend	Wednesday
embarrass	mathematics	reference	withhold

13 doubling consonants

In American English, when you add a suffix to a two-syllable word whose final syllable is not stressed, you do not double the 'l'. For example, American English uses the spellings **traveling** and **marvelous**, whereas British English uses the spellings **travelling** and **marvellous**.

If the final syllable is stressed, the final consonant is doubled in both British and American English. For example, both use the spellings **admitting** and **admitted**.
A few verbs have a single consonant in the base form and '-s' form in British English, but a double consonant in American English. For example, British English uses the spellings **appal** and **appals**, but American English uses **appall** and **appalls**. Both British and American English use the spellings **appalling** and **appalled**.

appal	enrol	fulfil	instil
distil	enthral	instal	

ⓘ Note also the British spellings **skilful** and **wilful**, contrasted with the American spellings **skillful** and **willful**.

🇺🇸 Note that a few words have a double consonant in British English, and a single consonant in American English.
carburettor – carburetor
chilli – chili
jeweller – jeweler
jewellery – jewelry
programme – program
tranquillize – tranquilize
woollen – woolen

14 '-our' and '-or'

🇺🇸 Many words, mostly abstract nouns of Latin origin, have their ending spelled '**our**' in British English, but '**or**' in American English.
armour – armor
behaviour – behavior
colour – color
demeanour – demeanor
favour – favor
flavour – flavor
honour – honor
humour – humor
neighbour – neighbor
odour – odor
tumour – tumor
vapour – vapor

15 '-oul' and '-ol'

🇺🇸 Some words spelled with '**oul**' in British English are spelled with '**ol**' in American English.
mould – mold
moult – molt
smoulder – smolder

16 '-re' and '-er'

🇺🇸 Many words, mostly of French origin, have their ending spelled '**re**' in British English and '**er**' in American English.
calibre – caliber
centre – center
fibre – fibre
meagre – meager
reconnoitre – reconnoiter

TOPICS

sombre – somber
spectre – specter
theatre – theater

⇨ See also **Usage** entry at **metre - meter.**

17 'ae' or 'oe' and 'e'

Many words, mostly of Greek or Latin origin, are spelled with '**ae**' or '**oe**' in British English, but '**e**' in American English. However, the American spellings are now sometimes used in British English as well.

aesthetic – esthetic
amoeba – ameba
diarrhoea – diarrhea
gynaecology – gynecology
mediaeval – medieval

ⓘ Note that **manoeuvre** is spelled **maneuver** in American English.

18 '-ise' and '-ize'

Many verbs can end in either '**ise**' or '**ize**'. For example, **authorise** and **authorize** are alternative spellings of the same verb. The '**ise**' ending is more common in British English than American English, but British people are increasingly using the '**ize**' ending. In this book, we use the '**ize**' ending.

ⓘ Note that for the following verbs you can only use the '**ise**' ending in both American and British English:

advertise	circumcise	excise	revise	televise
advise	compromise	exercise	supervise	
arise	despise	improvise	surmise	
chastise	devise	promise	surprise	

19 small groups

Note also the following small groups of words that are spelled differently in British and American English. The British spelling is given first.

analyse – analyze
breathalyse – breathalyze
catalyse – catalyze
paralyse – paralyze
analogue – analog
catalogue – catalog
dialogue – dialog
defence – defense
offence – offense
pretence – pretense

Vice is spelled **vise** in American English when it refers to the tool used to hold a piece of wood or metal firmly.

⇨ See also **Usage** entries at **licence - license** and **practice - practise.**

20 individual words

Some individual words are spelled differently in British English and American English. In the list below, the British spelling is given first.

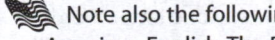

TOPICS

axe - ax	grey - gray
chequer - checker	nought - naught
dependence - dependance	plough - plow
distension - distention	pyjamas - pajamas
gelatine - gelatin	sceptic - skeptic
glycerine - glycerin	tyre - tire

⇨ See also **Usage** entries at **assure - ensure - insure, cheque - check, curb - kerb, dependent - dependant, disc - disk, draught - draft**, and **story - storey**.

With the following pairs there is also a slight change of pronunciation:
aluminium /ˌæluːˈmɪniəm/ – **aluminum** /əˈluːmɪnəm/
furore /fjʊˈrɔːri/ – **furor** /ˈfjʊərɔːr/
speciality /ˌspeʃiˈælɪti/ – **specialty** /ˈspeʃəlti/

21 two words or one word

In British English, some items are usually written as two words, but in American English they can be written as one word.
any more – anymore
de luxe – deluxe
per cent – percent

22 hyphens: compound nouns

Compound nouns can often be written as two separate words or with a hyphen. There are many differences between British and American practice, and you should check a Cobuild dictionary to be sure. In general, American English has fewer hyphenated compounds than British English. Speakers of American English are more likely to spell a compound as one word, or as two words without a hyphen.

At seven he was woken by the <u>alarm clock.</u>
She's the kind of sleeper that even the <u>alarm-clock</u> doesn't always wake.

ⓘ Note that you must always use a hyphen in words referring to relatives, for example **great-grandmother** and **mother-in-law**. You usually use a hyphen in compound nouns such as **T-shirt**, **U-turn**, and **X-ray** where the first part consists of only one letter. Words used together as compound nouns are often hyphenated when they are used to modify another noun, in order to make the meaning clearer. For example, you would refer to the **sixth form** in a school, but use a hyphen for a **sixth-form class**.

The <u>stained glass</u> above the door cast lozenges of yellow, green and blue upon the floor.
…a <u>stained-glass window.</u>
I did a lot of drawing in my <u>spare time.</u>
'Volunteering' for things was an accepted <u>spare-time occupation</u> for their particular social group.

23 compound adjectives

Compound adjectives can usually be written with a hyphen or as one word.

…any <u>anti-social</u> behaviour such as continuous lateness.
…the activities of <u>antisocial</u> groups.

Some adjectives are generally written with a hyphen in front of a noun and as two words after **be**.

He was wearing a <u>brand-new</u> uniform.
His uniform was <u>brand new.</u>

Prefixes that are used in front of a word beginning with a capital letter always have a hyphen after them.

TOPICS

…a wave of <u>anti-British</u> feeling.
…from the steps of the <u>neo-Byzantine</u> cathedral.

When you are describing something that is two colours, you use **and** between two adjectives, with or without hyphens.

…an ugly <u>black and white</u> swimming suit.
…a <u>black-and-white</u> calf.

If you are talking about a group of things, it is best to use hyphens if each thing is two colours.

…fifteen <u>black-and-white</u> police cars.

If each thing is only one colour, you cannot use hyphens.

… <u>black and white</u> dots.

A hyphen is used between two adjectives or noun modifiers that indicate that two countries or groups are involved in something.

<u>Swedish-Norwegian</u> relations improved.
…the <u>United States-Canada</u> free trade pact.

A hyphen is also used to indicate that something goes between two places.

If it was close to 6:27, they would amble to the train track and wait for the <u>New York-Montreal</u> train to roar through.

24 compound verbs

Compound verbs are usually written with a hyphen or as one word.
Take the baby along if you can't find anyone to <u>baby-sit</u>.
I can't come to London, because Mum'll need me to <u>babysit</u> that night.

25 phrasal verbs

Phrasal verbs are written as two (or three) words, without a hyphen.
She <u>turned off</u> the radio.
They <u>broke out of</u> prison on Thursday night.

However, nouns and adjectives that are related to phrasal verbs are written with a hyphen, if the first part ends in '**ing**', '**er**', '**ed**', or '**en**'.
Finally, he monitors the <u>working-out</u> of the plan.
One of the boys had stopped a <u>passer-by</u> and asked him to phone an ambulance.
Gold was occasionally found in the <u>dried-up</u> banks and beds of the rivers.
…selling <u>broken-down</u> second-hand cars at exorbitant prices.

Other nouns and adjectives related to phrasal verbs are written with a hyphen or as one word, or can be written in either way. For example, **break-in** is always written with a hyphen, **breakthrough** is always written as one word, and **takeover** can also be written as **take-over**.

Note that in American English, the solid form without a hyphen is more common than in British English.
Abbey National had fought off a <u>takeover</u> bid from Lloyds TSB.
The company fought off a <u>take-over</u> bid.

26 numbers

Numbers between twenty and a hundred are usually written with a hyphen, as in **twenty-four** and **eighty-seven**. Fractions are also often written with a hyphen, as in **one-third** and **two-fifths**. However, when you use **a** instead of 'one' you do not use a hyphen: **a third**.
Migraines can last <u>twenty-four</u> hours or more.
<u>Two-fifths</u> of the world economy is now in recession.
<u>A third</u> of the cost went into technology and services.

TOPICS

27 other points

In British English, if a word has two clear parts and the first letter of the second part is the same as the last letter of the first part, it is best to use a hyphen, especially if the letter is a vowel. For example, it is best to write **pre-eminent** and **co-operate**, not 'preeminent' and 'cooperate'. In American English, the hyphen is now usually omitted.

He agreed to co-operate with the police investigation.
Both companies said they would cooperate with the government.

When people are using a pair of hyphenated words which have the same second part, they sometimes just write the first part of the first word. However, it is clearer to write each word in full.

…the militants whose careers bridged the pre- and post-war eras.
… long- and short-term economic planning.

Compound words that are formed with the prefixes '**anti-**', '**non-**', and '**semi-**' are usually spelled with a hyphen in British English, but without it in American English. Adjectives formed by adding '**-like**' to a word are spelled without a hyphen in American English, unless the first part of the word is a proper noun or is rather long.

> anti-nuclear – antinuclear
> non-aggression – nonaggression
> semi-literate – semiliterate
> cloud-like – cloudlike

See a Cobuild dictionary for information on the usual way to write a particular compound word.

⇨ For the use of the hyphen to break a word at the end of a line, see **Topic** entry at **Punctuation**.

Suggestions

1 neutral suggestions	6 less firm suggestions
2 firm suggestions	7 very firm suggestions
3 less firm suggestions	8 suggestions about what would be
4 suggestions in writing and broadcasting	best
5 suggesting doing something together	9 replying to a suggestion

1 neutral suggestions

There are many ways of suggesting a course of action to someone.
You can say '**You could…**'.

You could make a raft or something.
You could phone her and ask.
'Well, what shall we do?' – 'You could try Ebury Street.'

You can also use '**How about…?**' or '**What about…?**', followed by an '-ing' form.

How about taking him outside to have a game?
What about becoming an actor?

ⓘ Note that you can also use '**How about…?**' or '**What about…?**' with a noun group, to suggest that someone has a drink or some food, usually with you, or to suggest an arrangement.

How about a steak and a couple of pints?
What about a drink?
'I'll explain when I see you.' – 'When will that be?' – 'How about late tonight?'

TOPICS

A more indirect way of suggesting a course of action is to use '**Have you thought of…?**', followed by an '-ing' form.

Have you thought of asking what's wrong with Henry?

2 firm suggestions

A firmer way of making a suggestion is to say '**Couldn't you…?**', '**Can't you…?**', or '**Why not…?**'

Couldn't you get a job in one of the smaller colleges around here?
Can't you just tell him?
Why not write to her?

You can also use '**Try…**', followed by an '-ing' form or a noun group.

Try advertising in the local papers.
Try a little methylated spirit.

A very firm way of making a suggestion is to say '**I suggest you…**'.

I suggest you leave this to me.

If you want to suggest persuasively but gently that someone does something, you can say '**Why don't you…?**'

Why don't you think about it and decide later?
Why don't you go to bed?

⇨ For other ways of saying firmly what course of action someone should take, see **Topic** entry at **Advising someone**.

3 less firm suggestions

If you do not feel strongly about what you are suggesting, but cannot think of anything better that the other person might do, you can say '**You might as well…**' or '**You may as well…**'.

You might as well drive on back to Famagusta by yourself.
You may as well go home and come back in the morning.

4 suggestions in writing and broadcasting

People who are writing or broadcasting make suggestions using expressions like '**You might like to…**' and '**It might be a good idea to…**'.

Alternatively, you might like to consider discussing your insurance problems with your bank manager.
You might consider moving to a smaller house.
You might want to have a separate heading for each point.
It might be a good idea to rest on alternate days between running.

5 suggesting doing something together

There are several ways of making a suggestion about what you and someone else might do.

If you want to make a firm suggestion which you think the other person will agree with, you say '**Let's…**'.

Come on, let's go.
Let's meet at my office at noon. All right?
Come on now. Let's be practical. How can we help?

You can make the suggestion seem persuasive rather than firm and forceful by adding the tag **shall we?**

I tell you what, let's slip back to the hotel and have a drink, shall we?
Let's do some of these letters, Mrs Taswell, shall we?

For a negative suggestion, you say '**Let's not…**'.

Let's not talk here.
We have twenty-four hours. Let's not panic.
Let's not go jumping to conclusions.

TOPICS

Speakers of American English sometimes say '**Let's don't…**' instead of 'Let's not…' in informal speech.

Let's don't talk about it.

Another way of making a firm suggestion is to say '**We'll…**'.

We'll talk later, Percival.
'What do you want to do with Ben's boat?' – 'We'll leave it here till tomorrow.'

Again, you can make the suggestion persuasive rather than forceful by adding the tag **shall we?**

We'll leave somebody else to clear up the mess, shall we?
All right, we'll change things around a bit now, shall we?

Another firm way of suggesting is to say '**I suggest we…**'.

I suggest we discuss this elsewhere.
I suggest we go to the hospital in St Johnsbury right away.

Another way of making a suggestion is to say '**Shall we…?**' You can make a suggestion like this sound firm or less firm by altering your tone of voice.

Shall we go and see a film?
Shall we make a start?
Shall we sit down?

6 less firm suggestions

When you want to make a suggestion without being too forceful, you use '**We could…**'. You use this form of suggestion when the issue of what to do has already been raised.

I did ask you to have dinner with me. We could discuss it then.
We could tow one of them in.
'I'm tired.' – 'Too tired for a walk, even? We could go to the Cave of Shulamit.'

You can also make a non-forceful suggestion in an indirect way, using '**I thought we…**' or '**I wonder if we…**' and a modal.

I thought we might have some lunch.
In the meantime, I wonder if we can just turn our attention to something you mentioned a little earlier.
I wonder whether we could have a little talk, after the meeting.

If you are unenthusiastic about your own suggestion, but cannot think of a better course of action, you say '**We might as well…**'.

We might as well go in.
We might as well go home.

7 very firm suggestions

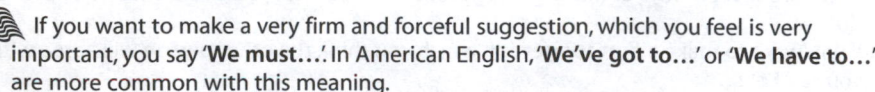 If you want to make a very firm and forceful suggestion, which you feel is very important, you say '**We must…**'. In American English, '**We've got to…**' or '**We have to…**' are more common with this meaning.

We must be careful.
We've got to go, now!
We have to hurry.

8 suggestions about what would be best

When you are suggesting doing something which you think is the sensible thing to do, you say '**We ought to…**' or '**We'd better…**'. People often soften this form of suggestion by saying **I think** or **I suppose** first, or adding the tag **oughtn't we?** or **hadn't we?**

We ought to give the alarm.
Come on, we'd better try and find somebody.
I think we'd better leave.
I suppose we'd better take a look through the bushes.

We ought to order, oughtn't we?
We'd better get going, hadn't we?

'**I think we should…**' is also used.

I think we should go back.
I think we should change the subject.

 If you are not sure that your suggestion will be accepted without argument, you say '**Shouldn't we…?**' or '**Oughtn't we to…?**'. Note that in American English, '**Oughtn't we…**' is followed by an infinitive without 'to'.

Shouldn't we have supper first?
Shouldn't we be on our way?
Oughtn't we to phone for the police?

You can also say '**Don't you think we should…**' or '**Don't you think we'd better…?**'

Don't you think we'd better wait and see whether or not the charges stand up?

9 replying to a suggestion

The usual way of replying to a suggestion that you agree with is to say '**All right**' or '**OK**'. You can also say something like '**Good idea**' or '**That's a good idea**'.

'Let's dance now.' – 'All right then.'
'Let's not do that. Let's play cards instead.' – 'That's all right with me.'
'Try up there.' – 'OK.'
'Let's sit down for a while.' – 'Good idea.'

You can reply '**Yes, I could**' to a suggestion starting with '**You could…**'.

'You could get a job over there.' – 'Oh yes, I could do that, couldn't I?'

A more casual way of replying is to say '**Why not?**'

'Shall we take a walk?' – 'Why not?'

People also sometimes say '**Fine**' or '**That's fine by me**' when replying to a suggestion about doing something together. If they are very enthusiastic, they say '**Great**'.

'What about Tuesday?' – 'Fine.'

If you do not agree with the suggestion, you can say '**I don't think that's a good idea**', '**No, I can't**', or '**No, I couldn't**'.

'You could ask her.' – 'I don't think that's a very good idea.'
'Well, can you not make synthetic ones?' – 'We can't, no.'

You can also give a reason for not accepting the suggestion.

'I'll ring her up when I go out to lunch.' – 'Why not do it here and save money?' – 'I like my calls private.'

Telephoning

In the examples in this entry, A is the person answering the phone, and B is the person who is making the phone call.

1 answering the phone

There are several ways of answering the telephone when someone phones you. Most people answer the telephone by saying '**Hello**'.

A: Hello.
B: Hello. It's me.

Some British speakers answer by giving their telephone number.

A: 76459.
B: Hello. Is that Carol?

ⓘ Note that you say each digit of the telephone number. For example, you would say **435 1916** as **four three five one nine one six**.

British speakers usually say **0** as **oh**. American speakers usually say **zero**. When a

TOPICS

number is repeated, British speakers use the word **double**. For example, they say **4335** as **four double three five**.

If you are at work, you can give the name of your organization or department, or your own name. You can say '**Good morning**' or '**Good afternoon**' instead of 'Hello'.

A: _Parkfield Medical Centre._
B: Hello. I'd like to make an appointment to see one of the doctors this morning please.

A: Hello. _Tony Parsons speaking._
B: Oh, hello. It's Tom Roberts here.

A: _Good morning._
B: Good morning. Who am I speaking to?
A: Er, my name is Alan Fentiman.

Some people say '**Yes?**' when answering a phone call, especially one within an organization, but this can sound abrupt and rude.

If you recognize the person's voice when they say 'Hello', you can say '**Hello**' followed by their name.

A: Hello.
B: Hello, Jim.
A: _Hello, Alex,_ how are you?

If you don't recognize the caller's voice, you can ask who it is. If you are at home, you say '**Sorry, who is it?**' or '**Who is this?**' Some people say '**Who's that?**', but this can sound rude.

A: Hello.
B: Hello.
A: _Sorry, who is it?_
B: It's me, Terry.

If you think you know who the caller is, you say, for example, '**Is that James?**' or '**That's James, isn't it?**'

A: Hello.
B: Hello. Can I speak to John?
A: I'm afraid he's just gone out. _Is that Sarah?_
B: Yes.

If you are at work, and the caller wants to speak to someone else, you say '**Who's calling?**' or '**Who's speaking?**'

B: Hello, could I speak to Mrs George, please?
A: _Who's calling?_
B: _The name is Pearce._
A: Hold on a minute, please.

If the caller has got through to the wrong number, you say something like '**I think you've got the wrong number**' or '**Sorry, wrong number**'.

A: Hello.
B: Mrs Clough?
A: _No, you've got the wrong number._
B: I'm sorry.

2 telephoning someone

When you are phoning a friend or relative, you can just say '**Hello**' when they answer the phone, if you think they will recognize your voice. You can add their name.

A: Hello.
B: _Hello!_ I just thought I'd better ring to let you know what time I'll be arriving.

A: Hello.
B: _Hello, Alan._
A: Hello, Mark, how are you?
B: Well, not so good.

ⓘ Note that after saying '**Hello**' friends and relatives normally ask each other how they are. If you need to make it clear who you are when you phone someone, you say '**It's…**' or '**This is…**' and your name.

A: Hello.
B: Hello. *It's Jenny.*

A: Hello.
B: Hello, Alan. *This is Eila.*

You can also say '**It's … here**'.

A: Hello.
B: *It's Maggie Turner here.*

Sometimes you do not need to give your name, for example when you are asking for general information.

A: Citizen's Advice Bureau.
B: Hello. *I'd like some advice about a dispute with my neighbours.*

If you are not sure who has answered the phone, you say '**Who am I speaking to?**' or, informally, '**Who's that?**'

A: Hello.
B: Hello. *Who am I speaking to, please?*

A: Yes?
B: I want to speak to Mr Taylor.
A: I'm afraid Mr Taylor's not in the office right now.
B: *Who's that?*

You can check that you have the right person, organization, or number by saying '**Is that…?**', or by just saying the name or number like a question.

A: Hello.
B: *Is that Mrs Thompson?*
A: Er, yes it is.
B: This is Kaj Mintti from Finland.

A: Hello.
B: Hello? *435 1916?*
A: Yes

 Note that speakers of American English usually say '**Is this…?**' instead of '**Is that…?**'

A: Hello.
B: Hello. *Is this the Casa Bianca restaurant?* I want to speak with Anna. Anna di Pietro.

3 **asking to speak to someone**
If the person who answers the phone is not the person you want to speak to, you say, for example, '**Can I speak to Paul, please?**' or '**Is Paul there?**'

A: Hello.
B: *Can I speak to Sue, please?*
A: Hang on – I'm sorry, but she's not in at the moment.
B: Can I leave a message?
A: Yes.
B: Would you tell her that Adrian phoned?

If you are making a business call, you say, for example, '**Could I speak to Mr Green, please?**' or just say the name of the person or department you want, followed by **please**.

A: William Foux and Company.
B: Er, good afternoon. *Could I speak to Mr Duff, please?*
A: Oh, I'm sorry, he's on another line at the moment. Can you hold?
B: No, it's all right. I'll ring later.

TOPICS

A: *British Gas.*
B: *Customer services, please.*
A: *I'll put you through.*

If the person you are speaking to is in fact the person you want, they sometimes say '**Speaking**'.

A: *Personnel.*
B: *Could I speak to Mr Wilson, please.*
A: *Speaking.*
B: *Oh, right. I wanted to ask you a question about sick pay.*

4 ending a phone call

When you end a phone call, you say '**Goodbye**' or, informally, '**Bye**'.

A: *I'm afraid I can't talk to you now.*
B: *OK, I'll phone back after lunch.*
A: *OK. Goodbye.*
B: *Goodbye.*

A: *I'll just check. Yes, it's here.*
B: *Oh, OK. Thanks. Bye.*

People sometimes also say '**Speak to you soon**' or '**Thanks for ringing**'.

A: *Speak to you soon. Bye.*
B: *Bye.*

Thanking someone

1 basic ways of thanking	**5** thanking someone for a present
2 emphatic ways of thanking	**6** thanking someone for an enquiry
3 more formal ways of thanking	**7** thanking someone in a letter
4 thanking someone for an offer	**8** replying to thanks

1 basic ways of thanking

You thank someone when they have just done something for you or given you something. You say '**Thank you**' or, more casually, '**Thanks**'.

'I'll take over here.' – 'Thank you.'
'Don't worry, Caroline. I've given you a marvellous reference.' – 'Thank you, Mr Dillon.'
'There's your receipt.' – 'Thanks.'
'Would you tell her that Adrian phoned and that I'll phone at eight?' – 'OK.' – 'Thanks.'

Some speakers, especially speakers of British and Australian English, say '**Cheers**' to thank someone in a casual way.

⇨ See **Usage** entry at **cheers - cheerio**.

Some British speakers also say '**Ta**' /tɑː/.

'You're pretty good at this.' – 'Cheers, mate.'
'This is all the material you need.' – 'Ta.'

If you need to indicate why you are thanking the other person, you say '**Thank you for…**' or '**Thanks for…**'.

Thank you for the earrings, Whitey.
Thank you for a delicious lunch.
Well, then, good-night, and thanks for the lift.
Thanks for helping out.

2 emphatic ways of thanking

People often add **very much** or **very much indeed** to be more emphatic.

TOPICS

'Here you are.' – *'Thank you very much.'*
'I'll ring you tomorrow morning.' – *'OK. Thanks very much indeed.'*

(i) Note that you can say **'Thanks a lot'**, but you cannot say ~~'Thank you a lot'~~ or ~~'Thanks lots'~~.
'All right, then?' – *'Yes, thanks a lot.'*

If you want to show that you are very grateful, you can say something like **'That's very kind of you'** or **'That's very good of you'**.

'Any night when you feel a need to talk, you will find me here.' – *'That's very kind of you .'*
'Would you give this to her?' – *'Sure. When I happen to see her.'* – *'That's very good of you, Rudolph.'*

You can also say something like **'That's wonderful'** or **'Great'**.

'I'll see if she can be with you on Monday.' – *'That's wonderful!'*
'Do them as fast as you can.' – *'Yes. OK.'* – *'Great.'*

Even more emphatic ways of thanking are shown below.

'All right, Sandra?' – *'Thank you so much, Mr Atkinson; you've been wonderful. I just can't thank you enough .'*
'She's safe.' – *'I don't know how to thank you.'*
I can't tell you how grateful I am to you for having listened to me.

3 more formal ways of thanking
People sometimes thank someone more formally by saying **'I wanted to thank you for…'** or **'I'd like to thank you for…'**, especially when expressing thanks for something that was done or given a little while ago.

I wanted to thank you for the beautiful necklace.
I want to thank you all for coming.
We learned what you did for Ari and I want to tell you how grateful I am.
I'd like to thank you for your patience and your hard work.

You can also express thanks more formally by saying things like **'I'm very grateful to you'** or **'I really appreciate it'**.

I'm grateful for the information you've given me on Mark Edwards.
I'm extremely grateful to you for rescuing me.
Thank you for coming to hear me play. I do appreciate it.

4 thanking someone for an offer
You can say **'Thank you'** or **'Thanks'** when accepting something that is offered.

'Have a cake.' – *'Thank you.'*

You say **'No, thank you'** or **'No, thanks'** when refusing something that is offered.

'There's one biscuit left. Do you want it?' – *'No, thanks.'*

(i) Note that you do not refuse something by just saying ~~'Thank you'~~.

⇨ See **Usage** entry at **Offers**.

5 thanking someone for a present
When you have been given a present, you say **'Thank you'**, or something like **'It's lovely'**.

'It's lovely. What is it?' – *'It's a shark tooth. The casing's silver.'*

People sometimes say **'You shouldn't have'** as a polite way of indicating that they are very grateful.

'Here. This is for you.' – *'Joyce, you shouldn't have.'*

6 thanking someone for an enquiry
You also say **'Thank you'** or **'Thanks'** when replying to someone who has asked how you are or how a member of your family is, or if you have had a nice weekend or holiday.

'How are you?' – *'Fine, thank you.'*
'How is Andrew today?' – *'Oh, Andrew's very well, thank you.'*
'Did you have a nice weekend?' – *'Lovely, thank you.'*

TOPICS

7 **thanking someone in a letter**

When thanking someone in a letter or email, you most commonly say '**Thank you for…**'. In a formal business letter or email, you can say '**I am grateful for…**'.

Dear Madam, <u>Thank you for</u> your letter replying to our advertisement for an assistant cashier. <u>I am grateful for</u> your prompt reply to my request.

If the letter or email is to a friend, you can say '**Thanks for…**'.

<u>Thanks for</u> writing.

8 **replying to thanks**

When someone thanks you for handing them something or doing a small service for them, it is acceptable not to say anything in reply in Britain.

However, people in the United States, especially employees in shops, often say something like '**You're welcome**' or '**No problem**'. When someone thanks you for helping them or doing them a favour, you reply '**That's all right**', '**Don't mention it**' or '**That's OK**'.

'Thank you, Charles.' – '<u>That's all right, David.</u>'
'Thanks. This is really kind of you.' – '<u>Don't mention it.</u>'
'Thanks. I really appreciate it.' – '<u>That's okay.</u>'

If you want to be both polite and friendly, you can say '**It's a pleasure**', '**My pleasure**', or '**Pleasure**'.

'Thank you very much for talking to us about your research.' – '<u>It's a pleasure.</u>'
'Thank you for the walk and the conversation.' – '<u>Pleasure.</u>'
'Thanks for sorting it out.' – '<u>My pleasure.</u>'

'**Any time**' is more casual.

'You've been very helpful.' – 'No problem. <u>Any time.</u>'

If someone thanks you in a very emphatic way, you can reply using the expressions below.

'He's immensely grateful for what you did for him.' – '<u>It was no trouble.</u>'
'Thanks, Johnny. Thanks for your trouble.' – '<u>It was nothing.</u>'
'I'm enormously grateful to you for telling me.' – '<u>Not at all.</u>'

Time

1	clock times	**5**	adverbs indicating time
2	prepositions indicating time	**6**	times as modifiers
3	approximate times	**7**	times as qualifiers
4	periods of the day		

⇨ For information on referring to days and longer periods of time, see **Topic** entry at **Days and dates**.
⇨ For information on time clauses, see **Grammar** entry at **Subordinate clauses**.

1 **clock times**

When you want to know the time at the moment you are speaking, you say '**What time is it?**' or '**What's the time?**'

<u>What time is it?</u>' – 'Three minutes past five.'
<u>What's the time</u> now?' – 'Twenty past.'

When asking about the time of an event, you usually use **when**.

<u>When</u> did you come?' – 'Just after lunch.'

You can also use '**What time**'.

<u>What time</u> did you get back to London?' – 'Ten o'clock.'
<u>What time</u> do they shut?' – 'Half past five.'

TOPICS

When you tell someone the time, you say 'It's...'.

It's ten to eleven now.

The table below shows different ways of referring to times.

Clock		Written/spoken	Digital
	four o'clock four 4.00	four in the morning 4 a.m. four in the afternoon 4 p.m.	`04:00` `16:00`
	nine o'clock nine 9.00	nine in the morning 9 a.m. nine in the evening nine at night 9 p.m.	`09:00` `21:00`
	twelve o'clock twelve 12.00	twelve in the morning 12 a.m. midday (*BRIT*) noon twelve at night 12 p.m. midnight	`12:00` `00:00`
	a quarter past twelve quarter past twelve twelve fifteen 12.15		`12:15` `00:15`
	twenty-five past two twenty-five minutes past two two twenty five 2.25		`02:25` `14:25`
	half past eleven half eleven (*BRIT*) eleven-thirty 11.30		`11:30` `23:30`
	a quarter to one quarter to one twelve forty-five 12.45		`12:45` `00:45`
	ten to eight ten minutes to eight seven-fifty 7.50		`07:50` `19:50`

TOPICS

(i) Note the following points:

- The twenty-four hour clock is used on some digital clocks and on timetables. In this system, five o'clock in the afternoon, for example, is expressed as 17.00.

In the United States, the 24-hour clock is not very common, and timetables use the 12-hour system, with a.m. and p.m.

You can use **o'clock** only when saying exact hours, not times between hours. For example, you can say **five o'clock**, but you do not say ~~'ten past five o'clock'~~ or ~~'a quarter past five o'clock'~~.

Come round at <u>five o'clock</u>.
I must leave by <u>eight o'clock</u>.

(i) Note that when using **o'clock**, people usually write the number as a word (for example **five**), not a figure ('5').

You do not have to use 'o'clock' when referring to an exact hour. People often just use a number.

I used to get up every morning at <u>six</u>.

● When saying times between hours, you can use **past** and **to**. You use **past** and a number when referring to a time thirty minutes or less after a particular hour. You use **to** and a number when referring to a time less than thirty minutes before a particular hour.

It's <u>twenty past seven</u>.
He returned to the house at <u>half past four</u>.
He got to the station at <u>five to eleven</u>.

(i) Note that you do not normally use the word 'minutes' in these expressions.

Speakers of American English often use **after** instead of 'past', and **of** instead of 'to'.

It was <u>twenty after eight</u>.
At <u>a quarter of eight</u>, he called Mrs. Curry.

● You only use the word **minutes** when you are talking about times between sets of five minutes, or when you want to show that you are being accurate and precise.

It was twenty-four <u>minutes</u> past ten.
We left Grosvenor Crescent at five <u>minutes</u> to ten.

● If it is clear what hour you are talking about, you do not need to add the hour after **past** or **to**.

'What time is it?' – 'It's <u>eighteen minutes past</u>.'
It's <u>quarter past</u>.
'What time's break?' – '<u>Twenty-five to</u>.'

● You can also express a time by saying the hour first and then the number of minutes past the hour. For example, you can say **7.35** as **seven thirty-five**.

(i) Note that if the number of minutes is less than 10, many people say '0' as **oh** before the number of minutes. For example, **7.05** can be said as **seven oh five** or **seven five**.

Note that you put a full stop after the hour when writing a time like this. Some people, especially Americans, use a colon instead.

At <u>6.30</u> each morning, the partners meet to review the situation.
By <u>3:34</u> p.m. the first thread had been removed.

● You can make it clear when a time occurs, if necessary, by adding a prepositional phrase. Note that you say **in the morning**, **in the afternoon**, and **in the evening**, but you say **at night**, not ~~'in the night'~~.

It was about four o'clock <u>in the afternoon</u>.
They worked from seven <u>in the morning</u> until five <u>at night</u>.

⇨ See sections on **exact times** in Usage entries at **afternoon, evening, morning,** and **night.**

You can also add **a.m.** to indicate a time between midnight and midday, or **p.m.** to indicate a time between midday and midnight. These abbreviations are not generally

used in conversation in British English.
The doors will be opened at 10 a.m.
We will be arriving back in London at 10.30 p.m.

⚠ **WARNING:** You do not use 'a.m.' or 'p.m.' with **o'clock**.

2 **prepositions indicating time**
The commonest preposition used to indicate the time when something happens is **at**.
The taxi arrived at 7.30.
They'd arranged to leave at four o'clock in Welch's car.
I'll be back at four.

Other prepositions are used in the following ways to indicate when something happens:

● If something happens **after** a particular time, it happens during the period that follows that time.
She complained that Hamilton was a very quiet place with little to do after ten at night.

● If something happens **before** a particular time, it happens earlier than that time.
I was woken before six by the rain hammering against my bedroom window.

● If something happens **by** a particular time, it happens at or before that time.
I have to get back to town by four o'clock.

● If something happens **until** a particular time, it stops at that time. **Till** is often used instead of 'until' in conversation.
I work until three.
I didn't get home till five.

● If something has been happening **since** a particular time, it started at that time and it is still happening.
He had been up since 4 a.m.

⇨ For information on other uses of these words, see separate **Usage** entries at each word.

3 **approximate times**
You can indicate that a time is approximate by using **about** or **around** in front of the time.
At about four o'clock in the morning, we were ambushed.
The device, which exploded at around midnight on Wednesday, severely damaged the fourth-floor bar.

At is sometimes left out.
He left about ten o'clock.

In conversation, people sometimes indicate an approximate time by adding '**-ish**' to the time.
Shall I ring you about nine-ish?

You can say that something happens **just after** or **just before** a particular time. You can also use **shortly after** or **shortly before**.
We drove into Jerusalem just after nine o'clock.
He had come home just before six o'clock and lain down for a nap.
Shortly after nine, her husband appeared.

When saying what the time is or was, you can also use **just gone** in British English, or **just after**.
It was just gone half past twelve.
It was just after 9pm on a cold October night.

4 **periods of the day**
The main periods of the day are:

| morning | afternoon | evening | night |

You can use the prepositions **in** or **on** with words referring to periods of the day. You can also use **last**, **next**, **this**, **tomorrow**, and **yesterday** in front of these words to form adjuncts.

I'll ring the agent <u>in the morning</u>.
<u>On Saturday morning</u> all flights were cancelled to and from Glasgow.
I spoke to him <u>this morning</u>.
He is going to fly to Amiens <u>tomorrow morning</u>.

⇨ For detailed information on how to use these words and which prepositions to use with them, see **Usage** entry at each word. See also see **Usage** entries at **last - lastly, next,** and **this - that**.

There are also several words which refer to the short period when the sun rises or sets:

| dawn | first light | dusk | sunset |
| daybreak | sunrise | nightfall | twilight |

You use **at** with these words when indicating that something happens during the period they refer to.

<u>At dawn</u> we landed for refuelling in Tunisia.
Draw the curtains <u>at sunset</u>.

5 **adverbs indicating time**

The adverbs and adjuncts in the two lists below are used to indicate that something happened in the past. Note that all these adjuncts can be put after the first auxiliary in a verb group.

The following adjuncts can be used with past tenses and with the present perfect:

| in the past | just | lately | previously | recently |

It wasn't all that successful as a deterrent <u>in the past</u>.
Her husband had <u>recently</u> died in an accident.

The following adjuncts can be used with past tenses but not normally with the present perfect:

| at one time | earlier on | once | sometime |
| earlier | formerly | originally | then |

The cardboard folder had been blue <u>originally</u> but now the colour had faded to a light grey.
The world was different <u>then</u>.

Before is not used with the present perfect when simply indicating that a situation existed in the past. However, it is used with the present perfect to indicate that this is not the first time that something has happened.

I'm sure I've read that <u>before</u>.

🏴 The tenses used with **already** are different in American English and British English.

⇨ See **Usage** entry at **already**.

You use the following adjuncts when referring to the future:

afterwards	in a minute	later on	sometime
at once	in a moment	one day	soon
before long	in future	one of these days	sooner or later
eventually	in the future	shortly	within minutes
immediately	later	some day	within the hour

We'll be free <u>soon</u>.
I'll remember <u>in a minute.</u>
<u>*In future*</u> *when you visit us you must let us know in advance.*

These adjuncts are usually put at the end or beginning of the clause.

Momentarily is used when referring to the future in American English, but not in British English.
⇨ See **Usage** entry at **momentarily.**

You use the following adjuncts to contrast the present with the past or the future, or to indicate that you are talking about a temporary situation in the present:

at the moment	just now	presently
at present	now	right now
currently	nowadays	these days

Biology is their great passion <u>at the moment.</u>
Well, we must be going <u>now.</u>

These adjuncts are usually put at the end or beginning of the clause.

(*i*) Note that **today** is used, mainly in newspapers and broadcasting, to refer to the present time in history as well as to the day on which you are speaking.

…the kind of open society which most of us in the Western world enjoy <u>today.</u>

⇨ See also **Usage** entries at **now** and **presently.**

(*i*) Note that **already** is used when referring to a present situation, as well as when referring to the past.

I'm <u>already</u> late.

⇨ See **Usage** entry at **already.**

6 | **times as modifiers**

Clock times and periods of the day can be used as modifiers.

Every morning he would set off right after the <u>eight o'clock</u> news.
Castle was usually able to catch the <u>six thirty-five</u> train from Euston.
But now the sun was already dispersing the <u>morning</u> mists.

(*i*) Note that people often refer to a train or bus by the time it leaves a particular place. They talk, for example, about **the six-eighteen**, meaning 'the train that leaves at six-eighteen'.

He knew Alan Thomas caught <u>the seven-thirty-two</u> most days.

Possessive forms of periods of the day can also be used as modifiers, when talking about a particular day.

It was Jim Griffiths, who knew nothing of <u>the morning's</u> happenings.

(*i*) Note that they are also used when saying how long an activity lasts.

He still had <u>an afternoon's</u> work to get done.

7 | **times as qualifiers**

You can use time adjuncts as qualifiers to specify events or periods of time.

I'm afraid the meeting <u>this afternoon</u> tired me badly.
No admissions are permitted in the hour <u>before closing time.</u>

Transport

1 prepositions

You can use **by** with most forms of transport when you are talking about travel using that form of transport.

Most visitors to these parts choose to travel by bicycle.
I never go by car.
It is cheaper to travel to London by coach.

⚠ **WARNING:** You do not use a determiner after **by.** For example, you do not say 'I never go by a car'. Note also that you cannot use 'by' when you are giving more detail about the vehicle. For example, you do not say 'I came by Tom's car'. You say 'I came **in** Tom's car'.

If you want to emphasize that someone walks somewhere, you say that they go **on foot.** In British English, you do not usually say 'by foot'.

They'd have to go on foot.

You can also use **in** when you are talking about travel using a car, taxi, ambulance, lorry, small boat, or small plane. Similarly, you can use **in** or **into** when talking about entering one of these vehicles and **out of** when talking about leaving one of them.

I always go back in a taxi.
She and Oliver were put into a lorry.
I saw that he was already out of the car.

However, you usually use **on, onto,** and **off** when you are talking about other forms of transport, such as buses, coaches, planes, trains, and ships.

…your trip on planes, ships and cross-channel ferries.
He got onto the bus and we waved until it drove out of sight.
Sheila looked very pretty as she stepped off the train.

ⓘ Note that **in, into,** and **out of** are sometimes used with these other forms of transport too.

He could hear the people in the plane screaming.
Just before I got into the bus, I went over to him.
We jumped out of the bus and ran into the nearest shop.

You can also say that someone is **aboard** or **on board** these other forms of transport, especially planes and ships.

He fled the country aboard a US Air Force plane.
…before the fish could be hauled on board his boat.

2 verbs

You usually use the verb **get** followed by a preposition to say that someone enters or leaves a vehicle.

Then I stood up to get off the bus.
They got on the wrong train.

The verbs **board, embark,** and **disembark** are used in formal English.
You use **board** to talk about getting on a bus, train, large plane, or ship.

…so that he could be the first to board the plane.

You can also use **embark on** to talk about getting on a ship and **disembark from** to talk about getting off a ship.

Even before they embarked on the ferry at Southampton she was bored.
…as they disembarked from the QE2 after their trip.

When you are talking about travel by public transport, you can use **take** instead of 'go by'. For example, instead of saying that you will 'go by' bus, you can say that you will **take** a bus.

We then <u>took a boat</u> downriver.
'I could <u>take a taxi,</u> 'I said.

Warning someone

1 warnings	**5** warnings on products and notices
2 strong warnings	**6** immediate warnings
3 explicit warnings	
4 warnings in writing and broadcasting	

1 **warnings**

There are several ways of warning someone not to do something.
In conversation, you can say '**I wouldn't … if I were you**'.
<u>I wouldn't</u> drink that <u>if I were you.</u>

A weaker way of warning is to say '**I don't think you should…**' or '**I don't think you ought to…**'.
<u>I don't think you should</u> try to make a decision when you are so tired.
<u>I don't think you ought to</u> turn me down quite so quickly, before you know a bit more about it.

You can also warn someone indirectly not to do something by saying what will happen if they do it.
You'll fall down and hurt yourself <u>if you</u> insist on wearing that old gown.

You can warn someone not to do something by accident or because of carelessness by saying '**Be careful not to…**' or '**Take care not to…**'.
<u>Be careful not to</u> keep the flame in one place too long, or the metal will be distorted.
Well, <u>take care not to</u> get arrested.

2 **strong warnings**

'**Don't**' is used in strong warnings.
<u>Don't</u> put more things in the washing machine than it will wash.
<u>Don't</u> turn the gas on again until the gasman tells you it's safe to do so.
<u>Don't</u> open the door for anyone.

You can emphasize **don't** with **whatever you do**.
<u>Whatever you do</u> don't overcrowd your greenhouse.
Don't get in touch with your wife, <u>whatever you do.</u>

You can mention the consequences of not doing what you say by adding **or** and another clause.
Don't drink so much <u>or you'll die.</u>

3 **explicit warnings**

People sometimes say '**I warn you**' or '**I'm warning you**' when warning someone, especially when preparing them for something they are going to experience.
<u>I warn you</u> it's going to be expensive.
<u>I must warn you</u> that I have advised my client not to say another word.
It'll be very hot, <u>I'm warning you.</u>

(*i*) Note that these expressions are also used as threats.
Much as I like you, <u>I warn you</u> I'll murder you if you tell anyone.
<u>I'm warning you,</u> if you do that again there'll be trouble.

4 **warnings in writing and broadcasting**

Never is used with an imperative as a warning in writing and broadcasting.

TOPICS

Never put antique china into a dishwasher.
Even if you are desperate to get married, never let it show.

'**Beware of…**' is used to warn against doing something, or to warn about something that might be dangerous or unsatisfactory.

Beware of becoming too complacent.
I would beware of companies which depend on one product and one man.

The expression '**A word of warning**' is sometimes used to introduce a warning. So are '**Warning**' and '**Caution**', in books and articles.

A word of warning: Don't have your appliances connected by anyone who is not a specialist.
Warning! Keep all these liquids away from children.
Caution. Keep the shoulders well down when doing this exercise.

5 **warnings on products and notices**

'**Warning**' and '**Caution**' are also used on products and notices. '**Danger**' and '**Beware of…**' are used on notices.

Warning: Smoking can seriously damage your health.
CAUTION: This helmet provides limited protection.
DANGER – RIVER.
Beware of Falling Tiles.

6 **immediate warnings**

When you want to warn someone about something that they might be just about to do, you say '**Careful**' or '**Be careful**', or, more informally, '**Watch it**'.

Careful! You'll break it.
He sat down on the bridge and dangled his legs. 'Be careful, Tim.'
Watch it! There's a rotten floorboard somewhere just here.
I should watch it, Neil, you're putting this on record.

In British English, you can also use '**Mind**', followed by a noun referring to something the other person might hit, fall into, or harm, or a clause referring to something they must be careful about.

Mind the pond.
Mind you don't slip.

'**Watch**' is sometimes used in a similar way, especially with a clause.

Watch where you're putting your feet.

Other warning expressions are '**Look out**' and '**Watch out**'. '**Look out**' is used only in urgent situations of danger. '**Watch out**' is used for urgent situations and for situations that are going to arise or might arise, or, in American English, as '**Mind…**' is used in British English.

Look out. There's someone coming.
Watch out for that tree!
'I think I'll just go for a little walk.' – 'Watch out – it's a very large city to take a little walk in.'

Words with alternative spellings

The following words can be spelled in two ways. The commonest spelling is given first. Where the second spelling is the preferred American English spelling, this is marked with the symbol †. In these cases, the second spelling is often the only acceptable American English spelling.

TOPICS

acknowledgement - acknowledgment †	dexterous - dextrous	kilogram - kilogramme
adrenalin - adrenaline	dispatch - despatch	likeable - likable †
adviser - advisor	douse - dowse	liquorice - licorice
ambience - ambiance	duffel coat - duffle coat	mackintosh - macintosh
annex - annexe	dyke - dike	mantelpiece - mantlepiece
artefact - artifact †	forego - forgo †	milligram - milligramme
balk - baulk	gram - gramme	movable - moveable †
banister - bannister	grandad - granddad †	Muslim - Moslem
by-law - bye-law	granny - grannie	nosy - nosey
caffeine - caffein	guerrilla - guerilla	OK - okay
carcass - carcase	gypsy - gipsy	phoney - phony
castor - caster	hiccup - hiccough	saccharine - saccharin †
caviar - caviare	hippie - hippy	sheikh - sheik
chaperone - chaperon	hooray - hurray	siphon - syphon
chilli - chili †	icon - ikon	swap - swop
cipher - cypher	impostor - imposter	Tsar - Czar †
conjurer - conjuror	inflection - inflexion	veranda - verandah
connection - connexion	jibe - gibe	whirr - whir †
curtsy - curtsey	judgement - judgment †	

Racket can be spelled **racquet** when used to refer to a bat with strings which is used for playing a game such as tennis or squash.

Two words have alternative spellings in British English only:

jail – gaol
wagon – waggon

In American English, the spellings **jail** and **wagon** are used.

Two words have three possible spellings:

hello – hallo – hullo
yoghurt – yoghourt – yogurt

Many verbs can end in either '-**ise**' or '-**ize**'.

⇨ For information on this, see section on '-**ise**' and '-**ize**' in **Topic** entry at **Spelling**. For information on differences between British and American spellings, see **Topic** entry at **Spelling**.

Words with the same pronunciation

There are many words in English that are pronounced the same but spelled differently. The following pairs and groups of words are explained at separate **Usage** entries in this book because they are often confused:

bass - base	fair - fare
bear - bare	here - hear
born - borne	pore - pour - poor
break - brake	principal - principle
chord - cord	role - roll
complement - compliment	sow - sew
council - counsel	stationary - stationery
curb - kerb	there - their
currant - current	waist - waste
die - dye	whether - weather
draught - draft	

The entries are usually at the pairs or groups of words given above, but see **Usage** entries at **there** and **whether** for information about words pronounced like these words.

ⓘ Note that in standard British English **paw** is pronounced the same as **pore** and **pour**, and **poor** is also often pronounced the same. **So** is pronounced the same as **sew** and **sow**.

There are many other pairs of words that have the same pronunciation in standard British English. Some of the commonest ones are listed below.

altar - alter	hair - hare	naval - navel	shear - sheer
berry - bury	hangar - hanger	none - nun	sole - soul
blew - blue	heal - heel	one - won	some - sum
boar - bore	heard - herd	packed - pact	son - sun
bough - bow	heroin - heroine	pain - pane	stair - stare
bread - bred	hoarse - horse	peace - piece	stake - steak
bridal - bridle	hole - whole	peal - peel	stalk - stork
caught - court	key - quay	pedal - peddle	steal - steel
cell - sell	knead - need	peer - pier	storey - story
coarse - course	knew - new	place - plaice	tail - tale
core - corps	knight - night	plain - plane	tear - tier
creak - creek	knot - not	pole - poll	threw - through
cue - queue	know - no	pray - prey	throne - thrown
cymbal - symbol	lain - lane	profit - prophet	toe - tow
dear - deer	leak - leek	raise - raze	too - two
dew - due	lessen - lesson	rap - wrap	vain - vein
earn - urn	loan - lone	raw - roar	wail - whale
feat - feet	made - maid	retch - wretch	wait - weight
fir - fur	mail - male	ring - wring	war - wore
flaw - floor	main - mane	road - rode	warn - worn
flea - flee	maize - maze	root - route	way - weigh
flour - flower	medal - meddle	sail - sale	weak - week
fort - fought	miner - minor	sauce - source	which - witch
foul - fowl	moan - mown	scene - seen	whine - wine
gorilla - guerrilla	morning -	sea - see	
grate - great	mourning	seam - seem	

ⓘ Note that the verb **read** has the same pronunciation as **reed**, but its past form, also spelled **read**, has the same pronunciation as **red**. The noun **lead** has the same pronunciation as **led**, the past form of the verb **lead**.

There are also the following groups of words which are pronounced the same in standard British English:

awe - oar - ore	flew - flu - flue	rain - reign - rein
buy - by - bye	meat - meet - mete	rite - right - write
cent - scent - sent	pair - pare - pear	saw - soar - sore
cite - sight - site	peak - peek - pique	ware - wear - where

Words with two pronunciations

☐1 **different meanings**	☐4 **'-ate'**	
☐2 **different word classes**	☐5 **other pronunciations**	
☐3 **different stress**		

☐1 different meanings

Several words have different pronunciations when they are used with different meanings or in different ways. Some of these words are explained in other entries.

⇨ See **Usage** entries at **lead, read, use - used - used to, wind,** and **wound.** See **Usage** entry at **old** for a note on the pronunciation of **aged.**

The following words also have different pronunciations for different meanings:

TOPICS

● **Bow** is pronounced /ba͜ʊ/ when it is used as a verb or a noun to refer to the act of bending your body. It is also pronounced /ba͜ʊ/ when it refers to the front of a boat.

We bowed to one another across the room.
He made a little bow and closed the door.
Soon the canoe was cutting through the water with froth curling at her bow.

Bow is pronounced /bo͜ʊ/ when it refers to a looped knot, a weapon, or the object drawn across the strings of a musical instrument.

He tied a neat bow.
Then she picked up her bow and positioned her cello.

● **Buffet** is pronounced /bu͡feɪ/ or /bʌfeɪ/ when it refers to a meal.
Ruth's got a cold buffet for us later.

It is pronounced /bʌfɪt/ when it means 'to push something violently'.
We splashed back to the jeep, buffeted by the wind.

Note that in words with two syllables which have come from French (other common examples are **garage** and **ballet**), the words are pronounced with the strss on the first syllable in British English, and with stress on the second syllable in American English.

● **Contract** is pronounced /kɒntrækt/ when it is used to refer to a legal agreement.
I did not sign a contract with them.

It is pronounced /kəntrækt/ when it means 'to become smaller'.
Metals expand with heat and contract with cold.

● **Recess** is pronounced /rɪses/ when it refers to a break from working.
The judge announced a five-minute recess.

It is pronounced /riːses/ when it refers to an area in a room that is set back or hidden.
The bed is in a recess.

● **Relay** is pronounced /riːleɪ/ when it refers to a race or when it means 'to send on television or radio signals'.
They came second in the 4x100 metres relay.
The dense cloud prevented the BBC from using a helicopter to relay pictures of the event.

It is pronounced /rɪleɪ/ when it means 'to pass on something that was said'.
I have been asked to relay to you a number of messages.

● **Row** is pronounced /ro͜ʊ/ when it refers to a group of things in a line, or when it means 'to move a boat using oars'.
...a row of parked cars.
He began to row steadily out towards the middle of the river.

It is pronounced /ra͜ʊ/ when it refers to a quarrel or a great deal of noise.
She took an overdose after a row with her mother.

● **Second** is pronounced /sekənd/ when it refers to part of a minute, when it is used as an ordinal, or when it means 'to formally support a proposal'.
Could I see your book for a second?
...at the top of the second flight of stairs.
I'll second that proposal.

It is pronounced /sɪkɒnd/ when it means 'to move someone temporarily to perform special duties'.
I am being seconded abroad for two years.

● **Sow** is pronounced /so͜ʊ/ when it means 'to plant seeds'.
You can sow winter wheat in October.

It is pronounced /sa͜ʊ/ when it refers to a female pig.

● **Tear** is pronounced /tɪə/ when it refers to a drop of liquid produced when you cry.
A single tear rolls slowly down his cheek.

It is pronounced /teə/ when used with other meanings, for example when it means 'to pull cloth or paper apart' or 'to run somewhere very fast'.
She folded the letter, meaning to tear it up.
I used to tear up the ladder onto the stage with only seconds to spare.

2 different word classes

Many words have different pronunciations for different word classes – for example they are always pronounced in one way when they are used as a noun and always pronounced in a different way when they are used as a verb. Various groups of words which have different pronunciations for different word classes are explained below.

3 different stress

A number of words have stress on the first syllable when they are used as a noun or adjective and stress on the second syllable when they are used as a verb. For example, **record** is pronounced /rekɔːd/ when used as a noun or adjective and /rɪkɔːd/ when used as a verb. **Contest** is pronounced /kɒntest/ when used as a noun and /kəntest/ when used as a verb. The following words have this pronunciation pattern:

abstract	converse	extract	perfect	redress
accent	convert	ferment	permit	refund
ally	convict	fragment	pervert	reject
combine	defect	frequent	present	relapse
compound	desert	implant	produce	reprint
conduct	dictate	import	progress	subject
conflict	discharge	imprint	project	survey
conscript	discount	incense	prospect	suspect
console	dispute	incline	prostrate	torment
consort	entrance	increase	protest	transfer
construct	escort	insult	rebel	transplant
contest	exploit	intrigue	record	transport
contrast	export	object	recount	

Similarly, the verb **confine** is pronounced /kənfaɪn/ and the noun **confines** is pronounced /kɒnfaɪnz/. The verb **proceed** is pronounced /prəsiːd/ and the noun **proceeds** is pronounced /prəʊsiːdz/. **Compact** is pronounced /kəmpækt/ when used as a verb and /kɒmpækt/ or /kəmpækt/ when used as an adjective.

4 '-ate'

A number of words have their last syllable pronounced /ət/ when they are used as an adjective or a noun and /eɪt/ when they are used as a verb. For example, **delegate** is pronounced /delɪɡət/ when used as a noun and /delɪɡeɪt/ when used as a verb. The following words have this pronunciation pattern:

advocate	consummate	duplicate	intimate
appropriate	degenerate	elaborate	moderate
approximate	delegate	estimate	separate
articulate	deliberate	graduate	subordinate
associate	designate	initiate	

(*i*) Note that in the case of **alternate**, there is a stress change too in standard British English: it is pronounced /ɒltɜːnət/ when used as an adjective and /ɒltəneɪt/ when used as a verb.

TOPICS

5 '-se'

word	part of speech	pronunciation
use ab**use** exc**use** mis**use**	verb noun	/juːz/ /juːs/
diff**use**	verb adjective	/dɪfjuːz/ /dɪfjuːs/
refuse	verb noun	/rɪfjuːz/ /refjuːs/
close	verb adjective/adverb	/kləʊz/ /kləʊs/
house	noun verb	/haʊs/ (pl /haʊzɪz/) /haʊz/

6 other pronunciations

word	part of speech	pronunciation
attribute	verb noun	/ətrɪbjuːt/ /ætrɪbjuːt/
content	noun adjective/verb	/kɒntent/ /kəntent/
excess	adjective noun	/ekses/ /ɪkses/
implement	verb noun	/ɪmplɪment/ /ɪmplɪmənt/
invalid	noun/modifier adjective	/ɪnvəlɪd/ /ɪnvælɪd/
live	verb adjective/adverb	/lɪv/ /laɪv/
minute	noun adjective	/mɪnɪt/ /maɪnjuːt/
mouth	noun verb	/maʊθ/ /maʊð/
overall	adjective/adverb noun	/əʊvərɔːl/ /əʊvərɔːl/
overflow	verb noun	/əʊvəfləʊ/ /əʊvəfləʊ/
overlap	verb noun	/əʊvəlæp/ /əʊvəlæp/
overthrow	verb noun	/əʊvəθrəʊ/ /əʊvəθrəʊ/
overhead overheads	adjective adverb noun	/əʊvəhed/ /əʊvəhed/ /əʊvəhedz/
underground	adverb adjective/noun	/ʌndəgraʊnd/ /ʌndəgraʊnd/
upset	verb/adjective after verb noun/adjective in front of noun	/ʌpset/ /ʌpset/

TOPICS

804

Glossary of grammatical terms

abstract noun a noun used to describe a quality, idea, or experience rather than something which is physical or concrete. EG *joy, size, language*. Compare with **concrete noun**. See Grammar entry at **Nouns**.

active voice verb groups such as 'gives', 'took', 'has made', where the subject is the person or thing doing the action or responsible for it. EG *The storm destroyed dozens of trees*. Compare with **passive voice**.

adjectival clause another name for **relative clause**.

adjective a word used to tell you more about a thing, such as its appearance, colour, size, or other qualities. EG … *a pretty blue dress*. See Grammar entry at **Adjectives**.

adjunct a word or combination of words that is added to a clause in order to give more information about time, place, or manner. See Grammar entry at **Adjuncts**.

adverb a word that gives more information about when, how, where, or in what circumstances something happens. EG *quickly, now*. See Grammar entries at **Adjuncts** and **Adverbs**. Types of adverb include:
adverb of degree an adverb which indicates the amount or extent of a feeling or quality. EG *I enjoyed it enormously*… EG *She felt extremely tired*.
adverb of duration an adverb which indicates how long something lasts. EG *He smiled briefly*.
adverb of frequency an adverb which indicates how often something happens. EG *I sometimes regret it*.
adverb of manner an adverb which indicates the way in which something happens or is done. EG *She watched him carefully*.
adverb of place an adverb which gives more information about position or direction. EG *Come here*.
adverb of time an adverb which gives more information about when something happens. EG *I saw her yesterday*.

adjunct clause a subordinate clause which gives more information about the event described in the main clause. See Grammar entry at **Subordinate clauses**.

adverb phrase two adverbs used together. EG *She spoke very quietly*.

affirmative another name for **positive**.

affix a letter or group of letters that is added to the beginning or end of a word to make a different word. EG *anti-communist, harmless*. See also **suffix** and **prefix**.

agent the person who performs an action.

agreement the matching relationship between the forms of different words being used to refer to or talk about a person, thing, or group, which show whether you are talking about one person or thing, or more than one. EG *I look/She looks*… *This book is mine/These books are mine*… *one bell/three bells*. Also called 'concord'. See Grammar entry at **Singular and plural**.

apostrophe s an ending ('s) added to a noun to mark possession. EG … *Harriet's daughter*… *the professor's husband*… *the Managing Director's secretary*. See Usage entry at **'s**.

apposition the placing of a noun group after a noun or pronoun in order to identify someone or something or give more information about them. EG … *my daughter Emily*.

article see **definite article, indefinite article**.

aspect the use of verb forms to show whether an action is still continuing, is repeated, or is finished.

attributive used to describe adjectives that are normally only used in front of a noun. When any adjective is used in front of a noun, you can say that it is used attributively. EG *classical, outdoor, woollen*. Compare with **predicative**.

auxiliary one of the verbs 'be', 'have', and 'do' when they are used with a main verb to form tenses, negatives, questions, and so on. Also called 'auxiliary verb'. **Modals** are also auxiliary verbs. See Grammar entries at **Auxiliaries** and **Modals**.

bare infinitive the infinitive of a verb without 'to'. EG *Let me think*.

base form the form of a verb which has no letters added to the end and is not a past form. EG *walk, go, have, be*. The base form is the form you look up in a dictionary.

broad negative adverb one of a small group of adverbs, including 'barely' and 'seldom', which are used to make a statement almost negative. EG *I barely knew her*. See Grammar entry at **Broad negatives**.

cardinal number a number used for counting. EG *one, seven, nineteen*. See Topic entry at **Numbers and fractions**.

case the use of different forms of nouns or pronouns in order to show whether they are the subject or object of a clause, or whether they are possessive. EG *I/me, who/whom, Mary/Mary's*.

classifying adjective an adjective which is used to identify something as being of a particular type. These adjectives do not have comparatives or superlatives. EG *Indian, wooden, mental*. Compare with **qualitative adjective**. See Grammar entry at **Adjectives**.

clause a group of words containing a verb. See also **main clause** and **subordinate clause,** and grammar entry at **Clauses**.

clause of manner a subordinate clause which describes the way in which something is done, usually introduced with 'as' or 'like'. EG *She talks like her mother used to*.

cleft sentence a sentence in which emphasis is given to either the subject or the object by using a structure beginning with 'it', 'what', or 'all'. EG *It's a hammer we need*… *What we need is a hammer*.

collective noun a noun that refers to a group or set of people or things. EG *committee, team, family*. See Grammar entry at **Nouns**.

colour adjective an adjective which indicates what colour something is. EG *red, blue, scarlet*. See Grammar entry at **Adjectives**.

common noun a noun used to refer to a kind of person, thing, or substance. EG *sailor, computer, glass*. Compare with **proper noun**.

comparative an adjective or adverb with '-er' on the end or 'more' in front of it. EG *friendlier, more important, more carefully*. See Grammar entries at **Comparative and superlative adjectives** and **Comparative and superlative adverbs**.

complement a noun group or adjective which comes after a link verb such as 'be', and gives more information about the subject or object of the clause. EG *She is a teacher... She is tired*. See Grammar entry at **Complements**. See also **object complement**.

complex sentence a sentence consisting of a main clause and a subordinate clause. EG *She wasn't thinking very quickly because she was tired*. See Grammar entry at **Clauses**.

compound a combination of two or more words that function as a single unit. For example, 'self-centred' and 'free-and-easy' are compound adjectives, 'bus stop' and 'state of affairs' are compound nouns, and 'dry-clean' and 'roller-skate' are compound verbs.

compound sentence a sentence consisting of two or more main clauses linked by a coordinating conjunction. EG *They picked her up and took her into the house*. See Grammar entry at **Clauses**.

concessive clause a subordinate clause, usually introduced by 'although', 'though', or 'while', which contrasts with a main clause. EG *Although I like her, I find her hard to talk to*. See Grammar entry at **Subordinate clauses**.

concord another name for **agreement**.

concrete noun a noun which refers to something you can touch or see. EG *table, dress, flower*. Compare with **abstract noun**. See Grammar entry at **Nouns**.

conditional clause a subordinate clause usually starting with 'if' or 'unless'. The event described in the main clause depends on the condition described in the subordinate clause. EG *If it rains, we'll go to the cinema... They would be rich if they had taken my advice*. See Grammar entry at **Subordinate clauses**.

conjunction a word which links together two clauses, groups, or words. There are two kinds of conjunction - **coordinating conjunctions,** which link parts of a sentence which are the same grammatical type ('and', 'but', 'or'), and **subordinating conjunctions,** which begin subordinate clauses ('although', 'because', 'when'). See Grammar entry at **Subordinate clauses**.

continuous tense a tense which contains a form of the verb 'be' and a present participle. EG *She was laughing... They had been playing* badminton. Also called 'progressive tense'. See Grammar entries at **Tenses** and **Continuous tenses**.

contraction a shortened form in which an auxiliary verb and 'not', or a subject and an auxiliary verb, are joined together and function as one word. EG *aren't, she's*. See Grammar entry at **Contractions**.

contrast clause another name for **concessive clause**.

coordinating conjunction see **conjunction**.

coordination the linking of words or groups of words which are of the same grammatical type, or the linking of clauses which are of equal importance. See Grammar entry at **Conjunctions**.

copula the verb 'be', when used with a complement. In this book, the term **link verb** is used for 'be' and for a few similar verbs such as 'seem', 'look', and 'become' used with complements.

count noun a noun which has a singular form and a plural form. EG *dog/dogs, lemon/lemons, foot/feet*. Also called 'countable noun'. See Grammar entry at **Nouns**.

declarative mood A clause in the declarative mood has the subject followed by the verb. Most statements are made in the declarative mood. EG *I saw him yesterday*. Also called 'indicative mood'.

defective verb a verb which does not have all the inflected forms that regular verbs have. For example, all modals are defective verbs.

defining relative clause a relative clause which identifies the person or thing that is being talked about. EG *I wrote down everything that she said*. Compare with **non-defining relative clause**. See Grammar entry at **Relative clauses**.

definite article the determiner 'the'.

delexical verb a verb which has very little meaning in itself but is used with an object to describe an action. 'Give', 'have', and 'take' are commonly used as delexical verbs. EG *She gave a small cry... I've had a bath*. See Grammar entry at **Verbs**. EG *She gave a small cry... I've had a bath*.

demonstrative one of the words 'this', 'that', 'these', and 'those'. They are used as determiners. EG *... this woman... ... that tree*. They are also used as pronouns. EG *That looks interesting... This is fun*. See Usage entries at **that - those** and **this - these**.

dependent clause another name for **subordinate clause**.

determiner one of a group of words including 'the', 'a', 'some', and 'my' which are used at the beginning of a noun group. See Grammar entry at **Determiners**.

direct object a noun group referring to the person or thing directly affected by an action, in a clause with an active verb. EG *She wrote her name... I shut the windows*. Compare with **indirect object**. See Grammar entry at **Objects**.

direct speech speech reported in the words actually spoken by someone, without any changes in tense, person, and so on. See Grammar entry at **Reporting**.

disjunct another name for **sentence adjunct**.

ditransitive verb a verb such as 'give', 'take', or 'sell' which can have both an indirect and a direct object. EG *She gave me a kiss*. See Grammar entry at **Verbs**.

dynamic verb a verb such as 'run', 'fight' or 'sing' which can be used in continuous tenses. Compare with **stative verb**. See Grammar entry at **Continuous tenses**.

'-ed' adjective an adjective ending in '-ed'. EG *I was amazed*. See Grammar entry at **'-ed' adjectives**.

'-ed' form another name for **past participle**.

ellipsis the leaving out of words when they are obvious from the context. See Grammar entry at **Ellipsis**.

emphasizing adjective an adjective such as 'complete', 'utter' or 'total' which stresses how strongly you feel about something. EG *I feel a complete fool*. See Grammar entry at **Adjectives**.

emphasizing adverb an adverb which adds emphasis to a verb or adjective. EG *I simply can't do it... I* was **absolutely** amazed. See Grammar entries at **Adjuncts** and **Adverbs**.

ergative verb a verb which can be used either transitively to focus on the person who performs an action, or intransitively to focus on the thing affected by the action. EG *He had boiled a kettle… The kettle had boiled.* See Grammar entry at **Verbs**.

exclamation a sound, word, or sentence which is spoken suddenly and loudly in order to express surprise, anger, and so on. EG *Oh God!* See Topic entry at **Reactions**.

finite a finite verb shows person, tense, or mood. A finite clause contains a finite verb group. EG *He **loves** gardening… You **can borrow** that pen if you want to.* Compare with **non-finite**.

first person see **person**.

focusing adverb an adjunct which indicates the most relevant thing or the only relevant thing involved in something. EG *only, mainly, especially.* See Grammar entry at **Adjuncts**.

fronting a structure in which you put a topic which is not the subject of a clause at the beginning of the clause. EG ***Lovely hair** she had.*

general determiner a determiner which is used when you are talking about people or things in a general or indefinite way. EG *a, some.* See Grammar entries at **Determiners** and **Quantity**.

gender a grammatical term referring to the difference between masculine and feminine words such as 'he' and 'she'. See Topic entry at **Male and female**.

genitive the possessive form of a noun. EG *man's, men's.* See Usage entry at **'s**.

gerund an '-ing' form used as a noun. See Grammar entry at **'-ing' forms**.

gradable A gradable adjective can be used with a word such as 'very' or in a comparative or superlative form, in order to say that the person or thing referred to has more or less of a quality. **Qualitative adjectives** such as 'big' and 'good' are gradable. EG *very boring, less helpful, the best.*

group noun another name for **collective noun**.

headword the main word of a noun group. EG *… a soft downy **cushion** with tassels.*

identifying relative clause another name for **defining relative clause**.

idiom a group of two or more words which have a special meaning that cannot be understood by taking the meaning of each individual word. EG *to kick the bucket, a new broom.*

if-clause a **conditional clause**, or reported question beginning with 'if'.

imperative a clause in the imperative mood has the base form of the verb without a subject. It is the mood used especially for giving commands, orders, and instructions. It is also used for making offers and suggestions. EG ***Come** here… **Take** two tablets every four hours… **Enjoy** yourself.* See Grammar entry at **Imperatives**.

impersonal 'it' 'It' is called an impersonal subject when it is used to introduce or comment on a fact, or when it is used in a cleft structure. EG *It's raining… It was you who asked.* See Usage entry at **it**.

indefinite article the determiners 'a' and 'an'.

indefinite place adverb a small group of adverbs including 'anywhere' and 'somewhere' which are used to indicate location or destination in a general or vague way. See Topic entry at **Places**.

indefinite pronoun a small group of pronouns including 'someone' and 'anything' which are used to refer to a person or thing in a general or vague way. See Grammar entry at **Pronouns**.

indicative mood another name for **declarative mood**.

indirect object a second object which is used with a transitive verb to indicate who or what benefits from an action, or receives something as a result of it. EG *She gave **me** a rose.* See Grammar entry at **Verbs**.

indirect question another name for **reported question**.

indirect speech another name for **reported speech**.

infinitive the base form of a verb. It is often used with 'to' in front of it. EG *(to) take, (to) see, (to) bring.* See Grammar entries at **Infinitives** and **'To'- infinitive clauses**.

inflection the variation in the form of a verb, noun, pronoun, or adjective to show differences in tense, number, case, and degree. EG *come/came, cat/cats, small/smaller/smallest.*

'-ing' adjective an adjective which has the same form as the '-ing' form of a verb. EG *… a smiling face.* See Grammar entry at **'-ing' adjectives**.

'-ing' clause a clause beginning with an '-ing' form. EG ***Realising that something was wrong**, I stopped.* See Grammar entry at **'-ing' forms**.

'-ing' form a verb form ending in '-ing' which is used, for example, to form continuous verb tenses. Also called 'present participle'. See Grammar entries at **'-ing' forms** and **'-ing' adjectives**.

'-ing' noun a noun which has the same form as the '-ing' form of a verb. EG *swimming, laughing.* See Grammar entry at **'-ing' forms**.

intensifier a submodifier which is used to reinforce an adjective and make it more emphatic. EG *very, exceptionally.*

interjection another name for **exclamation**.

interrogative adverb one of the adverbs 'how', 'when', 'where', and 'why' when they are used to ask questions. EG ***How** do you know that?* See Grammar entries at **Questions** and **Reporting**.

interrogative mood a clause in the interrogative mood has part or all of the verb group in front of the subject. Most questions are in the interrogative mood. EG ***Is it** still raining?* See Grammar entry at **Questions**.

interrogative pronoun one of the pronouns 'who', 'whose', 'whom', 'what', and 'which' when they are used to ask questions. EG ***Who** did you talk to?* See Grammar entries at **Questions** and **Reporting**.

intransitive verb a verb which is used to talk about an action or event that only involves the subject and so does not have an object. EG *She arrived… I was yawning.* See Grammar entry at **Verbs**.

inversion changing the word order in a sentence, especially changing the order of the subject and the verb. See Grammar entry at **Inversion**.

irregular not following the normal rules for inflection. An irregular verb has a past form and/or past participle which is formed in a different way from the regular '-ed' ending. See Grammar entries at **Comparative and superlative adjectives, Comparative and superlative adverbs, Irregular verbs,** and **Plural forms of nouns**.

lexical verb another name for main verb.

linking adjunct a sentence adjunct used to introduce a related comment or reinforce what you are saying. EG *moreover, besides.* See Grammar entry at **Linking adjuncts**

link verb a verb which links the subject and complement of a clause. Also sometimes called **copulas**. EG *be, become, seem, appear.* See Grammar entries at **Complements** and **Verbs**.

'-ly' words words ending in '-ly', such as adverbs of manner. See Grammar entry at **'-ly' words**.

main clause a clause which is not dependent on, or is not part of, another clause. See Grammar entry at **Clauses**.

main verb all verbs which are not auxiliaries or modals. Also called 'lexical verb'.

manner clause a subordinate clause, usually introduced with 'as', 'like', or 'the way', which describes the way in which something is done. EG *She talks **like her mother used to**.* See Grammar entry at **Subordinate clauses**.

mass noun a noun which is usually an uncount noun, but which can be used as a count noun when it refers to quantities or types of something. Some people call all uncount nouns mass nouns. EG *... two **sugars**. ... cough **medicines**.* See Grammar entry at **Nouns**.

measurement noun a noun which refers to a unit of measurement EG *metre, pound.* See Topic entry at **Measurements**.

modal an verb which is used with the base form of another verb to express a particular attitude, such as possibility, obligation, prediction, or deduction. Also called 'modal auxiliary' or 'modal verb'. EG *can, could, may, might.* See Grammar entry at **Modals**.

modifier a word or group of words describing a person or thing which come in front of a noun. EG *... a **beautiful** sunny day. ... ... a **psychology** conference.* See Grammar entry at **Modifiers**.

mood The mood of a clause is the type of structure it has, which indicates whether it is basically a statement, command, or question. See **declarative mood, imperative mood,** and **interrogative mood**. See also **subjunctive**.

negative A negative clause uses a word such as 'not', 'never', or 'no-one' to indicate the absence or opposite of something, or to say that something is not the case. EG *She did **not** reply... I'll **never** forget.* Compare with **positive**. See Grammar entries at **not, no, none, no-one, nothing, nowhere** and **never**.

negative word a word such as 'never', 'no-one', and 'not' which makes a clause negative.

nominal group another name for **noun group**.

nominal relative clause a clause beginning with a 'wh'-word which functions as a noun group. EG *I wrote down **what she said**.*

non-defining relative clause a relative clause which gives more information about someone or something, but which is not needed to identify them because we already know who or what they are. EG *That's Mary, **who was at university with me**.* Compare with **defining relative clause**. See Grammar entry at **Relative clauses**.

non-finite A non-finite verb group is an infinitive, a participle, or a verb group beginning with a participle, which cannot be the only verb group in a sentence. A non-finite clause is based on a non-finite verb group. See Grammar entries at **'To'-infinitive clauses, '-ing' forms,** and **Past participles**.

noun a word which refers to people, things, and abstract ideas such as feelings and qualities EG *woman, Harry, guilt.* See Grammar entry at **Nouns**.

noun clause another name for **nominal relative clause**.

noun group a group of words which acts as the subject, complement, or object of a clause, or as the object of a preposition. Also called 'nominal group' or 'noun phrase'. See Grammar entry at **Noun groups**.

noun phrase another name for **noun group**.

noun modifier a noun used in front of another noun, as if it were an adjective. EG *... a **car** door. ... a **steel** works.* See Grammar entry at **Noun modifiers**.

number the way in which differences between singular and plural are shown. EG *flower/flowers, that/those.* See Grammar entry at **Singular and plural**. See also **cardinal number** and **ordinal number**.

object a noun group which refers to a person or thing, other than the subject, which is involved in or affected by an action. See also **direct object** and **indirect object**. Prepositions are also followed by objects. See Grammar entry at **Objects**.

object complement an adjective or noun group which gives more information about, for example what the object becomes or is thought to be. EG *It made me **tired**... They consider him **an embarrassment**.* See Grammar entry at **Complements**.

object pronoun a personal pronoun which is used as the object of a verb or preposition. The object pronouns are 'me', 'us', 'you', 'him', 'her', 'it' and 'them'. See Grammar entry at **Pronouns**.

ordinal number a number that is used to indicate where something comes in an order or sequence. EG *first, fifth, tenth, hundredth.* See Topic entry at **Numbers and fractions**.

participle a verb form used for making different tenses. See **past participle** and **'-ing' form**.

particle an adverb or preposition which combines with verbs to make phrasal verbs EG *out, on.*

partitive a word which is used before 'of' to give information about the amount of a particular thing. EG *pint, loaf, portion.* See Grammar entry at **Quantity**.

passive voice verb forms such as 'was given', 'were taken', 'had been made', where the subject is the person or thing that is affected by the action. EG *Dozens of trees **were destroyed**.* Compare with **active voice**. See Grammar entry at **The Passive**.

past form the form of a verb, often ending in '-ed', which is used for the simple past tense.

past participle a verb form such as 'disappointed', 'broken', or 'watched' which is used, for example, to form perfect tenses and passives, or in some cases as an adjective. Also called the '-ed' form, especially when used as an adjective. See Grammar entries at **Past participles** and **'-ed' adjectives**.

perfect tense a tense made with the auxiliary 'have' and a past participle. EG *I **have met** him… We **had won**.*

person a term used to refer to the three classes of people who are involved in something that is said. They are called the first person (the person who is speaking or writing), the second person (the person who is being addressed), and the third person (people or things that are being talked about).

personal pronoun one of a group of words including 'I', 'you', 'me', and 'they', which are used to refer back to the people or things you are talking about. See Grammar entry at **Pronouns**.

phase a structure in which you use two verbs in a clause in order to talk about two processes or events that are closely linked. EG *She **helped to clean** the house… They **remember buying** the tickets.* See Grammar entries at **Infinitives**, **'-ing' forms** and **'To'-infinitive clauses**.

phrasal modal a phrase which forms a single verb group with another verb, and affects its meaning in the same way as a modal verb. EG *had better, would rather.* See Grammar entry at **Phrasal modals**.

phrasal verb a combination of a verb and an adverb or preposition, or a verb, an adverb, and a preposition, which together have a single meaning. EG *back down, hand over, look forward to.* See Grammar entry at **Phrasal verbs**.

phrase a group of words which is not a complete clause. Also another name for **idiom**.

place clause a subordinate clause which is used to talk about the location of something. EG *I left it **where it fell**.* See Grammar entry at **Subordinate clauses**.

plural the form of a count noun or verb which is used to refer to or talk about more than one person or thing. EG ***Puppies chew** everything… The **women were** ouside.* Compare with **singular**. See Grammar entry at **Singular and plural**.

plural noun a noun which is only used in the plural form. EG *trousers, scissors, vermin.* See Grammar entry at **Nouns**.

positive A positive clause is one that does not contain a negative word. Compare with **negative**.

possessive a **possessive determiner** or a noun with 's added to it, which shows who or what something belongs to or is associated with. EG *your bicycle, **Jerry's** house.* See Usage entry at **'s** and Topic entry at **Possession and other relationships**.

possessive determiner one of the words 'my', 'your', 'his', 'her', 'its', 'our' and 'their', which show who or what something belongs to or is connected with. They are also sometimes called 'possessive adjectives'. See Grammar entry at **Possessive determiners**.

possessive pronoun one of the words 'mine', 'yours', 'hers', 'his', 'ours', and 'theirs'. See Grammar entry at **Pronouns**.

postdeterminer one of a small group of adjectives which can be used after a determiner and in front of any other adjectives to make a reference clear and precise. EG *The **following** brief description.* See Grammar entry at **Adjectives**.

predeterminer a word which comes in front of a determiner, but is still part of the noun group. EG *… **all** the boys. … **double** the trouble. … **such** a mess.*

predicate what is said about the subject of a clause.

predicative used to describe adjectives that are normally only used after a link verb such as 'be'. When any adjective is used after a link verb, you can say that it is used predicatively. EG *alive, asleep, sure.* Compare with **attributive**.

prefix a letter or group of letters added to the beginning of a word in order to make a new word. EG *semi-circular.* Compare with **affix** and **suffix**.

premodifier another name for **modifier**.

preposition a word which is always followed by a noun group or an '-ing' form. EG *by, with, from.* See Grammar entry at **Prepositions**.

prepositional phrase a structure consisting of a preposition and its object. EG *… on the table. … by the sea.*

prepositional verb a verb that is always or usually followed by a preposition. See Grammar entries at **Phrasal verbs** and **Verbs**.

present participle another name for the **'-ing'-form**.

progressive tense another name for **continuous tense**.

pronoun a word which you use instead of a noun, when you do not need or want to name someone or something directly. EG *it, you, none.* See Grammar entry at **Pronouns**.

proper noun a noun which refers to a particular person, place, or institution. EG *Nigel, Edinburgh, Christmas.* Compare with **common noun**. See Grammar entry at **Nouns**.

purpose clause a subordinate clause, usually introduced by 'in order to', 'to', 'so that', or 'so', which indicates the purpose of an action. EG *I came here **in order to ask you out to dinner**.* See Grammar entry at **Subordinate clauses**.

qualifier any word or group of words describing a person or thing which comes after a noun or pronoun. EG *… a book **with a blue cover**. … the shop **on the corner**.* See Grammar entry at **Qualifiers**.

qualitative adjective an adjective which is used to indicate a quality, and which is gradable. EG *funny, intelligent, small.* Compare with **classifying adjective**. See Grammar entry at **Adjectives**.

quantifier a phrase ending in 'of' which allows you to refer to a quantity of something without being precise about the exact amount. EG *some of, a lot of, a little bit of.* See Grammar entry at **Quantity**.

question a structure which typically has the verb in front of the subject and which is used to ask someone about something. EG *Have you lost something?… When did she leave?* Also called 'interrogative'. See Grammar entry at **Questions**.

question tag a structure consisting of an auxiliary verb followed by a pronoun, which is used at the end of a **tag question**. EG *She's quiet, **isn't she?***

quote the part of a **quote structure** which indicates what someone has said, using the words they themselves used. EG *I said **'Why not come along too?'**.*

quote structure a structure containing a reporting clause and a quote. EG *She said 'I'll be late'.* Compare with **report structure**. See Grammar entry at **Reporting**.

reason clause a subordinate clause, usually introduced by 'because', 'since', or 'as', which gives the reason for something. EG ***Since you're here,*** *we'll start.* See Grammar entry at **Subordinate clauses**.

reciprocal pronoun 'each other' and 'one another', which are used to show that two people do or feel the same thing. EG *They loved **each other***.

reciprocal verb a verb which describes an action which involves two people doing the same thing to each other. EG *They **met** in the street.*

reflexive pronoun a pronoun ending in '-self', such as 'myself' or 'themselves', which is used as the object of a verb when the person affected by an action is the same as the person doing it. See Grammar entry at **Pronouns**.

reflexive verb a verb which is typically used with a reflexive pronoun. EG *Can you **amuse yourself** until dinner?* See Grammar entry at **Verbs**.

regular verb a verb that has four forms and follows the normal rules. See Grammar entry at **Verbs**.

relative clause a subordinate clause which gives more information about someone or something mentioned in the main clause. See also **defining relative clause** and **non-defining relative clause**, and Grammar entry at **Relative clauses**.

relative pronoun a 'wh'-word such as 'who' or 'which' that is used to introduce a relative clause. EG *... the girl **who** was carrying the bag.*

reported clause the part of a report structure which describes what someone has said. EG *She said **that I couldn't see her**.*

reported question a question which is reported using a report structure rather than the exact words used by the speaker. Also called 'indirect question'. See Grammar entry at **Reporting**.

reported speech speech which is reported using a report structure rather than the exact words used by the speaker. Also called 'indirect speech'.

reporting clause a clause which contains a reporting verb, which is used to introduce what someone has said. EG *They **asked** if I could come.*

reporting verb a verb which is used with a quote or a reported clause to describe what people say or think. EG *suggest, say, wonder.*

report structure a structure which reports what someone has said by using a reporting clause and a reported clause rather than repeating their exact words. EG *She told me she'd be late.* Compare with **quote structure**. See Grammar entry at **Reporting**.

result clause a subordinate clause introduced by 'so', 'so that' or 'such that' which gives the result of something. EG *The house was severely damaged, **so that it**

is now uninhabitable. See Usage entries at **so** and **such**.

rhetorical question a question which you use in order to make a comment rather than to obtain information. Rhetorical questions can end in an exclamation mark or a question mark. EG *Wouldn't it be awful with no Christmas!... Oh, isn't it silly?*

second person see **person**.

semi-modal the verbs 'dare', 'need', and 'used to' which behave rather like modals.

sentence a group of words which expresses a statement, question, command, or exclamation. A sentence usually has a verb and a subject, and may be a simple sentence, consisting of one clause, or a complex sentence, consisting of two or more clauses. A sentence in writing has a capital letter at the beginning and a full-stop, question mark, or exclamation mark at the end. See Grammar entry at **Sentences**.

sentence adjunct an adverb or adverbial expression which applies to the whole clause, rather than to just a part of it. EG ***Fortunately,*** *he wasn't seriously injured.* See Topic entry at **Opinions**.

's' form the base form of a verb with 's' on the end, used in the simple present tense. EG *She **likes** reading.*

simple tense a tense formed without using an auxiliary verb. EG *I **waited**... She **sang**.*

singular the form of a count noun or verb used to refer to or talk about one person or thing. EG *A growing **puppy needs** milk... That **woman is** my **mother**.* Compare with **plural**. See Grammar entry at **Singular and plural**.

singular noun a noun which is typically used in the singular form. EG *sun, business.* See Grammar entry at **Nouns**.

specific determiner a determiner which is used when referring to someone or something that has already been mentioned, or whose identity is obvious. EG *the, that, my.* See Grammar entry at **Determiners**.

split infinitive a 'to'-infinitive which has a word or phrase separating 'to' and the base form of the verb. EG *... **to** boldly **go** where no man has gone before.* See Grammar entry at **Split infinitives**.

stative verb a verb which describes a state, and which is not usually used in continuous tenses. EG *be, own, know.* Compare with **dynamic verb**. See Grammar entry at **Continuous tenses**.

strong verb another name for **irregular verb**.

subject the noun group in a clause that refers to the person or thing who does the action expressed by the verb. In a statement, the subject comes before the verb. EG ***We** were going shopping... **He** was murdered.* See Grammar entry at **Subjects**.

subject pronoun a personal pronoun which is used as the subject of a clause. The subject pronouns are 'I', 'we', 'you', 'he', 'she', 'it', and 'they'. See Grammar entry at **Pronouns**.

subjunctive a verb form which is used to express attitudes such as wishing, hoping, and doubting. The subjunctive mood is not very common in English, and is used mainly in conditional clauses such as 'If I were you...'. See Grammar entry at **The Subjunctive**.

submodifier an adverb which is used in front of an adjective or another adverb in order to strengthen or weaken its meaning. EG *… very interesting… … quite quickly.*

subordinate clause a clause which begins with a subordinating conjunction such as 'because' or 'while' and which must be used with a main clause. See Grammar entry at **Subordinate clauses**.

substitution the special use of pronouns and other words to replace part or all of a clause. EG *'Are you going to the party?' — 'I hope so'.*

suffix a letter or group of letters added to the end of a word in order to make a different word, tense, case, or word class. EG *slowly, childish*. Compare with **affix** and **prefix**.

superlative an adjective or adverb with '-est' on the end or 'most' in front of it. EG *thinnest, quickest, most wisely*. See Grammar entries at **Comparative and superlative adjectives** and **Comparative and superlative adverbs**.

tag a clause consisting of a pronoun and an auxiliary, which is added to a reply. EG *'Do you like it?' - 'Yes, I do.*' See also **question tag**.

tag question a statement to which a **question tag** (an auxiliary verb and a pronoun) has been added. EG *She's quiet, isn't she?*

tense the form of a verb group which shows whether you are referring to the past, present, or future. See Grammar entries at **Tenses, The Future, The Past** and **The Present**.

future 'will' or 'shall' used with the base form of the verb to refer to future events. EG *She will come tomorrow.*

future continuous 'will' or 'shall' with 'be' and a present participle, used to refer to future events. EG *She will be going soon.*

future perfect 'will' or 'shall' with 'have' and a past participle, used to refer to future events. EG *I will have finished by tomorrow.*

future perfect continuous 'will' or 'shall' with 'have been' and a present participle, used to refer to future events. EG *I will have been walking for three hours by then.*

simple past the past form of a verb, used to refer to past events and situations. EG *They waited.*

past continuous 'was' or 'were' with a present participle, used to refer to past events. EG *They were worrying about it yesterday.*

past perfect 'had' with a past participle, used to refer to past events. EG *She had finished*. Also called 'pluperfect'.

past perfect continuous 'had been' with a present participle, used to refer to past events. EG *He had been waiting for hours.*

simple present the base form and the 's' form, usually used to refer to present events and situations. EG *I like bananas… My sister hates them.*

present continuous 'am', 'are' or 'is' with a present participle, used to refer to present events. EG *Things are improving.*

present perfect 'have' or 'has' with a past participle, used to refer to past events which affect the present. EG *She has loved him for ten years.*

present perfect continuous 'has been' or 'have been' with a present participle, used to refer to past situations which still exist in the present. EG *We have been sitting here for hours.*

'that'-clause a clause starting with 'that' which is used

mainly when reporting what someone has said. 'That' can be omitted when the clause is used after a reporting verb. EG *She said that she'd wash up for me*. See Grammar entry at **'That'-clauses**.

third person see **person**.

time clause a subordinate clause which indicates the time of an event. EG *I'll phone you when I get back*. See Grammar entry at **Subordinate clauses**.

title a word used before a person's name which shows their position or status. EG *Mrs, Lord, Queen*. See Topic entry at **Names and titles**.

'to'-infinitive the base form of a verb preceded by 'to'. EG *to go, to have, to jump.*

'to'-infinitive clause a subordinate clause based on a 'to'-infinitive. EG *I wanted to see you*. See Grammar entry at **'To'-infinitive clauses**.

transitive verb a verb which is used to talk about an action or event that involves more than one person or thing, and therefore is followed by an object. EG *She's wasting her money.*

uncount noun a noun which refers to a general kind of thing rather than to an individual item, and so has only one form. EG *money, furniture, intelligence*. Also called 'uncountable noun'. See Grammar entry at **Nouns**.

verb a word which is used with a subject to say what someone or something does, or what happens to them. EG *sing, spill, die*. See Grammar entry at **Verbs**.

verbal noun another name for **'-ing' noun**. See Grammar entry at **'-ing' forms**.

verb group a main verb, or a main verb preceded by one or more auxiliaries or a modal, which combines with a subject to say what someone does, or what happens to them. EG *I'll show them… She's been sick.*

verbless clause a group of words that has the same function as a main clause or a subordinate clause, but does not contain a verb. EG *What about some lunch?… I stood with my hands behind my back*. See Grammar entry at **Verbless clauses**.

vocative a word used when speaking to someone, just as if it were their name. EG *darling, madam*. See Topic entry at **Addressing someone**.

'wh'-clause a clause starting with a 'wh'-word. See Grammar entries at **'Wh'-clauses** and **Reporting**.

'whether'-clause a clause beginning with 'whether' that is used to report a 'yes/no'-question. EG *I asked her whether she'd seen him*. See Grammar entry at **Reporting**.

'wh'-question a question which expects an answer mentioning a particular person, place, thing, amount, and so on, rather than just 'yes' or 'no'. Compare with **'yes/no'-question**. See Grammar entry at **Questions**.

'wh'-word one of a group of words starting with 'wh-', such as 'what', 'when' or 'who', which are used in 'wh'-questions. 'How' is also called a 'wh'-word because it behaves like the other 'wh'-words. See Grammar entry at **'Wh-' words**.

'yes/no'-question a question which can be answered simply with either 'yes' or 'no'. EG *Would you like some more tea?* Compare with **'wh'-question**. See Grammar entry at **Questions**.

Index